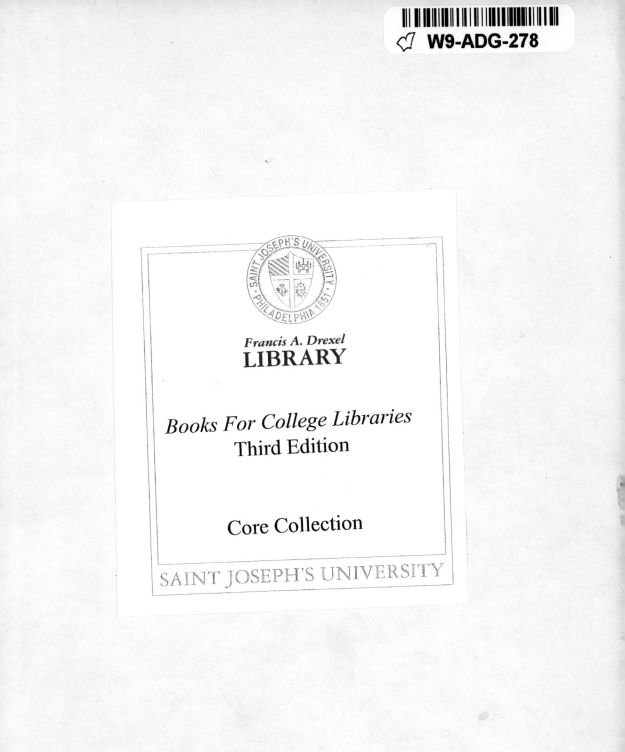

Francis A. Drexel
LIBRARY

Books For College Libraries
Third Edition

Core Collection

SAINT JOSEPH'S UNIVERSITY

UNITED STATES ARMY IN WORLD WAR II

The War in the Pacific

STRATEGY AND COMMAND: THE FIRST TWO YEARS

by

Louis Morton

MILITARY INSTRVCTION

OFFICE OF THE CHIEF OF MILITARY HISTORY
DEPARTMENT OF THE ARMY
WASHINGTON 25, D.C., 1962

This volume, one of the series UNITED STATES ARMY IN WORLD WAR II, is the tenth to be published in the subseries THE WAR IN THE PACIFIC. The volumes in the over-all series will be closely related and will present a comprehensive account of the activities of the Military Establishment during World War II. A list of subseries is appended at the end of this volume.

Library of Congress Catalog Card Number: 61–60001

Reprinted 1969

For sale by the Superintendent of Documents, U.S. Government Printing Office
Washington, D.C., 20402 – Price $10.25

UNITED STATES ARMY IN WORLD WAR II

Stetson Conn, General Editor

Advisory Committee
(as of 5 April 1961)

Fred Harvey Harrington
University of Wisconsin

Maj. Gen. Louis W. Truman
U.S. Continental Army Command

William R. Emerson
Yale University

Maj. Gen. Evan M. Houseman
Industrial College of the Armed Forces

Oron J. Hale
University of Virginia

Brig. Gen. Bruce Palmer, Jr.
U.S. Army War College

W. Stull Holt
University of Washington

Brig. Gen. William A. Cunningham III
U.S. Army Command and General Staff College

Bell I. Wiley
Emory University

Col. Vincent J. Esposito
United States Military Academy

C. Vann Woodward
Johns Hopkins University

Office of the Chief of Military History

Brig. Gen. James A. Norell, Chief of Military History

Chief Historian
Chief, Histories Division
Chief, Publication Division
Editor in Chief

Stetson Conn
Col. Leonard G. Robinson
Lt. Col. James R. Hillard
Joseph R. Friedman

The History of
THE WAR IN THE PACIFIC
prepared under the direction of Louis Morton

. . . to Those Who Served

Foreword

For the United States, full involvement in World War II began and ended in the Pacific Ocean. Although the accepted grand strategy of the war was the defeat of Germany first, the sweep of Japanese victory in the weeks and months after Pearl Harbor impelled the United States to move as rapidly as it could to stem the enemy tide of conquest in the Pacific. Shocked as they were by the initial attack, the American people were also united in their determination to defeat Japan, and the Pacific war became peculiarly their own affair. In this great theater it was the United States that ran the war, and had the determining voice in answering questions of strategy and command as they arose. The natural environment made the prosecution of war in the Pacific of necessity an interservice effort, and any real account of it must, as this work does, take into full account the views and actions of the Navy as well as those of the Army and its Air Forces.

These are the factors—a predominantly American theater of war covering nearly one-third the globe, and a joint conduct of war by land, sea, and air on the largest scale in American history—that make this volume on the Pacific war of particular significance today. It is the capstone of the eleven volumes published or being published in the Army's World War II series that deal with military operations in the Pacific area, and it is one that should command wide attention from the thoughtful public as well as the military reader in these days of global tension.

Washington, D. C.
5 April 1961

JAMES A. NORELL
Brigadier General, U.S.A.
Chief of Military History

The Author

Louis Morton, now Professor of History at Dartmouth College, was a member of the Office of the Chief of Military History from 1946 to 1959. During that time, he served as chief of the Pacific Section, responsible for the preparation of the 11-volume subseries on The War in the Pacific, deputy to the Chief Historian, and historical adviser for the post-World War II program. The present volume is the second he has written for the series UNITED STATES ARMY IN WORLD WAR II. The first, *The Fall of the Philippines,* was published in 1953. In addition, he has contributed substantially to other publications of this office, including *Command Decisions,* and has published numerous articles in professional military and historical journals.

A graduate of New York University, Mr. Morton received his doctorate from Duke University in 1938 in the field of American colonial history. After a brief teaching career, he joined the Williamsburg Restoration, which published his study, *Robert Carter of Nomini Hall,* and then in May 1942 volunteered for military service. Most of his Army career was spent in the Pacific on historical assignments, and it was during this period that his interest in military history began. He has served as consultant and lecturer at a number of military and civilian institutions and teaches military history at Dartmouth.

Preface

Strategy is a many-sided word, connoting different things to different people. The author of any work on strategy, therefore, owes it to his reader to define at the outset his own conception of this ambiguous term. For it is this conception that underlies the shape of his work and largely determines what belongs to it and what does not, what emphasis will be accorded certain subjects, and how they will be treated.

In the present volume, the author has viewed strategy broadly, including within it not only the art of military command—the original meaning of the term—but all those activities associated with the preparation for and the conduct of war in the Pacific. Strictly speaking, this book is not about military operations at all (though it includes operational strategy), for these belong in the realm of tactics and are covered fully in the other volumes of the Pacific subseries. It is focused rather on the exceedingly complicated and difficult, if less dangerous, tasks that are necessary to bring men with all that they need to the chosen field of battle at a given moment of time. These may be less glamorous endeavors than those usually associated with war, but they are as vital and were particularly important and complex in the Pacific, often determining the outcome of battle.

Viewed thus, the arena of Pacific strategy is the council chamber rather than the coral atoll; its weapons are not bombs and guns but the mountains of memoranda, messages, studies, and plans that poured forth from the deliberative bodies entrusted with the conduct of the war; its sound is not the clash of arms but the cool voice of reason or the heated words of debate thousands of miles from the scene of conflict. The setting for this volume, therefore, is the war room; its substance, the plans for war and the statistics of shipping and manpower. It deals with policy and grand strategy on the highest level—war aims, the choice of allies and theaters of operations, the distribution of forces and supplies, and the organization created to use them. On only a slightly lower level, it deals with more strictly military matters— with the choice of strategies, with planning and the selection of objectives, with the timing of operations, the movement of forces and, finally, their employment in battle.

Strategy in its larger sense is more than the handmaiden of war, it is an inherent element of statecraft, akin to policy, and encompasses preparations for war as well as the war itself. Thus, this volume treats the prewar period in some detail, not in any sense as introductory to the main theme but as an integral and important part of the story of Pacific strategy. The great lessons of war, it has been observed, are to be found in the events preceding the outbreak of hostilities. It is then that the great decisions are made and the nature of the war largely determined. Certainly this was the case in World War II, and the years before Pearl Harbor are rich in lessons for our own day.

The original design for the Pacific subseries of the UNITED STATES ARMY IN WORLD WAR II envisaged a single volume on strategy covering the entire period of the war as well as the prewar period. But it subsequently became evident that it would be impossible to tell so large a story in any meaningful way in so brief a span. An additional volume was therefore allocated to Pacific strategy. The terminal date for the present volume, December 1943, was selected partly for reasons of length but also because that date provided a logical dividing point in the story of Pacific strategy for a variety of reasons. Other volumes will deal with the final year and a half of the war, from December 1943 to August 1945.

Even so, it has been necessary to condense much of the story of Pacific strategy and to omit some things that perhaps should have been included. In each instance of this sort, the author has based his decision on the significance of the subject and its relevance to the larger theme of the book. Thus, the author emphasized the organization for planning on the higher levels at the expense of the organization of theater headquarters because it seemed to him that the area of decision deserved the greater attention. Similarly, he avoided a detailed account of theater organization for its own sake, since a *pro forma* account would shed little light on the major problems of the Pacific war. But when theater organization emerges as a major factor, as it does in the account of joint command or Army-Navy relationships, it receives considerable attention.

The temptation to deal in this book with the larger problems of global strategy became at times almost irresistible. Constantly the author had to remind himself that his subject was the Pacific war and that global strategy was treated in full elsewhere in this series. He attempted, therefore, to include only so much of the larger picture as was necessary to put the Pacific into its proper perspective. The same is true of logistics and of operations. UNITED STATES ARMY IN WORLD WAR II is a large series with volumes on a great many subjects, many of them closely related to one another and to this one. Thus, the author had constantly to skirt a narrow path between those volumes dealing with the higher echelons of the War Department and those dealing with operations in the theater. When he trespassed, he did so because it seemed necessary for an understanding of the story of Pacific strategy; to do otherwise would have been a disservice to the reader.

Every author who sets out to write a book incurs numerous obligations. But none owes more than one whose book is part of a larger series and who works within the framework of an organization in which many people contribute to the volume in the course of their daily work. This is such a book, and the debts of the author to his colleagues and associates are heavy indeed, even though he alone is responsible for interpretations made and conclusions drawn in this volume as well as for any errors of omission or commission. The list of those whose assistance eased the author's task extends from the Chiefs of Military History and the Chief Historians, past and present, to the typists who deciphered penciled scribblings and the file clerks who saved the author many valuable hours. Included in this long list are editors and cartographers, librarians and archivists, participants in the events described, and observers, supervisors, and subordinates. But the heaviest debts are to my fellow historians in this adventure in co-operative history, and especially to the authors of the other volumes in the Pacific subseries. The references to their work, which appear so often on the pages that follow, are only a partial acknowledgment of their contribution. Full acknowledgment would have to include also the less tangible but equally important benefits derived from close association and frequent conversation. For this aid, the author owes much to his colleagues, civilian and military, but he owes more perhaps to their encouragement and to the support and friendship they gave so freely during the years it took to write this book.

Hanover, New Hampshire   LOUIS MORTON
20 September 1960

Contents

Introduction

PART ONE

The Road to War

PART TWO

The Defensive: Pearl Harbor to Midway

PART THREE

Seizing The Initiative

PART FOUR

Emerging Patterns

Tables

Charts

Maps

Maps I–V are in inverse order inside back cover

Illustrations

Illustrations are from the following sources:

National Archives: pages 49, 52, 53, 117, 142, 196, 428.
Captured Japanese films: pages 95, 96, 116, 183, 268, 369, 551.
Life photograph taken by McAvoy: page 125.
The Netherlands Department of Defense: pages 167, 170, 173.
Australian War Memorial: page 368.

All other photographs are from Department of Defense files.

INTRODUCTION

THE PACIFIC WORLD

The theater of war is the province of strategy.

SIR EDWARD BRUCE HAMLEY

The Mediterranean is the ocean of the past, the Atlantic, the ocean of the present, and the Pacific, the ocean of the future.

JOHN HAY

The Pacific World

Much that has been written about the Pacific area is a mixture of romanticism and exaggeration. But for those who seek an understanding of the Pacific as a theater of war, a knowledge of the ocean, its islands, its peoples, and its history is a prerequisite. It was these factors which in large measure determined where and how the war would be fought, shaped strategy, complicated logistics, and conditioned tactics. Before his return journey came to an end under the Golden Gate Bridge, the World War II soldier who had fought his way across the Pacific had seen many strange sights and heard stranger tales. Nowhere did the grim reality of life in the Pacific correspond with the idyllic existence pictured in romantic literature.

The Pacific Ocean is the world of Melville and Maugham, of white whales and long-extinct animals and birds, of Lilliput and Brobdingnag, and of the long-sought continent of the South Seas, *Terra Australis Incognita*. In its vast reaches lie countless islands ranging in size from the tiniest coral outcroppings, so low they barely break the rays of the setting sun, to continental Australia, three million square miles in extent. It has every kind of clime from sweltering heat to polar cold, and a startling variety of physical settings—steaming and noisome jungles, foggy, frozen, wind-swept islands, deserts, palm-covered coral atolls, grassland pla-teaus, parched treeless plains, and live volcanoes throwing up new islands and destroying old ones.

Racially and culturally the Pacific world is a bewildering patchwork woven out of millenia of isolation and migration, when small bands of black and brown men, the "Vikings of the Sunrise," pushed their way eastward in fragile canoes across the whole wide Pacific to populate its far-flung islands. The white explorers, when they ventured into these waters centuries later, found there an astonishing variety of peoples and cultures. In the mountainous interior of New Guinea, in the Indies, and in the Philippines, were the dark, woolly haired, pygmy Negritos, who, like the aborigine of Australia, existed in almost neolithic state, traveling naked in migrant bands and living on roots, grubs, reptiles, and game; in Papua the fuzzy-haired natives lived much like the Negrito but had a primitive political and social organization in which prestige often depended upon the number of heads a man could collect; in the Solomons, the Fijis, and New Guinea, were the dark-skinned Melanesians, fierce fighters who carved intricate and grotesque patterns in wood, ate human flesh, and were as addicted to exclusive men's clubs and secret societies as the American of today; and in the lush, beautiful islands of the eastern Pacific, where the Europeans came first, dwelt the tall, gold-skinned Polynesian who, with more time for leisure in a land where food abounded, created complex mythological and religious rites, and developed intricate social patterns.

In the wake of the European explorers came the treasure seeker and trader, the scientist and map maker, the whaler and planter, the beachcomber and missionary. They were of all nationalities—Portuguese, Spanish, Dutch, English, French, American, German, and Japanese—and they brought with them the doubtful blessings of a superior technology and civilization. Some exploited the native mercilessly, cheated and robbed him, others altered and destroyed his institutions, pushed him off the land, took away his few possessions and enslaved him. In the interests of progress, they converted islands into pastures, plantations, and mines; ceremonial halls into schoolhouses; and, with firearms, gin, and white man's diseases, depopulated large areas and annihilated whole tribes.

When the less savory aspects of this era of "discovery" and exploitation could no longer be ignored, the great powers stepped in to stem lawlessness and control trade. National prestige and power and the acquisition of strategic bases became the touchstones of policy; colonial administrators and naval officers the symbol of the new authority. Under official sponsorship the annexation of the islands, begun almost four hundred years earlier with Magellan's great voyage, went forward so rapidly that by the end of the nineteenth century all of the Pacific world, "every exposed volcanic crust and coral outcrop,"[1] had been divided among

the powers. Henceforth, they could gain additional land there only at each other's expense. The islands of the Pacific had become pawns in the great game of international rivalry and their fate rested on the moves dictated in the great capitals of the world.

Even in the twentieth century the Pacific world has lived up to its reputation for vastness and variety. The first World War and the subsequent reshuffling of control under the mandate system passed almost unnoticed by the islanders, who, like the natives of Rabaul, were only bewildered by pronouncement "No more 'um Kaiser; God save 'um King." But the surprise attack on Pearl Harbor opened a war which was fought all the way from Hawaii and Australia to Japan and the coast of Asia. It was a war waged in all the elements. Large fleets ranged the vast ocean searching for the enemy, aircraft flew hundreds and thousands of miles over water to drop their bombs, submarines hunted secretly in the lanes of empire for their prey, and troops fought desperately for islands with strange and unpronounceable names. Solomon Islanders helped carve airstrips out of jungle, Fijian and Tongan scouts performed heroic feats behind the Japanese lines on Bougainville, Papuans carried supplies over the Owen Stanley Range to the troops in New Guinea, and Filipino guerrillas met MacArthur on the beaches at Leyte. Volcanic wastes and coral atolls rising in a lonely ocean were scrutinized from the air and sea and charted with all the meticulous care of modern science. Islands where few white men had ever been were the subject of serious and lengthy debate at the council tables in Washington and London before they became major battlegrounds of the

---

[1] Douglas L. Oliver, *The Pacific Islands* (Cambridge: Harvard University Press, 1952), p. 253.

war and then, overnight, great bases on the road to Japan.

The war came to an end with the loudest man-made explosion the world had yet heard. It was in the Pacific—last to be settled by primitive man, last to be divided among the colonial powers, and last to witness the terrible ferocity and devastation of modern war — that the atom age opened. The Pacific world, the home of the head hunter, had, by the middle of the twentieth century, become the proving ground of the H-bomb.

The Ocean and Its Islands

The Pacific is the biggest and the deepest body of water on the earth. With a total area of 68,634,000 square miles, it is twice as large as the Atlantic and covers more than one-third of the surface of the entire globe. Measured along the equator it is about 10,000 miles wide, but its greatest width, 12,500 miles, is between Panama and Malaya where it extends half the distance around the earth. From Bering Strait on the north, where the ocean is only 56 miles wide and 300 feet deep, to the Antarctic Circle, the Pacific measures 9,300 miles.[2] So vast is its extent that if a giant bulldozer scraped off all the land on the surface of the earth to sea level and dumped it into the ocean, the Pacific would still have an average depth of two miles.

The best way to get a true picture of the immensity of the Pacific world is to

imagine yourself on Mars, observing the planet Earth through a telescope more powerful than any yet built. From this vantage point, the most prominent feature on the globe before you, dwarfing the mountains and the continents, is the Pacific Ocean. But to the earth-bound, who see their planet most often in Mercator projection on a flat map, the great ocean shrinks in size and takes on distortions which seriously limit an appreciation of its actual dimensions. By showing meridians of longitude as parallel—actually they converge at the poles—and by increasing the spread between the parallels of latitude in proportion to their distance from the equator, the Mercator projection produces a double distortion which has the effect of blowing up the size of the areas to the north and south. Thus, Greenland appears larger than the continental United States on a map drawn to Mercator projection, whereas it is actually less than one-third the size. Conversely, New Guinea, which lies just below the equator, appears on a flat map to be only as large as New Zealand, 2,000 miles to the south, but its total area is actually three times greater and its 1,300-mile length would reach almost halfway across the United States.

Though practically all the islands of the Pacific were formed by violent upheavals of the earth's crust and volcanic activity and consist essentially of hardened lava, their origin is often masked by a coating of coral rock, the remains of once-living plants and animals. The most familiar of these is the coral polyp, a tiny marine animal that builds its own shell by extracting lime from sea water, thus providing the aviation engineers of World War II with the base for many of their airfields.

[2] Unless otherwise indicated, this section is based upon O. W. Freeman, ed., *Geography of the Pacific* (New York: John Wiley & Sons, 1951), pp. 1–34; Fairfield Osborn, ed., *The Pacific World* (New York: W. W. Norton & Co., 1944), pp. 21–42; Don Leet, *Causes of Catastrophe* (New York and London: McGraw-Hill, 1948), pp. 150–53, 189; R. W. Robson, *The Pacific Islands Handbook* (New York: The Macmillan Company, 1946).

The coral polyp creates not only islands but atolls and reefs as well. The atoll, so characteristic of the eastern Pacific, consists of a chain of coral-encrusted islets, usually roughly circular or horse-shoe-shaped in formation and enclosing a shallow lagoon; the reefs—in this case, fringing reefs—are platforms built upon the shoulders of volcanic peaks and extending between the shore and deep water. Reefs which are separated from the shore by a stretch of open water are called barrier reefs, and the largest of these, the 1,200-mile-long Great Barrier Reef off the northeast coast of Australia, is probably the greatest monument left by the tiny polyp.

The coral atoll with its many islets and reefs is actually the visible portion of a single land mass resting on a subterranean mountain. It is a haven in a wilderness of ocean that forever rolls high to boil whitely against the fringing reefs. In the lagoon, where the waters are blue and calm and where fish abound, lie safety and sustenance. Troops stationed on a coral atoll during the war admired its beaches of dazzling sand where thousands of birds nest, and its rows of graceful palm trees whose fruit is the lifeblood of the atoll. And everywhere they saw coral, shaped and colored in infinite variety, and incomparably beautiful.

It is the coral atoll that has become for many the typical South Sea island. Actually there is no typical Pacific island. Some are made of the same stuff as continents, some of volcanic rock, and some of coral. In climate, size, height, and shape; in distribution of plant and animal life; in population, culture, and political affiliation, they vary so widely as to defy any simple classification. Any grouping of the islands, whatever the basis chosen,

must of necessity be a compromise. But since it is necessary, for convenience of description, to adopt some system, perhaps the most suitable would be that which was most familiar to the soldier of World War II, the division of the Pacific world into five groups—Australia, Indonesia, Micronesia, Melanesia, and Polynesia. *(Map I)**

Before examining this grouping more closely, it would be well to understand clearly the meaning of certain geographic terms frequently used in connection with the Pacific world. One of these is the South Seas. As used by its originator, the Spanish explorer Balboa who first sighted the Pacific from his well-publicized peak in Darien, it referred to the waters off Panama, then to the trade routes followed by the Spanish galleons. More recently, it has been used loosely to refer to that portion of the ocean south of the equator. Oceania is another term that is loosely used. Generally it is taken to mean all the islands of the Pacific but some authorities exclude Australia and the Indies, and others reserve the term for the French possessions in the southeast Pacific. There is no disagreement, however, about the international date line where one moves mysteriously from one day to another and which rarely failed to confuse the soldiers who sailed across it. It is the line which, except for zigzags to place politically related areas in the same time zone, coincides with the 180th meridian. When it is Sunday to the east of the line, it is Monday to the west.

Of the five regions of the Pacific, Australia is the smallest in terms of ocean area covered, but the largest in terms of

---

* Maps numbered in Roman are placed in inverse order inside the back cover.

land mass. About 7,000 statute miles of ocean separate it from San Francisco and 8,000 from the Panama Canal, and, whether one travels east or west, London is 12,000 miles distant. These facts alone explain why for centuries Australia, closer to but ignored by Asiatic countries, was for Europeans and Americans an isolated continent.

The area of Australia is approximately the same as that of the continental United States, but most of it is flat and much of the western and central region is a desert. The coast line is regular—no continent has a more compact or smoother form—with few large natural harbors. The climate varies from tropical to temperate, and, since it lies entirely in the southern hemisphere, its seasons are the reverse of those in the United States. The most favorable year-round temperature is in the east and south, and it is there that the Europeans first settled, where industry and agriculture flourish, and where American troops were first stationed during the war.

Second of the major divisions of the Pacific world is Indonesia, the world's largest archipelago and the treasure house of the Pacific.[3]

The islands of Indonesia are divided into three groups. *(Map II)* The largest and most important of these, and the one that contains the bulk of the land in the archipelago, is the Greater Sunda group, which includes Sumatra, Java, Borneo, and the Celebes. Extending eastward from Java toward Australia is a double chain of smaller islands known as the Lesser Sunda group in which lie Timor and the famed island of Bali. To the north, between the Celebes and New Guinea, lie the Moluccas or Spice Islands. The entire archipelago, from the tip of Sumatra on the west to the Moluccas on the east, is almost 3,000 miles long, and from Borneo to Bali, about 1,000 miles wide. To the south is the Indian Ocean and to the north the Pacific Ocean and the South China Sea, that vital water route to the ports of Asia and Japan. Thus, lying between two continents and two oceans, Indonesia is the key to the control of the lines of communication in one of the most strategic areas in the world.

Few regions of the world are so rich in resources, have so even and comparatively pleasant a climate, and so much natural beauty and variety as Indonesia. The islands have mountainous spines skirted by extensive plains of great fertility, and a variety of plant and animal life equaled nowhere on earth. Gold, silk, spices, tea, and precious stones attracted adventurers and merchants from India and China to Indonesia centuries before the Portuguese and the Dutch ventured there in search of the luxuries of the Orient. Since then it has become one of the chief sources of the world's supply of rubber and quinine, kapok, pepper, and tea. It is one of the few places in the Far East where petroleum is found and its mineral resources are enormous. Little wonder that the islands of Indonesia have been coveted by the nations of Europe and Asia since earliest times.

North of Indonesia, fringing the coast of Asia, are several large groups of islands which some geographers consider, with Indonesia, as part of the Asiatic land mass. To the American troops the best known of these were the Philippines. Comprising almost 7,100 islands, only one-third of them named, and extending

---

[3] Indonesia as a geographical and cultural unit is not to be confused with the political entity, the recently established Republic of Indonesia.

FUJIYAMA, *sacred mountain of Japan, dominates the Tokyo Bay area. (Photo taken in 1945 with American warships in the harbor.)*

for 1,150 miles from Borneo to Formosa, the Philippine archipelago is strategically situated in the geographic heart of the Far East, athwart the trade routes between Japan and China to the north and Indonesia and southeast Asia to the south. Only eleven of the islands have an area greater than 1,000 square miles and two of these, Luzon and Mindanao, together comprise more than two-thirds of the 115,600 square miles of land in the archipelago.

Between the Philippines and Japan, forming a series of stepping stones northward, are Formosa and the Ryukyus. Named by Portuguese navigators the "Beautiful Island" and occupied briefly by the Dutch and the Japanese, Formosa has been largely under the control of the Chinese, who named the land Taiwan, or terrace bay, for its giant green terrace-like cliffs. The island has an area of 13,887 square miles, almost twice that of the state of Maryland. About a hundred miles to the west, across Formosa Strait, lies the southeast coast of China, and Hong Kong is only 360 miles away.

The Ryukyu Islands, scene of one of the last great battles of World War II, separate the East China Sea from the Pacific Ocean and extend in a wide arc from Formosa to Japan. In ancient times the land was ruled by native dynasties, but after the fourteenth century the is-

ON BOARD THE POWHATAN. *Commodore Perry entertains the Japanese Commissioners in July 1854.*

lands paid tribute to China and then, in the twentieth century, to the Japanese, who finally took over control of the country.

The Japanese archipelago consists of four main islands, Hokkaido, Honshu, Shikoku, and Kyushu, and hundreds of smaller islands which extend in a 1,250-mile-long arc off the coast of Asia. The total land area of the archipelago is about the same as that of the state of Montana, 147,000 square miles, over half of which is accounted for by Honshu, the so-called Japanese mainland and site of the capital and chief cities. The structure of the islands is volcanic and mountainous, but there are few mineral resources and only 20 percent of the land is arable. Most of Japan's people live on the plains, the most notable of which is the Kanto Plain, which includes Tokyo and has a population density of 750 to 900 persons to the square mile. It is on these plains that the rice, barley, and millet needed to feed the people is grown and so intensive is the system of cultivation that as many as four crops are produced in a year. Fishing boats swarm over the waters around Japan and provide that other staple of the Japanese diet. Meat, milk, and dairy products are scarce and little used in Japan, and cheese is so little liked that it is said even the Japanese rats will not eat it.

The Japanese islands are the only ones in the Pacific that have retained their independence and integrity since earliest times. According to legend, Japan was founded by the goddess of the sun and its rulers are her direct descendants. Before the middle of the sixteenth century the islands had a loosely organized feudal government headed by a shogun, or military leader, and virtually independent lords. After a period of internal conflict in the sixteenth century, the country came under new rulers who reformed the government and followed a policy of complete isolation from the rest of the world. It was not until Admiral Perry's visit in 1853 that Japan entered the community of nations, began to adopt western customs and techniques, and embarked on a policy of expansion.

Eastward across the Pacific, the direction taken by the successive waves of migration from Asia, lie the three remaining major divisions of the Pacific world: Micronesia and Melanesia, lying side by side along the equator, and Polynesia, whose islands fall within a vast triangle extending from Hawaii to Easter Island to New Zealand. These names, so deceptively alike, include areas of wide variation in climate and physical environment, and a great diversity in racial and cultural patterns.

The islands of Micronesia (meaning tiny islands in Greek) lie north of the equator, between the Philippines and the date line, an ocean area larger than the continental United States. The amount of land in this huge expanse of ocean, however, totals only 1,260 square miles, about as much as Rhode Island. Most of this land consists of low coral atolls, but many of the islands are volcanic in structure with peaks as high as

3,000 feet. Farthest north and closest to the Bonins, scene of the bloody battle for Iwo Jima, are the Mariana Islands, resting on the edge of a vast submerged mountain chain jutting deeply into Micronesia. It is on the southern extremity of this group that Guam, the largest island of Micronesia and an important American base in World War II, is located. Westernmost of the Micronesian islands and about 500 miles off the coast of Mindanao are the Palaus where soldiers and marines also fought during the war. From here the islands stretch eastward, south of the Marianas, for about 2,000 miles through the mysterious Caroline Islands, where lie Yap and Truk. Along the eastern border of Micronesia, roughly parallel to the date line, are two other island groups: the Marshall Islands, to which belong Bikini and Eniwetok, and the Gilbert Islands, where lie Makin and Tarawa, the scenes of important battles in the war against Japan.

The importance of the tiny islands of Micronesia is far out of proportion to their size. For the prehistoric settlers from Asia they provided malaria-free homes and, for those who followed later, stopping places on the voyage farther eastward. Since Magellan's time they have been a vital link in Pacific trade and communication, and a source of critical materials such as phosphate and bauxite. Guam served the Spanish galleons, and, 300 years later, the U.S. Navy and Pan-American aircraft. Truk, once a Spanish and then a German possession, became later the nerve center for the Japanese Imperial Navy in the central Pacific. Today, naval bases, airports, and cable and weather stations are scattered throughout the area and it is here that the latest models of the atom and hydrogen bombs have been tested.

South of Micronesia, parallel and almost equal to it in extent, is Melanesia, the black islands, so named for the complexion of its people. The islands of Melanesia form a broad-curving arc that stretches east and south from Indonesia to the date line. Though these islands have certain characteristics in common —climate, location, and structure—they represent the widest diversity of cultural and racial patterns in the Pacific and are grouped together only because it would be more confusing to group them separately.

Melanesia is probably the poorest place in the world to live, to work, or to fight, a verdict with which all soldiers unlucky enough to be stationed there heartily agreed. For convenience, it may be divided into a western and an eastern area. The first includes dragon-shaped New Guinea, second largest island in the world and almost continental in the variety of its climate, structure, and plant and animal life; the islands of the Bismarck Archipelago, New Ireland, and New Britain with its magnificent natural harbor at Rabaul; and, guarding the northern approaches to the Bismarck Archipelago, the Admiralty Islands. Together, these islands comprise one of the most backward and least-known regions of the world, peopled largely by the primitive black, fuzzy-haired Papuans, and a strange variety of bird life—the ostrich-like cassowary, the brilliantly hued but raucous bird of paradise, and the snow-white cockatoo. But their shore lines contain anchorages large enough to accommodate the combined fleets of the world, and their position adjacent to Indonesia and north of Australia gives

them great strategic importance.

The eastern portion of Melanesia consists of six major groups of islands: the Solomons, Santa Cruz, New Hebrides, New Caledonia, Loyalty, and Fiji. The Solomon Islands, which stretch in a double northwest-southeast chain for 700 miles to the east of New Guinea, include seven major and many small islands, whose names sound the roll of notable American battles: Guadalcanal, Tulagi, New Georgia, Vella Lavella, and Bougainville. With their damp, hot climate, malarial mosquito, and well-nigh impenetrable jungle they constitute one of the most forbidding areas on earth.

Southeast of the Solomons lie the New Hebrides, and below them, New Caledonia. To the east and forming the eastern limit of Melanesia are the Fiji Islands, whose remarkably well-built natives were once the most famous cannibals of the South Seas.

Last and largest of the regions of Oceania and the most homogeneous of its cultural and racial groupings, is Polynesia. It extends from New Zealand, far to the south and 1,200 miles east of Australia, to lonely Easter Island, outpost of Polynesia and home of an ancient and still unknown civilization, a distance of 4,000 miles. And from Easter to Midway and Kure, northernmost of the Hawaiian chain, is almost 1,000 miles more. In this vast ocean area, four times larger than the continental United States, are scattered innumerable bits of land whose total area, exclusive of New Zealand, is no larger than the state of Vermont.

The southern apex of Polynesia consists of two large mountainous islands and their outlying clusters of land known collectively as New Zealand. The islands, which became a rest area for American troops during the war, measure about 1,000 miles from north to south and extend from the subtropical to the subarctic regions with seasons comparable to but reversed from those in the United States.

Northernmost of the Polynesian islands is the Hawaiian chain and the island outposts nearby. The chain extends for almost 2,000 miles in a northwest-southeast direction. Located 2,100 miles from San Francisco, 3,400 miles from Yokohama, and midway between Panama and Manila, the Hawaiian Islands stand at the crossroads of the air and water routes of the central Pacific.

Only eight of the Hawaiian islands are inhabited. The most important are Hawaii, Maui, and Oahu, where the capital city and most of the islands' military and naval installations are located. At the opposite end of the Hawaiian chain, 1,300 miles northwest of Honolulu, is Midway, a lonely coral atoll six miles in diameter, where the United States won its first important victory after Pearl Harbor. Together with Wake and Johnston Islands, Midway is important chiefly as a civil air station and military base.

The remaining islands of Polynesia, with a few minor exceptions, lie below the equator and east of the Fijis, an area to which few American troops found their way. The most important of these are Tonga, Samoa, and the islands of French Oceania. The Tonga, or Friendly Islands as Captain Cook called them, lie to the east of the Fijis and extend for 200 miles north and south. There are about 150 islands in the group, the largest of which, Tongatabu, is about 100 square miles in extent. The Samoa Islands to the north extend in an east-west direction for about 300 miles. Western Samoa, which includes the two largest islands, is under the control of New Zealand, and the eastern portion, including Tutuila with its splendid harbor of Pago Pago, is American and was administered by the U.S. Navy until 1951.

French Oceania is comprised of seven separate groups of islands, the most important of which are the Marquesas, Society, and Tuamotu. The Society Islands are probably the most storied islands of Oceania. Almost all of the eighteenth century explorers of the Pacific stopped there and wrote glowing accounts of the people and the land. The largest island in the group and the one most often associated with tales of adventure and romance is Tahiti. The Tuamotu group is one of the largest archipelagoes in the Pacific, consisting of seventy-six atolls and stretching southeast of the Societies for about 1,300 miles. Remote from Asia, America, or Australia, subject to destructive hurricanes, and lacking fresh water or a fertile soil, the Tuamotu Islands have never attracted as much interest as other Polynesian islands.

Far to the north of Polynesia, separating the Pacific Ocean from the Bering Sea, lie the Aleutian Islands. From Alaska they sweep eastward for over 1,000 miles, like a finger pointing at Asia. Poor in resources and scene of some of the most disagreeable weather in the world, the islands were for many years almost ignored by the great powers. But their strategic location between America and Asia marked them as outposts for the defense of Alaska and a target for the Japanese early in the war.

The Great Powers in the Pacific

The exploitation and settlement of the Pacific world by Europeans had begun with the first voyages of the Portuguese and Spanish.[4] Under the papal Line of Demarcation, these two nations had in 1494 divided the world between them, Spain claiming exclusive rights to all land 370 leagues west of the Cape Verde Islands and Portugal all land to the east. The main objective of Magellan's voyage had been to find a shorter, western passage to the Spice Islands, which the Portuguese held, and thus prove that these islands fell within Spain's half of the world. Though he found the western passage, Magellan failed to establish Spain's rights to the Spice Islands and the Portuguese continued to enjoy exclusive control of the highly profitable trade of the Indies. There was none to challenge Spain's rights to the rest of the Pacific world, however, and Spanish galleons sailed regularly between ports in the new world and the outposts of empire in the Marshalls, the Carolines, the Marianas, and the Philippines.

The Dutch empire in the Far East was exclusively economic. The Portuguese and Spanish sought converts to Christianity as well as spice and gold; the Dutch wasted no energy on saving men's souls or on settlements. With single-minded persistence they sought economic advantages in the Far East and ultimately established a flourishing commercial empire extending as far as Formosa and Japan.

The English and French entered the Pacific much later. Following the precedent set by Sir Francis Drake, they first sought the wealth of the Pacific in the holds of Spanish galleons and in weakly defended Spanish settlements. In the years from 1675 to 1726 alone there were over a hundred English and French voyages into the Pacific, most of them officially sponsored buccaneering expeditions. But, despite the weakness of Spain, neither government showed any inclination to extend its sovereignty into the Pacific. Instead, it was the whalers, the traders, and the blackbirders who first brought western civilization to Oceania.

The establishment of trading posts, plantations, and missions was the prelude to annexation. As a result of the explorations of the eighteenth century, England and France had established conflicting claims to most of the Pacific world, but because of trouble in Europe and the belief that these islands were scarcely worth the risk of war neither government had pushed its claims. England, it is true, had established a penal colony in Australia shortly after the American Revolution, but no one opposed British claims to the isolated continent. Nor was there any serious opposition when France established a protectorate over Tahiti, then over all the Society and Marquesas Islands. But under the urging of the planters, merchants, and missionaries who now had an important stake in the Pacific, the

---

[4] For accounts of the exploration and exploitation of the Pacific, see J. C. Beaglehole, *The Exploration of the Pacific* (London: A & C Black, Ltd., 1934); Oliver, *The Pacific Islands*, pp. 63–103; Freeman, ed., *Geography of the Pacific*, pp. 61–87; Robson, *The Pacific Islands Handbook;* Samuel Eliot Morison, *The Maritime History of Massachusetts, 1783–1860* (Boston: Houghton Mifflin Company, 1921); Christopher Lloyd, *Pacific Horizons, The Exploration of the Pacific Before Captain Cook* (London: Allen & Unwin, 1946); James A. Williamson, *Cook and the Opening of the Pacific* (New York: The Macmillan Company, 1948).

attitude of the governments changed and each sought to establish its claims. To these interests was added later in the century the need for coaling stations and strategic bases, a need created by the use of steamships and the increased importance of Japan, Australia, and New Zealand in world politics and economics.

By the middle of the nineteenth century, the fight for the most desirable islands in the Pacific was on in earnest. England's efforts to settle New Zealand in the 1820's and 1830's had met strong opposition from the French and its was not until 1840 that the British felt their claim to the islands sufficiently strong to annex them. The French in their turn barely nosed out the English in New Caledonia, which Captain Cook had discovered, and annexed the island with its rich mineral resources in 1853.[5]

When German vessels began appearing in the Pacific, the race became three-cornered. In 1868 the Hamburg firm of Godeffroy began operations from Samoa and before long had branches in Hawaii, Fiji, and New Guinea. Though these activities were not official, they worried the British enough to make them annex the Fijis when German vessels began showing an undue interest in these islands. The French then strengthened their position in French Oceania by making Tahiti a colony and formally annexing the Tuamotus.

The German Government began acquiring land in the Pacific in 1884, after Bismarck had endorsed a strong expansionist policy. In that year the Germans seized the Bismarck Archipelago and the northeast coast of New Guinea. The Dutch had already added western New Guinea to their empire in 1828 and the British took the remaining portion of New Guinea for themselves. The next year the Germans seized control of the northern Solomons and, with splendid disdain for Spanish rights, hoisted the imperial flag over Yap and established a protectorate over the Caroline and Marshall Islands. The English and French thereupon proceeded to help themselves to additional slices of the Pacific pie. The two nations in 1887 established joint dominion (condominium) over the New Hebrides and the following year England established a protectorate over the Cook Islands. Before the end of the century, Samoa, the Gilbert and Ellice Islands, the Southern Solomons and Tonga had been divided among the powers, with England getting the lion's share.

The United States embarked on a colonial career in the Pacific comparatively late. With its energies absorbed in the settlement of a continent and in the Civil War, the United States was unable to take advantage of the early interest of the whalers and traders who had ventured so daringly and profited so enormously in the Pacific. But the ambition to establish mastery of the ocean and its commerce was almost as old as the republic, and formed a consistent pattern in the patchwork of westward expansion to the Pacific coast. Americans had discovered the mouth of the Columbia River in 1792, and had

[5] For the rivalry of the Western Powers in the Pacific, see: Jean I. Brookes, *International Rivalry in the Pacific Islands, 1800–1875* (Berkeley, Calif.: University of California Press, 1941); Foster R. Dulles, *America in the Pacific* (Boston: Houghton Mifflin Company, 1932); Sylvia Masterman, *The Origins of International Rivalry in Samoa, 1845–1884* (Palo Alto, Calif.: Stanford University Press, 1934); Richard W. Van Alstyne, "Great Britain, the United States, and Hawaiian Independence, 1850–1855," *Pacific Historical Review,* IV (1935), 15–24.

taken the lead in the whaling industry and the China trade. During the War of 1812, Captain David Porter raised the American flag in the Marquesas and established happy relations with the natives, a relationship which "with the common sailors and their girls all was helter skelter."[6]

But the government showed little inclination to follow up Porter's action and no claim was made to the island. Forty years later another naval officer, Commodore Matthew G. Perry, met the same reception to his proposals to establish bases in the Ryukyus, the Bonins, and Formosa. Ironically, the most significant result of his expedition to Japan was to promote the development of a nation which in time was to become America's chief rival in the Pacific.

Despite the hopes and initiative of many who dreamed of an American empire in the Pacific, the government moved slowly. In 1856 it passed the Guano Act which permitted U.S. claims to unoccupied islands for the purpose of working the guano deposits. These deposits were much in demand as fertilizer, and claims were laid to forty-eight islands, largely in the Line and Phoenix groups. But the guano, which had required thousands of years and countless millions of birds to create, was exhausted in twenty-five years and with it disappeared American interest in the islands. Most of the islands finally went to England, but the United States did establish claims to Howland, Baker, Palmyra, and other small islands which proved useful later in building a military air route across the south Pacific.

The acquisition of Alaska, Midway, and Samoa also came in this period. The first was acquired, with the Aleutians, by purchase from Russia in 1867 and gave the United States many more thousands of miles of Pacific coast line as well as an arc of islands extending far across the north Pacific. Midway, which was discovered by an American vessel in 1859, was formally annexed the same year as the Alaska purchase, and about the same time other small islands between it and Hawaii were acquired. But all proposals to take over the Hawaiian Islands, where the Americans held a dominant position, were rejected by Congress. The United States did, however, at the urging of the Navy acquire the right to establish a naval station at Pearl Harbor in 1884. It was also largely through the efforts of the Navy, backed by commercial groups, that the United States gained the harbor of Pago Pago in 1877. More than twenty years later the United States acquired Tutuila in eastern Samoa while Germany took the western half of the islands. England, in return for German concessions in Tonga and the Solomons, withdrew altogether from Samoa.

American expansion into the Pacific reached its peak with the annexation of the Hawaiian and Philippine Islands at the end of the century. As early as 1843 there were more Americans in Hawaii than all other foreign nationals, and the value of their property was over one million dollars. They held posts of responsibility in the government and virtually controlled the political and economic life of the island. For years they urged annexation by the mother country and by 1860 the issue was being debated hotly in the United States. Finally in 1893 the Americans in Hawaii overthrew the native monarch, established a republic, and requested annexation to the Unit-

---

[6] Quoted from Captain David Porter's *Journal* by Dulles, *America in the Pacific*, p. 100.

ed States. The offer was rejected, largely because of President Cleveland's opposition, but the new republic of Hawaii was recognized as the rightful government and, with support from important interests in the United States, continued to press for annexation. The Spanish-American war and the increasing interest of the Japanese in the islands led to a change of attitude. On 11 July 1898, by a joint resolution of Congress, the Republic of Hawaii was annexed by the United States.

The great prize of the Spanish-American War, which ousted Spain from the Pacific and made the United States a full-fledged colonial power, was the Philippine islands. But having won the islands by force, the American Government still had to decide what to do with them. Germany, fishing in troubled waters, had a fleet in Manila Bay and was ready to take over if the United States defaulted. McKinley's decision was for annexation, and formal cession of the islands, as well as of Guam, was made on 10 December 1898 with the signing of the Treaty of Paris. Few considered the other Marianas and the Carolines worth taking and Germany purchased them from Spain soon after.

The construction of the Panama Canal completed the transformation of the United States into a Pacific power. The first Spanish explorers had searched eagerly for a way around America and had found the westward passage far to the south. But this route was a long one, and Americans during the California gold rush had as often gone overland across the disease-ridden Isthmus of Panama to save time. A water route across the isthmus from the Atlantic to the Pacific would cut off almost 10,000 miles from

the journey, and the French began work on a canal in 1880. This effort failed, but American engineers took up the task in 1902 and when the canal opened in 1914 the United States gained control of the eastern gateway to the Pacific.

Last to enter the Pacific in search of empire, though itself a Pacific power, was Japan. In the years after Commodore Perry's visit, Japan, emulating the Western Powers, began to extend its control over weaker neighbors and to push its boundaries north and south. Between 1875 and 1880 the Japanese acquired the Kurils (Chishima), the Bonins, and the Ryukyus. The Sino-Japanese War in 1894–95 gave Japan Formosa and the Pescadores, accorded Korea a nominal independence, and demonstrated to a surprised world that Japan was a factor to be reckoned with in the Far East. In the treaty ending the war China also ceded to Japan the Liaotung Peninsula in southern Manchuria, but Russia, France, and Germany forced Japan to disgorge the peninsula.[7]

American annexation of Hawaii and, next year, of the Philippines aroused strong hostility in a Japan which was already angered by the French, Russian, and German interference with the provisions of the treaty with China. Many Japanese were convinced that the aims of the nation could only be achieved by force, and the influence of the Army and Navy, already considerable, increased sharply. As a result Japan embarked on a military and naval expansion program designed to make the nation so strong

---

[7] It is interesting to note that acceptance of the Russian, German, and French terms was decided by a *seidan*, that is, a sacred or personal decision of the Emperor Meiji, and was the only precedent for Hirohito's personal decision to end the war in 1945.

that it would never again suffer so humiliating an experience.[8]

Japan's first opportunity to test its new strength came in 1904 when, without the formality of a declaration of war, it attacked Russia. Despite unqualified success on land and sea, the Japanese were anxious to end the war within a year because of the heavy drain on the nation's resources. When President Theodore Roosevelt offered to mediate the dispute, therefore, both nations promptly accepted and some months later the Treaty of Portsmouth was signed. By this treaty, Russia recognized Japan's paramount interests in Korea and transferred to Japan the lease on the Liaotung Peninsula, railway and mining privileges in southern Manchuria, and the southern half of Sakhalin. Five years later Japan added Korea to its empire, and, by secret agreement with Russia, made southern Manchuria a Japanese sphere of influence.

Japan's opportunity to expand into the Pacific came with the outbreak of war in Europe in 1914. Using the pretext of the alliance with England signed in 1902, Japan declared war on Germany and seized the Marshall, Caroline and Mariana (except Guam) Islands, thus extending the Japanese empire almost 3,000 miles into the Pacific. Other Pacific powers, it should be noted, did not let this opportunity for expansion

go by without gain to themselves. Australia took over the German possessions in New Guinea, the Solomons, and the Bismark Archipelago, and New Zealand troops occupied western Samoa. Japan, not content with expansion into the Pacific, took over Germany's interests in the Shantung Province of China and the port of Tsingtao as well. The following year, 1915, in the Twenty-One Demands, Japan requested from China enormous additional economic and political concessions which, had they been granted, would have brought that nation under Japanese domination. But a vigorous protest from the United States, and other reasons, forced Japan to withdraw the most drastic of the demands.

By the Treaty of Versailles, Japan's wartime acquisitions, already approved by secret agreements with Britain, France, Russia, and Italy, were formally sanctioned. President Wilson opposed strongly the cession of the German islands to Japan, asserting that their only value was military and that their control by Japan would make the defense of the Philippines virtually impossible. But he failed to win over the Allies and Japan was granted under a mandate the islands it had seized, while England and Australia secured similar sanction for their actions.

With the Treaty of Versailles, the division of the Pacific world was complete. Japan was the dominant power in the western Pacific, north of the equator, and held almost all of Micronesia. The United States controlled the northeast Pacific with Hawaii and the Aleutians, and held outposts deep in Japanese-controlled territory in Guam, Wake, and the Philippines. The British Empire was dominant in the central and

---

[8] For Japanese expansion and Japan's relations to other powers in the Pacific, see Roy H. Akagi, *Japan's Foreign Relations, 1542–1936* (Tokyo: Hokuseido Press, 1937); Payson J. Treat, *Diplomatic Relations Between the United States and Japan, 1853–1895*, 2 vols. (Palo Alto, Calif.: Stanford University Press, 1932); Kenneth Scott Latourette, *The History of Japan* (New York: The Macmillan Company, 1947); Paul Clyde, *The Far East* (New York: Prentice-Hall, 1947).

southwestern Pacific, from Samoa westward to Australia and New Guinea, including almost all of Melanesia. France held most of the southeast Pacific, French Oceania, as well as New Caledonia, and, jointly with the English, the New Hebrides. The Dutch still had their rich empire in the East Indies, and in addition held the western portion of New Guinea. No nation could expand in the Pacific except at the expense of another and in violation of existing treaties. For Japan, this meant conflict with the stronger Western Powers. But on the Asiatic continent lay a weakened China and it was there that Japan sought the fulfillment for her dreams of empire. And it was there, in China and Manchuria, that the seeds for conflict with the United States were sown.

PART ONE

THE ROAD TO WAR

Am I deceived, or was there a clash of arms? I am not deceived, it was a clash of arms; Mars approaches, and, approaching, gave the sign of war.

OVID

For as the nature of foul weather lieth not in a shower of rain but in an inclination thereto of many days together; so the nature of war consisteth not in actual fighting but in the known disposition thereto during all the time there is no assurance to the contrary. THOMAS HOBBES

CHAPTER I

The Beginnings of Pacific Strategy

Covenants without swords are but words.
HOBBES, *Leviathan*

At the turn of the twentieth century, after the war with Spain, the United States for the first time in a hundred years found itself involved closely in the affairs of other nations. Possession of the Philippine Islands, Guam, Hawaii, and part of the Samoan archipelago had made the United States a world power and imposed on it the grave responsibility of defending outposts far from its shores. Such a defense rested, as Admiral Alfred Thayer Mahan had demonstrated, on sea power, on the possession of naval bases and a powerful fleet. Without these, no island garrison could hope to prevail against a naval power strong enough to gain supremacy in the Pacific.

Theodore Roosevelt, a close friend and student of Admiral Mahan, understood the importance of sea power and it was no accident that during his administration steps were taken to strengthen the Navy and to build the Panama Canal. But the work begun by him was not pushed vigorously in the years that followed. The American people were overwhelmingly isolationist and unwilling to pay the price of colonial empire. Thus, almost from the beginning of America's venture into imperialism the nation committed itself to political objectives but would not maintain the naval and military forces required to support these objectives. It is against

this background that American strategy in the Pacific and plans for the defense of U.S. island outposts must be viewed; it explains many of the seeming inconsistencies between policies and plans.

Early Plans for Defense

The defense of the 7,100 islands in the Philippine archipelago, lying in an exposed position 7,000 miles from the west coast of the United States, was for over thirty years the basic problem of Pacific strategy. From the start it was apparent that it would be impossible to defend all or even the major islands. A choice had to be made, and it fell inevitably on Luzon, the largest, richest, and most important of the islands. Only a few months after his victory in Manila Bay, Admiral Dewey, asserting that Luzon was the most valuable island in the Philippines, "whether considered from a commercial or military standpoint," recommended that a naval station be established there.[1] In the years that followed there was never any deviation from this view. Down to the outbreak of World War II that island, and

---

[1] Ltr, Dewey to John D. Long, Secy Navy, 29 Aug 98, quoted in O. J. Clinard, "Japan's Influence on American Naval Power, 1897–1917," *University of California Publications in History*, vol. XXXVI (Berkeley: University of California Press, 1947), p 27.

especially the Manila area with its fine harbor and transportation facilities, remained the chief problem for American strategic planners.

Though the basic element of Pacific strategy was a strong Navy with supporting bases, this alone would not suffice. Successful defense of an insular position like the Philippines required an Army garrison, coastal fortifications, and mobile forces to resist invasion. And perhaps as important as any of these was the close co-operation of the Army and Navy. In a sense, this was the vital element that would blend the ingredients of defense into a strategic formula for victory.

The mechanism devised for Army-Navy co-operation was the Joint Board, established in 1903 by the two service Secretaries. The board, consisting of eight members—four from the Army's General Staff and four from the General Board of the Navy—had a modest task initially. To it came all matters that required co-operation between the two services. It had no executive functions or command authority, and reported to the War and Navy Secretaries. Its recommendations were purely advisory, and became effective only upon approval by both Secretaries, and, in some cases, by the President himself.[2]

Almost from the start, the main task of the Joint Board was the development of war plans. The impetus was provided by Lt. Gen. Adna R. Chaffee, Army Chief of Staff, who proposed in April 1904, shortly after Japan's attack on Russia, that the Joint Board develop a series of plans for joint action in an emergency requiring the co-operation of the services. These plans, he suggested, should be based upon studies developed by the Army General Staff and the General Board of the Navy.[3]

From General Chaffee's proposal stemmed a series of war plans known as the color plans. Each of these plans was designed to meet a specific emergency designated by a color corresponding usually to the code name of the nation involved—RED for Great Britain, BLACK for Germany, GREEN for Mexico, ORANGE for Japan. On the basis of these joint color plans each of the services developed its own plan to guide its operations in an emergency, and Army and Navy field and fleet commanders drew up the plans to carry out these operations. In some cases, the early war plans were little more than abstract exercises and bore little relation to actual events. But in the case of Japan, the ORANGE plans were kept under constant review and revised frequently to accord with changes in the international scene.

The first serious examination of plans to resist a Japanese attack came in the summer of 1907. At that time tension between the United States and Japan, which had begun with the Japanese victory over Russia in 1905 and the San Francisco School Board segregation order in 1906, reached the proportions of a war scare. War seemed imminent and the protection of American interests in the Far East, especially of the newly

[2] The board initially had no staff and its membership was by individual appointment rather than by office. In 1919, is was reorganized, given a Joint Planning Committee which functioned as a working group, and its membership reduced to six—the chiefs of the services, their deputies, and the chiefs of the two War Plans Divisions.

[3] Ltr, Chaffee to Secy War, 22 Apr 04; Mins, JB Mtgs, 23 May and 24 Jun 04; Ltr, Brig Gen Tasker H. Bliss to Secy JB, 10 Jun 04, all in JB 325 (1903–1905), ser. 16.

acquired Philippine Islands, became an urgent problem. On 18 June 1907, in response to an inquiry from President Theodore Roosevelt, the Joint Board recommended that the fleet be sent to the Orient as soon as possible and that Army and Navy forces in the Philippines be immediately deployed in such a manner as to protect the naval station at Subic Bay. Because of Japan's strength, the Joint Board stated, "The United States would be compelled . . . to take a defensive attitude in the Pacific and maintain that attitude until reinforcements could be sent. . . . "[4] This view, adopted by necessity in 1907, became finally the keystone of America's strategy in the Pacific and the basis of all planning for a war against Japan.

The crisis of the summer of 1907, though it passed without incident, brought into sharp focus two weaknesses of America's position in the Pacific: the need for a major naval base in the area and the fact that the Philippine Islands could not be held except at great expense and with a large force. The islands, wrote Roosevelt at the height of the crisis, "form our heel of Achilles. . . . I would rather see this nation fight all her life than to see her give them up to Japan or to any other nation under duress."[5]

The question of naval bases was debated by the Joint Board and by Congressional committees during the months that followed. Two questions had to be decided: first, whether America's major

VIEW FROM MANILA BAY, *showing Corregidor Island at center with Caballo Island at lower left and a portion of Bataan Peninsula at upper right.*

base in the Pacific should be located in the Philippines or Hawaii; and second, whether the Philippines base should be in Subic Bay or Manila Bay. Though strong representation was made — especially by the Army — for locating the major base in the Philippine Islands, the Joint Board in January 1908 selected Pearl Harbor. The Hawaiian base, the board pointed out, was not designed to defend the Hawaiian Islands alone but to provide "a buffer of defense" for the entire Pacific coast and to lay the basis for American naval supremacy in the Pacific. In May of that year Congress authorized construction of the Pearl Harbor base and appropriated $1,000,000 for the purpose. This step, the House Naval Affairs Committee believed, would constitute in the future "one of the strongest factors in the prevention of

[4] A summary of the Joint Board's views is contained in Ltr, Maj Gen Fred C. Ainsworth, TAG, to Maj Gen Leonard Wood, CG Philippines Div, 6 Jul 07, AG 1260092, National Archives.

[5] Ltr, Roosevelt to Taft, 21 Aug 07, quoted by Henry F. Pringle, *Theodore Roosevelt* (New York: Harcourt, Brace and Company, 1931), pp. 408–09.

war with any powers in the Far East." [6]

Though the decision had been made to locate America's Pacific bastion in Hawaii, it was still necessary to provide for the defense of the Philippines, 5,000 miles away. A naval repair station and a secondary fleet base would have to be constructed in the islands, but there was strong disagreement even on this question. The Navy favored Subic Bay but the Army asserted that a base there would be indefensible against land attack and that Manila Bay, for a variety of reasons, should be selected. The Joint Board finally decided in favor of Cavite, on the south shore of Manila Bay, and the Army adopted a plan to concentrate its defenses in and around that bay on the islands in its narrow neck—Corregidor, Caballo, El Fraile, and Carabao—thus screening the naval base as well as the capital and chief city of the islands. It was this concept—the defense of the Manila Bay area and the fortification of Corregidor and its neighboring islands—that guided American planners until the outbreak of war in 1941.[7]

But no system of fortifications could guarantee the defense of the islands. The essential thing, as Maj. Gen. Leonard Wood pointed out at the time, was a strong fleet based in the Philippines. "Once sea control is lost," he asserted, "the enemy can move troops in force and the question then becomes one of time." [8] Congress and the Joint Board,

by concentrating fleet facilities in Hawaii, had, in effect, relegated the Philippines to a secondary place in strategic plans for the Pacific and made all hopes for its defense dependent upon the security of Hawaii and the ability of the fleet to move westward from Pearl Harbor.

The ORANGE Plan

The first ORANGE plans were hardly plans at all but rather statements of principles, which, it was hoped, could be followed in the event of war with Japan. By 1913, the strategic principles of the plan had been exhaustively studied and were well understood. In case of war with Japan, it was assumed that the Philippines would be the enemy's first objective. Defense of the islands was recognized as dependent on the Battle Fleet, which, on outbreak of war, would have to make its way from the Caribbean area around the Cape — the Panama Canal was not yet completed—and then across the wide Pacific. Along the way the fleet would have to secure its line of communication, using the incomplete base at Pearl Harbor and the undeveloped harbor at Guam. Once the fleet was established in Philippine waters, it could relieve the defenders, who presumably would have held on during this period, variously estimated at three and four months. Thereafter, Army forces, reinforced by a steady stream of men and supplies, could take the offensive on the ground while the Navy contested for control of the western Pacific.[9]

[6] *House Reports*, No. 1385, 60th Cong., 1st sess., 4 Apr 08, pp. 2–3.

[7] Cable, Wood to Ainsworth, 1 Nov 07; Ltrs, Lt Col Frederic V. Abbot and Capt Stanley D. Embick to Wood, 27 Nov 07, both in AG 1260092, National Archives; Memos, JB for Secys War and Navy, 31 Jan and 5 Mar 08, JB 325.

[8] Ltr, Wood to Ainsworth, 23 Dec 07, AG 1260092, National Archives.

[9] Memo, Brig Gen Montgomery M. Macomb, Chief, War College Div, for Chief of Staff, 13 Apr 15, sub: Plan for War With Japan, WCD 7820–16; Army Plan in Case of War in the Pacific Before the Panama Canal Is Completed, 19 May 13, approved by CofS, 20 May 13, by order of Secy War, WCD 7820–13.

During World War I planning for war in the Pacific was discontinued except for a brief flurry of activity in 1916, when Japanese vessels appeared off the Philippine Islands. And in the postwar period, the planners faced a situation considerably different from that of the earlier years. Then, Germany had been the chief threat to the peace in Europe. Now, with Germany in defeat and Russia in the throes of revolution, only Great Britain was in a position to engage the United States in war with any prospect of success. But economically and financially, England was in no condition for another conflict and there was no sentiment for war on either side of the Atlantic.

The situation in the Pacific and Far East was different. Between Japan and the United States there were a number of unresolved differences and a reservoir of misunderstanding and ill will that made the possibility of conflict in that area much more likely than in the Atlantic. Moreover, Japan's position had been greatly strengthened as a result of the war and the treaties that followed. In the view of the planners, the most probable enemy in the foreseeable future was Japan. Thus, U.S. strategic thought in the years from 1919 to 1938 was largely concentrated on the problems presented by a conflict arising out of Japanese aggression against American interests or territory in the Far East.

The strategic position of the United States in the Far East was altered fundamentally by World War I. Military aviation had proved itself during the war and though its enormous potentialities for naval warfare were not yet fully appreciated it was still a factor to be considered. Of more immediate impor-

tance was the transfer to Japan of the German islands in the Central Pacific. President Wilson had opposed this move at Versailles, arguing that it would place Japan astride the U.S. line of communications and make the defense of the Philippines virtually impossible. But Wilson had been overruled by the other Allied leaders, and Japan had acquired the islands under a mandate from the League of Nations which prohibited their fortification. "At one time," wrote Capt. Harry E. Yarnell, one of the Navy planners, "it was the plan of the Navy Department to send a fleet to the Philippines on the outbreak of war. I am sure that this would not be done at the present time . . . it seems certain that in the course of time the Philippines and whatever forces we may have there will be captured." [10]

Japan's position was further strengthened during these years by the agreements reached at the Washington Conference of 1921–22. In the Five-Power Naval Treaty concluded in February 1922, Japan accepted the short end of the 5:5:3 ratio in capital ships in return for a promise from the other powers that they would preserve the *status quo* with regard to their bases in the western Pacific. This meant, in effect, that the United States would refrain from further fortifying its bases in the Philippines, Guam, the Aleutians, and other islands west of Hawaii, and that Great Britain would do the same in its possessions. The net result of this bargain was to give Japan a strong advantage over the Western Powers in the Pacific, for the agreement virtually removed the threat

---

[10] Ltr, Yarnell to Col John McA. Palmer, 25 Apr 19, JB 325, ser. 28 C.

WASHINGTON CONFERENCE, 1921–22. *Seated at table, from left: Prince Iyesato Tokugawa (Japan), Jules Jusserand (France), Albert Sarraut (France), René Viviani (France), Aristide Briand (France), Oscar W. Underwood (U.S.), Elihu Root (U.S.), Henry Cabot Lodge (U.S.), Charles Evans Hughes (U.S.), Lord A. J. Balfour (Britain), Lord Lee of Fareham (Britain), Sir Aukland Geddes (Britain), Sir Robert Borden (Canada), G. F. Pearce (Australia), Sir John Salmond (New Zealand), and Srinivasa Sastri (India).*

posed by the Philippines, Guam, and Hong Kong. The British still had Singapore, but the United States had lost the opportunity to develop adequate base facilities in the far Pacific. With that loss, wrote Capt. Dudley W. Knox, went all chances of defending the Philippines and providing a military sanction for American policy.[11]

[11] Capt Dudley W. Knox (USN), *The Eclipse of American Sea Power* (New York: American Army & Navy Journal, Inc., 1922), pp. 135–36.

The Washington Conference brought the Philippines to the fore in a way apparently neither intended nor foreseen. Of the bases available for operations in the western Pacific they alone had facilities capable of supporting a naval force large enough to challenge Japanese supremacy in that region. Guam, which up to this time had been regarded as a more desirable base site than the Philippines but which had not yet been developed, now became of secondary importance. The Aleutians and Samoa were too remote to serve the purpose. The Philippines were, therefore, in the words of the recently formed Planning Committee, set up in 1919 to assist the Joint Board, "our most valuable strategic possession in the Western Pacific." So long as the Five-Power Naval Treaty remained in effect, they argued, the islands' fleet facilities and coastal defenses should be maintained to the extent permitted. At the same time, the Philippine garrison should be so strengthened, urged the planners, as to make the capture of the islands by any enemy "a costly major operation." [12]

By now the situation in the Pacific had so invalidated the assumption of earlier planning for a war with Japan as to require a complete review of strategy and the preparation of new plans. This need was emphasized by the Army planners when they submitted to the Joint Planning Committee in December 1921 a "Preliminary Estimate of the Situation," together with a recommendation for a new joint Army-Navy ORANGE plan. "It may safely be assumed," they declared, "that Japan is the most probable enemy." That nation's policy of expansion and its evident intention to secure a dominant position in the Far East, argued the Army planners, were bound to come into conflict sooner or later with American interests and policy in that region. Unless either or both countries showed some disposition to give way, a contingency the planners regarded as unlikely, this conflict of interests would lead ultimately to war. [13]

The Navy planners had by this time completed their own estimate of the situation in the Pacific. Their conclusion, submitted at the end of July 1922, was that the Japanese could, if they wished, take both the Philippines and Guam before the U.S. Fleet could reach the western Pacific. The role of the Philippine garrison, as the Navy planners saw it, would be to hold out as long as possible and to make the operation as costly as possible for the enemy. What would happen to the garrison thereafter the planners did not specify, but they hoped that the sacrifice of American forces would be justified by the damage done to the enemy. [14]

But Leonard Wood, Governor-General of the Philippines, disagreed strongly with the Navy estimate. A former Chief of Staff of the U.S. Army and commander of the Philippine Department, with influential friends in Washington, his word carried considerable weight. In his view, the "assumption on the part of the Navy that in case of war with Japan the Philippine Islands could not be defended, must be abandoned, and a long war waged to take them back and re-establish ourselves in the Far East" was a fatal error. Such a course, he told the Secretary of War with feeling, would damage the prestige of the United States in the eyes of the world, would have a "disintegrating and demoralizing effect upon our people," and could end only in national dishonor. "I feel sure," General Wood told the Secretary, "that when you and the President realize the effect of this on our future . . . , steps will be taken at once to see that the Army and Navy assume that the Philip-

---

[12] Ltr, JPC to JB, 13 Apr 22, sub: Defense of Phil, JB 303, ser. 179.
[13] Preliminary Estimate of the Situation, War Plan ORANGE, 3 Dec 21, WPD 368.

[14] Ltr, Secy War to CG Phil Dept, 27 Jul 22, cited in Ltr, Wood to Secy War, 5 Feb 23, JB 305, ser. 209.

pine Islands must not only be absolutely defended but succored by the Fleet." And in words reminiscent of a later day he warned the Secretary that the American people would not stand for a policy that required "abandonment of American posts, American soldiers, an American fleet, American citizens in the Far East. . . ." [15]

Just how the fleet would come to the rescue of the Philippines in the event of war, Governor Wood did not specify, but he felt sure the planners in Washington could solve the problem. They had undoubtedly reached their conclusions, he observed sympathetically, when faced by seemingly impossible tasks. But American ingenuity was equal to any task, declared General Wood, and the planners "should be directed to keep alive that problem and work it out to show just what could be done to make it possible." And as a starting point, he recommended that the Navy take for its mission: "First, the relief of the Philippines and the establishment of its base in Manila as an essential preliminary to the accomplishment of our main objective. . . . Second, the destruction of the Japanese fleet." [16] That the Navy would agree to so flagrant a violation of the first canon of naval strategy, that the primary mission of a fleet was always to destroy the enemy fleet, was, to say the least, doubtful.

Whether as a result of Governor Wood's intervention or for other reasons, the final estimate presented to the Joint Board as a basis for the preparation of a war plan carefully skirted the question of the abandonment of the Philippines. A war with Japan, the Joint Planners now

declared, would be primarily naval in character and would require offensive sea and air operations against Japanese naval forces and vital sea communications. The first concern of the Army and Navy in such a war, therefore, would be "to establish at the earliest possible date American sea power in the Western Pacific in strength superior to that of Japan." To accomplish this, the United States would require a base in that area capable of serving the entire U.S. Fleet. Since the only base west of Pearl Harbor large enough for this purpose was in Manila Bay, it would be essential, said the planners, to hold the bay in case of war and be ready to rush reinforcements, under naval protection, to the islands in time to prevent their capture. An additional mission recommended by the planners was the early capture of bases in the Japanese-mandated islands along the line of communications to the Philippines. [17]

Within two weeks the Joint Board had taken action. On 7 July 1923, General of the Armies John J. Pershing, senior member of the board, noted the board's agreement with the study made by the planners and recommended to the Secretaries of War and Navy that it be approved as the basis for the preparation of a war plan. The Joint Board, Pershing told the Secretaries, had reached the following conclusions with regard to the Philippines:

1. That the islands were of great strategic value to the United States for they provided the best available bases for military and naval forces operating in defense of American interests in the Far East.

[15] Ltr, Wood to Secy War, 5 Feb 23, JB 305, ser. 209.
[16] Ibid.

[17] Memo, JPC to JB, 25 May 23, sub: Synopsis of the Joint Army and Navy Estimate of the ORANGE Situation, JB 325, ser. 207. See also General Board 425, ser. 1136, 26 Apr 23.

2. That their capture by Japan would seriously affect American prestige and make offensive operations in the western Pacific extremely difficult.

3. That the recapture of the islands would be a long and costly undertaking, requiring a far greater effort than timely measures for defense.

4. That the national interests and military necessity require that the Philippines be made as strong as possible in peacetime.[18]

With the Secretaries' approval, given three days later, work on Joint War Plan ORANGE moved forward rapidly. As a matter of fact, the planners had by this time already adopted the basic strategic concept to guide American forces in a war with Japan. Such a war, they foresaw, would be primarily naval in character. The United States, in their view, should take the offensive and engage in operations "directed toward the isolation and harassment of Japan." These operations they thought could be achieved by gaining control of Japan's vital sea communications and by offensive air and naval operations against Japan's naval forces and economic life. If these measures alone did not bring Japan to her knees, then the planners would take "such further action as may be required to win the war." The major role in a war fought as the planners envisaged it would be played by the Navy. To the Army would fall the vital task of holding the base in Manila Bay until the arrival of the fleet. Without it, the fleet would be unable to operate in Far Eastern waters.

The concept of "an offensive war, primarily naval" was firmly embodied in the plan finally evolved. From it stemmed the emphasis placed on sea power and a naval base in the Phillipines. The first concern of the United States in a war with Japan and the initial mission of the Army and Navy, declared the Joint Planners, would be to establish sea power in the western Pacific "in strength superior to that of Japan." This, they recognized, would require a "main outlying base" in that region. Manila Bay, it was acknowledged, best met the requirements for such a base and its retention would be essential in the event of hostilities. Thus, the primary mission of the Philippine Department in the ORANGE plan was to hold Manila Bay.[19]

One notable aspect of the ORANGE plan was its provision for a unified command and a joint staff. Normal practice dictated separate Army and Navy commanders, acting under the principle of co-operation in joint operations. But the planners had come to the conclusion that such operations required "that all Army and Navy forces . . . form one command and that its commander have the whole responsibility and full power."[20] They therefore included in the plan provision for a single commander, to be designated by the President and to have full power commensurate with his responsibility.

In making this proposal the planners were far ahead of their time. Neither of the services was ready to operate in this way and there was as yet no doctrine or set of principles to guide commanders with such wide authority. The Joint Board, therefore, though it accepted without question most of the provisions of the ORANGE plan submitted by the Joint Planning Committee, returned

---

[18] Memo, Pershing to Secy War, 7 Jul 23, sub: Defense of Phil, JB 305, ser. 208. A similar memorandum went to the Secretary of the Navy.

[19] Draft, Joint Army-Navy Basic War Plan ORANGE, 12 Mar 24, JB 325, ser. 228.

[20] *Ibid.*

that portion dealing with command. The planners, the board instructed, were to eliminate the objectionable paragraphs.[21]

Surprisingly enough, the planners balked at these instructions and tried once more to convince their superiors of the necessity for unity of command. The plan, they pointed out, was the product of over three years of intensive study during which the problem of command in joint operations had been considered carefully and from every viewpoint. On the basis of their exhaustive study of the subject, the planners told the Joint Board, they could not recommend that operations on so large a scale and of such grave importance as those contemplated in the ORANGE plan "could be entrusted to co-operation alone." [22]

This stand availed the committee little for the Joint Board returned the plan again, this time with a more strongly worded injunction to remove the offending references to unity of command.[23] The planners had no choice now but to make the required changes. Striking out all references to unity of command and a supreme commander and substituting the familiar formulas of "mutual co-operation" and "paramount interest," they resubmitted the plan on 16 July. This the board accepted and on its recommendation the Secretary of War and the Secretary of the Navy gave their formal approval.[24]

[21] Ltr, Secy JB to JPC, 7 Jun 24, JB 325, ser. 228.
[22] Ltr, Col John L. De Witt, and Capt William H. Standley (USN) to JB, 20 Jun 24, sub: Joint Army-Navy Basic War Plan ORANGE, JB 325, ser. 228.
[23] Memo, Secy JB to JPC, 10 Jul 24, sub: Joint Army-Navy War Plan ORANGE, JB 325, ser. 228.
[24] Ltrs, Col Walter Krueger and Standley, 16 Jul 24; Rear Adm Edward W. Eberle, JB to Secy War, 15 Aug 24, sub: Joint Army-Navy Basic War Plan ORANGE, JB 325, ser. 228.

The final approval of War Plan ORANGE in September 1924 gave the United States for the first time since the end of World War I a broad outline of operations and objectives in the event of war with Japan. But the plan was really more a statement of hopes than a realistic appraisal of what could be done. To have carried out such a plan in 1925 was far beyond the capabilities of either service. The entire military establishment in the Philippines did not then number more than 15,000 men. The 50,000 men who, according to the plan, were to sail for the Philippines from the west coast on the outbreak of war, represented more than one third the total strength of the Army. Moreover, naval facilities in Manila Bay were entirely inadequate to support the fleet. The station at Cavite along the south shore of the bay had been largely neglected by the Navy and the facilities at Olongapo in Subic Bay dated from the early years of the century. Neither was capable of providing more than minor repairs. Only at Pearl Harbor, 5,000 miles to the east, was there a base even partially capable of servicing the major surface units of the Battle Fleet.

The advantages of distance and location, which gave the Philippines their strategic importance, were all on the side of the Japanese. Japan's southernmost naval bases were less than 1,500 miles from the Philippines, and Formosa was only half that distance away. An expeditionary force from Japan could reach Manila in three days; one mounted from Formosa on the Ryukyus could make the journey in a much shorter time. An American force, even assuming it reached the Philippines safely in record time, would require several weeks for the journey. By that time, the Japanese flag might be waving over Manila and the U.S. Fleet with its bunkers depleted would be "forced to fight under the most disadvantageous conditions or to beat an ignominious retreat."[25]

RED and RED-ORANGE

The ORANGE plan was based on a situation that never came to pass, that is, a war between the United States and Japan alone. Neither side, the planners assumed, would have allies or attack the territory of a third power. The ORANGE war, as envisaged by the planners, was a war that was to be fought entirely in the Pacific, with the decisive action to take place in the waters off the Asiatic coast.

These assumptions by the military strategists of the Army and Navy were entirely justified by the existing international situation and reflected a reasonable estimate of the most probable threat to American interests, an estimate that was shared by most responsible officials during these years. But the planners did not, indeed could not, ignore other possibilities, no matter how remote. Thus, during the same years in which they labored on ORANGE, the Joint Board Planners considered a variety of other contingencies that might require the use of American military forces. The most serious if not the most likely of these was a war with Great Britain alone (RED) arising from commercial rivalry between the two nations, or with Great Britain and Japan (RED-ORANGE). The latter contingency was conceded by all

to present the gravest threat to American security, one that would require a full-scale mobilization and the greatest military effort.

In their study of these two contingencies the military planners came to grips with strategic problems quite different from those presented by ORANGE. A war with Japan would be primarily a naval war fought in the Pacific. So far as anyone could foresee, there would be no requirement for large ground armies. There was a possibility, of course, that Japan would attack the Panama Canal, Hawaii, and even the west coast, but no real danger that Japan could seize and occupy any of these places. But in the unlikely event of a conflict between Great Britain and the United States, there was a real possibility of invasion of the United States as well as attacks against the Canal and American interests in the Caribbean area. In such a war, the major threat clearly would lie in the Atlantic. Plans developed to meet this remote danger, in contrast to ORANGE, called for the immediate deployment of the bulk of the U.S. Fleet to the Atlantic and large-scale ground operations, defensive in nature, to deprive the enemy of bases in the Western Hemisphere. As in ORANGE, it was assumed that neither side would have allies among the great powers of Europe and Asia, and no plans were made for an invasion of the enemy's homeland by an American expeditionary force. This was to be a limited war in which the United States would adopt a strategic defensive with the object of frustrating the enemy's assumed objective in opening hostilities.

The problems presented by a RED-ORANGE coalition, though highly theoretical, were more complicated. Here

---

[25] Hector Bywater, *Sea Power in the Pacific: A Study of the American-Japanese Naval Problem* (Boston: Houghton Mifflin Company, 1921), pp. 256–57.

the American strategists had to face all the possibilities of an ORANGE and a RED war—seizure of American possessions in the western Pacific, violation of the Monroe Doctrine, attacks on the Panama Canal, Hawaii, and other places, and, finally, the invasion of the United States itself. Basically, the problem was to prepare for a war in both oceans against the two great naval powers, Great Britain and Japan.

As the planners viewed this problem, the strategic choices open to the United States were limited. Certainly the United States did not have the naval strength to conduct offensive operations simultaneously in both the Atlantic and Pacific Oceans; it must adopt a strategic defensive on both fronts or else assume the strategic offensive in one theater while standing on the defensive in the other. The recommended solution to this problem—and it was only a recommended solution, for no joint war plan was ever adopted—was "to concentrate on obtaining a favorable decision" in the Atlantic and to stand on the defensive in the Pacific with minimum forces. This solution was based on the assumption that since the Atlantic enemy was the stronger and since the vital areas of the United States were located in the northeast, the main effort of the hostile coalition would be made there. For this reason, the initial effort of the United States, the planners argued, should be in the Atlantic.

A strategic offensive-defensive in a two-front war, American strategists recognized, entailed serious disadvantages. It gave the hostile coalition freedom of action to attack at points of its own choosing, compelled the United States to be prepared to meet attacks practically everywhere, exposed all U.S. overseas possessions to capture, and imposed on the American people a restraint inconsistent with their traditions and spirit. Also, it involved serious and humiliating defeats in the Pacific during the first phase of the war and the almost certain loss of outlying possessions in that region.

But the strategic offensive-defensive had definite advantages. It enabled the United States to conduct operations in close proximity to its home bases and to force the enemy to fight at great distance from his own home bases at the end of a long line of communications. Moreover, the forces raised in the process of producing a favorable decision in the Atlantic would give the United States such a superiority that Japan might well negotiate rather than fight the United States alone. "It is not unreasonable to hope," the planners observed, "that the situation at the end of the struggle with RED may be such as to induce ORANGE to yield rather than face a war carried to the Western Pacific." [26]

The strategic concept adopted determined the missions, theaters of operation, and major tasks of U.S. forces. The Navy's main task, in the event of a simultaneous attack in both oceans would be to gain control of the North Atlantic and to cut the enemy's line of communications to possible bases in the New World, in Canada and the Caribbean; the Army's task would be to capture these bases, thus denying Britain the opportunity to launch attacks against the United States. The principal theater of

[26] Proposed Joint Estimate and Plan—RED-ORANGE, prepared in WPD (Army) and approved by CofS, 3 June 1930, as basis for joint plan, G–3 Obsolete Plans Reg Doc 245–C. Additional material on RED-ORANGE may be found in the same file, 245–A through F and in WPD 3202. No joint plan was ever approved.

operations in a RED-ORANGE war, assuming Canada would side with Britain, would be, for the Navy, the Western North Atlantic, the Caribbean and West Indian waters; for the Army, those areas that could be used by RED or ORANGE to launch an invasion. Operations in the main theater would eventually bring about the defeat of enemy forces in North America, the economic exhaustion but not the total defeat of Great Britain, and finally a negotiated peace with Japan on terms favorable to the United States.

This plan for a RED-ORANGE war was admittedly unrealistic in terms of the international situation during the 1920's and 1930's. The military planners knew this as well as and better than most and often noted this fact in the draft plans they wrote.[27] But as a strategic exercise it was of great value, for it forced the military planners to consider seriously the problems presented by a war in which the United States would have to fight simultaneously in the Atlantic and Pacific Oceans. In an era when most war planning was focused on the Pacific and when Japan seemed the most likely enemy, this experience may have seemed irrelevant. But it was to prove immensely useful in the plans developed for World War II.

Strategic Dilemma

Between 1924 and 1938 the ORANGE plan was revised many times in response to changes in the international situation,

the mood of Congress, and military necessity. And with each change the gap between American commitment to the defense of the Philippines and the forces the United States was willing to commit to this defense became wider. By 1938 the dichotomy between national policy and military strategy in the Far East had made the task of the planners charged with the defense of America's position in that region all but impossible.

The first revision of ORANGE came in November 1926 and was designed to correct ambiguities in the original plan and to clear up the confusion in regard to timing and forces. This was done by designating M-day, the date on which a general mobilization would go into effect, as the starting point for the plan. On that day, the actions required to implement the plan would begin, and from that day were measured the phases specified in the plan.

The 1926 plan clearly specified Hawaii as the point of assembly for troops and supplies. Convoys were to be formed there for the journey westward. But the assumption of the earlier plan that reinforcements would sail directly to the Philippines—a doubtful assumption—was dropped in the 1926 plan. The Marshall, Caroline, and Mariana Islands, it was recognized, would have to be brought under American control first, and bases established in one or more of these island groups to guard the line of communications.[28]

---

[27] In 1923, the Army draft of RED-ORANGE started with the statement, "Under existing conditions a coalition of RED and ORANGE is unlikely," and twelve years later the Director of Naval Intelligence, commenting on another draft plan, stated that a RED-ORANGE combination was "highly improbable" in the next decade, if at all. Army Draft RED-ORANGE, 1923,

Reg Doc 245–F; Ltr, Dir ONI to Dir WPD, 27 Jun 35, sub: Jt Estimate of Situation, RED-ORANGE, copy in WPD 3202. By 1935, planning for such a war had virtually ended.

[28] Joint Army-Navy Basic War Plan ORANGE, 6 Oct 26; Ltr, JPC to JB, 11 Oct 26, sub: Revision of Plan ORANGE; Mins, JB Mtg, 14 Oct 26, all in JB 325, ser. 280.

Not satisfied with these changes, the planners proposed additional revisions in November of 1926, with the result that the Joint Board directed the preparation of an entirely new plan.[29] A difference of opinion became apparent almost immediately as the planners searched for a strategic formula that would produce victory in a war with Japan. One group argued for a strategic offensive in the western Pacific as the only way to exert sufficient pressure on Japan to win the war, and the other for a strategic defense, that is, the retention of the bulk of America's naval strength east of Hawaii, as the preferable course.

The advocates of the defensive hoped to gain victory over Japan by economic pressure and raids on Japanese commerce, but conceded that this strategy would expose the Philippines, Guam, and Samoa to attack and would probably cut off trade to the Far East. The strength of a defensive strategy, it was argued, lay in the fact that it would make the west coast and Hawaii "impregnable against attack," would cause little interference in the economy of the United States, "and would still permit our government to employ the political and industrial power and the great wealth of the country in an attempt to cut off Japanese world markets to both export and import."[30] Faced with this choice of strategies, the Joint Board elected the former and on 26 January 1928 directed the planners to prepare a plan based on the concept of a strategic offensive.[31]

Within three months, the new plan was completed. Though it retained the original concept of a naval advance across the Pacific, it allowed more time to assemble reinforcements and paid more attention to securing the line of communications. Forces in the Philippines were assigned the primary mission of holding the entrance to Manila Bay (Bataan and Corregidor), and the secondary mission of holding the bay area "as long as consistent with the successful accomplishment of the primary mission."[32]

That there was even then little expectation that the Philippines could be held is evident in the Army's estimate of the enemy's capacities as compared to its own. Japan, it noted, could raise and transport to the Philippines a force of 300,000 men in 30 days. Within 7 days of an attack, it could have 50,000 to 60,000 men off Luzon, within 15 another 100,000. The Americans would have to meet this attack with the forces then present in the Philippines: 11,000 troops of which 7,000 were Filipinos, a native constabulary numbering about 6,000 men, and an air component consisting of nine bombers and eleven pursuit planes. So great a discrepancy made any hope for a successful defense mere illusion. The best that could be hoped for under such circumstances was a delaying action that might buy enough time for the fleet to arrive with reinforcements.

The move to grant the Philippines their independence, which was finding increasing support among the American people and in Congress in the early

---

[29] Ltr, JPC to JB, 26 Nov 26, sub: Revision of ORANGE, JB 325, ser. 280.

[30] Ltr, JPC to JB, 9 Jan 28, sub: Joint Estimate of Situation Blue-ORANGE, and Joint Army-Navy War Plan ORANGE, JB 325, ser. 280.

[31] Memo, JB for JPC, 26 Jan 28, sub: Joint Army-Navy Basic War Plan ORANGE, JB 325, ser. 280.

[32] Joint Basic War Plan ORANGE, 24 Apr 28, JB 325, ser. 280. Other papers relating to the plan are in the same file. The plan was approved by the Secretary of the Navy on 19 June 1928, and by the Secretary of War on 10 July.

1930's, complicated enormously the problems of Pacific strategy and precipitated a number of reviews and studies by the planners of the effect of such a step. The conclusion of these studies was that the islands represented a powerful military asset to the United States and that their retention was necessary to support American policy in the Far East. The withdrawal of the United States from these islands, asserted the joint planners, would upset the balance of power in the Far East, give Japan a free hand in the western Pacific, and force the abandonment of the open-door policy. Though inadequately defended and far removed from the nearest American base in Hawaii, the Philippines were, in the opinion of the Washington planners, of great strategic importance, indispensable in a war against Japan. "We should relinquish our bases," they concluded, "only when we are prepared to relinquish our position as a nation of major influence in the affairs of Asia and the Western Pacific." [33]

From the Philippines came a strong dissenting voice. To the officers stationed in the islands, the plan to hold out against a powerful Japanese attack until reinforcements arrived seemed nothing less than self-delusion. "To carry out the present ORANGE plan," wrote the commander of the Corregidor defenses, "with its provisions for the early dispatch of our fleet to Philippine waters, would be literally an act of madness." [34] Corregidor, he admitted, could probably hold out for about a year and thus deny Japan

the use of Manila Bay. But the enemy could reach Manila from the land side and deny the U.S. Fleet a sheltered harbor in which to overhaul and repair major fleet units. It would be necessary, therefore, for the fleet to seize and develop bases as it moved across the Pacific, and this process, he estimated, would take two or three years. Certainly the small garrison in the Philippines could not resist that long. Unless the American people were willing to spend large sums for the defense of the islands—and there was in 1933 not the slightest hope that they would—the Corregidor commander and his superior, the commander of the Philippine Department, both advised that the United States arrange for the neutralization of the Philippines, withdraw its forces from the Far East, and adopt the line Alaska-Oahu-Panama as the "strategic peacetime frontier in the Pacific."

The planners in Washington, whatever their personal convictions may have been, did not accept this view. Indeed, they could not, for national policy dictated that the Philippines must be defended, no matter how hopeless the assignment seemed to those responsible for its defense. The withdrawal of United States forces from the Philippines and from China was a political question and the decision rested with the President and Congress.

From the military point of view, the Army planners in Washington found the assumptions of the Philippine commanders unwarranted. The field commanders, they maintained, had stressed the concept of an offensive in the western Pacific, but the plan did not require the immediate advance of the fleet westward "unless the situation existing . . . justifies such

---

[33] Ltr, JPC to JB, sub: Independence of Phil Is, 28 Feb 34, JB 305, ser. 525. See also JB 305, ser. 499 for earlier views.

[34] Memo, Brig Gen Stanley D. Embick for CG Phil Dept, 19 Apr 33, sub: Mil Policy of U.S. in Phil Is, and 1st Ind, Hq Phil Dept, 25 Apr 33, WPD 3251–15.

action." [35] Instead, the fleet would advance step by step through the mandates, taking such islands as it needed and constructing advance bases before moving on. It was just this course, the Army planners pointed out, that the Navy now favored.

To the Washington experts the idea that the Philippines could be neutralized by agreement with other powers was completely unrealistic. They thought it "highly improbable of attainment," at least so long as the United States retained military and naval bases in the islands. When the Philippines became fully independent, it might be possible to follow this course, provided that the United States withdrew all of its forces.

The Army planners in Washington dismissed also the fear that Japan would attack the United States in the near future. In their view, Japan was too dependent upon trade with the United States to risk a war that would place all her gains on the Asiatic mainland in jeopardy. "Only by adoption on the part of the United States of a policy of armed intervention," they concluded, "would ORANGE be justified in bringing on a war." [36]

In March 1934, when the Tydings-McDuffie act granting the Philippines their independence by 1946 was passed, the Army and Navy commanders in the Philippines reopened the question of American strategy in the Far East. In a joint letter to their respective chiefs the two commanders asserted that, in view of the reductions in military and naval strength in the Philippines, they could

not carry out their missions under the ORANGE plan. The "spectacular rise" of Japan as a military power, together with the improvement of military aviation, and increases in the speed and armament of surface vessels, nullified, in their judgment, the value of Manila Bay as a base. The time had come, it seemed to them, to make a decision on American policy. If the United States intended to defend the islands—and their defense was basic to the ORANGE plan—even after they were granted independence, then naval and land forces would have to be increased, those treaties prohibiting its fortification abrogated, and a base adequate for maintaining the fleet constructed. If the United States intended to withdraw and relinquish its control over the Philippines and responsibility for their defense, then, said the two commanders, only such American forces as would be needed to maintain order during the transition period should be kept in the islands. [37]

The decision of the Joint Board settled none of the questions raised by the Asiatic Fleet and Philippine Department commanders. National policy was not within its province and it could only assert that the Philippines would be defended and that reinforcements would be forthcoming, as planned in ORANGE, in the event of war. The board was fortified in this view by the Army planners who felt that the existing force in the Philippines was large enough to give "reasonable assurance" that Manila Bay could be held, and by the belief of the naval planners that reinforcements could

[35] Memo, Chief, WPD for CofS, 12 Jun 33, sub: Mil Policy of U.S. in Phil Is, WPD 3251–15.
[36] Ibid.

[37] Ltr, CinC Asiatic Fleet and CG Phil Dept to CNO and CofS, 1 Mar 34, sub: Inadequacy of Present Mil and Naval Forces in Phil Area . . . , JB 325, ser. 533.

be convoyed across the Pacific in time to avert disaster.[38]

Hardly had this decision been made when the ORANGE plan came under scrutiny again. This time it was General Douglas MacArthur, then Chief of Staff, who called for its revision to bring it into conformity with the new mobilization plan and the 4-army organization of the field forces. These changes did not affect the basic concept of the plan, but during the discussions the Navy planners proposed a new line of action, foreshadowed in 1928, calling for an advance in progressive stages across the Pacific through the mandated islands, seizing in turn the Marshalls and Carolines and developing there the bases needed to secure the line of communications to the western Pacific. The Marine and Army troops to carry out these operations were to sail from the west coast in echelons, the first leaving for the Marshalls twelve days after M-day. Incorporated into the 1935 revision of the ORANGE plan, this concept underscored the importance of holding Manila Bay to provide a base for the fleet when it finally fought its way through with reinforcements.[39]

Despite the careful plans to hold the Philippines in case of a Japanese attack, the view that the islands could not be held and that it would take several years to establish naval superiority in the western Pacific spread rapidly among the Army planners. Japan had revealed its expansionist aims in Manchuria and in China, had placed a veil of secrecy over the mandated islands, withdrawn from the League of Nations and from the naval limitations agreements of 1922 and 1930, and was rapidly building up its military strength and naval forces. The situation in Europe was threatening, too, with Hitler and Mussolini beginning to test their new found strength. Under the circumstances, the Philippine Islands might well prove a liability, draining off the forces needed to defend Hawaii, the Panama Canal, and the continental United States.

In recognition of the growing threat in Europe and the Far East, the Secretaries of the War and Navy Departments in the fall of 1935 called upon the Joint Board to re-examine America's military position in the Far East. At the same time, they asked Secretary of State Cordel Hull to designate a State Department representative to meet with the board. How seriously the Secretaries regarded the situation may be judged by their note to Hull. "The cumulative efforts of successive developments during the past two decades have so weakened our military position vis-à-vis Japan," they wrote, "that our position in the Far East is one that may result not only in our being forced into war but into a war that would have to be fought under conditions that might preclude its successful prosecution." [40]

The Secretaries' action set off another round of discussions over strategy that

---

[38] Memo, Brig Gen C. R. Kilbourne for Army Members, JPC, 1 May 34, sub: Mil Policy in Phil Is, WPD 3251–18; Ltr, JB to Secy War, 20 Jun 34, sub: Inadequacy of Present Mil and Naval Forces..., JB 325, ser. 533.

[39] Ltrs, MacArthur to JB, 18 Jun 35; JPC to JB, 23 Apr 35; JB to Secy War, 8 May 35, all titled Revision of Joint Army-Navy Basic War Plan ORANGE and filed in JB 325, ser. 546. The Secretaries of War and Navy approved the revised plan on 9 May 1935.

[40] Ltr, Actg Secy War and Secy Navy to Secy State, 26 Nov 35, JB 305, ser. 573. Stanley K. Hornbeck, Chief of the Division of Far Eastern Affairs, was appointed the State Department representative. Ltr, Hull to Woodring, 27 Nov 35, same file.

GENERAL MACARTHUR

ended in one more revision of ORANGE. The case for the Army planners was summarized by Brig. Gen. Stanley D. Embick, Chief of the War Plans Division and long associated with the Philippines and Pacific strategy. Reliance on a base that was inadequately defended, he observed, was to invite disaster. American strategy in the Pacific, he insisted, should concentrate on holding the strategic triangle, Alaska-Hawaii-Panama. Such a course would place the United States in an invulnerable position and permit its military and naval forces to conduct operations "in such a manner that will promise success instead of national disaster."[41]

The naval planners were of a different opinion. All their plans were based on

the use of the fleet in offensive operations west of Hawaii, and the acceptance of the strategic triangle would leave the Navy with little to do other than patrol the critical area and fend off an enemy attack.

These differences were fundamental and the planners, unable to reach agreement, submitted separate reports. The Army members recommended that, when the Philippines became independent, the United States should withdraw entirely from the islands and from China; the Navy members, that no decision on America's future military policy in the Far East should be made at this time but should await a complete re-examination of the ORANGE plan.

This was hardly an acceptable basis for decision by the Joint Board, and again they referred the problem to their planners. This time the planners agreed by avoiding the issue, and in May 1936 submitted a revision of ORANGE which restricted the mission of the Philippine garrison to holding the entrance to Manila Bay, that is, Corregidor and its neighboring islands. Up to that time it had been required to hold the Manila Bay area as long as possible. The naval concept of a progressive movement through the mandates remained unchanged.

Though the Army planners had failed to win their point, their efforts did result in a review of the Hawaiian defenses and to an emphasis on their importance in the revised ORANGE plan. The mission of the Hawaiian garrison was stated simply: to hold Oahu "as a main outlying naval base," and provision was made for a defense reserve for seventy days, the maximum time required for the fleet to reach Hawaiian waters. Prophetically,

[41]App. A to Memo initialed S.D.E., 2 Dec 35, sub: Mil Aspects of . . . Retention of U.S. of . . . Phil Is, JB 305, ser. 573.

the plan recognized the danger of a surprise raid and pointed out that a successful defense would depend "almost wholly upon our not being totally surprised by the enemy," and would "require an efficient intelligence service, not only in the Hawaiian Islands but elsewhere." [42]

It was abundantly clear by now that the Philippine garrison would not be able to hold out until such time—variously estimated at from two to three years—as the fleet could arrive with reinforcements. This fact was never explicitly stated but, significantly, the Army's 1936 ORANGE plan, unlike earlier plans, made no provision for reinforcements. The defense would have to be conducted by the peacetime garrison, a force of about 10,000 men, plus the Philippine Army then being organized by General MacArthur. [43]

The debate over Pacific and Far East strategy continued through 1936, when Japan joined Germany and Italy in the Anti-Comintern Pact, and into 1937. In the fall of that year, after Japan embarked on its war of aggression in China, the Joint Board again ordered a re-examination of existing plans, which it considered "unsound in general" and "wholly inapplicable" to the international situation. What it wanted from its planning committee was a new ORANGE plan that would provide for "a position of readiness" on the line Alaska-Hawaii-Panama —the so-called "strategic triangle." In addition, the planners were to make "exploratory studies and estimates" of the various courses of action to be followed after the position of readiness had been assumed. [44]

In less than two weeks the Joint Planning Committee reported its inability to reach an agreement. The Army members, reading their instructions literally, wanted to restrict themselves to the area specified by the board and draw up a plan, defensive in nature, which would provide for the security of the continental United States and the Pacific Ocean as far as Hawaii. A war plan, they reasoned, must take into account political and economic factors and it was impossible at this time to determine whether the United States would be willing to fight an unlimited war against Japan. With the European Axis clearly in mind they pointed out that political considerations might require limited action and purely defensive operations in the Pacific. Moreover, the forces available at the outbreak of war would hardly be adequate for assuming the defense of vital areas in the Western Hemisphere. To uncover these positions for an offensive in the far Pacific, the Army planners declared, would be foolhardy indeed. [45]

The Navy members of the Joint Planning Committee took the position that American strategy could not be limited to a purely defensive position of readiness but should aim at the defeat of the

[42] Memo, Krueger for CofS, etc, 14 Feb 36, sub: Mil and Naval Position in Far East, with Incls dated 6 Feb and 5 Mar 36, JB 305, ser. 573; Ltr, JB to Secy War, 19 May 36, sub: Revision of Joint Army and Navy Basic War Plan ORANGE, JB 325, ser. 570; Ltrs, JPC to JB 13 May 26, sub: US Forces, Hawaiian Is, and JB to Secy War, 19 May 36, same sub, JB 325, ser. 580; Ltr, JB to Secy War, 9 Dec 36, sub: Changes in ORANGE, JB 325, ser. 594.

[43] Army Strategical Plan ORANGE, 1936 Revision, JB 325, sers. 546 and 325. For MacArthur's plans to build a Philippine Army, see Louis Morton, *The Fall of the Philippines*, UNITED STATES ARMY IN WORLD WAR II (Washington, 1953), pp. 8–13.

[44] Memos, JB for JPC, 10 Nov 37, sub: Joint Basic War Plan ORANGE, JB 325, ser. 617; Embick to WPD, 3 Nov 37, same sub. AGO 225.

[45] Draft Memo, Krueger, 22 Nov 37, sub: Some Thoughts on Joint War Plans, AGO 225.

enemy. If it failed to do that, it was not, in the view of the naval planners, a realistic guide for the services in time of war.[46]

Once war began, the Navy members argued, production would be quickly increased to provide the means required for both the security of the continental United States and for offensive operations in the Pacific. While these forces were being assembled, the Navy was prepared to take the offensive beyond Hawaii into Japanese territory. Should the European Axis give aid to the enemy, the planners assumed that the United States would have allies to provide the assistance needed by the U.S. Fleet to maintain naval superiority over Japan and to permit the projection of American naval power into the Western Pacific. "The character, amount, and location of allied assistance," they added, "cannot be predicted."[47]

The separate reports submitted by the Army and Navy members of the Joint Planning Committee put the choice between the opposing strategies squarely up to the Joint Board. The board avoided this choice by issuing a new directive to the planners on 7 December 1937. Suggested by the Chief of Naval Operations, Admiral William D. Leahy, this directive attempted to compromise the differing interpretations of the Army and Navy planners, but gave the edge to the latter. The new plan, the board now specified, should have as its basic objective the defeat of Japan and should provide for "an initial temporary position

GENERAL EMBICK, *Chief, Army War Plans Division, 1935.*

in readiness" for the Pacific coast and the strategic triangle. This last, the board further directed, was to be the Army's job; the Navy's task would consist of "offensive operations against ORANGE armed forces and the interruption of ORANGE vital sea communications." Finally, the planners were to recommend the forces and materiel which would be required by each of the services to accomplish its mission in the new plan.[48]

Even under these revised instructions, the planners were unable to agree on the best way to protect American interests in the Pacific and Far East in the event of war with Japan. The Army planners, thinking possibly of the situation in Europe, wished to maintain a defense position east of the 180th meridian—the

---

[46] Ltrs, Army and Navy Members JPC to JB, 29 and 30 Nov 37, sub: Joint Basic War Plan ORANGE, JB 325, ser. 617. The Army plan is in Appendix A, the Navy's in Appendix B.

[47] *Ibid.*

[48] Directive, JB to JPC, 7 Dec 37, sub: Joint Basic War Plan ORANGE, JB 325, ser. 618.

outermost limits of the Hawaiian chain. Offensive operations to the west of that line, they believed, should be undertaken only when necessary and they only with the specific authorization of the President. Naval operations alone, they asserted, could not ensure the defeat of Japan and ultimately the maximum efforts of the two services would be required.

Throughout their version of the plan, the Army planners emphasized the defensive mission of the Army to defend the United States and its possessions. Though they did not exclude the Philippines, neither did they provide for augmenting the forces there as they did for American territory east of the 180th meridian. The defense of the Islands would have to be conducted by the forces already assigned plus whatever additional troops were available locally.[49]

The naval planners, still offensive-minded so far as the Pacific was concerned, emphasized in their version of the plan operations designed to bring about the defeat of Japan. Thus, they made the destruction of ORANGE forces the primary mission of joint and separate Army and Navy forces. Nor did they place any limits on operations in the western Pacific, merely repeating the time-honored formula that victory would be won by establishing "at the earliest practicable date, U.S. naval power in the western Pacific in strength superior to that of ORANGE and to operate offensively in that area."[50] This preference for the offensive was clearly reflected in his testimony to the Senate Naval Affairs Committee the following February when

Admiral Leahy asserted that "the only way that war, once begun, can be brought to a successful conclusion is by making the enemy want to stop fighting. . . . Prompt and effective injury to an enemy at a distance from our shores is the only correct strategy to be employed."[51]

Faced with another split report, the Joint Board turned over the task of working out a compromise to General Embick and Rear Adm. James O. Richardson. These two, after a month of discussion, finally submitted on 18 February 1938 a new ORANGE plan. This plan embodied the essential points of each of the services with the result that its provisions were sometimes less than clear. In return for the Army's removal of the proviso that operations west of the Hawaiian Islands would require Presidential authorization, the Navy took out its references to an offensive war, the destruction of the Japanese forces, and the early movement of the fleet into the western Pacific. The result was a broad statement of strategy calling for "military and economic pressure," increasing in severity until "the national objective," the defeat of Japan, was attained. Initial operations under this concept were to be primarily naval but would be coupled with measures required to ensure the security of the continental United States, Alaska, Oahu, and Panama.[52]

Though each of the services retreated from its original position, each won recognition of principles it held important.

[49] Ltr, JPC to JB, 27 Dec 37, sub: Joint War Plan ORANGE, JB 325, ser. 618.

[50] Ibid.

[51] Joint Committee on the Investigation of the Pearl Harbor Attack, 79th Cong., 1st sess., Hearings, pt. I, p. 294.

[52] Joint Basic War Plan ORANGE, 21 Feb 38, JB 325, ser. 618. The plan was approved by the Secretary of the Navy on 26 February and by the Secretary of War two days later.

The Navy retained its concept of a progressive advance across the Pacific, but avoided commitment on the time required for such a move — an essential point in any plan for the defense of the Philippines. The Army, on its side, gained recognition of the primary importance of the strategic triangle formed by Alaska, Oahu, and Panama to the defense of the United States. The earlier provision for the defense of Manila Bay was retained, but the omission of any reference to the reinforcement of the Philippine garrison or to the length of time it would take the fleet to advance across the Pacific was a tacit admission that the planners did not believe the position could be held.

A war with Japan, the ORANGE plan of 1938 assumed, would be preceded by a period of strained relations, during which the United States would have time to prepare for mobilization. No formal declaration of war was expected; when war came the planners expected it to come with a sudden surprise attack—an assumption that had been made in every ORANGE plan since the Russo-Japanese war. They thought, too, that American forces at the start of the war would be strong enough to permit naval operations west of Pearl Harbor, and that no assistance Japan could receive—presumably from Germany and Italy — would materially affect the balance of naval power in the Pacific.

On the outbreak of a war, the United States would first assume a position of readiness to meet all emergencies that might arise, a point the Army planners had insisted upon. During this initial period, the Army and Navy would place priority on such measures as were required to defend the west coast, the strategic triangle, the coastal defenses of the United States, and oversea possessions. At the same time, the Navy would make preparations, in co-operation with the Army, to open the offensive as soon as possible.

The plan outlined also the specific measures that would have to be taken to support offensive operations. These included the following:

1. Mobilization of Army forces, initially 750,000 men, excluding strategic reserves ready if needed to support the Navy.

2. Mobilization of naval vessels and an increase in personnel strength to 320,000 (including marines).

3. An increase in the strength of the Marine Corps to 35,000 men.

4. Additional increases in all services at a later date if necessary.

5. Plans for the movement of troops to vital areas for their defense and to ports for overseas movement.

Having assumed a position of readiness and completed initial preparations, the military and naval forces of the United States would then be free to meet any unexpected situation that might develop, including, presumably, an attack in the Atlantic. If none did, the Navy could then proceed to take the offensive against Japan with operations directed initially against the mandated islands and extending progressively westward across the Pacific. These operations combined with economic pressure (blockade) would, it was believed, result in the defeat of Japan and a settlement that would assure the peace and safeguard American interests in the Far East.[53]

The prospective loss of the Philippine

---

[53] *Ibid.*

base in 1946 and the abrogation by Japan of the Washington Treaty limitations on fortifications led after 1936 to a renewed interest in Guam. The whole problem of naval bases came under Congressional scrutiny when a board headed by Rear Adm. Arthur J. Hepburn submitted its report on naval bases in December 1938. The findings of the board, which had been appointed by Congress, reflected clearly the naval strategy of the day. Guam, it declared, should be developed into a fully equipped fleet base with air and submarine facilities. Such a project, it reminded the Congress, had been prepared earlier, but had been put aside because of the Washington Treaty. That treaty had now expired and there was no longer any restriction on the military fortification of Guam.[54]

The advantages of establishing a strong base at Guam were enormous, in the view of the board. For one thing, it would greatly simplify the task of defending the Philippine Islands. In the opinion of "the most authoritative sources," such a base would make the islands practically immune from attack, would create "the most favorable conditions . . . for the prosecution of naval operations in the western Pacific," and would contribute greatly to the defense of Hawaii and the continental United States.[55] By limiting hostile naval operations to the south, a fortified base at Guam would also serve to protect the trade routes to the Netherlands Indies and greatly simplify naval problems

"should the fleet ever be called upon for operations in the Far East."[56] And even if the United States withdrew from the western Pacific, the base at Guam, as Admiral Leahy pointed out, would have great value as a deterrent to any nation "contemplating a hostile move from the general area towards the Hawaiian Islands."[57] But Congress, after a heated debate, rejected the board's recommendations for fear of offending Japan, with the result that Guam, lying exposed at the southern end of the Marianas, was left virtually undefended.

The failure to fortify Guam, like the refusal to strengthen the forces in the Philippines, reveals strikingly the dilemma of America's position in the Pacific and Far East. National policy dictated the defense of an insular position which, in the opinion of the military planners, could not be defended with existing forces. The ORANGE plan of 1938, with the compromise between an offensive and defensive strategy, was merely a reflection of this contradiction between American interests and commitments in the Pacific. The nation would not abandon the Philippines but neither would it grant the Army and Navy funds to ensure their defense. Nowhere in the country, even where feeling against Japanese aggression in Asia ran highest, was there firm support for military appropriations. Strong isolationist sentiment supported a Congressional economy which by 1938 had so reduced the effectiveness of the nation's armed forces as to make its outposts in the Pacific "a distinct and exceedingly grave liability." American policy had created a wide gap

---

[54] House Doc. 65, 76th Cong., 1st sess., *Report on Need of Additional Naval Bases To Defend the Coast of the United States, Its Territories, and Possessions* (Hepburn Board Report), pp. 27–28.
[55] *Ibid.*, p. 28.

[56] *Ibid.*, p. 27.
[57] Hearings, House Committee on Naval Affairs, 25 Jan–17 Feb 1939, p. 55.

between objectives and means and forced on its planners a compromise strategy and the virtual abandonment of Guam and the Philippines. Already there was a shift in sentiment, a recognition of the danger ahead, and a disposition to prepare the country's defenses, but the neglect of almost two decades could not be overcome in the three years of peace that remained.

CHAPTER II

Japanese Policy and Strategy,
1931 – July 1941

It may even reasonably be said that the intensely sharp competitive preparation for war by the nation is the real war, permanent, increasing; and that battles are only a sort of public verification of mastery gained during the "peace" intervals.　WILLIAM JAMES

In the period between the two world wars, Japan sought to establish control first of east Asia and then of the southwest Pacific. After a decade of liberal ascendancy and acquiescence in the post-World War I agreements, the extremists in Japan gained power and embarked on a program of military preparation and territorial aggrandizement. First the Japanese moved into Manchuria and then into China, where they soon became involved in a war that dragged on interminably and from which they could extract neither victory nor honor. Having scrapped the Washington Treaty system, they withdrew from the League of Nations and from the naval disarmament system established in 1922 and 1930. Gradually they moved toward a closer understanding with Germany and Italy, and, in 1940, turned south to the rich British, French, and Dutch colonies of southeast Asia in search of raw materials they needed to carry on the war in China.

The United States opposed all these moves as vigorously as circumstances permitted. Since the turn of the century, when it had annexed the Philippines, the United States had been inextricably drawn into the confused politics and imperialist rivalries of the Far East. Despite the nation's traditional preference for remaining aloof from world affairs, it was abundantly clear that America could not remain indifferent to any change in the *status quo* in the Pacific or in Asia. John Hay had defined America's position in China in 1899, and his statement—that there must be equal opportunity for trade, or an open door, in China — remained the keystone of American policy in the years that followed. It was inevitable, therefore, that the United States would challenge the efforts of any power to gain a dominant position on the mainland of Asia.

America's opposition to Japanese expansion in Asia, its insistence on the open-door policy and the integrity of China, led to mutual distrust and suspicion. No Japanese government could accept America's solution for the deepening crisis and remain in power; nor would the United States accede under any conditions to the dismemberment of China. There was no escape from this dilemma and by mid-1941, despite the utmost efforts of men of good will on both sides of the Pacific, Japan was moving rapidly down the road that led to Pearl Harbor.

Japanese Expansion

The impulse to expansion and domination of East Asia had its roots deep in Japanese tradition, patriotism, and economic necessity; its strongest support came from the militarists and extreme nationalists. In marked contrast to the position of the armed forces in democratic countries, the Army in Japan had a tradition of political leadership and enjoyed a position high in the esteem of the people. It was not, as in the United States and Great Britain, the servant of the government, controlled through responsible civil officials and by the power of appropriation. Under the Japanese Constitution the Emperor commanded the Army and Navy, and the Diet had little control over the organization of the military forces.[1]

Military control in prewar Japan was exercised by the War and Navy Ministers and the General Staffs of the Army and Navy, not by the civil government. The services were in a peculiarly independent position. The War and Navy Ministers, though members of the Cabinet, could go over the head of the Premier and appeal directly to the throne in military or naval matters of great importance. Moreover, they could, by resigning from the Cabinet, force the resignation of the Premier and the formation of a new government, for under the Constitution, no Cabinet could exist without the War and Navy Ministers.

An even more significant aspect of the relationship of the services to the government of prewar Japan was the control of the Army and Navy over their respective Ministers. By custom, and after 1936 by law, the War and Navy Ministers were chosen from among the senior officers (3-star officers or higher) on the active list. Thus, the Army selected the Minister, who, if not himself a member of the General Staff, was almost certain to reflect its views. Opposition of the civil authorities could be quickly overcome by the threat of withdrawing the service Ministers from the Cabinet. The Chiefs of the General Staffs had the right also to report directly to the Emperor and had considerable freedom of action. So great was their prestige and influence in political matters and so unlimited their ability for independent action, that they could virtually commit the government to a course of action, and the nation to war.[2]

Despite the enormous power and prestige of the Army, the liberal and moderate elements in Japan were not without influence. The decade of the 1920's was theirs and during these years Japan followed a moderate course. This

---

[1] Under Articles 11, 12, and 62 of the Japanese Constitution, the Diet had partial control of the budget and this gave it some leverage over the military.

[2] E. E. N. Causton, *Militarism and Foreign Policy in Japan* (London: G. Allen and Unwin, Ltd., 1936), pp. 75–82; R. K. Reischauer, *Japan, Government and Politics* (New York: Ronald Press Company, 1939), pp. 90–93. For a general description of the Japanese high command, see Yale Candee Maxon, *Control of Japanese Foreign Policy: A Study of Civil-Military Rivalry, 1930–1945* (Berkeley: University of California Press, 1957).

course was based on the belief that the limits of profitable armed expansion had been reached and that the future of the nation lay in peaceful economic expansion and co-operation with the United States and Great Britain. It was this view that made possible the signing of the Washington Treaties in 1921–22, which established the *status quo* in the Pacific, recognized the sovereignty and territorial integrity of China, forbade additional fortification of certain islands in the Pacific, and limited capital ship construction.

As the decade of the 1920's came to an end, the popular discontent arising from the poverty and despair of worldwide depression was channeled into national and fascist movements. American exclusion of Japanese immigrants in 1924, although balanced by generous and ready sympathy during the Tokyo earthquake, had strengthened the hand of the discontented. Further, the acceptance by the liberal government in 1930 of the extension of naval limitation to cruisers, destroyers, and submarines provided the advocates of expansion with strong arguments for scrapping the entire Washington Treaty system, as well as the pretext for the assassination of the Premier. Nationalist groups readily joined forces with the supporters of the Army and the extreme right to demand a reversal of the liberal program and a return to the policy of expansion.

Events in China gave strong support for the aggressive policy urged by the expansionists. Under Chiang Kai-shek the Chinese were displaying symptoms of a nationalism and unity which boded ill for Japanese interests in Manchuria

and dreams of expansion in Asia. By 1931 the Chinese had already regained partial eonomic control of Manchuria and were seeking to remove foreign influence from China. The liberal government of Japan had made clear its intention of maintaining Japanese rights in Manchuria, but by peaceful means. The Army, doubtful of the efficacy of such means and acutely aware of the strategic importance of Manchuria, decided on bolder measures and in September 1931 seized control of key cities in Manchuria by force.

The seizure of Manchuria was the work of the Army extremists acting on their own authority and in defiance of government policy. Presented with a *fait accompli* and fearing open revolt, the government gave its reluctant consent to the Army's action and the Foreign Office did its best to justify to the rest of the world this violation of the Washington Treaties, the Kellogg Peace Pact, and the Covenant of the League of Nations. But the Japanese troops in Manchuria, the Kwantung Army, did not stop there. Despite opposition in the Cabinet and even from the throne, the Kwantung Army extended its control over the rest of Manchuria, established a puppet regime there, and began to move into the northern provinces of China. Nor did opposition from the United States, whose Secretary of State, Henry L. Stimson, informed Japan that his country could not recognize as legal this infringement on existing treaties or the violation of the open door policy in China, halt the Japanese Army. In 1933, after the League of Nations adopted the strongly critical report of the Lytton

Commission, Japan withdrew from the League.[3]

The Manchurian incident was but the first step in the Army's rise to power. Having defied the government and set the nation on a course opposed by the Cabinet, the Army gained virtual control the following year, 1932, as a result of the celebrated incident of 15 May when a group of young Army and Navy officers terrorized Tokyo for several hours and assassinated Premier Inukai.

With the death of the Premier, party rule in Japan virtually ceased. The Emperor's advisers, recognizing that either outright opposition to or complete acceptance of the Army's program would be equally disastrous, urged a middle course. The result was a series of compromise Cabinets in which the moderate and liberal elements opposed the dangerous policies of the militarists as far as prudence would allow and yielded to them when necessary.[4]

The balance thus achieved lasted only five years, years in which Japan renounced its adherence to the naval disarmament agreements of 1922 and 1930 and made abundantly clear its opposition to the Nine-Power Treaty of 1922 guaranteeing the sovereignty and territorial integrity of China. In 1935 a lib-

eral movement opposed to fascism and militarism and calling for a return to full parliamentary government began to take form. Liberals in the Diet attacked sharply the government's policy and criticized the War Ministry so strongly that it felt constrained to discipline some of the extremists in the Army. The extremists retaliated in February 1936, after the victory of the liberals in the elections of that month, with a full-scale armed revolt against the government. The mutineers, numbering 1,500 soldiers led by twenty-two junior officers of the 1st and Guard Divisions (supported, there is reason to believe, by other high-ranking officers), attacked members of the Cabinet, high court officials, and even senior Army officers thought to be lukewarm to the cause. The Finance Minister and one of the most important members of the high command were killed, while the Premier himself narrowly escaped assassination.

The government and the high command reacted with vigor. Army leaders, fearing that the forces they had raised might destroy them as well as their enemies, made serious efforts to restore discipline. The revolt was soon suppressed and the leading offenders court-martialed and punished, though lightly. Then followed an effective purge of the

[3]*The Japan Year Book, 1934* (Tokyo: Foreign Affairs Association of Japan, 1934); Henry L. Stimson, *The Far Eastern Crisis* (New York: Harper & Brothers, 1936); International Military Tribunal for the Far East (IMTFE), Defense and Prosecution Cases of Japanese Aggression in Manchuria, Japanese War Crimes Files, National Archives; Political Strategy Prior to Outbreak of War (in 5 parts), pt. I, Japanese Studies in World War II, 144, pp. 1–9, Mil Hist Sec, Far East Command (FEC). This series was prepared by former Japanese Army and Navy Officers under the supervision of G–2, FEC. Both the original Japanese version and translations are on file in OCMH.

[4]Reischauer, *Japan, Government and Politics*, pp. 154–57; Clyde, *The Far East*, pp. 600–604, 664; Judg-

ment, International Military Tribunal for the Far East, November 1948 (hereafter cited as IMTFE, *Judgment*), pt. B, pp. 98–103, copy in OCMH. Unless otherwise noted, the account which follows is based on these sources, *passim*, and on Herbert Feis, *The Road to Pearl Harbor, The Coming of the War Between the United States and Japan* (Princeton: Princeton University Press, 1950); Joseph W. Ballantine, "Mukden to Pearl Harbor: The Foreign Policies of Japan," *Foreign Affairs*, XXVII, No. 4 (July, 1949), 651–64; and Maxon, *Control of Japanese Foreign Policy*, *passim*.

NEW ARMY-CONTROLLED JAPANESE CABINET, MARCH 1936. *At left, War Minister Terauchi in uniform, with Navy Minister Nagano at his left.*

Army, directed by the War Minister and the General Staff and designed to prevent unauthorized or untimely revolts which the high command itself did not favor.[5]

The 26 February incident marked one more step in the Army's rise to power. Ten days after the mutiny, the Premier resigned and a new government more favorably disposed to the Army's program took office. From this time on, Japanese policy must be read in terms of military strategy.

To determine just who made Army policy is extremely difficult. Not even the leading civilian statesmen of Japan seem to have known, and Prince Ayamaro Konoye, thrice Premier and a politician who made co-operation with the Army the keystone of his career, complained that he never knew where Army opinion originated.[6] But there was no doubt about the essentials of this program. Its basic objective was to make Japan strong enough to become the un-

[5] IMTFE, *Judgment*, pt. B, pp. 113–19; Hugh Byas, *Government by Assassination* (New York: Alfred A. Knopf, 1942); Latourette, *The History of Japan*, p. 219; *The Japan Year Book, 1939*, pp. 134–36.

[6] Memoirs of Prince Konoye, in *Pearl Harbor Attack: Hearings Before the Joint Committee on the Investigation of the Pearl Harbor Attack* (Washington, 1946), 39 Parts, (hereafter cited as *Pearl Harbor Attack Hearings*), pt. 20, exhibit 173, p. 4014.

challenged leader of Asia. This could be accomplished, the Japanese military leaders believed, only by the expansion of the heavy industries necessary to support a modern war machine, the integration of the economic resources of Manchuria into the Japanese economy, the establishment of a firm position on the Asiatic continent, and the acquisition of the strategic raw materials needed to make the nation self-sufficient. Without these materials, most of which could be found in the East Indies and Malaya, Japan's pretensions to leadership in Asia were empty shadows.

The Army's program became the official policy of the Japanese Government in August 1936. At that time the most important members of the Cabinet, including the Premier and the War, Navy, Foreign, and Finance Ministers, met to fix the program of the new administration. The agreement reached at that meeting gave the Army and the nationalists all they wanted. Japan, the five Ministers agreed, must acquire a "firm position" on the Asiatic continent—a euphemistic way of saying that China must be conquered; expand into southeast Asia to secure the bases and raw materials needed to make the nation strong; and take steps to counter the Russian menace to the north. The Ministers had no difficulty in agreeing on the measures required to achieve these objectives: the Army (including its air arm) and the Navy would have to be strengthened, trade and industry expanded, and air and sea transportation improved. Finally, the Ministers agreed that to steel the national will and unify public opinion for the coming emergency, it would be necessary "to establish good living conditions for the people,

increase their bodily strength and foster sound thinking."[7]

The five Ministers carefully avoided any reference to military action. Rather, they stated explicitly that the expansion southward was to be gradual and peaceful, that every care would be exercised "to avoid aggravating friendly relations with other nations" and "to allay the Great Powers' suspicion and apprehension toward the Empire."[8] But the goals these Ministers set for Japan clearly implied military action. The Soviet Union would certainly oppose expansion in the north, and Great Britain and the United States could be expected to dispute any violation of the territorial integrity of China. To these opponents could be added the French and the Dutch, who would challenge Japan's expansion southward. Basic, therefore, to the new administration's program was the success of the effort to increase the nation's military and naval might and its capacity to wage war.

With agreement on the aims and methods of national policy, the Army-dominated Japanese Government moved closer to its natural allies, Germany and Italy, and on 25 November 1936 signed the Anti-Comintern Pact directed principally against Soviet Russia. The next move came in July 1937 when Japanese military forces, after a trumped-up incident near Peiping, marched into northern China. This action, like the Manchurian incident, was taken by the Army alone, without the knowledge or approval of the Cabinet, but no difficul-

---

[7] IMTFE, exhibit 216; Political Strategy Prior to Outbreak of War, pt. I, Japanese Studies in World War II, 144, app. 1.
[8] *Ibid.*

ties developed on that account in the first phase. The government readily supported the Army, on condition that it exert every effort to prevent the spread of the incident.[9]

The vigor of the Chinese reaction soon led to full-scale war, an eventuality the Japanese military leaders neither expected nor desired.[10] With command of the sea and air and with overwhelming superiority in men and equipment, the Japanese were able to occupy quickly the capital and the large coastal cities of China. But they were never able to extend their control much beyond the navigable rivers and the railroads or to bring the China incident to a successful close. It became an increasingly heavy drain on the nation's resources and a constant source of embarrassment to the Army.

The United States, like the other powers with interests in China, could hardly be expected to acquiesce in this new venture and in the destruction of the Nine-Power Treaty. In unmistakable terms it made clear to Japan that it still stood by the open-door policy and the territorial integrity of China, and that it considered Japan's action in China a violation of existing treaties. At the same time the United States Government acted with extreme caution and restraint, resisting public pressure to boycott the shipment of oil and scrap iron to Japan and declining all offers to mediate in the dispute.

Japan was just as anxious to avoid an open break and when the *Panay* was sunk in December 1937, quickly apologized and made indemnity. But so long as Japan persisted in its efforts to conquer China and the United States continued to insist on the territorial integrity of China and to aid that nation, no real solution of the China incident or restoration of good relations between the two countries was possible.

As the area of disagreement with the United States and Great Britain grew larger, Japan moved closer to the Axis. To the military, the future of Japan was closely tied to the destiny of Nazi Germany. The Anti-Comintern Pact had already paid dividends. Hitler had refused to participate in the Brussels Conference of November 1937, called to seek a settlement of the conflict in China, and had kept the Western Powers so preoccupied with European problems that they were unwilling to take any coordinated action in the Far East. But when the Japanese sought a full political and military alliance which would free them from the danger of Russian interference and recognize their special position in China, Hitler countered with a demand for military aid against Britain and France. This the Japanese were not prepared to promise and for two years the negotiations hung fire.

Meanwhile the relations between Japan and the United States steadily worsened. Six months after the sinking of the *Panay*, the United States placed a "moral embargo" on the export of aircraft and aircraft equipment to Japan, the first in a series of economic measures designed to deter Japanese aggression. Japan responded in November by announcing its intention of establishing

---

[9] Political Strategy Prior to the Outbreak of War, pt. I, app. 5, Japanese Studies in World War II, 144.

[10] Diary of Marquis Koichi Kido, submitted as an affidavit to IMTFE, p. 34. For a full account of the China incident from the Japanese point of view, see Political Strategy Prior to Outbreak of War, pt. I, Japanese Studies in World War II, 144.

JAPANESE TROOPS MARCHING THROUGH THE PEIPING GATE, *September 1937.*

a "Co-Prosperity Sphere" in east Asia and expressing a pious hope that other nations would "understand the true intentions of Japan and adopt policies suitable for the new conditions."[11] Both the United States and Great Britain recognized this policy for what it was and countered with loans to the Chungking government.

By the spring of 1939 the Army was ready to commit Japan fully to the Axis. But there was sharp disagreement in the Cabinet. The Navy and Foreign Ministers insisted on an agreement directed primarily against the Soviet Union and refused to accept any commitment which might involve Japan in a war against the Western Powers. They

were willing, however, to agree to lesser commitments in the hope that the United States and Great Britain might thus be forced to accept the situation in China. But the Army pressed for the full military agreement demanded by Germany, and even planned to negotiate separately to secure such an alliance. Neither side would give way.

On 23 August 1939 Germany, without Japan's knowledge, concluded a neutrality pact with Russia. A week later Germany invaded Poland and the war in Europe began. The German-Soviet Pact was a stunning blow to Japan's program for expansion and to the Army's prestige. The Japanese felt betrayed and bewildered and the Premier promptly offered his resignation to the Emperor, asserting bitterly that the failure of Japan's foreign policy had resulted from

[11] *United States Relations with China,* Dept of State Pub 3573 (Washington, 1949), p. 21.

KONOYE CABINET OF JUNE 1937. *Circled faces are, from left, Admiral Yonai, Premier Konoye, and General Sugiyama.*

"the unreasonableness of the Army."[12] A combination of civilian statesmen and Navy leaders, taking advantage of the Army's political eclipse, then attempted to reorient national policy toward better relations with Great Britain and the United States. The Cabinet formed for this purpose lasted only four months and was succeeded by a compromise Cabinet headed by Admiral Mitsumasa Yonai, the former Navy Minister.

All efforts to win over America and Britain foundered on the issue of China. On 26 July the United States had served notice on Japan of its intention to abrogate the commercial treaty which had governed the trade relations between the

two countries since 1911, and in December of 1939 prohibited Americans from furnishing Japan with technical information and manufacturing rights for the production of high-grade aviation gasoline. After January 1940, when the commercial treaty lapsed, the United States was free to employ economic sanctions against Japan. Congress, in June of that year, passed the National Defense Act which made it possible for the President to prohibit exports to Japan and on 2 July President Franklin D. Roosevelt put the export license system into effect by restricting the shipment of arms and ammunition, certain strategic materials such as aluminum, and airplane parts.

Japanese sentiment, which had veered toward the Western Powers after the German-Soviet Pact, shifted back toward

---

[12] Saionji-Harada Memoirs, 1931–1940 (24 parts with appendixes), Civil Intel Sec, G–2 FEC, copy in OCMH, quoted in Feis, *The Road to Pearl Harbor,* p. 34.

Germany in the spring of 1940 as the Axis gained one victory after another in quick succession. Once more the Army point of view found favor and support. The German-Soviet Pact had ruled out, at least temporarily, expansion northward, but the opportunities for easy conquest in the south were better than ever once Holland and France had fallen. The forces behind a full military and political alliance with Germany could now argue that such an alliance would secure Japan on the north, discourage American interference in China, and smooth the paths of empire to the south.

Once more overtures were made to the Germans. This time Hitler asked as payment for supporting Japan's ambitions in southeast Asia a Japanese commitment to hold the United States at bay by threatening Hawaii and the Philippines if America entered the war in Europe. The Premier thought the price too high, and the Army, now fully restored to its former prestige and political influence, brought about the fall of the Cabinet on 16 July 1940. Prince Konoye, who had been Premier in 1938 and was favorable to the Army's program, took over the reigns of government next.

In July 1940 Japan stood ready to embark on a course of unreserved expansion to establish the new order in Greater East Asia on the ruins of the crumbling British, Dutch, and French Empires. Only the United States was in a position to check Japan's ambitions, but such opposition, the Japanese believed, could be overcome with the assistance of Germany and Italy. Once a military pact with the Axis Powers had been signed and the war in China ended, then Japan would be free to establish the new order in Asia. All this, the Japanese leaders hoped, could be accomplished peacefully, but if not, the Japanese intended to be ready, for since 1931 they had been preparing the nation for war.

Economic and Military Preparations

In the decade 1930–40, industrial production in Japan increased at a phenomenal rate. In the opening year of the decade, Japanese industrial output was valued at six billion yen and the emphasis was on the light industries; by 1941 production had increased fivefold and heavy industry constituted 72.7 percent of the total.[13]

The military significance of this sensational rise in industrial production can be found in the emphasis on heavy industries, the basis of any modern military machine, and a measure of its importance lies in the increase in annual steel production from 1.8 to 6.8 million tons. In 1930 Japan had produced only 500 vehicles and 400 aircraft. Ten years later the annual production of vehicles was 48,000 units, and the Japanese aircraft industry was manufacturing over 5,000 planes annually. Shipbuilding in Japan showed a similar increase during these years. Deliveries under the naval construction program in this period totaled 476,000 tons, and construction of merchant ships rose from 92,093 tons in 1931 to 405,195 tons in 1937.[14]

---

[13] Jerome B. Cohen, *Japan's Economy in War and Reconstruction* (Minneapolis, Minn.: University of Minnesota Press, 1949), p. 1; United States Strategic Bombing Survey (USSBS), *The Effects of Strategic Bombing on Japan's War Economy* (Washington, 1946), p. 12.

[14] Cohen, *Japan's Economy in War and Reconstruction*, pp. 2–3; USSBS, *Japanese Naval Shipbuilding* (Washington, 1946), p. 1; USSBS, *Japanese Merchant Shipbuilding* (Washington, 1947), pp. 4–5.

TABLE 1 — JAPANESE MILITARY BUDGET, 1931–1940
(in millions of yen)

Year	Military Budget	Military Budget as Percent of Total Expenditures
1931	434	29.4
1932	733	37.6
1933	873	39.2
1934	955	44.2
1935	1,032	46.8
1936	1,105	48.4
1937	3,953	71.6
1938	6,097	75.4
1939	6,417	71.7
1940	7,266	65.9

Source: Cohen, *Japan's Economy in War and Reconstruction*, p. 5.

Much of this increase in industrial production, especially in the heavy industries, was due to government expenditures for military purposes which rose sharply after 1936 as a result of the February 1936 incident and the Army's ascendancy. (*Table 1*) Military expenditures after 1936 reflected military domination of political life. The entire economy of the nation was rigidly controlled and oriented toward war; the armament industries were expanded, and every effort was made to stockpile strategic raw materials.[15]

The production of armaments after 1936 increased rapidly to meet the demands of the China war. This increase was accomplished under a 5-year plan developed by the Army in 1937 and officially adopted by the Cabinet two years later. Separate programs were established for Japan, Manchuria, and northern China, and certain industries considered essential for war were select-

ed for rapid expansion.[16] Some success was achieved in Manchuria under the 5-year plan but the program for Japan had to be modified several times. The aviation and munitions industries made rapid progress, the steel industry achieved a remarkable success, and the production of machine tools surpassed the goals established. But other basic industries, such as the production of synthetic oil and hydroelectric power, were limited by the shortage of raw materials, and, despite the most strenuous efforts, failed to reach the goals set by the Army.[17]

During these years the Japanese armed forces also began building up stockpiles of essential supplies. Reserves of weapons, ammunition, and other important military equipment were adequate, but those of certain strategic materials were

[15] IMTFE, *Judgment*, pt. B, pp. 114ff.

[16] *Ibid.*, p. 353.
[17] History of the *Army Section, Imperial General Headquarters, 1941–1945*, Japanese Studies in World War II, 72, p. 5; Cohen, *Japan's Economy in War and Reconstruction*, ch. I.

not. The quantity of bauxite on hand in 1941 totaled 254,740 tons, which represented a 9-month supply. Also, since 1938, Japan had been forced to draw upon its stockpile of iron ore for the war in China, and at the end of 1941 had only a few months' reserve.[18]

The shortage of petroleum production was the key to Japan's military situation. It was the main problem for those preparing for war and, at the same time, the reason that the nation was moving toward war. For the Navy, the shortage of oil was critical; for the Army it was always a limitation. To secure reserves of this precious commodity, Japan imported heavily during the decade of the 1930's, the amount reaching 37,160,000 barrels in 1940. During that year Japan produced only 3,163,000 barrels, less than 12 percent of the nation's peacetime requirements. To increase the amount available for military use, civilian consumption of oil was curtailed sharply after 1937, and practically all civilian motor traffic was abolished or required to use wood and charcoal burners. Despite these measures, Japan had only 43,000,000 barrels of oil reserves in 1941, an amount sufficient at most for two years of war under the most favorable conditions, if supplemented by resources within the empire.[19]

The growth of Japan's military forces matched its industrial growth during these critical years. Between 1936 and 1941, the number of men conscripted for the Army doubled. At the end of 1937 Japan had 24 divisions, 16 of which were stationed in China; three years later the total had risen to 50: 27 in China, 12 in Manchuria, and the remainder in Korea and the home islands. The Army Air Forces showed the greatest proportionate growth, increasing from 54 squadrons in 1937 to 150 in 1941. Pilots were well trained and about half of them had actual combat experience in China or in border fighting with Soviet Russia.[20] (*Table 2*)

Japan's naval forces, which had been limited first by the Washington Naval Conference (1921) and then by the London Naval Conference (1930), grew rapidly after 1936 when Japan withdrew from the naval conference of that year. In 1937, twenty new vessels with a tonnage of 55,360 tons were completed; the next year this amount increased to 63,589 tons, and by 1941 had reached the prewar peak of 225,159 tons. This tonnage represented one battleship of the *Yamato* class, 10 carriers of unspecified tonnages, 7 cruisers, and 37 destroyers.[21] By 1941, Japanese combat tonnage had risen to 1,059,000 tons, more than twice that of 1922, and Japan's fleet was more powerful than the combined United States–British fleets in the Pacific.

Despite these preparations for war, the Japanese Army and Navy had no military or naval plans to guide them. There were in the files of the supreme command statements dealing with national defense policy and with the employment of troops, but these dated from 1930 and were expressed in general principles rather than in terms of specific operations. Moreover, they provided only for a defensive war against either

---

[18] Cohen, *Japan's Economy in War and Reconstruction*, p. 48.

[19] USSBS, *Oil in Japan's War* (Washington, 1946), p. 1.

[20] Hist of *Army Sec, Imperial GHQ*, Japanese Studies in World War II, 72, pp. 2–3; USSBS, *Japanese Air Power* (Washington, 1946), pp. 4–5.

[21] USSBS, *Japanese Naval Shipbuilding*, app. A.

TABLE 2—JAPANESE ARMY GROUND AND AIR FORCES
AND NAVY AIR FORCES
1937–1941

Year	Army Ground Forces Divisions	Army Air Forces (First-Line Aircraft)			Navy Air Forces				
		Bombers	Fighters	Rcn	Carrier-Based	Land-Based			
						Bombers	Fighters	Torpedo	Others
1937	24 (plus 6 Reserve Divisions)	210	210	120	216	204	132	108	178
1938	34	330	240	130	269	228	132	132	200
1939	41	450	280	180	201	288	132	156	228
1940	50	500	360	200	167	264	132	180	306
1941 (8 Dec)	51	660	550	290	684	443	252	92	198

Source: Japanese Opns in SWPA, GHQ Hist Series, II, p. 54.

the United States or the Soviet Union, and emphasized that in no case should Japan fight more than one of these countries at the same time. There was no mention in these statements of a possible war with Great Britain or the Netherlands, or of war against a combination of these powers. They were, in the words of one Japanese officer, "outdated writings" and "utterly nonsensical from the standpoint of authority and contents."[22]

The lack of a concrete strategical plan was partially overcome by the Army and Navy's annual operations plans. Each year the two services worked out their own plans for operations against the two named enemies separately and then submitted them for Imperial approval. These plans made no provision for total war, and so long as the government refused to decide which was the most likely enemy or to admit the possibility of war with more than one nation, it was im-

possible to establish priorities, for a war against Russia would require strengthening the Army and a war against the United States would call for larger naval appropriations. The Navy's 1940 plan for a war with the United States, therefore, simply declared that the Imperial Navy, in co-operation with the Army, would destroy American strength in the Far East and maintain command of Far Eastern waters "by intercepting and crushing American fleets."[23] How America was to be defeated was never even considered.

The Army's annual plan for 1940 emphasized defensive operations against the Soviet Union from Manchuria. Operations to the south were "secondary and supplementary in importance."[24] In case of war with the United States, the planners expected that Japanese forces would

---

[22] Political Strategy Prior to Outbreak of War, pt. IV, Japanese Studies in World War II, 150, pp. 1–2.

[23] *Ibid.*, p. 2.
[24] Deposition of former Lt. Gen. Shinichi Tanaka, Chief of Operations, Japanese General Staff, IMTFE, exhibit 3027.

take the Philippines and Guam, but made no concrete plans for their seizure or for countering American reaction. The main objective of the Army, they believed, was to prepare against attack, not to fight a war against the United States. The 1940 plan was equally vague about Great Britain and the Netherlands. In case of war the plan provided for the seizure of Hong Kong and Singapore, but not for the Netherlands Indies, Burma, India, or Australia. Japan, said the Army's Chief of Operations, "had no capacity to meet the need of a crisis . . . with drastic measures on a grand scale."[25]

Thus, throughout the decade of the 1930's, the Japanese leaders had no military strategy for a war against a coalition such as they later faced, and their policy was based almost entirely on political considerations and on what one officer called their "exceedingly conceptual and common sense understanding of war strategy." Deliberations of the Cabinet and of the Liaison and Imperial Conferences,[26] though attended by Army and Navy officers, were not limited by precise studies and plans outlining the course of military and naval action to be taken in every conceivable situation. They were guided, rather, by political strategy "pushed without any consideration of a definite war strategy plan."[27]

Japan Moves South

The program of the Konoye Cabinet, which took office on 22 July 1940, set the course of Japanese policy for the next critical year. This program was drawn up on 19 July, even before the Cabinet had been organized, and was accepted by the four principal ministers — the Premier, Prince Konoye, War Minister Hideki Tojo, Navy Minister Zengo Yoshida, and Foreign Minister Yosuke Matsuoka, whom Cordell Hull called "as crooked as a basket of fishhooks." The new administration, it was agreed, would make its main objective the establishment of a new order in east Asia, known as the Greater East Asia Co-Prosperity Sphere. Included in this sphere at first were Hong Kong, Burma, French Indochina, Thailand, Malaya, the Netherlands Indies, the Philippines, and New Guinea; later India, Australia, and New Zealand were added to the list. Specific measures designed to gain this grand objective included a closer alliance with the Axis, a nonaggression pact with the Soviet Union, and every effort necessary to bring the China war to an end. While there were some differences among the four ministers over the nature and timing of the actual measures to be taken, there was no question about basic objectives. And all were agreed that any nation that opposed this program was the enemy of Japan.[28]

---

[25]*Ibid.*

[26] The Liaison Conference was an informal body consisting of the service chiefs, the principal civilian ministers, and other high government officials, and served as a link between *Imperial General Headquarters* and the Cabinet. The same body when it met with the Emperor on more important occasions and under more formal circumstances was known as the Imperial Conference.

[27] Political Strategy Prior to Outbreak of War, pt. IV, Japanese Studies in World War II, 150, p. 3.

---

[28] Political Strategy Prior to Outbreak of War pt. II, Japanese Studies in World War II, 146, pp. 10–16. Unless otherwise indicated, this section is based upon Feis, *The Road to Pearl Harbor, passim;* Ballantine, "Mukden to Pearl Harbor," *Foreign Affairs* (July, 1949), pp. 658–61; IMTFE, *Judgment,* pt. B, pp. 487–520, pp. 864–903, and the Japanese sources cited above.

The program outlined on the 19th was discussed and approved by the full Cabinet on the 26th and, the following day, by a Liaison Conference. The decisions of this last conference, which became, in effect, the policy of the Japanese Government, differed only slightly from the preliminary program drawn up by the four ministers on the 19th. They were embodied in a document entitled General Principles To Cope With the Changing World Situation, laying down four specific measures designed to end the war in China and to give Japan a dominant position in southeast Asia:

1. The elimination of all aid to the Chungking government by third powers.

2. Adoption of "a firm attitude" toward the United States and, at the same time, the strengthening of political ties with the Axis and a drastic readjustment of relations with Russia.

3. Stronger diplomatic measures against the Netherlands Indies in order to secure vital raw materials.

4. Intensification of political, economic, and military preparations for war.

Japan hoped to gain these objectives by peaceful means but was prepared where necessary to use force. "In employing armed strength," it was agreed at the Liaison Conference, "efforts will be made to limit the war adversary to Great Britain insofar as possible. However, thorough preparations for the commencement of hostilities against the United States will be made as it may prove impossible to avoid war with that country." [29]

The first and most pressing problem for the new Konoye Cabinet was the conflict in China. Already the United States had indicated that it was in no mood to discontinue its support of Chiang. On 25 July, only three days after Prince Konoye had taken office, President Roosevelt added scrap iron and oil to the list of items whose export was subject to license. But the Japanese, undeterred by this warning and by the prompt rejection of fresh peace overtures to the Chungking Government, sought to take advantage of the weakness of Vichy France by demanding, first, the right to send troops into northern Indochina, adjacent to the China border, to intercept supplies to Chiang Kai-shek; and second, control of the airfields there to provide bases from which to bomb the Burma Road and Chungking. These demands had been specifically outlined in the "General Principles" adopted on 27 July and Japan was ready to resort to force to gain them. But military action proved unnecessary, for on 29 August, after the Germans had brought pressure on Vichy France, the French yielded. A month later Japanese troops entered Indochina.[30] Despite the explanation of Foreign Minister Matsuoka that this action was a normal military measure against China, the United States entered a formal protest. This was an empty gesture; more tangible was the loan of another twenty-five million dollars to Chiang Kai-shek and extension of the embargo on scrap iron and steel.

The effort of the Konoye Cabinet to secure strategic raw materials from the Netherlands Indies, an effort which

[29] IMTFE, exhibit 1310; Political Strategy Prior to Outbreak of War, pt. II, Japanese Studies in World War II, 146, app. 2.

[30] Political Strategy Prior to Outbreak of War, pt. II, Japanese Studies in World War II, 146, pp. 7–9, app. 2.

American economic measures had made more urgent, met with little success. On 16 July the Japanese had notified the Dutch that they wished to send a mission to discuss the relations between the two countries, and, after an exchange of notes limiting the scope of the mission to economic matters, the Minister of Commerce, Ichizo Kobayashi, and a staff of twenty-four experts, left for Batavia. The talks began early in September with the Japanese demanding large oil concessions in the Indies and three million tons of oil annually for five years, an amount that represented about three-fifths of Japan's normal requirements. The Dutch companies with whom the Japanese dealt, urged on by the British and the Americans, refused to meet these large demands. They were willing to send only half the amount requested and that on a 6-month contract basis. Kobayashi left Batavia on 22 October, and, though the conversations continued for some months more, the Japanese were never able to get what they wanted. But they took what they could—a slight increase in the amount of rubber, tin, and bauxite, and an agreement with the oil companies for the quantities offered.

On 27 September, four days after the dispatch of troops into French Indochina, Japan concluded the Tripartite Pact with Germany and Italy, thus achieving one more objective in the program outlined by the Liaison Conference. Under the terms of this agreement, Germany and Italy recognized the leadership of Japan in bringing a new order to Asia, and Japan, on its part, recognized the new order in Europe. More important was the commitment of the signatories to come to each other's aid "with all political, economic, and military means" should any of them be attacked by a power with which it was not then at war. Since Germany and Italy were at war with the western European nations, and since the pact was not to have any effect on the existing relations of the signatories with Soviet Russia, it was evident that the Tripartite Pact was a warning to the United States to remain neutral.

The decision to conclude the Tripartite Pact had been made on 19 September at the Imperial Conference. The agreements reached at this meeting constitute an important guide to what Japan hoped to achieve from the alliance with Germany and Italy and what the policy of the nation would be in the months to come. Clearly, the ministers expected support in their efforts to expand southward and end the war in China. With the co-operation of the Axis they hoped to induce the Russians to advance toward the Persian Gulf, and possibly India, that is, in a direction that would not threaten Japan. They hoped also, with the co-operation of Germany and Italy, to bring pressure on the United States to accept Japan's claims in the south and in China.

But the four ministers did not expect to pay for this support with military action, except where it was necessary to gain their own objectives. They agreed that they would assist the Axis against Great Britain by measures short of war, but reserved the right to make their own decisions on the use of armed force against that nation and the United States. If the war in China were near a conclusion, the four ministers decided, then Japan might resort to force to gain its objectives, waiting only for the right moment. But until that time, they agreed, Japan would not go to war against Great Britain or the United States unless the situation permitted no delay.[31]

It is clear that Japan did not interpret the Tripartite Pact as a commitment to war, and, as a matter of fact, the Emperor agreed to it with misgivings and only after he had been assured that it would not lead to hostilities.[32] The Konoye Cabinet evidently believed that the United States (and the Soviet Union) would not intervene in the Far East if the advance southward was achieved gradually and by diplomatic means. They hoped that the United States would be forced by the Tripartite Pact to remain neutral and that the issue would be between Japan and the British, Dutch, and French who were in no position to dispute Japanese expansion southward. Soviet opposition was to be overcome through the intervention of Germany.[33]

These hopes were entirely unrealistic. The United States had never retreated from its position on China and had declined time and again to recognize Japan's interpretation of treaties to which the United States was a party. Instead of showing any timidity or weakness, the United States Government on this occasion adopted a firm but cautious atti-tude. Cordell Hull announced to news-men that the pact did not substantially alter the situation, but his statement was belied by the announcement on 8 Octo-ber 1940 that consuls in the Far East had been instructed to advise American citi-zens to return home, and that three lin-ers had been sent to the Orient to hasten their evacuation.[34] Already the Pacific Fleet, which was normally based on the west coast, had been ordered to remain at Pearl Harbor indefinitely, and prepa-rations were being made to strengthen American garrisons in Alaska, Hawaii, and Panama.[35]

While maintaining a firm attitude to-ward Japan, the United States Govern-ment adopted a policy designed to "avoid an open struggle in the Pacific" so that American resources would not be divert-ed from the main tasks—strengthening the nation's military forces and aiding Britain. Japan, it was agreed, was not to be pushed "to the point where her military elements would demand war."[36] The door was to be left open for discus-sion and agreement, but the United States was to maintain its treaty rights in the Far East, continue to exert eco-nomic pressure against Japan, and pro-vide aid to China. The Tripartite Pact, in the view of the United States, had placed Japan in the Axis camp and Japan was to be treated as one of the

[31] IMTFE, exhibit 541; IMTFE, *Judgment*, pp. 504–508. Takushiro Hattori, The Complete History of the Greater East Asia War, translated from Japa-nese by FEC, Doc. 78002, I, 42–45, OCMH.

[32] Political Strategy Prior to the Outbreak of War, pt. II, Japanese Studies in World War II, 146, app. 4 and pp. 20–25. The latter reference contains an ac-count of the 26 September conference with the Em-peror to discuss the treaty.

[33] German-Japanese Relations From 1936 to 1943, MIS237954, Mil Intel Div Library; IMTFE, exhibits 551, 552.

[34] Cordell Hull, *The Memoirs of Cordell Hull*, 2 vols. (New York: The Macmillan Company, 1948), I, 914–15; Robert E. Sherwood, *Roosevelt and Hopkins: An Intimate History* (New York: Harper & Brothers, 1948), p. 271. See also Ltr. Joseph C. Grew, formerly U.S. Ambassador to Japan, to author, 19 Jun 49, copy in OCMH.

[35] *Pearl Harbor Attack Hearings*, pt. I, exhibit 9, p. 943. Mark Skinner Watson, *Chief of Staff: Prewar Plans and Preparations*, UNITED STATES ARMY IN WORLD WAR II (Washington, 1950), ch, XIV.

[36] Hull, *Memoirs*, I, 911.

Axis Powers. The last chance of settling Japanese-American conflicts as a separate problem, divorced from European affairs, was gone. In his Fireside Chat of 29 December 1940, President Roosevelt emphasized that the Tripartite Pact represented a threat to the United States and that the nation for its own defense must increase its aid to the free nations and make greater efforts to rearm.[37]

In spite of the fact that the Tripartite Pact had failed to convince the United States that acceptance of Japan's program for expansion was desirable, the Konoye Cabinet continued along the path laid out by the Liaison Conference of 27 July. Every effort was made to bring the war in China to an end; when air bombardment failed, the Japanese solicited the support of German diplomacy. The only result of these measures was another American loan to Chiang Kai-shek, this time for a hundred million dollars. Japanese policy was no more successful in the Indies. The conversations begun in September dragged on, with a new special envoy taking Kobayashi's place in January 1941. The Dutch so stoutly resisted Japanese pressure for economic co-operation that the new envoy reported that force alone would produce the desired results. "How can we compromise," complained one of the Japanese delegates, "when you refuse to accept our views."[38] But Japan was not yet ready for war and rather than lose prestige by breaking off the negotiations Konoye instructed the delegates to remain in Batavia.

In Indochina and Thailand the Japanese made important gains. Seizing the pretext of a border dispute between the two countries, Japan offered its services as mediator, after prior arrangement with Thailand, "on the ground of maintaining stability in Greater East Asia."[39] Britain was particularly concerned over Japan's entry into the dispute and the possibility of Japanese military intervention in an area so close to Burma, Malaya, and Singapore, and urged the French to negotiate. Neither British nor American efforts to end the dispute proved successful, and on 20 January 1941 Japan made a formal offer of mediation. It was accepted by both parties, the Vichy Government acceding only after German persuasion, and on the last day of the month a truce was signed. But a final settlement was still to be reached.

Japan's aims in the border dispute between Thailand and French Indochina were defined at the Liaison Conference of 30 January, when it was decided that Japan would use its position as mediator to obtain from the French naval bases in Camranh Bay and air bases near Saigon for a possible attack later against Singapore, an attack which the Germans were urging with vigor. Both countries would be required to sign agreements with Japan and promise not to conclude with any third power pacts affecting that nation. If either proved intractable it was agreed that force would be used, and for this purpose a large naval force was ordered to take up positions along the coasts of Indochina and Thailand. To the rest of the world, which noted these naval movements with considerable con-

---

[37] U.S. Department of State, *Foreign Relations of the United States, Japan: 1931–1941*, 2 vols. (Washington, 1943), II, 173–81.

[38] Joseph C. Grew, *Ten Years in Japan* (New York: Simon and Schuster, 1944), p. 213.

[39] Political Strategy Prior to Outbreak of War, pt. III, Japanese Studies in World War II, 147, p. 12.

cern, Japan protested that its only interest in the affair was to bring about peace in east Asia.

Conversations for the settlement of the boundary dispute were to open in Tokyo at the beginning of February, but the Vichy Government, though it had agreed to the armistice, would not agree so readily to Japanese mediation. Unfortunately, neither the United States nor Great Britain was in a position to affect the outcome, and the French finally agreed on 11 March, under the combined pressure of Germany and Japan, to accept mediation of the dispute and not to enter into any agreement inimical to Japan. The boundary controversy was settled on 9 May when the French ceded to Thailand most of the land in dispute, but Japan did not receive its wages until the end of July.

The date on which Vichy France acceded to the Japanese mediation plan, 11 March, was by coincidence the day on which the American Congress approved and the President signed the Lend-Lease Act. The stated purpose of this law was to promote the defense of the United States, but its real meaning lay in the aid it offered to the nations fighting the Axis. It was clearly a declaration of cold war against the Axis Powers, and was taken by them as such. There was no longer any doubt for those who could read American opinion rightly that the United States had taken its stand with Britain and China and would push all measures short of war to prevent their defeat.

The Konoye Cabinet, indifferent to or unable to comprehend the extent of American opposition, persisted in its efforts to push through the program laid down on 27 July 1940 in the General Principles To Cope With the Changing World Situation. One of the objectives of this program, it will be recalled, was "the readjustment of diplomatic relations with Soviet Russia."[40] Until the beginning of 1941 the Konoye Cabinet had been too involved in other matters to act on this front, but at that time, as Mr. Matsuoka, the Foreign Minister, was preparing to visit Europe, the question of an agreement with the Soviet Union came up again. The trip to Europe was approved and Matsuoka was instructed to seek Soviet recognition of Japanese supremacy in east Asia but to avoid military commitments. Matsuoka left Tokyo on 4 March. His first stop was Moscow where he talked with Molotov about the possibility of a nonaggression pact. Nothing tangible resulted from these conversations and Matsuoka went on to Berlin. Hitler had already decided to attack Russia, and urged that Japan take aggressive action in the Far East, specifically against Singapore, to bring about the final collapse of England. Not a word was said about the forthcoming attack on Russia, although Matsuoka may have surmised it; instead, the Germans hinted darkly about worsening relations with the Soviet Union when the Japanese Foreign Minister explained the nature of his talks with Molotov.

On his return trip Matsuoka stopped again in Moscow. The Russians had had a month to consider his proposals. Persuaded perhaps by foreknowledge of the impending German attack, as well as a willingness to encourage Japan's drive southward, Molotov and Stalin proved remarkably amenable to Matsuoka's proposals. On 13 April, after only a week

[40] Political Strategy Prior to Outbreak of War, pt. II, Japanese Studies in World War II, 146, app. 2.

of deliberation, an agreement that pledged Japan and the Soviet Union to respect each other's territorial integrity and to remain neutral in case of attack by a third power was signed.

The Japanese were jubilant over the pact with Russia and immediately made plans to push the program for expansion to the south, a program to which the Army and Navy were already heavily committed. It had been decided earlier that this expansion was to be achieved by diplomatic means, but that preparations for military action must be rushed if peaceful methods failed. On 6 December 1940 the Army had designated three divisions, then in south China, to be trained for operations in tropical areas, and ten days later had directed commanders in China and Formosa to study the problems involved in such operations and to prepare area studies of the Indies, Malaya, Indochina, Thailand, Burma, the Philippines, and Guam.[41] Next month the Japanese had begun aerial reconnaissance of the Malayan coast and the War Ministry and Foreign Office began to print military currency for use in the southern area.

Among the military preparations the Japanese undertook in the early spring of 1941 was a plan to take Singapore, a step the Germans favored highly for their own purposes. The Japanese were not averse to German support and were using this support to wrest from the Vichy Government advance bases in Indochina from which, presumably, they would attack the British Far Eastern bastion. Repeatedly the Japanese assured the Germans that they hoped to take Singapore, probably in May, but refused to commit themselves beyond the occupation of Saigon. They also assured the Germans that they were making preparations for a possible war against the United States, but had actually developed no plans for such a war other than a personal study initiated in January by Admiral Isoroku Yamamoto, commander of the *Combined Fleet* and an ardent advocate of carrier-based operations, for an attack against Pearl Harbor.[42]

Japan's position in Indochina had been greatly strengthened in May when an economic and political agreement with the Vichy Government was concluded. But in southern Indochina, where there were no Japanese troops, there was strong anti-Japanese sentiment supported by the de Gaullists, the Chinese, the British, and the Americans. The economic results of this sentiment were most disadvantageous to the Japanese and were reflected in the decreased quantity of rice exported from Indochina to Japan and the threat that other vital Indochinese resources such as rubber, tin, coal, and manganese would find their way into other markets. The occupation of southern Indochina, therefore, became an urgent matter for the Japanese and one which was to have an important effect on their relations with other nations.

Nor were Japanese efforts to wrest concessions from the Dutch meeting with success. The conversations had been going from bad to worse, although the Dutch had increased slightly the

---

[41] Imperial GHQ Army Dept Directives, 791, 6 Dec 40; 810, 16 Jan 41; and 812, 18 Jan 41, copies in OCMH.

[42] Apparently this study was kept a secret from the authorities, and even Yamamoto's staff, except for Rear Adm. Ohnishi, knew nothing of it. Statement of Rear Adm. Tomioka, then Chief of the Operational Section, Navy General Staff.

amounts of rubber, tin, bauxite, and nickel promised the Japanese earlier. But the requests for more oil and for concessions in the Indies had not yet been granted. Finally, on 17 June, Japan broke off the conversations and ordered its delegates home. Though the Japanese sought to minimize its meaning, this action was clearly an admission of defeat.

By this time Japan was feeling the pinch of shortages created by the controls the United States had instituted over shipments to Japan, and the relations between the two countries had improved not at all. Efforts to settle the outstanding disagreements between them had begun in February, when Ambassador Kichisaburo Nomura arrived in the United States.[43] After a series of preliminary talks with President Roosevelt and Mr. Hull, Nomura, on 18 April, handed the Americans a 7-point proposal as the basis for an agreement. Essentially, this proposal called for the United States to provide, or assist Japan in securing, strategic raw materials, and to persuade Chiang to reach agreement with Japan. In return, Japan would agree not to start war in the southwest Pacific and to interpret the Tripartite Pact as meaning Japan would support Germany only if that nation were the object of aggression. The proposal was not acceptable to the Americans and was made even less so by revisions from Tokyo. On 30 May, Mr. Hull presented an interim American proposal to Nomura and on 21 June a second draft, to which was

attached a "verbal memo" containing a delicate reference to the lack of confidence the Americans had in the pro-Axis Japanese Foreign Minister, Mr. Matsuoka. The negotiations had reached a deadlock and the only hopeful sign was the trouble brewing within the Japanese Cabinet where a change might produce a shift in the direction of Japanese policy.

The impending crisis in the Japanese Government was rapidly accelerated by the German invasion of the Soviet Union on 22 June, the day after Hull handed his note to Nomura. Though the Japanese had expected the attack, they were greatly upset when it came for it changed the entire complexion of world events and strengthened America's hand in the Pacific. The Japanese were oriented toward the south and seeking to obtain from Vichy France, with Germany's help, control over southern Indochina. This new development opened up the possibility of an advance northward, and thus required a thorough review of Japan's position and a reconsideration of the program established a year before.

The course charted by the Liaison Conference in July 1940 had by the middle of June 1941 brought Japan few of the advantages so optimistically expected. More by military pressure than diplomacy Japan had obtained from a defeated and subjugated France the right to occupy Tonkin Province in Indochina and the use of French air bases and military facilities there. Hopes for a base in southern Indochina had not yet been realized; the results of the economic agreement were proving disappointing, and important opposition to the new order in Asia was developing in Indochina. Efforts to secure from the

---

[43] These conversations were initiated unofficially by two clergymen. IMTFE, exhibit 3441, Ltr, Joseph C. Grew to author, 19 Jun 49, OCMH. A full account from the American side can be found in Hull, *Memoirs.*

Dutch the oil and other resources needed so desperately to support operations in China and to prepare for war had yielded meager results and ended in a serious diplomatic defeat. Negotiations with the United States had produced as yet no easy formula for peace and there was no sign that America would yield to the minimum Japanese demands. The Tripartite Pact had paid dividends, but, as events turned out, had proved unnecessary and had created a formidable obstacle to an agreement with the United States. But the Japanese were never able to resolve the deadlock in China, and it was this failure that forced them to adopt in desperation a course that led almost irresistibly to war.

CHAPTER III

Europe Versus the Pacific

> The second rule is to concentrate your power as much as possible against that section where the chief blows are to be delivered and to incur disadvantages elsewhere. CLAUSEWITZ

Since 1938, when the last revision of ORANGE was completed, American military strategists had made every effort to bring their plans into line with the rapidly changing situation in Europe and Asia. The world was dividing into two armed camps. On one side were Germany and Italy, associated with Japan by the Anti-Comintern Pact. For three years, these powers had been pursuing their aggressive policies in the Rhineland, Ethiopia, Austria, and China. On the other side were the democratic powers, Great Britain and France. Still suffering from the prolonged economic crisis of the early 1930's and weakened by domestic conflicts, these two had remained passive in the face of Axis threats and sought to avert armed conflict by a policy of appeasement. While such hopes did not seem entirely without foundation at the time, American leaders could no longer ignore the possibility of becoming involved in a two-ocean war.

The 1938 revision of ORANGE, with its emphasis on flexibility, represented an effort to bring strategy into line with the international situation. The Navy's single-minded insistence on an advance into the western Pacific was still reflected in the plan, but it was modified by an increasing awareness of the uncertainties of a world threatened by the rising tide of Axis aggression. The Army, with its concern for the defense of the United States, was shifting away from the Pacific orientation that had dominated strategic planning since World War I and was turning anxious eyes toward Europe. A RED or a RED-ORANGE war was no longer within the realm of probability, but the Atlantic area occupied more and more of the attention of the strategists after 1938.[1]

---

[1] The material covered in this chapter has been treated more fully from different points of view and with different emphases in a number of works in the series UNITED STATES ARMY IN WORLD WAR II: Maurice Matloff and Edwin M. Snell, *Strategic Planning for Coalition Warfare, 1941–1942* (Washington, 1953), chs. I–III; Watson, *Chief of Staff: Prewar Plans and Preparations*, chs. IV, X, and XII; Richard M. Leighton and Robert W. Coakley, *Global Logistics and Strategy, 1940–1943* (Washington, 1955), pt. one; Stetson Conn and Byron Fairchild, *The Framework of Hemisphere Defense* (Washington, 1960), chs. I–V; and also in William L. Langer and S. Everett Gleason, *The Undeclared War, 1940–1941* (New York: Harper & Brothers, 1953). The present account is based on the original sources, except where otherwise indicated, and has appeared in slightly different form in Kent R. Greenfield, gen. ed., *Command Decisions* (New York: Harcourt, Brace and Company, 1959).

Strategic Adjustment, 1938–1940

Though it was the Army planners who seemed most aware of the danger from Europe, it was the Navy that made the first move to strengthen America's Atlantic defenses. In December 1937, shortly after the *Panay* incident, the Director of the Navy War Plans Division, Capt. Royal E. Ingersoll, was sent to London to discuss informally with the British Admiralty the new construction programs of the two navies and the conditions of U.S.-British naval co-operation in the event both nations were involved in a war against Japan. During the course of these discussions, the possibility of a German war inevitably arose. The British viewed this possibility with real concern, for the Germans could be expected to attack British trade routes in the Atlantic. Should Italy join Germany, the prospects were even more alarming. The French, if they entered the war, would hold the western Mediterranean, but the British would still have to place the bulk of their forces in the Atlantic. They would have little, therefore, to send to the Far East. Here the United States could perform a valuable service in the common cause by taking up the slack in the Far East in return for the security the Royal Navy would provide in the Atlantic. Even if the United States became involved in the European conflict, Great Britain could still be relied upon to man the Atlantic barrier so long as the U.S. Fleet assumed responsibility for the Pacific. It is perhaps for this reason that the Navy members of the Joint Planning Committee, in their discussions over ORANGE in 1938, seemed less concerned about the Atlantic and more interested in the Pacific than the Army planners.[2]

Events in Europe in the fall of 1938 fully justified the concern of American policy makers and planners, and the Munich crisis in September of that year provided the impetus to a comprehensive review of American strategy. Taking the lead from the public statements of President Roosevelt and Secretary of State Hull, the Joint Board directed its planning committee in November to make a study of the course the United States should follow if German and Italian aggression in Europe and Japanese expansion in the Far East should threaten American security and interests in both the Atlantic and Pacific simultaneously.[3]

Here, for the first time, was a specific directive to the planners to study, within the context of the current international situation, the problems presented by a two-ocean war in which the United States, acting in concert with allies, would be opposed by a coalition. These problems had been studied before in the ORANGE-RED plans, but under entirely different assumptions and in a completely different situation. They had been considered briefly and tangentially also in the latest revision of ORANGE with its provision for a position of readiness and co-operation with allies. The informal naval conversations in London in January 1938 were a clear recognition of the possibility of such a war and the first step toward the intimate military collaboration that marked the Anglo-

---

[2] For an account of the staff conversations in London early in 1938, see *Pearl Harbor Attack Hearings*, pt. 9, pp. 4272–78 and Capt. Tracy B. Kittredge, *U.S.-British Naval Cooperation, 1939–1945*, sec. I, pt. C, pp. 37–38, MS in OCMH.

[3] Mins, JB Mtg, 9 Nov 1938.

American relationship during World War II.

For almost six months the planners of the Joint Board considered the problem presented by simultaneous Axis aggression in the Atlantic and Pacific areas and finally in April 1939 submitted their report. In it they reviewed the world situation, estimated the likelihood of war, calculated the probable objectives of the Axis in Europe and Japan in the Far East, discussed the effects of concerted action by these powers on the United States, and analyzed the strategic problems involved in the various situations that might result from such action. So comprehensive was the report, such a model of strategic analysis, that it was characterized by the Joint Board as "a monument" to its planning committee and became the basis for much of the strategic planning before Pearl Harbor.[4]

In their effort to arrive at a sound military strategy for the United States, the joint planners examined the various contingencies that might arise as a result of Axis aggression. Based on this examination, they concluded:

1. Germany and Italy would take overt action in the Western Hemisphere only if Great Britain and France remained neutral or were defeated.

2. Japan would continue to expand into China and Southeast Asia at the expense of Great Britain and the United States, by peaceful means if possible but by force if necessary.

3. The three Axis Powers would act together whenever the international situation seemed favorable. If other countries, including the United States, reacted promptly and vigorously to such action then a general war might well follow.

The reaction of the United States to these or any other situations that might arise, the planners pointed out, would depend in large measure on the forces available and the extent to which American interests were involved. In the event of a threat in both oceans simultaneously, the United States, they maintained, should assume the defensive in the Pacific, retaining adequate forces based on Hawaii to guard the strategic triangle. Arguing further in a manner reminiscent of RED-ORANGE planning, the strategists of the Joint Board declared that priority in a two-ocean war must go first to the defense of vital positions in the Western Hemisphere—the Panama Canal and the Caribbean area. From bases in that region, the U.S. Fleet could operate in either ocean as the situation demanded, but its primary obligation must always be to control the Atlantic approaches to the Western Hemisphere, especially to the south where the continent was most exposed. This task would not be difficult if Great Britain and France actively opposed Axis aggression, but if they did not the security of the South Atlantic would become the major concern of U.S. forces. In this situation, the active co-operation of the Latin American states was indispensable.

In their studies the planners also considered the possibility of a war with Japan alone. The United States would have to expect to lose all its possessions west of 180 degrees early in such a war, which, the planners prophetically pointed out, might well begin with a Japanese effort "to damage major fleet units with-

[4] Mins, JB Mtg, 6 May 1939; Ltr, JPC Rpt, Exploratory Studies, 21 April 1939, JB 325, ser. 634. The discussion of the report is based on the Exploratory Studies and related papers in the same file.

out warning," or a surprise attempt "to block the fleet in Pearl Harbor." It would be necessary, then, for American forces to fight their way back across the Pacific in a series of amphibious operations using one of four routes: (1) the Aleutians; (2) Pearl Harbor–Midway–Luzon; (3) the Marshalls–Carolines–Marianas–Yap–Pelileu; and (4) Samoa–New Guinea–Mindanao. The planners favored the second and third routes and thought that a combination of the two would have to be used. The garrisons in Hawaii, Alaska, and Panama were to be reinforced, but not the Philippines, apparently on the assumption that their loss was certain. The planners were astute enough to recognize, however, that "emotionalized opinion rather than . . . a reasoned adjustment of operations to the means at hand" might ultimately dictate the choice of battleground.

American military forces in 1939 seemed sufficiently strong to accomplish the minimum tasks required under the strategic concept proposed by the planners—defense of U.S. vital interests in the Western Hemisphere and in the Atlantic area. After hostilities began, American forces could be strengthened sufficiently to defeat the enemy operating in the Atlantic, even without the aid of Great Britain and France. If, at the same time, the United States maintained adequate defensive forces in the Pacific, Japan could probably be restricted to the western Pacific. It was even possible, in such a situation, that the Japanese leaders might prefer peace with the United States, hoping thereby to reap a profit from the war without cost to themselves. If, on the other hand, Japan initiated hostilities and the United States adopted a position of readiness but re-

frained from an advance to the western Pacific, the European Axis would probably not undertake any aggressive adventures in the Western Hemisphere. Thus, on all accounts, the planners held that a defensive strategy in the Pacific was preferable to any other course.

On the basis of their study the joint planners recommended that a series of war plans be prepared, each of them to be applicable to a different situation. Priority in these plans, they held, must be given to the defense of the United States, and this would require safeguarding the security of the Western Hemisphere. To hold firm to these objectives would be no easy task, the planners recognized. Not only must strategy be linked to policy, but it must also take cognizance of such intangibles as tradition, the spirit of the nation, and "emotionalized public opinion."

The pioneering study by the joint planners in 1939 raised sharply and dramatically the question of American policy in the event of concerted aggression by Germany, Italy, and Japan. By focusing on the threat to the Caribbean and South America, the planners challenged strongly the long-standing orientation of American strategy toward the Pacific and gave weight to the Army's arguments against offensive operations in the western Pacific.

The planners raised another issue that needed to be resolved before the course of national policy could be charted. All the color plans had been based on the assumption the United States would act alone. Was this assumption valid in terms of the international situation and in the face of a threatening Axis coalition? Should the strategists in drawing up their plans therefore assume that the

United States would have allies? And if so, who would they be and what would the United States be expected to do for them and they for this nation? Like the Atlantic vs. Pacific issue, this question of allies involved political matters and would have to be resolved by the President himself.

It was perhaps as well that no firm answers were forthcoming in the spring of 1939, for the course of events was still far from clear. The planners recognized this when they proposed that alternative plans be prepared to meet different situations in which the United States would have to meet the combined threat of Germany, Italy, and Japan. The Joint Board, in approving the work of the planners, accepted this recommendation and in June 1939 laid down the guide lines for the development of these war plans, aptly designated RAINBOW to distinguish them from the color plans.[5]

There were ultimately five RAINBOW plans in all, each of them based on a different situation. The objective of all was the same—to defend the United States and the Western Hemisphere from Axis aggression and penetration, overt or concealed. In each of the plans the planners "set forth the specific co-operation that should be sought from allied or neutral Democratic Powers, with respect to specific Theaters of Operations to render our efforts fully effective." Common to all of the plans was the

assumption that the United States would face a coalition rather than a single power.

The five specific situations forming the basis of the five RAINBOW plans were defined by the Joint Board as follows:

RAINBOW 1 assumed the United States to be at war without major allies. United States forces would act jointly to prevent the violation of the Monroe Doctrine by protecting the territory of the Western Hemisphere north of latitude 10° south, from which the vital tasks of the United States might be threatened. The joint tasks of the Army and Navy included protection of the United States, its possessions and its seaborne trade. A strategic defensive was to be maintained in the Pacific, from behind the line Alaska–Hawaii–Panama, until developments for offensive action against Japan.

RAINBOW 2 assumed that the United States, Great Britain, and France would be acting in concert, with limited participation of U.S. forces in continental Europe and in the Atlantic. The United States could, therefore, undertake immediate offensive operations across the Pacific to sustain the interests of democratic powers by the defeat of enemy forces.

RAINBOW 3 assumed the United States to be at war without major allies. Hemisphere defense was to be assured, as in RAINBOW 1, but with early projection of U.S. forces from Hawaii into the western Pacific.

RAINBOW 4 assumed the United States to be at war without major allies, employing its forces in defense of the whole of the Western Hemisphere, but also with provision for United States Army forces to be sent to the southern part of South America, and to be used in joint operations in eastern Atlantic areas. A strategic defensive, as in RAINBOW 1, was to be maintained in the Pacific until the situation in the Atlantic permitted transfer of major naval forces for an offensive against Japan.

RAINBOW 5 assumed the United States, Great Britain, and France to be acting in

---

[5] The first directive of the Joint Board was dated 11 May 1939, but on further study was revised and amended instructions issued on 30 June. Mins, JB Mtg, 6 May 39, and 30 June, JB 325, ser. 634; Ltrs, JB to JPC, 11 May 39, sub: Joint Army and Navy Basic War Plans, RAINBOW's 1, 2, 3, and 4; JPC to JB, 23 Jun 39, same sub; JB to JPC, 30 Jun 39, same sub. All in JB 325, ser. 642 and 642–1.

concert; hemisphere defense was to be assured as in RAINBOW 1, with early projection of U.S. forces to the eastern Atlantic, and to either or both the African and European continents; offensive operations were to be conducted, in concert with British and allied forces, to effect the defeat of Germany and Italy. A strategic defensive was to be maintained in the Pacific until success against European Axis Powers permitted transfer of major forces to the Pacific for an offensive against Japan.[6]

Of the five plans, RAINBOW 1 was basic, though most limited. Providing for the defense of the Western Hemisphere from the bulge of Brazil to Greenland and as far west as Midway in the Pacific, it established the necessary conditions that had to be met before any of the other plans could be executed. RAINBOW's 2 and 3 called for offensive operations into the western Pacific, the former on the assumption that Great Britain and France would be allies, and the latter that they would not. In this respect, RAINBOW 3 established virtually the same conditions as the ORANGE plan. RAINBOW 4 also assumed that Great Britain and France would be neutral, presumably as a result of Axis military action, and therefore emphasized the defense of the Western Hemisphere against external aggression. Emphasis in this plan as in RAINBOW 1 was on limited action to fend off any Axis threat to the American republics. In neither RAINBOW 1 nor 4 were major U.S. forces to be sent to Europe or to the far Pacific.

The situation envisaged in RAINBOW 5 came closer to the conditions of World War II than any of the others, though these were not foreseen at the time. Like RAINBOW 2, it assumed the active collaboration of Great Britain and France. But unlike that plan, which called for the United States to make the major effort in the Pacific, RAINBOW 5 envisaged the rapid projection of American forces across the Atlantic to Africa or Europe "in order to effect the decisive defeat of Germany, Italy, or both." Clearly implied in this statement was the concept that finally emerged as the basic strategy of World War II: that in a war with the European Axis and Japan, Germany would be the major enemy and the main effort would be made in Europe to secure the decisive defeat of Germany at the earliest possible date.

The summer of 1939 was one of tense expectancy. Europe was on the verge of war and Japan showed no disposition to abandon aggression in Asia. During these months, a joint RAINBOW 1 plan, which had first priority, was completed and the two services hurriedly pushed forward completion of their own plans for hemisphere defense.[7]

There were important organizational changes, too, at this time. In an effort to keep in close touch with his military advisers, President Roosevelt on 5 July 1939 placed the Joint Board under his immediate "supervision and direction." Up to that time, the board, it will be recalled, had reported to the two service Secretaries, under whose authority the board functioned. It had now a broader basis, but still sent its recommendations through the Secretaries, for the President had no desire to alter existing proce-

---

[6] Kittredge, U.S.-British Naval Cooperation, sec. I, Part D, Notes pp. 42–46; Memo, JPC to JB, 23 Jun 39; Mins, JB Mtg, 30 Jun 39, JB 325, ser. 642.

[7] Joint War Plan RAINBOW 1, JB 325, ser. 642–1. Approved by the Joint Board on 9 August, by the Secretary of War and Secretary of Navy on 14 August 1939, and by the President orally two months later.

GENERAL MARSHALL.   *(1944 photo.)*

ADMIRAL STARK

dures.[8] This change coincided with a change in the high command. On 1 August, Admiral Harold R. Stark was appointed Chief of Naval Operations to succeed Admiral Leahy, and a month later General George C. Marshall formally succeeded General Malin Craig as Chief of Staff of the Army after two months as Acting Chief.

The outbreak of war in Europe early in September 1939 gave a fresh urgency to RAINBOW planning. RAINBOW 2 seemed to fit the situation of the moment best and while work went forward on the development of plans, the President took measures to strengthen the nation's defenses and to keep America out of war by keeping war away from America. Immediately on the outbreak of hostil-

ities he proclaimed the neutrality of the United States, while ordering the Army and Navy to bring their strength up to the full authorized level. On his initiative, the Foreign Ministers of the American Republics met at Panama at the end of September to proclaim their neutrality and to devise measures for their joint defense. American security zones were proclaimed in the western Atlantic and eastern Pacific, and plans made to patrol these zones to keep war away from the Americas.

Throughout the winter of 1939–1940, the period of the "phony war," the joint planners sought to develop plans to meet the RAINBOW 2 contingency. The task proved a formidable one, indeed, for the range of possibilities was wide. Moreover, each proposed course of action in the Pacific had to be co-ordi-

---

[8] Mil Order, 5 Jul 39; Memo of Secy JB, 20 Jul 39, JB 346, ser. 646.

nated with that of the Allies. But without specific knowledge of the plans of their allies, the planners were faced with many uncertainties. In April 1940, therefore, they proposed that conversations should be held with the British, French, and Dutch "as soon as the diplomatic situation permits." By that time, the Army planners had prepared four drafts of a proposed RAINBOW 2 plan, on each of which the Navy had commented in detail.[9]

The Critical Summer of 1940

The planners were still trying to solve the problems posed by RAINBOW 2 when the nature of the war in Europe changed abruptly in the spring of 1940. Early in April, German forces invaded Denmark and Norway and by the end of the month had occupied both countries. On 10 May, the German campaign against France opened with the attack on the Netherlands and Belgium, and four days later German armor broke through the French defenses in the Ardennes. At the end of the month the British began the evacuation from Dunkerque, and on 10 June, Italy declared war. A week later, the beaten and disorganized French Government sued for peace. With France defeated and England open to attack and invasion, the threat from the Atlantic looked real indeed.

Nor was there any consolation to be found in the situation in Asia. In China, the Japanese had succeeded in occupying North China, the coastal area as far south as Canton, and the principal river and rail lines. Tokyo diplomats were speaking of a Japanese "Monroe Doc-

trine," and there was every indication that Japan intended to exploit the Axis victories in Europe and take over the French, British, and Dutch possessions in Asia and the Southwest Pacific. Only the United States was in a position to challenge Japan, and on 10 April 1940 the Joint Board instructed its planners to give priority to the development of plans based on RAINBOW's 2 and 3, both of which called for offensive operations in the Pacific.[10] That same month, the Pacific Fleet moved into Hawaiian waters for maneuvers, and despite the protests of its commander was kept there throughout the spring as a deterrent to Japanese aggression. Finally in June, when a Soviet-Japanese pact freed Japan for further aggression to the south, the fleet was ordered to remain indefinitely in Hawaiian waters. So tense was the situation that on the 17th of the month, as a result of reports of possible attacks on Pearl Harbor or Panama Canal, General Marshall sent alerts to the Army commanders in Hawaii and Panama.[11]

In this crisis, American strategy underwent a critical review. Clearly the greater danger was in Europe, and RAINBOW's 2 and 3 with their orientation toward the far Pacific were scarcely applicable. The defeat of France in June and

---

[9] The various drafts of RAINBOW 2 can be found in the Army files of the JPC, JB 325, ser. 642–2.

[10] Mins, JB Mtgs, 22 Feb and 10 Apr 1940; JPC to JB, 9 Apr 40, sub: Joint War Plans RAINBOW, approved 10 April, JB 325, Ser. 642–1. The priorities established for RAINBOW planning at this time were
1. Complete RAINBOW 2.
2. Develop RAINBOW 3 as far as the main courses of action.
3. Develop RAINBOW 5 as far as the main courses of action.
4. Complete RAINBOW 3.
5. Complete RAINBOW 5.
RAINBOW 4 was assigned the lowest priority and no planning for it was scheduled.

[11] The alert message is reproduced in *Pearl Harbor Attack Hearings*, pt. 15, p. 1594.

the possibility that Great Britain might soon fall outweighed any danger that Japanese aggression could present to American security. Calling for an early decision from higher authority, the Army planners argued that since the United States could not fight everywhere —in the Far East, Europe, Africa, and South America—it should limit itself to a single course. Defense of the Western Hemisphere, they held, should constitute the main effort of American forces. In any case, the United States should not become involved with Japan and should concentrate on meeting the threat of Axis penetration into South America.[12]

The Army's concern about America's ability to meet a possible threat from an Axis-dominated Europe in which the British and French Navies might be employed against the United States was shared by the Navy. As a result, the joint planners began work on RAINBOW 4, which only a month earlier had been accorded the lowest priority, and by the end of May had completed a plan. The situation envisaged now in RAINBOW 4 was a violation of the Monroe Doctrine by Germany and Italy coupled with armed aggression in Asia after the elimination of British and French forces and the termination of the war in Europe. Under these conditions, the United States was to limit itself to defense of the entire Western Hemisphere, with American forces occupying British and French bases in the western Atlantic.[13]

Acceptance by the Joint Board of the RAINBOW 4 plan was the beginning rather than the end of the comprehensive review of strategy precipitated by Germany's startling success in Europe. Still in doubt was the fate of Great Britain and the French Navy, and American policy depended to a very large degree on these two unknowns. Possession of the British and French Fleets would give the European Axis naval equality with the U.S. Fleet and make possible within six months, the time required to make the captured fleets operational, hostile Axis operations in the Western Hemisphere. Since considerable time would be required to mobilize, equip, and train American forces, the planners asserted that "the date of the loss of the British or French Fleets automatically sets the date of our mobilization."[14]

During the dramatic weeks of May and June 1940, the President met with his military advisers frequently and discussed with them every major development of the war. On 13 June, shortly before the fall of France, he called in the intelligence chiefs of the Army and Navy for an evaluation of the situation, posing a number of specific questions. This request precipitated an interim review of the various courses of action open to the United States in the light of the rapidly changing situation. As the planners saw it, there were three alternatives:

1. To maintain a strong position in the Pacific and to avoid commitment everywhere else.

---

[12] Memos, WPD for CofS, 22 May 40, sub: National Strategic Decisions; CofS for WPD, 23 May 40, no sub; *Aide Mémoire*, Maj Matthew B. Ridgway, 23 May 40. All in WPD 4175–10.

[13] Ltr, JPC to JB, 31 May 40, sub: Joint Army and Navy Basic War Plan RAINBOW 4. The Joint Board approved the plan early in June and the Secretaries

soon after. It was not approved by the President until 14 August. Relevant papers are in JB 325, ser. 624–4.

[14] Joint War Plan RAINBOW 4, JB 325, ser. 642–4.

GENERAL STRONG

2. To make every effort, including belligerent participation, to sustain Great Britain and France.

3. To take whatever measures were required to prevent Axis penetration into the Western Hemisphere.[15]

All three possibilities had already been considered in one or another of the RAINBOW plans, but, as the planners pointed out, the essence of the problem now was time. RAINBOW 4 was the best course to follow in this situation, in their view, and the end of British or French resistance, they held, should be the signal for American mobilization.

On the morning of 17 June, the day after the planners had submitted their report, General Marshall discussed the problem with his immediate assistants. "Are we not forced," he asked, "into a

question of reframing our national policy, that is, purely defensive action in the Pacific, with a main effort on the Atlantic side? We have to be prepared," Marshall told his staff, "to meet the worst situation that may develop, that is, if we do not have the Allied fleet in the Atlantic." The time had come, he thought, to mobilize the National Guard and to discontinue shipments to England of munitions that would be needed for American mobilization.[16]

On the basis of this discussion, the Chief of the War Plans Division, Brig. Gen. George V. Strong, recommended that same day that the Chief of Staff and the Chief of Naval Operations propose to the President as the basic policy of the United States: first, a purely defensive position in the Pacific; second, no further commitments for material aid to the Allies; and third, immediate mobilization for hemisphere defense. These recommendations reflected the pessimistic and strongly conservative outlook of the Army staff at the time, a view the Army planner made no effort to conceal. His proposal, Strong stated frankly, was "a recognition of the early defeat of the Allies, an admission of our inability to furnish means in quantities sufficient to affect the situation, and an acknowledgement that we recognize the probability that we are next on the list of Axis powers. . . ."[17]

General Marshall and Admiral Stark approved General Strong's recommendations in principle on 18 June and directed their planners to outline the measures required "to effect an imme-

---

[15] Memo, Sr Army and Navy Members JPC to Dirs WPD, 16 Jun 40, WPD 4250–3.

[16] Notes on Conf in OCofS, 17 Jun 40, Misc Confs, binder 3.

[17] Memo, WPD for CofS, 17 Jun 40, sub: National Defense Policy, WPD 4250–3.

diate mobilization of national effort for Hemisphere Defense." The result was a comprehensive review of national policy during the latter part of June by the War and Navy Departments, the State Department, and the President. With the study of the questions proposed by Roosevelt on the 13th, this review furnished an estimate of probable war developments and outlined the action required for full-scale mobilization and for aid to Britain and her allies. Though never approved by the President, the conclusion of the planners nevertheless reflected his views and constituted an important milestone in the development of U.S. strategy for World War II.[18]

The critical point at issue in the discussions was the fate of the French Fleet and the future of Great Britain. Military leaders wished to base their plans on the worst of all possible contingencies— that England, if not the British Empire, would be forced out of the war and that the French and British Fleets would fall to the Axis. The President, on the other hand, believed that American action should be based on the assumption that Great Britain would remain an active belligerent and that the military situation in Europe would not alter appreciably in the next six months. He did not feel, either, that aid to Britain should be cut off entirely, and countered the planner's arguments with the observation that if a small amount of aid would see the British through without seriously retarding American preparations, then that aid should be furnished. Nor was the President willing to put the armed forces on a wartime basis or

to support full mobilization of manpower and industry. He agreed on the necessity for defense of the Western Hemisphere and the protective occupation of European colonial possessions as well as other strategic positions in the Caribbean area and in Central and South America, but only after consultation and negotiation with the Latin American nations concerned.

As a result of these discussions, the planners recommended that American policy be based on the following:

1. That the British Empire would continue to exist in the fall and winter of 1940, though Great Britain itself might not remain an active combatant.

2. That France would be occupied by German forces, and even if the French in North Africa and elsewhere continued resistance, U.S. aid would not alter substantially the French position.

3. That U.S. participation in the war as an active belligerent could not prevent the defeat of France or of Great Britain at this time.

This estimate of the situation at the end of June, which incorporated the President's views, led the planners to recommend as the "Basis for Immediate Decisions Concerning the National Defense" a defensive in the Pacific, irrespective of the fate of the French Fleet. But if that fleet did fall into German hands, the planners recognized they would have to consider the question of whether to move the major portion of the U.S. Fleet to the Atlantic. The planners thought, too, that the further release of war materials needed for American forces would seriously weaken the United States. But they did not rule out altogether aid to Britain and stipulated, in accordance with Roosevelt's

---

[18] The relevant papers are filed in WPD 4250–3.

wishes, that aid would be given "under certain circumstances." [19]

During the summer of 1940, American policy and strategy were shaped in large measure by President Roosevelt's conviction that Britain must be encouraged to resist and that the British Fleet must not be permitted to fall to Germany. In a real sense, therefore, American strategy was dependent upon British fortunes. Only "one force," said Henry Stimson on the day after France's surrender, "remained between the Nazis and the Western Hemisphere—the British Fleet." Faced with this "appalling prospect," the United States would stand alone if that fleet were lost." [20]

Reassurances from the British that they had no intention of giving up the fight were gratifying to a President so closely committed to British support, but a more objective estimate of Great Britain's ability to resist invasion and detailed information on which to base plans were needed. To fill this need as well as to see for themselves how the British were fighting and what they needed most, the Army and Navy sent special observers to London in the summer of 1940 at Mr. Churchill's invitation. The Army observers were General Strong, Chief of the War Plans Division, and Maj. Gen. Delos C. Emmons of the Air Corps. Both would remain for only a few weeks, but the Navy observer, Rear Adm. Robert L. Ghormley, was to remain in London on extended duty. Already, the British had appointed their own Admiralty Committee to consider "naval cooperation with the United States Navy" in the event of American entry into the war, and had made clear to the Americans in a general way how they intended to fight the war. [21]

With the arrival of the special observers in London in August 1940, the conversations which had been carried on informally by the Navy since December 1937 were broadened to include Army representatives and enlarged in scope to include basic questions of strategy, command arrangements, and matériel requirements. None of the observers doubted the determination of the British people to continue their resistance. In their month in England, Generals Emmons and Strong were greatly impressed by the coolness and confidence of the British under attack, and by the organization, training, and techniques for defense against air attack. [22] British faith in the efficacy of air bombardment, and the independent position of the Royal Air Force had an effect also on the two Army observers. Implicit in their report was a reflection of the British belief that Germany could be so weakened ultimately by air bombardment as to make ground operations on the Continent feasible.

The American observers also learned much about British strategy for the conduct of the war. In broad terms, the British Chiefs outlined for the Americans their policy for the conduct of war:

1. The security of the United King-

[19] Memo, CofS and CNO for President, 27 Jun 40, sub: Basis for Immediate Decisions . . . ; see also preliminary studies by the planners, with the President's comments, in WPD 4250–3.

[20] Henry L. Stimson and McGeorge Bundy, *On Active Service in Peace and War* (New York: Harper & Brothers, 1948), pp. 318–19.

[21] For a complete account of these developments and naval conversations, see Kittredge, U.S.-British Naval Cooperation, sec. III, pt. A and B.

[22] Memo, Emmons and Strong for CofS, 22 Sep 40, sub: Observations in England, WPD 4368.

dom and Imperial possessions and interests.

2. Command of the home waters and the eastern Mediterranean, combined with an attempt to regain command of the entire Mediterranean.

3. An intensified air offensive and economic pressures against both Germany and Italy.

4. Development of resources for major offensive ground operations when opportunity offered.[23]

In the Far East, the British admitted frankly, their interests would be best served if the U.S. Fleet remained in the Pacific. Their original plan had been to send a naval force to the Far East in the event of a Japanese attack, but that was no longer possible. On the other hand, if Japan came into the war and if the United States sent a portion of the fleet into the Atlantic, British surface vessels from the Home Fleet and the force at Gibraltar could be sent to the Far East. "The support of the American battle fleet," observed the British Chief of the Air Staff, "would obviously transform the whole strategical situation in the Far East."

On the question of American material aid, the British were equally frank. In response to a question from Admiral Ghormley as to whether the British were relying on economic support and eventual co-operation of the United States, they replied that in the plans for the future "we were certainly relying on the continued economic and industrial co-operation of the United States in ever-increasing volume." American supply, they declared, was "fundamental to our whole strategy." But on the question of

the "eventual active cooperation" of the United States, the British Chiefs were somewhat evasive. "No account had been taken" of this possibility, they told the Americans, "since this was clearly a matter of high political policy."

For the British, Germany was clearly the main enemy and the "mainspring" of the Axis effort in Europe. Arguing from this basis, the British insisted that "whatever action may be necessary against any other country must, therefore, be related to our main object, which is the defeat of Germany"—a statement that came very close to the basic strategic decision of World War II. And when Admiral Ghormley asked the British how they expected to defeat Germany and whether the final issue would be decided on land, they replied that "in the long run it was inevitable that the Army should deliver the *coup de grace*." But they hoped that the Army's task could be made considerably easier by "a serious weakening in the morale and fighting efficiency of the German machine, if not a complete breakdown." How this would be accomplished, the British did not specify, but their emphasis on bombardment indicated that air power would certainly play a leading role in the defeat of Germany.

Shift to the Atlantic, September 1940–January 1941

Events in Europe after June 1940 gave hope for a brighter future than had seemed possible after the German offensive in April and May. The success of the British in beating off the attacks of the Luftwaffe and the reports of the special observers led to a more favorable program of support for the British war

[23] Minutes of the meetings with the British are in WPD 4402–1.

effort and to other measures such as the transfer of fifty old destroyers in return for a lease on British air and naval base sites in British possessions in the western Atlantic. For the moment, the Axis threat in Europe seemed to be blunted.

Meanwhile, the situation in the Far East had taken a turn for the worse. On 22 September, Japanese troops entered northern Indochina, and five days later the Japanese Government announced its adherence to the Rome-Berlin Axis. Just two days before the signing of the Tripartite Pact, the Army planners had completed a report on the ability of the United States to cope with the problems presented by the Axis threat. After reviewing the possibilities in Europe, the planners pointed out that the United States might soon face renewed advances in the Far East, possibly against the Netherlands Indies or the Philippines, but that it would not be possible to oppose such moves by a major effort in the Pacific in view of the greater danger in the Atlantic. Operations in the Pacific, they maintained, should be held to the minimum.[24]

There was general agreement in Washington with this view. The main problem was how to avoid a conflict with Japan and at the same time maintain American interests and defend American possessions in the Far East. The answer perhaps lay in Europe, for there was strong reason to believe that Japan would take no overt military action against the United States or Great Britain until German victory seemed assured. This line of reasoning served to strengthen the view that as long as Great Britain was in danger, the United States should remain on the defensive in the Pacific. It was also a powerful argument for continued aid to Britain, and for opposition to any move that might risk serious hostilities with the Japanese.

Early in October, the entire subject of American policy toward Japan was reviewed on the highest level in Washington. Inevitably the question of British co-operation arose. The military chiefs opposed strong action on the ground that the British would be unable to send any forces into the area and that the United States could not undertake to assume Allied obligations in the Far East. Despite the well-known views of the American staff, the British continued their efforts to persuade the Americans to join the defense of their Far Eastern possessions by sending naval units to Singapore. In May 1940, Churchill had offered to let the Americans use Singapore "in any way convenient" in order, as he put it, to "keep the Japanese quiet in the Pacific." On 4 October he tried again. In a strong personal message to President Roosevelt discussing the Far Eastern situation, he asked, "Would it not be possible for you to send an American Squadron, the bigger the better, to pay a friendly visit to Singapore? There they would be welcomed in a perfectly normal and rightful way."[25]

Both Admiral Stark and General Marshall were opposed to the dispatch of an American naval force to Singapore and agreed that the greater danger was in the eastern Atlantic. Secretary Hull also opposed the move. As he told the British Ambassador, "It will not be wise,

---

[24] Memo, WPD for CofS, 25 Sep 40, sub: Problem of Production . . . , WPD 4321-9.

[25] The message is quoted in Winston S. Churchill, *Their Finest Hour* (Boston: Houghton Mifflin Company, 1949), pp. 497-98.

even from the British standpoint, for two wars to be raging at the same time, one in the East and the other in the West. If this country should enter any war, this would immediately result in greatly cutting off military supplies to Great Britain." [26] The move would be politically inexpedient also, for this was an election year and Roosevelt was already in the midst of a campaign for election to a third term. A military gesture such as Churchill had proposed was likely to lose more votes than it would gain. Thus, on grounds of political expediency as well as strategy, the President turned down Mr. Churchill's invitation.

Yet developments since the summer of 1940 had made the need for a closer co-ordination of British and American plans increasingly evident. Almost every important problem faced by the military planners raised questions that could not be settled without an intimate knowledge of British capabilities and plans. But the hectic months of a Presidential campaign and the uncertainty of the outcome discouraged any serious effort to lay the basis for such co-ordination. By early November, President Roosevelt's re-election seemed certain and on the eve of the election Admiral Stark made the first bid for a firm and clear statement of American policy that would provide the basis for co-ordinated U.S.-British plans. [27] It was the strongest and most comprehensive analysis thus far of the various courses of action open to the United States, the military effect of developments in Europe and Asia, and the close relationship between British fortunes and American policy. Known as the "Plan Dog" memorandum because the recommended course of action if the United States became a belligerent was contained in paragraph D ("Dog" in military parlance), Admiral Stark's study constitutes perhaps the most important single document in the development of World War II strategy.

The central point of Admiral Stark's analysis was the recognition that American security depended to a very large extent on the fate of Great Britain. This note he sounded at the very outset with the assertion that "if Britain wins decisively against Germany we could win everywhere; but that if she loses the problems confronting us would be very great; and while we might not *lose everywhere*, we might, possibly, not *win* anywhere." Should the British Empire collapse, it seemed probable to Stark that the victorious Axis powers would seek to expand their control, economically at first and then politically and militarily, into the Western Hemisphere. The military consequences of a British defeat were so serious for the United States, Stark declared, that the British ought to be assisted in every way possible. He did not believe, either, that Britain had the manpower or material resources to conquer Germany alone. Assistance by powerful allies would be necessary ultimately, and to be ready for this eventuality Britain "must not only continue to maintain the blockade, but she must also retain intact geographical positions from which successful land actions can later be launched."

---

[26] Memoirs of Cordell Hull, I, 906.

[27] Memo, Stark for Secy Navy, 12 Nov 40, no sub. This is a revision of the original 4 November memorandum, no copies of which are in the Army file, revised to include the Army WPD comments and sent to the President. All papers relevant to this memo are filed in WPD 4175–15.

In facing the consequences of close co-operation with the British, Admiral Stark boldly raised the possibility—thus far avoided—of active American participation in the war. Since Britain could not herself defeat Germany, the question was how American resources in men and supplies could be employed in combination with the British to achieve this end. Admiral Ghormley, it will be recalled, had raised this question with the British in London in August, asking whether large-scale ground operations would be necessary. He had received an affirmative reply from the British then, and Stark now returned to this point. Blockade and bombardment, the means favored by the British, he did not think would do the job. The only certain way of defeating Germany was "by military success on shore," and for that, bases close to the European continent would be required. "I believe," Stark declared, "that the United States, in addition to sending naval assistance, would also need to send large air and land forces to Europe or Africa, or both, and to participate strongly in this land offensive."

Considering the importance of the Atlantic to American security, Stark argued strongly against major commitments in the far Pacific that would involve the United States in an all-out effort against Japan, as envisaged in ORANGE. Such a course would have the effect of drawing resources away from the Atlantic and cutting down aid to Britain. Even a limited war against Japan would require strong reinforcements in the Southwest Pacific and Southeast Asia to defend British and Dutch possessions. Also, it might prove very difficult indeed to prevent a limited war from becoming unlimited, as the Japanese later found out. Nor did Stark see how the defeat of Japan, even if this could be accomplished, would contribute materially to the more important objectives of the defense of the Western Hemisphere and the continued existence of the British Empire. To perform all the tasks required to achieve these objectives, the United States could "do little more in the Pacific than remain on a strict defensive."

The major alternative courses of action open to the United States, as Stark viewed the possibilities, were four, and he stated them as questions:

A. Shall our principal military effort be directed toward hemisphere defense and security in both oceans? (Similar to RAINBOW's 1 and 4.)

B. Shall we prepare for a full offensive against Japan, premised on assistance from the British and Dutch forces in the Far East and remain on the strict defensive in the Atlantic? (Similar to RAINBOW 2, or RAINBOW 3 and ORANGE with allies.)

C. Shall we plan for sending the strongest possible military assistance both to the British in Europe and to the British, Dutch and Chinese in the Far East? (In effect, this would call for an equal effort on two fronts while defending the Western Hemisphere.)

D. Shall we direct our efforts toward an eventual strong offensive in the Atlantic as an ally of the British, and a defensive in the Pacific? (Similar to RAINBOW 5.)

There was no doubt in Admiral Stark's mind that the alternative outlined in paragraph "Dog" would best serve the national interests. It would enable the United States to exert all its effort in a single direction, make possible the greatest assistance to Britain, and provide the strongest defense of the Western Hemisphere. The one great disadvantage of the Plan Dog, of course, was that it would leave Japan free to pursue her program of expansion in Asia and the Southwest Pacific. Therefore the United States, while making every effort to avoid war with Japan, should seek to keep that nation from occupying British and Dutch possessions in the Far East.

Plan Dog was the course to be followed in the event of war—and Stark seemed to have little doubt that the United States would soon be involved in the European conflict. But if war did not come, or, as he put it "until such time as the United States should decide to engage its full forces in war," the best course to follow would be that outlined in paragraph A, that is, to build up the defenses of the Western Hemisphere and stand ready to fight off a threat in either ocean.

Admiral Stark also had a program for carrying out the policy he proposed. The first step would be to prepare a joint plan as a guide for Army and Navy planning, and at least the "skeleton" of alternative plans for other situations that might develop. Such plans, however, would be of limited value, he pointed out, if there was not a "clear understanding between the nations involved as to the strength and extent of the participation which may be expected in any particular theater. . . ." For this reason, therefore, Stark recommended that secret staff talks be initiated with British military and naval authorities "to reach agreements and lay down plans for promoting unity of allied effort should the United States find it necessary to enter the war."[28]

The reaction of General Marshall and the Army planners to Plan Dog was entirely favorable. As a matter of fact, the Army had argued substantially along these lines in June 1940, when the prospect of an Axis victory in Europe had seemed so great, and General Marshall had then asked whether it would not be advisable to reframe U.S. naval policy so as to place the main effort in the Atlantic with "purely defensive action in the Pacific."[29] Thus, except for minor comments, the Army planners endorsed the Stark proposals, which went forward to the President on 13 November. On the 18th, the Joint Board instructed its planning committee to study the questions raised by Admiral Stark and prepare recommendations for submission to the President and the two service Secretaries.[30]

The British, who presumably learned of Plan Dog from Admiral Ghormley, also agreed with Admiral Stark. Since the plan was based so largely on the need to maintain the British Empire, this is not surprising. Churchill thought the plan "strategically sound" and "highly adapted to our interests," as indeed it was, but only because of the identity of British and American interests. He was "much encouraged by the American naval view," and cautioned his staff "to strengthen the policy of Admiral Stark"

---

[28] The British had already suggested such conversations on various occasions. The most recent suggestions were made in October by the British

Ambassador to Secretary Hull in Washington, and by Admiral Sir Dudley Pound to Ghormley in London.

[29] Notes of Conf in OCS, 17 Jun 40, sub: Defense Problems, OCS Misc Confs.

[30] Ltr, CofS to JB, 18 Nov 40, sub: National Defense Policy for the United States, JB 325, ser. 670; Memos, WPD for CofS, 13 Nov 40, sub: National Policy of the U.S.; Secy, Gen Staff for WPD, same date, no sub; CofS for Secy War, same date, no sub. All in WPD 4175–15.

and "not use arguments inconsistent with it."[31] Apparently the British Chiefs took this advice seriously for on 23 November Admiral Ghormley reported to Stark that in the view of the Admiralty, which he believed to be the view of the British Government, "the primary objective of the war is the defeat of Germany and Italy," and that in case Japan and the United States should enter the war, U.S.-British strategy in the Pacific should be to contain the Japanese and prevent extension of the operations to the south and to the Indian Ocean.[32] But the British clung to their faith in Singapore, and still hoped the United States would send a naval force there to hold it against the Japanese.

While arrangements went forward for conversations with the British, the joint planners continued their efforts to produce a statement of national defense policy based on Admiral Stark's recommendation. If acceptable, this document was to be submitted for approval to the President by the Secretaries of State, War, and Navy, and serve as the basis for instructions to the American representatives in the forthcoming staff conversations. On 21 December 1940, the joint planners completed their work. In all essential respects, their recommendations were similar to those of Admiral Stark. The major objective of U.S. defense policy, they said, was the security of the Western Hemisphere, and this was to be secured by full cooperation with the British Common-

wealth. Until forced to enter the war, the United States should follow the course advocated in paragraph A of Stark's memorandum; if forced into war with Japan, the United States should at the same time enter the war in the Atlantic and limit operations in the mid-Pacific and Far East so as "to permit prompt movement to the Atlantic of forces fully adequate to conduct a major offensive in that ocean."[33] American policy and strategy, therefore, would be designed to defeat Germany and her allies in order to prevent the extension of Axis influence into the Western Hemisphere, while seeking to keep the Japanese from entering the war or from attacking British and Dutch territory in the Far East.

The Joint Board approved the work of its planners on 21 December, and the Secretaries of War and Navy gave their approval soon after. The original intention was to have the Secretary of State join the two service Secretaries in submitting these recommendations to the President for his approval as the basis for future action by all agencies of the government. But Mr. Hull refused. He was in general agreement with these policies, he declared, but was doubtful of the propriety of "joining in the submission to the President of a technical military statement of the present situation."[34]

Arrangements for staff conferences with the British were completed early in January 1941, and on the 15th of the month the British delegation left for the

---

[31] Churchill, *Their Finest Hour*, pp. 690–91. The quotations are from his message of 22 November 1940 to the First Sea Lord.

[32] Ghormley to Stark, 23 Nov 40, quoted in Kittredge, U.S.British Naval Relations, se. III pt. D, p. 313, and Notes, app. B. Records of Admiralty Meeting, 22 Nov 40.

[33] Ltr, JPC to JB, 21 Dec 40, sub: National Defense Policy for the U.S., JB 325, ser. 670. Earlier drafts and directives are in the same file. See also relevant papers in WPD 4175–15 and JB 325, ser. 674.

[34] Memo, Brig Gen Leonard T. Gerow for CofS, 3 Jan 41, sub: Conf with Secy State, WPD 4175–15.

United States. There had been preliminary exchanges of view by cable and a
proposed set of instructions had been
prepared for the American representatives. But the military authorities still
did not have President Roosevelt's
approval of the recommended national
defense policy, which was to constitute
the guide lines for the American delegates. Finally, on 16 January, the President met with his military advisers, the
two Secretaries and the service Chiefs.
Present at the meeting also was the Secretary of State, who, with the others
constituted a group known informally
as the "War Council."

The meeting opened with a consideration of the problems raised by the possibility of simultaneous action by Germany
and Japan against the United States.
The President thought there was only
"one chance in five" of such an attack
but he avoided any commitment on the
basic question of whether to plan for
a major effort in the Atlantic or Pacific.
On one point, though, he left no doubt.
There was to be no curtailment of aid
to Britain, even in the event of a concerted attack in the Atlantic and Pacific.
Clearly, the President's major concern
was with Great Britain. In that sense,
he was of the same mind as his chief
military and civilian advisers. He
thought the Navy should be prepared
to convoy shipping in the Atlantic and
continue to patrol the coast. But he was
equally anxious that the Army should
not be committed to any operations until
it was fully prepared, and that American
military policy should be "very conservative" until its strength had been greatly
increased. In Latin America, the United
States would have to be prepared, the
President declared, to provide forces,

properly trained, to assist the governments in their resistance to subversive
Axis activity.

The President's view of American policy in the Pacific coincided closely with
that of the military authorities. There
the United States would stand on the
defensive with the fleet based on Hawaii.
There was to be no naval reinforcement of the Philippines, and the Commander of the Asiatic Fleet, based in
the Philippines, was to have discretion-
ary authority in the event of attack to
withdraw when he thought it necessary.
The choice was his and it would be up
to him to decide whether to sail east
toward Pearl Harbor or south to
Singapore, as the British wished.[35]

By the middle of January 1941, the
major lines of American strategy in
World War II had emerged and the re-
election of President Roosevelt assured
a continuation of the policy established
during the critical summer months of
1940. While hoping to achieve his aims
by measures short of war, the President
had publicly stressed during the preceding months America's unreadiness for
war and the danger from Europe and
the Far East. Army and Navy planners
had defined the problem facing the
United States in a series of studies, and
had made plans to meet various situations which might arise. The most likely
contingency in early 1941 was that the
United States, allied with Great Britain,
might be involved in a two-ocean war
against a combination of Germany, Italy,
and Japan. In such a contingency, it
was generally agreed, the United States
would adopt a defensive role in the
Pacific and make its main effort against

---

[35] Memo, CofS for WPD, 17 Jan 41, sub: White
House Conf of 16 Jan 41, WPD 4175–18.

the most powerful and dangerous enemy, Germany. But before firm plans could be made, it was first necessary to reach agreement with Great Britain on the broad aims of the war and the major outlines of strategy.

RAINBOW 5

During the first three weeks of January 1941 the planners of the Joint Board completed their arrangements for the American-British staff conference. On 21 January, they submitted to the board a proposed agenda for the meetings and a statement of the American position. The meetings were to be nonpolitical; no specific commitments were to be made "except as to technical method of cooperation," and agreements reached would be subject to approval by the two governments. Within this framework, the delegates were to determine the best methods by which the forces of both nations could defeat Germany and its allies should the United States be "compelled to resort to war"—a phrase introduced by the President; reach agreement on the methods and nature of military co-operation; and co-ordinate plans for the use of their forces.

As a guide for the delegates, American national objectives were defined in virtually the same terms used by Admiral Stark: (1) protection of the Western Hemisphere against military or political encroachment by any other power; (2) aid to the British Commonwealth; (3) opposition by diplomatic means to Japanese expansion. In the event of war, the "broad military objective" of the United States and Britain would be the defeat of Germany, which would be "most effectively attained" by placing the principal military effort in the Atlantic, or "navally in the Mediterranean"—another Presidential phrase. In the way of practical advice in negotiating with the British, the delegates were to keep the following in mind:

It is believed that we cannot afford, nor do we need, to entrust our national future to British direction. . . .

United States Army and Navy officials are in rather general agreement that Great Britain cannot encompass the defeat of Germany unless the United States provides that nation with direct military assistance. . . .

It is to be expected, that proposals of the British representatives will have been drawn up with chief regard for the support of the British Commonwealth. Never absent from British minds are their postwar interests, commercial and military. We should likewise safeguard our own eventual interests.[36]

The Joint Board gave its approval to these instructions and procedures on 22 January, submitting them in turn to the Secretaries of War and the Navy with the suggestion that the statement defining the military position and strategy governing the action of U.S. forces be approved by the President. As a result Secretary of the Navy Frank Knox personally submitted the report to the President on the 23d and three days later Roosevelt approved it with minor changes in wording.[37]

The American-British staff conversations opened in Washington on 29 January 1941 and continued through fourteen sessions to 29 March, when the dele-

---

[36] JPC to JB, 21 Jan 41, sub: Joint Instr for Army and Navy Representatives . . . , JB 325, ser. 674. The Presidential changes were made on 26 January; see note 37.

[37] Memo, FDR for Secy Navy, 26 Jan 41, JB 325, Ser. 674; Mins, JB Mtg, 22 Jan 41.

gates submitted a final report, commonly known as ABC–1.[38]

At the outset, the British stated their position clearly and fully:

1. The European Theater is the vital theater where a decision must first be sought.
2. The general policy should therefore be to defeat Germany and Italy first, and then deal with Japan.
3. The security of the Far Eastern position, including Australia and New Zealand, is essential to the cohesion of the British Commonwealth and to the maintenance of its war effort. Singapore is the key to the defense of these interests and its retention must be assured.

In line with this strategy, U.S. naval forces, after appropriate dispositions for defense of the Western Hemisphere, should be employed mainly in the Atlantic and Mediterranean, the British stated. But they also declared that the United States should maintain in the Pacific a fleet large enough to prevent the Japanese from prejudicing the main effort in the Atlantic.

There was no disagreement between the Americans and the British on the first two points. Both sides were agreed that Germany was the main enemy and the first objective of the allies. They agreed further that the Atlantic would be the decisive theater of the war and the principal effort of the two nations would be made there. The delegates also recognized the legitimate interests of each side, an indispensable basis for co-operation. On the American side, the security of the United States and the defense of the Western Hemisphere were

considered of paramount interest, with first call on American forces. British interests were broader, encompassing the security of the British Commonwealth of Nations. "A cardinal feature of British strategic policy," the delegates agreed, "is the retention of a position in the Far East such as will insure cohesion and security of the British Commonwealth and the maintenance of its war effort."

The third point of British strategy, the importance of Singapore, involved the whole question of Far Eastern strategy. On this, there was a fundamental disagreement between the British and American delegates. This disagreement stemmed partly from different national interests. The British had to deal with problems of imperial security, and in their view Singapore was essential to the defense of India, Australia, and New Zealand. American interests in the Far East, though substantial, were not as vital. The only American possession of importance in the area, the Philippines, had virtually been written off as indefensible in a war with Japan.

There was a basic difference in outlook also between the British and Americans. Reflecting their insular position and long tradition in wars against Continental powers, the British placed their main emphasis on sea and air power rather than large-scale ground forces. The reduction of Germany by these means would be a slow process, but the British were accustomed to long wars and had no doubt of ultimate victory. The final blow, they expected, would be delivered by ground armies, but to prepare for that eventuality they would first secure or regain the strategic positions required for the offensive—Singapore, the Mediterranean—and then con-

[38] Papers relating to the meeting are located in OPD Exec Files, item 11, Exec 4 and WPD 4402–1 *passim.* The report itself is found in several files, but is available in printed form in *Pearl Harbor Attack Hearings,* exhibit 49, pt. 15, pp. 1485–1542.

centrate on weakening the enemy's war machine. Victory with minimum losses and minimum risks, exploitation of superior naval power, and avoidance of large-scale continental operations — that was the classic British strategy.

The Americans, conscious of their overwhelming material resources and unwilling to face the prospects of a long war, wished to concentrate all their power at the earliest possible moment against the main enemy. To achieve this aim and end the war quickly with fewer casualties in the long run, they were willing to face the temporary loss of strategic positions like the Philippines and to risk substantial casualties initially rather than disperse their forces or adopt a purely defensive or delaying strategy.

These differences emerged sharply in the discussions over Singapore. What the British were asking the Americans to do was to underwrite the defense of the Empire and incorporate, as a central feature of Allied strategy, the British concept of the importance of Singapore as the key to defense of the Far East, even at the expense of concentrating for a decisive blow against Germany at the earliest possible date. Though the Americans appreciated the political, economic, and symbolic significance of Singapore for the British Empire, they doubted its strategic value and the wisdom of underwriting its defense. To accept the British proposal would not only have been contrary to their instructions but would constitute, the American delegates believed, "a strategic error of incalculable magnitude."[39] They therefore refused to budge from the position that the British must look after

their own special interests, as the United States would look after its own in the Philippines, and that the two nations should act together where their interests coincided—in the North Atlantic and the British Isles.

The report submitted by the American and British delegates laid down the basic guide lines of Allied co-operation in World War II. It defined clearly the policies, the "paramount interests" of both countries, and the general strategic concepts designed to support these policies. Among the major strategic objectives accepted by both sides were the following:

1. The early defeat of Germany as the predominant member of the Axis, with the principal military effort of the United States being exerted in the Atlantic and European area, the decisive theater. Operations in other theaters to be conducted in such a manner as to facilitate the main effort.

2. The maintenance of British and Allied positions in the Mediterranean area.

3. A strategic defensive in the Far East, with the U.S. Fleet employed offensively "in the manner best calculated to weaken Japanese economic power, and to support the defense of the Malay Barrier by directing Japanese strength away from Malaysia."

To secure these objectives, the delegates agreed on a number of specific measures, including economic pressure, a sustained air offensive against German military power, the early elimination of Italy from the war, raids and minor offensives at every opportunity, and the support of resistance movements in Axis-dominated countries. All these would be preparatory to the final offensive

[39] Memo, Army Delegates for CofS, 12 Feb 41, sub: Dispatch of U.S. Forces to Singapore, WPD 4402–3.

against Germany. For that it would be necessary to secure bases in the Mediterranean and on the west and northwest shores of Europe, and to gather "maximum land forces, composed largely of mobile armored divisions" to defeat and destroy the German Army.

The agreements reached between the American and British staffs and embodied in ABC–1 were not intended to be binding on the two nations or to have any political or official character, but only to determine the way in which the United States and the British Commonwealth could defeat Germany "should the United States be compelled to resort to war." From the start it was understood that conclusions reached by the conferees would have to be confirmed by the Chiefs of Staff of both nations and were contingent upon political agreements by the two governments. In line with this understanding, General Marshall and Admiral Stark gave their tentative approval to the report and advised the British Chiefs that they would present it to the President for approval at an appropriate time.[40] At the same time, the Joint Board issued a new directive for the preparation of RAINBOW 5, the situation most closely meeting the requirements laid down in ABC–1.

Work on RAINBOW 5 had been initiated originally in May 1940, after the German offensive in the west but before the fall of France. The situation envisaged then in RAINBOW 5 was a war in which the United States, allied with Great Britain and France, would project its armed forces "to either or both of the African and European continents as rapidly as possible" to accomplish the decisive defeat of Germany. The planning done in May on this basis was rendered obsolete within a month by the fall of France. Moreover, it seemed doubtful at the time that Great Britain would survive, and the planners turned their efforts to other RAINBOW situations —first RAINBOW 4 (hemisphere defense), and then RAINBOW 3 (United States alone in a major effort against Japan). By the end of 1940, when it appeared that Britain would survive and a revised RAINBOW 5 situation was the most likely contingency for which to plan, arrangements were already under way for the American-British staff conversations.

Once the Chief of Staff and Chief of Naval Operations had given their approval to ABC–1, work on RAINBOW 5 progressed rapidly. By 30 April, the Army and Navy had agreed on a joint plan and on that date submitted their work to the Joint Board. For the purposes of this plan, the Allies—Associated Powers, they were called—were assumed to be the United States, the British Commonwealth (less Eire), the Netherlands Indies, Greece, Yugoslavia, China, the Governments-in-Exile, and the Free French; the Axis nations, Germany, Italy, Rumania, Hungary, Bulgaria, and possibly Japan and Thailand. These last two, even if they were not in the war initially, were potential enemies and the possibility of their intervention was therefore taken into account in the plan.[41]

RAINBOW 5 was virtually identical with ABC–1. As a matter of fact, one of the first assumptions of the plan was

---

[40] Ltr, CofS and CNO to Special Army and Navy Observers in London, 4 Apr 41, sub: Tentative Approval of ABC–1, WPD 4402–18. See notation on Copy 98, *Pearl Harbor Attack Hearings*, pt. 15, 1485.

[41] Ltr, JPC to JB, 30 Apr 41, sub: Joint Basic War Plan RAINBOW 5, incl A, JB 325, ser. 642–5.

that the Allies would conduct the war "in accord with ABC–1." Thus, the strategic concepts, supporting measures, and missions enumerated in ABC–1 were repeated almost verbatim in RAINBOW 5. For the U.S. Army, "the primary immediate effort" would be to build up large land and air forces "for major offensive operations against the Axis powers" and other operations were to be restricted to those that would "not materially delay this effort." Just what these operations would consist of was not specified, although reference was made, as in ABC–1, to a large-scale attack by ground forces against Germany and to the capture of bases from which to launch such an offensive. As one of the Army planners explained at the time, " a plan must be formulated upon a situation and no prediction of the situation which will exist when such a plan can be implemented should be made." [42]

RAINBOW 5 was neither a blueprint for victory nor a plan of operations. It merely outlined the objectives and missions of American forces in case of war on the basis of assumptions that seemed sound at the time. Specific plans to achieve these objectives were still to be made. The first step was to secure authority to proceed.

Joint Board authority came on 14 May when the board formally approved both RAINBOW 5 and ABC–1, which it had tentatively approved early in April. Approval by the Secretaries came on 28 May (Navy) and 2 June (Army), at which time both plans went to the President, with the explanation that the Brit-ish Chiefs of Staff had approved ABC–1 provisionally and submitted it to their government for approval. The President apparently read the two documents carefully but withheld approval of ABC–1 on the ground that the British had not yet approved it. Nor would he approve RAINBOW 5, presumably because it was based on ABC–1, that is, on arrangements with the British which had not yet been accepted by that government. He did request, however, that "in case of war" the two plans be returned to him for his approval. [43]

The President's ambiguous response to the carefully worked out arrangements with the British, and to the American plans based on these arrangements, raised the question of whether the Army and Navy were authorized to proceed with their own planning for war on a RAINBOW 5 contingency. This question was resolved on 10 June at a meeting in Mr. Stimson's office. General Marshall's view was that since the President had not disapproved the plan, the Army could proceed with its own arrangements. This seemed reasonable, and it was on that basis that the services proceeded to make detailed plans for the employment of their forces. [44]

By the middle of 1941 American policy and military strategy had subordinated the Pacific to a secondary position, while maintaining that the United States would defend its overseas possessions and its interests in the Far East. The danger of war with Japan was a real one, but

---

[42] Memo, WPD for CofS (May 1941), sub: Analysis of Plans for Overseas Expeditions, cited in Matloff and Snell, *Strategic Planning 1941–1942*, pp. 45–46.

[43] Mins, JB Mtg, 14 May. The correspondence relating to the approval by the Secretaries and the statement recording the President's reaction are filed in JB 325, ser. 642–5.

[44] Mins, Conf Office, Secy War, 10 Jun 41, WDCSA, Secy of War Confs, I.

in the face of the greater threat from Germany it had been decided to place the main effort in the Atlantic and to restrain Japan by political and economic means. If Japan did attack, the United States would have to limit itself to the defense of that area in the Pacific vital to its security, Alaska-Hawaii-Panama, and accept the loss of the Philippines, Wake, and Guam. But there were some who still believed that the Philippines could and should be reinforced and that the obligation of the United States to the Filipinos and its position in the Far East transcended the logic of the military strategists.

The circumstances under which a war with Japan would begin were not yet known and, except for local defense plans, there was no settled solution on a plan to defeat Japan. The general pattern of the war and the courses of action open to American forces had been fixed over a long period of time. That the fleet would advance step by step across the Pacific through the Mandated Islands, specifically the Marshalls and the Carolines, to the Philippines, and that it would then seek to establish supremacy in the western Pacific was well understood and accepted. But beyond the general statement that Japan would be brought to her knees by economic pressure, blockade, and air bombardment, there was no specific plan for operations to defeat the enemy. Moreover, though it was assumed that British, Dutch, and Chinese forces would fight the common enemy, there were no plans for concerted action and there was still disagreement between the American and British planners over the role of Singapore. There was much still to be done—forces to be raised, weapons produced, and plans written. Until then, the United States would have to restrain an increasingly aggressive Japan by all means short of war.

CHAPTER IV

The Fatal Turn

Be audacious and cunning in your plans, firm and persevering in their
execution, determined to find a glorious end.

CLAUSEWITZ

The summer of 1941 was a crucial one for both Japan and the United States. Over a period of several years American planners had devised a strategy designed to protect the Western Hemisphere against Axis aggression and, if the United States was forced into war, to throw the bulk of its resources against Germany. But this strategy assumed, first, that Japan could be deterred from aggression by means short of war, and second, that in the event hostilities in the Far East could not be avoided, the United States would accept the loss of American territory in that area. The planners, unwilling to face the unpleasant prospect of large-scale military operations in the western Pacific, accepted these assumptions. But there were many, including the President and his Secretary of War, who found the conclusions of military logic distasteful and sought a way out of the dilemma. The solution provided by the advocates of air power turned American eyes once more to the Far East.

The crisis facing the Japanese leaders was more serious. In their view the very existence of the nation depended on their decisions. There seemed to be no way to end the war in China and economic restrictions were crippling their

efforts to stockpile strategic materials and prepare the nation for any eventuality. Japan was truly at the crossroad.

The July Crisis

Negotiations to settle the issues between Japan and the United States had been in progress since February 1941 when Ambassador Nomura had arrived in Washington. By summer, little progress had been made. The American position had been defined early in the conversations by Mr. Hull:

(1) Respect for the territorial integrity and the sovereignty of each and all nations.

(2) Support of the principle of noninterference in the internal affairs of other countries.

(3) Support of the principle of equality, including equality of commercial opportunity.

(4) Nondisturbance of the *status quo* in the Pacific except as the *status quo* may be altered by peaceful means.

But so long as the Japanese persisted in pursuing an aggressive policy in China and in southeast Asia there was not, in Mr. Hull's words, "one chance in twenty or one in fifty or even one in one hundred of reaching a peaceful settlement."[1]

In the year since Prince Konoye had become Premier (16 July 1940), the Japanese had achieved two of the four objectives outlined in the "General Principles."[2] The Tripartite Pact had been signed on 27 September 1940, and a neutrality pact concluded with Russia on 13 April 1941. Expansion by diplomacy had failed everywhere, except in Thailand. By agreement with Vichy France, Japan had obtained the right to military occupation of Tonkin Province and the use of air bases and military facilities in northern Indochina. But the Dutch, backed by the Americans and British, had stubbornly resisted Japanese efforts to gain economic concessions, and the Chinese showed no disposition to lay down their arms and accept Japanese terms for a settlement.

The German invasion of the Soviet Union on 22 June 1941 had a profound effect on the international situation and led the Japanese to re-examine the policy established only a year earlier. There was much heated discussion among Japanese political and military leaders of the probable effect of the Russo-German war, discussions which the Americans learned about through the medium of MAGIC[3] and which President Roosevelt characterized as "a real drag-down and knock-out fight . . . to decide which way they are going to jump—attack Russia, attack the South Seas . . . [or] sit on the fence and be more friendly with us." Foreign Minister Matsuoka favored the first course, the Army the second, and Premier Konoye inclined toward the third course. Finally, on 2 July 1941, an Imperial Conference, consisting of the chief members of the government and the armed forces meeting with the Emperor, made the final decision on Japan's future course.[4]

The question of a Soviet attack was put to rest by the Imperial Conference which decided that, regardless of any change in the international situation, Japan would adhere to the Tripartite Pact and to its plan for expansion to the south. If a favorable opportunity arose to take advantage of the war between Germany and the Soviet Union, Japan would be ready to do so. The negotiations with the United States were to be continued while preparations to place the nation on a war basis and strengthen its defenses were to be pushed forward with vigor. Also, steps were to be taken to bring about Chiang's surrender, and plans for the domination of Thailand and Indochina were to be executed immediately. "We will not be deterred," the Imperial Conference decreed, "by the possibility of being involved in a war with England and America."

---

[1] *Pearl Harbor Attack: Report of the Joint Committee on the Investigation of the Pearl Harbor Attack,* Doc. 244, 79th Cong., 2d sess. (hereafter cited as *Pearl Harbor Report*), p. 294. Unless otherwise noted this section is based on the *Pearl Harbor Report; Pearl Harbor Attack Hearings,* pt. 20, Memoirs of Prince Konoye; IMTFE, *Judgment,* pp. 924–35; Department of State, *Foreign Relations of the United States, Japan,* II, 342, 527–38, 549–55; Political Strategy Prior to Outbreak of War, pt. IV, Japanese Studies in World War II, 150. The most detailed accounts in secondary sources are Langer and Gleason, *The Undeclared War,* and, on the Japanese side, Feis, *The Road to Pearl Harbor.*

[2] See above, ch. II.

[3] Code name given to the interception and decoding of the Japanese messages.

[4] Ltr, Roosevelt to Harold L. Ickes, 1 Jul 41, cited in Langer and Gleason, *The Undeclared War,* p. 646. The 2 July decision is included among IMTFE Exhibits, 588. See also Ltr, Grew to author, 19 Jun 49, OCMH.

The problems posed by Germany's attack on the Soviet Union were hardly settled and the decision made to abide by the Tripartite Pact and continue the drive southward when a new crisis arose. Still unanswered was the note Hull had handed Nomura on 21 June, asking for some clear indication of a genuine desire for peace and making allusions to the pro-German attitude of certain members of the Japanese Government. Matsuoka, the foremost advocate of the alliance with Germany, insisted on an outright rejection of the note and the termination of the talks. Premier Konoye, fearful that a flat rejection would end the negotiations, wished to reply with counterproposals already prepared by the Army and Navy. Matsuoka would not budge from his position and Konoye, given the nod by Tojo and after consultation with the Emperor, moved to oust the pro-German Foreign Minister. First, on 16 July, he submitted the resignation of the entire Cabinet to the Emperor. Two days later he received the Imperial mandate to form a new Cabinet. This he did by selecting the same ministers as before except for Matsuoka, whom he replaced with Admiral Toyoda. The Japanese could now go ahead with the program outlined at the Imperial Conference of 2 July.

The first move of the new government was the virtual occupation of French Indochina. Protesting that Indochina was being encircled, Japan issued what was in effect an ultimatum to the Vichy Government on 19 July. On the 24th, Roosevelt offered to guarantee to the Japanese equal access to the raw materials and food of Indochina in return for the neutralization of that country Nothing came of the proposal. The fol-lowing day Japanese troops moved into the southern portion of Indochina. Japan now possessed strategically located air and naval bases from which to launch attacks on Singapore, the Philippines, and the Netherlands Indies.

Although the French acquiesced in this raid on their empire, the United States was not so obliging. In the view of the State Department, this fresh Japanese aggression constituted a threat to American interests in the Far East and justified the imposition of additional economic restrictions, then being considered by the President, as a warning to Japan. These restrictions were finally put into effect on 26 July when the President issued an order freezing Japanese assets in the United States. Since Japan no longer had the dollars with which to purchase the urgently needed materials of war, the effect of this measure, which the British and Dutch supported, was to create an economic blockade of Japan. The "obvious conclusion" of the "vicious circle of reprisal and counterreprisal," wrote Ambassador Grew, "is eventual war," and Admiral Stark took so serious a view of the situation that he warned Admiral Thomas C. Hart, commander of the Asiatic Fleet, on the 25th, to take "appropriate precautionary measures against possible eventualities."[5]

The sharp American and British reaction to their move into Indochina

---

[5] Rad, CNO to CINCAF, 25 Jul 41, in *Pearl Harbor Attack Hearings,* pt. 14, pp. 1400–1401; Grew Diary, July 1941, cited in Langer and Gleason, *The Undeclared War,* p. 654. Admiral Stark opposed a total embargo on oil at this time, but did favor a partial embargo that would provide Japan with enough for essential peacetime needs, but none for military purposes. Ltr, Stark to Col Warren G. Hoover, Actg Chief of Mil Hist, 5 Aug 59, OCMH.

GENERAL SUZUKI, *president of the Japanese Planning Board, 1941.*

came as a surprise to the Japanese and precipitated an intensive review of the nation's readiness to wage war. The picture was not encouraging. The powerful Planning Board which co-ordinated the vast, complex structure of Japan's war economy found the country's resources meager and only enough, in view of the recent action of the United States, for a quick, decisive war to gain the riches of the Southern Area. "If the present condition is left unchecked," asserted Teiichi Suzuki, president of the board, "Japan will find herself totally exhausted and unable to rise in the future." The blockade, he believed, would bring about Japan's collapse within two years, and he urged that a final decision on war or peace be made

"without hesitation." [6] The Navy's view was equally gloomy. There was only enough oil, Admiral Nagano told the Emperor, to maintain the fleet under war conditions for one and a half years and he was doubtful that Japan could win a "sweeping victory" in that time. His advice, therefore, was that every effort should be made to reach a peaceful settlement with the United States.

By the middle of August the two services had agreed on a broad line of strategy. The impetus came from a series of studies presented by the Total War Research Institute, a subordinate body of the Cabinet.[7] Forecasting the course of events during the next six months, the institute called for the invasion of the Netherlands Indies in November, followed the next month by surprise attacks on British and American possessions in the Far East. Anticipating that the United States and Great Britain would utilize Soviet bases in a war against Japan, the institute predicted that Russia, too, would become involved in the war, probably between April and October 1942. The bulk of the institute's studies, however, dealt with the problems of economic mobilization; military planning, except in the most general sense, was left to the services.[8]

These studies, as well as others, were used as reference material by the General Staffs in developing their own plans during the tense days that followed the embargo. From these discussions emerged four alternative lines of strat-

[6] Political Strategy Prior to Outbreak of War, pt. IV, Japanese Studies in World War II, 150, pp. 73–77.
[7] This group was established in October 1940 to conduct research into wartime measures, in co-operation with the Planning Board.
[8] IMTFE, exhibits 870, 870–A, and 871.

ADMIRAL NAGANO

egy, all of them designed to accomplish the swift destruction of Allied forces in the Far East and the early seizure of the Netherlands Indies. The first was based on the institute's studies and provided for the seizure of the Indies and then of the Philippines and Malaya. The second called for a step-by-step advance from the Philippines to Borneo, then Java, Sumatra, and Malaya. The reverse, from Malaya to the Philippines, constituted a third line of action and one which would have the advantage of delaying attack against American territory. The fourth plan proposed at this time consisted of simultaneous attacks against the Philippines and Malaya followed by a rapid advance along both axes to the Indies. Admiral Yamamoto's plan for an attack against Pearl Harbor, work on which had begun in January, did not

enter into the calculations of the planners at this time.

Army and Navy planners agreed that the first plan was too risky for it would leave Japanese forces exposed to attack from the Philippines and Malaya. The Navy preferred the second plan; it was safe, provided for a step-by-step advance, and created no serious problems. The Army objected to it, however, on the ground that by the time the main objectives in the Netherlands Indies and Malaya were reached the enemy would have had time to strengthen his defenses. The third plan, with its early seizure of Malaya and bypassing of the Philippines, appealed greatly to the Army planners, who hoped in this way to gain Southeast Asia and delay American entry into the war. But this course, as the Navy pointed out, also placed American naval and air forces in the Philippines in a strategic position athwart Japan's line of communication and constituted a risk of the utmost magnitude. The fourth course, simultaneous attacks and advance along two axes, created serious problems of co-ordination and timing and a dangerous dispersion of forces. But because it was the only course which compromised the views of both groups, it was finally adopted. For the first time the Japanese had a strategic plan for offensive operations designed to achieve the goals of national policy against a coalition of enemies.[9]

America Faces the Far East

By mid-August 1941, American military strategy for the Pacific and Far

---

[9] Political Strategy Prior to Outbreak of War, pt. IV, Japanese Studies in World War II, 150, pp. 9–10.

East—which reflected the determination to avoid war with Japan and to remain on the defensive even if it meant the loss of the Philippines, Guam, and Wake— no longer reflected the policy of the U.S. Government. There had been signs even before RAINBOW 5 was completed that American policy toward Japan was stiffening. The President's action in May making China eligible for lend-lease had marked the beginning of a shift in Far Eastern policy. Though it proved difficult to find any munitions to furnish China because early plans for lend-lease had been made entirely in terms of aid to Britain, by July the principle of arming a compact Chinese Army and Air Force with American weapons had been accepted with all the implications this had for relations with the Japanese. In addition, a mission under Brig. Gen. John Magruder was dispatched to China to aid in delivery of materials over the Burma Road and to assist the Chinese both in using the materials received and in placing orders properly. Magruder did not, however, have authority to discuss military plans with the Chinese, nor was he told what he should do if war broke out between the United States and Japan.[10]

The order of 26 July freezing Japanese assets in the United States and establishing a *de facto* oil embargo gave further confirmation of America's stiffening policy toward Japan. The planners had objected to the move on the ground that it might force Japan into war to gain the oil it so badly needed and thus imperil American interests in the Atlantic.[11] The President believed too, as he had written Secretary of the Interior Harold L. Ickes earlier in the month, that "it is terribly important for the control of the Atlantic for us to help to keep peace in the Pacific," but felt, after the German attack on the Soviet Union had in effect lessened the immediate danger in the Atlantic and freed Japan to move south, that the United States could take a stronger stand in the Pacific.[12] This conviction, shared by Stimson and others, was a basic factor in the decisions made during the months before Pearl Harbor.

A strong policy called for larger forces and for a revision of military plans. These were not long in coming. On the same day the oil embargo was imposed, General MacArthur, since 1936 the Military Adviser of the Philippine Commonwealth and architect of the Philippine Army, was recalled to active duty and given command of all U.S. Army Forces in the Far East (USAFFE). At the same time, by executive order, the Philippine Army was called into the service of the United States.[13] But it was the RAINBOW strategy and not the President's desire to strengthen American defenses that dictated the instructions sent to MacArthur. Except for approximately 400 reserve officers to assist in training

---

[10] Rpt, JPC to JB, Aircraft Rqmts for Chinese Govt, 9 Jul 41, JB 355, ser. 691; U.S. Mil Mission to China, 12 Sep 41, JB 354, ser. 716; Mins, JB Mtg, 12 Jul 41. For a full account of prewar policy toward China, see Riley Sunderland and Charles F. Romanus, *Stilwell's Mission to China*, UNITED STATES ARMY IN WORLD WAR II (Washington, 1953), ch. I.

[11] Memo, Turner for Stark, 19 Jul 41, sub: Study of Effect of Embargo . . . , *Pearl Harbor Attack Hearings*, pt. 5, pp. 2382–84.

[12] Ltr, Roosevelt to Ickes, 1 Jul 41, cited in Langer and Gleason, *The Undeclared War*, p. 646.

[13] For an account of these measures, and of the reinforcement of the Philippines which followed, see Morton, *The Fall of the Philippines*, chs. II and III.

the Philippine Army, he was told, he would not receive any reinforcements.

On the last day of July, only two days after he had told MacArthur not to expect any reinforcements, Marshall radically altered the Army position "to go to no further expense for permanent improvements unless savings will result." American policy, he told his staff, was to defend the Philippines, and presumably to reinforce them, but not to such an extent as to "jeopardize the success of the major efforts made in the theater of the Atlantic."[14] This scarcely constituted a reversal of the RAINBOW 5 strategy, but it did justify approval of a proposal to reinforce the Philippines with guns, tanks, and ammunition.

This shift was not as sudden as it appeared. There had been earlier proposals to reinforce the Philippines, most of which had been rejected only because of a lack of funds. The previous year President Manuel Quezon, with the support of the Philippine Department commander, had sought to secure additional money for Philippine defense by using the sugar excise funds—a project which required Congressional approval—and early in 1941 the strength of the Philippine Scouts had been doubled. Moreover, Secretary Stimson, who had served as governor-general of the Philippines and had long advocated a firm attitude toward Japan, favored the reinforcement of the islands, as did other men in high places. But it was the airmen's argument that their long-range bomber, the B-17, could do what the Navy could not that convinced the more skeptical and paved the way for a new view of the

defense of the Philippines. A force of these bombers based in the Philippines, it was contended, would not only serve to defend the islands but would constitute such a threat to Japanese movements southward toward the Netherlands Indies as to deter Japan from further aggression in that direction.

The air staff proposal was approved early in August and on the 14th the War Plans Division of the General Staff submitted a program for reinforcing the Philippines with antiaircraft artillery, modern combat planes, and tanks "to enhance the probability of holding Luzon, and, in any event, giving a reasonable assurance of holding Manila Bay."[15] General Marshall gave the plan his approval and then notified MacArthur that he would receive 1 coast artillery regiment, 1 battalion of tanks, an ordance company, and 31 P-40's sometime in September, and shortly after that another 50 P-40's directly from the factory. At the same time the Air Corps allocated 4 heavy bomber and 2 pursuit groups to MacArthur's Far East Air Force and ordered a provisional squadron of 9 B-17's from Hawaii to the Philippines. These planes, after a historic pioneer flight from Oahu by way of Midway, Wake, Port Moresby, and Darwin, reached Clark Field on 12 September. By this time the reinforcement of the Philippines enjoyed the highest priority in the War Department.

During the months that followed, aircraft, weapons, supplies, and men in increasing numbers were marked for shipment to the Philippines. But it took time to get orders filled, pack and ship them to the ports, find the vessels

[14] Gerow's Office Diary, entry of 31 Jul 41, OPD Exec Files; Phil Dept Def Proj, 1940, May 41, OPD Reg. Docs.

[15] Memo, Gerow for CofS, 14 Aug 41, sub: Reinforcement of Phil, WPD 3251-55.

to transport them, and sail them across the ocean. At every step of the way there were delays, but none so serious as the shortage of cargo ships. By November the backlog in U.S. ports of equipment marked for the Philippines amounted to approximately one million tons. Though a shipping schedule that provided for additional sailings in the next two months was established, a considerable quantity of supplies and a large number of men destined for the Philippines never got there.

The decision to reinforce the Philippines brought into sharp focus the problem of developing a trans-Pacific air route less exposed than the one via Midway and Wake. Airmen had long urged such a project, which had the additional advantages of guarding the line of communication to Australia and New Zealand and providing protection for surface vessels along the sea lanes of the South Pacific, but did not gain approval until August 1941. Construction was begun in October, when funds were made available, and by the time war came the route across the South Pacific by way of Christmas, Canton, Samoa, Fijis, and New Caledonia was nearing completion.[16]

The prevailing mood in Washington in the fall of 1941 was one of optimism over the possibility of defending the Philippines. It was the opinion of the Joint Board, expressed at the meeting of 19 September, that the reinforcements planned would have a profound strategic effect in a Pacific conflict and might well be the decisive element in deterring Japan from opening hostilities.[17] All that was needed was time to prepare. The general estimate was that preparations would be completed by March 1942. Until that time there was a risk that the Japanese would attack, but it was a risk the Army planners were apparently willing to take.

The view that Japan would not strike until the spring of 1942 was based on careful studies of the Far Eastern situation. Japan, it was assumed, wished to gain control of Asiatic Russia, China, and Malaysia, and would, if conditions were favorable, resort to war to gain its aims. The Philippines, strategically located along the path of Japan's southward course, would be one of the early objectives in a war with the United States. Thus far Japan had hesitated to seize these territories, the Army planners believed, because of Soviet Russia's unexpected and successful showing against the Wehrmacht, because of economic pressure from the United States, Great Britain, and the Netherlands, and because of the continued resistance of the Chinese Nationalists. Moreover, in the opinion of the planners, the conquest of the Philippines would be so costly an operation that Japan "will hesitate to make the effort except as a last resort." The more formidable the Philippine defenses, therefore, the less likelihood was there of a Japanese war. "Air and ground units now available or scheduled for dispatch to the Philippine Islands in the immediate future," concluded the

---

[16] For a full account of the development of this route, see Wesley Frank Craven and James Lea Cate, eds., *Plans and Early Operations—January 1939 to August 1942*, "The Army Air Forces in World War II," vol. I (Chicago: The University of Chicago Press, 1948) (hereafter cited as *AAF I*), pp. 180–82; AAF, Hist Study 9. The Development of the South Pacific Air Route, pp. 23–28, Air Hist Office.

[17] Mins, JB Mtg, 19 Sep 41.

planners, "have changed the entire picture in the Asiatic Area."[18]

Though the major assumptions and conclusions of RAINBOW 5 were still valid, its provisions for the defense of the Philippines were obviously in need of revision. Drawn up on the assumption that the islands could not be reinforced and that their loss was probable, it called for a limited defense of the entrance to Manila Bay by the existing garrison and local forces. MacArthur's recall to active duty and the induction of the Philippine Army into the service of the United States, and the new view of the defensibility of the islands and their role as a base for air operations against Japan, were eloquent testimony that events had once more outrun plans. In a strong letter to the War Department General MacArthur pointed out these facts, asserting that he would soon have a force of approximately 200,000 men organized into eleven divisions and a greatly strengthened air force. The time had come, he believed, to reject the "citadel type defense" of the ORANGE and RAINBOW plans in favor of an active defense of the entire archipelago.[19]

This proposal, so in accord with the new optimism over the defense of the Philippines, met with favor in the War Department and then in the Joint Board which on 21 November approved a revision of RAINBOW 5. In this revision, the mission of the Philippine garrison was expanded to include "all the land and sea areas necessary for the defense of the Philippine Archipelago," that is, of the entire Philippines and not only

Manila Bay. Moreover, the existence of a greatly enlarged air force in the Philippines was recognized by the provision for air attacks against "Japanese forces and installations within tactical operating radius of available bases." How far some of the planners had moved from their original defensive concept is perhaps most strikingly revealed in the first draft of a letter to MacArthur which the planners prepared for General Marshall. Air reinforcements, they wrote, had modified the conception of purely defensive operations "to include strong offensive air action," a phrase which Marshall prudently changed to "strong air operations in the furtherance of the strategic defensive."[20] But words could not gloss over the fact that the B–17 was an offensive weapon and that a force of heavy bombers in the Philippines had only one purpose—offensive operations. Marshall himself acknowledged this fact in an off-the-record press interview when he indicated "that though the last thing the United States wants is a war with the Japanese," it was preparing for "an offensive war against Japan," a war which would be waged "mercilessly everywhere in the Pacific.[21]

Though the Japanese did not wait until the spring of 1942 to open hostilities and MacArthur did not receive all that had been promised him, the Philippine garrison constituted in December 1941 a far stronger force than it had six months earlier. The strength of the ground forces, exclusive of the Philip-

<hr>

[18] Memo, Gerow for Secy of War, 8 Oct 41, sub: Strategic Concept of the Phil Is, WPD 3251–60.

[19] Ltr, MacArthur to TAG, 1 Oct 41, sub: Opns Plan R–5, WPD 4178–18.

[20] Ltr, CofS to CG USAFFE, 21 Nov 41, sub: U.S.-British Cooperation in the Far East, with Incl, extract of changes in RAINBOW 5, WPD 4402–112.

[21] Notes on Conf in OCofS, 15 Nov 41, copy in OCMH. The quotation is not General Marshall's but is from the notes of the meeting.

pine Army, had been increased by 8,563 men and now numbered 31,095. The ten reserve divisions of the Philippine Army had been two-thirds mobilized but were still poorly equipped and inadequately trained. The air force had been strengthened and reorganized. At Clark Field were 35 B-17's and scattered among the various fields on Luzon were over 100 P-40's. Much remained to be done to create a balanced air force, but the Philippines had nevertheless a larger number of modern combat aircraft than any other overseas base, including Hawaii and Panama.

Even the Asiatic Fleet had been reinforced, despite the Navy's assertion earlier in the year that it would not be. No major surface elements, it is true, had been added but Admiral Hart had received an additional squadron of PBY's for a total of 32, 6 motor torpedo boats, and 18 submarines, most of them of the latest type, giving him all together a fleet of 29 underwater craft. In addition, he had 1 heavy and 2 light cruisers, 13 old destroyers of World War I vintage, 6 gunboats, and miscellaneous vessels. Also under his command was the 4th Marine Regiment, withdrawn from China at the end of November.

The most powerful American force in the Pacific was the Pacific Fleet, based at Pearl Harbor and consisting of 9 battleships, 3 aircraft carriers, 12 heavy and 8 light cruisers, 50 destroyers, 33 submarines, and 100 patrol bombers. In addition, British and Dutch vessels in Far Eastern waters could be expected, in the event of war with Japan, to fight the common foe. Thus, the Allies could muster a naval force of considerable strength to oppose the Japanese *Combined Fleet.* Unfortunately, all efforts to work out a plan for concerted naval action in the Far East proved unsuccessful.

American bases along the line of communications between Hawaii and the Philippines had also been strengthened in 1941, but still represented little more than token forces. Guam, whose fortification had been recommended by the Hepburn Report in 1938 but denied by Congress, was still "practically defenseless against determined attack."[22] Its garrison was composed of 365 Marines, a small force of natives, and a navy consisting of three patrol boats; weapons included nothing larger than the .30-caliber machine gun. The defense of Wake Island, for which Congress had appropriated funds on the recommendation of the Hepburn Board, was a case, like that of the Philippines, of too little and too late. Construction was still in progress on 7 December but there was one Marine fighter squadron of twelve Grumman Wildcats on the island, and a 388-man detachment of the 1st Marine Defense Battalion armed with 5-inch coastal guns, 3-inch and .50 caliber antiaircraft guns, .30-caliber machine guns, and small arms. The largest group on the island were civilians, 70 Pan American Airway employees and over 1,000 construction men. Midway, the "sentry for Hawaii" and, in the opinion of the Hepburn Board, second in importance only to Pearl Harbor, had since mid-1940 been garrisoned by a small Marine force. In the summer of 1941 a naval air station was established on the island and in September the 6th Defense Battalion with 784 officers and men relieved the original garrison. The planes destined for Midway were embarked on the

---

[22] *Hepburn Report,* p. 27.

GENERAL SHORT

Lexington on 5 December, to be delivered on the morning of the 7th, but other events intervened and they did not arrive until the 17th.[23]

While the Navy, with Army air forces, provided the first line of defense in the Pacific, the Army, with certain exceptions, provided the forces to defend those bases from which ships and planes operated. The most important of these lay along the triangle Alaska-Hawaii-Panama. Not only were they vital bases but they constituted the strategic frontier of the United States and the outer defenses of the west coast. Of these, only Hawaii, 2,000 miles distant from San Francisco,

lay in the Pacific and figured in the plans for offensive operations against Japan in the event of war; Alaska and Panama, though fully as important, were more closely associated with hemisphere defense plans.

The planners had recognized early that the chief danger to Hawaii lay not so much in an effort by the Japanese to capture the islands, but rather in a sudden and unexpected attack, probably from the air, on the great naval base at Pearl Harbor. This thought had appeared from time to time in studies and estimates and was included in the local plans for defense.[24]

The transfer of the U.S. Fleet to Pearl Harbor in April 1940 and its retention there on the President's orders, a move designed to deter the Japanese, increased enormously the problems of defending the naval base and the growing number of airfield installations. During the summer and fall of 1940, Maj. Gen. Charles D. Herron repeatedly urged that heavy bombers and antiaircraft defenses, including artillery, and air warning equipment, be sent to Hawaii, and that bomb-proof shelters be built. The Navy, too, was concerned about the protection of its base from a surprise carrier-based air attack, and Secretary Knox gave strong support to Herron's requests in a letter to Stimson in January 1941. All were agreed on the danger and sought, within the limitations imposed by appropriations, to provide what was needed. But at that time Hawaii was the best equipped American base and had high priority for modern aircraft, antiaircraft guns, air warning

---

[23] Lt. Col. Robert D. Heinl, Jr., *The Defense of Wake* (Washington: U.S. Marine Corps Historical Section, 1947), pp. 4–11; *Marines at Midway* (Washington: U.S. Marine Corps Historical Section, 1948), pp. 3–9, 16.

[24] Watson, *Prewar Plans and Preparations*, pp. 465–75.

ADMIRAL KIMMEL

equipment, and barrage balloons. There was little more, Stimson assured Knox, that could be done except to provide for closer co-ordination between the Army and Navy.

When Lt. Gen. Walter C. Short assumed command of the Hawaiian Department in February 1941—at the same time that Admiral Husband E. Kimmel took over the Pacific Fleet—General Marshall carefully defined his mission for him as the protection of the naval base and the fleet, and warned against allowing service feuds to interfere with joint defense plans. Short continued along the lines already marked out, pushing construction of airfields, the air warning system, dispersal areas, and gun installations. In April he and Kimmel submitted a revised plan for the defense of Oahu which carefully specified the

responsibilities of each of the services. Included with the plan was the Army and Navy air commanders' estimate which, with remarkable prescience, outlined the probable course of a Japanese attack as a sudden air raid against ships and installations on Oahu, coming without warning and originating from carriers not more than 300 miles distant. "In a dawn attack," they foretold, "there is a high probability that it could be delivered as a complete surprise in spite of any patrols we might be using." [25]

By December 1941, the Army garrison in Hawaii had been considerably reinforced and was in many respects the strongest base in the Pacific. Assigned to its ground defense were 2 understrength infantry divisions, 4 antiaircraft artillery regiments, almost 4 complete coast artillery regiments, and 1 company of light tanks, with supporting service troops. Of the total of 234 aircraft, only about half were operational. Included in this total were a large number of obsolescent types and only six B–17's. The air warning system, though not yet completed, consisted of six mobile radar sets and three fixed stations in place but not completely installed.

The Plan for War

Despite repeated assertions of a willingness to go to war to gain its objectives, the Japanese Government in July had drawn back quickly in the face of the unexpectedly strong reaction from the United States. Contributing to this

---

[25] Joint Estimate of Army and Navy Air Action, 31 Mar 41, *Pearl Harbor Attack Hearings*, pt. 15, exhibit 44, p. 1437; *Pearl Harbor Report*, pp. 83–84; ltr, Marshall to Short, 7 Feb 41, WPD 4449–1.

JAPANESE MOCK-UP OF FORD ISLAND AND BATTLESHIP ROW, *Pearl Harbor, used in Japanese table-top maneuvers.*

lack of resolution was the slowing down of Germany's advance in Russia and the Japanese Navy's concern over the shortage of oil reserves. From the end of July until his resignation in October, Premier Konoye sought to persuade his Cabinet colleagues to adopt a less aggressive policy in an effort to reach agreement with the United States.

The first sign of this new policy was a proposal, delivered by Admiral Nomura in Washington on 6 August, for a personal meeting, a "leaders' conference," between the Premier and President Roosevelt. War Minister Tojo had agreed to this proposal only on the understanding that Konoye would use the occasion to press the program for expansion to the south. The American reply on the 17th that a prerequisite to such a meeting was the settlement of the issues between the two countries confirmed Tojo and the Army leaders in their view that the United States would never yield to the Japanese demands and that war should begin as soon as the Army and Navy were ready.

The difference between Konoye's and Tojo's views was temporarily resolved early in September and formalized at an Imperial Conference held on the 6th of the month. The agreement was characteristically Japanese and expressed in language both sides could accept and interpret in their own way. The negotiations with the United States, it was agreed, would be continued, as Konoye wished. But at the same time, military preparations would be pushed to completion so that the nation would be ready for war by the end of October, that is, in six weeks. "If by the early part of October," the conferees decided, "there is no reasonable hope of having our demands agreed to in the diplomatic negotiations . . . we will immediately make up our minds to get ready for war. . . ." [26]

The Imperial Conference also fixed the minimum demands Japan would make and the maximum concessions it would grant in the negotiations with the United States and Great Britain. The minimum demands Japan asked were, first, both the Western Powers would promise to discontinue aid to China, close the Burma Road, and "neither meddle in nor interrupt" a settlement between Japan and China; second, America and Britain would recognize Japan's special position in French Indochina and agree not to establish or reinforce their bases in the Far East or take any action which might threaten Japan; and third, both nations would resume commercial relations with Japan, supply the materials "indispensable for her self-existence," and "gladly cooperate" in Japan's economic program in Thailand and Indochina. In return for these "minimum demands" the Japanese were willing to agree not to use Indochina as a base for further military advance, except in China; to withdraw from Indochina "after an impartial peace" had been established in the Far East; and, finally, to guarantee the neutrality of the Philippine Islands. [27]

While negotiations went forward, the Army and Navy General Staff continued their preparations for war and the troops earmarked for operations in the south intensified their training, usually under conditions approximating those of the areas in which they would fight. Since agreement had already been reached on the strategy for war, General Sugiyama, Chief of the Army's General Staff, was able shortly after the 6 September Imperial Conference, to direct that detailed operational plans for the seizure of Malaya, Java, Borneo, the Bismarck Archipelago, the Netherlands Indies, and the Philippines be prepared. [28] The Army planners immediately went to work and the next two months witnessed feverish activity in the General Staff.

By the end of August the Navy staff had worked out plans for seizing bases in the western Pacific, and had from Admiral Yamamoto a separate plan for an attack on Pearl Harbor. "Table-top maneuvers" at Tokyo Naval War College between 10–13 September resulted in agreement on operations for the seizure of the Philippines, Malaya, the Netherlands Indies, Burma, and islands in the South Pacific. But there was still some doubt about Yamamoto's plan. The exercise had demonstrated that a Pearl Harbor strike was practicable, but many felt that it was too risky, that the U.S. Pacific Fleet might not be in port on the day of the attack, and that the danger of

---

[26] Konoye Memoirs, *Pearl Harbor Attack Hearings*, pt. 20, pp. 4022–23. The wording of this important statement varies in different documents. IMTFE Doc. 1579 gives a slightly different wording as does IMTFE *Judgment*, ch. VII, p. 939. The Japanese phrase "kaiseno ketsui su" may be translated literally "decide to open hostilities." Konoye apparently did not interpret the phrase as meaning that it was a decision for war; Tojo did.

[27] *Ibid.*, IMTFE Doc. 1652, exhibit 588.
[28] IMTFE exhibit 2244, Deposition of Tanaka.

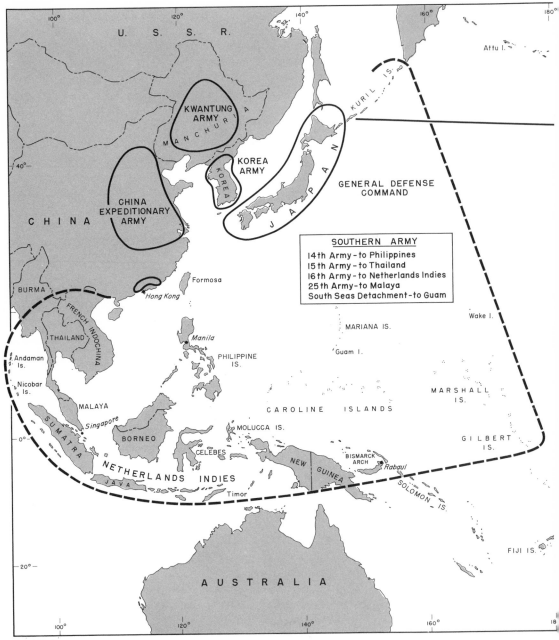

KWANTUNG
ARMY

KOREA
ARMY

GENERAL DEFENSE
COMMAND

CHINA
EXPEDITIONARY
ARMY

CHINA

BURMA

Formosa

Hong Kong

SOUTHERN ARMY
14th Army - to Philippines
15th Army - to Thailand
16th Army - to Netherlands Indies
25th Army - to Malaya
South Seas Detachment - to Guam

THAILAND

FRENCH INDOCHINA

Andaman
Is.

Nicobar
Is.

MALAYA

Singapore

SUMATRA

BORNEO

CELEBES

JAVA

NETHERLANDS INDIES

Timor

MOLUCCA IS.

NEW GUINEA

BISMARCK
ARCH

Rabaul

SOLOMON IS.

CAROLINE ISLANDS

MARIANA IS.

Guam I.

Wake I.

MARSHALL
IS.

GILBERT
IS.

FIJI IS.

AUSTRALIA

Attu I.

Manila

PHILIPPINE
IS.

KURIL IS.

U. S. S. R.

MANCHURIA

KOREA

JAPAN

MAP 1

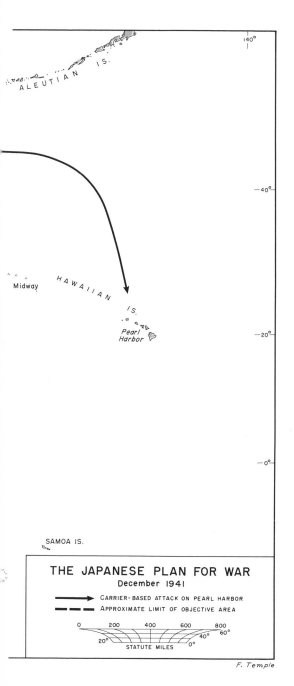

THE JAPANESE PLAN FOR WAR
December 1941

→ CARRIER-BASED ATTACK ON PEARL HARBOR
▬ ▬ APPROXIMATE LIMIT OF OBJECTIVE AREA

F. Temple

discovery during the long voyage to Hawaii was too great. But Admiral Yamamoto refused to give up his plan and finally, when he failed to convert his colleagues, offered to resign from the Navy. The combination of his strong argument that the success of the southward drive depended on the destruction of the American fleet, his enormous prestige, and his threat to resign were too much for opponents of the plan. In mid-October, a month after the maneuvers, the Navy General Staff finally adopted his concept of a surprise carrier-based attack on Pearl Harbor and incorporated it into the larger plan for war.[29]

This larger plan, which was virtually complete by 20 October and was the one followed by the Japanese when war came, had as its immediate objective the capture of the rich Dutch and British possessions in southeast Asia, especially Malaya and the Netherlands Indies. To secure these areas, the Japanese believed it necessary to destroy or neutralize the U.S. Pacific Fleet at Pearl Harbor, and to deprive the United States of its base in the Philippines. America's line of communications across the Pacific was to be cut by the seizure of Wake and Guam. Once the coveted area to the south had been secured, Japan would occupy strategic positions in Asia and in the Pacific and fortify them immediately. These bases were to form a powerful defensive perimeter around the newly acquired southern area, the home is-

---

[29] For a full account of the evolution of the Pearl Harbor plan see Robert E. Ward, "The Inside Story of the Pearl Harbor Plan," *U.S. Naval Institute Proceedings*, LXXVII, No. 12 (December 1951), pp. 1272–81.

lands, and the vital shipping lanes connecting Japan with its sources of supply.[30]

The area marked for conquest formed a vast triangle, whose east arm stretched from the Kuril Islands on the north through Wake, to the Marshall and Gilbert Islands. The base of the triangle was formed by a line connecting the Marshall and Gilbert Islands, the Bismarck Archipelago, Java and Sumatra. The western arm extended from Malaya and southern Burma through Indochina, and thence along the China coast. (Map 1)

The acquisition of this area would give to Japan control of the resources of Southeast Asia and would satisfy the national objectives in going to war. Perhaps later, if all went well, the Japanese believed, the area of conquest could be extended. But there is no evidence in the Japanese plans of an intention to defeat the United States. Japan planned to fight a war of limited objectives and, having gained what it wanted, expected to negotiate for a favorable peace.

Operations to secure these objectives and others would begin on the first day of war, when Japanese military forces would go into action simultaneously on many fronts. Navy carrier-based aircraft would attack the U.S. Pacific Fleet in the Hawaii area. Immediately after, joint Army and Navy air forces would strike American air and naval forces in the Philippines, while other Japanese forces hit British Malaya. After these simultaneous attacks, advance Army units were to be landed at various points in Malaya, the Philippines, and British

Borneo. The results thus obtained were to be immediately exploited by large-scale landings in the Philippines and in Malaya, followed by the rapid occupation of those areas. At the same time, Thailand was to be "stabilized," Hong Kong seized, and Wake and Guam occupied. The conquest of the Bismarck Archipelago would follow the seizure of the last two islands.

During this first period, Army and Navy forces were to seize advance air bases in the Celebes, Dutch Borneo, southern Sumatra, the Moluccas, and Timor. The bases thus seized were to be immediately utilized for air attacks on Java, while other preparations for the invasion of that island were speedily completed.

With the U.S. Fleet and the Philippines neutralized, and with advance bases in the Netherlands Indies, the Japanese would move against Java and Sumatra. Taking Singapore under fire from the land side, that is, from Malaya, Japanese forces would first invade and occupy this British bastion. Once that fortress was reduced, the Japanese would move on to northern Sumatra, in preparation for the drive on Java. Meanwhile, other Japanese forces moving southward through the Netherlands Indies were to join those in Sumatra in the final attack on Java.

While Java was being occupied, the Japanese would complete their seizure of Sumatra and capture air bases on the southern tip of Burma at the earliest possible moment. If conditions were favorable they would then push on in Burma and occupy the Andaman and Nicobar Islands in the Indian Ocean. Operations in China would be continued throughout this period in order

---

[30] This account of the Japanese plan is based on a number of documents which, together with the plan, are described in Morton, *The Fall of the Philippines*, pp. 51–55.

to maintain "the present strategic situation."[31]

The occupation of the Netherlands Indies would complete the first period of the war and would, the Japanese estimated, require five months. The Philippines they expected to take in 50 days, Malaya in 100, the Indies in 150. After that time the Japanese would consolidate their position and strengthen the bases along the perimeter of their newly gained empire in order to repulse any Allied effort to penetrate this defensive ring or threaten the vital area within it. During this period the Army would continue its operations in China and Burma and establish a system of administration for the southern area.

The Navy's plan for the period after the initial operations was to intercept with a strong force anticipated trans-Pacific operations of U.S. naval forces. Its plan lists as "areas expected to be occupied or destroyed" eastern New Guinea, New Britain, the Fiji Islands, Samoa, the Aleutians, Midway, and "strategic points in the Australia area."[32] But operations to seize these objectives were not authorized by *Imperial General Headquarters* until the spring of 1942.

Japanese planners anticipated that certain events might require an alteration in their strategy and outlined alternative courses of action. The first possibility was that Japanese-American negotiations then in progress would prove successful. If this unexpected success was achieved, all operations were to be suspended, even if the final order to attack had been issued. The second possibility was that the United States might take action before the attack on Pearl Harbor by sending elements of the Pacific Fleet to the Far East. In that event, the *Combined Fleet* would be deployed to intercept American naval forces. The attacks against the Philippines and Malaya were to proceed according to schedule.

If the Americans or British launched local attacks, Japanese ground forces were to meet the attack and air power was to be brought into the area to destroy the enemy. These local operations were not to interrupt the execution of the general plan, but if the United States or Great Britain seized the initiative by opening operations first, Japanese forces were to await orders from *Imperial General Headquarters* before beginning their assigned operations. The possibility of a Soviet attack, or of a joint United States–Soviet invasion from the north, was also considered by the Japanese planners. To meet such a contingency, Japanese forces in Manchuria were to be strengthened. Should this attack materialize the Philippine and Malay operations were to proceed as planned, while air units were to be immediately transferred from the home islands or China to destroy Russian air forces in the Far East. Ground forces were to be deployed to Manchuria at the same time to meet Soviet forces on the ground.

The forces required to execute this vast plan for conquest were very carefully calculated by *Imperial General Headquarters. (Chart 1)* A large force had to be left in Manchuria, and an even larger one in China. Garrisons for

---

[31] Hist of *Army Sec, Imperial GHQ,* Japanese Studies in World War II, 72, p. 16.

[32] *Combined Fleet* Top Secret Operational Order 1, 5 Nov 41, in *Pearl Harbor Attack Hearings,* pt. 13, p. 438.

CHART 1—DISPOSITION OF MAJOR JAPANESE FORCES FOR WAR, DECEMBER 1941

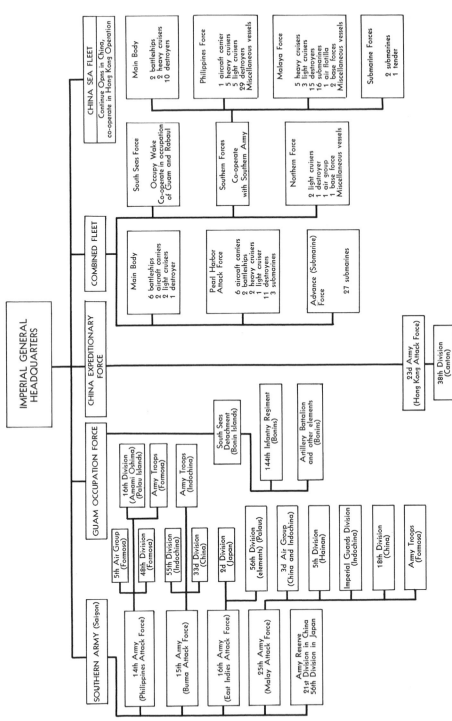

Source: Japanese Opns in SWPA, II, pp. 60–64

Korea, Formosa, Indochina, and the defense of the home islands required additional forces. Thus, only a small fraction of the Japanese Army was available for operations in the south. Of the total strength of the Army's 51 divisions, 1 cavalry group, 59 mixed brigades, and 1,500 first-line planes, *Imperial General Headquarters* could give the *Southern Army*, which had the mission of carrying out all these operations, only 11 divisions and the bulk of 2 air groups with approximately 700 planes.

The Japanese allocated their forces for the initial operations only after a careful estimate of the enemy forces.[33] In the Philippines, the Japanese correctly estimated there was a U.S. Army garrison (exclusive of Scouts) of 22,000 men and 110,000 Philippine Army troops. The air strength in the islands was thought to consist of 270 planes of all types, 70 of which were heavy planes. The British were thought to have in Malaya alone 90,000 troops, and in Burma another 35,000. Dutch ground forces in the Indies were estimated to number 85,000 men. The total enemy ground strength was placed at 447,000 men, including British, American, Dutch, and Thailand troops. This figure did not include Chinese, Indian, Australian, and New Zealand troops. The total enemy air strength, the Japanese estimated, consisted of 1,249 aircraft distributed as follows: Malaya, 330; Burma, 60; Philippine Islands, 270; Netherlands Indies,

312; Thailand, 177; China, 130. The Hawaiian air force was not included in the Japanese estimates.

American naval strength was overestimated. The Japanese believed there were 5 carriers in the Pacific area. They placed 2 cruisers, 1 heavy and 1 light, in the Asiatic Fleet, and another 3 in the Pacific Fleet, which was thought to contain also 11 battleships, 84 destroyers, and 30 submarines. The submarine force in Philippine waters was estimated at 17 underwater craft. Their estimate of British and Dutch naval forces was equally inaccurate.

In the execution of this complicated and intricate plan, the Japanese planners realized, success would depend on careful timing and on the closest co-operation between Army and Navy forces. No provision was made for unified command of all services. Instead, separate agreements were made between Army and Navy Fleet commanders for each operation. These agreements provided simply for co-operation at the time of landing and for the distribution of forces.

In addition to supporting the Army's operations in the south, the *Combined Fleet* had other important missions. Perhaps the most important, and certainly the most spectacular, was that assigned the *Pearl Harbor Striking Force*. Later, this force was to support operations of the *4th Fleet* and then assist in the southern operations. The *6th Fleet* (submarines) was to operate in Hawaiian waters and along the west coast of the United States to observe the movements of the U.S. Pacific Fleet and destroy lines of communication by surprise attacks on shipping. The *5th Fleet* was to patrol the waters east of Japan, in

[33] Army estimates are based on Hist of *Army Sec, Imperial GHQ*, Japanese Studies in World War II, 72, pp. 12, 18–22; Navy estimates on Political Strategy Prior to Outbreak of War, pt. V, same series, 152, pp. 19–20. The estimates are for November 1941: the first source.

readiness for enemy surprise attacks, and, above all, to keep on the alert against Russia.

The Japanese plan for war was complete in all respects but one—the date when it would go into effect. That decision awaited another more important decision: whether or not Japan would go to war. The answer was not long in coming.

CHAPTER V

The Decision for War

One would have lingering wars with little cost;
Another would fly swift, but wanteth wings;
A third thinks, without expense at all,
By guileful fair words peace may be obtained.

SHAKESPEARE, *Henry VI*

By the fall of 1941 relations between the United States and Japan had reached a critical stage. American leaders had made it clear that so long as Japan adhered to the Tripartite Pact and to its efforts to conquer China there was little chance for compromise. But they needed time to complete their preparations.

For the Japanese, most of whom were unwilling to pay the American price for peace, time was of the essence. They were convinced that acceptance of American peace terms would only lead to further demands and ultimately leave Japan dependent on the United States and Great Britain. To them the gambles of war seemed preferable to the ignominy of a disgraceful peace.

The necessity for a prompt decision on Japan's future course was pressing, the Japanese leaders believed. The economic blockade was slowly depriving the nation of the power to fight. Signs of military co-operation among the Allies and of their intention to reinforce their Far Eastern bases were too clear to be ignored. Failure to seize the right moment for action might lose for Japan the vital resources of Malaya and the Netherlands Indies without which the

nation would be dependent upon the United States and Great Britain. Thus, the Japanese were in the unenviable position—or thought they were—of either making concessions or going to war. They could not afford delay. "Time had become the meter of strategy for both governments. But one did not mind its passing, while the other was crazed by the tick of the clock."[1]

Tojo Takes Over

The six weeks' reprieve Prince Konoye had won on 6 September to

---

[1] Feis, *The Road to Pearl Harbor*, p. 270. Unless otherwise noted, this chapter is based on this work and upon the Konoye Memoirs, *Pearl Harbor Attack Hearings*, pt 20; The Japanese intercepts in pt. 12, pp. 1–254; *Pearl Harbor Report*; IMTFE, *Judgment*, ch. VII, pp. 935–95; *U.S. Foreign Relations, Japan: 1931–41*, II, 549–58, 709–16, 766–70; U.S. Department of State, *Peace and War, United States Foreign Policy, 1931–1941* (Washington, Government Printing Office, 1943). Other works of value for this period are Langer and Gleason, *The Undeclared War*; Walter Millis, *This is Pearl! The United States and Japan—1941* (New York: William Morrow and Company, 1947); Stimson and Bundy, *On Active Service in Peace and War*; Sherwood, *Roosevelt and Hopkins*, Hull, *Memoirs*; Samuel Eliot Morison, *The Rising Sun in the Pacific, 1931–April 1942*, vol. III, "History of United States Naval Operations in World War II" (Boston: Little, Brown and Company).

settle the outstanding issues between the United States and Japan by diplomacy went by quickly without producing a settlement. A new proposal, which Ambassador Nomura delivered to Hull on 27 September, was rejected by the Americans. On 10 October, Nomura, who had renewed the request for a meeting between Roosevelt and Konoye, wrote Foreign Minister Soemu Toyoda that there was not "the slightest chance on earth" of a leader's conference "so long as Japan refused to compromise." The negotiations, in the words of Toyoda, had "slowly but surely . . . reached the decisive stage."[2]

The domestic situation was no better. Even more insistently, the Army and Navy pressed for a quick decision on the question of war. Oil stocks, the services pointed out, were steadily diminishing, the United States was rapidly reinforcing the Philippines, and the most favorable season of the year for operations was rapidly approaching. Failure to act soon, they declared, might result in a delay of many months and expose the Japanese to a Soviet attack in Manchuria. Finally, on 24 September, General Sugiyama and Admiral Osami Nagano, the Army and Navy Chiefs of Staff, submitted a joint letter calling attention to the shortage of supplies, the effect of the weather on operations, and the problems of mobilizing, staging, and deploying their forces. "With all the force of their position" they asked for a quick decision "by 15 October at the latest," so that they could start operations by mid-November.[3]

With no agreement in sight Konoye sought to win an extension. On 12 October he invited War Minister Tojo, the Navy and Foreign Ministers, and the president of the Planning Board to his home for a final conference on the question of war and peace. At the meeting the Premier argued strongly for continuing the negotiations beyond the deadline, then set at 15 October. The Navy Minister would not commit himself but General Tojo, on the ground that success in the negotiations would require concessions in China, refused to go along with Konoye. The issue had now been narrowed to the withdrawal of Japanese troops from China and on the morning of the 14th the Premier again sought Tojo's consent. "On this occasion," he urged the War Minister, "we ought to give in for a time . . . and save ourselves from the crisis of a Japanese-American war." Tojo again refused, and at a Cabinet meeting later in the day demanded that the negotiations be terminated. Finally, late that night, he sent Konoye a message stating that the Cabinet ought to resign, "declare insolvent everything that has happened up to now, and reconsider our plans once more."[4]

Without Tojo's support Konoye had no recourse but to resign. The Army, seeking possibly to avoid responsibility for the decision which must soon be made, suggested as his successor a member of the Imperial family, Prince Naruhiko Higashikuni. The suggestion was rejected as contrary to tradition and the Marquis Kido, together with the council of senior statesmen (former pre-

---

[2] *Pearl Harbor Report*, p. 322.
[3] Political Strategy Prior to Outbreak of War, pt. IV, Japanese Studies in World War II, 150, pp. 13–15.

[4] Konoye Memoirs, *Pearl Harbor Attack Hearings*, pt. 20, p. 4010.

miers), recommended that Tojo himself be named premier. The Emperor accepted this recommendation. On the 18th Tojo took office with an Imperial mandate to reconsider Japan's policy in relation to the world situation without regard for the 6 September decision. The fate of Japan was in the hands of its generals.

In Washington where every Japanese move was carefully weighed and analyzed, the Cabinet crisis was cause for real concern and Ambassador Grew's cables did little to lessen it. On the 16th when Konoye resigned, Admiral Stark told Pacific and Asiatic Fleet commanders that there was "a strong possibility" of war between Japan and the Soviet Union. Warning them that Japan might also attack the United States, Stark instructed the two commanders to take "due precautions." This message Hart and Kimmel passed on to their Army colleagues who a few days later received quite a different message from Washington informing them that they need not expect an "abrupt change in Japanese foreign policy."[5] Apparently the Army did not agree with the Navy's estimate of the international situation, and neither mentioned the possibility of an attack on Pearl Harbor.

The period from 18 October to 5 November was one of mounting tension and frantic preparations on both sides of the Pacific. In Tokyo the Tojo Cabinet and the high command, meeting in an almost continuous series of Liaison Conferences, considered every aspect of Japan's position and completed the plans for war. Finally, on 5 November a decision was reached and confirmed by an Imperial Conference. This decision was substantially the same as that reached on 6 September: to continue negotiations in an effort to reach an agreement with the United States, and, if no settlement was reached, to open hostilities. The deadline first set was 25 November, later extended to the 29th of the month. The significance of this decision was revealed in a message the new Foreign Minister, Shigenori Togo, sent Admiral Nomura on the 4th telling him that relations between the two countries had "reached the edge." Next day he wrote that time was "exceedingly short," and the situation "very critical." "Absolutely no delays can be permitted. Please bear this in mind and do your best," Togo said. "I wish to stress this point over and over."[6]

The Imperial Conference of 5 November agreed that Japan should make proposals to the United States. The first, Proposal A, was an amendment to the latest Japanese proposal and provided for a withdrawal from China and French Indochina, when and if a peace treaty had been signed with Chiang Kai-shek. In certain areas in China, to be specified in the treaty, Japanese troops would remain for a "suitable period," vaguely and informally estimated at about twenty-five years. Further, the Japanese Government would interpret its obligations under the Tripartite Pact independently of the other Axis Powers. Lastly, Japan would agree not to dis-

[5] Memo, Gerow for CofS, 18 Oct 41, sub: Resignation of Japanese Cabinet; Rad, CNO to CINCPAC and CINCAF, 16 Oct 41, both in *Pearl Harbor Attack Hearings*, pt. 14, pp. 1389, 1402. See also Ltr, Grew to author, 19 Jun 49, OCMH.

[6] Dispatch, Togo to Nomura, 4 and 5 Nov 41, in *Pearl Harbor Attack Hearings*, pt. 12, exhibit 1, p. 92.

GENERAL TOJO

ral resources in the Netherlands Indies. Finally, the United States was to resume commercial relations with Japan, and to provide that nation with oil.[7]

With the decision made and the deadline set, the Army and Navy drew up an agreement embodying the objectives of the war and an outline of operations. On the same day the Navy Chief of Staff sent the *Combined Fleet* orders outlining the Navy's operations for war, with the explanation that "anticipating that war with the United States, Great Britain, and the Netherlands will begin in the early part of December, for self-preservation and self-defense, the Empire has decided to complete the various preparations for war."[8] During the remainder of the month, the fleet was assembled, and on the 21st all forces, including the *Carrier Striking Force* scheduled to attack the Pacific Fleet, were ordered into operational waters. Most of the submarines for the Hawaiian area left Japan around 20 November.

On the 6th, the Army Chief of Staff issued instructions to the *Southern Army* to prepare detailed plans for operations in the event that the negotiations failed. At a meeting in Tokyo on 10 November, the Army and Navy commanders reached agreement on the details of their plans. At the same time, the major field commanders received orders to proceed with their preparations. On 20 November, the actual order for the attack was issued, but with the proviso that it would be

criminate in trade, provided all other nations did the same. In his instructions to Nomura, Foreign Minister Togo emphasized that while other matters could be compromised in his negotiations with the United States, Japan could not yield on the question of China.

In Proposal B, to be made if the first was rejected, no mention was made of the Tripartite Pact or the removal of Japanese troops from China. Japan would withdraw its troops from southern Indochina immediately and from the northern part of that country only after the negotiation of a peace treaty with Chiang Kai-shek, or after the conclusion of a "just peace" in the Pacific. In return, the United States was to agree not to interfere in the negotiations with China, and to co-operate with Japan in the acquisition and exploitation of natu-

---

[7] The text of the two proposals is reproduced in IMTFE exhibit 779.

[8] USSBS, *The Campaigns of the Pacific War*, (Washington, 1946), app. 12, pp. 43–46, app. 14, p. 49. The *Combined Fleet* Top Secret Order 1 is reproduced in *Pearl Harbor Attack Hearings*, pt. 13, pp. 431–84.

held until the results of the diplomatic negotiations were known.[9]

In Washington, the privileged few followed each diplomatic move of the Japanese in the mirror of MAGIC while observing in reports from all parts of the Far East increasing evidence of Japanese military preparations. Japanese ship movements toward Malaya and the concentration of shipping at Formosa, staging area for an attack on the Philippines, were quickly detected by American observers. Mr. Grew, who had reported as early as 27 January 1941 that there was talk in Tokyo of a surprise attack on Pearl Harbor, warned on 3 November that recent troop movements placed Japan in a position to start operations "in either Siberia or the Southwest Pacific or in both," and that war might come with "dramatic and dangerous suddenness." "Things seem to be moving steadily toward a crisis in the Pacific," wrote Admiral Stark to his Pacific Fleet commander on 7 November. "A month may see, literally, most anything. . . . It doesn't look good."[10]

The Progress of Negotiations

The first proposal agreed upon at the Imperial Conference of 5 November was handed to Mr. Hull by Ambassador Nomura two days later. On the 12th, the Secretary of State told the Japanese Ambassador that the proposal was being studied and that he hoped to have a reply ready within three days. When it

JAPANESE SIGNS *proclaiming an economy drive in Tokyo.*

came it proved to be a rejection of Proposal A on the ground that the offer to withdraw troops from China and Indochina was indefinite and uncertain, and that the United States could not agree to the Japanese definition of nondiscrimination in trade.

On 20 November, Admiral Nomura, who now had the benefit of the advice of his newly arrived colleague Saburo Kurusu, presented Proposal B, virtually a restatement of the "minimum demands" and "maximum concessions" of the 6 September Imperial Conference. Intercepted Japanese messages had already revealed to Mr. Hull that this was to be Japan's last offer for a settlement. To the Secretary, the Japanese offer "put conditions that would have assured Japan's domination of the Pacific, placing

[9] Hist of *Southern Army,* 1941–45, Japanese Studies in World II, 72, pp. 4–8; Hist of *Army Sec. Imperial GHQ,* revised ed., same series, 72, pp. 29–39.

[10] Telgs, Grew to Hull, 27 Jan and 3 Nov 41, in *Pearl Harbor Attack Hearings,* pt. 14, exhibit 15, pp. 1042, 1045–60; Ltr, CNO to Kimmel, 7 Nov 41, G–3 Exec Files.

us in serious danger for decades to come." The commitments which the United States would have had to make were, in his opinion, "virtually a surrender." [11]

The problem faced by American political and military leaders was a serious one. An outright rejection of Proposal B might well provide Japan with the pretext for war. Full acceptance was out of the question. The only way out of the dilemma was to find a "reasonable counterproposal" or a basis for temporary agreement. In support of this point of view, Admiral Stark and General Gerow pointed out to the Secretary of State that a *modus vivendi* would "attain one of our present major objectives— the avoidance of war with Japan." "Even a temporary peace in the Pacific," Gerow, who was acting for Marshall, urged, "would permit us to complete defensive preparations in the Philippines and at the same time insure continuance of material assistance to the British—both of which are highly important." [12]

During the next four days, various drafts of a *modus vivendi* were prepared, and a final draft was completed on the 25th. This document provided that both nations would refrain from "any advance by force" into any areas in eastern Asia or the Pacific, and that Japan would withdraw from southern Indochina, reduce the number of troops in that country, and not send any reinforcements there. In return, the United States agreed to modify its economic restrictions to permit the shipment of $600,000

worth of cotton a month, medical supplies, and oil "for civilian needs." The *modus vivendi* was to remain in force three months. [13]

The *modus vivendi* and the reply to Japan's Proposal B were the subjects of a lively discussion by the War Council on 25 November. The general view was that the *modus vivendi* should be adopted, but Hull was pessimistic and expressed the view that the Japanese might "break out any time with new acts of conquest by force" and that national security now "lies in the hands of the Army and Navy." [14] Nor could the U.S. Government ignore the unfavorable reaction of other powers to the *modus vivendi*. Great Britain, China, the Netherlands, and Australia felt that it represented a move in the direction of appeasement. The Chinese reaction was especially sharp, and from Chiang came a bitter protest, supported by a cable from Churchill.

The President was faced with a fateful decision. The Army and Navy wanted time to prepare for war, and were willing to buy it with minor concessions. But the slight prospect of Japanese acceptance of the *modus vivendi* was, in the view of the Secretary of State, hardly worth the risk of lowering Chinese morale and resistance, and opening the way for appeasement. At a meeting in the White House on 26 November, the President and Mr. Hull agreed that the small results expected from the *modus vivendi* did not justify the risks.

---

[11] Hull, *Memoirs*, II, 1069.

[12] Memos, Stark and Gerow for Secy State, 21 Nov 41, in *Pearl Harbor Attack Hearings*, pt. 14, pp. 1104–07.

[13] *Pearl Harbor Attack Hearings*, pt. 14, exhibit 18, pp. 1085–1201. Mr. Hull characterized the economic concessions as "chicken feed." *Pearl Harbor Report*, p. 381.

[14] Hull, *Memoirs*, II, 1080.

That afternoon, therefore, when the Secretary of State handed the Japanese Ambassador his 10-point reply to Proposal B, he omitted the *modus vivendi* which had been intended as an introduction to these points outlining the basis for a peaceful settlement.

Though the military leaders were informed on the evening of the 26th of the decision to abandon the *modus vivendi*, they were apparently not advised of the action taken on the ten points. Consequently, the discussions on the morning of the 26th in General Marshall's office, and in the Joint Board later in the day, were held without knowledge of the final rejection of Japan's last proposal.[15] On the following morning, 27 November, Marshall and Stark summarized for the President their view of the situation. A Japanese offensive seemed imminent to them, but the direction of the attack "cannot now be forecast." "The most essential thing, from the United States point of view," they declared, "is to gain time" to complete the preparations for war. Military action before the completion of the reinforcement of the Philippines, they urged, should be avoided "so long as consistent with the national policy," and should be considered "only if Japan attacks or directly threatens United States, British, or Dutch territory."[16]

In view of the seriousness of the situation, the Army and Navy chiefs felt that commanders in the Pacific should be warned immediately. Already, the Navy had sent out word on the 24th—to be passed on to the Army commanders—that prospects for an agreement with Japan were slight and that Japanese troop movements indicated that "a surprise aggressive movement in any direction, including attack on Philippines or Guam" was a possibility.[17] Now, on the 27th, Stimson asked General Gerow—Marshall had left for the Carolina maneuvers—whether the Army should not send a warning. Gerow showed him the Navy message of the 24th, but this failed to satisfy Stimson who observed that the President wanted a warning message sent to the Philippines. After a number of hurried meetings of the War Council, the 27 November war warning was drafted. Considered by the War Department as a "final alert," the message was sent to Hawaii, the Philippines, Panama, and San Francisco. The commander of each of these garrisons was told of the status of the negotiations with Japan, the imminence of hostilities, and the desirability of having Japan commit the "first overt act." Each was instructed to "undertake such reconnaissance and other measures" as he thought necessary and to carry out the tasks assigned in RAINBOW 5 if hostilities occurred. With the exception of MacArthur, each of the commanders was also warned not to alarm the civilian population or to "disclose intent." At the same time G–2 of the War Department sent an additional and briefer message to Hawaii and Panama, but not to the Philippines, warning against subversive activities.

---

[15] OCofS Conf, 26 Nov 41, WDCSA 381 Phil (12–4–41); *Pearl Harbor Attack Hearings*, pt. 15, pp. 1641–43; Langer and Gleason, *The Undeclared War*, pp. 898–99.

[16] Memo, Marshall and Stark for President, 27 Nov 41, sub: Far Eastern Situation, *Pearl Harbor Attack Hearings*, pt. 14, p. 1083.

[17] Rad, OPNAV to Comdrs Pacific and Asiatic Fleets, 2005, 24 Nov 41, *Pearl Harbor Attack Hearings*, pt. 14, p. 1405.

JOINT BOARD MEETING, NOVEMBER 1941. *This is the first photograph taken of the Joint Board. Seated around the table, from left: Brig. Gen. Harold F. Loomis, Maj. Gen. Henry H. Arnold, Maj. Gen. William Bryden, General Marshall, Admiral Stark, Rear Adm. Royal E. Ingersoll, Rear Adm. John H. Towers, Rear Adm. Richmond K. Turner.*

The Navy warning of the 27th, which was passed on to the Army commanders, was more strongly worded and was definitely an alert for war. "This dispatch," it read, "is to be considered a war warning. . . . An aggressive move by Japan is expected within the next few days." Navy commanders were alerted to the likelihood of amphibious operations against either the Philippines, the Kra Peninsula, or Borneo and instructed to "execute an appropriate defensive deployment" preparatory to carrying out the tasks assigned in their war plans. The possibility of attack on Pearl Har-

bor was not mentioned in either of the messages.[18]

The response to these warnings was immediate. From MacArthur, who had promptly alerted his command, came the report that air reconnaissance had been extended and intensified "in conjunc-

[18] Memo, Gerow for Marshall, 27 Nov. 41, sub: Far Eastern Situation; Rads, Marshall to CG USAFFE, Hawaiian Dept, and Caribbean Defense Comd, Nos. 624, 472, 461, 27 Nov 41, OCS 18136–118 and WPD 4544–16; Brig Gen Sherman Miles to G–2 Hawaiian Dept. No. 472, 27 Nov 41. Most of these are published in *Pearl Harbor Attack Hearings*, pt. 3, p. 1021, pt. 14, pp. 1328–30. Stimson's account of these events is in pt. 39, p. 84. The Navy message is in pt. 14, p. 1406. See also *Pearl Harbor Report*, pp. 199–201.

tion with the Navy," and that measures for ground security had been taken. "Within the limitations imposed by present state of development of this theater of operations," he told the Chief of Staff, "everything is in readiness for the conduct of a successful defense." The reply from General Short in Hawaii, where both the war warning and the G–2 message had arrived at about the same time, read simply: "Report Department alerted to prevent sabotage." This clear indication of confusion in Hawaii went unnoticed in the Munitions Building. To General Marshall and his chief aides Hawaii was the only base "reasonably well equipped," its commanders had been fully alerted, and they "felt reasonably secure at that one point." Their eyes were focused on the Philippines and Southeast Asia.[19]

The Die is Cast

The day 29 November, the deadline set by the Japanese, found the force scheduled to attack Pearl Harbor already on its way and elements of the *Southern Army* assembling for their various tasks. Since Hull's note of the 26th—which a Liaison Conference had summarily rejected the next day—it had been clear to the Japanese leaders that no agreement was possible. But a few more days were needed, so on the 28th Nomura and Kurusu were instructed to do their best to keep the conversations open. The next day the council of senior statesmen met with members of the Cab-

inet. Tojo presented the Cabinet view for war, but several of the senior statesmen expressed doubts about the wisdom of a war with the United States. Prince Konoye asked why it was not possible to continue "with broken economic relations but without war," to which Tojo replied that the final consequence of such a course would be "gradual impoverishment."[20] Later that day, the same group met with the Emperor, and each man presented his views.

The Liaison Conference, which met in Tokyo at the Imperial Palace on 29 November 1941, was the conference at which the final details for the opening of hostilities were decided. Agreement was reached on the form and substance of a note to the United States which, in effect, would end the negotiations. The conferees agreed that a declaration of war would not be necessary. The timing of the note to be delivered in Washington was discussed, and it was finally decided to allow the Army and Navy to fix the interval between the delivery of the note and the opening of the attack.[21]

The decisions of the Liaison Conference were formalized and sanctioned by the Imperial Conference on 1 December. Tojo, who presided at this meeting, explained the purpose of the conference, and then the Cabinet ministers and the Chiefs of Staff discussed the question of war with the United States, Great Brit-

---

[19] Rads, MacArthur to Marshall, No. 1004, 28 Nov 41, OCS 18136–118; Short to Marshall, 27 Nov 41, WPD 4544–13. For testimony of Generals Marshall and Gerow on this question, see *Pearl Harbor Attack Hearings*, pt. 3, pp. 1036, 1423; pt. 27, p. 2191; *Pearl Harbor Report*, pp. 150–51.

[20] Konoye Memoirs, *Pearl Harbor Attack Hearings*, pt. 20, p. 4012.

[21] IMTFE, exhibits 2954 and 2955, Depositions of Tojo and Togo. On 4 December, Admiral Ito, Vice Chief of the Navy General Staff, conferred with Mr. Togo, Foreign Minister, in regard to the time interval between the delivery of the note and the opening of the attack. The Navy at first insisted on a 15-minute interval, but finally agreed to thirty minutes. Statement by Rear Adm. Tomioka, then Chief of the Operational Section, Navy General Staff.

ain, and the Netherlands. The decision was in favor of war. "Our negotiations with the United States regarding the execution of our national policy, adopted 5 November, have finally failed," reads the record of the meeting. "Japan will open hostilities against the United States, Great Britain, and the Netherlands." The Emperor spoke not a single word during the meeting.[22]

All was in readiness; only the date for the start of war remained to be fixed and that was quickly decided. The 8th of December (Japanese Standard Time) was the date selected and on the 2d the Army and Navy Chiefs passed the information on to the forces already moving into position for attack. But on the slim chance that by a miracle the United States would agree to the Japanese terms, the naval Chief of Staff added that should an amicable settlement be reached "all forces of the Combined Fleet are to be ordered to reassemble and return to their bases." From Admiral Yamamoto's flagship went the message *Niitaka Yama Nobore* 1208 (Climb Mount Niitaka 1208), the prearranged signal to carry out the attacks as scheduled.[23]

Various considerations underlay the choice of date and the decision to strike without warning. Both the Army and Navy held that delay would be disastrous and that surprise was an essential pre-requisite to the success of the plan. The Navy, moreover, feared that America's potential naval superiority would, by

March 1942, make the execution of the Japanese plan extremely hazardous, if not impossible. The Army was anxious to start operations immediately, to prevent the United States and Great Britain from completing preparations in the Philippines and Malaya. Weather was a decisive consideration also. December and January were favorable months for amphibious operations, with the tide and moon in favor of landings. Sunday morning was selected with a full knowledge of American weekend activities.[24]

The first week of December 1941 was one of strain and nervous tension in Tokyo and of suspense and somber watchfulness in Washington. The signs of an early break were too clear to be missed by those who could read the intercepted Japanese messages and intelligence reports. Nomura and Kurusu saw Hull several times, but both sides knew nothing could come of these meetings. On the 4th, Thursday, Congress adjourned for a long weekend. Next day the Japanese Embassy staff began to leave Washington and Nomura reported the partial destruction of codes.

On 6 December, President Roosevelt composed a last-minute plea for peace to the Emperor. On the same day a Liaison Conference in Tokyo approved the decision to have Nomura deliver Japan's final note at 1300 the next day, thirty minutes before the scheduled launching of the attack on Pearl Harbor. This note, in fourteen parts, began to arrive in Washington later in the day. Thirteen of the fourteen parts of the message were in American hands that night, together with reports of two large

---

[22] IMTFE exhibit 588, Doc. 1652, Record of Imperial Conferences.

[23] These messages are reproduced in USSBS, *The Campaigns of the Pacific War* (Washington, 1946), p. 51; Morison, *The Rising Sun in the Pacific*, p. 93. The message went out to all Navy forces at 1730, 2 December, as *Combined Fleet* Radio Operational Order 6.

[24] Hist of *Army Sec, Imperial GHQ*, Japanese Studies in World War II, 72, p. 36; IMTFE, exhibit 3646, Deposition of Togo.

Japanese convoys off Indochina, headed south. Unidentified aircraft, presumably Japanese, had been observed over Luzon where by this time a full air alert was in effect and where the troops had already moved into defensive positions along the beaches. In Manila, Admiral Sir Tom Phillips, commander of the British Far Eastern Fleet, was just leaving for his flagship *Prince of Wales* after concluding arrangements with Hart and MacArthur for concerted naval action in the event of an attack. From Hawaii came a reassuring message that work on the South Pacific ferry route was progressing satisfactorily. Fourteen B–17's left San Francisco that night for Oahu, after a personal inspection by Maj. Gen. Henry H. Arnold, on the first leg of their run to the Philippines. Their ground crews were already on the high seas in a heavily loaded convoy of seven vessels carrying aircraft, artillery, ammunition, fuel, men, and supplies to General MacArthur.

That same day, 6 December, Japanese forces were rapidly approaching their various destinations. The Pearl Harbor force after a voyage across the North Pacific was heading southeast and at 2300 (Washington time) was about 600 miles north of Oahu. On Formosa airfields the planes for the attack on Clark Field were lined up, and the troops scheduled to seize advance airfields in the Philippines had already left staging areas in Formosa and the Pescadores. The invasion force for Guam was in position fifty miles north, on the island of Rota, and the Wake force stood ready at Kwajalein. Advance units of the Japanese *25th Army* had left Hainan in two convoys on 4 December on their way to Malaya and on the 6th were nearing

southern Thailand and Kota Bharu in British Malaya.

On the morning of the 7th, Sunday, the fourteenth and last part of the final Japanese note was intercepted and decoded. The War Department had its copy by about 0900. Though it did not indicate when or where war would start, its intent was clear. A short time later two additional messages were intercepted. Taken with the 14-part note breaking off the negotiations, they were starkly revealing. One instructed the Japanese ambassador to destroy the code machines and secret documents; the other to deliver the 14-part message at 1300 (Washington time). At 1030 that morning Stimson and Knox went to Hull's office where they were closeted for well over an hour and at 1230 the President received the Chinese Ambassador to whom he read his note of the day before to the Emperor. "This is," he told Hu Shih, "my last effort for peace. I am afraid it may fail." [25]

General Marshall spent Sunday morning on the bridle path and reached his office before 1100. The intercepted message giving the 1300 deadline (0730 Hawaiian time) for delivery of the 14-part note struck him as significant and he suggested to Admiral Stark that an additional warning be sent to the Pacific. He then composed a message to the commanders in Hawaii, the Philippines, Panama, and San Francisco telling them that the Japanese were destroying their coding machines and would present at 1300 "what amounts to an ultimatum." "Just what significance the hour set may have," he added, "we do not know, but be on alert accordingly."

---

[25] Feis, *The Road to Pearl Harbor*, p. 340.

Declining an offer from Admiral Stark for the use of the Navy's radio, Marshall turned the message over to an officer for transmission over the Army's network and was assured shortly before noon that it would be delivered in thirty minutes. By a series of ironical circumstances and unexpected delays the message to Hawaii was in turn entrusted to commercial telegraph and radio and then to a bicycle messenger who, on his way from Honolulu to Fort Shafter, was caught in the attack with his still encoded message.[26]

President Roosevelt's personal note to the Emperor reached Tokyo at noon of the 7th (Tokyo time), but was not delivered to Ambassador Grew until 2100 that night. Shortly after midnight (about 1100 of the 7th, Washington time), he called on the Foreign Minister to request an audience with the Emperor, but Togo said he would deliver the message himself. Meanwhile Ambassador Nomura had made an appointment to see Mr. Hull at 1345. He and Kurusu arrived at the State Department a half hour late and were admitted to Hull's office at 1420, only a few minutes after the Secretary had received a telephone call from the President telling him of the attack on Pearl Harbor. The Japanese emissaries handed the secretary the 14-part note, which he already had on his desk. "In all my fifty years of public service," he said with feeling, "I have never seen a document that was more crowded with infamous falsehoods and distortions—infamous falsehoods and distortions on a scale so huge that I never imagined until today that any Government on this

planet was capable of uttering them."[27] The Japanese left without making any comment.

In Tokyo, Ambassador Grew received from Foreign Minister Togo the Japanese note breaking off the negotiations about four hours later (approximately 0800, Tokyo time). Later that morning, after Japanese bombs had fallen on Hawaii, Guam, and Wake, after Japanese forces had attacked the Philippines, Hong Kong, and Shanghai, and Japanese troops had landed in Malaya, Mr. Grew received an announcement that a state of war existed between Japan and the United States. Around noon, Premier Tojo read to "a stunned and silent nation" the Imperial Rescript declaring war. The broadcast closed on the martial strains of *"Umi Yukaba"*:

Across the sea, corpses in the water;
Across the mountain, corpses in the field;
I shall die only for the Emperor,
I shall never look back.[28]

Conclusion

From the vantage point of hindsight, Japan's decision to go to war appears as a supreme act of folly. By this decision, the Japanese leaders appear to have deliberately committed their country to a hopeless struggle against a coalition vastly superior in potential industrial and military strength. The Pearl Harbor attack, which brought the United States into the war, has been characterized as politically "disastrous" and strategically "idiotic." "One can search military history in vain," writes the historian of naval operations in World

---

[26] *Pearl Harbor Report*, pp. 219–28.

[27] *Pearl Harbor Report*, p. 41.

[28] Japanese Opns in Southwest Pacific Area, Hist series II, p. 41, OCMH.

War II, "for an operation more fatal to the aggressor."[29]

To the Japanese the decision to go to war was a difficult choice, made only under the greatest necessity and with an awareness of the danger involved. But, after calculating all the risks, the Japanese believed they had a fair chance of success. They fully appreciated the industrial potential of the United States and that nation's ability to fight a major war on two fronts. But they had to accept this risk, as General Tojo said, "in order to tide over the present crisis for self-existence and self-defense."[30] They recognized, too, that victory would have to be won quickly and that the longer the war lasted the more disadvantageous would Japan's position vis-à-vis the United States become. Their plans provided for such a victory, but made no provision for the defeat of the United States or Great Britain. The Japanese intended to fight a limited war for limited objectives and having once secured these objectives they planned to set up a defense in such depth and of such strength that the Allies would prefer a settlement to the long and costly war that would be required to reduce these

KURUSU AND NOMURA *in Washington, December 1941.*

defenses. To the Japanese leaders, this seemed an entirely reasonable view.

Perhaps the major error of the Japanese was their decision to attack the United States when the main objective of the war was to gain the strategic resources of Southeast Asia. Had they bypassed the Philippines and rejected Yamamoto's plan for the strike against Pearl Harbor, it is possible that the United States might not have gone to war, or, if it had, that the American people would have been more favorably disposed toward a negotiated peace. While the Japanese would have had to accept certain risks in following such a course, they would not have forced the United States to declare war. The President and his chief advisers were prepared to ask Congress for a declaration of war if Japan attacked Great Britain. The

---

[29] Morison, *The Rising Sun in the Pacific*, p. 132. Admiral Stark later recalled a conversation with Nomura, to whom he said, prophetically: "If you attack us we will break your empire before we are through with you. While you may have initial success due to timing and surprise, the time will come when you too will have your losses but there will be this great difference. You not only will be unable to make up your losses but will grow weaker as time goes on; while on the other hand we not only will make up our losses but will grow stronger as time goes on. It is inevitable that we shall crush you before we are through with you." Nomura made no reply. Ltr, Stark to Hoover, 5 Aug 59, OCMH.

[30] Political Strategy Prior to Outbreak of War, Japanese Studies in World War II, 150, p. 37.

Japanese knew this, but they did not know, or seriously miscalculated, the strength of isolationist sentiment in the United States. To a large part of the American people, a war with Japan over Malaya or the Netherlands Indies would have appeared as an effort to pull British and Dutch chestnuts out of the fire. Such a war would have split the country and made difficult the full mobilization of American and industrial might. "I don't know," Hull remarked later to Admiral Stark, "whether we would have been in the war yet if Japan had not attacked us."[31]

The United States Government was in a difficult position in the winter of 1941. It was committed to a major effort in the Atlantic and the support of the British Isles but had drawn a line in the Far East beyond which it would not permit Japan to go. At the same time, it was preparing for offensive operations against Japan, preparations that would be completed within several months. Had Japan, without abandoning its aims in Southeast Asia, sedulously avoided any overt act against the United States—a course that was debated in Tokyo until the end of November—the administration would have been faced with a distasteful choice: (1) to declare war against Japan and risk an unpopular war, or (2) to stand idly by while the Japanese secured the rich resources of Malaya and the Indies which would enable them to push the war in China. The Japanese, by attacking Pearl Harbor, made a choice unnecessary and unified the American people as nothing else could have done. "Like Adam and Eve," says the British military historian, Maj.

Gen. John F. C. Fuller, "the Americans discovered they were naked. Their eyes were most unexpectedly opened, and they suddenly realized that they had been living in a fool's paradise. . . ."[32]

The Japanese placed great reliance for the success of their plans on the situation in Europe. Even if Germany did not defeat England or Soviet Russia they thought there was little possibility of peace. They did not expect an early invasion of England, but did anticipate that Germany would establish control of the European continent in the near future. And even if Germany did not defeat England or the Soviet Union, both those nations would be too preoccupied to make a major effort in the Far East. The possibility of Soviet action in Manchuria or American use of Soviet bases in Asia was not discounted and provision was made in the plan for either contingency. But such action, it was believed, would not come until after the southern area had been seized.

---

[31] Ltr, Stark to Hoover, 5 Aug 59, OCMH.

[32] Maj. Gen. J. F. C. Fuller, *The Second World War, 1939–1945* (New York: Duell, Sloan and Pearce, 1949), p. 133. Evidence on public opinion is not conclusive. A Gallup poll reported in the New York *Times* for 23 February 1941 found that although 56 percent of those polled were in favor of an effort "to keep Japan from seizing the Dutch East Indies and Singapore," only 39 percent supported risking war in such an attempt. Again, in August 1941, a *Fortune* poll showed that 33.7 percent of those polled were in favor of defending the Philippines, East Indies, and Australia, and only 22.3 percent favored the defense of an unspecified portion of this area. The conclusion of John W. Masland, writing in 1941, was that "powerful commercial interests and articulate isolationist pressure groups" opposed American opposition of Japan. John W. Masland, "American Attitudes Toward Japan," *Annals of the American Academy of Political and Social Science* (May 1941), p. 165. See also *Public Opinion, 1935–1946*, prepared by Mildred Strunk under editorial direction of Hadley Contril (Princeton, N.J.: Princeton University Press, 1951), p. 1077, items 33–35, 38, 39.

Considering the alternatives, the international situation in the fall of 1941, and the risks, the Japanese plan was not altogether as unrealistic as it has appeared to many. The seizure of Southeast Asia and the time allotted did not seem too difficult, and with the resources of this area the Japanese believed they could wage a defensive war along their outer perimeter for a long time. Certainly this course, even with its risks, was preferable from their point of view to submission.

In the view of the leaders of Japan, there was no honorable choice but war.

The United States and Great Britain, they were convinced, were bent on destroying Japan or reducing it to a minor power. Submission was unthinkable and Japan had no alternative, "but to resolutely plunge into war" while it still had the power to do so. The nation entered the war, wrote a prince of the Imperial family, "with a tragic determination and in desperate self-abandonment." If it lost, "there will be nothing to regret because she is doomed to collapse even without war."[33]

[33] Statement of Prince Higashikuni, 9 Jun 49, ATIS, G-2 FEC, copy in OCMH.

PART TWO

THE DEFENSIVE: PEARL HARBOR
TO MIDWAY

With broken heart and head bowed in sadness but not in shame, I report to your Excellency that today I must arrange terms for the surrender of the fortified islands of Manila Bay. . . . With profound regret and with continued pride in my gallant troops, I go to meet the Japanese commander.

General Wainwright to President Roosevelt, 6 May 1942

Why, victor, dost thou exult? The victory will be your ruin.

OVID

CHAPTER VI

The First Weeks of War, 7 – 26 December

Mars, unscrupulous god of war, rages throughout the world.
VERGIL

When the Japanese opened hostilities in the Pacific they struck with such dramatic suddenness, at so many points, and over so vast an area that the Americans, whose eyes were fixed on the Philippines and Southeast Asia, were taken completely by surprise. Almost simultaneously the Japanese attacked Hawaii, the Philippines, Wake, Guam, Singapore, Hong Kong, Malaya and Thailand. All these assaults, even the one against Pearl Harbor, had been foreseen but no one had anticipated that they would all be made at once, on the first day of war.

The Japanese Offensive: First Phase

In the Japanese plan for war, the 5-month period allotted to the seizure of the southern area, supporting operations, and the capture of positions necessary to establish a strong defensive perimeter was divided into three phases. The first phase consisted of six separate and widely scattered operations, synchronized to obtain the maximum advantage of surprise, and timed to begin simultaneously on the date set for war. On that day Japanese forces would launch the attack on Pearl Harbor to destroy or neutralize the U.S. Pacific Fleet; cut the line of communications to the Philip-

pines by occupying Guam, Wake, and the Gilberts; destroy American air power in the Philippines to remove the threat to their own right flank and as a prelude to the invasion of the islands; occupy Thailand to secure a base for operations against Malaya and Burma; land in northern Malaya and on the Isthmus of Kra to begin the drive toward Singapore off the base of the Malaya Peninsula; and take over the British outpost at Hong Kong. (*Map III*)

The force assigned to the Pearl Harbor attack—4 heavy and 2 light carriers supported by 2 fast battleships, 2 heavy cruisers, a destroyer squadron, submarines, tankers, and supply ships—left the assembly area in Tankan Bay in the desolate, snowbound Kurils on 26 November, Tokyo time. Following a northerly route across the Pacific, well off the shipping lanes and beyond the range of patrol planes from Wake and Midway, Vice Adm. Chuichi Nagumo took his formidable fleet eastward through fog and rough sea and early on the 4th of December, after the weather had moderated sufficiently to permit refueling, reached a point about 900 miles north of Midway. There the fleet turned southeast until it was about 500 miles north of Oahu. Then it shifted course due south for the final run to the target at a speed of twenty-four knots. It was now 2100 of the 6th, Hawaiian time (1700 of the 7th Tokyo time). In less than nine hours, just before 0600 of the 7th, the carriers had reached their launching point some 200 miles north of Oahu, having come 3,000 miles across the Pacific, much of it by dead reckoning, without detection. Immediately the heavy cruisers sent up four reconnaissance planes. Except for the richest prize, the three carriers and their escort, the entire Pacific Fleet was in port.[1]

It was still dark when the Japanese pilots, cheered by shouts of "Banzai" from their comrades, took off from the carriers. The first wave of 183 planes was formed and headed for Oahu by 0615, to be followed an hour later by a second wave of 167 planes. Already a force consisting of Japan's most modern submarines, based on Kwajalein in the Marshalls, had taken up positions covering the entrance to Pearl Harbor, and five midget submarines were making their way toward the open submarine net.

Flying at 9,000 feet, above a dense but broken layer of clouds, into a magnificent sunrise, the first wave of aircraft reached Oahu, "still asleep in the morning mist," at 0750. Part of the formation headed for the Army's Wheeler and Hickam airfields; the rest for the fleet anchorage at Ford Island. Five minutes later, after at least three of the midget submarines had penetrated into the har-

bor, the Japanese planes dropped their first bombs.

The next two hours of that Sabbath morning on Oahu, where all attention up to then had been focused on the possibility of sabotage, were a nightmare. Bombs and torpedoes dropped everywhere, on ships in the harbor, on Army installations, on depots, and other targets. Dive bombers machine-gunned parked planes and the ground crews rushed pell-mell to their battle stations. Within a half hour almost all the great ships lined up in "Battleship Row" had been hit. *Oklahoma* capsized, *West Virginia* sank, *Arizona* was aflame, and *California* was going down. Hickam and Wheeler Fields, hit in the first attack, suffered badly. The Army planes, parked in close order, wing tip to wing tip, were perfect targets.

By 1000 the raid was over and the Japanese planes were heading north toward the carriers. Three hours later the carriers were speeding away to the northwest, still undetected, leaving behind them on Oahu death and destruction. Some of the submarines remained in Hawaiian waters until early January, a few venturing as far as the west coast, to report on the movements of the Pacific Fleet and to attack American shipping.

The results achieved by the raid were a complete vindication of Admiral Yamamoto, originator of the plan. The Japanese pilots had studied their charts and intelligence reports well and knew exactly what to go after. Though there were 94 naval vessels in the harbor, they concentrated on the battle force of the Pacific Fleet, sinking or putting out of action in less than two hours 8 battleships, 3 light cruisers, 3 destroyers, and

---

[1] The account which follows is based on Japanese Opns in SWPA, pp. 68–71; Japan's Decision to Fight, ATIS Research Rpt No. 131; Morison, *The Rising Sun in the Pacific*, pp. 88–95; Craven and Cate, *AAF I*, pp. 194–201; Morton, *The Fall of the Philippines*, pp. 78–79.

a number of auxiliary vessels. They also destroyed 92 naval planes and damaged 31 more. The Army lost a total of 96 aircraft, including those destroyed in depots and those later cannibalized. American casualties for the day were 2,403 men killed and 1,178 wounded, most of them naval personnel.[2]

Despite the enormous damage they wrought, the Japanese had failed to take full advantage of their opportunity. For some unaccountable reason they overlooked entirely the installations at Pearl, the repair shops, the dry dock, and the oil tanks then filled to capacity. And even less understandable is their failure to seek out and destroy the American carriers at sea, which, with the cruisers, destroyers, and submarines, constituted an effective striking force. Both these failures cost the Japanese dearly later, but for the moment they had good reason to rejoice. With the loss of only about fifty planes and five midget submarines, they had inflicted on the United States what an official Congressional report described as "the greatest military and naval disaster" in the nation's history.[3]

While Admiral Nagumo's carrier-based planes were immobilizing the U.S. Pacific Fleet at Pearl Harbor, other Japanese forces were moving to cut the American line of communications to the Philippines and to knock out General MacArthur's air force. Planes from Saipan hit Guam shortly after the Pearl Harbor attack, and at about the same time planes based on Kwajalein began the bombardment of Wake. These attacks marked the opening of softening-up operations which continued for two days and on the 10th the invasion force moved up. Against Guam, Vice Adm. Shigeyoshi Inouye, commander of the *Fourth Fleet,* sent the Army's *South Seas Detachment* plus supporting naval units, all together about 5,000 men. Landing before dawn on the northwestern and eastern shores of Guam, this force quickly overcame the small Marine garrison and the native police and gained possession of the island in a matter of hours. That same day, the Japanese also occupied Makin and Tarawa in the British-held Gilbert Islands without resistance.

At Wake, where the defenders were more numerous and better prepared, the Japanese sent a smaller force and with quite different results. Led by Maj. James P. S. Devereux, the marines, on the morning of the 10th, beat off the first landing attempt by about 500 special naval landing troops. The weak Japanese force, less two destroyers sunk by Marine aircraft, withdrew to Kwajalein to await reinforcements and was back on the 22d with 500 more men and additional naval and air support, including two carriers diverted from the retiring Pearl Harbor force. Early the next morning the Japanese landed and before the day was over the garrison, after a bitter resistance, was forced to surrender. A naval expedition, sent to

[2] Morison, *The Rising Sun in the Pacific,* p. 126. These figures are revised estimates and are slightly higher than those given in *Pearl Harbor Report,* pp. 64–65. Other figures are used in Stetson Conn, Rose C. Engelman, and Byron Fairchild, Guarding the United States and Its Outposts, ch. VII, a volume now in preparation for the series UNITED STATES ARMY IN WORLD WAR II. The reader should consult this work for a fuller treatment of the Army's role in the Pearl Harbor attack.

[3] *Pearl Harbor Report,* p. 65. Admiral Stark wrote later, "Had the Japs devoted some of their attack to our shops, oil storage, etc.—it would have been a lot rougher going for a considerable period." Ltr, Stark to Hoover, 5 Aug 59, OCMH.

"BANZAI!" *Japanese sailors cheer the Pearl Harbor attack force as the airplanes take off from a carrier, 7 December 1941.*

relieve the island, had approached to within 425 miles of Wake by the morning of 23 December. But when news of the surrender reached Hawaii, it was ordered to return to Pearl Harbor, to the bitter disappointment of the Marine aviators aboard the *Saratoga*. With the capture of Wake the Japanese gained control of the line of communication across the Central Pacific.[4]

As at Pearl Harbor, the keynote to the Japanese attack against the Philippines was surprise. The first aim was to de-

stroy the Far East Air Force, then land advance units to build airstrips for the short-range Army fighters which would cover the landing and subsequent operations of the main invasion force when it came ashore later. The task of conquering the Philippines was assigned to Lt. Gen. Masaharu Homma's *14th Army;* naval support would be provided by the *3d Fleet* assisted by elements of the *2d Fleet;* air support, by the *5th Air Group* and *11th Air Fleet.* The main staging area for the invasion force was Formosa, but units staged from the Ryukyus, Pescadores, and Palau as well. Naval aircraft of the *11th Air Fleet* based on Formosa were to deliver the main attack on American air installations in central

[4] Heinl, *The Defense of Wake*; Morison, *The Rising Sun in the Pacific*, pp. 184–86. A Japanese account of these actions is contained in Japanese Opns in SWPA, p. 71; a fuller account of the Guam action is in Opns of the *South Seas Detachment*, Japanese Studies in World War II, 36.

PEARL HARBOR, 7 DECEMBER 1941

Luzon and Army aircraft, which had a shorter range, would strike targets to the north.[5]

The opening air offensive was planned for daylight of the 8th—the 7th east of the date line—about three hours after the raid on Pearl Harbor. Simultaneous action was impossible, for the sun rose earlier in Hawaii. But even this plan for a 3-hour delay went awry, for at dawn of the 8th dense clouds of heavy fog blanketed the Formosa airfields. The Japanese were filled with dismay. As the early morning hours rolled by, their anxiety increased. The Americans, they

were sure, would by now have news of the Pearl Harbor raid and would have taken precautions against air attack. Even more frightening was the possibility that this delay would enable the heavy bombers of the Far East Air Force to attack Formosa. Indeed, after an erroneous report and a misunderstood radio message, the alarmed Japanese began passing out gas masks.

News of the Pearl Harbor attack had indeed reached Manila, as the Japanese feared. The Navy radio picked up the message announcing the raid at 0230 of the 8th (0800, 7 December, Hawaiian time), and within two hours all commanders had been alerted and troops ordered to battle positions. At about

[5] For a full account of this plan and of the events which followed, see Morton, *The Fall of the Philippines*, ch. V, *passim.*

0500, Maj. Gen. Lewis H. Brereton, commander of the Far East Air Force, was waiting outside MacArthur's office for permission to send his B–17's, half of which had been moved south to Del Monte airfield in Mindanao, against Formosa. The events which followed have been obscured by the conflicting statements of the several participants, but this much is clear: (1) That an attack against Formosa was proposed; (2) that it was deferred in favor of a photo reconnaissance mission; (3) that at about 1100 the strike against Formosa was finally authorized; and (4) that the heavy bombers at Clark Field, which had been ordered aloft at about 0800 were called in to make ready for the raid on Formosa.[6]

Despite the fog a few Japanese Army aircraft had taken off from Formosa and bombed targets in northern Luzon between 0930 and 1030. Finally at 1015, as the fog began to lift, the *11th Air Fleet* sent its planes out for the attack on Clark Field. The assignment was an important one and the pilots of the 192 aircraft assigned to the mission were the best and most experienced men available. They arrived over the target at about 1220 to find the B–17's lined up on the field below and the fighters readying for a take-off. After the delay in getting started and the lapse of time since the Pearl Harbor attack, the Japanese had not expected to find so rich a harvest. But they did not question their good fortune and went in for the attack.

The raid lasted for more than an hour, the first flights concentrating on the hangars, barracks, and warehouses. The greatest casualties were inflicted by the low-level attacks of the Zeros, which destroyed and damaged 17 or 18 B–17's and 18 P–40's—almost the entire force based at Clark—on the ground. Casualties were fifty-five killed and more than a hundred wounded. Japanese losses could not have been more than six fighters. The two squadrons of B–17's which had been transferred to the Del Monte airfield in Mindanao escaped the attack.

Simultaneously with the raid on Clark Field the Japanese struck the fighter base at Iba, to the west, destroying all but two of the P–40's there as well as the radar station, barracks, warehouses, and equipment. Before dawn the next day they hit Nichols Field near Manila, and on the 10th the naval yard at Cavite, which they practically destroyed. Thus, in two days and with insignificant casualties the Japanese virtually wiped out America's air power in the Far East and removed the threat to the flank of their advances southward.

At the start of war most of the surface strength of the small U.S. Asiatic Fleet was based south of Manila Bay, in the Visayas. By evening of the 8th, the fleet, except for the submarines and auxiliary craft, was steaming south out of Philippine waters. On the 14th, Patrol Wing 10 and three tenders followed, and two days later the remaining B–17's flew from Mindanao to Darwin in northwest Australia.

The Japanese began their landings in the Philippines on the first day of war on Batan Island, 150 miles north of Luzon. On the 10th, they made two more landings, one at Aparri and one at Vigan, in northern Luzon, and two days later more

---

[6] A full account of the events preceding the attack on Clark Field can be found in Morton, *The Fall of the Philippines*, pp. 79–84.

Japanese came ashore at Legaspi, on the southeast tip of the island. These were not the main landings and were designed only to secure airfields and to cut communications between Luzon and the islands to the south. General MacArthur read the meaning of these moves right and refused to shift his forces to meet them, but waited instead for the main landings to come.

The Japanese landings in the southern Philippines had as their primary purpose the acquisition of bases for the attack on Borneo. Two landings were made: one at Davao in Mindanao on 20 December by a force from Palau; and another, by elements of the same force, on Jolo Island in the Sulu Archipelago four days later. In neither case were the Americans or Filipinos able to offer more than a token resistance. Within a short time the Japanese had moved two naval air flotillas from Formosa to Davao and Jolo, and the *3d Fleet* began assembling in Davao harbor for the invasion of Borneo.

The main landings of the *14th Army* came on 22 December at Lingayen Gulf 120 miles north of Manila, with a secondary effort at Lamon Bay, southeast of the capital, two days later. Opposition was slight and by Christmas Day General Homma had secured a firm lodgment and was ready to drive on Manila from two directions. Next day General MacArthur declared the capital an open city and transferred his headquarters to Corregidor. Already General Brereton, commander of the Far East Air Force, had left for Australia; Admiral Hart was on his way south to join his fleet; and the American and Filipino troops on Luzon were falling back to the Bataan Peninsula.

The Japanese had achieved remarkable successs thus far in their campaign to take the Philippines. Within a period of three weeks they had established complete aerial and naval supremacy, cut the line between the Philippines and Australia, and now they stood ready to move in force on Manila.

In the China area, the Japanese met with equal success. Their plans called for the occupation of the British base at Hong Kong, and the seizure of the foreign concessions in Shanghai and Tientsin. The latter were taken without difficulty, but the British and Canadian garrison at Hong Kong put up a stiff resistance. On the morning of 8 December Japanese planes from Canton bombed the Kowloon airfield on the mainland just across the strait from Hong Kong. The Japanese *38th Division,* also based at Canton, moved out at about the same time and by 14 December had penetrated the British defenses on the mainland to reach the Kowloon Peninsula. On the night of the 18th, the *38th Division,* aided by the *Second China Expeditionary Fleet,* began to cross the strait and by morning of the next day was firmly entrenched on the island of Hong Kong. The next week witnessed bitter fighting, but the odds against the British and Canadians were too great. On Christmas Day the garrison surrendered.[7]

---

[7] Despatch by Maj Gen E. M. Maltby, "Operations in Hong Kong, 8–25 December 1941," *Supplement to the London Gazette*, January 29, 1948: Japanese Opns in SWPA, p. 75. For full account of the battle for Hong Kong, see the official British volume, Maj. Gen. S. Woodburn Kirby, C. T. Addis, J. F. Meiklejohn, G. T. Wards, and N. L. Desoer, *The Loss of Singapore*, vol. I, "History of the Second World War: The War Against Japan" (London: Her Majesty's Stationery Office, 1957).

The success of the Japanese at Pearl Harbor, in the Philippines, and in China was, in a sense, meaningless without similar successes in the principal theater of operations, Southeast Asia. It was there that the strategic resources Japan needed so badly were and it was there that the Japanese concentrated their main strength—three armies, with supporting air and naval forces. Malaya and Singapore were to be taken by Lt. Gen. Tomoyuki Yamashita's *25th Army;* the Netherlands Indies by the *16th Army,* and Burma by the *15th.* The *3d Air Group,* based in south China and northern Indochina, and the *Southern Expeditionary Fleet* were to support the forces in Malaya.

Advance units of the *25th Army* left Hainan Island on 4 December and on the morning of the 8th began landing at Singora and Pattani in southern Thailand, and at Kota Bharu, just across the border, in British Malaya. At the same time Japanese aircraft in Indochina bombed military installations in Singapore. The first two landings were unopposed, and even assisted by local Thai authorities, but the Kota Bharu force came under strong attack from British aircraft and beach defense guns and withdrew with heavy losses. Later in the day, with stronger air protection, the Japanese tried again and this time succeeded in establishing a beachhead. On the evening of the 9th, the main body of the *25th Army* began to arrive, and next day Japanese land-based naval aircraft removed the last danger to the beachhead by sinking the *Prince of Wales* and *Repulse,* which had ventured forth from Singapore without air cover. The loss

of these two warships signaled the end of British naval power in the Far East.

With the occupation of Singora, Pattani, and Kota Bharu, General Yamashita was soon able to gain control of the air over Malaya and close support for his ground forces. Deployed in parallel columns along the east and west coasts of the peninsula, the *25th Army* began its drive toward Johore Bharu just across the strait from Singapore. By Christmas it was only 150 miles from its objective.

While the campaign for Malaya was moving forward rapidly, the Japanese took steps to gain control over Thailand. On the first day of war, elements of the *Imperial Guards Division,* stationed in Indochina and attached to the *15th Army,* moved across the border into Thailand while other elements of the division were landed at points along the narrow Kra Isthmus. The Thailanders offered no opposition and, after consolidating their position the Japanese began to assemble their forces in Thailand for the invasion of Burma.

Japanese operations in Indonesia, which in this phase included only the seizure of positions in Borneo, met with the same success as had operations elsewhere. From Camranh Bay in French Indochina came the force which made the first landings in British Borneo. Composed of three battalions of infantry and special naval troops, covered by 1 carrier, 1 battleship, 3 cruisers, and 4 destroyers, this force embarked on 13 December and three days later landed near Miri where it promptly occupied an airstrip and seized the partially destroyed oil fields. On the 24th it made an amphibious hop to Kuching, capital of Sarawak, a native state in northwest Borneo ruled by a British rajah.[8]

Their success in the opening weeks of the war exceeded the expectations of even the most optimistic Japanese leaders. By Christmas they had achieved all of the objectives outlined in their plan for the first phase of the war and were well on their way to completing the second phase. Except for the temporary setbacks at Wake and Kota Bharu, operations had proceeded with a smoothness rare in war. American and British forces everywhere had been decisively beaten and were on the defensive; the safety of the home islands was assured, and the resources of Southeast Asia were within grasp. Never were Japan's self-esteem and its prestige in Asia so high; the fortunes of the Allies so low.

The amazing success of the Japanese can be attributed as much to the unpreparedness of the Allies and the suddenness of the attack as to the superiority of Japanese tactics, troops, and equipment. By concentrating overwhelming air and naval power for the attack and striking with a swiftness that gained for them the full advantage of surprise, they were able to win their objectives with a minimum of losses. From each new base they moved forward in the same manner, always achieving local air and naval supremacy before landing their troops. They avoided direct assault against forti-fied positions, using flanking maneuvers where possible. And when they could not avoid direct assault they struck at night and pushed on, regardless of loss. Their first objectives were always airfields, and air power (land- and carrier-based) dominated their operations during these first weeks of war, as it would dominate Allied operations later in the war.

Meeting the Emergency

The first reaction in Washington to Admiral Kimmel's message—"Air raid on Pearl Harbor. This is not drill"—received at 1350 of the 7th, was one of surprise and shock. "My God," exclaimed Secretary Knox incredulously, "this can't be true. This must mean the Philippines." He immediately telephoned the White House where Mr. Roosevelt, who was lunching with Harry Hopkins, remarked that "the Japanese had made the decision for him." Hull had the news before the Japanese Ambassadors arrived for their final meeting and expressed himself, when they appeared, in "pretty strong Tennessee mountain language." Stimson, who received the startling report a short time later, was astonished that the Japanese should have chosen Hawaii as "the point of attack."[9]

As soon as confirmation of the first report was received by telephone from Oahu, the Army and Navy put into effect their war plans. Messages went out to all commanders informing them that Japan had opened hostilities and directing them to carry out the tasks

[8] Operations in Malaya, Thailand, and Borneo are described in Kirby, et al, The Loss of Singapore; Japanese Opns in SWPA, pp. 72–75; Morison, The Rising Sun in the Pacific, pp. 187–92; Despatches of Lt Gen A. E. Percival and Air Chief Marshal Sir Robert Brook-Popham in the Supplement to the London Gazette, January 22 and February 26, 1948; Borneo Opns, 1941–42, Japanese Studies in World War II, 22; and 25th Army Opns in Malaya, same series, 85.

[9] Quotes are from Pearl Harbor Report, p. 439; Stimson and Bundy, On Active Service, p. 391; Sherwood, Roosevelt and Hopkins, p. 431.

assigned in RAINBOW 5, so far as they pertained to Japan. In Hawaii there was confusion over references to a warning about a Japanese attack, and it was not until 1500 that the confusion was resolved by the receipt of the long-delayed message Marshall had sent shortly before noon.[10] The command there made a quick recovery from the attack and before the end of the day had instituted martial law in the islands, taken stock of its losses, and sent off an urgent plea for heavy bombers and fighters.[11]

With the War Department's message to General MacArthur invoking RAINBOW 5 went assurances of confidence and "every possible assistance and support within our power." No word had been received from the Philippines and when this message failed to evoke any response General Marshall sent still another asking whether the Philippines had yet been attacked. Finally, General Gerow was able to establish telephone communications with Manila and talk to MacArthur. He had known since about 0300 (Manila time) of the Pearl Harbor raid, MacArthur said, but there had been no attacks as yet and, he told Gerow, "our tails are up." General Arnold, too, talked by telephone with his air commander in the Philippines, General Brereton, and warned him specifically against a surprise Japanese attack.[12] A short time later came news of the Japanese attack against Clark Field.

That day and the next, more news, all of it bad, continued to trickle into Washington. The Japanese bombings of Guam, Wake, Hong Kong, and Singapore and their landings in Malaya and Thailand were noted but without much surprise. Most of these attacks had been expected and none had the impact of Pearl Harbor and Clark Field. What was most alarming was the lack of information on the size and location of the force which had hit Pearl Harbor. For all anyone knew it might return to Pearl Harbor to bomb the installations overlooked before. Or it might be on its way to the Panama Canal or the unguarded west coast of the United States. Seattle had only one 3-inch gun and one automatic weapons battery; San Francisco, an antiaircraft brigade, and Los Angeles a regiment— and all those cities and many others were clamoring for more protection. Hawaii needed more planes, guns, and men; help would have to be sent to General MacArthur; and Panama was too vital to be ignored. Between San Francisco and Hawaii were three transports carrying men and supplies and farther west was a large convoy headed for Manila. All these problems and many more had to be solved at once, in an atmosphere of frenzied activity and deep concern over where the blow would fall next.

Complicating the task of commanders in Washington and in the Pacific was the inevitable flood of rumors and speculations, some of which were given credence in the highest official circles. Japanese aircraft were reported over Los Angeles, San Francisco, and other west

---

[10] Affidavit of Capt. William B. Cobb, cited in History of United States Army Forces, Middle Pacific and Predecessor Commands During World War II (hereafter cited as USAFMIDPAC Hist), pt. I, vol. 1, p. 58, copy in OCMH.

[11] Rad, Short and Martin to TAG, No. 1068, 7 Dec 41, AG 381 (11–27–41 Gen) Far East.

[12] Rads, Marshall to MacArthur, Nos 736 and 737, 7 Dec 41, AG 381 (11–27–41 Gen) Far East; Record

of Tel Conv between Gerow and MacArthur, WPD 4622; Henry H. Arnold, *Global Mission* (New York: Harper & Brothers, 1949), p. 272.

coast cities on the first day of war and for days thereafter. Pilots mistook floating logs for submarines and every vessel for a Japanese carrier. On the day following Pearl Harbor there was an alert in San Francisco and the schools in Oakland were closed on the basis of a report that enemy carriers were off the coast of California. Another report, which came from the Chief of Staff, alerted the Western Defense commander to the presence of a hostile force believed to be only 400 miles away.

In Hawaii, where "invasion fever" ran high, the rumors were even wilder. There were at least a dozen reports of paratroop landings in different places on the 7th, and Japanese voices were heard constantly on short wave radio. People saw flashing signal lights, flares, swatches cut in sugar cane fields to form arrows pointing at vital installations. Word that the water supply of Honolulu had been poisoned spread rapidly, and Japanese landing parties were observed at various points. The wildest tales were believed. A truck that had been delivering milk for months to Hickam Field became, on the morning of the 7th, a Japanese armored vehicle, complete with troops and machine guns. Japanese cars and trucks were supposed to have deliberately created traffic jams on the roads leading to military installations. Japanese pilots wore civilian clothes, it was thought, so that they could mingle with the civil population if they were shot down. Finally, it was reliably reported that on a specified kilocycle a message—"Chopsticks, I don't want to set the world on fire. Why can't it happen again tonight"—was heard, and all preparations were made for another attack on Pearl Harbor.

The excitable Filipinos saw as many specters as did the Hawaiians and Americans. Many of the Japanese bombers which hit Clark and Nichols Fields were believed to be piloted by Caucasians—presumably Germans. Arrows, like those in the sugar fields of Oahu, but formed by headlights, pointed at military targets; Japanese voices were heard over short wave. There were reports, as in Hawaii, of landings, of Japanese carriers off the coast, of paratroopers, poisoned water supply, and of active fifth columnists. As elsewhere, these reports had to be checked, and the staff kept busy searching for the grain of truth in the wild rumors that came in over the wires.[13]

Matters of grand strategy required little attention during the first days of the war. There was no disagreement about them, and they had little relevance to the immediate problems facing the Army and Navy. The staff conversations with the British early in the year had provided a global strategy and a basis for concerted action "so that at the very beginning," as General Marshall later explained, "we had a fair understanding of what we had best do rather than the necessity of engaging in prolonged conversations. . . ."[14] This understanding, which included a recognition that Germany was the main enemy and that the major effort would be made initially in Europe, was obviously not applicable in the present situation. Of first importance now was the necessity to check the Japanese, to unify and co-ordinate "the

<hr>

[13] USAFMIDPAC Hist, pt. I, vol. 2, app. 3E; Craven and Cate, *AAF I*, pp. 278–79; Morton, *The Fall of the Philippines*, p. 115. For rumors received in Washington see OCS 21105–3 and WPD 4622–13.
[14] *Pearl Harbor Attack Hearings*, pt. 3, p. 1222.

PRESIDENT ROOSEVELT *signs the Declaration of War, December 1941.*

tinuing shipments of war materials to Britain and the Soviet Union, and discussed at length the specific measures required to redress the naval balance in the Pacific and to defend vital installations in the United States and overseas. The President also told his advisors during the meeting that he would go before Congress next day to ask for a declaration of war.

Relations with the European Axis was one of the most troublesome questions facing the President. Japan alone had attacked the United States, but American strategy was oriented toward Europe and the nation was committed to the support of the powers fighting Germany and Italy as well as Japan. A declaration of war against the European Axis, without provocation, might arouse opposition in Congress and in the country. That there was no intention of abandoning England and the Soviet Union had been made clear in the meeting of the War Council, and again, later in the day, when Mr. Churchill telephoned the President to offer his support and say that he intended to go before the House of Commons to ask for a declaration of war against Japan. He proposed also that he come to Washington with his principal military advisers to discuss the changed situation now that "we are all in the same boat." To this, Roosevelt had promptly agreed.[16]

The question of relations with the European Axis was discussed on the evening of the 7th in a Cabinet meeting which Roosevelt termed the most serious "since Lincoln met with his Cabinet at the outbreak of the Civil War."[17] The

forces of all opposition to Japan in the Far East, with special reference to the South Seas area."[15]

It was to this task and to the immediate measures required to put the nation on a war footing that the President and his chief military and naval advisers addressed themselves on the outbreak of war. On the afternoon of the 7th, only a few hours after the Pearl Harbor attack, the President met with his War Council to consider what must be done. Those present at the meeting—Hull, Stimson, Knox, Marshall, and Stark— agreed that America's position in the Far East had been greatly weakened but that the Japanese attack had mobilized the nation as nothing else could have. They recognized the necessity for con-

---

[15] Hull, *Memoirs*, II, 1113.

[16] Sherwood, *Roosevelt and Hopkins*, pp. 432–33, 439; Hull, *Memoirs*, II, 1059–1100.

[17] Sherwood, *Roosevelt and Hopkins*, p. 433.

draft message he read to the Cabinet members contained no mention of Germany or Italy. Evidently, in the belief that these nations would support Japan, he preferred to wait and let them declare war first. Later that night the President reviewed the situation with Congressional leaders and the next day went before Congress which, with only one dissenting vote, approved the declaration of war against Japan. Great Britain, the Netherlands Government-in-exile, the British Dominions, and various Central American republics followed suit soon after. It was not until the 11th that Germany and Italy declared war against the United States, thus ending the uncertainty of America's relations with the European Axis.

Hawaii

The significance of the damage inflicted on the Pacific Fleet on the first day of war was apparent almost immediately. The offensive power of the fleet, it seemed, had been shattered and its ability to defend Hawaii and to provide a screen for the west coast and the Panama Canal greatly reduced. In fact, there was a "grave possibility," the Navy planners thought, that "the Japanese might capture the Hawaiian Islands."[18] On the 8th, therefore, the Navy changed Admiral Kimmel's instructions, and, in effect modified RAINBOW 5 and ABC-1.

The new mission of the Pacific Fleet was now almost entirely defensive. Deleted were the provisions for the support of British naval forces, operations against the Caroline and Marshall Islands, and the diversion of Japanese forces from the Malay Barrier. Kimmel was to limit himself largely to the defense of the islands and sea communications east of the date line. This decision was approved by the Joint Board the same day and about a week later, after further study by the naval planners, was communicated to the British.[19]

More than a change in mission was required to remedy the damage at Pearl Harbor. The first step in re-establishing American power in the Central Pacific and sharpening the badly dulled edge of the "strategic triangle" was to strengthen the Pacific Fleet. This was accomplished by ordering back to the Pacific those warships that had been sent to the Atlantic in the spring and summer to protect the convoys to England — the carrier *Yorktown*, 3 battleships, 9 destroyers, and 12 old submarines. This action, too, constituted a revision of the existing war plan, which provided for the transfer of units of the Pacific Fleet to the Mediterranean in the event of war so that the British could reinforce their Far Eastern fleet.[20] Such a step was obviously out of the question.

The Pearl Harbor attack had not only

---

[18] Mins, JB Mtg, 8 Dec 41. Admiral Stark, though he did not minimize the seriousness of the damage at Pearl Harbor, reminded the President on the morning of the 8th that the striking force of the fleet —the carriers, cruisers, destroyers, and submarines— had largely escaped damage and that shore base facilities were intact. Ltr, Stark to Hoover, 5 Aug 59, OCMH.

[19] Rad, CNO to CINCPAC, 0139, 9 Dec 41; Ltr, Secy for Collab to Chief Staff Officer, British Staff Mission, 16 Dec 41, sub: ABC-1 Modification, both cited by Lt. Grace P. Hayes, USN, in Hist of JCS in World War II: The War Against Japan, vol. I, ch. II, p. 10; Mins, JB Mtg, 8 Dec 41.

[20] Mins, JB Mtg, 8 Dec 41; Rad, CNO to CinC Atlantic, 8 Dec 41, copy in WPD Msg File, No. 116; ABC-1, pars. 55 and 57, *Pearl Harbor Attack Hearings*, pt. 15, pp. 1526–27.

revealed the weakness of American defenses in the Pacific but had brought into the open, with dramatic suddenness, the inadequacies of command by mutual co-operation and the danger of divided responsibility. These weaknesses had been recognized before the war, General Marshall complaining in February 1941 that "old Army and Navy feuds" in Hawaii were becoming confused with questions of national defense.[21] But all efforts to establish unity of command in those areas where the Army and Navy were jointly responsible for defense had foundered on the sharp crags of service jealousies and rivalries.

The disaster at Pearl Harbor aroused the President to the dangers of divided command. Determined that there should be no repetition of the confusion of responsibility that had existed in Hawaii, he ordered his military and naval advisers on the 12th to establish a unified command in Panama under the Army. Though some of the naval members of the Joint Board were opposed to the move, they had no choice but to accept it, for, as the minutes recorded, "unless unified control was effected by joint agreement between the Army and Navy, the establishment of a Department of National Defense . . . might be considered a certainty." In Hawaii, the Navy was given command effective 17 December. "For your confidential information," Marshall explained to the Army commander in Hawaii, this action had been taken because "the Secretary of War and the Secretary of the Navy were determined that there would be no question of future confusion as to re-

sponsibility. . . . Both Stark and I were struggling to the same end. . . ."[22]

The establishment of unity of command coincided with a complete turnover in the high command in Hawaii. As early as the 12th demands for an inquiry into the causes of the disaster at Pearl Harbor were being made in Congress, but they were staved off until the 14th when Secretary Knox returned from Hawaii after a quick inspection. His description of the situation there in the days preceding the attack did nothing to lessen the demand for an inquiry and the next day the President appointed a 5-man board headed by Supreme Court Justice Owen J. Roberts to make an official investigation. With the public explanation that it was acting to "avoid a situation where officials charged with responsibility for the future security of the vital base would otherwise at this critical hour also be involved in a searching investigation," the Navy on the 17th relieved Admiral Kimmel, General Short, and Maj. Gen. Frederick L. Martin, the air commander. Rear Adm. Chester W. Nimitz was jumped two grades and appointed in Kimmel's place. Pending his arrival in Hawaii, Vice Adm. William S. Pye took over command of the Pacific Fleet and of all forces in the area under the principles of unified command. Short's replacement, Lt. Gen. Delos C. Emmons, an air

---

[21] Ltr, Marshall to Short, 7 Feb 41, WPD4449–1; Ltr, Stark to Hoover, 5 Aug 59, OCMH.

[22] Ltr, CofS to CG Hawaiian Dept, 20 Dec 41, *Pearl Harbor Attack Hearings*, pt. 15, p. 1483; Mins, JB Mtgs, 13 and 17 Dec 41; Memo, Stark for Marshall, 17 Dec 41, sub: Unity of Command, WPD 2917–38. Ltr, Emmons to Hoover, 10 Jul 59, OCMH. General Emmons recalled that on the morning of 8 December he and Maj. Gen. Lesley J. McNair called on Marshall for instructions, and recommended that unity of command be established immediately in the Pacific. General Marshall told them that he intended to take the matter up with the Navy.

ADMIRAL KING   GENERAL EMMONS   ADMIRAL NIMITZ

force officer, was in San Francisco when he received Marshall's telephone call to proceed to Hawaii at once and take command of the Department. He arrived on the night of the 16th and the following morning relieved General Short. Brig. Gen. Clarence L. Tinker flew out the same day to take over command of the air forces.[23] General Marshall survived this crisis but his naval colleague, Admiral Stark, was ultimately replaced by Admiral Ernest J. King.

The safety of the fleet base in Hawaii continued to be the main preoccupation of the Navy and the chief subject of debate between the Navy and Army planners during the first weeks of the war. The former believed that all available resources should be sent to Oahu immediately. The latter, harassed by calls for protection from civilian agencies and military commanders and fearful of attacks against the west coast and Panama, resisted these demands, but did agree with their naval colleagues on the strategic importance of Hawaii and the need for reinforcements. The question was how much of the slender resources then available should be sent and how much should be allotted to other commands and for civilian defense.

The problem of Hawaii's defenses was thoroughly discussed at the Joint Board meetings on 8 and 9 December. Already the War Department had received General Short's estimates of the equipment, supplies, and troops needed for his command, and had approved most of his requests, including those for 60 heavy bombers and 100 pursuit craft, 10,000,000 rounds of .50-caliber ammunition, and a large number of bombs.[24] But the Navy did not regard these reinforcements— which were scheduled to leave the west coast after 12 December—as adequate. It wanted all available antiaircraft artillery and a large force dispatched to Oahu immediately, even, Admiral Stark de-

---

[23] New York *Times*, December 18, 1941; Memo, Deputy CofS for TAG, 16 Dec 41, no sub; Tel Conf of CofS and Emmons, 16 Dec 41, both in OPD Exec Files. Ltr, Emmons to Hoover, 10 Jul 59, OCMH.

[24] Rad, Short to Marshall, 8 Dec 41, AG 381 (11–27–41 Sec 1) Far East.

clared, "at the risk of taking a chance on leaving some installations in the United States unprotected." So serious was the danger, in Stark's estimation, that he advised Kimmel not to use Pearl Harbor as a base, except for submarines and patrol craft, until it was reinforced.[25]

The position taken by Stark and his naval planners was not an unreasonable one. Disaster had followed disaster in the Pacific. The naval base at Cavite in the Philippines had been virtually destroyed and Admiral Hart on the 10th had reported that Manila was no longer tenable as a naval base and that he was sending the rest of his fleet, except the submarines and patrol craft, south, a decision which Admiral Stark approved.[26] Hard on the heels of this news came word that the *Prince of Wales* and *Repulse* had been sunk. Added to the loss of American strength in the Pacific and Far East, these fresh disasters had a profound effect on naval thinking and strategy.

Oddly enough, the naval commander in Hawaii, Admiral Kimmel, did not share the pessimism of his Washington superiors, though he pressed for reinforcements as vigorously as any and yielded to none in his view of the seriousness of the situation. But he also saw the bright side of the picture. For one thing, the workshops and depots at Pearl Harbor were still intact. And more important, the three carriers had escaped the attack and were available for limited missions. Certainly the strategy for the use of the fleet would have to be changed, Kimmel told Secretary Knox when he visited Hawaii on the 11th, but he added,

"a very powerful striking force of carriers, cruisers and destroyers survives. These forces must be operated boldly and vigorously on the tactical offensive in order to retrieve our initial disaster." [27]

The Army planners, though they were unwilling to reinforce Hawaii to the extent desired by their naval colleagues or by Admiral Kimmel, did not minimize the danger to that outpost. In an estimate of 10 December, G–2 pointed out that the Japanese were striking out "in all directions simultaneously" and that their next objectives might include major elements of the fleet, installations and factories on the west coast, Alaska, and Panama. Of these the most serious, G–2 thought, would be the loss of the Panama Canal and of major elements of the fleet. An Army War Plans Division estimate two days later listed five possible lines of Japanese action: continued operations in the Philippines and Malaya; attacks against Hawaii, seizure of a base in the Aleutians; air strikes on the Panama Canal; and raids against shipping and installations on the west coast. To counter these the United States would only be able first, to resist Japanese attacks in the Philippines with the forces already there; second, reinforce Hawaii and defend it against attack, with the knowledge that "the naval situation in the Pacific is such that a successful defense of Hawaii cannot be absolutely assured"; and, finally, defend Alaska, the west coast, and the Panama Canal.[28]

The Navy's estimates differed from the

---

[25] Mins, JB Mtg, 9 Dec 41; Morison, *The Rising Sun in the Pacific*, p. 219.

[26] Rad, CINCAF to OPNAV, 1330, 10 Dec 41; Mins, JB Mtg, 10 Dec 41.

[27] Quoted in Morison, *The Rising Sun in the Pacific*, p. 220. The original of Kimmel's report has not been found in the Navy's files.

[28] Memos, G–2 for GHQ, 10 Dec 41, sub: Brief Estimate of the Situation, WPD 4544–28; Gerow for CofS, 12 Dec 41, sub: Brief Current Strategic Estimate, WPD 4622–37.

Army's mainly in the emphasis placed on Hawaii. Admiral Kimmel had admitted, even while urging boldness, that the most probable enemy action in his theater was a raid by fast striking forces against Oahu, Midway, or the Aleutians. But Admiral Stark took a more serious view. The Japanese, he told Marshall on the 11th, had the ships and men to land on any of the outlying islands in the Hawaiian chain, blockade Oahu, or attack the west coast, Alaska, and Panama. "This picture," he declared, "is not overdrawn. The Hawaiian Islands are in terrible danger of early capture. Every resource of the United States in ships, troops, aircraft, and material should be considered available for use in this emergency. . . ."[29] He proposed, therefore, that the equivalent of three divisions, as many planes as possible, a large naval force, and a large amount of supplies—altogether 100,000 men and 500,000 tons of shipping—be dispatched immediately to Hawaii. And until these reinforcements arrived, he declared, the Navy would discontinue the use of Pearl Harbor as a base.

Such grand-scale reinforcement was impossible, even if the shipping could be found, without abandoning the defense of other vital points and endangering the safety of the Atlantic sea lanes. General Marshall reminded Stark of these obligations, while admitting the importance of Hawaii and agreeing to send additional reinforcements to the islands if it could be done without "jeopardizing the security of the Panama Canal and Continental United States."[30]

Finally, after a week of discussion, the two Chiefs collaborated on a joint estimate for the President that reflected Stark's view of the seriousness of the danger, but made allowance for the needs of other areas and listed the measures already taken.[31]

By this time the danger to Hawaii, though not ended, was waning. Reports of enemy landings and imminent attacks had all proved false. In General Short's opinion there was, by 15 December, little danger of a hostile landing; raids, he thought, were still possible. His successor, General Emmons, added to Short's requests for reinforcements two square divisions, two antiaircraft regiments, and 10,000 service troops. He was given only one of the divisions, the 27th, and told that reinforcements would reach him over an extended period of time, priority for emergency shipments having already passed to the Southwest Pacific.[32] By Christmas it was clear that Hawaii was no longer in immediate danger of invasion, a view endorsed by the British planners who believed that the main Japanese effort was in Southeast Asia, and that, while raids and hit-and-run attacks in the eastern Pacific were still possible, a large amphibious operation in that area was most unlikely.[33]

---

[29] Memo, CNO for CofS, 11 Dec 41, sub: The Dangerous Strategic Situation, OPD Exec Files.

[30] Memo, CofS for CNO, 12 Dec 41, sub: Defense of Oahu, WPD 4544–29.

[31] Memo, CofS and CNO for President, 20 Dec 41 (?), sub: Dangerous Strategic Situation, WPD 4449–6.

[32] Rad, Short to Marshall, 15 Dec 41, AG 381 (11–27–41 Sec 1) Far East; memos, WPD for CofS, 23 Dec 41, sub: Hawaiian Defenses, and WPD for TAG, 25 Dec 41, sub: Reinf for Hawaii, both in WPD 3444–19; Ltr, Emmons to Hoover, 10 Jul 59, OCMH.

[33] ABC–4, 24 Dec 41, ann. 2 ARCADIA Proceedings. For reinforcements to Hawaii during this period, see Leighton and Coakley, *Global Logistics and Strategy*, ch. VI, and ABC 381 (11–27–41 Gen) Far East, WPD 3444–14 and 15, 4622–39, and 3674–74.

The Philippines

The shift in focus of interest from Hawaii to the western Pacific evidenced by the higher priority given Australia and the Philippines on 24 December was the culmination of a dispute that had begun on the first day of war. The issue had been raised by the necessity for deciding the fate of a convoy of seven ships, escorted by the cruiser *Pensacola* and carrying men and munitions to Manila via the South Pacific route. The Navy had, on the 8th, ordered the *Pensacola* convoy to put in at Suva in the Fijis to await further orders, and on the 9th, at a meeting of the Joint Board, proposed that the ships be brought back to Hawaii to reinforce that badly battered garrison. The Army members of the board, notably General Gerow, supported this view and suggested further that a portion of the convoy might be returned to the United States. Following discussion the board agreed that the convoy should be ordered back to Hawaii. General Marshall concurred without comment.[34]

This decision of the Joint Board represented virtually the abandonment of the Philippines. There was ample precedent for such a policy in the prewar studies of the planners, approved by the Joint Board, demonstrating that the Philippines could not be held in the face of a determined Japanese attack. But between July and December 1941 there had been a reversal of that view and the inauguration of a large-scale program of reinforcements designed to make the islands strong enough to resist invasion. The program was still incomplete when war came and it was evident at once that the defense of the islands had become, as Secretary Stimson wrote, "once more the desperate and losing struggle which had been forecast in the planning of earlier years."[35]

Though the action of the Joint Board in ordering the *Pensacola* convoy back to Hawaii may have been necessary for military reasons, it overlooked the moral, phychological, and political considerations which affected the attitude of America toward the Philippines and its position in the Far East. Though these considerations were not, perhaps, strictly within the province of the Army and Navy planners, their existence and potential importance had been recognized in some of the early studies. As late as December 1940 the two service Secretaries and the President had approved a Joint Board study that made the point that in the event of war with Germany and Japan, the decision to make the main effort in the Atlantic initially might well be endangered "should Japanese success seem imminent." Public opinion, the board had suggested then, might lead to heavy pressure "to support the forces engaged in the Far East instead of leaving them to their fate" and result in stronger effort in that area than provided for in the plans.[36]

Though no war plans that took into full account the moral and political factors of the situation in the Far East were ever made, it was these factors that ultimately decided the strategy of the United

---

[34] Mins, JB Mtg, 8 and 9 Dec 41. In the convoy was a field artillery brigade, eighteen P–40s, fifty-two A–24's, a large quantity of ammunition and miscellaneous equipment, many vehicles and about 5,000 troops. Rad, Marshall to MacArthur, No. 776, 12 Dec 41, WPD 4628.

[35] Stimson and Bundy, *On Active Service*, p. 395.
[36] Memo, CNO for CofS, 15 Dec 41, Incl: Extract from JB 325, ser. 670, 21 Dec 40, WPD 4561–10.

SECRETARY STIMSON *confers with General Marshall, January 1942.*

States during the opening months of the war. The President, Secretary Stimson, and General Marshall all felt strongly with the American people that the United States had an obligation to do all in its power to aid the Philippine people and support General MacArthur whatever the risks. Moreover, General Marshall had already assured MacArthur that he could expect "every possible assistance," and he was reluctant to tell him now, after the Joint Board's decision, that the *Pensacola* convoy had been turned back. He wanted "to send some news," he told Stimson on the morning of the 10th, "which would buck General MacArthur up." [37]

Secretary Stimson was thoroughly in sympathy with the Chief of Staff's views. A former governor-general of the Philippines and one of the foremost advocates

of a strong policy in the Far East, Mr. Stimson needed no urging to do all in his power for the Filipinos and General MacArthur, and immediately went to the White House with the problem. There, where there was a sensitive appreciation for the moral and political consequences of the Joint Board decision, he found ready support and a promise of aid. This assistance took the form of a request by the President that the Joint Board reconsider its decision on the fate of the *Pensacola* convoy. Thus, when the Board met that afternoon, 10 December, it had little choice but to reverse itself, though the naval members still felt that there was little hope of getting the supplies to MacArthur. The Army members followed the lead of their chief and argued that the vessels should proceed to Brisbane, after which some means would be sought to convoy them northward. Two days later, the senior Army officer in the convoy, Brig. Gen. Julian F. Barnes, was placed under MacArthur's command and told that his principal task was to get the men, planes, and munitions in the holds of the seven ships to the Philippines by any means available and as quickly as possible. [38]

The news that reinforcements were on the way was received with enthusiasm in Manila. But Admiral Hart's response to MacArthur's request for help in bringing the convoy in dampened this enthusiasm. Like Admirals Stark and Turner, and like many Army planners as well, Hart thought the cause of the Philip-

[37] Mins, CofS Conf, 10 Dec 41, WDCSA CofS Conf, II.

[38] Mins, JB Mtg, 10 Dec 41; Rad, OPNAV to CTF 15, 10 Dec 41, WPD Msg File; Memo, CofS for Comdr D. H. Harries, Australian Naval Attaché, 12 Dec 41, sub: Msg for Transmission; Rad, Marshall to MacArthur, No. 776, 12 Dec 41, both in WPD 4628.

pines was a hopeless one. The Japanese, he believed, would have established a complete blockade of the Philippines before the convoy could arrive, and he could not, he told MacArthur, take the responsibility for protecting the convoy if it tried to make the journey between Australia and the Philippines.[39]

MacArthur took strong exception to Hart's view that the convoys could not be brought in safely, but the admiral found firm support in Washington. The Chief of Naval Operations not only agreed with Hart's estimate but urged him to leave the Philippines as soon as possible "to support the defense of the Netherlands East Indies and Australia." Foreseeing the loss of Singapore and Luzon and unwilling to risk the loss of its warships in a hopeless cause, the Navy wished to concentrate Allied resources on the defense of the Malay Barrier and northwest Australia. The artillery and ammunition earmarked for MacArthur, it proposed, should be retained in Australia and used for the defense of Darwin. The Army planners did not differ with the naval estimate of the probable loss of the Philippines or of the importance of the Malay Barrier, but they did oppose any effort to divert aid from MacArthur. And so did naval officers in Australia, who asserted their belief that the *Pensacola* convoy could still reach the Philippines, provided that there was "adequate cooperation" between the Army and Navy.[40]

MacArthur not only refused to accept the view that the Philippines were doomed, but warned that "if the suspicion of such action ever materializes the entire structure will collapse over my head." What he wanted was a review of the accepted strategy in the Pacific and Far East "lest a fatal mistake be made." To him "the locus of victory or defeat" lay in the Philippines. If they and the Indies fell, so would Singapore and the Asiatic continent. The defense of the islands, therefore, justified, in his view, the allocation of the combined resources of the Allies to the Pacific. "If the Western Pacific is to be saved," he told the Chief of Staff in language similar to that used by Admiral Stark in describing the plight of Hawaii, "it will have to be saved here and now."[41] Constantly he urged on the Chief of Staff a bold course of action against an over-extended enemy. On the 10th, asserting that there existed a "golden opportunity . . . for a master stroke," he suggested a strong carrier-based air attack against the Japanese home islands which, he declared, would "at once relieve pressure from objectives of Japanese drive to southward" for Japan itself was weakly defended. "Definite information available here," he added significantly, "shows that entry of Russia is enemy's greatest fear." A few days later he advanced the idea that aircraft carriers be used to bring in 300 pursuit planes, a proposal the Navy vigorously and successfully opposed.[42]

---

[39] Rads, MacArthur to Marshall, 13 and 14 Dec 41, OPD Exec Files; CNO to CINCAF, 1958, 10 Dec 41, WPD 4622–30.

[40] Rad, Milid Melbourne to WD, No. 40, 18 Dec 41, WPD 4622–38; CNO to CINCAF, 14 Dec 41, copy in AG 381 (11–27–41 Gen) Far East; MacArthur to Marshall, 14 Dec 41, OPD Exec Files.

[41] Rad, MacArthur to Marshall, 13 Dec 41, OPD Exec Files.

[42] Rads, MacArthur to Marshall, No. 198, 10 Dec 41, WPD 4544–26; 14 Dec 41, OPD Exec Files; memo, CNO for CofS, 23 Dec 41, sub: Transportation of Short Range Aircraft, AG 381 (11–27–41 Gen) Far East.

Additional weight was given MacArthur's pleas by the arguments of Francis B. Sayre, High Commissioner for the Philippines. Stressing the moral and political aspects of the Philippine campaign and the importance of that campaign to America's position in the Far East, he urged the President to send MacArthur the reinforcements and supplies he had requested. Rumors that the United States was leaving the Filipinos to their fate were circulating in Manila, Sayre told Mr. Roosevelt, and if reinforcements did not arrive soon the Filipinos might abandon all resistance and submit passively to the Japanese.[43]

MacArthur's and Sayre's requests were received sympathetically in Washington, where they brought immediate results. The President had already ordered the Army and Navy to make every effort to aid the Philippine garrison, but the latter was noticeably lacking in enthusiasm for the program. This reluctance Roosevelt sought to overcome by calling in Acting Secretary of the Navy, James V. Forrestal, and telling him that "he was bound to help the Philippines and the Navy has got to help in it."[44] To Sayre the President sent reassurances that he was keeping directly in touch with the situation in the Far East. At the same time Marshall sent a separate message to MacArthur explaining that the problem of getting supplies to him had been "complicated by Naval losses," but that reinforcements were being "rushed" to the Philippines. "The strategic importance of the Philippines is fully recognized," the Chief of Staff told

MacArthur, "and there has been and will be no repeat no wavering in the determination to support you."[45]

This pledge was no empty promise. Marshall was doing everything possible to give MacArthur what he needed and had only the day before assigned the newly arrived deputy chief of the War Plans Division, Brig. Gen. Dwight D. Eisenhower, the task of co-ordinating and directing this program of reinforcement. Like Stimson and Marshall, Eisenhower believed that it was necessary to make every effort to reinforce the Philippines, even if the hope of success was slim. The program would have to be based on Australia, he believed, and work should begin at once to construct military bases there from which to send supplies and men northward. "We must take great risks," he wrote, "and spend any amount of money required."[46]

Eisenhower's plan, which Marshall quickly approved, was to use the forces in the *Pensacola* convoy, due in Brisbane on the 22d, as the nucleus of the new command. Designated U.S. Army Forces in Australia (USAFIA), this command would be essentially an air and supply base. General Barnes, when he arrived in Brisbane, was to be relieved as commander of the forces in the convoy by an air officer from the Philippines. Eventually, Maj. Gen. George H. Brett, then in Chungking, would take over command of USAFIA, with Col. Stephen

---

[43] Rad, Sayre to President, No. 628, 15 Dec 41, WPD 4622–38.

[44] Stimson and Bundy, *On Active Service*, p. 396.

[45] Rads, Marshall to MacArthur, No. 787, 15 Dec 41; President to Sayre, 15 Dec 41, both in WPD 4622–38.

[46] General Dwight D. Eisenhower, *Crusade in Europe* (New York: Doubleday and Company, 1948), p. 18.

J. Chamberlin, later to become Mac-Arthur's G–3, as chief of staff.[47] The primary task of the Australian command would be the support of the Philippines and for this purpose its commander would take his instructions from General MacArthur. In addition, the USAFIA commander was to arrange for the flight of the planes in the *Pensacola* convoy northward, loaded with all the ammunition they could carry, and to co-operate with the Navy in securing the sea lanes. Any course that would achieve these results, the Chief of Staff directed, was authorized.[48]

General MacArthur was kept fully informed of these developments and on the 18th Marshall undertook to summarize for him the measures being taken to send him help. Two transports, he told him, were to be loaded with aircraft and ammunition and dispatched shortly from San Francisco. Two additional shipments were scheduled to reach Brisbane early in January and would give that base 230 aircraft. Via the South Atlantic–Africa route, two Pan American clippers loaded with 50-caliber ammunition were heading for Australia. Fifteen heavy bombers were being diverted from their original destinations and ordered to the Southwest Pacific on a flight schedule which would see the arrival of three planes a day between Christmas and the New Year. Finally, Marshall said, the War Department was making available to the USAFIA commander the sum of $10,000,000 to finance blockade-runners

between Australia and the Philippines.[49] These measures added up to an impressive program of reinforcement and represented considerable staff work in Washington, but to MacArthur in the Philippines it was only a paper program. Until the aircraft and supplies reached him, he and his men could find little consolation in such summaries.

On 22 December, the same day that the bulk of the Japanese *14th Army* landed at Lingayen Gulf, the *Pensacola* convoy with its valuable cargo of aircraft, artillery, and ammunition arrived in Brisbane. Already General Mac-Arthur had instructed the USAFIA commander to send the convoy (less the aircraft, which were to be unloaded, assembled, and flown north) to the Philippines, and the Joint Board had provided for co-ordination between the Army and Navy forces in the area. This co-ordination it hoped to achieve by directing General Brett and Rear Adm. William A. Glassford, Hart's representative, to meet "for the purpose of agreeing upon common action" to transport the supplies MacArthur needed, and, in co-operation with the Australians, establish a base at Darwin and defend northwest Australia.[50] Marshall had done all he could to assure the transshipment of the convoy to the Philippines, and, on the day the convoy reached its destination, once again reminded the Army commanders in Australia to spare neither effort nor expense to accomplish their task. At the same time, the Navy instructed its representatives in Austra-

[47] Memo, WPD for CofS, 17 Dec 41, sub: Plan for Australian Base, WPD 4628–1.

[48] Ltr, Maj Gen Richard C. Moore to Brett, 19 Dec 41, OCS 18136–161; Rad, Marshall to Mil Attaché Melbourne for Brett, No. 31, 17 Dec 41, WPD 4628–1.

[49] Rad, Marshall to MacArthur, No. 824, 18 Dec 41, WPD 4622–28.

[50] Rad, Marshall to Brett, 21 Dec 41, WPD 4622–38; JB 325, ser. 783.

lia to assist in every way and Admiral Stark asked Hart, who was to leave Manila shortly, to impress on the Australians the importance of keeping open the Torres Strait route for supplies to Darwin and the Philippines.[51]

Despite these elaborate preparations and the efforts of the small group of officers in Australia, none of the planes, men, or munitions of the *Pensacola* convoy ever reached the Philippines. When the planes were assembled it was discovered that they lacked vital parts needed in combat. Before the missing parts could be found or shipped from the United States, the fields on which the planes would base had fallen to the enemy. The field artillery brigade, together with other reinforcements and supplies from the convoy, left Brisbane on the 28th on two fast ships. By the time the ships got to Darwin the Japanese had already established themselves in Borneo athwart the line of communication northward and the convoy was halted. "It now appears," General Marshall wrote the Far East commander, "that the plans for reaching you quickly with pursuit plane support are jeopardized. Your day to day situation and

that of Borneo will determine what can be done at any moment. . . ."[52]

Though there was no relaxation in the determination to reinforce the Philippines, it was evident by the last week in December that these efforts had but slight chance of success and that the men and supplies in and en route to Australia might be available for another cause. The President wanted them to be used "in whatever manner might best serve the joint cause in the Far East"; the British wanted them for Singapore, and the Navy pushed for the establishment of a strong base at Darwin. The Army planners, who were reluctantly coming to share the pessimism of their naval colleagues about the fate of the Philippines, limited their plans to the development of a strong air base in Australia from which to project air operations forward for the defense of Singapore and the Malay Barrier.[53] It was to this problem that the American planners in Washington and their British allies turned their attention during the weeks that followed.

[51] Rads, Marshall to Mil Attaché, Melbourne, No. 36, 22 Dec 41, WPD 4630–2; OPNAV to CINCAF, 2302, 22 Dec 41, Office of Naval Records.

[52] Rad, Marshall to MacArthur, 879, 24 Dec. 41, AG 381 (11–27–41 Gen) Far East; Morton, *The Fall of the Philippines*, p. 154.

[53] Notes on White House Mtg, 24 Dec 41, OPD Exec Files; Ltr, Marshall to Lt Gen H. C. B. Wemyss, British Mission, 24 Dec 41, AG 381 (11–27–41 Gen) Far East; Rad, Marshall to Mil Att Melbourne, No. 41, 25 Dec 41, WPD 4628–3.

CHAPTER VII

The Malay Barrier

Defensive warfare, therefore, does not consist of waiting idly for things to happen.

CLAUSEWITZ, *Principles of War*

Though the program to reinforce the Philippines and establish an American base in Australia developed almost accidentally from the improvisations of the first day of the war, it clearly foreshadowed the direction of American strategy in the Pacific. But no clear statement of this strategy, let alone specific plans to put it into effect, existed when the program was adopted. Before either could be developed it would be necessary to correlate American and Allied strategy in the Pacific and to develop a program of action against the common enemy.

Allied Strategy

When General MacArthur told Marshall on 10 December that what Japan feared most was Soviet entry into the war, he emphasized a fact well understood in Washington. That did not mean, however, that military authorities were unanimously in favor of Soviet participation. Admiral Stark, for example, seriously questioned the advisability of such a move because of the effect it would have on the war in Europe. General Marshall agreed fully that any move that would weaken Soviet resist-

ance on the eastern front would be disastrous to the Allied cause. But it was undeniable, he pointed out, that a Soviet attack against Japan would improve America's position in the Pacific. The fact that Japan had not attacked the Maritime Provinces seemed to him significant. "If immediate fighting in the Manchukuo front is disadvantageous to Japan," Marshall declared, "it is, for that reason, immediately advantageous to us."[1]

But participation by the Soviet Union in the war against Japan was not the only way that nation could aid the Allied cause in the Far East. In the Maritime Provinces were bases that lay within bombing distance of the industrial heart of Japan. In the hands of American forces, these bases would constitute a formidable threat to the Japanese enemy.

The possibility that the Soviet Union would allow the United States to base its forces in the Maritime Provinces was a specter that haunted the Japanese and was always a factor in their planning. The Americans had considered this possibility in their prewar plans and esti-

---

[1] Memos, Gerow for Marshall, 17 Dec 41, sub: Memo for President (not used); Stark for President, 3 Dec 41, no sub, both in WPD 4557.

mates, and had sought to make the necessary arrangements with the Soviet Union. These efforts had been unsuccessful, but as late as November 1941, General Marshall was still optimistic and confided to a group of newsmen that "arrangements are being made to provide landing fields for flying fortresses in Vladivostok" and that the Philippine-based B–17's would shuttle between Clark Field and Vladivostok in the event of war, dropping their bombs en route on the "paper cities of Japan."[2]

The Pearl Harbor attack gave impetus to the efforts to complete arrangements with the Soviet Union for American use of the Maritime Provinces. On the day after the attack Secretary Hull sounded out Maxim Litvinov, the Soviet Ambassador, on this question and Marshall raised it in military conference. But Litvinov, on instructions from his government, quickly put an end to such hopes. To the President, during a visit to the White House, and to Mr. Hull later, he made it perfectly clear that the USSR would have to maintain a neutral position in the Far East. His country, Litvinov explained, was too heavily committed in the war against Germany and "could not risk an attack by Japan."[3]

Stalin's reluctance to engage in discussions dealing with the Far East was in marked contrast to Chiang Kai-shek's eagerness for concerted action. China had not been included in the prewar discussions of strategy and no plans had been made for the use of Chinese bases or troops in the event of war with Japan. The first suggestion that China become an active partner in such a war came from Chiang who, when he heard of the Pearl Harbor attack, summoned the American and Soviet ambassadors and told them of his hopes for a military alliance of all the anti-Axis nations under American leadership. This thought the Ambassadors passed on to their governments, but it was not until the 11th that the Generalissimo formally proposed such an alliance, as well as the preparation of comprehensive plans for concerted action against Japan and the formation of a military mission headed by an American, with headquarters at Chungking.[4]

In Washington, the desirability of international military collaboration was fully recognized and plans for a meeting were already being made. Chiang's suggestions, therefore, though they were not entirely in accord with American views, were readily accepted by Roosevelt, but with the proviso that several conferences, not one, be held to co-ordinate the efforts of the Allies. All together there would be three: one in Chungking, one in Singapore, and one in Moscow, and invitations went out immediately. Chiang quickly agreed, as did the British, who were scheduled to meet separately with the Americans in Washington later in the month. But Stalin asked that his country not be pressed into any action against Japan, and Roosevelt's invitation

---

[2] Notes on Mtg of newspaper correspondents with Gen Marshall, 15 Nov 41. The notes were made by the correspondents, one of whom supplied the author with his copy.

[3] Hull, *Memoirs*, II, 1111; Mins, CofS Mtg, 10 Dec 41, WDCSA Conf II.

[4] Telg. U.S. Ambassador, Chungking, 8 Dec 41, WPD 4389–42; Memo, Laughlin Currie for Pres, 11 Dec 41, WPD 4389–46; Rad, Magruder to Secy War, No. 95, 11 Dec 41, WPD Msg File. For full story of this incident, see Charles F. Romanus and Riley Sunderland, *Stilwell's Mission to China*, UNITED STATES ARMY IN WORLD WAR II (Washington, 1953), ch. II.

for a meeting in Moscow trailed off in a series of inconclusive messages.[5]

Preparations for the other two meetings, to be held concurrently and to consider ways to halt the Japanese, were quickly completed. Representing the United States at Chungking would be Generals Brett, then in India, and Magruder, head of the mission to China. Lt. Col. Francis G. Brink, military observer in Singapore and an old hand in the Far East, would attend the meeting there. The results of these conferences, Roosevelt stipulated, were to be forwarded to Washington by 20 December so that they could be used in the forthcoming meeting with Churchill and the British Chiefs of Staff, scheduled for 22 December.

When the Chungking Conference convened on 17 December neither Lt. Gen. Sir Archibald Wavell, the British delegate, nor Brett was present. Nevertheless the Generalissimo took the opportunity to present his plans for the formation of an Allied general staff at Chungking, and for the prosecution of the war against Japan. On the 22d, Brett, who had just received orders to go to Australia and take command of U.S. Army forces there, arrived with Wavell and the conversations with the Chinese began in earnest. Brett's instructions from Washington were to join with the others in seeking ways to take advantage of Japan's "present over-extension"—MacArthur's thesis—and to reassure the Chinese that the United States was not abandoning the Philippines or its partners in Asia. After considerable discussion, a plan that placed control in Washington and called for only limited operations in Asia was evolved by the delegates and sent to Washington. The Generalissimo thought it unsatisfactory and sent his own. Neither contained any concrete suggestions on command or logistics, two problems that would plague the Allies in China for the next three years. The conference ended on the 23d, having produced, one of the planners wrote, "very little in the way of concrete results."[6]

The Singapore Conference (18–20 December), though it produced no plan to halt the Japanese drive, was more fruitful, for from it came the first concrete proposal for an Allied command in the Southwest Pacific. Colonel Brink's instructions were to present MacArthur's views on Far East strategy, which General Marshall summarized for him as follows:

American, Australian, and Dutch air and naval forces should cooperate to keep open line of communications from Australia to Philippines. Successful defense of Philippines considered essential to maintenance of Allied defensive structure in the Western Pacific. Plans for immediate Philippine reinforcement definitely dependent for success upon establishment of air traffic between Philippines and bases south. Every effort should be made to supplement air supply by reestablishment of limited sea communications between Australia and Philippines.

These views, Marshall added "are generally concurred in by the President." At the same time he informed MacArthur

---

[5] Rads, Roosevelt to Chiang, 12 and 14 Dec 41; to Stalin, 13 Dec 41; Stimson to Magruder, 13 Dec 41; Stalin to Chiang, 12 Dec 41, OPD Exec Files; Romanus and Sunderland, *Stilwell's Mission to China*, pp. 50–52.

[6] Romanus and Sunderland, *Stilwell's Mission to China*, p. 57; Rads, Marshall to Brett, No. 71, 15 Dec 41, and Brett to Marshall, 27 Dec 41, WPD 4389–54 and 58, and other related papers in this file.

of the forthcoming meetings and of his instructions to the American delegates, adding the suggestion that he correspond directly with them "if practicable from the viewpoint of secrecy." [7]

With these instructions and with the additional statement from MacArthur and Hart, couched in MacArthurian language, that "the Far East area is now the dominant locus of the war," Colonel Brink presented to the Singapore conferees the American view of the importance of the Philippines and the necessity for keeping open the lines of communication. But the British view of the importance of Singapore predominated. The report of the conferees, therefore, while it called for large reinforcements to the Southwest Pacific and adopted all of MacArthur's suggestions for the protection of the air and sea lanes between Malaya and the Philippines, gave second place to the defense of the Philippines. Japanese conquest of Singapore, the conferees thought, would be a disaster of the first order. Not only would it make certain the loss of the Netherlands Indies with is vast resources in oil and rubber, but it would also place the enemy in position to isolate Australia and New Zealand and to separate the British and American fleets in the Far East. The importance of the Philippines was limited, in the report of the Singapore Conference, to its use "as an advanced and flanking base for offensive action against Japanese lines of communication." [8]

The most important result of the Singapore meeting was the proposal made by Brink for a unified command. The conference, he told the Chief of Staff, "clearly indicated the need for one supreme head over a combined allied staff" to co-ordinate the efforts of the American, British, Australian, and Dutch forces in the area and to make plans for the future. The "unofficial opinions" of the conferees, he added, indicated that the appointment of an American familiar with the Pacific area to this post "would not only be acceptable but desirable." If such an appointment were made and a headquarters established, Brink suggested that it be located in Java. But he did not fail to point out that the majority of the delegates believed the major base of Allied operations in the Southwest Pacific should be in Australia, with an advance base in the Indies. [9]

Brink's suggestion was quickly picked up in Washington. In the Army War Plans Division, where it went first for comment, the idea of a unified command in the Far East was described as "an absolute essential for the successful prosecution of the war effort in this theater," and a matter that ought to be discussed with the British. Action in the division ended with the note, "This matter is being considered by the Chief of Staff. It has been discussed at the White House." [10]

---

[7] Rads, Marshall to Brink, No. 59, 15 Dec 41; Marshall to MacArthur, same date, both in WPD 4544-31.

[8] Rad, Brink to Marshall, 21 Dec 41, OCS 18136-179; Ltr, Brink to Marshall, 25 Dec 41, sub: Singapore Conf, WPD 4544-31; Rad, Duff Cooper, British

Chairman of the Conf, no addressee, 20 Dec 41, WPD 4402-137.

[9] Rad, Brink to Marshall, 21 Dec 41, OCS 18136-179; comments by Brink on Singapore Conf, attached to Rpt of Conf, WPD 4544-31.

[10] Memo, Maj Elmer J. Rogers, Jr., for ACofS WPD, 22 Dec 41, sub: Rpt of Singapore Conf, WPD 4544-31;

By the time the reports of the Singapore and Chungking Conferences reached the War Department, Churchill and his Chiefs of Staff had arrived in Washington for the first of the many wartime conferences which marked the most successful military alliance in the history of warfare. This meeting, which lasted from 22 December 1941 to 14 January 1942 and is known by the code name ARCADIA, was in many respects the most important of the conferences held during the war. It established an organization for the conduct of coalition warfare that survived all the stresses and strains of conflicting national interests; reaffirmed the basic decision to make the major effort in Europe at a time when the American people had not yet recovered from the shock of Pearl Harbor and when disaster threatened in the Pacific and Asia; established the first Allied command of the war; and laid down a broad program for the future as well as a plan for immediate action.[11]

The divergence between British and American views, which had been plainly evident at the ABC meetings early in 1941, was again apparent at the ARCADIA conference. The Americans believed that their national interests would best be served and the security of the United States best assured by the early defeat of Germany and Japan. This objective they put ahead of all others and made the measuring rod for every problem put before them. The British, too, sought the early defeat of the enemy, but they differed with the Americans on how to do it. Further, their national interests encompassed the security and future of a far-flung empire with its long lines of communication. Their task was more complex than that of the Americans and their path to victory more circuitous. For them, the Middle East, Singapore, Malaya, Australia, India —all held an importance the Americans could not grant on purely military grounds. The British pressed hard for the allocation of Allied resources to the defense of these positions, not only at ARCADIA but at the conferences that followed, while the Americans pushed single-mindedly for those operations that would bring about the defeat of the enemy. But determination to agree and good will on both sides overcame all differences.

About one thing, the major objective of Allied strategy, there was no disagreement. The principals subscribed to a basic statement of war aims that served as the strategic objective for the year 1942 and the basis for the division of the resources of the two nations. "Much has happened since February last," the conferees noted, "but notwithstanding the entry of Japan into the War, our view remains that Germany is still the prime enemy and her defeat is the key to victory. Once Germany is defeated the collapse of Italy and the defeat of Japan must follow." [12] It was agreed therefore, as "a cardinal principle" of American and British strategy, "that only the minimum of force necessary for the safeguarding of vital interests in other thea-

---

[11] The minutes of the ARCADIA conference are bound separately and, with the records of the conference, are filed in ABC 337, ARCADIA. For accounts of the work of the conference, see Matloff and Snell, *Strategic Planning, 1941–42*, ch. V: Hayes, The War Against Japan, ch. I, pp. 45–72; Winston S. Churchill, *The Grand Alliance* (Boston: Houghton Mifflin Company, 1950), chs. 15–17; Sherwood, *Roosevelt and Hopkins*, ch. XX.

[12] ABC–4/CS1, 31 Dec 41. The original British version of the final phrase reads "must speedily follow."

ters should be diverted from operations against Germany."

In terms of the existing situation, this "cardinal principle" meant that the production of armaments would have to be stepped up; that essential positions would have to be defended; that the vital lines of communication would have to be held; and that, by a combination of bombing, blockade, and propaganda, German resistance would have to be reduced so that the Allies could land on the Continent in 1943. But the principle of minimum force in the Pacific was one that could be interpreted variously and usually was, depending on the situation. There were always those who could justify additional forces for the Pacific on the ground that they were required to safeguard vital interests there. This was the Navy's position, argued forcefully and consistently by Admiral King.

In the Pacific and Far East, the Americans and the British Chiefs of Staff agreed, it would be necessary to maintain the security of Australia, New Zealand, and India; to support China; and to gain "points of vantage" from which an offensive against Japan could "eventually be developed." These were long-range objectives; the "immediate object" was to hold Hawaii, Alaska, Singapore, the Malay Barrier, the Philippines, Rangoon, and the route to China.

As a general statement of strategy, the objectives outlined by the U.S. and British Chiefs of Staff had little relevance to the immediate emergency in the Far East where the Japanese were advancing rapidly on every front. What was needed was agreement on the apportionment of the resources of both nations to that area, and, specifically, the amount to be

assigned each of the vital positions still in Allied hands but defended by a variety of national forces and independent commanders. Both sides were apparently reluctant to enter into detailed discussions of this subject, but they agreed that the planners should study the question of the disposition of the forces in and en route to the Southwest Pacific. This study, the Chiefs stipulated, should be based on three alternative assumptions; first, that the Allies would hold both the Philippines and Singapore; second, that they would hold Singapore and the Netherlands Indies but lose the Philippines; and third, that they would lose Singapore and the Philippines.

The planners went to work on the problem immediately and quickly produced a report the Chiefs approved on the last day of the year. Recognizing that the forces then in the area could not hold the positions prescribed and that immediate reinforcements would have to be provided, the planners framed the following statement of Allied aims:

1. Hold the Malay Barrier, that is the Malay Peninsula, Sumatra, Java, and the islands stretching eastward to northwest Australia, "as the basic defensive position"; and Burma and Australia "as essential supporting positions."

2. Re-establish communications with the Philippines and support the garrison there, while maintaining communications to Burma and Australia and within the Far East area.

Appended to the report were lists of the forces already in the theater and scheduled to arrive by 1 February. These the planners recommended be deployed "as now arranged," if the Philippines and Singapore held. If they did not, the reinforcements should be used to defend the Malay Barrier, Burma, and Australia, with American troops being used on the east side of the barrier (Australia), British and Commonwealth forces on the west (Burma and India). Should the Philippines alone fall to the Japanese—an admission the Americans were not yet willing to make to the British who firmly believed that Singapore would hold—then U.S. reinforcements would be employed along the barrier and the lines of communication to the east.[13]

By the time this study was approved, the Chiefs of Staff had already decided to set up a unified American command in the Far East. The dangers and disadvantages of command by co-operation had been made abundantly clear by the disaster at Pearl Harbor, and Marshall felt very strongly that unity of command was perhaps even more important than the allocation of resources or the assignment of troops. On the 25th, after he had Brink's report on the Singapore Conference, he raised the problem with his American and British colleagues. "The matters being settled here," he told them, "are mere details which will continuously reoccur unless settled in a broader way. . . . I am convinced that there must be one man in command of the entire theater. . . . If we make a plan for unified command now, it will solve nine-tenths of our troubles." Without minimizing the difficulties of establishing such a command over the forces of four nations, Marshall believed that it could be done and was willing "to go the limit" to achieve it. "A man with good judgment and unity of command,"

he said, "has a distinct advantage over a man with brilliant judgment who must rely on cooperation." But the consensus of the meeting was not in Marshall's favor and the subject was dropped after polite comment.[14]

The next day Mr. Roosevelt, apparently after discussion with Marshall and King, raised the question of a unified command in the Far East at a White House meeting with Churchill and others. The Prime Minister, like his military advisers, did not favor the idea and there the matter rested for the moment. But neither the President nor General Marshall abandoned their fight and both privately did their utmost to change Churchill's mind.[15] In this they were successful so far as the principle of unified command was concerned but agreement on the officer who would exercise such a command and the limits of his authority was not so easily reached. Oddly enough, the British wanted an American and the Americans favored a British officer, specifically General Wavell, then Commander-in-Chief, India, for the post. Finally on 28 December, Churchill agreed to the American proposal and Wavell was alerted to his coming appointment. It was decided also that Wavell, when he assumed command, would report to the Combined Chiefs of Staff, then being established, and that his headquarters would be located in Java.

Meanwhile U.S. Army planners had been working on a directive designed

---

[13] ABC–4/3, 31 Dec 41; JPC Rpt, 28 Dec 41, sub: Supporting Measures for SWP, ABC–4/3; Rad, Marshall to MacArthur, 1 Jan 42, WPD 4639.

[14] Mins, ARCADIA Mtg, 25 Dec 41; Memo for File by Eisenhower, 28 Dec 41, sub: Notes of Chiefs of Staff Conf, 25 Dec 41, WPD 4639.

[15] Gerow, Notes on White House Conf, 26 Dec 41, OPD Exec Files; Mins of White House Conf, 26 Dec 41, WDSCA Conf I; Sherwood, *Roosevelt and Hopkins*, p. 457.

primarily to show whether one could be drawn "which would leave the Supreme Commander with enough power to improve the situation and still not give him power to destroy national interests or to exploit one theater without due consideration to another." [16] The task was a difficult one and the results were not entirely satisfactory, the British Chiefs objecting on the ground that the limitations placed on the commander were too heavy. It was sent to the Allied planners, therefore, for further study and a revised draft was prepared. This one, with slight modifications, proved acceptable and was finally approved, though with some reluctance, by all the governments involved on 10 January 1942.[17]

The new command Wavell was to head was to be known as ABDACOM, for the initials of the national forces involved (American, British, Dutch, and Australian) and included Burma, Malaya, the Netherlands Indies, and the Philippines. The inclusion of the Philippines in Wavell's command was a formal gesture and one Wavell himself wished to avoid.[18] Significantly, neither China nor Australia was included in the ABDA area. (Map 2) As much for political as military reasons the former was organized as a separate theater commanded by Chiang Kai-shek, but independent of Allied control. The Australians, though they protested their

omission from the discussions in Washington and their lack of representation in the Combined Chiefs of Staff, accepted the terms of the directive and permitted their troops in the ABDA area to become a part of Wavell's command. USAFIA (U.S. Army Forces in Australia), however, was not included in the new command on the ground that its primary responsibility was to MacArthur and its main task to support the defense of the Philippines. Soon after Wavell assumed command, when it became apparent that only limited aid could be sent to the Philippines, the mission of USAFIA was broadened to include the support of operations in the ABDA area. And the northwest portion of Australia was also added to ABDACOM at General Wavell's request.[19]

The staff of the new command, it was understood, would represent all the nations concerned. The American and British Chiefs of Staff did not attempt to name Wavell's staff, but they did seek to guard against the preponderance of one nationality in his headquarters. Thus, they stipulated that his deputy and the commander of the naval forces would be Americans, and that a British officer would command the air forces and a Dutch officer the ground forces.

The problem of protecting the interests of each nation represented in ABDACOM without unduly restricting the commander was resolved by limiting Wavell's authority to the "effective coordination of forces." He was given command of all forces "afloat, ashore,

---

[16] Mins, ARCADIA, 27 Dec 41.

[17] ABC–4/5, Directive to Supreme Comdr in ABDA Area, 10 Jan 42. An earlier version of the directive can be found in the 30 December meeting of the conference, and the directive actually issued to Wavell is dated 2 January, the day after the President and Prime Minister approved it.

[18] Rad, Marshall to MacArthur, No. 930, 12 Jan 42, WPD 4639–14. For additional papers on this subject, see WPD 4639–19.

[19] Romanus and Sunderland, *Stilwell's Mission to China*, pp. 61–63; Rads, Marshall to Barnes, Nos. 206 and 223, 27 and 30 Jan 42, both in WPD 4628–25; CCS 8, 24 Jan 42, sub: Inclusion of Darwin in ABDA, ABC 323.31 POA (1–29–42).

THE ABDACOM AREA
January–February 1942

——————	Original Abda Area
• • • • • •	Darwin Sub-command
– – – – –	Air Sub-command

CHINA

JAPAN

BURMA
NORGROUP

THAILAND

FRENCH INDOCHINA

Formosa

Hong Kong

Hainan

Andaman Is.

Nicobar Is.

MALAYA
WESGROUP

Manila

PHILIPPINE IS.

SUMATRA

Singapore

BORNEO

CENGROUP

Batavia

EASGROUP

CELEBES

JAVA

TIMOR

ANZAC

NEW GUINEA

AREA

Darwin

AUSTRALIA

F. Temple

MAP 2

and in the air," but was permitted to exercise that control only through subordinate commanders whom he could not relieve and who had the right to appeal to their governments if they considered their orders and national interests to be in conflict. Though he could assign missions to his forces, form task forces for specific operations, and appoint their commanders, he was prohibited from altering the tactical organization of the national forces in his command, using their supplies, or controlling their communications with the home government. And in matters of logistics and administration he could exercise only the most general control.

The severe limitations placed on General Wavell's authority were in marked contrast to the heavy responsibilities laid upon him by the chiefs in Washington. Not only was he given the task of maintaining "as many key positions as possible" under the strategic objectives already outlined (that is, to hold the Malay Barrier, Burma, and Australia), a formidable enough undertaking in itself, but he was also enjoined "to take the offensive at the earliest opportunity and ultimately to conduct an allout offensive against Japan." "The first essential," the Chiefs told him, "is to gain general air superiority at the earliest possible moment." With the lesson of the first Japanese successes still fresh in mind, they cautioned Wavell against dispersing his air forces or using them in piecemeal fashion.[20]

These instructions, with their emphasis on offensive operations, were probably

motivated by an understandable reluctance in Washington to dedicate a command to defensive action, but there was a clear realization that the forces in the theater were then and for some time would be hard pressed even to hold their own. And even as these instructions were being written the enemy was moving swiftly and in force toward those "key positions" Wavell was to hold.

Having established the ABDA area and appointed General Wavell its commander, the American and British staffs in Washington had still to settle the problem of reinforcements to the Southwest Pacific, for it was obvious with each passing day that the situation there was rapidly worsening. This problem brought the assembled planners up against the hard fact, which was to plague them throughout the war, that there were not enough ships to do all the jobs required. They had earlier in the conference agreed that American troops would be sent to Iceland and northern Ireland, and that landings might be made in North Africa later in the year. The shipping requirements for these operations alone were so great that the North Atlantic sailings were approved only on the understanding that they would be discontinued "if other considerations intervened."[21] The necessity for speeding up the schedule of reinforcements to the Southwest Pacific created an additional and immediate demand for the ships already allocated to the North Atlantic projects and led to a re-examination of the entire shipping shortage.

The debate over Atlantic versus Pacific priority on shipping was precipi-

---

[20] ABC–4/5, Directive for the Supreme Commander, 2 Jan 42. A copy is printed in General Wavell's account entitled "ABDACOM," app. A, copy in OCMH.

[21] Notes on White House Mtg, 1 Jan 42, WDCSA 334 Mtgs and Confs.

tated by Admiral Stark, who, on 11 January, a day after General Wavell arrived in Batavia but before he assumed command, reviewed the critical situation in the Far East and raised the question of diverting ships from the less critical North Atlantic route to the Pacific. In this he had the support of General Marshall and Admiral King, but the British, in the belief that Singapore would hold and anxious for the Americans to relieve then in Iceland and Ireland, sought other ways to find the ships. The matter was finally referred to the shipping experts who reported the next day that by delaying the North Atlantic sailings one month, which would have the effect also of delaying the proposed North African operation, and by reducing lend-lease shipments to the Soviet Union, it would be possible to send aircraft, gasoline, artillery, and about 22,000 men across the Pacific on 20 January and an additional 23,300 British troops shortly after. The Chiefs accepted this solution, as did the President and Prime Minister when Mr. Hopkins assured them that ships would be found to keep supplies moving to the Soviet Union.[22] The minimum force principle for allocation of resources to the Pacific had now been stretched so far as to justify the postponement of troop movements to Iceland and northern Ireland and, in part at least, the delay of the North African landings. In the days to come it was to be stretched even further.

The conference scored one other major achievement before its close on 14 January. Last on the agenda the British had

submitted before the meeting was an item calling for the establishment of "joint machinery" for collaboration. Just what the British had in mind was not clear, but in preparation for the coming discussion the Americans studied the matter and decided they would seek as their solution to the problem of collaboration the establishment of a Supreme Allied War Council, patterned on the World War I model, and of two committees to support the council—a Military Joint Planning Committee and a Joint Supply Committe.[23]

The idea of a Supreme Allied War Council came up early in the conference. It quickly became apparent that the World War I model would hardly meet the requirements of a global war, and action was deferred until the more urgent problems were disposed of. Finally, on the 13th, the British returned to the subject of the organization of the alliance. By this time the ABDA command had been created and Admiral Sir Dudley Pound suggested that the same pattern be followed on a global scale. This was entirely agreeable to the Americans, as was the British suggestion to avoid confusion between Allied and national activities by adopting a standard nomenclature. *Joint* was to be used for interservice collaboration of one nation; *combined,* for collaboration between two or more nations.[24]

One further matter remained to be settled—the location of the Allied command post. The British, naturally,

---

[22] Mins, ARCADIA, 11 and 12 Jan 42; ann. 1 to 10th Mtg, 12 Jan 42; CofS Conf, 12 Jan 42, ABC 337 ARCADIA; White House Conf, same date, OPD Reg. Docs.

[23] JB 325, ser 729. For full discussion of this subject, see Vernon E. Davis, Origins of the Joint and Combined Chiefs of Staff, vol. I, Organizational Development, ch. V, History of the JCS in World War II.

[24] Mins, ARCADIA Mtg, 13 Jan 42; Post Arcadia Collaboration, 10 Jan 42, an. 4 to Mins, ARCADIA, 10 Jun 42.

wanted it in London; the Americans, in Washington. There had been some consideration earlier in the conference of a dual system operating out of both capitals, but this idea was quickly discarded. By the 13th it had been virtually decided that the headquarters of the alliance would be in Washington. The British therefore proposed to leave in the American capital Field Marshal Sir John Dill to represent Mr. Churchill on the highest levels, and the heads of the Joint Staff Mission, the organization established after the ABC–1 meetings in March 1940, to represent the Chiefs of Staff. Similarly, the Americans were to designate their own officials to represent the President and the Chiefs of Staff in London.

The Americans did not favor this solution. Though they did not object to Sir John Dill's appointment and even preferred him to anyone else, they felt that British representation in Washington should be limited to the level of the Chiefs of Staff. The assignment of a high-ranking British officer in Washington with access to the President would, they believed, create many problems. The proposal also seemed to them to suggest the dual command post concept. To General Marshall, "there could be no question of having any duplication of the Combined Chiefs of Staff organization in Washington and London." Though he had no objection to parallel subordinate committees, "there could be," he asserted, "only one Combined Chiefs of Staff who would give broad directions on the allocation of materiel." [25]

The final details for U.S.-British collaboration were settled at the last meeting of the conference. On the evening of the 13th the Americans prepared a draft of the arrangements already agreed upon, which with some modifications was accepted by the British and became the basis for the organization of the Combined Chiefs of Staff during the war. [26] As defined by the conferees, the Combined Chiefs of Staff consisted of the British Chiefs of Staff or their representatives in Washington, and the U.S. Chiefs, who, in the accepted terminology, were designated as the U.S. Joint Chiefs of Staff. The Combined Chiefs were to sit in Washington only and to meet weekly, or more often if necessary. They were to have a secretariat to maintain their records and prepare and distribute their papers, and a staff of planners designated the Combined Staff Planners (consisting of the chief American planners and their British opposite numbers). This latter group was "to make such studies, draft such plans, and perform such other work" as directed by the Chiefs.

The authority granted to the Combined Chiefs was broad. They were to "develop and submit recommendations" for the ABDA area and for the other areas "in which the United Nations may decide to act in concert . . . modified as necessary to meet the particular circumstances." To perform these functions, they were given responsibility for recommending to their political superiors "a broad program" of the requirements for implementing strategic decisions and for preparing general directives establishing policy governing the distribution of the weapons of war. Such weapons and war equipment were to be allocated "in ac-

---

[25] Mins, ARCADIA Mtg, 13 Jan 42.

[26] ABC–4/CS 4, 14 Jan 42, sub: Post- ARCADIA Collaboration; Mins, ARCADIA Mtg, 14 Jan 42, an. 2.

cordance with strategical needs" through appropriate groups in Washington and London under the authority of the Combined Chiefs. Finally, the Combined Chiefs were given responsibility to settle the broad issues of priority for overseas military movements.

The combined organization established at the ARCADIA Conference, though it stemmed in large measure from the efforts to meet the crisis in the Southwest Pacific, was patterned on the ABC–1 arrangements and on British practice. Under the former, an effective and well-manned British Joint Staff Mission had been established in Washington, and it was this body that provided the basis for a Combined Chiefs of Staff organization in the American capital. British experience with committe organization provided the other key to the combined system established at ARCADIA. Thus, the Combined Chiefs were responsible to the President and Prime Minister in much the same way as the British Chiefs were already responsible to Churchill in his dual capacity as Prime Minister and Minister of Defense.[27] And the organization of the U.S. Joint Chiefs of Staff that emerged during the months after the ARCADIA Conference was shaped in large degree by the necessity for providing American counterparts to the highly developed system of committees and secretariats under the British Chiefs and the War Cabinet.

The ABDACOM Interlude

While the American and British heads of state with their military staffs were in Washington establishing the strategic

basis and the organization for the conduct of the war, the Japanese Army and Navy had continued their drive into Southeast Asia and the Southwest Pacific with unabated vigor. Operations during the first phase of their plan for seizing the southern area had been remarkably successful and in the first week of January 1942 they opened the second phase. The objectives of this phase of the plan included the seizure of the Bismarck Archipelago and Malay Peninsula; the capture of Singapore; and, in preparation for the final assault on Java, heart of the Indies, the acquisition of air and naval bases in southern Sumatra, Dutch Borneo, the Celebes, Amboina, and Timor. The occupation of Java itself and of northern Sumatra was scheduled for the third phase, after which the Japanese would complete their operations in Burma and consolidate their position in the conquered area. All these operations were to be completed by the end of April, in time to meet possible attack from the Soviet Union, which, the Japanese believed, would come in the spring, if it came at all that year.

In Malaya there was no clear demarcation between the first and second phase. There the Japanese, driving in two columns down the east and west coasts of the peninsula, continued to advance without halt. Combining amphibious encirclement with frontal assault, General Yamashita was able to force the stubborn British defenders back time after time until by 10 January he stood at the gates of Kuala Lumpur, on the west coast of Malaya, which his *5th Division* captured the next day. His eastern column meanwhile had advanced to within 100 miles of Singapore. By the middle of the month, he had united his

---

[27] Davis, *Origins of Joint and Combined Chiefs of Staff,* I, p. 269.

GENERAL TER POORTEN *greets General Wavell (left) on his arrival at Batavia.*

thus making possible the invasion of Java a month earlier than planned. At *Imperial General Headquarters* the Terauchi-Kondo proposal met a favorable reception, for it would not only speed operations in the south and keep the enemy off balance but it would also make available at an earlier date the troops needed in Manchuria if the Soviet Union should enter the war—a danger that continued to haunt the Japanese. Early in January, therefore, *Imperial General Headquarters* approved the recommendation and advanced the timetable for the seizure of the southern area.[29]

The first signs of the increased tempo of Japanese operations in the Netherlands Indies came very quickly. Late in December the Japanese had gained control of British Borneo and the South China Sea approaches to the Malay Barrier. Now, in the first week of January, the *16th Army*, which had been given the *38th Division* to accelerate its drive into the Indies, completed its preparations for the advance. At Davao in the southern Philippines it organized two task forces, one to take the important oil center of Tarakan in northern Borneo, and the other Menado in the Celebes. Both left Davao at the same time, 9 January. The first landed at Tarakan on 11 January and, after overcoming slight resistance from the Dutch defenders aided by American B–17's based near Surabaya, took that town the same day. The second force, reinforced by about 330 naval paratroopers and supported by the seaplane tenders *Chitose* and *Mizuho* and three heavy cruisers, took Menado at the same time.

two columns and was preparing to attack the single line the gallant defenders had formed before the plain which constitutes the southern tip of the peninsula.[28]

So rapidly had their forces moved and so light had been resistance that even before the end of the year Japanese commanders in the field were urging their superiors in Tokyo to speed the timetable of conquest. In the last week of December, Field Marshal Hisaichi Terauchi, commander of the *Southern Army,* and Vice Adm. Nobutake Kondo, *2d Fleet* commander, jointly recommended advancing the schedule of operations against Sumatra and Borneo,

[28] *25th Army* Opns in Malaya, Japanese Studies in World War II, 85; Despatch by Lt Gen A. E. Percival, Opns of Malaya Command, 8 Dec 41–15 Feb 42, *Supplement to the London Gazette,* February 20, 1948. Kirby, *et al, The Loss of Singapore,* chs. XIV, XVII.

[29] *Hist of Army Section, Imperial GHQ* (rev. ed.), Japanese Studies in World War II, 72, pp. 42–43.

The seizure of these two points completed the Japanese control of the Celebes Sea and the northern approaches to Makassar Strait. Through that strait lay one of the routes to Java.[30]

It was at this juncture, on 10 January, that General Wavell reached Batavia, capital of the Netherlands Indies, located on the northwest coast of Java. Already there or soon to arrive were his deputy, General Brett, and the commanders of his ground and naval force, Lt. Gen. H. ter Poorten and Admiral Hart. In the absence of Air Marshal Sir Richard E. C. Peirse, General Brereton was appointed deputy commander of the air forces. On the 15th, General Wavell formally assumed command of the ABDA area (ABDACOM) with headquarters at Lembang, inland from the capital and about ten miles north of Bandoeng.[31] (Chart 2)

From the start it was apparent that the defense of the ABDA area, even in the unlikely event that the promised reinforcements arrived in time, had little chance of success. Already the Japanese had taken Hong Kong, isolated the Philippines, landed in Borneo and the Celebes, and were making rapid progress down the Malay Peninsula. To oppose their advance Wavell had, in addition to the British forces fighting a losing battle in Malaya and the American forces in the Philippines, two Dutch divisions in Java and small Dutch garrisons else-

where in the Indies; a naval force—including the U.S. Asiatic Fleet—of 1 heavy and 8 light cruisers, 23 destroyers, and 36 submarines; and an air force of 4 fighter and 6 bomber squadrons, including the remnants of the Far East Air Force, plus 250 more planes in Burma and Malaya. With these meager forces General Wavell could only try to hold back the Japanese tide while waiting for reinforcements which never came.[32]

The urgent need for reinforcements was only one of Wavell's problems. Keeping the peace within his own small international headquarters, unraveling the confused command relationships between his forces, and reconciling conflicting national interests and strategic concepts were others almost as serious. Even so minor a matter as the location of the headquarters could not be settled amicably and it was only after he had overridden the strong objections of his naval commanders that Wavell established his headquarters at Lembang.[33]

The relationship between Wavell and MacArthur, though it created no difficulties, illustrated the confused situation in ABDACOM. In addition to the task of holding the Malay Barrier, Wavell had also been instructed to re-establish communications with Luzon and to support the Philippine garrison. Before assuming command, he objected to this assignment and proposed that the islands be excluded from the ABDA area. President Roosevelt, without consulting his military advisers, approved this suggestion to avoid any delay in Wavell's assumption of command. When General Marshall learned of this action he saw

---

[30] Hist of *Southern Army*, Japanese Studies in World War II, 24, pp. 16, 19; Naval Opns in Invasion of NEI, Japanese Studies in World War II, 17, pp. 18–20; Morison, *The Rising Sun in the Pacific*, pp. 280–281; Craven and Cate, *AAF I*, p. 380. The tenders were later converted into light carriers.

[31] Rads, Marshall to MacArthur, No. 930, 12 Jan 42; to Brereton, No. 52, same date, both in WPD Msg File; Wavell, "ABDACOM," pp. 1–2.

[32] Wavell, "ABDACOM," pp. 16–18.

[33] Narrative of Events, Asiatic Fleet, Leading up to War, 8 Dec 41 to 15 Feb 42, pp. 54–55, OCMH.

CHART 2—ORGANIZATION OF ABDACOM, JANUARY–FEBRUARY 1942

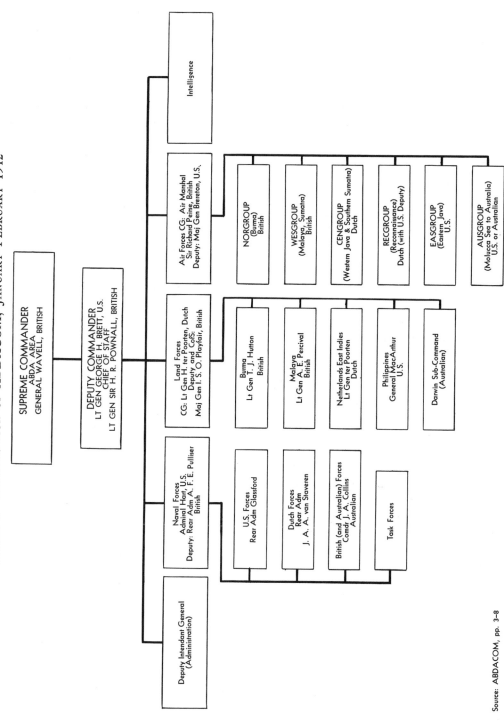

Source: ABDACOM, pp. 3–8

ABDA COMMAND *meeting with General Wavell for the first time. Seated around the table, from left: Admirals Layton, Helfrich, and Hart, General ter Poorten, Colonel Kengen, Royal Netherlands Army (at head of table), and Generals Wavell, Brett, and Brereton.*

that it might well have an adverse effect upon morale in the Philippines and was contrary to the ABDA agreement. An important reason for the establishment of Wavell's command had been the desire to co-ordinate the efforts of the Allies in the Far East, and the United States had allocated to the defense of ABDA aircraft which had been under MacArthur's command or sent out originally for his use. With King's support, therefore, Marshall recommended to the President that he rescind his earlier message. The President saw the point immediately, and Wavell was told the day after he assumed command that the Philippines would remain in his area.[34]

[34] Rad, Wavell to British Chiefs of Staff, ABDA 48, 14 Jan 42; Memo, WPD for U.S. Secy CCS, 16 Jan 42, both in WPD 4639–19; Ltr, U.S. Secy CCS to Brig V. Dykes, 16 Jan 42, sub: Responsibility of Supreme Commander ABDA, ABC 381 SWPA (1–12–42).

The establishment of the ABDA area made necessary also a reshuffling of the U.S. Army commands already in existence in the Southwest Pacific and Southeast Asia. Although MacArthur was assured by the War Department that the establishment of ABDACOM would not alter his position or affect his forces, he actually lost a part of his command. The U.S. Army Forces in Australia were then a part of USAFFE (U.S. Army Forces, Far East) and under MacArthur's direction. Now he was told that these forces would be formed into a separate command on a level with USAFFE and placed under General Brereton, who had been selected because of his "intimate knowledge of your situation and needs." The reason for this move was that the Japanese advance into the Indies had made control by MacArthur of the forces in Australia and the Netherlands

Indies impractical. But, he was assured, "when satisfactory communications with the Philippines have once been reestablished your resumption of actual command of all American Army forces in the Far East will be easily accomplished."[35]

Other than the paper changes in command, the establishment of ABDACOM had no effect on operations in the Philippines. MacArthur reported formally by radio to his new superior and sent representatives from Mindanao to Java to solicit what aid they could, but the relationship between the two headquarters was never more than nominal.

General Brereton's assignment as air commander in the ABDA area, pending the arrival of Air Marshal Pierse, complicated an already confusing situation. Brereton was also commander of U.S. Army Forces in Australia (USAFIA), a post General Brett had held before him, and in this capacity also came under Wavell's control. But this control was only partial, for, as the War Department explained to Brereton, "U.S. troops in Australian territory come under the control of General Wavell only when specifically allotted for service in the ABDA area."[36]

The physical difficulties of exercising command simultaneously over USAFIA, a logistical and administrative headquarters in Australia, and over ABDAIR, an operational headquarters in Java, as well as the conflicting missions of the two, made it imperative to clarify Brereton's status. On the 16th, therefore, a day after he assumed command,

General Wavell, at Brereton's request, asked Marshall to relieve Brereton of his responsibilities in Australia so that he could concentrate on the full-time job of directing his air forces. This was quickly done, and General Barnes, who had in effect been directing the activities of USAFIA since the 12th, was authorized to assume command of base facilities in Australia.[37]

Barnes himself seems to have been somewhat confused about his status and responsibilities for he was never formally designated as a commander of USAFIA and Brereton continued to receive messages addressed to him with that title. Moreover, when Brereton had difficulty getting logistical support from Australia that he wanted, he complained to the War Department, which promptly informed Barnes that he was to provide that support as best he could. At the same time, the War Department made it clear to Barnes that he was not under Brereton's but Wavell's command, and that General Brett, as Wavell's deputy, could issue orders to him. So far as the War Department was concerned this ended the matter, but General Barnes, even at the end of January, was apparently not clear on his relationship to ABDACOM "in general" and to General Brett "in particular regarding troops and supplies in Australia."[38]

Not only was there confusion over command in the ABDA area, but national commanders differed with one

[35] Rad, Marshall to MacArthur, No. 930, 11 Jan 42, WPD 4639–14.
[36] Rad, WD to Brereton, No. 52, 12 Jan 42, WPD 4628–20; Marshall to MacArthur, No. 930, same date, WPD 4639–14.

[37] Rads, Brett to Marshall, ABDA 7 and 22, 15 and 16 Jan 42, WPD Msg File; Wavell to Marshall, ABDA 71, 16 Jan 42; Marshall to Wavell, No. 25, same date; both in WPD 4639–19.
[38] Rads, Barnes to Marshall, No. 130, 29 Jan 42; No. 138, 31 Jan 42, WPD Msg File; Marshall to Barnes, No. 206 and 223, 27 and 30 Jan 42; Marshall to Brett, No. 48, 27 Jan 42, all in WPD 4628–25.

another and with the Supreme Commander over the conduct of operations and the allocation of resources. To the American, Dutch, and Australian officers, it seemed that General Wavell was devoting far too much attention, as well as a disproportionate share of Allied resources, to the defense of Malaya, Singapore, and Burma, an attitude that seemed to them to reflect British rather than Allied interests. The American commanders, Admiral Hart and General Brereton, free from any territorial interest in the area, wished to protect the lines of communication and air and naval bases along the Malay Barrier, which they believed essential links in defensive structure of the Southwest Pacific and the starting points for offensive operations. The Dutch desired above all else to concentrate Allied resources on the defense of their territories. And the Australians, concerned over the defense of the homeland, continually pressed for a greater share of the theater's resources on the east. If General Wavell made any effort to reconcile these views, the records do not show it. Despite the representations of the national commanders to their governments—in Washington Brett's were refuted by the Army planners, as was his proposal to break up the new theater—Wavell continued to act on the assumption that the security of the Netherlands Indies and Australia depended on the defense of Malaya and Singapore.[39]

These difficulties were brought out sharply in the discussion of naval rein-

forcements. Most of the British and Dutch vessels in the area were assigned to convoy duty, leaving only the U.S. Asiatic Fleet, based on Surabaya, free for operations. The Dutch, whose naval forces were under the operational control of the British, were none too happy over this assignment, preferring to employ their vessels in the defense of Dutch territory. Their irritation was further increased by the British announcement of the transfer of some of their cruisers and destroyers to the Indian Ocean and American refusal to provide naval reinforcements for convoy duty. Ultimately the Australians were persuaded to send additional vessels into the area, but the damage had been done and the Dutch resentment persisted.[40]

The Dutch were displeased also with the way naval operations were being conducted. Admiral Hart, they felt, had his forces too far back and was showing more concern over Darwin and the supply routes to Australia than over the progress of the enemy through Makassar Strait and the Molucca Sea. They were disappointed, too, over their failure to gain command of the naval elements in ABDA. Their interests, they felt, were predominant and their knowledge of the area greater than that of the Americans. This attitude, which Dutch naval officers made little effort to conceal, added to Hart's already considerable burdens and complicated his task enormously.

By the end of January, relations between Admiral Hart and the Dutch naval commander had become so strained that they could no longer be ignored. It was then that General Wavell suggested to the Prime Minister that Hart

---

[39] Hart, Narrative of Events, *passim*; Lewis H. Brereton, *The Brereton Diaries* (New York: William Morrow and Company, 1946, pp. 88–89; Memo, WPD for TAG, 17 Jan 42, sub: Comd in ABDA, WPD 4639–29; Rad, Brett to Marshall, ABDA 95, OPD Exec Files.

[40] Hayes, The War Against Japan, ch. III, pp. 17–20.

be relieved on account of his age and that a Dutch officer, or, if the United States would send naval reinforcements to the ABDA area, a younger American be given command. The suggestion was passed on to Washington and finally to Hart himself who replied that he did not consider himself too old to discharge his duties and did not wish to be relieved. Though both Admirals King and Stark supported the Asiatic Fleet commander, the President decided to adopt Wavell's suggestion. His decision was influenced largely by the fact that the United States had refused to send naval reinforcements to the area and by the hope that the Dutch would assume a more active role in the naval defense of ABDA. There was never any feeling, Admirals King and Stark later recalled, that Hart had proved unfit or that he was too old to exercise command. After the President had made his decision Hart had no recourse but to step down, which he did on the 5th by asking to be relieved on account of ill health, a course Admiral Stark had recommended to him. Six days later the Secretary of the Navy ordered him home.[41] His place was taken by Vice Adm. Conrad E. L. Helfrich, Dutch naval commander.

With the relief of Admiral Hart, ABDACOM lost its last American force commander. Air Marshall Pierse had taken over from General Brereton on 28 January, as originally intended, and the Dutch continued to command the ground forces. The U.S. Chiefs, anxious to secure direction of one of the major elements in ABDACOM in the interests of "homeland support," put forward Brett's name as commander of the

ADMIRALS HELFRICH AND HART

Allied air forces. Both the President and the Prime Minister supported the nomination, but Brett seems to have had larger ambitions and argued that such a "drastic change" would be unsettling. The matter was dropped.[42]

While the Allies sought to solve the problem of command and bring reinforcements into the area, the Japanese continued to advance almost without interruption. In Malaya General Yamashita forced the British back from line after line until on 27 January Lt. Gen. A. E. Percival, the British commander in Malaya, withdrew his forces to Singapore. The causeway connecting the fortress to the mainland was blown on 31 January. Only the waters of Johore Strait lay between Yamashita and his goal.

For a week, while the Singapore gar-

[41]*Ibid.*, pp. 20–22; Hart, Narrative of Events; Mins, CCS Mtg, 10 Feb 42.

[42]Rads, Marshall to Brett, No. 73, 4 Feb 42, WPD 4628–27; Brett to Marshall, 3 Feb 42, AB 371 (2–3–42).

rison desperately prepared its defenses, Japanese aircraft and artillery paved the way for the final assault. Shortly before midnight of 8 February, under cover of an extremely heavy artillery bombardment, the Japanese began to cross the straits. By the morning of the 9th, they had established a firm position on the island and were pouring reinforcements into the lodgment area. From there the Japanese spread over the island, infiltrating the defender's lines and isolating them into small pockets of resistance. On the 15th General Percival, with his water, food, and ammunition gone, decided that further resistance was impossible. That afternoon, he met Yamashita at the Ford Motor Factory and formally surrendered his command, an act which symbolized the end of British imperial power in the Far East.[43]

The loss of Singapore was a major blow to the Allied cause in the Far East and a disaster of the first magnitude for the British who had long regarded it as an impregnable fortress and the key to the defense of Australia, New Zealand, and India. Fortunately, the British estimate of the importance of Singapore to the security of the Dominions proved incorrect, but that did not lessen the immediate shock or minimize the seriousness of the blow to the British Far Eastern Fleet, which had already suffered the loss of the *Prince of Wales* and *Repulse*. With its base gone, the British Navy now had to retire to Sydney in Australia and to Ceylon, and when Ceylon was threatened briefly in April, to the east coast of Africa.

For ABDACOM, which had been established only a month before, the fall of Singapore was a crushing blow. In anticipation of this disaster, General Wavell had warned the Chiefs of Staff on the 13th that a drastic change in plans might soon be necessary. It was doubtful, he wrote, that Sumatra, obviously the next Japanese objective, could be held, and if it were not, then Java would fall. Though he told the Chiefs he intended to continue his present plans for the defense of Java "until situation enforces changes," it was apparent by the 13th that he had no real hope for success, a view that was reinforced by his recommendation to divert reinforcements, two Australian divisions, already en route from the Middle East to Java, to Australia or Burma, preferably the latter.[44]

The Dutch took violent exception to Wavell's estimate. They insisted that Java must be defended, regardless of the fate of Sumatra. To them and to the Netherlands Government-in-exile Java had an even greater political, moral, and sentimental significance than Singapore had for the British. Wavell's proposal seemed to them an abandonment by their Allies and confirmed their worst fears that ABDACOM was a device to use Allied resources for the defense of Singapore and of British interests in the Far East.

Unpalatable as it was to the Dutch, Wavell's estimate had to be accepted for not only was Singapore about to fall into Japanese hands, but Java was clearly threatened from three directions—the South China Sea, Makassar Strait, and Molucca Sea. Following up the Borneo

---

[43] Percival, Opns in Malaya; *25th Army* Opns in Malaya, Japanese Studies in World War II, 85, pp. 58–110; Wavell, "ABDACOM," pp. 32–42; Kirby, *et al, The Loss of Singapore*, ch. XXIV.

[44] Rads, Wavell to CCS, 13 Feb 42, CCOS 7; Wavell to CCS, 15 Feb 42, CCOS 8, OPD ABDA Msg File.

landings of late December and early January, the Japanese, moving by water through Makassar Strait, had landed at Balikpapan on the 24th. The landings had been made only after a battle with U.S. naval forces—their first of the war —in which the American destroyers won a tactical victory but failed to stop the enemy. The Japanese took Balikpapan easily but failed to capture the oil refineries there. These, the Dutch had already gutted.

From Balikpapan, the Japanese moved on to Bandjermasin, along the southeast coast of Borneo, which they took on 10 February. Only a day before, another Japanese force had sailed through the Molucca Sea to land at Makassar on the southwest tip of Celebes Island, facing Makassar Strait. By 10 February that strait and the north shore of the Java Sea were under Japanese control.

The Molucca Sea approach to the Malay Barrier fell into Japanese hands as a result of amphibious hops and naval-air engagements in which the Allies fought a desperate but losing battle. From Menado, which they had taken on 11 January, the Japanese moved on to Kendari on the 24th, the same day they landed at Balikpapan. Amboina Island was occupied a week later by a strong force which overcame the small Dutch and Australian garrison with little difficulty. By the end of the month the Japanese controlled the Molucca Sea and were in position to cut the line between Java and Australia and to breach the east flank of the Malay Barrier.

On the western flank of the barrier, the Japanese had early secured the South China Sea approaches and on 9 February, without waiting for the fall of Singapore, launched their attack on southern Su-matra. From Camranh Bay in Indo-china came a strong naval force to support the transports headed for Palembang with its airfield and oil refinery. On the 14th about 700 paratroopers were dropped in the Palembang area, but achieved only a limited success against the Dutch and British defenders. At the end of the day Allied troops were still in control, but next morning, when the main Japanese force landed upshore and began to move toward Palembang, they withdrew. Two days later, the Japanese were in control of southern Sumatra, leaving the northern part of the island to the conquerors of Singapore. Only the Straits of Sunda now separated the Japanese from their main objective, Java.[45]

By 16 February, three days after Wavell had told the Combined Chiefs in Washington that he might not be able to hold Sumatra, the situation in the ABDA area had rapidly worsened. There was no longer any chance of holding Java, Wavell now told the Chiefs. Its loss would be serious, he asserted, and would deprive the Allies of their only base in the South China Sea. But, he pointed out, the fall of Java would not be fatal to the Allied cause. Burma and Australia, not Java, he declared, were the "absolutely vital" positions in the war against Japan. He therefore recommended again that the two Australian divisions be diverted to Burma, with

[45] For accounts of these operations, see Wavell, "ABDACOM," pp. 52–67; Morison *The Rising Sun in the Pacific*, pp. 280–311; Craven and Cate, *AAF I*, ch I, ch X; Hist of *Southern Army*, Japanese Studies in World War II, 24, pp. 16, 19; Naval Opns in Invasion of NEI, Japanese Studies in World War II, 17, pp. 18–20, 22–23, 26–27; Ambon and Timor Invasions, Japanese Studies in World War II, 30, pp. 1–15.

Americans providing reinforcements for Australia.[46]

Washington agreed with Wavell's estimate of the probable loss of Java. Reinforcement was evidently futile and the wisest course, the Combined Chiefs thought, would be to send at least one of the Australian divisions to Burma and the other to Australia. It was clear also that the fall of Java would split the ABDA area and make a co-ordinated defense of its eastern and western extremities impossible. The British therefore suggested that Burma be taken out of ABDACOM and transferred to their command in India, a proposal that the U.S. Chiefs and General Wavell, who had always believed Burma was an integral part of the Indian command, readily accepted. This was accomplished formally on 21 February.[47] The plan for sending the Australian divisions to Burma, however, came to naught. Concerned over the defense of their own country, the Australians persistently refused, despite strong appeals from Churchill and Roosevelt, to permit the diversion of these divisions to Burma, and finally, on 23 February, they were ordered home.[48]

Though the loss of Java was conceded by all except the Dutch, there was a reluctance to act on this assumption. To do so would create the impression that the Americans and British were deserting their Dutch allies. On the 20th, therefore, the Combined Chiefs, asserting that "every day gained is of importance," directed Wavell to defend Java "with the utmost resolution" and not to withdraw or surrender any of the troops there. To minimize the loss of Allied troops in Java, the Chiefs specifically prohibited Wavell from reinforcing that island further, but did give him discretion to use his naval forces and American planes in Australia as he thought best.[49]

Even as these fresh instructions were being received at ABDACOM, the Japanese were making their execution impossible. On the 19th, they landed on the southern tip of Bali, immediately to the east of Java. Next day they landed on Timor, half of which was Dutch and half Portuguese. Control of these islands, lying between Java and northwest Australia, completed the isolation of Java, placed Japanese land-based fighters within bombing range of the Dutch base at Surabaya, and made further reinforcements from Australia impossible.

With the Japanese making ready for the final assault on Java, General Wavell turned to his superiors for new instructions. Their orders were to transfer command of Java to the Dutch and withdraw, but to maintain ABDACOM and keep his headquarters intact. When and where he would go was left to him. Ground forces "for whom there are arms" were to remain and continue the fight, but air forces that could operate from bases outside Java and other troops "who cannot contribute to defense" were to be withdrawn, the Americans and Australians to go to Australia. General Brett was to return to Australia, when

---

[46] Rad, Wavell to Prime Minister and Dill, 16 Feb 42, OPD ABDA Msg File.

[47] Mins, CCS Mtg, 17 Feb 42; Rads, CCS to ABDACOM, 17 and 21 Feb 42; ABDACOM to CCS, 19 Feb 42, OPD ABDA Msg File.

[48] For a full discussion of this matter, see Lionel Wigmore, *The Japanese Thrust*, ser. I, vol. 4, "Australia in the War of 1939–1945" (Canberra: Australian War Memorial, 1957), pp. 442–65. Churchill's account of this incident is somewhat different. Winston S. Churchill, *The Hinge of Fate* (Boston: Houghton Mifflin Company, 1950), pp. 155–66.

[49] Rad, CCS to ABDACOM, DBA 19, 20 Feb 42, OPD ABDA Msg File.

released by Wavell, to command the U.S. forces there.[50]

The ABDA commander did not agree with the program. What he wanted was the dissolution of ABDACOM, all reason for its existence having disappeared. Burma, he pointed out, had already been separated from the ABDA theater and Java's defense was a local problem, best handled by the Dutch themselves. If the Philippines, which had never really been under his control, were taken over by the Americans again and northwest Australia by the Australians, he told the Chiefs, he could turn over his remaining forces to the Dutch and leave the area by 25 February.[51]

This recommendation was in line with the solution being proposed by the British Chiefs of Staff for the establishment of two areas in the Far East, one to be under American control and to include Australia; the other a British area encompassing India and the Indian Ocean. The Dutch opposed such a solution for fear it would mean the end of Allied assistance in the Netherlands Indies. 'For God's sake,' wrote the Dutch governor-general to Marshall, "take the strong and active decisions and don't stop sending materials and men."[52]

Still anxious to avoid the appearance of abandoning their allies, the U.S. Chiefs continued to oppose the dissolution of ABDACOM. But in recognition of the fact that Wavell had lost the confidence of the Dutch and obviously wanted to pull out, they agreed to the dissolution of his headquarters and his transfer to India, leaving control of the ABDA area to the Dutch. And lest the Dutch should think that the Americans had made this arrangement to shirk their commitments, Marshall assured the Dutch governor that the forces then assembling in Australia were "seeking opportunity to enter the ABDA battle" and would "continue their full support of the Dutch commanders in their magnificent fight."[53]

On the 25th General Wavell turned over command to the Dutch and left for India where General Brereton had already gone to organize an American air force. This move placed MacArthur technically under the Dutch, but he had already been told that "because of your special situation all procedures in your case remain as heretofore."[54] The burden of defending Java was now squarely on the Dutch. Their forces, with the exception of minor ground units (including an American artillery battalion), American and British naval units, and a small U.S.-Australian fighter force, composed the entire command.

There was still a chance that fighters could be brought in by sea, though the air ferry route had been closed by the Japanese seizure of Timor. To this task was assigned the aircraft tender *Langley*, which on 23 February had been ordered to Tjilatjap, on the south coast of Java,

---

[50] Rads, CCS to ABDACOM, DBA 20 and 22, 21 and 22 Feb 42, OPD ABDA Msg File; Marshall to Brett, No. 185, 21 Feb 42, WPD 4639–48; Mins, CCS Mtg, 21 Feb 42.

[51] Rads, ABDACOM to CCS, CCOS 19 and 20, 22 and 23 Feb 42, OPD ABDA Msg File.

[52] Rad, H. J. Van Mook to Marshall, 22 Feb 42, OPD ABDA Msg File.

[53] Rad, Marshall to Van Mook, 24 Feb 42, WPD 4639–55; British COS to Joint Staff Mission, No. 76, 23 Feb 42, ABC 323.31 POA; Mins, CCS Mtg, 23 Feb 42; CCS to ABDACOM, DBA 23, 23 Feb 42, OPD ABDA Msg File.

[54] Rad, Marshall to MacArthur, No. 1083, 24 Feb 42, WPD 4639–54.

with its cargo of thirty-two assembled P–40's and their pilots. On the 27th, almost within sight of Java, it was spotted by Japanese patrol planes and sunk. The freighter *Seawitch* with 27 P–40's in her hold had left Fremantle at the same time, but sailed separately and made its way successfully to Java. It arrived there on the eve of invasion and the P–40's, still crated, were dumped into the sea to prevent their capture.[55]

Meanwhile the Japanese had completed their preparations for the invasion of Java. D-day was set for 28 February. Supporting the invasion was the largest force of warships the Japanese had yet assembled for an amphibious operation. In it were four battleships, led by Admiral Kondo, a carrier group led by Admiral Nagumo of Pearl Harbor fame, and the two attack forces, each now considerably reinforced.

The approach of the Japanese was carefully traced by the Allies, and Admiral Helfrich, Hart's successor as Allied naval commander, estimated that the convoys would reach Javanese waters early on the 27th. Hurriedly he made his plans to meet the attack with a woefully inferior naval force led by Rear Adm. K. W. F. M. Doorman. All Doorman had were 2 heavy cruisers, one of them the USS *Houston,* 3 light cruisers, and 11 destroyers. Contact between the opposing forces came shortly after 1500 of the 27th, and the fight that began then raged throughout the afternoon and into the night. By the time the battle of the Java Sea was over the Allies had lost half their ships, including the flagship

and Admiral Doorman. The Japanese had not lost a single vessel.[56]

During the next few days the Japanese completed their control of the air and sea approaches to Java. From their circle of bases surrounding the island patrol planes kept constant watch while bombers completed the destruction of Allied airfields and military installations. At the same time the powerful battle fleet ranged the waters of the Java Sea to hunt down the remnants of the Allied fleet which were split between Surabaya and Batavia, seeking some way to make their escape into the Indian Ocean. The last fight began on the night of 28 February when the heavy cruisers USS *Houston* and H.M.S. *Exeter,* accompanied by the light cruisers H.M.A.S. *Perth* and two destroyers, tried to slip through Sunda Strait, between Java and Sumatra. The Japanese had already closed the strait and the Allied warships sailed into a trap. That night, in a vigorous battle which lasted past midnight, the *Houston* and *Perth* went down. Next day, 1 March, the *Exeter* was sunk off the coast of Borneo.

Meanwhile the Japanese convoys had come in for the landing. On the way the convoy was attacked by three submarines and the remaining planes of the Allied air force, about ten light bombers and fifteen fighters, and suffered some damage. But the landing was accomplished without serious difficulty, and by morning of the 1st the Japanese were consolidating their positions and rapidly expanding the beachheads.

---

[55] Morison, *The Rising Sun in the Pacific*, pp. 359–63; Craven and Cate, AAF I, 396–98.

[56] For an exciting account of the battle, see Morison, *The Rising Sun in the Pacific*, pp. 342–59. An analysis of the battle is contained in Rear Adm William A. Glassford, Narrative of Events in the SW Pacific, 14 Feb–5 Apr 42, WDCSA 210.72 (5–20–42) SPA.

Though the Dutch had concentrated their remaining ground forces in Java, mostly in the western portion of the island, the issue was never in doubt. The Japanese moved inland rapidly, splitting the Dutch Army on the island and isolating the defenders into small groups. Batavia fell on the 2d without a struggle, after the government moved inland to Bandoeng. It was not safe even there, for the Japanese closed in on this mountain retreat and by the 8th were in position to attack the remnants of the Dutch Army defending it. The next morning the Dutch surrendered and the fight for Java was over.[57]

For the Japanese, the conquest of the Indies was the crowning achievement of the war. It realized their long-cherished dream of empire. The rich resources of Southeast Asia, the oil, rubber, and manganese needed for war and for the control of Asia, were now in their possession. And all this had been won in three months.

For the Allies the fall of Java marked the loss of the Malay Barrier, "the basic defensive position" in the Far East. The strategic significance of this loss was enormous. Not only did the Allies lose the resources of the Indies and their lines of communications northward, but they found themselves in a perilous position, split into two areas and threatened by invasion. The gateway to the Indian Ocean lay open and Australia and India were in dire danger. And the Allies could ill afford to lose the ships, planes, and men that went down in the heroic defense of Malaya, Singapore, and the Indies.

The defeat of ABDACOM was, in a sense, the inevitable outcome of Allied weakness. There was no time to assemble in an area so remote from the sources of supply sufficient aircraft to contest Japanese domination of the air. Although reinforcements adequate for this task were allocated by the Combined Chiefs of Staff, only a trickle, barely enough to replace losses, reached its destination. The warships that might have challenged the invaders were engaged in other tasks, and when they were finally organized into a combined striking force it was already too late. In the six weeks of its existence ABDACOM never had a chance to test the validity of General Marshall's contention that a unified command would "solve nine-tenths of our troubles." But important lessons about Allied command could be learned from the disagreements and differences which marked the brief existence of ABDACOM and these were not lost when the time came to establish other commands later in the war.

While the campaign for Java was in progress, the Japanese had pushed on to take northern Sumatra and central Burma, thus consolidating their control of the southern area and cutting China off from its Allies. From Singapore, ten days after that fortress had fallen, came the troops to take northern Sumatra. With their arrival the defenders of the island fled to Java in time to join the fight there, and eventually to surrender. Burma was to have been seized in two phases and its occupation completed only after operations to the south were over. But early in January the schedule had been speeded up and before the end of the month the *15th Army* had pushed across the Thai-Burma border and seized

[57] Invasion of the NEI, Japanese Studies in World War II, 16; Morison, *The Rising Sun in the Pacific*, pp. 363–75; Craven and Cate, *AAF I*, 397–98.

Moulmein. On 8 March, after the battle of Sittang Bridge where the Japanese destroyed two Indian brigades, they captured Rangoon, southern terminus of the supply line to China and the port of entry for lend-lease supplies. Pushing on to the north, they had by mid-March reached the Toungoo-Prome line in central Burma, and though they did not finally gain victory there until early in May they had effectively blockaded China by the time the Indies had fallen.[58] By the end of March, the vast area of sea and land from New Guinea and northwest Australia to central Burma, which had formed ABDACOM, was under Japanese control. Only to the north, in the Philippines, where American and Filipino troops still stood fast, had the Japanese failed to meet their timetable of conquest.

[58] For an account of the campaign in Burma, see Romanus and Sunderland, *Stilwell's Mission to China*, chs. III and IV.

CHAPTER VIII

The Philippines

Posterity, thinned by the crimes of the ancestors, shall hear of those battles.
HORACE

In the period when the Japanese were overrunning Malaya and the Indies their campaign in the Philippines progressed slowly. Their initial success had been spectacular. First they had knocked out the Far East Air Force, established air and naval supremacy in the Philippines, and seized advance airfields on Luzon. Then, on 22 December, General Homma put the bulk of his *14th Army* ashore at Lingayen Gulf, north of Manila. The remainder landed two days later at Lamon Bay, south of the capital, to form the southern arm of a giant pincer movement converging on Manila. But Homma quickly discovered he was dealing with a determined and able foe. MacArthur did not, as Homma and *Imperial General Headquarters* expected, stay to fight it out on the central plain of Luzon. Instead he put into effect the long-standing ORANGE plan and withdrew his forces to the Bataan Peninsula in a skillful and dangerous double retrograde movement, made in two weeks under the most difficult circumstances and constant pressure. At the same time he proclaimed Manila an open city and transferred his headquarters to Corregidor. Thus, when Homma, on 2 January, reached his objective, the capital city, he was able to take it without opposi-

tion. But his victory was a hollow one. The enemy army was still intact and in control of the entrance to Manila Bay. So long as it maintained its hold on Bataan and Corregidor Homma would be unable to use the great port of Manila or to claim victory in the Philippines.

South of Luzon, the Japanese had made only one important conquest in the Philippines when they occupied the harbor of Davao in Mindanao, as a base for the invasion of Borneo. But the American and Philippine forces on that island were undefeated. Well-organized and led, they still held the airfield at Del Monte. In the central Philippines the Japanese had as yet made no landings. There the scattered garrisons on Panay, Cebu, Bohol, Leyte, and other islands, strengthened their defenses and made plans for the day when the enemy would appear off their shores.

The Siege of Bataan

In the Japanese scheme of conquest, the Philippines occupied only a secondary place and *Imperial General Headquarters* had not been generous with General Homma. All it had given him to take the islands, a job that was scheduled to be completed in fifty days, were two divisions, the *16th* and *48th*, two tank regiments, an air group, and service and supporting troops. One other unit, the *65th Brigade*, consisting of three 2-battalion regiments, was to come in later to mop up and garrison the islands. But Homma was not allowed to keep even this force, for *Imperial General Headquarters*, having decided late in December to speed up operations in the southern area, took from him his best unit, the *48th Division*, as well as the air group. Word of this decision reached Homma via *Southern Army* headquarters on 2 January, the day he occupied Manila.

Fortunately for the Japanese cause, Homma, for reasons entirely unrelated to the decision of *Imperial General Headquarters*, had already ordered the *65th Brigade* to the Philippines, three weeks earlier than intended. The brigade, which in the opinion of its commander was "absolutely unfit for combat duty," reached Luzon on New Year's Day, just in time to replace the *48th Division* in the coming battle for Bataan.[1]

Despite this weakening of his forces, Homma felt certain of an early victory. On the basis of faulty intelligence he concluded that resistance would be weak, and that the American and Filipino troops would make their stand around Mariveles, near the tip of the peninsula, then withdraw to Corregidor. Japanese operations on Bataan would therefore take the form of a pursuit

rather than an assault against a strongly fortified position. Such operations, Homma felt, could be safely entrusted to the inexperienced and untrained *65th Brigade*, reinforced with seasoned troops of the *16th Division* and aided by supporting artillery and armor.

General Homma's optimism was entirely unfounded. Arrayed against him on a line extending across the northern part of the jungled mountain fastness of Bataan were two corps, one led by Maj. Gen. Jonathan M. Wainwright and the other by Maj. Gen. George M. Parker, Jr. In Wainwright's corps on the left (west) were three of the recently-inducted Philippine Army divisions, the 26th Cavalry of Philippine Scouts (Filipino citizens forming part of the Regular Army of the United States), and other troops, for a total of 22,500 men. On the right (Manila Bay side) of the peninsula, in Parker's corps, were four more Philippine Army divisions, a Philippine Scout regiment, plus supporting troops, all together 25,000 men. To the rear were the regular U.S. Army Philippine Division (composed largely of Philippine Scouts), two battalions of light tanks, a 75–mm. SPM group, together with corps and USAFFE artillery. The southern tip of the peninsula, designated the Service Command Area, was defended by a heterogeneous force composed of constabulary, Philippine Army troops, grounded airmen, bluejackets, and marines.[2] Control of the two corps and of the elements to the rear was retained by General MacArthur's headquarters on Corregidor, with an advance echelon on Bataan.

Despite this considerable force, num-

---

[1] *65th Brig* Opns Rpt, Mt. Natib, p. 3; *14th Army* Opns, Japanese Studies in World War II, 1, I, 39, 60–62, 73–76. Most of the material covered in this chapter is treated at greater length in Morton, *The Fall of the Philippines*, chs. XV–XXII. For the convenience of the researcher, footnote references are to the original sources rather than to the author's earlier volume.

[2] USAFFE Field Orders 1 and 2, 6 and 7, Jan 42 and GO 3, 7 Jan 42, copies in OCMH.

GENERAL HOMMA COMES ASHORE

bering about 90,000 men, the American position was not a strong one. There had been little time to build fortifications; communications were inadequate, and many of the troops were untrained and poorly equipped. Food was scarce and there was a shortage of supplies of all types. Moreover, the main battle position was not a continuous line. Separating the two corps was the 4,222-foot-high Mt. Natib which made physical contact and mutual support virtually impossible.

The Japanese opened the battle for Bataan on 9 January with an artillery barrage that "shook the northern portion" of the peninsula, after which the infantry moved out to the attack. The main force, which attacked first, was repulsed in a series of bloody battles and was finally forced to shift to the west in search of an opening in the American lines, while another column sought to turn Parker's left flank on the slopes of Mt. Natib. Finally, on the 15th, the Japanese found an opening and drove through. By the evening of the 16th they were in position to outflank the corps. Hastily a counterattack was organized with troops from the Philippine Division, but to no avail.[3]

Meanwhile the Japanese on the other side of the peninsula, traversing the jungled height near the center, had cut

[3] 65th Brig Opns Rpt, Mt. Natib, apps. 3 and 20, p. 15.

behind Wainwright's line on 21 January and established a block along the only road in the area. Unable to reduce the block, the troops in Wainwright's corps withdrew, pulling back along the coast. At about the same time, 24 January, MacArthur ordered a general withdrawal to the reserve battle position.

The first battle was over but Homma was still far from victory. He had won this round but at such heavy cost that the *65th Brigade,* in the words of its commander, had "reached the extreme stages of exhaustion."[4] The American and Filipino forces had disengaged successfully and occupied their new line across the waist of the peninsula on 26 January. They had saved Bataan for another day. But there was no further retreat from this line. "With its occupation," MacArthur wrote, "all maneuvering possibilities will cease. I intend to fight it out to complete destruction."[5]

During the next two weeks Homma committed the remainder of the *16th Division* and, by a series of frontal attacks combined with amphibious assaults behind the enemy line, sought to gain the victory which had thus far eluded him. Again he failed, this time with such heavy casualties that he had to break off the fight and call on *Imperial General Headquarters* for reinforcements. From 6 January to 1 March, *14th Army* had suffered almost 7,000 casualties, 2,700 killed and over 4,000 wounded. Between 10,000 and 12,000 more men were down with malaria, beriberi, and dysentery. So depleted was the *14th Army* that the American and Filipino troops, had they chosen that

moment to attack, could, in Homma's words, have walked to Manila "without encountering much resistance on our part."[6]

But by this time MacArthur's troops were showing the alarming effects of reduced rations, lack of quinine, and continuous combat. Almost the first official action on Bataan had been an order cutting the ration in half. This meant the Americans would theoretically receive 36 ounces of food a day, the Filipinos 32.[7] Actually they never received even that amount. The ration varied from day to day and was based solely on the amount of food on hand. From an average of about 30 ounces a day it decreased steadily until it was barely enough to sustain life. Not only was the diet inadequate, but it was unbalanced as well, deficient in vitamins and lacking the minor luxuries which might have compensated for its bareness and monotony. There was no butter, coffee, tea, jam, fresh milk, or vegetables, and precious little sugar, fruit, and tobacco. Deprived of the solace of cigarettes and coffee, the soldier living on little more than 20 ounces of food a day could be very miserable indeed.[8]

The consequences of the inadequate and unbalanced ration and other shortages soon became evident in the high incidence of malnutrition and vitamin deficiency diseases and a marked decrease in combat efficiency. Signs of

---

[4] *65th Brig Opns* Rpt, Mt. Natib, pp. 33, 38.
[5] Rad, MacArthur to Marshall, No. 108, 23 Jan 42, AG 381 (11–27–41 sec. 1) Far East.

[6] United States of America *vs.* Masaharu Homma, pp. 3062–63, testimony of Homma; pp. 2450, 2457, 2576, testimony of Lt. Gen. Takaji Wachi and Col. Yoshio Nakajima, National Archives; *14th Army Opns,* Japanese Studies in World War II, 1, I, 116.
[7] Rad, MacArthur to CG Bataan Service Comd, 5 Jan 42, AG 430 (25 Dec 41); Inventory of Rations, 3 Jan 42, AG 430.2 (3 Jan 42) both in Phil Rcds.
[8] See Rpts of the QM Phil Dept in AG 319.1 (29 Jan 42) Phil Rcds.

serious muscle waste and depletion of fat reserve were plain in the thin bodies and hollow cheeks of the hungry men. Night blindness, swelling, diarrhea, and dysentery became common, and beriberi in its incipient stages was almost universal among the troops. The men had lost the capacity to resist even the most minor ailment, and any disease, warned the Bataan surgeon, would assume epidemic proportions.

These fears were soon justified in the rapid spread of malaria. For a time the disease had been kept under control by prophylactic doses of quinine, but the supply was limited and its use, except for those already infected, was discontinued at the end of February. Within a week the number of daily malaria admissions to the hospitals jumped to 500 and a month later was approaching the fantastic figure of 1,000. Despite every expedient it proved impossible to obtain a large enough supply of quinine to bring the disease under control or permit its use as a prophylaxis.[9] By the end of March the two general hospitals, designed to accommodate 1,000 patients each, had about 8,500 patients, and another 4,000 were being treated in a provisional hospital. Undetermined numbers were hospitalized in their units, and all medical installations on Bataan were bursting with patients.[10]

The effects of disease and starvation upon combat efficiency were disastrous. A month after they reached Bataan, the men were only about 75 percent effective; six weeks later this figure dropped

to 25 percent. The condition of the troops, wrote an inspecting officer, "was utter nightmare." In one regiment the men "were just able to fire a rifle out of the trench, and no more." [11]

The one great hope that fortified the men on Bataan and Corregidor was their belief that somehow large reinforcements and shiploads of food and supplies would break through the Japanese blockade and come to their rescue. This belief was based partly on the desperate desire to believe it and partly on MacArthur's promise in January that "thousands of troops and hundreds of planes" were on the way.[12] President Quezon and High Commissioner Sayre had given the same promise in public statements earlier, based on Roosevelt's broadcast of 29 December, which the New York Times headlined with, "All aid promised. President pledges protection." Sustaining the faith of the troops on Bataan also was the conviction that their country would never abandon them to the enemy and that somehow they would be rescued.[13] These hopes were badly shaken when President Roosevelt, in his February 23d Fireside Chat, placed the Philippines in their proper perspective "in the big picture of the war." His listeners on Bataan could find no hope for relief in the President's remarks about the nature of global warfare, the tremendous tasks facing the American people, and the volume of production. What they needed was food, clothing, and medicine, and they needed them im-

[9] Material on the prevalence of disease can be found in AG 440 (26 Jan 42) and AG 710 (24 Mar 42) Phil Rcds; Col Wibb E. Cooper, Med Dept Activities in the Phil, ann. XIV of USAFFE—USFIP Rpt of Opns, copy in OCMH.

[10] Cooper, Med Dept Activities, pp. 32–33, 55, 57–61.

[11] Col Harry A. Skerry, Comments on Engineer Hist, No. 18; Col Ray M. O'Day, Hist of 21st Div (PA), II, 39, both in OCMH.

[12] Ltr Order, USAFFE to All Unit Comdrs, 15 Jan 42, sub: Msg from Gen MacArthur, copy in OCMH.

[13] Ltr, MacArthur to Hoover, 21 Jul 59, OCMH. New York Times, December 21, 1941.

mediately. "Plain for all to see," wrote one officer, "was the handwriting on the wall, at the end of which the President had placed a large and emphatic period. The President had—with regret—wiped us off the page and closed the book." [14]

Strategy and Logistics

If the troops on Bataan thought—mistakenly—they had been abandoned, they could be sure that they had in General MacArthur an eloquent and powerful champion to plead their cause in the councils of war. Constantly and persistently, in the strongest terms, he urged the President and Chief of Staff on to bolder measures and stronger efforts for the relief of the Philippine garrison. The support of the Philippine Islands, he asserted time and again, was the most important objective of the Allied cause in the Far East and no effort should be spared to achieve this end. The arrangements and plans made for the defense of the Malay Barrier and the establishment of a base in Australia, while contributing to this cause, did not, MacArthur held, materially affect his own situation.

What MacArthur wanted was a major Allied effort in the Southwest Pacific that would have as its objective the relief of the Philippines. This effort, he believed, should take the form of an advance, by air and naval forces, from Australia through the Netherlands Indies and Borneo to Mindanao. Once air and naval supremacy had been established, an Army corps could be landed on Mindanao, and from there, projecting air and naval forces northward,

reinforcements could be brought into Luzon and the enemy driven from the Philippines. "Enemy appears to have tendency to become overconfident," he wrote, "and time is ripe for brilliant thrust with air carriers." [15]

So important were these operations, in MacArthur's view, so vital were they to the Allied position in the Far East and the defense of Allied territory that he did not hesitate to urge that the resources of Great Britain, as well as those of the United States, be placed at his disposal. After all, he pointed out, the British Empire would benefit most from these operations. Singapore, Australia, and India would be saved and the British line of communications in the Far East made secure. England itself would be free from attack during the winter months and could safely release forces and lend material aid to a cause which was so greatly to its benefit.[16]

But this effort, if it was to be undertaken, must be made soon, MacArthur warned Marshall. Already his food supply was low and his munitions, especially in antiaircraft ammunition, limited. The Corregidor garrison, whose existence depended on its vulnerable water and power supply, could not hold out indefinitely. Unsupported, he told the Chief of Staff on 1 January, he would be able to resist serious attack at most for three months. Pending the arrival of the expeditionary force it would be necessary therefore to restore his line of communication to the United States "by aggressive air and naval action," a course he

---

[14] Col Richard C. Mallonée, Bataan Diary, II, 69, copy in OCMH.

[15] Rad, MacArthur to Marshall, No. 20, 7 Jan 42, AG 381 (11–27–41 Gen) Far East. See also his messages of 27 December and 1 January to the Chiefs of Staff, in same file and in WPD 4639–2.

[16] Rad, MacArthur to Marshall, Nos. 2 and 3, 1 Jan 42, WPD 4639–2.

had urged before and continued to urge.[17]

MacArthur's pleas for a major Allied effort in the Southwest Pacific reached Washington at a time when the ARCADIA Conference was in session and while the U.S. and British Chiefs of Staff were themselves considering how best to halt the Japanese advance. But the sympathetic response to his messages and the assurance that "the President and Prime Minister, Colonel Stimson and Colonel Knox, the British Chiefs of Staff and our corresponding officials" were doing everything possible to strengthen Allied forces in the Far East could not disguise the fact that Washington and London did not attach the same importance to the defense of the Philippines as MacArthur did. "Our great hope," General Marshall told him, "is that the rapid development of an overwhelming air power on the Malay Barrier will cut the Japanese communications south of Borneo and permit an assault on the southern Philippines."[18]

The emphasis in such a strategy, as MacArthur well knew, was not on the drive northward but on holding the Malay Barrier and its east and west anchors, Burma and Australia. The support of the Philippine garrison and the re-establishment of the line of communications to Luzon, though included as one of the objectives of Allied strategy, clearly came after these. MacArthur agreed that the Japanese drive southward must be halted, but believed that this objective could best be accomplished by holding the Philippines. To him the

islands were "the locus of victory or defeat," and if they fell so would the Malay Barrier and the entire Asiatic continent. This view the Washington planners, whose perspective encompassed a war on many fronts, never accepted.

What MacArthur did not know was that the Army planners in Washington had on the 3d of January submitted a study proving that the Philippines could not be reinforced and that his plan for an offensive northward from Australia to Mindanao would constitute "an entirely unjustifiable diversion of forces from the principal theater—the Atlantic." It would require, they noted, about 1,500 aircraft of various types, at least half of which would have to come from other areas, service and construction units to build airfields along the line of advance, a large logistical organization, and the transfer from the Atlantic and Mediterranean of 7–9 capital ships, 5–7 carriers, about 50 destroyers, 60 submarines, and the necessary auxiliaries. The greatest effort that could be justified in terms of global strategy, the planners stated, was to hold the Malay Barrier while projecting operations as far north as possible. Since this view was essentially that already accepted by the Combined Chiefs, the effect of the Army planners' study was to confirm the decision already made when ABDACOM was established.[19]

The conclusions of the Army planners, however valid they were, did not affect the determination of the President, Mr. Stimson, or General Marshall

---

[17] *Ibid.*; Rad, MacArthur to Marshall, No. 20, 7 Jan 42, AG 381 (11–27–41 Gen) Far East.
[18] Rad, Marshall to MacArthur, 2 Jan 42, WPD 4639–2.

[19] Memo, Gerow for CofS, 3 Jan 42, sub: Relief of Phil, WPD 4639–3. There is no record of formal approval of this study. Both Stimson and Marshall noted it, but made no comment.

to send MacArthur all possible aid. That program was already under way and everything possible was being done in Washington to ensure its success. Thus, when MacArthur on the 4th, the day after the planners had submitted their study, suggested, first, that a plan for blockade running be developed and put into effect immediately; and second, in a tart reference to the Navy, that "some relief be obtained on use of submarine transportation," Marshall took what action he could. Already the funds to initiate blockade running had been allocated, but the program would have to await further arrangements in Australia. Meanwhile he asked Admiral Hart to send MacArthur by submarine the anti-aircraft ammunition he needed so badly. The response was discouraging. Hart replied that he could not spare any of his submarines for such a mission and it was not until the end of the month, after Marshall had enlisted the aid of Admiral King, that the submarine was dispatched. There was nothing Mac-Arthur could do, for Hart's fleet was not under his control, but he did not hesitate to express his feelings. "I urge," he wrote Marshall, "steps be taken to obtain a more aggressive and resourceful handling of naval forces in this area." [20] In this view he would soon have the support of the Dutch.

But assurances and messages from Washington did not get supplies to the Philippines. That task was the responsibility of commanders in Australia and the Netherlands Indies, who, beset with problems of their own, had not the same sense of urgency as impelled MacArthur to insist that failure to reach him with supplies would have "monumental" and "disastrous" results. This sense of urgency Marshall undertook to impart to these officers after MacArthur had given his "professional" assurance that the blackade could easily be pierced. To Brereton and Brett he dispatched similar messages on 17 January calling for "comprehensive efforts" to run the blockade. "To insure utmost energy" in carrying out these efforts, Marshall made ten million dollars of the Chief of Staff's funds available to Brereton and promised more if needed to induce ship's masters and their crews to undertake the hazardous journey. "Risks will be great," he wrote. "Rewards must be proportional." At the same time he made another million available to Mac-Arthur and sent Col. Patrick J. Hurley, former Secretary of War and an old friend of the Philippine commander, to Australia immediately to lend his "energetic support" to the blockade-running program. "Only indomitable determination and pertinacity will succeed," wrote Marshall, "and success must be ours." [21]

Under the impetus of Marshall's urgent instructions for a comprehensive program and the use of "bold and resourceful men," General Brereton began to draw up elaborate and ambitious plans. But there was no time for such plans and when Marshall learned of them he quickly registered his disappro-

[20] Rads, MacArthur to Marshall, No. 9, 4 Jan 42; AG 381 (11–27–41 Sec. 1) Far East; Marshall to Brett, No. 671, 5 Jan 42; COMINCH to CINCAF, same date; MacArthur to Marshall, No. 26; COMINCH to CINCAF; Brett to Marshall, No. 485, all dated 9 Jan 42 and in WPD Msg File.

[21] Rads, MacArthur to Marshall, No. 72, 17 Jan 42; Marshall to CG USAFIA, same date, both in AG 381 (11–27–41 sec. 1) Far East; Marshall to Brett, ABDA No. 26, same date, WPD 4560–9; Marshall to Mac-Arthur, No. 949, same date, OCS 18136–196.

val. Action and results were needed, he wrote, not plans.[22]

Thus urged, the commanders in Australia concentrated on getting ships and supplies, but it was a long, hard job, beset with many obstacles, including the reluctance of the Dutch and British to risk the loss of precious shipping. By 2 February, despite the high rewards and frantic efforts, only five vessels had been enlisted in the cause. One was already en route to Corregidor with 700 tons of rations and ammunition; the other four were loading in Brisbane and were scheduled to leave in the near future. All but one would sail directly for the Philippines. The *Mormacsun*, under orders from Washington not to go further north than the Netherlands Indies, would transfer its cargo at a Dutch port to smaller vessels for the last leg of the journey.[23]

These efforts were satisfactory as far as they went but they did not add up to the aggressive strategy MacArthur felt should be followed in the Far East. Early in February he again presented his views on this subject in a message to the Chief of Staff with the hope that they would be shown "to the highest authority." The message opened with the startling statement that the present strategy, aimed at building up forces before the Japanese advance, was "a fatal mistake on the part of the Democratic Allies." The plan to build a base and acquire air supremacy in the Southwest Pacific, he predicted, would fail and, as

a result, the war would be indefinitely prolonged. The only way to defeat the enemy was to seek combat with him. "Counsels of timidity based upon theories of safety first," he warned, "will not win against such an aggressive and audacious adversary as Japan." "What the Allies ought to do," he asserted, was attack the Japanese line of communications "stretched over 2,000 miles of sea." The argument that naval forces for such an attack were not available he brushed aside with the observation that a great naval victory was not necessary; "the threat alone would go far toward the desired end."[24]

General Marshall's reply, though sympathetic, made it perfectly clear that the Allies were doing all they could in the Pacific. No one denied the advantages of an attack against Japan's line of communication, he pointed out, but neither the naval forces nor the bases for such an attack were available. Moreover, MacArthur's proposal did not take into consideration the need to keep open the Allied line of communication. The course the Allies had adopted, he explained, was all that could be done with existing forces. Until additional forces could be accumulated the Allies had little choice but to "limit the hostile advance so as to deny him [the enemy] free access to land and sea areas that will immeasurably strengthen his war-making powers or will be valuable to us as jump off positions when we can start a general offensive."[25]

---

[22] Rads, Brereton to TAG, 19 Jan 42; Marshall to Brereton, same date, both in AG 381 (11–27–41 sec. 1) Far East.

[23] Rad, Brereton to Marshall, No. 88, 22 Jan 42; Barnes to TAG, No. 154, 2 Feb 42, both in AG 381 (11–27–41 sec 2A) Far East.

[24] Rad, MacArthur to Marshall, No. 201, 4 Feb 42, WDCSA 381 (2–17–42) Phil. This message, as well as many others from MacArthur, was forwarded to the President.

[25] Rad, Marshall to MacArthur, 8 Feb 42, WDCSA 381 (2–17–42) Phil.

On the same day that the Chief of Staff dispatched his reply to MacArthur, President Quezon, who had moved the seat of the Commonwealth Government to Corregidor, offered a plan to bring hostilities in the Philippines to a close. This plan was based on the assumption that the Japanese were in the Philippines only because the United States was there. If the United States Government would grant the Philippines their independence immediately and withdraw its forces, Quezon explained to President Roosevelt, then he would seek to persuade Japan to do the same. If Japan agreed, as he thought it would, then he would disband the Philippine Army and leave his country without fortifications of any kind. The major powers could then neutralize the Philippines and save it from the ravages of a war in which it had no real interest.

Quezon's disquieting proposal, which the American High Commissioner supported, was accompanied by an estimate from General MacArthur painting a dark picture of the military situation in the Philippines. "So far as the military angle is concerned," MacArthur wrote, "the problem presents itself as to whether the plan of President Quezon might offer the best possible solution of what is about to be a disastrous debacle." He did not believe it would affect the ultimate fate of the Philippines; that, he thought, would be decided by the outcome of the war in other theaters. "If the Japanese Government rejects President Quezon's proposition," he told Marshall, "it would psychologically strengthen our hold because of their Prime Minister's public statement offering independence. If it accepts it, we lose no military advantage because we would still secure at least equal delay." [26]

The reaction from Washington to Quezon's proposal was prompt and emphatic. President Roosevelt repudiated the scheme outright and declared, in a personal message to Quezon, that the American Government would never agree to such a solution to the war in the Philippines. But he softened the blow by pledging that "so long as the flag of the United States flies on Filipino Soil . . . it would be defended by our own men to the death." To MacArthur the President sent strict instructions to continue the fight without surrender of American troops "so long as there remains any possibility of resistance." [27] There was no misunderstanding the meaning and tone of this message.

Both Quezon and MacArthur accepted the President's decision without question. Quezon wrote that he fully appreciated the President's position and would abide by the decision. MacArthur, in his reply, explained that his message had been misunderstood, that he never had any intention of surrendering and would fight "to destruction" on Bataan and Corregidor. [28]

This matter was hardly settled when events in the Pacific, gloomy at best, took a turn for the worse. Already the Japanese had taken Malaya, Borneo, and the Celebes, and on 15 February Singapore fell. Its loss provided MacArthur with the occasion for still another plea

[26] Rads, Ft. Mills to Marshall, Nos. 226 and 227, 8 Feb 42, CofS Phil Sit File. The first part of the message is addressed to Roosevelt and signed Quezon; the second to Marshall signed MacArthur. Ltr, MacArthur to Hoover, 21 Jul 59, OCMH.
[27] Rad, Roosevelt to MacArthur for Quezon, No. 1029, 9 Feb 42, CofS Phil Sit File.
[28] Rads, MacArthur to Roosevelt, No. 252, 11 Feb 42; Quezon to Roosevelt, No. 262, 12 Feb 42, both in OPD Exec Files.

for an attack against the Japanese line of communications. "The opportunities still exist for a complete reversal of the situation," he declared with characteristic optimism. "It will soon, however, be too late for such a movement." [29]

To the planners in Washington and the officers of USAFIA and ABDACOM, the loss of Singapore and the rapid Japanese advance into the Netherlands Indies was hardly the occasion for attack. To them it forecast the invasion of Sumatra and Java and an end to blockade-running. Pat Hurley, who had arrived in Australia on 8 February, reported from Java on the 17th that "movements are progressing as expeditiously as can be expected under existing condition." But he also warned that the sea routes north of Australia were becoming increasingly hazardous. A few days later he told the Chief of Staff that there were "almost insuperable difficulties" in getting supplies to MacArthur. [30]

The former Secretary of War did not exaggerate. Despite the elaborate preparations and large funds, the five vessels reported on 2 February were all that ever joined the blockade-running program. Of these only three, the Coast Farmer, Dona Nati, and Anhui, got through. The first, a 3,000-ton Army freighter with a speed of 10 knots, left Australia on 4 February and put in at a Mindanao port fifteen days later. The other two left later and arrived at Cebu in mid-March. All together, they brought in more than 10,000 tons of rations, 4,000 rounds of small arms am-

munition, 8,000 rounds of 81–mm. ammunition, and miscellaneous medical, signal, and engineer supplies. [31]

But the delivery of these supplies left them far from the battlefield of Bataan. From Mindanao and Cebu they still had to be transported northward through the inland seas to Manila Bay. For this leg of the journey, fast interisland motor ships with a capacity of 300 to 1,000 tons were used. Cebu was the headquarters for these vessels and from there thousands of tons went northward. The Legaspi was the first to make the journey safely, arriving at Corregidor on 22 January with a cargo of rice and other food. Two other vessels, the Princessa and Elcano, performed the same feat in February, the latter carrying rations unloaded from the Coast Farmer. Three other vessels carrying the remainder of that ship's cargo were sunk as were others carrying the supplies brought in by the Dona Nati and Anhui. Of the 10,000 tons of rations that had reached the Philippines, only about 1,000 tons—a 4-day supply for the 100,000 soldiers and civilians on Bataan—ever reached Manila Bay. [32]

Before the end of February it was already evident that the blockade-running program from Australia was a failure, but it was not until the Japanese landed in Java that the officers in charge of the program admitted their inability to supply the Philippines. This admission came to General Marshall in a joint message from Brett and Hurley recom-

[29] Rad, MacArthur to Marshall, No. 297, 16 Feb 42, WDCSA 381 (2–17–42) Phil.

[30] Rads, Hurley to Marshall, ABDACOM No. 2, 17 Feb 42, AG 381 (11–27–41 sec. 2B) Far East; 21 Feb 42, OPD 381 SWPA, sec. 1 case 21.

[31] Maj Gen Julian F. Barnes, Rpt of Orgn of USAFIA; Maj Richard M. Leighton and Elizabeth Bingham. Development of U.S. Supply Base in Australia, both in OCMH.

[32] Rpt of QM Opns in Phil Campaign, ann. of USAFFE–USFIP Rpt of Opns, pp. 29–40, 69–70, and app. A, Rpt of Opns, Cebu Depot, OCMH.

mending that the program be abandoned and that the Philippines be supplied directly from the United States via Hawaii "through open sea areas in which the chance of reaching destination is much greater than through narrow channels between island and blockade areas of the Southwest Pacific." [33]

The Brett-Hurley proposal was a sound one; it had already been made by MacArthur who, on 22 February had expressed strong dissatisfaction with the efforts being made in Australia. The program, he had asserted, should be controlled from Washington and other routes, including that across the central Pacific from Hawaii, be utilized. "If it is left as a subsidiary effort," he told Marshall, "it will never be accomplished." [34] Immediately the supply experts in the War Department, on the basis of the President's request, made a quick survey of the problem. Their conclusion was that direct supply of the Philippines from the United States by way of Hawaii was "practical and desirable." Six World War I destroyers, they pointed out, could be converted to cargo vessels for this purpose. The plan was quickly approved. [35]

The schedule established under the new program called for six sailings, the first vessel to leave New Orleans on 28 February, the last on 22 March. But there were delays in assembling the cargoes, selecting the route, and finding gun crews, and it was not until 2 March that the first ship sailed. The others followed later in the month, two sailing from New Orleans through the Panama Canal to Los Angeles and then Honolulu, the others directly from the west coast. But they had left too late and none ever reached their destination. [36]

Submarines and aircraft as well as surface vessels were utilized in the desperate attempt to supply the beleagured garrison. The underwater craft could carry rations and ammunition directly to Corregidor but in such limited amounts that the ten trips made netted a total of only 53 tons of food (less than one meal for the men on Bataan), 3,500 rounds of badly needed 3–inch antiaircraft ammunition, over 1,000,000 rounds of .50 and .30–caliber ammunition, and about 30,000 gallons of diesel oil for the power plant on Corregidor. The aircraft, with more limited space, were used largely for medical supplies. They succeeded in bringing their cargoes as far as Del Monte in Mindanao, but most of the quinine and morphine so critically needed on Bataan remained there. [37]

By mid-March the opportunity to bring supplies to Bataan and Corregidor had been lost. The Japanese were in control of the air and sea routes and

---

[33] Rad, Hurley and Brett for Marshall, 483, 4 Mar 42, AG 381 (11–27–41 sec. 3) Far East.

[34] Rad, MacArthur to Marshall, 344, 22 Feb 42, WPD Ready Ref File, Phil.

[35] Memos, Somervell for Marshall, 22 Feb 42, sub: Supply of U.S. Forces in Phil, OCS 18136–258; Marshall for Roosevelt, 24 Feb 42, no sub, WPD 4560–26, Marshall for Roosevelt, 28 Feb 42; sub: Blockade Runners, OCS 18136–268. Vice Adm. Bernhard H. Bieri (ret.), then one of the naval planners, recalled later that he never heard of this plan to use World War I destroyers and doubted that it had been submitted to the Navy. Anyone familiar with the steaming characteristics of these 1,000–ton destroyers and with the distances in the Pacific, he wrote, "would have crossed it out as a practical operation." Ltr, Bieri to Hoover, 17 Jul 59, OCMH.

[36] Messages dealing with these vessels can be found in AG 384.3 GHQ SWPA and in the Hist Br, OCT, SWPA, Phil Shipping.

[37] Rpt, CTF 51 to CINCSWPA, 15 May 42, sub: Submarine Relief Activities, ser. FF6–4, A 16–3, copy in OCMH; Ltr, GHQ SWPA to CG US. Air Service, 14 May 42, sub: Phil Relief Shipments, AG 384.3M.

had blocked the passage between Mindanao and the Visayas to Manila Bay. The total effort and large sums expended by that time had produced negligible results in terms of tonnages delivered to the troops. But it was an effort that had to be made, no matter how high the cost or slim the chance of success. The American people owed at least that much to the gallant Philippine garrison.

Command

From the beginning there was little doubt in Washington that the Philippine garrison was doomed. After the Japanese victory in Malaya and in the Netherlands Indies, the outcome in the Philippines was certain. It was only a question of time and there were many who thought the battle would be over very soon. But if the garrison was doomed, what would happen to General MacArthur? Was he to be allowed to fall into Japanese hands, lost forever to the Allied cause? The answer was self-evident. MacArthur's services were too valuable to be sacrificed in a hopeless cause and he must be rescued to lead other forces in the war against Japan.

There were difficulties to this solution. A command commensurate with his rank and seniority must be found for him. The timing and circumstances of his departure must be arranged with great care to avoid the appearance of abandoning the Filipinos to whom he was the symbol of resistance. And MacArthur himself might show an understandable reluctance to leave his troops in the midst of battle. If he was ordered out, Colonel Hurley said, it would have to be by the President and in such a way

that his reputation, "his honor and his record as a soldier," would not be compromised.[38]

The first reference to this matter came on 4 February when General Marshall, undoubtedly at the direction of the President, mentioned to MacArthur the possibility of his transfer to another command should Bataan fall, leaving only Corregidor in American hands.[39] "Under these conditions," he told MacArthur, "the need for your services there might well be less pressing than at other points in the Far East." There were, Marshall explained, two possibilities. One was for MacArthur to go to Mindanao to direct guerrilla operations and to await the supplies which would make a counterattack possible. The other was to go directly to Australia and there resume command of all U.S. Army forces in the Far East. No decision had yet been made on his future employment, Marshall went on, and before one was he wanted the confidential views of the Philippine commander. "It is to be understood," he concluded, "that in case your withdrawal from immediate leadership of your beleaguered force is to be carried out it will be by direct order of the President to you."[40]

Whatever MacArthur thought about this proposal he kept his own counsel

---

[38] Memo, Hurley for Marshall, 21 Feb 42, OPD 381 SWPA, sec. 1, case 21.

[39] Rear Adm. Charles A. Moore, one of the Navy planners in February 1942, served on the panel that reviewed the present manuscript before publication. At that time, July 1959, he recalled that on several occasions he had mentioned to Secretary of State Cordell Hull the necessity for getting MacArthur out of the Philippines, and that it was Hull who finally went to the President with this suggestion. Notes of Panel Meeting, 17 July 1959.

[40] Rad, Marshall to MacArthur, 4 Feb 42, WDCSA 370.5 (3–17–42) Phil.

and carefully avoided the subject in the days that followed. But he did say to the President, a week later and in another connection, that he and his family—his wife and young son were still on Corregidor with him—would "share the fate of the garrison."[41] Marshall picked up this statement and a few days later, in a message dealing with the need for antiaircraft ammunition, urged MacArthur to send his family to safety for his next assignment might separate them "under circumstances of greatly increased peril" and "poignant embarrassment." MacArthur answered the inquiry about ammunition but pointedly omitted any reference to the personal aspects of Marshall's message.[42]

Nothing further was said about the matter for another week, though it must have been discussed more than once at the White House where MacArthur's worth was rated by one officer as the equivalent of five Army corps. Finally, on 21 February, when it was already evident that ABDACOM was doomed and that a new command would have to be established in the Southwest Pacific, MacArthur received word that the President had tentatively decided to order him to Mindanao, but was not "sufficiently informed as to the situation and circumstances to be certain that the proposal meets the actual situation."[43]

The next day, without waiting for a reply from Corregidor, the President made his decision and ordered Mac-

Arthur to leave for Australia as soon as possible, stopping at Mindanao only long enough "to insure a prolonged defense." On his arrival in Australia he would assume command of a new theater of operations in the Southwest Pacific, arrangements for which were then in progress. So urgent was this new assignment that he was to make ready immediately and not to "delay in Mindanao" longer than a week. Washington would provide the transportation.[44]

MacArthur's first reaction was to refuse the assignment and remain with his men. But after consultation with the senior members of his staff, who pointed out that he could do more for the Philippine garrison in Australia than on Corregidor, he decided to accept.[45]. He did not, however, accept the injunction to leave immediately. Pointing out that his abrupt departure might have an adverse effect on morale, he asked for permission to delay his departure until, as he put it, the "psychological time" presented itself. "Please be guided by me in this matter," he urged the President. "I know the situation here in the Philippines and unless the right moment is chosen for this delicate operation, a sudden collapse might occur." This permission was readily granted as was authority to call on the Army and Navy commanders in Australia for the transportation he would require.[46]

[41] Rad, MacArthur to Roosevelt, No. 252, 11 Feb 42, OPD Exec Files.

[42] Rads, Marshall to MacArthur, 14 Feb 42; MacArthur to Marshall, 15 Feb 42, both in WDCSA 370.05 (3–17–42) Phil.

[43] Rad, Marshall to MacArthur, 21 Feb 42, WDCSA 370.05 (3–17–42) Phil; Eisenhower Personal Notebook, entry of 23 Feb 42, copy in OCMH.

[44] Rad, Marshall to MacArthur, No. 1078, 22 Feb 42, CofS folder entitled MacArthur's Move to Australia.

[45] Frazier Hunt, *MacArthur and the War Against Japan* (New York: Charles Scribner's Sons, 1944), p. 64. In this connection, see Jonathan M. Wainwright, *General Wainwright's Story* (New York: Doubleday and Company, 1945), pp. 1–5.

[46] Rads, MacArthur to Marshall, No. 358, 24 Feb 42; Marshall to MacArthur, No. 1087, 25 Feb 42, both in WDCSA 370.05 (3–17–42) Phil.

The "psychological time" arrived in the second week of March. It was then that MacArthur judged the situation on Bataan stable enough for him to leave without risking "a sudden collapse." Arrangements for transportation were quickly made and the officers to accompany him and his family carefully selected. On the 11th all was ready and as darkness settled over Manila Bay, MacArthur stepped into the first of the four PT boats that would take him and the rest of the group, all together twenty-one persons, to Mindanao.[47]

The trip to Mindanao took two nights. On the first the group reached a small uninhabited island in the central Philippines (Cuyo Island). The small craft had broken formation during the night and became separated, one of them dumping its spare fuel when it mistook another PT boat for an enemy vessel. The next night the group continued south in the three remaining vessels, reaching Mindanao at daybreak. There they were met by Maj. Gen. William F. Sharp, commander of the Mindanao Force, and driven to Del Monte airfield to board the three B–17's which should have been waiting there to take them to Australia. But there was only one on the airfield and MacArthur considered that unfit for passengers. Incensed, he dispatched two messages, one to General Brett in Australia asking for other planes immediately and the other to General Marshall calling for "the best three planes in the United States or Hawaii" with veteran crews. "To attempt such a des-

perate and important trip with inadequate equipment," he wrote, "would amount to consigning the whole party to death and I could not accept such a responsibility."[48]

Three B–17's were dispatched from Australia immediately. Two of them reached Del Monte on the night of the 16th, the other soon after. That night the entire group took off and arrived at Darwin at 0900 the next morning. From there MacArthur proceeded to Melbourne, where his arrival was greeted with wild enthusiasm by the Australians. He had made the hazardous journey, "undoubtedly unique in military annals" he told General Marshall, in safety, but it would be more than two and a half years before he would redeem his pledge to return to the Philippines.[49]

The departure of General MacArthur had no immediate effect on operations in the Philippines, but it resulted in a complete change in the top command in the islands. This change was not MacArthur's doing. He fully intended to retain his control of the forces in the Philippines as commander of USAFFE from his new headquarters 4,000 miles away. The headquarters itself as well as its most important staff officers he took to Australia with him. But he left behind an advance echelon and it was through this small staff headed by his G–4, Col. Lewis C. Beebe, whom he designated deputy chief of staff of USAAFE and recommended for promotion, that he intended to exercise his control. Beebe's main task would be to get supplies for Corregidor and Bataan; the di-

[47] Rads, Marshall to MacArthur, 6 Mar 42, WDCSA 370.05 (2–17–42) Phil; Brett to Marshall, No. 760, 19 Mar 42, AG 371 (3–19–42); Rear Adm Francis W. Rockwell, Rpt on Gen MacArthur's Evacuation, Office CNO, Naval Hist Div.

[48] Rad, MacArthur to Marshall, No. 482, 14 Mar 42, WDCSA 370.05 (2–17–42) Phil.

[49] Rad, MacArthur to Marshall, No. 5, 21 Mar 42, OPD Exec Files.

GENERAL MACARTHUR WITH GENERAL HURLEY *after arriving in Australia.*

rection of operations would be handled in MacArthur's own headquarters.[50]

MacArthur realized full well the disadvantages of exercising command so far from the battlefield. These he sought to overcome by organizing his forces into four major commands and giving to each greater control over its operations. For the troops on Bataan, and those still holding out in the mountains of Luzon, he established the Luzon Force and named General Wainwright as its commander. Wainwright's old job as I Corps commander was given to Maj.

Gen. Albert M. Jones. Thus, for the first time in the campaign the fighting on Bataan came under a separate command, which was, in effect, an army headquarters directing the operations of two corps. Previously this direction had been provided by USAFFE.[51]

The task of holding Corregidor until his return, MacArthur assigned to Maj. Gen. George F. Moore, commander of the Harbor Defense of Manila Bay. His last instructions to Moore were to set aside enough food to maintain 20,000 men on half-rations until 30 June 1942 in the expectation that if Bataan fell the Philippine Division would be brought to Corregidor to make a last stand there. When he could hold out no longer, MacArthur told him, he was to destroy Corregidor's formidable armament so that it could not be used against the Americans when they returned.[52]

The other two commands MacArthur left behind included the remaining forces in the Philippines. Previously these forces had been organized into the composite Visayan–Mindanao Force under General Sharp. On 4 March, MacArthur split this command and created a separate Visayan Force under Brig. Gen. Bradford C. Chynoweth. Sharp remained in command of Mindanao, the only island south of Luzon on which a major Japanese force had landed.[53] This move was probably designed to permit General Sharp to devote all his energies to the defense of Mindanao, the base from which MacArthur still hoped to mount a counteroffensive against the Japanese.

But careful as he had been in making

[50] Rpt of Harbor Defense of Manila Bay, ann. VIII of USAFFE–USFIP Rpt of Opns, p. 42.

[51] Wainwright, *General Wainwright's Story*, p. 2.
[52] Rpt of Harbor Defense, pp. 33, 42ff.
[53] USAFFE–USFIP Rpt of Opns, p. 55.

these arrangements (to go into effect the day after his departure), and briefing the force commanders and new deputy chief of staff, MacArthur neglected one thing—to inform the War Department. Whatever the reasons, the result was utter confusion. The War Department assumed that Wainwright, the senior officer in the islands, was in command of all forces in the Philippines as MacArthur had been, and addressed him as such. But the messages, intended for Wainwright and marked for the commander in the Philippines came to Beebe who had no recourse but to refer them to MacArthur, then en route to Australia. Beebe's position was an embarrassing one and he urged his chief repeatedly to clear up the matter with Washington. But to no avail. MacArthur remained silent and the War Department uninformed.[54]

Events finally overwhelmed General Beebe. On the 20th came messages from the President and Chief of Staff, addressing Wainwright as commander in the Philippines and telling him of his promotion to lieutenant general. No confusion was possible. "Upon the departure of General MacArthur," wrote Marshall, "you become commander of U.S. forces in the Philippines."[55] Beebe had no choice but to turn over the messages to Wainwright, who, next morning, formally assumed command of U.S. Forces in the Philippines (USFIP), the name of his new headquarters, and designated Beebe his chief of staff. Like

MacArthur, he commanded the naval forces as well as those of the Army, and was therefore a joint commander.[56]

It was only when MacArthur learned of Wainwright's assumption of command on the 21st that he informed the War Department of his own arrangements. To Marshall these seemed unsatisfactory for a variety of reasons, and he told the President so. Wainwright, he felt, should continue in command. The President accepted this advice and MacArthur was advised that unless he had strenuous objections, Wainwright would retain his new post.[57] MacArthur made no objections. He understood thoroughly Marshall's difficulties, he said, and would accommodate himself to the arrangements already made. "Heartily in accord with Wainwright's promotion to lieutenant general," he radioed, "His assignment to Philippine command is appropriate."[58]

Thus ended the uncertainty and confusion. Wainwright was now confirmed as the commander of all forces in the Philippine Islands with the large authority and heavy responsibilities formerly possessed by General MacArthur. But he was not independent of his former commander, for MacArthur, though not yet officially appointed to his new office, had acquired even greater responsibilities than before and command over an area stretching from Melbourne to Manila.

---

[54] Rad, Marshall to USAFIA, No. 740, 18 Mar 42, OPD 381, Phil, sec 1, case 13. The correspondence between Beebe and MacArthur is filed in AG 311.23 (4 Feb 42) GHQ SWPA.

[55] Rads, Roosevelt to CG USAFFE, No. 1198; Marshall to Wainwright, No. 1204, both dated 19 Mar 42, and No. 1203, 20 Mar 42, OPD Exec Files.

[56] MacArthur had acquired this control on 30 January 1942. Rad, Marshall to MacArthur, 30 Jan 42, WPD 3251–75.

[57] Rad, MacArthur to Marshall, No. 3, 21 Mar 42, AG 311.23 (4 Feb 42) GHQ SWPA; Memo, Marshall for Pres, 22 Mar 42, sub: Comd in Phil; Rad, Marshall to MacArthur, No. 810, 22 Mar 42, both in OPD Exec Files.

[58] Rad, MacArthur to Marshall, No. 19, 24 Mar 42, AG 311.23 (4 Feb 42) GHQ SWPA.

CHAPTER IX

Australia and the Line of Communication

Logistics comprises the means and arrangements which work out the plans of strategy and tactics.

BARON DE JOMINI, *The Art of War*

When in December the War Department established in Australia the command known as USAFIA it had no intention of using its ground forces to defend that subcontinent or of creating a theater of operations. All it wanted to do was to provide a base from which to supply the Philippines. That purpose was soon enlarged to include the support of ABDACOM, but not to the extent of committing large ground forces. The American contribution in that area, General Marshall told Brett before he assumed command of USAFIA, was to be "predominantly air, with other elements limited to those necessary for efficient air operation and the security of the bases."[1]

The advance of the Japanese into the Bismarck Archipelago, New Guinea, and the Solomons, combined with their success along the Malay Barrier in December and January, brought into sharp relief the danger to Australia and the necessity of enlarging its defenses. This task was assumed, somewhat reluctantly, by the United States, and with it went the additional burden of defending the islands stretching across the South Pacific—the life line to Australia. The results, largely unforseen and never anticipated in prewar plans, were to have a profound effect on the war in the Pacific.

The Northeast Area

North of Australia, "like a prehistoric monster, half bird and half reptile,"[2] lies New Guinea, separating Indonesia to the west from the islands of Melanesia to the east. The eastern half of New Guinea (except for the Papuan Peninsula), with the islands of the Bismarck Archipelago—New Britain, New Ireland, and the Admiralties—and those of the northern Solomons—Buka and Bougainville—compose the Australian Mandated Territory. The Papuan Peninsula, which formed the tail of the New Guinea monster, was Australian colonial territory. To the east of Papua lay the southern Solomons, constituting a British colony.

The strategic significance of the inaccessible and inhospitable region compris-

---

[1] Rad, Marshall to Brett, No. 41, 25 Dec 41, WPD 4628–3.

[2] Samuel Eliot Morison, *Breaking the Bismarcks Barrier, 22 July 1942 – 1 May 1944,* vol. VI, "History of United States Naval Operations in World War II" (Boston: Little, Brown and Company, 1957), p. 27.

ing the southeast portion of New Guinea and the Solomons lay in the fact that its straits and seas and its isolated communities provided a double path to the important east coast of Australia and the line of communications to the United States. Both paths began at the Bismarck Archipelago. The western route led along the New Guinea coast, from Lae and Salumaua to the tip of the Papuan Peninsula, and then through the Coral Sea to the developed and industrialized east coast of Australia. The second route extended from the Bismarck Archipelago in a southeasterly direction through the Solomons to the New Hebrides, New Caledonia, the Fijis, and the island chain stretching eastward to Hawaii. Far to the south lay New Zealand, like Australia a British Dominion and a vital link in the imperial system.

At the apex of these two routes, on the island of New Britain, lay Rabaul, capital of the Australian Mandated Territory and key to the defense of the Northeast Area. With its first-rate harbor and airfield sites, Rabaul was potentially the finest base in the region for an enemy advance along either or both routes. Conversely it could be used as a springboard from which to attack with air or naval forces the Japanese stronghold at Truk, which lay only 640 miles to the north, and to drive in the right flank of the Japanese position in the Central Pacific. The other key Allied base in the Northeast Area was Port Moresby, which faced northeastern Australia across the Gulf of Papua and Torres Strait. To its rear, providing a measure of security, lay the towering Owen Stanley range.

With their limited forces, many of which were serving in the Middle East

and elsewhere, the Australians could do no more than place token garrisons in the Northeast Area. At Port Moresby was a brigade group of about 3,000 men, a handful of planes, and some artillery. The rest of New Guinea was defended by a local militia called the New Guinea Volunteer Reserve, while Rabaul was garrisoned by a mixed force numbering about 1,500 men.[3]

The Japanese had no plan to invade Australia when they went to war, but they recognized fully the importance of Rabaul and the Bismarck Archipelago as a base for offensive operations and as an outpost for the defense of Truk and their own line of communications. In their plans, therefore, they provided for the "seizure of strategic points in the Bismarck Archipelago."[4] This task was to be accomplished after the occupation of Guam and by the same force which took that lonely American outpost—a joint force consisting of the Army's *South Seas Detachment* and the Navy's *South Seas Force.*

Vice Adm. Shigeyoshi Inouye, *4th Fleet* commander, began making his plans for an advance into the Bismarck Archipelago immediately after the occupation of Guam on 10 December. It was not until 4 January, however, that Maj. General Tomitaro Horii, commander of the *South Seas Detachment,* was told by *Imperial General Headquarters* to make

---

[3] Dudley McCarthy, *Southwest Pacific Area—First Year: Kokoda to Wau* (Canberra: Australian War Memorial, 1959), ch. II; Samuel Milner, *Victory in Papua,* UNITED STATES ARMY IN WORLD WAR II (Washington, 1957), ch. I; USSBS, *The Allied Campaign Against Rabaul* (Washington, 1946), p. 6.

[4] Army-Navy Central Agreement, Nov 1941, in USSBS, *The Campaigns of the Pacific War,* app. 12.

ready for the invasion of Rabaul, to be undertaken around the middle of the month. Inouye and Horii, who was directly under the control of *Imperial General Headquarters,* quickly made arrangements for the coming operations. The *South Seas Detachment* would take Rabaul; the *South Seas Force* of the *4th Fleet,* Kavieng in New Ireland. D-day was set for 23 January. With a full appreciation of the importance of Rabaul to the Allies, the Japanese anticipated a naval reaction, either from Australia or Hawaii, and took every precaution to meet such a contingency. But they had an accurate knowledge of the defenses of Rabaul and Kavieng and did not foresee any difficulty in overcoming either garrison. Nevertheless they made their plans carefully, reconnoitered thoroughly, and began softening up the target three weeks before the invasion date.[5]

On 14 January the *South Seas Detachment,* a heavily reinforced regimental combat team numbering about 5,000 men, left Guam escorted by units of the *4th Fleet.* Additional protection was furnished by three carriers and supporting warships detached from the Pearl Harbor force and led by Admiral Nagumo himself; a scouting force of four heavy cruisers; and a separate submarine force of six large underwater craft. At dawn of the 20th and again on the 21st, Nagumo sent his carrier planes against Rabaul and nearby points along the New Guinea coast to complete the

destruction begun on the 4th by Truk-based bombers. Then, while the carriers and cruisers stood off to the north to repel a counterattack and the submarines took up positions before St. George's Channel between New Britain and New Ireland, the convoys moved toward the target. An hour before midnight of the 22d the invasion force hove to in Rabaul Harbor.

The weeks of bombing had accomplished their purpose and Rabaul was virtually without air or coastal defenses when Horii took his *South Seas Detachment* ashore in the early hours of the 23d. The Australians put up only a nominal defense. Hopelessly outnumbered and outgunned, they retreated into the hills and jungle behind the town. Four hundred men of the garrison made good their escape; the rest were captured or killed. By noon the Japanese were in control of Rabaul.[6]

Meanwhile, the force designated for the occupation of Kavieng, two companies of special naval landing troops, had left Truk on the 20th and under separate escort sailed directly to New Ireland. On the morning of the 23d this force landed at Kavieng without opposition, the defenders having been captured as they sought to make their escape in small boats. Thus, in a few hours, with almost no casualties, the Japanese had gained control of the strategic Bismarck Archipelago and uncovered the outer defenses of the Northeast Area.

In the weeks that followed the Japanese consolidated their hold on the area and began to convert Rabaul into a formidable base. Mopping-up operations

---

[5] This account of the planning and seizure of Rabaul and Kavieng is based on Hist of the *South Seas Detachment,* Japanese Studies in World War II, 36; Japanese Opns in SWPA, series II, ch. V; Southeast Area Air Opns and Southeast Area Naval Opns, Japanese Studies in World War II, 38 and 48.

[6] For an account of the Rabaul operation, see Wigmore, *The Japanese Thrust,* ch. XVIII.

were completed by the end of the month and troops posted on adjacent islands to establish an outer ring of defense. In the invasion convoy had been a large number of construction troops and these were put to work immediately to repair and improve existing airfields, build new ones, and construct naval facilities. On 30 January 9 Zeros from Truk moved to Rabaul, and soon after 20 medium bombers landed at the Vinakauan airfield outside the town. By the end of February an entire air group—48 medium bombers, a similar number of fighters, and 12 flying boats—was based at Rabaul.[7]

The fall of Rabaul alarmed the Australians as nothing else had. General Wavell's ABDACOM still provided some measure of protection against invasion from the northwest, but the Northeast Area was now virtually unprotected. This possibility had been foreseen when the ABDA area was created and the British had then suggested that the U.S. Pacific Fleet assume responsibility for the defense of the northeast approaches to Australia and for the line of communication. Still reeling from the blow at Pearl Harbor, the Navy refused this additional burden, but Admiral King had on 1 January directed his planners to study the problem. The result was a recommendation to establish the ANZAC area envisaged a year before in ABC–1, but to enlarge it on the north and east to include the Fijis, New Hebrides, and New Caledonia. Air and naval forces in this area would be supplied by Australia and New Zealand, assisted by the United States, and would be under the direction of an American flag officer responsible to the Commander in Chief of the Pacific Fleet.[8]

This proposal, as finally amended by Admiral King and the British First Sea Lord, Admiral Pound, was submitted to the Australian Government on 8 January. For reasons that are not clear, the Australians, though extremely concerned over the defense of the Northeast Area, took no action for two weeks. Finally, on 23 January, the day the Japanese took Rabaul, the Australian Prime Minister, John Curtin, agreed to the establishment of the ANZAC area under American command, but with assumptions about the responsibilities of the Pacific Fleet commander that took another week to remove. It was not until the end of the month, therefore, that ANZAC was formally established, with Vice Adm. Herbert F. Leary in command. His task was to cover the eastern and northeastern approaches to Australia and New Zealand; protect Allied shipping and support the defense of the islands in the area; and, finally, destroy enemy forces and attack enemy positions in the area.

The ANZAC command, like ABDACOM, was short-lived, but unlike that ill-fated command did not disintegrate under Japanese pressure but because it had outlived its usefulness. Nor did Admiral Leary have responsibility for the defense of the land areas included in ANZAC; his was exclusively a naval and air command. Initially it consisted of three Australian cruisers, plus some destroyers and corvettes. To

---

[7] USSBS, *The Allied Campaign Against Rabaul*, pp. 6–7, 11–12.

[8] CCS 15, The ANZAC Area, 29 Jan 42, ABC 323.31 (1–24–42) POA 1; Mins, White House Conf, 1 Jan 42, WDCSA 334 Mtgs and Conf; Hayes, The War Against Japan, vol. I, ch. I, pp. 61–64; ABC–1, ann. 3, in *Pearl Harbor Attack Hearings*, pt. 15, p. 1516.

these were added the USS *Chicago* and two destroyers from the Pacific Fleet. A squadron of B–17's from Hawaii was assigned and it reached Townsville in northeast Australia on 17 February. Several days later these bombers hit Rabaul in the first blow of a long campaign of attrition to neutralize that rapidly growing Japanese base.[9]

The establishment of ANZAC was only one of the measures taken to meet the danger created by Japanese occupation of Rabaul.[10] It was at this time, too, that the Australians approved a proposal the Combined Chiefs had made on 11 January to include Darwin and the northwest coast of Australia in General Wavell's ABDA area. This approval came on 23 January, the same day that the Australians agreed to the establishment of ANZAC, and the Combined Chiefs immediately notified Wavell of his new responsibilities.[11]

While this change gave some hope for the security of Darwin (which the U.S. Navy was then using as a base, but which it abandoned after the attack of 19 February), it did not meet the problem of defending Port Moresby in the Northeast Area. The ANZAC force alone could not, the Australians believed, give them the protection they needed and they so informed the British while requesting 250 more fighter planes and

a squadron of the American P–40's allotted to General Wavell. Neither the British nor the American Chiefs could meet this new and unexpected request, but offered as an alternative to include Port Moresby in the ABDA area. General Wavell argued strongly against this solution as well as the suggestion that he divert some of his planes to the Australians, and the matter was dropped.[12]

But the problem of meeting Australia's demand for fighter planes was still not solved. After considerable discussion, General Marshall agreed to divert one American squadron to the defense of Port Moresby. This solution, though it failed to satisfy the Australians, was one which, perforce, they had to accept.[13] But by the time this decision was made the ANZAC force had taken over responsibility for the air and naval defense of the Northeast Area.

It was now early February and the signs of disintegration along the Malay Barrier to the northwest were clearly evident. Here was another threat to an Australia already concerned over the security of the northeast flank. Two of its divisions, the 6th and 7th, were due from the Middle East this month and the next. Under existing plans they were to be used in the defense of the Netherlands Indies, and thus, indirectly, of Australia itself. To this arrangement the Australian Government had no objections. But on 13 February General Wavell raised another possibility. In

---

[9] G. Harmon Gill, *Royal Australian Navy, 1939–42*, ser. 2, vol. 1, "Australia in the War of 1939–1945" (Canberra: Australian War Memorial, 1957), p. 519; Milner, *Victory in Papua*, p. 8.

[10] The measures discussed in the remainder of this section are covered fully in Hayes, The War Against Japan, ch. II, pp. 7–12; Matloff and Snell, *Strategic Planning, 1941–42*, pp. 128–31.

[11] CCS 8, Inclusion of Port Darwin in ABDA, 24 Jan 42, ABC 323.31 (1–29–42); Wavell, "ABDACOM," p. 4; Rad, CCS to Wavell, DBA 2, 24 Jan 42, OPD ABDA Msg File; Gill, *Royal Australian Navy*, p. 517.

[12] Memo, Gerow for Marshall, 27 Jan 42, sub: Msgs for Australia, WPD 4628–24; Rads, CCS to ABDA COM, DBA 5, 29 Jan 42; Wavell to CCS, 00649, 1 Feb 42; all in OPD ABDA Msg File; Mins, CCS Mtgs, 23 and 27 Jan 42.

[13] Mins, CCS Mtg, 3 Feb 42; Rads, CCS to Wavell, DBA 8, 3 Feb 42; Marshall to Wavell, 5 Feb 42, OPD ABDA Msg File.

view of the early loss of Singapore and the prospects of an invasion of Sumatra and Java he suggested to the Combined Chiefs that at least one of the two Australian divisions be sent instead to Burma.[14]

In Washington there was a full appreciation of the seriousness of the situation along the Malay Barrier. It was recognized, too, that, in the event ABDACOM fell, the United States could best defend the right (east) flank and the British the left in Southeast Asia.[15] But the British could ill spare the troops to send there and the Australians had already made it evident that they would not permit their divisions to serve in Burma. Moreover there was in the Middle East a third Australian division, the 9th, which was scheduled to return home soon. If the British were to have the use of any of these troops, then the United States, it was becoming increasingly clear, would have to provide more than air or service troops for the defense of Australia.

It is against this background that the action that followed Wavell's message of the 13th can be best understood. Up to that time the policy of the War Department, reiterated time and again, had been to send out only aircraft and the necessary service and supporting troops to Australia. Now, on 14 February, the War Department suddenly reversed itself and decided to send an infantry division — the 41st — as well as additional supporting troops, all together about 25,000 men, for the ground defense of Australia. Two days later, with the help of Harry Hopkins, the ships required for most of these troops had been found. In a period when shipping space was the most precious of Allied resources, this rapid action was indeed remarkable.[16]

The Americans and British now turned to the Australian Government for aid in Burma. On the 16th, after the fall of Singapore, Wavell had come out flatly for the diversion of both the 6th and 7th Australian Divisions to Burma on the ground that they would have a "very great effect on Japanese strategy and a heartening effect on China and India."[17] Reinforcements for Australia, he said, unaware of the decision made in Washington two days earlier, should be provided by the United States. The United States and British Governments, unwilling to go as far as Wavell and believing that Australia would never consent to his proposal, asked Curtin for only one of the divisions for Burma. To these official requests were added the personal appeals of Churchill and Roosevelt, the latter enjoining the Australian Prime Minister to "have every confidence that we are going to reinforce your position with all possible speed."[18] But the Australians were adamant. They had contributed much to the imperial cause and would neither risk the loss of their men in Burma nor jeopardize the security of

[14] Rad, Wavell to CCS, CCOS 7, 13 Feb 42, OPD ABDA Msg File.

[15] Rad, Roosevelt to Prime Minister, 18 Feb 43, ABC 323.31 (1–29–42 sec. 1A) POA; Sherwood, *Roosevelt and Hopkins*, pp. 502–03.

[16] Rad, Wavell to Prime Minister, 16 Feb 42, OPD ABDA Msg File; Memo, Marshall for Eisenhower, 14 Feb 42, no sub, WPD 4630–64; Churchill, *Hinge of Fate*, pp. 140, *passim*; Matloff and Snell, *Strategic Planning, 1941–42*, pp. 128–30; Leighton and Coakley, *Global Logistics and Strategy*, p. 174.

[17] Rad, Wavell to Prime Minister, 16 Feb 42, OPD ABDA Msg File.

[18] Rad. Roosevelt to Curtin, No. 330, 20 Feb 42, OPD ABDA Msg File; Churchill, *Hinge of Fate*, p. 157.

the homeland to grant the British the use of their 7th Division.[19]

This refusal did not affect the movement of American ground troops to Australia. The first echelon of the 41st Division left the west coast early in March and the rest sailed from San Francisco later in the month and during April.[20] Thus, the United States had committed itself, less than three months after the attack on Pearl Harbor, to the ground defense of Australia, with all that such a defense implied.

The Line of Communications

Intimately associated with the defense of Australia as well as the larger problems of future strategy in the Pacific was the line of communications between that country and the United States. The islands along this line lay generally south of the equator, far from the well-traveled air and sea routes to the north. Their strategic significance lay in the fact that once the Central Pacific was lost, they offered the only route to the sister Dominions of Australia and New Zealand. Should this South Pacific line be cut these Dominions would be isolated and the island possessions of the Allies lost to the enemy.

This fact was thoroughly understood by the Japanese naval planners. The lessons taught by Admiral Mahan had not been lost on these officers and they looked on the islands of the South Pacific with an envious eye. Fortunately for the Allied cause, they were unable to in-

clude these islands in their war plans for the timetable of conquest was too close and the initial operations too numerous and scattered. But they did not overlook them either. In his order to the *Combined Fleet* setting out the tasks to be accomplished, Admiral Yamamoto listed among the "areas expected to be occupied or destroyed as quickly as operational conditions permit the Fijis...and Samoa," as well as "strategic points in the Australian Area."[21] Taken in conjunction with the occupation of the Bismarck Archipelago and the islands of the Central Pacific, this statement of intentions had large implications for the war in the Pacific.

The United States had recognized early the importance of the islands of the South Pacific and in October 1941 had begun building airfields on some of them to provide an alternate air ferry route to the Philippines. But the work had only just begun when war came and, except for local defense forces, none of the islands had been garrisoned. This lack was partially remedied in the days following Pearl Harbor when General Short in Hawaii sent token forces consisting of a few gun crews to Canton and Christmas Islands, both of which were under his jurisdiction. He could do no more until his own urgent needs were filled.[22]

Primary responsibility for the local defense of the islands of the Pacific rested with the governing nations— Great Britain, New Zealand, the Free French, Australia, and, in the case of

---

[19] Rad, Curtin to Churchill, 21 Feb 42, OPD ABDA Msg File.

[20] Memos, WPD for G–3, 17 and 19 Feb 42, sub: Movement of Troops to SUMAC, WPD 4630–66 and 70; Leighton and Coakley, *Global Logistics and Strategy*, p. 174.

[21] *Combined Fleet* Opn Order No. 1, 5 Nov 41, copy in *Pearl Harbor Attack Hearings*, pt. 3, p. 438.

[22] See above, p. 99; Mins, JB Mtg, 26 Nov 41; Msgs in AG 381 (11–27–41 sec. 1) Far East; K. Williams, The South Pacific Air Route, USAF Hist Studies, No. 45.

Hawaii, Samoa, and other small islands, the United States. But the task of guarding the sea lanes to Australia and New Zealand—a separate though related problem to that of local defense—was the responsibility of the Pacific Fleet and British naval forces. Under ABC–1 and the RAINBOW plan, the former was responsible for the defense of the area east of the 180th meridian, that is, up to but not including the Fijis and New Zealand; the latter for the region to the west as far as longitude 155° east. The Pacific Fleet had the additional mission of supporting the British in their area of responsibility which included the east coast of Australia and the southeast portion of the Papuan Peninsula.[23]

This arrangement was invalidated almost immediately on the outbreak of war when the Chief of Naval Operations had declared that the Pacific Fleet could do no more than defend the area east of the 180th meridian. The result of this decision, which the British and Australians accepted only because they had to, left a vacuum in the Allied defenses, which, it was apparent, the Japanese would soon fill if the Allies did not. Late in December, therefore, when the initial shock of the Pearl Harbor attack had worn off, Admiral King ordered the recently appointed Commander in Chief of the Pacific Fleet, Admiral Nimitz, to maintain the line of communication to Australia by extending his control of the line Hawaii-Samoa westward to include the Fijis "at earliest practicable date." This task, King told Nimitz, was second and "only in small degrees less important" than the protection of the line of

communication from Midway to Hawaii and the west coast.[24]

This decision did not ensure the security of the line of communications, however, for it still left the area west of the Fijis uncovered and made no provision for local defense. The problem was therefore laid before the first U.S.-British conference then in session in Washington. No one there disagreed with the necessity for holding the islands, which it was recognized not only furnished an air route across the Pacific but provided bases for Allied air and naval forces and outposts for the defense of Hawaii and Australia as well. (Map 3) The real problem for the planners was to find the troops to do the job and the shipping to support them. The formula finally agreed upon, on 10 January, was to allocate responsibility for the defense of the islands east of the 180th meridian to the United States, and those west of that line to New Zealand and Australia.[25]

Even before this agreement was reached, the Americans had been assembling the forces needed to garrison the islands in their area of responsibility. The Army, it had been decided, would provide the garrisons for Christmas, Canton, and Bora Bora; the Navy, for Palmyra and Samoa. These garrisons would be small, for it was recognized that the security of the islands depended ultimately on air and naval power, rather than on the strength of the ground forces. To convert each island into an impregnable

---

[23] ABC–1, copy in *Pearl Harbor Attack Hearings*, pt. 15; Mins, JB Mtg, 8 Dec 41.

[24] Ltr, Secy for Collab to Br Staff Mission, 16 Dec 41, sub: Modification of ABC–1; Rad, COMINCH to CINCPAC, 1740, 30 Dec 41, both cited in Hayes, The War Against Japan, ch. I, pp. 11, 58.

[25] ABC–4, 31 Dec 41; ABC–4/8, 10 Jan 42, sub: Defense of Island Bases, both in ARCADIA; Memo, WPD for CofS, 4 Jan 42, sub: Troop Movements to Pacific Bases, WPD 4571–22.

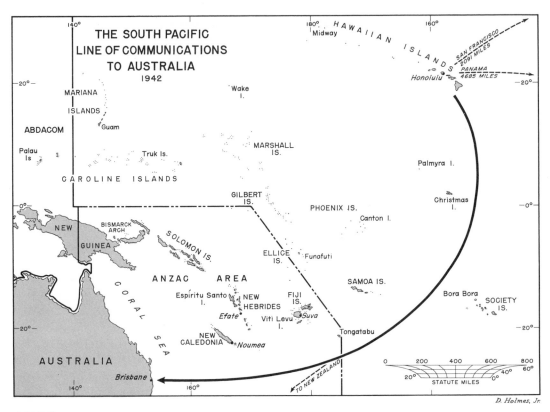

THE SOUTH PACIFIC
LINE OF COMMUNICATIONS
TO AUSTRALIA
1942

MAP 3

fortress would not only be wasteful of precious troop strength and shipping, but would probably be less effective than defense by mobile air and naval forces. Thus the strength of the Canton and Christmas garrisons was set at about 2,000 men each, chiefly infantry and artillery, and a squadron of pursuit planes. Bora Bora, which the Navy planned to use as a refueling station, was given an Army garrison of 4,000 consisting largely of an infantry and an antiaircraft artillery regiment.[26]

Palmyra, between Hawaii and Canton, was an essential link in the new air ferry route. The Navy had begun, a year before the war, to develop a seaplane base there but wished now to enlarge its facilities and to garrison the island. For this purpose it sent out a Marine detachment and naval construction units, while the Army supplied a pursuit squadron for local protection. Plans for the expansion of military facilities in American Samoa, which had been under naval administration since its acquisition

[26] Relevant papers on the planning and organization of these garrisons are filed in WPD 4571–22 and 24. The story of the establishment of the base at Bora Bora, with emphasis on the logistical problem, is told in Leighton and Coakley, *Global Logistics and Strategy*, ch. VII; see also, Craven and Cate, *AAF I*, p. 431.

in 1899 and already possessed air and naval installations, were also pushed vigorously by the Navy. Its defenses were provided by a Marine brigade which left San Diego on 6 January, escorted by a naval force including the carriers *Enterprise* and *Yorktown*, and which reached the island seventeen days later.[27]

The defense of Hawaii was a special case. In the first days of war its reinforcement had seemed perhaps the most urgent task facing the Army and Navy, but by Christmas 1941 concern for its safety had somewhat abated. Priority for troops and equipment had then shifted to the Southwest Pacific. But General Emmons, the new commander of the Hawaiian Department, had been promised in December large reinforcements, including one square division, an armored regiment, aircraft of all types, and service troops. These, he had been told at the time, would be shipped later, after the emergency in the Southwest Pacific had passed. The threat in that area, however, had increased rather than diminished, and, with the additional necessity of reinforcing the line of communications, had made the prospect of strengthening Hawaii's defenses more remote than ever.[28]

In February, therefore, when Emmons requested reinforcements above those already authorized, the whole question of the defense of Hawaii and its troop requirements came up for review. By this time it was clear that the major part of the Japanese forces was committed to the Southwest Pacific and that Hawaii was no longer in danger of invasion. The Japanese were still capable of air and naval raids against the islands, but this threat could be met by the Pacific Fleet and the air strength already allotted. It was recognized, moreover, that the assignment of additional air and ground forces to Hawaii would play into Japan's hands for it would pin down American strength and consume valuable shipping space without any appreciable effect on Japanese military forces. The Joint Chiefs therefore turned down Emmons' new requests and decided to send him only what had been promised earlier.[29]

This decision made, the Army hastened the shipment of the promised but long-overdue reinforcements to Hawaii. In mid-February an advance party of the 27th Division left the west coast to make preparations for the arrival of the rest of the division. In ships loaned by the British, the New York National Guard division was moved to Hawaii in three echelons during March. But at the end of the month there were still 40,000 troops allocated to the Hawaiian garrison in the United States awaiting shipment.[30]

Providing forces for the islands west of the 180th meridian was not initially an American responsibility. For the

---

[27] Department of the Navy, *Building the Navy's Bases in World War II*, (Washington, 1947), pp. 121–22, 190–95, 208–13; Morison, *The Rising Sun in the Pacific*, p. 259; Craven and Cate, *AAF I*, p. 437.

[28] Rad, Marshall to Emmons, No. 1013, 16 Jan 42; Emmons to TAG, No. 1677, 13 Jan 42, both in WPD Msg File; Memo, Gerow for Eisenhower, 20 Feb 42, sub: Reinforcements for Hawaii, WPD 3444–19. See also Matloff and Snell, *Strategic Planning, 1941–42*, p. 152; Conn, Engelman, and Fairchild, Guarding the United States and Its Outposts, ch. VIII.

[29] JCS 11 and 11/1, Hawaiian Defense Forces, 12 Feb 42, ABC 381 (2–12–42) Hawaii.

[30] Edmund G. Love, *The 27th Infantry Division in World War II* (Washington: Infantry Journal Press, 1949), p. 18. Relevant papers are filed in AG 370–5 (12–26–41).

Fijis, which many thought to be seriously threatened, the United States agreed to provide air and antiaircraft forces. But it was New Zealand which furnished most of the air as well as the ground defenses of the island, a contribution which exceeded 8,000 men, including the native Fijian troops who later acquired an awesome reputation as jungle fighters.[31]

The security of New Caledonia was one of the most bothersome problems of the Pacific area. Second in size only to New Zealand among the islands in the South Pacific and an important station along the air ferry route, New Caledonia had a dual strategic significance. Not only did it lie at the end of the long line of islands stretching across the Pacific, but it flanked the northeast approaches to Australia from New Guinea and the Solomons. Moreover it contained valuable deposits of nickel and chrome, which would undoubtedly make it a tempting prize, Admiral King thought, for the metal-hungry Japanese.

The defense of New Caledonia was complicated by political factors. Sovereignty was exercised by the Free French Government in London through a High Commissioner, Admiral Georges Thierry d'Argenlieu, but responsibility for its defense was assigned by the Allies to Australia. Neither could spare the large forces required to make this vital outpost secure. The French had on the island 1,400 poorly equipped, ill-trained troops, mostly natives, and the Australians could contribute only a single company of commandos. Reinforcements were urgently needed, and it was this need that

projected the United States into the confused politics of New Caledonia and made that island one of the major American bases in the Pacific.[32]

American interest in New Caledonia predated the war. Since October 1941 the United States had been actively negotiating with the Free French for the right to construct an airfield there. Work on the field was well along on 7 December, despite conflict between the French and the Australians who were building the airstrip. Pearl Harbor gave an added impetus to this effort and an urgency to the island's defense that was heightened when General Charles de Gaulle threw in his lot with the powers arrayed against Japan and offered to make available to the Allies the Free French islands of the Pacific.[33] Neither Australia nor the United States, however, was yet ready to assume responsibility for the defense of the island.

The progress of negotiations soon hit a snag. General de Gaulle and his Pacific representative, Admiral d'Argenlieu, had approved American plans for the development of airfields in New Caledonia with the understanding that these fields would be under a French commander who would in turn be subordinate to any Allied command established in the Southwest Pacific. Such an Allied com-

---

[31] Craven and Cate, *AAF I*, pp. 430–31, 434.

[32] This account of the reinforcement of New Caledonia is based on OPD Hist MS, Delaying and Containing Action in the Pacific, pp. 28–35; Matloff and Snell, *Strategic Planning, 1941–42*, pp. 115–17; Hayes, The War Against Japan, ch. II, pp. 59–60; Capt. Francis D. Cronin, *Under the Southern Cross* (Washington: Combat Forces Press, 1951), ch. I. Valuable material is contained in WPD 3718, AG 381 (11–27–42) (1–19–42), and folder entitled Political Disturbances, New Caledonia, OCMH.

[33] Capt Tracy B. Kittredge, Evolution of Global Strategy, pt. II, ch. II, pp. 29–30, JCS Hist Div.

mand, they had assumed, would be American. By arrangements between the Americans and British, however, New Caledonia fell into the British area of responsibility, and had been delegated by them to the Australians. When D'Argenlieu learned of this arrangement he insisted that the French command all Allied forces and installations on the island and demanded that he be informed of plans for the area. He permitted the Australians to continue work on the airfield, but on a temporary basis.[34]

Weeks passed and D'Argenlieu received no word of plans for the defense of the island or of the decisions reached by the Americans and British then meeting in Washington. Increasingly nervous over the safety of the island, where Japanese submarines had already been sighted, and unable to get any satisfaction from the Australians, the French turned to the Americans—to General Emmons in Hawaii and to officials in Washington—with their complaints. Finally, on about 15 January, D'Argenlieu told Emmons that if reinforcements were not sent immediately it would be necessary to stop all work on the airfields because they would, when completed, provide the Japanese with a strong inducement for attacking New Caledonia.[35]

Already a decision on the defense of New Caledonia had been made, based not on D'Argenlieu's thinly veiled threats but on a sober review by the Combined Chiefs of the needs of the

islands along the line of communications. By that decision, which was kept a carefully guarded secret from the French, the United States agreed to assume Australia's obligations in New Caledonia. The size of the force it agreed to send there was the largest yet allocated to the Pacific, except for Hawaii and Australia, and consisted of one division (reinforced), two air squadrons, and service troops. So large an undertaking strained an already overloaded shipping schedule and made even more marked the discrepancy between a strategy that placed the war in Europe first and a program that sent the bulk of the troops to the Pacific.

The Army planners recognized—and deplored — this and other diversions from the main theater but could not deny the necessity that had created them. Immediately they set to work assembling the forces required and making arrangements for their shipment. Instead of selecting a division already organized and trained the planners put together a force, under the command of Brig. Gen. Alexander M. Patch, Jr., of about 15,000 men, many of them from the recently triangularized 26th and 33d National Guard Divisions. Though this force, designated Task Force 6184, consisted of an "odd conglomeration" of units that gave it the appearance, at first glance, of a "military stew of men and equipment," it had many of the marks of an infantry division. There was a brigade headquarters from the 26th Division, two infantry regiments, the 132d and 184th, a field artillery regiment with 155-mm. howitzers, and the usual service elements, strengthened by attachments. But it included also a battalion of light tanks, a pursuit squadron, an antiair-

[34] Ibid., pp. 31–33.
[35] Memo, CofS for Secy State, 20 Jan 42, sub: Defense of New Caledonia, WPD 3718–14. Many of the papers dealing with New Caledonia are located in this file.

craft regiment, and a coast artillery battalion.[36]

The mission given General Patch was brief: to hold New Caledonia, in cooperation with the military forces of the United Nations, against all attacks. Presumably he would receive no reinforcements. He was an independent commander, responsible only to the War Department and reporting directly to Washington. But his authority was more restricted than it appeared on the surface. He had, for example, no control over the airfields which were causing so much difficulty with the French. That was the responsibility of General Emmons, over 3,000 miles away, and of the Australians who were doing the construction work. Also, responsibility for the supply of his force was shared by the San Francisco Port of Embarkation and General Barnes in Australia, who had also to meet the demands of Brereton and Brett for the ABDA area and MacArthur for the Philippines. Finally, as Patch soon learned, the question of French participation in the command of forces on the island was still far from settled.[37]

In the record time of two weeks, not without considerable difficulty and confusion, Task Force 6184, including about 4,000 air and service troops for Australia, was organized, equipped, and loaded aboard seven transports, all that could be assembled on the east coast at that time. On 23 January it sailed from New York and reached Melbourne, via the

GENERAL PATCH *being greeted by Admiral d'Argenlieu.*

Panama Canal, on 26 February. In Australia, where there was considerable anxiety over the safety of the homeland and where American ground forces had not yet made their appearance, envious eyes were cast upon this large force, not only by the Australians but by the American commanders as well. But there was no mistaking the destination of Task Force 6184 or General Marshall's injunction that this force was to be used along the line of communications, not as reinforcements for Australia or the ABDA area.[38]

Meanwhile Admiral d'Argenlieu had become more and more insistent in his demand for troops and equipment. Fearing premature disclosure through Free French channels of the movement of so large a force, General Marshall was ada-

---

[36] Cronin, *Under the Southern Cross*, p. 4. For a list of the units in TF 6184, see p. 422; Matloff and Snell, *Strategic Planning*, 1941–42, p. 149, N. 10.

[37] Memo, WPD for TAG, 22 Jan 42, sub: Defense of New Caledonia, WPD 3718–17.

[38] Rad, Marshall to Brett, No. 69, 2 Feb 42, AG 381 (11–27–41 sec. 2A), Far East.

FORWARD ECHELON OF THE 41ST DIVISION *en route to Australia unloading at Oro Bay, New Guinea.*

mant in his refusal to do more than authorize General Emmons to tell the admiral that the Allies would provide for the defense of New Caledonia. The nationality, composition, size, and time of arrival of the force were kept secret and d'Argenlieu, perforce, had to content himself with Emmons' assurances that the island would be defended.

The transshipment of Task Force 6184 from Melbourne to New Caledonia was a heavy task. The troops had to be debarked and those intended for use in Australia sent to their destinations with their equipment. The remainder of the men had to be housed and fed in nearby camps while the cargo was sorted, rearranged, and loaded.[39] General Patch had left for Australia by air via the South Atlantic route to make these arrangements, carrying with him the manifests and other documents. But he fell ill in Trinidad and had to return to Washington for hospitalization. Later he flew directly across the Pacific to New Caledonia, stopping only at Hawaii to consult with General Emmons. Meanwhile Barnes made whatever preparations he could until another courier arrived.

[39] Leighton and Coakley, *Global Logistics and Strategy*, p. 150 *passim*. The documents on this shipment are well summarized in Matloff and Snell, *Strategic Planning, 1491–42*, p. 150, n. 14.

Laboring in the heat of the Australian summer, the dock workers at Melbourne completed their task by 6 March and on that date the seven transports of Task Force 6184, with naval escort, set sail for New Caledonia. After an uneventful voyage they entered the harbor of Noumea at the southwest tip of the cigar-shaped island six days later. There arrangements for their unloading had already been made by an advance party flown in from Melbourne. General Patch had arrived on the 5th, bringing with him the information that d'Argenlieu had been seeking for so long and the news that a large force would soon reach the island. This news and the arrival of Task Force 6184 put to rest the uncertainty and fears of the French, but, unfortunately, did not end the difficulties that had plagued the planners and diplomats and now rested on Patch's shoulders.

Although General Patch had been told he could expect no reinforcements, these were soon on the way. In mid-April, he received a third infantry regiment, the 164th, and authority to organize from his force an infantry division. This was done in May when the Americal Division, which was to fight its way from Guadalcanal to Tokyo, was created.

By the time Task Force 6184 arrived in New Caledonia the 41st Division was on its way to Australia and the garrisons organized early in January to defend the line of communications had already reached their destinations. In the Fijis was the 70th Pursuit Squadron. The Bora Bora garrison, which left Charleston on 27 January, completed its journey in three weeks but so hastily had it been assembled and shipped that it did not complete its unloading until almost

two months later. The Christmas Island and Canton garrisons left San Francisco on 31 January and were at their stations before the middle of February.[40] The line of communications between the United States and Australia, which had lain so nakedly exposed to Japanese attack in the dark days after Pearl Harbor, was, three months later, rapidly being converted into a chain of island bases linking the two countries. But it was still only a thin line of defense, weakly held and easily pierced, and the danger of attack was still a live threat. (*Table 3*)

The Japanese Threat

The Japanese had not been idle during these months. Even before the war their naval planners had contended that they could not stop with the seizure of Rabaul but must go on to establish control over the Solomons and the northeast coast of New Guinea. Such action would not only secure the Japanese position in the Bismarck Archipelago with the least cost through air attrition, but would, the naval planners noted, provide a springboard for further advances to the Fijis, Samoa, and "strategic points in the Australia Area." Though they were unable to win approval for this scheme in the prewar plan, the naval planners did not abandon the project but placed it on their agenda, to be accomplished "as quickly as operational conditions permit."[41]

Hardly had Rabaul fallen when the

---

[40] Matloff and Snell, *Strategic Planning, 1941–42*, p. 150; Leighton and Coakley, *Global Logistics and Strategy*, ch. VII.

[41] Combined Fleet Operational Order No. 1, 5 Nov 41, *Pearl Harbor Attack Hearings*, pt. 3, p. 438.

TABLE 3—MAJOR ARMY COMBAT FORCES FOR THE PACIFIC, PRESENT AND PROJECTED, APRIL–MAY 1942

Base	Infantry	Artillery	Aircraft
Hawaii	Divisions: 24th Division 25th Division 27th Division (Additional Division projected.)	AA Regiments: 6 Present 1 Projected CAC Regiments (155-mm. Gun), 2	Heavy Bombers: 41 Present 96 Projected Medium and Light Bombers: 26 Present Pursuit: 179 Present 225 Projected
Australia	Divisions: 32d ⎱ En route 41st ⎰	AA Regiments, 3 AA Battalions, 3	Heavy Bombers: 41 Present 80 Projected Medium and Light Bombers: 152 Present and En route 207 Projected Pursuit: 477 Present and En route 640 Projected
New Caledonia	Divisions, Americal	AA Regiment, 1 CAC Battalion, 155-mm. Gun, 1	Pursuit: 40 Present 75 Projected
Fijis	Division, 37th, Projected		Pursuit, 25
Bora Bora	Regiments, 102d Infantry (less one Battalion)	AA Regiment, 1	
Christmas	Battalion, 1	CA Battalions, 2	Pursuit, 25
Canton	2 Companies	CA Battalions, 2	Pursuit: 40 Present 50 Projected
Tongatabu	147th Infantry reinforced (less one bn)	AA Regiment, 1	Pursuit, 25 Present
Efate	24th Infantry (reinforced)		

Navy high command raised the question of a further advance into the area northeast of Australia. "Operational conditions," the naval officers thought, were ripe for an extension of the original perimeter into the Solomon Islands and northeast New Guinea, to Lae and Salamaua in the Huon Gulf, and even to Port Moresby. Such a move, they argued, would not only strengthen Japan's defensive position but would deny the Allies key bases for counterattack. From airfields in this area the Imperial Navy could keep a close watch on enemy naval movements far to the south and at the same time "intensify pressure on northeastern Australia," hindering its use for air operations by the Allies. These large results, naval officers did not fail to point out to their Army colleagues, could be achieved at slight cost and with few troops.[42]

While the Army planners were digesting this tempting morsel, the Navy presented them with still another dish—one on which they nearly choked. Since the main reason for advancing beyond the original perimeter was to delay an Allied counteroffensive from the south, why not, the Navy asked, seize the main enemy base by taking Australia itself? Apparently carried away by its own boldness the Navy went even further—there were no limits to this kind of strategy—and proposed that India, too, be taken as a means of forestalling Allied recovery and reorganization. Clearly the naval staff, as one of the Japanese ad-

mirals put it, had succumbed to the "so-called Victory Disease."[43]

No decision was reached on the invasion of Australia or India at this time. At least twelve divisions would be required to invade Australia, the Army planners said, as well as supplies and shipping in such magnitude as to make the operation "a reckless undertaking far in excess of Japan capabilities."[44] Similar reasons ruled out the move against India. The Navy did not push these projects—though it had its own plans for carrier strikes in the Indian Ocean —and was satisfied to let the matter rest for the time being.

To the proposal to advance into New Guinea and the Solomons the Army could find few objections. It was a feasible operation, would have significant results, and would require relatively few Army troops. Agreement was quickly reached. On 29 January *Imperial General Headquarters* issued orders directing Army and Navy forces in the Bismarcks to occupy the Lae-Salamaua area in New Guinea and then, "if possible," move on to take Port Moresby. Operations to seize air bases in the Solomons and capture Tulagi, just north of Guadalcanal, were authorized at the same

[42] Japanese Opns in SWPA, SWPA Series II, ch. V, pp. 6–7; Hist of *Army Sec, Imperial GHQ, Japanese Studies in World War II*, 72, pp. 33–34; Lt Gen Seizo Arisue, formerly intelligence chief of the General Staff, reply to author's questions, 14 Jul 49, ATIS Doc No. 49157, p. 27, copy in OCMH.

[43] Statement of Rear Adm Tadaichi Hara, cited in Samuel Eliot Morison, *Coral Sea, Midway and Submarine Actions, May 1942 – August 1942*, vol. IV, "History of United States Naval Operations in World War II" (Boston: Little, Brown and Company, 1949), p. 4; Japanese Opns in SWPA, ch. V pp. 10–11; Arisue Questionnaire, pp. 28–29; Interrog of Lt Gen Shinichi Tanaka, 25 Oct 47, copy in OCMH; Statements of Rear Adm Sadatoshi Tomioka, *Navy Sec, Imperial GHQ*, 2 Aug 50, ATIS Doc 61232; Col Takushiro Hattori, *Army Sec, Imperial GHQ*, 29 Aug 49, ATIS Doc 50307, both in Statements of Japanese Officials, IV, 314 and I, 331, copy in OCMH.

[44] Arisue Questionnaire, p. 29.

time but would be carried out by naval forces alone.[45]

Plans for the invasion of Lae and Salamaua, like those for the Bismarck area, were made by General Horii, commander of the *South Seas Detachment*, and Admiral Inouye, *4th Fleet* commander. With a full knowledge of the weakness of the Australian garrisons in New Guinea, the two commanders assigned only small forces to the operation. Salamaua was to be taken by one battalion of Horii's detachment, supported by an artillery battery and other smaller units; Lae by a naval landing force of battalion size. Naval escort and support, including four heavy and two light cruisers, would be provided by Inouye's *4th Fleet*, and air cover by the *4th Air Group* based at Rabaul. These plans were completed on 16 February, with the landing scheduled for the end of the month.[46]

The concentration of Japanese forces at Rabaul had not gone unnoticed and Admiral Nimitz had sent the carrier *Lexington* into the area. With Admiral Leary's B–17's at Townsville, this carrier force was to meet the enemy and, if possible, destroy it. On 20 February the *Lexington*, accompanied by four heavy cruisers and ten destroyers, reached a point about 350 miles south of Rabaul where it was detected and attacked by Japanese aircraft. The battle that followed was inconclusive. The American carrier force drove off the Japanese planes, but abandoned any further effort against Rabaul because all chance of sur-

prising the Japanese had been lost and the ships were running short of fuel. Two days later the ANZAC B–17's made their first attack on Rabaul.[47]

These raids, while they did not alter the Japanese plan, did postpone its execution. Finally, on 5 March, all was in readiness and the invasion force sortied from Rabaul harbor to reach Huon Gulf two days later. There it split, one group heading for Lae, the other for Salamaua. Early next morning, 8 March, the troops went ashore, covered by aircraft from Rabaul and Gasmata which had been bombing the target area as well as Port Moresby since the 2d. There was no opposition at the beaches or in the towns, and during the next two days the Japanese unloaded their supplies and began to build the bases. Thus, at almost no cost, the Japanese acquired control of the straits between northeast New Guinea and New Britain and positions from which they could support a further advance southward and prevent the Allies from breaking out into the open seas north of the Bismarck Archipelago.[48]

The absence of opposition did not mean the Allies would take this fresh assault without reprisal. Since the inconclusive raid of the *Lexington* on 20 February, Admiral Nimitz had assembled another force, almost double that of the first, in an effort to halt the Japanese advance into Australia's Northeast

---

[45] *Navy Sec, Imperial GHQ*, Directive No. 47, 29 Jan 42. The order is quoted in Japanese Opns in SWPA, ch. V, pp. 7–8.

[46] Southeast Area Naval Opns, Japanese Studies in World War II, 48, pp. 19–20; Japanese Opns in SWPA, ch. V, pp. 8–9; Milner, *Victory in Papua*, ch. I.

[47] Early raids in the Pacific Ocean, 1 Feb – 10 Mar 42, Combat Narrative, ONI, pp. 35–40. See General Marshall's warning of probable enemy carrier operations northeast of Australia in his letter to Barnes, undated, but written early in February, WPD 4630–57.

[48] Japanese Opns in SWPA, ch. V, p. 9; Hist of *South Seas Detachment*, Japanese Studies in World War II, 36, I, 10–11; Naval Invasion of Eastern New Guinea, Japanese Studies in World War II, 101.

Area. This time he used two carriers, the *Lexington* and the *Yorktown*, supported by more cruisers and destroyers plus elements of the ANZAC force. These vessels sortied northward toward Rabaul early in March, too late to intercept the convoys headed for Lae and Salamaua. But they were not too late to do damage, and on 10 March, from positions in the Gulf of Papua, the carriers sent their planes aloft toward Huon Gulf. The strike apparently came as a complete surprise to the Japanese, who lost four vessels sunk, three more damaged, and almost 400 men killed and wounded. Next day the B–17's from Townsville came over Lae and Salamaua, but with less effect. That attack marked the last serious effort made during this period against the Japanese, who by this time had brought aircraft into the area and declared it secure. They were now within 170 air miles of Port Moresby.[49]

Operations against Port Moresby and Tulagi, which the Japanese intended to use as air bases, were to have begun immediately after the capture of Lae and Salamaua, according to the 29 January directive from *Imperial General Headquarters.* But by the time those bases had been taken more than a month later, Admiral Inouye had revised his view of the seriousness of the next step. His original plan had been based on the assumption that the Allies would be unable to bring air power to the target and that therefore he would need only the long-range planes from Rabaul as support. In view of what had happened since 20 February, and the growing strength of Allied air power in Australia, that assumption was no longer valid. The seizure of Port Moresby and Tulagi would be far riskier than anticipated, Inouye concluded, and would require carrier support. But the carriers that he needed were no longer available, for the striking force of the *Combined Fleet* with five carriers and four battleships was making ready for a raid against Ceylon, scheduled for early April. Admiral Inouye had no choice, therefore, but to await the return of the fleet from the Indian Ocean. In the interim he consolidated his position in the Bismarck Archipelago and advanced into the northern Solomons — to the Shortland Islands and Bougainville.[50]

Meanwhile in Tokyo the question of an invasion of Australia had come up again. The Navy pushed more vigorously for its plan this time, arguing that the U. S. Fleet would be unable to take offensive action in the western Pacific until the end of 1942. In the meantime, the naval planners warned, the Allies were pouring airplanes, men, and supplies into Australia and converting it into a base for offensive operations. The Army's desire to consolidate along the original perimeter and concentrate on the war in China and preparations for a possible attack by Soviet Russia, the naval planners argued, constituted a defensive and negative policy. "Such a policy," asserted Yamamoto's chief of staff, "would in effect render futile all our military successes" and put Japan "in the position of waiting for her enemies to attack without any special ad-

---

[49] Morison, *The Rising Sun in the Pacific,* p. 387; *Early Raids in the Pacific,* ONI Combat Narrative, pp. 57–68; Hist of *South Seas Detachment,* Japanese Studies in World War II, 36, I, 11–12.

[50] Japanese Opns in SWPA, ch. V, p. 10; Southeast Area Naval Opns, Japanese Studies in World War II, 48, I, pp. 1–2; Hist of *South Seas Detachment,* Japanese Studies in World War II, 36, p. 8.

vantage to herself. . . ."[51] The wisest course, therefore, was to continue on the offensive, with Australia as the ultimate objective.

The Army remained adamant in its opposition to this plan. Its original conception of operations in the Southwest Pacific had been defensive and the Navy's proposal for an aggressive policy in that area was alarming. Army forces, already widely scattered throughout the Netherlands Indies, Malaya, Burma, Indochina, the Philippines, and elsewhere, would have to be spread dangerously thin if Japan embarked on new and costly adventures. Moreover, the fear of Russia, which had dictated the time of attack and the speed of the advance, had not abated and the Army was anxious to adhere to the original plan to deploy its forces to the north. All these considerations, plus the size of the force required and the difficulties of supplying and maintaining this force, convinced the Army that the invasion of Australia was a "ridiculous operation."[52]

The outcome of this debate, which lasted through March and April, was a compromise plan, approved on 28 April, to cut the line of communications and isolate Australia. Under this plan, the long-deferred Port Moresby and Tulagi operation would be speedily concluded and would be followed by the occupation of important points in New Caledonia, the Fijis, and Samoa. From these newly acquired bases, Japanese aircraft and submarines could interrupt if not cut off entirely the flow of weapons, men, and supplies to Australia and prevent the development on that continent of a base for an Allied counteroffensive. Obviously this was a compromise which favored the Navy point of view.[53]

Preparations for the Tulagi and Port Moresby invasions were already complete when *Imperial General Headquarters* issued its new plan on 28 April. The *South Seas Detachment* and the naval landing troops of the *4th Fleet* were standing by, ready to embark; three days earlier Rabaul-based bombers had begun to strike northeast Australia. D-day for Tulagi was set for 3 May; for Port Moresby, a week later. On 29 April the *5th Carrier Division* (two carriers) and the *5th Cruiser Division* reached Truk. At long last, Admiral Inouye could begin the Port Moresby operation.

On 4 May, the day after Inouye moved his headquarters from Truk to Rabaul and a naval force landed at Tulagi, the Port Moresby invasion force set sail. Already the joint staff in Tokyo was making plans for the invasion of New Caledonia, the Fijis, and Samoa.

Pacific Build-up

At the same time the Japanese were heatedly debating their future course, the American planners in Washington were reviewing the twin problems of strategy and deployment in the Pacific in the light of the decision to make the main effort against Germany. Despite every effort to halt the movement of troops, planes, and weapons to the Pacific and every argument that these movements and the precious shipping they

---

[51] Private Papers of Rear Adm Mutome Ugaki, quoted in Japanese Opns in SWPA, ch. V, p. 11, n. 30; Hist of *Army Sec, Imperial GHQ*, Japanese Studies in World War II, 72, pp. 45–50.

[52] Hist of *Army Sec, Imperial GHQ*, p. 50; Japanese Opns in the SWPA, ch. V, pp. 11–13.

[53] Hist of *Army Sec, Imperial GHQ*, pp. 50–51; Arisue Questionnaire, pp. 28–29; Deposition of Shinichi Tanaka, IMTFE Exhibit 2676.

consumed were in violation of the accepted strategy, this flow continued and even increased. And with each shipment of troops came increased demands for additional troops, for more planes, and for supplies.

No one could deny the necessity that created these demands. The Japanese were not pursuing a plan that fitted into the Allied blueprint, and it was the Japanese advance, not Allied strategy, which dictated what must be done. But the mounting drain of the Pacific war on the limited resources of the Allies could, by the end of February, no longer be ignored. "Through a combination of circumstances," observed General Eisenhower, the Chief of the War Plans Division, "we are being drawn into a deployment in the Southwest Pacific that far exceeds original planning objectives and which in the absence of powerful air and naval forces . . . is not warranted."[54]

The immediate occasion for a review of the entire problem by the staff in Washington was the demand from almost every quarter for planes and more planes. Aircraft, especially heavy bombers, were, after shipping, perhaps the most critical of the Allied resources. The Australians wanted about 200 P–40's to meet the threat to Port Moresby; the New Zealanders asked for bombers for the protection of the Fijis; Admiral Leary needed a squadron of B–17's for his ANZAC force; and the Dutch, who were making ready for a last-ditch defense of Java, pressed hard for 72 fighters.[55]

In addition to these requests, there were other demands to be met by the Army. Its obligation in Hawaii had not been fulfilled, and there was from Admiral King a request that the Army furnish garrisons for two more islands in the South Pacific—Tongatabu in the Tonga Group, southeast of the Fijis, and Efate in the New Hebrides, between New Caledonia and the Solomons. The first would provide protection for the southern route from Samoa to Australia, the second an outpost for the defense of New Caledonia and the Fijis. "The Navy," complained General Eisenhower, "wants to take all the islands in the Pacific—have them held by Army troops, to become bases for Army pursuit and bombers. Then! the Navy will have a safe place to sail its vessels."[56]

Eisenhower's comment was indicative of a difference in view between the Army and Navy over the importance of the Pacific and the priority it should enjoy in the constant struggle for men and matériel. The Army planners recognized fully the importance of Australia and the line of communications but considered their retention as desirable rather than vital operations. Their support should be accomplished, they believed, with a minimum of effort, and priority should go to Europe to make possible an early offensive against Germany. "We've got to go to Europe and fight," wrote Eisenhower, "we've got to quit wasting resources all over the world—and still worse—wasting time."[57]

For the Navy, with its traditional in-

---

[54] Memo, Eisenhower for Marshall, 28 Feb 42, sub: Strategic Conceptions, OPD 384 PTO sec. 1, case 11.

[55] The material in this section is treated fully in Hayes, The War Against Japan, ch. V, pp. 1–48; Matloff and Snell, Strategic Planning, 1941–42, pp. 156–64, 210–16, 221–27.

[56] Eisenhower Notations, 17 Feb 42, copy in OCMH; Memo, King, no addressee, 18 Feb 42, noted in Memo, Marshall for King, 24 Feb 42, sub: Garrison for Efate, OPD Exec Files.

[57] Eisenhower Notations, 22 Jan 42, copy in OCMH.

terest in the Pacific, that area held a greater importance than for the Army and its reinforcement had first priority. The safety of the line of communications was essential to the fleet and until the Japanese threat to the islands along that line had been met—and for the Navy this threat was still a very live one —the naval planners considered the Allied position in the Pacific precarious. They did not wish to abandon the efforts to launch an early offensive in Europe, but felt strongly that until the danger was over the Pacific should have first call on American resources. There were extremists on both sides, too, some who were willing to risk the loss of the Southwest Pacific for the advantage of an early offensive against Germany, and others who would concentrate entirely on the Pacific, even if it meant the abandonment, for the time being, of the Atlantic theater.[58]

Despite this difference, Admiral King finally secured the garrisons he wanted for Efate and Tongatabu. For the former the Army furnished a reinforced infantry regiment, the 24th, numbering about 5,000 men, and the Navy the aircraft and artillery (both Marine). This force arrived early in May to relieve the small detachment Patch had sent up from New Caledonia to guard this important outpost. Later, a portion of the Efate garrison moved up to Espiritu Santo to build a bomber strip there. The Tongatabu garrison, composed of an infantry regiment (less one battalion), a regiment of antiaircraft artillery, and a pursuit squadron, plus a naval contingent, amounted to 8,200 men. It reached its destination on 14 May and began work

immediately to construct a naval base and airfield. Like the Bora Bora force, which it greatly resembled, it was assembled and loaded in haste and paid the penalty in the difficulties it met when it began to debark.[59]

Meanwhile the review of strategy and deployment, which had begun on 11 February with a directive from the Combined Chiefs, had almost run its course. The results were far from conclusive. About all the planners could agree on after a month of intensive study was a recommendation that the Joint Chiefs decide immediately "on a clear course of action," and then follow that course "with the utmost vigor." They did, however, suggest three possibilities, each representing substantially a view held at the outset of the debate, for the Joint Chiefs to choose from, thus leaving to their superiors the decision they were themselves unable to make. The Chiefs made their choice two days later, on 16 March. The United States, they then agreed, should assemble in the United Kingdom the forces needed for an offensive "at the earliest practicable time," and provide for the Pacific only those forces allocated under "current commitments." This meant, in effect, that the Joint Chiefs would thereafter test the demands from the Pacific against the needs of the European theater and the priority of operations there.[60]

---

[58] For these views and others, see the JPS 2 series, ABC 370 (1–28–42).

[59] Memos, Marshall for King, 24 Feb 42, sub: Garrisons for Efate; King for JCS, 2 Mar 42, sub: Defense of Tongatabu and Efate, ABC 381 (3–2–42).

[60] JPS 2/1 Directive to JUSSC, 11 Feb 42; Mins, CCS Mtg, 10 Feb 42; JPS 2/2, Review of Strategic Situation in Japanese Theater, 18 Feb 42, with minority report JPS 2/2 (A); Mins, JPS Mtgs, 19, 21, 24 Feb 42; JPS 2/4 (D) Strategic Deployment, 24 Feb 42; JPS 2/5 and 2/6, same title, 6 Mar 42; JCS 23, same title, 14 Mar 42; Mins, JCS Mtg, 16 Mar 42. All in ABC 370 (1–28–42) and CCS 281 (1–30–42).

This policy had hardly been formulated when it became necessary to depart from it. On 5 March, when the situation in the Middle East appeared critical, Winston Churchill had asked Roosevelt if the United States would, among other things, send a division to Australia and one to New Zealand. In this way he hoped to retain in the Middle East those troops the Dominions wanted brought home for their own protection. After consulting his military advisers, Roosevelt agreed to the Prime Minister's proposal, subject to approval by the Australian and New Zealand Governments. The Australians, who had correctly diagnosed the Japanese plan to take Port Moresby and cut the line of communications, accepted this arrangement as a temporary solution to their difficulties. The War Department thereupon selected the 32d Division, already alerted for shipment to Ireland, for assignment to Australia. It would arrive in May, and, with the 41st, scheduled to leave within the month, would place two American divisions in the Southwest Pacific.[61]

For New Zealand the Army planners picked the 37th Division (Ohio National Guard). Already that division's 147th Infantry Regiment (less one battalion) had been sent to Tongatabu, and in mid-April an advance detachment of eighty men left for New Zealand. The division itself was scheduled to sail late the next month. But before it left the President precipitated another comprehensive review of deployment to the Pacific by raising the question early in April of the defenses of Fiji and New Caledonia, a review that led to a change in the destination of the 37th Division.

The discussions that followed the President's query made it clear that the differences which had split the planners before were still unresolved. The Navy, with a clear appreciation of Japanese intentions, persisted in its belief that the strength allocated to the Pacific, especially in aircraft, was inadequate to meet the danger there. The Army took a more optimistic view. While admitting the inadequacy of Allied air defenses in the Pacific, the Army planners asserted —at a time when the enemy was preparing to move to Port Moresby, Tulagi, New Caledonia, the Fijis, and Midway —that the danger in the Pacific was not great enough to warrant the diversion of aircraft from the planned major effort in Europe. Failure to reinforce the Pacific, Army planners admitted, involved risks, but such risks, they insisted, must be taken in order to move against Germany.

To these differing views were now added those of General MacArthur, recently arrived in Australia, reinforced by the representations of the Dominion governments. The second front, MacArthur held, should be in the Pacific. Not only would an offensive there aid Russia by releasing the forces held down in Manchuria, he argued, but it would also protect Australia and India and have the enthusiastic support of the American people.[62] This proposal and

---

[61] Memo, WPD for CofS, 5 Mar 42, sub: Answer to Prime Minister, OPD Exec Files; CCS 56 and 56/1, Prime Minister Msg, 5 and 6 Mar 42, ABC 311.5 (1–30–42); Rad, Marshall to MacArthur, No. 739, 18 Mar 42, OPD MacArthur File.

[62] Rad, MacArthur to Marshall, No. 176, 8 May 42, CM–IN 2333; Memo, Capt John L. McCrea, naval aide to President, to JCS, 2 Apr 42, with JPS 21 ser., ABC 381 (1–22–42) Pacific Bases. The views of the Army and Navy planners can be found in the same file. Mins, JPS Mtgs, 4 and 6 Apr 42.

others like it all added up to a strong plea for priority in the Pacific.

The month-long debate that ensued raised sharply the entire question of strategy in the Pacific and its relation to the war against Germany. On the assumption that Japanese forces were capable of attacking the line of communications and that their next move would be in that direction, the Navy wished to strengthen each of the bases along that line with bombers and fighters. Mobile forces in Hawaii and Australia, the naval planners believed, would be unable to concentrate at the point of attack in time to prevent an enemy landing. The Navy had another reason for wanting to build up the forces along the line of communications. Already it was planning to use these islands as bases for offensive operations and for the support of the fleet. "Given the naval forces, air units and amphibious forces," Admiral King told the President, "we can drive northwestward from the New Hebrides into the Solomons and the Bismarck Archipelago after the same fashion of step by step advances that the Japanese used in the South China Sea." [63]

The position taken by the Army and Air Force planners was that the area should be defended by mobile forces, with bombers based on the flanks, in Australia and Hawaii. There would thus be no necessity to pin down large forces on each of the islands. The line of communications, it was true, lacked defense in depth but that was preferable, the Army planners believed, to scattering the bombers needed for the projected air offensive against Germany. [64]

MacArthur went even further than the Navy in his demands on Allied resources. Not only did he want reinforcements to hold his present position and a 100 percent increase in aircraft but also the forces required to conduct operations northward from Australia—three more divisions and aircraft carriers. In Washington there was no intention of undertaking the kind of campaign MacArthur contemplated, which consisted esentially of an active and aggressive defense from Port Moresby rather than Australia itself. His requests, therefore, were politely but firmly denied. But MacArthur was not one to accept defeat easily and with Prime Minister Curtin's support continued to press for reinforcements through other channels. Though this procedure brought him a reprimand—which the President softened by a gracious letter—it also brought the problem forcibly to the attention of the highest authority. [65]

Plans for war against Germany had by early May created heavy requirements for men and matériel in the European theater that threatened to put a strong brake on Pacific deployment. In mid-April at a conference in London between American and British representatives, it had been agreed, largely at American insistence, that the Allies would begin planning immediately for an invasion of the Continent in 1943 (ROUNDUP). It was recognized, however, that action against Germany might have to be under-

---

[63] Memo, King for President, 5 Mar 42, no sub, OPD Exec Files.

[64] JPS 21/7, Defense of Island Bases, 18 Apr 42, and attached OPD Notes on JPS 13th Mtg, 22 Apr 42, ABC (1-22-42 sec. 2) Pacific Bases.

[65] Rads, Marshall to MacArthur, Nos. 739 and 1499, 18 Mar and 26 Apr 42, OPD MacArthur File; MacArthur to Marshall, Nos. 70470 and 588, 4 and 25 Apr and 1 May 42, CM-IN-6643 and 0186; Marshall to MacArthur, No. 31, 6 May 42, CM-OUT-1136; MacArthur to Marshall, No. 176, 8 May 42, CM-IN-2333.

taken earlier in the event of disastrous Soviet reverses or some unexpected favorable development that would present the Allies with an opportunity to exploit a weakness in the German position. To meet such a possibility, the Allies agreed on a contingency operation for the invasion of the Continent in the fall of 1942 (SLEDGEHAMMER), by which time Pacific deployment would be largely completed. Forces for the invasion in 1943 would be assembled in the British Isles on a schedule, worked out in great detail after the London Conference, that would place sufficient forces in Britain in time to meet the requirements of an emergency operation in the fall of 1942 should that prove necessary or desirable. This build-up in the British Isles, which was known by the code name BOLERO, became the basis for the planned deployment of forces to Europe.[66]

The competing demands of Europe and the Pacific came into sharp conflict early in May, after the President had expressed a desire, presumably in response to pressure from the Australian Prime Minister, to raise the number of ground troops planned for Australia from 25,000 to 100,000.[67] This proposal created serious concern among the Army planners, and General Marshall, immediately on his return from a tour of inspection, protested directly to the President, pointing out that this diversion from BOLERO would imperil the plans so recently made for the invasion

of the Continent.[68] On 4 May, the entire problem was discussed at a meeting of the Joint Chiefs of Staff. General Marshall held firmly to the position already stated by the Army planners that any increase in the forces already allotted to the Pacific would make BOLERO impossible. The Joint Chiefs, he asserted, must therefore stoutly resist all demands from that theater, no matter how legitimate. Admiral King argued strongly against this view. Without denying the desirability of an early offensive in Europe, he insisted that the reinforcement of the Pacific was fully as important as BOLERO, and more urgent. "We must not permit diversion of our forces to any proposed operation in any other theater," he argued, "to the extent that we find ourselves unable to fulfill our obligation to implement our basic strategic plan in the Pacific theater." This strategy he stated simply as holding "what we have against any attack" the Japanese could launch.[69] The implications of such a strategy were clear.

Unable to reach agreement, the Joint Chiefs could only refer the matter to the President himself for decision, and on 6 May General Marshall, after outlining his own and King's position, asked the Commander in Chief in effect to make the choice. The answer came two days later: "I do not want 'BOLERO' slowed down."[70] The issue had finally been decided in favor of the Army.

---

[66] For a full discussion of the London Conference and the planning that followed, see Matloff and Snell, *Strategic Planning, 1941–42,* pp. 183–91, *passim,* and Leighton and Coakley, *Global Logistics and Strategy,* ch. XIV.

[67] Memo, McCrea for JCS, 1 May 42, sub: Aircraft and Troops for Australia, OPD Exec Files.

[68] Memo, CofS for President, 4 May 42, no sub, OPD Exec Files.

[69] Memo, King for JCS, 4 May 42, sub: Defense of Island Bases, JCS 48, app, to JCS Mins of that date.

[70] Memo, President for Marshall, 6 May 42, no sub; CofS for President, same date, sub: Pacific Theater vs BOLERO, JCS 48, ABC 381 (1–22–42) sec. 2 Pacific Bases.

Though the President's decision meant that the Navy and General MacArthur would have to shelve, temporarily at least, their plans for offensive operations and a strong defense in depth, it did not halt the movement of troops and planes to the Pacific. Rather, it speeded up these movements, for the Army, having won the victory, was anxious to meet its commitments promptly. "Since we have won our point," Eisenhower wrote General Arnold on 8 May, "it is my opinion we should reach and maintain the amounts indicated . . . as quickly as possible." Arnold agreed and listed the number of planes he expected to have in the Pacific by 1 July.[71]

This determination to bring the forces in the Pacific to their authorized strength did not solve all the problems that had been raised during the course of the debate. One of these was the defense of the Fijis, then garrisoned by New Zealand troops and an American pursuit squadron. It was General Marshall who proposed a solution which would meet the need for stronger forces in the Fijis without requiring additional troops. The 37th Division, which had been promised to New Zealand in return for the retention of the Dominion's troops in the Middle East, could be sent instead to the Fijis, Marshall suggested, thus releasing almost 10,000 New Zealand troops for the defense of the Dominion. Admiral King raised no objections to this proposal and it was quickly adopted by the Joint Chiefs and approved by the President. The New Zealand Government accepted this arrangement, too, in return for an agreement that the United States would assume strategic responsibility for the defense of the Fijis. Orders for the 37th Division were hurriedly changed, and early in June the first detachment landed at Suva. Since it had proved impossible to collect in so short a time the additional troops required for a balanced garrison force, the rest of the 37th went on to New Zealand where an Army port detachment had already gone to handle its debarkation.[72]

New Zealand's demands had been satisfied without altering the basic strategy but there was no way of meeting the demands from Australia without abandoning or delaying BOLERO. All of Mr. Curtin's appeals to Washington and London, and MacArthur's requests to the War Department came up against the hard fact that the planners did not believe Australia was in imminent danger of invasion or that the time had come for offensive operations in that theater. The best that Churchill and Roosevelt could offer was admiration for the aggressive spirit which prompted the requests for troops and assurances of support if a real threat developed. Meanwhile, the President told MacArthur, every effort would be made to send him "all the air strength we possibly can." To do more, as Marshall had pointed out, would make the Southwest Pacific the principal theater of operations. MacArthur would have to do with what he had, at least for the present.[73]

Though the President's decision of 8

---

[71] Memos, Eisenhower for Arnold, 8 May 42, no sub, OPD 381 case 62; Arnold for Eisenhower, 14 May 42, no sub, OPD 381 PTO, case 21.

[72] Mins, JCS Mtg, 4 May 42; Joint Army-Navy Plan for Fijis, 13 May 42; Memo, COMINCH for N. Z. Minister, 9 May 42, same sub, both in OPD 381 Fiji. See also Leighton and Coakley, *Global Logistics and Strategy*, p. 178.

[73] Rad, MacArthur to Marshall, 3 May 42, CM–IN–0667; Ltr, Marshall to Dill, 22 May 42, OPD Exec Files; Milner, *Victory in Papua*, pp. 29–32.

TABLE 4—ARMY STRENGTH IN PACIFIC, APRIL 1942[a]

Base	Present		En Route		Projected	
	Ground	Air	Ground	Air	Ground	Air
Totals_____	102,920	29,760	37,700	------------	231,060	44,140
Hawaii_____	62,700	8,900	7,300	------------	100,000	15,000
Christmas_____	1,700	320	------------	------------	1,700	490
Bora Bora_____	3,850	------------	------------	------------	3,850	------------
Canton_____	1,300	40	------------	------------	1,300	50
Fijis_____	10	700	------------	------------	15,000	720
Australia_____	16,900	17,100	30,400	------------	60,000	24,000
New Caledonia_____	16,000	2,000	------------	------------	23,000	2,500
Suva_____	10	700	------------	------------	10	720
Tongatabu_____	0	0	------------	------------	6,300	660
New Zealand_____	0	0	------------	------------	15,000	0
Efate_____	450	0	------------	------------	4,900	0

[a]Excludes strength in Philippines where forces surrendered in May 1942.

Source: Adapted from Chart 2, Matloff and Snell, Strategic Planning, 1941–42.

May, made two days after the Port Moresby invasion force had left Rabaul, had eased temporarily the heavy drain of the Pacific on Allied resources, it was, in a sense, a tribute to the enormous progress made by the Army and Navy under the most adverse conditions in building up the defenses of the Pacific in the short period of five months. At the start of the war, the United States had in the Pacific only two garrisons of any size, Hawaii and the Philippines. By the beginning of May, despite defeat and disaster and the decision to concentrate on the war in Europe, Hawaii had been considerably reinforced, the defenses of Australia and New Zealand bolstered with American ground troops and aircraft, and a chain of island bases established along the line of communications. In the area, or scheduled soon to arrive, were over 250,000 Army ground and air troops (exclusive of the Philippine garrison). Ground forces included six divisions and Task Force 6184, soon to be organized into the Americal Division, the equivalent of almost three separate infantry regiments, a large number of coast and antiaircraft artillery units, and service troops of all types. (Table 4) Each of the island bases had at least one pursuit squadron, but most of the air as well as the ground strength in the Pacific was concentrated in Australia and Hawaii. The former had 41 heavy bombers, 150 light and medium bombers, and about 475 fighters; the latter about 30 heavy bombers and considerably fewer aircraft of other types. Both were still short of the authorized goals, especially in heavy bombers. This weakness constituted the main complaint of the Navy and was to be one of the chief problems in the Pacific in the months to come.

CHAPTER X

The U.S. and Japanese High Commands

An army is of little value in the field unless there are wise counsels at home.
CICERO

During the early months of the war, while the Japanese tide of victory was flowing strong, the Allies had already begun to look to the future. Though the effort to defend the Malay Barrier had failed, the Allies had hurriedly sent reinforcements to hold Australia, Hawaii, and the island chain across the Pacific. Already, plans were maturing to build a base in Australia and to develop air and naval bases along the line of communications. It was still too early to predict the course of operations once the Allies were in a position to take the initiative, but it was not too soon to prepare for that time. Thus, while bases were being established and forces deployed to the Pacific, the Allies began to organize for the offensive ahead.

The first step in preparing for an offensive was to develop an Allied organization to co-ordinate the efforts of the Allies, and within this framework to devise a mechanism for planning and co-ordinating operations on many fronts. In this the British had the advantage of an early start, and a combined staff was quickly formed. The American counterpart of this organization, the Joint Chiefs of Staff, took shape more slowly. Utilizing existing organizations and staffs, the Americans developed during the months after Pearl Harbor a mechanism for directing the U.S. war effort that lasted, with modifications, until the end of the war. For the Pacific, which was to become an area of U.S. responsibility, this Washington organization became in effect a supreme command.

The organization of the Japanese military high command, perfected before the war, was, on the surface, not unlike that of the United States. The commander in chief of the Japanese armed forces was the head of the state, the Emperor. Under him was *Imperial General Headquarters* with its Army and Navy Sections—there was no separate air service —which prepared and co-ordinated the operations of forces in the field. The Army and Navy Ministers sat in the Cabinet and civilian agencies directed the war effort on the home front. But this organization, superficially so similar to the American, could not conceal the fact that Japan was a military dictatorship in which the civilian officials exercised little real authority and the Emperor was but a symbol.

The Washington Command Post

At the ARCADIA Conference in Washington, it will be recalled, the first steps had been taken toward establishment of a combined U.S.–British organization for the conduct of the war.[1] It had been decided then that the Combined Chiefs of Staff would be located in Washington, where the British Chiefs would be represented by a Joint Staff Mission. During the months that followed the combined organization began to take shape and the functions of the Combined Chiefs were more clearly delineated. By the early summer of 1942 this process was largely completed.

The American side of the Allied high command developed more slowly. The old Joint Board with its Joint Planning Committee had neither the authority nor the organization to meet the challenges of global war (or of the British committee system), and it gave way gradually to the emergent Joint Chiefs of Staff. Membership in the two bodies, though similar, was not identical. The former had consisted of the service chiefs, their deputies, and the heads of the War Plans Division and air arms of the two services. Since December 1941, Admiral King as commander of the U.S. Fleet, though not a member, had also sat with the Joint Board, whose presiding officer at the time was the Chief of Naval Operations, Admiral Stark. During the ARCADIA meeting the term U.S. Chiefs of Staff, employed to designate a group comparable to the British Chiefs, had referred to four men—Admiral Stark, General Marshall, Admiral King, and General Arnold. The last two were not chiefs of a service and one of them was not even a member of the Joint Board, but their inclusion was considered necessary to balance the British representation.

Within the next few months, the membership of the Joint Chiefs, which was established on 9 February, was re-examined and took final form. General Marshall's position was not affected, except that as a result of the reorganization of the War Department in March 1942 his authority as Chief of Staff, U.S. Army, was enhanced. General Arnold's position as commander of the newly formed semiautonomous Army Air Forces also increased his stature in the Joint Chiefs, although he remained Marshall's subordinate and thus not in the same position in combined councils as the British air chief who was head of a separate service.

The Navy also underwent reorganization in March designed to streamline it for the war ahead. One of the effects of this reorganization was to consolidate the functions of the Chief of Naval Operations and Commander in Chief, United States Fleet, and at Admiral Stark's behest Admiral King was placed in supreme command of all professional activities of the Navy.[2] This change was formally recognized in an Executive Order of 12 March which assigned King to both commands, designated him as the principal naval adviser to the President, and gave him a greater degree of control over the bureaus than had ever been exercised by any Chief of Naval Operations.[3] In addition, he was given two strong assistants, a Vice Chief of Naval Operations, and a Deputy Commander for the U.S. Fleet.

The effects of these moves, though

---

[1] See above, pp. 164–66.

[2] Davis, Origins of JCS and CCS, I, 350–51.

[3] Admiral Stark was relieved as Chief of Naval Operations on 26 March 1942 and appointed Commander, U.S. Naval Forces, Europe.

they greatly increased the authority of the Chiefs within their services, was to reduce the membership of the Joint Chiefs by one. But already a move was under way to add another, one who would represent the President much as Maj. Gen. Sir Hastings Ismay represented Churchill on the British Chiefs, and because he represented no service, could serve as an impartial chairman. The President, at first cool to the idea, was finally convinced of the advantages of such an arrangement and on Marshall's suggestion designated Admiral William D. Leahy as his own chief of staff.[4] No appointment could have been better calculated to add weight to the Joint Chiefs and to cement relations with the White House. Admiral Leahy, after serving as Chief of Naval Operations, had retired from the Navy in August 1939. Since then he had served as Governor of Puerto Rico and Ambassador to the French Government at Vichy. In June 1942, he returned to the United States, and on 18 July was recalled to active duty and designated Chief of Staff to the Commander in Chief—a post without precedent in American history. With this appointment, the membership of the Joint Chiefs of Staff was fixed for the duration of the war.

The charter of the Combined Chiefs approved at ARCADIA had specifically provided for a planning staff, the Combined Staff Planners, and had even named the officers who would compose that body.[5]

The senior members on the American side, the Joint Staff Planners (JPS), were Brig. Gen. Leonard T. Gerow and Rear Adm. Richmond K. Turner, Chiefs of the Army and Navy War Plans Division—both members of the Joint Board and, simultaneously, of that agency's Joint Planning Committee. In this latter capacity, they directed the work of the Joint Strategic Committee, composed of at least three officers from each of the War Plans Divisions, whose task it was to work on joint war plans, and of various ad hoc committees formed to study other problems as they arose. It was natural that this organization should be taken over bodily by the Joint Chiefs, and for a time it served both bodies equally.

This system had its disadvantages, and membership of the Joint Staff Planners was soon changed. The Navy kept its chief planner, Admiral Turner, on the committee, but gave him two assistants, one of them an air officer. Probably because of the heavier burdens of the Chief of the Army's War Plans Division, Gerow's successor, General Eisenhower, designated the head of the division's Strategy and Policy Group, Col. Thomas T. Handy, as the Army member of the Joint Staff Planners instead of assuming the post himself.[6] The air representative

---

[4] For an account of this appointment, see Davis, Origins of JCS and CCS, pp. 378–85; William D. Leahy, *I Was There* (New York: Whittlesey House, 1950), pp. 96–97; Ltr, Secy of War to President, 20 Mar 42, WDCSA 032.

[5] U.S. ABC–4/CS4, 14 Jan 42, sub: Post-ARCADIA Collaboration. This description of the joint organ-

ization for planning is based upon Davis, Origins of JCS and CCS, pp. 324–85, and its sequel, vol. II in Hist of JCS Organization in World War II, Development of the JCS Committee Structure, pp. 386–590; Ray S. Cline, *Washington Command Post: The Operations Division* UNITED STATES ARMY IN WORLD WAR II (Washington, 1951), chs. VI and VIII; Craven and Cate, *AAF* 1, pp. 251–56.

[6] Admiral Turner was replaced as chief naval planner by Rear Adm. Charles M. Cooke, Jr., in June when Turner left to command the South Pacific Amphibious Force. General Handy's successor was Brig. Gen. Albert C. Wedemeyer.

JOINT CHIEFS OF STAFF. *From left: Admiral King, General Marshall, Admiral Leahy, and General Arnold.*

initially was Maj. Gen. Carl Spaatz, and, after the March reorganization of the War Department, the Assistant Chief of Staff for Plans of the new Army Air Force. Other members were added from time to time—an additional member in August to even the Army and Navy representation, and then seven more members with varying status to represent logistical interests. Clearly this was not a committee of equals. The senior Army and Navy planners were its leading members and by virtue of seniority, official position, and access to the chiefs of their services their views were generally binding on the other members of the committee.

The work of the Joint Staff Planners was broad and varied, ranging from global strategy to the allocation of minor items of supply and encompassing not only strategic but also operational, logistic, and administrative aspects. Obvi-

ously, the group was too unwieldy and too diverse in its composition to handle all the problems that came before it. Most of its work was farmed out to subordinate committees, the two senior members controlling the assignments. Most of these subcommittees were *ad hoc*, formed for a particular task and composed of planning officers and staff experts drawn from the two services by the chief Army and Navy planners. Only the Joint Strategic Committee, which had been taken over from the Joint Board and redesignated the Joint U.S. Strategic Committee (JUSSC), had a recognized status and membership as the working group for the Joint Planners. Assigned to it full time were eight senior and highly qualified officers, four each from the Army and the Navy War Plans Divisions. One of the Army representatives was an Air Forces officer and the Navy's contingent usually included a

Marine officer. The committee's charter, as defined by the Joint Chiefs, called upon it to "prepare such strategical estimates, studies and plans" as the JPS directed, and, in addition, to initiate studies at its own discretion.[7] It was natural, therefore, for the Joint Staff Planners to rely heavily on the JUSSC, especially in the field of broad strategy, and to invite its members to sit with them from time to time.

The role of the JUSSC in planning proved to be quite different from that envisaged by those of its members who placed somewhat more emphasis on their strategic responsibilities than did their superiors. Much of the committee's work proved to be routine, concerned with relatively minor matters, and so heavy was the load that it had no time left to study problems it considered more important in the conduct of the war. Moreover, some of its members thought it would be more appropriately and profitably employed in the study of future strategy than in routine matters of troop deployment, production priorities shipping schedules, and the like.[8]

There was much merit in this view. Certainly there was a need for long-range studies, for a group of senior and experienced Army and Navy planners, free from the burdens of day-to-day problems, who would devote their time to the larger issues of the war, to future strategy and political-military questions. But who was best qualified to advise the Joint Chiefs on these high-level matters? One view was that this should be done by a reconstituted JUSSC reporting directly to the Joint Chiefs and consisting of four flag or general officers representing the Army, Navy, Army Air Forces, and the Navy air arm. Another proposal for utilizing the JUSSC more effectively in strategic planning was to reduce its membership to four senior officers with two assistants for each of its members and charge it with responsibility, under the Joint Staff Planners, for co-ordinating the preparation of plans in support of the basic strategy, reviewing these plans, and developing recommendations for changes in the basic strategy. If neither of these proposals was acceptable, then the JUSSC, said one of its members, ought to be redesignated the "Joint Working Committee" of the JPS in frank recognition of its present function.

The Joint Chiefs considered this problem very carefully over a period of several meetings in the fall of 1942. There was no disagreement with Marshall's assertion of the need for "an organization, with sufficient prestige and disassociated from current operations, which can obtain a good perspective by being allowed time for profound deliberations."[9] In his view, an entirely new organization should be created to meet this need. The possibility of using the deputy chiefs of the services for this purpose, an arrangement that would permit the Joint Chiefs to leave decisions on minor matters to the new committee, was discussed at some length. The solution finally adopted represented a combination of the various proposals. To satisfy the need for a

---

[7] JCS 14, 27 Feb 42, sub: Proposed Directive to JIC and JUSSC; Mins, JCS Mtg, 9 Mar 42.

[8] Memo, Col. Ray T. Maddocks for Handy, 9 Jul 42, sub: The JSSC, ABC 020 (13 Jul 42) sec. 3–J–A.

[9] Quoted in Davis, Development of the JCS Committee Structure, p. 553. These discussions are recorded in the JCS minutes of 20 and 27 October, 3 November, 8 and 10 December 1942.

high-level group of planners, the Joint Chiefs formed a new committee, called the Joint Strategic Survey Committee (JSSC)—not related to the JUSSC—consisting of three flag or general officers, assigned to full time duty. Reporting only to the Joint Chiefs, these officers would have no duties other than to reflect on basic strategy and the long-range implications of immediate events and decisions. No sources of information were to be denied them and they could, if they desired, attend any meeting of the Joint or Combined Chiefs of Staff and of Joint or Combined Staff Planners.[10]

This was to be truly a committee of "elder statesmen," and the appointments made fully bore out this intention of the Joint Chiefs. Representing the Army was Lt. Gen. Stanley D. Embick, who had been associated with strategic planning throughout a long and distinguished career. Vice Adm. Russell Willson represented the Navy, though he had to be relieved of his important duties as Deputy Commander in Chief, U.S. Fleet, to serve on the committee. The Army Air Forces member was Maj. Gen. Muir S. Fairchild, recognized as an officer of exceptional ability and breadth of view. With this membership, unchanged throughout the war, the Joint Strategic Survey Committee began its existence in November 1942.

The creation of the JSSC solved only one of the problems facing the Joint Chiefs. Still needed was a group that could act for them on minor matters and could represent them on various governmental bodies where military advice was required. The idea of a committee consisting of the Deputy Chiefs of Staff, originally proposed as an alternative to the JSSC, seemed an admirable solution to this problem. Thus came into existence the Joint Deputy Chiefs of Staff (JDCS), consisting initially of Lt. Gen. Joseph T. McNarney, Vice Adm. Frederick J. Horne, and Maj. Gen. George E. Stratemeyer.[11]

But the problem of the Joint U.S. Strategic Committee was still unresolved. The role the members of the committee had envisaged for themselves had now become the province of the elder statesmen of the Joint Strategic Survey Committee. Moreover, the former had been engaged since August 1942 on future strategy for the defeat of Japan. In addition, it was directed late in November to prepare a long-range study for the employment of United Nations forces for the defeat of both Germany and Japan, to be coordinated with British studies on the same problem. Since the Joint Strategic Survey Committee was engaged in similar studies, the need for a review of the duties of the JUSSC was more urgent than ever. Various proposals had been put forward, but by the end of 1942 no change had been made. When it came in May 1943, it was accompanied by a reorganization of the entire JCS structure.[12]

The work of the Joint Chiefs was supported by a variety of other committees, some of which functioned purely in a joint capacity and some as the U.S. component of committees of the Combined Chiefs. Intelligence activities were under

---

[10] JCS 149/D, 7 Nov 42, sub: Charter of the JSSC. The charter authorized four members, two from the Army and two from the Navy, but the Navy never named a fourth member.

[11] JCS 164/D, 11 Dec 42, sub: Functions of the JDCS.
[12] See below, p. 455.

the purview of the Joint Intelligence Committee (JIC), which had been taken over from the Joint Board at the same time as the JUSSC. In recognition of the role of psychological warfare in modern war, a separate committee (JPWC) was formed to advise the Joint Chiefs on this subject. The Office of Strategic Services was also a part of the joint committee system, directly responsible for certain matters to the Joint Chiefs and for others to the JIC and the JPWC. Additional committees advised on communications, weather, new weapons and equipment, and transportation. *(Chart 3)*

Within the War Department, strategic planning and the co-ordination of military operations were centered in the Operations Division of the General Staff, successor to the old War Plans Division whose functions it absorbed in March 1942. In a very real sense, the Operations Division was General Marshall's command post, the agency through which he exercised control over and co-ordinated the vast activities of the Army in World War II. All strategic planning in the War Department was done within the Operations Division, or funneled through it, and its officers represented the Army on virtually every major combined and joint committee. Any matters that might affect strategy or operations came to it, and its roster included logisticians as well as ground and air officers. So varied were its functions that General Wedemeyer was able to inform a British officer of the Joint Staff Mission that "your Washington contact agency is now the Executive Officer, Operations Division, War Department General Staff. He will be able to refer you directly to the proper section for solution of any prob-

lems presented."[13] In effect, it was a general staff within the general staff.

The organization of the Operations Division was tailored closely to its duties and the needs of the Chief of Staff. Under Eisenhower, its chief from February to June 1942, it was organized into three major groups—planning, operations, and logistics—and an Executive Office. The first, called the Strategy and Policy Group, was the one most intimately concerned with joint and combined planning, and was responsible for matters of general strategy, the preparation of studies, plans, and estimates, and the issuance of directives for theater and task force commanders. Its chief was the Army member of the Joint Staff Planners and from it came the representatives of the JUSSC. It had a section that dealt with future operations only, another with strategy, and one with subjects that came up for discussion at the combined level.

The co-ordination of operations within the Operations Division was handled by the Theater (Operations) Group. This was the largest of the groups, and was organized ultimately into sections corresponding to the various theaters of operations and serving in effect as Washington echelons of these theater headquarters. It was this group that kept in close touch with theater problems, directed the movement of troops overseas, and co-ordinated all War Department activities relating to theater requirements. For Pacific matters there were two sections, the Pacific and the South-

[13] Ltr, Wedemeyer to Maj E. H. Baume, BJSM, 15 Jun 42, quoted in Cline, *Washington Command Post*, p. 122. This account of the Operations Division is drawn very largely from this volume, especially Chapter VIII.

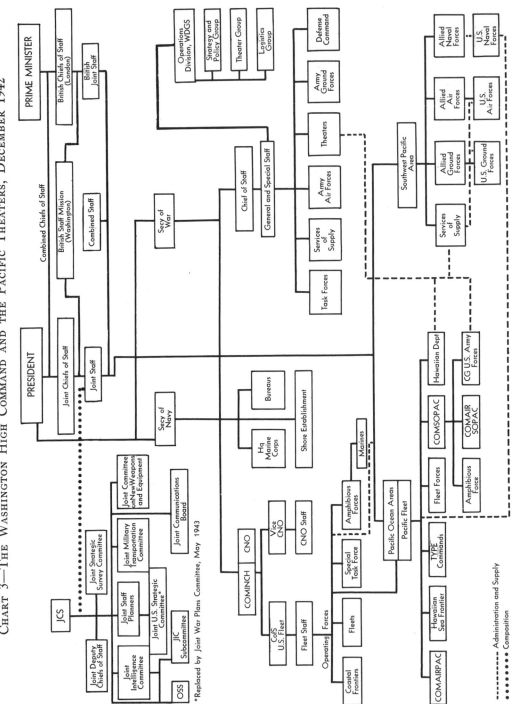

CHART 3—THE WASHINGTON HIGH COMMAND AND THE PACIFIC THEATERS, DECEMBER 1942

*Replaced by Joint War Plans Committee, May 1943

west Pacific Theater Sections, headed from mid-1942 to mid-1944 by Cols. Carl D. Silverthorne and William L. Ritchie. Both these officers made frequent trips to the theaters and were constantly called upon by the theater commanders and by the planners in Washington for assistance and advice on theater problems.

In recognition of the intimate relationship between logistics and strategy, and the dependence of operations on manpower, weapons, equipment, and transportation, the Operations Division had a Logistics Group. This group did not participate in logistical planning or in the manifold activities related to supply of Army forces; these were the functions of G–4 and of the Army Service Forces under General Somervell. What it did instead was to view these matters from the strategic level in order to advise General Marshall on their implications when decision by the Chief of Staff became necessary. It was in a unique position to do so because of its access to the planners and theater experts in the division, and its members represented the Army on a variety of committees, both military and civilian.

The Navy Department organization for strategic planning and direction of operations was not as highly centralized as the War Department organization. The reason for this difference lay partly in Admiral King's dual status as Chief of Naval Operations (CNO) and Commander in Chief, United States Fleet (COMINCH). In the former capacity he was responsible for "the preparation, readiness and logistic support of the operating forces" of the Navy—its fleets, shore establishments, sea frontiers, and all seagoing forces. But as COMINCH,

in which capacity he was the supreme commander of all operating forces of the Navy, Admiral King was responsible for execution of the plans he helped to shape. To meet his dual responsibilities, King formed two separate staff organizations, each of which maintained its own planning office.[14]

In his role as CNO, Admiral King had ultimately six principal assistants, a Vice Chief of Naval Operations, a Sub Chief, a Deputy for Air Operations, and three assistant chiefs. One of these last officers was Director of the War Plans Division and the principal strategic adviser of the Chief of Naval Operations. This office, comparable in prewar days and in the first months of the war to the Army's War Plans Division, was responsible for the preparation of basic war plans, and of plans for the development and maintenance of naval forces for war. In prewar days, its director had been a member of the Joint Board, and its officers had represented the Navy on the Joint Planning Committee, the Aeronautical Board, and other joint groups. When war came most of its strategic planning functions were assumed by other offices. Finally in 1943, it was redesignated the Logistical Plans Division in recognition of the fact that its functions were limited to logistical planning and co-ordination. Thus, the Navy War Plans Division developed in a way quite different from the Army's War Plans Division and, instead of becoming a super general staff, diminished in importance to become ultimately an office under the Assistant Chief of Naval Operations for Logistic Plans.

---

[14] This account of naval organization is drawn principally from The National Archives, *Federal Records of World War II,* vol II, *Military Agencies* (Washington, 1951), pp. 571–602.

It was in his role as Commander in Chief, United States Fleet, that Admiral King performed most of his duties as a member of the Joint and Combined Chiefs. Thus, it was the fleet staff, under a Deputy Commander and Chief of Staff, that assumed most of the burdens of strategic planning and direction of naval operations. For each of these functions, planning and operations, there was a separate division—the Plans Division and the Operations Division. The last, as the name implies, was concerned with the operations of fleets and naval forces and kept a constant check on their organization, combat readiness, and movements. Through this division, Admiral King maintained close contact with his fleet and force commanders, both surface and air, and exercised control over their operations. In general, this office performed the same functions as the Theater Group of the Army's Operations Division but none of the other functions of that division.

The chief responsibility for strategic planning in the Navy resided in the Plans Division, Headquarters, Commander in Chief, United States Fleet. Like the Logistic Plans Division, CNO, it had its origins in the prewar War Plans Division, part of whose functions were transferred to the fleet staff in January 1942. When the two offices of CNO and COMINCH were combined in March 1942, the Plans Division was assigned additional responsibilities. Thus, it became the source for current and long-range strategic plans for the Navy, and its officers became the chief naval representatives on the various joint and combined committees. It was the director of this division, first Admiral Turner and then Admiral Cooke, who was the

naval member of the Joint and Combined Staff Planners, as was his chief planner, usually a naval air officer. Other officers in the division sat on the Joint U.S. Strategic Committee and on various joint *ad hoc* committees as they were formed. The division's main task was the preparation of estimates, studies, and plans for joint and combined forces, but it served also, much as did the Army's Operations Division, as the co-ordinating agency for implementing joint plans and for liaison with other planning offices in the Navy Department and with the War Department General Staff.

The Japanese High Command

The Japanese high command, centered in Tokyo, was headed by the Emperor. Under the Japanese constitution, the Army and Navy were responsible solely to the Emperor, and the Chiefs of Staff of the two services, as imperial advisers, had direct access to the throne. The Emperor also received military counsel from two advisory bodies, the Board of Marshals and Fleet Admirals and the Supreme War Council. But the first exercised little influence and the second was consulted only on administrative matters. Real authority and control lay in the hands of the general staff and was exercised solely through the Chiefs of Staff. They alone were responsible for strategy and planning, and for the direction of operations.[15]

---

[15] This section is based on a study prepared for the author by Stanley L. Falk, OCMH. The major sources used in its preparation included: *Imperial GHQ Army High Command Record*, Japanese Studies in World War II, 72; Hattori, *The Greater East Asia War;* Japanese Operations in SWPA; Maxon, *Control of Japanese Foreign Policy.*

The organization of the Army and Navy General Staffs, with certain important exceptions, was similar. The Army staff was the larger, reflecting the greater power of its Chief of Staff and his control over training and other activities not shared by his naval colleague. It was organized into bureaus, the most important of which were the 1st (Operations), 2d (Intelligence), 3d (Transportation and Communications), and General Affairs Bureau. The main Navy staff consisted also of numbered bureaus, but the numbers did not correspond to those in the Army. The bureaus of both services, corresponding to G-Sections of Western general staffs, were usually headed by general and flag officers who exercised considerable influence on strategy and operations.

The conduct of the war was nominally in the hands of *Imperial General Headquarters,* acting directly under the authority of the Emperor. Representing the Army and Navy Chiefs of Staff and the War and Navy Ministries, *Imperial General Headquarters* was divided into the Army and Navy Sections, each acting independently. Army Section met in the Army General Staff offices, Navy Section in its own offices. At joint meetings, held about twice a week on the Imperial Palace grounds, both Chiefs of Staff presided. The Emperor occasionally attended these meetings, but rarely those of the individual service staffs.

The main weakness of *Imperial General Headquarters* was that it was not a single joint command, even an imperfect one. Rather it was a facade to cover two separate organizations with strong competing interests and rivalries. Army and Navy plans were developed separately in the Operations Bureaus of the General Staffs, and plans and operations orders were issued not from *Imperial General Headquarters* as such but rather from its Army Section or its Navy Section. Joint operations were conducted by means of agreements between the Army and Navy, and separate orders were issued to Army and Navy commanders. Often Army-Navy disagreement over a proposed joint operation might result in delay or even the abandonment of the operation. Even when agreement was reached, the operation would normally be carried out not by a joint commander, but by separate Army and Navy commanders who would "co-operate" with each other under the terms of an Army-Navy "agreement." On the rare occasions that saw the establishment of a joint operational command, supplies were still delivered through separate service channels, with consequent duplication, oversights, and mutual recriminations.

In the absence of any leadership on the part of the Emperor, the Army and Navy went their separate ways. But the Army was clearly the leading service. The position of General Tojo as both Premier and War Minister, along with his other Cabinet positions, undoubtedly lent the Army increased prestige, and Admiral Shigetaro Shimada, the Navy Minister during most of the war, followed a policy of trying to co-operate with the Army. There was, nevertheless, no co-ordinated Army-Navy policy. As one former Navy Minister put it, "As far as questions of Army operations are concerned, if the Chief of the Army General Staff says that we will do this, that is the end of it; and as far as the Navy operations are concerned, if the Chief of the Navy General Staff says we will do this, that fixes it; and should there develop difference of opinion between the two chiefs, then nothing can be accomplished."[16] This division was a major weakness in Japan's military establishment. The Japanese were well aware of this, and late in the war General Tojo proposed a real merger of Army and Navy Sections, a proposal that came to naught.

The link between *Imperial General Headquarters* and the Cabinet was the Liaison Conference. This conference, initiated briefly in 1937 after the re-establishment of *Imperial General Headquarters,* was resumed in 1940 and continued throughout the war. It had no formal status or authority, but was merely a framework for discussions between the civil government and the military authorities. The participants were the Chiefs of Staff, the Army and Navy Ministers (themselves active duty officers and largely under the control of the Chiefs of Staff), the Premier, and such other ministers as might be necessary. Also present were the Cabinet secretary and the chiefs of the Military Affairs Bureaus of the Army and Navy Ministries. These last three functioned as a secretariat, and by their choice of agenda and their role in briefing the participants, they exercised a very strong influence on the outcome of the Liaison Conferences. Their presence, also, meant that the conference proceedings would soon become known to other members of the General Staffs, and the civilian participants were fully aware of the danger of assassination for any one who raised too strong a voice against the plans of the military.

The Liaison Conference usually met twice a week, in a small conference room in one of the Imperial Palace buildings. There was no presiding officer, but the Premier occupied an armchair at the far end of the room and the others sat grouped around him. A variety of subjects was discussed at these meetings: war plans, diplomatic moves, the administration of occupied areas, and the assignment of national resources. Once a decision was reached at the Liaison Conference, it became in effect national policy by virtue of the official position of conference members, though the conference itself had no legal status.

On the surface the Liaison Conference appeared to be a meeting of equals. But appearances were deceptive. The military dominated the conference and dictated policy. "Imperial General Headquarters was in the Liaison Conferences," explained General Tojo after the war, "and after they got through deciding things, the Cabinet, generally speaking, made no objection. Theoretically, the Cabinet members could have disagreed . . . , but, as a practical matter, they agreed and did not say anything."[17] *Imperial General Headquarters* was thus the source of Japanese national policy. "The Cabinet, and hence the civil government," wrote former Premier Konoye in

[16] Adm Mitsuma a Yonai, in USSBS, *Interrogations of Japanese Officials,* II, 328. This discussion of IGHQ is based on Maxon, *op. cit.,* pp. 21, 59–62, 126–27, 167–68, 185–86, 189, 191, 255 n. 7; Hattori, *op. cit.,* pp. 239–40; Japanese Opns in SWPA, p. 52; Tsuruzo Akisada, History of Conflicts Between Army and Navy, and Clique Struggles, GHQ FEC, MIS, Hist Div, Translation of Japanese Documents, III; Morison, *Breaking the Bismarcks Barrier,* pp. 15–22.

[17] Quoted in Maxon, *op. cit.,* p. 150. This discussion of the Liaison Conference is based on *ibid.,* pp. 127–29, 132, 149–56, 168, 181–83; Imperial GHQ Army High Command Record, Japanese Studies in World War II, No. pp. 6–9, and Chart I; Japanese Opns in SWPA, p. 52 n. 24.

his memoirs, "were manipulated like puppets by the Supreme Command...."[18]

On extremely important occasions, the Liaison Conference became an Imperial Conference, or a Conference in the Imperial Presence, by adding to its membership the Emperor, the President of the Privy Council, and other high officials. These meetings were much more formal that the Liaison Conferences. The participants made set speeches, previously written and rehearsed, all differences of opinion having been carefully resolved beforehand. The Emperor listened in silence, seated on a raised dais before a long, rectangular table, where the major participants sat facing each other. The three secretaries were grouped around a small table in the corner of the room. The Premier presided over the meeting, and each participant rose in turn, bowed to the Emperor, and stood stiffly in front of his chair while speaking. No one entered or left the room during the conference. At the conclusion of the presentations, the President of the Privy Council asked questions designed to elicit further information for the Emperor. These questions and answers were unrehearsed, but none of the representatives of the Cabinet dared deviate from the prearranged conclusions of the group. The Emperor, whose role was normally a passive one, did not speak. Only on very rare occasions, such as at the Imperial Conference on 6 September 1941 and the one in August 1945 that led to the Japanese surrender, did he venture to exercise his authority.[19]

Beneath the military high command structure in Tokyo, the Japanese had an extensive field organization. (Chart 4) In theory, field commanders were directly responsible to the Emperor, the commander in chief of the armed forces, but in fact came under the control of Imperial General Headquarters, acting for the commander in chief. There was no direct communication between the throne and the field. Basic orders were issued to field commanders as Imperial General Headquarters Army or Navy Section Orders, signed by the appropriate Chief of Staff, "by Imperial Command." The detailed instructions necessary for the implementation of these orders, called Imperial General Headquarters Army or Navy Section Directives, were issued by the appropriate Chief of Staff without any reference to the throne. Recommendations of the field commanders to the throne or request for review of headquarters decisions had to be submitted to Imperial General Headquarters through the appropriate Chief of Staff.[20]

Unlike the Allies, the Japanese did not ordinarily organize their ground, air, and naval forces in the field under a single joint commander. Nor did they establish theaters of operations corresponding to geographical areas under a theater headquarters. Normally, the forces of each service in an area were placed under a separate Army or fleet headquarters whose commanders received orders through separate channels and worked together under the principle of co-operation. The highest Japanese command, equivalent to a U.S. Army overseas command or perhaps to

---

[18] Quoted in Maxon, op. cit., p. 182.

[19] Ibid., pp. 63–64, 66, 156–59, 161–62, 172, 182–83, 204–09; Hattori, op. cit., pp. 243–45.

[20] Imperial GHQ Army High Command Record, p. 2. Examples of Imperial General Headquarters Army and Navy Orders and Directives are to be found in several volumes of these documents prepared by FEC Mil Hist Sec, copies of which are on file in OCMH.

Chart 4—The Japanese High Command

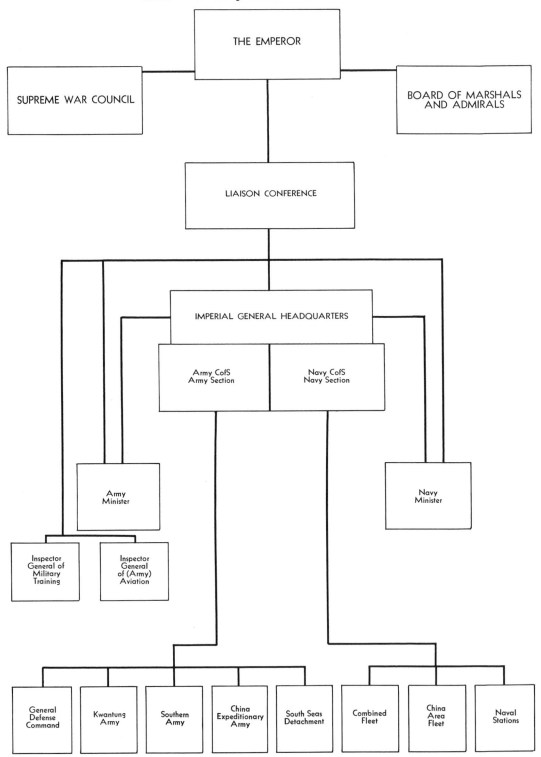

an army group, was the general army, the size of which might vary widely, and which operated directly under the Army Section of *Imperial General Headquarters* in Tokyo. There were three such armies during the early period of the war: *Southern Army, Kwantung Army,* and *China Expeditionary Army.* In each of these were usually one or more area armies, equivalent to U.S. field armies and consisting of units equivalent to a U.S. corps but called armies by the Japanese. There was no unit called a corps in the Japanese Army, Japanese divisions, brigades, and other separate units being assigned directly to armies. (An exception was the *South Seas Detachment* which served directly under Army Section, *Imperial General Headquarters.*) Thus, *Southern Army,* which conducted the opening operations of the war, consisted of four armies, two air groups, and several smaller units.

Unlike the Army, the Japanese Navy placed most of its combat forces under a single command, the *Combined Fleet,* which controlled all naval operations in the Pacific area and was roughly comparable to the U.S. Pacific Fleet. During the early months of the war, this fleet

had under its command six numbered fleets, two numbered air fleets, and the *Southern Expeditionary Fleet.* The numbered fleets, depending on their mission, contained surface, submarine, and air units as well as service and support elements and base forces. Most of the carrier-based air power of the *Combined Fleet* was concentrated in the *1st Air Fleet,* which included four of Japan's five carrier divisions. Land-based naval air power was for the most part assigned to the *11th Air Fleet,* submarines to the *6th Fleet,* and battleships to the *1st Fleet.*[21]

This was the organization of the Japanese high command during the first year of the war. As the war progressed, adjustments were made, old organizations expanded and shifted, and new commands created to meet the needs of the changing strategic situation. But the basic structure, except for the creation of a Supreme Council in August 1944 to take the place of the Liaison Conference, remained unchanged throughout the war.

---

[21]*Imperial GHQ* Army High Command Record, *passim;* Japanese Opns in SWPA, pp. 52–56; The Imperial Japanese Navy in World War II, Japanese Studies in World War II, 127, *passim.*

CHAPTER XI

Organization and Command of the Pacific

The general who advances without coveting fame and retreats without
fearing disgrace, whose only thought is to protect his country and do
good service for his sovereign, is the jewel of the kingdom.

SUN TZU

At the outbreak of war the United
States had in the Pacific four major
commands, USAFFE and the Asiatic
Fleet in the Philippines, the Pacific Fleet
and the Hawaiian Department in Hawaii. All quickly proved inadequate to
deal with a situation that had not been
anticipated in prewar plans. They had
no time to do more than improvise,
sending forces where they were most
urgently needed and establishing bases
and commands as they were required
and as troops and shipping became
available.

As American responsibilities in the
Pacific were extended and U.S. forces
there increased, the need for centralized
direction and control of the scattered
and often independent garrisons which
had developed helter-skelter became
more urgent. There was no single agency
in the Pacific to supply these forces, no
plan to unify their efforts, and no single
commander to mold them into an effective force capable of offensive as well as
defensive operations. The fashioning of
such an organization and the selection
of a commander presented many problems, not the least of which was the delicate adjustment of the conflicting claims

of the Army and Navy to command in
the Pacific. By midsummer of 1942 the
task was substantially completed and
the Army and Navy organization in the
Pacific had taken the form it would
retain for almost three years of war.

The Problem of Responsibility

Responsibility for the defense of Allied
interests in the Far East and in the vast
Pacific Ocean was divided at the start
of war among the powers most directly
concerned and there was little or no
provision for common action. The British held the predominant interest in
Southeast Asia, China on the Asiatic
mainland, the Dutch in the Indies, Australia and New Zealand in the Southwest and South Pacific, and the United
States in the western Pacific and the
ocean reaches from the date line to the
shores of the western hemisphere.

Before the war was a month old the
need for co-ordinated effort against the
Japanese had produced agreement, somewhat unwillingly on the part of the Australians and the Dutch, for the establishment of ABDACOM. This agreement
was limited to that portion of the

Pacific and Far East that lay between Burma and Australia and in no wise affected the responsibilities of each nation for the defense of its own interests and territory outside the ABDA area.

The fall of Singapore on 15 February, foreshadowing the loss of Sumatra and Java, made virtually certain the split of the ABDA area in two. The military staffs as well as their political chiefs began therefore to seek a substitute for the doomed ABDACOM. With the Japanese in control of the Malay Barrier, interposed between the Pacific and Indian Oceans, it was evident that the operations of those forces assigned to the Southwest Pacific and Southeast Asia could no longer be co-ordinated under a single commander. That responsibility would now have to be divided.[1]

There was no disagreement over the division of responsibility. Even before the fall of Singapore it was generally accepted that the United States had the primary interest in the Pacific Ocean, Great Britain in the Indian. China, because of political difficulties, was already recognized as a special problem. Talking with Harry Hopkins on the evening of 15 February, President Roosevelt clearly indicated that the United States should assume responsibility for the reinforcement of Australia and New Zealand, as well as China. The British, he thought, were in a better position to support India and Burma where their

political and economic influence was paramount. These thoughts Roosevelt included in a message to Churchill three days later, with expressions of sympathy for the loss of Singapore.[2]

The same or similar ideas were advanced independently about the same time in other quarters. The day after Singapore's surrender Admiral King suggested that the east (Australian) flank of ABDACOM be combined with the ANZAC Area to form a single theater. While admitting that there were other ways to solve the problem of organization, he made it clear that the United States had the predominant interest in the area and that the operations of the Pacific Fleet required the defense of Australia and the line of communications. The British, he stated, should assume responsibility for China, Burma, and India.

This same idea was advanced also by the Joint U.S. Strategic Committee on the 18th. A few days later the Joint Staff Planners themselves suggested that a separate Australian command, to include part of New Guinea, be established, and that ANZAC be retained to defend the Northeast Area. Finally, on 23 February, the British Chiefs in London, apparently in response to the President's message to Churchill, declared in favor of establishing two areas of strategic responsibility: one a United States area to comprise the Pacific Ocean, including Australia and New Zealand, and the other a British area encompassing the Indian Ocean and Southeast Asia. The countries within these areas would

---

[1] The material in this section is covered in part in Matloff and Snell, *Strategic Planning, 1941–42*, pp. 164–73; Hayes, The War Against Japan, ch. IV; Leighton and Coakley, *Global Logistics and Strategy*, ch. IX; History of U.S. Army Forces in the South Pacific Area (USAFISPA), MS prepared by the author and associates in 1944–45 at Hq USAFISPA, copy in OCMH. Besides using these works as necessary, the author has closely examined the sources on which they were based and has drawn his own conclusions.

[2] Sherwood, *Roosevelt and Hopkins*, pp. 502–03; Mins of the War Council, 16 Feb 42, Secy War Conf II, WDCSA; Rad, President to Churchill, No. 106, 18 Feb 42, ABC 323.31 (1–29–42 sec. 1A) POA.

provide for their own defense, but the United States and Great Britain would furnish the forces and exercise strategic control "in accordance with the general policy agreed between London and Washington for the conduct of the war as a whole."[3]

Pending formal agreement between the British and American Governments, the Combined Chiefs in Washington discussed the practical problem of drawing the boundary line between the areas for which each nation would assume strategic responsibility when the time came. The British Chiefs had suggested on the 23d a line extending southeast from Singapore through the Java Sea to Timor, then south to Australia, thus placing most of the Malay Barrier in the British area. The planners in Washington objected to this division on the ground that those islands in the Netherlands Indies that were within range of Australia were vital to its defense and should be under its control. Moreover, they pointed out, submarine and air operations along the Malay Barrier could be more effectively based on Australia than on India, where the British Far Eastern Fleet was stationed. The line they proposed, therefore, placed all of the Indies except Sumatra, as well as the Philippines and Australia,. within the American area, and it was this line, slightly modified, which was finally accepted by the Combined Chiefs early in March.[4]

Acceptance by the Combined Chiefs of the principle of strategic responsibility and of a line separating the Pacific and Indian Oceans did not in itself constitute formal authority for allocation of areas of responsibility or the establishment of new commands. These measures would have to wait agreement on the political level and formal dissolution of ABDACOM, a step that would not be taken so long as the Dutch continued to fight in Java. In the interim, adjustments were made in command to meet the changing situation and prepare for the reorganization that was certain to come. On 22 February General MacArthur was ordered to Australia to command what was euphemistically called "a reconstituted ABDA Area" and three days later Wavell left for India where Brereton had already gone. At the same time General Brett returned to Australia to command U.S. forces there until MacArthur's arrival.

These adjustments had scarcely been made when the news from Java gave increased urgency to the need for an early decision on the establishment of areas of responsibility and the formation of a new command in the Pacific. The problem was discussed at the White House on 7 March, and on the 9th, the day the Dutch in Java laid down their arms, Roosevelt broached the subject to Prime Minister Churchill. Starting with the obvious need to replace ABDACOM, the President suggested a three-way division of the Allied world into American and British areas. In the Pacific, where the United States would have responsibility, command would be exercised by an American officer responsible to the U.S. Joint Chiefs. The British, Roosevelt suggested, should assume similar

---

[3] Rad, BCOS to JSM, 23 Feb 42, ABC 323.31 (1–29–42 sec. 1–A) POA; Memo, King for CCS, 17 Feb 42, sub: Changes in ABDA, ABC 381 (1–12–42) SWPA; JUSSC, Review of Strategic Situation, 18 Feb 42, CCS 381 (1–30–42); Mins, CCS Mtgs, 17, 22, and 23 Feb 42.

[4] CCS 53, Demarcation of New Strategic Areas, 28 Feb 42, CCS 381 (1–24–42 sec. 1); Mins, CPS Mtg, 25 Feb 42; CCS Mtg, 3 Mar 42.

responsibility in a "middle area" stretching from Singapore to the Mediterranean. A third area comprising Europe and the Atlantic would be jointly administered by the United States and Great Britain through the Combined Chiefs of Staff. This body, under Roosevelt's plan, would also co-ordinate operations in all three areas, allocate Allied resources, and formulate grand strategy.[5]

Substantially the same proposal was made the same day by General Marshall, acting at the President's behest, to the Joint Chiefs of Staff. This step introduced the plan officially into military channels and placed it ultimately before the Combined Chiefs. Though it produced no formal agreement, Marshall's statement to the Joint Chiefs is instructive for in it he undertook to clarify the control of the U.S. and British Chiefs over the proposed spheres of responsibility. Where strategic responsibility was assigned to a single nation, he stated, the government of that nation would make arrangements with the other governments in the area for its organization and command, and the Chiefs of Staff of that nation would exercise jurisdiction over operations and "minor strategy"— presumably the strategy relating to that area alone. In those spheres where joint responsibility was established, strategic responsibility would devolve on the Combined Chiefs.[6]

While Marshall's memorandum was making its way upward through official channels and while the Joint Chiefs were working out an organization for the Pacific area, negotiations on the political level continued. On 18 March Churchill responded to the President's proposal with a hearty indorsement of the idea for American and British spheres, and of a single American commander for the Pacific responsible to the Joint Chiefs. The Combined Chiefs under his and Roosevelt's direction would see to it, Churchill assumed, that operations in each theater conformed to a common strategy. Both the Australian and New Zealand Governments, to whom Churchill had forwarded the President's proposals, favored the principle of spheres of responsibility also, but had serious objections to the command arrangements Roosevelt had suggested. They were willing, even anxious, to have an American commander but wanted a voice in the formulation of strategy and a seat on the Combined Chiefs of Staff when that body deliberated on Pacific matters.[7]

Reasonable as this request seemed, it was greeted in Washington with the same objections that had been offered to similar representations when ABDACOM was created. To the Joint Chiefs, the adoption of this arrangement, plus some other suggestions made at the same time, was inadvisable because it would slow up and complicate their work. This discussion, like the formal paper on spheres of responsibility, led nowhere, for already a new organization of the

---

[5] White House Conf, 7 Mar 42, summarized in JCS 19, 9 Mar 42; Mins, JCS Mtg, 9 Mar 42; Memo, Eisenhower for JCS, 8 Mar 42, sub: Strategic Responsibility, JCS 19/1, 9 Mar 42; Rad, President to Churchill, No. 115, 9 Mar 42, CCS 381 (3–5–42).

[6] Memo, Marshall for JCS, 9 Mar 42, sub: Strategic Responsibility, JCS 19/1; Mins, JCS Mtg, 9 Mar 42, CCS Mtgs, 17 and 24 Mar 42; CCS 57/2, Strategic Responsibility, 24 Mar 42; Memo, Secy JCS to JCS, 15 Jul 42, sub: Status of Agreements on Strategic Responsibility, CCS 381 (1–24–42 sec. 3).

[7] Rads, Churchill to President, Nos. 46, 54, and 58, 18, 20, and 24 Mar 42, filed with JCS 19/1 and CCS 57/1, ABC 371 (3–5–42) and CCS 381 (1–24–42).

Pacific theater, which the establishment of areas of responsibility would presumably authorize, had been created.[8] Military exigency had outpaced political decision.

The Southwest Pacific and Pacific Ocean Areas

In the weeks that had passed since the fall of Singapore, the Army and Navy planners had been hard at work fashioning an organization in the Pacific that would satisfy both services as well as the governments involved. The task was a difficult one and resulted finally in a compromise that worked reasonably well and produced in three years the victories which took Allied forces from Australia and Hawaii to the Philippines and Okinawa.

From the start the discussion over organization assumed that two theaters would be established in the Pacific despite the fact that the President evidently had in mind a single commander for the entire area and had so stated in his recent message to the Prime Minister. The appointment of a single commander had so many obvious advantages and was so close to General Marshall's belief in the importance of unified command that the failure of the Joint Chiefs and their planners to consider it is indeed surprising. One can only conclude that this omission was deliberate, but the record provides no clue to the reason. The answer may lie in the fact that everyone recognized that no officer could

be found who would be acceptable to all. The outstanding officer in the Pacific was General MacArthur, who, if he had the support of the President, the Army, the American people, and the Australians, did not have the confidence of the Navy. There was a widespread feeling in the Navy that the Pacific was peculiarly its province. Certainly the Navy would never have entrusted the fleet to MacArthur, or to any Army officer. Admiral Nimitz, the chief naval candidate for the post, had not yet acquired the popularity and prestige he later enjoyed and was, moreover, considerably junior to MacArthur in length of service and seniority. There was no escape from this impasse except the creation of two commands.[9]

As in the discussion over spheres of responsibility, the decision on organization would have to await the outcome in Java. Suggestions made before that time, though helpful, could receive no official sanction. In that category fell Admiral King's proposal to combine that portion of the ABDA area still in Allied hands with ANZAC into a single command. The remainder of the Pacific, including the Philippines, King thought, could then be integrated into a separate command and subdivided into three areas, a north, south, and central Pacific. His proposal and others were studied by the planners but never got beyond that stage.[10]

---

[8] Memo, Marshall for Pres, 24 Mar 42, ABC 323.31 (1–29–42 sec. I–B) POA; Mins, JCS Mtg, 23 Mar 42. See also WDCSA 381 Australia.

[9] Memo, Turner for King, 19 Mar 42, Office of Naval Records, cited in Hayes, The War Against Japan, ch. IV, p. 18.

[10] Memo, King for JCS, 16 Feb 42, sub: Changes in ABDA, ABC 381 (1–12–42) SWPA; Mins, CCS Mtg, 17 Feb 42; WPD Notes on Demarcation of New Strategic Areas CPS 19/D and CCS 53, ABC 323.31 (1–29–42 sec 1–A) POA; Mins. JCS Mtg, 2 Mar 42.

Meanwhile the Australian and New Zealand Governments had joined forces to develop plans for their own defense. For four days, from 26 February to 1 March, their Chiefs of Staff met in Melbourne to discuss this problem as well as the related problem of organization and command in the Southwest Pacific. General Brett was present at these meetings and reported fully to the War Department, urging at the same time that the United States take immediate action to reorganize the area. The Dominion Chiefs of Staff, he told Marshall at the end of the conference, favored the establishment of a new area encompassing their own territory as well as Timor, Amboina, and New Guinea, and the appointment of an American officer to command it. (Brett was the man they had in mind.) This officer, the Australians and New Zealanders thought, should be responsible to the U.S. and British Chiefs, rather than the U.S. Chiefs alone.

Though this arrangement differed in several important respects from those already under consideration in Washington, Marshall seized this fresh opportunity to force a decision on the organization of the Pacific. "I should like to see the question of command settled quickly and specifically . . . ," he wrote to Brett, "but the definite proposal to that effect should be made by the local governments." What he suggested was that the Australians and New Zealanders make their recommendations formally to the British who would eventually forward them to the Combined Chiefs. If this was done, he thought "the whole matter could be settled expeditiously." But, he warned Brett, "you must be careful not to give the impression that you

are acting under instructions from the War Department."[11]

The Australian and New Zealand proposal reached Washington on 7 March, whereupon Marshall advised Brett to do nothing more until he received fresh instructions. "The Combined Chiefs of Staff," he explained, "are studying the subjects covered . . . which involve far-reaching readjustments."[12] But the Combined Chiefs, having agreed only a few days before, on 3 March, that if the Pacific area was made an American responsibility, control would be vested in the U.S. Chiefs of Staff, did not consider the ANZAC proposal at all but passed it on to the Joint Chiefs. There it met serious criticism from Admiral King who had strong objections to placing Australia and New Zealand in a single theater. New Zealand, he insisted, was a link in the line of communications and an integral part of the system of island bases stretching east and north to Hawaii. The defense of this line, King declared, was essentially a naval problem and intimately associated with the operations of the Pacific Fleet. Australia and its approaches through the Netherlands Indies and New Guinea formed a separate strategic entity and should, King asserted, be placed under another command.[13] Here was a clear exposition, based on strategic considerations, for a twofold division of the Pacific.

[11] Rads, Brett to Marshall, Nos. 87 and 467, 27 Feb and 3 Mar 42, WPD Ready Ref File Australia; Marshall to Brett, No. 543, 5 Mar 42, WPD Msg File Australia.

[12] Rad, Marshall to Brett, No. 589, 8 Mar 42, WPD Msg File Australia; Memo, British COS for JSM, 7 Mar 42, Governmental and Strategical Control, CCS 57, 323.31 (1–29–42 sec. 1–A) POA.

[13] Comments of Adm King on Hayes, The War Against Japan, ch. IV, p. 21; JCS 18, Governmental and Strategical Control, 8 Mar 42.

The differences between the Army's and Navy's views emerged clearly in the next two days during which the naval staff members, following up King's lead, developed one plan and their Army colleagues another. The Navy's plan called for an Australian area whose western limits followed the line of demarcation between the Pacific and Indian Oceans accepted by the Combined Chiefs. The eastern boundary, the 160th and 165th meridian east as far as the equator, placed all of the Solomons in the Australian area, but excluded the New Hebrides, New Caledonia, and New Zealand. On the north the area was bounded by an irregular line drawn to include New Guinea and the Indies, but not the Philippines. The rest of the Pacific, from New Zealand and New Caledonia eastward, the naval planners organized into a Pacific Ocean area subdivided into three parts and placed under the Commander in Chief, Pacific Fleet. Operational control of both the Australian and Pacific Ocean areas, the naval planners recommended, should rest with the Joint Chiefs.[14]

The Army planners led by General Eisenhower accepted the twofold division of the Pacific but not Admiral King's claim that New Zealand belonged with the line of communications rather than Australia. Their arrangement followed closely the one proposed by the Dominions and provided for a Southwest and North Pacific area. The first would comprise all of the Pacific south of the line Philippines–Samoa. The supreme commander for this area, which would include New Caledonia, the Fijis, New Guinea, Australia and New Zealand, was to be selected by the governments in the area, but it was already understood that he would be an American, probably MacArthur. The North Pacific area, everything north and east of the Philippines and Samoa, would be commanded by a naval officer.[15]

The differences between the Army and Navy plans were reconciled by the Joint Chiefs between 9 and 16 March. In the 9 March meeting, at which the two plans were first discussed, Admiral King firmly defended the Navy solution, emphasizing the need for preserving freedom of action for the fleet. General Marshall, apparently convinced by King or unwilling to risk a deadlock that would require Presidential action, did not insist on the adoption of the Army's plan but only that the Philippine Islands, for "psychological reasons," be included in the Australia, or Southwest Pacific Area, as it came to be called. To this Admiral King agreed and the Navy's plan, with some slight modifications, was approved by the Joint Chiefs.[16] Curiously enough, this action, which anticipated American and British approval of the division of the world into spheres of responsibility, had no official basis then or thereafter, for the British Government never took action on the proposal to establish these spheres of responsibility. The reason for this failure is not clear, but there is no doubt that the planners of both nations as well as their military and civilian chiefs favored the proposal and always acted as though it had official sanction.

Having reached agreement on the organization for the Pacific, the Joint

---

[14] JCS 18, Governmental and Strategical Control, 8 Mar 42.

[15] Memo, Marshall for JCS, 9 Mar 42, sub: Creation of SWPA, JCS 18/2.

[16] Mins JCS Mtgs, 9 and 16 Mar 42; CCS Mtg, 17 Mar 42.

Chiefs proceeded to the task of selecting the commanders and preparing directives for them. Theoretically this task presented few difficulties but it was complicated by commitments already made and instructions previously issued. Though MacArthur's name had not been mentioned in the Joint Chiefs' discussions, he had been virtually promised the post of supreme commander in the Southwest Pacific Area even before such an area had been established. On 10 March, while he was still negotiating with King on the future organization of the Pacific, Marshall had instructed Brett to notify the Australian Prime Minister "within the hour" of MacArthur's arrival in Australia and of his assumption of command of U.S. forces there — the post Brett himself held. "You will propose," Marshall further instructed Brett, "that the Australian Government nominate General MacArthur as the Supreme Commander of the Southwest Pacific Area, and will recommend that the nomination be submitted as soon as possible to London and Washington simultaneously."[17]

General Brett followed his instructions faithfully. When MacArthur's plane reached Darwin on 17 March, Brett telephoned Prime Minister Curtin and in the President's name put forward MacArthur's nomination for the post for which the Australians had earlier nominated Brett himself. This was the first indication Curtin had of MacArthur's presence and he fell in with Brett's suggestion readily and with enthusiasm. That same day he named MacArthur as his government's choice for supreme commander. In Washington this request

was the signal for an unusually prompt War Department press release announcing the news of MacArthur's arrival in Australia and his impending appointment "in accordance with the request of the Australian Government." To the British Prime Minister, Roosevelt explained that he had authorized this public statement to forestall Axis propaganda that MacArthur's departure from the Philippines meant that the United States had abandoned the Filipinos. MacArthur's nomination, the President assured Churchill, would "in no way interfere with procedure of determining strategic areas and spheres of responsibility through established channels."[18]

Whether by design or not, the effect of Marshall's instructions to Brett, which the President approved, was to present the British with a *fait accompli*. It also made any discussion by the Joint Chiefs of a commander for the Southwest Pacific entirely academic. The legal forms were preserved, however, and officially the Southwest Pacific Area was still to be established and its commander designated. These actions presumably would be completed only after agreement between the United States and Great Britain on spheres of responsibility. Thus it was that on 18 March, two days after the Joint Chiefs had agreed on an organization for the Pacific and the day after MacArthur reached Australia, Marshall dispatched a long message to MacArthur explaining the situation to him and assuring him that when the negotiations with the British and Australians were completed his appointment would be

---

[17] Rad, Marshall to Brett, 613, 10 Mar 42, OPD Exec Files.

[18] Milner, *Victory in Papua*, p. 18; Rads, Brett to Marshall, No. 736, 17 Mar 42, President to Churchill, same date, OPD Exec Files; WD Press Release, 17 Mar 42.

made official. Until that time he would be, for all practical purposes, the supreme commander in the Southwest Pacific. As such, Marshall told him, he would be ineligible to command directly any national force and would therefore have to relinquish command of U.S. Army Forces in Australia to Brett from whom he had taken over only the day before. Ultimately, Brett would command the air forces, Admiral Leary the naval forces (ANZAC would cease to exist when the new organization went into effect), and an Australian officer the ground forces.[19]

MacArthur's position was anomalous. He commanded neither the Southwest Pacific Area nor U.S. Army Forces in Australia, but only USAFFE, which, since Wainwright's assumption of command in the Philippines, consisted only of the handful of officers he had brought with him. Until he received official authority, his control of the forces in Australia would be difficult and his relationship with the Australian Government would have to be conducted on an unofficial and informal basis. Despite these handicaps, MacArthur quickly took hold. By the end of the month he had secured Brett's appointment as commander of the air forces, which he had found "in a most disorganized condition," placed American and Australian ground combat forces under an "appropriate Australian general," and American service troops in USAFIA under General Barnes. This arrangement, he told Marshall, would "free the combat echelons of all administrative, supply, and political considerations, permit-

ting uninterrupted concentration on combat." [20]

Meanwhile the planners in Washington, spurred on by the necessity of regularizing MacArthur's position, were drafting the directives and completing their arrangements for the organization of the Pacific theater. Though there was no urgency in the Pacific Ocean Area, the naval planners wished to establish both areas simultaneously. Failure to do this, Admiral Turner thought, might open the way for an Army effort to enlarge the Southwest Pacific at the expense of the South Pacific along the lines laid down in the Army plan or in the ANZAC proposals. The naval planners feared also that the Army might raise objections, if the opportunity arose, to placing its forces under naval control. Thus, on the 19th, Admiral Turner, the chief naval planner, submitted to King draft directives for the Southwest and Pacific Ocean Areas with the recommendation that both be acted on at the same time.[21]

At this point Admiral King departed from the procedure usually followed in such matters and instead of processing the draft directives through the Joint Chiefs' committees sent them directly to General Marshall with the explanation that he was doing so "in order to save the time that might be lost through possible prolonged discussions of the

---

[19] Rad, Marshall to MacArthur, No. 739, 18 Mar 42, OPD Exec Files.

[20] Rads, MacArthur to Marshall, No. 19, 24 Mar 42; Brett to Marshall, No. 792, 21 Mar 42; Marshall to MacArthur, No. 791, 21 Mar 42; MacArthur to Marshall, No. 3, 21 Mar 42; Marshall to MacArthur, No. 81, 22 Mar 42, all in OPD Exec SWPA—MacArthur File.

[21] Memos, Turner for King, 19 Mar 42; King for Marshall, same date, sub: Command Areas in Pacific, both cited in Hayes, The War Against Japan, ch. IV, p. 25.

GENERAL MACARTHUR AND ADMIRAL NIMITZ

Planning Staff." He and Marshall, King suggested, should settle the problem between themselves.[22] Apparently the Army Chief of Staff passed these draft directives to his own planners who found little to object to and at the next meeting of the Joint Chiefs on 30 March they were accepted and forwarded to the White House. Final approval by the President was given on the last day of the month.[23]

The directives thus approved—they were dated 30 March—established the two Pacific areas, set their geographical limits, named the commanders, and assigned their missions. MacArthur, as expected, was appointed Supreme Com-

mander (a title he himself changed to Commander in Chief) of the Southwest Pacific Area; Admiral Nimitz, Commander in Chief, Pacific Ocean Areas.[24] The boundaries of the two areas conformed to the earlier agreement: MacArthur's domain included Australia, the Philippines, New Guinea, the Solomons, the Bismarck Archipelago, and all of the Netherlands Indies except Sumatra. Admiral Nimitz' command, though it had less land area, was even larger in extent and encompassed the remainder of the Pacific except for a broad band of ocean off the coast of Central and South America.[25] It was divided into three subordinate areas, two of them, the Central and North Pacific, under Nimitz' direct control, and the third, the South Pacific, under a naval officer responsible to Nimitz. The dividing line between the first two was at 42° north, thus placing Hawaii, the Gilberts and Marshalls, the Mandated Islands, and Japan itself in the Central Pacific. The South Pacific Area, which extended southward from the equator, between the Southwest Pacific and longitude 110° west, included the all-important line of communications. (*Map IV*)

Unlike the ABDA Area, in which each of the participating powers had equal responsibility and representation, the two areas established by the 30 March directives were the exclusive responsibility of the United States. The authority granted the commanders under this new arrangement was broader than that

[22] Memo, King for Marshall, 20 Mar 42, sub: Proposed Directives, cited in Hayes, The War Against Japan, ch. IV, p. 26.

[23] Memos, Marshall and King for Pres, 30 Mar 42, no sub; U.S. Secy CCS for Marshall and King, 1 Apr 42, both in ABC 323.31 (1–29–42 sec. 3) POA; Mins, JCS Mtg, 30 Mar 42.

[24] First designated in the singular, Pacific Ocean Area.

[25] This band included the area east of the 110th meridian, and south of latitude 11° north and was designated the Southeast Pacific Area. It was under separate command and never became an active theater.

exercised by General Wavell, and they were not bound by many of the restrictions that had limited the authority of the ABDA commander. ABDACOM had reported to the Combined Chiefs; MacArthur and Nimitz reported to the Joint Chiefs, which had jurisdiction over operational strategy subject to the grand strategy formulated by the Combined Chiefs. In its relations with the Pacific commanders, the Joint Chiefs would act through the chiefs of each of the services as executive agents, so that MacArthur would receive his orders from Marshall, Nimitz from King.

This organization, it should be noted, did not establish a unified command for the Pacific, but rather two separate area commands. Control over the theater as a whole was vested in the Joint Chiefs of Staff, which became in effect the directing headquarters for operations in the Pacific. But that body lacked a single head—except the President himself—and operated under a committee rather than a staff system so that even in Washington command was diffused and decentralized and decisions on strategy and theater-wide problems could be reached only by debate and compromise. Within the theater itself there was no single authority which could choose between strategic plans, resolve the conflicting claims of MacArthur and Nimitz for troops and supplies, assign priorities, shift forces from one area to another, or concentrate the resources of both areas against a single objective. Such an arrangement complicated the problems of war in the Pacific. It led to duplication of effort and keen competition for the limited supply of ships, landing craft, and airplanes; and it placed on the Joint Chiefs the heavy burden of decision in

many matters that could well have been resolved by lesser officials.

Of all the faulty decisions of the war [General MacArthur wrote] perhaps the most unexplainable one was the failure to unify the command in the Pacific. The principle involved is perhaps the most fundamental one in the doctrine and tradition of command. In this instance it did not involve an international problem. It was accepted and entirely successful in the other great theaters. The failure to do so in the Pacific cannot be defended in logic, in theory or even in common sense. Other motives must be ascribed. It resulted in divided effort, the waste of diffusion and duplication of force and the consequent extension of the war with added casualties and cost. The generally excellent cooperation between the two commands in the Pacific supported by the good will, good nature and high professional qualifications of the numerous personnel involved was no substitute for the essential unity of direction of centralized authority.[26]

Though superficially alike, the directives to the Pacific commanders differed in some fundamental respects. As supreme commander in an area that presumably would include large forces of other governments, MacArthur, like Wavell, was specifically enjoined from directly commanding any national force or interfering with its internal administration. Nimitz was not thus restricted for it was anticipated that his forces would be mostly American and his operations more closely related to the fleet. Thus, he was permitted to exercise direct command of the forces in the North and Central Pacific, and, through a subordinate commander, those of the South Pacific. Furthermore, he exercised direct control of the Pacific Fleet (CINCPAC), in which capacity he was directly respon-

---

[26] Ltr, MacArthur to Maj Gen Albert C. Smith, Chief, Mil Hist, 5 Mar 1953, OCMH.

sible through naval channels to Admiral King. Undoubtedly the difference in the authority granted the two men, as well as the wording of the tasks assigned to each, was based partially on the Navy's conviction that MacArthur had a limited conception of the use of naval as well as air power. If he was given command of these forces, Turner told King, "I believe that you will find the Supreme Commander will tend to use . . . [them] in a wrong manner, since he has shown clearly unfamiliarity with proper naval and air functions."[27]

There were significant differences, too, in the tasks assigned each of the Pacific commanders. MacArthur's mission was mainly defensive and included only the injunction to "prepare to take the offensive." Combined with the statement that he was to "hold the key military regions of Australia as bases for future offensive action against Japan," it was possible to derive from it, as MacArthur quickly did, authorization for offensive operations based on Australia. This does not seem to have been the intention of the Army planners in Washington. At the time, they apparently had no thought of opening such an offensive, though the Navy did hope to launch operations in the Southwest Pacific, but not from Australia.

Admiral Nimitz' directive assigned a defensive mission, too, but it clearly envisaged offensive operations for the future by instructing him to "prepare for the execution of major amphibious offensives against positions held by Japan, the initial offensives to be launched from the South Pacific Area

and Southwest Pacific Area."[28] This wording implied that Admiral Nimitz would command not only the offensive in his own area, but that in MacArthur's area as well. And this may well have been the intent of the naval planners who drafted the directives, for in their view all amphibious operations — and any operation in the Pacific would be amphibious — should be under naval command. But the major offensive when it came, the Navy believed, would be across the Central Pacific along the route marked out in the prewar ORANGE plan.

Presidential approval of the directives to MacArthur and Nimitz did not constitute authority for assumption of command. The other governments involved would have to give their consent, too, and in view of the difference between the present version and the plan the Australians and New Zealanders had proposed, that consent might not be readily granted. The British and the Dutch raised the first objection, but it was a minor one and was easily met by a change in wording of the first paragraph of the directives. Their approval was won by the first week of April.

The objections of the Australians and New Zealanders were not so easily met. They were understandably dissatisfied with the separation of the Dominions and reiterated the arguments for a single strategic entity incorporating their own territory, the Fijis, and New Caledonia. To this Admiral King replied, in a memorandum for the President, that "The defense of Australia is primarily a land-air problem for which the best possible naval support is a fleet free to maneuver without restrictions imposed

---

[27] Memo, Turner for King, 19 Mar 42, cited in Hayes, The War Against Japan, ch. IV, p. 30.

[28] JCS Directive to CINCPOA, 30 Mar 42, ABC 323.31 (1–29–42 sec. 1 B) POA.

by the local situation." New Zealand's defense was primarily a naval problem, and "has no relation," King insisted, "to the defense of Australia." Though they were not convinced, the Australians and New Zealanders finally accepted this separation "because of the necessity of an immediate decision." [29]

But the Dominion governments had other objections to the new organization. They found no guarantee in the new directive, they said, that their forces would not be moved out of Australian and New Zealand territory, or that the local commanders would be able to communicate freely with their governments, as had been the case in ABDACOM. These arguments King answered—Marshall was in London—by pointing out that the actions of the Joint Chiefs were subject to review by the President to whom the governments involved had recourse through diplomatic channels. "The interests of the nations whose forces or whose land possessions may be involved in these military operations are further safeguarded," Admiral King explained, "by the power each nation retains to refuse the use of its forces for any project which it considers inadvisable." This statement apparently settled the fears of the Australians. Approval of the directives followed not long after and on 18 April General MacArthur officially assumed command of the Southwest Pacific Area. [30]

The size of the area under MacArthur's command after 18 April can perhaps be appreciated by superimposing a map of the United States over one of the Southwest Pacific. Miami would fall on Townsville and Seattle on Sarawak in Borneo; San Francisco would fall in Java and New York on Rabaul. Thus, the headquarters in Melbourne would be equivalent to one in South America directing operations against Boston and New York, and planning for an invasion against northwest Canada.

The logistical difficulties in a theater of this size and in this part of the world were enormous. The line of communications to the United States (San Francisco to Sydney), the main source of supply, was over 4,000 miles long. This fact combined with the scarcity of ships constituted a major problem in the shipment of men and supplies from the United States, as well as within the theater. Ports, bases, airfields, and roads had to be carved out of jungle, and there was rarely enough equipment and men to do the job without extraordinary measures. "Forced risks" and "crisis management" were common parlance among the logisticians in the theater. Climate, terrain, and tropical diseases were an ever-present factor in planning and operations, imposing additional burdens on the supply system.

It would take time to overcome these difficulties but in the meantime General MacArthur could begin to organize his forces, provide for their administration and supply, and plan for future operations. The Australian commanders had been notified on the 17th that orders issued by him were to be considered "as emanating from the Commonwealth

---

[29] Memo, King for President, 5 Apr 42, CCS 57/2, ABC 323.31 (1–29–42 sec. 2) POA; Hayes, The War Against Japan, ch. IV, p. 331.

[30] General Order 1, GHQ SWPA, 18 Apr 42; Rad, MacArthur to Marshall, No. 327, 18 Apr 42, CM–IN–4719. The correspondence between the Dominion governments and Admiral King, who acted for the Joint Chiefs in Marshall's absence, is in ABC 323.31 (1–29–42 sec. 2) POA and CCS 381 (1–24–42 sec. 2).

ADMIRAL LEARY

Government," and MacArthur could therefore formally establish the three commands, Allied Land, Air, and Naval Forces, which, with the existing American commands, USAFIA, USAFFE, and Wainwright's USFIP in the Philippines, constituted his entire force. General Sir Thomas Blamey, recently returned from the Middle East, became Commander, Allied Land Forces; General Brett, Allied Air Forces; and Admiral Leary, Allied Naval Forces. All American units, with the exception of certain air elements, were assigned to USAFIA, the administrative and service agency for U.S. Army forces, which on 20 July was redesignated the U.S. Army Services of Supply under the command of Brig. Gen. Richard J. Marshall. But for operational employment, all American ground troops, soon to number two divisions, as well as those of the Australians, who contributed in addition to the militia

two more seasoned divisions from the Middle East, came under General Blamey. Similarly, General Brett and his successor, Maj. Gen. George C. Kenney, commanded the American, Australian, and Dutch air elements and Admiral Leary (soon succeeded by Rear Adm. Arthur S. Carpender) the naval units which included four cruisers, destroyers, submarines, and auxiliary craft.[31]

MacArthur organized his own headquarters, located initially in Melbourne, along traditional U.S. Army lines. (*Chart 5*) There was nothing in his directive requiring him to appoint officers of the participating governments, as General Wavell had been required to do. General Marshall urged strongly that he do so and the President indicated that he would like to see Australian and Dutch officers in high position on the Supreme Commander's staff.[32] But MacArthur did not follow these suggestions and the staff named on 19 April was almost entirely American with a few Australian and Dutch officers serving in subordinate posts. The top positions went to those USAFFE officers who had come from Corregidor; Maj. Gen. Richard K. Sutherland, Chief of Staff; Brig. Gen. Richard J. Marshall, Deputy Chief of Staff; Col. Charles P. Stivers, G–1; Col. Charles A. Willoughby, G–2; Brig. Gen. Spencer B. Akin, Signal Officer; and Brig. Gen. Hugh J. Casey, Engineer Officer. The others came from the USAFIA staff: Brig. Gen. Stephen J. Chamberlin, G–3; Col. Lester J. Whit-

[31] GO 1, GHQ SWPA, 18 Apr 42; Rads, MacArthur to Marshall, Nos. 381 and 415, 20 Apr 42, OPD MacArthur File.
[32] Rad, Marshall to MacArthur, No. 1178, 9 Apr 42, CM–OUT–1495.

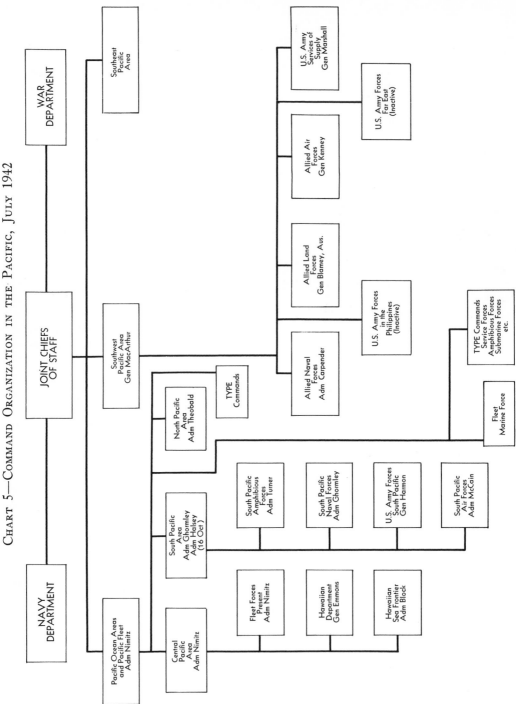

CHART 5—COMMAND ORGANIZATION IN THE PACIFIC, JULY 1942

lock, G–4; and Col. Burdette M. Fitch, Adjutant General.[33]

The most serious problem confronting MacArthur was the defense of Australia. The Australian Chiefs of Staff, recognizing the impossibility of defending so vast an area with their small force, had in February decided to concentrate their strength in the Brisbane-Melbourne area, outposting the rest of the country as well as the Northeast Area.[34] This concept MacArthur later characterized as passive and defeatist, strategically unsound and "fatal to every possibility of ever assuming the offensive."[35] Speaking at an off-the-record press conference just one year after he had reached Australia, he declared that within three days of his arrival he had decided to scrap the Australian concept and to adopt instead an active defense far to the north in New Guinea. There at Port Moresby he would wage the battle for Australia on ground of his own choosing and on his own terms. This decision, in his view, "was one of the most decisive as well as one of the most radical and difficult decisions of the war."[36]

The Australians did not let MacArthur's characterization of their strategy or his claim to omnipotence go unchallenged. Their own plans, they claimed, did make provision for the defense of the forward area in New Guinea and they had reinforced Port Moresby to the fullest extent possible. They could find no evidence, either, that MacArthur had issued any directives or altered their troop dispositions in such a way as to indicate any fundamental change in strategy at that time. The change that was made came later, they claimed, and was made possible by the arrival of reinforcements from the Middle East and the United States. All these considerations John Curtin, the Australian Prime Minister, called to MacArthur's attention after the press conference of March 1943, but MacArthur again asserted flatly, "It was never my intention to defend Australia on the mainland of Australia. That was the plan when I arrived, but to which I never subscribed and which I immediately changed to a plan to defend Australia in New Guinea."[37]

Whether the matter was as represented by MacArthur or by Curtin, the fact was that the forces required to put into effect an active defense in New Guinea were simply not available in April 1942. MacArthur's naval force was small and unbalanced and lacked aircraft carriers. The only combat troops he had were the 41st U.S. and two Australian divisions (less two brigades in Ceylon); the 32d Division was not due until May. And although he had 17 Australian air squadrons and American units consisting of 2 heavy and 2 medium bomber groups and 3 fighter groups (not all of them had yet arrived), his air component was below standard in organization and training. But all his efforts to secure more at that time were unavailing, and it was with this force that MacArthur

---

[33] GO 2, GHQ SWPA, 19 Apr 42.

[34] Australian Chiefs of Staff, Appreciation, 27 Feb 42, G–3 Jnl, GHQ SWPA.

[35] Ltr, MacArthur to Smith, response to question by the author, 5 Mar 53, OCMH.

[36] Ibid; Ltr, Curtin to Blamey, 16 Nov 43, copy in OCMH.

[37] Ltrs, MacArthur to Curtin, 6 Nov 43; Curtin to Blamey, 16 Nov 43; Blamey to Curtin, 28 Jan 44; Rowell to Maj. Gen. Orlando Ward, Chief, Mil Hist, 6 Apr 51, all in OCMH; Milner, Victory in Papua, pp. 24–25; McCarthy, Southwest Pacific Area–First Year, pp. 25–33.

in April made preparations to hold Port Moresby.[38]

The organization of the forces of the Pacific Ocean Areas, where Admiral Nimitz assumed command on 8 May, was far more complicated than in the neighboring theater. Already in the area was the old prewar Army command, the Hawaiian Department, whose primary responsibility was the defense of Oahu, and especially the Pearl Harbor base of the Pacific Fleet. The unified command established on 17 December 1941, ten days after the Japanese attack, was limited to the Hawaiian area and did not include the chain of islands which had since been garrisoned by Army forces. In the absence of any other Army command, responsibility for the supply and administration of some of these island garrisons had fallen on General Emmons, the Hawaiian Department commander. But he did not have the broad authority that his naval colleagues had at the time for the control of forces along the line of communications.

As Commander in Chief, Pacific Ocean Areas (CINCPOA), Admiral Nimitz exercised considerably more direct control over his forces than did General MacArthur in the Southwest Pacific. In addition to his command of the Pacific Fleet, he also commanded directly two of the three areas established in the 30 March directives. (Later he relinquished personal command of the North Pacific.) Like MacArthur, he was prohibited from interfering in the internal administration of the forces in his theater, but as a fleet commander he remained responsible for naval administration as

well as operations. He was thus answerable to himself in several capacities and it was not always clear whether he was acting as area commander, fleet commander, or theater commander responsible to the Joint Chiefs in Washington. This fact and the failure to define precisely the relationship between Admiral Nimitz and General Emmons led to the numerous misunderstandings that marked Army and Navy operations in that area during the war.

The South Pacific Area

Of the three subordinate areas of Admiral Nimitz' command the one whose organization presented the greatest problem was the South Pacific where the Allied offensive would come first. Admiral Ghormley, who was in London when he received his appointment as Commander, South Pacific Area (COMSOPAC), on 13 April, did not assume command for two months although he arrived in Auckland, New Zealand, the site of his new headquarters, on 21 May. On the way out, he had stopped in Washington where King told him that his was "a most difficult task" and that the offensive against Japan would probably start from the South Pacific "possibly this fall."[39] His next stop was Pearl Harbor, where he stayed for a week to confer with Nimitz and his staff. There he was told again to prepare for an amphibious offensive and met his air commander, Rear Adm. John R. McCain. His command, Nimitz told him, would include all the garrisons already in the area (about 60,000 Army troops plus three fighter and two medium bombardment groups), the remnants of

[38] The Campaigns of MacArthur in the Pacific, SWPA Series, I, p. 40; McCarthy, *Southwest Pacific Area–First Year*, p. 82.

[39] Morison, *Coral Sea, Midway and Submarine Actions*, p. 251.

the ANZAC naval force, a marine division already en route to New Zealand, plus whatever forces might be allocated by the United Nations. Exempted were those forces concerned with the land defense of New Zealand, a task that remained a responsibility of the New Zealand Chiefs of Staff.[40]

Ghormley's organization closely paralleled Admiral Nimitz'. Retaining for himself control of all naval units in the area and of their administration as well, he exercised command through a staff that was essentially naval. Of 103 officers assigned in September 1942 only three wore the Army uniform. Thus his headquarters became the center for naval administration as well as joint operations and planning. He quickly established air, amphibious, and service commands, all under naval officers and predominantly naval staffs, but not a ground command, as General MacArthur had done. Instead, his own headquarters did the planning for and retained control of Army and Marine Corps elements in the theater.

The amphibious command was organized on 18 July and the Navy gave Ghormley one of its ablest—and most contentious—officers, Admiral Turner, chief of the War Plans Division, to command it. All air units in the theater were under Admiral McCain, soon to be replaced by Rear Adm. Aubrey W. Fitch. His responsibilities included not only operational control of all aircraft, but training and indoctrination as well. It was this latter responsibility that was to cause so much difficulty.

The first logistical agency for the South Pacific was the Service Force in New

Zealand, but on his arrival Ghormley established the Service Squadron, South Pacific. Charged with responsibility for the procurement and delivery of all supplies in the theater, except those exempted from naval control, this headquarters quickly took charge of the transportation and base facilities of the Navy and Marine Corps in the area under a logistical plan issued on 15 July. As the highest supply agency in the South Pacific, Service Squadron co-ordinated all service organizations in the theater, controlled all ships and shipping, distributed all supplies obtained locally, designated ports of call, and established priorities.

The establishment of the South Pacific coincided with the opening of offensive operations and made more urgent the solution of the problems presented by the absence of a comparable Army command. There were Army troops in New Zealand, New Caledonia, Efate and Espiritu Santo in the New Hebrides, the Fijis, Tongatabu, and Bora Bora. These troops had been rushed out so quickly that there had been no opportunity to perfect arrangements for their support and control. Some commanders, like General Patch, were responsible directly to the War Department; others, to General Emmons in Hawaii. Administration therefore was complicated and command confused. Moreover the supply of these forces was cumbersome and inefficent with responsibility divided among the San Francisco Port of Embarkation, USAFIA, and the Hawaiian Department. Complicating the situation even more was the fact that responsibility for the airfields along the line of communications belonged to General Emmons, so that a base commander might report directly to the War Department, get his

---

[40] Unless otherwise noted this section is based on Hist of USAFISPA.

ADMIRAL GHORMLEY

ADMIRAL McCAIN

supplies from the San Francisco port, and take his orders for airfield construction, possibly his most important task, from General Emmons.

Allocation of aircraft to the South Pacific Area constituted another major problem. Admiral King and his naval planners had long argued for heavy bombers in the area, contending that B–17's in Hawaii and Australia could not meet the threat of invasion along the line of communications. The army and air planners, backed by Presidential authority, had firmly resisted demands for a South Pacific heavy bombardment force as well as an increase in the air units already authorized, arguing for the same mobility for aircraft that the Navy insisted on for warships. Though the

Navy lost the argument it did get a group of heavy bombers—the 11th Bombardment Group—for the South Pacific late in June by an arrangement which established an Hawaiian Mobile Air Force of B–17's that could be used anywhere in the Pacific subject to approval by the Joint Chiefs of Staff.

The assignment of the Army Air Forces' most precious weapon, the B–17, to the South Pacific brought into sharp focus the question of control of aircraft. The area command, despite its theoretically joint character, was naval and the air commander was a naval officer. Army aircraft thus came under naval control for operations, a fact that could not be avoided, distasteful as it may have been to the airmen. But when it

ADMIRAL FITCH

ADMIRAL TURNER

became apparent that Admiral McCain would also be responsible for the training and indoctrination of Army air units, the air planners expressed strong objections. Their forces, they felt, should retain their identity, be assigned appropriate missions, and execute them under their own commanders in accordance with Army Air Forces doctrine. Under no circumstances, they insisted, should air units be integrated into a naval force and commanded by naval officers.[41]

While this debate was in progress, the problem of administration and supply

was becoming more acute. Admiral King's proposal on 10 April that a Marine officer be appointed as commander of the South Pacific bases and a joint supply organization established to take over responsibility for their logistic support only precipitated another disagreement between the Army and Navy. The idea of a separate commander for all the bases was rejected, but the proposal for an interservice logistical organization was the subject of discussions throughout April and May. The Navy favored a joint organization to supply all forces in the South Pacific on the ground that this arrangement would result in the greatest economy in shipping and avoid duplication of effort. This organization would function in the theater

---

[41] Wesley Frank Craven and James Lea Cate, eds., *The Pacific—Guadalcanal to Saipan: August 1942 to July 1944*, vol. IV, "The Army Air Forces in World War II" (Chicago: University of Chicago Press, 1950), pp. 29–30.

under the Service Squadron in the South Pacific and in San Francisco under a comparable naval headquarters. The Army, fearing naval control over Army supplies, opposed this proposal and insisted on parallel Army and Navy supply organizations. "We have so dominant an interest . . . ," wrote Maj. Gen. Brehon B. Somervell, "so clear a responsibility in the supply of our large forces; we must definitely control the means."[42] Agreement proved impossible and all that remained of the proposal when the debate ended was a joint purchasing office for local procurement in New Zealand.

Another solution to the problem of administration and supply was that recommended by General Emmons who wanted an Army commander for the South Pacific, stationed in the Fijis and subordinate to him, to co-ordinate the operations, supply, and maintenance of Army forces in that area.[43] A month later, when the War Department had still failed to act on his proposal, Emmons asked for a clarification of his responsibilities, pointing out that confusion was resulting from the conflicting requests he was receiving from the base commanders. The clarification was not long in coming for already the War Department had decided to establish a separate Army command in the South Pacific, but along different lines from those suggested by Emmons.[44]

The solution arrived at in Washington was designed as much to meet the problem of the control of Army aircraft as it was to create a more orderly system of supply and administration. At the same time that the B–17's had been sent to the South Pacific the Army had decided to appoint an air officer as commander of all Army forces placed under Ghormley. This arrangement had been worked out, apparently, between General Eisenhower and Maj. Gen. Millard F. Harmon, Chief of Air Staff. After certain modifications, Admiral King finally accepted this arrangement on 2 July and five days later the new command, U.S. Army Forces in the South Pacific Area, was created. Harmon himself was the officer Marshall selected for this new and difficult assignment.[45]

General Marshall's instructions to Harmon were detailed and specific. His first task was to take over the administration and training of all U.S. ground and air troops in the South Pacific, and secondarily to assist Ghormley in the preparation and execution of plans then under consideration for the employment of Army forces. On his arrival in the theater, Marshall instructed, Harmon was to inspect the Army bases in the area and submit to Washington recommendations for "the rearrangement, reduction or augmentation of the personnel and materiel . . . with a view to establishing a balanced, cohesive and efficient Army contingent."[46] This done he would take over responsibility for the logistic support of the Army bases in the area, utilizing to the full local resources. Through COMSOPAC he would procure whatever he could from the Joint

---

[42] Cited in Leighton and Coakley, *Global Logistics and Strategy*, p. 189.

[43] Ltr, Emmons to Marshall, 20 May 42, sub: Army Com in South Pacific OPD 384 PTO case 18.

[44] Rad, Emmons to TAG, 27 Jun 42, CM–IN–9002; Marshall to Emmons, 4 Jul 42, CM–OUT–1179.

[45] Relevant Papers, all of which the author consulted, are filed in OPD 384 PTO case 18 and are listed in Matloff and Snell, *Strategic Planning, 1941–42*, p. 265.

[46] Ltr, Marshall to Harmon, 7 Jul 42, sub: Instruction to CG USAFISPA, with amendment dated 12 Jul 42, OPD 384 PTO case 18.

Purchasing Board, established by Ghormley in June 1942 and consisting of three American officers—one from each of the services. Other supplies, except for petroleum products, which were a naval responsibility, he would procure from the San Francisco port.[47]

Unlike Ghormley, General Harmon had no operational control over his forces. Though he did later acquire such command it was by delegation from COMSOPAC, for limited periods and for specific purposes. His instructions, too, limited his authority. They lacked, he later said, "simplicity and directness," and by particularizing his duties had the effect of restricting his command. He had no power over the employment of Army forces, and could only plead his instructions to assist COMSOPAC in the preparation and execution of plans as authority for a voice in the discussions and decisions involving Army and Air Force units. So vague was this provision, that he commented to a Washington colleague later that "anyone could interpret [it] in any way they desired."[48] His own interpretation was as broad as he could make it, with the result that he played a far more active role in operations than was ever intended.

Many of the officers General Harmon chose for his staff were highly trained airmen whose selection reflected the War Department's intention that the new headquarters would uphold the Army Air Forces' interests in this predominantly naval area. His chief of staff was Brig. Gen. Nathan F. Twining, later to become commander of the Thirteenth

Air Force; his supply officer, Col. Robert G. Breene; his operations officers Cols. Frank F. Everest, Dean C. Strother, and Thomas D. Roberts; and his Signal officer, Col. Francis T. Ankenbrandt. On 16 July these men left Washington by air. After a brief stopover in San Francisco, where they met General Kenney, on his way to Australia to replace General Brett, they reached Hawaii on the 22d and Suva in the Fijis on the 26th. From there Kenney reported to Admiral Ghormley and assumed command of U.S. Army forces in the area by radio. His headquarters, he announced, would be in Noumea, capital city of New Caledonia. Until he could issue further instructions on administration and supply, Harmon told the Army commanders, they were to handle such matters as before.

The headquarters in New Caledonia was opened on 29 July. Already Admiral McCain was established there and Ghormley soon moved his own headquarters, located aboard the USS *Argonne,* to the port of Noumea. Thus, the major Army and Navy headquarters were quickly brought together so that a close working relationship could be established. "There has been no suggestion of any lack of harmony," General Harmon told Arnold. "Neither Ghormley or McCain are inclined to demand or suggest tasks beyond the capabilities of our units and freely consult unit commanders and members of my staff on matters of technique.... All commands, forces, and units in this area are working full out, and in full accord to the common end; and this relationship will be preserved."[49]

---

[47] See Leighton and Coakley, *Global Logistics and Strategy*, pp. 190–92.

[48] Ltr, Harmon to Handy, 4 Nov 43, copy in OCMH.

[49] Ltr, Harmon to Arnold, 5 Aug 42, copy in OCMH.

The logistical problems that faced General Harmon were, like those of other commanders in the Pacific, perhaps the most difficult. His command covered a tremendous area, over one million square miles, practically all of it ocean. The most distant bases were 3,000 miles apart. Unlike a continental theater of operations with debarkation facilities, road nets, and railways, the South Pacific had almost no communications or developed industrial facilities except in New Zealand. Harbors and docks were scarce. In the entire area there were only four ports, Auckland, Wellington, Suva, and Noumea, with usable terminal installations, and of these only the first was adequate to support a major military effort. Before any of these ports could accommodate large shipments of troops and supplies it would be necessary to enlarge and improve harbors, docks, and warehouses. Roads and the other requirements for a large supply base were nonexistent or entirely inadequate. To add to this difficulty, Harmon had to impose order on an already complicated and confusing situation and deal with a naval supply organization which performed many of the functions his own would. "Our own Army logistic problem," he explained to Marshall, "is sufficiently difficult in itself. The one of coordination with the Navy to avoid duplication, economize on transportation and insure availability of surpluses in one service to meet deficiencies of the other is doubly so."[50] He had been in the area only a month when he told a Washington colleague that "logistics is

still, and for a long time will be in a muddle."[51]

It was not until 15 October, about two and one-half months after his arrival, that General Harmon assumed responsibility for supply and administration of Army forces in the South Pacific.[52] This responsibility he delegated to a Service Command headed by his G–4, Colonel Breene, soon to be promoted to brigadier general, thus leaving himself free to concentrate on operational matters. All Army commanders were instructed to send their requisitions as well as all reports and requests, to the new headquarters, soon reorganized and redesignated the Services of Supply, where they would be consolidated and forwarded to Washington. In this way central control and standard procedure for all Army units in the area were established for the first time.

Harmon's control of Army air units in the South Pacific was less direct. From the outset he insisted, as did his superiors in Washington, that their administration, supply, and training were his responsibility, though Admiral McCain exercised operational control. Moreover, even in operations he did not concede that McCain's control was complete. It was his responsibility, he asserted, to see that the Army's aircraft were employed in a way that was consistent with doctrines and techniques of the Air Forces. Very early he came to the conclusion that this could only be achieved by a centralized Army air organization for the South Pacific. Failure to create such an organization, he told General Arnold, would soon place the Army "in the posi-

---

[50] Ltr, Harmon to Marshall, 9 Sep 42, copy in OCMH.

[51] Ltr, Harmon to Brig Gen St. Clair Streett, 27 Aug 42, copy in OCMH.
[52] GO 6F, Hq USAFISPA, 15 Oct 42.

tion of being unable to refute an assertion to the effect: "You do not have in the Army any senior officer with operational experience of large Air Forces in this type of warfare."[53] The organization Harmon wanted was finally established in January 1943 when the Thirteenth Air Force was activated, but already the major issue had been resolved.

Almost the first problem Harmon raised with Admiral Ghormley when he reached Noumea was that of Army control over the operations of the B–17's and B–26's based on Efate and Espiritu Santo. The solution worked out during several conferences with Ghormley and McCain late in July gave to Harmon responsibility for the training and indoctrination of Army air units, but left to McCain the formulation of doctrine for the employment of aircraft and their

assignment to operations. In routine operations such as patrolling, the aircraft were to be controlled by the base commander through his air officer, who might be an Army or Navy officer. But the missions and objectives were to be assigned by McCain. In short, General Harmon received, in large measure, supervision over the administration of Army air units as well as control over their employment in normal and routine situations. But he had little to say in their assignment, the strategy that dictated their employment, and the organization under which they would operate.

By the time these problems had been solved and the organization of the South Pacific worked out, the forces in the area were already engaged in offensive operations. These operations had been made possible by a series of naval battles which had turned the balance in the Pacific and given the initiative for the first time since 7 December to the Allies.

---

[53] Ltr, Harmon to Arnold, 12 Oct 42, copy in OCMH.

CHAPTER XII

Transition

There are only three principles of warfare—Audacity, *Audacity*, and AUDACITY.

GENERAL PATTON

The story of the first four months of the war in the Pacific was one of unrelieved tragedy and disaster. Everywhere, from Hawaii to Burma, the Allies had suffered humiliation and defeat at the hands of a foe who seemed almost superhuman, able to traverse unbelievable distances and impossible terrain on a handful of rice and quick to take advantage of every Allied weakness. Only in the Philippines, where American and Filipino forces still held out, had the implacable foe been thwarted, and even there the end was clearly in sight.

But the next two months of 1942 would tell a different story. Already the tide of Japanese victory was receding as the Allies recovered from their momentary confusion and sought to overcome their initial weakness. In April the raid came against Tokyo, a fitting retaliation for Pearl Harbor and the first good news the American public had had in four months of war. Next month the Allies struck another blow in the Coral Sea to give pause to the overconfident and jubilant Japanese. Finally, early in June, came the great American naval victory off Midway, which marked the turning point of the war and made possible the offensives that followed later in the year.

During these months the only dark spot in an otherwise brightening scene was the loss of the Philippines and the tragic fate of its gallant defenders. But this isolated victory had little strategic significance for the Japanese who in two brief and bitter months had seen the initiative they had thought so firmly in their hands slip away from them. The sunshine-filled days of victory had indeed been short.

The Fall of the Philippines

When Wainwright moved to Corregidor to take over MacArthur's post on 21 March, the lull which had settled over the Bataan battlefield in mid-February was already coming to an end. Since 8 February when he had abandoned his fruitless attempts to reduce the Bataan defenses, General Homma had received large reinforcements, almost two divisions as well as artillery, aircraft, and individual replacements. By the end of March his plans were ready and most of his troops in position to attack. But before he gave the signal he offered Wainwright one last chance to surrender, urging him to be sensible and follow "the defenders of Hongkong, Singapore, and the Netherlands East Indies in the acceptance of an honorable defeat."[1] Wainright did not even reply to this message, and on 3 April, Good Friday, after almost two weeks of intensive air and artillery attacks, the final Japanese offensive began.

From the start the attack went well for General Homma who, on the basis of his earlier disappointments, was prepared for the worst. The 80,000 Americans and Filipinos crowded into the southern tip of the Bataan Peninsula were too weak from hunger, their combat efficiency too low to withstand the ferocity of the Japanese attack. In short order Homma's forces pierced the center of the American line, outflanked the defenders, and forced them back from the main line of resistance. By the night of the 8th, General King's Luzon Force had virtually disintegrated. Philippine Army troops were in complete rout and units were melting away "lock, stock, and barrel." Headquarters had lost contact with the front-line troops and the roads were jammed with soldiers who had abandoned arms and equipment in their frantic haste to escape. Three months of malnutrition, malaria, and intestinal infections had left the Americans and Filipinos weak and disease-ridden, totally incapable of the sustained physical effort necessary for a successful defense. There was nothing for General King to do but surrender.

The battle for Bataan was ended; the fighting was over. The men who had survived the long ordeal could feel just-ly proud of their accomplishment. For three months they had held off the Japanese, only to be overwhelmed finally by disease and starvation. In a very real sense they had suffered "a true medical defeat."[2]

The events that followed General King's surrender present a confused and chaotic story of the disintegration and dissolution of a starved, diseased, and beaten army, a story climaxed by the horrors and atrocities of the infamous Death March. Denied food and water, robbed of their personal possessions, forced to march under the hot sun and halt in areas where even the most primitive sanitary facilities were lacking, clubbed, beaten, and bayoneted by their Japanese conquerors, General King's men made their way into captivity. Gallant foes and brave soldiers, the battling bastards of Bataan had earned the right to be treated with consideration and decency, but their enemies had reserved for them even greater privations and deeper humiliation than any they had yet suffered.[3]

Though the fall of Bataan ended all organized opposition on Luzon, it did not give the Japanese the most valuable prize of all, Manila Bay. So long as Corregidor and its sister forts lying across the entrance to the bay remained in American hands, the use of the finest natural harbor in the Orient was denied them. And before General Homma could report to his already impatient superiors in Tokyo that he had accom-

---

[1] The text of the surrender message is in the exhibits of the trial of General Homma, Prosecution exhibit 421. This section is based on Morton, *Fall of the Philippines*, ch. XXIII–XXXII.

[2] Rpt, Luzon Force Surgeon to CG, Luzon Force, 30 Jun 42, sub: Medical Aspects of the Surrender, copy in OCMH.

[3] For an account of the Death March, see Stanley L. Falk, *Bataan: The March of Death* (New York: W. W. Norton & Company, 1962).

plished his mission, he would also have to occupy Mindanao to the south as well as the more important islands in the Visayan group in the central Philippines.

It took the Japanese another month to accomplish these tasks. While his troops were making ready for the assault on Corregidor, General Homma launched the offensive in the south. On 19 April a detachment recently arrived from Borneo took Cebu in the Visayas and next day another from Malaya occupied the neighboring island of Panay. Both detachments then joined the one at Davao to begin the campaign on Mindanao. In a concerted drive beginning on 29 April, the Emperor's birthday, the Japanese advanced rapidly on all fronts and within a week had virtually gained control of the island. "North front in full retreat," reported General Sharp. "Enemy comes through right flank. Nothing further can be done. May sign off any time now."[4]

Meanwhile the Japanese had turned their attention to Corregidor. With the southern tip of Bataan in their possession they could now emplace artillery on the heights of the Mariveles Mountains and along the Manila Bay shore, only two miles across the channel from the island fortress. By thus massing their artillery they were able to pour on Corregidor so steady and heavy a volume of fire that the intermittent air attacks of the preceding three months paled into insignificance. "One day's shelling," remarked one officer, "did more damage than all the bombing put together."[5]

For twenty-seven days, from 9 April to 6 May, this bombardment continued, increasing in intensity as the days went by. By the evening of 5 May there was little left on the island to stop the Japanese. The beach defenses had been demolished, the huge seacoast guns silenced, and the antiaircraft batteries reduced to impotence. All wire communication had been destroyed and every effort to restore it unavailing. "Command," observed General Moore, "could be exercised and intelligence obtained only by use of foot messengers."[6]

Even the topography of the island had changed. Where once there had been thick woods and dense vegetation only charred stumps remained. The rocky ground had been pulverized into a fine dust, and the coastal road had been literally blown into the bay. Deep craters, empty shell cases, and huge fragments of concrete pockmarked the landscape. Gone were the broad lawns, impressive parade grounds, spacious barracks, and pleasant shaded clubs and bungalows of peacetime. By 5 May Corregidor lay "scorched, gaunt, and leafless, covered with the chocolate dust of countless explosions."[7]

By this time the 10,000 men on Corregidor—soldiers, marines, and sailors alike—knew that a Japanese assault was imminent. "It took no mental giant," as Wainwright observed, "to figure out by May 5, 1942, that the enemy was ready to come against Corregidor."[8] And most of the men knew as well as their commander that they stood little chance.

---

[4] Rad, Sharp to MacArthur, 9 May 42 GHQ SWPA G–3 Jnl, Phil Is, Opns Rpts.

[5] The Siege of Corregidor, Mil Rpts on UN, No. 12, 15 Nov 43, p. 50, MID WD.

[6] Rpt of Harbor Defenses of Manila and Subic Bays, an. 8, USAFFE USFIP Rpt of Opns, p. 72.

[7] Maude R. Williams, The Last Days of Corregidor, supp. p. 1, typescript diary in OCMH.

[8] Wainwright, *General Wainwright's Story*, p. 114.

There had been six hundred casualties since 9 April, and those who escaped injury were beginning to feel the effects of malnutrition. Men were living on nerve alone, and morale was dropping rapidly. All hopes for reinforcement had long since disappeared. There was only enough water to last four more days at most and no prospect that the pipes and pumps for the artesian wells could be repaired. In any event, the power plant on which the Corregidor garrison was entirely dependent would not last more than a few weeks.

Life in Malinta Tunnel, where those who could had taken refuge, had become almost unbearable. Dust, dirt, great black flies, and vermin were everywhere, and over everything hung the odor of the hospital and men's bodies. On the haggard faces of the men could be seen the effects of the continuous bombardment. There was a limit to human endurance and that limit, General Wainwright told the President, "has long since been passed."[9]

The long-awaited and dreaded attack came late on the night of 5 May, after a particularly intense artillery concentration on the tail of the tadpole-shaped island. The full moon, "veiled by streaks of heavy black clouds," was just rising when, shortly before midnight, Japanese artillery fire suddenly ceased, and its bass roar was replaced "by the treble chattering of many small arms."[10] Barges were observed approaching the tail (east) end of the island, and at 2230 the order went out to prepare for a hostile landing. A few minutes later a runner from the beach defense command post arrived at Moore's headquarters in Malinta Tunnel with the news that the Japanese had landed.

The fight for Corregidor lasted only ten hours. Though the Japanese suffered heavy losses during the landing and came ashore in the wrong place, they recovered quickly. One group cut across the tail of the island while the bulk of the Japanese turned west, advancing in the darkness along the axis of the island toward Malinta Tunnel. At Battery Denver on a ridge near the east entrance of the tunnel, the Japanese ran into the first serious opposition and it was there that most of the fighting took place that night and during the early hours of the morning. The defenders threw everything they had into the battle, including coast artillery men and a provisional battalion of 500 sailors, but their efforts were doomed to failure. Finally, at 0800, after the Japanese had brought tanks and artillery ashore for a concerted attack, General Wainwright committed his last reserves.

The final blow came soon after when the Japanese sent three tanks into the action. The first appearance of armor on the front panicked the defenders and caused some to bolt to the rear. It took the combined efforts of commissioned and noncommissioned officers to calm the troops and prevent a rout. "The effect of the tanks," the Japanese noted with satisfaction, "was more than had been anticipated."[11]

By 1000 on the morning of 6 May the situation of the American troops on Cor-

---

[9] *Ibid.*, pp. 122–23.
[10] Maj John McM. Gulick, Memoirs of Btry C, 91st CA (PS), p. 188, copy in OCMH.

[11] Statement of Col Yoshida, 9 Feb 50, ATIS Doc 62644, Statements of Japanese Officials on World War II, GHQ FEC, IV 553–57, OCMH.

regidor was critical. The troops on the front line, pinned down by machine gun and artillery fire, could move neither forward nor back and had no weapons with which to meet the tanks. Already between 600 and 800 men had been killed and about 1,000 more wounded. All reserves had been committed and practically all the guns destroyed. The Japanese were apparently preparing for another landing at the opposite end of the island, and, in any case, would reach Malinta Tunnel with its 1,000 wounded men in a few hours. When they did there would be a wholesale slaughter.

It was on this basis that General Wainwright made his decision to surrender, to trade one day of freedom for several thousand lives. By 1200, all arms larger than .45-caliber were destroyed, codes and radio equipment smashed, classified papers burned, and the surrender message broadcast in English and Japanese. At that time, the American flag on Corregidor was lowered and burned and the white flag hoisted. "With broken heart and head bowed in sadness but not in shame," Wainwright wrote the President, "I report . . . that today I must arrange terms for the surrender of the fortified islands of Manila Bay. . . . With profound regret and with continued pride in my gallant troops, I go to meet the Japanese commander."[12] The five-month-long struggle for control of the Philippine Archipelago was over; the victory which Homma had hoped to win by the middle of February was finally his, three months later. It was a victory without honor and for this delay and

GENERAL WAINWRIGHT *broadcasts surrender instructions.*

loss of face Homma was relieved of command and spent the rest of the war on the side lines, as an officer on inactive status.

In the context of global war, the Philippines did not in mid-1942 possess great strategic significance. The Japanese tide had already swept around the islands and over Southeast Asia and the Indies, through the Bismarck Archipelago into the Solomons and New Guinea, and eastward across the Pacific as far as the Gilbert Islands. Only in the Philippines had the enemy been halted, and in this successful though hopeless resistance lay the real importance of the bitter defense. It demonstrated that the Japanese were not invincible, and that they could be stopped by determined men, ably led. For an Allied world surfeited on gloom, defeat, and despair, the epic of Bataan and Corregidor was

---

[12] Rad, Wainwright to Roosevelt, 6 May 42. A copy of this message is reproduced in Wainwright, *General Wainwright's Story*, pp. 122–23.

a symbol of hope and a beacon of success for the future.

The Tokyo Raid

To balance the bad news of the loss of the Philippines, the American public could look back with satisfaction to the recent announcement of the spectacular raid against Tokyo on 18 April. Conceived during the dark days of January as a retaliation for Pearl Harbor, this bold strike, coming only nine days after the surrender of Bataan, was a powerful boost to morale at home and a grim warning of American determination to carry the war into the enemy's territory.

The idea for the raid is credited variously to the President, to Stanley K. Hornbeck of the State Department, and to others. Apparently it was first considered seriously in the Navy Department by Capt. Francis L. Low, Admiral King's operations officer, and King in January 1942. The problem, King and Low agreed, was to get planes within striking distance of Tokyo Bay without putting the carriers within range of the enemy's air and naval defenses. This meant the launching position would have to be at least 500 miles off the Japanese coast. Where would the planes put down after the attack? Certainly the aircraft carriers would not be able to await their return. Vladivostok was only 600 miles from Tokyo, but the Soviet authorities would not provide a haven for the American fliers for fear of risking hostilities with Japan. They would have to land somewhere in eastern China, thus adding 1,500 miles to the minimum of 500 required to reach Tokyo. Only the Army Air Forces could provide a plane with the range and bomb load required. But would army bombers be able to take off from aircraft carriers?[13] Obviously the Army Air Forces would have to study the problem.

General Arnold, when the idea was presented to him, was enthusiastic. While Capt. Donald B. Duncan, King's air operations officer, worked out the naval details of the plan, Arnold's staff studied the air problems presented by this daring scheme. The first task was to select an airplane that would meet the requirements. Three types were considered and the planners finally chose the twin-engine medium bomber, the B–25. For this mission, the planes would have three auxiliary fuel tanks and additional gasoline inside for a capacity of 1,141 gallons, cameras, a 2,000-pound bomb load, a simple bombing device called the Mark Twain, and two dummy tail guns which, it was hoped, would discourage Japanese fighters from attacking from the rear.[14] The choice of planes, all of which came from the 17th Bombardment Group, determined the choice of crews. Twenty-four were needed and it was decided to get them all, if possible, from this group. More than enough volunteered to make up the force required for the assignment. General Arnold himself chose the leader of the expedition, Lt. Col. James H. Doolittle.

[13] Vice Adm Donald B. Duncan, Account of Tokyo Raid Planning, written for Samuel E. Morison, historian of U.S. naval operations. A detailed study of the Tokyo raid was prepared by Lt. Col. S. L. A. Marshall during the war and is on file in OCMH. This study was the basis for the accounts in Morison, *The Rising Sun in the Pacific*, pp. 389–98, and Craven and Cate, *AAF I*, 438–44. This author used these narratives as well as many of the records used by Colonel Marshall.

[14] The Norden sight was not used because the planes were to bomb from low altitude and because of the danger of enemy capture.

There were many problems, the most important of which was to train the pilots in carrier take-offs, still to be solved. These were worked out during March when the crews trained at Eglin Field, Florida, on a strip the size of a carrier's deck. Before the month was over all the pilots had taken off twice with fully loaded planes in a distance of 700 to 750 feet. There was, unfortunately, no time for practice with live bombs or for gunnery training. All the younger pilots, however, were required to make an extended overwater flight from Eglin to Houston, Texas. On 24 March, after less than a month's training, the entire group was ordered to Alameda Naval Air Station in San Francisco Bay where the naval task force which would carry the B–25's across the Pacific was already assembling.

The plan for the impending raid on Tokyo was one of the best kept secrets of the war. Only a handful of men knew the entire plan at this time. Neither the pilots nor the ships' crews had yet learned their ultimate destination, though many may have guessed it by then. Not even the highest staff officers in Washington had anything to do with the project. This secrecy is strikingly illustrated by the response from the Military Intelligence Division of the War Department General Staff to the suggestion of an unidentified State Department official for a surprise blow against Japan on the Emperor's birthday, 29 April. Except for the date, the State Department's proposal, forwarded to General Marshall by Hornbeck, was by coincidence identical in every respect to the operation already under way. The response from Military Intelligence, which was asked to comment on the proposal, was generally unfavorable and revealed a complete ignorance of the project.[15]

This secrecy extended even to the Chungking government which would have to make arrangements for the reception of the crews once they had completed their mission. Chiang Kai-shek and Lt. Gen. Joseph W. Stilwell, commander of U.S. Army forces in China, Burma, and India, were told only that certain fields in eastern China would be required for the use of American bombers and that a quantity of aviation gasoline and other stores must be available by 19 April. Chiang gave his assent on 28 March without knowing what would happen, and it was not until 2 April, after the task force had already put to sea, that he was told that at least twenty-five B–25's were involved. After that date arrangements were quickly made for the arrival of the planes, the procurement of personnel and supplies, and for communications—no information was to be relayed over Chinese signal channels. But already bad weather had settled over eastern China.

Meanwhile Colonel Doolittle and his group had arrived at Alameda on 31 March. There waiting was the carrier *Hornet*, Capt. Marc A. Mitscher commanding, with two cruisers, four destroyers, and an oiler. Next morning sixteen of the B–25's—all there was room for—were hoisted to the carrier's flight deck and lashed down securely. At 1000 of the 2d, under cover of a thick fog, the *Hornet* and its escort steamed

---

[15] Ltr, Hornbeck to Marshall, 14 Mar 42; Memo, Col. Oscar N. Solbert, MI to WPD, 16 Mar 42, sub: Possible Double Play in Opns Against Japan, AG 381 (3–14–42).

COLONEL DOOLITTLE AND CAPTAIN MITSCHER *on the Hornet.*

days at sea, the *Hornet* force rendezvoused with a similar force out of Pearl Harbor at a point north of Midway at the date line. Led by Vice Adm. William F. Halsey, Jr., who flew his flag from the *Enterprise*, the entire expedition steamed westward toward Japan at sixteen knots, the 4 cruisers and 8 destroyers in the van and on the flanks, *Hornet* in the center, with the 2 oilers and the flagship in column behind.

For four days, from 13 to 17 April, the task force nosed its way silently through the heavy seas of the North Pacific.[16] Overhead the planes of the *Enterprise* maintained constant vigil. On the 16th the Army bombers were spotted for the take-off. There was no space to spare on the crowded flight deck; the leading bomber (Doolittle's) had 467 feet clearance, the last hung precariously over the edge of the ramp. About 1,000 miles east of Tokyo, on the 17th, the carriers and cruisers refueled and speeded ahead at twenty knots, in the face of winds which had increased to gale force, toward the Japanese coast. Barring accident or interception the *Hornet* would be in launching position by sundown the next day.

Unknown to Halsey and Doolittle, there had been a hitch in the plans. Fearing Japanese reprisal, Chiang had urged early in April, when the *Hornet* had already put to sea under radio silence, that the operation be postponed, or even canceled, but it was too late for such drastic measures. On the 15th he gave reluctant assent to the final plans and for the use of the fields in eastern

down San Francisco Bay and through the Golden Gate. Once away from shore the loud-speakers announced what the men already suspected—that the target was Tokyo. "Cheers from every section of the ship greeted the announcement," records the *Hornet* action report, "and morale reached a new high." Now for the first time it was possible to provide the bomber crews with target data and other information they would need.

Weather during this first leg of the voyage was foul. Though the high winds, heavy seas, and frequent squalls reduced the danger of detection they also subjected the B–25's to damage from vibration and exposure to the elements. *Hornet*'s machinists checked the planes frequently to make certain the lashings were secure and to repair mechanical difficulties. On 13 April, after eleven

---

[16] Since the task force crossed the date line, it lost one day on the way out.

China, excepting only the one at Chu-chow which could not be made ready because of bad weather. It was just this field that all the crews had chosen for their landing, but there was no way to get the information to the task force without giving away its position to the enemy.

Halsey and Doolittle had changed their plans too. To minimize the danger of interception, the plan originally called for a nocturnal attack, launched about 500 miles off the Japanese coast on the afternoon of the 19th, with Doolittle taking off about three hours ahead of the others to light up Tokyo with incendiaries. This would bring the crews over Chuchow during daylight of the 20th. But Halsey for some unaccountable reason was a day ahead of schedule and there was no way to alert the Chinese so that the fields would be ready. Colonel Doolittle was not unduly concerned. The Chinese, he felt certain, would receive ample notice of his arrival from Radio Tokyo.

More serious were the developments of the 18th which forced a change in the hour as well as the day of the attack. At 0210 that morning *Enterprise* picked up two ships on its radar screen and altered course. The search flight sent out at first light confirmed the bad news that the task force had apparently struck the enemy's first line of patrol ships some two hundred miles further off the coast than expected. Worse than that, one of the search planes reported at 0715 that it had been sighted. Again course was changed, but about a half hour later another enemy patrol ship was observed, this time from the deck of the *Hornet*. There could be little doubt that the task force had been discovered and reported.

Enemy counteraction could be expected at any time.

Halsey was now faced with the most critical decision of the entire voyage. Should he push on toward the Japanese coast to bring the B–25's to the position originally planned, withdraw to safety, or launch the bombers immediately? Whichever course he chose, he would have to strike a delicate balance between the risks to his carriers and the risks to the Army bombers. Japan was still 670 miles away, more than 100 miles further than the air planners had considered safe for the bombing run. It was evident to Halsey that he could take his carriers no further without exposing them to attack. The bombers would have to take off now or not at all—the carriers must withdraw. His decision, made with Colonel Doolittle's concurrence, was to launch the bombers and risk attack, though Tokyo was still five hours' flight away and the prospect of the crews reaching the fields in China slim. At 0800 Halsey gave his orders: *Hornet* to turn at twenty-two knots into the wind and prepare to launch; *Nashville* to sink the patrol ship sighted fifteen minutes earlier.

Aboard the *Hornet* the next hour and a half was full of excitement and ordered confusion. The wind was at forty knots and the sea so rough that the green waters washed over the carrier's ramps. After a few last-minute instructions the bomb racks were loaded and the planes readied for the take-off. It was 0818 when Colonel Doolittle began his run down the flight deck and then roared upward to circle the *Hornet* once before heading west. The rest of the pilots followed quickly and without incident except for one "who hung on the brink of a stall until," wrote Admiral Halsey, "we nearly catalogued his effects."[17] By 0924 the entire group was airborne and the task force reversed course and speeded for home at 25 knots, all radios tuned in for news from Tokyo.

The flight of the bombers toward Tokyo Bay was uneventful, though they flew over warships and past Japanese aircraft. Apparently the patrol boat warnings had not yet been broadcast. In their favor also was the fact that Tokyo that morning was holding a full-scale air drill which was just ending when Colonel Doolittle's plane reached the city, coming in from the north at rooftop level, shortly after noon. Not a shot had been fired at his plane when at 1215 (Tokyo time) he and Lt. Travis Hoover in the second plane dropped their incendiaries and bombs. One antiaircraft battery answered the attack, apparently on the initiative of the gunners, but there was as yet no general alarm or understanding that an enemy raid was in progress.

After this first bombing there was an interlude of about twenty minutes during which the air raid warning finally sounded. Then at 1240 eleven more bombers, which had reached the target by different courses, came in over the enemy capital, hitting factories, oil tanks, power plants, and military installations. The remaining three planes, loaded with incendiaries, hit Nagoya, Yokohoma, the Yokosuka Navy Yard, and Kobe. Though all the crews had been cautioned against striking nonmilitary targets it was inevitable that they should and for this three of the fliers later paid with their lives. Fifteen of the sixteen bombers success-

fully completed their missions. Not a single plane had been shot down, but the last and most dangerous portion of the voyage still lay ahead.

Behind them the American pilots left a surprised and confused enemy. By later standards damage was slight, but the Japanese people could not doubt that the enemy had broken through the Empire's inner defenses to strike at the heart of the homeland. How it had been done the authorities did not yet know. The patrol boats had alerted them to the presence of the carriers, but they were puzzled by the fact that the aircraft which struck Tokyo had been Army bombers, not the carriers planes. they expected. The Japanese did not apparently associate Doolittle's attack with the carriers. The bombers, they thought, had come from Midway and they were still expecting a carrier-based attack the next morning, when the ships reported by the patrol boats would have come within launching position. It was some time before the Japanese accepted the truth that the carriers and the bombers were part of the same force.

The rest of the story of the Tokyo raid—the landing of the fliers in China and their flight to safety—is one of heroism, suffering, and tragedy. Of the sixteen crews, fifteen made China with the help of a providential tail wind; the sixteenth landed near Vladivostok and its crew was interned by the Russians, escaping later to Iran. The planes over China, except one which came down along the coast, made their way through the darkness and rain until their fuel was exhausted without finding the designated fields. Four of the bombers crash-landed and the crews of the remainder bailed out. Eight of the men

---

[17] William F. Halsey and Joseph Bryan, *Admiral Halsey's Story* (New York: Whittlesey House, 1947), p. 103.

fell into Japanese hands and 1 of those who had parachuted was killed in descent. Thus 71 of the 80 men who had started on the hazardous journey finally made their way to safety.[18]

The naval task force made good its escape also, evading the planes and ships the Japanese sent in pursuit and sinking several small vessels in the bargain. Once beyond the outer picket line, the voyage home was uneventful, and on 25 April, a week after the President had announced that planes from Shangri-La had bombed Tokyo, Halsey led his fleet into Pearl Harbor. All hands were looking forward to an extended shore leave, but already a new crisis was developing in the Coral Sea.

Coral Sea and Midway

Ever since early March, when the *4th Fleet* and the *South Seas Detachment* had jointly occupied Lae and Salamaua along the northeast coast of New Guinea, the Japanese had been preparing for a seaborne invasion of Port Moresby, a move that would take them into the Coral Sea between Australia and the New Hebrides. The carriers and cruisers required for that operation had finally arrived at Truk on 29 April at which time orders for the long-delayed invasion were issued.[19]

The landings at Port Moresby—there were to be two of them—were to be made at dawn, 10 May, by General Horii's *South Seas Detachment* and a battalion of special naval landing troops. Both units were to leave Rabaul on the 4th in a convoy whose maximum speed,

fixed by the old Army transports carrying the *South Seas Detachment*, was only six and a half knots. Since these slow ships would expose the convoy to air and naval attack, the Japanese made careful provision to protect their troops. Direct support would be provided by a naval escort force comprising the small carrier *Shoho*, 4 heavy cruisers, and a destroyer squadron. Ranging farther afield, free to strike any Allied air and naval units, was a carrier division comprised of 2 large carriers, the *Shokaku* and *Zuikaku*, 3 heavy cruisers, and 7 destroyers under the command of Vice Adm. Takeo Takagi. In addition, 2 submarines were to take up positions in the Coral Sea and 4 others along the eastern coast of Australia to intercept any Allied naval warships hastening to the scene. Finally, long-range bombers based at Rabaul were to strike targets in northeast Australia and interdict air and naval traffic in the Coral Sea and Torres Strait.[20]

For this venture, the Japanese, who had acquired considerable caution since the Allied reaction to the Lae-Salamaua landings, left nothing to chance. As a prelude to the invasion of Port Moresby by this sizable force, there would be two preliminary operations: first, the occupation of Tulagi in the southern Solomons on 3 May; and second, the seizure two days later of Deboyne Island just off the east coast of Papua. With these islands in their possession, the Japanese would

---

[18] Four of the men who were captured by the Japanese were recovered after the war.

[19] See above, p. 217.

[20] This account of the plans and of the action which follows is based on the following sources: Japanese Opns in SWPA, 125–29; Hist of *Army Sec, Imperial GHQ*, pp. 51ff; Hist of *South Seas Detachment*, pp. 12–14; Southeast Area Naval Opns, I, pp. 2, 4, 15; Bismarck—Solomons Landing Opns, pp. 36–42; *18th Army* Opns, I, p. 7; ONI Combat Narrative, The Battle of the Coral Sea OCMH; Morison, *Coral Sea, Midway and Submarine Actions*; Craven and Cate, *AAF I*, pp. 448–50.

be able to provide shore-based air support for the landings at Port Moresby and to cover the east flank of the invasion force during its approach.

Even before the arrival of the large carriers at Truk on 29 April, the Japanese had already put the first part of this plan into effect. Four days earlier, aircraft from Rabaul had begun to bomb fields in northeast Australia. The Tulagi force moved out of Rabaul a few days later and on 2 May stood off the island. There was no opposition to the landing next day; the small Australian detachment had been warned and after destroying what it could had pulled out for Efate in the New Hebrides. On the 5th the Japanese occupied Deboyne Island. Thus far everything had come off on schedule, exactly as planned.

While these preliminary operations were in progress, the Port Moresby invasion force was moving into position for the landing. The *South Seas Detachment* and the special naval troops began loading on 2 May and on the 4th sailed out of the harbor to meet the naval escort. That same day the *Shokaku* and *Zuikaku,* steaming south from Truk, received reports of an Allied carrier-based attack on Tulagi and set course for the island at full speed.

Despite continued reports of Allied naval forces in the Coral Sea, the Port Moresby convoy, reinforced by the *Shoho* group, which had supported the Tulagi landing, continued on its way. But on the 7th, when it was clear that the invasion force had been spotted, the transports and a portion of the escorting and supporting naval elements were ordered back to safety. Remaining to take up position for the impending battle were the carriers *Shokaku* and *Zuikaku* with their cruiser and destroyer escort in the open waters south of the Solomons, off San Cristobal.

The presence of Allied naval forces in the Coral Sea was no accident. Ever since February, reports of Japanese concentrations in the Northeast Area and in the mandated islands had been coming into Washington. By mid-April the time and place of attack had been fairly well determined from intercepted and decoded messages and both Nimitz and MacArthur warned to expect a seaborne invasion of Port Moresby.[21] Thus alerted, both Pacific commanders made preparations to frustrate this fresh Japanese venture, which, if successful, would prove disastrous to MacArthur's plans for the defense of Australia and would create a serious threat to the line of communications.

General MacArthur's slender naval resources were no match for the formidable Japanese fleet entering his theater but he did what he could. His chief weapon was the land-based Allied Air Forces, and under his direction Brett assembled all the planes that he could at bases in northeast Australia. From there, long-range bombers struck Rabaul, Lae, Buka, and Deboyne during the first week of May while reconnaissance planes kept constant vigil along the sea approaches leading into the Coral Sea. It was these aircraft that discovered the Port Moresby invasion force on 6 May in the vicinity of Jomard Passage off the coast of Papua.[22]

---

[21] JIC Daily Summary, 19 and 24 Feb 42; Rad, King to Nimitz and Leary, No. 2032, 18 Apr 42, both cited in Hayes, The War Against Japan, ch. IV, p. 50.

[22] Allied Opns in SWPA, SWPA Series, I, pp. 46–47; Rad, MacArthur to Marshall, No. 719, 13 May 42, OPD Exec Files.

Most of the naval forces to meet the Japanese threat came from Admiral Nimitz' Pacific Fleet and were under his command. By noon 29 April he had made his plans. These called for the organization of a task force built around the carriers *Yorktown* and *Lexington* and under the command of Rear Adm. Frank J. Fletcher to rendezvous west of the New Hebrides and south of the Solomons. Fletcher's orders were simply to "operate in the Coral Sea commencing 1 May."[23] By that time, his force would include an attack group of cruisers and destroyers, a support group of three cruisers—two of them Australian—from the Southwest Pacific, a search group, and a destroyer screen for the carriers. All together Admiral Fletcher would have in his command 2 carriers, 1 light and 7 heavy cruisers, 13 destroyers, 2 tankers, and a seaplane tender. The submarines were not included in the task force; they would operate independently and patrol the coastal waters off northeast Australia and New Guinea. Thus, while the Japanese had a unified command for this operation the Allies were divided, with the bulk of the naval forces under Nimitz and the submarines and land-based aviation under MacArthur.

This array of Allied naval strength was hardly large enough to warrant any great optimism over the outcome. But it was the best Nimitz could do at the moment. He had other forces—Halsey's two carrier groups, each with one carrier, had returned to Pearl Harbor on the 25th—but it would take time to overhaul the vessels and make the 3,500-mile journey to the Coral Sea. On the off-chance that the battle would be delayed and that

Halsey could reach the scene, Nimitz made provision for the two additional carriers in his plans and ordered Halsey to make ready for the action.

The Japanese landing at Tulagi on 3 May took the Allies by surprise and found Fletcher's force some 500 miles to the south, still refueling. Immediately, Admiral Fletcher, who flew his flag from the *Yorktown,* made for Tulagi at high speed. Next morning, he launched his planes against the Japanese in the harbor, crippling a destroyer and sinking some small boats, and then returned to join the *Lexington.* The damage wrought by the raid was minor and had little effect on Japanese activities other than to alert them to the presence of American carriers and to bring the *Shokaku* and *Zuikaku* down to the area at full speed.

During the next few days, as the Port Moresby invasion force moved toward the target, search planes from the American carriers sought the enemy without success. Early on the morning of 6 May, when Brett's B-17's finally located a large force approaching Jomard Passage, word was flashed to Fletcher who at once ordered his fleet to set course for the enemy. All that day the fleet steamed northwest and the next morning Fletcher sent in the attack group of cruisers and destroyers to block the southern end of Jomard Passage through which the *Shoho* and the convoy's screen would pass.

Unknown to Fletcher, the main carrier strength of the Japanese was nowhere near Jomard, but off to the south and east. Early on the 7th, Japanese scout planes spotted two American vessels, a tanker and a destroyer, and mistakenly reported the former as a carrier. The *Shokaku* and *Zuikaku*'s bombers moved

[23] CINCPAC Opn Plan 23-42, 29 Apr 42; Morison, *Coral Sea, Midway and Submarine Actions*, p. 16.

in for the attack. Against such easy prey the Japanese pilots had little difficulty, sinking the destroyer at once and fatally damaging the tanker.

Meanwhile American aircraft had sighted the *Shoho* group and moved in for the kill, sinking the *Shoho* and a mine layer at 0930 of the 7th. But still neither side had definitely located the main force of the other. Throughout that day and into the night each searched feverishly for the other without success.

On the morning of the 8th, the opposing carriers, about 235 miles apart, located each other. The *Shokaku* and *Zuikaku* immediately launched their attack planes which made contact at 0920. At about the same time aircraft from the *Lexington* and *Yorktown* hit the Japanese in an attack that lasted less than two hours. The results seemed to be fairly even. Both the American carriers were damaged, the *Lexington* seriously. Only one of the Japanese carriers, the *Shokaku*, was hurt badly, but the enemy had lost more planes. Of the original complement of almost 100 aircraft, the Japanese had less than forty. Neither side was in condition to continue the fight.

Deprived of carrier protection and naval escort for the Port Moresby convoy, which had remained out of the way throughout the battle, the Japanese commander decided to call off the invasion and turn back to Rabaul. From Admiral Yamamoto came swift disapproval and an order to resume the fight and "annihilate the remnants of the enemy fleet."[24] But it was too late. For two days he tried to re-establish contact, but finally had to give up.

<hr>

[24] Japanese in SWPA, 129.

Explosion on the Lexington *during the Coral Sea Battle.*

Admiral Fletcher's problem was more serious. The *Lexington* was burning badly and he must try to save it. Shortly after noon of the 8th an internal explosion rocked the "Lady Lex." Soon there were more explosions and by late afternoon the *Lexington*'s fires were beyond control. Fletcher realized that he could no longer hope to save the Lady and made ready to pick up her crew when the time came to abandon ship. All hope of returning to the battle was already gone when he received Nimitz' message to retire. That night the *Lexington* went down. Not a man was lost, and even the captain's dog was saved.

The loss of the *Lexington* gave the victory to the Japanese, if victory is measured in ship losses alone. But the Japaneses did not so consider it. Their plan to take Port Moresby had been frustrated; strategically the victory belonged to the Allies. Coming as it did on 8 May, two days after the gloomy news of Corregidor's surrender, this victory gleamed all the more brightly as an augur of the future.

The defeat in the Coral Sea had little immediate effect on Japanese plans. These plans had originally called for the seizure of strategic positions in New Caledonia, the Fijis, and Samoa once the Port Moresby operation was over.[25] But the staff at *Imperial General Headquarters,* which approved this plan on 28 April, had hardly begun to prepare for operations against the Allied line of communications when the Navy proposed instead an attack against Midway and the western Aleutians. The Aleutians strike had already been discussed during March and the Army favored it. But Admiral Yamamoto who had first raised the possibility of such an attack against the Aleutians, regarded it as only one part of a larger plan whose main objective was Midway. Admiral Nagano, Chief of the Navy General Staff, did not raise that aspect of Yamamoto's plans in the discussions with the Army planners. Apparently he was not convinced at this time of the wisdom of an attack against Midway, but Yamamoto soon brought him around to his point of view. On 16 April, Nagano issued orders calling for a simultaneous attack on Midway and the Aleutians early in June, followed by the New Caledonia–Fiji–Samoa operation.

These orders were merely a statement of naval intentions and would not become approved war plans until the Army gave its consent. But Nagano for some unexplained reason did not mention Midway during the debate over the in-

vasion of Australia which led to the agreement of 28 April. Once again Yamamoto turned the powers of his persuasion on Nagano. Now he had the Tokyo raid, which the Japanese then thought had originated from Midway, to bolster his argument. Unless that island was occupied, he warned, there might be more American air raids against the homeland. Again Admiral Nagano bowed to the wishes of his forceful subordinate.

Thus, at the beginning of May, the Army planners received from their naval colleagues a plan for operations against Midway and the Aleutians. General Sugiyama, Chief of the Army General Staff, thought the plan overbold and opposed it, but the Navy was united. Nagano, stoutly backed by Yamamoto, insisted that Midway must be taken and if the Army refused to go along, the Navy would have to act independently. After a brief struggle, General Sugiyama finally gave in, influenced no doubt by Nagano's assurance that only a very small Army force, about one regiment, would be required. On 5 May, before the Coral Sea battle, *Imperial General Headquarters* issued orders for the Midway–Aleutians operation, to take place early in June. The New Caledonia–Fiji–Samoa operation would be postponed until after Midway and the western Aleutians had been occupied.[26]

The decision of 5 May was, in a real sense, a victory for Admiral Yamamoto. In the five months since the start of the

[25] See above, p. 217.

[26] Hist of *Army Sec, Imperial GHQ,* pp. 48, 50; Aleutians Naval Opns, Mar 42–Feb 43, pp. 2, 5–6; Midway Opns, pp. 3–5, 27, Japanese Studies in World War II, 53 and 96; Japanese Opns in SWPA, 124–25; Interrog of Generals Tanaka and Arisue; Statements of Admiral Tomioka and Colonel Hattori, Statements of Japanese Officials, IV, 315, I, 331–32.

war, the *Combined Fleet* had moved back and forth across the waters of the Pacific from Pearl Harbor to Ceylon, destroying everything in its path. It had sunk 5 of the enemy's battleships, 1 aircraft carrier, 2 cruisers and 7 destroyers; damaged a number of capital ships; and destroyed thousands of tons of merchant shipping and fleet auxiliaries. The cost had been small: 3 of the carriers had lost heavily in planes and skilled pilots; 23 small naval vessels, of which the largest was a destroyer, and about 60 transports and merchant ships had been sunk. The time was ripe, Yamamoto firmly believed, for a decisive blow. Pearl Harbor had only crippled the U.S. Pacific Fleet; the attack on Midway, by forcing Nimitz into a fleet engagement, would give the Japanese an opportunity to destroy it.[27]

The Battle of the Coral Sea did not alter Yamamoto's views, though it meant that the *Shokaku* and *Zuikaku* would not be available for the Midway operation and that there would have to be another try for Port Moresby. But that was placed on the bottom of the list, to be made after New Caledonia, the Fijis, and Samoa had been taken. Midway and the Aleutians now had first priority and planning for them went forward rapidly.

Concurrently with the planning for Midway and the Aleutians, the Army and Navy staff in Tokyo made preparation for the operations which would follow, and on 18 May established the *17th Army* under Lt. Gen. Haruyoshi Hyakutake. His orders were to co-operate with the *Combined Fleet* in the capture of New Caledonia, the Fijis, and Samoa, in order to "destroy the main enemy bases

in those areas, establish operational bases at Suva and Noumea, gain control of the seas east of Australia, and strive to cut communications between Australia and the United States."[28] Early July was the date tentatively selected for the start of these operations, provided that the fleet was ready.

General Hyakutake lost no time in getting ready. His total force consisted of about nine infantry battalions and support would be furnished by the *2d Fleet*, with attached carriers, and the *11th Air Fleet*. The *South Seas Detachment*, scheduled to take New Caledonia, was to assemble at Rabaul in the latter part of June; the two detachments selected to seize the Fijis and Samoa were to be ready at Truk early in July. When these operations were concluded, the Japanese would make a second try for Port Moresby.[29]

Meanwhile Admiral Yamamoto had completed his plans for the Midway–Aleutians campaign. The Aleutians force was built around the carriers *Junyo* and *Ryujo* and included, in addition to the landing force, submarines to patrol the west coast.[30] For the Midway operation, Yamamoto organized the most formidable force the Japanese had assembled since Pearl Harbor. The occupation force numbered about 5,000 Army and Navy troops whose transports would be protected by a strong escort. The main body of the fleet with which Yamamoto hoped to destroy the U.S. Pacific Fleet comprised a carrier force of 4 large carriers, the *Akagi, Kaga, Hiryu,* and *Soryu,*

[27] Morison, *The Rising Sun in the Pacific*, pp. 285–86, and *Coral Sea, Midway and Submarine Action*, pp. 5, 74–76.

[28] *Imperial GHQ* Army Order 19, 18 May 42, in Japanese Opns in SWPA, 125.

[29] *17th Army* Opns, I, pp. 4, 6; Statement of Admiral Tomioka.

[30] One of the submarines stood off Seattle while one of its planes scouted the harbor.

together with battleships, cruisers, destroyers, and auxiliaries; an attack force of 3 battleships, including the 60,000-ton *Yamato*, flagship of the expedition, a light carrier, tenders, miscellaneous vessels, and a screen of 16 submarines. Yamamoto's plan was to open the campaign on 3 June by an attack on Dutch Harbor followed by the occupation of the western Aleutians. The carriers then would soften up Midway, while the attack force, led by Yamamoto himself, would move in and finish off the Pacific Fleet if it challenged the carriers. Finally, on the night of 6 June, the landing force would take Midway. But the success of the plan depended, as Yamamoto well knew, on the defeat of the American fleet. So long as that fleet was intact, victory at Midway or in the Aleutians would at best be a hollow one.[31]

In the last week of May the Japanese began moving into position. The Aleutians force left Japan first, followed on 27 May by the carriers, led by the same Admiral Nagumo who had commanded in the strike on Pearl Harbor. The next day the landing force, which had been assembled at Saipan, completed loading and sailed for the rendezvous point, accompanied by the covering cruisers and destroyers. The following morning (0600 of the 29th), Admiral Yamamoto left Tokyo Bay with the main body of the fleet.

Again, as in the Coral Sea, the Japanese found the American fleet waiting for them. As before, the warning had come from intelligence sources which had broken the Japanese codes and thus acquired advance information on the next Japanese move. The Battle of the Coral Sea had barely closed when these intelligence sources revealed that the Japanese were collecting a large task force in home waters for an operation scheduled for late May or June. Just where the attack would come was not yet known but Admiral King thought it might be another attempt at Port Moresby or against New Caledonia and the Fijis.[32]

In support of this view King could turn to the estimate made by General MacArthur some days earlier and without reference to intelligence sources. The end of resistance in the Philippines —the message was dated two days after the surrender of Corregidor—and the British defeat in Burma, MacArthur had written, would probably release Japanese forces for use elsewhere. Unlike the British who feared the Japanese would move in force into the Indian Ocean after the strike against Ceylon early in April, he thought the enemy would probably strike against New Guinea and the line of communications. Thus far he and King were in agreement, while the Army planners were inclined to minimize the threat in the Pacific and side with the British. The Japanese, MacArthur pointed out, had the bases for an offensive in the Pacific but not for large operations against India. To guard against the next Japanese attack, therefore, he recommended "adequate security for Australia and the Pacific Area . . . followed at the earliest possible moment by offensive action or by at least a sufficiently dangerous initial

---

[31] Morison, *Coral Sea, Midway and Submarine Actions*, pp. 74–79, 87–90.

[32] Rad, Nimitz to King, No. 2347, 10 May 42, cited in Hayes, The War Against Japan, ch. V, p 51; Memo, King for Marshall, 12 May 42, sub: Sit in SPA and SWPA, OPD Exec Files.

threat of offensive action to affect the enemy's plans and dispositions." [33]

This estimate, when taken with intelligence of Japanese concentrations, combined to produce in Washington a change in plans. At the insistence of Admiral King, Generals Marshall and Arnold finally agreed to an increase in the air strength of New Caledonia and the Fijis, despite the earlier decision not to do so. Heavy and medium bombers en route to Australia were to be diverted to these two garrisons, together with an antiaircraft regiment for the Fijis, to come from the Hawaiian force. MacArthur, it was realized, would probably protest this diversion of his heavy bombers, but Marshall and Arnold decided they would meet that contingency when it arose. [34]

Before this program of reinforcement began, the cryptanalysts learned that the enemy objectives would be Midway and the Aleutians. [35] This information was immediately passed to Nimitz and MacArthur, and orders went out to keep the heavy and medium bombers scheduled for New Caledonia and the Fijis in Hawaii. The Marine garrison at Midway was reinforced and began feverishly to prepare the ground defenses of the island against invasion. The Marine air group there was brought up to strength

(64 aircraft) and 15 Army B-17's were flown in at the end of May. With other reinforcements and exclusive of the Marine air group, the air strength at Midway by 3 June consisted of 30 PBY's, 4 B-26's, 17 B-17's, and 6 TBF's. [36] In the North Pacific, a task force of four heavy cruisers and eight destroyers was organized to meet the naval threat and all air elements in the area, including a few B-17's that were rushed out, were quickly mobilized for the defense of Alaska and the Aleutians.

To meet the threat of the main force of the Japanese fleet off Midway, Admiral Nimitz had only limited naval forces. The *Lexington* was gone, the *Yorktown* damaged. All the fleet's battleships were on the west coast. The *Saratoga* and *Wasp* were on orders for the Pacific, but were not scheduled to arrive until late June. Only the *Enterprise* and *Hornet* (Task Force 16), lately returned from the South Pacific after the Tokyo raid and now commanded by Rear Adm. Raymond A. Spruance during Halsey's hospitalization, were ready at Pearl Harbor on 26 May, the day Nagumo took his carriers out of the Inland Sea. Next day Fletcher brought his *Yorktown* force in and the repair crews at Pearl performed the miracle of getting it ready for action in about two days. Thus Nimitz had at the end of the month a force of 3 carriers, 1 light and 7 heavy cruisers, 13 destroyers, and 25 submarines. On 2 June these vessels rendezvoused at a point 350 miles northeast of Midway, where Admiral Fletcher assumed command of the entire force. Next day the fleet was waiting 200 miles north of Midway for the appearance of the enemy. Fletcher's orders

---

[33] Rad, MacArthur to Marshall, No. 176, 8 May 42, OPD Msg File.

[34] Memos, King for Marshall, 12 May 42, sub: Sit in SPA and SWPA; Marshall for Eisenhower, same date, both in OPD Exec Files; Marshall for King, 13 May 42, sub: Sit in South Pacific, OPD 381 Australia; Rad, King to Nimitz, No. 2410, 13 May 42, OPD 381 PTO sec. 1 case 22.

[35] Rads, Emmons to Marshall, 16 May 42, CM-IN-5477; Nimitz to King, No. 0639, 14 May 42, ABC 381 (1–22–42 sec. 2) Pacific Bases; Memo, King for Marshall, 18 May 42, sub: Hawaiian and Alaskan Defenses, OPD Exec Files.

[36] Craven and Cate, *AAF I*, 455–56.

were to avoid a surface engagement with the more powerful Japanese fleet and to seek a decision by air action.[37]

Meanwhile, the Seventh Air Force in Hawaii had been making its own preparations for the battle. On the 18th the air force had been placed on a special alert and thereafter intensified its search missions. In the days that followed, Maj. Gen. Clarence L. Tinker, commander of the Seventh Air Force, received a steady stream of reinforcements and by the end of the month had in commission 44 B–17's, 4 B–18's, and 101 P–40's, with more planes arriving almost daily.[38]

But these measures did not satisfy General MacArthur, who was still concerned over the security of Australia and asking for reinforcements, including aircraft carriers. In justification, Marshall carefully explained the reasons for this concentration at Midway, pointing out the enemy was "endeavoring to maneuver our Pacific Fleet out of position. . . . The future of Australia will hinge on our preliminary deployment to meet this situation and our countermoves."[39] Should the Japanese move against Australia instead of Midway, Marshall assured his former chief, then the reinforcements diverted to Hawaii "will immediately be dispatched to your assistance." "Your needs," he went on, "are being given every consideration possible in light of developing situation."

MacArthur took quick advantage of this opportunity to point out again that "lack of seapower in the Pacific is and has been the fatal weakness in our posi-

tion since the beginning of the war."[40] Since the enemy's intentions were known, he thought the "Indian and Atlantic Oceans should be temporarily stripped in order to concentrate in sufficient force for this special occasion." Failure to do this, he warned, might well result in "such disasters and a crisis of such proportions" as the United States had never before faced.

General Marshall was away on an inspection of the west coast defenses when MacArthur's message came in and it went to Admiral King for reply. Apparently King saw merit in MacArthur's proposal, for he himself suggested next day that the British Far Eastern Fleet be moved up to Colombo in Ceylon and that the Pacific Fleet be reinforced with carriers, battleships, cruisers, and destroyers from the Atlantic. At the same time he recommended that the movement of aircraft to the Pacific be given priority "even over BOLERO."[41] These proposals struck at the heart of the decision of 6 May to limit Pacific reinforcements to aircraft already authorized,[42] and evoked from the Army planners strong opposition. General McNarney, acting for Marshall in his absence, immediately informed his chief of this newest development, but withheld official reply until Marshall's return on 27 May. The Chief of Staff was willing to support King's plan for naval reinforcements, but, like McNarney, opposed the allocation of additional aircraft to the Pacific, or, as a matter of fact, any move that would interfere with the build-up for

---

[37] Morison, *Coral Sea, Midway and Submarine Actions*, pp. 81–82, 97; Ltr, Spruance to Hoover, 17 Jul 59, OCMH.

[38] Craven and Cate, *AAF I*, 454–55.

[39] Rad, Marshall to MacArthur, No. 109, 22 May OPD 381 Gen, sec. 1.

[40] Rad, MacArthur to Marshall, No. 119, 23 May 42, CM–IN–6409.

[41] Memo, King for Marshall, 24 May 42, sub: Sit in Pacific, WDCSA, SWPA.

[42] See above, p. 222.

BOLERO.[43] This answer did not satisfy Admiral King or meet MacArthur's and Nimitz' demands for reinforcements of the Pacific, but there the matter rested until the crisis presented by the Japanese move against Midway and the Aleutians had been met.

The Japanese, blissfully unaware of the reception being prepared for them, were meanwhile closing in on their objectives. Far to the north, under cover of heavy fog and rough weather, the Aleutians force had by the 3d of June reached a point about 180 miles southwest of Dutch Harbor, from where the *Junyo* and *Ryujo* sent their planes aloft. Though alerted the day before when a PBY had spotted the two carriers, the aircraft at Dutch Harbor had been unable to locate the enemy and forestall the strike that followed. In addition to the damage to barracks and installations, the Americans lost about twenty-five men. Next day the weather was worse but the Japanese, now less than 100 miles away, struck again at Dutch Harbor, this time with more effect. But they did not get away unscathed; they lost five planes out of twenty-six to P-40's from Umnak.

While the *Junyo* and *Ryujo* planes were striking Dutch Harbor, American aircraft were groping in the fog and mist for the enemy carriers. A PBY sighted the Japanese force at 0845 of the 4th, but it was not until midafternoon that any of the bombers were able to locate the target. And when they did they had to bomb almost blind through the fog. By this time the carriers had completed their task and were already withdrawing to a point from where they could screen the

landings in the western Aleutians, at Attu and Kiska, on 7 June.[44]

At Midway the Japanese had met disaster. Sighted on 3 June by one of the Midway search planes, the occupation force had come under attack from B-17's later in the day but had escaped. That night PBY's equipped with radar attacked again, this time hitting one of the tankers and strafing the transports. But this was only a preliminary to the real battle that came the next day when Admiral Nagumo's carrier force, which had already discharged its planes for the attack, was discovered to the northwest of the island. B-17's, B-26's, and Marine planes were already aloft and these sped to the scene while the remaining aircraft on Midway as well as those on the three American carriers made ready to take off. When the Japanese aircraft, seventy-two bombers and thirty-six fighters, moved in to the attack they met a warm reception. Badly hit, the Japanese nevertheless managed to inflict severe damage before they made their escape.[45]

Meanwhile, the Japanese carriers had come under heavy attack from the Americans. Bunched together, the *Akagi, Kaga,* and *Soryu* proved vulnerable targets and all were fatally hit. The *Soryu* was dealt the last blow by the submarine *Nautilus* and went down at 1610; the *Kaga* joined her a few minutes later, and that evening the *Akagi,* which had been

---

[43] Rad, McNarney to Marshall, No. 1096, 24 May 42, AG 381 (5-24-42); Memo, Marshall for King, n.d., sub: Sit in Pacific, OPD 381 PTO sec. 1.

[44] Craven and Cate, *AAF I,* 462-70; Morison, *Coral Sea, Midway and Submarine Actions,* pp. 175-85.

[45] The B-17's bombed one of the surfaced American submarines by mistake, but, fortunately, missed the target. General Emmons apologized to Admiral Nimitz for the error and asked him what should be done. "Have your air commander meet the sub on arrival at Pearl Harbor," replied Admiral Nimitz, "and invite the crew to have a drink." Ltr, Emmons to Hoover, 10 Jul 59, OCMH.

set afire and was burning fiercely, was abandoned. Nagumo's fourth carrier, the *Hiryu,* launched its own attack on *Yorktown,* dealt her a lethal blow, and then was herself hit by dive bombers from the other two American carriers. Like the *Akagi,* the *Hiryu* was set afire and finally abandoned on the morning of the 5th.

The fate of the Japanese carriers decided the issue. Yamamoto's vain effort on the night of the 5th to snatch victory from defeat by an attack against the island was a measure of desperation and only resulted in fresh disaster. Two of his cruisers collided and had to retire, only to be hit the next day by planes from the *Enterprise* and *Hornet.* One was sunk and the other badly damaged. Yamamoto's main body—the battleship division, three destroyer divisions, and the Aleutians force—was still intact and, in a final effort to destroy the Pacific Fleet, Yamamoto sought to lure Admiral Spruance into a trap off Wake Island. But Spruance, though tempted, refused to take the bait. By the afternoon of the 7th Yamamoto knew his last hope was gone and started for home. The surprise he had hoped to achieve had been gained by the enemy instead; he had been outmaneuvered, outsmarted, and, worst of all, had lost four carriers with their planes and pilots, the main striking force of the *Combined Fleet.* It was a blow from which the Japanese fleet never fully recovered.[46]

This disaster, the full extent of which was concealed from the Japanese public, had a decisive effect on General Hyaku-

take's plans for the seizure, early in July, of New Calednoia, the Fijis, and Samoa. Four days after the battle ended, on 11 June, *Imperial General Headquarters* postponed the operations for two months and later canceled them altogther.[47] The capture of Port Moresby was now more urgent than ever to meet the threat of counterattack from Australia. An amphibious operation was no longer possible, however, and *Imperial General Headquarters* canceled the project at the same time it called off the New Caledonia–Fiji–Samoa operation. But it did not give up the idea of taking Port Moresby. Instead it directed Hyakutake to make plans for an overland drive from the east coast of New Guinea across the towering Owen Stanley Range. On the basis of this order and a naval survey for airfield sites, General Hyakutake ordered Horii, the *South Seas Detachment* commander, to land at Buna and reconnoiter the land route for an advance on Port Moresby. Finally, on 11 July, a month after it had canceled a seaborne invasion of Port Moresby, *Imperial General Headquarters* gave its blessing to this new scheme for an overland attack. Ten days later the Japanese landed at Buna.[48]

For the period between mid-March, the high-water mark of Japanese expansion, and late July the Japanese had precious little to show for their efforts other than a victory, already assured, in the Philippines. They had acquired a seaplane base at Tulagi on 3 May and soon thereafter began building an airstrip on the neighboring island of Guadalcanal. A month later they had seized

---

[46] For the naval side of the battle, see Morison, *Coral Sea, Midway and Submarine Actions,* 101–55; for the Air Forces account, Craven and Cate, *AAF I,* 456–62. The author used these accounts as well as many of the sources cited in both works.

[47] *Imperial GHQ,* Navy Order 20, 11 Jul 42; Japanese Opns in SWPA, 129.

[48] For a full account of these plans and the operations that followed see Milner, *Victory in Papua.*

BATTLE OF MIDWAY. *Japanese heavy cruiser of the Mogami class after being bombed by carrier-based aircraft.*

two islands in the bleak Aleutians, and then a beachhead at Buna from where they hoped to launch an attack against Port Moresby. The cost of these scattered holdings in planes, trained pilots, and carriers had been enormous. Until these losses were replaced and the superiority lost at Midway regained, as it never could be in a race against American production, the Japanese would have to go on the strategic defensive. The tide of victory had finally turned.

PART THREE

SEIZING THE INITIATIVE

The passage from the defensive to the offensive is one of the most delicate operations of war.

NAPOLEON, *Maxims*

In war, the only sure defense is the offense.

GENERAL PATTON

CHAPTER XIII

Planning the Offensive

Strategy is a system of expedients. It is more than knowledge; it is the application of knowledge to practical life, the art of action under the most trying circumstances.

VON MOLTKE

Though the decisive and far-reaching effects of the victory at Midway were not immediately apparent, it was clear that the Allies had temporarily gained the initiative in the Pacific. For the first time since the outbreak of war, they were in a favorable position to take the offensive.

The prewar decision to concentrate Allied resources on the defeat of Germany and to pursue a defensive strategy in the Pacific—confirmed more than once since 7 December—did not preclude offensive action in this secondary theater. RAINBOW 5 provided for limited offensives by the Pacific Fleet, and the Navy, once the shock of Pearl Harbor had worn off, showed no inclination to interpret the strategic defensive as a mandate for inaction. Under the leadership of King and Nimitz, the Navy sought eagerly and willingly every opportunity to strike at the enemy whenever and wherever possible. Perforce, these operations, conducted with small forces, were largely hit-and-run affairs which had little more than nuisance value. Stronger measures were called for if the victory gained at Midway was to be exploited. The problem was to settle on an opera-

tion that could be undertaken with the limited forces available and within the accepted strategic concept for the Pacific but which would produce more enduring results than earlier raids and strikes.

Availability of forces and the direction of the Japanese advance rather than abstract strategic calculations ultimately determined the choice of Allied objectives. The Midway victory had ensured the security of Hawaii, and, in any case, the fleet was not yet strong enough for an advance across the Central Pacific. So that possibility was ruled out. Similarly, an advance by way of the Aleutians, where the danger was considered remote and the possibility of strategic gain small, was discarded. Only in the South and Southwest Pacific was the danger real and imminent. There the Japanese had advanced along the New Guinea coast and down the Solomons ladder until in May they reached Tulagi. And though frustrated in their attempt to take Port Moresby, there was little likelihood that they would abandon altogether their effort to gain control of Papua, and with it of the Coral Sea and Torres Strait. Should they succeed, and should they be allowed to retain control of the southern Solomons, then Australia and the line of communications would be in jeopardy. Thus, the choice of objectives quickly narrowed down to an operation in the southern Solomons. The removal of the threat there was clearly an objective of the first importance. *(Map 4)*

Offensive action in the Solomons was attractive for other reasons also. Not only was it believed that such an operation would fall within the capabilities of the Allied forces en route or already in the theater, but, more important, that it would open the path for a drive on Rabaul, the major Japanese base in the South Pacific. The capture or neutralization of that base, only 700 miles from Truk and the focal point of the Japanese advance southward, would make it possible for the Allies to support a drive later across the Central Pacific and to initiate an offensive that would bring the forces of MacArthur and Nimitz back to the Philippines. Once there they could cut the Japanese off from the strategic resources to the south and make ready to storm the citadel of Japan itself, if that should prove necessary.

Early Plans

The Navy, with its traditional interest in the Pacific, took the lead early in the war in the development of plans to meet the immediate Japanese threat and ensure ultimate victory. Like their Army colleagues, the naval planners believed that before an all-out offensive against Japan could be undertaken it would be necessary to build American defenses in the Pacific and assemble large forces there. It was in the application of this principle, in timing and in the allocation of resources, that differences arose.

The Army planners wanted to establish a line that could be held with minimum forces, and generally opposed large reinforcements to the defense of this line unless vital American interests were involved. Short of such a challenge, they were willing apparently to accept the loss of territory rather than divert to the Pacific the resources allocated to the war against Germany.

The naval planners never fully accepted this view, even when it was indorsed by the President, and were willing to risk the delay of BOLERO in order to hold the Pacific. Firmly and with conviction they consistently argued that until such time as the all-out offensive against Japan could begin, the United States must maintain and improve its strategic position in the Pacific while taking every opportunity to strike at the enemy to prevent him from becoming so firmly entrenched that it would be extremely difficult to dislodge him.[1] It was this view that prompted Admiral King to instruct Nimitz shortly after the Pearl Harbor attack to extend his operations westward toward the Fijis and to undertake raids and limited offensives wherever possible.[2]

The desirability of offensive action in New Guinea and the Solomons became apparent early in February after the Japanese began to move southward from Rabaul. The necessity for defensive measures was still paramount, but the Navy, in recommending the establish-

---

[1] The clearest statement of the naval view is to be found in Memo, King for JCS, 4 May 42, sub: Defense of Island Bases, JCS 48; the Army view in Memo, WPD for CofS, 28 Feb 42, sub: Strategic Conception . . . , OPD Exec Files.

[2] See above, p. 205; Hayes, The War Against Japan, ch. VI, p. 2.

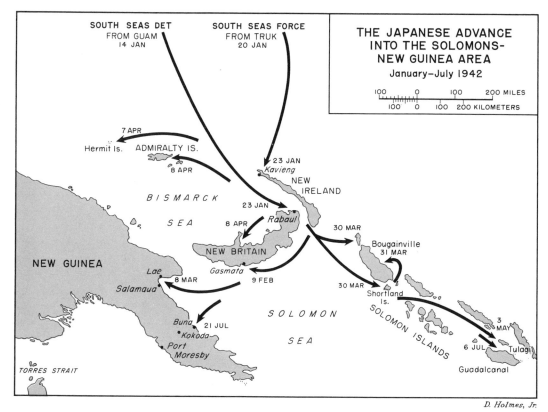

MAP 4

ment of an outpost at Funafuti in the Ellice Islands, did not fail to point out that the island could also serve as a base for future offensive operations. The Army planners opposed this measure, arguing that until the United States was ready to open a sustained offensive "our island commitments should be limited to those necessary to secure our routes to critical areas." Every additional garrison, General Gerow pointed out, meant the further diversion of air and ground forces and the use of critical shipping.[3] The Joint Chiefs finally gave

[3] Memo, Gerow for CofS, 10 Feb 42, sub: Advance Base in Ellice Islands, and related papers in ABC 381 Ellice Is (2–5–42).

their approval to the Funafuti project on 16 March.

While this project was still under discussion, Admiral King, it will be recalled, had proposed on 18 February that bases be established also at Efate in the New Hebrides and Tongatabu. Offered primarily as a defensive measure to secure Australia and the line of communications, the proposal to establish a base at Efate, like that for Funafuti, carried clearly the implication of an early offensive in the area. This implication was not lost on the Army planners and was confirmed some weeks later when Admiral King explained, in support of his proposal, that current naval strategy included a drive northwest from bases ("strongpoints," he called them) in the New Hebrides through the Solomons and New Guinea to the Bismarck Archipelago. A garrison at Efate, therefore, would serve the double purpose of protecting the line of communication and providing a spring-board for a "step-by-step general advance." Marine forces, King thought, would make the landing and capture each position after which Army troops could move in to occupy the islands, thus relieving the marines for the next step forward.[4]

Not only did Admiral King's exposition of naval strategy fail to evoke any objection from the Army planners who had only a short time before expressed strong views on the subject, but within a few days it received the powerful sanction of Presidential approval. At a White House meeting on 5 March dealing, among other matters, with the impending loss of Java and the security of the line of communication to Australia, Roosevelt made it clear that Australia and New Zealand would have to be held and that the Navy's concept of operations in the Pacific would prevail. The President's understanding of the Navy's concept was based on a memorandum King had written for him. In it the admiral had repeated substantially the same points he had made to Marshall in defense of the Efate proposal—the establishment of strongpoints along the line of communications and an advance into the Solomons and New Guinea similar to the one made by the

Japanese in the South China Sea. "Such a line of operations," King told the President, "will be offensive rather than passive — and will draw Japanese forces there to oppose it, thus relieving pressure elsewhere."[5]

This victory for the naval point of view was only one round in the long debate over BOLERO versus Pacific priorities which ended temporarily in early May with the President's decision in favor of BOLERO.[6] But while this debate was in progress, the Navy staff continued to develop plans for an offensive in the Pacific. By 16 April it had produced a plan which called for an offensive in four stages or phases. The first, already in progress, was the one in which the Allies would build up their forces and secure positions in the South and Southwest Pacific for an offensive, while engaging in minor action against the enemy "for purposes of attrition." The next phase of the Navy plan consisted of the New Guinea–Solomons operations already described by Admiral King. Also called for in this period were "heavy attrition attacks" against Japanese bases in the Carolines and Marshalls, a move that would inaugurate the long-delayed Central Pacific offensive envisaged in the old ORANGE plan. This offensive would reach more formidable proportions in the third phase of the Navy plan, when both the Carolines and Marshalls would be captured and converted into advanced naval and air bases. From these newly won positions as well as those gained in the Bismarck Archipel-

---

[4] Memo, King for Marshall, 2 Mar 42, sub: Establishment of Garrisons at Efate and Tongatabu, ABC 381 (3–2–42). See also Memo, Marshall for King, 24 Feb 42, same sub, OPD Exec Files; JCS Mins, 2 Mar 42. For the occupation of Efate and Tongatabu, see above, ch. IX.

[5] Memo, King for Pres, 5 Mar 42, no sub, ABC 323.31 (1–29–42 sec. 1A) POA; See also Mins, White House Mtg, 5 Mar 42, CCS 031 (3–5–42); Hayes, The War Against Japan, ch. VI, pp. 7–8; Morison, *Coral Sea, Midway and Submarine Actions*, pp. 146–47.

[6] See above, p. 222.

TRAINING ON AUSTRALIAN BEACHES *for assault operations.*

ago during the second phase, the Allies would then advance into the Netherlands Indies or the Philippines, "whichever offers the most promising and enduring results."[7] Beyond that point the naval planners did not go.

Nothing was done about this naval plan at the time; Coral Sea and Midway fully occupied the Navy's attention. But, interestingly enough, among the measures proposed to meet the danger at Midway was one from Admiral Nimitz to General MacArthur for a landing at Tulagi by the 1st Marine Raider Battalion, then in Samoa, supported by the naval forces of the Southwest Pacific.

Such an operation, Nimitz told Mac-Arthur, would accomplish two results: It would throw the enemy off balance at a moment when he was preparing a major blow in a distant area; and it would blunt his drive southward toward the New Hebrides and New Caledonia.[8]

With the objectives of this bold maneuver, General MacArthur was entirely in sympathy. Unfortunately, he explained, he did not have the forces to support such a move or to ensure the permanent occupation of the island, which was in his area, once it was taken. But he did have, he told General Marshall, his own plans for an offensive in the Solomons and suggested that, until

[7] Memo, WPD (Navy) for COMINCH, 16 Apr 42, sub: Pacific Ocean Campaign Plan, cited in Hayes, The War Against Japan, ch. VI, pp. 7–8.

[8] Rad, Nimitz to MacArthur, No. 0351, 28 May 42, cited in Hayes, The War Against Japan, ch. VI, p. 11.

such time as he was ready to put them into effect, Admiral Nimitz might well assist him by using his forces in the South Pacific for a push northward through the New Hebrides to the Santa Cruz group east of the southern Solomons.[9]

Admiral King, too, thought Nimitz' scheme impractical and recommended that he employ his forces in raids against whatever worthwhile objectives he could find in the area. Under no circumstances, King warned Nimitz, should he engage in any operations that would involve the permanent occupation of a base without first getting approval from Washington. MacArthur would not even concede the advisability of raids. The Japanese, he pointed out, had a full regiment at Tulagi and could, from Rabaul, send troops into the southern Solomons a good deal faster than the Americans.[10]

General Marshall, to whom MacArthur had forwarded Nimitz' proposal, agreed that the time had not yet come for an offensive. But, he reported to Mac-Arthur, the Navy was "impressed with the possibilities of an early attack" on Tulagi and would try to assemble the forces required. Though the question of command had not been raised, Marshall assured the Southwest Pacific commander, who might have wondered why the Navy should be seeking forces for an operation in his area, that if such an assault was undertaken, it would be under MacArthur's direction. "All decisions, including the extent to which you accede to any further proposals by CINCPAC [Nimitz]," he assured his former chief on 1 June, "rest with you."[11]

If this was the case the Navy apparently did not know it. At the same time Marshall was reassuring MacArthur, Admiral Nimitz was telling Ghormley that he would continue to control elements of the South Pacific force, even when they were operating in the Southwest Pacific Area.[12] Thus, the Navy served notice that it would retain control of the forces required for amphibious operations, and therefore of the operations themselves, wherever they occurred. The Army for its part made it equally clear that the theater commander was the supreme authority in his own area, and, once an operation was approved and the forces assigned, would control those forces and command the operation.

Strategy and Command

Plans for an early offensive in the Pacific received their greatest impetus from the victory at Midway. The smoke of battle had scarcely cleared when General MacArthur took the center of the stage with an urgent appeal for an immediate offensive to exploit the opportunity presented by the Japanese defeat. What he had in mind was not a raid on little Tulagi but a full-scale assault against New Britain and New Ireland to gain control of Rabaul and the strategic Bismarck Archipelago. If his superiors in

---

[9] Rads, MacArthur to Nimitz, 29 May 42; Mac-Arthur to Marshall, Nos. 840 and 217, 28 May and 2 Jun 42, CM–IN–8352 and 0469; Memo, Marshall for King, 6 Jun 42, sub: Early Attacks on Japanese Bases, OPD 381 (PTO) case 41.

[10] Rad, MacArthur to Marshall, No. 217, 2 Jun 42, CM–IN–0469, contains the text of King's message to Nimitz of 1 June; Rad, King to Nimitz, No. 0100, 1 Jun 42, WDCSA Files, SWPA (6–3–42).

[11] Rad, Marshall to MacArthur, No. 161, 1 Jun 42, CM–OUT–0095.

[12] Instr, Nimitz to Ghormley, 1 Jun 42, copy in WDCSA files, SWPA (6–1–42).

Washington would give him, in addition to the three divisions he already had, a division trained for amphibious operations (presumably marines) and the two carriers he had asked for so often, he was ready, he announced, to move out immediately. With confidence, he predicted he would quickly recapture the Bismarcks and force the Japanese back to Truk, 700 miles away, thus winning "manifold strategic advantages both defensive and offensive" and making "further potential exploitation immediately possible."[13]

The initial reaction in Washington to MacArthur's characteristically bold plan was favorable. The Navy already had plans of its own for operations in the Solomons, which, though more limited in scope, had similar objectives. The Army was also considering an offensive, and General Marshall, only a few days earlier, had directed his planners to study the problems posed by operations in the New Britain–New Ireland area, assuming the use of a Marine division and two carriers.[14] Thus, during the days that followed, the Army and Navy planners to whom was entrusted the task of studying MacArthur's proposals were able to reach substantial agreement on the outlines for an offensive in the Southwest Pacific.

The plan developed in Washington called, like MacArthur's, for a quick campaign against Rabaul. Landings in the Bismarck Archipelago, the planners recognized, would have to be preceded by intensive air bombardment of the enemy's bases in New Guinea and the Solomons. Only in this way could air support for the invasion force, an indispensable condition for success, be assured. But where would the aircraft come from: B–17's could reach any target in the area, but the Allies had no fields within fighter range of Rabaul. Carrier aircraft was the answer and the planners asserted that three carriers with necessary escorts would have to be provided, as well as the B–17's from Hawaii. The landing itself, the planners stated, could be made by the amphibiously trained 1st Marine Division, which, it was estimated, could be ready in Australia by 5 July. Once Rabaul was taken, it could be garrisoned by Army troops already in Australia—the 32d and 41st U.S. Divisions and the 7th Australian—and the area cut off reduced at leisure. On the touchiest question of all — command — the planners recommended that the operation be placed under General MacArthur with a naval officer in tactical control of the assault force.[15]

Agreement on the planning level was no assurance that Admiral King, who was in favor of an offensive but under different conditions, would accept this plan. That General Marshall expected opposition is evident in his warning to MacArthur, in reference to the aircraft carriers required for the operation, not to take any action until he, Marshall, had had an opportunity "to break ground

[13] Rad, MacArthur to Marshall, No. 913, 8 Jun 42, CM–IN–2264. The development of plans for the offensive after Midway is treated also in Matloff and Snell, *Strategic Planning, 1941–42*, pp. 258–267, and John Miller, jr., *Guadalcanal: The First Offensive*, UNITED STATES ARMY IN WORLD WAR II (Washington, 1949), pp. 8–21.

[14] Rad, Marshall to MacArthur, 10 Jun 42, CM–OUT–2319.

[15] Memo, Marshall for King, 12 Jun 42, sub: Opns in SWPA; Memo, Street for Ritchie, 23 Jun 42, sub: Offensive Operations in SWPA, OPD 381 (SWPA) case 73 and 80.

with Navy and British. . . ." "I comprehend fully the extreme delicacy of your position," replied MacArthur, "and the complex difficulties that you face there."[16]

Neither the effort to secure aircraft carriers for MacArthur from the Navy and the British nor the strategic concept of the plan was the main issue in the debate which ensued. It was the fight over command that became the crucial question. Admiral King struck the first blow when he remarked to Marshall almost as soon as he learned about MacArthur's plan that the forthcoming offensive would be "primarily of a naval and amphibious character"—and therefore, by implication, should be under naval command.[17] Marshall ignored this remark. The success of any operation against the Japanese stronghold in the Bismarck Archipelago, he asserted, depended on speed and close co-operation between the Army and Navy forces involved. After enumerating these forces —including the carriers—he declared that a quick decision and unity of command were the essential prerequisites to success. Further delay might wreck the entire project.

Everyone agreed on the desirability of the operation and the need for speed. But MacArthur, staunchly supported by the Chief of Staff, insisted that it be under Army command; King and his senior advisers that it be under naval command. MacArthur's argument was a geographic one. Since the objectives were in his area, he declared, operational control should be in his headquarters.[18] The naval position was based on the concept that amphibious operations should be under naval command. But behind this view was Admiral King's reluctance to give MacArthur any of the Navy's precious aircraft carriers, and with them the battleships, cruisers, destroyers, and auxiliaries that would be needed for their support.[19] On that point he was adamant and not once during the war did MacArthur ever have any large carriers under his command.

Although the naval planners, with their Army colleagues, looked with favor on MacArthur's plan and thought to solve the command problem by placing the operation under a naval task force commander subject to MacArthur's control, they were unable to win over their immediate superior, Rear Adm. Charles M. Cooke, Chief of the Navy War Plans Division, or Admiral King. The planners, these two believed, had placed too much reliance on air power. The enemy's bases in New Guinea and the Solomons, both King and Cooke asserted, could not be knocked out entirely by bombing, and until they were it would be foolhardy to send aircraft carriers into the area, within the range of Japanese land-based aircraft. It would be safer, they argued, to go slowly and by stages up the Solomons to Rabaul, eliminating the enemy's bases and air power as they went along.[20]

When MacArthur learned of the objections to his proposal he quickly shifted

---

[16] Rads, Marshall to MacArthur, 10 Jun 42, CM–OUT–2319; MacArthur to Marshall, 11 Jun 42, CM–IN–3328.

[17] Memo, King for Marshall, 11 Jun 42, sub: MacArthur Dispatch of 8 Jun 42, WDCSA File (SWPA).

[18] Rad, MacArthur to Marshall, No. 16, 18 Jun 42.

[19] Hayes, The War Against Japan, ch. VI, p. 15.

[20] Memo, Ritchie for Street, 23 Jun 42, sub: Offensive Opns in SWPA, OPD 381 (SWPA) case 80; Rad, Marshall to MacArthur, No. 277, 23 Jun 42, CM–OUT–5704; Hayes, The War Against Japan, ch. VI, pp. 15–16.

ground. Admiral King, he protested, had misunderstood his plan and was laboring under a misapprehension.[21] In his original message, he said, he had purposely sketched only the broad outlines of the plan and deliberately omitted the preliminary steps of an invasion of Rabaul. Certainly, he agreed, it would be necessary to gain positions in the Solomons and along the north coast of New Guinea before committing any forces in the Bismarck area. He had never had any other idea.

But on the matter of command MacArthur would not yield. Repeating the now-familiar arguments for placing the operation under his general direction he, like General Marshall, contended that "the very purpose of establishment of the Southwest Pacific Area was to obtain unity of command." The point was doubly emphasized by his protest, at the same time, to the procedure followed by Admiral King in sending instructions on operational matters directly to Admiral Leary, the commander of naval forces in the Southwest Pacific. Correct procedure would have been for King to forward these instructions to Marshall, as executive agent for the Joint Chiefs, who would in turn send them to MacArthur for Leary. Failure to follow the regular channels, MacArthur pointed out, made "a mockery" of the concept of unity of command, and of the organization established for the Pacific less than three months earlier.[22]

If Admiral King had misunderstood his plan, as MacArthur claimed, so, too, had the Army planners. Not only had they construed it as a quick blow directly

against Rabaul but, with their naval colleagues, had found it entirely acceptable and superior to the much slower process of attacking successively Tulagi and other Japanese bases in the Solomons and New Guinea before assaulting Rabaul. To do that, the Army planners pointed out, would expose Allied forces to continuous attack from Rabaul during each stage of the advance. MacArthur's original plan they thought superior to King's for it avoided that danger and, in addition, eliminated the necessity for taking many preliminary positions. These, the planners believed, would fall of their own weight once Rabaul was seized.[23]

Actually, no one had misunderstood MacArthur, as is clear from the detailed plans prepared in his headquarters at this time. His objectives were the same as King's, but there were important differences in emphasis and timing. MacArthur, it is true, admitted the necessity of capturing intermediate positions in New Guinea and the Solomons, a step King asserted was an essential condition to the advance on Rabaul. But King placed much more emphasis than MacArthur on the capture of Tulagi and adjacent positions, and envisaged a much slower advance than did the Southwest Pacific commander. MacArthur's Tulsa I plan, completed on 27 June, three days after his second message, provided for the seizure of Rabaul in about two weeks, including the time required for the occupation of bases along the way. Obviously this plan, which never went to Washington, could hardly be characterized as a step-by-step advance such as King had in mind. Even the

---

[21] Rad, MacArthur to Marshall, No. 248, 24 Jun 42, CM–IN–7976.

[22] *Ibid.*

[23] OPD Memo, 22 Jun 42, sub: Estimate SWPA Offensive, 381 OPD (SWPA) sec. 2.

GENERAL HANDY

planning officers on MacArthur's staff thought the timing of TULSA too rapid, and recommended revision. The second draft of the plan, therefore, completed on 1 July, provided for a slower schedule, but one which hardly met the objection. Rabaul was now to be taken in eighteen days instead of the fourteen originally allocated, and this time the plan called for an airborne operation— though there were no paratroopers in Australia—and the seizure of Buna as a staging point for the assault against Lae and Salamaua. Just how these places, as well as others, would be taken and developed into forward air bases in time to support the final attack on Rabaul—all in less than eighteen days— was not explained in the plan. Nor did General Chamberlin, MacArthur's G–3, yet know the answer.[24]

Despite the significant differences between MacArthur's concept of operations and that of Admiral King, it was assumed in Washington that the debate over strategy had been settled. The only issue remaining was that of command and on that Admiral Cooke, the Chief of the Navy War Plans Division, would not give way. To all appeals from his own and the Army planners, Cooke turned a deaf ear. The Navy, he insisted, must command and the logical solution was to turn the operation over to Admiral Ghormley, commander of the South Pacific Area. Finally, on 24 June, General Handy made one last effort to persuade his naval opposite number to go along with the recommendation of the planners. But Cooke stood firm and Handy had to report that he had made no progress whatever and that the Navy would not consent to MacArthur's control. "Cooke," he told Marshall, "was very emphatic and stated that he was expressing Admiral King's decision as well as his own view."[25] The issue, Handy concluded, would have to be settled between King and Marshall. He could do no more.

Admiral King had not only made up his mind, but before the day was out had taken it on himself to direct Nimitz to make ready for the forthcoming operations. This alert, sent without consulting Marshall and at a time when operations themselves were still under discussion, took the form of a draft directive from the Joint Chiefs of Staff. Though the directive, King explained, set forth only "contemplated" arrangements, it made perfectly clear his views

---

[24] Extracts of TULSA I and II are in OCMH.

[25] Memo, Handy for Marshall, 24 Jun 42, sub: Opns in SWPA, OPD 381 (SWPA) case 76.

ADMIRAL COOKE

on how the offensive should be conducted, and by whom. Nimitz would command; that was categorically stated. For the offensive he would have not only his own and Ghormley's forces, but also aircraft, ships, and submarines from MacArthur's Southwest Pacific Area. The Army, in King's plan, would have no share in the assault; its role would be limited to furnishing garrisons for the islands taken by the Navy and Marine troops.[26] The next day, 25 June, King submitted this draft directive to the Joint Chiefs for approval, and with it a letter to Marshall stressing the need for action before the Japanese recovered from the defeat at Midway and this "golden opportunity" was lost.[27]

On the assumption that there was no real difference between MacArthur's and King's concept of the offensive, Marshall restricted his comments to the Navy's arrangements for command. These he found neither practical nor logical. In an appeal for a genuine acceptance of the principle of unity of command he asked King to reconsider. He appreciated fully, he wrote, the Navy's concern for the safety of its vessels and the great difficulty of co-ordinating land, sea, and air action, but he suggested that these objections to Army command might be eliminated if the Joint Chiefs defined the manner in which naval forces were employed and the waters in which they would operate. The "lines drawn on a map"—the geographical argument for MacArthur's command—Marshall conceded, should not govern the choice of commander, but he felt, nevertheless, that the operation which "is almost entirely in the Southwest Pacific Area and is designed to add to the security of that area," should be entrusted to MacArthur. He and his staff, including Admiral Leary, had been in the Southwest Pacific for months, Marshall pointed out, during which time they had learned much about the islands and the problems involved in operations there. To bring in another commander at this time, Marshall concluded, would be most unfortunate.[28] At the same time he told MacArthur, who was growing impatient at the delay, not to concern himself with the question of command. "I am now engaged," he explained, "in negotiations looking to settlement of the

[26] Rad, King to Nimitz, 2306, 24 Jun 42, OPD 381 (SWPA) case 80.
[27] Ltr, King to Marshall, ser. 00544, 25 Jun 42, OPD 381 (SWPA) case 80.

[28] Memo, Marshall for King, 26 Jun 42, sub: Offensive Opns in the South and Southwest Pacific Area, OPD 381 (SWPA) case 80.

question of unity of command under your direction." [29]

Admiral King showed no disposition to abandon his claim to naval control over the operations against Rabaul. The original directive to Nimitz, he pointed out to Marshall, had authorized him to "prepare for the execution of amphibious operations to be launched from the South Pacific Area and Southwest Pacific Area"—just such an operation as was then under consideration. He reminded Marshall, too, that he had recommended an Army command for Europe where most of the forces would be ground troops. And by the same reasoning, he observed, the operation in the Solomons, which would involve primarily naval and amphibious forces, should be under naval control. Permanent occupation of the area could be delegated to the Army, but the landings and the assault, King asserted, would have to be under Nimitz' direction; indeed, in his view, they could "not be conducted in any other way." MacArthur, he thought, could contribute little initially. Bluntly he warned General Marshall that he was ready to open the offensive, "even if no support of Army forces in the Southwest Pacific is made available." [30] And the next day he gave point to this threat by instructing Admiral Nimitz to go ahead with his preparations for the campaign, even though there would probably be some delay in reaching a decision on the extent of the Army's participation. Meanwhile, King wrote, Nimitz could proceed with his plans on the basis that

he would have the use of only naval and Marine forces. [31]

Resisting his first impulse to reply in kind to King's impolitic note, General Marshall waited instead for several days to compose a suitable answer. But while tempers in Washington cooled, General MacArthur found fresh cause for irritation. First came a copy of King's message to Admiral Nimitz, then Nimitz' reply setting forth the forces, which included elements of MacArthur's own air and naval forces, that he would need for the operation. Finally, MacArthur found that King was again corresponding directly with Admiral Leary. All these, MacArthur saw as clear warning of the Navy's intentions. To him, it was quite evident, as he told Marshall, that the Navy intended to assume "general command control of all operations in the Pacific theater." If the Navy succeeded in this effort, the role of the Army in the Pacific, he warned, would become subsidiary and would consist "largely of placing its forces at the disposal and under the command of Navy or Marine officers." This objective, he pointed out, was the real purpose of the Navy's insistence on controlling operations in the Pacific, using marines as the assault force, and relegating the Army to occupation duties. It was all part of a master plan, which he had learned about "accidentally" when he was Chief of Staff, MacArthur told Marshall. Under this plan, he asserted, the Navy hoped to gain complete control over national defense and reduce the Army to a training and supply organization. Having alerted his chief to the far-reaching implications of this perfidious scheme, MacArthur pledged

---

[29] Rad, Marshall for MacArthur, 26 Jun 42, CM–OUT–6596.

[30] Ltr, King to Marshall, ser. 00555, 26 Jun 42, sub: Offensive Opns in South and Southwest Pacific Area, OPD 381 (SWPA) case 80.

[31] OPD Cover Sheet, 27 Jun 42, sub: Offensive Opns Pacific Theater, OPD 381 (PTO) case 64.

that he would take "no steps or action with reference to any component of my command" except under direct orders from Marshall.[32]

MacArthur's attitude was no more helpful in reaching agreement than Admiral King's and Marshall made it clear immediately that he was more interested in fighting the Japanese than the U.S. Navy. Whatever the outcome of the negotiations (and he hoped it would be in MacArthur's favor), it would be necessary, he told the Southwest Pacific commander, to throw all forces, Army and Navy, into the battle. MacArthur responded immediately with the assurance that he would use all the resources at his command against the enemy "at all times and under any conditions." Once the decision was made, he declared, he would co-operate to the fullest extent.[33]

Compromise: The 2 July Directive

By the end of June, it was evident that neither MacArthur nor King would give in on the question of command. A compromise had to be found, and it was up to Marshall to find one and then persuade both parties to accept it. He made his first move on 29 June, when he replied at last to Admiral King's strong note of the 26th. In a calm and moderate tone, he observed that at least on the essential thing, the necessity for speedily mounting an operation against the Japanese and pushing it through to a successful conclusion, he and King were in

agreement. But neither did he ignore King's scarcely veiled threat of unilateral action by the Navy. The implications of that statement disturbed him greatly and he told the admiral, in language almost identical to that he had used with MacArthur, that "regardless of the final decision as to command, every available support must be given to this operation, or any operation against the enemy." Finally, he asked King to meet with him at his earliest convenience to discuss the problem.[34]

It was as a result of the meetings between the two men—they met apparently on the 29th and 30th—that a basis for compromise on the troublesome question of command was finally evolved. Two solutions were offered by King. The first was a modified version of the suggestion made earlier by Admiral Cooke, to give command to Admiral Ghormley who would operate under the control of Nimitz. It was King's idea that this arrangement would hold only for the Tulagi operation; thereafter MacArthur would have control of the rest of the campaign against Rabaul. While this proposal was being studied, King made another: to give command of the entire Rabaul offensive to Ghormley, but to make him responsible directly to the Joint Chiefs in Washington rather than to Nimitz. This move would, in effect, put Ghormley on the same level as Nimitz and MacArthur and create a third command in the Pacific.[35]

[32] Rad, MacArthur to Marshall, No. 254, 28 Jun 42, CM–IN–9329.

[33] Rads, Marshall to MacArthur, 28 Jun 42, CM–OUT–7356; MacArthur to Marshall, 29 Jun 42, CM–IN–9591.

[34] Memo, Marshall for King, 29 Jun 42, no sub, OPD 381 (SWPA) case 80.

[35] Rad, Marshall to MacArthur, 29 Jun 42, CM–OUT–7501 with attached informal Memo from Marshall to Handy, OPD Exec Files; Memos, Marshall for King 1 Jul 42, OPD 381 (SWPA) case 80; King for Marshall, 2 Jul 42, OPD 384 (PTO) sec. 2.

General MacArthur, whose comments the Chief of Staff solicited, thought the proposal to shift command after Tulagi a poor one from the "standpoint of operational application." The entire offensive, he thought, must be considered as a whole and not in parts. Moreover, its success would depend upon the "complete coordination of the land, sea and air components," a condition difficult to attain, he thought, under the arrangements proposed. To change command in the midst of operations, at a time when it was impossible "to predict the enemy's reaction and consequent trend of combat," MacArthur warned, "would invite confusion and loss of coordination."[36] The conclusion was obvious. MacArthur should be in command from the start and be responsible for co-ordination through the responsible air, ground, and naval commanders.

King's second proposal was not even sent to MacArthur for comment. Marshall found it unsatisfactory and apparently did not consider it seriously as a basis for discussion. Instead, he offered King a counterproposal that skillfully combined the first proposal with an arrangement designed to meet MacArthur's objections to it. The major feature of this compromise was the division of the offensive into three separate tasks whose objective was the seizure and occupation of the New Britain—New Ireland area. Task one was the Tulagi assault and would be under the control of Admiral Nimitz; Ghormley was not even mentioned but presumably would exercise direct command. It would start about 1 August, at which time the boundary of MacArthur's area would be moved westward one degree to longitude 159° east to put the southern Solomons in the South Pacific, thus meeting the objections of the proponents of the geographic argument. As before, the Army would furnish the garrison for the island after it was taken but the forces would come from the South, not the Southwest Pacific. Task Two called for the seizure of Lae, Salamaua, and the northeast coast of New Guinea; Task Three, for the final attack on Rabaul and adjacent positions. Both would be under General MacArthur's control, but the Joint Chiefs would reserve for themselves the right to determine when command would pass from Nimitz to MacArthur, what forces would be used, and the timing of the tasks.[37]

Admiral King met this compromise plan, which Marshall thought the only way "we can successfully and immediately go ahead," in the same spirit in which it was offered. He still believed that the offensive should be entrusted to Ghormley under the direct control of the Joint Chiefs "whose authority cannot properly be questioned by either principal—General MacArthur . . . or Admiral Nimitz." But he was willing to forego this point "to make progress in the direction in which we are agreed that we should go," if Marshall would agree to defer a decision on Tasks Two and Three until a later time. Task One, which favored the Navy, King accepted, though he preferred placing it under the

---

[36] Rad, MacArthur to Marshall, No. 261, 1 Jul 42, CM–IN–0088.

[37] Memo, Marshall for King, 1 Jul 42, sub: Joint Draft Directive for Offensive Opns in SWPA, OPD (SWPA) Case 80.

Joint Chiefs rather than Nimitz. Marshall refused to accept this change and later in the day persuaded Admiral King to accept his original compromise.[38]

The Joint Chiefs approved the plan that same day, 2 July. There was only one change. Task Two, which originally mentioned only the seizure of Lae, Salamaua, and northeast New Guinea, now called for the capture of the "remainder of the Solomon Islands" as well.[39] Thus, MacArthur was made responsible, without any preliminary notice or discussion, for an area which would witness some of the bitterest fighting of the Pacific war.

At the same time that the directive for operations in the Solomons and New Guinea was approved, Admiral King gave his consent to two proposals he had long opposed. The first of these was the creation of an Army command for the South Pacific Area, the post which went to General Harmon.[40] The second was the Army's plan for the formation of two mobile air forces in the Pacific theater, consisting of heavy bombers and stationed at each end of the line of communications in Hawaii and Australia. For months King had been insisting that heavy bombers must be stationed along the line of communications as well as in Hawaii and Australia, but he now suddenly abandoned his position and agreed to the Army's scheme under which the bombers would be available for operations anywhere in the Pacific "as may be directed by the U.S. Chiefs of Staff."[41]

These arrangements completed, Admiral King set off for San Francisco to meet Admiral Nimitz — who was slightly injured in an air accident on the way— to explain personally to him the plans that had been made and his hopes for the future.

Thus was ended the debate that had consumed much of the time of the Washington and Pacific staffs and their chiefs for almost a month. Marshall, who had never given up the fight for the principle of unity of command, had displayed throughout a high order of military statesmanship. Avoiding the extreme position of both King and MacArthur, he had ably defended the point of view of his own service and fashioned a compromise that offered an effective instrument for the prosecution of the war. His satisfaction with the outcome was evident when, on the 3d, he told MacArthur that "a workable plan has been set up and a unity of command established, without previous precedent for an offensive operation."[42] That there would be further difficulties he did not doubt, but so long as there was the will to co-operate he was optimistic about the future. "I wish you to make every conceivable effort to promote complete accord in this affair," he told MacArthur. "There will be difficulties and irritations inevitably, but the end in view demands a determination to suppress these manifestations."[43]

To this plea MacArthur replied with assurances that he would co-operate fully. And as a mark of this co-operative

---

[38] Memo, King for Marshall, 2 Jul 42, OPD 384 (PTO) Sec 1.

[39] Joint Directive for Offensive Opns in SWPA, 2 Jul 42, OPD 381 (SWPA) case 83.

[40] See above, Chap. XI.

[41] Ltr, King to Marshall, ser. 00580, 2 Jul 42; OPD Memo for record, 4 Jul 42, sub: Pacific Theater Mobile Air Force, both in OPD 384 (PTO) sec. 1.

[42] Rad, Marshall to MacArthur, No. 334, 3 Jul 42, CM–OUT–0677.

[43] *Ibid.*

spirit he pointed to his invitation to Ghormley and Maj. Gen. Alexander A. Vandegrift, commander of the 1st Marine Division, to come to Melbourne to arrange for the co-ordination of their efforts in the coming operation. Finally, he suggested that Ghormley, after he completed Task One, should be retained as commander of forces afloat during Tasks Two and Three.[44] The prospects of a harmonious relationship between the Army and Navy were never brighter, but the task of making ready for the offensive to come would soon create fresh problems and renew their earlier disagreements.

[44] Rad, MacArthur to Marshall, No. C–121, 4 Jul 42, CM–IN–1306.

CHAPTER XIV

Preparations and Problems

> A plan of campaign should anticipate everything which the enemy can do, and contain within itself the means of thwarting him. Plans of campaign may be infinitely modified according to the circumstances, the genius of the commander, the quality of the troops and the topography of the theater of war.
>
> NAPOLEON, *Maxims*

In the South Pacific, preparations for the coming offensive had begun even before the Joint Chiefs had given their approval. Before he left Washington on 1 May, Admiral Ghormley had been alerted to the possibility of operations and since then had been kept informed of the discussions between the Army and Navy planners. Finally, on 25 June, he received word through Admiral Nimitz that the time had come to make his plans. Immediately he called General Vandegrift and his staff from Wellington, where the 1st Marine Division was located, to a conference in Auckland. It was then that the marines, who had not expected to go into action until the end of the year, learned for the first time of the plans to invade the Solomons and of their role in the campaign. They would have to be ready on 1 August, the tentative date for the landing. There was little time and the division was far from ready, but the marines did the best they could, cloaking their preparations under the guise of amphibious training.

Logistics and Strategy

Assembling the troops earmarked for the landing presented considerable dif-

ficulties. Only the 5th Marines, division headquarters, and miscellaneous elements of the 1st Division were actually in the theater. Of the other two infantry regiments, one, the 1st Marines, was at sea, and the other, the 2d, attached to the 1st Division for the operation, had not yet left San Diego. The division's artillery component, the 11th Marines, was with the 1st, en route to Wellington, where it was scheduled to arrive on 11 July. The large fleet of warships, transports, and cargo vessels required for the operation was scattered from Brisbane to San Diego.[1]

The logistical difficulties facing General Vandegrift were imposing. With the limited dock facilities at Wellington, it was necessary to combat-load the 5th Marines before the 1st and 11th Marines arrived. These last two, organi-

---

[1] This account of preparations is based on a manuscript history of U.S. Army Forces in the South Pacific prepared by the author during the war and filed in OCMH. See also, Miller, *Guadalcanal: The First Offensive*, ch. II; Morison, *Coral Sea, Midway and Submarine Actions*, ch. XIII; John Zimmerman, *The Guadalcanal Campaign* (Washington: Historical Division, Headquarters, U.S. Marine Corps, 1949). The 1st Marine Division at the time consisted only of two infantry regiments, the 7th having been detached for service with the 1st Provisional Marine Brigade in Samoa.

zation-loaded before they had left the United States, would have to be completely reloaded for combat when they reached Wellington. The first task, combat loading the 5th Marines, was accomplished without difficulty, but the second proved a nightmare. Plans for handling the cargo of the eight vessels carrying the second echelon of the division could not be made in advance for there were no manifests. It was necessary, therefore, to unload, sort the cargo, requisition the rations and other supplies needed, and combat-load the eight vessels in about ten days. The marines themselves, with the help of a few skilled operators and limited equipment, had to do the job working in 8-hour shifts around the clock. Tired and in poor physical condition after the month-long voyage, the marines had to work under disheartening conditions and in a steady cold rain —this was the winter season in New Zealand—which disintegrated the paper cartons and spilled cans all over the docks. In spite of these difficulties the division was loaded with sixty days' supplies and ready to sail on 22 July. On that day the twelve transports with escort left Wellington to rendezvous with the remainder of the invasion force coming from San Diego, Pearl Harbor and Noumea.

Long before the 1st Marine Division had completed its preparations, it had become apparent that the task ahead would be more difficult than originally thought. At the time the Joint Chiefs had approved the directive for an offensive in the South and Southwest Pacific, the Japanese had not yet begun to consolidate their positions in the southern Solomons and New Guinea. Some Japanese activity had been observed in the area and reported by the former planters and civil servants who had remained behind to serve in the Coastwatching Service of the Australian intelligence. But it was not until early July, when the enemy landed troops on Guadalcanal, just south of Tulagi, and began to build an airfield there at Lunga Point, that the meaning of this activity became clear. The news was passed on to Washington on 6 July, where the threat posed by the new airfield combined with the existence of the seaplane base at Tulagi was fully appreciated. Additional information on Japanese shipping in the vicinity and the progress of construction on Guadalcanal did nothing to lessen the fear. Time was of the essence and obviously Guadalcanal would be as important an objective of Task One as Tulagi.[2]

It was while this disquieting news was coming in that MacArthur and Ghormley held their meeting in Melbourne on 8 July. The result was a joint message to Marshall and King representing, the two Pacific commanders declared, their own opinions "arrived at separately and confirmed by decision."[3] With particular emphasis, they called attention to the "marked change in the enemy situation," their own shortage of planes, the scarcity of shipping to move men and material, and the absence of airfields and port facilities. The Japanese, they pointed out, were building airfields and developing their bases at Kavieng, Rabaul, Lae, Salamaua, Buka, and Guadalcanal. Both MacArthur and Ghormley

---

[2] Rad, MacArthur to Marshall, 6 Jul 42, CM–IN–2068. For an account of the Coastwatching Service, see Eric A. Feldt, *The Coast Watchers* (Melbourne: Oxford University Press, 1946).

[3] Rad, MacArthur and Ghormley to JCS, 1012, 8 Jul 42, OPD Exec Files.

doubted that the Allies with their piti-
fully inadequate resources and lack of
airfields would be able to gain and maintain air supremacy in the objective area.
"The successful accomplishment of the
operation," they told the Joint Chiefs,
"is open to gravest doubts."

Ghormley, like MacArthur, disliked
the idea of breaking up the operation
against Rabaul into separate parts and
joined him in opposing it before the
Joint Chiefs. Once begun, the two men
argued, the entire offensive should be
carried forward to its conclusion in one
continuous movement. Failure to do so
would expose the assault forces to counterattack from Rabaul and constitute a
danger of the greatest magnitude. Task
One, therefore, should be postponed, the
Pacific commanders told Marshall and
King, until the means required to execute all three tasks had been assembled.
Admiral Nimitz, in commenting on the
proposal, argued against postponement.[4]

The MacArthur-Ghormley message
created a most unfavorable impression
in Washington. Admiral King expressed
the views of many when he pointed out
that MacArthur, who only a short time
before was proposing to strike out boldly
and swiftly for Rabaul, "now, confronted
with the concrete aspects of the problem," claimed with Ghormley that even
the much more limited operation against
Tulagi could not be undertaken without
considerably more air power and shipping.[5] To the naval planners, the fact
that the Japanese were consolidating

their positions in the Solomons seemed
to call for speed, not delay. Rather than
wait until all three tasks could be pushed
through in one continuous movement,
they thought that Task One was now
more urgent than ever and that the
enemy must be ejected from the southern Solomons before he could move
against the Allied line of communication. MacArthur, it was admitted, did
not have the means at hand for Tasks
Two and Three, but these, they felt,
would have to be provided later by the
Army. Task One must be launched
without delay; planning for the other
two should be completed as soon as
possible.

General Marshall accepted the Navy
view without argument and agreed that
MacArthur would need more aircraft
and transportation before he could begin
his own operations. In his reply to the
Southwest Pacific commander, therefore,
he held out the promise of additional
support for Tasks Two and Three, but
made it clear that even if this support
was not forthcoming because of conditions elsewhere he was to push vigorously
the preparations and detailed planning
for these tasks. Task One, King and
Marshall announced, was to proceed as
planned. They did not, they told Mac-
Arthur and Ghormley, "desire to coun-
termand operations already under way,"
but, in recognition of the limited means
in the Pacific, they asked the two commanders to submit requests for the means
"absolutely essential to the execution of
Task One."[6]

---

[4] Ltr, Spruance to Hoover, 17 Jul 59, OCMH.
Spruance was chief of staff to Nimitz at the time.

[5] Memos, King for Marshall, 10 Jul 42, sub: Mac-
Arthur-Ghormley Dispatch, and Cooke to King, 9
July 42, same sub, both in OPD 381 (PTO) sec. 2.

[6] Rad, JCS to MacArthur and Ghormley, 2100, 10
Jul 42, OPD 381 (PTO) sec 2. The Joint Chiefs
meeting of this date, their 24th, was the first one in
which the coming offensive was discussed.

The Pacific versus Europe

At the same time that the Army and Navy chiefs in Washington were resisting the appeals from their Pacific commanders for additional support and a more massive offensive, they found themselves arguing, by a curious twist of circumstances, for a reversal of the Europe-first strategy developed before the war and confirmed at the ARCADIA Conference in December 1941–January 1942. The background of this startling proposal lies in the decision, reaffirmed in June, (a) to invade the European continent in the fall of 1942 in the event the Red Army suffered disastrous reverses (SLEDGEHAMMER) and (b) to mount a major invasion of the Continent in 1943 (ROUNDUP). BOLERO, the concentration of forces in England for the invasion, applied to both operations.[7] Upon this project General Marshall and his staff had put most of their energies for months and when early in July the British, faced with threats of disaster in the Middle East and North Africa, proposed that plans for the possible invasion of the Continent in 1942 (SLEDGEHAMMER) be abandoned and North Africa be invaded instead, the Chief of Staff reacted with considerable vigor. He had opposed such an invasion earlier and still did on the ground that it was an indecisive operation that would scatter American forces, drain away Allied re-

sources, and jeopardize both the main assault in Europe in 1943 (ROUNDUP) and the American position in the Pacific. If the British refused to go through with SLEDGEHAMMER, therefore, the United States should, Marshall argued, turn its full attention to Japan. Tearing a page from MacArthur's book, he pointed out that such a move would have many advantages, that it would receive the strong support of the American people, and, after a second front in Europe, would be the most effective way to relieve pressure on Russia.[8] The Joint Chiefs, he concluded, should unite in recommending this course to the President.

Admiral King was more than willing to join forces with his Army colleague. Though he accepted and supported the strategy which gave priority to the war in Europe, King had always placed greater emphasis than Marshall on the importance of holding and maintaining a strong position in the Pacific. Moreover, his conception of a defensive strategy in the war against Japan included active measures and much larger forces than the Army was willing to put into that theater. Early in May, before Coral Sea and Midway and when the threat in the Pacific had loomed so large, Admiral King had argued unsuccessfully against the build-up in Britain. Though that crisis had passed, King, like MacArthur, saw in the renewed Japanese activity a fresh threat which would require larger efforts in the Pacific. It was natural therefore that Admiral

---

[7] Though the 1942 operation was contingent on a major Soviet defeat, President Roosevelt had virtually promised Molotov at the end of May that the Allies would open a second front that year. The British were far from sanguine about such an operation, and there was considerable doubt in the American staff about the feasibility of the operation. Sherwood, *Roosevelt and Hopkins*, pp. 568–70, 577; Matloff and Snell, *Strategic Planning, 1941–42*, pp. 233–34.

[8] Mins, JCS Mtg, 10 Jul 42; Rad, MacArthur to Marshall, No. 176, 8 May 42, cited in ch. IX above; Churchill, *The Hinge of Fate*, p. 434. For a more detailed account of these discussions, see Matloff and Snell, *Strategic Planning, 1941–42*, pp. 187–90, 232–49.

King should welcome the strange reversal of roles that made Marshall champion of the Pacific cause. Readily he accepted, with minor modifications, the memorandum Marshall had prepared urging on the President a change in the basic strategy of the war if the British persisted in their refusal to undertake SLEDGEHAMMER.[9]

This threat of a shift away from Europe and toward the Pacific, used later as a strategem in debate with the British, was apparently seriously intended at this time. The "Hitler-first" strategy and the build-up of forces in the British Isles for an early invasion of the Continent, which General Marshall had consistently advocated and defended, was based on the recognized military principle of concentration of force. Rather than violate that principle and open a major and costly offensive that could produce no decisive results against Germany, Marshall was willing to turn temporarily to the lesser enemy and the secondary theater. It was not the course he preferred, but at least it would avoid the dispersion of American resources and manpower and would bring about the defeat of one of the Axis Powers. He hoped, he told the President frankly, that the British would give in rather than see the United States go its own way but he was ready, if they did not, "to turn immediately to the Pacific with strong forces and drive for a decision against Japan."[10]

To President Roosevelt at Hyde Park, this unexpected recommendation from his chief military and naval advisers for a drastic revision in American strategy came as a complete surprise. Immediately he asked for a detailed and comprehensive statement of the plans they had made for such a shift, to be ready "this afternoon"—it was then Sunday, 12 July.[11] This statement, he directed, should include estimates of the time required to transfer ships, planes, and men to the Pacific and the effect of the move on the war in every theater. The request was an impossible one, and perhaps the President knew that. No one had forseen so sudden and basic a reversal in strategy and there were no studies of the kind now required. Nevertheless, while their staffs worked feverishly to produce the information desired, the Joint Chiefs submitted a preliminary and hasty study to the President. After outlining the adjustments that would have to be made and the effect of the proposed strategy on the military efforts of the British and Russians, the Joint Chiefs recommended that, after the capture of Rabaul, the United States should concentrate its forces in a drive northwest through Truk, Guam, and Saipan. As a substitute, or, simultaneously, if conditions were favorable, they suggested the route through the Malay Barrier and Borneo to the Philippines. This program was admittedly an inadequate response to Roosevelt's request for the Pacific alternative, but it was the best that could be done in the short time allotted.[12]

[9] Memo, Marshall and King for Roosevelt, 10 Jul 42, no sub, OPD 381 (Gen) case 73.

[10] Memo, Marshall for Roosevelt, 10 Jul 42, sub: British Proposal Relative to BOLERO, OPD Exec Files. See also, Stimson and Bundy On Active Service, p. 424.

[11] Tel Msg, President to Marshall and King, recorded in Memo, Col John R. Deane for King, 12 Jul 42, OPD Exec Files.

[12] Memo, JCS for President, 12 Jul 42, sub: Pacific Opns, OPD 381 (Gen) case 73.

The merits of the Joint Chief's proposal and of the staff studies initiated by the President's request were to prove shortly a matter of no consequence. By 14 July the President had made up his mind. "I want you to know," he told Marshall then, "that I do not approve the Pacific proposal."[13] Instead Marshall and King were to go to London with Hopkins immediately—the 16th was suggested—to work out some arrangement with the British. A North African invasion, he gave Marshall to understand, was a definite possibility if the British could not be persuaded to adhere to SLEDGEHAMMER.

The next morning, after Roosevelt's return to Washington, Marshall saw the President at the White House and was left in no doubt about his views. The proposal to turn to the Pacific, Mr. Roosevelt said, was "a red herring" whose purpose, he implied, was something other than that stated in the Marshall-King memorandum. So strongly did he feel on this subject that he even suggested that "the record should be altered so that it would not appear in later years that we had proposed what had amounted to the abandonment of the British."[14] That night he told Hopkins, "If we cannot strike at SLEDGEHAMMER, then we must take the second best—and that is not the Pacific. There we are conducting a successful holding war."[15]

Thus, when Marshall and King left for London with Hopkins they did so with the clear understanding that the

President would support their efforts to gain acceptance of SLEDGEHAMMER but would not tolerate any ultimatum to the British. "It is of the utmost importance," he told the three delegates, "that we appreciate that defeat of Japan does not defeat Germany and that American concentration against Japan this year or in 1943 increases the chance of complete German domination of Europe and Africa."[16] The defeat of Germany, on the other hand, would surely result, Roosevelt believed, in the defeat of the Japanese enemy, "probably without firing a shot or losing a life." Again, the basic strategy of the war had been confirmed.

What course would the United States have followed in the Pacific had the President accepted the recommendation of his military advisers in July 1942? No definite answer is possible, of course, but in the studies initiated by the President's request for a comprehensive statement of the Pacific alternative can be found a clear statement of the strategy contemplated. Obsolete before they were completed on 15 July, these studies are, nevertheless, of interest in revealing the Army planners' views and the estimates on which these views were based.[17]

First, the planners considered possible alternatives to BOLERO — North Africa, Norway, the Middle East, and others— and dismissed them all for various reasons. The Pacific, they decided, offered the greatest possibilities and in support of this view they attributed to the Japanese a strength that was so far from real-

---

[13] Tel Msg, Roosevelt to Marshall, 14 Jul 42, WDCSA Files (BOLERO). Churchill's attitude is stated in a letter of 12 July to Field Marshal Dill in Churchill, *The Hinge of Fate*, p. 438.

[14] Memo, Marshall for King, 15 Jul 42, no sub, WDCSA 381 (War Plans).

[15] Sherwood, *Roosevelt and Hopkins*, p. 602.

[16] Memo, Roosevelt for Hopkins, Marshall, and King, 16 Jul 42, sub: Instrs for London Conf, WDCSA 381, printed in Sherwood, *Roosevelt and Hopkins*, pp. 603–05.

[17] OPD, Statement of Present Basic Strategy, with Incls, 15 Jul 42, OPD Exec Files.

ity as to suggest that they had little appreciation of the far-reaching significance of the Midway victory. The Japanese, they thought, were capable of extending their hold in the Aleutians, attacking eastern Siberia, and seizing British positions in India. An attack against Australia and the line of communications they considered a real possibility. Even an all-out assault on Hawaii was not ruled out. And if the Japanese were successful in that, they would, the planners believed, make a determined effort to drive the United States from the Pacific. "It is possible," the planners concluded, "that, if undeterred, the enemy may consolidate and prepare defenses so effectively that he cannot be defeated by the forces which we will be able to operate against him."

To avert this disaster, the Army planners proposed a 5-phase plan to step up the war against Japan. The first was Task One, already in preparation. Phase 2 included Tasks Two and Three which, with the forces formerly allocated to BOLERO, could begin in November and be carried through as a continuous operation under MacArthur. In April 1943, when naval forces would be available, the third and fourth phases would begin, the former consisting of the seizure of the Caroline and Marshall Islands, the latter of a drive through the Netherlands Indies. Phase 5 called for the reoccupation of the Philippines at an undetermined date.

This 5-phase plan offered little that was new and was much like the one developed by the Navy staff in April. Though the planners overestimated Japanese strength they, like many others, totally underestimated the vigor of the Japanese reaction to the Solomons offensive. American weakness in the Pacific was fully appreciated in these Army studies, however, and implicit in them was the realization that the diversion of troops and planes from Europe would not greatly accelerate operations in the Pacific where the role of the Navy was so decisive. Thus, the Army planners were unable to schedule operations in the Central Pacific before April 1943, contingent on the availability of naval forces. Finally, they had no plans for operations once the Philippines were reoccupied. Where to go after that and what measures to take for the defeat of Japan were problems which none of the planners, Army or Navy, had yet faced seriously. Later, these problems would become the focal point of the debate over Pacific strategy.

MacArthur Prepares

Completely unaware of events in Washington, the theater comanders continued their preparations for the task ahead. Under the Joint Chiefs' directive of 2 July, MacArthur was required to supply naval reinforcements and land-based air support for the Solomons invasion, and to interdict enemy air and naval operations in his area. This he readily agreed to do and during the weeks that followed his Melbourne meeting with Ghormley, MacArthur's staff worked out the details for co-ordinating the efforts of two theaters with officers from the South Pacific. From his small navy, MarArthur turned over to Ghormley virtually his entire striking force, 4 heavy cruisers (3 of them Australian), 1 light cruiser, and 9 destroyers. On 14 July these warships sailed from Brisbane under the flag of Rear Adm. V. A. C. Crutchley, RAN, to join the South Pacific forces for the coming cam-

GENERAL MacARTHUR AND GENERAL KENNEY

GENERAL EICHELBERGER AND GENERAL BLAMEY

paign. The submarines in the Southwest Pacific, though not reassigned, were also to be used in support of the coming offensive. Operating out of Brisbane, the underwater craft would have the task of interdicting enemy shipping off Rabaul. The role of MacArthur's Allied Air Forces was perhaps the most vital of supporting operations. Before the landings its planes would reconnoiter eastern New Guinea and the Bismarck Archipelago; thereafter they were to patrol the north and northwest approaches to the objective area, while making every effort to neutralize enemy aircraft in New Guinea and the Solomons.[18]

While plans were being made to provide support for Task One, responsibility for which rested on Admiral Ghormley, General MacArthur made preparations for the tasks to follow. Airfields in northern Australia and New Guinea were rushed to completion and planes dispatched as rapidly as the fields became available. These would serve in Task One and were needed as quickly as possible. To direct the training and later the operations of the two U.S. divisions in his area, General MacArthur asked for and was given a corps headquarters in July. Maj. Gen. Robert C. Richardson, Jr., who was in Australia on an inspection trip for General Marshall, was the first candidate for the post, but because of his strong feelings about serving under Australian command (Allied Land Forces was under General Blamey) the assignment finally went to Maj. Gen. Robert L. Eichelberger. Command of the Allied Air Forces, with which Mac-

Arthur had expressed some dissatisfaction, underwent a change too, when General Kenney relieved Brett late in July. About the same time, Brig. Gen. Richard J. Marshall, MacArthur's deputy chief of staff and one of that small band which had come out of Corregidor with him, took over the supply headquarters (designated on 20 July U.S. Army Services of Supply) from Barnes who returned home, like Brett, for reassignment. That same day, General MacArthur moved his headquarters further up the coast of Australia but still far from the scene of operations. Effective 1 August the boundary between the South and Southwest Pacific was moved west to the line agreed upon, longitude 159° east. (Map 5)

The Joint Chiefs' directive of 2 July made necssary also another revision of MacArthur's TULSA Plan, last revised on 1 July. The objectives of the plan were the same as those of the directive, but the timing and the forces were different. For one thing, MacArthur's planners could now assume, somewhat optimistically, that they would have the Marine division, the carriers, and the support of the South Pacific land-based aircraft for their own operations when Task One was completed. Also, they would assume that the Guadalcanal-Tulagi area would be in Allied hands before their own forces went into action. There was no need, however, to revise the scheme of operations already developed. As before the campaign against Rabaul was envisaged as a two-pronged advance in five stages through the Solomons and along the northeast coast of New Guinea. The first three phases, which would take his troops as far as Lorengau in the Admiralties and Buka in the northern Solo-

---

[18] GHQ SWPA Opns Instr No. 14, 26 Jul 42, Hist Rec Index Cards, OCMH; The Campaigns of MacArthur in the Pacific, SWPA Series, I, ch. II; Milner, *Victory in Papua*, pp. 47–48.

MAP 5

THE BATTLE AREA

August 1942

50   0   50   100
STATUTE MILES

Buka I.

S O L O M O N

Ontong Java

BOUGAINVILLE

Kieta

Buin

Shortland Is. Ballale
Faisi   I.

Treasury Is.

CHOISEUL

I S L A N D S

Rekata
Bay

Vella Lavella

Kolombangara

SANTA
ISABEL

THE

Gizo

NEW
GEORGIA

Rendova

Vangunu

S
L
O
T

Russell
Is.

Savo I.

Florida
I.

MALAITA

Cape Esperance

Tulagi I.

Lunga Pt

GUADALCANAL

SAN
CRISTOBAL

D. Holmes, Jr.

592496 O–62—22

mons, would complete Task Two; the next two, which called for the seizure of Kavieng (New Ireland) by the force moving up the Solomons and a combined assault by both forces against Rabaul, would complete the tasks assigned by the Joint Chiefs.[19]

An important feature of MacArthur's TULSA plan from the start was the establishment of airfields at Milne Bay at the southeast tip of the Papuan Peninsula and at Buna. These would be required for the assault against Lae and Salamaua, and plans for the former were made even before the Joint Chiefs' directive of 2 July. Work at Milne Bay began early in July and continued without interruption from the Japanese who were apparently unaware of the project. When they did learn of it, they landed troops there late in August and made a determined effort to seize the base, but it was already too late.[20]

The effort to build an airdrome in the Buna area developed in a way that was entirely unforeseen and involved General MacArthur's forces in a long and costly battle at a much earlier date than anticipated. Plans for construction of the airstrip were issued on 15 July after a reconnaissance of the area, and a special task force was organized for the project. The plan was a complicated one. From Port Moresby would come one group, mostly Australian infantry, traveling to Buna by foot over the Kokoda Trail, the one passable route across the Owen Stanley Range. There it would meet a smaller group coming in by boat and forming a beachhead to protect the main convoy carrying the construction and garrison units.[21]

The plan had hardly been completed and orders issued when reconnaissance revealed that the Japanese had assembled a large convoy and appeared to be moving on Buna. This supposition was entirely correct. Frustrated at Coral Sea and Midway and forced to cancel operations against Samoa, New Caledonia, and the Fijis, the Japanese had nevertheless refused to give up their plans to take Port Moresby. Since a seaborne invasion was no longer possible, *Imperial General Headquarters* on 11 June had ordered the *17th Army* commander, General Hyakutake, to make plans for an overland assault from the east coast of the Papuan Peninsula, first determining by reconnaissance whether such an operation was feasible. This task was assigned to the *South Seas Detachment,* and the starting point selected was Buna. But when General Horii had almost completed his plans, *Imperial General Headquarters* decided that a reconnaissance was not necessary; Port Moresby was to be captured by overland assault. Thus, on 18 July the *South Seas Detachment* was directed to "speedily land at Buna, push forward on the Buna-Kokoda road, and capture Port Moresby and adjacent airfields."[22]

The final Japanese plan for the Port Moresby operation called for a landing

[19] TULSA II–A, Joint Basic Plan for . . . New Britain–New Ireland–Admiralties Area, no date but probably prepared at the end of July, abstract in OCMH.

[20] The Campaigns of MacArthur in the Pacific, SWPA Series II, pp. 50–51, 65–68; Milner, *Victory in Papua,* pp. 77–88.

[21] GHQ SWPA, Instr to Comdrs AAF, ALF, ANF, Occupation and Construction at Buna Bay, 15 Jul 42, Hist Rec Index Cards, OCMH.

[22] Japanese Opns in SWPA, p. 132. This account of the Japanese landing at Buna is based on this work, pages 132–36, and the sources cited therein.

at Buna on 21 July by a joint force of 3,300 men. Support would be provided by planes from Rabaul and a naval force of two light cruisers and three destroyers. On 20 July the convoy left Rabaul and, despite air attacks from B–17's which damaged one of the three transports, reached its destination on schedule, at 1900 of the 21st. There was no resistance and by the morning of the 22d the village of Buna was in Japanese hands. The construction troops and the garrison immediately began to convert Buna into an advance base, under steady bombardment from the planes of the Allied Air Forces. At the same time, about 1,000 men, the so-called *Yokoyama Force,* moved out toward Kokoda, which they occupied on 29 July after defeating an Australian contingent of about equal strength. To General Hyakutake at Rabaul they sent back word that the overland assault against Port Moresby was a feasible operation and that firm plans could now be made. But they had failed to reckon with the difficulties still to be overcome in the long hard pull across the Owen Stanley Range.

Beaten to the punch at Buna and faced with a new threat to Port Moresby, General MacArthur put aside thoughts of Task Two to concentrate on the job of driving the enemy back along the Kokoda Trail and out of his newly won position along the coast. Until this was accomplished, he would be unable to begin the assault against Lae and Salamaua and inaugurate Task Two of the Joint Chiefs' directive.

There was concern in Washington also over this fresh Japanese advance. With the invasion already on its way to the Solomons, the Navy was especially anxious that the Japanese in New Guinea

be contained and that the Allies retain control of the vital sea lanes in the area. General MacArthur, the naval planners felt, had not displayed any great enthusiasm for the Joint Chiefs' directive and, in the absence of any information on his activities and plans, they were fearful that he might not appreciate fully the importance of supporting the Solomons offensive. These anxieties Admiral King passed on to Marshall with the suggestion that MacArthur be asked what plans he had to hold the Japanese advance in New Guinea. The Chief of Staff, though he felt that King's assumption that MacArthur had not taken all measures to counter the Japanese threat was scarcely justified, accepted the suggestion and that same day, 31 July, queried MacArthur on the subject.[23]

MacArthur's response was long and detailed. In it he explained what he had done and was doing to stop the Japanese and outlined his plans for the development of bases in New Guinea. Unfortunately, he explained, he did not have enough transports to move the needed troops forward from Australia as quickly as he would wish—the 7th Australian Division and three brigades were under orders for New Guinea—but if the ships could be furnished he would speedily regain Buna. The remainder of the message was devoted to an explanation of the TULSA plan. Task One, he believed, would be completed by the time he reached Buna—it was, but at a much later date than anyone else had estimated—and he would then start Task

<hr>

[23] Memos, King for Marshall, 31 Jul 42, sub: Japanese Opns in New Guinea; Marshall for King, 1 Aug 42, same sub; Rad, MacArthur to Marshall, No. 384, 31 Jul 42, all in OPD 381 (SWPA) case 92.

Two, "if the Marines with their amphibious equipment can be used." [24] Also needed, he made clear, would be the carriers and the land-based bombers of the South Pacific. With them he was confident he could complete Tasks Two and Three rapidly.

Final Preparations

The brief crisis brought on by the British proposal to substitute a North African invasion for SLEDGEHAMMER, coming as it did in the midst of preparations for the Solomons offensive, had momentarily held out the possibility of a greatly enlarged effort in the Pacific and an end to the Army's reluctance to commit its forces there. The President's decision abruptly restored the *status quo* so far as the claims of the Pacific theater in relation to the requirements of other theaters were concerned, but left unresolved the problem of reinforcements for the offensive ahead. This problem, first raised by MacArthur and Ghormley on 8 July and suspended briefly while the Pacific alternative was under discussion, was reopened by Admiral King on 14 July when he sent to General Marshall a request from Nimitz for three antiaircraft regiments to be used in the Solomons. Next day, in the conviction that the situation was too serious to permit delay and that the powerful Japanese forces assembling at Rabaul spelled trouble for the South Pacific commander, King urged General Marshall to reconsider the Army's decision. In addition to the antiaircraft regiments he wanted Marshall to order MacArthur to make additional garrison troops available if

needed to reinforce those from the South Pacific. [25]

The request for garrison forces from MacArthur's area was turned down flatly, that for antiaircraft units was met by the offer of a regiment to replace those at Bora Bora and Tongatabu, which would be moved forward to the Solomons. Though King had accepted this offer conditionally before his departure for London with Marshall, it brought strong objections from Ghormley and Nimitz, who wanted a steady flow of troops and planes to replace those lost when the battle began. Unless this was done, Nimitz wrote, "not only will we be unable to proceed with Tasks Two and Three of this campaign, but we may be unable even to hold what we have taken." [26] The Army was adamant in its opposition and maintained steadfastly that it could not send reinforcements to the South Pacific Area without cutting deeply into commitments elsewhere. [27]

Actually, nothing done at this time could have had any immediate effect on Admiral Ghormley's plan or on the campaign ahead; already the forces for the invasion were assembling in the South Pacific. Ever since his return from Melbourne on 9 July, Ghormley and his staff had been perfecting their plans and completing their preparations. On the 10th he had received his orders from Nimitz together with a list of the ground, air, and naval forces he would have for the

[24] Rad, MacArthur to Marshall, Q–147, 2 Aug 42, OPD 381 (SWPA) case 92.

[25] Memos, King for Marshall, 15 Jul 42, sub: Garrison Forces for Solomons; 14 Jul 42, sub: AAA Units in South Pacific, both in WDCSA Files (SWPA).

[26] Memo, Vice Adm Russell Willson for Lt Gen Joseph T. McNarney, (both acting for their chiefs in London), 22 Jul 42, sub: Reinforcements for South Pacific, WDCSA File (SWPA).

[27] For the papers dealing with this decision, see WDCSA Files (SWPA) and OPD 320.2 (PTO) cases 21 and 30.

operation. These included, in addition to the 1st Marine Division, three carrier task groups built around the *Saratoga, Enterprise,* and *Wasp* (the first two were at Pearl, the *Wasp* at San Diego), the additional B–17's from the Hawaiian Mobile Air Force, the land-based aircraft of the South Pacific Area (altogether 291 aircraft of various types), and a large number of warships, transports, and cargo vessels.[28]

On receipt of Nimitz' order, preparations for the coming offensive were intensified. The development of airfields in the New Hebrides, where the B–17's would base, was given highest priority. By the end of the month two strips, each 5,000 feet long and 150 feet wide, were almost ready. The one at Efate had been built in three weeks; the one at Espiritu Santo in twelve days. Both were within striking distance of the objective.

Meanwhile the planning staff had completed its work and on 16 July Admiral Ghormley issued the basic plan for the seizure of Guadalcanal and Tulagi. Two major task forces were organized, the Expeditionary Force under Admiral Fletcher and the Air Force under Admiral McCain, both responsible directly to Ghormley. Fletcher's force included virtually all the ships and troops assigned to the operation, with responsibility for the amphibious forces and the landing itself going to Admiral Turner who was under Fletcher. The three carrier groups were also a part of Fletcher's force but were commanded directly by Rear Adm. Leigh Noyes. Admiral McCain's Air Force included all land-based Army,

Navy, Marine, and New Zealand planes in the area. Organized into seven groups and scattered throughout the South Pacific, this force had the double task of reconnaissance and bombardment of the objective. Neither General Harmon nor any other Army officer was given any responsibility for the operation; the top command was entirely naval.

Admiral Ghormley divided the operation into three phases. In the first, starting about 27 July, the Expeditionary Force was to rendezvous in the Fiji Islands for rehearsal. Phase Two called for the seizure of Tulagi and Guadalcanal on 7 August, Ghormley having secured a week's delay in the start of the campaign. The final phase, later canceled, provided for the seizure of Ndeni in the Santa Cruz group as an air and seaplane base. Five submarines of the Pacific Fleet were to provide support from 22 July through 20 August by patrolling the waters around Truk, and Allied aircraft were to cover the approaches and support the operations once they began.

In the three weeks remaining after receipt of Ghormley's plan, each of the task force commanders assembled his force and made his own plans for D-day. Admiral Noyes's carriers came by separate ways. The *Wasp* had left San Diego on 1 July with the transports carrying the 2d Marines. The *Saratoga* group sailed from Pearl a week later, followed shortly after by the *Enterprise.* That same day, the last of the Marine units, the 3d Defense Battalion, left Hawaii aboard two transports. On the 21st Admiral Fletcher ordered the Expeditionary Force to assemble southeast of the Fijis by 1400 of the 26th for rehearsal. The 1st Raider Battalion, which

---

[28] This account of plans and preparations is based on the author's manuscript history of the South Pacific cited above, as well as Miller, *Guadalcanal: The First Offensive,* ch. II.

A–20 skip-bombing an enemy freighter.

had transferred earlier from Samoa to New Caledonia, was picked up by four destroyer-transports and got to the rendezvous in time, but the 3d Defense Battalion in Hawaii had to join the rest of the force on its way to the objective.

From the 28th through the 31st, the invasion rehearsed off Koro Island in the Fijis. It was the first time that the naval, air, and ground commanders had met to arrange the details of the operation, but the rehearsals were unrealistic and General Vandegrift thought them a loss of valuable time. When they were over, the entire force—eighty-two vessels— sailed for the Solomons, the carriers heading for a point southwest of Gua-

dalcanal. Turner's Amphibious Force, in three great concentric circles with the destroyers on the outside, made for Sealark Channel between Tulagi and Guadalcanal.

As this assembly of ships made its way slowly toward the still-unsuspecting Japnese, the land-based aircraft of Admiral McCain's force went into action. From the hardly completed airstrips at Efate and Espiritu Santo, the Army B–17's of the 11th Bombardment Group, only recently arrived from Hawaii, began their daily bombardment of the objective area. Off to the west and north, over New Guinea and the Bismarck Archipelago, MacArthur's Allied Air Forces kept close

B-17 *heading home from a bomb run over the Solomons.*

watch over the Japanese. Any unexpected Japanese move now might well spell the difference between success and failure.

To assemble, mount, and support the invasion force had taken all the resources of the theater commanders and left them with precious little to meet an emergency. MacArthur's requests for future operations could be deferred, but the demands from Nimitz and Ghormley for the task at hand were becoming even more insistent. And these could not so easily be put aside. At the end of July, Admiral Nimitz and General Emmons, who had repeatedly asked for more aircraft, joined forces to request two heavy bombardment groups to replace the B-17's of the 11th Bombardment Group, which left for the South Pacific on the 26th of the month. They were badly needed, Nimitz reported, to follow up the invasion of Guadalcanal and, in the absence of most of the Pacific Fleet from Hawaiian waters, to support the defense of that area[29]

General Harmon, when he arrived in the South Pacific on 26 July, also found many deficiencies in his command and

[29] Rad, Emmons to Marshall, 26 Jul 42, CM-IN-9215 and associated papers in OPD 320.2 (Hawaii). Nimitz' message is attached to Memo, King for Marshall, 1 Aug 42, sub: Reinforcement of South Pacific, OPD 320.2 (PTO) case 37.

added his voice to the growing chorus of complaint. His first requests for service and supporting units were turned down in Washington with the reminder that the forces in the South Pacific were to be held to the "minimum consistent" with the defensive role of the theater. Meanwhile his requests for air service units and transports were forwarded to the Army Air Forces. Arnold was willing to comply with these requests but, unfortunately, would not be able to provide the units until the fall.[30]

The position taken by the Army on reinforcements for the Pacific was challenged strongly by Admiral King on his return from London at the end of July. The occasion was furnished by the agreement made with the British and by Marshall's own statement that the substitution of the North African operation (Torch) for the invasion of the Continent would release planes and shipping for use in the Pacific. Citing Admiral Nimitz' need for heavy bombers, Admiral King asked Marshall to review the Army's decision against air reinforcements "in the light of recent decisions reached in London." [31] The Army planners were all for turning down this fresh demand with the statement that there were no air units available and that it was impossible to say when any would be. But General Marshall held off. It was now 5 August, two days before the invasion and he decided rather than turn

down the request, to withold his answer.[32]

But Admiral King had no intention of letting the matter rest there. Already he was preparing a list of needed reinforcements for the Pacific that would make earlier requests appear modest by comparison. This latest proposal was based on a report by General Harmon after his first inspection of the Army bases in the South Pacific and a study of the plans for the forthcoming offensive. The minimum Army ground reinforcements needed in the area to comply with the Joint Chiefs' directive, Harmon had told Admiral Ghormley, were 2 divisions plus 2 infantry regiments, 4 regiments of coast artillery (3 antiaircraft and 1 harbor defense), and 2 battalions each of coast artillery and 105–mm howitzers. Air reinforcements, he estimated, should consist of 6 fighter squadrons (3 with the new P–38's), 2 squadrons of heavy, 1 of medium, and 3 of dive bombers. These Harmon knew perfectly well were not available then or likely to be soon, and he limited his request for immediate shipment to 3 squadrons of P–38's and replacements for heavy bombers lost in action and attrition. The remainder, he added, should be sent as soon as possible.[33]

Admiral Ghormley lost no time in forwarding Harmon's estimate, in which he heartily concurred, to his chief in Washington. Taken with MacArthur's most recent statement of his plans, this estimate seemed to King to represent the minimum requirements for the completion of Task One and the initiation of Task Two. He did not expect that so

---

[30] Rad, Harmon to Marshall, 30 Jul 42, CM–IN–10727. Other relevant papers are filed in OPD 320.2 (PTO) case 5.

[31] Memo, King for Marshall, 1 Aug 42, sub: Reinforcements for the South Pacific, OPD 320.2 (PTO) case 37. The agreement referred to was CCS 94, par. e, 24 Jul 42.

[32] Informal Memo, Marshall for Handy, undated, attached to Memo, Handy for Marshall, 5 Aug 42, sub: Reinforcement for South Pacific, OPD 320.2 (PTO) case 37.

[33] Ltr, Harmon to Ghormley, 4 Aug 42, OCMH; Rad, Harmon to Marshall, 5 Aug 42, CM–IN–1252.

large an order could be filled immedi-ately—shipping was too scarce for that—but 'it would appear prudent," he told Marshall, "to commence assembly and planning for first, the air reinforcements and second, ground reinforcements in strengths required to execute plans for the immediate future." [34]

This time the Army planners could not deny the necessity for reinforcements. The marines had landed on Guadalcanal and Tulagi on the 7th, the day before King had penned his note, but already the Japanese were gathering forces for a determined counterattack. Boldly and quickly they moved down to the threat-ened area and on the night of 8–9 Au-gust, off Savo Island, dealt the invading fleet a mortal blow. In one of the brief-est and most disastrous naval engage-ments of the war, the Allies lost a total of four heavy cruisers, one of them Aus-tralian, and suffered other damage which forced them to retire, leaving the marines stranded on the beaches without air or naval support and with only mea-ger supplies. All of the dire predictions from Admiral King and the commanders in the field had come true; all their esti-mates of what would be needed for the invasion, made, it should be noted, after the operation had been decided upon, would soon prove to be painfully accu-rate. The Japanese were evidently de-termined to hold on to what they had, and at Rabaul were the reinforcements they needed. Allied reinforcements were still a long way off, and before they could reach the battlefield, there would be other crises both in the Solomons and New Guinea.

---

[34] Memo, King for Marshall, 8 Aug 42, sub: Mini-mum Army Reinforcements, OPD 320.2 (PTO) case 37.

CHAPTER XV

Crisis in the Pacific, August – November 1942

When a general makes no mistakes in war, it is because he has not been at it long.

TURENNE

The Allied disaster off Savo Island on the night of 8–9 August created so serious a situation that for almost four months the fate of the Allied offensive hung in the balance. The Japanese, though they did not at first grasp the full meaning of the Marine landings, were determined to maintain their hold on the Solomons and New Guinea. Skillfully utilizing every means at their disposal and the advantages of interior lines of communication, they sought time and again during these months to oust the invaders from Guadalcanal. It was not until mid-November, after a series of fierce aerial and naval battles which gave the Allies control of the air and sea, that the issue was decided. But the Japanese fought on for two more months in the vain hope that they might yet snatch victory from defeat. In the end they lost, but the six months' campaign gave them time to strengthen their positions further up the Solomons ladder, in the Bismarck Archipelago, and along the northeast coast of New Guinea. Never again would the Allies underestimate the Japanese will to resist or the capacity and skill of the Japanese soldier.

Few men in Washington had anticipated so vigorous a reaction from the Japanese. Though every senior commander in the Pacific, with the strong support of Admiral King, had warned of trouble ahead if more planes, ships, and men were not quickly dispatched, the Army and air planners had stoutly resisted their demands and maintained that no more could be spared for what was, after all, a secondary and defensive theater of operations. But so strong was the desire to exploit the advantages of Midway and check the Japanese advance toward the Allied line of communications that the commanders in the field acquiesced in the decision to attack. Once the offensive was begun, it was no longer possible to deny the resources needed for victory. Against the arguments for European (and North African) priorities for a future offensive were now posed the immediate and compelling demands of the Pacific. The consequences of failure were too serious to be accepted and again, despite the oft-affirmed "Germany first" strategy, the proponents of stronger measures and larger forces for the Pacific won another round in the never-ending contest for the resources of war.

Emergency Measures

Hardly had the 17,000 men of the 1st Marine Division (reinforced) taken Tulagi and the neighboring small islands and seized the partially completed airstrip at Lunga Point (promptly named Henderson Field) on Guadalcanal, than they found themselves isolated—without air or naval protection and with less than half of the supplies they had brought with them. The aircraft carriers had gone first. Short of fuel and faced with the prospect of hostile air attack, Admiral Fletcher, on the evening of the 8th, had requested and been given permission by Ghormley to withdraw his carriers to safety the next morning. Admiral Turner, perforce, decided that he would have to pull out his amphibious force of warships, transports, and cargo vessels also, and so informed General Vandegrift. This decision had hardly been made when the disastrous Battle of Savo Island provided additional impetus for a hasty withdrawal. By evening of the 9th the amphibious force was steaming southward, carrying with it the heavy construction equipment needed to complete the airfield at Lunga Point, the 5-inch guns of the 3d Defense Battalion, the barbed wire so sorely needed for defense, and large quantities of ammunition and food. Virtually a besieged garrison, the marines were in a desperate plight.[1] The offensive opened so hope-

fully only a few days earlier already seemed in jeopardy.

In Washington there was consternation at the unexpected withdrawal of the fleet and the disastrous consequences of the Battle of Savo Island. From Admiral Nimitz came an urgent request, strongly supported by King, for more planes, and from General Harmon came a similar request for reinforcements together with a pessimistic report on the situation on Guadalcanal. "We have seized a strategic position from which future operations against the Bismarcks can be strongly supported," he wrote. "Can the Marines hold it?" He was doubtful that they could. The Japanese, he thought, could assemble their forces quickly and recapture the island before the Allies could reinforce. Only "the resourcefulness and determination of our own forces," he told Marshall, would be able to "foil this attempt."[2]

The first problem, everyone recognized, was to provide the isolated marines with air support. There was no time to collect the planes in the United States and ship them out. They would have to come from resources already in the theater. But from where? Admiral Nimitz had the answer: divert to the South Pacific the heavy and medium bombers allocated to MacArthur and already en route. Marshall accepted this proposal immediately and author-

---

[1] Miller, *Guadalcanal: The First Offensive*, p. 81. Unless otherwise noted the material in this chapter dealing with ground operations on Guadalcanal is based on this volume; that dealing with naval and air operations on Samuel Eliot Morison, *The*

Struggle for Guadalcanal, August 1942–February 1943, vol. V, "History of United States Naval Operations in World War II" (Boston: Little, Brown and Company, 1950); Craven and Cate, *AAF IV*, ch. II, and the Marine Corps account, Zimmerman, *The Guadalcanal Campaign*.

[2] Ltr, Harmon to Marshall, 11 Aug 42, copy in OCMH; Ltr, King to Marshall, 9 Aug 42; OPD Memo for Record, 10 Aug 42, sub: Aerial Reinforcement of South Pacific. Last two in OPD 452.1 (PTO), case 6.

ized Harmon to retain these planes temporarily if he felt they could be used more effectively in his area than in the Southwest Pacific. At the same time, the Chief of Staff urged MacArthur to intensify his own efforts to neutralize the enemy's airfields and to make plans to send a pursuit squadron to Guadalcanal. Marshall was interested, too, in the extent of co-ordination between the South and Southwest Pacific Areas and asked MacArthur for a report on that matter as well as the feasibility of the plan to rush fighters to Henderson Field.[3]

MacArthur's reply was both disappointing and reassuring. The plan to send fighters to Guadalcanal would be a hazardous undertaking and the chances of success slim. But if Marshall thought the measure necessary he would be willing to risk it. His report on relations with Ghormley was much more encouraging. Co-ordination between the two theaters, he told the Chief of Staff, was excellent. He had made arrangements with Ghormley, he reported, to provide air support on request, but thus far had received no requests. This was not the understanding in Washington, but Ghormley and Harmon, when queried, confirmed MacArthur's assertions of harmonious relations.[4]

Reassuring as such reports were, they did not lessen the seriousness of the situation in the Solomons or diminish the need for planes and supplies. General Harmon's estimates of the force needed for victory, made on the eve of the invasion, were now strengthened, and he used the occasion to impress them once more on his superiors in Washington. Admiral King, too, pressed hard for reinforcements, reminding Marshall on the 13th that his earlier requests were still unanswered and asking for immediate action to meet the demands from Hawaii and the South Pacific.[5]

The real question at issue between Marshall and King was the disposition of fifteen of the air groups (including three of heavy bombers) originally allocated to BOLERO. At the London meeting with the British Chiefs of Staff in July, Marshall had insisted that, since SLEDGEHAMMER had been canceled in favor of TORCH, these air groups plus the shipping for one division be set aside "for the purpose of furthering offensive operations in the Pacific."[6] King accepted this statement at face value and used it as a basis for his demands on the Army. General Marshall, however, apparently never intended that this provision should be interpreted literally. "I regarded the list of withdrawals for the Pacific," he told Eisenhower soon after his return from London, "as one which gave us liberty of action though not necessarily to be carried out in full, and no dates were mentioned."[7] One of the heavy bomber groups, he did admit, would probably have to be sent to the

---

[3] Rads, Marshall to Harmon, 9 and 10 Aug 42, CM–OUT–2792 and 3043; Rad, Marshall to MacArthur, 10 Aug 42, CM–OUT–3042.

[4] Rads, MacArthur to Marshall, 12 and 13 Aug 42, Nos. C–253 and 341; Rad, Harmon to Marshall, 12 Aug 42, No. 768. All in OPD Exec Files.

[5] Ltr, Harmon to Marshall, 11 Aug 42, copy in OCMH; Memo, King for Marshall, 13 Aug 42, sub: Reinforcements for South Pacific and Hawaii, OPD 320.2 (PTO), case 37.

[6] CCS Memo, 24 Jul 42, sub: Opns in 1942–43, CCS 94, ABC 381 (7–25–41), sec. 1.

[7] Ltr, Marshall to Eisenhower, 20 Jul 42, cited in Matloff and Snell, *Strategic Planning, 1941–42,* pp. 301–02; Mins, JPS Mtg, 16 Sep 42.

Pacific but the disposition of the others would depend on the situation. Thus, when Admiral King asked for more planes on the 13th, Marshall readily agreed to release one heavy bomber group, but refused to accede to King's earlier requests. And he stipulated, moreover, that the bombers—the 90th Bombardment Group (H) was selected —were to go to Hawaii, not to the South Pacific. For the South Pacific, Marshall told King, the Army was readying 44 fighters and had already authorized General Harmon to retain for his use any of the 29 B–17's, 52 B–25's, and 9 B–26's en route to Australia.[8]

To the commanders in the Pacific, these promised reinforcements—the 90th Bombardment Group was not scheduled to arrive until mid-September—could hardly be considered adequate. The position of the marines on Guadalcanal was precarious, with the Japanese bombarding the island almost at will, and in New Guinea the Australians along the Kokoda Trail were still retreating before the advancing enemy. Instead of changing their plans when the marines landed on Guadalcanal, the Japanese had intensified their campaign in New Guinea, bringing in more construction equipment, supplies, and infantry reinforcements. These moves were based on the view held in Tokyo, largely by the Army, that the Allied action in the Solomons was only a reconnaissance in force, a view that was confirmed by the failure of the Allies to reinforce the marines

or to make a determined bid for air and naval supremacy in the days after the landing. The recapture of Guadalcanal, the Japanese thought, would therefore not be too difficult and could be accomplished while the Port Moresby operation was in progress.[9]

If the Tokyo planners misread Allied intentions, so, too, did some planners in Washington apparently misread the aims of the Japanese. Because the enemy had failed to follow up his victory off Savo Island with a large-scale counteroffensive, they concluded that he would make no effort to do so and that the battle for Guadalcanal would soon be over. It was none too soon, they believed, to make plans for Task Two, and within a week of the Marine landings, on the basis of MacArthur's TULSA plan, General Marshall was proposing to Admiral King that they ask the Pacific commanders when Task One would be completed and Task Two begun.[10] King readily agreed and next day, 15 August, the theater commanders were queried about their plans for the future.

The response from the South Pacific put to rest any illusions about an early end to the battle for Guadalcanal. Though the Japanese had not yet made an effort to land troops on the island, the danger, Admiral Ghormley asserted, was still great. If he did not get reinforcements soon, he told Nimitz and King, he might lose not only Guadalcanal but other positions in the South Pacific as well. Until planes had been based on Henderson Field, the line of communi-

---

[8] Memo, Handy for Marshall, 15 Aug 42, sub: Reinforcements for South Pacific and Hawaii; Memo, Marshall for King, 20 Aug 42, sub: Reinforcements for South Pacific and Hawaii. These and other relevant papers are in OPD 320.2 (PTO), case 37; see also OPD 370.5 (Hawaii), cases 22–24.

[9] Japanese Opns in SWPA, II, pp. 136–38.
[10] Memo, Marshall for King, 14 Aug 42, sub: Early Initiation of Limited Task Two, OPD 381 (PTO) case 84.

cations to Guadalcanal restored, and men and supplies sent forward, any idea of further advances, Ghormley warned, was a delusion.[11]

General Harmon concurred in this view and filled in the details which made it painfully evident that much more was needed on Guadalcanal. The Japanese, he was certain, would make an effort to retake the island, either by direct assault or infiltration from New Georgia to the north. To guard against this contingency he called for large air and ground reinforcements and for a determined effort to break through with supplies for the marines and enough equipment and gasoline to start large-scale air operations at Henderson Field.[12]

Armed with these statements from the South Pacific commanders, Admiral King again called on the Army for reinforcements, as agreed at the London meeting. By this time Marshall had decided to send the 90th Bombardment Group to Hawaii and so informed King. But ground reinforcements in the quantity General Harmon had asked for earlier in the month, and which Ghormley and King now requested again, could not be sent without considerably more shipping than was available to the Army. Finally, after the Army had agreed to provide a balanced force of about 20,000 men, the Navy agreed for its part to contribute enough ships from its own September and October allotments to transport about half of the force. On this basis plans were made which ultimately saw the arrival of the 43d Division in the South Pacific — one regimental combat team, the 172d, going to Espiritu Santo to defend the heavy bomber base there, and the rest of the division to New Zealand. Shortly thereafter, the division was transferred to New Caledonia at a heavy cost in scarce shipping.

The movement of the division to the Pacific, completed in November, was not without incident. The *President Coolidge*, which was carrying the 172d Regimental Combat Team as well as a harbor defense battalion, blundered into a mine field at the end of its voyage in the harbor of Espiritu Santo and sank, taking with it all the desperately needed weapons and equipment of the units aboard. Fortunately, only two lives were lost in this tragic and unexplained accident.[13]

Long before these reinforcements had reached their destination, the situation in the Pacific had taken a turn for the worse. In the two weeks since the Marine landings, the Japanese had assembled a force of about 1,000 men and ferried them to Guadalcanal, where, on 21 August, they sought to penetrate the thin Marine line and overrun the airfield. This attack was easily repulsed, but the Japanese had other forces ready at Truk and these they immediately dispatched under naval convoy to Guadal-

[11] Rad, Ghormley to Nimitz and King, 17 Aug 42, 0230, cited in Miller, *Guadalcanal: The First Offensive*, pp. 82–83.

[12] COMGENSOPAC Summary of Sit, 20 Aug 42, OPD 381 (PTO), sec. 3.

[13] Lt. Gen. Millard F. Harmon, The Army in the South Pacific, pp. 3–4, a narrative prepared by General Harmon at the request of his historical officer, copy in OCMH. Memo, King for Marshall, 20 Aug 42, sub: Early Initiation of Limited Task Two; Memo, Marshall for King, 24 Aug 42, sub: Early Initiation of Limited Task Two. Both filed with related papers in OPD 370.5 (PTO), cases 9 and 14. Memo, King for Marshall, 27 Aug 42, sub: Transportation of 13,000 Army Troops, OPD 381 (PTO), case 84.

canal via Rabaul. Alerted in advance to the presence of a Japanese naval task force steaming south ahead of the transports, Admiral Ghormley sent his own naval forces, including two carriers, to meet it. In the Battle of the Eastern Solomons that followed (23–24 August) the Japanese lost the carrier *Ryujo,* a destroyer, and ninety planes; the Americans only twenty planes and the services of the *Enterprise,* which was badly damaged. Neither side could claim a victory, but the Japanese withdrew, only to return a few days later with the Guadalcanal reinforcements. More were already on the way and it was clear that the next few weeks would witness bitter fighting on Guadalcanal and along its sea and air approaches.

In New Guinea, General MacArthur was having troubles of his own. The reinforced Japanese garrison at Buna, despite attacks from the planes of the Allied Air Forces, was rapidly completing the airfield and other installations there. The *South Seas Detachment* had meanwhile continued its slow advance along the Kokoda Trail and by the end of the month had overcome Australian resistance and begun the long, hard climb up the Owen Stanley Range. Though faced with some of the worst terrain and weather in the world, the Japanese troops pushed on, moving ever closer to their goal. Meanwhile, on 25 August, another Japanese force had landed on the north shore of Milne Bay, at the southeast tip of New Guinea, where a combined Australian-American garrison was holding the partially completed air base there. This attack, which was part of the co-ordinated Japanese offensive against Port Moresby, was repulsed in less than a week, but the threat

of further Japanese offensives and naval action still remained.[14]

The crisis in the South and Southwest Pacific and the clear threat of further Japanese offensives produced in the last week of August renewed requests from the theater commanders for air reinforcements. On the day after the Battle of the Eastern Solomons, Admiral Ghormley asked once again for heavy and medium bombers, pointing to mounting losses and the critical situation in the Solomons as justification. King endorsed this request and passed it on to Marshall, who already had a similar message from Harmon before him.[15]

Since the 20th, when King had concluded, on the basis of Ghormley's and Harmon's estimates, that Task Two would have to be deferred and had asked for air and ground reinforcements, the Army staff had been studying air deployment in the Pacific. Ground reinforcements had been made available without question once the shipping was found, but there was strong opposition to sending more planes. General Arnold in particular objected to additional allocations of aircraft to the Pacific as a dangerous "tendency toward ever greater dispersion of Air Forces throughout the world." In his view, American aircraft should be concentrated in the United Kingdom for the planned bomber offensive against Germany, not scattered unprofitably throughout the Pacific. Some 300 Japanese planes in the South and Southwest Pacific, he pointed out, were holding down over 800 American planes. The

---

[14] This account of the New Guinea campaign is based on Milner, *Victory in Papua,* ch. VI; and Allied Opns in SWPA, I, chs. III–IV.

[15] Rad, Ghormley to Nimitz and King, 25 Aug 42, 0330, OPD Exec Files; Rad, Harmon to Marshall, 25 Aug 42, CM–IN–9889.

argument was a telling one and was endorsed by Admiral Leahy, who had recently joined the Joint Chiefs as the President's Chief of Staff.[16]

The Army planners, too, had been counting planes in the Pacific. Their figures, though differing slightly from Arnold's statistics, constituted an impressive list, showing a total of 161 heavy, 98 medium, and 42 light bombers, and 553 fighters in the theater. En route and being prepared for shipment were 66 more heavies, 22 mediums, and 257 fighters. Such a computation, combined with Arnold's cogent argument, confirmed Marshall in his decision not to allocate more aircraft to the Pacific. There were enough planes there to meet the present danger, he told King, if the theater commanders would pool their resources to get the most effective use out of what they had. MacArthur had already been instructed to provide aid to the South Pacific, and Ghormley, Marshall suggested, should call on him in the event of an emergency.[17] For the moment this ended the matter.

The quantity of planes in the Pacific was not the only question at issue; pilot training, combat fatigue, armament, armor, and performance of different types of aircraft were other equally pressing problems that had to be solved. There was much dissatisfaction with the P–400 fighter, the export version of the P–39. From Guadalcanal had come reports, through General Harmon, that the P–400 could not climb fast or high enough and was no match for the Japa-

nese Zero. The new twin-engine P–38 was what he needed, he said, but the only ones in the Pacific were in MacArthur's area. Twenty-one had recently reached Australia and forty-four more were being readied for shipment. If Harmon wanted any, Marshall suggested, he should negotiate directly with MacArthur; none were available in the United States.[18] When the request was made some days later, MacArthur had to refuse because he did not have enough for his own operations, but he stood by his earlier agreement to send thirty P–39's. "I want to do everything I can to help you even to the jeopardy of my own safety," he told Ghormley, "but my resources are practically negligible.[19]

By this time, MacArthur had revised his previous optimistic estimates for an early start on Task Two. So serious did the situation in the Pacific seem to him at the end of August that he urged, "with greatest reluctance," a complete review of the Army's policy on reinforcements. "I beg of you most earnestly," he wrote Marshall on 30 August, "to have this momentous question reviewed by the President and the Chiefs of Staff lest it become too late."[20] In the last two months, he pointed out, the situation in the Pacific had changed drastically. The Japanese had decreased their forces in China and in the recently occupied territories and were concen-

[16] Memo, Arnold for Marshall, 21 Aug 42, sub: North African Opns; Memo, Leahy for Marshall, 21 Aug 42. Both in WDCSA (SPA).

[17] Memo, Marshall for King, 25 Aug 42, sub: Air Reinforcements for South Pacific, OPD 452.1 (PTO), case 8.

[18] Rad, Marshall to MacArthur, 30 Aug 42, CM–OUT–9510; OPD Memo for Record, 30 Aug 42, sub: Fighter Support for Solomons, OPD 452.1 (PTO), case 10.

[19] Rad, MacArthur to Marshall, 3 Sep 42, CM–IN–0944.

[20] Rad, MacArthur to Marshall, 30 Aug 42, No. C–381, GHQ Hist Rec Index Cards, OCMH. Mr. Curtin sent a similar message to the President and Prime Minister the next day. CCS 660.2 (3–14–42), sec. 2.

trating their resources in the South and Southwest Pacific. The "main battle front" in the war with Japan, he asserted, had now definitely shifted to New Guinea and the Solomons. Far from planning for further offensives, the Allies, he thought, should be increasing their ground, air, and naval strength in that area to match the rapid Japanese build-up.

MacArthur understood entirely even if he did not agree with the strategy that assigned to him limited forces and a holding mission, but, he told Marshall, it was doubtful that even this task could be accomplished with the forces at hand. "Holding areas," he pointed out, must have "sufficient forces actually to hold," and their size could only be determined "by a constantly changing accurate appraisal of the enemy's power; an arbitrary predetermined strength figure will not insure safety." Failure to review the strategic situation and to meet the changing conditions, he warned, was to invite a disaster "similar to those that have successively overwhelmed our forces in the Pacific since the beginning of the war."

In Washington this urgent dispatch, soon supported by a similar if less eloquent warning from Ghormley, received immediate attention. One copy went to the President, who discussed it with Marshall, and another to the Joint Chiefs of Staff, who turned it and the Ghormley message over to their planners for study. Persuasive as MacArthur was, Marshall showed no disposition to change his views. In a carefully worded reply, sent out on the last day of the month, he expressed his understanding and sympathy but made clear his opposition, in the light of "recent decisions involving world-wide strategy," to further rein-

forcement of the Pacific. "The defense of the Pacific areas, particularly in air and naval matters," he told Mac Arthur, "will depend to a large degree upon the closeness of the cooperation and coordination of the forces now available to you, Nimitz, and Ghormley." There was no misunderstanding the Chief of Staff's meaning. MacArthur and the other Pacific commanders would have to get along with what they had and cooperate with each other to get the maximum use out of the forces already in the theater. No more would be forthcoming.[21]

Admiral King took a more serious view of the situation than Marshall, and, as so often before, sided with the Pacific commanders. Again, on 3 September, he presented the case for Ghormley and Harmon and repeated their requests for more aircraft, including the modern P-38. These needs must be met, he insisted, even if to do so would interfere with commitments in the Atlantic theater.[22]

Nor did General MacArthur accept Marshall's decision in this matter. In a strong response to the Chief of Staff's message, he rose to his own defense. Pointing to the Japanese advance along the Kokoda Trail, he emphasized his need for naval forces—practically all of his had been loaned to Ghormley for the Guadalcanal invasion—and for shipping to move ground reinforcements from Australia to New Guinea. These were essential defense moves, but more than that was needed. A defensive strategy, he argued, might lead to further defeats

[21] Rad, Marshall to MacArthur, 31 Aug 42, filed with JCS 96, Japanese Intentions in the Pacific, same date, ABC 384 (8–31–42) Pac.

[22] Memo, King for Marshall, 3 Sep 42, sub: Air Reinforcements for South Pacific, WDCSA (9–3–42) SWPA.

NEW P–38's *being hauled from the port area to the airfield at Noumea, September 1942.*

in New Guinea, with disastrous results for the Allied cause. What was needed were the means to open an offensive to clear the northeast coast of New Guinea —essentially Task Two, with the additional burden of taking Buna—as soon as possible.[23]

General Marshall was not moved by these arguments and appeals. Stoutly he maintained, and sought to prove with the statistics supplied by Arnold, that there were enough planes in the Pacific to meet the Japanese threat; that the fighters in the theater were adequate for operations; that more fighters could not be sent in time anyhow; and, finally, that to do so would have a drastic effect on the plans for TORCH. Naval forces and shipping, Marshall thought, could be supplied from the South Pacific and Australia, and he suggested to MacArthur that he refer his requests to Ghormley.[24]

From the Pacific came quick disagreement with this estimate of the performance of aircraft and the numbers needed. Admiral Nimitz pointed out that the total figures were misleading. The area covered was enormous, attrition high,

[23] Rad, MacArthur to Marshall, 3 Sep 42, CM–IN–0944; Rad, MacArthur to Marshall, 6 Sep 42, no number, GHQ Hist Rec Index Cards, OCMH; Rad, MacArthur to Marshall, 7 Sep 42, CM–IN–2633.

[24] Rad, Marshall to MacArthur, 9 Sep 42, CM–OUT–3025; Memo, Arnold for King, 5 Sep 42, sub: Air Reinforcements; Memo, McNarney, DCofS, for King, 5 Sep 42, same sub. Last two in WDCSA (9–3–42) SWPA.

replacement difficult and slow. Moreover, the dispersion of fighter planes along the line of communications, distant from the scene of operations, accounted for a large part of the total.[25]

General Harmon, too, took issue with his superiors in Washington on the performance of his fighter planes. It was discouraging to the pilots, he observed, to watch impotently while the high-altitude Japanese aircraft flew over to drop their bombs. Even two squadrons of P–38's in the forward area "would be a God-send." "Do you think it might be possible," he asked Marshall, "to whittle just a little bit from BOLERO? I do not like to unduly press this, and would not, but for my conviction that it is of real and continuing importance in the conduct of the Solomon-Bismarck action."[26]

Harmon's comments on attrition and replacement, and on the need to rest the pilots, gave strong support to Nimitz' observations, but Harmon also emphasized, as he had many times before, that the difficulty in bringing strong air support into the Guadalcanal area lay in the failure to develop the facilities at Henderson Field and in the shortages of heavy equipment and fuel needed for air operations.

Though Marshall followed up these and other questions Harmon and Nimitz had raised, the central problem was still the deployment of aircraft to the Pacific. Several committees of the Joint Chiefs of Staff had been studying this and related problems for some weeks but thus far had succeeded only in disagreeing. It

was evident now that before a decision could be reached the Joint Chiefs themselves would have to review the issues. It was to this task they turned after the first week of September.

The Debate Over Priorities

The decision of late July, affirmed during the first week of September, to launch an offensive in North Africa (TORCH) before the end of the year had a profound effect on almost every phase of the war. The cost of this venture had to be closely calculated, shipping set aside, troops, planes, and supplies furnished, and plans re-examined. The allocation of forces to the various theaters, established earlier on the basis of the ARCADIA Conference and BOLERO, had to be studied again and new priorities fixed in terms of the requirements for TORCH. And all this had to be done while the desperate battle for Guadalcanal and northeast New Guinea was raging and when the need for planes and ships in the Pacific was most urgent.[27]

Work on these problems began early in August and it soon became evident that, as in previous discussions, there was a wide difference of opinion between the Army and the Navy on the apportionment of resources, especially aircraft, to the Pacific. The question at issue again was the disposition of the fifteen air groups—actually fourteen since one heavy bombardment group was soon to be sent to Hawaii—originally allotted to BOLERO and to become available during the next six or seven months. General

[25] Rad, Nimitz to King, 6 Sep 42, 0199, WDCSA (9–3–42) SWPA.

[26] Ltr, Harmon to Marshall, 9 Sep 42, copy in OCMH. See also Rad, Harmon to Marshall, 8 Sep 42, No. 222, OPD Msg file; Memo, King for Marshall, 11 Sep 42, sub: Aircraft Sit, OPD 452.1 (PTO) case 19.

[27] For a full account of the cost of TORCH see Matloff and Snell, *Strategic Planning, 1941–42*, ch. XIV; Leighton and Coakley, *Global Logistics and Strategy*, ch. XVII.

Marshall and General Arnold took the view that until the requirements of TORCH, the Middle East, and the United Kingdom were met, no decision could be made on the disposition of these planes. Admiral King, while admitting the priority of TORCH and even the Middle East, countered with the argument that the planes should go where the need was greatest. Thus, the debate was really one of priorities.

It was the Joint Staff Planners who first reviewed this problem. Responding to a suggested order of priority from the British Chiefs of Staff, the planners took the position held by their respective service chiefs. Expanding on the theme propounded by Admiral King, the Navy members argued that there was no reason why the United Kingdom should have a greater claim on Allied resources than the Pacific. Against the needs for a future offensive from the British base they placed the urgent requirements of the South and Southwest Pacific where the situation was critical and where planes might well make the difference between victory and defeat.[28]

The Army and Air Force planners were equally convinced than an early offensive against Germany with the full power of Allied ground and air forces was the most effective way to bring about the defeat of the Axis. Moreover, they argued, the Pacific would have approximately 5,000 planes by April 1943, as opposed to an estimated total of 4,000 for the Japanese. And these 4,000 included the air complements of Japan itself and the neighboring islands. The commanders in the Pacific, the Army planners thought, should certainly be able, with a superiority of 1,000 planes, to carry out their defensive mission.[29] This argument by numbers overlooked a number of important factors: the performance of American aircraft, the vast extent of the Pacific area, the number of planes immobilized but required in Hawaii, Australia, and along the line of communications, and the more technical problems of replacements, attrition, untrained crews, and others which the air officers in the theater were finding so frustrating.

Unable to resolve their differences, the planners submitted the dispute to their superiors for a decision on 5 September. But the views on which the Army and Navy planners had split were held as strongly by their chiefs, and the discussion at the next meeting of the JCS simply reflected and extended the arguments of the subordinate committees.[30] The Navy members insisted on the literal interpretation of the July agreement relative to the fifteen air groups and stressed the urgency of sending air reinforcements to the South Pacific, at the expense of TORCH if need be. The Army refused to accept this view, pointing out that the July agreement "had been recorded only as an agreement for the transfer of planes from one jurisdiction to another." On the priority of TORCH and the Middle East Marshall refused to budge, though he was willing, like

---

[28] Memo, Handy for Marshall, 6 Aug 42, sub: TORCH OPD Exec Files; Mins, CPS Mtg, 7 Aug 42; Min, JCS Mtg, 11 Aug 42; Mins, CCS Mtg, 13 Aug 42.

[29] JPS 48, 28 Aug 42, sub: Deployment of Air Forces in Pacific; OPD Notes on 32d JPS Mtg, 2 Sep 42, sub: Deployment of Air Forces in Pacific. Both in ABC 381 (9–25–41), sec. 3.

[30] JCS 97, 5 Sep 42, sub: Deployment of Air Forces in Pacific, ABC 381 (9–25–41), sec. 3; Mins, JCS Mtg, 8 Sep 42.

Leahy, to reserve judgment on the United Kingdom. But, he reiterated, the Atlantic was the area in which the United States could get "the greatest return for the investment of forces."[31]

General Arnold took an even stronger position than his chief. Though ordinarily silent in the deliberations of high strategy, he was eloquently articulate on the deployment of aircraft. The build-up in Britain of a strong air force with which to bomb Germany out of the war was his chief interest and, in his view, took precedence over all other matters. TORCH, he argued, was the beginning of the offensive against Germany and was closely related to the air offensive from the United Kingdom which would divert German aircraft from North Africa. Both, therefore, should have the same priority, General Arnold asserted, and he cited messages from Eisenhower, Spaatz, Maj. Gen. George S. Patton, Jr., and Maj. Gen. Mark W. Clark, in support of this view. The Pacific, he believed, had enough planes, if only they were properly used, and he opposed sending more until the needs for TORCH, the United Kingdom, and the Middle East —which bore the same relation to TORCH as the bomber offensive from Britain— were met.[32]

When challenged by Admiral King, Arnold went even further and asserted that the diversion of aircraft from TORCH or the United Kingdom constituted a violation of the accepted Allied strategy for the war and would seriously jeopardize the success of the North African venture. To this King replied that since TORCH had not yet been launched and the Middle East did not seem to be in danger—a view that Marshall and Leahy seemed to support—the Pacific ought not to be relegated to the bottom of the priority list. Finally, after a fruitless discussion at the 15 September meeting of the Joint Chiefs, when Arnold argued that facilities in the Pacific were hardly adequate for the planes already in the area, much less the reinforcements King was asking for, Admiral Leahy suggested that the matter be dropped until General Arnold had had an opportunity to inspect these facilities for himself. The suggestion was immediately accepted and the debate over priorities tabled for almost two weeks.[33]

Meanwhile the joint planners had produced another split report. Given MacArthur's 30 August warning of disaster and Ghormley's supporting message, the planners had been directed to review the situation in the Pacific and make recommendations on the best course to follow. The job was handed over to a subcommittee whose Army members reported a week later. Their findings, informally concurred in by Brig. Gen. Albert C. Wedemeyer and Col. Orvil A. Anderson, the chief Army and Air Force planners, added nothing new to the debate. MacArthur and Ghormley, they asserted, had exaggerated the danger. No additional forces were needed beyond those already

---

[31] Mins, JCS Mtg, 8 Sep 42; Memo, Admiral Willson (Deputy for King) for JCS, 7 Sep 42, sub: JCS 97, ABC 381 (9–25–41), sec. 3.

[32] JCS 97/1, 11 Sep 42, sub: TORCH and Air Opns from the Middle East and United Kingdom, ABC 381 (9–25–41), sec. 3. For statement of Arnold's general views, see his *Global Mission*, pp. 337ff.

[33] Memo, King for Arnold, 5 Sep 42, sub: Aircraft for the Solomons; Memo, Arnold for King, 14 Sep 42, sub: Aircraft for the Solomons. Both atched to JCS 97/2, 15 Sep 42, ABC 381 (9–25–41), sec 3. Mins, JCS Mtg, 15 Sep 42.

allocated, and if neither commander believed he had sufficient resources to undertake the operations called for in Task Two, then these operations ought to be deferred. The Joint Chiefs, they suggested, should explain again to the commanders in the Pacific the strategic policy of the Allies.[34]

The Navy's case was prepared by the senior naval planner himself, Admiral Cooke. Squarely he met the argument of his Army and Air Force colleagues by challenging the thesis that preparation for operations in the European theater had an overriding priority. He was not opposed to such measures or to those operations which would contribute to the defeat of Germany, but he felt that they should be undertaken only after steps had been taken to ensure the security of the Western Hemisphere, Hawaii, Alaska, and the line of communications to Australia and New Zealand. To accomplish the last it would be necessary, Cooke asserted, to send air reinforcements, especially fighters, to the South Pacific. What the Pacific commanders needed most, he said, was reassurance that their area was not forgotten, not an explanation of Allied Strategy. And with this reassurance should go, Cooke concluded, a promise of reinforcements in the near future.[35]

In the discussion that followed, Wedemeyer moved closer to Cooke's position, largely because of his opposition to TORCH. But the Air Force planner, Colonel Anderson, continued to argue that the employment of aircraft in

the Pacific was uneconomical and failed to take advantage of the mobility of the air arm. All efforts to change his views proved unavailing, and the planners finally decided to refer the matter back to the subcommittee for further study. There it remained until December despite attempts to drop it altogether from the agenda.[36]

General Arnold's trip to the Pacific, at the end of September, though brief, gave him an opportunity to observe at first hand the conditions under which the war in the Pacific was being fought and to talk with the commanders. Only recently a Japanese counteroffensive on Guadalcanal had been thrown back in the battle of Bloody Ridge and reinforcements and supplies were just beginning to trickle into the marine perimeter. But conditions at Henderson Field were still far from satisfactory and the lack of fighter planes of modern design to fight off the almost daily attacks from Japanese bombers was still the most serious weakness in the South Pacific. Naval forces, too, were considerably reduced. The carrier *Wasp* had been sunk on 15 September, and the *Saratoga*, damaged by torpedo action on 31 August, was in Pearl Harbor for repair, as was the *Enterprise*. Only the carrier *Hornet* remained in action in the South Pacific. And already coast-watchers and reconnaissance aircraft were reporting large Japanese forces at Rabaul and in the northern Solomons. A major Japanese effort to retake Guadalcanal was clearly impending.

During this same period the Japanese in New Guinea had advanced along the Kakoda Trail until on 16 September

---

[34] Memo, Maj Robert W. Davis for Lt Col R. L. Vittrup, JPS Secy, 8 Sep 42, sub: Japanese Intention in Pacific.

[35] Memo, Cooke for Vittrup, 14 Sep 42, sub: Japanese Intention in Pacific.

[36] Mins, JPS Mtg, 16 Sep 42.

they had reached a point on the Australian side of the Owen Stanley Range, only twenty air miles from Port Moresby. There they halted, worn out by starvation, disease, and the hardships of an incredibly difficult journey, to await reinforcements and supplies and to consolidate their position for the final assault.[37] That assault never came, for on 23 September *17th Army Headquarters* at Rabaul, faced by the more serious threat at Guadalcanal and the possibility of Allied landings on the northeast coast of New Guinea, ordered its troops back toward Kokoda with orders to secure future offensive key points on the north side of the Owen Stanley Range, as well as a strong rear base at Buna. By the end of the month the Japanese were retracing the path they had so lately traveled, with the Australians in pursuit. It was at this time that two regiments of the 32d Division reached Port Moresby by air to join the Australian 7th Division and MacArthur issued his plans for a general offensive designed to clear the Japanese out of the Papuan Peninsula.

By accident or design, Arnold's trip to the Pacific coincided with a previously scheduled visit by Admiral Nimitz to Noumea. The advantages of a conference of the theater commanders with Arnold prompted General Marshall to suggest to the Air Forces commander that he arrange his itinerary so as to be present in Noumea on the 27th, the date when Nimitz would be there. This suggestion Arnold readily accepted.[38] Marshall also wanted MacArthur to attend the Noumea conference but the Southwest Pacific commander declined because, he said, "pending the completion of the operations I am now developing in New Guinea I can not leave here." [39] Instead he invited Nimitz to meet him in Brisbane and, on Marshall's suggestion, sent his Chief of Staff and air commander, Generals Sutherland and Kenney, to Noumea.[40]

The visit to the Pacific and the conference at Noumea did not alter General Arnold's belief that the South Pacific already had as many planes as it could support and that the solution to the problem lay in a more effective distribution, not an increase in the number of aircraft assigned to the theater. This was the position he took on 6 October when he reported to the Joint Chiefs, and again it was Admiral King who challenged him with the oft-repeated arguments and with references to the fresh threat of a Japanese offensive. The only new note in the meeting was that interjected by Admiral McCain, just returned from the South Pacific, who emphasized some of the practical problems faced by the air commanders in a theater where maintenance and spare parts were not always available and where ground crews often did not have the equipment to service new planes when they arrived. No closer to agreement than before Arnold's trip, the Joint Chiefs again referred the problem back to their planners, this time with instructions to study the distribution of aircraft and the number required to reach the "saturation point"

---

[37] Msg of Instr to *South Seas Detachment*, 20 Sep 42, ATIS GHQ SWPA, Current Translation 2.

[38] Rad, Marshall to Arnold, 22 Sep 42, CM–OUT–7355. For Arnold's account of the trip, see his *Global Mission*, pp. 336–50.

[39] Rad, MacArthur to Marshall, 22 Sep 42, CM–IN–9515.

[40] Rad, Marshall to MacArthur, 22 Sep 42, CM–OUT–7382; Rad, MacArthur to Marshall, 23 Sep 42, CM–IN–9987.

GENERAL ARNOLD *(center) confers with (from left) General Twining, General Patch, Admiral McCain, and General Streett at Noumea, September 1942.*

of the facilities in the Pacific. This time they were to have the help of General Arnold and Admiral McCain.[41]

Within ten days a preliminary report covering the South Pacific Area was ready. At Guadalcanal and Espiritu Santo, where the possibility of "inflicting attrition losses" on the enemy was greatest, the planners agreed, the airfields should be kept at the saturation point, with 100 percent replacements at Efate, New Caledonia, and the Fijis. In the rear areas, the planners stipulated, there should be a 50 percent reserve for losses by attrition. Marshall and King approved the report quickly and the staff began immediately the detailed work required to put it into effect.[42]

The full story of the joint planners, incorporating the computations of Arnold and McCain, was completed on 22 October and approved five days later. As finally revised it provided for increases for the South Pacific: 30 heavy

---

[41] Mins, JCS Mtg, 6 Oct 42.

[42] JCS 97/4, 16 Oct 42, sub: Deployment of Air Forces in Pacific, and related papers filed with it in ABC 381 (9–25–41), sec. 3. See also OPD 320.2 (PTO), case 64.

ADMIRAL NIMITZ *discusses the Solomons campaign with (from left, standing) General Patch, Admiral Ghormley, and General Harmon at Noumea, October 1942.*

and 32 medium bombers, 34 fighters, 14 Navy patrol and 12 torpedo bombers, and 24 observation planes. Assignment of these planes to specific islands was to be made by Admiral Nimitz, and for this purpose he was authorized to deploy and distribute air units within the theater at his discretion and without specific permission, as had been the case before, from the War and Navy Departments.[43]

[43] JCS 97/5, 22 Oct 42, sub: Deployment of Air Forces in Pacific; Memo, King for JCS, 6 Nov 42, same sub; Memo, Marshall for Deane, 11 Nov 42, same sub, all in ABC 381 (9–25–41), sec 3; Mins, JCS Mtg, 27 Oct 42.

This late October solution to the problem of air deployment left unanswered the basic question: what to do with the air groups remaining from the BOLERO commitment. That question had served Admiral King well as a lever to raise the authorized level of Pacific allocations and to gain for the theater commanders a portion of the air reinforcements they were asking for. Now, when the question came up again at the last October meeting of the Joint Chiefs, King agreed without argument that the twelve remaining groups, which were not yet available anyhow, should be considered as part of the U.S. strategic reserve.[44] Thus was ended, temporarily, the debate begun almost three months earlier by the cancellation of SLEDGEHAMMER and the decision to invade North Africa.

The October Crisis

The decision in mid-October to send air reinforcements for the South Pacific was undoubtedly due, in part at least, to the threat of a new and larger Japanese assault in the Solomons and New Guinea. The signs of such a threat were too clear to be mistaken. From intelligence sources had come news of the movement of enemy forces from China, the Netherlands Indies, the Philippines, and Truk to the South Pacific, and as early as mid-September Allied aircraft had reported the massing of Japanese ships, planes, and troops at Rabaul and in the northern Solomons. The transfer of these troops southward to Guadalcanal, by destroyer and landing craft, begun in late August, was by the end of September in full swing. On the basis of the evidence Admiral Ghormley could not help but conclude that the enemy would soon make a major effort to recapture Guadalcanal.

General Harmon not only agreed but also believed that the Japanese would probably succeed unless considerable reinforcements were forthcoming and air operations intensified. And from MacArthur came similar warnings and a plea not to lose this "golden opportunity" to anticipate the enemy and clear the northeast coast of New Guinea.[45]

The estimates of the Pacific commanders were entirely correct. After their initial miscalculation of Allied intentions, the Japanese had quickly revised their views and on 31 August *Imperial General Headquarters* had given first priority to the recapture of Guadalcanal. Both the Army and Navy commanders at Rabaul had been ordered to assemble the forces required and push preparations for a general offensive in the Solomons. Between 30 August and 7 September they had put enough troops ashore on Guadalcanal to launch their mid-September attack. The failure of this attack only spurred the Japanese on to greater efforts and convinced them that they must defer the Port Moresby operation and concentrate their forces for a major offensive in the Solomons. It was at this time, it will be recalled, that the troops on the Kokoda Trail in the Ioribaiwa area had been ordered back to Kokoda and Buna and the reinforcements originally intended for New Guinea, plus additional troops allotted by *Imperial General Headquarters,* were ordered to Guadalcanal. The new offensive was to open on 21 October, later postponed to the 23d, and was to be made by one full division and supporting troops, about 20,000 men, and all the naval forces the *Combined Fleet* could spare.[46]

Allied intelligence sources first thought that this Japanese activity portended an attack against Hawaii, the Aleutians, or even Siberia, but these possibilities were soon ruled out. New Guinea or the Solomons, King told Marshall and Leahy on 3 October, were the probable objectives, and he recommended "additional

[44] Mins, JCS Mtg, 27 Oct 42.

[45] Rad, MacArthur to Marshall, 27 Sep 42, GHQ Hist Rec Index Cards; Ltr, Harmon to Arnold, 15 Sep 42, with entries dated 19 Sep, both in OCMH.

[46] Japanese Opns in SWPA, pp. 136, 139, 152.

forces and logistic support . . . to meet this situation."[47] No action was taken at the time other than to refer the matter to the planners, but within ten days the Japanese were moving in force down the "Slot"—the narrow waters between the double Solomon chain—with large reinforcements and supplies. Though attacked by American aircraft and opposed by a naval force of cruisers and destroyers in the Battle of Cape Esperance (11–12 October), the Japanese succeeded in putting ashore over 3,000 troops and large quantities of supplies for the attack later in the month.

With this additional evidence of Japanese intentions, it became clear that the situation in the South Pacific was critical and that emergency measures were required. Immediate warning went out to General MacArthur on the 16th relaying the information picked up from intercepts that the Japanese were concentrating large naval forces—three carriers, five or six battleships, together with cruisers and destroyers—in the vicinity of the Shortland Islands, and asking him again to do everything possible to support operations in the Guadalcanal area. Most useful, Marshall told MacArthur, would be air attacks against the Japanese naval forces assembling in the northern Solomons.[48]

To this call from Washington for assistance to the beleaguered marines—one in a long series of similar requests—MacArthur tartly responded by pointing out that he had been supporting the South Pacific as much as he could and that Ghormley had on three separate

occasions "radioed his appreciation." Moreover, he was in constant communication with Ghormley, was co-ordinating his air operations with South Pacific requirements, and "three times within the week" had sent out bombing missions specifically at Ghormley's request.[49] Nor did MacArthur miss the opportunity to remind the Chief of Staff that not only had he been aware of the situation in the Solomons for some time, but had, in fact, anticipated it. In a reference to his message of 30 August, he reminded the Chief of Staff that he had called attention to this new Japanese threat sometime before and "begged review of the question by the President and the Chiefs of Staff lest it become too late."

Having thus set the record straight, MacArthur then went on to provide a picture of the situation in his own area and the disadvantages under which his forces were required to operate. Supply, he pointed out, was the controlling factor, and until he had overcome the incredible difficulties of transportation to and in the battle area, the outcome would remain in doubt.

MacArthur's solution to the crisis in the Pacific would require a sweeping reversal of the carefully calculated and delicately balanced U.S.-British program for global warfare. Nothing less was required, he declared, than that shipping "from any source" must be made available to the Pacific; that the Army corps promised him earlier should be "dispatched immediately"; that all heavy bombers must be "ferried here at once"; that his air strength be increased; "immediate action taken" to establish naval bases along the east coast of Australia;

[47] Memo, King for Leahy and Marshall, 3 Oct 42, sub: Mil Sit in Pacific, OPD 381 (PTO), case 102.

[48] Rad, Marshall to MacArthur, 16 Oct 42, CM–OUT–05130.

[49] Rad, MacArthur to Marshall, 17 Oct 42, No. C–731, GHQ Hist Rec Index Cards.

and that the British Eastern Fleet should be moved to the west coast of that continent. In short, MacArthur was proposing that the entire resources of the United States and Great Britain should be diverted to the Pacific to meet the critical situation in the Solomons and New Guinea.[50] And to make certain that his views reached the highest authority he sent a personal message to Secretary Stimson the next day calling attention to his message and appealing for a complete review of Pacific strategy.[51]

Other commanders, though more modest in their demands, were pessimistic also about the prospects. On 6 October, before the Battle of Cape Esperance, Harmon had declared that it was his personal conviction that the enemy was capable of retaking Guadalcanal and would do so "in the near future" unless Allied air, ground, and sea forces were greatly increased. If they arrived in time, these reinforcements, he thought, would make a Japanese offensive so costly to the enemy that he would not attempt it.[52]

Among the measures Harmon proposed to meet the Japanese threat was the immediate shipment to Guadalcanal of one Army regimental combat team. Admiral Ghormley accepted this recommendation, and on 8 October the 164th Infantry of the Americal Division, formed in May from Task Force 6184, left New Caledonia to reinforce the tiring marines. The move was completed five days later when the Army troops landed at Lunga Point. So great was the need for fresh troops that Vandegrift immediately assigned them a portion of the defense perimeter around Henderson Field.

The day the 164th Infantry reached Guadalcanal was the one selected by the Japanese to begin intensive preparations for the coming offensive. Late that afternoon, thirty-seven Japanese bombers came down to hit Henderson Field, after which the enemy on the ground opened up with his 150–mm. howitzers. Finally, shortly before midnight, a Japanese naval force, including two battleships, stood off the island and leisurely dropped 14–inch shells on the field for over an hour while a cruiser plane overhead kept the target well illuminated. Clearly, this was a prelude to the expected offensive, and Admiral Ghormley asked MacArthur again to send his bombers against Rabaul and Japanese bases in the northern Solomons in order to relieve the pressure on Guadalcanal. And when the Japanese continued their bombing and shelling of the island, he told Nimitz on the 15th that the big push was on and that he was doubtful whether the marines would be able to hold out. Air and naval reinforcements were desperately needed, as was another division in the Fijis, which might well be the next Japanese objective if Guadalcanal fell.[53]

If any support was needed for this gloomy prediction it could be found in General Harmon's report on the 17th. Japanese activity during the last ten days had strengthened Harmon's conviction that the enemy would be able to take Guadalcanal. Like MacArthur, who had stated that the Allies faced disaster in the Solomons "unless the Navy accepts successfully the challenge of the enemy

[50] *Ibid.*

[51] Rad, MacArthur to Stimson, 18 Oct 42, GHQ Hist Rec Card Index.

[52] Memo, Harmon for Ghormley, 6 Oct 42, sub: Occupation of Ndeni, OCMH.

[53] Rad, Harmon to Marshall, 15 Oct 42, CM–IN–06202, in which Harmon reports Ghormley's message to Nimitz.

surface fleet," Harmon asserted that Guadalcanal could not be held "without more naval support."[54] It was time, he told Marshall, to consider the consequences of defeat and to strengthen the islands along the line of communications to Australia. Fiji, the most important base on that line, would be most vulnerable to attack and he recommended to Marshall, as Ghormley had to Nimitz, that another division, in addition to the 43d, which was already en route, be sent there.

The transfer of one of the four divisions in Hawaii had, in fact, already been discussed and decided upon in Washington. Still pending was the selection of unit and destination. The first was settled quickly with the choice falling on Maj. Gen. Lawton Collins' 25th Division, which was alerted for shipment on 19 October. Fixing its destination presented more serious problems, for at this moment the Australian Prime Minister, John Curtin, was pressing for the return of his 9th Division from the Middle East. His claim was a strong one, and to satisfy him the 25th Division was tentatively earmarked for Australia. The President and Joint Chiefs hoped in this way to meet Australia's demands and at the same time allow General Sir Bernard L. Montgomery, who was then preparing his counteroffensive against El Alamein, to keep the 9th Division under his command. It was with this idea in mind that President Roosevelt told Curtin that he was releasing an American division. Carefully avoiding any commitment on its destination, Roosevelt said only that the division would go to the South or Southwest Pacific wherever "its employment will be of greater advantage to the defense of Australia." Final decision on the destination of the 25 Division was not made until the end of November, when the Joint Chiefs compromised by directing the division to Guadalcanal, instead of the Fijis, to relieve the 1st Marine Division for shipment to Australia. Thus MacArthur would get a combat-tested amphibious division, the marines a well-earned rest, and the South Pacific a fresh Army division.[55]

Meanwhile Admiral Nimitz was doing what he could to help Ghormley. Securing permission from Washington to strip the defenses of the Central Pacific, he rushed fighters and bombers to the danger zone. And by pushing repairs on the damaged vessels in Pearl Harbor he found naval reinforcements for Ghormley. On 16 October, the carrier *Enterprise,* repaired in record time, left for the South Pacific in company with the battleship *South Dakota* and nine destroyers. But Nimitz had grave doubts that Admiral Ghormley was the best man to meet the crisis in the Solomons. Someone more aggressive, he thought, might do better, and, after a meeting with his staff on the evening of the 15th, he asked King for authority to replace Ghormley with Admiral Halsey. Permission was readily granted and on 18 October, when Halsey reached Noumea to take over his old task force with the *Enterprise* as his flagship, he received orders to take over

[54] Rad, Harmon to Marshall, 17 Oct 42, CM–IN–07191; Rad, MacArthur to Marshall, 17 Oct 42, No. C–731, GHQ Hist Rec Index Cards, OCMH.

[55] Rad, Marshall to Emmons, 19 Oct 42, CM–OUT–06063; Rads, Curtin to Churchill, 17 Oct 42, and Roosevelt to Curtin, 28 Oct 42, filed with Memo, Leahy for Roosevelt, 27 Oct 42, CCS 320.2 (10–22–42) Australia; OPD Memo for Record, 30 Nov 42, sub: Destination of 25th and 1st Marine Division, with other related papers in OPD 370.5 (11–30–42), PTO, case 45.

command of the South Pacific area.[56] No one thereafter had cause to complain about a lack of aggressiveness in the South Pacific.

President Roosevelt, too, was viewing the situation in the Solomons with increasing concern. Undoubtedly he had followed the debate over priority with keen interest, but it was not until 24 October, when the Japanese offensive had already begun, that he took a hand. "My anxiety about the Southwest Pacific," he wrote in an urgent message jointly to Leahy, King, Marshall, and Arnold, "is to make sure that every possible weapon gets in that area to hold Guadalcanal, and that having held it in this crisis, that munitions and planes and crews are on the way to take advantage of our success." Soon Allied ground troops would be engaged in North Africa and they, too, Roosevelt reminded his military advisers, would need air support. Matters would have to be so arranged that both fronts could be supported "even though it means delay in our other commitments, particularly to England." What the President wanted the chiefs to do over the weekend—it was then Saturday—was to prepare for him a report on the status of all combat aircraft in the United States and to check every possible source for the temporary diversion of munitions."[57]

This was a large order for a short weekend, but by Monday, the 26th, both

Marshall and King had their separate replies ready. Both dealt primarily with the situation in the South Pacific, outlining the forces each service had in the area and the measures being taken to meet the crisis. Neither could find any air reinforcements in the continental United States, where there were barely enough planes for tactical training and security. The only practicable source from which to draw on for the Pacific was the United Kingdom or TORCH.

Shipping, Marshall and King agreed, was the critical problem. In the final analysis, reinforcements to the Pacific and support of the troops there were limited by the number of cargo vessels and transports available. In the next three months, Marshall pointed out, the Army and Navy would be short twenty-five ships a month for the Pacific route. Only by halting troop movements to England, the Middle East, and India, discontinuing the Persian Corridor project, and canceling the five-ship allotment to Russia for west coast shipments and other lend-lease commitments could they find the ships required to move the needed supplies and equipment to the Pacific. Another critical shortage was in ammunition, and that lack, too, Marshall observed, could not be overcome without cutting into other commitments. "Regardless of the strength of combat units we deploy in the area," he concluded, "we cannot effectively consolidate our gains unless we secure appropriate logistic support."[58]

[56] Morison, *The Struggle for Guadalcanal*, p. 183. Halsey, who was promoted to full admiral soon after his assumption of command, had had no inkling of the change when he left Pearl Harbor. Ltr, Spruance to Hoover, 17 Jul 59, OCMH. At the time, Spruance noted, Admiral Turner was doubtful of the ability of the Allies to hold Guadalcanal.

[57] Memo, Roosevelt for Leahy, King, Marshall, and Arnold, 24 Oct 42, OPD 381 (PTO), case 107.

[58] Memo, Marshall for Roosevelt, 26 Oct 42, sub: Sit in South Pacific; Memo, King for Roosevelt, 26 Oct 42, sub: Diversion of Munitions to South Pacific. Both in OPD 381 (PTO), case 107. See also Leighton and Coakley, *Global Logistics and Strategy*, ch. XV.

Whether or not Roosevelt read these reports is not clear in the record, but that afternoon Marshall apparently discussed their contents with Admiral Leahy. The admiral then passed on to Roosevelt the gist of the reports and later in the day, on the President's authority, Leahy instructed the War Shipping Administration to "provide without delay twenty additional ships . . . for use in the South Pacific, not at the expense of Russia or the new expedition (TORCH) ."[59]

By this time the Japanese offensive on Guadalcanal had virtually run its course without disaster for the Allies, and though the Japanese on the island were still capable of offensive action, the crisis was over. The ground offensive had begun on the night of the 23d. Under the leadership of Lt. Gen. Masao Maruyama, commander of the *2d Division,* the Japanese sought for three days to penetrate the line around Henderson Field. But the marines and Army troops of the 164th Infantry held firm, and on the 26th Maruyama called off the assault, having lost at least 2,000 men.

Hardly had this threat ended when a Japanese naval force built around four carriers and led by Admiral Nagumo was discovered near the Santa Cruz Islands, southeast of Guadalcanal. The approach of this formidable fleet had been noted earlier and preparations made to meet it. But all Halsey had were two carriers, *Hornet* and the recently repaired *Enterprise,* which had reached the area on the 24th. It was this force which met and engaged the formidable Japanese fleet on the morning of the 26th in the Battle of the Santa Cruz Islands. Fought at long range by carrier aircraft, this battle, like the one that preceded it, proved indecisive. The *Hornet* went down and the *Enterprise, South Dakota,* and several smaller vessels were damaged. Japanese surface losses were less severe—2 carriers, 1 heavy cruiser, and 2 destroyers damaged—but their loss of aircraft and trained pilots, combined with the losses at Midway, was serious.

The battle over, Admiral Nagumo withdrew northward to Truk, not because he had been defeated but because General Maruyama had failed and there was nothing more he could do until another offensive was launched. Behind him he left a badly crippled American fleet guarding an island on which American troops still held precarious possession of a battered and pock-marked airfield. The immediate crisis on Guadalcanal was over, but the final .battle for possession of the airstrip and for air and naval mastery of the southern Solomons was still ahead. "I feel that the Jap can win now in the Solomons only by bold aggressive action of heavily superior forces," General Harmon reported optimistically on 1 November. "The picture has materially changed."[60]

The Shipping Crisis

The scarcity of shipping, which both Marshall and King had stressed in their report to the President on 26 October and which the commanders in the Pacific had complained about frequently, was a problem of long standing. MacArthur had attributed most of his difficulties in New Guinea to a total lack of light ship-

---

[59] Memo, Leahy for Deane, 26 Oct 42.

[60] Ltr, Harmon to Marshall, 1 Nov 42, copy in OCMH.

SHIPS AT NOUMEA *waiting to be unloaded.*

ping and made clear that he could not begin Task Two without assurance of continuing logistical support and a secure line of communications. In the South Pacific, supply was only second in importance to air reinforcements. His "most vexing problem," Harmon told Marshall on 9 September, was logistics. "Army, Navy, and Marines all mixed in the jungle, mountains of supplies piling up on the beach, and a road-stead full of ships, bombs and fuel drums scattered through the coffee and cocoa," he wrote, "was a fine picture of war *as she is* but not as it should be."[61]

Much of the difficulty was the result of the world-wide shipping shortage or,

as at Espiritu Santo where the confusion derived from the hasty withdrawal of troops and supplies from Guadalcanal, of unexpected and unanticipated developments. But Pacific geography, climate, and the absence of any well-developed transportation system, combined with the shortage of service troops and the waste and duplication of a divided command, aggravated and enlarged the logistical problems. The enormous distances in an oceanic theater of operations almost completely dependent upon water transportation created an insatiable demand for ships, the most precious of Allied commodities. And once committed to the Pacific route, with its primitive or nonexistent ports and discharge facilities, a vessel would be a long time returning to home port. More than

---

[61] Ltr, Harmon to Marshall, 9 Sep 42, copy in OCMH.

twice as many ships, General Somervell estimated, would be required to move the same number of troops to Australia as to England, and to maintain them there.[62]

Undertaken on a shoestring despite warnings from MacArthur and Ghormley, the Guadalcanal campaign absorbed more and more men and equipment. No provision had been made for the receipt and storage of the supplies that reached the area in response to the urgent requests from Army and Navy commanders. Soon these emergency shipments, together with those normally required for the support of the garrisons in the area, were piling up at the forward bases, where the supplies originally scheduled for Guadalcanal were still awaiting shipment.

None of the ports in the South Pacific had the docks, labor, equipment, or storage areas to handle this traffic. Except for Auckland, Suva, Noumea, and one or two others, none of the ports could handle large ocean-going vessels, and even these were suited more for the normal peacetime conditions of a leisurely sugar and copra economy than for the heavy shipments of modern war. There had been no time, even if there had been the will, to build docks, storage areas, and roads, and to bring in the modern equipment and machinery required for the rapid discharge of large vessels. In all of the South Pacific there was in July 1942 only one port company. It was stationed in New Zealand—far from the scene of battle.

- The heaviest burden fell on the Free French port of Noumea where by 23 September there were eighty-six ships in the harbor. Not all the supplies on these vessels were earmarked for the troops in New Caledonia. Some of the ships were destined for Guadalcanal and other ports in the forward area which could not receive them; others were naval vessels in need of provisions. With the few berths available in Noumea (shared with French commercial interests), it is not surprising that unloading could not keep pace with the arrival of new ships. The situation was hardly improved by the lack of co-ordination between the Army and Navy, each of which requisitioned separately, had its own shipping, and received its own supplies, leaving those not needed aboard ship in the harbor. Ships thus became, in a sense, floating warehouses, a use never intended. Moreover, the vessels destined for Guadalcanal and other advance bases had to remain in the harbor of Noumea until such time as they could sail freely into the forward area and be unloaded promptly. In this way, vessels that could have been used to carry vitally needed supplies and reinforcements were immobilized for considerable periods of time, thereby aggravating the already critical world-wide shipping shortage.

So wasteful a system could hardly be tolerated, and emergency measures were taken to reduce the congestion. General Patch, commander of the New Caledonia base as well as of the Americal Division, was told to add more men to a provisional port company he had organized earlier, and the Navy considered a proposal to move 600 longshoremen to Noumea by air. In October, General Somervell sent his chief planner, Maj.

---

[62] Leighton and Coakley, *Global Logistics and Strategy*, ch. XV. Unless otherwise noted, this section is based to a large extent on this excellent volume, although the author consulted most of the documents there cited.

Gen. Leroy Lutes out to the Pacific to look into the situation. Appalled at what he saw, Lutes urged Harmon to push through plans for a strong, centralized supply and service organization, and one was formally established under Brig. Gen. Robert G. Breene in mid-November. "General Lutes' visit," Harmon reported to the Chief of Staff, "was a definite help." [63] The solution to the confusion and waste in the South Pacific, Lutes believed, lay in the establishment of a truly co-ordinated interservice logistical organization which could control and supervise all supply activities in the theater. This was the solution he proposed in general terms to the theater commanders and in specific terms on his return to Washington in November. He also impressed on the Washington planners the need for additional service troops in the South Pacific, and was successful in increasing the allotment.[64]

Though General Lutes' proposal held out the promise of a more efficient supply system in the future—a joint logistical plan was approved in March 1943—it did not relieve the congestion at Noumea. That job was done by Halsey and Harmon whose success was, in part, attributable to the improvement in the tactical situation on Guadalcanal. By 16 November, when Halsey gave General Breene's Services of Supply responsibility for loading and discharge at Noumea, the danger from Japanese air and naval attack had lessened and it was possible to send forward many of the vessels

waiting in the harbor. Thus, when the New Caledonia service commander, Brig. Gen. Raymond E. S. Williamson, assumed control of port operations on the 20th, there were only thirty-seven vessels awaiting discharge. This total jumped rapidly during the next month when the Americal Division was moved to Guadalcanal, and the 43d Division plus New Zealand troops moved in to take its place. These shipments, with the supplies destined for the 25th Division, then moving from Hawaii directly to Guadalcanal, soon crowded the port at Noumea again.

General Williamson met this challenge bravely. Utilizing combat troops, Navy longshoremen, native labor, and experienced civilians from New Zealand, in addition to the regular port detachment, he was able to move the cargoes much more rapidly. He also had the use of the so-called Nickel Dock—the dock reserved for the French Nickel Company —for three months. During his first month of command, sixty of the vessels in the harbor were unloaded, leaving a backlog of only twenty-nine. The port was not yet cleared, nor would it be for some months to come, but by the end of the year there was little likelihood of a repetition of the September–November congestion. The measures already adopted or under consideration gave promise of that, and of a more efficient and coordinated theater-wide logistical program.

Relieving the congestion in South Pacific ports was one way of getting more cargo vessels and transports for the Pacific run; another was to take the ships from other theaters. During the October crisis, when the need was greatest and congestion at its peak, President Roose-

[63] Ltr, Harmon to Marshall, 1 Nov 42, copy in OCMH.

[64] For his account of the trip, see Leroy Lutes, "Supply: World War II." *Antiaircraft Journal*, Nos. 4 and 5 (July–October 1952); Leighton and Coakley, *Global Logistics and Strategy*, p. 413.

velt, it will be recalled, had directed the War Shipping Administration to furnish twenty vessels for November sailings to the South and Southwest Pacific with the stipulation that they must come from projects other than TORCH and the Soviet aid program.[65] The War Shipping Administration, unable to find twenty commercial vessels, declared that commitments elsewhere would have to be cut if Pacific requirements were to be met. But this was a task for the military, not the War Shipping Administration, and at the end of October the problem was turned over to the Joint Planners.[66]

Within the week the planners had come up with a solution. Since there was no time to divert vessels from the Atlantic, they left commitments to that area undisturbed. Six ships, they proposed, should be taken from the Hawaiian, Alaskan, and Panamanian runs, and another six from lend-lease shipments to India and the Middle East. A few more could be provided by economies in existing schedules.

The Joint Chiefs accepted these recommendations informally, but the War Shipping Administration pointed out that the cut in lend-lease shipments violated priorities established by the Combined Chiefs of Staff. Action by that body was a clear prerequisite to approval of the plan and the matter was therefore referred to one of the combined committees for study as a matter of urgency —it was already mid-November. But before that committee could meet, the War Shipping Administration suddenly announced that it had found the vessels required for the Pacific without cutting into British requirements for the Middle East, thus meeting the minimum shipping needs for November in the Pacific.[67] But the shortage of cargo vessels was still serious and an even more serious shortage in personnel carriers was soon to develop.

The Crisis Ends

By the time the shipping crisis had passed, the Guadalcanal campaign had reached its final stage. Having failed in October to wrest control of the southern Solomons from the Allies, the Japanese were only more determined to succeed next time. There were still large Japanese forces on Guadalcanal, and to these General Hyakutake decided to add the *38th Division*, recently arrived at Rabaul, for his second attempt. As before, the ground assault would be co-ordinated with air and naval action, and Admiral Yamamoto at Truk furnished the forces designed to gain undisputed and final mastery of the Solomons. In early November these forces assembled at Rabaul and in the northern Solomons while destroyers brought in additional troops and equipment to Guadalcanal.

Allied intelligence faithfully recorded these movements, reporting by 12 November the presence of 2 carriers, 4 battleships, 5 heavy cruisers, 30 destroyers,

---

[65] See above, p. 345.

[66] Ltr, Lewis Douglas, WSA, to Leahy, 28 Oct 42, with Memo, Vice Adm Emory S. Land and Douglas for Roosevelt, 27 Oct 42, sub: Rqmts for Additional Tonnage. These and other relevant papers in CCS 540 (10–26–42) SWPA.

[67] Memo, Deane for Leahy, Marshall, and King, 5 Nov 42, sub: Allocation of Twenty-Nine Additional Ships for SWPA; Ltr, Douglas to Leahy, 9 Nov 42; Ltr, Douglas to Leahy, 17 Nov 42. Mins, JCS Mtg, 17 Nov 42; JCS 143 ser. 5, 16, and 19 Nov 42; Leighton and Coakley, *Global Logistics and Strategy*, pp. 396–98.

and a large number of transports and cargo ships in the northern Solomons. To meet this threat Admiral Halsey had 24 submarines, which had been temporarily assigned to the South Pacific during the October crisis, the carrier *Enterprise,* 2 battleships, 3 heavy cruisers, plus some light cruisers and more than 20 destroyers. On Guadalcanal itself, reinforcements brought in since the October crisis included artillery, a Marine regiment, and on 12 November, when the battle opened, another regiment, the 184th Infantry, of the Americal Division.

The naval and air engagements between 12 and 15 November, known collectively as the Battle of Guadalcanal, decided the issue. They began with a simultaneous effort by the Americans and Japanese to reinforce their troops on the island. In the van of the Japanese convoy was a strong battleship force with orders to neutralize Henderson Field and clear the way for the landing to follow. Guarding the American transports unloading the 184th Infantry was a naval task force of five cruisers and eight destroyers under Rear Adm. Daniel J. Callaghan, a friend and former aide of the President. It was this force that met the Japanese battleships off Savo Island on the night of 12–13 November and in one of the wildest naval engagements in modern times drove back the superior enemy force and foiled the Japanese plan. Losses on both sides were severe.

On the 14th, the Japanese, freshened and reinforced, came in again, but this time they were met by two battleships and destroyer escort. The ensuing battle, fought at long range by radar, was a clear victory for the Americans. The Japanese lost one battleship and then

withdrew, leaving four of their transports to be destroyed at leisure the next day. The Battle of Guadalcanal was over; the Japanese had made their last major effort to retake the island and had lost. Air and naval mastery of the southern Solomons was now in Allied hands and though the grinding task of destroying the Japanese on the island continued for almost two more months, the final outcome was no longer in doubt. In their pidgin English, the natives summed up the general feeling in a song with the refrain "Me laugh along Japani, ha, ha!"[68]

The Allied situation in New Guinea had also improved considerably by mid-November. Since the end of September the Australian 7th Division had pursued the Japanese back across the Owen Stanley Range through Kokoda and on toward Buna. By this time two regiments of the U.S. 32d Division had moved into the area and stood ready with the Australians to begin a co-ordinated attack against the Buna beachhead. The Japanese offensive in New Guinea, begun so hopefully four months before, was clearly marked for disaster. Virtually cut off by Allied air and sea power from their base at Rabaul and pinned down along a narrow strip with the sea at their backs and with Allied troops pressing in on them, the Japanese in Buna, like their fellows on Guadalcanal, were indeed in desperate straits.

Not only in the Pacific but elsewhere also fortune favored the Allied cause. At Stalingrad the Germans had been

---

[68] *Among Those Present, Official Story of the Pacific Islands at War,* prepared for the Colonial Office by the Central Office of Information (London: His Majesty's Stationery Office, 1946), p. 37.

checked and the great Russian winter offensive was already beginning to unfold; in North Africa General Montgomery had defeated Rommel at El Alamein and was in full pursuit of Rommel's army when, on 8 November, U.S. and British troops landed at Oran, Algiers, and Casablanca. "It would seem," said President Roosevelt, "that the turning point in this war has at last been reached." [69]

---

[69] Address to the New York *Herald-Tribune* Forum, 17 Nov 42, quoted in Sherwood, *Roosevelt and Hopkins,* p. 656.

CHAPTER XVI

Command and Co-operation

Nothing is more important in war than unity in command.

NAPOLEON, *Maxims*

The Guadalcanal campaign provided the first real test of the organization established at the end of March 1942 for the conduct of joint operations in the Pacific. Though the troops on Guadalcanal had survived each crisis and were, by the end of the year, in sight of final victory, the margin of safety had been too narrow, the moments when the issue seemed in doubt too numerous to permit a repetition of those grueling and heartbreaking six months. Haste, inexperience, a failure to assess accurately the enemy's reaction and the forces required for speedy victory undoubtedly accounted for much of the difficulty and would be corrected in the future. But from the reports of commanders in the field and observers sent out from Washington it was evident that these facts did not account for all that had gone wrong. Misunderstandings and disagreements between the services had had an important effect upon the conduct of the campaign and would, unless quickly resolved or removed, continue to plague operations and hinder the effectiveness of future offensives against Japan.

Army-Navy Relations in the South Pacific

In the South Pacific, the most serious disagreements between the Army and Navy commanders arose from differing views on the role of the air arm and the proper utilization of Army aircraft. Operational control of all aircraft in the theater was in the hands of naval officers, first Admiral McCain and then Admiral Fitch. General Harmon, himself a senior air officer with a staff of experienced airmen headed by General Twining, had little or nothing to say about how his planes would be employed. Through Admiral Ghormley he could make recommendations and suggestions, which might or might not be accepted, but his authority extended little further than his personal influence. And though his relationship with Ghormley and the air commander was cordial and even friendly, it could not overcome the differences between Air Forces and Navy doctrine.

From the first Harmon felt that not enough emphasis had been given to air power. In his report to Marshall on the

Guadalcanal landing he called attention to the fact that no air construction units had been included in the invasion force, and that even when Henderson Field was completed it would be impossible to base bombers there until fighter and antiaircraft protection was provided. Since the prospect for the early completion of the field was slim, he did not push the matter. More urgent was the need for airfield construction personnel and equipment, ground crews, fuel, bombs, and ammunition. Only if the Navy could send these up to Guadalcanal, together with Marine fighter and scout bombers, Harmon told Marshall, would he be able to send in his own bombers. "If all this were done," he wrote, "I believe the position can be held. It is the procedure I propose to recommend to Admiral Ghormley."[1]

On Harmon's recommendation Ghormley did make the effort to send forward construction equipment, but progress was disappointingly slow. Still Harmon was optimistic and felt that Ghormley was doing all he could. So gratifying was the naval effort that Harmon reported to General Marshall on 9 September that he was very pleased and that he was getting along fine with the Navy. "My Chief of Staff [Twining] and I," he wrote, "confer with Admiral Ghormley and his Staff almost every day and decisions are made and action taken without delay."[2] Once the field on Guadalcanal was made suitable for "continuous, effective bomber operations on a reasonable scale"—which he then expected to be by the 15th—he felt he would be "out of the thick woods."

Within the week Harmon's mood had changed. In a note to General Arnold dated 15 September he recited a long list of grievances. Henderson Field was still not usable by medium or heavy bombers, and by fighters only in dry weather. The steel mats required for construction had not arrived and there was only enough fuel to last four more days. He was sending more P-400's and P-39's up to Guadalcanal, but wanted Arnold to know that "they simply cannot function at the altitude at which Jap bombers operate, and are of limited value as medium altitude fighters."[3]

Without criticizing Ghormley — "no man could have more conscientiously endeavored to carry out a most difficult directive" — Harmon made it perfectly clear that the Navy's failure to give first priority to airfield construction on Guadalcanal was the most serious error of the campaign and the reason why the situation there was so critical. From the very beginning he and his staff had stressed that point, he said, and he was beginning to wonder "if the Navy really and fully appreciated this necessity in the beginning. They seemed to as we talked to them but the positive action was not taken. . . . The point is that it was not the consuming thought in every Naval Commander's mind and the plan did not have as its first and immediate objective the seizure and development of Cactus [Guadalcanal] *as an Air base.*"[4]

The Navy's failure to appreciate the importance of airfield construction was, in Harmon's view, a reflection of the Navy's concept of air power as a sup-

---

[1] Ltr, Harmon to Marshall, 11 Aug 42, copy in OCMH.

[2] Ltr, Harmon to Marshall, 9 Sep 42, copy in OCMH.

[3] Ltr, Harmon to Arnold, 15 Sep 42, copy in OCMH.

[4] *Ibid.*

porting arm for naval and ground forces. To Harmon, and he assumed to Arnold as well, air power was the dominant element in the war, surface and ground forces the supporting elements. Moreover, it was the land-based, not carrier-based aircraft, that would have to make the main effort.

Even the Navy's conduct of its own naval operations, Harmon felt, was open to criticism. Though he protested that he found it difficult "to charge lack of aggressiveness," he made it evident that he held no high opinion of the Navy's accomplishments in the South Pacific. "Boats go in, start to unload and then run out on threat of attack," he observed. "No naval surface forces have been in the Cactus-Ringbolt area [Guadalcanal-Tulagi] since Turner departed with what was left of his outfit after the 'battle' of Savo Island, August 9th."[5]

Overcaution and a defensive spirit dominated the Navy's operations, Harmon believed. He appreciated the necessity for " a line of action tempered with reasonable caution," but pointed out at the same time that most of the Navy's surface losses had come when it was operating "in a role other than offensive." As an example he cited the case of the *Wasp* sunk by torpedoes while on patrol south of the Solomons. Assigning a patrol mission to the carrier and the surface forces required to protect it did not impress him as sound doctrine. "I may be entirely wrong," he wrote, "but if I owned any CVs I would surely leave them safely tucked away a thousand or more miles back or I would use them on a deliberate offensive thrust."[6] Vigorous offensive action he insisted was the best

defense, regardless of the strategic role assigned the Pacific in global strategy.

Although General Harmon's criticism of the Navy's failure to appreciate the importance of air power or to employ its surface forces offensively left much to be said on the other side, it did make strikingly clear his strong dissatisfaction with the conduct of the campaign. General Arnold, to whom these comments were directed, soon had the opportunity to judge for himself the truth of Harmon's assertions. His voyage to the Pacific later in September took him to Noumea where he conferred with Ghormley and Nimitz as well as Harmon. His conclusions, presented to General Marshall on his return to Washington, were, first, "that the Navy had not demonstrated its ability to properly conduct air operations," and, second, that the Navy's failure to appreciate the importance of logistics had led to a shortage of the supplies required to support military operations.[7]

The Navy had some criticisms of its own. Especially disappointing to it was the performance of the Army's heavy bomber, the B–17, which, the Navy contended, bombed from too high an altitude to be effective against shipping and surface craft, the prime naval targets. General Harmon readily agreed that his B–17's were having trouble in this respect, but attributed it to the green crews and the fact that the strikes were often made at extreme range. He hoped to do better, he told his naval colleagues, but despite his insistence on low-altitude bombing the performance of the B–17 against maneuvering surface targets con-

---

[5] *Ibid.*
[6] *Ibid.*

[7] Memo, Arnold for Marshall, 6 Oct 42, sub: One Comdr for Pacific, OPD 384 (4–3–42).

DAMAGE TO SUPPLIES *caused by improper packing, dunnage, and handling.*

tinued to be disappointing. There was no getting around the fact that the B–17 was not the ideal plane for such missions.[8]

Logistical matters, too, provided cause for dissatisfaction, and on this subject Marshall received numerous reports which supported the complaints from General Harmon and the conclusions of General Arnold. A résumé of the information supplied by four Army officers recently returned from the Solomons listed as the major shortcomings in the campaign there the supply system, im-

proper loading, and the failure to expand the airfield facilities sufficiently to support heavy bomber operations. In the latter part of September, these officers reported, supplies on Guadalcanal had been so scarce that had it not been for the captured Japanese rations and gasoline, the lot of the troops would have been "extremely desperate." Their conclusion, after reviewing other effects of the supply shortages, was that 'long range supply planning for the operation could have been improved upon," and they suggested that the logistical organization established in Australia be used as a model. These comments, edited to remove any statements that might unnec-

[8] Craven and Cate, *AAF IV*, pp. 63–70; Ltr, Harmon to Marshall, 9 Sep 42, copy in OCMH. Memo, Marshall for Handy, 8 Sep 42, OPD 452.1 (PTO), case 13.

essarily offend the Navy, Marshall passed
on to Admiral King "for whatever the
information may be worth to your
people."[9]

Admiral Halsey's assumption of command in mid-October and the offensive
spirit that marked operations thereafter
brought warm approval from Harmon.
The two men worked well together and
Halsey's insistence on the "one force"
principle did much to eliminate misunderstanding, as did his willingness to
give the Army more responsibility and
a greater share in the conduct of operations. This attitude was apparent almost
immediately when General Harmon,
whose opposition to the seizure of Ndeni
in the Santa Cruz Islands Ghormley had
overruled, recommended to the new
commander that the operation be canceled and the forces earmarked for Santa
Cruz be sent to Guadalcanal instead.
Halsey accepted this proposal with the
result that the Army's 147th Infantry
from Tongatabu landed at Guadalcanal
the following month. "Where disposition of Army forces is involved," Harmon told General Marshall, "the Commander South Pacific makes his decision
only after conference with me."[10]

Despite the improved relations
between the two commanders in the
Pacific—Harmon was pleased to report
that Halsey was establishing his headquarters ashore at Noumea, close to his
—there was little improvement in the
airfield at Guadalcanal. By the middle
of November the field there was still

HENDERSON FIELD *in November 1942.*

not adequate to support medium and
heavy bombers. Harmon was optimistic
about the future but had to confess that
the failure to develop the airdrome at
Lunga Point was "one of the biggest
disappointments of this campaign."[11]

Nor had the performance of the B–17
against surface targets improved. Halsey, himself an airman, understood the
difficulties and appreciated the fact that
the B–17 was most effective in high-
altitude mass bombing against fixed
targets, but so long as the Japanese continued to send their ships into the southern Solomons he had to employ the
bombers against them.[12] Necessity here
overrode doctrine and Harmon, while
suggesting more profitable targets, did

[9] Memo, Marshall for Somervell, 16 Oct 42, no sub;
Memo, Marshall for King, 20 Oct 42, no sub. Both in
WDCSA (Solomons).

[10] Ltr, Harmon to Marshall, 1 Nov 42; Memo, Har-
mon for Ghormley, 6 Oct 42, sub: Occupation of
Ndeni; Harmon, Army in the South Pacific, p. 3.
All in OCMH.

[11] Ltr, Harmon to Streett, 16 Nov 42, copy in
OCMH.

[12] Ltrs, Harmon to Halsey, 22 Oct and 20 Nov 42,
cited in Craven and Cate, *AAF IV*, pp. 63–64.

ADMIRAL HALSEY AND GENERAL HARMON

his best to better the B–17 score in attacks against shipping.

The Southwest and Central Pacific

MacArthur's use of the heavy bombers also came under criticism from the Navy, but for a different reason. He was employing his B–17's primarily against enemy airfields rather than shipping, as the Navy desired. When queried about this, General MacArthur explained that it was necessary to gain air superiority in New Guinea and that he had, in fact, achieved this objective. Moreover, it was this superiority that enabled him to support Ghormley's operations in the Solomons. His earlier efforts to bomb surface craft, he pointed out, had proved disappointing because of the training and leadership of his air forces. This was the view also of an observer sent out by

General Marshall who reported that the bombardiers "could not hit anything from any altitude principally because they lacked necessary training." [13] But these difficulties, MacArthur believed, would be overcome soon and better results against Japanese shipping achieved under the newly arrived air commander, General Kenney.

Another disturbing factor in the relationship between the Army and Navy in the Pacific was the co-operation, or lack of it, between the South and Southwest Pacific Areas. General Marshall's frequent references to this problem are a measure of the importance he attached to it, and, perhaps, of his doubts about assurances of harmonious relations. He had raised this question very early in the campaign, apparently on the basis of unofficial reports, and had received from MacArthur, Ghormley, and Harmon strong denials of any differences. Yet, at the end of August, Harmon told General Arnold that he was doing his best to co-ordinate the air effort of the two areas. "It is a rather delicate assignment," he wrote. "Bring it up in conference every few days and once in a while hand Ghormley a message suggesting he might want to send it to MacArthur. He usually does." [14]

There is little doubt that MacArthur provided support to the South Pacific when asked to do so. Usually this support took the form of bomber strikes against Rabaul and the northern Solomons, and more than once he alluded

[13] Rad, Ritchie to Marshall, 21 Sep 42, CM–IN 9230. See also Memo, King for Marshall, 11 Sep 42, sub: Aircraft Sit, OPD 452.1 (PTO), case 19; Rad, MacArthur to Marshall, 16 Sep 42, CM–IN 6695; Rad, Marshall to MacArthur, 14 Sep 42, CM–OUT 4694.
[14] Ltr, Harmon to Arnold, 28 Aug 42, copy in OCMH.

to grateful acknowledgements from Admiral Ghormley for this assistance. Still the rumors of a lack of co-operation persisted and as late as 19 October, in response to a query from the White House, General Marshall had to assure the President that MacArthur was doing all he could to support the Guadalcanal campaign.[15]

But MacArthur also had his hands full, and with justice complained that his own operations were considerably hampered by the lack of naval forces. Since these had been loaned to Ghormley for the Guadalcanal invasion MacArthur asked late in August that the South Pacific commander be given the additional responsibility of covering the sea approaches to the Milne Bay area where the Japanese had recently landed. Apparently Ghormley and Nimitz opposed this suggestion, but Marshall was able with King's help to arrange for the return of the Southwest Pacific naval units to MacArthur.[16] This transfer had hardly been effected when another crisis on Guadalcanal brought from Nimitz a request that the submarines in the Southwest Pacific be placed under his control. Feeling possibly that the co-operation between the two theaters was a one-sided affair, MacArthur rejected the proposal, only to find late the following month that the Joint Chiefs had assigned twelve of his submarines to the South Pacific.[17]

Marshall's efforts to secure the co-ordination of forces in the South and Southwest Pacific during the Guadalcanal campaign seemed to the Army planners in Washington to have had little effect. The same officer who had served as the Chief of Staff's observer in MacArthur's area, and who had been given the task of briefing Brig. Gen. Walter Krueger before his departure for Australia, summed up the difficulties ahead as follows:

The problem most urgently in need of immediate solution is that of unity of command of the forces now operating from the Southwest and South Pacific Areas against the same enemy force based on Rabaul. . . . The operations of two large and powerful forces are being conducted concurrently with no coordination other than lateral liaison. As long as this continues it is allowing the enemy to take fullest advantage of his unity of control and interior lines. A solution to this problem would also help in simplifying some of the logistical complications now existent in the support of these separate forces.[18]

In the Central Pacific Area, which Nimitz commanded as a part of his larger Pacific Ocean Areas, relations between the Army and Navy commands also caused some concern in Washington. Fortunately, since the area was not yet the scene of active operations, the disagreements there had no serious consequences. But some of these differences dated from prewar days and their persistence was not a hopeful sign for co-operation in the future. In July, for example, the Navy expressed concern over the latest Army defense plan because it failed to make provision for certain important

---

[15] Memo, Capt John L. McCrea (Naval Aide to President) for Marshall, 14 Oct 42, OPD Exec Files; Memo, Marshall for Roosevelt, 19 Oct 42, WDCSA (SPA).

[16] Rad, MacArthur to Marshall, 28 Aug 42, No. C–367, GHQ Hist Rec Index Cards, OCMH; Rad, Marshall to MacArthur, 31 Aug 42, OPD Exec Files.

[17] Memo, King for Roosevelt, 26 Oct 42, sub: Diversion of Munitions to South Pacific, OPD 381 (PTO), case 107; Rad, MacArthur to Marshall, 16 Sep 42, No. C–504, OPD Msg File.

[18] Ritchie, Notes for Krueger, 20 Jan 43, cited in Draft MS Hist of OPD, OCMH.

naval installations. Rather than order General Emmons to alter the plan, Admiral Nimitz referred the matter to Washington with the request that his responsibility for assignment of defense missions be clarified. King took the view that Nimitz had that right under the principle of unity of command, and General Marshall agreed with him. But Marshall made the distinction between the assignment of a mission and the employment of forces for its accomplishment. The former was the responsibility of the theater commander, the latter of the service commander.[19] The distinction was a fine one, not always understood, and the problem became the subject of dispute again at a later date.

Another example of a lack of singleness of purpose in the Central Pacific was the difficulty in establishing a joint Army-Navy command post. This project dated from October 1941 when the proposal was made by the Chief of Naval Operations. General Short opposed the scheme vigorously but his successor, on orders from the War Department, gave his consent. The Navy drew up plans for the command post in January, revised them to meet the wishes of the Army headquarters, and then submitted revised plans. These elicited further objections, and six months passed without any visible progress. It was apparent by now that the entire matter would have to be referred to a joint board for a decision on the location of the proposed command post. Such a board was finally appointed in September, but its members could reach no agreement. It was not until December 1942, more than a year after the initial proposal had been made, that a site was finally selected. The building itself was still in process of construction at the end of the war.[20]

Joint Staffs

Long aware of the differences in doctrine and training between Army and Navy officers, General Marshall sought in various ways to overcome the obstacles to genuine unity of command. Constantly he impressed on his staff and on

---

[19] Hist, USAFMIDPAC and Predecessor Commands in World War II, pt. IV, pp. 839–40, copy in OCMH. General Emmons, when he read this volume in manuscript, commented that he did not recall any differences of opinion between Admiral Nimitz and himself, except in the case of Canton Island, a refueling point for aircraft. His account of this incident is worth noting:

The defense of this small coral reef [Emmons wrote], with an exposed width of from 50′ to 400′, was simple. I believed it impossible to invade it from the sea and a very difficult operation to invade from the air. We had approximately 2,000 troops on Canton including one pursuit squadron with another quickly available from Xmas Island and some AA artillery. Furthermore, there was another route via Xmas Island and still another to the east. The defense of Canton Island was my responsibility.

We had plenty of troops available in Hawaii but they were being trained for offensive combat operations.

Admiral Nimitz threatened to order me to send more troops to Canton. I told him that, if he did, I would have to appeal to the Chief of Staff. A day or two later I sent a few additional men to Canton to prevent further argument and informed Admiral Nimitz of my action. He seemed happy about that and I thought that was the end of the matter. The Japs reconnoitered Canton early in the war, dropped a few bombs that caused no damage, and never returned. Ltr, Emmons to Hoover, 10 Jul 59, OCMH.

[20] Hist, USAFMIDPAC and Predecessor Commands in World War II, pt. IV, pp. 806–09, copy in OCMH. Emmons recalled later that the site was in the rear of the Army command post and that when he left in June 1943 the tunneling work had been largely completed. Work was apparently discontinued after his departure. Ltr, Emmons to Hoover, 10 Jul 59, OCMH.

Army commanders in the field the necessity for subordinating service interests to the larger interests of the war. Concession and compromise were the principles that guided his relations with Admiral King, and co-operation was a recurring theme in the messages he sent to his subordinates.

One of the major obstacles to a unified command, General Marshall recognized early, was the service point of view, the inevitable result of a lifetime spent in learning the business of being a soldier or a sailor or an airman. Since there was no way of eliminating this obstacle short of an extended period of training, Marshall sought to diminish its effect by placing Army officers on the staff of Naval commanders and sponsoring the appointment of Naval officers to staffs headed by Army commanders. This exchange, he felt, would result in a better understanding by each of the services of the others' problems and practices and alert the commanders to potential areas of disagreement.

It was this thought that prompted Marshall, when the South Pacific Area was established, to secure the assignment of two Army officers to Admiral Ghormley's staff. With the formation of an Army headquarters in the area some months later and General Harmon's arrival in Noumea, there seemed to be little need for Army representation on Ghormley's staff and both officers were reassigned. Instead Harmon himself and the senior members of his staff consulted frequently with their naval colleagues. "Twining and myself are on board [the *Argonne*, Ghormley's headquarters] almost daily," Harmon reported to General Arnold. "Breene has been contacting Admiral Turner and his staff on logistic

matters and was on board today getting some problems of supply coordinated." At Espiritu Santo were other officers "practically serving on McCain's staff." [21]

In Hawaii there was no comparable co-ordination between the Army and Navy commanders, none of the frequent and informal exchanges of views which marked the relationship between Harmon and Ghormley. When General Emmons complained that the Navy did not appreciate the importance of logistics, Marshall suggested as a means of overcoming the difficulty, the assignment of Army officers to Admiral Nimitz' staff. "I am inclined to believe," he told Emmons, "that the constant presence of a capable Army staff officer in a G–4 capacity with a naval staff would have rapidly tended to correct such lack of realization." In Marshall's view, liaison between the commanders was not a satisfactory substitute for a joint staff that would assure the commander of competent and disinterested advice. "Higher commanders talk things over in generalities. Staff officers plan in intimacy over long periods." To this assertion he added General Arnold's view that "until Naval commanders of joint forces have qualified Army officers as working members of their staffs the maximum effectiveness of the combined arms cannot be secured." [22]

During the next few days Marshall discussed this problem with Admiral King. The admiral quickly accepted his colleague's suggestion that Army officers be assigned to the staff of a naval officer exercising unity of command and

---

[21] Ltr, Harmon to Arnold, 28 Aug 42, copy in OCMH.

[22] Rad, Marshall to Emmons, 15 Oct 42, WDCSA (10–15–42) SWPA.

proposed that General Marshall should select the officers for such assignment. On his part, Marshall proposed that King detail naval officers to Army commands to ensure the close co-operation "we have both striven constantly to attain."[23] Both men thereupon informed the designated theater commanders — MacArthur was not included — of their decision and proceeded to select officers for these assignments.

In the South Pacific, this move was not greeted with much enthusiasm. Harmon thought his method of working with Halsey entirely adequate, but when Marshall directed him to name an air officer for assignment to Halsey's staff he did so promptly. Other officers were similarly assigned later under urging from Washington, but in the fall of 1943, there were only six Army officers on Halsey's staff.[24] Their value, Harmon thought, was questionable. "As good and possibly better results would have been obtained," he wrote, "had planning activities continued on the initial basis of close daily association of opposite numbers on the Army and Navy staffs."[25]

A Unified Command for the Pacific

One other solution to the difficulties in the Pacific was to place the entire theater under one command. This proposal was first put forward by General Arnold on his return from the Pacific early in October and reflected the Air Forces view that Army aircraft under naval control were not being employed effectively. Only by establishing a single command for the entire theater and placing an Army officer in charge could these problems be resolved, Arnold asserted. That there would be powerful opposition to such a move, he readily conceded. As a matter of fact, he thought a "Presidential decree" would be required to bring about the change. And for General Marshall's information, he nominated three officers for the post: General MacArthur, Lt. Gen. Joseph T. McNarney, and Lt. Gen. Lesley J. McNair, all of whom he thought "perfectly capable of conducting the combined operations . . . in this area."[26]

What General Marshall thought of Arnold's suggestion we do not know. All he did was pass it on to the Operations Division without comment, at least none that was recorded. There it was studied by General Streett, an air officer, and General Wedemeyer, each of whom prepared a separate memorandum on the subject. Streett, who had apparently drafted Arnold's paper in the first instance, naturally approved of the whole idea and thought that Marshall would support it, "regardless of the difficulties." What he and Wedemeyer ought to do now, he declared, was to draft a study on the subject for General Marshall, one that "will not be entirely unpalatable for the Navy nor do violence to our feelings." The problem would come in selecting a commander; that task, Streett thought, ought to be done by the President himself.[27]

[23] Memo, Marshall for King, 22 Oct 42, sub: Detail of Officers to Duty on Staffs of Naval and Army Officers; Memo, King for Marshall, 18 Oct 42, same sub. Both in WDCSA 210.72 (10–22–42).
[24] Hist of USAFISPA, pt. II, p. 293.
[25] Harmon, The Army in the South Pacific, p. 19, OCMH.

[26] Memo, Arnold for Marshall, 6 Oct 42, sub: One Comdr for Pacific Theater, OPD 384 (4–3–42).
[27] Memo, Streett for Wedemeyer, 9 Oct 42, sub: One Comdr in Pacific Theater, OPD 384 (4–3–42).

Though he was more cautious about taking action, General Wedemeyer supported the idea of a single commander for the Pacific. The present organization with its "divided responsibility and chopped-up areas" he agreed was wasteful and inefficient. The consolidation of the theater would make possible the concentration of resources where they were most needed. In his opinion, command should be vested in the Air Forces, the service that would exercise the strongest influence in the Pacific. On this basis, Wedemeyer recommended as his first choice General Arnold, McNarney as his second.[28]

That General Marshall saw these studies is doubtful; nor is there any evidence that either Wedemeyer or Streett ever discussed the subject with him. But when the President on 24 October inquired about the situation in the Solomons, Marshall took the occasion to list, under "measures to be taken," the need "for a further unification of command in the entire Pacific Theater," especially in the South and Southwest Pacific Areas. "The present complications in the employment of air in the Pacific," he concluded, "emphasize this necessity."[29] When the President failed to respond to this suggestion, Marshall dropped the matter.

The postscript was written by General Streett five days later when he outlined for his chief, General Handy, his views on command in the Pacific. "At the risk of being considered naive and just plain

country-boy dumb," he could not help feeling that the major obstacle to a "sane military solution" of the problem was General MacArthur himself. Only with MacArthur out of the picture would it be possible to establish a sound organization in the area. Streett appreciated fully the political implications of removing MacArthur, but thought it could be done safely if the general were given some high post such as the ambassadorship to Russia, "a big enough job for anyone." Then, depending on whether the Navy or the Air Forces was considered to have the dominant role in the war, the post of supreme commander in the Pacific could be given either to Admiral Nimitz or General McNarney. The South and Southwest Pacific, Streett thought, should be combined under General Eichelberger, I Corps commander, with Brig. Gen. Patrick J. Hurley, former Secretary of War, as his "Chief of Civilian Affairs." The organization of the remainder of the theater could be left to the supreme commander who would "draw his own lines, designate subordinates, and select his own command post."[30] General Handy's comments on this proposal, if he made any, are not recorded. Streett left the Operations Division about a month later and ultimately became one of MacArthur's senior air commanders.

The problems arising from the organization of the Pacific into two major commands (one predominantly Army, the other predominantly Navy) continued to be a major concern of the Joint Chiefs and the basis for misunderstanding and disagreement between the serv-

---

[28] Memo, Wedemeyer for Streett, 11 Oct 42, sub: Supreme Comdr in Pacific Theater, OPD 384 (4-3-42).

[29] Memo, Marshall for Roosevelt, 26 Oct 42, sub: Sit in South Pacific, OPD 381 (PTO), case 107. General Streett prepared the draft of this memorandum for the Chief of Staff.

[30] Memo, Streett for Handy, 31 Oct 42, sub: Comd in the Pacific, OPD 384 (PTO), sec. 2.

ices. The fact that they had little effect on operations and the vigor and speed with which the war against Japan was conducted is a tribute to the determination of all concerned to make common cause against the enemy.[31]

---

[31] In this connection, it is worth noting the reaction of Vice Adm. Bernhard H. Bieri, one of the wartime naval planners, to this chapter when he read it in manuscript:

By its stress on the divergence of the services on command, one would get the impression from reading this history that all the services did was fight each other and not the Japs!

As a matter of fact while these problems were always here present, and were not lacking in other theaters, the war against the Japs was won and the *fighting men* were not too disturbed or delayed by matters of high command. It is a matter of great question whether this part of the war would have been better prosecuted under a single *supreme* commander. Certainly both MacArthur and Nimitz profited by the wise decisions of the JCS, and if one or the other had been SC, there would still have been those decisions to make, and by the JCS. As to administration, perfection in war was hardly attained anywhere under any system.

On the whole there was great cooperation and without this even a unified command is not effective.

Ltr, Bieri to Hoover, 17 Jul 59, OCMH.

CHAPTER XVII

Japanese and American Plans

The blow, wherever struck, must, to be successful, be sudden and heavy.

GENERAL ROBERT E. LEE

In late November 1942, when the tide of battle in the southern Solomons and the Papuan Peninsula turned in favor of the Allies, the Joint Chiefs of Staff in Washington and the American commanders in the South and Southwest Pacific began to consider once more how best to continue the offensive against Rabaul. The offensive inaugurated by the Joint Chiefs' directive of 2 July 1942, it will be recalled, consisted of three tasks. The first of these, the seizure of Guadalcanal and Tulagi, was now almost completed. With its completion and the seizure of Buna the Allies would have forward bases in the Solomons and New Guinea from which to launch the operations required by Tasks Two and Three: the conquest of the remainder of the Solomons, of the northeast coast of New Guinea, and, finally, of New Ireland and New Britain in the Bismarck Archipelago. It was essential, if the impetus of the Allied drive was to be maintained, that plans for the execution of these two tasks be made quickly. The Japanese would not stand idly by if the Allies did not follow up their advantage. Already they were making plans of their own.

The Japanese Regroup

Although the mid-November air and naval battles virtually assured an Allied victory on Guadalcanal, the Japanese were not yet ready to admit defeat. With a full recognition of the seriousness of their situation in the Solomons and New Guinea—which together they designated as the Southeast Area—the Japanese made preparations to recoup their losses and to repulse any further Allied offensives. Their first step was to establish on 18 November a more effective command in the area. The *17th Army*, which had hitherto been responsible for operations in the Solomons and New Guinea, was restricted by order of *Imperial General Headquarters* to the Solomons alone. At the same time a new headquarters, *18th Army*, was established for operations in New Guinea, with Lt. Gen. Hatazo Adachi, chief of staff of the *North China Area Army*, in command. In addition, the *8th Area Army*, a theater command comprising the two armies, was created, and Lt. Gen. Hitoshi Imamura, commander in Java, was ordered to Rabaul to take over the new post. These arrangements, which the

Navy paralleled by placing the *11th Air Fleet* and the *8th Fleet* under a *Southeast Area Fleet*, were to go into effect on 26 November.[1]

Orders from Tokyo to Imamura and to Admiral Yamamoto, commander of the *Combined Fleet* at Truk, made it clear that the high command was determined to maintain and reinforce the Japanese position in the Southeast Area. In the Solomons, both commanders were instructed to strengthen air bases and intensify air operations against Allied shipping and ground forces. At the same time they were to reinforce the troops on Guadalcanal who would meanwhile "secure key positions in preparation for offensive operations, while recovering their strength."[2] Once these measures had been completed, then the Army and Navy commanders would unite their forces in a joint offensive to retake Henderson Field, Tulagi, and other key positions in the Solomons.

The program *Imperial General Headquarters* laid out for its forces in New Guinea was as ambitious as its plans for the Solomons. Buna, which had not yet been taken by MacArthur, was to be strengthened, as were the bases at Lae and Salamaua. In addition, Japanese forces were to occupy Madang, Wewak, and other unspecified strategic areas in New Guinea. "Preparations for future operations . . . ," decreed the high command, "will embrace every possible plan

for the capture of Port Moresby. . . ."[3] (*Chart 6*)

To carry out these tasks, *Imperial General Headquarters* gave to Imamura strong ground and air reinforcements. The former included three divisions and as many brigades. Air reinforcements consisted of the *12th Air Brigade* and the *76th Squadron*, which, with air units already in the area, were placed under the newly established *6th Air Division* to provide support for both the *17th* and *18th Armies*. On activation late in November, the air division had fifty-four light bombers, eighty-four fighters, and some reconnaissance planes, but it did not begin active operations until a month later.

After a hasty journey by air from Tokyo via Truk, where he conferred with Admiral Yamamoto, General Imamura reached Rabaul on 22 November 1942, just a few days before Adachi, the *18th Army* commander, arrived from China. On the 26th, Imamura formally assumed command of the *8th Area Army*, established his headquarters, and issued his first directive governing operations of the two armies under him. Based on the *Imperial General Headquarters* order of 18 November, this directive required the *17th Army* to recapture Guadalcanal and the *18th*, in co-operation with naval forces, to hold and consolidate its position at Buna while preparing for future operations, presumably against Port Moresby. Operations in the Solomons were given first priority and for this purpose Imamura assigned his main strength to the Guadalcanal operation, which would begin about the middle of January. With these orders went a mes-

---

[1] This section is based on Japanese Opns in SWPA, 158–90, and the following monographs in the series, Japanese Studies in World War II: Southeast Area Air Opns, 1942–44, No. 38; *17 Army Opns*, vols. I and II, Nos. 39 and 40; *18th Army Opns I*, No. 41; Southeast Area Naval Opns, vol. I, No. 48; Southeast Area Opns, pt. IV (rev.); *8th Area Army*, No. 110. All in OCMH.

[2] *Imperial GHQ* Navy Directive 159, 18 Nov 42, OCMH.

[3] *Ibid.*

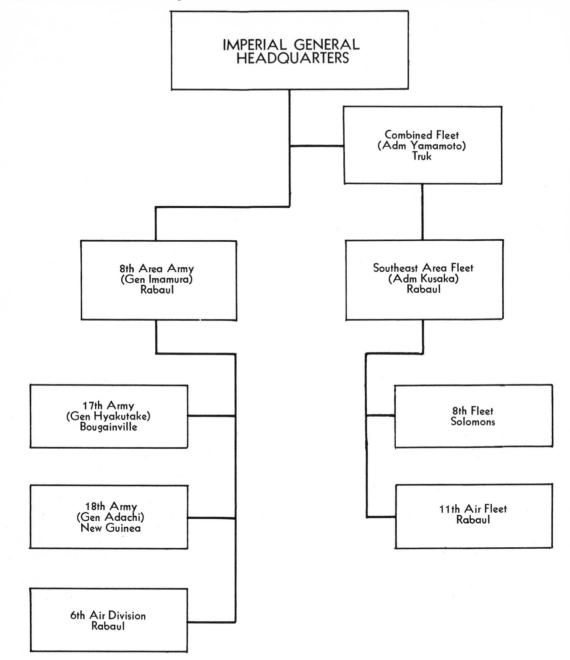

Source: Southeast Area Operations, pt. IV, Japanese Studies in World War II, 127, pp. 12–14; Imperial Japanese Navy Organization, Japanese Studies in World War II, 116.

sage of sympathy for those who had survived the "hard and painful battle" and an injunction to the officers and men, whose bravery was "enough to make even the gods weep," to "set His Majesty's heart at ease" by winning through to victory.[4]

These orders for offensive operations, issued at a time when Allied air and naval forces had gained control in the battle area and when Allied ground forces had seized the initiative and were pressing the Japanese on every side, proved entirely unrealistic. Buna fell early in January, after Adachi had ordered his troops to withdraw up the coast a short distance to Sanananda. On Guadalcanal, where the American Division commander, General Patch, had assumed control of operations on 9 December, the Americans were already making plans for a final offensive. The signs of a Japanese defeat were too clear to be ignored even by the optimistic planners in Toyko, and at the end of December, scarcely more than a month after it had ordered the offensive *Imperial General Headquarters* decided the time had come to withdraw Japanese forces from Guadalcanal and the Buna area.[5]

The Japanese decision, conveyed personally to Rabaul by one of the senior Army officers in *Imperial General Headquarters*, reached Imamura on 4 January. Immediately he made plans for the evacuation of those troops that could still be saved and during the next few weeks Japanese destroyers under cover of darkness brought out large numbers of men from Guadalcanal undetected. On 23

January MacArthur announced that the campaign for Papua was over, and on 9 February General Patch made a similar announcement for Guadalcanal. Thus ended the 6-month campaign to halt the Japanese drive toward Port Moresby and the South Pacific. The Allied line of communications to Australia and New Zealand was finally secure.

The decision to withdraw from Guadalcanal and Buna did not signify that the Japanese intended to abandon the Solomons and New Guinea. It emphasized rather their determination to retain their hold in the Southeast Area and was the prelude to a regrouping of forces and the strengthening of defenses. "Hereafter," read the 4 January order from *Imperial General Headquarters*, "the Bismarck Archipelago and the Solomons Islands north of New Georgia and Santa Isabel will be secured . . . , operational bases such as Lae, Salamaua, Madang and Wewak will be strengthened at once and strategic points north of the Owen Stanley Range in northeast New Guinea will be occupied and secured."[6]

Even before he received these instructions, General Imamura had begun to strengthen his position in the Southeast Area. His orders when he assumed command had called for such a program, and one of his first official acts had been to initiate plans for the occupation of Madang and Wewak. This task he had assigned to the *18th Army*, and General Adachi had occupied both places in mid-December with three infantry battalions recently arrived from the Netherlands Indies. Work on airstrips and roads began immediately. About the same time a special naval landing force moved

---

[4] Order is quoted in Southeast Area Opns, pt. IV, *8th Area Army*, p. 14.

[5] *Ibid.*, p. 17.

[6] *Ibid.*

GENERAL ADACHI   GENERAL HYAKUTAKE

into Finschhafen, off the tip of the Huon Peninsula, opposite New Britain.

The garrisons at Lae and Salamaua were reinforced early in January by the *Okabe Detachment*, a reinforced regiment of the *51st Division* stationed at Rabaul. It was Adachi's plan to bring the entire division to Lae, where he planned to establish his headquarters, and to put the *20th* and *41st Divisions* at Madang and Wewak, thus making both areas strong enough to meet the expected Allied attack. The plan went awry, however, thanks largely to the activity of Allied bombers. The convoy carrying the *51st Division* was attacked and almost destroyed by Kenney's Allied Air Forces in the Battle of the Bismarck Sea between 1 and 3 March, and the division virtually annihilated. Adachi

did succeed during January and February in putting ashore at Wewak the bulk of the *20th* and *41st Divisions*. But so effective was the Allied air blockade that the Japanese had to make their way by land and small boats to Madang where they sought to open up a land route to the base at Lae.

Japanese defenses in the Solomons were also considerably strengthened during this period. The airfield at Munda in New Georgia, originally intended as a base from which to support operations on Guadalcanal, was completed on 15 December, when work was begun on a new airstrip at Vila on nearby Kolombangara. Other bases further up the Solomons ladder, in the Shortlands, on Bougainville, and on Buka, were strengthened and additional

ADMIRAL YAMAMOTO

GENERAL IMAMURA

troops brought in to replace the decimated units evacuated from Guadalcanal. On Bougainville, where General Hyakutake had his *17th Army* headquarters, was the *6th Division*, and on New Britain was the *38th*, reorganized after its experience on Guadalcanal. The three infantry battalions in New Georgia and Santa Isabel, now the most forward Japanese positions in the Solomons and by agreement between Imamura and Yamamoto an area of naval responsibility, were reinforced in February and March with naval troops and in April with two infantry regiments.

In air power, which had been so critical a factor for both sides in the campaigns just ended, the Japanese had clearly lost the lead to the Allies. During the struggle for Guadalcanal alone

they had sacrificed about 900 naval planes, one-third of them carrier-based. At the end of February 1943, they had only 200 Navy and 100 Army combat aircraft of modern design, mostly Zero fighters and twin-engine land-based bombers. Three months later, after every plane that could be spared had been sent to the Southeast Area, the strength of the *6th Air Division* numbered 217 aircraft — 77 bombers, 114 fighters, and 26 reconnaissance planes.[7] With the Navy's *11th Air Fleet*, numbering about 200 operational planes, and with the 200 carrier-based planes of the *3d Fleet* at Truk, this total represented the peak strength in aircraft of the Japanese command in the Southeast Area in

[7] Southeast Area Opns, pt. IV, *8th Area Army*, p. 25.

the period before the Allies resumed the offensive.

Tasks Two and Three: The Indivisibility of Strategy and Command

American planning for operations against Rabaul began almost immediately after the last threat of a successful Japanese counterattack against Guadalcanal had ended. The spark was provided by General Marshall who, on 1 December, sent Admiral King for comment the draft of a directive for the theater commanders telling them to go ahead with Tasks Two and Three. Substantially the same as the Joint Chiefs' directive of 2 July 1942, which had inaugurated the Allied offensive, Marshall's draft specified that the forces required would come from those already assigned to the South and Southwest Pacific Areas, subject to the approval of the Joint Chiefs. Fully aware of Admiral King's concern for the mobility of the fleet, Marshall also reserved to the Joint Chiefs the right to withdraw naval units in the event of an emergency. Like the original plan, this new directive gave to MacArthur strategic direction of the campaign against Rabaul during Tasks Two and Three but specified that direct control of the naval and amphibious phases of the campaign would be exercised by a naval officer. MacArthur, thus, would have the authority to select the objectives, allocate the forces, and fix the timing and sequence of the operations.[8]

With this proposal, Marshall precipitated anew the long-standing debate over command in the Pacific, disguised at first as a discussion of strategy. The initial reaction of the naval planners to the draft directive was favorable, but Admiral King, who had for some time been pressing for a revision of the July 1942 directive, did not give his consent so readily. He had other ideas that he thought might make Tasks Two and Three unnecessary and give to the Navy control of the offensive against Rabaul. Why continue up the Solomons and assault the Japanese bastion frontally, he asked? On the basis of the Guadalcanal experience it would take years to reach Rabaul that way. Instead, why not outflank the Japanese by seizing the Admiralties, northwest of Rabaul, and bypass the Solomons altogether?[9]

Nimitz and Halsey showed no enthusiasm for this idea when King put it up to them. To the former the relative merits of a frontal versus a flanking assault against Rabaul seemed academic. In his view, Task One would not be finished until air and naval bases had been established on Guadalcanal and the area firmly secured. Moreover, it was impossible to start on Task Two until Washington made larger forces available. Those in the theater were not adequate to do the job. And when the offensive was resumed it should be directed by Halsey, not MacArthur, declared Admiral Nimitz, giving as his reason the fact that since operations in the Solomons would require most of the surface forces of the Pacific Fleet, command should be vested in a flag officer. "Any change of command of those forces which Halsey has welded into a working

---

[8] Memo, Marshall for King, 1 Dec 42, sub: Proposed Joint Directive . . . , OPD 381 (SWPA), case 83.

[9] Rads, King to Nimitz and Halsey, 1915, 30 Nov 42, cited in Hayes, The War Against Japan, ch. X, p. 32.

organization," he told King, "would be most unwise."[10]

These views Admiral Nimitz expanded in a letter to King a week later. In it he met his chief's posposal for a flanking operation against Rabaul by way of the Admiralties with the argument that the capture of the Japanese bastion would not give the Allies control of the Solomons. The enemy's bases there and in New Britain and New Ireland, he pointed out, were mutually supporting and there was no assurance that the seizure of Rabaul would reduce their effectiveness or induce the garrisons to surrender. Moreover, if the Japanese retained control of the straits and seas south and east of Rabaul, the Allies would only expose their flanks to attack if they bypassed the bases in that region. Thus, Nimitz concluded, the planners would have to accept a step-by-step frontal attack up the Solomons, with the next objective the Munda air base on New Georgia or Buin on the southeast coast of Bougainville. The choice would depend on the size of the force provided and the state of Japanese defenses. And again he urged that Halsey be given command of operations in the Solomons.[11]

In the South Pacific, both Admiral Halsey and General Harmon fully subscribed to the concept of a progressive step-by-step advance up the Solomons ladder as a prerequisite to the seizure of Rabaul. "To be able to attack the Bismarcks simultaneously from New Guinea and the Solomons," wrote Harmon, "would be ideal." But he did not believe that the South Pacific could do much to aid MacArthur's advance along the northeast coast of New Guinea. "To send surface forces into the western areas of the Solomons Sea with the Jap air as heavily entrenched as it is," he told Marshall, "would be taking a risk beyond the gain to be anticipated even with the best of fortune."[12]

It was primarily to meet the danger of Japanese air attack on Allied surface forces as well as to support naval operations in the Solomons that Admiral Halsey conceived the idea of seizing Woodlark Island between New Guinea and the Solomons as the site for an air base. That island, as well as the neighboring Trobriand group, lay outside the bad weather belt. Its possession would provide the Allies with a fighter and medium bomber base site within range of Rabaul as well as a staging point for aircraft midway between the South and Southwest Pacific. Since Woodlark lay in MacArthur's area, Halsey suggested to him in mid-December that it be seized, offering at the same time to furnish some of the troops required. Although MacArthur did not take up the suggestion then, Admiral King, who had received a copy of Halsey's message, apparently looked on the proposal with favor and asked Halsey to consider also the possibility of taking Kiriwina and other islands in the Trobriand group. There the matter rested for the time.[13]

Though he was willing to shelve Admiral Halsey's suggestion temporarily, King thought Nimitz' ideas important enough to pass on to Marshall and

[10] Rad, Nimitz to King and Halsey, 0235, 2 Dec 42, cited in Hayes, The War Against Japan, ch. X, p. 33.

[11] Ltr, Nimitz to King, 8 Dec 42, sub: Future Opns in Solomons, OPD Exec Files.

[12] Ltr, Harmon to Marshall, 25 Nov 42, copy in OCMH.

[13] Rads, Halsey to MacArthur and King, No. 0510, 17 Dec 42; King to Halsey, No. 2159, 18 Dec 42, cited in Hayes, The War Against Japan, ch. XI, p. 11.

Leahy. Only Marshall's comments are on record. The admiral, Marshall pointed out, had failed to include in his calculations the forces of the Southwest Pacific, whose air component would be "a most important factor in whatever plan is adopted." This failure, as well as the absence of information in the War Department on Navy and Marine aircraft, observed the Army Chief of Staff, constituted "the most compelling argument against the continuance of divided command for future operations in the Solomon Islands — Bismarck Archipelago."[14]

The arguments that Nimitz had presented in favor of a step-by-step advance up the Solomons under Halsey's command Marshall used to support a unified command under General MacArthur. The Japanese positions in the Solomons and New Guinea, he pointed out, resembled an inverted **V** with the point at Rabaul. Against each leg of the **V** the Allies had placed two strong but separate forces, one controlled from MacArthur's headquarters and the other from Nimitz', thousands of miles away, and each independent of the other. "Skillful strategic direction, coordinating the employment of the two strong Allied forces available," Marshall insisted, "appears mandatory to offset the Japanese advantages of position and direction." Only in this way could the Allies exploit quickly success against either leg of the **V** and at the same time use their forces, especially the bombers with their strategic mobility, where they were most needed and where

they could achieve the most decisive results.

With Nimitz' contention that Admiral Halsey's command in the South Pacific should not be disturbed, General Marshall agreed. He did not intend that it should. The plan he had in mind, he pointed out, would leave to Halsey the tactical control of his forces and would not affect the efficiency of his command. All that he wanted to do, Marshall told King, was to give MacArthur strategic control of Tasks Two and Three. Moreover, he reminded the Chief of Naval Operations, the projected operations against Rabaul would all take place in MacArthur's Southwest Pacific Area and should therefore be under the control of the area commander.

Admiral King, who had not yet replied to Marshall's initial proposal of 1 December, delayed two more weeks after receiving this new note. In the meantime the Army and Navy planners continued to discuss the matter in the hope of reaching a settlement acceptable to their chiefs. On 23 December, two days after they had received Marshall's memorandum, the Navy planners had the draft of a reply ready. They accepted the principle of unified command without argument but expressed doubts about the advisability of turning over to MacArthur the direction of operations in the Solomons at that time. To them, command was inseparable from control of the Pacific Fleet. The Navy, they argued, could not discharge its responsibilities unless the fleet commander was free to shift his forces from one area to another as the situation changed and in accordance with naval doctrine. What the naval planners feared was the improper employment of the fleet by an

---

[14] Memos, Marshall for King, 21 Dec 42, sub: Strategic Direction of Opns in SWPA; Comdr Victor D. Long to Marshall, Leahy, *et al*, 15 Dec 42, same sub, with copy of Nimitz' letter, OPD Exec Files.

Army commander or the loss of its mobility by assignment to a limited theater of operations, a point Marshall had made in connection with the employment of bombardment aviation. "If the Pacific Fleet is seriously weakened," they asserted, "the whole Pacific campaign will collapse. We must therefore be careful to insure that the Fleet is not so handled as to risk serious loss without commensurate damage to the enemy."[15]

Though the Navy planners opposed giving to MacArthur strategic direction of the campaign against Rabaul on the terms proposed by the Army, they were willing to do it if Nimitz was appointed the supreme commander for the entire Pacific theater. Nimitz, thus, would be MacArthur's superior and the guardian of the Navy's interests in the Pacific. It was an offer to trade, a *quid pro quo* arrangement by which the naval planners offered the Army command over operations against Rabaul in return for control of the Pacific, or, as they put it, for an arrangement that would guarantee "the strategic flexibility" of the Pacific Fleet.

The Army planners refused to trade on this basis. All that Marshall had proposed, commented General Handy, was a unified command for operations already projected in the Solomons and New Guinea. That question could be settled quickly by action of the Joint Chiefs of Staff. The larger problem of command for the entire Pacific had "political, international, and organizational implications" that would make a solution much more difficult. For this reason alone Handy urged that the Navy

accept Marshall's proposal, which would not only speed up operations against Rabaul but would constitute also "a positive step toward eventual unification."[16] Nor did Handy miss the opportunity to point out that the principle of strategic flexibility applied equally to the Air Forces and that ground troops, too, played a vital role in the Pacific war. "The Fleet," he observed tartly, "would be as helpless without air and land forces as the latter would be without the Fleet."

General Handy's appeal for quick action left the naval planners unmoved. Several times during the next week they prepared rebuttals to the Army argument and restatements of their own case, but never sent them. Finally, on 6 January, Admiral King took the matter into his own hands and made formal reply to General Marshall. Stressing, as his planners had, the vital role of the Pacific Fleet and Nimitz' broad responsibilities, Admiral King argued that it was impossible to divorce these from control of the immediate task at hand. "The nature of these Pacific tasks," he declared, "is so vital and so compelling I feel that they must be given precedence over lesser considerations that may be in conflict."[17]

Despite this strong stand, Admiral King showed more disposition to compromise than his planners. What he proposed was a continuation of the command established for Task One, with MacArthur and Halsey each directing operations in his own sphere while coordinating their efforts and supporting each other when required. Only when Rabaul itself became the objective would

[15] Draft Memo, King for Marshall, 23 Dec 42, sub: Strategic Direction of Opns in SWPA, OPD Exec Files.

[16] Memo, Handy for Capt Richard L. Conolly, USN, 24 Dec 42, no sub, OPD 384 (PTO) case 43.

[17] Ltr, King to Marshall, 6 Jan 43, OPD Exec Files.

a single command be required. At that time, King suggested, MacArthur could be given strategic direction of the operations against Rabaul, provided that, first, Nimitz' control was extended to include the waters of the Southwest Pacific, and second, that the naval forces involved remained under Nimitz' "general command" so that he could meet any sudden emergency. Though he thought it "psychologically undesirable," King suggested also that the boundary line between the South and Southwest Pacific might be moved to solve this troublesome problem of command.

General Marshall apparently thought as little of this last solution as did King and in his rejoinder made no mention of it. Following the line laid down by General Handy the Army Chief of Staff drew a sharp distinction between unified command for the Pacific theater and "the immediate and urgent problem of unified control" of current operations.[18] The first, he agreed, was desirable if not imperative but could hardly be attained by merely extending Nimitz' authority. The "international and organizational implications" Handy had referred to would first have to be carefully considered and the solution finally adopted "based fundamentally more upon the selection of the commander as an individual rather than upon his specific military or naval qualifications."

The second problem, that of establishing unified control for the operations against Rabaul, could not, in Marshall's opinion, be left for the future. The Guadalcanal campaign had demonstrated only too clearly the shortcomings of the existing arrangements. To continue

them, as King wanted to do, would be foolhardy. But he was willing to accept other features of the admiral's plan, so he suggested a compromise along the following lines:

1. That MacArthur exercise strategic control of the operations against Rabaul from the start.

2. That Halsey exercise direct command of the naval forces.

3. That Nimitz retain sufficient general control of the Pacific Fleet elements assigned to the operation so that he could withdraw them when necessary for use in another area.

4. That the Joint Chiefs themselves exercise control over the strategic movement of air forces.

This latest proposal by General Marshall did not differ in any essential respect from his first proposal made more than a month before. Clearly, General Marshall intended to stand firm and King must have recognized that further efforts to persuade him to accept the Navy view would be fruitless. He therefore dodged the issue by observing that until more was known about how Tasks Two and Three were to be carried out it would be impossible to reach a decision on command. MacArthur should be directed to get in touch with Nimitz and Halsey and then submit his detailed plans to Washington. "I will agree with your likely comment that I should have made the above point months ago," he observed wryly, "—however, I make it now." [19]

Marshall readily acceded to this request as he had to King's request the day before for MacArthur's views on the desirability of making the Admiralties

---

[18] Memo, Marshall for King, 8 Jan 43, sub: Strategic Direction of Opns in SWPA, OPD 384 (PTO) case 43.

[19] Ltr, King to Marshall, 8 Jan 43, OPD Exec Files.

rather than Rabaul the main objective.[20] MacArthur's reply, copies of which went to Nimitz and Halsey, presented virtually the same scheme of operations he and Ghormley had submitted the previous July, after their meeting in Melbourne. His plan then and now was to advance progressively in five successive phases under cover of land-based aircraft through the Solomons and up the northeast coast of New Guinea until his converging forces had isolated Rabaul. Only then would he make the final assault, which, he thought, would require long preparations and great resources "and might well prove to be the decisive action of the Pacific war." King's suggestion that naval action against the Admiralties be substituted for the assault against Rabaul he found unacceptable

because it would have to be undertaken without land-based air support.[21]

This reply was far from satisfactory. What Marshall and King wanted now were detailed plans based upon a complete exchange of views among the Pacific commanders, not a concept of operations. They therefore pressed MacArthur to get in touch with Nimitz and Halsey and submit something more concrete which the Joint Chiefs could use as the basis for a directive covering such matters as target dates, command, and logistics.[22] Before General MacArthur could meet this new request the Joint Chiefs and the President had already left for Casablanca in French Morocco to meet with the British.

---

[20] Rads, Marshall to MacArthur, Nos. 164 and 192, 7 and 8 Jan 43, CM–OUT 2273 and 2833.

[21] Rad, MacArthur to Marshall, 10 Jan 43, CM–IN 4574.
[22] Rad, Marshall for MacArthur, 11 Jan 43, CM–OUT 3664.

CHAPTER XVIII

The Pacific in Grand Strategy

A great country cannot wage a little war.

DUKE OF WELLINGTON

The victories that had given a new urgency to plans for the Pacific, together with the Soviet stand at Stalingrad and the landings in North Africa, signaled a radical alteration in the relative position of the Allies and the Axis. The days of crisis, of shortages in critical war materials were past; the initiative throughout the world was passing into Allied hands. New and important questions had to be answered. Where should the Allies strike next? How could they best use their advantage? How should they distribute their resources?

Almost everyone agreed that Germany was the main enemy and its defeat the key to victory, but that broad principle did not provide the answer to the problems ahead. It was neither a plan for victory nor a working basis for the many decisions that had to be made from day to day. Allied forces, engaged with the enemy in the Pacific and in the Mediterranean, were competing with each other for aircraft and munitions. The Soviet Union and China had to be supplied and the Middle East reinforced. And, most important of all, a decision had to be made on the cross-Channel invasion, deferred in July 1942 for the landings in North Africa. Despite the increase in Allied resources and trained troops during the past year, there was not enough for all theaters and for every purpose. It was time to take a new look at strategy and reach the decisions that would provide a guide for the future.

Strategic Concepts

Efforts to produce a long-range plan for victory as a realistic basis for the allocation of resources between Europe and the Pacific had been under way since mid-1942. The cancellation of SLEDGEHAMMER (the plan for an emergency operation in Europe in 1942), which had the effect of abandoning the principle of concentration in the British Isles in favor of the invasion of North Africa, combined with additional commitments to the Pacific to meet the Guadalcanal emergency, had virtually voided these early efforts. One of the more interesting of these, in the light of the cancellation of SLEDGEHAMMER, was the study made to determine what effect the collapse of Soviet resistance would have on Allied strategy. The conclusion, accepted by the Joint Chiefs, was that in such an event the United States would have to reverse its strategy and go on the defensive in Europe.[1] After the victory at Stalingrad this possibility became so remote that the subject retained only an academic interest.

The search for a strategic concept on which to base long-range plans continued throughout the fall of 1942. Finally, late in November, the problem was referred to the Joint Strategic Survey Committee, which, it will be recalled, consisted of three distinguished senior officers, one each from the Army, Navy, and Army Air Forces, whose function it was to advise the Joint Chiefs of Staff on matters relating to global strategy and national policy.[2] The solution of the elder statesmen of the joint committee, submitted on 11 December, was to make more flexible the "Beat Germany First" concept by specifying that though "maximum forces" would be employed for the offensive in Europe, the size of these forces would be limited by whatever "offensive-defensive operations" might be required in the Pacific and elsewhere. As the strategists viewed it, the primary effort was to be made against Germany, first by air bombardment and then by a co-ordinated large-scale invasion to be launched in 1943. Operations in the Pacific they limited to those required for the security of Australia, New Zealand, Hawaii, Alaska, and the line of communications.[3]

The response of the Joint Chiefs was, on the whole, favorable. Maj. Gen. George E. Stratemeyer, substituting for General Arnold, could find nothing to quarrel with in the committee's emphasis on the bomber offensive against Germany, and General Marshall heartily approved the goal of a 1943 cross-Channel assault. Admiral King accepted the emphasis on operations in Europe without question but objected to the role assigned the Pacific. The term "offensive-defensive," he pointed out, was subject to varying interpretations, and he proposed, in a clear reference to the British, that it be changed to "offensive" so that there would be no misunderstanding the intention of the United States to exert constant and steady pressure in the Pacific. Only in this way, he argued, could the Japanese be prevented from consolidating their position and the war in the Pacific brought to an early close. He thought, too, that the strategists had failed to give sufficient weight to the fact that stronger forces than those already allocated would be required in the Pacific during the coming year. A fixed percentage of the resources of the Allies, 25 or 30 percent, King suggested, should be set aside for the war in the Pacific.[4] Just how King arrived at these figures and how he expected them to be used in allocating Allied resources is impossible to determine. But they did serve to dramatize his plea for the Pacific war, and to set some limits to the priority of Europe and the Mediterranean.

Instructed by these views, the three members of the Joint Strategic Survey Committee retired for further study and discussion. Nine days later, on 20 December, they presented to the Joint Chiefs the fruit of their labors. The strategic concept outlined earlier re-

[1] JCS 85, 24 Aug 42, JUSSC Rpt, Strategic Policy of UN and U.S. on Collapse of Russia.

[2] See above, p. 230.

[3] JCS 167, 11 Dec 42, JSSC Rpt, Basic Strategic Concept for 1943. The revisions of this study described below are located in the same file.

[4] The JCS minutes of this meeting, 15 December, went to the JSSC and are not on file. This account is derived from Hayes, The War Against Japan, ch. X, pp. 19–21.

mained unchanged, except for the phrase "offensive-defensive" to which King had objected. In the new version it became "offensive and defensive."[5] The committee had also taken to heart King's animadversions on the Pacific and now stipulated that "until such time as major offensive operations can be undertaken against Japan, we must prevent her from consolidating and exploiting her conquests." Thus, the committee recommended that in the Pacific the United States conduct those "offensive and defensive operations necessary for the security of Alaska, Hawaii, New Zealand, Australia, and the line of communications, as well as those required to maintain the initiative in the Solomons and New Guinea and inflict heavy losses on the enemy.

The Joint Chiefs subjected this new statement to the same searching scrutiny it had given its predecessor. First it modified the committee's statement on the war in Europe by limiting the forces there to those "consistent with maintaining the accepted strategic concept in other theaters." Indicative, perhaps, of the changed role of the Pacific in global strategy is the fact that the term "strategic defensive," though it was applied to other areas, was not once used in connection with the Pacific. Instead, the Joint Chiefs accepted Admiral King's statement calling for offensive and defensive operations there and in Burma. In other theaters, not specific, operations would be limited to those required to maintain "the strategic defensive."[6] With these changes, the report of the

Joint Strategy Survey Committee was approved by the Joint Chiefs, who then passed it on to the British Chiefs of Staffs for comment.[7]

The British planners meanwhile had worked out their own ideas on strategy. Like the Americans, they favored the early defeat of Germany, but their conception was closer to the formula adopted at the ARCADIA meeting, and they gave to the war against Germany a priority on Allied resources much greater than that allowed by the Americans. In recognition of Germany's strength on the Continent they favored an intensive air campaign against the Nazis before invasion and thought that the main effort in 1943 ought to be devoted to operations in the Mediterranean. All Allied resources, except the minimum necessary to safeguard "interests in the East," should be devoted to this primary objective. .

Only after the defeat of Germany, the British contended, should the Allies turn to Japan. In support of this position they pointed to the logistical advantages of fighting in Europe as compared to the Pacific war and to the superiority of the Soviet Union over China as an ally. Nor did they fail to observe that once Germany was defeated the Soviet Union might well be persuaded to join the Allies in their war against Japan.[8]

Though they minimized the significance of the Pacific in global strategy, the British planners were not blind to their imperial obligations. Starting from the same premise as the Americans—

---

[5] JCS 167/1, 20 Dec 42, JSSC Rpt, Basic Strategic Concept for 1943.

[6] JCS Mtg, 22 Dec 42; draft of suggested changes in JCS 167/1, 22 Dec 42.

[7] CCS 135, 26 Dec 42, Basic Strategic Concept for 1943.

[8] Ltr, Dill to King, 7 Nov 42, with incl entitled, American-British Strategy. See also, Memo, Handy for Marshall, 8 Nov 42, same sub, ABC 381 (9–25–41), sec. 3.

that Allied bases and the line of communications in the Pacific must be made secure—they concluded that offensive action against Japan should be limited to those operations that would "contain the Japanese forces and so prevent her liquidating China or successfully attacking the Western Coast of America, Russia, India, Australia, or New Zealand." No mention was made of operations then in progress or projected in the Solomons and New Guinea.

Aware that their formula for the Pacific, first advanced in November, had been sharply though informally criticized by the Americans, the British planners had a modified version ready when the Joint Strategic Survey Committee's report reached them late in December. Still asserting that the Japanese were incapable of expanding their war effort significantly or becoming unbeatable, as Germany could if left alone, the British reiterated their preference for limited and containing actions against Japan. But they expressed this idea in more general terms and gave less emphasis to purely British interests in the hope, apparently, that their strategic concept would be acceptable to the Americans. Omitting their earlier references to the necessity for action to hold India, Australia, and New Zealand, they proposed instead that operations in the Pacific be on a limited scale, "sufficient only to contain the bulk of the Japanese forces in that area." [9] On the necessity of keeping China in the war and conducting operations in Burma to keep open the line of communications, there was no disagreement between the Allies, and the British included a statement to this effect in both versions of their study on strategy.

The reaction of the American strategists to this study and to the British comments on their own report was, so far as the Pacific was concerned, unfavorable.[10] The difference over Pacific strategy, they told the Joint Chiefs, was fundamental, and they recommended that the problem be studied anew. This recommendation the Joint Chiefs accepted after a discussion in which General Marshall again expressed his feelings about operations in the Mediterranean, and Admiral King urged once more that the Pacific be allotted a fixed percentage of the total resources of the Allies.[11]

With the Casablanca meeting only a week away, the American planners had little time to re-examine their own ideas and seek to reconcile them with those of the British. Two groups worked on the problem and both came to the same conclusion: that the British had underestimated the Japanese. There were other differences between the Allies, deriving mostly from the different emphasis given by each to operations in the Mediterranean and to the build-up of forces in England for the cross-Channel assault.[12] Before firm plans could be made, production schedules fixed, and Allied resources allocated for the coming year, the U.S. and British heads of state and their military advisers would have to

---

[9] CCS 135/2, 3 Jan 43, American-British Strategy in 1943. This paper, like the others in this series, deals primarily with the war against Germany and Italy.

[10] JCS 167/3, 5 Jan 43, JSSC Rpt, Basic Strategic Concept for 1943.

[11] Mins, JCS Mtg, 5 Jan 43. King claimed at this point that only 10 percent of Allied resources were being used against Japan; later he raised this to 15 percent.

[12] JCS 167/5, 10 Jan 43, Rpt of JSSC, Basic Strategic Concept for 1943; JPS 106, 7 Jan 43, same sub.

reconcile these basic differences and reach agreement on a long-range strategic plan for the defeat of the Axis in Europe and Asia. It was at the Casablanca Conference that the Allies sought to solve these momentous problems.

The Casablanca Conference

Second of the great wartime U.S.-British meetings that marked the most successful coalition in the history of modern warfare, the Casablanca Conference resolved only imperfectly the differences between the Allies and failed to produce the blueprint for victory the Americans had hoped for. In the ten days between 14 and 23 January, the political and military chiefs of both nations found themselves separated—as they had been a year earlier at the ARCADIA Conference in Washington—by national interest, outlook, and divergent strategic concepts. That they resolved these differences even imperfectly and agreed upon a common program was evidence of a mutual confidence and singleness of purpose that their enemies never achieved.

Pacific strategy occupied a subsidiary place in the discussions at Casablanca; the major problem was how to defeat Germany and where to strike after North Africa had been secured. Both sides were agreed on the goal but each wished to reach it by a different path. The Americans, led by General Marshall, argued strongly for the concentration of Allied air and ground forces on a cross-Channel invasion to defeat Germany at the earliest possible moment. Any diversion from this program Marshall likened to a suction pump siphoning away the resources needed for the main effort and delaying

the inevitable clash with the main body of the German Army.

The British, poorer than their allies in manpower, natural resources and productive capacity, were understandably less anxious to formulate a long-range strategy or to invade the Continent and take on the Wehrmacht. They wanted first to so weaken Germany that the struggle would not leave England in an exhausted state. By conducting offensives on the periphery of Fortress Europe and striking at the heart of Germany from the air, they hoped to make the final blow less costly and perhaps unnecessary. Thus, they argued for an extension of operations in the Mediterranean to knock Italy out of the war and to force Hitler to scatter his forces. From this basic difference with the Americans stemmed other differences and the varying emphasis each side placed on the problems before it.[13]

The solution reached was in large measure a victory for the Mediterranean cause, which the President had always found more attractive than did his military advisers. Sicily was to be the Allied objective in Europe in 1943. Meanwhile, preparations for the cross-Channel attack would continue. Ground forces and landing craft would be assembled in the United Kingdom during the next year and a combined staff formed to plan for the invasion. Until that time, Germany's industrial and economic system was to be progressively destroyed, and the morale

---

[13] The records of the conference are bound in a separate volume entitled Casablanca Conference: Papers and Minutes of Meetings. See also, Sherwood, *Roosevelt and Hopkins*, ch. 27; Churchill, *The Hinge of Fate*, pp. 674–96; Matloff, *Strategic Planning for Coalition Warfare, 1943–44*, UNITED STATES ARMY IN WORLD WAR II (Washington, 1959), ch. I.

of its people undermined "to a point where their capacity for armed resistance is fatally weakened," by a combined bomber offensive from the United Kingdom.[14]

It is in the context of the cross-Channel debate that the Casablanca discussions of Pacific strategy and the decisions reached there must be read. Unwilling to tie their hands in Europe by adopting a long-range strategic program for the defeat of Germany, the British were even more reluctant to commit themselves to a broad plan for the defeat of the secondary enemy, Japan. Until Germany was defeated the Allies should limit themselves in the Pacific, they argued, to the defense of a fixed line in front of those positions that must be held. To do otherwise, the British feared, might involve the Allies in a major effort against Japan and thus curtail or make impossible the concentration of forces against Germany. Such arguments, they knew, might well raise some doubt in the minds of the Americans about the intentions of the British to participate in the war against Japan once the war in Europe was over. It was to allay this suspicion that Churchill offered, "for the effect on the people of the United States," to enter into a treaty committing his government to turn all its resources and effort toward the defeat of Japan, "if and when Hitler breaks down." [15] The word of a great English

gentleman, the President assured him, was enough for the American people.

Though reassured about the future, the U.S. Chiefs of Staff could find little cause for present satisfaction. Certainly the Prime Minister's statement did not represent any change in the British view of Pacific strategy. That view the Americans could not accept. It would impose on the nation a passive role in a part of the world the American people considered peculiarly their own and in which national interest and tradition dictated a positive and active program. National pride and sentiment also colored the American view. Pearl Harbor, Bataan, Midway, and Guadalcanal were symbols that stirred the imagination, and the one great American hero to emerge thus far from the war was General MacArthur, whose name was inseparably linked with the Pacific. There were other more practical considerations that the Joint Chiefs had to weigh. The Pacific was an area of U.S. military responsibility where American forces were already engaged. To do as the British wanted might make the final effort more costly and stretch the war out indefinitely, a contingency that neither the American people nor their political and military leaders would accept.

There were strategic reasons, too, why the course proposed by the British was unacceptable. Japan was now on the defensive and sound strategy dictated continued offensives to keep the enemy off balance and retain the initiative. Constant pressure must be exerted on the Japanese to keep them from consolidating their hold over the territory so recently captured. Moreover, the U.S. Chiefs argued, there were already in the Pacific large air, naval, and ground

---

[14] CCS 166/1/D, 21 Jan 43, The Bomber Offensive from the U.S.; Mins, 65th CCS Mtg, 21 Jan 43. See also Wesley Frank Craven and James Lea Cate, eds., *Europe: Torch to Pointblank: August 1942 to December 1943*, vol II, "The Army Air Forces in World War II" (Chicago: University of Chicago Press, 1949), pp. 277–93.

[15] Mins, CCS Mtg, 18 Jan 43.

forces. To allow them to remain idle while the war raged on other fronts was unthinkable, a shameful waste of Allied resources and manpower. Nor did the Americans take as lightly as the British the possibility of Japanese attack. The enemy, in their view, was still capable of limited offensive action and, given the opportunity, could be expected to do his best to improve his position.

It was at the Casablanca Conference that the Americans first used the Pacific as a counterbalance to the Mediterranean. Both bore somewhat the same relationship to global strategy. The British considered the Pacific, the Americans the Mediterranean, as the theater that threatened to drain away from the area of primary interest the resources of both allies. General Marshall was well aware of this and deliberately linked the two when he warned the British that the threat of "another Bataan" in the Pacific "would necessitate the United States regretfully withdrawing from the commitments in the European theater." [16] In doing so he served notice on the British that proposals for further offensives in the Mediterranean would be met with similar proposals for the Pacific. Thus used, Pacific strategy became a lever by which the Americans could exert pressure on the British to bring them back to the cross-Channel assault.

The debate over the Pacific at Casablanca began at the very first meeting of the military chiefs. General Marshall led off with the suggestion, first advanced by Admiral King at meetings of the Joint Chiefs, that Allied resources be divided between Europe and the Pacific, on a fixed percentage basis, 30 percent

---

[16] Mins, CCS Mtg, 17 Jan 43.

going to the Pacific. No proposal could have been better calculated to bring out sharply the fundamental difference between the two sides. But the British shied away from the issue then, and at the next meeting sought to avoid it by asking for a review of the situation in the Pacific. This gave Admiral King an opportunity to explain American strategy in concrete terms and to present his own views. The operations in the Solomons and New Guinea, he reminded the British, were designed to protect Australia and its lines of communication. That task could not be considered complete until Rabaul, "the key to the situation," was taken. Where to go after that was a problem the U.S. Chiefs had not yet considered but King thought the Philippines rather than the Netherlands Indies should be the next objective. Of the three avenues of approach to the Islands—North, Central, and South Pacific—he favored the middle one by way of the Marshalls, Marianas, and Carolines.

This review—and preview—concluded, Admiral King returned to the issue Marshall had raised earlier. Only 15 percent of the resources of the Allies, King estimated, was going to the Pacific, barely enough to hold the present line. Another 15 percent would be required to continue the offensive. General Marshall, who took the floor next, gave point to King's remarks by describing the status of American forces in the Pacific. The only way to defeat the Japanese, he told the British, was to keep them off balance, force them to fight without pause or rest.

The British could no longer evade the issue, which by now had merged with the plan for an offensive in Burma to open the supply line to China. Rather than oppose directly the American proposals, however, the British Chiefs sought to limit them by stressing the difficulties and problems while expressing apprehension over the diversion of Allied resources. Their position on an offensive in Burma, which lay within their own theater, was no more encouraging and was conditioned as much by political as by military considerations. Not only did they fear that it would affect operations in Europe, despite King's assurance that the resources required would come from the 30 percent requested, but they were concerned also over the effect of a Burma offensive on the fate of India. Nor did they share the American view on the importance of China as an ally. So trying was this British lack of enthusiasm that Admiral King was moved to ask, somewhat unfairly, "on whom would fall the principal burden of defeating Japan once Germany had been knocked out." [17] Obviously, nothing was to be gained by continuing the discussion and the whole matter was turned over to the planners with instructions to report "what situation . . . we wish to establish in the Eastern Theater in 1943, and what forces will be necessary to establish that situation." [18]

The planners were no more able to agree than their chiefs, and though they did narrow down the area of disagreement, each side presented its own report. The Americans laid out an ambitious program, which, in addition to the operations in Burma, called for the capture

of Rabaul, followed by an advance across the Central Pacific as far as Truk and up the New Guinea coast to the border of the Dutch portion of the island. All this, as well as the capture of Kiska in the Aleutians, was to be accomplished in 1943.

The British planners played the role of critics, disposing of the American proposals. Guided by the rule that any project that might prejudice the defeat of Germany at the earliest possible moment was unacceptable, they reduced the American program to two offensives: the capture of Rabaul and limited operations in Burma. Hoping, perhaps, to soften their criticism, they suggested that later, if additional operations proved necessary or desirable, the Americans might submit detailed plans to the Combined Chiefs for a decision "as to the right course of action." [19]

This last statement, with its assumption that the Americans had to submit their plans for the Pacific to the British for approval, had an effect quite different from that intended. The Pacific theater was an area of American responsibility, as India-Burma was British, and by agreement was understood to be under the exclusive jurisdiction of the U.S. Joint Chiefs, subject to the Combined Chiefs (that is, the Americans acting with the British) only in matters of grand strategy and therefore not a matter for discussion with the British. In a sense, this argument was an evasion. The basic question was the division of resources between the Atlantic and Pacific theaters, and the British were certainly within their rights in objecting to operations

---

[17] Mins, CCS Mtg, 14 Jan 43. For a full account of the role of Burma in these discussions, see Romanus and Sunderland, *Stilwell's Mission to China*, pp. 269–74.
[18] Mins, CCS Mtg, 15 Jan 43.

[19] CCS 153, 17 Jan 43, Situation To Be Created in Eastern Theater; CCS 153/1 (British), same date and subject.

PLENARY SESSION AT CASABLANCA. *From left, standing: unidentified British officer, General Ismay, Lord Louis Mountbatten, General Deane, Field Marshal Dill, Air Chief Marshal Sir Charles Portal, Harry Hopkins. Seated, General Arnold, Admiral King, Prime Minister Churchill, President Roosevelt, General Sir Alan Brooke, Admiral of the Fleet Sir Dudley Pound, General Marshall.*

that would, in their judgment, divert resources from the main effort. By taking the position they did, the Americans reserved to themselves the right to decide what commitments they would undertake in the Pacific, and thereby limit the resources available for the war against Germany.

These sentiments, expressed at a separate meeting of the U.S. Chiefs on 18 January, did not make the discussions with the British which followed any easier. Opposed at every turn and reminded repeatedly that no offensive must be undertaken that would prejudice

the main effort against Germany, Admiral King finally asserted flatly that the Combined Chiefs' authority extended only to the broad issue of deciding on "the balance between the effort to be put against Germany and against Japan."[20] The U.S. Chiefs themselves would determine where and when to use their forces in the Pacific.

This was plain talk, and if the meeting was inconclusive it at least cleared the air and removed some misunderstanding. By the time the Combined Chiefs met

---

[20] Mins, CCS Mtg, 18 Jan 43.

with the President and Prime Minister in plenary session that evening, 18 January, the planners had worked out a tentative agreement, phrased in the most general terms, fixing Allied objectives in all theaters for 1943. Accepted by Roosevelt and Churchill, this agreement became the basis for the general plans developed for the Pacific theater in the remaining days of the conference.[21]

Strategy for 1943

In several important respects this broad statement of objectives was most disappointing. It contained no clue as to how Japan was to be defeated but merely stated that the object of operations in the Pacific and Far East would be to attain "a position of readiness"—left undefined—for the all-out offensive to come after Germany's downfall. Moreover, these operations—the capture of Rabaul, an offensive in the Marshall and Caroline Islands "if time and resources allow," and the capture of Burma—were to be undertaken only if, in the opinion of the Combined Chiefs, they did not "jeopardize the capacity of the United Nations to take advantage of any favorable opportunity that may present itself for the decisive defeat of Germany in 1943." The Americans could not quarrel with this restriction but might very well disagree with the British on what constituted a "favorable opportunity."

The general terms in which the agreement was couched made it subject to different interpretations and promised to lead to disagreements in the future. "Adequate forces" were to be provided but no word was said about what they

would consist of, who would furnish them, and at what time. And still unresolved was the problem of dividing Allied resources between the two major theaters which Marshall and King had raised at the start of the conference.

But the Americans had to be satisfied with what they could get and on 22 January presented their plans for the Pacific together with a very general statement of how they expected to defeat Japan.[22] This last they hoped to accomplish by blockade, bombardment, and assault by sea—"measures which greatly resemble those which would be effective against the British Isles." But assault from the sea, that is, the invasion of the Japanese home islands, was a contingency the Americans hoped might ultimately prove unnecessary. And it was too early to make plans for this contingency in any event.

It was the second of these measures, air bombardment, that appealed most to the Joint Chiefs as a guide to planning in the immediate future. The problem as they saw it was to secure bases within reach of the enemy and their plans for 1943 were designed with that end in view—"to work toward positions from which land-based air can attack Japan." Just what these positions were they did not yet know. Admiral King spoke of the Philippines; General Arnold of China and the B–29's still in production. Nor would they know until they had settled on a long-range plan for the defeat of Japan.

---

[21] CCS 155/1, 19 Jan 43, Conduct of the War in 1943; Mins, CCS Mtg, same date.

[22] CCS 168, 22 Jan 43, Conduct of the War in the Pacific Theater in 1943. No approval was requested of the British; the CCS merely "took notice" of the paper and included it in the report submitted next day to the President and Prime Minister. Mins, CCS Mtg, Mtg, 22 Jan 43; CCS 170/1, 23 Jan 43. Rpt to President and Prime Minister.

Lacking such a long-range plan and ultimate objectives, the Joint Chiefs could not afford to overlook any possibilities or ignore any route of advance. Moreover, their forces in the theater were not concentrated but divided among the several areas and under separate command. None could be permitted to remain idle. With all this in mind and after a comprehensive review of Japanese capabilities, the Joint Chiefs decided on three separate offensives for 1943: in the North Pacific to move into the Aleutians, in the South and Southwest Pacific to capture Rabaul, and in the Central Pacific to gain the line Truk-Guam. But under the restrictions imposed by the Combined Chiefs, the advance in the Central Pacific was made subject to the requirements for Burma and contingent on the release of forces after the Rabaul offensive. Everyone assumed, despite the experience of Guadalcanal and the pessimistic estimates of MacArthur and Nimitz, that Rabaul would be captured by May of 1943.

Precise as this plan was about objectives, it was pointedly silent on several important matters. There was in it no mention of the dates on which these operations would occur or their sequence; nor did it contain any estimates of the forces that would be required. These omissions were deliberate. To have submitted this information to the British would have been a tacit admission of their right to participate in the detailed planning for an area of U.S. responsibility and opened up the possibility of prolonged debate. Such matters were for the Joint Chiefs to decide and would be settled in American councils.

Though the effect of this move was to shut the British out of any voice in the allocation of resources to the Pacific, they accepted the American plan without recorded dissent. Next day, 23 January, both sides presented this plan together with the plan for operations in Europe, to the President and Prime Minister. The heads of state accepted the two plans almost without question and the conference came to an official close. The military chiefs on both sides could take considerable satisfaction in their accomplishments, and in Churchill's extravagant praise of their work, unsurpassed in its "professional examination of the whole scene of the world in its military, its armament production and its economic aspects." [23] They had, at least, compromised their differences and produced a program for the next twelve months. But this agreement was an illusion, achieved by semantic means and by an overcommitment in Burma, in the Pacific, and in Europe. The differences remained, hidden behind a cloak of generalities. The very first test would tear it apart and reveal the failures of Casablanca.

---

[23] Quoted in Sherwood, *Roosevelt and Hopkins*, p. 684.

CHAPTER XIX

Means and Ends: The March 1943 Directive

When two people ride the same horse, one must sit behind.

ANONYMOUS

Hardly had the U.S. Chiefs of Staff returned to Washington than the united front they had presented to the British at Casablanca fell apart. The family quarrels they had put aside for the visit they resumed in the privacy of their own chambers, picking up the dispute over command and strategy where they had left it some weeks before. But now the problem was complicated by agreements made with the British at Casablanca and by new and unexpected demands from the Pacific. Spurred on by the necessity of maintaining the offensive against Japan, the Joint Chiefs finally reached agreement on the course to follow, but it fell far short of the goal set at Casablanca and was, like almost all other arrangements made for the Pacific, a compromise that neither side accepted as final.

Theater Plans

Before leaving for Casablanca, Marshall and King had agreed to suspend their discussion of command for Tasks Two and Three pending the receipt of detailed plans from MacArthur. These plans, they had told him, were to be co-ordinated with Admirals Nimitz and Halsey, by personal conference if possible, or, failing that, by staff conversations. MacArthur's plan, when it came, proved to be virtually a restatement of earlier proposals and a request for many more men and planes. Nor had he discussed these proposals with Nimitz and Halsey, as the Joint Chiefs had requested, but instead had sent copies to each. On the basis of their replies—which he had not yet received—he and the two naval commanders, he explained, would make their decision. Staff officers could then arrange the details. "Meanwhile," he told Marshall, "I am continuing with the development of detailed plans." [1]

MacArthur's proposals hardly provided the basis for decision in Washington. To Admiral King they seemed to constitute more a concept than a plan and gave no concrete idea of what MacArthur intended to do, "how he expects to do it or what the command set-up is to be." If the Joint Chiefs could not get this information King recommended they ask Nimitz and Halsey to furnish their own plans for the Solomons. The Joint Chiefs themselves could then co-ordinate

---

[1] Rad, MacArthur to Marshall, 27 Jan 43, CM–IN 12553.

these plans with those MacArthur made for New Guinea.[2]

Admiral King's dissatisfaction with the lack of co-ordination in the Pacific was further increased when MacArthur failed to respond to a request from the South Pacific for air reinforcements early in February. Mistaking increased air activity and a concentration of Japanese vessels formed to evacuate troops from Guadalcanal as the prelude to another attack, Admiral Halsey asked MacArthur for the loan of some heavy bombers to meet the emergency, while initiating action from Washington toward the same end. MacArthur, concerned with the security of his own area, refused the request but promised to give what aid he could by support missions if Halsey would give him more information. "I am in complete ignorance of what you contemplate," he told Admiral Halsey, adding that until he had such knowledge he could not justify the diversion of his air forces or the dislocation of his plans. "Moreover," he concluded, "effective support can only be given if sufficient information is available to me to permit coordination."[3] Despite intercession from Washington, Halsey did not receive any bombers from MacArthur and the matter was dropped when the Japanese threat failed to materialize.[4]

Although this incident seemed to confirm the worst fears of those in Washington who were concerned over the lack of co-ordination in the Pacific, it hardly disturbed the cordial relations between MacArthur and Halsey. Both had by now virtually completed their plans and were ready to arrange the final details. Halsey's next operation, the occupation of the Russell Islands between Guadalcanal and New Georgia, was scheduled for 21 February, and the forces assigned for the invasion were already assembling at Guadalcanal. Authorized by Admiral Nimitz on 29 January, the Russells operation was really an extension of Task One and designed to gain an advance base for later operations against New Georgia. The 43d Division, with attached Marine troops, would make the landing and construction troops would follow closely to put in the air and naval facilities. No support was requested from General MacArthur and none was needed, for the Japanese had abandoned the island and the operation was concluded without bloodshed.[5]

Even before the seizure of the Russells, Halsey had apparently decided upon New Georgia as his next objective. Nimitz had suggested earlier the possibility of bypassing New Georgia and going directly to Bougainville, but this was clearly out of the question now. Japanese preparations to defend New Georgia and the construction of airfields there, fully reported by the coast watchers, and by air reconnaissance, made its capture an essential step in the advance on Rabaul. On this assumption Halsey's staff had drawn up plans for the seizure of New Georgia, with the tentative target date of 1 April.

It was these plans that Rear Adm. Theodore S. Wilkinson, Halsey's deputy, carried to Brisbane on 11 February.

---

[2] Memo, King for Marshall, 6 Feb 43, sub: Opns in SWPA for Prosecution of Rabaul Campaign, OPD 381 (PTO) sec. 3; Draft Memo (not sent), Marshall for King, 13 Feb 43, same sub, OPD Exec Files.

[3] Paraphrase of Msg in Rad, MacArthur to Marshall, 9 Feb 43, CM–IN 4996.

[4] For material on the Washington side, see the WDCSA 452.1 (SPA) file and messages.

[5] Miller, *Guadalcanal: The First Offensive*, pp. 351–56.

Rather than reply to MacArthur's proposals by radio, the South Pacific commander had chosen this means to co-ordinate his plans with those of the Southwest Pacific. Agreement was reached almost immediately, for that same day MacArthur reported to General Marshall that co-ordination had been arranged and that he and Halsey, according to Wilkinson, were in complete agreement on the execution of Tasks Two and Three.[6]

By this time MacArthur had virtually completed the detailed plan so persistently requested by the Joint Chiefs. Dated 12 February and called ELKTON I to distinguish it from the revised versions that followed, this plan was basically the same as the earlier TULSA and the one submitted with Ghormley in July of the previous year. As before, the offensive against Rabaul was divided into five stages with the forces in the Solomons and New Guinea converging on the final objective. Each stage represented a separate operation or series of operations designed to gain a strategic position for further advances under cover of fighter aircraft. In the first, MacArthur's forces would take Lae by a combined airborne, ground, and amphibious assault, then Finschhafen and other bases in the Huon Gulf–Vitiaz Strait area, and, finally, Madang, to seal off the waters north of the strait. The South Pacific Force was to follow up with the capture of New Georgia and then, simultaneously with the Southwest Pacific assault on New Britain, would move into Bougainville. The seizure of Kavieng, the fourth step in the plan, would isolate Rabaul and pave the

way for the final stage, a combined effort by both theaters against Rabaul.[7]

ELKTON provided no dates. In MacArthur's view it would be unrealistic to put them in until he knew what forces he would have. The South Pacific, he contended, had sufficient strength to carry out its part of the plan, but he could not even undertake the campaign against Lae without reinforcements. Four of his six divisions—three were Australian—were worn out by the recent campaign in Papua, his naval forces were weak, and his air strength was far below the minimum required for the offensive. To put ELKTON into effect he would need, he estimated, 1,800 more planes, five divisions, and more cruisers, destroyers, and PT boats.

In view of the Joint Chiefs' desire to conduct the offensive with forces already allocated to the Pacific and their assumption that Rabaul would be taken in 1943, it was, perhaps, well that MacArthur decided to send his chief of staff, General Sutherland, and other members of his staff to Washington with the plan to explain it. These officers, he told Marshall, could leave at the end of February and on the return journey stop off at Pearl Harbor and Noumea to see Nimitz and Halsey. From this suggestion grew the idea of a full-scale conference in Washington. On 16 February invitations went out to the Pacific commanders. Each was asked to send representatives to the conference and each agreed. By early March a high-ranking

---

[6] Rad, MacArthur to Marshall, 11 Feb 43, CM–IN 5610.

[7] ELKTON I, 12 Feb 43, Photostat in OCMH; GHQ SPWA, Studies in the History of SWPA, (4 vols), II, New Guinea and Bismarck Campaign, 29–32, Hist Sec, G–3; John Miller, jr., *CARTWHEEL: The Reduction of Rabaul*, UNITED STATES ARMY IN WORLD WAR II (Washington, 1959), ch. II.

group including Sutherland, Kenney, Harmon, Emmons, Spruance, and Twining, was on its way.[8]

Before the delegates could assemble to settle Pacific affairs, Admiral King made one more last effort to gain for the Navy control of operations in the Solomons. This time he sought to accomplish his purpose by "modifying" the boundaries between the South and Southwest Pacific so as to place Bougainville and the New Georgia Group in Halsey's area. Such a modification, he assured Marshall, would "clarify the military situation." The Army Chief of Staff refused even to consider the proposal, responding briefly that it was not advisable to change the boundaries "in this critical area prior to the conference." [9] At this point King left for the west coast to meet Admiral Nimitz but was back before the conference began.

The Pacific Military Conference

The Pacific Military Conference opened on 12 March with an imposing array of admirals and generals in attendance. Admiral King led off with a brief summary of the Casablanca decisions, followed by General McNarney, acting for Marshall. The remainder of the session was devoted to a reading of MacArthur's long-awaited plan, now revised and bearing the title of ELKTON II. The concept and scheme of maneuver were unchanged, but the number of forces required had been raised since the original plan had been completed. Now MacArthur would require for himself and Halsey—he assumed the two tasks would be under his control—a total of twenty-two and two-thirds divisions, forty-five air groups, and whatever warships the Joint Chiefs could furnish. He did not specify the cargo ships, troop transports, landing craft, supplies, and replacements that he would need, but there was no doubt that they would reach imposing proportions. All this was to be supplied in advance of the first step.[10]

The Washington planners were completely unprepared for such large demands. Though a secondary theater in their view, the Pacific had larger American forces than any other theater of operations. Army strength alone, exclusive of Alaska, amounted to 374,000 men as compared to 298,000 in the Mediterranean and 107,000 in the United Kingdom. But this proportion was expected to change rapidly in the course of the year as operations in Europe expanded. Even without close study it was evident to those who heard General Sutherland read MacArthur's requirements for the capture of Rabaul that some serious adjustments would have to be made in their plans or his. It is little wonder, then, that Admiral Cooke, who presided over the conference, adjourned the meeting until the next day to give the plan-

[8] Rads, MacArthur to Marshall, 15 Feb 43, CM–IN 7418; Marshall to MacArthur to Emmons for Nimitz; Marshall to Harmon for Halsey, 16 Feb 43, CM–OUT 5656–60. Also included in the delegation were Brig. Gen. Stephen J. Chamberlin, G–3, GHQ SWPA; Brig. Gen. Dewitt Peck (USMC) and Capt. Miles R. Browning (USN), Halsey's war plans officer and chief of staff; and Capt. Forrest P. Sherman (USN) of Nimitz' staff. General Wedemeyer, who had been to Casablanca and was en route from China to Brisbane to explain the Casablanca decisions to MacArthur, accompanied the group.

[9] Memos, King for Marshall, 18 Feb 43, sub: Development of Opns in South-Southwest Pacific; Marshall for King, 19 Feb 43, same sub, OPD 381 (PTO) sec. 3.

[10] ELKTON II, 28 Feb 43, ABC 370.26 (6–8–42), sec. 2. The minutes of the conference are separately bound and located in section 4 of the same file.

ners time to recover and to make some rapid calculations.[11]

Next morning the Army planners had their figures ready. MacArthur, they had found, was scheduled to receive during the coming year only 2 more divisions (which would give him a total of 17) and enough additional aircraft to bring his strength up to 18 groups or 982 planes. Exclusive of Halsey's requirement, this was about half of what he wanted. Actually, these figures were somewhat misleading as to the strength of the Southwest Pacific. Of the total number of aircraft only 144 would be heavy bombers, the only planes capable then of striking Rabaul and targets in the northern Solomons. The count of divisions was also misleading, for it included 11 Australian divisions only 3 of which were trained and equipped for offensive operations. In any case and regardless of these deficiencies, MacArthur would be short at the end of the year, under existing plans, three and two-thirds divisions and 15 air groups.[12]

The prospects for the South Pacific were no better. It would get only 1 more division in 1943. With the 1 New Zealand, 2 Marine and 4 Army divisions already in the theater, Halsey would have a total of 8, 2 less than the number called for in ELKTON. And instead of the recommended 15 air groups, he would have only 6, including 72 heavy bombers. With the reduction in fighter strength envisaged by the War Department, there would be fewer Army air-

craft in the South Pacific at the end of the year than there were at the time of the conference. The difference, then, between MacArthur's requirements for the capture of Rabaul and what the War Department was ready to give him and Halsey amounted to a total of five and two-thirds divisions and 24 air groups.

Actually these differences were not as great as they seemed. Both MacArthur and Halsey had other forces than those allocated by the War Department. Of the 1,000 aircraft MacArthur had in March, only 750 were American, the rest were Australian. And John Curtin, the Australian Prime Minister, was pressing for more on his own account. The figures for the South Pacific are much more revealing. There the Army had only about 700 planes and no intention of sending many more during the year. But when the number of Navy and Marine land-based aircraft to be sent was added, the total would amount to almost 1,800. Despite these adjustments, there would still be a shortage of heavy bombers in both areas, and neither the Army nor the Navy could provide the forces needed for all five stages of ELKTON at the start of the offensive.[13]

With the presentation of both sets of figures—those in ELKTON and those in the Washington schedules—the task of the conference became clear: provide MacArthur the forces he required, persuade him to lower his estimates, or cancel the decision to take Rabaul in 1943 and substitute a less ambitious program.

---

[11] Mins, 2d Mtg, Pacific Mil Conf, 12 Mar 43. Strength figures are from Matloff, *Strategic Planning for Coalition Warfare, 1943–44*, p. 92.

[12] Memo, Handy for Pacific Conferees, 13 Mar 43, sub: Deployment of Forces, OPD Exec Files; Mins, 3d Mtg, Pacific Mil Conf, 13 Mar 43.

[13] For estimates of Navy and Marine aircraft, see Memo, Cooke for Pacific Conferees, 13 Mar 43, sub: Availability of Navy Forces, Incl. to Mins, 4th Mtg, Pacific Mil Conf, 15 Mar 43.

For two days the alternatives were debated. The Pacific delegates, Army and Navy alike, insisted that ELKTON represented the absolute minimum required to accomplish Tasks Two and Three and that all of the forces requested would have to be made available before the campaign could begin. Admitting that they could seize their initial objectives with what they had—or, in the case of the Southwest Pacific, with what they would have by September—the theater planners maintained that it would be unwise to do so without the means to follow up. To do otherwise, declared General Harmon, would create a "very delicate situation." Speaking for the South Pacific delegation, he joined with Sutherland in asserting "that the estimate of forces required as shown in the ELKTON plan cannot be reduced."[14]

The Washington planners, though they could see no way of meeting the ELKTON requirements, were not nearly as united as the theater representatives. There was no disagreement about ground forces; the shortages could be met from reserves in the United States. The problem was to find the ships to transport the additional troops and to keep them supplied once they reached their destination. Shipping affected also the number of aircraft that could be sent to the Pacific, but the real disagreement arose over the interpretation of the Casablanca decision and its application to the Pacific. The

position taken by the Air Forces representative, Brig. Gen. Orvil A. Anderson, was that the combined bomber offensive against Germany had been given the highest priority at Casablanca and that, therefore, the requirements for Europe would have to be filled first. The Pacific commanders would have to be satisfied with what was left. Admiral Cooke, the chief naval planner, challenged this interpretation sharply. The Casablanca agreement, he pointed out, called also for the capture of Rabaul and for "adequate forces" to maintain the offensive against Japan. Germany, he admitted, was the main enemy and its defeat was the first aim of the Allies. But requirements elsewhere had to be met and it was the job of the planners to allocate their resources—notably shipping and aircraft—in such a way as to carry out all the tasks agreed upon at Casablanca unless it could be clearly established that they would jeopardize the capacity of the Allies to seize any unexpected opportunity to defeat Germany in 1943.

The exchange that followed is one of the few debates recorded fully in the record. While the Pacific representatives sat by silently and General Wedemeyer sought vainly to steer the proceeding into calmer waters, Admiral Cooke proceeded, in a series of pointed questions directed at Anderson, to challenge the Air Forces allocations to Europe and to demonstrate that it was not meeting its obligations in the Pacific. What was the purpose of the combined bomber offensive, he asked? Were the results "an effective contribution to the war effort?" How many planes did the Air Forces estimate would be needed for the bombings? Had the requirements of the of the South and Southwest Pacific been

---

[14] Memo, Sutherland and Harmon for Joint Planners, 14 Mar 43, no sub, ann. A to Mins, 4th Mtg, Pac Mil Conf, 15 Mar 43. The South Pacific planners also took into account naval and Marine forces, but they still needed twenty-four heavy bombers and additional fighters, half of which, they said, should be P–38's.

considered when these estimates were made? Did the Air Forces base its allocations to the Pacific on what was left after European allotments had been made? Or did it believe that the air offensive could be increased if it gave less planes to the Pacific? How many planes were needed in Europe, in the Pacific?

Several of these questions Anderson answered by simply citing the Casablanca decision calling for "the heaviest possible bomber offensive against the German war effort." Several went unanswered. But throughout General Anderson maintained that it was not his job to make estimates or to deploy aircraft. The first was the responsibility of the theater commanders, the second of the Joint Chiefs of Staff. All he was concerned with was availability, and he had given the Pacific what was available "after aircraft had been otherwise allotted" on the basis of the Air Forces' interpretation of the Casablanca decision.[15]

With this exchange the Navy placed itself squarely on the side of the Pacific delegates, an alliance that illustrates nicely that curious contradiction in the relationship between the services. When the needs of the Pacific were balanced against those of Europe and North Africa the Army and Navy commanders in the Pacific, supported by King and the naval planners in Washington, stood together in a formidable alliance. But when the time came to decide on the use of the forces in the Pacific and the role to be assigned to the Army and Navy, the alliance fell apart. Interestingly enough, Generals Harmon and Kenney, both senior air officers and longtime associates of General Arnold

(Harmon had been his chief of staff), also found themselves aligned with the Navy. General Wedemeyer's position was in between. He recognized the priority of operations against Germany, but he also appreciated the necessity for providing the forces required to meet commitments in the Pacific. "The position of the War Department representatives," he told Marshall, "has been rather difficult. . . ." The theater delegates, he added tartly, were determined to get all they could and the Navy, "for obvious reasons," was lending its support.[16]

Although the conferees had failed thus far to reach agreement they had at least succeeded in defining the areas of disagreement. There was no recourse now but to place the problem before the Joint Chiefs and this Cooke and Wedemeyer did on 16 March. There was enough shipping, they told their superiors, to warrant an increase in the scheduled allocations to the Pacific, but not enough to meet the ELKTON requirements. The Joint Chiefs themselves would have to decide just how much could be spared without jeopardizing the effort in Europe. Neither Wedemeyer nor Cooke believed that Rabaul could be taken in 1943 unless the forces requested by MacArthur were furnished, and they recommended therefore that the objectives of the South and Southwest Pacific for the year be fixed in terms of what could be achieved with the forces available rather than in terms of the Casablanca agreement.[17]

The Joint Chiefs had no sooner begun

---

[15] Mins, 4th Mtg, Pacific Mil Conf, 15 Mar 43.

[16] Memo, Wedemeyer for Marshall, 16 Mar 43, sub: Conf on Opns in Pacific, ABC 370.26 (7–28–42) sec. 4.

[17] Memo, Cooke and Wedemeyer for JCS, 16 Mar 43, sub: Plan for Opns for Solomons–New Guinea–New Ireland Area, JCS 238.

to consider the problem when they too were faced with the necessity of interpreting and applying the decisions made at Casablanca. And they succeeded no better. Admiral King took the same position as Cooke—too literal an interpretation of the European provisions of the Casablanca agreement would leave nothing for any other theater and make impossible the operations envisaged in the Pacific and Far East. Marshall's approach was based not on principle but on practical considerations. First, he said, the Joint Chiefs should find out what forces were in the theater and how they could be used. When this was done they would then be able to determine what other forces would be needed. Stratemeyer, acting for General Arnold, insisted that any reduction of the bomber offensive was contrary to the Casablanca agreement. The Pacific delegates, he thought, should be told what they could have and make their plans on that basis. Admiral Leahy's view was broader and he refused, like King, to consider the bomber offensive except in relation to operations elsewhere. American forces and interests in other areas, he observed, must be considered equally. Thus, no matter how they approached the problem, the Joint Chiefs always came back to the same question: What was the intent of the Casablanca agreement? Unable to answer it they directed the planners to investigate further the possibility of sending more to the Pacific than was then allotted and to come up with concrete proposals on how this could be done.[18]

After discussion with the theater representatives, who by now were showing some disposition to modify their requirements, the Joint Staff Planners found that the shipping available by October would indeed permit an increase in the forces sent to the Pacific. But they were still far from agreement on what these forces should consist of, so they submitted two plans. The first, which reflected the Army's concentration on the war against Germany, provided for the shipment of two divisions to the Southwest Pacific and one to the South Pacific and a "modest increase" in air units to both areas. A variant of the plan, based on Harmon and Kenney's willingness to do with fewer service units, provided for 25 percent more planes. The second plan, which embodied the Navy's view, used the shipping space allotted to the South Pacific division for additional aircraft for both theaters. Since neither would provide the forces MacArthur estimated would be required to take Rabaul, the planners joined in recommending that his instructions be changed.[19]

The choice was now up to the Joint Chiefs. The Army's preference for the first plan was clear. That plan was consistent with the Casablanca agreement to make the major effort against Germany and at the same time furnish "adequate forces" to the Pacific. True, these forces were not adequate to capture Rabaul, but they would suffice to retain the initiative. Adoption of the second plan, the Army planners pointed out, would result in "an unwarranted weakening of the bomber offensive against Germany without producing the compensating advantage of taking Rabaul." [20] This last point

---

[18] Mins, JCS Mtg, 16 Mar 43.

[19] JCS 238/1, 18 Mar 43, Plan for Opns for Solomons–New Guinea–New Ireland Area.
[20] Ibid.

was disputed by the naval planners who doubted that the diversion of aircraft from Europe would be large enough to affect seriously the strategy adopted at Casablanca. It was the preference of the representatives from the Pacific that finally prevailed. If it came to a choice between aircraft and ground troops there was no doubt which they would take. And it was on this basis that the Joint Chiefs, except for General Stratemeyer, voted for the second plan. "The conference," observed an unidentified naval officer, "was satisfactory from the Navy viewpoint." [21]

The acceptance of the Navy's plan by the Joint Chiefs brought the theater delegates much closer to their goal. What it meant in concrete terms was two more divisions, additional heavy bombers, plus six and one-half Army air groups. This was far less than the ELKTON plan called for but more than the Air Forces had been willing to grant initially. With what they already had and the Navy's allotments to the South Pacific, Mac-Arthur and Halsey together would have 2,500 planes, of which 240 would be heavy bombers. [22]

The decision of the Joint Chiefs had settled the question of forces, or means, for the South and Southwest Pacific. Still to be decided were the objectives, or ends, to be achieved in 1943 with these means. Before making that decision the Joint Chiefs solicited the views

of the theater delegates, with the understanding that the Pacific commanders themselves would not be committed thereby. [23]

As always throughout the conference, the officers from the Pacific, regardless of service or area, displayed an astonishing unanimity. With the three chiefs of staff, Sutherland, Spruance, and Capt. Miles R. Browning, as their spokesmen they agreed that, with the forces allotted, only Task Two could be carried out in 1943. The completion of that task, which corresponded roughly to the first three stages of ELKTON, would place MacArthur's forces at Cape Gloucester in New Britain and Halsey's in Bougainville.

But there were significant differences between this limited plan and ELKTON. The seizure of New Georgia, which everyone at the conference knew was already scheduled as the next move by South Pacific forces, was conspicuously absent from the new plan. Instead the plan now called for the occupation by the Southwest Pacific of Woodlark and Kiriwina, a move Admiral Halsey had suggested some months earlier and which had been incorporated in the first draft of ELKTON but not in the version presented to the conference. [24]

The Joint Chiefs readily accepted on 21 March the judgment of the theater representatives that operations in 1943 would have to be limited to Task Two, a view that had been expressed a month earlier by some of the Washington planners. They approved also the Woodlark and Kiriwina operation when Sutherland

---

[21] Outline History of the Pacific Military Conference, cited in Hayes, The War Against Japan, ch. XI, p. 38; Mins, JCS Mtg, 19 Mar 43. See also George C. Kenney, *General Kenney Reports* (New York: Duell, Sloan and Pearce, 1949), pp. 215–16, which implies that the President exercised some influence on the final decision.

[22] Miller, *CARTWHEEL*, MS ch. II, p. 19.

[23] Mins, JCS Mtg, 19 Mar 43.

[24] Memo, Sutherland, Spruance, Browning for JCS, 20 Mar 43, sub: Offensive Opns in South and SWPA. JCS 238/2.

explained that the War Department's inability to furnish the heavy bombers called for in ELKTON made it necessary to seize these islands, which lay within medium bomber range of targets in the northern Solomons, for use as air bases. The fact that their possession would give the South and Southwest Pacific "a stepping stone for the interchange of air units" was undoubtedly a strong argument also in favor of the operations.[25]

General Sutherland's explanation of the sequence of operations in the plan, and of the minor role given to the forces of the South Pacific, was not so readily accepted by the Joint Chiefs. Harmon had remonstrated mildly, but since the other delegates seemed to find the arrangement satisfactory he had acquiesced. Not so Admiral King. He had no intention of immobilizing the strong naval forces in the South Pacific and thus freeing the Japanese Fleet for operations elsewhere. If Halsey's fleet was not to be used in the Solomons for many months yet, then it might be employed with profit, he felt, against the Gilberts and Marshalls in the Central Pacific. Both Spruance and Browning opposed this suggestion, thus demonstrating again the unity of the theater representatives. After a lengthy discussion the Joint Chiefs went into closed session from which they emerged with agreement in principle to the theater plan and instructions to their own planners to prepare a new directive to the Pacific commanders.[26]

Still to be heard from were the commanders themselves. Presumably they had been kept informed of the progress of the meetings but on 23 March the Joint Chiefs notified them officially of the decision made in Washington. "Prevailing opinion here," they were told, "indicates desirability of deferring projected Munda operation . . . until after establishment of air base on Woodlark and possibly after seizure of Lae and Huon Peninsula."[27] Comments were requested from all three.

MacArthur's response was a vigorous support of the position taken by Sutherland. The two areas, he asserted, must be regarded, "for operational purposes," as a single unit and since neither was strong enough for independent action, neither should undertake "divergent action" simultaneously. He was, he told Marshall, already committed to the campaign in New Guinea, which had been "temporarily suspended because of a lack of resources,'' and ought to be allowed to complete it as soon as possible to provide a "defensive cover" for northeast Australia. Until that was accomplished and Huon Gulf, Madang, and Vitiaz Strait secured, he said, operations against New Georgia should be postponed.[28]

Admiral Halsey, like his chief of staff, accepted the postponement of the New Georgia operation, which he had planned to start early in April. The seizure of Woodlark and Kiriwina, he conceded, could come first. But he would not accept a purely passive role. His statement that he would continue to exert pressure against the enemy and to hit him whenever and wherever he could was the reassurance Admiral King needed. More-

---

[25] Mins, JCS Mtg, 21 Mar 43.
[26] Mins, JCS Mtg, 21 Mar 43.

[27] Rad, Marshall to MacArthur, No. 2226, 23 Mar 43, OPD Log.
[28] Rad, MacArthur to Marshall, C–1162, 25 Mar 43, CM–IN 13827.

over, said Halsey, he would seize any position in New Georgia or Bougainville that he could if such action would not involve him in a major struggle.[29]

Before a directive could be drafted for the theater commanders one more problem, that of command, had yet to be solved. It was perhaps the most difficult of all and by common consent had been avoided officially during the discussions over means and ends. But it had not been forgotten and now that all other major questions had been settled the planners returned to the debate that had marked their first discussions over Pacific strategy.[30]

Admiral King opened the final round in this debate with the now familiar proposal to adjust the boundaries so as to place the Solomons in Halsey's area, leaving to the Joint Chiefs the co-ordination of operations in the two areas. When this effort met the same fate as had similar schemes, Admiral Cooke suggested a complicated arrangement by which Halsey would command operations in the Solomons and co-ordinate all naval operations in the area while MacArthur would direct the operations in New Guinea and co-ordinate the air effort. Cooke revised this plan almost immediately, after a conversation with General Handy, but the revision dealt only with the method of securing coordination and still left to Halsey control of the operations in the Solomons.[31]

The Army refused to budge from the position it had taken earlier, that strategic direction of the campaign against Rabaul should go to MacArthur, as provided in the directive of July 1942. The Navy mustered all the old arguments as well as some new ones, but without success. This repeated rejection of all attempts at a compromise finally moved Admiral Cooke to remark:

When commands were set up in England for operations in France and for the invasion of North Africa . . . the Navy recognized that. this was an Army matter and accorded unified command to the Army upon its own initiative. . . . The Pacific . . . is and will continue to be a naval problem as a whole. If, to meet this problem we are to have unified command . . . , it is, in my opinion, up to the War Department to take the steps necessary to set it up as a unified Naval command.[32]

Cooke's plea produced no results. The Army planners studying the problem of command in the Pacific had already come to the conclusion that all the proposals and arguments could be summed up in three propositions: (a) give command to MacArthur, (b) give it to Nimitz or his representative, or (c) provide for separate commands and the co-ordination of operations by co-operation between the two commanders. On this basis the Army planners had drafted three separate plans, each embodying one of the alternative solutions, which they now passed on to the Navy. Meanwhile, on 26 March, General Marshall formally submitted to the Joint Chiefs in the form of a draft directive the plan that would

---

[29] Miller, *CARTWHEEL*, p. 18.

[30] Though the official records contain no mention of command problems during the meeting of the Pacific Conference, General Kenney states that there were heated discussions about it with the delegates. Kenney, *General Kenney Reports*, p. 213.

[31] Memo, King for Marshall, 19 Mar 43, sub: Offensive Opns in Solomons-New Guinea Area, with com-

ments, ABC 370.26 (7–28–42) sec. 4; Cooke for Wedemeyer, 22 Mar 43, no sub, and Cooke for Handy, same date, no sub, both in OPD Exec Files.

[32] Memo, Cooke for Handy, 23 Mar 43, sub: Comd in Pacific, OPD Exec Files.

give MacArthur command. In addition to outlining the tasks already agreed upon, the draft directive specified that Halsey, under MacArthur's general direction, would command operations in the Solomons and that the naval units assigned to these operations would remain under Nimitz' control.[33]

It was the last provision that disturbed the Navy most. Sensitive to any limitations on the control or strategic mobility of the fleet, Admiral King saw in Marshall's proposed directive a restriction on Admiral Nimitz' freedom to use naval units wherever they were most needed. He preferred for that reason to give command to Nimitz instead of MacArthur but did not press the point, offering instead a revision of the statement relating to naval units. He did insist, however, that operations in the Solomons should not be postponed until after the landing in New Britain and proposed that a statement to that effect be added to the directive.[34]

These differences were thrashed out in a special meeting of the Joint Chiefs on 28 March. This time King, for reasons that can only be guessed at, did not even raise the question of command. The discussion, therefore, was confined to the wording of the directive. On this basis, Marshall was perfectly willing to give ground and the differences were amicably settled by revising the directive to

give Nimitz control of those forces in the Pacific Ocean Areas not specifically assigned to the offensive by the Joint Chiefs of Staff. But King found no support, either from his colleagues in the Joint Chiefs or from Admiral Halsey, for his proposal enjoining MacArthur not to delay operations in the Solomons.

These matters settled, the Joint Chiefs formally approved General Marshall's directive and next day sent copies by radio to the Army and Navy commanders in the Pacific. Written in crisp and simple language, the directive that had taken four months to complete consisted of six brief paragraphs. First it canceled the previous directive of 2 July 1942 which called for the capture of Rabaul, and then it outlined the command arrangements under which operations would be conducted. Other than the statement that forces would be provided by the Joint Chiefs, there was no reference to the means required to carry out the tasks, listed as follows:

1. The establishment of airfields on Kiriwina and Woodlark.

2. The seizure of Lae, Salamaua, Finschhafen, Madang, and western New Britain (Cape Gloucester).

3. The seizure of the Solomon Islands "to include the southern portion of Bougainville."

The objectives of these operations were, in general, the same as those fixed at Casablanca: "to inflict losses on Japanese forces, to deny these areas to Japan, to contain Japanese forces in the Pacific by maintaining the initiative." To them was added the further objective of preparing for the "ultimate seizure of the Bismarck Archipelago." Finally, MacArthur was to submit to the Joint Chiefs his general plans "including composition

---

[33] Memos, Marshall for JCS, 26 Mar 43; Handy for Cooke, 25 Mar 43, both in OPD Exec Files; Deane for King and Marshall, 27 Mar 43, sub: Directive for Opns in South and Southwest Pacific; Handy for Marshall, same date and subject, ABC 370.26 (7–28–42) sec. 1.

[34] JCS 238/4, 27 Mar 43, Opns For Seizure of Solomons–New Guinea–New Britain–New Ireland, ABC 370.26 (7–28–42) sec 1.

of task forces, sequence, and timing of major offensive operations.[35]

Thus, almost anticlimactically, was ended the debate begun on 1 December 1942 when General Marshall first proposed a directive, which in all essential respects was similar to the one approved on 28 March. For four months Admiral King and the naval planners had opposed it strongly and sometimes bitterly. At the end they finally accepted it, almost without question. The key to this strange about-face lies, perhaps, in the following observation, written by an unidentified naval officer:

I have come to the conclusion that Admiral King considers his relations with General Marshall on such a successful plane . . . that there are some matters in which he will not proceed to their logical accomplishment believing that even if he succeeded he would damage the relationship mentioned beyond repair. One of these items is the unification of command in CINCPAC, including the efforts of General MacArthur up the New Guinea coast.[36]

[35] JCS 238/5/D, 28 Mar 43, Opns for Seizure of Solomons–New Guinea–New Ireland Area; Rads, JCS to MacArthur, Nimitz, and Halsey, 29 Mar 43, CM–OUT 11091–92–93; Mins, JCS Mtg, 28 Mar 43.

[36] Outline History of the Pacific Military Conference, cited in Hayes, The War Against Japan, ch. XI, p. 52.

CHAPTER XX

CARTWHEEL and the I-GO Operation

Secrecy and celerity are the life of dispatch in all military operations.

FRANCIS BACON

The Joint Chiefs' directive gave to the planning in the Pacific a new urgency and an immediate goal that had been absent before. Until agreement on forces and objectives had been reached in Washington the plans developed in the theater had of necessity been tentative. Now, for the first time since July of the previous year, realistic plans with specific targets, forces, and dates could be made, and it was to this task that the Pacific planners turned in the spring of 1943.

Meanwhile, the Japanese had not been idle. Determined to retain Rabaul, they spared no effort to strengthen their bases in the Solomons and New Guinea. If they could not hold the outposts to Fortress Rabaul, at least they could make every Allied advance a costly and time-consuming task. While they did what they could to disrupt Allied preparations, they sought to improve their position in the threatened area. When these efforts failed, the Japanese assembled all their resources for an ambitious and desperate attempt to smash Allied air power and cut the enemy's line of communications. Thus, even before the offensive called for by the Joint Chiefs began, the Solomons–New Guinea area became the scene of violent air attacks on whose out-

come depended the fate of the plans then being prepared.

CARTWHEEL

Although much work had been done by both the South and Southwest Pacific staffs on plans for the operations called for in the new directive, it was more than a month before this task was completed and two months more before the first operation began. Drafting the over-all plan was not difficult. All that was required was to revise ELKTON to bring it into line with the forces made available and the objectives set by the Joint Chiefs.

The chief problem before the theater planners was still the co-ordination of operations in the Solomons with those in New Guinea. So far as the Solomons were concerned the directive called only for the occupation of southern Bougainville, but, as Harmon later wrote, "it was obvious that . . . a long jump could not be made from Guadalcanal and the Russells into Bougainville." [1] An intermediate base within fighter range of Bougainville would have to be secured first, and for the South Pacific planners this

---

[1] Harmon, Army in the South Pacific, p. 6, OCMH.

meant the seizure of New Georgia and the Munda airstrip. True, Admiral Halsey had accepted the ELKTON timetable but had made it clear that he intended to take advantage of any opportunity to seize favorable positions in the central Solomons. Thus, despite MacArthur's assertion that the forces of the South Pacific could move directly into Bougainville once MacArthur had landed at Cape Gloucester, Halsey and Harmon still clung to their belief that New Georgia would have to be taken. Their job was to convince MacArthur they were right.

That task fell to Halsey and early in April he flew to Brisbane to talk with MacArthur. It was their first meeting, but five minutes after he had reported, Halsey later wrote, "I felt as if we were life long friends." [2] Perhaps MacArthur felt so, too, for the admiral seems to have had little difficulty in persuading him of the necessity of seizing New Georgia and of doing it as quickly as possible. Before the meeting was over MacArthur had not only given his consent to the New Georgia plan but had agreed that the operation be conducted simultaneously with the occupation of Woodlark and Kiriwina, the first objectives of the southwest Pacific.

This meeting between the two commanders was the first test of the command arrangement so recently established by the Joint Chiefs. So far as Halsey was concerned, his new assignment gave him two "hats," one as a subordinate to Nimitz who controlled his forces and the other as a subordinate to MacArthur who dictated his strategy. But after the

meeting he remarked that this arrangement was both "sensible and satisfactory." Nor did he later have reason to change his mind, for as the war progressed his relationship with MacArthur grew ever more friendly. "Not once did he, my superior officer, ever force his decisions upon me," he wrote later. "On the few occasions when I disagreed with him, I told him so, and we discussed the issue until one of us changed his mind." [3]

This problem settled, the planners completed their work and on 26 April ELKTON III was issued. Known by the code name CARTWHEEL, this plan called for thirteen separate operations in a period of eight months during which the forces of the South and Southwest Pacific would advance by successive stages, always in support of each other and under cover by land-based fighters, to positions from which they could converge on Rabaul. The operations fell into two groups: those along the western or New Guinea axis and those in the Solomons along the eastern axis. (Map V) In the first place the Southwest Pacific would occupy Woodlark and Kiriwina (with Halsey furnishing the garrison troops for the former), while forces from the South Pacific moved into the New Georgia group. While this last was still in progress MacArthur's forces would embark on the second phase: the capture of Lae, Salamaua, Finschhafen, and Madang. By the time Madang was taken, Halsey would have captured Faisi in the Shortlands and Buin in southern Bougainville. The third and final phase of CARTWHEEL would see the landing at Cape Gloucester in western New Britain, the capture of Kieta on the east

[2] Halsey and Bryan, *Admiral Halsey's Story*, pp. 154–55.

[3] *Ibid.*

coast of Bougainville, and the neutralization of Buka, a small island off the northern tip of Bougainville.[4]

The timetable for this complicated series of operations was carefully worked out so that the final objective would be won by the end of the year. The first phase would begin in June, one month being allotted for the occupation of Woodlark and Kiriwina Islands and five for New Georgia. By the time New Georgia was taken in October, MacArthur's forces in the Southwest Pacific would have seized Lae, Salamaua, and Finschhafen and begun the offensive against Madang. Meanwhile, the forces of the South Pacific would have gone on to take Buin and Faisi, and then Bougainville in January 1944. By that time Southwest Pacific forces would have concluded operations on New Britain. But carefully as this sequence of operations was worked out, everyone recognized it was only tentative and subject to change, depending, as MacArthur remarked, on the "fluctuation of tactical circumstances."[5]

The forces for each of these operations were as carefully computed as the timing. In the first phase MacArthur would use two regimental combat teams, in the second, five Australian divisions and one tank regiment, and in the third, one Marine division. With service and supporting troops, reserves, and naval and air forces, this schedule would place a heavy drain on MacArthur's resources. Phase Two alone, MacArthur estimated,

would require almost 170,000 air and ground troops. South Pacific requirements, though not as great, would call for the utilization of all the resources of that theater in the coming year.

Such large requirements called for the closest co-operation between the two areas and the most effective and economical use of their forces. Thus, Halsey would furnish the garrison and construction troops for Woodlark, while supporting that operation with his naval and air forces. During the second and third phase of CARTWHEEL, he would continue to provide air and naval support to MacArthur's forces in their drive along the New Guinea coast. At the same time, South Pacific aircraft would assist in the neutralization of Rabaul, freeing a portion of MacArthur's air forces for tactical missions in New Guinea. In addition, the two areas would share intelligence information, exchange operational summaries, link radio communications, and pool their resources for air reconnaissance.

Profiting from the experience of Guadalcanal and Buna and in anticipation of the tasks ahead, both MacArthur and Halsey had tightened their organization, created new headquarters, and adopted more effective methods for planning and controlling their operations. The South Pacific's plans for New Georgia, for example, were worked out by a planning committee consisting of Army, Navy, and Marine commanders. It was they who reviewed with Halsey's chief planning officers the tactical plans for the campaign in a series of conferences during the latter part of May and resolved the numerous tactical and organizational problems that arose in the days that followed.

[4] ELKTON III, 26 Apr 43, Plan for Seizure of Lae–Salamaua–Madang–New Britain–Solomons Area, OCMH. For an account of the detailed planning and execution of these operations, see Miller, *CARTWHEEL*. This work has been used freely in the present chapter.

[5] Rad, MacArthur to Marshall, 5 May 43, CM–IN 3409.

The forces of the South Pacific also underwent reorganization during this period.[6] *(Charts 7–9)* No single ground commander was appointed, as in the Southwest Pacific, though Halsey had demonstrated during the Guadalcanal campaign his willingness to give the Army commander tactical control even though that officer had no tactical mission. But the air organization had been considerably modified since August 1942 on the basis of experience in the Guadalcanal campaign. Air Command, Solomons, had been established to exercise operational control, under the Commander, Aircraft (land-based), South Pacific Force (COMAIRSOPAC), over aircraft in the forward area and in January the Thirteenth Air Force had been activated with General Twining in command, to provide administrative control over Army air units. Naval forces in the area were placed under the Third Fleet organized in March, at the same time that the Seventh Fleet was created for the Southwest Pacific. Halsey himself was named commander of the Third Fleet, which had no organic naval units but consisted of whatever warships were assigned from time to time by Admiral Nimitz. Supply in the area remained, as before, under Service Squadron, South Pacific, but the Army's Services of Supply created in November 1942 and headed by General Breene was assuming ever larger responsibilities. The South Pacific Amphibious Force, under Admiral Turner, retained its importance as the directing tactical headquarters for landing operations, which meant, in effect, all operations in the area.

The organization of MacArthur's command conformed more closely to the familiar Army pattern, with an Allied headquarters (GHQ) on top of the structure and air, ground, and naval forces under separate operational commands directly beneath it. Administrative control was exercised by each national force through its own headquarters. Thus, the American Fifth Air Force and Sixth Army were under one of the three major tactical commands for operations and training, but in matters of administration and supply reported to USAFFE, re-established in February 1943, with MacArthur in command, as the highest American headquarters in the area. The U.S. Army Services of Supply (USASOS), commanded by Maj. Gen. Richard J. Marshall, continued to serve as the logistical agency for Army forces under USAFFE, controlling the various supply bases in Australia and New Guinea. American naval forces in the area were under the operational control of Allied Naval Forces and the administrative control of the Seventh Fleet, which, like the Third Fleet, was a part of Nimitz' Pacific Fleet. Both General Kenney and Vice Adm. Arthur S. Carpender, commanders of the Fifth Air Force and Seventh Fleet respectively, functioned as national and Allied force commanders.

The organization of the ground forces was somewhat more complicated. Under the Australian General Sir Thomas A. Blamey, who also commanded the Australian military forces, Allied Land Forces was to exercise tactical control through task forces created for each operation. Thus, in the Papuan campaign Australian and American troops had been under a predominantly Australian

[6] For a description of the South Pacific command, see above, chapter XI.

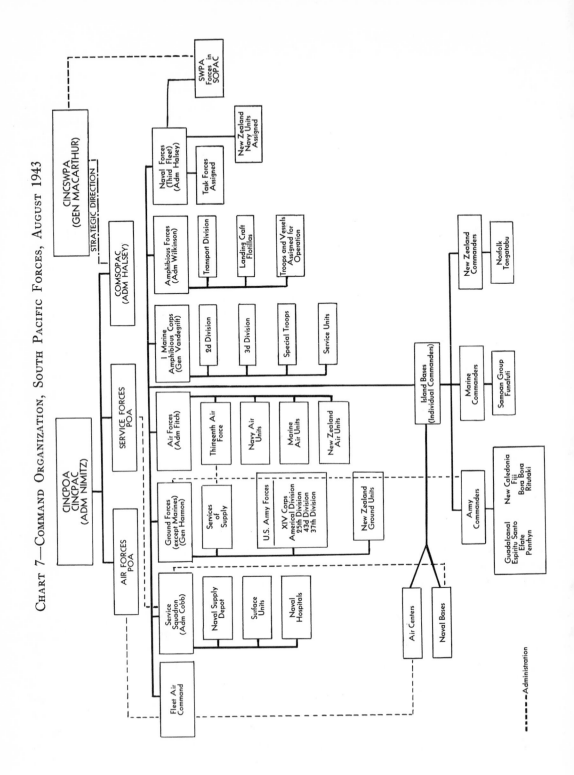

CHART 7—COMMAND ORGANIZATION, SOUTH PACIFIC FORCES, AUGUST 1943

CINCPOA
CINCPAC
(ADM NIMITZ)

CINCSWPA
(GEN MACARTHUR)

STRATEGIC DIRECTION

AIR FORCES POA

SERVICE FORCES POA

COMSOPAC
(ADM HALSEY)

Naval Forces
(Third Fleet)
(Adm Halsey)

SWPA Forces in SOPAC

Task Forces Assigned

New Zealand Navy Units Assigned

Amphibious Forces
(Adm Wilkinson)

Transport Division

Landing Craft Flotillas

Troops and Vessels Assigned for Operation

I Marine Amphibious Corps
(Gen Vandegrift)

2d Division

3d Division

Special Troops

Service Units

Air Forces
(Adm Fitch)

Thirteenth Air Force

Navy Air Units

Marine Air Units

New Zealand Air Units

Ground Forces
(except Marines)
(Gen Harmon)

Services of Supply

U.S. Army Forces

XIV Corps
Americal Division
25th Division
43d Division
37th Division

New Zealand Ground Units

Service Squadron
(Adm Cobb)

Naval Supply Depot

Surface Units

Naval Hospitals

Fleet Air Command

Island Bases
(Individual Commanders)

New Zealand Commanders

Norfolk
Tongatabu

Marine Commanders

Samoan Group
Funafuti

Army Commanders

New Caledonia
Fiji
Bora Bora
Ritutaki

Guadalcanal
Espiritu Santo
Efate
Penrhyn

Air Centers

Naval Bases

- - - - - Administration

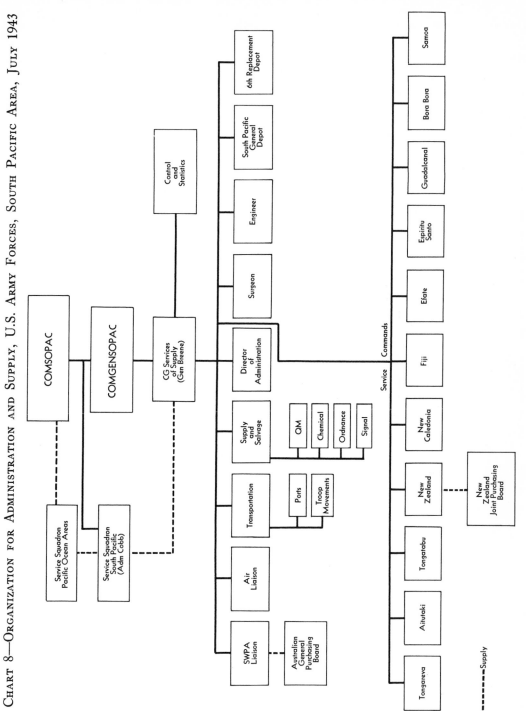

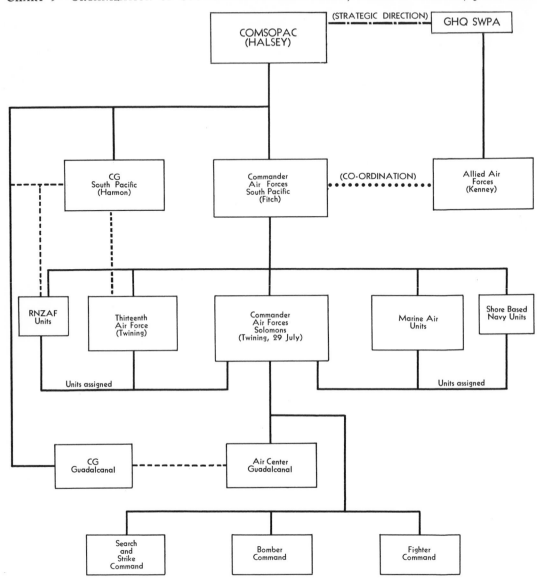

CONFERENCE AT ALAMO HEADQUARTERS. *From left, Generals Chamberlain, Krueger, and MacArthur, Brig. Gen. Edwin D. Patrick, Rear Adm. Thomas C. Kinkaid, and Maj. Gen. Ennis C. Whitehead.*

headquarters called New Guinea Force, which was, in turn, under Allied Land Forces. But conditions had changed since this arrangement had been adopted. Throughout the winter of 1942–43, U.S. Army combat troops had reached the theater in larger numbers and more were expected. A corps headquarters under General Eichelberger had been formed in Australia in September, and in February 1943 the first echelon of Lt. Gen. Walter Krueger's Sixth Army headquarters reached Australia.[7] MacArthur

7 February 1943. When he assumed command of Sixth Army ten days later, it consisted of the following units, all of which were already in the area:

Headquarters, 1 Corps at Rockhampton
    32d Division, in Australia near Brisbane
    41st Division, Dobodura area, New Guinea
    1st Marine Division (under Army operational control only), Melbourne
    158th Infantry Regiment, Port Moresby, New Guinea
    503d Paratroop Infantry Regiment, near Brisbane
    40th Antiaircraft Brigade, New Guinea
    41st Antiaircraft Brigade, Queensland
    98th Field Artillery Battalion (Pack), Port Moresby
    2d Engineer Special Brigade, Australia

The second echelon of Sixth Army headquarters arrived in Brisbane by ship on 17 April 1943. The 24th Infantry and 1st Cavalry Divisions were assigned to Sixth Army when they arrived in Australia in May and July of the year.

---

[7] General Krueger arrived in Brisbane with his chief of staff and a few other staff officers by air on

therefore created for CARTWHEEL an independent task force called first New Britain Force and then ALAMO Force, which was to operate under the control of GHQ rather than Allied Land Forces. Consisting entirely of American troops, ALAMO Force was virtually identical with Sixth Army and was commanded by General Krueger. New Guinea Force remained under Blamey but became almost exclusively an Australian command with U.S. troops attached only for special purposes. The practical result of this arrangement was to remove American forces from Blamey's control and to make Allied Land Forces a paper organization.[8]

All of the headquarters involved participated in the planning for CARTWHEEL, with GHQ providing a centralized direction and co-ordination, in marked contrast to the system used in the South Pacific. (*Charts 10 and 11*) There the commander of the force charged with responsibility for the operation rather than Halsey's headquarters co-ordinated the activities of the units involved. MacArthur described his own organization to General Marshall in this way:

Complete and thorough integration of ground, air, and naval headquarters with GHQ is the method followed with marked success in the SWPA. . . . Naval, air commanders and their staffs are in the same building with GHQ. The land commander and his staff are nearby. These commanders confer frequently with the CinC and principal members of GHQ. In addition

to their functions as commanders they operate, in effect, as a planning staff to the CinC. When operating in forward areas the same conditions exist.

The personal relationships established and the physical location of subordinate headquarters makes possible a constant daily participation of the staffs in all details of planning and operations. Appropriate members of GHQ are in intimate daily contact with members of the three lower headquarters. . . .

GHQ is, in spirit, a headquarters for planning and executing operations each of which demands effective combinations of land, sea, and air power. . . . It is only the determination that GHQ shall act as a GHQ rather than as the headquarters of a single service that will produce the unanimity of action and singleness of purpose that is essential for the successful conduct of combined operations.[9]

While MacArthur and Halsey were making the detailed plans called for by the Joint Chiefs' directive, Admiral King in Washington was growing increasingly restive at the apparent delay. MacArthur sent few reports of his plans during this time, even when ELKTON III was completed, and though Halsey informed his superiors of his own plans it seemed to King that nothing was being done except to hold conferences and exchange messages. Requests from the Southwest Pacific for additional naval units only increased his concern and on 2 May he finally expressed his impatience to General Marshall. The Pacific theater, he observed, had been inactive for two months and still MacArthur had not submitted the "general plans" asked for in the directive of 28 March. The Joint Chiefs, he felt, should not wait any longer but should prod MacArthur immediately. Marshall had no objections

---

[8] In this connection, see the report by General Richardson of his inspection of the Southwest Pacific Area in June 1942, much of which dealt with the status of U.S. Army combat forces under Australian command. Memo, Richardson for CofS, 9 Jul 42, sub: Australia, OPD Exec Files, SWPA, IV. This same file contains records of the discussions of Richardson's report.

[9] Rad, MacArthur to Marshall, No. C–4369, 31 Jul 43, GHQ Hist Records Index Cards, OCMH.

CHART 10—COMMAND ORGANIZATION, SOUTHWEST PACIFIC AREA, JULY 1943

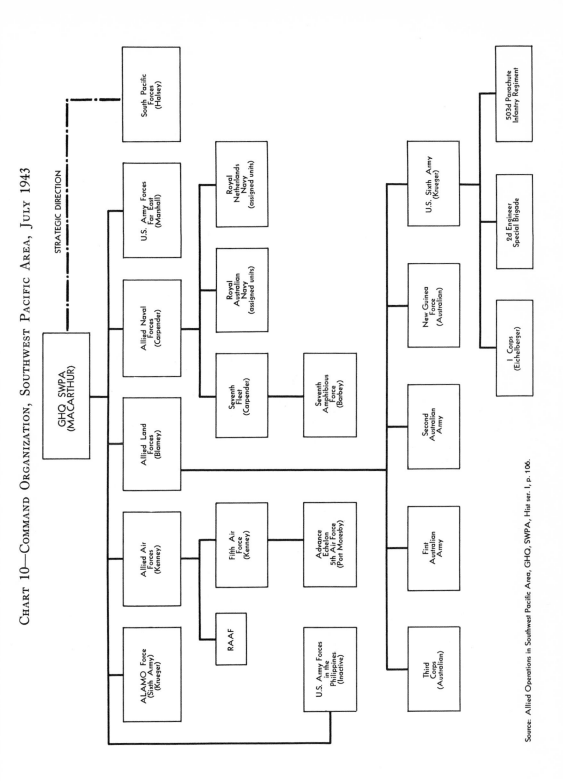

Source: Allied Operations in Southwest Pacific Area, GHQ, SWPA, Hist ser. I, p. 106.

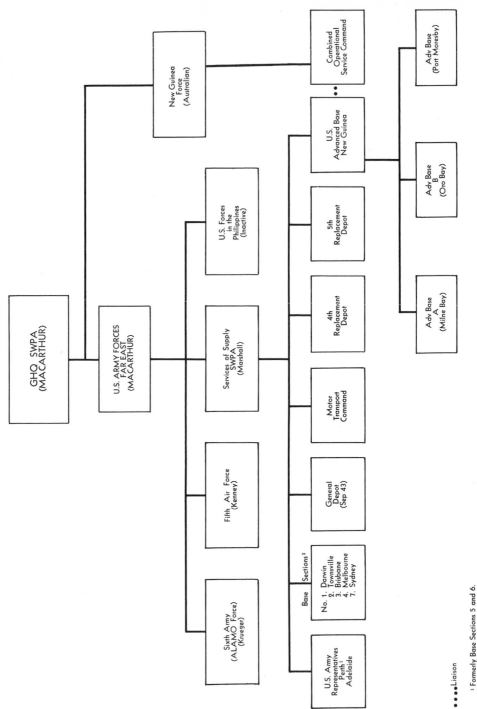

•••••Liaison

[1] Formerly Base Sections 5 and 6.

[2] Base Sections were redesignated and moved forward as the war in the Southwest Pacific progressed. Thus, the numbers and locations varied for different periods.

and next day a message asking MacArthur for his plans went out.[10]

The reply put an end to any fears that time had been wasted. MacArthur explained CARTWHEEL in some detail and gave the sequence and timing of the major operations for the coming year. The offensive, he told Marshall, would start about 15 June and would continue thereafter in rapid order for the next six months until his forces and those of Admiral Halsey converged for the final assault on Rabaul. But with the exception of the opening date, the dates listed, he cautioned the Chief of Staff, were still tentative. Within three weeks he had changed even the first date and set the occupation of Woodlark and Kiriwina and the invasion of New Georgia for the end instead of the middle of June.[11] Already the men and supplies were moving into the forward area, to the southern Solomons and the Papuan Peninsula, for the first phase of CARTWHEEL.

The I-GO Operation

By coincidence, *Imperial General Headquarters* in Tokyo was reviewing its own strategy for the Southeast Area at the same time that the Americans were discussing this question. The American debate was sparked by the victory at Guadalcanal and Buna; the Japanese review by defeat and the increasing effectiveness of Allied air and sea operations. After the Battle of the Bismarck Sea early in March, when a large part of the *51st Division* was virtually destroyed, neither General Imamura, the *8th Area Army* commander at Rabaul, nor his superiors in Tokyo could deny any longer the seriousness of the Allied threat. It was time, the Japanese planners concluded, for a fresh look at their strategy and for renewed efforts in the Southeast Area.

The discussions that took place in Tokyo in mid-March brought out clearly the differing points of view of the Army and Navy. The former considered the New Guinea area as the more important, first because it was vital to the defense of the Philippines and the Netherlands Indies, and second because it was more suitable for large-scale Army operations than the smaller islands of the Solomons. The Navy, interested primarily in the security of the *Combined Fleet* base at Truk, wished to concentrate on the Solomons approach to Fortress Rabaul for that avenue seemed to them to lead naturally to their position in the Caroline Islands. The Solomon Islands, moreover, offered advantageous sites for naval bases and lent themselves to operations for which the Navy was best suited.

The reconciliation of these views was the task of the Tokyo planners. Neither side would give way though the Army brought in Imamura's chief of staff, Lt. Gen. Rinpei Kato, and several of his assistants, who were in Tokyo to get more planes for their area, to bolster its case. The naval planners were not impressed but the Army had its way in the end, for the issue was decided not on its merits but on the influence of the contending parties. The decision, embodied in an Army-Navy Central Agreement issued to Imamura and Yam-

[10] Memo, King for Marshall, 2 May 43, OPD 381 (Security) case 109; Rad, Marshall to MacArthur, 3 May 43, CM–OUT 1108.

[11] Rads, MacArthur to Marshall, 5 and 27 May 43, CM–IN 3409 and 17166.

amoto on 25 March, was a clear victory for the Army. First priority thereafter would go to operations in New Guinea.

The Army-Navy Central Agreement, a Japanese euphemism for strategic directive, called for a major effort by the two services, "working together as a single body," to extend and consolidate their operating bases in New Guinea while securing their position in the Solomons and in the Bismarck Archipelago.[12] Operations in New Guinea would consist of strengthening the bases at Lae and Salamaua and maintaining control over New Guinea and western New Britain. Airfields and roads were to be built, units reinforced, supplies stockpiled, and every measure taken to repulse the expected Allied offensive when it came. The only offensive mission assigned was the destruction of enemy air power in order to disrupt the obvious Allied preparations for the attack and to protect the Japanese supply routes. This task under the new directive would fall largely on the Navy whose air arm was not only to interdict the enemy's shipping but also "to wage aerial annihilation operations in concert with the Army." [13]

The burden of defending the Solomons was divided between the Army and the Navy, the former taking responsibility for the northern portion of the area and the latter for New Georgia and

Santa Isabel. The Bismarck area was a joint responsibility, and special emphasis was given to strengthening the western sector of New Britain, facing the Huon Peninsula. Offensive operations in the Solomons, as in New Guinea, were to be conducted largely by the Navy, which, in addition to its aircraft, was to employ submarines to check the flow of enemy supplies and reinforcements.

The Japanese had only limited resources with which to achieve this ambitious design. General Imamura's Army air forces at this time consisted of about 170 planes, of which 74 were fighters, 54 light bombers, and half that number heavy bombers. By September, *Imperial General Headquarters* promised Imamura, he would have another 150 aircraft, but September was a long way off. The Navy was in better shape. It had 240 planes and was scheduled to receive another 100 sometime during the summer. In addition, Vice Adm. Jinishi Kusaka, commander of the *Southeast Area Fleet,* could also expect reinforcements if they were needed from the carriers of the *Combined Fleet.*

In establishing a command for the area, the Japanese faced the same problems as did the Americans. (*Chart 12*) Unlike their enemies, however, they were never able to establish a unified command even for a limited period of time. As senior Army commander in the area, General Imamura had under him the *17th* and *18th Armies* and the *6th Air Division* but exercised no control over naval forces. These included the *8th Fleet* and the *11th Air Fleet,* both of which were under Admiral Kusaka's control as commander of the *Southeast Area Fleet.* Kusaka in turn reported to Admiral Yamamoto, the

---

[12] *8th Area Army* Opns, pt. IV of Southeast Area Opns Record, rev. ed., Japanese Studies in World War II, 127, p. 23, OCMH. This section is based on this source and on the following: Southeast Area Naval Opns, pt. II, Japanese Studies in World War II, 49; Southeast Area Naval Air Opns, pt. III, Japanese Studies in World War II, 122, pp. 34–36; Japanese Opns in World War II, GHQ SWPA Series II, pp. 188–90; Hattori, *The Greater East Asia War*, II, pt. 5, pp. 4–12.

[13] *8th Area Army* Opns, pt. IV, p. 25.

Combined Fleet commander at Truk. Other than to direct the services to "act in concert"—an injunction that was largely ignored—*Imperial General Headquarters* made no effort to establish a unified command for the Southeast Area. Only when Army and Navy forces operated together in ground operations, would there be a single commander "for purely operational purposes" and the choice then would be made entirely on the basis of seniority.[14]

On receipt of the Army-Navy Central Agreement, both General Imamura and Admiral Yamamoto issued fresh instructions to their commands. The Army's instructions, issued on 12 April, simply assigned the tasks set out by *Imperial General Headquarters* to the various forces in the area: the *18th Army* was to strengthen and defend Japanese bases in New Guinea; the *17th Army* was to do the same in the northern Solomons, and the *6th Air Division*, while shifting base from Rabaul to New Guinea, was to conduct reconnaissance, cover the movement of supplies, support ground operations if required, and co-operate with naval air forces in the destruction of Allied air power. Aside from this last provision, Imamura's program did not hold any great threat for the Allies who by this time had acquired aerial supremacy in eastern New Guinea.

Admiral Yamamoto's plan was much more ambitious and potentially more dangerous for the Allies. His orders from Tokyo were to destroy Allied air power in New Guinea and the Solomons, and he made plans to accomplish just that. The operation, designated *I-GO*, was to be in two parts, the first lasting

from 5 to 10 April in the Solomons and the second from 11 to 20 April in New Guinea. That it was to be a major effort was evident by Yamamoto's transfer of about 150 carrier-based planes from the *3d Fleet* to the Southeast Area and his own voyage to Rabaul with the *3d Fleet* commander on 3 April to take personal charge of the operation.[15]

After a preliminary and unprofitable attack against the Russells on 1 April, Yamamoto launched the *I-GO* Operation on the 7th with an attack against Guadalcanal. The target was a tempting one for in the vicinity were about a dozen warships, fourteen transports, and about forty smaller vessels. Ashore were large quantities of supplies stored for the coming invasion of New Georgia. With the 224 fighters and bombers he assigned to this strike—the largest since Pearl Harbor—Yamamoto expected great results. The reports of vast damage brought back by his pilots justified his hopes but were actually far from the truth. The Allies, alerted by the coast watchers, had sent 76 fighters, all that were available at Henderson Field, to meet the Japanese and had succeeded in knocking down 21 planes. Their own loss was seven fighters and a few small vessels.

On 11 April, Admiral Yamamoto turned his attention to New Guinea, the second phase of the *I-GO* Operation, with an attack by 71 fighters and 216 bombers against Allied shipping in Oro Bay, south of Buna. Next day he sent 124 fighters and 43 bombers over Port Moresby, and on the 14th delivered the final

---

[14] *8th Area Army*, pt. IV, p. 27.

[15] For accounts of the *I-GO* Operation, see, in addition to the sources cited above, Miller, *CARTWHEEL*, pp. 42–45, and Morison, *Breaking the Bismarcks Barrier*, pp. 117–29.

CHART 12—ORGANIZATION OF JAPANESE FORCES, SOUTHEAST AREA, JULY 1943

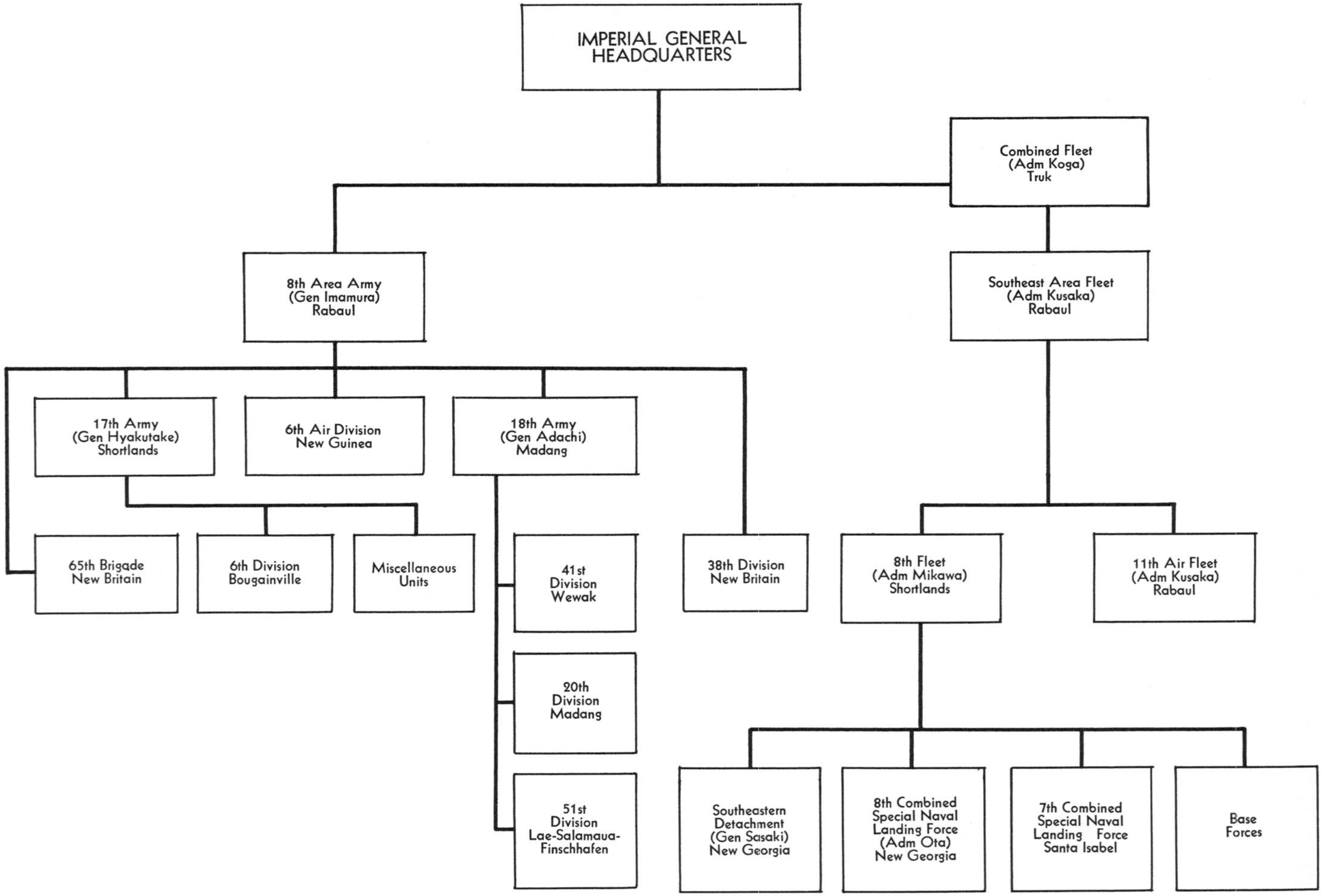

Source: Miller, CARTWHEEL, p. 33.

attack of the *I-GO* Operation with a 196-plane strike against shipping in Milne Bay. The reports that reached Yamamoto of the damage inflicted on the Allies in all these attacks were highly gratifying and it was with the conviction that *I-GO* had proved a great success that the *Combined Fleet* commander called off the operation and sent the carrier-based planes of the *3d Fleet* back to Truk.

The success of the *I-GO* Operation was an illusion based on greatly exaggerated claims of damages by the Japanese fliers, a bitter truth that Admiral Yamamoto did not live long enough to learn. His undoing was the work of American cryptanalysts who learned that he was planning to visit the Buin area in southern Bougainville with his chief of staff and several other officers on 18 April to inspect the naval air bases there and congratulate those who had taken part in the *I-GO* Operation. The visit of so august a personage prompted a rash of messages between Buin and Rabaul which gave the American cryptanalysts all the details of the journey—the exact time of departure and arrival, the course, and the number and type of planes in the entourage. Thus, when the two bombers carrying Yamamoto and his party approached Buin and as the nine accompanying fighters started to leave, a flight of eighteen P–38's from Guadalcanal appeared on the scene. "All of a sudden," says one Japanese writer,

"a great disaster took place." [16] The P–38's came in low, concentrating on the bombers, and in a matter of minutes had disposed of both of them. One crashed into the dense Bougainville jungle carrying Yamamoto and several of his staff to their deaths; the other landed in the sea close by, fortunately for the chief of staff who survived.

The death of Admiral Yamamoto, author of the Pearl Harbor plan and perhaps the ablest officer in the Imperial Japanese Navy, was a major victory for the Allies. It was a source of particular satisfaction for those who remembered the admiral as author of the boast that he would dictate peace in the White House, a statement he never made. To the Japanese the loss was "an almost unbearable blow," and they showed their grief in the full-dress public funeral they gave the admiral's ashes in Tokyo on 5 June. Less than three weeks later the Allied offensive Yamamoto had sought to forestall began. Between 23 and 25 June MacArthur's forces seized Woodlark and Kiriwina Islands without opposition and on the last day of the month another force seized a beachhead in Nassau Bay, only about ten miles south of Salamaua. Simultaneously, Halsey's forces landed at Rendova across the channel from Munda airfield on New Georgia. CARTWHEEL was on.

---

[16] Hattori, The Greater East Asia War, II, pt. 5, p. 11.

PART FOUR

EMERGING PATTERNS

Now the general who wins a battle makes many calculations in his temple ere the battle is fought. The general who loses a battle makes but few calculations beforehand. Thus do many calculations lead to victory and few calculations to defeat.

SUN TZU

CHAPTER XXI

The North Pacific and the Soviet Union

Generals with their armies and admirals with their fleets are mere weapons wielded by the hand of the statesman. It is for him to decide when to strike, where to strike, and how to strike.

SIR JOHN FORTESCUE

American interest in the North Pacific as a potential theater of operations in a war against Japan antedated Pearl Harbor. Based originally on the hope of gaining air bases in the Soviet Maritime Provinces within easy reach of Japan, this interest was reinforced later by the desire for an air ferry route to facilitate the delivery of lend-lease planes. But those pushing for air operations based on Soviet territory made little headway against Stalin's determination to maintain a neutral position in the Far East.[1] Moreover, the requirements from other parts of the Pacific and the plans for an offensive in Europe left little for an area that was not in urgent need and where operations did not hold out the promise of decisive results.

Strategic Background

By the spring of 1942 the Army planners in Washington, despite strong arguments from the commanders in the theater and from the Army Air Forces, were beginning to view the idea of bombing Japan from Siberia with increasing skepticism. To the argument that such air attacks would relieve the pressure on Russia, the Army planners replied that the Soviet Union would benefit more if the Allies undertook an offensive in the South Pacific. Such action, they thought, would have the effect of containing Japanese forces, thus removing the danger of a Japanese attack against Siberia.[2]

This was a view that General MacArthur could support warmly. Writing from Australia in May 1942, he argued that the Soviet Union could best be helped by opening a second front, but that the second front should be in the Pacific. An offensive there would relieve Japanese pressure on Siberia, he argued, and permit Marshal Stalin "either to utilize the Siberian resources in direct support of his European front or to join his allies in the Pacific attack."[3] But since Stalin had no intention of getting involved in the Far East or permitting U.S. aircraft to base in the Maritime Provinces, this entire discussion was academic. Without the active co-operation of the Soviet Union a North Pacific offen-

---

[1] See above, pp. 154–56.

[2] Memo, Capt John H. Caughey for Eisenhower, 11 Mar 42, sub: Assistance to Russia, JPS 19/D, ABC 381 (1–23–42).

[3] Rad, MacArthur to Marshall, No. 176, 8 May 42, GHQ, SWPA Hist Rec Index.

sive against Japan was out of the question at this time and General Marshall, on 18 March 1942, restricted the role of Army forces in Alaska to the strategic defensive. And at the end of the month, he and the other members of the Joint Chiefs agreed to discontinue planning for operations in the north until arrangements could be made with Russia for "a more complete military collaboration." [4]

Though the President took no action at that time, he did act early in June when information pointing to a Japanese attack on Siberia was received in Washington. The seizure of Attu and Kiska on 6 and 7 June, combined with the movement of Japanese air forces to Paramushiro in the Kurils, seemed ample confirmation of this information. Moreover, it was feared that as a preliminary step in their invasion of the Maritime Provinces the Japanese would seize additional positions in the North Pacific in order to cut the line of communications between Siberia and Alaska. To this fear was added the real concern felt by officers in the theater and in Washington and by the American people that Japan would use its newly acquired bases in the Aleutians as a springboard for invasion of the United States. Thus, the planners had to anticipate the possibility of additional operations in Alaska as well as a Japanese attack on Siberia, a step that would bring the Soviet Union into the war against Japan. [5]

In these circumstances the first and most pressing need was to strengthen the Alaskan defenses and measures were immediately taken to that end. The second and almost equally urgent matter requiring attention was to provide for co-ordination between U.S. and Soviet operations in the event of a Japanese attack. But no plans could be made until agreement with the Soviet Union was reached on the political level, a step that the Joint Chiefs had recommended in March and now urged again. This time the President acted upon the recommendations of his military advisers and on 17 June appealed personally to Marshal Stalin for "an immediate exchange of detailed information" on military facilities in Siberia and Alaska. "We are prepared to come to your assistance with our air power," Roosevelt told the Soviet leader, "provided suitable landing fields are available in Siberia." Secret military staff conversations, the President added, were essential to the common interest and ought to be initiated at once. [6]

Roosevelt's personal intervention accomplished its purpose and Stalin consented, somewhat reluctantly, to U.S.-Soviet staff conversations to be held in Moscow. Maj. Gen. Follett Bradley was chosen for the assignment and in July left for Russia on a mission that would prove both barren and frustrating so far as acquiring information about Siberian bases and concerting plans for action against Japan were concerned. The Russians were more interested in securing

---

[4] Mins, JCS Mtg; 30 Mar 42, Memos, Marshall and King for Roosevelt, 30 Mar 42; Marshall for WPD, 18 Mar 42; both in ABC 381 (1–23–42); JCS 16/1, 29 Mar 42, sub: UN Action in Case of War Between Russia and Japan.

[5] Memo, G–2 for OPD, 21 May 42, OPD 381 Japan (3–7–42), sec. 1, and related papers in this file; JCS 61, 14 Jun 42, sub: Estimate of Sit in North Pacific.

[6] Rad, Roosevelt to Stalin, 17 Jun 42, OPD Exec Files; Mins, JCS Mtg, 15 Jun 42; JCS 61, 14 Jun 42, sub: Estimate of Sit in North Pacific. For the measures taken to defend Alaska, see Conn, Engelman, and Fairchild, Guarding the United States and Its Outposts, ch. X.

lend-lease aircraft than in military collaboration.[7]

The Aleutians

Though the fear of a Japanese offensive in the north—a fear the Russians, judging from their actions, apparently did not share—ultimately proved groundless, the task of expelling the Japanese from the Aleutians remained. Operations in this area promised to be extremely difficult. The islands seemed, on the map, to provide an easy route across the Pacific to the Kurils and Japan, but in actuality this region was one of the most forbidding in the world. (Map 6) Sustained air and naval operations would be impossible during certain seasons of the year and difficult even at more favorable times. There were few developed areas suitable as bases, the distances between them were great, and almost all supplies would have to be brought from the United States.[8]

Command of the Aleutians, which fell within the North Pacific Area, was assigned to Admiral Nimitz who exercised his responsibility through his representative, Rear Adm. Robert A. Theobald. But the situation was complicated by the fact that the bulk of the forces in the region were Army troops assigned to the Alaskan Defense Command, under Maj. Gen. Simon B. Buckner, Jr., which, in turn, was a part of Lt. Gen. John L. DeWitt's Western Defense Command. At the time of Midway the Alaska garrison consisted of about 30,000 men—more than half in antiaircraft units—and the Eleventh Air Force (Brig. Gen. William O. Butler), all together almost 51,000 troops. Admiral Theobald's authority extended only to operations, but for this purpose the planes of the Eleventh Air Force came under his control, a situation that led to considerable difficulty.

Planning for active operations against the Japanese in the Aleutians began in mid-June, within a week of the occupation of Attu and Kiska. At that time General DeWitt proposed to Marshall that he be given additional troops to retake the islands as the first step in a counteroffensive aimed at reaching Japan through the North Pacific. But the Army planners in Washington saw little profit in such an undertaking, especially when the resources of the Allies were already being strained to the utmost. They therefore vetoed Dewitt's suggestion but did approve his request for additional air and ground forces for the defense of Alaska.[9]

Not easily discouraged, General DeWitt continued to press for an offensive in the North Pacific, submitting to General Marshall various plans to drive the enemy from the Aleutians. All of these proposals, coming in the midst of preparations for the Guadalcanal and North African invasions, were rejected. A more modest plan, submitted by DeWitt on 18 July, did meet a favorable response. According to this plan,

---

[7] For an account of the Bradley mission, see Matloff and Snell, *Strategic Planning, 1941–42*, pp. 343–46.

[8] In the preparation of this section, the author used freely the following works: Conn, Engelman, and Fairchild, Guarding the United States and Its Outposts, chs. IX and X; Matloff, *Strategic Planning for Coalition Warfare, 1943–44*; Craven and Cate *AAF I*, ch. 8, and *AAF IV*, ch. 11; Hayes, The War Against Japan. In most cases, however, the author has consulted the source materials and drawn his own conclusions.

[9] Rads, DeWitt for Marshall, 8 and 15 Jun 42, Nos. 583 and 630, OPD 381 (Alaska), case 24; Notes on War Council, 15 Jun 42; Gen Council Mins, 16 Jun 42.

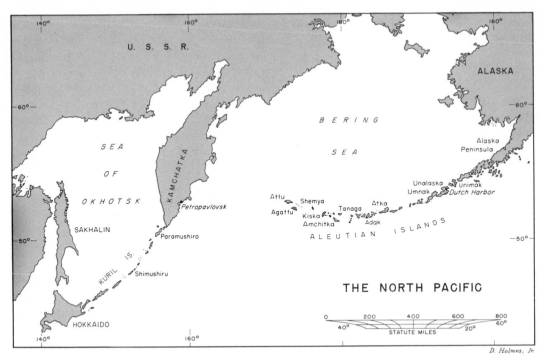

MAP 6

D. Holmes, Jr.

Tanaga Island, about 160 miles from Kiska, would be occupied and converted into an air base, thus neutralizing the Japanese base at Kiska. General DeWitt had already conducted a reconnaissance and was able to assure the Chief of Staff that the island possessed adequate airfield sites and harbor facilities to make the scheme practicable.[10]

What impressed the Washington planners most was DeWitt's assertion that he could accomplish this task with troops already under his command (3,000 for the assault and 5,000 for the garrison), and with resources available on the west coast and in Alaska. All he needed, he said, was naval support, and he asked that he be allowed to arrange for that with Admiral Nimitz. "Urge details of operation be left to me and I be given freedom of action," he wrote. "Early decision essential to success of this operation."[11]

This request for naval support led to complications DeWitt had not foreseen. To secure the naval support he required, it was necessary to gain the Navy's approval of the project and to issue a joint directive to DeWitt and to the naval commander in the area, Admiral Theobald. Almost immediately the plan ran into trouble. In proposing the project to the Navy, the Army planners men-

---

[10] Ltr, DeWitt to Marshall, 16 Jul 42; Rad, Marshall to DeWitt, 18 Jul 42, CM–OUT 5106; Memo, OPD for Marshall, 27 Jul 42, sub: Plans for Opns in Alaska, OPD 381 (Alaska), case 24.

[11] Rad, DeWitt for Marshall, 19 Jul 42, OPD 381 (Alaska), case 25.

tioned Adak, a small island near Tanaga, as an alternative but expressed a preference for Tanaga. This created the first obstacle, for the Navy decided it would first have to conduct its own reconnaissance. It appeared also that approval would have to await Admiral Theobald's return from a brief journey. And finally, naval officers in Alaska were reporting that the naval support needed for the operation would not be available until September.[12] The Navy, therefore, while approving the plan in principle, asked that a decision be deferred.

Though General DeWitt protested this delay, there was little to be done. His difficulties were increased when Admiral Theobald, on his return, expressed opposition to the Tanaga project because of navigational hazards. Adak, he thought, would be preferable on account of its harbor facilities. DeWitt and General Buckner continued to favor Tanaga for its advantageous airfield sites. The Joint Chiefs' approval on 5 August of the Tanaga project failed to bring the field commanders into agreement and finally in mid-August the dispute was referred to Washington for settlement.

The compromise worked out in Washington was a victory for the naval point of view. Admiral King not only stood solidly behind Theobald but also withdrew his earlier approval of the seizure of Tanaga, substituting Adak Island in its stead. If this substitution was not acceptable to the Army, he told Marshall, then the entire project should be dropped.

With far more important operations in progress or in prospect, the Army planners were not inclined to take a strong stand on so relatively unimportant a matter. They therefore counseled General Marshall to accept King's proposal, with the proviso that Tanaga might be taken at a later time. Marshall accepted this solution and so informed General DeWitt. On 30 August Army troops from Alaska occupied Adak and two weeks later the first Adak-based planes hit Kiska.[13]

Although the Tanaga-Adak debate had finally been settled and the operation successfully concluded, relations between the Army and Navy officers in the area were such that there was grave doubt in Washington that joint operations in the theater would be conducted with the degree of co-operation required for success. Many factors contributed to this lack of harmony, not the least of which was the personality of some of the senior commanders. Unified command, difficult to attain under ideal conditions, was impossible without a determination on the part of all commanders to subordinate their individual convictions to the common good. As viewed from Washington, this "predisposition to agree" was not evident among the commanders in the Alaskan theater and by August had produced such strong feelings as to bring from General Handy a recommendation that the War and Navy Departments inform the senior officers in the theater

---

[12] Memos, Actg CofS for CNO, 23 Jul 42, sub: Occupation of Tanaga or Adak; CNO for Actg CofS, 25 Jul 42, same sub, OPD 580.82 (Alaska), case 13. See other papers in this file for additional correspondence on this matter.

[13] JCS 42/D, 5 Aug 42, sub: Japanese Capabilities in Aleutians; Memos, King for Marshall, 18 Aug 42, sub: Tanaga Island Development, OPD Exec Files; OPD for Marshall, and Marshall for King, same date and sub, OPD 580.82 (Alaska), case 15; Rads, DeWitt to Marshall, 20 and 31 Aug 42, CM–IN 7583 and 12123.

that there could be no excuse "for with-holding whole-hearted support of the Service or the Commander exercising unity of command." "Strong notice of this conviction . . . ," he believed, "would do much to force essential co-operation and reduce much fruitless controversy between the two Services." [14]

When the situation did not improve the following month, the Army pro-posed a separate Alaskan Department independent of General DeWitt and headed by an air officer. This arrange-ment would also make it possible to shift the three top commanders in Alaska—Theobald, Buckner, and Butler — to other assignments quietly and without any unpleasantness. But even while this proposal was under discussion, DeWitt and Theobald were involved in a dis-pute over a small garrison in the Pribilof Islands. "What is it," General Marshall was moved to remark when he learned of this new conflict, "that produces so many complete misunderstandings?" [15] If he was seeking an answer he failed to receive one then, but since the imme-diate disagreement was soon settled, he

and Admiral King decided to make no change in command at that time. [16]

Less than a year later, after the test of active operations and after the relief of Admiral Theobald, King wrote:

In the North Pacific Area no complete unified command has been established. Naval Forces, amphibious operations, and a portion of the Army Air Forces have been placed under the Commander North Pacific, to operate under the principle of mutual cooperation with the ground forces and other Air Forces. The Commander North Pacific has carried out operations under joint directives not directly from the Joint Chiefs of Staff, but from the Commander in Chief, Pacific Ocean Areas, and the Com-manding General, Western Defense Com-mand. This arrangement, made last year, has, for the ADAK, AMCHITKA, ATTU, and the prospective KISKA operations, worked extremely well in practice, largely due to excellent cooperation between the responsible commanders concerned. I have not seen fit to press for a change in this set-up, nor do I wish to do so now. In fact, it is working so well that I believe a change would be a mistake. [17]

Meanwhile General DeWitt, far from abandoning his original proposal for the occupation of Tanaga, had begun again to urge the seizure of that island. But with Adak in American hands, the plan-ners in Washington could see no advan-tage in occupying Tanaga and suggested Amchitka Island, only fifty miles from Kiska, as the next objective. DeWitt did not favor this plan. Pointing to the in-conclusive findings of a reconnaissance

---

[14] Memo, Handy for McNarney, 8 Aug 42, sub: Army-Navy Co-operation in Alaska, OPD 384 (WDC), case 9. In commenting on this chapter in manuscript, General DeWitt wrote: "Too much emphasis is being placed on an incident that had no appreciable effect on operations as far as local commanders were concerned. It seems to have ap-peared more serious on paper than it actually was. There was a personality clash between Admiral Theobald and General Buckner, but it was super-ficial and had no lasting effect on the mutual co-operation that followed. It was forgotten after Admiral Theobald was relieved and General Buckner promoted." (Comments of DeWitt, July 1959, OCMH.)

[15] Memo, Marshall for Handy, 8 Sep 42, no sub, OPD Exec Files; Ltr, Marshall to DeWitt, 3 Sep 42; Memo, Marshall for King, 3 Sep 42, last two in WDCSA (Alaska).

[16] Memo, Marshall for King, 22 Sep 42, sub: Comd in Alaska, WDCSA (Alaska). See also correspondence between Marshall and DeWitt in this file and in "GCM" Personal File.

[17] Memo, King for Marshall, 19 Jul 43, sub: Relief by Army Troops of Marine Corps Ground and Avia-tion Units now on Garrison and Defense Duty at Tutuila, Wallis, Upolu, and Palmyra, OPD 384 PTO, case 55.

made at the end of September, he empha-sized the difficulties of constructing an airfield on the island. Moreover, the seizure of Amchitka would require larger naval forces than would be available, in view of an impending transfer of destroy-ers and other ships from the North Pacific to Guadalcanal. Operations against Amchitka, DeWitt asserted, were impractical, and unless otherwise di-rected he intended, he told Marshall on 17 October, to go ahead with the Tanaga project. If the Joint Chiefs approved, he hoped to go on to Kiska, then possibly to Attu and finally to Amchitka.[18]

The Kiska plan to which DeWitt referred in his message to Marshall was one he had submitted almost two weeks earlier. The occasion for this new move to open up the question of a general offensive in the North Pacific had been provided by Admiral Nimitz. As com-mander of the Pacific Ocean Area (which included the North Pacific), Nimitz was legitimately concerned over the fact that a portion of his naval strength was being immobilized in North Pacific waters without any visible effect on Japanese operations at Kiska and Attu. This strength, Nimitz felt, could profitably be employed elsewhere in the Pacific where it was badly needed. He did not believe, either, that the newly con-structed base at Adak would achieve decisive results, or that the Japanese could be driven from the Aleutians by air power alone. Nothing less than the seizure of both Japanese-held islands by American troops could accomplish that, said Nimitz, and he recommended that

the Army begin training a force capable of doing the job.[19]

Here was strong support indeed for Dewitt, who had long been pushing for an offensive against Kiska, and he lost no time sending to Marshall a plan for the seizure of the island. This plan called for the use of troops already in Alaska and accustomed to the climate, their place to be taken by additional troops provided by the War Department. In this way, DeWitt pointed out, the troops for the invasion could be assem-bled quickly in one place for training and equipped there for the coming as-sault. But, if this plan was not accept-able, DeWitt expressed a willingness to employ troops from the United States. In either case, the equivalent of a division, trained and equipped for am-phibious operations, would be required. These same troops, DeWitt added, could be employed later for operations against Attu and Amchitka.[20]

There was no disagreement in Wash-ington about the desirability of driving the enemy from the Aleutians. President Roosevelt had even suggested, during a visit to the west coast, that old battleships be used "to blast the Japs out of Kiska." But Admiral King, when this suggestion reached him, saw little merit in the Pres-ident's idea. Like Nimitz and DeWitt, he thought the job could be done only by amphibious troops. And he agreed also with DeWitt's scheme to use troops already in Alaska for the landing. But he did not agree with DeWitt's opti-

---

[18] Rads, DeWitt to Marshall, 20 Aug 42, CM–IN 7583; Marshall to DeWitt, 15 Oct 42, CM–OUT 5161; DeWitt to Marshall, 17 Oct 42; Memo, Streett for Handy, 9 Sep 42, OPD 381 (ADC), case 38.

[19] Ltr, Nimitz to King, 24 Sep 42, sub: Amphibious Training for Opns in Kiska, WDCSA (Alaska).
[20] Ltr, DeWitt to Marshall, 5 Oct 42, WDCSA (Alaska); Memo, DeWitt for Marshall, 12 Oct 42, sub: Plans for Reduction and Occupation of BOODLE (Kiska), OPD 320.2 (WDC), case 194.

mistic estimates of what he would need to capture Kiska. This matter, King felt, needed further study, and since the transports required for the operation could not be made available until January or February of 1943 no time would be lost by looking into the matter further.[21]

General Marshall also felt no purpose would be served by haste since weather in the fog-swept Aleutians was most difficult during the winter months. The spring of 1943, he thought, was the earliest date when an offensive could be launched in the North Pacific. He saw no necessity, therefore, for using troops already in Alaska, as DeWitt had suggested. There was ample time to select the troops needed and to train them in the United States where facilities for amphibious training already existed. For these reasons, plus the fact there was not then available or likely soon to be the assault shipping required for operations against Kiska, General Marshall thought it best to tell DeWitt his plan was not "favorably considered" at this time. And on the basis of reports on Amchitka, he suggested that another reconnaissance be made of the island to determine its suitability as an air base.[22]

General DeWitt did not accept this decision without protest. Though he ordered the reconnaissance Marshall requested he again asserted his objections to the occupation of Amchitka as a prelude to the seizure of Kiska. And convinced as he was of the possibility of a Japanese offensive in the Aleutians he could not agree that there was time to train the troops in the United States. He wanted the troops quickly for use in an emergency, and he wanted them readily available. "I appreciate the heavy responsibility and pressure under which you are working . . . ," he told Marshall, "but I hope you will find time to consider its [the Kiska plan] broader aspects and direct a favorable decision."[23]

This plea had no observable effect on Marshall's conviction that there was no real danger from the Japanese at Kiska, and therefore no pressing need to send troops to a theater whose mission was primarily defensive. Requirements elsewhere, in the Solomons, in New Guinea, in North Africa, and in Burma, were far more urgent and important.[24] Moreover, the Navy had by mid-November concluded that the most favorable target date for the seizure of Kiska would be 15 May 1943. If this date was acceptable, Admiral King proposed that the theater commanders be directed to prepare for the operation. On this basis, General Marshall was willing to agree tentatively to the Kiska invasion in mid-May. A final decision, he maintained, should not be made until March when he and King would be in a better position to determine what troops and assault shipping were needed and whether they could be spared. Admiral King accepted this condition without demur on 23 November, thus settling the problem temporarily for the Washington plan-

---

[21] Ltr, DeWitt to Marshall, 29 Sep 42; Memos, King for Marshall, 5 and 12 Oct 42, sub: Amphibious Opns Against Kiska, WDCSA (Alaska).

[22] Memos, Marshall for King, 17 Oct 42, sub: Amphibious Opns Against Kiska; OPD for Marshall, 15 Oct 42, same sub: Ltr, Marshall to DeWitt, 29 Oct 42, Memo, OPD for Marshall, same date, sub: DeWitt's letters of 19 and 23 Oct 42, all in OPD 381 (ADC) case 36.

[23] Ltr, DeWitt to Marshall, 5 Nov 42, WDCSA (Alaska).

[24] For expressions of this view, see the papers filed in OPD 381 (ADC), cases 36 and 44.

ners but leaving the theater commanders in doubt as to whether an offensive against Kiska would ultimately be launched.[25]

The temporary shelving of the Kiska offensive left unsettled the question of Amchitka. On receipt of Marshall's request for a new reconnaissance, General Buckner and Admiral Theobald had organized a survey party, but had delayed its departure because of the weather and the reported presence of Japanese on the island. So concerned was Admiral Nimitz over this report that he recommended on 22 November, the day before King and Marshall had reached agreement on Kiska, that an Army force be sent immediately to Amchitka to prevent the Japanese from constructing an air base there.[26] This was a step the Air Forces planners had already urged but which DeWitt continued to oppose persistently.

Under Rear Adm. Thomas C. Kinkaid, Theobald's successor and an experienced carrier commander who had fought the Japanese in the South Pacific, relations between the Army and Navy improved greatly. En route to his new assignment as commander of the North Pacific Area, he stopped off at Pearl Harbor to talk with Nimitz, who undoubtedly impressed on him the necessity for occupying Amchitka. He then went on to San Francisco where on 12 December he met General DeWitt and had a long talk with him about the situation in the

Aleutians. As a result of this discussion, DeWitt agreed to cancel his long-cherished design for occupying Tanaga and to use the troops already assembled for that purpose to seize Amchitka Island instead. Both Admirals King and Nimitz, who were in San Francisco at the time, immediately gave their consent to the cancellation of Tanaga.[27] Substitution of Amchitka would have to await formal approval by the Joint Chiefs.

Steps to gain this approval were initiated by Admiral King on his return to Washington. By 15 December he had already prepared and sent to General Marshall a proposed directive for the occupation of Amchitka, which he explained, was intended as preliminary to the expulsion of the Japanese "from Kiska and all of the Aleutians." At the same time, King suggested that the target date for Kiska be advanced to 1 March and that Admiral Nimitz be instructed to submit detailed plans for the seizure of both Amchitka and Kiska as well as an estimate of the forces required for both operations. Left to Nimitz also was the selection of a date for the occupation of Amchitka.[28]

General Marshall and the Army planners accepted this revised plan, but with two important reservations. First, they would not agree to the occupation of Amchitka until the results of the reconnaissance ordered in November were in; and second, they refused to commit themselves to any target date for the Kiska invasion. This refusal was based,

[25] Memos, King for Marshall, 15 Nov 42, sub: Amphibious Opns Against Kiska, WDCSA (Alaska) SS; OPD for Marshall, 17 Nov 42 and Marshall for King, 23 Nov 42, same sub, both in OPD 381 (ADC), case 45.

[26] Rad, Nimitz to King, No. 1041, 22 Nov 42, OPD 381 (ADC), case 47.

[27] Rad, Nimitz to Theobald, No. 2112, 17 Dec 42, OPD 381 (ADC), case 4.

[28] Memo, King for Marshall, 15 Dec 42, sub: Directive to occupy Amchitka, OPD 381 (ADC), case 50.

GENERAL DEWITT

Marshall explained, on "our serious logistical shortage" in the South and Southwest Pacific and on the possibility that once air forces were established on Amchitka the invasion of Kiska might prove unnecessary.[29]

Admiral King made no objection to the Army's conditions and the proposed directive authorizing the Amchitka and Kiska operations was quickly revised and approved by the Joint Chiefs on 17 December. Within a few days the first condition set by the Army was met when the reconnaissance group returned from Amchitka and reported that there were favorable airfield sites on the island.

This was the signal DeWitt was waiting for and he now acted with vigor and speed. By mid-January 1943, American troops had landed on Amchitka, occupied the island without resistance, and begun the construction of an airfield. Before the end of February, fighter planes based on the island were flying over Kiska as often as the foul weather permitted.[30]

Planning for the occupation of Kiska had meanwhile run a checkered course and come to a standstill. The Joint Chiefs directive, though it failed to set a target date for the operation, called for plans and these General DeWitt hastened to supply. Immediately on receipt of the directive he conferred with Nimitz, Kinkaid, and others about the Army's participation in the campaign and on 19 December forwarded to Washington an estimate of what he would need. Included was one division, two infantry regiments, and service and support troops, all together 25,000 men. Though this estimate was less than Admiral Nimitz' by one division, it still called for more troops than Marshall was ready to commit to the Aleutians. He was willing to give DeWitt the division, but no additional infantry strength beyond that. And to be certain that there was no misunderstanding he reminded DeWitt that the final decision on Kiska was still to be made. But the assurance of one division was enough for DeWitt and on that basis he made his plans. These were approved by Admiral Nimitz on 9 January, when

[29] Memo, Marshall for King, 16 Dec 42, sub: Directive To Occupy Amchitka; OPD Memo for Record, same date and sub, OPD 381 (ADC) case 50.

[30] Memo, Conolly for Handy, 18 Dec 42; Ltr, Marshall to DeWitt, 17 Dec 42; Rpt of OPD Observer on Amchitka Opn, all in OPD 381 (ADC), cases 50 and 61; Rads, DeWitt to Marshall, 20 and 25 Dec 42, CM–IN 8656, 8937, 11265.

preparations for the operation began in earnest.[31]

Selected to lead the assault was Rear Adm. Francis W. Rockwell, who had come out of the Philippines with General MacArthur. With Army and Navy officers assigned to the operation, Rockwell formed a joint planning staff at San Diego, site of the Marine Corps Amphibious Training Center and in close proximity to the major forces and headquarters that would participate. While this group developed its plans, the 7th Division, selected to make the assault, was reorganized, brought up to full strength, and put through an intensive training program. In its amphibious phase, this program was directed by Marine officers. At the same time, the Eleventh Air Force stepped up its operations against Kiska, bombing the island as often as weather permitted.

These preparations did not change General Marshall's views on Kiska. Never enthusiastic about a North Pacific offensive unless the Soviet Union entered the war against Japan and fearful of its effect on other more important areas, he had given reluctant consent to the invasion of Kiska. At the same time, he sought to keep to a minimum the forces required for the operation while hoping that ultimately it would prove unnecessary. Thus, at the Casablanca Conference in January 1943 he had taken the lead in modifying the original statement of U.S. intentions in the Aleutians — seizure and occupation of the western Aleutians — to the milder "make the Aleutians as secure as may be" with the

ADMIRAL KINKAID

forces available. Though the change was made ostensibly to allay British fears of large-scale operations in the North Pacific, there was never real danger of such operations in the light of Marshall's conviction.[32]

The limitations placed on the North Pacific offensive by General Marshall and confirmed at Casablanca led ultimately to a change in the plans for Kiska. By early March, when these plans were already far advanced, it had become apparent to Admiral Kinkaid that he would not be able to get the ships he needed or to launch the planned air offensive against Kiska in time to mount

[31] Rads, Marshall to DeWitt, 20 Dec 42, CM–OUT 7134; DeWitt to Marshall, 19 and 21 Dec 42, 11 Jan 43, CM–IN 8228, 9548, 5161; Nimitz to CTF 3 and 8, No. 0342, 9 Jan 43.

[32] Mins, JCS Mtg, 22 Jan 43; CCS 168, 22 Jan 43, sub: Conduct of the War in Pacific in 1943; CCS 170, 23 Jan 43, Rpt to President and Prime Minister.

the operation before the pea-soup fogs of the summer season set in. After consultation with DeWitt and Buckner, he proposed, therefore, a less ambitious undertaking against Attu, which, he believed, could be carried off with the forces and shipping already available. The Joint Chiefs readily agreed to this change, but Admiral King made it clear to both Nimitz and DeWitt that this acceptance did not constitute a directive for the operation but only authorization to plan and train for it. Final approval would wait the outcome of the Pacific Military Conference, then only two days away.[33]

While Pacific strategy was being debated in Washington, Admiral Rockwell's joint staff in San Diego started to plan for the seizure of Attu, the new but still unapproved objective. On 17 March General DeWitt, hoping perhaps to force a decision, submitted to Nimitz a draft directive setting 7 May as the target date for the invasion. No action followed this recommendation, but a few days later word reached Washington that the Japanese were building an airfield on Attu. "If they are allowed to complete this, and go further in the consolidation of their position there by establishment of airfields on Shemya and Agattu," wrote Admiral King, "our eventual recapture of these areas will be rendered very much more difficult." Since by that time the Pacific Military Conference had reached the conclusion that operations in the South and Southwest Pacific during 1943 would have to be limited to Task Two, King recom-

mended that the Joint Chiefs give Nimitz and DeWitt the green light on Attu. On the understanding that no additional forces would be required, Marshall consented and the same day, 22 March, King issued, in the name of the Joint Chiefs of Staff, the joint directive for the seizure of Attu.[34]

Preparations for the coming invasion now moved forward rapidly. Detailed plans were drawn up by Rockwell's staff and by the troop commanders. On 31 March, Admiral Nimitz and General DeWitt jointly issued the operational directive outlining the tasks—seizure of Attu and Shemya Islands—and setting the date for the assault as 7 May. Kinkaid, as commander of the North Pacific, was to command the entire operation; Admiral Rockwell, the amphibious phase. Once the troops were established ashore, command was to pass to the 7th Division commander, Maj. Gen. Albert E. Brown. The relationship between the Army and Navy commanders, DeWitt assured General Marshall on 1 April, was excellent and all the officers concerned were showing a commendable unity of purpose. Preparations were being completed rapidly and he expected, he told Marshall, that his greatest enemy would be the weather and not the Japanese.[35]

This easy assumption proved less than accurate for almost immediately on landing the troops ran into all sorts of

---

[33] Rads, Kinkaid to Nimitz, Nos. 0103 and 0115, 7 Mar 43; King to Nimitz and DeWitt, No. 1221, 10 Mar 43, OPD 381, case 39. For an account of the Pacific Military Conference, see above, ch XIX.

[34] Memos, King for Marshall, 22 Mar 43, sub: Opns Against Attu; Handy for King, same date and sub; Rad, DeWitt to Nimitz, No. 2239, 19 Mar 43, all in OPD 381, case 54 and 39; Rad, King to Nimitz, No. 1939, 22 Mar 43, OPD Exec Files.

[35] Rads, Nimitz to Kinkaid and Rockwell, No. 1839, 1 Apr 43; Kinkaid to Nimitz, No. 0323, 31 Mar 43, OPD 381, case 54; Ltr, DeWitt to Marshall, 1 Apr 43, WDCSA (Alaska).

difficulties. By 12 May it was evident that the reduction of the Japanese defenses would be a longer and tougher job than anyone had anticipated. As the campaign dragged on the Navy became increasingly apprehensive over the safety of the naval supporting force and on 16 May Admiral Kinkaid, after consultation with DeWitt and Buckner, relieved General Brown, the ground commander, and appointed Maj. Gen. Eugene M. Landrum in his stead. Fortunately, this drastic move did not impair the harmony between the services, but neither did it accomplish the miracle of ending the stalemate ashore. It was not until two weeks later that the island was secured and construction begun on an airfield. By that time a small force had landed on Shemya Island, thirty-five miles to the east, to begin work on an airfield there.[36]

Still on the docket was the seizure of Kiska, deferred in favor of Attu because of the lack of shipping and other resources. Thought to be the main Japanese stronghold in the Aleutians and garrisoned by a force of about 10,000 men, this island had always been De-Witt's preferred objective. Now there was no further reason for delay and even before the Attu campaign was over DeWitt joined with Admiral Nimitz in urging the Joint Chiefs to give their consent to the invasion of Kiska early in September. Failing to receive

approval, they tried again at the end of the month. This time they furnished a detailed operational plan and moved the target date up to 15 August, in accordance with Admiral King's wishes.[37]

While the Navy supported the Kiska project, the Army planners continued to express doubts about the advisability of the operation. Some were concerned over the diversion of critical resources to this indecisive area; others thought a war of attrition in the Aleutians might pay better dividends than outright seizure of the island. Finally, Nimitz and DeWitt were authorized to prepare for the invasion, but permission to make the assault was withheld.[38]

The second week of June saw the resolution of the differences over Kiska. On the heels of a study by the Army planners, General Marshall expressed a willingness to leave the decision to the Navy. But Admiral King refused to act on this suggestion and recommended instead that they turn the problem over to the Joint Staff Planners. Marshall agreed, and during the next few days the planners reviewed the entire project. Their recommendation, made on 11 June, was that Nimitz and DeWitt be authorized to invade Kiska at a date to be chosen by themselves. August, the planners pointed out, was the best month of the year for operations in the Aleutians. Moreover, the force required for the invasion—five regimental combat

---

[36] For General Brown's account of his relief, see his account of the operation entitled "The Attu Operation," undated but written after the war, in OCMH. See also Samuel Eliot Morison, *Aleutians, Gilberts and Marshalls, June 1942–April 1944*, vol VII, "History of United States Naval Operations in World War II" (Boston: Little, Brown and Company, 1951), pp. 47–49; ONI Combat Narrative, The Aleutians Campaign, pp. 83ff; Conn, Engelman, and Fairchild, Guarding the United States and Its Outposts, ch. XI.

[37] Rads, DeWitt to Nimitz, No. 2345, 19 May 43; Nimitz to King, No. 0247, 21 May 43; DeWitt and Nimitz to JCS, 30 May 43, CM–IN 19422; Memos, King for Marshall, 23 May 43, no sub; OPD for Marshall, 22 May 43, sub: Reduction of Kiska, all in OPD 381, case 132.

[38] The various papers dealing with this discussion are filed in OPD 381, case 132, and ABC 381, Japan (5–31–42).

PLANNING THE KISKA OPERATION. *From left, seated: Admiral Rockwell, Admiral Kinkaid, Maj. Gen. Charles H. Corlett, General Buckner, General Butler, and Maj. Gen. G. R. Pearkes of the Canadian Army Pacific Command; standing: Commander Dennison, Captain Colclough, Colonel Jones, General Ready, General Post.*

teams, a specially equipped and trained U.S.-Canadian force of regimental size, and an artillery battalion—was available, or would be by 15 August, the planners observed. There was, therefore, in their opinion no reason to delay, especially since the operation would have a favorable psychological effect on the American people. The Joint Chiefs accepted this recommendation and gave their approval immediately, despite the fear that the operation would be a costly one and the island once taken would require a large garrison. Three days later the theater commanders were notified of the decision.[39]

The next two months were busy ones for the commanders in Alaska. While final preparations were being made, the Eleventh Air Force in July stepped up its operations, to drop a total of 424 tons of bombs on Kiska. During the same month the Navy hit the island with an additional 330 tons of explosives. On 2 August, a joint air and naval force struck Kiska with devastating blows, followed two days later by the heaviest air raid to date. Thereafter the island was subjected to daily bombings, with increased intensity until D-day, 15 August.

The absence of strong enemy opposition to these attacks had been noted, but no one had put the correct interpretation

---

[39] Supp Mins, JCS Mtg, 8 Jun 43; OPD Brief, 8 Jun 43, sub: Notes on JCS 91st Mtg, JCS 346, ABC 381 Japan (5–31–42); JCS 346/2, 11 Jun 43, sub: JPS Rpt Opn Cottage; Rad, JCS to DeWitt, 14 Jun 43, CM–OUT 5847. For Canadian participation in

Aleutian operations, see Col. Stanley W. Dziuban, *Military Relations Between the United States and Canada, 1939–1945,* UNITED STATES ARMY IN WORLD WAR II (Washington, 1960).

on this fact. Actually there had been no enemy opposition at all after July. The Japanese garrison had evacuated under cover of fog and mist. But despite this fact, pilots and observers had continued to report antiaircraft fire and Japanese activity. It was only when the troops landed on 15 August fully expecting to meet strong resistance that the Allies learned there were no Japanese on the island. For almost three weeks Allied air and naval forces had been pounding an empty island. If this fact was embarrassing to those entrusted with the direction of the campaign, it was none the less welcome to the foot soldier on whom would have fallen the nasty job of wiping out the Japanese garrison.

The decision by the Japanese to withdraw the Kiska garrison of almost 6,000 men had been made shortly after the Attu landing in May. The first reaction of *Imperial General Headquarters* to the American invasion had been to order Army and Navy forces in the area to rush to the scene and "annihilate the enemy," a favorite Japanese phrase. Mature second judgment dictated another course and within a week these orders were countermanded. The Aleutians, *Imperial General Headquarters* now decided, could not be defended with the forces available. These forces, it reasoned, could be employed more effectively in the Kurils and Hokkaido and on 21 May *Imperial General Headquarters* issued orders for the evacuation of both Attu and Kiska.

The withdrawal of the troops on Attu proved an impossible task, though at least one submarine made the attempt. But on Kiska, the evacuation went forward smoothly under an elaborate and detailed plan. Thirteen submarines assigned to the task first took off the sick and wounded and then the civilians early in June. The loss of two of the submarines led to a change in plan. A naval task force of the *5th Fleet* was to move in and take off the entire garrison, with its supplies and equipment, in one operation. Delayed by bad weather, the task force (consisting of three cruisers and eleven other warships) finally anchored in Kiska Harbor at 1340 on 29 July. It took only fifty-five minutes to embark over 5,000 men and by 1 August the force was back in the Kurils (Paramushiro) after a calm and safe voyage.[40]

Though the anticlimax at Kiska rang down the curtain on the campaign to expel the Japanese from the Aleutians, it did not end consideration of the use of these bleak islands for further offensives against Japan. Rather it increased the urgency of the problem for there were now in the Alaska-Aleutians area almost 150,000 troops. Until a decision was reached, these troops would remain idle.

---

[40] The Aleutians Island Campaign; Naval Opns in the Northern Area; Northern Area Monthly Combat Reports; Naval Opns, Mar 42–Feb 43, all in Japanese Studies in World War II, Nos. 51–54; Hattori, The Greater East Asia War, II, pt. 5, 51–57.

CHAPTER XXII

The Revival of ORANGE

You don't kill men with guns you're not using.

GENERAL MATTHEW B. RIDGWAY

After mid–1942 and throughout most of 1943, while American naval, air, and ground forces were engaging the Japanese in desperate battle in the Solomons, in New Guinea, and in the Aleutians, relative calm reigned over the Central Pacific. In this region, stretching westward across the ocean from the Hawaiian Islands to the Philippines, Japanese fleets and merchant vessels roamed freely, subject only to the attacks of Pacific Fleet submarines, which were taking an ever-increasing toll of enemy ships. Scattered Japanese garrisons leisurely built airstrips and prepared their defenses, scarcely aware of the war that raged to the north and south. But even while these battles were being fought, plans were being laid at Pearl Harbor and in Washington for an offensive that would ultimately reach the coast of Japan itself. Before the year 1943 was out the Central Pacific would see some of the bitterest fighting of the war.

The Central Pacific War

The scene of impending conflict was Micronesia, an ocean area larger than the continental United States. Scattered throughout this vast expanse of ocean are tiny islands, numbering over 1,000 and clustered into four major groups whose total land area is about 1,200 square miles. (*Map 7*) Most easterly of the groups are the Gilberts, low-lying coral atolls located just west of the date line and almost on the equator. To the northwest are the Marshall Islands, a double chain of atolls, reefs, and islets, none of which rises more than a few feet above sea level. Stretching almost due west from the Marshalls, in a long irregular string about 2,000 miles in length, are the 550 islands of the Caroline group. In the center of the group lies Truk and at the western extremity is Palau, pointing a finger at the Philippines. The Marianas, fourth of the island groups of Micronesia, lie above the Carolines and extend for more than 400 miles from Guam in the south to within 500 miles of Iwo Jima.[1]

Strategically located across the main sea lanes between the United States and the Philippines and dominating the most direct avenue of approach to the western Pacific, the islands of Micronesia played a vital role in Japanese war plans. Forehandedly, the Japanese had gained

---

[1] See the Introduction, above, for a description of these islands.

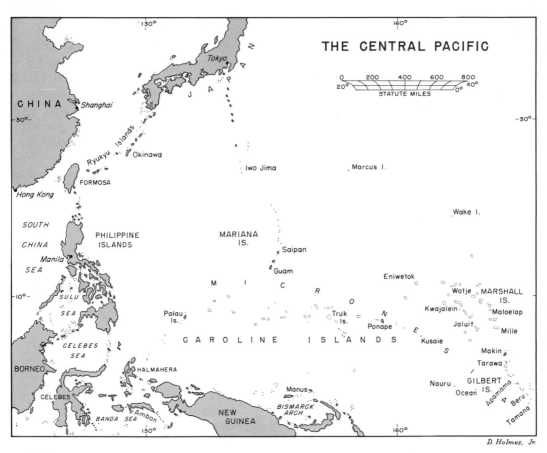

MAP 7

control of most of these islands before the war. The Carolines, Marshalls, and Marianas (except for Guam), they had seized from Germany during World War I and held under a mandate from the League of Nations. The rest—Guam, the Gilberts, and the two phosphate islands, Ocean and Nauru—they occupied shortly after Pearl Harbor, thus extending the outer perimeter of the empire's defenses almost to the date line and placing Japanese forces in position to cut the Allied line of communications in the South Pacific. Only the disaster at Midway kept them from pushing on to Samoa and the Fijis, as they had every intention of doing.[2]

Vital as the Central Pacific was to the Japanese in the defense of the home islands, it was equally important to the Americans, who recognized it as a separate area of responsibility under Admiral Nimitz' direct command. Along it lay the line of communications to the Philippines and the traditional path of

[2] See Chapter XII, above, for an account of Japanese planning for this move and the effect of the Midway defeat.

advance against Japan marked out in the ORANGE plans of the 1920's and 1930's.[3] According to these plans, the Pacific Fleet with troop-carrying transports would venture from Pearl Harbor at the start of war and sail westward into the Mandates. The advance of this force was to be a progressive, step-by-step affair in which selected islands would be seized and developed as forward bases before the next move began. Thus would the United States project its naval strength ever westward until the Philippines were reached.

In prewar plans, the Philippine garrison had been assigned the mission of holding Manila Bay for an indefinite period, presumed to be six months. Though few responsible officers believed the fleet could fight its way through to Manila Bay in that time, the ORANGE plans made no provision for any other contingency, such as the recapture of the Philippines. Thus, according to these old plans, when the fleet reached Manila Bay with its reinforcements it would find the bay in friendly hands, available as a base for further operations.

It was this plan, modified and placed in the context of a global struggle in which Germany was the main enemy and Europe the main theater, that was in effect on the morning of 7 December.[4] But the Japanese attack on Pearl Harbor altered completely the balance of forces in the Pacific and rendered obsolete the ORANGE concept of a Central Pacific offensive. The Navy would have enough to do defending the Hawaiian outpost and the west coast of the United States.

Guam, Wake, and the Philippines lay beyond reach and all hopes for an early offensive into the Mandates lay at the bottom of the bay with the battleships of the Pacific Fleet. Until this loss was replaced and the Pacific Fleet strengthened, the Navy would have to husband its resources and fight a defensive war.

The adoption of a defensive strategy did not mean inaction and from the start the Pacific Fleet struck at the enemy whenever and wherever it could with the meager forces available. Thus in the period from February through March 1942, task forces built around the three carriers, fortunately absent from Pearl Harbor at the time of the attack, raided Japanese-held islands in a vain effort to divert Japanese forces in their drive southward. In April came the carrier-borne strike against Tokyo and in August the premature raid on Makin by the 2d Marine Raider Battalion led by Lt. Col. Evans F. Carlson. But perhaps the most profitable operations of the fleet during this period were those of the submarines, which in the first four months of the war sank 300,000 tons of Japanese shipping.[5]

Spectacular as these miscellaneous operations and hit-and-run raids were, they did not end the Japanese threat to Hawaii or ensure the security of the line of communications across the South Pacific. It was the victory at Midway that accomplished the first and opened

---

[3] For an account of prewar ORANGE planning, see above, Chapters I and III.

[4] This plan, RAINBOW 5, is described above, in Chapter III.

[5] The Makin raid is described in full in Philip A. Crowl and Edmund G. Love, *Seizure of the Gilberts and Marshalls*, UNITED STATES ARMY IN WORLD WAR II (Washington, 1955), ch. IV, and by Morison, who also covers submarine operations, in *Coral Sea, Midway, and Submarine Actions*, chs. X and XI. Early naval raids are covered in Morison, *Rising Sun in the Pacific*, ch. XIII, and ONI, Combat Narrative, Early Raids in the Pacific Ocean. For an account of the Tokyo raid, see above, Chapter XII.

the way for an offensive designed to achieve the second. That offensive opened with the landing of the marines on Guadalcanal in August 1942 and with the first encounters between Allied and Japanese troops on the heights overlooking Port Moresby. Both campaigns proved more difficult and costly than anticipated and consumed all the resources that could be spared for the Pacific. For four months the issue hung in the balance, but by the end of the year victory seemed assured. The time had come to plan the next move in the drive on Rabaul; perhaps there would be enough left over to open the long-delayed offensive in the Central Pacific.

The Philippines in Central Pacific Strategy

All prewar plans for war with Japan, whether alone or in concert with other powers, had been conditioned largely by the almost impossible task of defending the Philippines. It was this problem rather than the defeat of Japan that preoccupied the planners and produced the ORANGE concept for an advance across the Central Pacific and the successive capture of positions in the mandated islands. The objective of these operations, essentially naval in character, was the reinforcement of the Philippines. Japan would be defeated later by operations vaguely described in ORANGE as "military and economic pressure made progressively more severe." [6] If these did not produce the desired result, other means would be devised.

A whole generation of officers had learned their lessons in the ORANGE

school. As students at the Army and Navy War Colleges and during their tours in the Pacific and in Washington they had developed theoretical exercises and solved theoretical problems on the basis of the ORANGE assumptions. Now, as senior officers in wartime, they faced the cold reality of defeating an actual enemy. It is not surprising, therefore, that their first wartime planning for an offensive in the Central Pacific should follow the familiar pattern of the time-tested, Philippine-oriented ORANGE plan.

This pattern was clearly evident at the Casablanca Conference in January 1943. There, for the first time in Allied councils, the concept of a progressive advance across the Central Pacific was resurrected and an effort made to co-ordinate such an advance with the offensive already under way in the South and Southwest Pacific and in the Aleutians.[7] There was no thought of initiating a Central Pacific offensive immediately or substituting it for the drive on Rabaul, an objective never foreseen in prewar planning. Nor did the plans developed at Casablanca envisage operations beyond the Philippines. In this sense Pacific strategy after a year of war was still closely tied to the prewar ORANGE concept. The only difference was that the enemy had forced on the Allies a different route of advance. The objective was still the Philippines.

The spokesman for the Central Pacific at Casablanca was Admiral King. That he should speak out first was natural in view of the predominantly naval char-

---

[6] Ltr, JPC to JB, 27 Dec 37, sub: Joint Basic War Plan ORANGE, JB 325, ser. 618.

[7] For an account of the Casablanca Conference and Pacific strategy, see above, Chapter XVIII. See also John Miller, jr., "The Casablanca Conference and Pacific Strategy," *Military Affairs*, XIII (Winter, 1949) 209–15, and Crowl and Love, *Seizure of the Gilberts and Marshalls*, pp. 7–10.

acter of the area and the traditional interest of the Navy in this route of advance. His advocacy of a Central Pacific offensive, however, did not imply any lessening of the effort in the South and Southwest Pacific. Operations there were essential, he believed, for the security of Australia and the line of communications. But once that campaign was over and Rabaul captured, where would the Allies go next, King asked. He found his answer in ORANGE, his objective in the Philippines.

In choosing the Philippines, Admiral King did not rule out offensives elsewhere, in the North Pacific and on the Asiatic mainland. Nor did he overlook the Netherlands Indies as an alternative objective to the Philippines. The Japanese had gone to war primarily to obtain the rich natural resources of the Indies and were largely dependent on these islands for the prosecution of the war. Their loss would be a crippling blow for the Japanese and any effort by the Allies to seize them would meet with determined and desperate resistance. Moreover, as Admiral King pointed out, an operation against the Japanese in the Indies would constitute, in effect, a frontal assault on a strongly held position, a costly and difficult venture in any case. The Philippines, King asserted, could be taken with far less effort and at much lower cost. And from these islands, which lay along the main Japanese line of communications, the Allies would be able to cut off the vital flow of oil and other resources to Japan as effectively as from the Indies.[8]

To Admiral King, the most feasible approach to the Philippines was by way

of the Central Pacific. Though he did not commit himself at Casablanca to this route, he made it clear that he preferred it to the two other alternate approaches. The one in the south, he pointed out, was outflanked by enemy bases in the Mandates and unsuitable for large fleet engagements; the one to the north, starting from the Aleutians, he apparently never considered seriously. The advantages were clearly all on the side of a direct thrust across the Pacific. It was shorter than the southern route; it would take American forces along a path familiar to most naval officers from their studies at the Naval War College; and it would approach the Philippines from the flank by way of the Marshalls, Truk, and the Marianas.

General MacArthur would not have agreed with this reasoning. Writing in retrospect ten years after the war, he explained his view toward the Central Pacific as follows:

The so-called "Central Pacific Concept," as finally embodied in the Orange War Plans, had in mind the relief of the Philippines before those Islands fell to the Japanese in the event of attack. This necessitated securing the lines of communication and supply between the Philippines and the United States which were threatened so long as Japan continued to hold and occupy the flanking Central Pacific Islands mandated to her following World War I. The "Central Pacific Concept" consequently lost its validity when it was abandoned in favor of a "Europe First" policy as the Japanese actually struck the Philippines. That was the time which presented the golden opportunity, both in strategy and logic, for a Central Pacific drive by our combined fleets aimed at engaging and destroying Japan's naval power on the Pacific. Had we reacted in this manner as always theretofore intended we would have brought the war to a speedy and victorious close and saved the

---

[8] Mins, CCS Mtg, 14 Jan 43.

Philippines and other areas on the Pacific from the long travail of enemy occupation, while at the same time sparing our own nation the terrible sacrifice exacted during the ensuing years of conflict.

Apologists for the "Europe First" concept point to our Pearl Harbor losses as having so weakened the Navy as to prevent such a Central Pacific drive. This argument has little or no validity for the diversion of the naval power engaged in the relatively unproductive North African campaign could have enabled the massing of a combined fleet capable of overpowering any combination of naval strength the axis powers were able to mount in the Pacific. This evaluation flows from the facts that the enemy European fleets by that time had been reduced to little more than a nuisance value, the German threat to the middle east had been eliminated by Rommel's defeat at El Alamein, the German offensive in Russia had been stopped at Stalingrad and the great Russian ground counter-offensive had been successfully launched. Having missed this initial opportunity, the belated Central Pacific drive toward the Marianas in July 1944 could at best produce local tactical successes without bringing to bear any decisive influence upon the course of the war.[9]

For different reasons than MacArthur might have advanced had he attended the Casablanca Conference, the British were doubtful of the virtues of an advance across the Central Pacific to the Philippines. As a matter of fact, they were opposed in principle to any Pacific venture that might threaten the primary effort against Germany. But when Admiral King readily agreed, at least in principle, that the recapture of the Philippines should come after Germany was defeated, the British did not pursue the subject. They doubted also the advisability of scheduling preliminary operations in the Central Pacific as far as Truk before the final blow in Europe, but on this question King maintained a discreet silence.

During the next few days, while the American and British Chiefs discussed other matters, their planners worked out a program for the Pacific for the year ahead. Included in the ambitious plan submitted on 17 January[10] was the seizure of the Gilberts, Marshalls, and Caroline Islands, including Truk, as preparatory steps in the recapture of the Philippines. These operations were to begin after the capture of Rabaul, also scheduled for that year, but at least one of the planners—Admiral Cooke— thought the advance in the Central Pacific might open even earlier.[11]

To the British this plan, which included also the recapture of Burma, seemed more extensive than was warranted by the resources available for the Pacific in 1943. Once begun, they feared these operations might divert Allied strength from the main effort in Europe. They sought, therefore, to restrict Pacific operations and suggested that the Allies limit themselves in 1943 to Rabaul and Burma. Admiral King thought this restriction entirely unnecessary. The proposed drive into the Central Pacific, he declared, was not a commitment on Allied resources but a desirable course of action that would utilize whatever forces were available. It might include only action in the Marshalls during the year or it might extend as far as Truk, depending upon events that could not then be foreseen. If Rabaul was taken in May

---

[9] Ltr, MacArthur to Maj Gen A. C. Smith, Chief, Mil Hist, 7 Jan 55, OCMH.

[10] For the other provisions of this plan, see above, Chapter XVIII.
[11] Mins, JCS Mtg, 17 Jan 43.

then the drive into the Mandates might make considerable progress before the opening date of the Burma offensive in November. Certainly, King argued, it would be unwise to limit the Pacific program to Rabaul and Burma alone. Such a restriction might well have the effect of imposing on Allied troops in the Pacific an enforced idleness for a period of months and was contrary to the Allied aim of keeping the Japanese under "continual pressure."

The British actually had little choice but to accept the American assurance that the Central Pacific would not drain off resources intended for Europe. Whether they actually believed this is doubtful; they were fully aware that operations once begun generate demands for additional resources. But to argue on this basis would raise questions about their own operations. Once this position had been reached, agreement came quickly. If all the Americans wanted was to ensure the fullest use of available forces and to be ready to exploit any opportunity that arose, the British were willing to accept General Marshall's suggestion that the matter be settled by specifying that if any operations were launched in the Central Pacific in 1943 they would be made "with the resources available in the theater."[12] This qualification, taken with the proviso that such operations would not be undertaken until Rabaul had been reduced or at the expense of the Burma campaign, gave adequate assurance that operations in the Pacific would not jeopardize the Allied effort in Europe.

With agreement on the broad outline of Pacific strategy, the Americans at Casablanca were free to consider in more detail Pacific prospects for the coming year. So far as the Central Pacific was concerned, the outlook was bright. Japan, it was true, might launch an offensive of its own from bases in the Mandates, either by way of Midway against Hawaii or by way of New Caledonia, Fiji, and Samoa against the vital line of communications to Australia. The first the Japanese had already attempted, without success, and the Joint Chiefs thought another attempt would also fail. The second line of action, a drive toward the line of communications, had been partially forestalled by the Allied invasion of the Solomons, but there still remained the possibility, the Joint Chiefs believed, of a Japanese attack against Samoa from the Gilbert and Ellice Islands. Such a move, if successful, would expose the Fijis to direct invasion and cut the South Pacific line as effectively as the earlier Japanese drive southward through the Solomons had threatened to do.

To counter these potential Japanese moves in the Central Pacific, the Americans considered two possible courses: an advance westward from Midway by way of Wake and the Marshalls to the Truk-Guam line; or northwest from Samoa through the Ellice and Gilbert Islands into the Marshalls. Both would serve the purpose of forestalling an enemy attack, would keep the Japanese off balance, and divert their forces away from Rabaul, where the Allies expected to make their major effort. In addition, the second course would ensure the security of the Fiji-Samoa portion of the line of communication. If this course was

---

[12] Mins, CCS Mtg, 18 Jan 43. The final wording of the plan is in CCS 155/1, 19 Jan 43, sub: Conduct of the War in 1943.

adopted, it would be possible to advance to the Truk-Guam line by way of Rabaul once that bastion was reduced, either in concert with a drive from the east or alone.[13]

These were the courses open in January 1943, but it was still too early to make a choice that might prove unnecessarily restrictive at a later date. The decision of the Joint Chiefs, therefore, was one calculated to leave them free to seize any opportunity that might arise. It called for an advance west from Midway "as practicable," northwest from Samoa, and north from Rabaul — the last to be undertaken only if there were sufficient forces at hand to occupy and exploit the Truk-Guam line. The British, it will be recalled, accepted this statement of U.S. intentions without comment and on 23 January it was adopted as part of the final report of the conference.[14]

With the sanction of the Casablanca decision, Admiral King set his staff to work in February 1943 on plans for an early assault against the Ellice and Gilbert Islands, followed, perhaps, by the seizure of the Marshalls.[15] Undoubtedly influenced by the delay in getting Task Two of the Rabaul offensive under way,

he wanted now to take up the slack in Pacific operations with an offensive in the Central Pacific. In this way, he thought, the Allies would be able to retain the initiative while, at the same time, diverting Japanese forces from the defense of Rabaul.

Before presenting this proposal to his colleagues on the Joint Chiefs of Staff, Admiral King sounded his chief naval subordinates in the Pacific, Admirals Nimitz and Halsey. The response was anything but encouraging.[16] Admiral Halsey, who was then preparing for further operations in the Solomons, thought he had enough to do without taking on another job. Far from supporting his operations in the South Pacific, this new task would drain away forces from the central effort and make Task Two more difficult and time-consuming. All the forces available should be thrown into the Solomons, he told King, for the Japanese were consolidating their positions there and delay might well prove costly. In this view he was strongly supported by his superior, Admiral Nimitz, who felt that until the Americans gained a marked superiority over the Japanese in naval and air strength, it would not be advisable to strike out in the Central Pacific.

Admiral King was not convinced by these arguments and thought his two most experienced commanders, each preoccupied with his own problems, had missed the point. An offensive in the Central Pacific, conducted simultaneously with the offensive in the South,

---

[13] JCS Memo, 22 Jan 43, sub: Conduct of the War in Pacific Theater in 1943, CCS 168; Mins, CCS Mtg, 22 Jan 43.

[14] CCS 170/1, 23 Jan 43, sub: Final Rpt to President and Prime Minister. The discussions at Casablanca are discussed more fully above in Chapter XVIII.

[15] Funafuti in the Ellice group, it will be recalled, had been occupied early in October 1942 by marines from Samoa, but this fact was a closely guarded secret, even in the Navy. Morison, *Aleutians, Gilberts, and Marshalls*, pp. 78–79. The Marshalls plan, dated 12 February 1943, contemplated the occupation of Kwajalein, Wotje, and Maloelap. CNO (WPD) File Marshall Islands Plan, case 183, cited in Hayes, The War Against Japan, ch. II, p. 4.

[16] Rads, King to Halsey, 9 Feb 43; Halsey to King, info Nimitz, 11 Feb 43; Nimitz to King, 11 Feb 43, all in Navy files. Cited in Hayes, The War Against Japan, ch. XI, pp. 12–13.

would, he believed, support that effort and at the same time draw strength from it. What he had in mind, he explained, was to "whipsaw" the Japanese to prevent them from concentrating their forces in one area.[17]

But Halsey persisted in his opposition to the scheme. While recognizing the advantages of mutually supporting operations in two separate areas, he thought an attack such as King was proposing would be both unprofitable and costly. It would constitute a frontal assault, and, even if successful, would gain for the Allies no important objective. On the other hand, the islands, once seized, would prove a continuing drain on Allied resources and virtually require further advances in the same direction, which may have been precisely what Admiral King wanted. To Halsey, Rabaul was the prime objective, the key to the Japanese defenses, and he was all for striking at it as soon as possible and with everything he had and could get.[18]

At this stage, General MacArthur indicated his readiness to discuss plans for the capture of Rabaul, and the planners, meeting with Nimitz' and Halsey's representatives in Washington at the Pacific Military Conference, devoted almost the entire month of March to this problem.[19] But even during this period Admiral King did not abandon altogether his hopes for an early drive against the Ellice and Gilbert Islands. At one point in the conference, when General Sutherland, MacArthur's chief of staff, presented the plan agreed upon by the theater representatives, King again

raised the possibility of an offensive in the Central Pacific.[20] The plan proposed, he pointed out, would immobilize naval forces in the South Pacific for some time and he suggested that they be used during this interval in the Central Pacific, specifically in the Gilberts and Marshalls. Why he preferred the Marshalls to the Ellice Islands, he did not say.

Again the main opposition came from naval officers in the Pacific. Vice Adm. Raymond A. Spruance, Nimitz' representative at the conference, agreed that naval forces could not be allowed to remain idle while MacArthur advanced up the New Guinea coast to New Britain, but he did not believe the time was yet ripe for an attack against the Gilberts and Marshalls. It would be necessary, first, to seize advance positions from which to support such an attack; and, second, to assemble a large enough force to continue the advance across the Central Pacific after the islands were captured. Like Halsey, he did not think the Gilberts and Marshalls a sufficiently important objective to warrant attack unless it was followed up. So far as the fleet was concerned, Spruance thought it might best be employed, if not needed in the South Pacific, in the Aleutians and in the Hawaiian area.

Captain Browning, Halsey's chief of staff and the officer most directly concerned, was not even willing to grant that the naval forces of the South Pacific, even if temporarily idle, should be transferred to another area. The South Pacific, he pointed out, was the decisive

---

[17] Rad, King to Nimitz, info Halsey, 13 Feb 43.

[18] Rad, Halsey to King, 17 Feb 43.

[19] For an account of the Pacific Military Conference, see above, Chapter XIX.

[20] Mins, JCS Mtg, 21 Mar 43; Memo, Sutherland, Spruance, and Browning for JCS, 20 Mar, 43, sub: Opns in South and SWP Areas During 1943, JCS 238/2.

theater of operations for the Japanese and Halsey's warships constituted the greatest menace to their lines of communication southward from Rabaul. So long as the Allies maintained a naval striking force there, the Japanese would be forced, Browning asserted, to keep a strong naval force of their own in the vicinity. Thus, the mere existence of a South Pacific fleet would, in a measure, ensure the security of Hawaii. It should therefore remain where it was, Browning concluded, unless its employment elsewhere would contribute to the main offensive mission of the theater, the capture of Rabaul.

At this point in the conference Admiral King dropped the subject. With his two top commanders in the Pacific and their representatives in Washington—all senior naval officers—arrayed in opposition to his plan, King must have realized that he had no chance of success. Clearly the weight of opinion was against him. The Central Pacific offensive would have to await the capture of Rabaul, postponed by the Pacific Military Conference to 1944, or an increase in the forces available and projected for the Pacific.

By his decision to abandon temporarily the proposal for a Central Pacific offensive, Admiral King unknowingly avoided a head-on conflict with General MacArthur over basic strategy. For MacArthur, too, had a plan, appropriately called RENO, for divorcing the Japanese from their Philippine prize but by a route altogether different from that favored by King.[21] And in view of Mac-

Arthur's strong ties in the Philippines and his dramatic promise in March 1942 to return, it was unlikely he would agree to any plan that did not permit him to keep his pledge. In his eyes, the liberation of the Philippines was a personal as well as a national obligation. He would not yield the privilege of fulfilling that obligation to any other.

But MacArthur did not base his RENO plan on these political and personal grounds—valid as they may have been. He had sound military reasons for the course he advocated. The Philippine Islands, he contended, were the most important strategic objective in his theater, promising results far more decisive than any that could be achieved by the capture of Rabaul. This importance the islands derived from their position athwart the major sea routes linking Japan with the vital oil and raw materials to the south. Control of the islands, therefore, would enable him to sever "the main artery of supply to Japan's factories" and so reduce her capacity to wage war as to make her vulnerable to direct assault. Thus far, he and King were in agreement.

It was on the choice of routes to the objective that they parted company. To MacArthur looking northward from Australia there seemed to be four possible approaches to the Philippines:

1. Westward from Hawaii through the Central Pacific by way of the Marshalls and Carolines.

2. Northwest from Australia along the north coast of New Guinea to Halmahera and then to Mindanao.

3. Due north through the Netherlands Indies by way of the Banda Sea and Molucca Passage.

4. Westward from Australia to Macas-

---

[21] Estimate of the Situation and Rough Draft, RENO Plan, 28 Feb 43, GHQ SWPA, Hist Rec Index Cards. The plan was under constant revision, each succeeding version receiving a higher Roman numeral for identification. The last was RENO V, 15 June 1944.

sar Strait or the South China Sea, then north.

Of these four routes, MacArthur favored the second. For him it was the shortest, and the one that most effectively utilized the power of land-based aircraft, exploited the enemy's principal weakness, and took full advantage of the positions won in the advance on Rabaul. The danger of attack from the flanks to which his forces would be exposed when they reached the tip of New Guinea could be obviated, MacArthur believed, by the neutralization or occupation of Palau to the north by Nimitz' forces and of Ambon in the Netherlands Indies by his own forces. One great advantage of this route that MacArthur stressed was the fact that it led directly to Mindanao, where there were excellent airfield sites and where Allied operations would be supported by a strong guerrilla force and by heavy and medium bombers based on northwest Australia and New Guinea. The advance to Luzon, the ultimate objective, would follow the occupation of Mindanao.

In MacArthur's opinion none of the other routes offered comparable advantages. Both routes through the Indies (Nos. 3 and 4) would meet major Japanese ground forces, would be exposed to flanking attacks, and would fail to utilize the full strength of Allied forces. The Central Pacific route (No. 1) so strongly favored by Admiral King, was subject to even more serious criticism, MacArthur thought. It was the longest of the four routes, would require large naval forces, and would have to be made without the support of land-based air power. But perhaps the most telling argument against the Central Pacific route was the fact that an offensive west-

ward from Hawaii would require "a re-orientation of front" in the Pacific. There was little doubt that in his view such a change would represent a basic shift in strategy and vitally affect his own plans for recapturing the Philippines.

With these convictions, it was certain that MacArthur would oppose the concept of a Central Pacific offensive. That he did not at this time was due simply to the fact that he was not officially informed of King's plans. Nor, for that matter, was King or any other member of the Joint Chiefs aware of RENO. At the Pacific Military Conference General Sutherland had presented only the ELKTON plan for the recapture of Rabaul; he had made no mention of RENO although he was present during King's discussion with Spruance and Browning. So long as others were able to postpone the Central Pacific offensive, Sutherland apparently saw no need to reveal MacArthur's plans. But the question was not yet settled and would not be until MacArthur had presented his case. That time was not far off.

The Japanese

The development by the Japanese of an integrated and mutually supporting defensive system in the Central Pacific dates from the spectacular raid on Makin by Colonel Carlson's marines in August 1942. Heroic and daring as it was, the raid had consequences never foreseen by those who proposed it. It had been designed to confuse the enemy, divert his forces from Guadalcanal, and gain information and prisoners. All these it accomplished, but it also demonstrated to the Japanese suddenly and dramatically how weak were their defenses in the Central

Pacific. More than any other single event it alerted them to the danger of attack in an area they considered secure and because of it they committed far heavier forces there than they had originally intended. In this sense, the Makin raid proved a costly venture and made the task for those who followed much more difficult.[22]

Up to the time of Makin, the Japanese paid scant attention to their Central Pacific outposts. Though the Navy, which had responsibility for the area, fully appreciated the strategic value of these islands, it consistently overestimated their defensive strength and assigned to them only token garrisons. Thus, it entrusted the safety of the seaplane base at Makin to a detachment consisting of less than fifty men and commanded by a warrant officer. To its other outposts in the Gilberts, the Navy sent garrisons of comparable size, secure in the belief that the islands were safe so long as Japanese planes and ships controlled the skies and seas of the Central Pacific.

Their illusions of safety shattered by the Makin raid, the Japanese moved with vigor and speed to overcome their earlier neglect. From Jaluit in the Marshalls, headquarters of the *6th Defense Force*, came a company-sized unit, part of it flown into Makin on 20 August and the rest following by ship. It was reinforced on 15 September by a company

of the newly activated *Yokosuka 6th Special Landing Force*, bringing the strength of the Makin garrison to 500.[23]

These reinforcements were only part of a general program by the Japanese to strengthen their position in the Gilberts. On 25 August they occupied Nauru and the next day Ocean Island, both to the west of the Gilbert chain. During the first week of September they took over Apamama in the central Gilberts and in the middle of the month they landed in force on Tarawa.

The promptness of the Japanese reaction can be surmised from the fact that the unit that occupied Tarawa on 15 September, the *Yokosuka 6th Special Naval Landing Force*, had come directly from Japan. Consisting of about 1,500 officers and men, the *6th Special Naval Landing Force* took over responsibility for all of the Gilberts, sending detachments to Apamama and Makin. With two additional companies that had meanwhile reached Ocean and Nauru from the Carolines, the Japanese had almost 2,000 troops in the Gilberts at the end of September.

Though the islands had been abandoned months earlier by the Allies, they were not yet entirely clear of their former white residents. Those who remained, mostly Australians and New Zealanders, had fled to the small islets and atolls in the southern Gilberts where they could observe and report Japanese air and surface movements throughout the group.

The removal of this embryo intelligence net was the first task the Japanese

---

[22] This section is based on Hattori, The Greater East Asia War, II, pt. V, ch. 3, and Crowl and Love, *Seizure of the Gilberts and Marshalls*, ch. IV. Admiral Turner as Chief of the Navy War Plans Division had rejected a proposal before the war to place a defense battalion at Makin, an action he later regretted. Comments of Rear Adm. Charles J. Moore, Jul 59, OCMH.

[23] Inner South Sea Islands Area Naval Opns, pt. I, Gilbert Islands Opns, p. 9, Japanese Studies in World War II, 161.

turned to once they had sufficient troops in the area. On 26 September a detachment from Tarawa landed on Beru Atoll and destroyed the radio station there, thus depriving the coast watchers of their vital link with the outside world. Next day the detachment moved on to the neighboring atoll, Tamana, where it found additional radio equipment, a radio operator, and two Allied soldiers. Raids on other atolls netted more equipment and prisoners. By 6 October the job was completed and the Japanese could report the Gilberts cleared of the enemy.

The next task the Japanese turned to was the construction of airfields and ground defenses. In October they began building air bases on Nauru and Tarawa. The strips were completed by the end of January 1943, and in late March, when adequate ground defenses and supporting installations were put in, a portion of the *22d Air Flotilla* from the Marshalls flew in to take over the air defense of the area.

If the Makin raid had alerted the Japanese to the threat of a Central Pacific offensive, the experience on Guadalcanal convinced them that their defenses in the area were still inadequate. Certainly the garrisons so recently established in the Gilberts could scarcely hope to withstand a determined assault such as the Allies had launched in the Solomons. "The Navy," one former Japanese officer noted, "lost confidence in the ability of the local air base to maintain air superiority, and it realized that the defense of the islands was far weaker than it had expected." [24] A review of the situation

in February and March led to a changed concept of operations emphasizing land defenses and co-ordinating air and ground operations with those of the fleet. This concept was approved on the highest levels in Tokyo and promulgated in orders issued on 25 March 1943. "The defense of strategic points," these orders directed, "will be strengthened promptly, and in the event of an enemy attack, the first [Japanese] attack will be launched . . . to destroy the enemy in close co-ordination with surface and air forces." At the same time the *Combined Fleet* commander was instructed to keep the main body of his carrier forces in the Pacific and "to annihilate the enemy fleet with interception operations." [25]

On the basis of this revised strategy, the Japanese proceeded during the spring and summer of 1943 to strengthen their position in the Gilberts and Marshalls. The naval ground forces in the Gilberts were reorganized and designated the *3d Special Base Force*, additional units and laborers were brought in, and ground and antiaircraft defenses expanded. Interception areas were marked out to provide a defense in depth, and arrangements made to bring reinforcements from Truk and Rabaul in the event of attack. The Army contributed to the defense of the area also by organizing special garrison units built around an infanry battalion and artillery battery for duty in the Central Pacific. One of these went to Wake, another to Marcus, but the one earmarked for the Gilbert Islands met disaster at sea. A fourth unit was thereupon organized to replace it,

---

[24] Hattori, The Greater East Asia War, II, pt. V, 42–43.

[25] Imperial Navy Opns Plan in Third Phase of the Greater East Asia War, 25 Mar 43; Opnl Policy To Be Followed by the Combined Fleet. Both cited in *ibid.*, p. 43.

but the need in the Solomons proved greater and it was diverted to Bougainville. The unit finally sent was a regiment of the *65th Brigade* in the Philippines, but it got no further than the Marshalls, thus leaving the defense of the Gilberts in the hands of the Navy.

The Central Pacific in Long-Range Strategy

In the spring of 1943, American planning for the Central Pacific assumed a new and broader meaning in the strategy of the war against Japan. Throughout 1942, Central Pacific strategy had been narrowly conceived in terms of the prewar ORANGE plan as the route to the Philippines. But as the tide of war turned, the planners in Washington began to look further into the future in search of a strategy by which to defeat Japan. The immediate objectives— Rabaul, the Truk-Guam line, and Burma —remained the same, but the objectives beyond changed. Scrutinized in terms of a broader frame of reference than envisaged in ORANGE, the recapture of the Philippines seemed to be less urgent than it was before. Within this context, the role of the Central Pacific acquired a significance it had never had in the prewar period.

Work on a long-range plan for the defeat of Japan had begun in August 1942 but it was not until April of the following year that the Joint U.S. Strategic Committee, which had responsibility for the task, submitted its plan to the Joint Staff Planners.[26] In it the commit-

tee recognized frankly and apparently for the first time that to achieve the objective of unconditional surrender set at Casablanca it might prove necessary to invade the Japanese home islands. How this would be done and what would be required, it was still too early to say. But the planners did hold out the hope that the Japanese might capitulate under other circumstances: (a) if they lost control of the sea lanes in the Far East and therefore the ability to wage war, or (b) if their centers of production were destroyed and their will to resist broken by "a sustained, systematic, and large-scale air offensive." In any case, control of the sea and the intensive air bombardment of Japan were indispensable prerequisites to an invasion of the home islands.

To the planners of the JUSSC, the key to Pacific strategy lay in the air offensive against Japan, for the choice of an area from which to launch this offensive would largely determine the direction of the advance and the selection of objectives. Siberia, the Kurils, and Formosa were considered but the planners finally chose China as the best base for the air offensive. It met the requirements of proximity to the target, provided areas for widely dispersed airfields, could be used to mount an invasion of Japan if one proved necessary, and contained friendly forces with a potential for offensive action. As Admiral King remarked, "China's geographical position and manpower were vital to the defeat of Japan and must be used. A collapse of China would vastly prolong

---

[26] JUSSC 40/2 Apr 43, and JPS 67/4, 28 Apr 43, Strategic Plan for the Defeat of Japan. The Joint U.S. Strategic Committee (not to be confused with the Joint Strategic Survey Committee) went out of existence on 24 April 1943 and was succeeded by the Joint War Plans Committee (JWPC). See above, Chapter X, for a description of these committees, and below, Chapter XXIII.

the war and vitally affect the whole situation vis-a-vis Japan." [27]

The choice of China created certain problems. Airfields would have to be developed, equipment and supplies in large quantities brought in, and a large American force maintained in China. The Chinese were incapable of doing the job and the existing land and air supply lines were clearly inadequate to support so great an effort. What was needed, the planners concluded, was a port such as Hong Kong on the east coast of China. With Hong Kong in Allied hands, it would be possible to ship directly to China from the United States all the men, supplies, and equipment required to launch the air offensive and, if necessary, invade Japan. Here for the first time was a clear statement of the concept behind the China coast strategy, which became so persistent a theme in American planning for the war against Japan.

The logic of their reasoning now took the planners step by step back across the Pacific. If the capture of Hong Kong was necessary to mount the air offensive against Japan, the Allies would have to gain control of the South China Sea. The best way for American forces to reach this body of water, the planners thought, was through the Sulu Sea, lying between the Philippines and Borneo. And the Sulu Sea, in turn, was best approached by way of the Celebes Sea, a route that could have the advantage of cutting off Japan from the supplies in the Netherlands Indies.

At this point the problem became more practical. There were two routes that might be followed to reach the Cel-

ebes Sea: one by way of Pearl Harbor through the Mandates to Mindanao in the Philippines, the other by way of the Solomons and New Guinea to Halmahera. Which should they choose? After considerable deliberation the Joint Staff Planners finally decided that both routes should be followed, but the Central Pacific route, they thought, would produce more decisive results and they therefore recommended that the main effort be made there.[28]

In their analysis of the most favorable route to the Celebes Sea, the planners weighed carefully the relative merits of the approaches through the Central and the South–Southwest Pacific Areas. The first, they thought, was more desirable for a variety of reasons. It was shorter and more direct, and therefore would be logistically more economical. Also, the Allies would encounter fewer problems in maintaining troops and developing air bases on the islands and coral atolls of the Central Pacific than in the damp, malaria-infested jungles of New Guinea and the Solomons.

But more important than these were the strategic advantages of the Central Pacific. There the Allies would be able to strike the Japanese on their vulnerable eastern flank, at points where the Japanese could bring to bear only such limited air and ground forces as they

---

[27] Mins, 84th CCS Mtg, 14 May 43, Trident Conference Book, p. 349.

[28] One of the naval planners, Capt. Charles J. Moore, disagreed with this recommendation on the ground that "the relative merits" of the two routes had been compared "with primary consideration of relative position only . . . " Memo, Moore for JSP, 27 Apr 43, sub: Strategic Plan for the Defeat of Japan, ABC 381 (8–27–42) Japan. In commenting on the present manuscript, Admiral Moore explained that his objection may have been based on his long-standing opposition to the capture of Truk, at this time an integral part of the Central Pacific concept. Comments of Admiral Moore, Jul 59, OCMH.

could base on the small and widely separated islands in that region. Against such forces the Allies could concentrate the full power of their rapidly growing naval and naval air strength. In amphibious operations, the Allies could expect by their concentration of power to overcome the disadvantages imposed by the great distances in the area and the limited opportunities they would have to utilize land-based aircraft. And finally, U.S. naval power in the Central Pacific, if employed successfully against the main body of the Japanese fleet, might open up the way for an attack against Japan itself.

One of the most persuasive reasons for emphasizing the Central Pacific as the planners did was the huge shipbuilding program in the United States. This construction program dated from July 1940, when Congress had passed the so-called Two-Ocean Navy Bill authorizing an expansion of about 70 percent in combat tonnage. Thus, when the Japanese attack on Pearl Harbor came, the construction of naval shipbuilding facilities required to meet the exigencies of war was already under way. Thereafter, expansion continued at an accelerated rate and by the early part of 1943 had reached full production capacity.[29] Other problems remained, and the shifting tides of war created new demands and priorities but these were largely solved as they arose. By the spring of 1943, the ships whose hulls had been laid in 1940 and 1941 were reaching completion. Of the 10 battleships authorized in 1940, 6 were

in service by the end of 1943. Carrier strength, which on 7 December 1941 consisted of 7 first-line vessels and 1 escort, increased in the same period to 50 carriers of all types. Most of these were escort carriers but among the new ships commissioned were 7 carriers of the *Essex* class as well as 9 light carriers. Warships of other types in corresponding numbers reached completion during the year 1943, including landing craft and auxiliary vessels. Of these last, perhaps the most important for amphibious operations were the attack transports and cargo vessels.[30]

The promise of this large fleet of carriers, battleships, cruisers, and destroyers, many already completed or close to completion in the spring of 1943, created its own pressure for a strategy that would exploit to the full this potential naval superiority. Only in the open waters of the Central Pacific could the United States employ such a fleet to its fullest extent. There it could be used as an offensive weapon to seek out and destroy the enemy fleet and to support amphibious operations that would not only bring U.S. forces closer to Japan but would also create situations that would bring the enemy's fleet into action. No other areas in the Pacific offered similar opportunities, and if U.S. strategy failed to

---

[29] Admiral King's First Report, 1 Mar 44, in *The War Reports of General of the Army George C. Marshall, General of the Army H. H. Arnold, and Fleet Admiral Ernest J. King* (Philadelphia and New York: J. B. Lippincott Company, 1947), pp. 484–85.

[30] *Ibid.*, pp. 488–94. Major combatant ships added to the U.S. Fleet between December 1941 and December 1943 were as follows:

Battleships (BB)	8
Heavy Cruisers (CA)	4
Light Cruisers (CL)	15
Destroyers (DD)	207
Destroyer Escorts (DE)	199
Aircraft Carriers (CV)	7
Light Aircraft Carriers (CVL)	9
Escort Carriers (CVE)	29
Submarines (SS)	88

Ibid., pp. 738–63, app. B.

seize them, then how, asked the planners, could they justify the costly naval construction program already approved.

In comparing the southern with the central route, the planners of the Joint U.S. Strategic Committee noted that an advance from the east by strong American naval and air forces in the Central Pacific would outflank Japanese positions on the north coast of New Guinea and sever Japan's line to the Indies. On the other hand, a drive northward by MacArthur's forces up the north coast to New Guinea, would have no effect on the Japanese in the Central Pacific whose position rested on local air and naval superiority and an unchallenged line of communications to the home islands. As a matter of fact, the planners observed, the Japanese in the Central Pacific would be able to attack MacArthur on his flank and rear as he advanced northward, an ability they would not possess if the Allies elected to make their drive from the east. Moreover, the southern route followed a longer and more circuitous course than the central route and would require the seizure of Japanese positions whose strength, unlike those in the Mandates, was limited only by the availability of troops and shipping. And in contrast to the widely separated Japanese garrisons in the Central Pacific, the Japanese in the South and Southwest Pacific had established a system of mutually supporting bases providing defense in great depth.

Though the central route was clearly preferred by the planners, they saw many reasons why the road up through the Solomons and New Guinea merited consideration. MacArthur's forces, supported by an extensive system of bases stretching back to Australia and the islands of the South Pacific, were already engaged with the enemy. To shift them now to the Central Pacific would free large enemy forces for use elsewhere and impose a considerable strain on the logistical organization in the theater. So great would be the loss of time and the waste of shipping required to shift front in the Pacific that the planners doubted there would be any saving in the long run.

General MacArthur, though he was not consulted at this time, could have advanced additional advantages for the Southwest Pacific route. Comparing it with the Central Pacific, he wrote in 1955:

The main distinction between the concept underlying Southwest Pacific operations and the Central Pacific Concept was that the former embodied a series of flanking movements around enemy held strong points leaving them impotent with the severence of their supply lines to the north, while the latter envisioned the reduction of enemy strong points across the Central Pacific by costly frontal assaults. The relativity in the casualty rate historically speaks for itself.

Under our strategic conception in the Southwest Pacific we sought as we advanced north to maintain land based air support for our operations—the drive across the Central Pacific was, on the other hand, dependent upon support from carrier based aircraft. The limited potential of carrier bases due to non-continuous operations, occasioned by the necessity for periodic return to land bases for resupply and maintenance, was demonstrated when for the first and only time the Southwest Pacific command departed from the principle against out-distancing its land based air support in the attack upon Leyte. Then we placed our dependence for air support upon carriers whose limitations threatened to a dangerous degree the success of the operations.[31]

---

[31] Ltr, MacArthur to Smith, 7 Jan 55, OCMH.

Though MacArthur did not refer to them, political considerations also argued against abandonment of the southern route. Australia and New Zealand could not be expected to look with favor on any strategy that relegated them to a secondary role in an area where they had a primary interest. Undoubtedly they would feel that they had been abandoned by their American allies after bearing the brunt of the enemy's attack during the dark days of 1942. Such an attitude might well cancel out the military advantages of a greater effort in the Central Pacific. Nor could the planners ignore the great potential oil reserves on the Vogelkop Peninsula, the birdlike head of the monster-shaped island of New Guinea. In any advance from the south these could be expected ultimately to fall into Allied hands.[32]

It was for these reasons that the planners, while emphasizing the decisive advantages of the Central Pacific route, recommended that the southern route also be used. They did not fail to note, moreover, that a simultaneous advance toward the Sulu Sea along both routes would give the Allies important advantages. The two forces, as they converged on the objective, would be able to support each other by air and naval operations. Each would keep the enemy in its area pinned down, uncertain where the next blow would fall and unable to shift his forces. By timing their blows skillfully and selecting their objectives carefully, the Allies could neutralize the advantages the Japanese possessed in their interior lines of communication

while exploiting fully their own advantages. Strategically off balance, the Japanese would have to guard every point in their vast perimeter, from the Aleutians to the Indies. The Allies, under no such compulsion, would be free to move their forces freely and to concentrate at the point of attack.

On the basis of this reasoning, the Joint U.S. Strategic Committee envisaged the defeat of Japan in a series of operations divided into five broad phases. Assuming the co-operation of the British and Chinese, Allied forces in Southeast Asia would recapture Burma and the Burma Road during the first phase. In the Pacific, operations during this phase would be directed toward opening the line of communications to the Celebes Sea. These were to be exclusively American operations utilizing both MacArthur's and Nimitz' forces, but making the main effort in the Central Pacific. In the second phase, U.S. forces would recapture the Philippines while British forces in Southeast Asia sought to wrest control of Indochina from the Japanese. The capture of Hong Kong was to be accomplished by Chinese forces in the third phase, after the British and Americans had gained control of the South China Sea. Thereafter, the three nations would seize such airfields in China as would be required in the final air offensive against Japan (Phase IV), with China taking the major role in ground operations. The bombing of Japan (Phase V) would be primarily an American effort, but no provision was made in this general scheme to follow up the air bombardment with the invasion of the enemy's home islands. Though the planners recognized that to secure Japan's surrender it might prove necessary to

[32] On this last point, see Robert Ross Smith, *The Approach to the Philippines*, UNITED STATES ARMY IN WORLD WAR II (Washington, 1953), pp. 426–27.

invade, that decision had yet to be made.

The discussions that followed the submission of this ambitious and long-range plan in April produced no significant change in the fundamental strategy outlined in the plan. The Joint War Plans Committee, which succeeded the Joint U.S. Strategic Committee as the working group of the Joint Staff Planners, was the first to review the plan. In general, the committee accepted both the reasoning and conclusions of the JUSSC, and its own plan, submitted on 5 May, was largely based on the earlier one. The war planners, however, placed less emphasis on the air offensive against Japan than had their predecessors and more on control of the seas as a means of securing the unconditional surrender of Japan.[33] In addition, they added to the earlier plan a sixth phase providing for the invasion of Japan and gave to U.S. forces the primary role in this last operation. The idea of a simultaneous offensive in the Central and in the South–Southwest Pacific, with the major effort in the former area, the war planners accepted without question. Three days later, the Joint Chiefs of Staff approved this plan with minor modification.[34]

At the same time that they submitted their strategic plan for the defeat of Japan, the joint war planners recommended specific objectives that should be taken in 1943–1944 to achieve the long-range aims set forth in the strategic plan.[35] For the Pacific, these objectives would include the completion in 1943

of Task Two (CARTWHEEL) by MacArthur's forces, followed the next year by the capture of the Bismarck Archipelago and Manus Island in the Admiralties. The only operation the war planners scheduled for the Central Pacific during this same period was the capture of the Marshall Islands.

Limited resources in the Pacific dictated the strategy behind this program. At the Pacific Military Conference in March 1943, it had been agreed that MacArthur could not take Rabaul that year with the forces available and projected. The war planners therefore limited his future tasks to what they estimated he could accomplish with these resources. Their selection of objectives was clearly designed to place MacArthur in position to project his air and naval power into the Central Pacific to support the advance there. Thus, the reduction of Rabaul would give him air supremacy in the New Ireland–Admiralties area; the occupation of Manus, airfields and a naval base within striking range of the western Carolines. Operations in the Central Pacific, the planners pointed out, were dependent upon resources already committed elsewhere. These, they estimated, would not be available until April 1944 and the Central Pacific offensive would therefore have to be delayed until that date. Thus, though they had established the strategical primacy of the Central Pacific, the planners were forced by practical considerations to recommend that the main effort during the remainder of 1943 and during the early part of 1944 be made in the South–Southwest Pacific.

Before this proposed plan reached the Joint Chiefs, a broader program dealing with operations throughout the world

---

[33] JWPC 15, 5 May 43, sub: Strategic Plan for the Defeat of Japan.

[34] JCS 287 and 287/1, 7 and 8 May 43, Strategic Plan for the Defeat of Japan; Mins, JCS Mtg, 8 May 43.

[35] JWPC 9/1, 5 May 43, sub: Opns in Pacific and Far East in 1943–44.

was approved.[36] Prepared by a different team of planners from the Joint War Plans Committee, this study called for a more ambitious program in the Pacific during 1943 and 1944 than was envisaged in the first study. To MacArthur was assigned the task of capturing Japanese-held New Guinea, as well as the Solomons and the Bismarck Archipelago. And during the same period, according to this plan, Admiral Nimitz' forces in the Central Pacific would go on to take the Caroline Islands after they occupied the Marshalls. Additional objectives in the war against Japan included the Aleutians, Burma, and the bombardment of Japan from bases in China.

On the basis of this world-wide study, the Joint War Plans Committee reviewed its own schedule of operations for the Pacific and on 12 May 1943 submitted a revised and more detailed plan.[37] MacArthur, the war planners now estimated, would not be able to complete operations in the Bismarck Archipelago before 1 April 1944. He could then proceed to the Celebes Sea by way of the north coast of New Guinea, or up from Darwin by way of Timor, Ceram, and the island of Celebes, a route that was not seriously considered.

Operations in the Central Pacific would begin, under this new plan, with the occupation of the Marshalls on a date the planners purposely left open. This job, they estimated, would require six

months and would be followed by the invasion of the Caroline Islands—first Ponape, then Truk, and finally the western islands in the group. With a main fleet base at Truk and airfields at strategic points in the area, the forces in the Central Pacific would be in position to move west toward the Philippines and the Celebes Sea or north via the Marianas to Japan.

Carefully, the planners avoided fixing a timetable or any established order of operations. Thus far, they reminded the Joint Chiefs of Staff, it had committed itself only to CARTWHEEL, which would carry MacArthur's forces as far as western New Britain. Thereafter the schedule was flexible and the Joint Chiefs might adopt any or all of the operations suggested. They could even cancel operations in the Bismarck Archipelago, the planners observed, if they thought the capture of Rabaul was no longer necessary and go directly into the Marshalls. In that case, the resources in the Pacific could be concentrated on the drive westward across the Central Pacific and operations in New Guinea relegated to a secondary place in line with the strategic concept of making the main effort in the Central Pacific. The decision was up to the Joint Chiefs and it would have to be made before CARTWHEEL was over. But first it would be necessary to re-examine the long-range strategic aims of the Allies and to review the decisions made at Casablanca. In recognition of this necessity, another meeting of the U.S. and British political and military chiefs had been scheduled, and already the British delegates were gathering in Washington, for the third of the wartime international conferences.

---

[36] JCS 290, 7 May 43, Conduct of the War in 1943–44.

[37] JWPC 9/2, 11 May 43, sub: Opns in Pacific and Far East in 1943–44; JCS 304, 12 May 43, same sub. This study was not discussed by the Joint Chiefs of Staff at this time, but was placed on the agenda for the TRIDENT Conference, which began that morning.

CHAPTER XXIII

Central Pacific Timetable

> By maritime strategy we mean the principles which govern a war in which the sea is a substantial factor. . . . The paramount concern, then, of maritime strategy is to determine the mutual relations of your army and navy in a plan of war.
>
> JULIAN CORBETT, *Some Principles of Maritime Strategy*

The spring of 1943 had seen a comprehensive review of Pacific strategy and a growing conviction among many that the time had come to open up an offensive in the Central Pacific. Still ahead was the task of translating this conviction into a firm decision and clearcut directive upon which the commanders in the field could act.

But before this decision could be made and the appropriate orders issued, it would be necessary to calculate the effect of this new offensive upon global strategy and on operations already scheduled in the Pacific and elsewhere. Resources were limited and ends, as always, would have to be fitted to means. Differences of opinion, in Washington and in the theater, would have to be considered, and, if possible, reconciled. The end result was bound to leave many dissatisfied. But dissatisfaction was better than inaction, and during the early summer of 1943 the Joint Chiefs of Staff and their planners moved slowly but surely toward a solution and a plan.

The TRIDENT Conference

The third formal U.S.-British conference of the war, known by the code name TRIDENT, opened in Washington on 12 May 1943 with a full-scale meeting of the political and military chiefs of the two nations.[1] On the American side, the preparations for this conference had been more thorough and comprehensive than for any of the preceding meetings. Thirty-one different studies covering a wide variety of subjects, including the strategic plan for the defeat of Japan, had been produced by the American planners in the three weeks preceding the conference. This time the Americans were determined not to be caught unprepared as at Casablanca, where Admiral King remarked that "the British had a

---

[1] Harry Hopkins attended this and other meetings. General Arnold was ill during the conference and Lt. Gen. Joseph T. McNarney, Marshall's deputy and an air officer, substituted for him. Minutes of the conference and the papers approved at the meetings are in the printed and bound volume entitled TRIDENT Conference, May 1943.

paper ready" on every subject raised for discussion.[2]

The thorough staff work that preceded the TRIDENT Conference was undoubtedly due in large measure to the reorganization of the joint staff. The need for this reform had been evident for some time, and in January 1943, immediately after the meetings at Casablanca, a special committee was established to study the problem.[3] The 60-page report of this committee, submitted on 8 March 1943, provided the basis for a thorough review of the entire JCS committee structure and the reorganization that followed. With respect to strategic planning, the chief weakness of the system, it was recognized, was the burden of responsibility placed on the Joint Staff Planners, who not only represented the United States on the combined level but also directed all planning activities on the joint level while occupying positions of responsibility within their own services. The problem of the Joint U.S. Strategic Committee had never been solved either, and its members were still dissatisfied with the role assigned them.

The organization that finally emerged in May 1943—preliminary measures had been adopted earlier—greatly increased the efficiency of planning on the joint level and made U.S. representation on the combined level much more effective than it had been. The membership of the Joint Staff Planners was reduced to four, two each from the Army and Navy, and the number of issues that came

before it was sharply reduced by the establishment of additional committees. The most important of these was the Joint Administrative Committee, later called the Joint Logistics Committee, which was given purview over logistical matters but had to channel its studies for the Joint Chiefs through the JPS. This provision applied to other joint committees as well, and was designed to ensure the co-ordination of all activities and plans with basic strategic concepts.

The reorganization of May 1943 solved the problem of the JUSSC by abolishing that body and creating the Joint War Plans Committee (JWPC). Unlike the JUSSC, this new group was not charged with responsibility for broad strategy or future planning—that function was now assigned to the Joint Strategic Survey Committee—but only for the preparation of joint war plans. Membership in the JWPC was large, to give it an adequate staff to do the job assigned. Three senior members representing the Army, Navy, and Army Air Forces, controlled the committee and assigned the work to planning teams designated by color, the Red Team handling all Pacific and Far East matters. The work of the teams was reviewed by the senior members who, in turn, reported directly to the Joint Staff Planners.

As part of the preparation for the TRIDENT Conference, the "elder statesmen" of the Joint Strategic Survey Committee had considered carefully the question of conference tactics and the basic position the Joint Chiefs should take in their meetings with the British. The British, they thought, would seek to increase the Allied effort in the Mediterranean, possibly to the east of

---

[2] Mins, JCS Mtg, 8 May 43.

[3] For a full account of the work of this committee and the discussions that followed, see Davis, Development of the JCS Committee Structure, pp. 590–683. A shorter, more general account can be found in Cline, *Washington Command Post*, pp. 235–39.

Sicily. Such action, the strategists contended, would divert from the main effort against Germany and they recommended that the U.S. Joint Chiefs oppose it as contrary to sound strategy. If the British wished to undertake operations in the eastern Mediterranean, then, said the strategic planners, the U.S. Chiefs should take the position that the United States could not support its allies there but would instead commit additional resources to the Pacific. An effort in the western Mediterranean would be less objectionable, the strategists believed and could be supported if the British agreed to mount the air offensive against Germany in 1943 and the cross-Channel attack the next year.[4]

In the view of the senior officers on the Joint Strategic Survey Committee, strategy in the Pacific and Far East could not be divorced from the strategy in Europe. They recommended, therefore, that at the forthcoming conference the U.S. Joint Chiefs should establish the interrelationship of the two, and, while upholding the priority of the war against Germany, emphasize American interest in the early defeat of Japan. By taking this position at the start, the strategists pointed out, the U.S. Chiefs would be able to counter the anticipated insistence of the British on Mediterranean operations, and their reluctance to undertake the cross-Channel invasion, with the requirements of the Pacific theater. Moreover, if the British refused to support the campaign in Burma in furtherance of the Allied effort to keep China in the war, a cardinal principle of American strategy, the Joint Chiefs could argue

that the United States would have to "expand and intensify its operations in the Pacific, in order to counteract the advantage which Japan gains by Allied failure adequately to support China."[5]

Though the Joint Chiefs did not formally approve these recommendations, it was evident throughout the conference that they had taken the advice of their strategic committee seriously. In his opening remarks to the Combined Chiefs on the morning of 13 May, Admiral Leahy, reading from a paper prepared by the committee, stressed the global aspects of the war and the relationship of European and Pacific strategy. Referring to the matters the Joint Chiefs considered most essential—the cross-Channel attack and the role of China—the admiral pointedly observed that the decision on operations to be undertaken during the next eighteen months should be based on the contribution of each to the early defeat of both enemies.[6] To give added point to this emphasis on the Pacific, Leahy proposed that the strategic aims of the Allies include the maintenance and extension of "unremitting pressure" against Japan while the war against Germany was still in progress. To the British, the addition of the word *extension*—used here for the first time—to the accepted formula to "maintain unremitting pressure" against Japan seemed to give the war in the Far East an unjustified "pride of place" and to open the way for extensive operations in the Pacific. These operations, they feared, might divert resources from the main effort against Germany by creating "a vacuum

---

[4] JCS 286, 6 May 43, sub: Recommended Line of Action at Coming Conf.

[5] *Ibid.*

[6] Mins, CCS Mtg, 13 May 43, an. A, JCS Memo, same date, sub: Global Strategy of the War.

into which forces would have to be poured." [7]

Admiral Leahy's emphasis on the Pacific and Far East as a foil to the British preoccupation with the Mediterranean was a recurrent theme of the conference. Marshall, for example, expressed this view frankly on the 13th at a meeting with the British. At a separate meeting next day, the Joint Chiefs agreed that if the British would not commit themselves to the cross-Channel invasion in 1944, then the United States as a "last resort," should increase its efforts in the Pacific.[8] Three days later, Admiral Leahy told the British Chiefs that under certain circumstances, U.S. interests might require an "extension of effort against Japan, if necessary, even at the expense of the European Theater." [9] This clear threat was made even more explicit when the Americans declared the Germany-first strategy might have to be reversed if it seemed "that the war as a whole can be brought more quickly to a successful conclusion by the earlier mounting of a major offensive against Japan." [10]

These statements, revealing as they were of the American attitude, were but the prelude to the discussion of Pacific problems, which began on 20 May, a week after the conference had opened. By that time, the two most troublesome and pressing matters before the Combined Chiefs of Staff—operations in the Mediterranean and in Burma—had been

virtually settled and the way cleared for discussion of American plans in the Pacific.

The strategic plan for the defeat of Japan was considered first. Revised to incorporate the concept of extending as well as maintaining "unremitting pressure" against Japan and to emphasize the importance of China, the plan presented by the U.S. Chiefs was basically the same 6–phase plan they had approved on 8 May.[11]

The British reaction was lukewarm. They thought the American proposals somewhat vague and general and felt the alternative courses of action should be analyzed more carefully. Since there was no need for an immediate decision, the U.S. Chiefs agreed to refer the problem to a combined committee of American and British planners for further study. Before the conference closed, arrangements were made for an exchange of visits between London and Washington by the planners working on the problem.[12]

The more pressing problem of deciding upon a schedule of operations for the Pacific during the coming year was not so easily settled. On the morning of the 21st, Admiral King explained the American program in some detail. After outlining the situation in the Pacific and the alternate routes of advance, King referred to the traditional interest of American planners in the Pacific. Ever since the acquisition of the Philippines, he said, they had studied intensively the

---

[7] Mins, CCS Mtg, 14 May 43. Leahy's proposal was first submitted to the British as a JSSC study, JCS 243/3, 9 Apr 43, sub: Survey of Present Strategic Sit. The British commented in CCS 199, 13 Apr 43, same sub; Memo by British COS, 23 Apr 43, same sub; CCS Supp Mins, 23 Apr 43.

[8] Mins, CCS Mtg, 13 May, and JCS Mtg, 14 May 43.

[9] Mins, CCS Mtg, 17 May 43.

[10] CCS 220, 19 May 43, sub: Strategic Plan for Defeat of Japan.

[11] CCS 220, 19 May 43, sub: Strategic Plan for Defeat of Japan. The 8 May plan was JCS 287/1 and bore the same title. See above, ch. XXII.

[12] Mins, CCS Mtg, 20 May 43; CCS 251/1, CPS Memo, 25 May 43, sub: Proposals for Improving Combined Planning.

problems involved in reinforcing and reconquering the islands in the event of a Japanese attack. The results of these studies showed, King maintained, that no matter which route was followed the essential conditions for success in the Pacific were, first, control of the lines of communication, and second, recapture of the Philippines. Essential to both were decisive action against the Japanese fleet and seizure of the Marianas. This last, in King's opinion, was the key to the situation because of the islands' location on the Japanese line of communications." [13]

The plan Admiral King presented to the Combined Chiefs was virtually the same as that developed by the American planners earlier in the month. Completed on 12 May, the day the meeting opened, the plan had never been approved by the U.S. Chiefs, and probably not all of them had had an opportunity to study it.[14] For the Pacific theater, the plan had set as objectives for 1943 and 1944 seizure of the Marshalls and Carolines, capture of the Solomon Islands, the Bismarck Archipelago, and Japanese-held New Guinea, and ejection of the Japanese from the Aleutians. To these Admiral King had added "the intensification of operations against the Japanese line of communications." He was most emphatic also about the necessity of maintaining and extending "unremitting pressure" against the enemy during the year ahead and suggested that, in deciding on any operation, the Chiefs ask themselves whether it would "further threaten or cut the Japanese line of communication" and "contribute to the attainment of positions of readiness" for the final asault on Japan.[15]

The British Chiefs accepted the American plan without discussion, and the remaining days of the conference were devoted to a careful study of the resources required to carry out this program. Seven divisions, it was estimated, would be needed to capture the Bismarck Archipelago and 2 more for the Marshalls, in addition to large air and naval forces. But if Rabaul could be neutralized by air bombardment, the number of divisions would be reduced by 2. An operation against the Carolines, which would involve the capture of Truk and Ponape, would require 3 more divisions, as well as additional heavy bombers, aircraft carriers, battleships, cruisers, and other warships. There were enough surface forces in the Pacific to meet these requirements, but 4 more divisions, 2 Army and 2 Marine, would be required to carry out the operations scheduled for the coming year.[16]

The final report of the conference, approved by Roosevelt and Churchill on 25 May, reaffirmed the determination of the Allies, in co-operation with the Soviet Union, to concentrate their resources against Germany in order to secure the surrender of the Axis in Europe as soon as possible. This effort would not preclude operations against Japan for, at the insistence of the Americans, the final report provided that sufficient resources would be made available to the Pacific and Far East commanders to maintain and extend "unremitting pressure" against Japan. Once Germany was defeated, the Allies, aided possibly by the

---

[13] Mins, CCS Mtg, 21 May 43.

[14] CCS 239, 20 May 43, sub: Opns in Pacific and Far East in 1943–44. For earlier action on the plan, see above, ch. XXII.

[15] Mins, CCS Mtg, 21 May 43.

[16] CCS 239/1, sub: Opns in Pacific and Far East in 1943–44, 21 May 43.

Soviet Union, would turn their full attention to Japan and seek to force her unconditional surrender at the earliest possible date.

Specific operations in the Pacific during 1943–1944 were designed to support this broad strategic concept by: (a) securing positions from which to force the ultimate surrender of Japan; (b) keeping China in the war; and (c) holding the lines of communication. Thus, the final report of the conference embodied the 5–point program developed by the American planners before the meeting and called for:

1. Air operations in and from China.

2. Ejection of the Japanese from the Aleutians.

3. Seizure of the Marshall and Caroline Islands.

4. Seizure of the Solomons, the Bismarck Archipelago, and that portion of New Guinea held by the Japanese.

5. Intensification of operations against the Japanese line of communications. No special significance or order of priority was intended by this listing of operations. The accomplishment of all five, it was agreed, was essential to the defeat of Japan, and any "conflict of interest" between them and other operations would be resolved by the Combined Chiefs.[17]

This ambitious program, which would witness the opening of a new front in the Pacific, seemed to the Combined Chiefs to be well within the capabilities of the Allies. Unless the rate of losses increased sharply, they told the President and Prime Minister, there would be enough troops and supplies in the theater in time to meet the requirements of this program. Under existing deployment schedules, General MacArthur would have 5 U.S. Army, 1 Marine, and 3 Australian divisions available for offensive operations by January 1944; Halsey in the South Pacific, 5 Army, 2 Marine, and 1 New Zealand divisions; and Nimitz, 3 Army and 1 Marine divisions. Still needed for the Central Pacific offensive were 2 divisions for the Marshalls and 2 for the Carolines, and these, the Combined Chiefs declared, could be made available from resources within the United States without cutting into the requirements of other areas.[18]

With the approval of the final report, the TRIDENT Conference came to an end. Much had been accomplished during these two weeks, and the prospects ahead were brighter than they had ever been. The Allies had agreed on a strategic concept for the conduct of the war and on the general objectives to support this strategy. Considerable progress had been made also in reaching agreement on a broad plan designed to secure the early defeat of the Axis Powers, and another meeting had been scheduled for August to complete the task begun in May. But the acceptance at TRIDENT of a cross-Channel attack, with a tentative target date of May 1944, and of the combined bomber offensive from the United Kingdom put the planning for the defeat of Germany on a firm basis. And while these plans matured, the offensive in the Mediterranean would continue, it was agreed at TRIDENT, with an invasion of the Italian boot to come after the scheduled capture of Sicily.

---

[17] CCS 242/6, Final Rpt to President and Prime Minister, 25 May 43.

[18] CCS 224/1, Implementation . . . for Conduct of the War in 1943–44, 25 May 43; Mins, CCS Plenary Session, 25 May 43.

On the Pacific side, the TRIDENT decisions reflected an increased emphasis on the importance of operations against Japan. On the basis of the agreements reached at the conference, the Americans could proceed confidently with their plans to open an offensive in the Central Pacific. The course for the year ahead had been charted, and with the operations in the Solomons, New Guinea, and the Aleutians already in progress, the Joint Chiefs could turn to the task of opening the long-deferred Central Pacific drive. Meanwhile, American and British planners, working together, would seek to develop a long-range strategy for the defeat of Japan in time for the next meeting of the two allies in August.

The Marshalls Plan

Hardly had the TRIDENT Conference ended than the Navy, anxious to employ the growing naval strength of the Pacific Fleet, began to press for early action in the Central Pacific. Though the conference had not fixed any timetable for Pacific operations, earlier plans had clearly implied, if they had not stated, that the offensive through the Mandates would begin only after the capture of Rabaul, presumably in the spring of 1944. But now the naval planners could see no reason to wait, and on 27 May, at Admiral Cooke's suggestion, the Joint Staff Planners directed the War Plans Committee to study the requirements for an invasion of the Marshall Islands and to prepare an outline plan for the operation, with recommended target dates.[19]

By 10 June, the joint war planners had done their job. The plan they submitted called for the invasion and seizure of the Marshalls in three steps: first, the simultaneous seizure of the central atolls, Kwajalein, Wotje, and Maloelap; second, the occupation of the outpost atolls, Eniwetok to the north and Kusaie to the south; and third, the reduction or neutralization of the remaining islands in the area, including Wake and those in the Gilbert group.[20] In this way, the invading forces would strike suddenly at the enemy's stronghold before he could disperse his forces, thereby avoiding a costly and slow step-by-step advance through the atolls of the Gilberts and Marshalls. The success of the attack, the planners believed, would be further enhanced if it was made at the end of October, during the dark of the moon and just a few days before the opening of the Burma offensive.

The forces required for the execution of this plan raised serious problems. For the first time American troops would have to assault a strongly defended coral atoll. Because of what the planners called "the serious implications of failure" and because this experience would serve as a guide for later atoll operations in the Pacific, it was "almost imperative," the planners declared, that only amphibiously trained, battle-tested "shock troops" should be used for this first venture into the Japanese Mandated Islands. A corps of two reinforced divisions, they estimated, would be required, in addition to assault shipping, amphibian trac-

---

[19] Memo, JPS for JWPC, 27 May 43, sub: Examination into Pacific Theater. The JWPC in turn delegated the task to its RAINBOW Team, which was to

submit a report by 5 June. JWPC 39/D, 28 May 43, sub: Opns Against Marshalls, both in ABC 384 Marshall Islands (6–10–43), sec. 1.

[20] JPS 205, Preliminary Rpt by JWPC, 10 Jun 43, sub: Opns Against Marshalls.

tors capable of hurdling the coral reefs, and two bomber groups (one heavy and one medium) for garrison duty.

There was only one way to meet these requirements and that was to draw upon the resources allocated to MacArthur and Halsey for CARTWHEEL. The two divisions which most closely met the criteria set by the planners were the 1st and 2d Marine Divisions, both blooded on Guadalcanal and scheduled for employment in New Guinea and the Solomons later in the year. Less experienced but possible substitutes were the Army's 7th Division, still in the Aleutians, and the unseasoned 3d Marine Division in the South Pacific. The planners, however, preferred the more experienced Marine divisions and recommended their use in the Marshalls invasion. They did this with a full awareness of the effect of such a move on CARTWHEEL. Deprived of their battle-tested amphibious troops and assault craft, MacArthur and Halsey would virtually have to abandon their drive toward Rabaul almost before it had begun—"not later than late July 1943" the planners estimated. By that time the two commanders would presumably have occupied Kiriwina and Woodlark Islands, infiltrated New Georgia, and captured the Lae-Salamaua-Finschhafen-Madang area of New Guinea. There they would have to stand, if the recommendations of the joint war planners were accepted, until the Marshalls were taken.

Damaging as this proposal would have been to MacArthur's plans, it was not as drastic as one made by Admiral King at the same time. Anxious to end the inactivity of American forces in the Pacific and ensure their most effective utilization, King recommended to the Joint Chiefs that they (a) establish a definite timetable for operations in the Central Pacific, starting with the Marshalls invasion on 1 November; (b) get from General MacArthur a list of the operations he planned, with "firm dates"; and (c) give to Admiral Nimitz the authority to co-ordinate and schedule all offensive operations in the Pacific. This last, he suggested, could be accomplished by adding to the original directive given Nimitz in March 1942 the mission to "coordinate the timing, under the general direction of the U.S. Joint Chiefs of Staff, of major amphibious offensives throughout the Pacific Theater."[21] And in an accompanying note to General Marshall, King added: "I now feel that the urgency of these problems will permit of no further delay in the taking of effective action to solve them."

Admiral King's proposal to give Nimitz co-ordinating authority in the Pacific was, in effect, a device to make that officer the supreme commander in the theater, for co-ordination and timing of operations were clearly the prerogatives of command. So controversial an issue could hardly be discussed without further study and the Joint Chiefs therefore referred it to the Joint Staff Planners, who already had the Marshalls invasion plan of their War Plans Committee, with instructions to report by 14 June. At the same time Marshall sent an inquiry to MacArthur asking for more specific information on his plans. MacArthur's response hardly added much to what was already known in Washington—Kiriwina and Woodlark would be invaded on 30 June, Lae and Salamaua on 1 September. Any esti-

---

[21] Memo, King for Marshall, 11 Jun 43, sub: Future Campaign Opns in Pacifiic Ocean Areas, ser. 001150, OPD 381 Security, case 163. Circulated as JCS 353, same date and title.

mates about the operations to follow, MacArthur declared, would be "pure guess work," and would depend to a large degree on Japanese reaction to the initial attacks.[22]

The deliberations of the Joint Staff Planners were somewhat more productive. Meeting on 13 June to consider the Marshall Islands invasion plans and Admiral King's recommendations on command, the planners quickly divided along service lines. From the Army point of view, an offensive in the Central Pacific was certainly desirable, provided it had a reasonable chance of success and would not prejudice MacArthur's CARTWHEEL operations. On this last point, the Army was adamant and stood ready to back its position with strong political and military arguments.[23] The Navy planners felt just as strongly about the Central Pacific, the area where the growing strength of the fleet could be most profitably employed. It was unthinkable, they said, that the fleet should remain relatively idle until CARTWHEEL was over. There had been too many delays and postponements already, said Admiral Cooke, and the time had come to open the Central Pacific offensive. He proposed, therefore, that the Marshalls operation be scheduled for about 1 November. And he was confident, moreover, that it could be carried out without disrupting MacArthur's schedule.

Despite the seeming disparity in their views, the planners were not too far apart. Both sides could agree at least that a Central Pacific offensive was desirable, that it should begin as soon as possible, and that it should not be made at the expense of operations in the South and Southwest Pacific. On that basis, they recommended to the Joint Chiefs of Staff that the Marshall Islands should be invaded about 1 November and that Admiral Nimitz be directed to submit his plans for the operation. At the same time, they instructed the Joint War Plans Committee to prepare a new plan based on a target date of 1 November or 1 December and on the assumption that there would be no interruption to CARTWHEEL. The Joint Chiefs, the planners further recommended, should direct General MacArthur to furnish "without delay" specific information, including targets, dates, and forces, on the operations he planned to conduct in his area. These recommendations the Joint Chiefs accepted without question at their meeting of 15 June and the necessary instructions were quickly drafted.[24]

But on the question of command raised by Admiral King, the Army and Navy planners were unable to reach agreement and presented the Chiefs with a split report. The Army maintained it would be inadvisable for the Joint Chiefs to delegate their control over coordination and timing of operations in the Pacific to Admiral Nimitz. The proper exercise of this function, they argued, required a global viewpoint that no theater commander could be expected to possess. More important was the fact that the authority to co-ordinate clearly

---

[22] Rads, Marshall to MacArthur, 11 Jun 43, CM–OUT 4580; MacArthur to Marshall, 12 Jun 43, CM–IN 7367. MacArthur's estimate was essentially the same as that he had submitted on 27 May. See above, ch. XXII.

[23] Mins, JPS Mtg, 13 Jun 43; OPD Brief, Notes on Preliminary Rpt by JWPC . . . , JPS 205, in ABC 384 Marshall Islands (6–10–43), sec. 1.

[24] JCS 353/1, 14 Jun 43, sub: Future Campaign Opns in Pacific Ocean Area; JWPC 54/1/D, 14 Jun 43, sub: Sequence of Certain Pacific Opns; Mins, JCS Mtg, 15 Jun 43.

implied control over the assignment and movement of forces in the area and therefore supreme command of the Pacific. The Navy denied that this was necessarily the case and argued the need for co-ordinating amphibious operations with the Pacific Fleet's responsibility for holding the line of communications, but the Army insisted that acceptance of King's proposal was tantamount to making Admiral Nimitz supreme commander in the Pacific. This they could not accept and the Joint Chiefs therefore decided to table the matter.[25]

The disagreement over command had no effect on the development of plans for the Central Pacific offensive. On the 15th a message went out to MacArthur informing him of the tentative plan for an invasion of the Marshall Islands on about 15 November by forces drawn largely from his and Admiral Halsey's areas. These forces, the Joint Chiefs told him, included the 1st Marine Division, then in Australia, and the 2d Marine Division in the South Pacific, together with their assault transports, cargo vessels, and the major part of Halsey's fleet. "Urgently needed for immediate planning purposes," the Joint Chiefs wrote, " is an outline of operations in the South and Southwest Pacific Areas giving dates that may affect present basis of planning for Central Pacific operations."[26] The next day the Joint Chiefs directed Admiral Nimitz to submit to them his plan for the seizure of the Mar-

shall Islands, including forces, shipping, and target dates.[27]

Alternate Proposals

The task now facing the joint war planners was a difficult one. What they had to do was produce a plan for the invasion of the Marshall Islands on 1 December that would not curtail MacArthur's CARTWHEEL operation. But they could see no better way of seizing the Marshalls than by direct invasion and this, they were convinced, would require trained and experienced combat troops. Since such troops would have to come from the South and Southwest Pacific, the planners did not see how the operation could be mounted by 1 December without affecting MacArthur's plans. Thus, their first solution to the problem was not a solution at all but a restatement of the original plan in which the effect on CARTWHEEL was implied rather than stated.[28]

Realizing full well that they had failed to solve the problem, the planners tried a completely different approach and on 18 June submitted a new plan. There were, they said, three alternate courses of action to a direct invasion of the Marshalls, which they still preferred if the forces could be found. The first alternative was to approach the Marshalls from the north through Wake Island; the second, from the east by way of the islands in the eastern chain of the Marshalls group; the third, from the south by way of Nauru and the Gilberts. The first two the planners rejected as unsatisfactory; the third they thought

[25] Mins, JPS Mtg, 13 Jun 43; JCS 353/1, 14 Jun 43, sub: Future Campaign Opns in Pacific Ocean Area; Mins, JCS Mtg, 15 Jun 43.

[26] Rad, JCS to MacArthur, No. 4769, 15 Jun 43, CM–OUT 6093. Copies went to Nimitz and Halsey through the Army commanders in each area, Generals Richardson in the Central Pacific and Harmon in the South Pacific.

[27] Rad, King to Nimitz, 16 Jun 43, CM–IN 9883.

[28] JPS 205/1, 17 Jun 43, sub: Opns Against the Marshalls.

was a feasible plan though "definitely inferior" to the 3-phase assault on the Marshalls they had recommended earlier.[29]

The Gilberts-Nauru plan, as presented by the Joint War Plans Committee, called first for the establishment of advance air bases and fleet anchorages in the Ellice group and on Howland Island east of the Gilberts for reconnaissance and air support. This phase completed, the assault forces, consisting of one Marine division and one regimental combat team mounted from the South Pacific, would land simultaneously on Nauru Island and on Tarawa and Makin in the Gilberts under the cover of carrier-based aircraft. These and other islands in the group would then be developed into air bases from which Allied planes could bomb the Marshalls and reconnoiter the Carolines. Finally, after the Gilberts-Nauru position had been consolidated, garrison units would move into the area to relieve the assault force. In addition to the Marine division and regimental combat team, the operation would require 2 or 3 amphibian tractor battalions and supporting units, 5 heavy bombardment squadrons, and 1 fighter group during the combat phase. To garrison the islands another division with support and service elements, and an air component of 2 bomber and 2 fighter groups would be needed.

This new plan no more met the requirements laid down by the Joint Staff Planners than either of the earlier plans. Moreover, the Joint War Plans Committee was itself lukewarm about the plan, as the Army member remarked,

"When we get the Gilberts, we still do not have the Marshalls."[30] The truth was that no one was enthusiastic about an operation in the Gilberts. But the Navy apparently felt that something had to be done with the fleet and that an invasion of the Gilberts was better than no action at all. "There seems to have grown up in our Navy," wrote one of the Army planners, "the fixation that any action by the Fleet must acquire territory."[31]

The Army, approaching the problem from a different point of view, refused to be stampeded into any course not based on a thorough study of the entire situation in the Pacific. The Marshalls operation, it found, was unsound and entirely unacceptable if it resulted in the postponement of CARTWHEEL; the Gilberts plan it thought feasible. But the wisest course, the Army believed, would be to "analyze all possible operations in the Pacific, east of the Philippine-Honshu line, select the desirable ones, determine the sequence, and set dates for planning purposes." If the Navy felt it must employ its fleet offensively then it should seek purely naval engagements.[32]

Still to be heard from was General MacArthur. Informed on the 15th of the operations projected in the Central Pacific, at the same time he was asked for specific information about his own plans, MacArthur's response five days later left no doubt about his position. As a matter of fact, he told the Chief

---

[29] JPS 205/2, 18 Jun 43, sub: Opns Against Marshalls.

[30] Memo, Col William W. Bessell, Jr., for Col Roberts, 18 Jun 43, sub: Opns Against Marshalls, JPS 205/2, in OPD Exec Files.

[31] Ibid.

[32] OPD Brief, no date, Summation of Memos on Opns in Central Pacific; JCS 115/1, 23 Jun 43, sub: Opns in Central Pacific, ABC 384 Marshall Islands (6–10–43), sec. 1.

of Staff, he found the news most "disturbing" and expressed great concern over the effect of an invasion of the Marshalls on his and Admiral Halsey's CARTWHEEL operations. These, he reminded his Washington superiors, were only preliminary to the final assault on Rabaul, the great strategic prize toward which South and Southwest Pacific forces had been driving since August 1942. To withdraw either the 2d Marine Division from the South Pacific or the 1st, which was scheduled to invade New Britain on 1 December, would not only rule out any campaign against Rabaul in the near future, MacArthur asserted, but would also jeopardize the success of CARTWHEEL itself.[33] Two days later, he backed up this contention with Halsey's statement that the loss of the 2d Marine Division with its assault craft and shipping would deprive him of a strategic reserve of manpower to meet any sudden emergencies and put a "severe strain" on logistics in the South Pacific.[34]

There were other reasons why, in MacArthur's view, the withdrawal of the two Marine divisions would be unfortunate. First, it would have, as he put it, "profound political repercussions," presumably on Australia's relations with the United States. Second, it would be wasteful of shipping to transfer forces from advanced bases in the South and Southwest Pacific back to Hawaii. And finally, it seemed to represent a radical shift in the strategy of the war in the Pacific,

a shift he assumed was made at TRIDENT. "I am entirely in ignorance regarding the discussions and decisions of the recent Washington Conference," he told Marshall, "and request that I be advised in this respect insofar as it affects the broad concept of operations in this theater."[35]

As MacArthur saw it, the main effort in the Pacific was the drive northward through the Solomons and New Guinea. An invasion of the Marshalls was therefore "a diversionary attack," which, he admitted, would be helpful in making the main effort, provided the troops came from the United States. To draw them from his and Halsey's theater, he declared, would only weaken the main attack "to an extent that may result in its collapse."

Though MacArthur had not been informed of the TRIDENT decision to initiate an offensive in the Central Pacific, it must have been perfectly apparent to him that the Marshalls invasion could presage nothing else. He took the occasion, therefore, to present his own views on strategy to the Chief of Staff. He was convinced that "from the broad strategic viewpoint" the drive northward from Australia through New Guinea to Mindanao offered the greatest advantages for the Allies. It would place them most quickly in position to cut the Japanese line of communications southward while permitting them to support their own advance with land-based aircraft. "By contrast," MacArthur declared, "a movement through the mandated islands will be a series of amphibious attacks with the support of carrier-based aircraft against objectives defended by naval units and

---

[33] Rad, MacArthur to Marshall, C–3302, 20 Jun 43, CM–IN 13149.

[34] Rad, MacArthur to Marshall, 22 Jun 43, 13605. For the views of the air commanders, see Rads, Arnold to Kenney and Harmon, 22 Jun 43, CM–OUT 9340 and CM–OUT 9341; MacArthur to Marshall, 24 Jun 43, CM–IN 15013; Harmon to Arnold, 25 Jun 43, CM–IN 15655.

[35] Rad, MacArthur to Marshall, 20 Jun 43.

ground troops supported by land-based aviation." This type of operation he thought was the most difficult and hazardous, and he cited the Japanese experience at Midway to make his point.

The Central Pacific route, in MacArthur's view, suffered from the further disadvantage of not offering any vital strategic objective. An offensive westward across the Pacific, therefore, would require a series of hazardous "amphibious frontal attacks" against islands of limited value. Only when the drive reached Mindanao would the forces of the Central Pacific be in position to make any large strategic gains, and this objective, MacArthur believed, he could reach more quickly and with less cost by way of New Guinea.

The fact that the Central Pacific advance had the sanction of the prewar ORANGE plan did not impress General MacArthur. He had worked on this plan and understood it thoroughly. But he did not believe it was applicable in the present situation. The Japanese conquest of Malaya and the Netherlands Indies, he observed, had partially invalidated the assumptions of ORANGE and made its execution impracticable. More important was the fact that ORANGE had assumed that Hawaii would constitute the only advanced base in a war against Japan once the Philippines were lost. The possibility that Australia might be used had not been foreseen, and its availability now, MacArthur asserted, altered the situation completely. A blind adherence to an outdated prewar plan whose assumptions were no longer entirely valid did not seem to MacArthur to justify a strategy that would involve U.S. forces in costly and time-consuming operations for objectives of little strategic value.

This forthright statement of strategy and vigorous protest against the Central Pacific advance, though it did not reverse the decision to launch an offensive westward from Hawaii, did have some effect in Washington. About a week earlier, Admiral King had proposed to Marshall that the 1st Marine Division be transferred from Australia to the Central Pacific. Marshall had postponed his reply, and now, on the basis of information from MacArthur, he turned down the request firmly. To accede to it, he told King would seriously affect the operational schedule established in CARTWHEEL.[36]

MacArthur's views also supported the Army's case for a more careful approach to the Central Pacific offensive and a thorough study of the alternatives. Thus, when the Joint Staff Planners met on 23 June to discuss the two plans submitted by their Joint War Plans Committee the Army member proposed and the group accepted the suggestion that the committee be directed to restudy the problem along broader lines, taking into consideration the views of General MacArthur and Admiral Halsey. As interpreted by the joint war planners, this new directive called for "determination of the most suitable and feasible operations in the Pacific, whether they apply to the Marshalls-Gilberts or not."[37] They were also authorized under their new instructions to consider the possibility of seizing a position in the Admi-

---

[36] Memos, King for Marshall, 14 Jun 43, sub: Withdrawal of 1st Marine Div, JCS 238/1; Marshall for King, 23 Jun 43, same sub, WDCSA South Pacific Area.

[37] JWPC 58/D, 24 Jun 43, sub: Opns in Central Pacific, Incl B; Incl A, JPS Directive, both in ABC 384 Marshall Islands (6–10–43), sec. 1; Mins, JPS Mtg, 23 Jun 43.

ralties instead of trying to take Rabaul and Kavieng, and to neutralize these last two strongholds by air bombardment. "By these means," it was thought, "the Bismarcks could be controlled instead of captured, our progress accelerated, and forces made available for the Central Pacific."[38]

The planners of the Joint War Plans Committee had hardly settled down to work on 28 June, when the elder statesmen of the Joint Strategic Survey Committee, on their own initiative, presented the Joint Chiefs with a new set of recommendations for the Pacific.[39] As they saw it, the Allied strategy in the South and Southwest Pacific was the same strategy in reverse that the Japanese had followed during the first six months of the war, less the advantages of surprise and superiority the Japanese had enjoyed. Such a strategy, they thought, held small promise of any striking success in view of the enemy's strong position in the area. Far more promising, now that the United States had recovered from its initial setback and restored the naval balance in the Pacific, was the Central Pacific offensive. This line of advance and not the advance northward from Australia, said the Joint Strategic Survey Committee, should constitute the main effort and be given the highest priority. Not only would operations along this axis prove most remunerative, but they would also make possible the most effective use of American naval strength and, perhaps, bring on a decisive engagement with the Japanese fleet. Further, an advance through the Mandates would shorten the long line of communications to the

Southwest Pacific, support the defense of Australia, and contribute to "the several objectives of the South and Southwest Pacific campaigns as now conceived." Among these was undoubtedly the opening of the Celebes Sea to Allied forces, a goal the strategists believed would be greatly enhanced by the seizure of the Marshalls and Gilberts in 1943.

Though this argument had been advanced earlier in connection with the strategic plan for the defeat of Japan and approved as the basis for discussion with the British at TRIDENT, the Joint Chiefs as a group were not willing at this time to give the Central Pacific priority over operations in MacArthur's area. Admiral King was the only member who favored such a policy and he proposed a full-scale strategic review on the basis of these recommendations. But none of the others agreed and the matter was disposed of by sending it to the Joint Staff Planners "for examination."[40]

The Army's reaction to the proposal of the Joint Strategic Survey Committee would have greatly encouraged MacArthur, the champion of the southern over the central route of advance. To the Army planners, the selection of one route over any other at this time seemed premature. How could anyone say which was the best route, they asked, until a plan for the defeat of Japan had been developed? Even then, the effect of any operation in the Pacific on operations elsewhere would have to be studied before it would be possible to decide which was the best course. Moreover, the Army planners did not believe it would be

---

[38] Incl. B, cited above.
[39] JCS 386, 28 Jun 43, sub: Strategy in Pacific.

[40] Mins, JCS Mtg, 29 Jun 43.

possible to bypass western New Guinea by following the Central Pacific route to Mindanao, and doubted that such an advance would bring on a decisive fleet engagement. The Japanese, they thought, would only risk such an action if a vital area was threatened or if their fleet had the advantage. As to the first, the planners thought that only a threat to the Japanese home islands and the sea approaches to the South China Sea would bring out the Japanese *Combined Fleet*. It might well accept action also during an invasion of the Marshalls and Carolines, but in these areas, the Army planners pointed out, the Japanese with land-based aviation would hold the advantage.[41]

On about 4 July there arrived in Washington still another plan for the Central Pacific, this one prepared at Pearl Harbor by Admiral Nimitz' staff. Directed by the Joint Chiefs on 15 June to prepare a plan for the invasion of the Marshalls about 1 November, Admiral Nimitz had come up with a scheme that differed from any thus far proposed though it resembled the Gilberts plan in its requirement for air bases in the Ellice group. The initial landings were to be made on Tarawa in the Gilberts and on Jaluit and Mille in the southern Marshalls. The remaining important atolls in the Marshalls—Maloelap, Wotje, Kwajalein, Eniwetok, and Kusaie—would have to be seized later, Nimitz declared, for the forces required to take them in the initial assault were not then available. Under this concept, carrier-based air cover would be needed not only for the initial assault, but also for the later phases of the campaign to coun-

ter the enemy's land-based aircraft in the Marshalls.[42]

Admiral Nimitz' plan, like the other proposals made for a Central Pacific offensive, was referred ultimately to the War Plans Committee of the Joint Staff Planners. Certainly the joint war planners could not complain for lack of guidance or suggestion, their instructions were clear and their authority broad. They had their own earlier studies on the Marshalls and Gilberts, General MacArthur's and Admiral Halsey's views, the recommendations of the Joint Strategic Survey Committee, and now Admiral Nimitz' plan. It was up to them to produce a plan acceptable to all parties concerned.

The Gilberts-Nauru Plan

By 10 July the planners had come up with their answer. They liked best, it seemed, their own plan for an invasion of the Gilberts, which they thought "the most suitable, feasible, and acceptable of those that can be undertaken with the forces and shipping available" by 1 December 1943.[43] In reaching this conclusion, the planners reviewed the three other courses already proposed—direct invasion of the Marshalls, the approach via Wake, and Nimitz' plan—but rejected them for tactical reasons or because sufficient forces were not available. The preferred plan, too, would require forces not then available in the Pacific, but the committee planners hoped to get them from the South and

---

[41] OPD Brief, 29 Jun 43, Strategy of Pacific, JCS 386.

[42] The information on this plan, which the author has not seen, is based on Hayes, The War Against Japan, ch. XVII, pp. 14–15.

[43] JPS 205/3, 10 Jul 43, sub: Opns Against Marshalls-Gilberts.

Southwest. This could be accomplished, they pointed out, by eliminating in the final phase of CARTWHEEL the seizure of western New Britain, thus freeing the 1st Marine Division. And if Rabaul was neutralized by air action rather than assaulted, then the 2d Marine Division also would become available. These changes, the planners believed, would give MacArthur control of the Bismarck Archipelago earlier and at less cost than under the existing plans.

To the planners on the Army General Staff, this reasoning had some obvious flaws. It provided for the capture of the Gilberts but made no provision for seizure of more important objectives in the Marshalls or Carolines. Nor did they believe that so limited an objective as the Gilberts justified the withdrawal of two divisions from the South and Southwest Pacific and the radical alteration of MacArthur's plans. The result, they thought, would be to leave the forces in both areas "in an exposed position without either having achieved a decisive objective and without resources to advance further for some time." [44] As Col. Frank N. Roberts, the Army member of the Joint Staff Planners, remarked, "To go into the Gilberts at the expense of pressure on Rabaul was not acceptable to the Army." [45]

The Navy planners did not view the problem in this light. Though they had no specific plans for continuing into the Marshalls or Carolines, they had no intention either of stopping with the Gilberts operation. Rabaul, they argued,

could be reduced more effectively by operations in the Marshalls than by other means. Thus, when the Joint Staff Planners met on 14 July, Admiral Cooke had ready a proposed directive for Nimitz to proceed with the capture of Nauru and the Gilberts on 1 December. And in anticipation of the Army's—and MacArthur's—objections to cancellation of the western New Britain operation and the withdrawal of the 1st Marine Division, he proposed instead that Halsey's southern Bougainville operation be canceled and that only the 2d Marine Division be transferred to the Central Pacific. This the Army countered with a proposal to invade Wake Island alone on 15 November, an operation that would require neither the 1st nor the 2d Marine Division, and to postpone other Central Pacific operations until the forces could be made available without interrupting CARTWHEEL. [46]

The task of reconciling these views did not present any great difficulty. Meeting informally during the next few days, the planners agreed that provision should be made for subsequent operations into the Marshalls and Carolines and that both the western New Britain and Bougainville operations should be retained in CARTWHEEL. [47] With these points settled, the Joint Staff Planners were able to reach agreement on a course of action they could submit to the Joint Chiefs. This they did on 19 July, recommending the seizure of Nauru and the

[44] OPD Brief, no date, Opns Against Marshalls-Gilberts, JWPC 58/2, filed with JPS 205/3, ABC 384 Marshall Islands (6–10–43), sec. 1.

[45] Mins, JPS Mtg, 14 Jul 43.

[46] Ibid.; Draft Memos, JPS for JCS, 12 Jul 43, sub: Strategy in Pacific; Reply to Cooke, 14 Jul 43, both in OPD 381 Security case 195.

[47] Draft Memo by JPS, 19 Jul 43, sub: Strategy in Pacific, with attached informal Memo, Roberts for Handy, filed with JPS 219/D, ABC 384 Pacific (6–28–43).

Gilberts, target date 1 December 1943, followed promptly by invasion of the Marshalls about 1 February 1944.[48]

In support of this recommendation, the planners reviewed carefully and fully the entire situation in the Pacific. The Japanese, they pointed out, were relatively strong in the Solomons and New Guinea, and with their network of airfields were capable of strong resistance despite the difficulty of supplying these garrisons. To relieve the pressure on the Japanese in this area by discontinuing CARTWHEEL would permit the enemy to deploy his strength, especially in aircraft, to other areas where Allied forces were not as strong. Operations in the South and Southwest Pacific, therefore, should be carried out as scheduled, the planners concluded, whether the final objective was the capture or the neutralization of Rabaul.

Any advance westward from Hawaii into the Japanese positions in the Central Pacific would not only support the drive northward from Australia but would also employ American naval strength most effectively. Faced by this double threat, the Japanese would have to disperse their air forces and defend a greatly expanded front under disadvantageous conditions. The Americans, on the other hand, could support operations in either area with their naval forces and, once the Gilberts were taken, would be able to advance further into the Central Pacific, thereby shortening and making more secure the lines of communication to the Southwest Pacific. But first it would be necessary, the planners observed, to secure an air base in

the Ellice group through which to stage aircraft into the Gilberts.

The planners did not foresee any great difficulty in supplying the forces required for the Gilberts operation. The South Pacific would provide shipping, combat vessels, and the 2d Marine Division as the assault force. Later, if the Joint Chiefs decided to go through with the capture of Rabaul, they could send Halsey another division. Meanwhile, for the Gilberts, the Central Pacific could provide an Army division to back the Marine troops in the assault or as a garrison, and the North Pacific could furnish additional forces after the scheduled invasion of Kiska. Air forces for the operation would come from the Navy, the Central Pacific's Seventh Air Force, and from the North Pacific. These should provide enough, the planners thought, to make it unnecessary to draw on MacArthur's or Halsey's air strength.

On the subject of the Marshalls invasion, the planners were somewhat vague. They did not doubt that the forces required would be available by 1 February, and mentioned specifically the assault units of the Gilberts operation. Additional air units would be required, but where these would come from the planners did not say. Apparently they were satisfied to leave the solution of this problem for a later date.

The Joint Chiefs of Staff, meeting on 20 July, received the report of its planners with favor. General Marshall recognized the risk of withdrawing the 2d Marine Division from the South Pacific in the event it was decided to capture Rabaul, but agreed with his staff advisers that the risk was worth taking. He agreed also that the Gilberts invasion would support CARTWHEEL, and should

---

[48] JCS 386/1, 19 Jul 43, sub: Strategy in Pacific.

therefore be approved.[49] General Arnold, too, supported the plan and thought the Army Air Forces could provide the four additional squadrons needed to ensure the success of this "important operation."[50] These statements reassured Admiral Leahy, who had expressed concern lest the proposed operations interfere with MacArthur's operations, and he also gave his consent. And Admiral King went even further than the planners. The target date for the Gilberts invasion, he suggested, should be moved up to 15 November, that for the Marshalls to 1 January, in order to profit from the operations scheduled under CARTWHEEL.[51] The Joint Chiefs accepted this amendment and that same day sent Admiral Nimitz a formal directive to open the Central Pacific offensive. In it they outlined the concept and purpose of the projected invasion, listed the forces he would have, and instructed him to accomplish the following:

1. Organize and train forces for amphibious operations in the Ellice and Gilbert groups and against Nauru.

2. Occupy and develop for use as air bases those islands required for support of the invasion.

3. Capture, occupy, defend, and develop bases on Nauru and in the Gilberts.

4. Prepare by 1 September plans and a detailed estimate of forces required for the invasion of the Marshalls.[52]

By this time the idea that it might prove unnecessary to capture Rabaul had taken firm root in Washington. The prospect of avoiding the long and costly effort that would be required to reduce this Japanese bastion was certainly attractive enough, the planners thought, to warrant serious consideration. Among the recommendations they made to the Joint Chiefs on 19 July, therefore, was one authorizing them to undertake such a study "with a view to gaining control of the Bismarck Archipelago through the seizure of Manus Island, Kavieng, and Wewak."[53] The inclusion of this seemingly irrelevant matter in a study dealing with the Central Pacific was a natural one, for the planners could not avoid the fact that there was an intimate relationship between MacArthur's operations and those in the Central Pacific. If forces were not needed for Rabaul, they could certainly be used in the Marshalls. And, in any case, operations in both areas would have to be co-ordinated and mutually supporting.

MacArthur's views on this subject were still unknown. As a matter of fact, the first indication he had that the cancellation of the Rabaul operation was being considered in Washington came on 21 July on the heels of the Nimitz directive, when Marshall told him of the proposal to take Kavieng, Manus, and Wewak, thus isolating Rabaul and making its capture unnecessary. "If you concur in this conception," wrote Marshall, "outline plans to cover these operations . . . are desired before 1 September for

---

[49] Mins, JCS Mtg, 20 Jul 43; OPD Brief, 20 Jul 43, Strategy in Pacific, JCS 386/1, ABC 384 Pacific (6–28–43.

[50] Mins, JCS Mtg, 20 Jul 43.

[51] Memo by King, 20 Jul 43, sub: Strategy in Pacific, JCS 386/2.

[52] Rad, JCS to Nimitz, No. 202204, 20 Jul 43, CM–IN 14465. Information copies of the message went to

MacArthur and Halsey. The directive as prepared by the JPS included as app. A in JCS 386/1, 19 Jul 43, sub: Strategy in Pacific.

[53] JCS 386/1, 19 Jul 43, sub: Strategy in Pacific.

Joint Chiefs of Staff consideration." [54]

MacArthur, most emphatically, did not concur. The capture of Wewak he considered so difficult that he had purposely planned to bypass it. He expected, moreover, that his advances north and west through the Solomons and along the New Guinea coast would be opposed by strong enemy naval forces. To meet these he would have to have the support of South Pacific fleet units and an advance naval base from which they could operate. Only Rabaul met the requirements for such a base, and its capture, he told Marshall, "is a prerequisite to a move in force along the north coast of New Guinea." [55]

With these views, it was hardly likely that MacArthur would look with favor on the projected withdrawal of the 2d Marine Division. His reaction, therefore, to Admiral King's request at this moment for the 1st and 3d Marine Divisions — the latter then in the South Pacific — for use in the Gilberts, may well be imagined. There was no need,

however, to solicit his views in the matter. The request was based solely on a desire to avoid "mixed forces" and on the presumed unique qualifications of the marines for island warfare. General Marshall refused the request on more substantial grounds. "However desirable from the Navy point of view to employ only Marine divisions in the operation," he observed, "it is my opinion that both the undoubtedly bad effect on the CARTWHEEL operation and the waste of shipping far outweigh the anticipated advantages." [56] Instead, he offered King the 27th Division, then in Hawaii, for use in the Gilberts campaign, an offer that was promptly accepted. [57] Thus, by the end of July, the Joint Chiefs had done all they could to launch the Central Pacific offensive at the earliest possible date without sacrificing any of the operations in the South and Southwest Pacific. Admiral Nimitz had his instructions and the forces with which to carry them out. The rest was up to him.

[54] Rad, Marshall to MacArthur, 21 Jul 43, CM–OUT 8604.

[55] Rad, MacArthur to Marshall, No. C–4183, 23 Jul 43, CM–IN 16419.

[56] Memo, Marshall for King, 29 Jul 43, sub: Release of 1st and 3d Mar Divs; Ltr, King to Marshall, 22 Jul 43, both in OPD 381 Security, case 196.

[57] Memo, Vice Adm Richard S. Edwards for Marshall, 31 Jul 43, sub: Designation of 27th Div to Gilberts Opn, OPD 381 Security, case 196.

CHAPTER XXIV

Organizing for the Offensive

Whereas the Success of this Expedition will very much depend upon an entire Good Understanding between Our Land and Sea Officers, We do hereby strictly enjoin and require you, on your part, to maintain and cultivate such a good Understanding and Agreement . . . as the Commander-in-Chief of our Squadron is instructed, on his part, to entertain and cultivate the same good Understanding and Agreement.

Royal Instruction to General Wolfe, 1759

The decision to open the Central Pacific offensive initiated in the Hawaiian area, where the major theater Army and Navy commands were located, a a burst of activity that had not been seen since before the Battle of Midway. Up to now, the mission of the Central Pacific Area had been largely defensive. Operations in the southern Solomons and in the Aleutians, it is true, were nominally under Admiral Nimitz' command, but the staff officers of the Central Pacific had played little or no part in the planning and conduct of these operations. They had no sooner begun to plan for active operations, therefore, than they ran into the familiar organizational and logistical problems that had beset the South Pacific staff during the Guadalcanal Campaign. Some had been anticipated and an effort made to solve them in advance. Others developed during the planning period and had to be resolved by the Army commander on the spot as best he could, or referred to higher headquarters for arbitration.

Often the solutions represented compromises that no one thought entirely satisfactory; the Army had one way of doing things, the Navy another. But at no time did the commanders permit their differences to delay or hazard the success of the offensive. On one thing all were agreed. The main job was to meet the enemy and defeat him with the least possible loss of life. Under the acid test of combat, most differences could be quickly resolved.

The Problem

Foremost among the problems facing Admiral Nimitz in preparing for the coming offensive was the organization of his forces. Nimitz' role as commander of the Pacific Ocean Areas was clear, but his additional positions as Commander in Chief, Pacific Fleet, and Commander of the Central Pacific Area created some confusion. Moreover, he used virtually the same staff while acting in all three capacities, and Army ground and air officers justifiably felt that their point of view could not be adequately represented on a staff consisting almost entirely of naval officers and functioning largely as a fleet staff.

The customary naval task force organization created further difficulties, for by placing ground and air units under task force or group commanders, usually naval officers, it obfuscated the lines of authority in areas where the Army normally retained control. These and other problems consumed much of Admiral Nimitz' time, but their importance fully warranted the effort. On their successful solution, he knew, depended the relationship between Army and Navy commanders in the area and the effective utilization of his forces in the operations to come.

The problems that now faced Admiral Nimitz had long plagued his superiors in Washington. So long as the Central Pacific theater remained quiescent, discussion of these problems could be deferred. But by the summer of 1943, as plans for the offensive began to take shape, the Army planners in Washington had apparently become convinced that the time had come to clarify Admiral Nimitz' status and to create a truly joint theater staff in which the Army would have representation commensurate with its responsibilities and the size of its forces in the area.

Two efforts had been made earlier in the year to meet some of the problems raised by joint operations of the Army and Navy in the Pacific. The first of these was the Basic Logistical Plan of March 1943, designed "to insure co-ordinated logistical effort and procedure in each command area . . . involving joint Army-Navy operations in which

unity of command and responsibility had been established. . . ."[1] Developed largely in response to conditions in the South Pacific, the plan had as its objective the most effective and economic utilization of trans-Pacific shipping and of the supply and service elements of each of the services in the theater. The joint commander, it stipulated, would determine the requirements of his theater for personnel and supplies and prepare a consolidated list, indicating shipping priorities. Presumably he would take into account the wishes of the major service commanders in his area, but the final decision would be his. The organization for supply in his theater was clearly the responsibility of the joint commander also, but under the Basic Logistical Plan he was to establish a unified system either through a joint logistical staff or through joint planning by separate staffs.

Though the plan was generally sound, its execution left much to be desired. In both the South and Central Pacific Areas, where its provisions were most directly applicable, few changes were made immediately. Neither Nimitz nor Halsey established a unified logistical system, electing instead to set up joint logistical boards. Because of the urgency of operational requirements, considerable progress was made toward co-ordination of supply activities in the South Pacific. But in the Central Pacific, where the services had long maintained separate supply systems, very little had been accomplished in development of an effec-

---

[1] Basic Logistical Plan for Command Areas Involving Joint Operations, 7 Mar 43, AG 381 (3–5–43). For a full discussion of the background and development of the plan, see Leighton and Coakley, *Global Logistics and Strategy*, p. 656–60.

tive and unified logistical system by the summer of 1943.

Even more important than the Basic Logistical Plan was the effort in April 1943 to define the principles of unified command in joint operations and to lay down the rules under which such command would be exercised.[2] The only existing guide was the *Joint Action of the Army and Navy*, published in 1935, supplemented by the separate directives issued to theater commanders on their appointment. This system had obvious shortcomings and as early as the fall of 1942 the Army planners had begun to study the problem. By the beginning of 1943, after the experience of operations in the South and Southwest Pacific and the prospect of additional operations in both areas and in the Central Pacific as well, it was apparent that unless some guide rules were established the conduct of joint Army-Navy forces in future operations might be adversely affected.[3]

Agreement on a set of rules for command of joint operations was not easily obtained. There were fundamental differences between the Army and Navy in doctrine and training. The nature of the forces each utilized and the way in which the Army and Navy organized and employed these forces differed also. It was natural, therefore, that each service should have its own concept of joint operations. Despite these differences, agreement was reached on 20 April 1943

and embodied in a Joint Chiefs of Staff directive entitled Unified Command for U.S. Joint Operations.[4] It was a brief document about a page in length, which, in clear concise language, defined unified command, fixed the limits of the commander's authority and responsibility, told him what he could and could not do in general terms, and specified how he would organize his forces and exercise his command.

As defined in the JCS directive, a unified command was one "in which a force composed of units of the Army and Navy operates as a single command unit under an officer specifically assigned by higher authority." In choosing the commander, the Joint Chiefs indicated they would be guided by the nature of the projected operations—air, ground, or surface—and the objectives sought. Whatever his service, the officer selected would be responsible to the Joint Chiefs alone and would exercise his command of Army and Navy forces assigned to his area through the commanders of these forces. In operations, this authority would ordinarily be limited to the assignment of missions to these forces, tactics and techniques being the province of the force commanders. Administrative matters the joint commander was to leave as far as possible to others, keeping his own participation to a minimum and exercising discipline through the commanders of the separate services.

Perhaps the most significant provisions of the JCS directive on unified command were those relating to organization. A joint commander, it specified, was not to assume command of any component of his force "unless so directed by the Joint

---

[2] The principle of unified command in combined operations had been established earlier by agreement with the British at Casablanca. System of Command for Combined U.S. British Operations, 11 Feb 43, JCS 215.

[3] For an account of early planning on this problem, see Matloff, *Strategic Planning for Coalition Warfare, 1943–44*, pp. 102–05.

[4] JCS 263/2/D, 20 Apr 43.

Chiefs." To this prohibition against acting in a dual capacity was linked the injunction to establish a joint staff consisting of representatives of the component parts of his force "in such a manner as to insure an understanding of their several capabilities, needs, and limitations, together with the knowledge essential to maximum efficiency in integration of their efforts." [5]

The directive for unified command in joint operations met its first real test late in June 1943 when Admiral King proposed to General Marshall that Army troops replace marines on garrison duty in rear areas of the Pacific. Marshall refused. The assignment of troops in the Pacific, he told King, was but one phase of the broader problem of co-ordination within the theater. The Joint Chiefs had given Nimitz authority and the means to carry out his mission; it should not, he declared, tell him where to assign his forces as well. What Nimitz did need, Marshall claimed, was "an adequate joint operational staff, as provided in the directive for unified command," to advise him as to the most effective use of his forces. The existing staff he characterized as "an excrescency" superimposed on the Pacific Fleet staff.[6]

As General Marshall saw it, the creation of a truly joint staff with adequate Army representation was only a partial remedy for the "lack of coordination and consequent inefficient use of all available means in the Pacific Area." The basic difficulty, he thought, stemmed from Nimitz' position as theater, area, and fleet commander. These jobs, Marshall felt, should be divorced and Nimitz, like MacArthur, should function only as commander of the theater.

General MacArthur, it will be recalled, had been specifically enjoined when he assumed command of the Southwest Pacific Area from commanding directly any component of his force, but Nimitz had not been so restricted. At that time — April 1942 — it had been assumed that operations in the Central Pacific would be primarily naval. Combining of the area and the fleet, therefore, had seemed both logical and natural.[7] It was logical also that the staff serving Nimitz while he was wearing his naval cap should also serve him when he donned his other hat. Thus had developed an organization which had served well for over a year but which the Army now thought inadequate for the operations ahead and inconsistent with the concept and practice of joint command.

Admiral King did not agree. He had hoped, he said, that his proposal to release the marines could be considered by itself "to help get on with the war in the Pacific," and he regretted the necessity for a review of the command arrangements in that area. But now that the problem had been raised he met it head on. He acknowledged readily that the projected offensive would impose greater demands on Nimitz' headquarters but stoutly denied any lack of co-ordination or inefficiency in the theater. "Without doubt," he told the Army Chief of Staff, "we are in accord as to the objectives to be attained and as to the general principles of command." [8] He was glad, he said, to have Marshall's views, but

---

[5] *Ibid.*

[6] Memos, Marshall for King, 13 Jul 43, sub: Relief by Army Troops . . . ; King for Marshall, 24 Jun 43, same sub, both in OPD 370.5, case 240.

[7] See above, ch. XI.

[8] Memo, King for Marshall, 19 Jul 43, sub: Relief by Army Troops . . . , OPD 370.5, case 240.

pointed out that he himself had only recently taken steps to increase both the Army and Navy membership on Nimitz' joint staff.[9] And at present, he added, he was "exploring the practical aspects of making changes in the Pacific that will produce the best results, not only in the immediate but in the more distant future. . . ." Marshall, he promised, would be kept informed "of these explorations" as they progressed.

On the matter of Nimitz' multiple command, King made no concessions whatever. Though he admitted that it might become necessary at a later date to relieve Admiral Nimitz from his duties as Pacific Fleet commander, he asserted that the present arrangement had worked well for the past 18 months and had "utilized our talents to the best advantage." But the possibility that King would turn over fleet command to one of Nimitz' subordinates was most unlikely in view of his statement that in the future "more or less the entire Navy will become incorporated in the Pacific Fleet." [10]

That the Navy would enter into discussions with the Army on so important a post in the naval hierarchy as the Pacific Fleet command, or assign to that command any but its senior representative in the theater, seemed most doubtful. As Army planners noted at the time, after discussion with their naval colleagues, the Navy would be most reluctant to make the Pacific Fleet "a unit under a Theater Commander" for this would in effect remove it from the direct control of Admiral King in his capacity as Commander in Chief, U.S. Fleet. Rather than limit Nimitz' operational control as fleet commander, the Navy Department, the Army planners believed, would seek to extend his—and thereby King's—authority to include the surface elements in MacArthur's area, on the ground that it was essential for the "maximum mobility" of the fleet.[11]

It did not seem to Admiral King, either, that Nimitz' multiple command violated the current doctrines on joint command, as Marshall had charged. Underlining the final clauses of the passage cited by Marshall—"unless so directed by the Joint Chiefs of Staff"—he argued that since the Joint Chiefs had established the Pacific Ocean Areas "with full cognizance" that Admiral Nimitz was already the Commander in Chief, Pacific Fleet, it followed that the Chiefs had in effect given their consent to this arrangement.[12]

Whatever the merits of King's argument, it was evident to the Army planners that if Admiral Nimitz was divested of his fleet command his relationship to Admiral King would be significantly altered. Functioning solely as the commander of an active theater of operations under the Joint Chiefs of Staff, he would no longer be responsible directly to King through naval channels for the operations and administration of the Pacific Fleet. In these circumstances, King's relationship to Nimitz would be limited to King's position as a member of the

---

[9] King was referring here to his request of 25 June for the assignment of two Army officers to the staff of the Pacific Fleet and two more to the staff of the projected Central Pacific Force. No mention was made of a joint staff. Memo, King for Marshall, 25 Jun 43, sub: Assignment of Army Officers, OPD 210.31, case 50.

[10] Ibid.

[11] OPD Memo For Record, 19 Jul 43, no sub, OPD 370.5, case 240.

[12] Memo, King for Marshall, 19 Jul 43, sub: Relief by Army Troops . . . , OPD 370.5, case 240.

Joint Chiefs of Staff. And as executive agent for that body, King would have no authority other than that granted by it to direct Nimitz on the employment of the fleet, which would become a subordinate force under the control of the theater commander. Thus, the authority King exercised over the Pacific Fleet and over Admiral Nimitz as its commander by virtue of his position as Commander in Chief of the U.S. Fleet would in large measure be lost if the Army's proposal to separate the theater and fleet commands was adopted.[13]

In one respect, General Marshall's criticism of Nimitz had been unjustified. Marshall had declared that the matter of shifting troops from one base to another should be left to Admiral Nimitz as theater commander exercising unity of command. His failure to do so had seemed to Marshall to indicate a lack of co-ordination in the theater stemming from the absence of an adequate joint staff. What Marshall and his advisors seem to have overlooked was that in May 1942 the Joint Chiefs of Staff had prohibited commanders vested with unity of command from permanently transferring units of a service to which they did not belong from one station to another without approval from the appropriate department in Washington.[14] Admiral Nimitz, therefore, did not have the authority to transfer Army units in his area, and it was for this reason, King pointed out to Marshall, that he, King, had requested Marshall's consent to the

replacement of Marine garrisons by Army units in the first place.

Admiral Nimitz' authority as theater commander was limited in other ways. Under the original directive establishing the Pacific Ocean Areas, Nimitz was required to exercise command of the South Pacific Area through a designated representative—first Admiral Ghormley and then Admiral Halsey—who functioned virtually as a theater commander. Thus, in the South Pacific, Nimitz did not have full command responsibility, and, as a matter of fact, did not wish to exercise such responsibility.[15]

The situation in the North Pacific Area was different. There, no real unified command had been established. The commander of the area, a naval officer, acted under directives from both Admiral Nimitz and the Commanding General, Western Defense Command, and his relations with the air and ground commanders were governed by the principle of mutual co-operation. This arrangement had worked so well that King believed "a change would be a mistake."[16]

Command arrangements in the Central Pacific were unlike those established for the other two areas of Nimitz' Pacific Ocean Areas. There was in the Central Pacific no designated commander and no separate area headquarters. Nimitz himself acted as Central Pacific commander when necessary, using the same staff that served him in his other capacities. Army forces in the area were under the old prewar Hawaiian Department whose commander served also as Military Gov-

---

[13] Memo for Record, 9 Nov 43, sub: Designation of CPA as a Theater of Opns, OPD 384 (PTO) sec. 2, case 54.

[14] Rad, JCS to CINCPAC et al., 041819, 4 May 42, copy in OPD 370.5, case 240. This directive was modified so far as AAF units were concerned on 30 October 1942.

[15] OPD, Memo for Record, 19 Jul 43, no sub, OPD 370.5, case 240.

[16] Memo, King for Marshall, 19 Jul 43, sub: Relief by Army Troops . . . , OPD 370.5, case 240. See above, ch. XXI.

ernor of Hawaii. Though under Nimitz in most matters, this officer functioned also as independent commander in certain specific fields, including military government, a situation that did nothing to ease the difficulties of unified command.[17] Even in operational matters, Nimitz did not exercise full control over Army forces. Under a Joint Chiefs directive of April 1942, when a situation calling for a "fleet-opposed invasion" arose, the Navy would exercise unity of command. But when a state of "Army-opposed invasion" was declared, unity of command was to be exercised by the Army commander. As interpreted by the Army planners, this meant that in an "Army-opposed invasion" of Hawaii, responsibility for the defense of the islands would rest with the commander of the Hawaiian Department, regardless of the disposition or movement of the Pacific Fleet.[18]

These restrictions on Nimitz' authority greatly complicated the problem of command in the Pacific Ocean Areas. Clearly, it would be no simple matter to relieve him of his command of the Pacific Fleet, as Marshall had suggested, and make him a theater commander with full responsibility for all three areas of his jurisdiction. General Marshall quickly realized this and did not press the matter further. He was willing, he told King, to send Army troops to relieve the marines on garrison duty. He was also willing to revoke the May 1942 directive so far as it applied to the South and Cen-

tral Pacific, but only "coincident with assumption by CINCPAC of the role of Theater Commander" with full responsibility for the two areas. The larger questions, he thought, should await the outcome of King's own investigations and of a joint study then in progress on the roles of the Army and Navy.[19]

Curiously enough, the question of a supreme commander for the entire Pacific was not raised at this time by either the Army or Navy. Heretofore in almost every debate over command, one side or the other had proposed this solution to the problem at hand. The advantages of a single command were conceded by both sides, but it was impossible to reach agreement on a commander. Clearly, the Navy would not agree to a solution that placed Nimitz under General MacArthur. And just as clearly, the Army would not accept a solution which made MacArthur subordinate to the Pacific Fleet commander. Various compromise candidates had been proposed—Arnold, McNair, McNarney—but none of these apparently had sufficient stature to overcome the Navy's claim to supreme command.[20]

In none of the discussions over command had the Army put forward the one candidate who might conceivably have been acceptable to the Navy as supreme commander in the Pacific. That man was George C. Marshall, the Army Chief of Staff, and in the fall of 1943 the possibility of his assignment to the Pacific was considered for the first time. The occasion was provided by a study of the more important problem of command

---

[17] For an account of these difficulties, see History of United States Army Forces, Middle Pacific and Predecessor Commands During World War II, pt. IV, Army-Navy Joint Action, OCMH.

[18] Rad, JCS to Comdrs Coastal and Sea Frontiers, 191630, 19 Apr 42; OPD Memo for Record, 19 Jul 43, no sub, both in OPD 370.5, case 240.

[19] Memo, Marshall for King, 12 Aug 43, sub: Relief of Army Troops . . . , OPD 370.5, case 240.

[20] For an earlier discussion of this problem, see above, Chapter XVI.

in Europe for the projected invasion of the Continent. General Marshall was the obvious choice for this assigment, and the task before the planners was to present an organization that would meet the political and military requirements of the situation and at the same time ensure the fullest utilization of General Marshall's services in the Allied war effort.[21]

This problem was studied with the greatest care in the War Department during September 1943, and on 5 October General Handy submitted to Marshall the views of the Army planners on command in Europe. On the assumption that Marshall would exercise this command—he had already been tentatively selected—Handy argued that the arrangements made at the forthcoming Cairo Conference should provide for Marshall's continued membership on the Combined Chiefs of Staff, at least in regard to matters relating to Europe. It was also desirable, Handy pointed out, to leave in abeyance the problem of a supreme commander in the Pacific. His reason, he stated frankly, was that "at some time in the future, when the European war is rapidly drawing to a successful conclusion, the availability of General Marshall might offer a solution, which would not be highly controversial, for an over-all Pacific commander."[22]

What Handy was saying, of course, was that command in Europe and command in the Pacific were intimately related and that a solution in one area

might well affect the situation in the other. And so long as General Marshall was the most likely candidate for the European command, his staff wished to defer decision in the Pacific until the shape of the war against Germany became clear. What would be Marshall's position, for example, if Germany surrendered shortly after the Chief of Staff's relief and reassignment, leaving him "with the form and not the substance of command?" Would the President call him back to Washington to replace a newly appointed Chief of Staff? Would he be available for duty in the Pacific? These and other questions lay behind the staff's desire to move slowly in the matter of Pacific command while keeping the arrangements for command in Europe as flexible as possible.

Further discussion threw no additional light on this subject. Thus, as the Cairo Conference drew near, the Army recommended that the question of a supreme commander for the Pacific not be raised at the conference lest it complicate the problem of selecting the commander for Europe. In support of this position, Handy pointed out that to do so would give the British a vote in the choice of commander in an area that was "almost 100 percent American."[23] Furthermore, there was no necessity for a decision in the Pacific, Handy said, until a plan for the defeat of Japan had been developed. In the meantime, operations in the area were going well and coordination between the two commanders appeared to be satisfactory. In any case, the selection of a supreme commander at this time, observed Handy, would

[21] For an exposition of the political and military considerations involved, see Forrest C. Pogue, *The Supreme Command*, UNITED STATES ARMY IN WORLD WAR II (Washington, 1954), pp. 23–28.

[22] Memo, Handy for Marshall, 5 Oct 43, sub: Comdr and System of Comd for War in Germany, tab A, OPD 384, case 15.

[23] Memo, Handy for Marshall, 10 Nov 43, sub: Problem of Over-all Comd, OPD Exec 5, item 15, folder 3.

force a choice between MacArthur and Nimitz, a choice, Handy observed, that would be both unpalatable and "politically impracticable." This was the view ultimately accepted by the Joint Chiefs of Staff, and on 19 November, aboard the *Iowa,* the President agreed not to bring up the matter of a supreme commander for the Pacific at the forthcoming meeting with the British at Cairo.[24]

Theater Organization

Admiral Nimitz' views on the subject of command were, of course, of primary importance in any decision relating to the organization of his theater. On him rested the responsibility for operations in the Pacific Ocean Areas. He, therefore, had the greatest stake in perfecting an organization for the most effective employment of his forces. Thus, Admiral King had requested Nimitz' ideas on command even before the Army had raised the question. On 2 July he had suggested to Nimitz that perhaps the time had come to take a close look at his own position and the organization of his theater. In view of the projected offensives in the Central Pacific, did Nimitz think, King asked, that a change would be desirable? Specifically, he wanted to know what Nimitz thought about the idea of distinguishing between his functions as area commander and as naval commander, and whether such a distinction ought to be extended to the staff that served him in both capacities. And he was interested further in Nimitz' recommendations on the relationship between the Pacific Ocean Areas command

and the command of the three areas that comprised it.[25]

Admiral Nimitz could see little advantage in a separation of his functions or the division of his staff. As a matter of fact, he thought that for the forthcoming offensive his control of the fleet should be tightened rather than weakened. This he hoped to achieve, he told King, by consolidating elements of the fleet into task forces under separate commanders, thus decreasing the number of coequal subordinates reporting directly to him. Specifically, he had in mind a Central Pacific Force for use in the Gilberts campaign and so recommended to Admiral King.[26] He wanted also to expand his planning staff, but opposed the creation of two separate staffs. The net effect of such a move, he thought, would be to slow down business and create a demand for more and more staff officers, files, and space. Inevitably, each of the headquarters would grow in size and ultimately become an organization less manageable and efficient than the small headquarters he now maintained.

Though Nimitz' response temporarily discouraged further efforts to create a joint staff, it held out the promise of a reorganization of the forces in the Central Pacific to meet the demands of the projected offensive. This reorganization was not long in coming. On 20 July Admiral Nimitz received the directive from the Joint Chiefs to seize the Gilberts and to plan for the Marshalls invasion. About two weeks later, on 5 August, he established a Central Pacific Force to

---

[24] Mins, JCS Informal Mtg, 19 Nov 43, 1500, OPD Exec 2, item 11.

[25] Rad, King to Nimitz, 021437, 2 Jul 43, cited in Hayes, The War Against Japan, ch. XIX, p. 16.
[26] Ltr, Nimitz to King, 12 Jul 43, sub: CINCPAC Comd and Staff Organization for POA, in Hayes, The War Against Japan, ch. XIX.

plan and conduct these operations, and appointed as its commander Admiral Spruance, his chief of staff.[27]

The Central Pacific Force was an operational headquarters. Its job was to plan for the operations ahead, supervise and coordinate the plans and preparations of the forces assigned, and carry out the operation at the appointed time. Nimitz himself retained control over the administration and supply of the naval and Marine units of the Central Pacific Force; the commander of the Hawaiian Department, of the Army ground and air elements.

Within the Central Pacific Force were three major commands, the Fifth Amphibious Force, the Carrier Force, and the Defense and Shore-Based Air Force. The first was established on 24 August with Rear Adm. Richmond Kelly Turner, who had led the invasion of Guadalcanal, in command. His job was to conduct the landing operations, and for this purpose he was given ultimately all the assault forces as well as the transports, cargo vessels, landing craft, and supporting warships. These Turner organized into two attack forces. A separate ground headquarters, V Amphibious Corps, was created on 4 September. Commanded by Maj. Gen. Holland M. Smith, USMC, this headquarters was to direct the training and control the operations not only of the troops assigned for the Gilberts invasion, but also for those that followed. (Chart 13)

The Defense and Shore-Based Air Force under Rear Adm. John H. Hoover included all the shore-based aircraft—

Army, Marine, and Navy—assigned to the operation. Consisting of more than 300 planes and organized into four groups, Hoover's force was to conduct search and photo reconnaissance missions, develop and defend U.S. air bases in the forward area, and attack enemy bases and shipping before, during, and after the landings.

The third and last major component of the Central Pacific Force was the Fast Carrier Force led by Rear Adm. Charles A. Pownall. Consisting of six large and five small carriers with supporting battleships, cruisers, and destroyers, this force had the twofold mission of providing long-range protection for the invasion force and direct support during the operation itself.

At the same time that Nimitz was organizing his forces for the offensive ahead, the Army commander in the area —Lt. Gen. Robert C. Richardson, Jr.— was also reorganizing his forces. General Richardson had arrived in Hawaii to relieve General Emmons on 26 May 1943, but he was even then no stranger to the problems of the Pacific. A year earlier he had made an extended tour of inspection of the theater as the personal representative of the Chief of Staff and talked at length with all the major commanders in the area.[28] Though the situation had changed greatly since that time, the familiarity with Pacific problems he had acquired then stood Richardson in good stead now. On 1 June he formally assumed command of the Hawaiian Department, becoming simultaneously the Military Governor of Hawaii. Almost immediately, he appointed a board of officers to make a study of

---

[27] Morison, *Aleutians, Gilberts and Marshalls*, p. 86; Crowl and Love, *Seizure of the Gilberts and Marshalls*, p. 25.

[28] General Richardson's Trip, OPD 333, case 15.

CHART 13—COMMAND ORGANIZATION, PACIFIC OCEAN AREAS, OCTOBER 1943

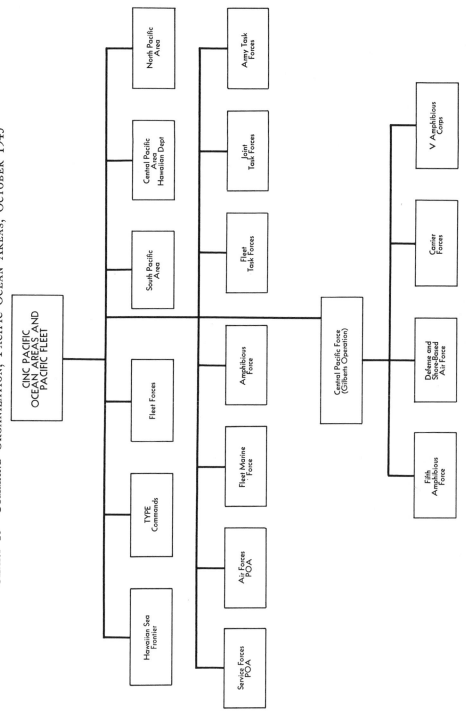

Source: Derived from Chart prepared by Navy and filed in 323.3 POA (1–29–42).

ADMIRAL SPRUANCE

GENERAL RICHARDSON

the existing organization of the Department. "It can be foreseen . . . ," he told the senior officer of the board, "that as the war against the Japanese develops the Hawaiian Islands and particularly the Island of Oahu will assume greater and greater importance. It is essential that this command be prepared and have foreseen the facilities which will be required in the operation of a large advance base." [29]

On the basis of the report and recommendations of this board, General Richardson on 29 July modified radically the

organization of his command, placing the major air and ground forces in the area under seven major commands, all under his direct control. In recognition of the importance of shipping in an oceanic theater, he abolished the old Service Forces and created instead an Army Port and Service Command. A Hawaiian Artillery Command was also established, and a Department Reserve designated. All the combat divisions in the area, as well as those expected, were placed under separate command and a task force headquarters was formed in anticipation of future needs. Finally Richardson appointed a deputy chief of staff for operations, who became in effect a War Plans officer since the Hawaiian Department

---

[29] Ltr, Richardson to Col. Ray E. Blount, 2 Jun 43, sub: Ltr of Instrs, copy in USAFMIDPAC Hist, pt. III, app. I to ch. II.

GENERAL SMITH   ADMIRAL HOOVER

did not have then or later acquire an operational mission.[30]

Though this reorganization increased the efficiency and flexibility of the Army organization in the Central Pacific and went far toward meeting the requirements for the expanding role of Army forces in the area, it did not take into account the fact that Richardson's responsibilities would soon extend far beyond the territorial limits of the prewar Hawaiian Department. The establishment of the Central Pacific Force on 5 August, by bringing all troops involved in the Gilberts operation under one headquarters, further emphasized the

need for a comparable Army organization encompassing all troops within the geographical limits of the Central Pacific Area. At Admiral Nimitz' suggestion, therefore, Richardson recommended to General Marshall that he be designated commander of all Army ground and air elements in the area "so that Army troops used in the forthcoming operations will have a commander toward whom they can look for supply, administration, and assistance." [31] At the same time, in response to Nimitz' request that the Army construct and defend a bomber base on Baker Island, he asked for authority to shift his forces within the theater with-

---

[30] USAFMIDPAC Hist, pt. III, pp. 296–301, 362.

[31] Rad, Richardson to Marshall, No. 4907, 6 Aug 43, CM–IN 3916.

out first requesting permission from the War Department. This authority, he explained, was necessary to meet Admiral Nimitz' operational requirements.

In Washington, Admiral King, no doubt prompted by Nimitz, supported Richardson's request on the ground that his appointment as commander of Army forces in the Central Pacific Area would create an organization similar to that in the South Pacific. Under such an arrangement, he pointed out, General Richardson's position vis-à-vis Nimitz would parallel the relationship between Harmon and Halsey. Richardson's appointment was desirable also, King told Marshall, "to insure co-ordination and effectiveness in the area for the forthcoming offensive," and he asked therefore that the change be made as soon as possible.[32]

Actually the War Department planners were already studying the problems of General Richardson's status and authority. With the exception of certain War Department restrictions relating to island garrisons (which the planners now recommended be removed) and an additional restriction on the use of aircraft imposed by Admiral Nimitz, they found that Richardson had full authority to employ the forces under his command, subject to agreement with Nimitz, as he wished. They saw no difficulty either in designating the Hawaiian Department commander as Army commander in the Central Pacific and recommended that this be done. Marshall quickly approved these recommendations, at the same time informing Admiral King that action was being taken to meet his request. Finally, on 14 August, Richardson received offi-

cial notification of this decision and on that day assumed the title Commanding General, U.S. Army Forces, Central Pacific Area "by direction of the President."[33]

The geographical extent of General Richardson's authority under this directive, as distinguished from his Hawaiian Department command, corresponded to the area delineated as the Central Pacific in Nimitz' original directive. It encompassed therefore all the land and sea areas of the Pacific between the equator (but including Canton Island) and the 42d parallel to the north, except for that portion of MacArthur's Southwest Pacific Area that lay north of the equator and a small strip off the coast of South America. Within this vast region, only a small portion of which was as yet in American hands, Richardson was responsible for the administration and training of all U.S. Army troops, whether ground or air. This responsibility included also supply, but the precise nature of these duties was left undefined pending his recommendations. And like Harmon, General Richardson had no responsibility for operations other than to assist "in the preparation and execution of plans" involving Army forces in the area, "subject to the direction of the Commander-in-Chief, Pacific Ocean Area."[34]

In designating Richardson Commanding General, U.S. Army Forces, Central Pacific Area, the War Department had said nothing about his duties as Hawai-

[32] Memo, King for Marshall, ser. 001594, 9 Aug 43, no sub, OPD 384 (PTO) case 54.

[33] OPD Memo For Record, 12 Aug 43, sub: Designation of CG Hawaiian Department as CG U.S. Army Forces in Central Pacific; Memo, Marshall for King, same date and sub, OPD 384 (PTO) case 54; Rad, Marshall to Richardson, 14 Aug 43, CM–OUT 5372.
[34] Rad, Marshall to Richardson, 14 Aug 43, CM–OUT 5372.

ian Department commander. Actually his responsibilities for both were about the same, but the older command, which carried certain additional legal responsibilities, had been established by Congress and could be altered only by that body. Did Richardson still retain those functions unique to the Hawaiian Department or had the new directive superseded the old? This confusion was settled quickly when the War Department on 18 September affirmed the continued existence of the Hawaiian Department under Richardson and stated explicitly what had been left implicit before—that its instructions to Richardson were not intended to affect the status of the Hawaiian Department or to impair his authority as commander of a territorial division as defined in regulations and in the Articles of War.[35]

With regard to supply, General Richardson recommended that his authority should be the same as that normally exercised by any overseas commander and should extend to all Army forces in the Central Pacific Area as well as Navy and Marine forces for certain classes of supply. (*Chart 14*) This authority, granted him on 25 October, confirmed an arrangement already in existence in the theater, for, under directives issued by Nimitz, Richardson's headquarters had become virtually the logistical agency for the support of the projected offensive.[36]

By this time, differences of opinion over the division of responsibility between the Army and Navy commands in the theater were beginning to affect planning for the forthcoming operations. In the task force organization established by Nimitz in August all land-based aircraft, whether Army, Navy, or Marine, had been placed under Admiral Hoover, a naval air officer. Since this arrangement placed virtually all the Army's combat air units in the Central Pacific under naval command, General Richardson proposed that the senior Army air officer in the area, Maj. Gen. Willis H. Hale, be given this command, subject to Hoover's control. Nimitz opposed this suggestion and insisted that, "in view of the over-all naval aspect of the operation," Admiral Hoover continue to exercise direct command over such shore-based aviation as was assigned to the Central Pacific Force. But if Richardson desired, Nimitz was willing to assign General Hale to Hoover's staff.[37]

This proposal hardly met Richardson's objections. What he wanted was an Army headquarters in close juxtaposition to Hoover's, not representation on the staff. General Hale, he insisted, should command directly the Army air units in the invasion of the Gilberts as a subordinate to Hoover. In this way Hoover would exercise control through Hale, who would be in a position to ensure the proper and effective employment of Army aircraft in accordance with Army Air Forces doctrines. This argument, which was similar to the one General Harmon had successfully impressed on Halsey during the Guadalcanal Campaign, apparently convinced Admiral Nimitz and on 25 October he agreed to appoint Hale commander, under

[35] USAFMIDPAC Hist, pt. II, Structural and Functional Development of the Army Command, p. 363.

[36] *Ibid.*, pp. 366–67; Rads, Ft. Shafter to WAR, No. W–6410, 17 Oct 43, CM–IN 10104; WAR to CG USAFCPA, 25 Oct 43, CM–OUT 12232.

[37] CINCPOA ser. 001299, 13 Oct 43, sub: Organization of Comd for GALVANIC, cited in USAFMIDPAC Hist, pt. IV, p. 844.

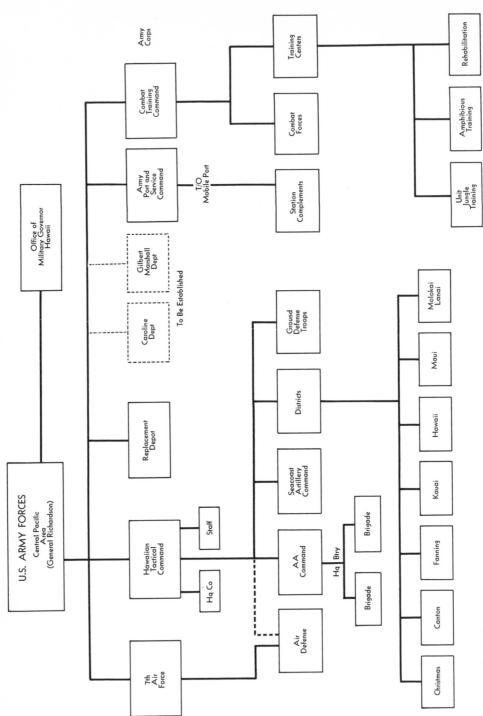

Hoover, of a task group composed of Army air units.[38]

Control of the 27th Division, scheduled to make the assault on Makin, and of other Army troops assigned to the Gilberts operation also created a problem during the period of planning and preparation. The V Amphibious Corps, established on 4 September as a permanent theater organization headed by a Marine officer, General Holland Smith, had responsibility for the amphibious training of all troops in the theater. But in addition, General Smith commanded the expeditionary forces for the Gilberts operation. In this latter capacity, Smith's responsibility for training Army troops was not clearly defined and his relationship to Admiral Turner, the assault force commander, was somewhat confusing. His control also over Army combat troops, who were attached to his corps in October while it was still in process of organization, raised some questions.

The 27th Division, under Maj. Gen. Ralph Smith, had been assigned to the Central Pacific Force for the Gilberts invasion early in September. Since that time it had remained under Richardson's headquarters for planning and training while co-ordinating these activities with Spruance's headquarters. The interposition of V Amphibious Corps headquarters in the chain of command in the midst of preparations for the coming invasion seemed to General Richardson a cumbersome and unnecessary arrangement, especially since he had responsibility, under the directive of 14 August,

GENERAL HALE

for the administration and training of all U.S. Army ground and air forces in the Central Pacific. He was aware also of the confusion over command between Turner and Holland Smith, and sought enlightenment from Admiral Nimitz. Who, he asked, would control Army ground troops during the invasion?

Nimitz' reply did not clarify the situation. The 27th Division, the admiral explained, was a part of the V Amphibious Corps, the theater organization formed to train troops for amphibious operations. But it was also a part of the Gilberts expeditionary force, and thus under Holland Smith in both his capacities. This explanation left Richardson with no recourse but to seek

[38] Ltr, Richardson to Nimitz, 20 Oct 43, sub: Organization of Comd for GALVANIC; CINCPOA ser. 00207, 25 Oct 43, same sub, both cited in USAFMIDPAC Hist, pt. IV, pp. 844–45.

from his superiors in Washington a clarification of his earlier instructions with regard to his responsibility for administration and training. The reply, received on 3 November, outlined the War Department's conception of his authority as follows:

In the fullest coordination with CINCPAC, you will continue the training of forces to the extent that time and facilities are available or are made available to you. Troops earmarked for specific operations should pass to the command of CINCPAC, Central Pacific Force, Fifth Amphibious Force, V Amphibious Corps, . . . at the time when, at the discretion of CINCPAC, they are required for specific operational training or rehearsal under the Force, Corps, Task Force commander in preparation for eventual utilization. The exact determination as to when such training responsibilities will pass from you to CINCPAC or his appropriate subordinate commander must, in all cases, be decided by CINCPAC after consultation with you as his Army adviser.[39]

General Richardson could find little solace in this fresh statement of his responsibility. It gave him no authority he did not already have and confirmed the action taken by Nimitz. But he accepted the decision gracefully and assured the Chief of Staff that "your conception of my responsibility for administration and training has been in effect continuously." His relations with Admiral Nimitz were excellent and there was, he further assured General Marshall, the "closest cooperation" between his office and that of CINCPAC, "with whom," he said, "I discuss daily the participa-

tion of Army troops in forthcoming operations."[40]

Though he gave these assurances, Richardson was not convinced of the need for a corps headquarters in the type of operations envisaged in the Central Pacific. To him it was just another echelon to deal with, for amphibious training, as he pointed out to General Handy, was conducted by Admiral Turner's amphibious force. The elimination of the V Amphibious Corps, in Richardson's opinion, would not affect the situation in any way. As a matter of fact, he remarked, "this Marine Corps headquarters gives me the impression of wanting to justify itself by extending its control to the maximum."[41] But this matter was Nimitz' responsibility, not the War Department's, and Brig. Gen. John E. Hull, acting for Handy, suggested to Richardson that he take it up with the admiral "in the interest of conservation of manpower, a problem most vital at this stage of our war effort."[42] By this time the problem had become academic so far as immediate operations were concerned, for already Army and Marine forces had invaded the Gilberts. At a later stage in the war, during the Saipan campaign, this problem of command and interservice relations would arise again, in a more acute form.

The Joint Staff

The proposal to establish a theater joint staff for the Pacific Ocean Areas, a proposal the Army had temporarily

---

[39] Rad, Marshall to Richardson, 2 Nov 43, CM–OUT 480. See also Ltr, USAFICPA, 17 Oct 43, sub: Clarification of Comd of 27th Division, CINCPOA ser. 00249, 25 Oct 43, same sub, both cited in USAFMIDPAC Hist, pt. IV, pp. 842–43.

[40] USAFMIDPAC Hist, pt. II, p. 364.
[41] Ltr, Richardson to Handy, 5 Nov 43, OPD 384 (PTO) sec. 2, case 54.
[42] Ltr, Hull to Richardson, 17 Nov 43, OPD 384 (PTO) sec. 2, case 54.

dropped in mid-July, had meanwhile been revived by General Marshall. The spark that kindled anew the interest in this project was a letter written by Brig. Gen. Edmond H. Leavey, one of Somervell's ablest assistants and recently assigned to the staff of Vice Adm. William L. Calhoun, Commander, Service Force, Pacific Fleet. In it, General Leavey recorded for his former chief, General Somervell, his impressions of the Navy's organization in the Pacific. His purpose, he declared, was to inform Somervell, in advance, of "the general nature of the situation" in case the official report he submitted later to Admiral Calhoun "causes any particular reaction in Naval circles." [43]

The picture Leavey painted of naval organization constituted a strong indictment and justified fully the general's concern about the reaction in "naval circles." So far as he could discern there was not even any theater staff in the area. Admiral Nimitz' headquarters, Leavey charged, was not a theater staff at all but merely a fleet staff for operations in the Central Pacific. Moreover, there·was no section or officer in Nimitz' headquarters or elsewhere, "either designed for, or capable of, co-ordinating and controlling the Service of Supply activities in the theater." Admiral Calhoun's responsibility as Service Force commander, declared Leavey, was for fleet supply only, and even in this field did not include Halsey's fleet in the South Pacific. For this reason Leavey believed his own assignment to Calhoun's staff was a mistake. "I would be in a much better position to help clear up the logistic picture," he told General Somervell, "if I were directly on Admiral Nimitz' staff, and expect to so report to Admiral Calhoun and Admiral Nimitz on my return to Pearl Harbor."

"Complete and coordinated" operations in the Pacific could be achieved, General Leavey believed, only by establishing what he called a GHQ type of theater headquarters. The staff of such a headquarters should consist of naval, air, and ground officers with adequate representation of the essential supply services. Thus, the staff would be qualified to co-ordinate tactical and logistical planning while exercising the necessary supervision over day-to-day operations in both fields. Leavey also believed that the area commanders under Nimitz should have similar joint staffs, and he recommended that separate commanders be appointed for the Central and North Pacific, as had been done for the South Pacific.

General Leavey's views surprised no one in Somervell's headquarters. They were much the same as those expressed about eight months earlier by General Lutes after a trip to the Pacific. As Somervell's operations officer, Lutes now gave strong support to Leavey's report, noting that he had himself recommended virtually the same reforms proposed by Leavey. Moreover, Lutes told his chief, Admiral Nimitz had agreed "to *initiate* a modified organization ·to provide for theater staff supervision of logistic supply matters in the entire Pacific area." [44] It was to assist in putting this plan into effect and to "sell" it to the Navy that Leavey had been sent to the Pacific in

---

[43] Ltr, Leavey to Somervell, 29 Jul 43, OPD 384 (PTO) sec. 2, case 55.

[44] Memo, Lutes for Somervell, 11 Aug 43, sub: Attached Ltr from Brig Gen Leavey, OPD 384 (PTO) sec. 2, case 55. (Underlining is by Lutes.)

the first place, Lutes reminded Somervell. But in view of Leavey's report
Lutes had his doubts that the Navy
would proceed as planned.

A week after writing this letter, General Lutes himself was in Hawaii. If
anything, his own report of conditions
there was even more critical than Leavey's. He found no arrangements for
logistical control in the theater headquarters, as provided in the Basic
Logistical Plan of March 1943, and no
machinery for resolving differences
within the Army-Navy Logistical Board,
which correlated supply matters common
to both services. More serious was his
contention that there was little exchange
of information between the Army and
Navy staffs. Richardson's staff, he noted,
had to "*solicit*" from the Navy the information it needed, and even then did not
learn enough "to plan supply and other
logistical requirements" for future
operations.[45]

As evidence of the need for a joint
staff to control and co-ordinate planning
and operations on the theater level, General Lutes pointed to the dual standard
of living of the Army and Navy. In some
instances soldiers and sailors stationed
almost within a few yards of each other
lived entirely differently. Where the
Army had built temporary shelters for
reasons of economy, the Navy had
constructed much better facilities
for its men. This difference, declared
Lutes, had created "a serious morale
situation."[46]

Planning for the projected offensive
in the Gilberts and Marshalls provided

an even better illustration, General Lutes
thought, of the defects of the organization of the Central Pacific. The Navy
staff, he found, had only a "very limited
knowledge" of the Army's logistical resources in the area and of the number
of service units that could be made available for future operations. This last was
a particularly sore point with the War
Department's supply experts, for they
had continually to fight for a larger share
of the Army's manpower. "If we could
get the backing of Admiral Nimitz on
such matters as Army Service Units,"
Lutes told General Somervell, with reference to the South Pacific, "we might
have more luck with our own General
Staff in obtaining such units. . . ."[47]

Both Leavey's and Lutes's reports ultimately reached General Marshall, who
had a deep and abiding conviction in
the necessity for a representative joint
staff. Leavey's report, which he described
as "a rather intimate picture of the logistical side of the Pacific theater as viewed
from Army eyes," he passed on to Admiral King on 10 August in the hope that
the Navy chief would give the matter
his "personal consideration."[48] More
than two weeks went by without reply
and on the 26th Marshall forwarded
Lutes's report to King. This time he
wrote a much stronger endorsement.
Both reports, he declared, pointed clearly
to "the urgent necessity of establishing
a joint staff for the theater and he could
see no reason why this matter "should
not be an immediate proposition." Certainly "in view of the coming events" in
the Central Pacific, the creation of such

---

[45] Memo, Marshall for King, 26 Aug 43, no sub,
OPD 384 (PTO) sec. 2, case 55. (Underlining is by
Lutes.)
[46] *Ibid.*

[47] *Ibid.*
[48] Memo, Marshall for King, 10 Aug 43, no sub,
OPD 384 (PTO) sec. 2, case 55.

a staff was, in Marshall's judgment, "an absolute requirement." [49]

Admiral King's response to this appeal was a strong protest against the action of both Leavey and Lutes in sending their reports directly through Army channels. First, he doubted that either officer was qualified to comment on the organization of the Central Pacific. They had had only a limited opportunity to observe "the overall situation," and, according to members of Nimitz' staff, General Lutes at least was not "completely and accurately informed on the matters which he discusses." [50]

A more serious indictment was Admiral King's criticism of the procedure followed by the two Army officers in presenting their views. General Leavey, he contended, had violated the first principle of the staff officer—loyalty to the commander and to the organization he served. As a member of Admiral Calhoun's staff, Leavey should have made "a forthright report through his responsible superior." By writing directly to General Somervell, King charged, Leavey had "violated proper, correct, and required military procedure." Lutes's error was not as clear. He did not know, King said, for what purpose Lutes had been sent to the Pacific. But if it was "to observe and report" on Admiral Nimitz' organization and command, then Nimitz should have been informed in advance. "I do not believe," King told Marshall, "that actions of this kind, even though they may be steps toward the formation of a joint staff,

will help to promote the unity of action which you and I are attempting to bring about." [51]

King's protest, it will be noted, did not deal at all with the substantive questions raised by the two officers involved. He ignored these questions also in a second communication of the same date in which he examined General Eisenhower's organization in North Africa with reference to its applicability in Nimitz' area. This possibility had first been raised by one of the naval planners and the Army had obligingly asked both Eisenhower and MacArthur to describe the organization of their headquarters. [52] MacArthur's reply, which King did not comment upon, emphasized the importance of "complete and thorough integration" of ground, air, and naval elements, close personal relationships, and the close physical location of the various headquarters. All these, he claimed, made possible "a constant daily participation of the staffs in all details of planning and operations" and "an attitude that is without service bias." But, he cautioned, the mere assembly of an approximately equal number of officers from the various services would not in itself produce an effective joint staff. [53]

General Eisenhower's response was fuller and to the point. Like MacArthur, he occupied a dual position as commander of an Allied theater of operations and as the commander of U.S. forces in that theater. In the latter capacity, Eisenhower exercised his functions, which consisted largely of supply,

---

[49] Memo, Marshall for King, 26 Aug 43, no sub, OPD 384 (PTO) sec. 2, case 55.
[50] Memo, King for Marshall, 30 Aug 43, no sub, ser. 001801, OPD 384 (PTO) sec. 2, case 55.

[51] *Ibid.*
[52] Rads, Marshall to MacArthur to Eisenhower, 26 Jul 43, CM–OUT 10477 and 10478.
[53] Rad, MacArthur to Marshall, 31 Jul 43, No. C–4369, CM–IN 22577.

personnel, and discipline, through a deputy theater commander, much as MacArthur did through a deputy chief of staff. And like MacArthur, he had organized his air and naval elements into separate forces with their own commanders and exercised command through them rather than through his own headquarters. However, instead of appointing a single ground commander as MacArthur had done in the case of Allied Land Forces, Eisenhower exercised this control himself through his senior ground officer, the British commander of the 15th Army Group, and when necessary, through the commanders of separate task forces or units. Later, the 15th Army Group commander became the deputy commander for ground operations.[54]

To the heads of the major staff divisions of his headquarters, Eisenhower entrusted the task of co-ordinating and supervising the corresponding staff divisions of the air and naval headquarters in the Mediterranean theater. In addition, he had a joint planning staff, which paralleled closely that of the Combined Chiefs in "organization, membership, and duties." This small staff was actually a part of the G–3 Section of Allied Force Headquarters and made its recommendations to G–3 rather than to Eisenhower directly.

Conferences between the officers of the various staffs were held frequently and on a regular basis. He himself, Eisenhower explained, met with his major

subordinate commanders at least once a week, and "in periods of operational activity" more often.[55] Furthermore, his chief of staff met three times a week with the senior American and British administrative and supply officers to co-ordinate nonoperational matters. Co-ordination was achieved also, Eisenhower pointed out, through the joint planning staff, a separate joint intelligence committee and daily G–3 conferences with representatives of the air and naval staffs.

One further agency established by Eisenhower to secure co-ordination and co-operation of the forces under his command was the so-called Chief of Staff Conference. This body consisted of his own chief of staff, G–2, and G–3, and the corresponding officers of the air and naval headquarters. Meeting daily, this group exchanged information on the activities and intentions of each of the headquarters with particular reference to the effect of operations by one service on those of the others. "This conference," Eisenhower explained, "is expected to develop points of friction or malcoordination in the details of operations," thus providing assurance for him and for the major force commanders that "operational co-ordination exists in details as well as in policy."[56]

In the organization of his headquarters, Eisenhower had followed in general the pattern he knew best, the U.S. Army staff organization, with such modifications as were necessary to meet conditions peculiar to the Mediterranean theater.

---

[54] Rad, Eisenhower to Marshall, W–6285, 1 Aug 43, CM–IN 814. It should be noted that this difference between MacArthur's and Eisenhower's control over ground operations was more apparent than real, for General Blamey, the Allied Land Forces Commander in the Southwest Pacific Area, did not actually function in that capacity. See above, ch. XX.

[55] Memo, Silverthorne for Capt Charles T. Joy, USN, 21 Oct 43, sub: Staff Organization in NATO, Incl, p. 3, OPD 384 (PTO) sec. 2, case 55.

[56] Rad, Eisenhower to Marshall, W–6710, 7 Aug 43, CM–IN 5102.

One important difference was in the composition of the staff. His was an Allied command consisting of U.S. and British forces, and the British were fully represented on the staff of Allied Force Headquarters. In addition, Eisenhower had two deputy chiefs of staff, both British, one for operations and one for supply. The first was charged with "the general co-ordination" of the G–2 and G–3 Sections of the headquarters. G–1 and G–4 were under the second deputy chief of staff, who, after January 1943, was also the British Chief Administrative Officer in the theater. As such he reported directly to the War Office in London, and held a position similar to that of the deputy theater commander, an American officer, through whom Eisenhower exercised his functions as commander of U.S. forces in the theater.

Other problems unique to the Mediterranean theater, such as military government and French rearmament, were handled by special staff sections which then had no counterpart in the War Department. In sections such as these and where specialized knowledge was required, assignment was on the basis of qualification rather than nationality and rank. Furthermore, in those sections dealing with administrative and supply matters there was a duplication of function and personnel that would not have been tolerated in the War Department. This was necessary, Eisenhower explained, because of the Allied nature of his command, "since the American channel goes back to Washington and the British channel to London." [57]

To Admiral King, the organization established by Eisenhower for the Medi-

terranean theater did not seem applicable to the Pacific, where the situation was quite different. He noted, for example, that co-ordination of air, ground, and naval plans and operations in the Mediterranean was effected through the commanders concerned rather than through the staff of Allied Force Headquarters. As a matter of fact, King pointed out, Eisenhower did not have a joint staff at all but an Allied staff of American and British officers, with little or no air or naval representation. Was this the kind of organization General Marshall wanted for the Pacific Ocean Areas, he asked? "If it is not," he told the Chief of Staff, "I would welcome a more or less specific outline of what you have in mind." [58] And, in what appeared to be an oblique reference to General Leavey, he again reminded Marshall that the effectiveness of any organization "is bound to depend upon the personalities and the loyal cooperation of those involved."

The task of outlining specifically the kind of organization the Army wished to recommend for the Pacific Ocean Areas was assigned to the Operations Division of the General Staff. Even here there was no unanimity of opinion.[59] But the necessity for reaching agreement was largely obviated when Admiral Nimitz on 6 September announced the formation of a joint staff. This staff, he told General Richardson, would consist of Army and Navy officers and would be organized into four sections—Plans,

[57] Rad, Eisenhower to Marshall, W–6285, 1 Aug 43, CM–IN 814.

[58] Ltr, King to Marshall, sec. 001800, 30 Aug 43, OPD 384 (PTO) sec. 2, case 53.
[59] Memos, Wedemeyer for Hull, 3 Sep 43, sub: Changes in Theater Boundaries and Comd Setup–Pacific; Ritchie for Handy, 28 Aug 43, same sub, OPD 370.5, sec. 7, case 240.

Operations, Intelligence, and Logistics. The first two would be headed by naval officers from the fleet staff; General Leavey would take the post of chief of the Logistics Section and another Army officer—to be recommended by Richardson—that of chief of Intelligence. "Have discussed this organization thoroughly with Admiral Nimitz and his advisers," Richardson reported with evident satisfaction to Marshall. "Both Admiral Nimitz and I are in full accord to solve in advance as many operational and logistic problems as possible." [60]

Admiral Nimitz' decision to establish a joint staff, just as discussions in Washington were approaching a climax, was not a sudden one. *(Chart 15)* Early in July, it will be recalled, King had suggested to him that in view of the coming offensive in the Central Pacific it might be desirable to reorganize his staff. At that time Nimitz had seen no need for a change. But the Navy planners in Washington had nevertheless continued to study the problem, and it was for this purpose that they had in late July asked their Army colleagues for information about Eisenhower's and MacArthur's staff.[61] The results of these studies, as well as the Army's criticism of Pacific organization, were passed on to Admiral Nimitz, who presumably had continued to give the matter his attention. General Richardson, too, had been exerting his influence on behalf of the joint staff, and it was General Somervell's opinion that the Hawaiian commander, by the use of a "tack hammer" rather than a "sledge

hammer" technique, had "undoubtedly been instrumental in securing Admiral Nimitz' consent to the creation of the joint staff." [62]

Thus, by the end of August, both the theater and the Washington staffs, spurred on by Admiral King who was himself being pressed by General Marshall, were working hard on the problem. On 6 September, the same day that Admiral Nimitz announced the formation of the joint staff in Pearl Harbor, Admiral King had sent him a proposed organization for the Pacific Ocean Areas. General Marshall, he explained, had been urging him for some months to separate the fleet and area commands in the Pacific and to establish in Hawaii a joint staff with greater Army representation. On the first issue, King had no intention of giving way. "I plan," he assured Nimitz, "to keep command of the Pacific Fleet and the command of the Pacific Ocean Areas vested in one person —you." [63] But in the matter of a joint staff he was apparently willing to make adjustments. These, he told Nimitz, were incorporated in the draft plan, which, in his view, represented the best efforts of the naval planners "to compromise the conflicting aspects of this problem."

Admiral Nimitz responded to this proposed reorganization by describing the system he had already put into effect. The new joint staff, he claimed, showed "a thorough appreciation of the necessity of amalgamating the interest" of the Army "with our own," and provided the machinery required to put into effect

[60] Rad, Richardson to Marshall, No. 5498, 7 Sep 43, CM–IN 5272.

[61] Memo for Record, 26 Jul 43, sub: Staff Organization in NATO and SWPA, OPD 384 (PTO) sec. 2, case 53.

[62] Memo, Somervell for Marshall, 12 Sep 43, OPD 384 (PTO) sec. 2, case 55.

[63] Ltr, King to Nimitz, ser. 001889, 6 Sep 43, cited in Hayes, The War Against Japan, ch. II, pp. 90–91.

CHART 15—HEADQUARTERS ORGANIZATION, CINCPOA–CINCPACFLEET, OCTOBER 1943

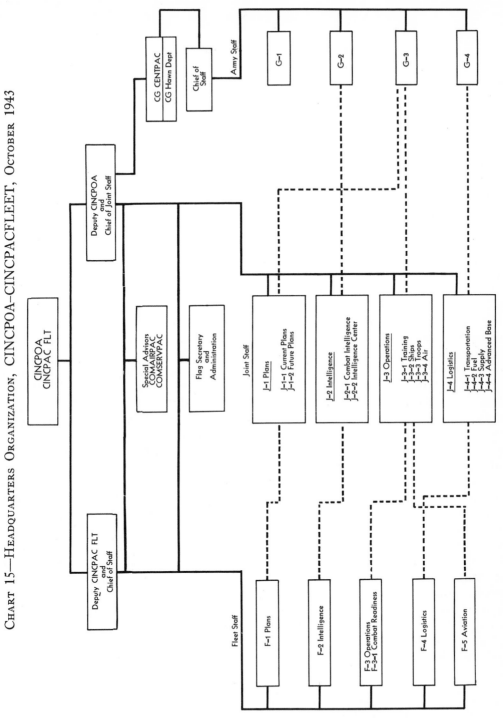

the principles of joint action.[64] The staff was to be headed by a Deputy Commander, Pacific Ocean Areas, a vice admiral, and would consist of officers from both services. But some of these officers, Nimitz pointed out, would serve in a dual capacity on the fleet or Army staff and on the joint staff, a provision that was to cause considerable dissatisfaction later.

In view of the Army's criticism of the organization for supply in the area and the failure to meet the requirements of the Basic Logistical Plan, Admiral Nimitz called special attention to the Logistics Section of the new staff. Headed by General Leavey, this section would establish priorities and supervise theater transportation, fuel supply, medical services, and the advance base sections. This last was a function hitherto assigned to the Service Force, Pacific Fleet, and likely to assume increasing importance as the Central Pacific offensive pushed westward into the Mandates. With logistical responsibility thus centralized Nimitz felt that his staff would be able to give "full and undivided consideration to joint logistical matters," and at the same time ensure that the Army's needs would be fully represented.[65]

Admiral Nimitz' optimistic view of the benefits that would result from this organization were not fully shared by General Somervell, who was in Hawaii from the 8th to the 12th of September. As he saw it, the formation of a joint staff, promising as it was, would not solve

the "still nebulous" command problem in the Pacific nor make any clearer the "rather tenuous and ill-defined" relationships between the various commanders and staffs.[66] There was no question that Nimitz was the theater commander and that Richardson, as Army commander, was his subordinate. The fact that this relationship was clear and that the working arrangements between these two officers and their staffs were "of the best" did not mean, Somervell pointed out, that the same was true elsewhere in the Pacific. It was not true, he declared, of the relationship between the area commands (the North, Central, and South Pacific) and the theater command, which, Somervell observed, was marked by a "lack of uniformity." And within each of the areas there were wide variations in organization, in the responsibility of the commanders, and in methods of operation. Thus, supply and logistics followed "a different pattern" in Hawaii than elsewhere.

Nimitz' command of the Central Pacific Area and of the fleet created an additional problem. By retaining both commands, Somervell declared, Admiral Nimitz had become so involved in details and so preoccupied with the local situation that he had lost sight of "the general picture" and thereby reduced his effectiveness as theater commander.

General Somervell's solution to the command problem in the Pacific Ocean Areas was similar to that proposed earlier by General Marshall. First, he would separate the fleet and Central Pacific commands, appoint separate commanders for each of the areas, and establish in

---

[64] Ltr, Nimitz to King, ser. 00168, 9 Sep 43, sub: Comd Relationships and Staff of CinCPOA and Pacific Fleet—Reorganization of, OPD 384 (PTO) sec. 2, case 53.

[65] Ibid.

[66] Memo, Somervell for Marshall, 12 Sep 43, OPD 384 (PTO) sec. 2, case 55. See also Memo, Somervell for Nimitz, 22 Sep 43, no sub, OPD 384, case 17.

each an organization parallel to that of the theater command. In addition, he would establish a base area comprising Hawaii and "perhaps a few of the islands immediately to the south." Because of the importance of these islands in the coming offensive, Somervell would make the commander of this area responsible for "the operation of supply and administrative system" and coequal with the other area commanders. With such an organization, said Somervell, Admiral Nimitz would be free from "the multitudinous problems which arise in any of the three sectors or with the details of handling the supply lines, the training of troops sent into the base area prior to their commitment to more active theaters, or the defense of the base area." Relieved of these heavy burdens and aided by an effective joint operating staff, Nimitz would be able, Somervell concluded, to give his full attention to theater-wide problems and to the prosecution of the war against Japan.

Meanwhile in Washington, the Army planners had continued to study the problem of Pacific command. As yet, they had not received any more information about Nimitz' reorganization than that contained in General Richardson's message of 7 September. All they knew, therefore, was that the Pacific Ocean Areas commander had initiated action to establish a joint staff and that this staff would consist of four sections. That much, they thought, was "a most fortunate step for Admiral Nimitz to take." [67]

General Somervell's report to the Chief of Staff arrived in Washington while these discussions over command were still in progress. With the earlier reports of Leavey and Lutes, it furnished the basis for a comprehensive review on 20 September of command arrangements in the Pacific Ocean Areas as seen through Army eyes. The Army's spokesman in this case was General Handy, chief of the Operations Division. Addressing his naval counterpart, Admiral Cooke, Handy expressed concern over Nimitz' apparent concentration on Central Pacific affairs. In the opinion of the Army, he said, the time had come for Nimitz to assume the functions of theater commander and, with the aid of a joint operational staff, exercise his responsibility equally in all three areas of his command. [68] The present organization, he admitted, was entirely adequate for the operations of the Pacific Fleet, but, asked General Handy, "was it adequate" to handle the operational and logistical planning essential to successful utilization of not only the Pacific Fleet afloat, but of its shore-based installations, and all of the Army forces—both combat and services—totaling over 300,000 in the Pacific Ocean Areas?

The question was rhetorical. Clearly, the Army planners had already answered the question in the negative. And, while disclaiming any desire "to force on Admiral Nimitz" their ideas as to how he should organize his staff, they had a number of specific suggestions to make. These Handy now presented to Admiral Cooke in the hope they might prove helpful. Without argument, the Army planners conceded that Eisenhower's organization was not "the ideal organization" for the Pacific. They also thought Nimitz' division of the joint staff into four sections "quite proper," as was the

---

[67] Memo, Handy for Cooke, 20 Sep 43, sub: Joint Staff for Adm Nimitz, OPD 384 (PTO) sec. 2, case 55.

[68] *Ibid.*

selection by Nimitz of his own chief of staff. There was little doubt in the minds of the Army planners that Nimitz should choose a naval officer as his chief of staff, but they expressed concern lest this officer become bogged down in detail. To avoid this unhappy condition they proposed that Nimitz, like Eisenhower, have two deputy chiefs of staff, one a flag officer, the other an Army general. Each could then co-ordinate "routine matters pertaining to his own service," while performing any other tasks the chief of staff might assign.

Tied to this proposal was the suggestion that Nimitz appoint to his joint staff representatives from the Army and Navy administrative and supply services, thus giving him, in effect, a special staff consisting of medical, signal, ordnance, engineer, quartermaster, transportation, civil affairs, and other sections. Each of these, while an integral part of the joint staff, would be supervised by one of the four main sections, but the job of co-ordinating the work of all would fall on the two deputy chiefs of staff. Theirs would be the responsibility of seeing to it "that the many angles of joint operations" received full consideration in planning and in operations. "With such a staff as outlined herein," concluded General Handy, "Admiral Nimitz would be in a much better position than he is at present to direct over-all planning and operations" for the entire theater.

At the time General Handy made these recommendations, the Army planners had not yet received a specific and detailed description of the actual organization put into effect by Nimitz on the 6th. This lack was remedied almost immediately from two different sources. From General Richardson came a copy

of the Nimitz directive and a letter praising it—and the admiral—highly.[69] The new joint staff, the Hawaiian commander told General Marshall, was already proving "most helpful" in furnishing information required for planning. In this respect, declared Richardson, Admiral Nimitz had been extremely co-operative, thus sparing the Army "the embarrassment of being confronted with a readymade plan."

The second copy of the Nimitz directive came from Admiral King on 22 September, the day he and Admiral Cooke left for Pearl Harbor to confer with the Pacific commander. Scribbled hastily on a piece of paper attached to the directive was the comment, "It would seem that we are in a fair way to setting up an adequate staff organization out there."[70] General Marshall agreed, but with reservations. The objective toward which he and his staff had been striving for months was a reorganization in which Nimitz would function solely as a theater commander, divorced from his area and fleet commands. The establishment of a joint staff was "definitely a step" toward that goal, but in Marshall's view, there was still room for improvement.[71] And lest King still had any doubt as to what the Army had in mind, Marshall referred him to General Handy's recommendations on the subject. These he declared were "directly in accord" with his own views "as to a desirable organization of this staff and

---

[69] Ltr, Richardson to Marshall, 19 Sep 43, OPD 384 (PTO) sec. 2, case 53.

[70] Penciled Note, King for Marshall, 22 Sep 43, attached to Ltr, Nimitz to King, 9 Sep 43, sub: Comd Relationship, ser. 00168, OPD 384 (PTO) sec. 2, case 53.

[71] Memo, Marshall for King, 24 Sep 43, no sub, OPD 384 (PTO) sec. 2, case 55.

as to a delineation of its responsibilities and relationships to other commands and staffs in the Pacific Ocean Theater."

This statement by General Marshall was apparently made more for the record than for the purpose of persuading King to make further changes in the organization of the Pacific Ocean Areas. The Admiral had conceded as much as he intended to, and the date for the Gilberts assault was rapidly approaching. Unless the Army planners wished to broaden the problem and relate it to matters of more immediate importance, they would have to accept the fact that the debate over Pacific command had reached a stalemate.

What had begun in early July as an effort by the Army to bring the organization of the Pacific Ocean Areas into line with its concept of joint command had finally resulted, after two months of discussion, in the establishment of a joint staff. Though this reform fell far short of the initial aim, it was apparently as far as the Navy was willing to go to meet the Army's criticism. Summarizing the situation for General Handy, one of the Army planners predicted on 9 October that Admiral Nimitz would make no effort to bring the South Pacific any more closely under his control or "that any conclusion can be had as to where the over-all command responsibility is going to rest" until the operations then scheduled were concluded.[72] His advice to the general, therefore, was that the Army should make no further atempt at that time to alter command relationships in the Pacific. There the matter rested for the next six months.

---

[72] Memo, Silverthorne for Handy, 9 Oct 43, sub: Observations on Organizations, OPD 384, case 17. Nimitz did, however, order Halsey to establish a joint staff in the South Pacific.

CHAPTER XXV

Operations and Plans, Summer 1943

The art of war is simple enough. Find out where your enemy is. Get at him as soon as you can. Strike at him as hard as you can, and keep moving on.

GENERAL GRANT

The intensive activity that marked the preparations of the Central Pacific Area during the summer and early fall of 1943 for the projected offensive into the Gilberts and Marshalls had little or no effect initially on operations in the Solomons and New Guinea. There the forces of General MacArthur and Admiral Halsey, operating under CARTWHEEL, had gone into action at the end of June. The objective was the line Lae–Salamaua–Finschhafen–western New Britain–southern Bougainville, to be reached in eight months. From there, the Allies would be in position finally to drive on Rabaul and gain control of the Bismarck Archipelago.

CARTWHEEL Begins

The Southwest Pacific

The first phase of CARTWHEEL, the occupation of Woodlark and of Kiriwina in the Trobriands, Nassau Bay, and New Georgia, began on the last day of June 1943.[1] (*Map V*) Seizure of the first two

objectives MacArthur assigned to General Krueger's newly formed ALAMO Force, Allied Air and Naval Forces furnishing support as required. This was the first amphibious operation in the Southwest Pacific Area and the planning was careful and complete. The VII Amphibious Force under Rear Adm. Daniel E. Barbey provided the ships to transport and land the assault troops; Allied Naval Force, the vessels to clear the sea lanes and protect the invasion force from enemy surface attack. General Kenney's Allied Air Force undertook to neutralize distant air bases and furnish close air support. The ground troops were organized into two separate task forces, each of regimental size, one to take Woodlark, the other Kiriwina.[2]

Preparations for the landings were thorough, and May and June were busy months at Milne Bay and Townsville, staging points for the operation. Re-

[1] For a description of the CARTWHEEL plan, see above, Chapter XX. The JCS directive of 28 March 1943 that fixed the objectives and command for CARTWHEEL is described in Chapter XIX.

[2] The Woodlark Force consisted of the dismounted 2-squadron 112th Cavalry, the 134th Field Artillery Battalion (105-mm. howitzers), a naval construction unit (Seabees), the 12th Marine Defense Battalion, plus service units; the Kiriwina Force, of the 158th Infantry (less the 2d Battalion), the 148th Field Artillery Battalion (105-mm. howitzers), and additional supporting and service elements. An account of this operation can be found in Miller, *CARTWHEEL: The Reduction of Rabaul*, Chapter V.

hearsals were held during the last days of June, though it was already known that there were no Japanese on either Woodlark or Kiriwina. As a matter of fact, advance parties landed at both places before D-day and began to prepare for the arrival of the main body. The actual landings on 30 June, therefore, came as an anticlimax, and, aside from the confusion caused by the darkness and the unfamiliar waters, were made without difficulty.

As events turned out, the seizure of Woodlark and Kiriwina was unnecessary. Intended originally to provide the Southwest Pacific forces with advance fighter and medium bomber bases within range of Japanese airfields in the northern Solomons and in the Rabaul area, these islands were never really utilized for that purpose. Other sites captured during the Allied drive provided better bases when the time came. But the operation was of value in another way, for it provided the forces in MacArthur's area with training and experience in amphibious operations they had not had before.

The landing at Nassau Bay, made simultaneously with the occupation of Woodlark and Kiriwina, was also unopposed. Situated on the New Guinea coast a short distance below the Japanese strongholds at Salamaua and Lae, Nassau Bay offered logistical advantages too good to miss. In Allied hands, it would open a water route along which supplies could be brought to the Australian troops then pushing forward from Wau, about twenty-five miles inland, toward Salamaua. Hitherto supplied by air and native carriers, the Australians had progressed slowly, building roads as they went. An operation against Nassau Bay had other advantages: it would give Mac-

Arthur a base from which to mount and support further advances up the New Guinea coast; and, if made at the same time as the Woodlark and Kiriwina landings, would serve to confuse the enemy. The drive to Salamaua from Nassau Bay would mask also the more important Allied drive against Lae, further up the New Guinea coast.

The operation itself, though it was unique in some respects, presented few difficulties.[3] A force known as the MacKechnie Force and consisting of the 1st Battalion, 162d Infantry, augmented by support and service troops, was organized for the landing under the control of New Guinea Force.[4] Staging out of Morobe, about forty miles south of Nassau Bay, the 1,000 men of the MacKechnie Force made the run to their objective in PT boats and landing craft on the night of 29 June. Despite the confusion created by rain and darkness, most of the men were ashore and ready for the enemy by daybreak of the 30th. The slight Japanese opposition that developed later was easily overcome and by 2 July the beachhead was secure and contact made with the Australians from Wau. The drive against Salamaua, about twenty miles to the north, could now begin in earnest.

South Pacific

Simultaneously with the landings at Nassau Bay and in the Trobriands, the forces of the South Pacific made their

---

[3] For an account of the operation, see Miller, *CARTWHEEL*, ch. V; Morison, *Breaking the Bismarcks Barrier*, pp. 134–37.

[4] Col. Archibald R. MacKechnie, Commanding Officer, 162d Infantry, 41st U.S. Infantry Division, commanded the force and gave it its name, a practice that the Japanese frequently followed.

FIJIAN COMMANDOS *with their New Zealand leader.*

first move into the New Georgia group in the central Solomons. This was by far the most ambitious undertaking of the first phase of CARTWHEEL and the forces allocated to the operation by Admiral Halsey were proportionately larger. Organized in accordance with the naval practice predominating in the South Pacific, these forces included Aubrey W. Fitch's Aircraft, South Pacific; submarines of the Seventh Fleet on loan from MacArthur's area; a naval covering force of carriers, battleships, cruisers, and destroyers commanded by Halsey himself; and, finally, the Attack Force, led by Admiral Turner and comprising all the ships, landing craft, supplies, and troops required for the initial landings.

The troops allotted to Admiral Turner for the invasion included the Army's 43d Division, a Marine Raider regiment

(less two battalions), a 155-mm. howitzer battalion and a Marine defense battalion, Fijian commandos, antiaircraft, construction, and service units, all organized into the New Georgia Occupation Force under Maj. Gen. John H. Hester, commander of the 43d Division. Hester, therefore, functioned in a dual capacity, as did most of the members of his staff—an arrangement that seemed to General Harmon to bode trouble for the future.[5]

The plan of operations for the conquest of New Georgia, designated TOE-NAILS, was dictated in part by geography and in part by enemy strength and dispositions. Composed of about a dozen comparatively large and hundreds of tiny islands extending in a northwest-southeast direction for 130 miles, the New Georgia group presents major problems for an invasion force. It is partially surrounded by a coral barrier, inside of which are large lagoons with shallow bottoms and dangerous coral outcroppings. Entrance into the group from the south is limited generally to narrow passages and channels calling for expert navigation. Munda Point on New Georgia Island, the largest of the group, is inaccessible to large vessels, but to the south, across Blanche Channel, lies Rendova and a sheltered harbor. To the northeast, extending the chain toward Bougainville, are Kolombangara and Vella Lavella.

Defending the central Solomons were about 10,000 Japanese Army and Navy troops, organized into two separate commands and operating under the direct control of Navy headquarters on Rabaul.

---

[5] Miller, *CARTWHEEL*, ch. VI. See also, Ltr, Harmon to Handy, 15 Jul 43, OPD 319.1 (PTO) sec. 3, case 146.

Army forces under Maj. Gen. Noboru Sasaki consisted of troops drawn largely from the *6th* and *38th Divisions*; naval forces, led by Rear Adm. Minoru Ota, of the *Kure 6th* and *Yokosuka 7th Special Naval Landing Forces*. Formed into scattered detachments these troops were strategically placed to repel any enemy attempt to seize the airfields and harbors in the area.[6]

Admiral Halsey's plan for gaining control of this complex of islands and reefs was a complicated one, but precise and detailed in all respects. Since the island of New Georgia could not be invaded directly, Halsey decided to gain first a foothold in the islands, from which he could mount and support the main assault. Rendova filled these requirements admirably and became the major objective of the preliminary landings to be made on D-day, 30 June. But it was not the only objective, for that same day South Pacific forces were to occupy three other positions in the New Georgia group—Segi Point, Wickham Anchorage, and Viru Harbor. The first was intended for use later as a fighter base, the last two as staging areas for supplies and reinforcements. (*Map 8*)

The invasion of New Georgia Island was scheduled to come four days after the preliminary landings. It was to be mounted from Rendova, in landing craft and small boats brought up for the purpose from Tulagi and Guadalcanal. The main force would land in the south and strike out for Munda, while a secondary force landed on the opposite side of the

airfield near Enogai Inlet in Kula Gulf, a move designed to cut the Japanese line of communications. Once Munda was captured, South Pacific forces would mop up and secure the island, then move on up the New Georgia chain to Vila airfield on Kolombangara in preparation for the later invasion of southern Bougainville.

With the experience of Guadalcanal still fresh in mind, Halsey and his staff took every precaution to ensure adequate supplies for the invasion force and the prompt development of logistical facilities. Virtually every agency in the South Pacific contributed to this effort, appropriately designated DRY GOODS. During the months preceding the invasion, supplies poured into Guadalcanal, there to be stockpiled for the day they would be needed. Despite the shortage of service troops and port facilities and the destruction caused by a severe tropical storm, thousands of tons were unloaded across the Guadalcanal beaches by the end of June in an effort characterized by heroic improvisations and effective use of the newly developed 2½-ton amphibian truck, the Dukw. Guadalcanal also served as the staging area for part of the assault force, and the location of the 37th Division, elements of which were to stand by as area reserve for the operation.

Detailed and exact as these plans were, they had to be revised at the last moment. Unexpectedly, the Japanese sent reinforcements toward Segi Point, one of the four preliminary landing sites of the Allied invasion earmarked for use as an advanced fighter strip. To avert the loss of this potential base, Halsey quickly altered his plans, moving up the date of the landing and substituting elements of

---

[6] For an account of Japanese plans and operations, see, in addition to the sources cited, Japanese Opns in SWPA, vol. II, ch. VII; Hattori, The Greater East Asia War, vol. II, pt. V, ch. 5, pp. 57–63; Southeast Area Operations Record, pt. II, *17th Army* Operations, vol. II, Japanese Studies in World War II, 40.

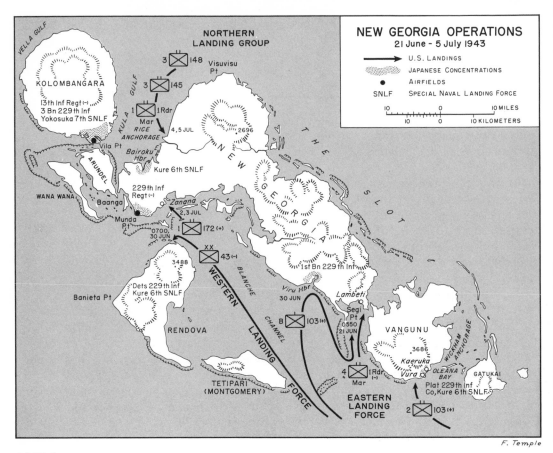

MAP 8

the 4th Marine Raider Battalion for the original landing force. No time was lost. By the night of 20 June, the marines were on their way toward Segi Point in two fast destroyer-transports. Next morning they landed without opposition, beating out the Japanese.

The remainder of the plan for the preliminary landings on 30 June, with one exception, was carried out as scheduled, but not without considerable confusion and unexpected difficulties. The night was dark, the weather foul, and the sea rough. At Wickham Anchorage, the troops started to land on the wrong beach and had to re-embark. On the second try, the small boats heading blindly toward shore were scattered by larger craft. Six were lost on the reef. The landing, when it was made, came at the wrong beaches and was marked by an "impressive disorganization." Fortunately, there were no Japanese on hand and the troops were able to re-form before the shooting began. By 4 July Wickham Anchorage was secure.

The Viru landing was not made at all. The Japanese were already in possession, and the assault force, after waiting outside the harbor for the Marines from Segi to take the place by overland assault, finally disembarked at the latter site, twelve miles away. The next morning, Viru Harbor was in American hands.

At Rendova, where the bulk of the troops were to land, the weather and darkness also had their effect. One ship ran aground on a reef, and the specially trained "Barracudas"—C and G Companies, 172d Infantry—who were to cover the major landing came ashore some miles from their destination at Rendova Harbor. Thus, when the first boats of the main assault force moved toward the beaches in the first light of dawn, they carried with them Turner's admonition, "You are the first to land—expect opposition." [7] But the warning proved unnecessary. The 120-man Japanese garrison, taken by surprise, offered only desultory opposition and by 0800 the assault force was safely ashore. The operation, remarked General Harmon, who was present during the landing, "was splendidly executed and reflects great credit on Admiral Turner and his Staff and Commanders. . . ." [8]

Though the Rendova garrison offered little opposition on the ground, Japanese air and artillery went into action promptly once the enemy realized what was happening. Coastal defense guns from Munda Point and from Baanga Island opened fire on Turner's naval escort, scoring a hit on the destroyer Gwin. At 1100 came the first of several air attacks, one of which resulted in the

loss of the flagship McCawley. But the Americans gave as much as they got and knocked down most of the attacking aircraft.

The chief obstacle to the landing came not from the Japanese but from the reefs, shallow waters, and soft red clay roads of Rendova. These combined to impede unloading operations and to create utter confusion on shore, where heavy mud-bound trucks clogged all routes to the supply dumps. Soaked radios, poor packaging, and inadequately marked containers added further to the troubles of the beach masters. Finally General Hester was forced to call a halt to the unloading of vehicles until the supply situation ashore was cleared up. But this measure proved inadequate and ultimately the supply experts revised their plans for a supply base at Rendova.

The main landing on the southern coast of New Georgia, west of Munda Point, came 2 July, after several false starts. Three days later, a second force came ashore on the west coast of the island at Rice Anchorage. While this force worked its way into position to cut off the Japanese defenders from their line of supply and reinforcements—a mission it never actually accomplished—the Army troops to the southeast began their arduous march through the jungles toward the Munda airfield.

From the start, the campaign went badly. Heat, tangled undergrowth, and the determined opposition of the enemy slowed the advance and brought heavy casualties to the inexperienced troops of the 43d Division. On 7 July, elements of the 37th Division on Guadalcanal were ordered forward, and three days later, in a vain effort to inject fresh spirit into the worst-hit of his two front-line

[7] CTF War Diary, entry of 30 Jun 43, quoted in Miller, CARTWHEEL, p. 87.

[8] Memo, Harmon for Halsey, 11 Jul 43, sub: Narrative Report of Observations on First Day of TOENAILS Operation, OPD 319.1 (PTO) sec. 3, case 146, Incl 1. Harmon came ashore with the second wave.

RENDOVA COMMANDERS. *From left, Brig. Gen. Leonard F. Wing, Admirals Wilkinson and Turner, and General Hester.*

RENDOVA LANDING FORCES *being carried to their objective in Higgins boats.*

regiments, General Hester relieved its commander and most of the regimental staff. Despite these efforts, the offensive ground slowly to a halt.

If General Hester was concerned with the speed of his advance, so also were his superiors. Harmon's misgivings that Hester "did not have enough command and staff . . . to watch the whole show as well as keep a close hold on his Division" had led him, before D-day, to instruct Maj. Gen. Oscar W. Griswold, XIV Corps commander on Guadalcanal, to be ready to take over if necessary. "Thought I would watch the operation," he later explained to General Handy, "and if it didn't go properly throw in Griswold and the advance echelon of XIV Corps staff." [9] Hester's conduct of the Rendova operation gave Harmon no reason to believe that such a change would soon be necessary. As a matter of fact, he had nothing but praise for the New Georgia Occupation Force commander.[10]

By 5 July, after the drive to Munda began, Harmon had apparently revised his views. Though he did not at that time feel that Hester should be replaced, he did believe that the New Georgia commander needed more staff officers so that he could devote his time to operations. He recommended to Halsey, therefore, that the forward echelon of the XIV Corps staff should move up to New Georgia about 8 July and that Griswold should take over the Occupation Force after the capture of Munda.[11]

Admiral Turner, commander of the entire New Georgia assault force and therefore Hester's immediate superior, was "in violent disagreement" with this proposal. It was Harmon's belief that the admiral "was inclined more and more to take active control of land operations," and he saw little hope of reaching agreement with him. He therefore appealed directly to Halsey, who, on 6 July, decided in favor of the Army commander. The relief of Hester as commander of the New Georgia Occupation Force—there was no thought of relieving him of his division—would be decided later.[12]

But Turner was not content to leave the matter there and presented his case directly to Halsey, as he had every right to do. Regretting the necessity for disagreeing with Harmon, Turner nevertheless argued strongly for the retention of Hester as commander of the Occupation Force. To replace him with Griswold, Turner contended, would deal "a severe blow" to the morale of troops on New Georgia. Moreover, he could see no reason for a change, in view of Hester's admirable conduct of operations. Harmon disagreed, and it was on his advise that Halsey acted. Thus, on 10 July, General Griswold received orders to go to New Georgia and at a date to be specified later—presumably after the capture of Munda, assume command of the Occupation Force. Turner would continue to support the operation but would no longer have authority over the ground forces.[13]

[9] Ltr, Harmon to Handy, 15 Jul 43, OPD 319.1 (PTO) sec. 3, case 146.

[10] Memo, Harmon for Halsey, 11 Jul 43, sub: Narrative Report . . . , OPD 319.1 (PTO) sec. 3, case 146, Incl 1.

[11] Rad, Harmon to Halsey, 5 Jul 43, cited in Miller, *CARTWHEEL*, p. 123.

[12] Ltr, Harmon to Handy, 15 Jul 43, cited above; Rad, Halsey to Harmon, 6 Jul 43; COMSOPAC War Diary, same date, both cited in Miller, *CARTWHEEL*, p. 123.

[13] Rads, Turner to Halsey, 7 Jul 43; Halsey to Turner, 9 Jul 43; Harmon to Griswold, 10 Jul 43; cited in Miller, *CARTWHEEL*, pp. 123–24.

This matter decided, Harmon remained at his headquarters in Noumea to await the capture of Munda. On the morning of the 13th, he dictated a letter to General Handy in Washington. His mood was optimistic and he forecast early success. "Hester," he reported, "is close to Lambeti Point and generally closing in on Munda. Liversedge [commander of the force that had landed at Rice Anchorage] holds Enogai Inlet and is astride the junction of the Munda-Bairoko-Enogai trails." [14] The letter was never sent, for that same morning brought alarming news from Griswold, recently arrived in New Georgia. The operation, Griswold reported, was going badly, with the 43d Division about ready "to fold up." In his opinion, the division would "never take Munda," and he advised that the 25th Division and the remainder of the 37th be sent quickly to New Georgia "if this operation is to be successful." [15]

The promptness with which higher headquarters acted on receipt of this news is a mark of the efficiency of the South Pacific command and the close co-operation between the Army and Navy commanders in the area. Harmon and Halsey went into conference immediately, and before the meeting was over Halsey had made his decision. Harmon was to assume complete control of ground operations in New Georgia with full authority "to take whatever steps were deemed necessary to facilitate the capture of the airfield." [16]

This was the second time that Halsey had thus expressed his confidence in the Army commander by making him virtually his deputy for ground operations,[17] and Harmon assumed his new duties with dispatch and in a confident spirit. First he ordered Griswold to be ready to assume command "on prompt notice," and to prepare plans for resuming the offensive. The reinforcements he needed, Harmon assured him, would be available at the proper time. Then at about noon of the 14th, Harmon left by plane for Guadalcanal, from where he could oversee the movement of reinforcements and reach the front lines in short order. That same day, a regimental combat team of the 25th Division was alerted for movement to New Georgia on twelve hours' notice.[18]

The next move was Halsey's. On 15 July, he relieved Admiral Turner of command in the South Pacific and transferred him to the Central Pacific, where he was to head the amphibious forces in the coming offensive. This transfer, based on orders from Nimitz and seemingly unrelated to events in New Georgia, effectively removed from the scene the chief architect of the New Georgia plan and Hester's most effective champion. His successor, Rear Adm. Theodore S. Wilkinson, assumed command that same day.

---

[14] Ltr, Harmon to Handy, 13 Jul 43, cited in MS History of the New Georgia Campaign, I, ch. III, p. 37, OCMH.

[15] Rad, Griswold to Harmon, 13 Jul 43, cited in Hist of New Georgia Campaign, I, ch III, 39, OCMH.

[16] Harmon, The Army in the South Pacific, p. 8; Admiral William F. Halsey, Jr., Narrative Account

of the South Pacific Campaign, p. 7. These accounts by the two South Pacific commanders were prepared before they left the theater in mid–1944. Copies in OCMH.

[17] The first occasion was in December 1942, during the Guadalcanal Campaign. See above, ch. XVI. As commander of U.S. Army Forces in the South Pacific, General Harmon had only administrative and supply responsibilities.

[18] Rad, Harmon to Griswold, 14 Jul 43, cited in Hist of New Georgia Campaign, I, ch. III, 40; Miller, CARTWHEEL, p. 124.

General Hester's relief as commander of the New Georgia Occupation Force followed only a few hours later. Even before Turner's departure, Griswold had his orders to assume command of the Occupation Force at 2400, 15 July. At that time, Griswold formally took over control of ground operations on New Georgia under Harmon. Hester's command of the 43d Division was not affected by this change.

The shift in command of the New Georgia operation accomplished no miracles. The jungle remained as impenetrable as ever, the heat as intense, and the Japanese as determined as before to hold Munda airfield. It took time to bring in reinforcements and reorganize the troops for a fresh assault. By 25 July, General Griswold was ready to resume the offensive. The attack opened on the morning of the 25th when air and naval forces went into action and Army artillery battered the Japanese in their dugouts. When the artillery lifted, the ground troops, after throwing back a Japanese counterattack that penetrated to the 43d Division command post, made their way forward slowly through the jungle. The going was tough and 43d Division troops, already tired, failed to keep pace with the advance. Finally, on 29 July, Harmon sent in Brig. Gen. John R. Hodge, Assistant Division Commander, 25th, to replace Hester. The general, he felt, was tired—"had lost too much sap." He had carried too much of a load from the start of the campaign and had lost touch with his own troops. For that Harmon was willing to take most of the blame. He had failed to see, he confided to his chief of staff, that one man could not handle both the division and Occupation Force, "that a Corps

commander and staff were necessary." [19]

The relief of Hester coincided with the Japanese decision to pull back to their final line in front of the airfield. Thereafter the advance of the American troops was more rapid, and Harmon was able to report to Halsey on 1 August that "there is no presently valid reason for doubting its success." [20] But he still expected to meet strong opposition and doubted that the fight would be over "in time for tea tomorrow." [21]

The end was closer than Harmon thought, for the Japanese were at the end of their rope. By 3 August, the Americans had reached the edge of the Munda airfield and circled it on the north. On the 4th they overran the field. "Open season in Nips today . . . ," Harmon wrote. "All are determined that tomorrow's action spells bad news for Tojo. The sun shines brightly." [22] Next day, despite the rain, the last enemy resistance was overcome. At 1410, Munda was in American hands.

The one great lesson of the New Georgia campaign was that it demonstrated strikingly the consequences of a failure to adhere to the principles of unity of command in joint operations. The relief of General Hester was the culmination of a series of events that had their origin in faulty command arrangements. Admiral Turner, as commander of the Attack Force, exercised his control of the ground forces in an active manner and showed no disposition to relinquish this control even after the troops were estab-

[19] Ltr, Harmon to Brig Gen Allison J. Barnett, 28 Jul 43, quoted in Hist of New Georgia Campaign, I, ch. V, 34.
[20] Ltr, Harmon to Halsey, 1 Aug 43, quoted in *ibid.*, p. 40.
[21] Ltr, Harmon to Stratemeyer, 1 Aug 43, *ibid.*
[22] Rad, Harmon to Halsey, 4 Aug 43, *ibid.*, p. 43.

MUNDA AIRFIELD *fell to American forces on 4 August 1943.*

lished ashore. And not only were the 43d Division commander and his staff improperly used, but ground units were shuffled in a manner that no experienced Army commander would have tolerated. "This incident," wrote General Hull some years after the event, "demonstrates the fallacy of placing forces of one service under the immediate control of an officer of another service who is not trained in the organization and tactics involved in the operation of that service." [23]

Strategic Forecast, August 1943

As American troops were making their way slowly through the jungles of New Georgia toward Munda airfield, the planners in Washington were preparing for their next full-scale conference with the British, to be held in Quebec in mid-August. The chief problems facing the

---

[23] A similar failure, Hull added, was later responsible for the Smith versus Smith controversy on Saipan. As a result of this controversy, according to General Hull, "General Marshall decided that

Army troops would not again serve under General Holland Smith; and they didn't thereafter." Ltr, Hull to Hoover, Jul 59. The relief of Maj. Gen. Ralph Smith, commander of the Army 27th Division, by Lt. Gen. Holland Smith, USMC, is described in Philip A. Crowl, *Campaign in the Marianas,* UNITED STATES ARMY IN WORLD WAR II (Washington, 1960), ch. X.

ON NEW GEORGIA. *Generals Twining (left), Harmon, Griswold, and Breene, and Brig. Gen. Dean C. Strother.*

Americans were those connected with the war in Europe; the time had come it seemed to them for a final decision on the cross-Channel attack.

But the war in the Pacific also required attention. There was as yet no approved long-range plan for the defeat of Japan, no clear decision on the area where the main effort would be made, or even whether the invasion of Japan would be necessary. However important these matters may have been, they were not, in the summer of 1943, urgent except insofar as they affected plans for the immediate future. Thus, though the planners continued their search for a long-range plan

and produced numerous valuable studies in the process, they did so with a recognition that final agreement on such a plan would probably have to await the settlement of numerous unresolved problems, not the least of which was the future role of the Soviet Union and China in the war against Japan.

Though handicapped by the lack of a long-range strategy into which to fit their plans for the immediate future, the planners proceeded as best they could to outline a pattern of operations to be followed in the Pacific during the next eighteen months, utilizing the studies already made and tentatively approved as the basis for planning. Central Pacific strategy, at least through the seizure of the Marshalls, was clear, but there was some doubt as to where Nimitz' forces would go after that. CARTWHEEL also set out a firm schedule for MacArthur and Halsey, but doubts had recently been expressed on the necessity for the capture of Rabaul. To clear up these and other matters, the planners turned to MacArthur for his advice.[24]

MacArthur's answer came early in August in the form of a revision of his RENO plan outlining the steps by which he intended to return to the Philippines.[25] These steps, or operations, were divided into six phases, the first of which was identical with CARTWHEEL. By March 1944, according to RENO II, forces of the Southwest Pacific would have secured the objectives outlined in Phase I—control of the Bismarck Archipelago, including the capture of Rabaul, and of eastern New Guinea. Phase II, which would begin on 1 August, would carry the advance into the Hollandia area of Dutch New Guinea, bypassing Wewak. This move was to be accompanied by the invasion of the Kai, Aroe, and Tanimbar Islands in the Netherlands Indies off the southwest coast of New Guinea, a move designed to guard the left flank of the main drive up the northwest coast of the dragon-shaped island. The remainder of 1944 and the early months of 1945 would be devoted to Phase III operations in northwest New Guinea and would culminate in the capture of the Vogelkop Peninsula, head of the New Guinea dragon.

During the next two phases of RENO, for which MacArthur set no dates, forces of the Southwest Pacific would continue their advance along the Netherlands Indies axis to seize the islands between New Guinea and the Philippines, thereby gaining control of the Celebes Sea. At the same time the Palau group in the western Carolines was to be captured, either by MacArthur or Nimitz, to protect the right flank of the advance into Mindanao, the final phase of RENO II.

In its general features, RENO II clearly reflected MacArthur's strategic and tactical concepts and his view of the importance of the Philippines in the war against Japan. It called for the capture of Rabaul as a necessary preliminary to control of the Bismarck Archipelago, and for bypassing Wewak, whose capture General Marshall had suggested in July. Implicit in the plan was the view that the New Guinea route was superior to the Central Pacific, and that the step-by-step advance under cover of land-based aircraft was the safest course to follow. And it repeated the familiar arguments for the concentration of Pacific resources on the drive up the New Guinea coast as the most effective way to exploit the Allied advantages in that area and to speed up the tempo of the war.

Though MacArthur's schedule of operations for 1943 and 1944 was generally acceptable in Washington, his views on broad Pacific strategy found little support. Not only had the Joint Chiefs of Staff and their planners become convinced of the desirability of the Central Pacific route, but they had also apparently made up their minds about Rabaul. Thus, the program drawn up by the

---

[24] Rad, Marshall to MacArthur, 19 Jul 43, CM–OUT 7555.

[25] RENO II, 3 Aug 43, Outline Plan for Operations of the Southwest Pacific Area, copy in OPD 381, case 214. For discussion of RENO I, See above, ch. XXII.

planners for the remainder of 1943 and 1944 gave full weight to the Central Pacific offensive and called for the neutralization rather than the capture of Rabaul. The reconciliation of this program with MacArthur's promised to be a difficult task.

In the opinion of the planners, Admiral Nimitz' forces, after they had completed the operations already scheduled in the Gilberts and Marshalls, should continue westward into the Carolines, taking first Ponape, then Truk, "the key Japanese position in the Central Pacific," and finally Yap and the Palau Islands.[26] From there, at some indefinite day, the forces of the Central Pacific would move into the Philippines. Though no operations were scheduled for the Marianas, the planners indicated their intention of preparing an outline plan for the recapture of Guam in the near future.

The strategic objective of the program developed in Washington early in August was the line Palaus–Vogelkop Peninsula. This aim fitted in perfectly with MacArthur's RENO plan, though the operations envisaged in Washington were not identical with those outlined by MacArthur. For one thing, the Washington planners ruled out the capture of Rabaul as an unnecessary move and "an intolerable drain" on resources and manpower. For another, they included in their program the seizure of Wewak, despite MacArthur's assertion that the operation "would involve hazards rendering success doubtful."[27] Finally, they omitted altogether the operations MacArthur had scheduled in the Netherland East Indies to protect the left flank of his advance along the New Guinea coast.[28]

The similarity of the Washington and RENO plans was more marked than the differences. In both, MacArthur's and Halsey's forces were to complete CARTWHEEL; next, they were to gain control of the Bismarck Archipelago. This last they were to accomplish, under the Washington plan, in three phases: first, seizure of the islands along the eastern border of the Archipelago (New Ireland, New Hanover, and St. Matthias); second, capture of the Admiralty Islands to the north and west; and, finally, occupation of the New Guinea coast line as far west as Wewak. These tasks completed, MacArthur was to continue along the northwest coast of New Guinea in a series of amphibious and airborne operations that would take him to the Vogelkop Peninsula by the end of 1944.[29] Or so the planners believed.

The timetable for this ambitious program—which also included operations in the China-Burma-India Theater—was carefully worked out to exploit the advantages inherent in an advance along two widely separate routes. (*Table 5*) Thus, while Nimitz prepared for the Gilberts invasion in November 1943, MacArthur and Halsey were to continue their own offensives in New Guinea and the northern Solomons. In January 1944 Nimitz would go into the Marshalls and

---

[26] JPS 235, 31 Jul 43, sub: Opns Against the Carolines; JPS 236, same date, sub: Opns Against the Palau Islands. These and other outline plans prepared by the Joint War Plans Committee became the basis for the over-all plans, JPS 245, 5 Aug 43, sub: Opns in the Pacific and Far East in 1943–1944. This plan was submitted to the Joint Chiefs on 6 August as JCS 446.

[27] Rad, MacArthur to Marshall, 23 July 43, CM–IN 16419.

[28] JPS 243, 5 Aug 43, sub: Opns in the New Guinea–Bismarck Archipelago–Admiralty Islands Area Subsequent to CARTWHEEL.

[29] JCS 446, 6 Aug 43, sub: Specific Opns in Pacific and Far East in 1943–1944.

TABLE 5—TIMETABLE OF PACIFIC OPERATIONS, AUGUST 1943

Target Date	Central and North Pacific	Southwest Pacific	South Pacific
15 August 1943	Kiska		
1 September		Lae, Madang	
15 October			Buin, Faisi.
15 November	Gilberts		
1 December		New Britain (Cape Gloucester).	Kieta, Buka (Neutralize).
11 January 1944	Marshalls		
1 February		Neutralize Rabaul Wewak	
1 May			Kavieng.
1 June	Ponape	Manus	
1 August		Hollandia	
1 September	Truk		
15 September		Wadke Island	
15 October		Japan Island in Crelvink Bay.	
30 November		Manokwari on the Vogelkop Peninsula.	
31 December	Palau		

the next month MacArthur would assault Wewak. These operations concluded, Halsey would occupy Kavieng in New Ireland in May, and then in June the forces of all three would go into action simultaneously against Ponape, Manus, and Hollandia. When Nimitz moved out against Truk in September, MacArthur was to start his advance toward the Vogelkop Peninsula. By the end of the year, if all went well, both commanders would have reached their objectives and would be standing on the Palaus-Vogelkop line.

The planners were entirely confident that the resources required to carry out this program could be made available in time. They expected also that if forces were idle in one area they could be transferred to the other so that the momentum of the drive would not be lost. But the Washington authorities were careful not to commit themselves in advance to such transfers or to any single theater, agreeing only that if there were any conflicts "due weight should be given to the fact that operations in the Central Pacific" promised a more rapid advance that operations elsewhere.

On 7 August, just one week before the scheduled Quebec Conference, the Joint Chiefs met to discuss, among other things, the program outlined by the planners.[30] On the whole, they thought it a sound plan and accepted most of it without question. The one important point relating to the Pacific that came up during the discussion was Admiral King's suggestion for greater flexibility in the Central Pacific so that Nimitz could advance north from the Carolines, toward Japan as well as west toward the Philip-

---

[30] Mins, JCS Mtg, 7 Aug 43.

pines. What he had in mind was the possibility of moving into the Marianas, either in conjunction with or instead of the seizure of the Palaus.

Capture of the Marianas was a project King had long favored. At the Casablanca Conference, seven months before, he had described these islands as "the key to the situation because of their location on the Japanese line of communication."[31] By the time of the TRIDENT Conference in May, he had found additional reasons for going into the Marianas but the program then approved had not included any operations for their capture.[32] Now, in August, he again emphasized the importance of these islands. This time he secured from his colleagues their assent to inclusion in the approved program for 1943–1944—the statement that "it may be found desirable or necessary to seize Guam and the Japanese Marianas, possibly the Bonins" after capture of Truk. Such a move, it was asserted, "would have profound effects on the Japanese because of its serious threat to the homeland."[33] These and other minor changes were quickly made and on 9 August the Joint Chiefs gave their approval to the program. Soon after, the American delegation left for Quebec.

The main business of the conference at Quebec was the war in Europe. The British, as a matter of fact, had momentarily hoped to avoid altogether any discussion of Japan, but the Americans would not let them do so. The war in the Pacific had an urgency for them it did not have for the British. Moreover, strategic plans in one theater were bound to affect plans in the other. As General Marshall observed early in the conference, "it was essential to link Pacific and European strategy." And Admiral King did not fail to point out that the inability of the Allies to take Rabaul in 1943, as originally planned, was a direct result of the failure at Casablanca to consider the requirements of the Pacific war in relation to the war in Europe.[34]

It was not until 17 August, after they had discussed the war in Europe at length, that the Combined Chiefs turned to the American program for operations against Japan in 1943–44.[35] The debate that followed dealt largely with the situation in Southeast Asia, the area in which American and British views differed most markedly. On the Pacific side, recognized by now as virtually an American domain, harmony prevailed. Only one important point did the British raise. Would it not be advisable, they asked, to curtail operations in New Guinea and make the main effort through the Central Pacific rather than advance equally up both fronts? The forces thus released, they suggested, could then be used in the cross-Channel attack for which the Americans were pushing so hard.[36]

---

[31] Mins, CCS Mtg, 14 Jan 43.

[32] Mins, CCS Mtg, 21 May 43.

[33] The revised version of JCS 446 was issued as CCS 301, 9 Aug 43, sub: Opns in the Pacific and Far East, 1943–1944; Supp Mins, JCS, 9 Aug 43.

[34] Mins, CCS Mtg, 14 Aug 43. Minutes of the Quebec Conference are bound separately, with all the papers there approved, in the volume titled QUADRANT, code name of the conference.

[35] CCS 288/3, 14 Aug 43, sub: Agenda. The order of business for discussions of the war against Japan was (1) the long-range plan for the defeat of Japan, (2) operations in the Pacific and Far East, and (3) operations and command in the China-Burma-India Theater.

[36] Mins, CCS Mtg, 17 Aug 43; Churchill, *Closing the Ring* (Boston: Houghton Mifflin Company, 1951), pp. 86–87.

AMERICAN STRATEGIC PLANNERS *at the Quadrant Conference. From left: Generals Handy, Wedemeyer, and Fairchild, and Admiral Willson.*

The idea that the main effort should be made in the Central Pacific was not a new one. The Americans had discussed it frequently among themselves and there were many, especially in the Navy, who favored it. King himself would have preferred such a strategy, but before the British he hewed firmly to the party line and championed the cause of the Southwest Pacific. The dual advance, he declared, was more advantageous than an advance along one route. Each complemented the other; together, they produced greater results than could either alone and opened up additional areas of exploitation. Thus the two forces could converge on the Philippines or, one could go north from Truk into the

Marianas. Furthermore, Marshall observed, the Japanese were losing heavily in New Guinea.[37]

The British suggestion that the savings effected by limiting operations in New Guinea be applied to OVERLORD held no appeal for the Americans, despite their desire to secure a commitment for the cross-Channel attack. The advocates of the Central Pacific strategy saw it as an opportunity to speed up the tempo of the war by concentrating on the area that promised the most decisive results, not as a means of providing additional forces for Europe. If the allocations to MacArthur were cut back, then these

---

[37] Mins, CCS Mtg, 17 Aug 43.

THE COMBINED CHIEFS AT QUEBEC. *From left foreground: Lord Louis Mountbatten, Admiral Pound, General Brooke, Air Chief Marshal Portal, Field Marshal Dill, General Ismay, Brigadier Harold Redmond, Comdr. R. D. Coleridge, Generals Deane, Arnold, and Marshall, Admirals Leahy and King, and Captain Royal.*

resources, declared King, should go to Admiral Nimitz for the advance across the Central Pacific. Moreover, General Marshall pointed out, most of the forces required for MacArthur's advance in New Guinea were already in or en route to the theater and, in any case, could not be employed in Europe. To curtail MacArthur's operations, therefore, would not produce additional forces for OVERLORD.[38]

Having stirred up this brief tempest, the British backed off. They did not mean, they said, that operations in New

Guinea should be discontinued. All they had in mind was to limit MacArthur's forces to a holding role and to assure themselves that the Americans did not intend to recapture all of New Guinea. With this latter point, MacArthur himself would have agreed; but certainly not with the former. Neither his plans nor those of the Washington planners contemplated such a role for the Southwest Pacific. But since the British did not pursue the question further at this time, the discussion was dropped.

Only one other time during the conference did the British seek to limit operations in New Guinea and that was when

---

[38] *Ibid.*

the Combined Chiefs were considering their interim report to the President and Prime Minister on 21 August. This time the British approached the matter from another angle. They had no objection to the American program in the Pacific for 1943–1944, they declared, but thought it should include a statement requiring the review of operations in New Guinea "to ensure that the results likely to be obtained are commensurate with the effort involved." [39] There was little reason for such a request since the Joint Chiefs, as a matter of course, kept all American operations under constant review. Moreover, such a statement might easily be interpreted as an expression of a lack of confidence in General MacArthur. Already, the Americans pointed out, MacArthur had been disappointed by the refusal to provide him with forces he had asked for. The British suggestion could serve only to add to his disappointment and to have "a disheartening effect upon him." When this was pointed out, the British promptly withdrew their suggestion, explaining that they had had "no idea" that the final report would be sent to General MacArthur.

Though the war against Japan continued to take up much of the time of the conferees at Quebec, there was no further discussion of the Pacific program for 1943–1944. The Combined Chiefs of Staff accepted the American plan *in toto* and incorporated it in the final report that the President and Prime Minister approved on the last day of the conference.[40] This action, in effect, placed the seal of approval on the specific operations outlined in the broad program. For the Central Pacific, this meant the seizure of the Gilberts, the Marshalls, Ponape and Truk in the Carolines, and, finally, either the Palaus or the Marianas, or both. For MacArthur, the decision of the Combined Chiefs meant the disapproval of his plans to take Rabaul. But it was also an assurance that he would not be limited to a holding mission and that operations in his theater would not be curtailed. Specifically, his task for the next sixteen months would be to complete CARTWHEEL, gain control of the Bismarck Archipelago, neutralize Rabaul, capture Kavieng, the Admiralties, and Wewak, then advance along the northwest coast of New Guinea to the Vogelkop Peninsula in a series of "airborne-waterborne" operations. Nothing was said about the Philippines, but presumably sometime in 1945 he could launch his invasion of the islands, in conjunction with a drive from the Central Pacific.

---

[39] Memo, British COS, 21 Apr 43, sub: Progress Rpt to President and Prime Minister; Mins, CCS Mtg, 21 Aug 43.

[40] CCS 319/5, 24 Aug 43, sub: Final Rpt to President and Prime Minister.

CHAPTER XXVI

Review and Adjustment

Strategy decides where to act; logistics brings the troops to this point; grand tactics decides the manner of execution and the employment of troops.

BARON DE JOMINI, *The Art of War*

No sooner had the program for the Pacific been approved on the highest level than it had to be adjusted to meet changed conditions. The stresses and strains created by limited resources as well as the conflicting interests and competing requirements of the theater commanders dictated other changes. Thus, in the period between August and December 1943, the plans so recently made were reviewed once more and revised as necessary. There was nothing unique or unusual in this fact. Planning was a continuous process and up to the moment of execution no plan was ever considered so firm that it could not be challenged and changed to attain a given objective more effectively or at less cost.

Ships and Plans

The men and means required to carry out the series of operations planned for the Pacific in 1943 and 1944 had been carefully computed at Quebec. The report of the planners had been optimistic, and it was partially on this basis that the ambitious program mapped out for

the coming year had been adopted.[1] The one item about which there was some doubt was shipping. Certainly there was ample evidence that the day of plenty had not yet arrived and that the chronic shortage of ships that had so plagued the Pacific commanders in the past would continue to affect planning. As a matter of fact, on the day the conference opened, General MacArthur had submitted to Washington his estimate of the shipping he would need during the coming months to meet the requirements of CARTWHEEL. The total came to seventy-one Liberty ships and ten freighters to move 150,000 men with their equipment.[2] In view of the requirements of other theaters, this was a big order to fill. But by permitting MacArthur to retain seventy-one Liberty ships for intratheater movements and providing some but not all of the troop transports requested, the Washington authorities were able to promise Mac-

---

[1] CCS 239/2, 26 Aug 43, sub: Implementation of . . . Specific Opns for Conduct of War, 1943–1944.
[2] Rad, MacArthur to Somervell, 14 Aug 43, CM–IN 10721.

Arthur that he would get most of what he needed.[3]

In the Central Pacific, where plans were being matured for the invasion of Nauru and the Gilberts in November and of the Marshalls in January 1944, there were other problems.[4] At the time the directive had been issued for the seizure of these islands, little was actually known about them. They had been selected as the initial objectives largely because of their location. It had been assumed that they could be seized with the forces available, but with the understanding that the commanders in the field would require more information about the targets before the invasion. It was for this reason that the Washington planners had emphasized the importance of preliminary operations to occupy and develop air bases in the Ellice group and elsewhere for reconnaissance as well as support. Thus, among the first steps taken in the theater to prepare for the Gilberts-Nauru invasion was the occupation of Baker Island, 480 miles east of the Gilberts, and of two additional islands in the Ellice group. Airfields were quickly built and by early September aircraft from these and other nearby islands were flying over the targets.[5]

The information received at Pearl Harbor as a result of this aerial reconnaissance, and from other sources, raised some doubts in the minds of the theater planners. The seizure of Nauru, it now appeared, would be a more formidable task than had been thought. The island's coast line was generally precipitous and the terrain favorable for defense. Certainly the 27th Division, which had the task of taking the island, would find it no easy job and could expect heavy losses.

There were other reasons why the Nauru operation did not appeal to Nimitz' planners. The island lay about 450 statute miles west of Tarawa, where the 2d Marine Division was to land. To assault both islands simultaneously would require splitting the supporting naval forces and create a situation favorable to Japanese counterattack against either of the supporting elements. Under these conditions, the dispersal of the fleet represented a risk the naval commanders had no wish to assume. Moreover, an assault against two widely separated targets would require more transports and cargo vessels than would otherwise be needed, and shipping facilities in the theater were already being strained to the utmost. Any plan that

---

[3] Rads, Hull to Handy and Somervell, 15 Aug 43, CM–OUT 6054; Somervell to MacArthur, 18 Aug 43, CM–IN 13773; MacArthur to Marshall, 19 Aug 43, CM–IN 14061; Marshall to MacArthur, 24 Aug 43, CM–OUT 18280. For a full discussion of this problem, see Richard M. Leighton and Robert W. Coakley, Global Logistics and Strategy: 1943–1945, MS ch. XX, "Shipping in the Pacific War." This is a forthcoming volume in the series UNITED STATES ARMY IN WORLD WAR II.

[4] See above, ch. XXII.

[5] For an account of the occupation and development of these islands see Crowl and Love, Seizure of the Gilberts and Marshalls, pp. 52–56. Admiral Spruance later recalled that when the directive for

the Gilberts and Marshalls was received at Pearl Harbor—he was then Nimitz' chief of staff—no one really knew how difficult the capture of a fortified atoll would be or what the Japanese had in the islands. At a conference in Nimitz' office, Spruance writes, "I strongly urged the necessity of an advance from our Hawaii–South Pacific line of communications through the Ellice and Gilbert Islands in order to establish air bases (and where possible bases for ships) as a necessary preliminary to the conquest of the Marshalls. Capt. Forrest Sherman, then Chief of Staff to COMAIRPAC, supported me as to the necessity for preliminary reconnaissance, except that he preferred Wake rather than positions to the southward." Ltr, Spruance to Hoover, 17 Jul 59, OCMH.

would result in a saving of precious shipping space was always welcome.

Fortunately, the theater planners had an alternative target that would solve all these problems. Why not take Makin Atoll, about 100 miles north of Tarawa, instead of Nauru? It was close enough to Tarawa to permit naval forces to support both operations from one area, and to effect economy in shipping. From the strategic point of view, it would serve as well as or better than Nauru as a base for future operations against the Marshalls; tactically, it would present fewer problems. It was neither as well defended by the Japanese nor as difficult to assault as Nauru.[6]

The arguments for the substitution of Makin for Nauru convinced Admiral Nimitz of the need for a change. He discussed the problem about 25 September with Admiral King, who was then at Pearl Harbor, and King, too, thought the idea a good one. The next day Nimitz formally requested the Joint Chiefs to authorize the change on the grounds that the occupation of Nauru "will involve losses of personnel and material, and a logistic burden which outweigh advantages."[7] Seizure of Makin, he asserted, was well within the theater capabilities in shipping and logistics and would reduce expected losses "to acceptable figures." And to allay any concern in Washington about the Japanese on Nauru, he explained that he planned to neutralize that island during the Gilberts and Marshalls operations. Thereafter, its position would be, as he put it,

"similar to that of Kiska after our capture of Attu."

Admiral Spruance, then Nimitz' chief of staff and commander-designate of the forces assigned to capture the Gilberts, later described the decision to substitute Makin for Nauru as follows:

Nauru was an uplifted circular atoll with no lagoon, no protection except on the lee side, a narrow beach and inshore of that a cliff about 100 ft. high. It lay about 380 [nautical] miles west of Tarawa toward Truk. The operation called for would have divided our fleet into two parts, out of supporting distance of each other, each one engaged in conducting a difficult amphibious operation. The Japanese Fleet at Truk was about equal to our own in strength, and, except for our submarines, we had no means of knowing what it was doing. I protested against this situation, but got no change. The more we studied the problem of how to capture Nauru, the less we liked it. Finally, Gen. Holland Smith wrote a letter recommending we not take Nauru. Admiral Turner and I both added our endorsements concurring, and I handed it to Admiral Nimitz at his morning conference, at which Admiral King and Admiral C. M. Cooke were present (about 25 Sept). Admiral King read the letter and then asked me what I proposed to take instead of Nauru. I replied "Makin," and said that Makin was in the direction we were going and would be of much more value to us than Nauru, that Nauru had been of value to the Japanese, but it would not be after we took the Gilberts. After some discussion Admiral King agreed to the change, and recommended it to the JCS.[8]

There was little objection to Nimitz' proposal. In view of Admiral King's advance approval, there was no comment at all from the Navy. The Army planners reviewed the problem briefly and concluded that on the whole Makin was

---

[6] Crowl and Love, *Seizure of the Gilberts and Marshalls*, p. 26.

[7] Rad, Nimitz to King, No. 260439, 26 Sep 43, CM–IN 20329.

[8] Ltr, Spruance to Hoover, 17 Jul 59, OCMH.

a more desirable objective than Nauru. As a matter of fact, they pointed out, they would have included it in the original plan themselves, "but for limitation of resources." [9] The only aspect of the problem that concerned the Air Forces was the fact that Makin had no air facilities and would require extensive development before it could be used by the Americans. Nauru, on the other hand, had been developed by the Japanese and its capture would provide the Americans with a ready-made air base. But having expressed this concern, General Arnold raised no objection to the substitution and on 27 September the Joint Chiefs gave their formal consent. A week later, Nimitz formally directed Admiral Spruance to seize Makin, Tarawa, and Apamama—target date, 20 November 1943.[10]

By the time this change was made the plan for the invasion of the Marshalls had also been reviewed and adjusted. Directed by the Joint Chiefs to have ready by 1 September an outline plan and an estimate of the forces required for the Marshalls operation, Admiral Nimitz had wasted no time. The plan was ready on 20 August and when the Joint Chiefs returned from Quebec it was waiting for them. With it was a proposed directive for the operation and a request for a firm planning date.[11]

The plan proposed by Nimitz called for the simultaneous seizure of the three Marshalls atolls—Kwajalein, Wotje, and Maloelap—and the neutralization of Jaluit and Mille. Forces for the operation—the 7th Infantry Division, the 4th Marine Division, and the 22d Marines reinforced—were to be mounted from the Hawaiian Islands and bases in the South Pacific, with the Ellice Islands and the Gilberts as staging points. Reconnaissance and air bombardment would precede the landings. Assuming the successful completion of the Gilberts operation, Nimitz thought he could launch the invasion of the Marshalls on 1 January 1944, the date set by the Joint Chiefs of Staff.

This plan was all right as far as it went, but the Washington planners did not think it went far enough. The goals set at Quebec called for a more ambitious plan that would place American forces in position to move next into the Carolines and, perhaps, into the Marianas. The objectives Nimitz had set himself would take him only into the eastern and central Marshalls. Eniwetok and Kusaie in the western Marshalls and Wake Island to the north were the goals Nimitz should strive for, the planners thought. Not only would the seizure of these islands consolidate U.S. control of the Marshalls, but the islands would also provide the bases for rapid advance westward or northward.[12]

When the planners sought to broaden the scope of Nimitz' plan, they ran up against the shortage of shipping—the perennial problem of Pacific planning. Ultimately the shortage was reduced to

[9] Memo, Col Frank N. Roberts for Handy, 27 Sep 43, sub: Substitution of Makin for Nauru . . . , OPD Exec Files (2, item 1b).

[10] Memo, Marshall for King, 27 Sep 43, sub: Substitution of Makin for Nauru, OPD Exec Files (2, item 1b); Rad, King to Nimitz, 271805, 27 Sep 43, CM–IN 19285; CINCPAC–CINCPOA Opns Plan 13–43, 5 Oct 43. The original target date was 19 November.

[11] Ltr, Nimitz to King, ser. 00151, 20 Aug 43, sub: Seizure of Marshalls, OPD Exec Files.

[12] Mins, JPS Mtg, 27 Aug 43, JPS 262, 28 Aug 43, sub: Seizure of Marshalls; JCS 461, 30 Aug 43, same sub. See also CCS 319/5, 24 Aug 43, sub: Final Rpt to President and Prime Minister, QUADRANT; and Crowl and Love, *Seizure of the Gilberts and Marshalls*, pp. 167–69.

nine transports and ten cargo vessels. If the planners wanted Nimitz to include Eniwetok, Kusaie, and Wake in the Marshalls operation and still retain the 1 January target date, they would have to find these additional vessels for him. The shipping experts, though they confirmed the shortage, thought it could be done. There was a chance that some ships from the Atlantic or from the South and Southwest Pacific might be available, or that other types of vessels could be used for the operations. This was enough for the Navy planners. Admiral Nimitz, they declared, should be directed to take the three additional objectives concurrently with or immediately after the seizure of Kwajalein, Wotje, and Maloelap.[13]

The Army planners also favored a broader Marshalls plan, but were less optimistic about the shipping prospects. They feared also that it might provide a justification for taking from the Southwest Pacific the additional ships required by Nimitz and thus adversely affect CARTWHEEL. As a safeguard against this danger, therefore, they proposed that the target date of 1 January be made contingent on the availability of shipping. In effect, this provision would introduce all sorts of possibilities for change and might well affect the long-range schedule for operations in the Central Pacific. For this reason, and because he wished to meet Admiral Nimitz' request for a firm planning date, General Marshall sided with the Navy planners. Thus, the directive that went to Nimitz on 1 Sep-

tember retained the target date of 1 January while adding the additional mission of taking Wake, Eniwetok, and Kusaie.

Though Marshall overruled his planners on the date of the invasion, he was as determined as they that operations in the South and Southwest Pacific should not be sacrificed to the Central Pacific drive. He insisted, therefore, that Nimitz be told that operations currently planned under CARTWHEEL would continue and that post-CARTWHEEL operations in New Guinea, New Ireland, and the Admiralties would begin about February 1944. The Joint Chiefs accepted this condition and it was included in the final directive sent to Nimitz.[14]

Agreement on a plan and target date for the invasion of the Marshalls did not signify that there was no further reason for concern over shipping. Rather it raised the possibility of new shortages, for, as General Marshall noted, Nimitz' plan called for more shipping than had been used to transport the 34,000 troops of Patton's force in the North African invasion. If Central Pacific operations continued to consume such vast quantities of ships, there was indeed reason for apprehension, Marshall thought. He therefore asked that Central Pacific shipping requirements be studied more closely to see what effect they would have on operations in other theaters, and whether they could be reduced. The other Chiefs gave their assent to this proposal and on 6 September the planners were directed to make the survey.[15]

[13] Leighton and Coakley, Global Logistics and Strategy: 1943–1945, MS ch. XX, "Shipping in the Pacific War," p. 15; Memo, Deputy Chief, Planning Div OCT, for Somervell, 31 Aug 43, sub: Shipping for Seizure of Marshalls, Hq ASF Folder Trans SOS 1943.

[14] Rad, JCS to Nimitz, 2 Sep 43, CM–IN 1123; JCS 461, 30 Aug 43, sub: Seizure of Marshalls; Mins, JCS Mtg, 31 Aug 43.
[15] Memo by CofS, USA, 6 Sep 43, sub: Pacific Opns and Availability of Shipping. This memo was prepared by General Somervell. JCS 471; Mins, JCS Mtg, 7 Sep 43.

The results were distinctly encouraging. There would be ample cargo space to meet all requirements, the planners reported. Moreover, the shortage in troop carriers created by the allocation to Nimitz of nine additional ships could be met by converting freighters to transports. By June of 1944, the planners estimated, the deficit of 33,900 spaces would have been converted to a surplus of 86,000 spaces for Pacific personnel. Thus, the planners concluded, the operations projected for 1943–1944 could go forward as scheduled, if all else went well.[16] The outlook for the future, so far as shipping was concerned, was brighter than it had ever been.

This optimistic forecast did not mean there were enough vessels of all types to take care of immediate needs. Assault ships such as the LST and other landing craft were still in short supply and would continue to affect operations in all theaters, especially as the date for OVERLORD approached. To provide MacArthur with sufficient craft of this type for CARTWHEEL, for example, it was necessary to authorize exchange between his and Halsey's area, and one War Department observer thought the speed of the New Guinea advance would be increased if MacArthur had more shipping.[17]

Nor were there sufficient ships in the fall of 1943 to enable the War Department to send to the Pacific the additional units requested by the theater commanders, even if these units had been available. General Harmon's request for an Army division early in November was turned down because of the shortage of shipping, and Richardson was told by General Handy, when he complained about the lack of ships, that "the extremely critical shipping situation" was not confined to the Pacific. Allocations to the Central Pacific, he was told, had been made only after careful consideration of the ships available and operational requirements. It was "in no sense," added Handy, "a hit-and-miss guess which fails to consider the needs of each area."[18]

Meanwhile, the date for the Marshalls invasion, which apparently had been firmly fixed on 1 September, had come under re-examination. The theater planners in Hawaii had tried to produce a plan that would meet the specifications laid down by the Joint Chiefs, but finally had to admit their failure. With the Gilberts campaign looming so close, they did not see how they could train the troops, reconnoiter the Marshalls, repair damage to vessels, and complete construction in the Gilberts—all in time to meet the scheduled date of 1 January. The only solution seemed to be to delay the invasion and on 25 October Admiral Nimitz so recommended, "with considerable regret." The new date, he proposed, should be 31 January. He would make every effort "to anticipate this date," he promised, but at the same time he warned Admiral King that if damage to ships during the Gilberts operations proved excessive it might be necessary

[16] JCS 471/1, 23 Sep 43, sub: Pacific Opns and Availability of Shipping; Mins, JCS Mtg, 28 Sep 43. For a further discussion of this problem, see Leighton and Coakley, Global Logistics and Strategy: 1943–1945, MS ch. XX, "Shipping in the Pacific War."

[17] Rads, Ritchie to Handy, 27 Sep 43, CM–IN 18992; Marshall to MacArthur, 8 Oct 43, CM–OUT 3401.

[18] Ltrs, Handy to Richardson, 28 Oct 43, sub: Central Pacific Opns and Deployment, OPD 381, case 257; Handy to Harmon, 8 Nov 43, no sub, OPD 381, case 261.

to postpone the Marshalls invasion still further.[19]

Short of providing Nimitz with additional ships and trained troops, neither of which were available, there was nothing to be done but accept Nimitz' recommendation and urge him to move as fast as possible. The joint planners, after studying the matter, concluded hopefully that the advantages of more thorough preparation outweighed the disadvantages occasioned by the delay. And they discovered unexpected benefit in the fact that a delay in the Marshalls invasion would place it close to MacArthur's scheduled attack against Wewak on 1 February. The two operations coming so close together, the planners reasoned, would work to the advantage of both.[20]

All of the Joint Chiefs except General Marshall seemed ready to accept this view and approve the delay without question. Theater commanders were always making such recommendations, General Marshall pointed out, and it was up to the Joint Chiefs, in considering these matters, "to decide the relation between urgency and perfection."[21] Reminded thus of their responsibilities, the Joint Chiefs reviewed the matter more carefully, and on Admiral King's suggestion approved the delay but with the proviso that the date of the invasion should not be later than 31 January. "You will spare no effort," King wrote in a separate communication to Nimitz, "to speed

up training and other preparations, and thus get on with the war."[22]

Strategic Role of the North Pacific

The role of the North Pacific in the strategy of the war against Japan had, by the fall of 1943, been studied exhaustively. From the outset, it had been apparent that the resolution of this question was largely dependent upon the role of the Soviet Union in the Far East and its willingness to co-operate with the United States, at least to the extent of making available bomber bases in the Maritime Provinces. Thus, the first studies of a possible offensive in the North Pacific had been sparked by the fear that Japanese troops would move into Siberia and bring Russia into the war under disadvantageous circumstances. Combined with this threat was the strong desire of the Air Forces to utilize Siberian bases for air attacks against the Japanese home islands at such time as Russia entered the war. In the face of Stalin's determination to maintain a scrupulous but armed neutrality in the Far East and avoid a two-front war, the first overtures for co-operation in the North Pacific had come to nought.

The occupation of Adak at the end of August 1942 raised again the question of a North Pacific offensive.[23] Though the means for such an offensive were not then available, the possibility of a Japanese attack against the Soviet Union could not be discounted. To prepare for such a contingency Admiral King proposed on 21 September that plans be

---

[19] Ltr, Nimitz to King, ser. 00247, 25 Oct 43; Crowl and Love, *Seizure of the Gilberts and Marshalls*, p. 168; Robert D. Heinl, Jr., and John A. Crown, *The Marshalls: Increasing the Tempo* (Washington: U.S. Marine Corps Historical Branch, 1954), pp. 9–11.

[20] JPS 205/5, 30 Oct 43, sub: Opns in Central Pacific; Mins, JPS Mtg, same date: JCS 559, 1 November 43, sub: Opns in Central Pacific.

[21] Mins, JCS Mtg, 2 Nov 43.

[22] Rad, JCS to Nimitz, 4 Nov 43; King to Nimitz, ser. 002415, 4 Nov 43, sub: Delay in FLINTLOCK, cited in Hayes, The War Against Japan, II, 86.

[23] See above, ch. XXI.

made not only to aid Russia but also to use Soviet territory—which would presumably be available in case of a Japanese attack. The whole problem of the North Pacific, King urged, should be carefully studied to determine "the potentialities of a campaign against Japan via Alaska, the Aleutians, and the Bering Strait into the Kamchatka Peninsula via northeast Siberia." [24]

The special committee of Army, Navy, and Marine officers formed to make this study, spent more than two months on the job. Its massive report, boiled down to essentials, called first for the expulsion of the Japanese from the Aleutians in order to build forward air bases there and to secure the line of communications to Siberia—a project already under way; second, the establishment of a supply and air base at Petropavlovsk on the Kamchatka Peninsula; and third, the capture of Paramushiro and Shimushu in the Kurils. These operations, and others, the committee made clear, were contingent upon the entry of the Soviet Union into the war and its willingness to permit U.S. forces the use of its territory. But even under these conditions, the committee believed, it would not be possible to mount large-scale operations against the Kurils or on the Asiatic mainland for some time. The committee recommended, therefore, that a division be readied for the occupation of Petropavlovsk, whose retention it considered essential for U.S.-Soviet co-operation; that air facilities in Alaska and the Aleutians be expanded; that small naval craft (two squadrons of PT boats) be earmarked for dispatch to Siberia; that the

Aleutians be cleared; and that plans be made for the operations outlined. [25]

There were numerous objections to this ambitious program. Not only would it immobilize a division, divert resources to Alaska, and initiate operations prematurely, but it was also based on the doubtful assumption that the Soviet Union would co-operate with the United States in the execution of these plans. Despite these objections, the committee finally submitted virtually the same recommendations to the joint planners. It did, however, stress the need for co-ordination with the Soviets and for obtaining information from them on the strength and disposition of their forces, the logistical support they could be expected to provide in case of operations in the Kurils or on Kamchatka, and the status of airfields, communications, and transportation in the area. These recommendations the joint planners passed on without modification to the Joint Chiefs on 30 December. They in turn approved the recommendations, but only as a basis for further planning. [26]

Though each of the services could and did prepare to carry out its share of this program, it was impossible to make any realistic plans involving the use of Soviet territory or combined action with Soviet forces until additional information was secured. The prospects for getting this information seemed bright at the time. Maj. Gen. Follett Bradley, who had gone

---

[24] Memo, King for JCS, 21 Sep 42, sub: Campaign Against Japan via the Northern Route, ABC 381 Japan (5–31–42), sec. 1.

[25] JPS 67/1, 30 Nov 42, sub: Campaign Against Japan via the Northern Route, summarized in OPD Memo for Handy, 1 Dec 42, sub: Brief on JPS 67/1, ABC 381 Japan (5–31–42), sec. 1.

[26] Mins, JCS Mtg, 30 Dec 42 and 5 Jan 43; OPD Brief, Notes on JPS Mtg, 2 Dec 42, sub: Campaign against Japan via the Northern Route, JPS 67/1, ABC 381 Japan (5–31–42), sec. 1; JCS 182, 1 Jan 43, same sub.

to Moscow in July 1942, had only lately arrived in Washington. Stalin, Bradley was convinced, would not agree to any action that could be interpreted as hostile to Japan so long as the Soviet Union was at war with Germany. But if Japan attacked the Soviet Union, Bradley believed that Stalin would permit the United States to base its planes in Soviet territory. As a matter of fact, Stalin had agreed in October to permit the Americans to conduct a survey of Eastern Siberia, but Bradley had preferred to wait. He still thought it better to wait and not press the Russians for information until the United States was ready to make a definite commitment of aircraft to the Russians. Such a procedure, he told General Marshall, would allay Stalin's suspicions and demonstrate America's resolution to stand firmly by its Russian ally if Japan attacked.[27]

On the basis of Bradley's report, and on Marshall's recommendation, the Joint Chiefs agreed that Stalin should be assured by the President that he would receive American support in case of a Japanese attack. This support, they further agreed, should consist of three heavy bombardment groups (105 planes), which Arnold was directed to provide. The Russians, in return, were to provide the airfields and certain items of supply, and permit General Bradley to make the survey already authorized. The President approved the recommendations and on 30 December sent Stalin a personal message covering these points.[28] Meanwhile, on the assumption that Stalin would give

his consent, Bradley began to make his preparations for the survey.

It was at this point that the recommendations made by the committee studying North Pacific strategy reached the Joint Chiefs. There seemed every reason then to believe that the information needed to carry out these recommendations would be forthcoming. But within a few days this optimism had given way to a growing pessimism, for Stalin had interpreted the message as an outright offer of 100 bombers, thereby giving to the American proposal a meaning never intended. He would be delighted, he said, to get these planes, but he needed them on the German front, not in Siberia. If the first message had been misunderstood, Roosevelt's second could not have been. This time Stalin's reply made it perfectly clear that he wanted no American planes in Siberia. More than that, he had changed his mind about permitting Bradley to make the survey. "It would seem obvious," he told the President, "that Russian military objects can be inspected only by Russian inspectors." Nor did he think any purpose would be served by having General Marshall come to Moscow, a suggestion Roosevelt had made earlier.[29]

With this exchange, the correspondence ended. And with it died the hope for any immediate arrangements with Stalin for concerted action in the Far East, a hope that for a brief moment had flickered so brightly. The Soviet Union, it was clear, wanted planes for the German front, not closer collaboration with the United States in the Far East. Thus, when the joint planners

[27] JCS 180, 27 Dec 42, sub: Bradley Mission, ABC 334.8; Ltr, Bradley to Marshall, 14 Dec 42, sub: Rpt of Bradley Mission to Russia, OPD Bradley Folder.

[28] Memo, Leahy for President, 30 Dec 42, sub: Survey of Air Force Facilities in Far East, filed with JCS 180 in ABC 334.8 Bradley Mission.

[29] Rads, Stalin to Roosevelt, 13 Jan 43; Roosevelt to Stalin, 8 Jan 43; Stalin to Roosevelt, 5 Jan 43, all filed with JCS 180.

were reviewing Pacific strategy in May 1943, they rejected the idea of an offensive against Japan from the Aleutians on the ground that such an offensive would have to await Soviet entry into the war.[30]

Though the Russians in the months that followed the Roosevelt-Stalin exchange gave no sign of any change in their attitude, the American planners were forced by events to turn once again to a consideration of the role of the North Pacific. Early in August 1943, General DeWitt forwarded to Washington a plan for the invasion of Paramushiro and Shimushu in the Kurils, one of the projects proposed eight months earlier by the planners. If the War Department would increase his ground forces and strengthen the bomber components of the Eleventh Air Force, DeWitt wrote, he stood ready to launch the invasion of the Kurils in the spring of 1944.[31]

DeWitt's optimism was not shared by Admiral Nimitz or the planners in Washington. The Pacific Fleet was fully engaged in the South Pacific and neither Nimitz nor King saw any possibility of making available the surface forces required for such an operation. Finding the troops and planes needed for the offensive DeWitt had in mind would be difficult enough, but even more difficult would be the task of finding the ships and building the bases from which to mount and support a Kurils invasion. Moreover, such an operation, if it was to prove of real value, would have to

be followed by operations against the Japanese home islands themselves. To accept DeWitt's proposal, therefore, the War Department would have to be prepared to commit forces of such size as to affect all other operations in the Pacific, and probably those in Europe as well, and to follow up with a major assault against the enemy's last citadel.[32]

But there were solid advantages to the proposal for an offensive across the North Pacific. For one thing, it would provide employment for the large ground and air forces already in the area. The very existence of such forces created a demand for their use. And few could dispute the strategic importance of the Aleutians. This importance derived from the position of the islands in the narrow seas between the American continent and Asia, a position that affected the Soviet Union as well as the United States and Japan. Except for China, the Aleutians provided the only bases then in American hands from which the new long-range B–29 bombers—still in the production stage — could reach Japan. Thus, when the proposal for an invasion of the Kurils by way of Paramushiro came up for discussion in August 1943 it was not rejected but referred to one of the planning committees for further study.

Before the committee had finished its work, General Marshall reopened the whole problem of the North Pacific early in September by proposing to the Joint Chiefs that they reduce the size of the garrison there during the next year to

---

[30] JWPC 9/1, 5 May 43, sub: Opns in Pacific and Far East in 1943–44.

[31] Ltr, DeWitt to Marshall, 2 Aug 43, with attached plan for offensive operations in the Northwest Pacific, dated 30 Jul 43, CCS 381 NWPac (7–30–43).

[32] Ltr, Nimitz to King, 18 Aug 43; Memo, King for Marshall, 30 Aug 43, both in WDCSA 381, sec. 2. For Army planners' view see OPD 370.5, case 264, and OPD 381, case 206.

about 80,000 men. There was little objection to this reduction but it raised inevitably the question of the future role of the forces in the North Pacific. Would they be required later to move into the Kurils? If so, then the garrison might later have to be increased. If not, then perhaps greater reductions were justified. At any rate, it was time, the Joint Chiefs decided, to get an answer to these questions. The joint planners were the ones who got the job. It was up to them to come up with the answers on the size of the Alaska garrison and "whether it would be preferable to keep large forces in the Aleutians and mount operations against Paramushiro from there, or whether such operations should be mounted from the United States." [33]

Before making their recommendations, the planners solicited the views of the theater's senior officers at a conference held in Washington. Present at the meeting, which began on 15 September, were General Buckner, the Army commander in Alaska, Rear Adm. John W. Reeves, his naval opposite, and Capt. Oswald S. Colclough, Admiral Kinkaid's representative. Buckner took the lead in presenting the case for an increase in the theater's forces and an offensive toward Japan. Emphasizing the logistical problem in the area and the difficulty of air and naval operations he estimated he would need 2 amphibiously trained divisions, in addition to the 2 he already had, plus 4 heavy bombardment squadrons and a chain of air bases. With these reinforcements, Buckner believed (and the others supported him) that offensive operations against Paramushiro could begin in the spring of 1944. This move, in his view,

was but part of a larger scheme which envisaged operations later against the Japanese home islands. Only in this way could decisive results be achieved. And once the offensive gained momentum, the Russians, Buckner believed, would join the other Allies fighting Japan, thereby bringing the war to an early close.[34]

Though the planners were not prepared to accept entirely the recommendations of the theater commanders, it was not because of a failure to appreciate the enormous strategic significance of the North Pacific for the future as well as the present. With prophetic insight, they pointed to Russia's traditional interest in the region and the uncertainty of "the pattern of future relationships." Aside from every other consideration, they believed that common sense and the interests of the United States dictated "that we properly organize this area for defense and for offense, and at the earliest practicable date." [35] On this basis the planners readily supported the development of a large supply base at Adak, the construction of airfields suitable for the B–29's, and the shipment of two groups of these bombers "if operational and available" to the Aleutians. These projects, they pointed out, would be useful in the future "come what may during or after the war."

On the more immediate questions—operations against Paramushiro and the size of the force to be assigned to the area — the planners had some doubts. Though the final answers would depend upon studies then in progress, they thought it unlikely that operations

---

[33] Mins, JCS Mtg, 7 Sep 43.

[34] Mins, JPS Mtgs, 15 and 20 Sep 43.
[35] JCS 474–1, 21 Sep 43, sub: Garrisons in Alaska.

against Paramushiro could be initiated until the spring of 1945 and that the strength in the theater should therefore be reduced to 80,000 men, as General Marshall had suggested. But if it was decided to open the offensive a year earlier, as the theater representatives urged, then the garrison would have to be maintained as its existing strength.[36]

The "elder statesmen" of the Joint Strategic Survey Committee — Admiral Willson and Generals Embick and Fairchild — were in substantial agreement with the planners. Having recently reviewed the "categories of defense" assigned to Alaska and the Aleutians and found them too high, the committee strongly supported the reduction of the garrison to a size commensurate with the mission assigned and the possibility of attack.[37] Like the Joint Staff Planners, the Strategic Survey Committee thought there was little chance of mounting an operation against Paramushiro before the spring of 1945 and therefore no necessity for retaining more than 80,000 men in the area. But the committee differed with the joint planners in the matter of base development. Construction, they believed, should be limited to those facilities necessary to support the assault on Paramushiro and the opera-

tion of B–29's, then scheduled for completion in the spring of 1944.[38]

The Joints Chiefs found these recommendations generally acceptable, differing with the planners only in minor matters. At General Arnold's request the number of B–29 groups that would be sent to the theater was not specified, and all concurred in the general statement that the reduction of troop strength in the theater should be accomplished as soon as possible. Admiral King objected mildly to the category of defense assigned the Aleutians, maintaining that the Japanese were still capable of an offensive in the area. None of the others agreed with this "concession of superhuman powers to the Japanese" and when General Handy pointed out that a failure to make the change in defense status would justify the retention of forces in the theater adequate to meet a major attack, Admiral King withdrew his objections.[39] The Joint Chiefs thereupon gave their approval on 5 October 1943 to the recommendation of the planners to reduce the size of the Aleutians garrison while preparing the base facilities and airfields for a future offensive in the Kurils, if one should be decided upon. Though that decision was left for the future, the theater commanders were directed to prepare for the Paramushiro operation, with the tentative target date set for the spring of 1945.[40]

---

[36] Ibid.

[37] Categories of Defense are defined in *Joint Action of the Army and the Navy* (1935) as the degree of preparation required to defend specific areas under specified circumstances. There are six such categories designated alphabetically A through F. Continental Alaska, which had been in Category B, defined as an area in which minor attacks were possible, the JSSC placed in Category A—attack unlikely but provided with nominal defenses for "political reasons." Other portions of the Alaska Theater were to be similarly downgraded for defense purposes, Adak from D (major attack possible) to C (minor attack probable) and Unalaska from D to B.

[38] JCS 474/2, 21 Sep 43 sub: Garrisons in Alaska; JCS 474/3, 25 Sep 43, same sub.

[39] Mins, JCS Mtgs, 28 Sep and 5 Oct 43; JCS 474/5, 5 Oct 43, sub: Change in Category of Defense in Hawaiian and Aleutian Is.

[40] Memo, King for Marshall, 5 Nov 43; Rad, Marshall to Buckner, 8 Nov 43, both in WDCSA 381 (1942–43).

If the Alaskan commanders could no longer look forward to strong reinforcements and offensive operations in 1944, they had at least a fair chance of getting two or more groups of the coveted B–29's as things stood. They had been instructed to have ready by the spring of the year airfields on which to base the long-range bombers when they came, and the commanders turned to this task with zeal. But all their efforts to secure a definite commitment from Washington on the number of planes they would receive and the date of arrival were unavailing. Plans for the use of the B–29's were only then being considered in Washington, and the Aleutians was but one—and the least important—of several possible theaters for B–29 operations.[41] The problem was an important one. closely related to the strategy for the defeat of Japan, and no decision was reached until well into 1944. But even before then it was clear that no B–29's would be sent to the Aleutians before the spring of 1945, if then. By that time the war against Japan had progressed so far that there was little or no prospect of active operations in the North Pacific.

CARTWHEEL and RENO

In the Southwest Pacific, General MacArthur, like Admiral Nimitz, was also revising his plans "to get on with the war." The Trobriands, Nassau Bay, and Munda airfield had been captured by early August, but much remained to be done to complete CARTWHEEL. Halsey's forces had still to extend their con-

trol to the remaining islands in the New Georgia group, after which they would move into the southern Bougainville area, seizing the Shortland Islands, Ballale, Faisi, Buin, Kahili, and Tonolei Harbor. The program MacArthur had laid out for himself in CARTWHEEL was no less ambitious and included the capture of Lae, Salamaua, Finschhafen, and western New Britain.

Planning for these moves began in the summer of 1943 when MacArthur ordered Admiral Halsey to prepare for the invasion of southern Bougainville and the commander of the New Guinea Force to make plans for the capture of the Markham Valley–Huon Peninsula area of New Guinea.[42] This latter task fell to General Blamey, who arrived at Port Moresby and assumed command of New Guinea Force on 20 August. Plans for the capture of Lae, Salamaua, and Finschhafen were by that time already well under way. The American and Australian troops in the vicinity of Salamaua were to continue to press the attack against that objective as a cover for the invasion of Lae. The 9th Australian Division was to take Lae, landing a few miles to the east on 4 September. The next day, the 503d U.S. Parachute Infantry Regiment was to drop on Nadzab in the Markham Valley, seize and develop the airstrip, and block enemy movements overland from Wewak to Lae. Australian troops, including eventually the 7th Division, would be flown up to Nadzab and from there advance eastward down the Markham Valley toward Lae at the mouth of the Mark-

---

[41] JPS 288, 4 Oct 43, sub: Plans for Defeat of Japan Within Twelve Months After Defeat of Germany; JPS 320, 9 Nov 43, sub: Early Sustained Bombing of Japan.

[42] GHQ SWPA Operating Instrs 13 Jun 43. For a comprehensive account of the plans and operations under CARTWHEEL, see Miller, *CARTWHEEL*, chs. XI and XII.

ham River in conjunction with the 9th Australian Division drive up the valley. Meanwhile, other Australian troops were to consolidate Allied control of the Markham Valley and secure additional airstrips by seizing other important sites in the area. The move to the north shore of the Huon Peninsula would begin with the assault on Finschhafen, set for mid-October.

Halsey's plans for the capture of southern Bougainville and the small islands immediately to the south were based originally on the availability of the 3d Marine and 25th Infantry Divisions. But the commitment of the 25th to New Georgia and the cancellation of the Rabaul campaign altered the situation radically. Experience in New Georgia also dictated adjustments in the initial concept of the Bougainville operation. At the end of July, therefore, Admiral Halsey proposed to MacArthur that the original plan be modified to relieve him of the necessity of taking Buin, Kahili, and Tonolei Harbor on the island of Bougainville itself. The major objectives of the operation could be achieved, he declared, by seizing the Shortlands and Ballale in the straits south of Bougainville.[43]

With MacArthur's approval, planning proceeded on this basis for more than a month. Then, early in September, Halsey came up with another idea—take the Treasury Islands and Choiseul south of the Shortlands, and there establish bases from which to neutralize the increasingly strong Japanese positions in the southern Bougainville area. After that he and MacArthur could decide,

on the basis of reconnaissance, whether a landing on Bougainville itself was necessary. From the Treasuries, he pointed out, he could move to Empress Augusta Bay on the west side of the island; from Choiseul, to Kieta on the east coast.[44]

Halsey's new plan, which Rear Adm. Robert B. Carney, South Pacific chief of staff, carried to Brisbane on 10 September, did not meet with MacArthur's approval. The most important objection to it was that it would not place Halsey's fighter aircraft in position to strike Rabaul in time to cover the Southwest Pacific advance to Cape Gloucester at the end of December. To do that, said MacArthur, Halsey would have to seize airfield sites on the island of Bougainville, specifically at Empress Augusta Bay, on 1 November. The Treasuries and Choiseul could be taken between 20 and 25 October to provide PT bases and radar sites. A week later, at a meeting attended by General Harmon, MacArthur reiterated these points but left the decision on where the Bougainville landing would take place to Admiral Halsey.[45]

Halsey had his orders; the only question he now had to decide was where on Bougainville he would land. The Washington planners had studied the change and recommended to the Joint Chiefs that they take no action. MacArthur was within his rights and the operation

---

[43] Ltr, Halsey to MacArthur, 26 Jul 43, sub: Bougainville Opn; Miller, *CARTWHEEL*, p. 226.

[44] Ltr, Halsey to MacArthur, 9 Sep 43, sub: ELKTON III—Bougainville Objectives, Miller, *CARTWHEEL*, p. 227.

[45] Halsey, Narrative Account of the South Pacific Campaign, p. 8; Harmon, The Army in the South Pacific, p. 9; Ltr, MacArthur to Halsey, 11 Sep 43, no sub: Notes for Memo on Conf Between Representatives of South and Southwest Pacific; Miller, *CARTWHEEL*, pp. 227–28.

within the terms of his directive.[46] By the end of September Halsey had made his choice. The landing would be made over the heavy surf at Empress Augusta Bay, 215 miles southwest of Rabaul, on 1 November 1943. "Enthusiasm for the plan," he later wrote, "was far from unanimous, even in the South Pacific, but, the decision having been made, all hands were told to 'Get going.' " [47]

Behind MacArthur's insistence on speeding up the pace of the advance was an apparent concern for the fate of his cherished plan to return to the Philippines. On 17 September, a general staff officer from Washington, Col. William L. Ritchie, had arrived in Brisbane with copies of the deliberations and decisions of the U.S. and British Chiefs at Quebec.[48] Colonel Ritchie, Marshall explained to MacArthur, would brief him on the conference, deliver to him the conference documents relating to the war against Japan, and explain fully the Joints Chiefs' plans for operations in the Pacific during the coming year. At the same time, Marshall asked MacArthur to forward to Washington by 1 November his plans for the neutralization of Rabaul, the capture of Kavieng and the Admiralties, and the subsequent advance to the Vogelkop Peninsula—all approved at the Quebec meeting.[49]

MacArthur's reaction to the Quebec decisions was not reassuring. The program approved there had set the objec-

tive of Southwest Pacific forces at the Vogelkop Peninsula; there was nothing in it about what would come after that. In view of the importance attached to the Central Pacific offensive by the Washington planners, MacArthur apparently felt he could not discount altogether the possibility that he would be pinched out of the war when the New Guinea Campaign was over. The recapture of the Philippines and the final defeat of Japan would then fall to Nimitz' forces and the Navy. This failure to define the role of the Southwest Pacific once the Vogelkop Peninsula had been reached, MacArthur felt, would not only have an adverse effect upon his own staff, but might well lead to a "let down" in the Australian war effort.[50]

Colonel Ritchie's efforts to allay MacArthur's fears for the future were unavailing and he finally called on General Marshall for help. What was needed, he said, was a statement of long-range objectives for Southwest Pacific forces that MacArthur could use as a basis for planning and show to the Australians. Acting for the Joint Chiefs, Marshall did his best to reassure the Southwest Pacific commander. The Quebec decision, he explained, had not projected operations beyond 1944 because there was not sufficient information to plan past that date and because much would depend on what the Japanese did in the interval. Meantime, said Marshall, the Joint Chiefs intended to apply "unremitting pressure"—a phrase that was used with increasing frequency—against Japan from every side, from Asia as well as the Pacific. If an advance toward Japan from the North Pacific seemed profitable, then

---

[46] JPS 275, 18 Sep 43, sub: Opns in the South-Southwest Pacific Area; JPS 725/1, 21 Sep 43, same sub.

[47] Halsey, Narrative Account of the South Pacific Campaign, p. 8; Rads, Halsey to MacArthur, 1 Oct 43, MacArthur to Halsey, same date; Miller, *CARTWHEEL*, p. 229.

[48] Rad, Ritchie to Handy, 18 Sep 43, CM–IN 13521.

[49] Rad, Marshall to MacArthur, 18 Sep 43, CM–OUT 9252.

[50] Rad, Ritchie to Marshall, 28 Sept 43, CM–IN 19656.

the Joint Chiefs might adopt a strategy directed toward that end. Certainly, they would utilize to the full the naval strength of the Central Pacific, a major asset in the war against Japan. It might even prove most advantageous ultimately, Marshall pointed out, to place the main effort in that theater. Only time could tell.

Having thus reminded MacArthur gently that the Joint Chiefs intended to retain their freedom of action, Marshall told him that Mindanao in the southern Philippines would probably be the next objective after Vogelkop. Would he, therefore, draw up plans as quickly as possible for the move into the Philippines? This was good news to MacArthur, but even more encouraging were the two assumptions Marshall gave him to guide him in his planning; first, that the main effort in the drive toward the Philippines would be made from the Southwest Pacific; and, second, that Southwest Pacific forces would be increased at the existing rate.[51]

MacArthur had long anticipated the drive to the Philippines and had a plan ready in his files. As RENO II, he had submitted it to Marshall in August; all he had to do now was bring it up to date. By 20 October RENO III was ready.[52] Like earlier versions of the plan, RENO III called for the successive advance westward along the north coast of New Guinea in a series of amphibious and airborne assaults made under cover of land-based aircraft. Wherever possi-

ble, strongpoints would be bypassed and enemy airfields and supply bases neutralized as the Allied bomb-line moved forward.

The schedule of operations outlined in RENO III was similar to that in the previous plans except where changes were required by the program approved at Quebec. Thus, Rabaul was to be neutralized rather than captured during Phase I, and the entire timetable was accelerated to permit the invasion of Mindanao in February 1945. But MacArthur evidently still intended to capture Rabaul at a later date, though he did not specify when or with what forces. Phase I, MacArthur estimated, would start on 1 February 1944 and would carry him through the Bismarck Archipelago and Hansa Bay by the spring of the year. From there he would launch the Phase II attack in the Humboldt Bay area of New Guinea (Hollandia) and in the Arafura Sea in June and August of the year. As before, Wewak was to be bypassed. Phase III operations would begin in mid-August with the advance to Geelvink Bay, to be followed in October with the capture of the Vogelkop Peninsula. In December, Southwest Pacific forces would move on to Halmahera, the Celebes, possibly the Palaus (Phase IV), and finally on 1 February 1945, to Mindanao.[53]

The forces needed for these operations were carefully listed. Phase I—the capture of Hansa Bay, Kavieng, and the Admiralties—would require 7 infantry divisions, 2 parachute regiments, and 59 air groups. Ten divisions would be needed for garrison duty. In the next

---

[51] Rad, Marshall (for JCS) to MacArthur, 2 Oct 43, CM–OUT 630. Drafts of the message and concurrence by the Navy are filed in OPD 381, case 192.

[52] RENO III, 20 Oct 43 sub: Outline Plan for Opns of SWPA to Re-Occupy Southern Philippines, ABC 384 Pacific, sec. 8–A.

[53] Cf. RENO I and RENO II, chs. XXII and XXV above.

two phases, MacArthur intended to employ 6 divisions and 1 parachute regiment in the assault, supported by 77 air groups and 13 divisions for garrison. No estimates were made for the final two phases of the advance. They were still more than a year away, and there was time enough, if the plan was adopted, to assemble the forces, shipping, and supplies that would be needed. That these would be considerable was already clear, for in the first three phases alone, even assuming his retention of South Pacific forces, MacArthur would need 6 more divisions, 18 air groups, and a large number of warships ranging in size from escort carriers to landing craft.

Against these requirements the planners in Washington had to place those of other commanders. Europe, of course, had first priority. Would there be enough left over to provide MacArthur with what he needed under the scheme outlined in RENO III and at the same time carry out the program already approved for the Central Pacific? Admiral Nimitz' estimate of assault and garrison forces was large. In or en route to his theater in September 1943 were 5 Army divisions, but only 2 of them would remain there. Army strength in the Central Pacific at this time was about 130,000, with over 100,000 more scheduled for shipment by June 1944. Total Army requirements for operational and garrison forces to that date, Richardson estimated, would come to 285,420 men, an excess of about 50,000 over current and allocated strength.[54]

It is interesting to note in this connection, in view of the priority of Europe, that the Army had a total of 826,672 men deployed in the Pacific and 92,929 in China-Burma-India as against 1,464,216 in the European, Mediterranean, and North African theaters in December 1943. More significant, perhaps, is the fact that the 13 Army and three and a half Marine divisions in the Pacific equaled the total number in Europe and the Mediterranean at that time. Of the Army divisions, MacArthur had 4 (1st Cavalry, 24th, 32d, and 41st); Halsey, 4 (25th, 37th, 43d, and American); and Nimitz 5 (6th, 7th, 27th, 33d, and 40th). The number of air groups in Europe was double the 34 groups available for operations against Japan. But to get an accurate picture of the American effort in the two theaters, it is necessary to add to the Army forces in the Pacific, the Pacific Fleet, comprising the bulk of U.S. naval forces; Marine Corps ground forces, including three divisions; and the air forces, shore and carrier-based, of the Navy and the Marine Corps.[55] (*Tables 6–8*)

By the time MacArthur's RENO III plan reached Washington—it was brought by his chief of staff, General Sutherland, on 4 November—the joint planners were in the midst of preparations for the coming conference at Cairo and Tehran. As a matter of fact, MacArthur had been asked on 27 October to submit his summary of the situation and a report on his plans in time for the scheduled conference. These Sutherland brought with

---

[54] Ltr, Nimitz to JCS 30 Sep 43, sub: Garrison Rqmts in Central Pacific Area; USAFMIDPAC Hist, pt I, vol. I, p. 115.

[55] Rad, Marshall to MacArthur, 4 Nov 43, CM–OUT 1289; Matloff, *Strategic Planning for Coalition Warfare, 1943–1944*, Table 3, presents a comparison of Army forces deployed overseas on 31 December 1942 with those deployed on 31 December 1943 in all theaters.

TABLE 6—STRENGTH, U.S. FORCES IN THE PACIFIC, 31 DECEMBER 1943[a]
(Compared to European and Mediterranean Theaters)

Area	Total	Army (Incl AAF)	Marines	Navy Shore-Based	Navy Ship-Based
Total	1,791,782	826,672	160,410	248,000	556,700
SWPA	353,945	297,055	22,090	34,000	800
South Pacific	383,874	208,382	71,692	99,000	4,800
Central Pacific	344,414	206,891	49,523	85,000	3,000
North Pacific	147,278	114,344	1,034	30,000	1,900
Pacific Ocean	562,271	—	16,071	—	546,200
Total	1,849,298	1,464,216	2,482	37,000	345,600
European Theater	866,541	830,423	1,118	21,000	14,000
Mediterranean and North Africa	652,093	633,793	—	16,000	2,300
Atlantic Ocean	330,664	—	1,364	—	329,300

[a]Figures are approximate and are derived not from statistical reports but from estimates of the Joint Staff Planners developed for planning purposes; actual strength of Army commands in Pacific areas was 818,482; in the European theater, 768,274; and in the Mediterranean–North African theater, 597,658.

Source: JCS 521/3, 4 Feb 44, sub: Strategic Deployment of U.S. Forces to 31 December 1944.

him together with full authority to speak for MacArthur and a request that he be allowed to present his views personally before the Joint and Combined Chiefs of Staff.[56]

About 8 November, Sutherland met with the joint planners. By this time, the planners had received from the Joint War Plans Committee a revised schedule for Pacific operations in 1944. For the Central Pacific this schedule included operations as far as the Palaus and even the still-tentative Marianas, but it took the forces of the Southwest Pacific only as far as the Vogelkop Peninsula, scheduled for invasion in August. The last two phases of RENO III it omitted entirely. Omitted also were the operations MacArthur had recommended in the Arafura and the Celebes Seas to protect the left flank of his advance along the north coast

of New Guinea.[57] Since the planners had evidently seen RENO III, these omissions could not have stemmed from ignorance of MacArthur's intentions. Rather, they were based on the considered judgment of the planners that these operations were neither feasible nor desirable, and that the resources required to carry them out could not be available in time.

General Sutherland did his best to change this view. He reviewed the situation in the Pacific in some detail and dwelt on the enemy's deployment during the past months, his capabilities and his intentions. The most profitable target for the Allies and the one that would best accomplish the objectives set at Quebec, he asserted, was the Philippines. Repeating the by now familiar arguments advanced by MacArthur for a return to the islands, Sutherland made a

[56] Rad, MacArthur to Marshall, 31 Oct 43, CM–IN 18860; Marshall to MacArthur, 27 Oct 43, 12164.

[57] JWPC 115/1, Rpt by JWPC, 7 Nov 43, sub: Specific Opns for Defeat of Japan, 1944.

TABLE 7—MAJOR U.S. COMBAT FORCES IN THE PACIFIC, 31 DECEMBER 1943[a]

Ground Forces

Army		Marine	
Division	13	Division	3½
Regiments	5	Regiments	1
Battalions	126	Battalions	18 2/3
Tank	7	Amphtrac	3 2/3
AA (Gun)	47	Defense	15
AA (AW)	46		
AA (SL)	26		

Total	
Divisions	16½
Regiments	6
Battalions	144 2/3

Aircraft

Army		Navy and Marine (Shore-Based)	
Bomber	745	Bomber	386
Heavy	346	Medium and Light	72
Medium and Light	399	Dive and Torpedo	314
Fighter	973	Patrol Bomber	660
Reconnaissance	118	Heavy	96
Troop Carrier	312	Medium	348
		Light	216
		Fighter	384
		Reconnaissance	36
		Photo	36
		Troop Carrier	72

Navy (Carrier-Based)	
Torpedo Bomber	519
Scout Bomber	432
Fighter	884
Miscellaneous	106

Total	
Bomber	2,241
Patrol Bomber	660
Torpedo and Scout Bomber	951
Fighter	1,131
Reconnaissance and Photo	190
Troop Carrier	384
Miscellaneous	106

Naval Vessels

Combatant		Miscellaneous	
Battleship, new[b]	6	Destroyer, escort	57
Battleship, old	7	Patrol Craft	85
Carrier, Large	7	Minelayer	9
Carrier, 10,000 ton	7	Minesweeper	47
Carrier, escort	14	Transport	54
Cruiser, Heavy	12	Cargo	14
Cruiser, Light	13	LST	125
Destroyer, new	175	LCM	99
Destroyer, old	13		
Submarine, new	105		
Submarine, old	18		

[a] Figures are approximate, developed for planning purposes by the Joint Staff Planners.

[b] The term *new* applies to vessels constructed after 1936.

Source: JCS 521/3, 4 Feb 44, sub: Strategic Deployment of U.S. Forces to 31 December 1944.

592496 O–62—36

TABLE 8—MAJOR U.S. COMBAT AND AIR FORCES IN PACIFIC AND EUROPEAN AREAS, 31 DECEMBER 1943[a]

Forces	Pacific Areas						European Areas			
	Total	Southwest Pacific	South Pacific	Central Pacific	North Pacific	Navy in Pacific Ocean	Total	European	Mediterranean-North African	Navy in Atlantic Ocean
Ground Units:										
Divisions, total	16+	5	5	6+	0	xxx	17	11	6	xxx
Army	13	4	4	5	0	xxx	17	11	6	xxx
Marine	3+	1	1	1+	0	xxx	0	0	0	xxx
Regiments, Infantry, total	6	3	3	0	0	xxx	2	2	0	xxx
Army	5	3	2	0	0	xxx	2	2	0	xxx
Marine	1	0	1	0	0	xxx	0	0	0	xxx
Battalions, Infantry, total	144+	33	43+	42+	26	xxx	113	37	67	xxx
Army	126	31	34	35	26	xxx	113	37	76	xxx
Marine	18+	2	9+	7+	0	xxx	0	0	0	xxx
Shore-Based Aircraft:										
Bombers, total	1,183	429	381	199	24	150	2,144[b]	1,216	928	----
Heavy, Army	346	144	108	70	24	0	1,460	988	472	----
Medium & Light, Army	423	285	57	57	0	24	684	228	456	----
Dive & Torpedo, Navy & Marine	414	0	216	72	0	126	----	0	0	----
Fighters, total	1,537	474	390	381	100	192	2,623	1,425	1,198	----
Day & Bomber	1,465	450	366	369	100	180	2,575	1,425	1,150	----
Army	925	450	150	225	100	0	2,575	1,425	1,150	----
Navy & Marine	540	0	216	144	0	180	0	0	0	----
Night	72	24	24	12	0	12	48	0	48	----
Army	48	24	12	12	0	0	48	0	48	----
Navy & Marine	24	0	12	0	0	12	0	0	0	----
Reconnaissance, Army, total	164	88	28	12	0	36	204	120	84	----
Troop Carrier, total	384	234	87	38	13	12	494	130	364	----
Army	312	234	39	26	13	0	494	130	364	----
Navy & Marine	72	0	48	12	0	12	0	0	0	----
Patrol Bomber, total	660	72	240	156	96	96	0	0	0	----
Heavy, Navy & Marine	96	0	24	36	0	36	0	0	0	----
Medium, Navy & Marine	348	60	120	60	48	60	0	0	0	----
Light, Navy & Marine	216	12	96	60	48	0	0	0	0	----

[a] Figures are approximate and represent informed estimates for planning purposes.
[b] Shore-based naval aircraft on Atlantic bases excluded; data not shown in source document.
Source: JCS 521/3, 4 Feb 44, sub: Strategic Deployment of U.S. Forces to 31 December 1944.

strong plea for the invasion of Mindanao. Its capture, he pointed out, might force the Japanese into a decisive fleet engagement, would place the Allies in a favorable position to strike a decisive blow at Japanese shipping, and permit them to move their land-based air strength in position to apply "maximum pressure" against the Japanese. "We thereby attack the enemy," he concluded, "in each of his four major points of weakness: oil, naval and merchant shipping, and the air." [58]

The best way to reach the Philippines was by way of the Southwest Pacific Area. No other route, said Sutherland, offered the same advantages. Systematically he considered the approaches through Southeast Asia and across the Pacific. The first, which no one seriously favored, he considered undesirable both tactically and logistically. The Central Pacific route was more difficult to discount, but it, too, Sutherland found undesirable as "a succession of independent seaborne attacks, supported by carrier-based aviation, against islands that are thoroughly organized for defense and supported by land-based aviation as well as by the carrier-based air of the Japanese Fleet." Such attacks, he declared, were not only "the most hazardous" of military operations but also of little value in maintaining "unrelenting pressure" against the Japanese. Each operation would be independent, would contribute little to the next, and would not materially weaken the enemy whose

ability to make war was based on the China–Philippines–Borneo–Netherlands Indies littoral. "All the rest of her holdings are merely outposts," and their capture would not, he believed, reduce Japan's capacity to fight.

Sutherland admitted that the Central Pacific advance would exploit America's growing naval power. But he qualified this endorsement by pointing out that such an advance would fail to utilize the equally important strength of land-based aircraft or employ decisively and in effective combination Allied land, sea, and air power. In short, the route across the Pacific, in Sutherland's view, would involve the Allies in a frontal assault and a war of attrition without promise of great strategic results.

The use of all avenues of approach to Japan's inner citadel in the Philippines was obviously the most desirable course. Were the forces for such a course available, then it should by all means be adopted, said Sutherland—provided, of course, that the offensive along one axis of advance did not require a lessened effort in the other. But until Germany was defeated, there was little likelihood that the Pacific commanders would have the forces needed for two or more simultaneous and equally powerful drives to the Philippines. "To attempt a major effort along each axis," Sutherland declared, "would result in weakness everywhere in violation of cardinal principles of war, and . . . in failure to reach the vital strategic objective at the earliest possible date, thus prolonging the war." For the present, he argued, a single strong attack along one axis, supported by forces in the other areas, was the only possible course. The Southwest Pacific was the route to follow; RENO III, the

---

[58] General MacArthur's Estimate of Pacific Sit and Concept of Over-all Plans for Defeat of Japan, no date, filed in folder labeled Notes on Particular Points that may be discussed in SW, S, and CP Areas, OPD Exec Files.

plan. All the Joint Chiefs had to do, concluded Sutherland, was approve the plan and provide the forces.[59]

The joint planners were apparently not convinced by Sutherland's arguments that all available resources be concentrated in the Southwest Pacific for the drive on the Philippines. Instead, they accepted the schedule of their planning committee and recommended to the Joint Chiefs a continuation of the existing strategy: concurrent and mutually supporting operations along both axes of advance, with the transfer of forces from one area to the other when required. MacArthur's plan for operations in the Netherlands Indies they rejected, as they did his hope of ultimately capturing Rabaul.[60] And faced by the inevitable question of deciding which of the two theaters should have the priority in a conflict, the planners fell back on the formula that in such an event "due weight should be accorded to the fact that operations in the Central Pacific promise a more rapid advance toward Japan." [61] The final decision on the drive to the Philippines as well as on the objectives for 1944 was still to be made. The coming conference at Cairo would provide the answer.

---

[59] General Sutherland in commenting on the present volume in manuscript form, stated that a more correct reflection of his position at the time would be "to *combine* the effect of converging forces from the Southwest Pacific, South Pacific, and Central Pacific along an axis to the Philippines." Sutherland Comments, Jul 59, OCMH.

[60] Shortly after the Cairo Conference, General Sutherland stated to the Joint Chiefs, according to the memory of Admiral Bieri who was present, that MacArthur believed the decision to bypass Rabaul "would go down in history as one of time's greatest military mistakes." Ltr, Bieri to Hoover, 17 Jul 59, OCMH.

[61] JCS 581, 9 Nov 43, sub: Specific Opns for Defeat of Japan, 1944; Memo, Col. George A. Lincoln for Chief, Strategy Sec, OPD, 8 Nov 43, sub: Reno III, ABC 381 Strategy Sec (7 Jan 43).

CHAPTER XXVII

The Japanese Revise Their Strategy

In war something must be allowed to chance and fortune, seeing it is in its nature hazardous and an option of difficulties.

GENERAL JAMES WOLFE, 1757

Viewed from Tokyo, the war by September 1943 had reached a critical stage. The defeat at Midway in June 1942 followed by the loss of Guadalcanal and Papua early in 1943 had been serious but not fatal blows. More serious had been the loss of ships and pilots, and these, it was hoped, would ultimately be replaced. But MacArthur's and Halsey's victories in the Solomons and New Guinea during the summer of 1943 cast a more serious light on the situation. Obviously the Allies were making a determined assault on the Solomons, eastern New Guinea, and the Bismarck Archipelago, which the Japanese called the Southeast Area. Failure to hold the outposts in New Guinea and the Solomons, they recognized, could have disastrous consequences and might well be the prelude to an Allied advance toward Truk and the Philippines.

The Allied drive from the south was not all the Japanese had to worry about; danger lay also to the north and to the east. In May 1943 they had lost Attu

and in July they had been forced to evacuate Kiska. Though there were no signs of an early offensive from the Aleutians, this was a possibility the Japanese could not overlook. The threat from the east, across the Central Pacific, was more immediate. American fast carriers had recently struck Marcus Island, Wake, and Japanese bases in the Marshalls, and American forces had occupied islands in the Ellice group, south of the Gilberts. All this activity, the Japanese reasoned correctly, could only mean the Allies were preparing to launch an offensive in the Central Pacific in the near future. Clearly, the time had come for a reassessment of Japan's military and political situation and a realistic appraisal of her prospects for the future.

The New Operational Policy

The review of Japan's position in mid-war was sparked by *Imperial General Headquarters* early in September with a comprehensive "Estimate of the

Enemy Situation."[1] The Allied offensive, the Japanese planners believed, would increase in intensity rather than diminish in the days ahead, and could be expected to reach its peak probably by the early summer of 1944. During the remainder of 1943 and through 1944, the Allies, they thought, would make a concentrated effort to capture Rabaul and other strategic positions in the South and Southwest Pacific, while opening offensives in Burma, Sumatra, and the Indian Ocean area. If the Allies succeeded in taking Rabaul, they would almost certainly drive next for the Philippines and the Mandated Islands, the Japanese believed. Oddly enough, they did not expect a "large-scale enemy offensive" in the Central Pacific, at least in 1943, because of the weakness in carrier strength.

Just what the Japanese meant by a "large-scale" offensive is not clear. Certainly it did not mean operations against the Gilberts, Nauru, Wake, or Marcus, for these were definitely considered possible Allied moves to be undertaken in

concert with the offensive against Rabaul. The Allies could be expected also, if the opportunity offered, to invade the Kurils and the Netherlands Indies, to disrupt Japanese sea communications, and to bomb the occupied areas and even Japan itself.

The situation on the Asiatic mainland was no better. On review, the Japanese planners could discern no reason to believe that the Soviet Union would change its policy toward Japan and join the Allies in the Far Eastern war. But they did think Stalin might permit the United States to use air bases in Eastern Siberia. For this reason the planners held that Japan would have to maintain strong forces in Manchuria as well as in China, where there was every prospect of increased Allied air activity.

In this situation, *Imperial General Headquarters* found little cause for optimism. The enemy had gained aerial supremacy in the Solomons and eastern New Guinea, and, despite the courageous efforts of Japanese troops in the area, was continuing to advance. Elsewhere, the outlook was no brighter; everywhere the Japanese turned they faced the prospect of actual or potential Allied offensives. "In short," the Deputy Chief of the Army General Staff predicted gloomily, "the situation will develop steadily toward the decisive stage and we are rapidly approaching a crucial stage which may well decide the fate of our country."[2]

Japanese estimates of Allied strength were fairly accurate. Ground and air forces arrayed against them they placed at 23 divisions and 2,500 planes of all types. This was only "front-line" strength; total strength, including re-

---

[1] This chapter, except where otherwise noted, is based on the following Japanese sources: Hattori, The Greater East Asia War, III, 1–34, 45–50; Japanese Opns in SWPA, chs. VII and VIII; the following Japanese Studies in World War II: *Imperial GHQ Army High Command Record* (No. 72), pp. 91–113; Hist of the *Southern Army* (No. 21) pp. 52–57; Hist of the *8th Area Army* (No. 37), pp. 32–46; Southeast Area Opns Record, pt. IV, *8th Area Army* Opns No. 110), pp. 85–136; Hist of *2d Area Army* (No. 31), pp. 1–26; Operations in the Central Pacific (No. 55) pp. 8–11; and *Imperial GHQ* Navy Directives 280, 284, 287; *Imperial GHQ* Army Directives 1652, 1653, 1699, 1701, all in OCMH. An excellent summary of the Japanese situation for part of this period may be found in Robert Ross Smith, *The Approach to the Philippines*, UNITED STATES ARMY IN WORLD WAR II (Washington, 1953), pp. 84–92; Miller, *CARTWHEEL*, pp. 212–14; and Crowl and Love, *Seizure of the Gilberts and Marshalls*, pp. 63–70, 206–12.

[2] Quoted in Hattori, The Greater East Asia War, III, 12.

serves, the planners at *Imperial General Headquarters* placed at 6,000 aircraft and 70 to 80 divisions. The rate of increase of these forces depended, the Japanese recognized, on a variety of factors: the situation in Europe, shipping, and U.S. production. But even assuming the Allies gave first priority to the war against Germany, the Tokyo planners reckoned that the Allies would have 4,000 aircraft and 35 divisions available for operations against Japan at the end of 1943. A year later, this total would have jumped to 7,000 aircraft and 60 divisions, assuming a shipping capacity of four to five million tons.

The main naval strength of the Allies, the Japanese knew, was concentrated in the U.S. Pacific Fleet operating out of Pearl Harbor. The nucleus of this fleet, they estimated correctly as consisting of about 6 large aircraft carriers, 15 battleships, and 15 cruisers, organized into several forces.[3] Separate task forces, including 10 converted aircraft carriers, were believed to be operating in the Alaska-Aleutians area and in the waters off Australia. Allied submarines, which were

responsible for the bulk of their shipping losses, the Japanese estimated at about 100. Of these, by far the greatest number, about 80, were believed to be American; the remainder, British. Operating bases for the underwater craft were correctly located in Hawaii, Dutch Harbor, Alaska, and Ceylon. No mention was made of the Australian submarine base.

This estimate of the enemy's intentions and capabilities did not hold out much promise for the future. And when the Japanese considered their own resources, the picture became even darker. Their great weaknesses, they recognized, were in aircraft and in shipping. Without an adequate supply of both, Japan could not hope to halt the Allied drive, much less open an offensive of its own. The total number of aircraft that would be required by the Army and Navy during 1944, it was estimated, was 55,000, an impossible figure in view of the fact that total Japanese aircraft production in August 1943 was only 1,360 and in September 1,470. And even if the Japanese could produce as many as 55,000 planes, the effort would so strain the economy of the nation that it would be impossible to try to match American and British naval forces, build up ground strength to a level adequate to meet a possible threat from the Soviet Union, or initiate large-scale offensive operations in China. But these goals the Japanese were apparently willing to sacrifice for air power, the Navy planners insisting only that they had to have special attack and antisubmarine craft.

The shipping problem was no less serious than the shortage of aircraft. In a period of less than two years 445 vessels totaling 1,754,000 tons had been sunk and another 414 (2,109,800 tons) dam-

---

[3] Admiral Nimitz' Pacific Fleet included the forces designated for the Central Pacific operations, Admiral Halsey's South Pacific Force, and the North Pacific Force. In the Central Pacific Force alone, there were, in November 1943, 6 heavy carriers (CV) and 5 light carriers (CVL). The *Essex* had joined the fleet in June 1943, followed a month later by the *Yorktown* and *Lexington*, both heavy carriers, and the light carriers *Independence, Belleau Wood,* and *Princeton*. The fast battleship *Alabama* joined in August, and during the next few months Nimitz received 5 new battleships, 7 old ones, 10 fast carriers, 7 escorts, 8 heavy and 4 light cruisers, 66 destroyers, 27 attack transports and cargo carriers, and 9 merchant vessels suitable for transport. Samuel Eliot Morison, *New Guinea and the Marianas, March 1944–August 1944,* vol. VIII, History of United States Naval Operations" (Boston: Little, Brown and Company, 1953) pp. 85–86.

TABLE 9—JAPANESE SHIPPING LOSSES, 7 DECEMBER 1941–20 SEPTEMBER 1943[a]

Caused By	Sunk		Damaged		Total	
	No. of Vessels	Tonnage (in thousands of tons)	No. of Vessels	Tonnage (in thousands of tons)	No. of Vessels	Tonnage (in thousands of tons)
Totals_____	445	1,757.4	414	2,109.8	859	3,867.2
Submarines_____	290	1,233.0	146	910.7	436	2,143.7
Aircraft_____	75	303.7	97	536.2	172	839.9
Mines_____	29	85.7	22	106.2	51	191.9
Sea Disasters_____	51	135.0	149	556.7	200	691.7

[a]Only ships with a gross tonnage of more than 500 are included.
Source: Hattori, The Greater East Asia War, III, 16.

aged. By far the largest toll, over two million tons, had been taken by Allied submarines; the action of Allied aircraft accounted for another 840,000 tons. (Table 9) And there was every reason to expect that the number of sinkings would increase sharply unless drastic measures were taken. At the present rate, the Japanese estimated, shipping losses from Allied submarines alone would total 100,000 tons a month by the end of the year.[4] Only a major effort to increase greatly the number of escort vessels and antisubmarine aircraft could avert this disaster.

The production of aircraft and ships would take time. The problem facing the Japanese, therefore, was to gain the maximum time with the minimum loss, to trade space for time. The solution proposed by the planners at Imperial General Headquarters was embodied in the "New Operational Policy." Convinced that the line eastern New Guinea–northern Solomons–Marshall and Gilbert Islands could not be held, and was, indeed, on the verge of collapse, they rec-

ommended that a new line encompassing the "absolute national defense sphere"[5] be established. Beyond this line there would be no retreat; along it would be built impregnable defenses. And while the Allies fought their way to this line, the Japanese could repair their losses in aircraft and shipping in preparation for a great counteroffensive.

The selection of a new defense line was based on the most careful calculation of Japan's resources and Allied capabilities. Extending from the Kuril Islands southward through the Bonins, Marianas, and Carolines, thence south and west to western New Guinea, the Sunda Islands in the Netherlands Indies, and finally to Burma, this line comprised the minimum area considered essential for the attainment of Japan's war aims. Possession of this area would give Japan the advantage of interior lines and the raw materials and food needed to meet military and civilian requirements. Since it corresponded also to the Greater East Asia Co-Prosperity Sphere, its security was an essential prerequisite to the political and economic control of the nations included

---

[4]During 1943, U.S. submarines sank 22 Japanese naval vessels of all types and 296 merchant ships, at a loss of 15 submarines. Morison, New Guinea and the Marianas, p. 16.

[5]The term the Japanese used was "Zettai Kokubo Ken–I."

within the Japanese orbit. Any reduction of the area, or the acquisition by the Allies of bases from which to strike important political and industrial targets within it, was bound to affect seriously Japan's political position and capacity to wage war.

Based on these considerations, the Japanese planners formulated a strategy whose primary objective was the defense of this vital area. First, in recognition of Japan's inability to hold the existing line in the Southeast Area, the Japanese would take a long backward step and establish a more restricted perimeter extending from the Carolines to western New Guinea. Next, they would erect an "undefeatable strategic position" along this new line, establishing advance bases in front of it to keep Allied air power at a safe distance and safeguard the line of communications. Finally, they would build up Japanese power within the absolute defense area, with special emphasis on air power. By utilizing the geographic advantages of this new line and of interior lines of communications, the Japanese hoped they would be able to repulse any large-scale enemy offensive and ultimately to launch a counteroffensive of their own. (Map 9)

In concrete terms, as enunciated by the Army Section of *Imperial General Headquarters* on 15 September 1943, this new strategy or "operational policy" would require the following:

1. Close cooperation with the Navy.
2. Strong delaying action in the Southeast Area. Allied forces advancing in this critical region were to be resisted fiercely, and delayed as long as possible. The time thus gained was to be used to build up the defenses along the new line from the Banda Sea to the Caroline Islands and to marshal the forces for a counteroffensive.

3. All-out defense in the Southwest Area, the Japanese designation for the region extending from the Banda Sea to Burma. This area was part of the absolute national defense sphere; therefore the complete destruction of any enemy forces seeking to invade the region was absolutely essential to Japan's successful prosecution of the war.
4. Preservation of the *status quo* in China, while increasing pressure against the enemy to destroy his will to fight. In North China, preparations would be made to meet the contingency of Soviet-American cooperation, but no step would be taken that might bring the Soviet Union into the war.
5. Strengthening the defenses of the home islands, the oil regions of the East Indies and the shipping lanes to Japan. These measures were vital to the conduct of the war and the execution of the new operational policy.
6. Raiding operations deep behind enemy lines in every area.
7. All possible measures of operations that would bring into full play the combined fighting power of the air, ground, and naval forces; in short, any operation that promised success.[6]

The Decision Is Made

Japan's military leaders had proposed a new operational policy, a strategy designed to trade space for time; her political leaders now put forward a foreign policy to match. First among the objectives of the Foreign Ministry was the preservation of peace with the Soviet Union. This was to be achieved in three ways: first, by maintaining Japanese military strength and, if possible, by winning military victories over the United States and Great Britain; second, by adopting positive measures designed to improve friendly relations with the USSR; and third, by exercising restraint but resolu-

---

[6] *Imperial GHQ* Army High Command Record, Japanese Studies in World War II, 72, pp. 94–96.

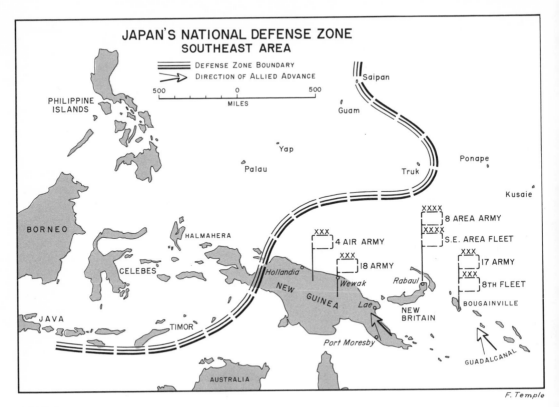

MAP 9

tion in dealing with the Soviet Union over controversial matters.[7]

The possibility that Germany and the Soviet Union might suddenly conclude a separate peace treaty was a contingency the Japanese could not ignore. Such a move, they recognized, would undoubtedly have a profound effect on Japan's situation. Therefore, to ensure that the effect was favorable and the dangers minimized, the Japanese agreed that they must follow the situation closely and be prepared at the first sign of peace to move in with an offer of mediation. The timing of this offer was considered of the utmost importance by the experts in Japan's Foreign Ministry. It should coincide, they said, with military success in the field, either by Germany or Japan, or with the successful completion of negotiations for a settlement of the China incident.

Co-operation with Germany was a political rather than a military objective for the Japanese. Thus, the measures proposed were limited to exchange of views and information, visits of dignitaries, and joint declarations of common aims and objectives in the war against the Allies. What the Japanese wanted

[7] For a full discussion of the political aspects of the Japanese situation at this time, see Morton, "Japanese Strategy and Policy in Mid-War," *United States Naval Institute Proceedings*, (February, 1959).

most from Germany were war materials and technical information. For these they were willing to exert their "utmost effort" to promote co-operation and even to hold out the possibility of German participation in the economic development of the Greater East Asia Co-Prosperity Sphere.

To cope with the political offensive being waged by the Anglo-American Allies in East Asia, the Japanese decided they must take stronger measures to convince the peoples of Asia that their destiny lay with Japan. The most effective argument, of course, was military victory, but the Japanese could not rely on that. They proposed therefore to secure the "voluntary" co-operation of the Asiatic people by fair and just treatment of the occupied nations and by propaganda emphasizing the evils of colonialism. The weakness in their argument, the Japanese realized, was the Japanese Army in China. Resistance by the Chungking government would by example encourage opposition to the Japanese everywhere in Asia. A primary aim of Japanese foreign policy, therefore, must be the settlement of the China incident.

The political program proposed by the Foreign Ministry was reviewed and accepted without dispute on 25 September at a meeting of the Liaison Conference, which, it will be recalled, consisted of the service chiefs and the Cabinet and served as a link between *Imperial General Headquarters* and the government. At this same meeting of 25 September the assembled political and military chiefs approved the strategic policy presented by *Imperial General Headquarters*. With agreement on the basic problems of political and military strategy, the leaders of the Japanese Government were ready to go before the Emperor. His assent would seal the decisions already made and give them the powerful sanction of imperial decree.[8]

The Imperial Conference that fixed the course Japan would attempt to follow during the next year and a half opened at 10 o'clock on the morning of 30 September 1943. Assembled for this meeting with the Emperor, the "August Mind" of Japan, were the highest officials of the government — the Premier and War Minister, Hideki Tojo; the Navy, Foreign Affairs, Finance, Agriculture, and Commerce Ministers; the Chiefs and Deputy Chiefs of the Army and Navy General Staffs; the President of the Privy Council, Director of the Cabinet Planning Board, and Minister for Greater East Asia Affairs; and the heads of various government departments. In accordance with custom Premier Tojo presided.

For most if not all those present at the Imperial Conference, the proceedings offered nothing new. The purpose of the conference was to secure the Emperor's sanction for decisions already made, not to present various proposals and policies for his decision. The Japanese constitutional system did not assign the role of policy-maker to the Emperor. As the personification of national unity and the supreme symbol of Japanese life and thought, the Emperor stood above party and faction. Ancient tradition limited his action to approval of the decisions of his ministers; precedent dictated silence. But by his presence alone, he set upon these decisions a finality and authority that could be achieved in no

---

[8] For a discussion of the proceedings of this meeting, see *ibid.*

other way. Thereafter, there was no turning back; only another Imperial Conference could alter or reverse the course approved by the Emperor. This was the significance of the meeting of 30 September; it witnessed, in solemn and historic fashion, a major shift in Japanese policy and strategy for the conduct of the war.

General Tojo opened the conference with a reading of the political estimate adopted at the Liaison Conference of 25 September. The Emperor listened gravely; there was no discussion. Next, the secretary read the proposed "General Outline of the War Direction Policy." Each of the more important officials then stood up in turn, with Tojo leading off, to elaborate on the program and explain to Emperor Hirohito how his department expected to achieve the goals set out in the new program. The President of the Privy Council asked several penetrating questions and when these were answered to his satisfaction Tojo closed the conference at 3:30 p.m., with a brief statement announcing that since there was no objection, the new policy was adopted unanimously. There is no record that the Emperor spoke once during the meeting.

The New Strategy in Action

Once the stamp of Imperial approval had been secured, the Army and Navy lost no time putting into effect the new strategy. In accordance with established practice, the basic strategy was embodied in an "Army-Navy Central Agreement," the Japanese equivalent of a U.S. Joint Chiefs of Staff directive. With this central agreement outlining the major objectives of the new policy, *Imperial General Headquarters* sent to the commanders in the field specific instructions on the course they were to follow in attaining these objectives. For the army commanders these instructions came from the Army Section of *Imperial General Headquarters* in the form of a GHQ numbered order. The Navy Section issued its own order to the fleet commanders, a procedure that led to different interpretations of the central agreement and left to the separate commanders responsibility for making arrangements for co-ordination and concerted action of joint forces.[9]

The central agreement promulgated after the Imperial Conference differed in no essential respect from the policy formulated by *Imperial General Headquarters* on 15 September. In general terms it called for the "utmost endeavor" by the Army and Navy, acting in close co-operation, to delay the enemy drive in the strategic Southeast and Central Pacific Areas as long as possible while preparing for a large-scale counteroffensive that would end the Allied threat from the south and east. Preparations for this counteroffensive would include airfield and base development, concentration of forces in the threatened area, stockpiling of munitions and critical supplies, and active operations to cut the Allied line of communications and keep the Allies off balance. Six months were to be allowed for these preparations on the assumption that the main Allied drive would begin in the spring or summer of 1944.

---

[9] Army-Navy Central Agreement on Operations in Central and South Pacific Areas, 30 Sep 43; *Imperial GHQ* Army Directive 1653, same date; *Imperial GHQ* Navy Directive 280, same date. All in OCMH.

The task of putting this plan into effect in the Southeast Area, which was outside the absolute national defense line, fell on the commander of the *8th Area Army*, General Imamura, and his naval colleague, Admiral Kusaka, commander of the *Southeast Area Fleet*. The first was to make every effort to hold the Bismarck Archipelago and Bougainville, in anticipation of an Allied drive on Rabaul. At the same time he was to support the forces on the New Guinea side of the Bismarck barrier to fend off the Allied offensive as long as possible. In this he was to have the help of the *Southeast Area Fleet*, whose air and naval forces were to attack Allied convoys, in co-operation with Army aircraft, and keep open the supply lines to Japanese forces in New Guinea and the Solomons.[10]

General Imamura's plans were based on the estimate that the Allied offensive in New Guinea and the Solomons was directed at the capture of Rabaul. The attack, he thought, would come in February or March 1944, after the Allies had gained control of Bougainville, and of Dampier Strait between New Guinea and New Britain. Imamura considered the possibility of an Allied encirclement of Rabaul by the seizure of the Admiralties and New Ireland, but finally decided that MacArthur would try to take Rabaul by direct assault, as, indeed, MacArthur wished to do. Enemy ground strength Imamura estimated at 19 to 22 divisions, four of which he placed in the Solomons and three in New Guinea; the remain-

ADMIRAL KUSAKA

der, though not in the combat area, he considered available for operations should the need arise. Of the 3,000 planes credited to MacArthur and Halsey, the Japanese commander thought only about half were located in the forward areas—700 in New Guinea and 600 in the Solomons.

On the basis of this estimate and his new mission, General Imamura saw his task as one of delaying the enemy drive. His main effort clearly would have to be directed toward holding Bougainville and the Dampier Strait area (Cape Gloucester in New Britain and the Huon Peninsula in New Guinea) as long as possible. This concept was much like the one he was already following, and Imamura's new plan differed from the old only in the emphasis it placed on the critical areas.

---

[10] Hist of *8th Area Army*, Japanese Studies in World War II, 37, pp. 32ff; Southeast Area Opns Record, pt. IV, *8th Area Army* Operations, Japanese Studies in World War II, 110, pp. 85–88.

To carry out this plan, General Imamura had 2 armies, the *17th* and *18th*, 2 independent divisions, some nondivisional units, support and service troops, and an air army. The *18th Army*, with headquarters at Madang, was responsible for the defense of eastern New Guinea and had assigned to it 3 divisions, the *20th*, *41st*, and *51st*. The *17th Army* in the Solomons had only 1 division, the *6th*, located on Bougainville, but a nondivisional strength consisting of the *4th South Seas Garrison Unit*, plus 1 artillery and 4 infantry battalions. To this *17th Army* strength must be added the naval ground units in the central and northern Solomons, which constituted a fairly large body of well-trained combat troops.

Troops in the Bismarck Archipelago, on New Britain, New Ireland and the Admiralties, were under the direct control of *8th Area Army*. The largest strength was concentrated on New Britain at whose eastern end stood Rabaul, the last stronghold of the Southeast Area. Guarding this critical area as well as western New Ireland was the *Rabaul Defense Unit*, composed of the *38th Division* and attached elements. The western end of New Britain, facing Dampier Strait, was held by the *65th Brigade*, while the central portion was reserved for the *17th Division*, scheduled to arrive shortly from Shanghai. In the Admiralties, with its strength concentrated on Los Negros, was the *51st Transport Regiment*.

The Army air strength of the Southeast Area, consisting of the *6th* and *7th Air Divisions*, was organized into the *4th Air Army*. Except for one air brigade assigned to the support of the *19th Army* in the Banda Sea area, this air force operated chiefly in eastern New Guinea and western New Britain, in defense of Dampier Strait. Air support for the Bismarck Archipelago and the northern Solomons was furnished largely by shore-based naval aircraft of the *11th Air Fleet* based at Rabaul and in southern Bougainville.

On 7 October 1943, General Imamura issued the revised plan for operations in the Southeast Area. The *18th Army* in New Guinea was to occupy and defend the coastal region along Dampier Strait, particularly Finschhafen, and the Ramu Valley in the interior. To the *17th Army* in the Solomons, Imamura assigned the task of holding Bougainville, and to the *65th Brigade* on New Britain the eastern shore of Dampier Strait. The *4th Air Army* was to provide support as required, with the primary mission of destroying any enemy forces attempting to land in the Dampier Strait region. If this proved impossible and if the enemy established a foothold on Bougainville or in the critical Dampier Strait area, then all Japanese troops under his command, ruled General Imamura, would "trade position for time, to the end that the enemy offensive will be crushed as far forward as possible under the accumulation of losses." [11]

The main burden of holding the Central Pacific rested on Admiral Mineichi Koga, *Combined Fleet* commander at Truk. Directed to push preparations for holding the Carolines and the Marianas, both of which were included in the absolute national defense sphere, Admiral Koga had to rely largely on

---

[11] Southeast Area Opns Record, pt. IV, *8th Area Army* Opns, Japanese Studies in World War II, 110, p. 95.

Army reinforcements to fortify the bases in his area. All together, *Imperial General Headquarters* allotted for this purpose approximately forty infantry battalions, as well as tanks, artillery and other support.[12] (*Table 10*) But many of these forces were lost at sea as a result of Allied submarine attacks and never reached their destination. Those that did, Koga used to reinforce the Gilberts and Marshalls, thereby weakening his defenses in the Marianas and Carolines.

From the Army point of view, the assignment of troops intended for the Marianas and the Carolines to outlying positions in the Marshalls was a serious error. But even more serious, many Army officers believed, was the fact that the Navy Section of *Imperial General Headquarters*, by emphasizing the naval mission to meet and engage the enemy fleet, failed to impress on Admiral Koga the necessity for husbanding his strength along the vital national defense line. Koga, the Army held, had not been given proper guidance, with the result that the new operational policy was never properly carried out in the Central Pacific.

Among the orders issued by *Imperial General Headquarters* on 30 September were those to the commander of the *Southern Army*, Field Marshal Hisaichi Terauchi, directing him to expedite preparations for the expected counteroffensive. Originally, the *Southern Army* headquarters had controlled Japanese operations in the entire Southern Area from Malaya to Guadalcanal, but its jurisdiction had been gradually restricted as new commands were formed in the Solomons and New Guinea to meet the Allied offensive in 1942 and 1943. It was time, *Imperial General Headquarters* decided in October 1943, to carve out another piece from Terauchi's domain. This piece, which extended from the *8th Area Army* boundary at longitude 140° east westward to Makassar Strait and from latitude 5° north southward to Australia, included most of Dutch New Guinea, Halmahera, the Celebes, Timor, and the Lesser Sunda Islands. In the view of *Imperial General Headquarters*, this area had now assumed a critical importance as the pivotal point for the projected counteroffensive. More important, perhaps, was the fact that the area included the sea approaches to the Celebes and South China Seas—objectives of the Allied drive across the Central Pacific—and covered the route to the Philippines favored by General MacArthur.[13]

Prompted by these considerations, the planners in Tokyo took steps to reorganize the defenses of this area. In a series of orders dated 29 October, they established a separate command under the direct control of *Imperial General Headquarters*, organized an area army headquarters to direct operations, and assigned to it an additional army and three more divisions. (*Chart 16*) The headquarters designated for the area was General Korechika Anami's *2d Area Army*, then in Manchuria. Under it would be the

---

[12] Operations in the Central Pacific, Japanese Studies in World War II, 55, pp. 10–13; *Imperial GHQ* Army High Command Record, Japanese Studies in World War II, 72, pp. 100–102; Crowl and Love, *Seizure of the Gilberts and Marshalls*, pp. 64–66, 209–10.

[13] *Imperial GHQ* Army High Command Record, Japanese Studies in World War II, 72, pp. 98–100, 102–104; Hist of *Southern Army, 1941–45*, Japanese Studies in World War II, 21, pp. 52–60; Hist of *2d Area Army*, Japanese Studies in World War II, 31, pp. 4ff; Japanese Opns in SWPA, II, ch. VIII, *passim*.

TABLE 10—JAPANESE ARMY REINFORCEMENTS, CENTRAL PACIFIC,
SEPTEMBER 1943–JANUARY 1944

Island	Unit	Date of Arrival
Carolines: Truk	52d Division: Division Headquarters 19th Infantry (less 2d Battalion) 3d Battalion, 150th Infantry (Remainder of division left Japan in January 1944)	December 1943–January 1944
Mortlock	4th Nanyo Detachment	January 1944
Ponape	3d Nanyo Detachment 2d Battalion, tank and machine cannon companies of KO Detachment	November 1943, January 1944
Kusaie	2d Nanyo Detachment KO Detachment (less elements)	November 1943, January 1944
Marshalls: Eniwetok	1st Amphibious Brigade (less 2d Battalion and Engineer Units)	September 1943–January 1944
Jaluit	2d Infantry Battalion (less 2 companies, Nanyo Detachment)	September 1943
Mille	1st Nanyo Detachment (less 2d Battalion) 3d Infantry Battalion, one Mountain Artillery Battalion (less one company), one engineer company (less one platoon) of KO Detachment	September–November 1943
Maloelap	One infantry company, 1st Amphibious Brigade One infantry company, 1st Nanyo Detachment	September 1943–January 1944
Wotje	One infantry company, 1st Amphibious Brigade One infantry company, 1st Nanyo Detachment One machine gun company	September 1943–January 1944
Kwajalein	1st Infantry Battalion (less 2 companies), 1st Amphibious Brigade Engineer Units	January 1944

Source: Hattori, Greater East Asia War, III, 52.

19th Army, already in the area, and the *2d Army*, which, like the *2d Area Army*, was to be transferred from Manchuria. To the former was assigned an additional division, the *46th* from Japan; to the latter the *3d* and *36th Divisions*, then stationed in China. With the arrival of these units, and others, General Anami would have under his control two armies and a total of five battle-tested and fresh divisions, one of which, the *36th*, was organized and equipped for amphibious operations.[14] Already in the area, was the *7th Air Division*.

The wholesale shifting of forces and supplies required by these orders placed a serious strain on the already overburdened Japanese shipping facilities. It was almost a month before General Anami established a provisional headquarters at Davao in the southern Philippines and only on 1 December did he assume operational control. At the time, *2d Army* had no combat units at all and the *19th Army*, for which reinforcements would not arrive until February 1944, had only two divisions whose elements were scattered among the islands west of New Guinea. Even if shipping had been available, it would have been impossible to concentrate forces for a sudden emergency. The arrival of the *36th Division* on 25 December and its subsequent assignment to the Geelvink Bay area made it possible at least to provide protection for what was considered the most important strategic position in the *2d Army* zone. But this still left the northeast New Guinea coast from Wewak to Sarmi virtually undefended.

---

[14] The *3d Division* orders were changed, and the *35th*, also in China, was transferred, instead.

If General Anami had reason to complain about the shortage of ground forces, he had even more reason to fear for his air defenses. His only air unit was the *7th Air Division*, then recuperating at Ambon from the heavy blows it had suffered in eastern New Guinea during the summer and early fall. When Anami assumed control of the division it had only about fifty planes operational, and virtually all these were involved in local defense and escort missions in the *19th Army* area. There were none to spare for the *2d Army*, and, in view of the critical shortage of planes everywhere, little prospect of getting more.

Nor could General Anami expect much help from his naval colleague, commander of the newly formed *4th Expeditionary Fleet*. This force was a fleet only in name, consisting largely of several naval special base units and some special landing troops, scattered throughout the area. There was a navy air unit at Kendari in the Celebes, but it, too, had only about fifty planes and most of its experienced pilots had been moved to Rabaul. The real strength of the Japanese Navy in this region lay in the *Southwest Area Fleet*, with headquarters at Surabaya. In the event of a naval threat from the south by way of the Indian Ocean, it was this organization rather than the *4th Expeditionary Fleet* that would go into action. Any threat from the east would presumably be met by the *Combined Fleet* at Truk.

Even without the strong protests from the field, the high command in Tokyo could not have failed to see how weak were the defenses of western New Guinea and the Central Pacific. There was no shortage of troops or munitions; Anami was promised reinforcements that would

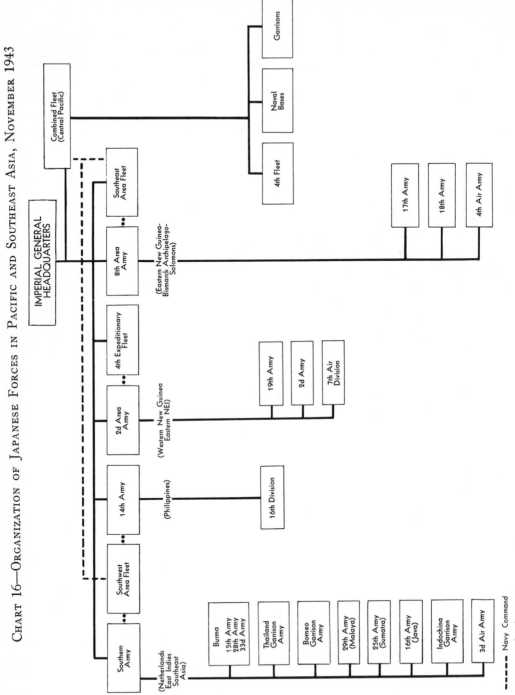

CHART 16—ORGANIZATION OF JAPANESE FORCES IN PACIFIC AND SOUTHEAST ASIA, NOVEMBER 1943

have given 2d *Area Army* a total strength of 320,000 men. Nor could Admiral Koga complain that *Imperial General Headquarters* refused to send him troops when he asked for them. The trouble was shipping. At the Imperial Conference of 30 September, the Army and Navy had asked for additional ships to move the troops and supplies needed to carry out the new operational policy.[15] They had received only 250,000 additional tons, barely enough as it turned out to meet the losses from enemy action. The rest had been allocated to civilian agencies for the war production program. Under these circumstances, the monthly requirements of 2d *Area Army* for 450,000 gross tons of large and medium-sized transports and 150,000 gross tons of smaller ships for a period of four months proved too heavy a drain on the resources of *Imperial General Headquarters*.

The shortage of shipping was not an absolute shortage; 2d *Area Army*'s requirements might still have been met had it not been for the competing demands of other theaters and the unexpectedly heavy losses from Allied submarines. From November on, the Central Pacific was regarded as the more critical area and enjoyed a higher priority than the Southeast Area. But the ship losses there proved most serious. In December, the total was 300,000 gross tons, and during the first month of the new year, the figure rose to 460,000 (including ships heavily damaged) —the highest yet recorded since the start of the war. It was largely for this reason that

shipments to the 2d *Area Army* were virtually discontinued during February and March 1944, even though an additional 300,000 tons of shipping was allocated to the armed forces in that period.

The Japanese were having trouble also meeting the goals set for aircraft production. By the end of the year it was evident these ambitious goals, though successively reduced, would not be met, partly because Japanese industry was not equal to the task and partly because of the shortage of shipping and shipping losses. Thus, instead of the 4,000 planes that should have come off the assembly lines each month, Japanese military forces received during the first quarter of 1944 only about half that number.

Essential also to the success of the new strategy adopted at the end of September was the airfield construction program designed to furnish bases from which to meet the Allied threat and support the planned counteroffensive in the spring of 1944. In General Anami's area alone, 100 new airfields, echeloned in depth and mutually supporting, were to be built. The task was a gigantic one and impossible of execution even though combat units were put to work as labor troops. The shortages of critical materials, and lack of mechanized equipment, labor, and engineering skill, combined with the difficulties of transportation brought the construction program to a grinding halt almost before it had got started. As a result, few of the projected air bases were ever completed.

In the final analysis, the success or failure of the plans so hopefully made in September depended on the ability of the Japanese forces in New Guinea,

---

[15] As of September 1943, the Army and Navy were allocated 2,842,000 gross tons of shipping; about 2,500,000 had been allocated for nonmilitary use. Japanese Opns in SWPA, ch. VIII, p. 5.

the Solomons, and the Central Pacific to halt the Allied drive, or at least hold long enough to permit the assembly of troops and supplies needed for an effective defense, and, ultimately, a counteroffensive. But even while these plans were being drawn and the forces required moved into the critical areas, General MacArthur, Admiral Nimitz, and Admiral Halsey had begun to push against the outposts of the absolute national defense line.

CHAPTER XXVIII

The Execution of Strategy: Pacific Operations, August – December 1943

> The conduct of war resembles the workings of an intricate machine with tremendous friction, so that combinations which are easily planned on paper can be executed only with great effort.
>
> CLAUSEWITZ

While plans for the future were being made in Tokyo and Washington, the war in the Pacific went forward rapidly on every front. Between the summer of 1943 and the end of the year, Allied forces in the Pacific hit the enemy from every direction in a bewildering variety of operations that set the pattern of Pacific warfare. These operations were everywhere marked by the employment of air, ground, and naval forces— American, Australian, and New Zealand —under a unified command and a timetable that called for the most careful planning and co-ordination. Whatever differences existed between the services or among the Allies, operations against the enemy were conducted in a spirit of co-operation and mutual good will.

New Georgia

Capture of the Munda airfield by Admiral Halsey's forces on 5 August had signified the end of only one phase, though an important one, of the New Georgia campaign.[1] There were still a large number of Japanese on New Georgia Island and they would have to be tracked down and captured or killed before the island could be considered secure. Then the remaining islands in the group — Arundel, Baanga, Gizo, Kolombangara, and Vella Lavella — would have to be occupied or neutralized. Only then would the campaign be ended and the forces of the South Pacific free to move on into the northern Solomons.

Even before Munda had fallen, General Griswold, XIV Corps commander, had taken steps to prevent the escape of the Japanese on New Georgia. Patrols had gone out to encircle the airfield and to cut all routes of escape. Following them had come stronger forces. Leaving the 43d Division to guard the airfield, Griswold had sent elements of the 25th Division north along the inland trail from Munda to Bairoko Harbor, where

---

[1] See above, ch. XXV.

a mixed force of Marine and Army troops had been trying unsuccessfully to overcome a small Japanese garrison. A second column, consisting of elements of the 37th Division, Griswold sent along the west coast of the island toward Zieta.[2]

The Japanese were not so easily trapped. Having withdrawn successfully from Munda on 3 August, the Army and Navy commanders in the central Solomons, General Sasaki and Admiral Ota, now decided they could no longer hold New Georgia with the troops at their disposal. Leaving a small force to harass the Americans and maintain a foothold on the island against the day of their return, they transferred their remaining troops to other islands in the group: to Baanga, which lay within artillery range of Munda; to Arundel, covering the narrow water route northward from Munda; and to Kolombangara, where Sasaki established his headquarters. Reinforcements had been promised from Rabaul, and with these Sasaki and Ota hoped ultimately to launch a counteroffensive and drive the enemy from New Georgia.[3]

The Americans required more than two weeks of hard fighting to clear the small Japanese force left behind by Sasaki on New Georgia. (Map 10) By that time, mid-August, all Japanese hopes for a counteroffensive had disappeared. The reinforcements sent by higher headquarters at Rabaul, about 1,500 Army and Navy troops, had been intercepted in Vella Gulf on the night of 6–7 August and virtually destroyed. Only about 300 men had survived to reach Vella Lavella. Next had come orders to withdraw from Baanga, where the Americans had already landed, and to cancel all plans for counterattack. Sasaki's mission now was to hold out as long as possible to give the Japanese in the northern Solomons time to make ready for the next Allied advance. No more reinforcements would be forthcoming; Sasaki would have to do the job with what he had—a mixed force of about 11,000 men, most of whom were concentrated on Kolombangara.

Meantime, Admiral Halsey had revised his own plans. The prospect of "another slugging match" such as the one at Munda to capture the airfield at Vila on Kolombangara, the objective set in the original plans, was not an attractive one.[4] No one wanted to do it, but how could it be avoided? With the advantage of hindsight, the answer seems simple enough—bypass it, neutralize it, and go on to Bougainville. The planners on Halsey's staff were thoroughly aware of the advantages of bypassing enemy strongpoints. Though not yet publicized by that name, the maneuver was a well-understood military principle. As General MacArthur wrote: "The system is as old as war itself. It is merely a new

---

[2] For a full account of operations covered in this section, see Miller, *CARTWHEEL*, ch. IX; Maj. John N. Rentz, USMC, *Marines in the Central Solomons* Historical Branch, Headquarters, U.S. Marine Corps (Washington, 1952); Morison, *Breaking the Bismarcks Barrier*, chs. XII–XIII; Craven and Cate, *AAF IV*, ch. VII. The author was assigned as Historical Officer in the South Pacific from 1943 to 1945 and directed the preparation of histories covering the operations in the theater. These have been used in the preparation of this and other chapters.

[3] Japanese plans and operations described in this chapter are based on the following: Hattori, The Greater East Asia War, III, 53–83; Japanese Opns in SWPA, vol. II, ch. VII; Southeast Area Opns Records, pt. III, *18th Army* Opns, pt. II, Japanese Studies in World War II, 42.

[4] Halsey and Bryan, *Admiral Halsey's Story*, p. 170.

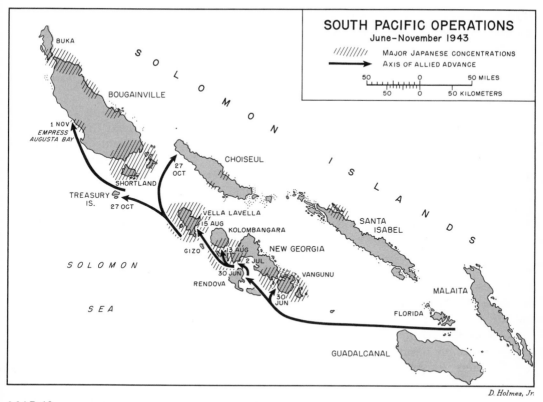

MAP 10

name, dictated by new conditions, given to the ancient principle of envelopment. . . . It has always proved the ideal method for success by inferior in number but faster moving forces." [5]

The idea of bypassing Kolombangara, therefore, was a natural one. The obvious alternative was Vella Lavella, fifteen miles to the northwest and defended by only a handful of Japanese. A landing there would certainly be easier, if intelligence estimates were correct, and would have the further advantage of placing South Pacific forces even closer to their next objective, Bougainville, than a landing at Kolombangara. Halsey liked the idea when it was proposed to him in July, but before he would buy it he wanted the answer to certain questions. Could fighter aircraft be based there to support the invasion of Bougainville? Could the Japanese field at Vila be interdicted by artillery during the landing and could Sasaki's line of supply be cut so that the Kolombangara garrison could safely be left "to die on the vine"? [6]

---

[5] Ltr, MacArthur to Gen Smith, Chief Mil Hist, response to questions by author, 5 Mar 53, OCMH.

[6] Rad, Halsey to Turner and Fitch, 11 Jul 43, cited in Miller, *CARTWHEEL*, Chap. X, p. 13; Ltr, Halsey to Gen Ward, Chief, Mil Hist, 27 May and 27 Aug 52, OCMH.

The answers were provided by a reconnaissance party, which reported at the end of July that a field could be built near Barakoma at the south end of the island. Also reassuring, though incorrect, was the news that there were no Japanese in the area. On the basis of this information and the recommendation of Admiral Wilkinson, Turner's successor, Halsey issued orders for the capture of Vella Lavella on 11 August. The invasion force would consist of a regimental combat team from the 25th Division, plus supporting and service troops, under Brig. Gen. Robert B. McClure. Army and Navy construction troops would go in shortly after the invasion to build the airfield and a small naval base.[7] Three separate naval forces, including aircraft carriers and submarines, would provide close support for the landing and stand ready to head off any Japanese attempt to interfere with the invasion. Aircraft from New Georgia would cover the landing also and in addition strike Japanese bases in the Shortlands and on Bougainville. Griswold's contribution to the operation would consist of the capture of Arundel Island, immediately to the south of Kolombangara. With artillery emplaced there he could take Vila airfield under direct fire and render it useless for the period of the campaign.

D-day for the Vella Lavella invasion was 15 August, and on the 12th an ad-vance party left Rendova to mark the beaches at the landing site. News had also come from the Australian coast watcher there that about forty Japanese had been taken prisoner by the natives, and the advance party was given the additional task of collecting these prisoners. It later developed that the Japanese, whose number had increased to about 300, had not been captured at all. Despite this disturbing news, the advance party held the beachhead for the main invasion force, capturing seven Japanese in the process.

D-day was a complete success. The assault troops landed without interference, and supplies were unloaded with a minimum of confusion. Ground operations thereafter consisted largely of mopping up small groups of Japanese, an activity that occupied the troops until almost the end of September. By that time Arundel had fallen to Griswold's troops after a long and unexpectedly difficult fight by the small Japanese garrison. But the major Japanese resistance came from the air, and for almost a month Allied and Japanese planes fought it out over the central Solomons.

While this battle was in progress, General Sasaki began to make plans for his escape. He had accomplished his mission and could now give up the central Solomons to the enemy. But to get his men through to southern Bougainville where they were needed to fight again was no easy task. The evacuation of Kolombangara began on 28 September. By transport, barge, landing craft, and other types of vessels, the Japanese troops made their way northward under cover of darkness. Of the 11,000 men Sasaki had gathered at Kolombangara, more than 9,000 made good their escape.

---

[7] The landing force consisted of Army—35th Infantry, 64th Field Artillery Battalion (105-mm. howitzers); Company C, 65th Engineer Battalion, 25th Cavalry Reconnaissance Troops, plus other elements of the 25th Division; Marines—4th Defense Battalion; Navy—58th Naval Construction Battalion and a naval base group.

Finally, on the night of 6 October a strong destroyer force came down with transports to pick up the last survivors. A small group of American destroyers, outnumbered three to one, intercepted the Japanese, but suffered heavy losses and was unable to prevent the rescue. With this engagement, known as the Battle of Vella Lavella, the New Georgia campaign came to an end. It had lasted more than four months and had required far larger forces than had been estimated. But at its conclusion, the forces of the South Pacific were at the threshold of Bougainville, whose invasion was less than a month away.

Salamaua to Sio

While Halsey was thrusting forward the right leg of the Allied advance toward the Bismarcks deep into enemy territory, MacArthur was pushing the left leg forward into the Huon Peninsula. (Map V) During July and August, when fighting raged the fiercest in the Solomons, Australian and American troops advanced slowly toward Salamaua. This was only a diversionary move, intended to deceive the enemy. Lae was the real objective and Allied Air and Naval Forces operations during this period were directed as much toward its seizure as to support of the Salamaua campaign. Thus, by the time Salamaua was captured on 12 September, General Kenney's air forces had struck a heavy blow at Japanese air power, and Admiral Kinkaid's destroyers and PT boats had cut deeply into the enemy's thin line of communications. Ground troops, too, had taken a heavy toll, for General Imamura, determined to hold Salamaua, had placed there the bulk of the 10,000 men

available for the defense of the Lae-Salamaua area.[8]

Operations against Lae began even before Salamaua had fallen. Allied Air Forces planes began the preassault bombardment on 1 September, while continuing to neutralize Japanese fields in New Guinea and New Britain. On the morning of the 4th, troops of the 9th Australian Division came ashore in the vicinity of Lae, one brigade landing sixteen miles east of the town and another four miles closer in. A Japanese effort to break up the landing with an air attack proved unsuccessful and by evening of D-day the Australians had secured the beachheads and begun the drive westward toward Lae.

Nadzab was captured the next day, 5 September, by the 503d Parachute Infantry Regiment in the first Allied airborne operation of the Pacific war. Flown in from Port Moresby in ninety-six C–47's, accompanied by over 200 bombers, fighters, and other aircraft, the paratroopers reached Nadzab without mishaps. At 1020 the jump began, and within five minutes the entire regiment was dropping gently toward the ground. Three men were killed and thirty-three injured during the drop, but once on land there were no further casualties. The Japanese had been taken completely by surprise, and had failed to provide any reception whatever.

With the strip at Nadzab in his possession, General MacArthur sent in the airfield engineers and then the 7th Australian Division. On the 10th, this division began its advance eastward

---

[8] For an account of operations in the Markham Valley and Huon Peninsula, see Miller, *CARTWHEEL*, ch. XI; Morison, *Breaking the Bismarcks Barrier*, ch. XIV; Craven and Cate, *AAF IV*, ch. VI.

AUSTRALIAN TROOPS GO ASHORE NEAR LAE

down the Markham Valley toward Lae, in concert with the westward drive of the 9th Australian Division along the coast. Lae was now virtually cut off, and the Japanese wisely decided to pull out and make their way overland as best they could to the north shore of the Huon Peninsula. Thus, the Australians met no strong organized resistance and on 15 September entered Lae, only to find the Japanese gone.

The rapid seizure of Lae put Mac-Arthur about a month ahead of the original CARTWHEEL schedule, which had set a mid-October target date for the Finschhafen operation. But before taking advantage of this stroke of good fortune, MacArthur ordered a comprehensive review of the Allied situation in New Guinea. The objective was control

of Vitiaz and Dampier Straits, separating the Huon Peninsula and New Britain. The capture of Finschhafen was only one step toward this goal; Madang, the Japanese stronghold on the north shore of the peninsula, and Cape Gloucester in western New Britain would have to be taken also to gain control of these strategic straits. The problem, therefore, was how to exploit the gains at Lae and Salamaua to achieve the final objective more rapidly.

In a sense, it was the Japanese who answered this question by drawing the absolute national defense line from the Marianas through the Carolines to western New Guinea, thereby placing the Solomons, Rabaul, eastern New Guinea, and the Gilberts and Marshalls in the category of areas whose retention

AIRBORNE OPERATIONS AT NADZAB

was not essential to Japanese victory.[9] But this decision by *Imperial General Headquarters* did not mean that those areas forward of the line were to be abandoned. Rather, Japanese positions there were to be strengthened and held as long as possible, and commanders in the field were enjoined to exert their utmost efforts to delay the enemy's drive toward the absolute defense line.

It was on the basis of these orders and the reinforcements sent by *Imperial General Headquarters* that the Japanese commanders in the Solomons and New Guinea made their plans for defense. An essential aspect of these plans, it will be remembered, was control of Dampier and Vitiaz Straits. To this end the Japa-

nese strengthened the defenses of Bougainville in an effort to stem the Allied drive up the Solomons, and reinforced Rabaul and the Cape Gloucester garrison in western New Britain to hold the east side of the straits.

The key position on the New Guinea flank was Finschhafen, an airfield site and staging point for men and supplies. No one knew better than Lt. Gen. Hatazo Adachi, *18th Army* commander in New Guinea, that the 1,000-man garrison at Finschhafen was inadequate, but, lacking the troops, there was nothing he could do to reinforce it. The Allied invasion of Lae changed the situation and led to a change in plans that freed the *20th Division* from its current assignment. One element of the division Adachi ordered inland to Kaiapit, stra-

[9] See above, ch. XXVII.

tegically situated near the source of the Markham and Ramu Rivers, to prevent the Allies from advancing down the Ramu Valley to Madang. The main body of the division, then located at Bogadjim about 25 miles south of Madang, he ordered to Finschhafen, 200 miles away.

When the *20th Division* left Bogadjim on 10 September, five days before the Australian occupation of Lae, Allied plans for the next advance had been laid. Estimating correctly that the Japanese would stubbornly resist the Allied drive along the Huon Peninsula, it was agreed that General Blamey's New Guinea Force should advance simultaneously along the coast to Finschhafen and Saidor and inland to Kaiapit, then down the Ramu Valley to Dumpu, in conjunction with the invasion of western New Britain by General Krueger's Alamo Force. The probable target date, it was then estimated, would be 1 December 1943.

This plan and the target date was set at a conference in Port Moresby on 3 September, before the Lae invasion and before the *20th Division* had begun its move toward Finschhafen. The absence of opposition at Lae combined with information on the enemy's movements forced a rapid change in the timetable. Now the Allies much reach Finschhafen before the *20th Division*. MacArthur waited only for the first troops to reach Lae. When they did, on 15 September, he ordered General Blamey to start the drive up the Markham Valley. Two days later, he issued his orders for the seizure of Finschhafen. The Madang operation was temporarily postponed in the hope that it might ultimately prove unnecessary.

The advance up the Markham Valley began almost immediately. On 19 September a company of Australian infantry, flown by transport planes to a point about eight miles from Kaiapit, seized that strategic village at the head of the valley. (*Map 11*) There it was joined two days later by elements of the 7th Division from Nadzab. The drive down the Ramu Valley began soon after and by 6 October Dumpu was in Allied hands.

The landing at Finschhafen came on 22 September, and was made by a brigade of the 9th Australian Division. After a week of hard fighting, the Australians captured the town and nearby airfield on 2 October. But the victory was, in a sense, a hollow one, for the bulk of the Japanese garrison, 4,000 men, had retreated to the 3,240-foot-high Satelberg, a peak that dominated Finschhafen and the surrounding area. There it was joined by the *20th Division* and on 16 October, the Japanese launched a co-ordinated ground and seaborne counterattack. This effort failed, but the Japanese kept trying until the end of October. Thereafter they went on the defensive. The Australians had now received reinforcements and it was their turn to take the offensive. But a month of difficult fighting was still required to drive the Japanese off Satelberg.

The Australians did not stop once they had taken the peak. Their orders were to take Sio, about fifty miles up the coast, so they pushed on, driving the remnants of the *20th Division* before them. On 15 January 1944, they reached their objective and seized the town, thereby bringing under Allied control a 60-mile-stretch of coast line extending from Finschhafen to Sio. Except for

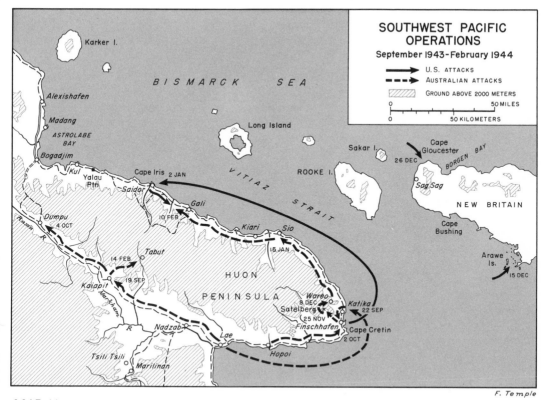

MAP 11

F. Temple

isolated centers of resistance, the New Guinea Force campaign in the Huon Gulf area was over.

The Gilbert Islands [10]

While MacArthur and Halsey were taking turns hitting the Japanese, Admiral Nimitz had moved into the Gilberts,

thus launching the long delayed offensive westward across the vast ocean reaches of the Central Pacific.

For this operation, Nimitz had the bulk of the Pacific Fleet, the Fleet Marine Force, the Army's Seventh Air Force, and the combat and logistical elements of General Richardson's command. All of these contributed to or directly participated in the Gilberts invasion.[11] The role of the Army was to furnish the assault element for Makin, land-based aircraft for Admiral Hoover's

---

[10] For an account of operations in the Gilberts, see Crowl and Love, *Seizure of the Gilberts and Marshalls;* Morison, *Aleutians, Gilberts and Marshalls;* Capt. James R. Stockman, USMC, *The Battle for Tarawa,* Historical Section, Headquarters, U.S. Marine Corps (Washington, 1947); Craven and Cate, *AAF IV,* ch. IX; Jeter A. Isely and Philip A. Crowl, *The U.S. Marines and Amphibious War* (Princeton, N.J.: Princeton University Press, 1951), ch. VI.

[11] For the organization of these forces, see above, ch. XXIV.

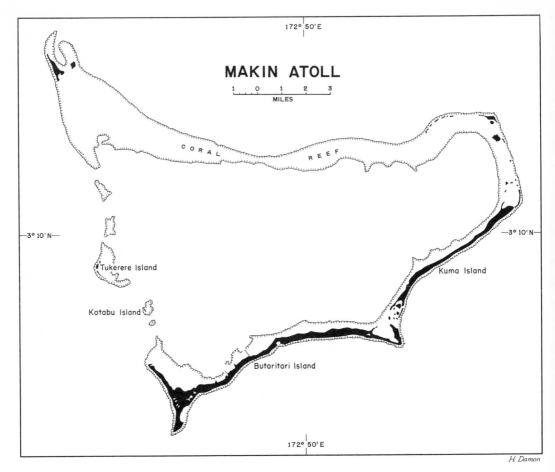

172° 50'E

MAKIN ATOLL

```
      1    0    1    2    3
      |----|----|----|----|
            MILES
```

CORAL   REEF

—3° 10'N—   —3° 10'N—

Tukerere Island

Kuma Island

Kotabu Island

Butaritari Island

172° 50'E

H. Damon

MAP 12

Defense and Shore-Based Air Force, logistical support, and part of the garrison force.

Preparations for the invasion of the Gilberts had begun in August 1943, when Nimitz received the directive for the operation from the Joint Chiefs of Staff. Since that time, the forces had been selected and trained, an organization established under Spruance for the conduct of this and succeeding amphibious operations, a joint staff provided for Nimitz, and the equipment and supplies needed for the assault and subsequent occupation of the islands assembled.

The task had not been easy. This was the first offensive effort in the Central Pacific Area and the transition from a defensive to an offensive role required many adjustments in organization and outlook. Preparations were complicated also by the problems of interservice relations and the fact that the major assault units were not only from different services and accustomed to operate in different ways but also were scattered throughout the Central and South Pacific Areas. The 27th Division, scheduled to take Makin, was in Hawaii; the 2d Marine Division, which was to seize Tarawa, was in New Zealand; and the three defense battalions were at Wallis, Samoa, and Pearl Harbor. To assemble, train, and rehearse these forces and bring them into position before the objective at the exact moment and in the right order was a complex and difficult task.

An additional factor that affected all preparations for the Gilberts invasion was that they had to be done concurrently with the planning for the Marshalls. There was simply not enough of everything to go around. Many of the vessels used for the first operation would have to be used again in the Marshalls two months later. But expendable supplies could not be reused, nor could the assault forces for the Gilberts be employed again in so short a time. Thus, two separate task forces, complete with all the equipment and supplies needed for amphibious warfare had to be assembled simultaneously. It was a job of the first magnitude for a headquarters that had not yet conducted a single amphibious attack.

One of the chief tactical problems of the Gilberts invasion as well as subsequent operations against coral atolls was to carry the assault troops and their supplies across the fringing reefs that encircled the objective and constituted a major hazard in the landing. To traverse this obstacle and to take the troops across the defended beaches, the assault forces had the shallow-draft amphibian tractors, officially designated LVT but more often called the amphtrac or Alligator. With the 2½-ton amphibian truck (the Dukw), used first in the Sicily and

New Georgia campaigns, the LVT rates as one of the great contributions of World War II to the art of amphibious warfare. Both were truly amphibious weapons of the most modern design and played a vital role in making possible the efficiency and success that marked amphibious operations in the Pacific during World War II.

At an early stage in the planning for the Gilberts campaign it was realized that LVT's would be required both at Tarawa and Makin. (*Maps 12 and 13*) Especially at Tarawa, where the water over the fringing coral reefs was extremely shallow and the beach defenses especially strong, was there need for the amphibian tractor. Since most of the amphtracs the 2d Marine Division had were of the early unarmored type, subject to mechanical failures and clearly inadequate for the job, the division requested 100 of the latest models, LVT(2). The request was granted but because of a shipping shortage, the division received only 50. This gave the Marines a total of about 125 of the vehicles, enough for the first three waves of the assault. The 27th Infantry Division, which would face less formidable obstacles at Makin, had 48 of the amphtracs, but received them only at the end of October, thirteen days before it embarked for the invasion.

The movement to the objective was itself a masterpiece of logistical planning. On 31 October, part of the garrison force left Oahu in six LST's with destroyer escort; five days later three more LST's carrying the amphibian tractors and special landing forces for the Makin invasion sailed for the Gilbert Islands. The first group, traveling more slowly and by a longer route, would reach its destina-

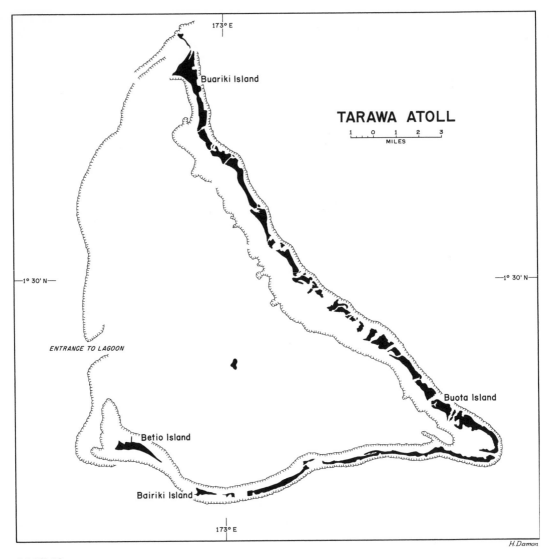

173° E

Buariki Island

TARAWA ATOLL

1   0   1   2   3
MILES

—1° 30' N—   —1° 30' N—

ENTRANCE TO LAGOON

Buota Island

Betio Island

Bairiki Island

173° E

H.Damon

MAP 13

tion later than the second, which was scheduled to arrive at the same time as the main body of Admiral Turner's Northern Attack Force. This last, consisting of the Makin assault troops and the expeditionary force, loaded in attack transports, and a carrier group under Rear Adm. Arthur W. Radford left Pearl

Harbor on 10 November in the company of the Carrier Interceptor Group. The carriers sailed a course parallel to and 350 miles northwest of the landing force until they were 800 miles from the target. There the carriers struck out in different directions to their assigned stations and the landing force turned south to meet Rear Adm. Harry W. Hill's Southern Attack Force. On 18 November, Hill and Turner rendezvoused at a point about 600 miles southeast of Makin and traveled toward the objective along a parallel course.

The elements constituting the Southern Attack Force, scheduled for the Tarawa invasion, came from the South Pacific. From New Zealand the 2d Marine Division went to Efate in the New Hebrides for rehearsal and from there sailed in attack transports for the Gilberts on 13 November. Next day it was joined by the Southern Carrier Group from Espiritu Santo, and a few days later by a small force of light cruisers from Bougainville.[12] Just south of Funafuti, the carriers parted company with Admiral Hill who headed for his rendezvous with Turner. The Relief Carrier Group under Admiral Sherman, which had supported Halsey in the Bougainville operation, fueled at Espiritu Santo and sailed north to Nauru, hit it on the 19th, then provided cover for the Makin and Tarawa garrisons en route to the objective. From Wallis Island, west of Samoa, came the garrison force for Apamama, and from Samoa came the LST's carrying the fifty new amphtracs for the 2d Marine Division.

Late on the night of 19 November, the two attack forces and the vast armada of warships, cargo vessels, transports, and other craft were in their assigned positions. During the early morning hours of the 20th, as the battleships and heavy cruisers moved into position for the opening bombardment and the carriers sent their planes off the flight decks to bomb and strafe the beaches, the transports took their assigned stations and prepared to debark the troops. The invasion of the Gilberts had begun; four months of planning and preparation were now to reach fruition.

The Japanese had offered comparatively little opposition to the approach of these various task forces from all parts of the Pacific. Some land-based planes had come out to strike at one of the LST groups, but without much effect. The *Combined Fleet* at Truk had not stirred. Twice before, once in September and again in October, when a fast carrier force under Rear Adm. Charles A. Pownall had struck the Gilberts and Wake, Admiral Koga had sallied forth to give battle. Both times he had failed to find Pownall's elusive carriers and had returned to Truk empty-handed. Apparently convinced by the Bougainville landing that the Americans would not strike now in the Central Pacific, Koga had sent 173 of his carrier-based planes and a strong force of heavy cruisers to Rabaul at the beginning of November. The result was disastrous. Without his cruisers and the carrier planes, Koga dared not venture out of Truk. Helpless, he had to stand by idly as the huge American fleet converged on the Gilberts. The one chance he had sought for a showdown with the Pacific Fleet was lost.

Though the main striking force of the *Combined Fleet* was immobilized at this critical juncture, the Japanese were by no means defenseless. Despite the attacks of Admiral Pownall's fast carrier force, Japanese aircraft in the Gilberts-Marshalls area were still capable of inflicting damage. And at Truk were submarines that could strike heavy blows if they could get within reach of the Allied

[12] For an account of the operations at Bougainville, beginning 1 November, see below, pp. 575–78.

LVT's AT TARAWA

invasion force. These Koga sent out as soon as he heard of the landing and one of them sank the escort carrier *Liscome Bay* on 24 November. Koga also sent ground and air reinforcements to Tarawa, but they got only as far as the southern Marshalls. By that time Tarawa had fallen and the troops were used to bolster the defenses of Kwajalein instead.

The defense plans of the local garrisons at Makin and Tarawa were little affected by events at Rabaul and Truk. Makin had the smaller force, about 700 men, and most of these were labor and service troops. Effective combat strength was probably no more than 300. Light defenses had been constructed along the lagoon side, and across the island were two tank barrier systems surrounded by ditches, pill boxes, and wire entangle-

ments. Gun emplacements and rifle pits, so placed as to provide mutual support and interlocking fields of fire, guarded the approaches to these barriers and offered additional protection against assault from the ocean side of the island. These were not formidable defenses, nor was the defending force large, but so narrow and restricted was the area of operations that the greatly outnumbered Japanese fully expected to give a good account of themselves.

On Tarawa, the defenders were not only more numerous but enjoyed also the advantage of strong fortifications. The total force numbered about 4,800 men, more than half of them effective combat troops. The island itself had been converted into a fortress, ringed with beach defenses whose 13-mm. and 7.7-mm. machine guns were carefully positioned to drive off the invaders. On the fringing reef were log and concrete obstacles to channelize approaching boats. In the water and on the beaches were additional obstacles and double-apron low-wire fences along which the defenders could lay down a barrage of antiboat fire calculated to halt the invaders before they could step ashore. Inland from the beaches were bombproof shelters of concrete and coconut logs for weapons and men alike, connected by a system of ditches and tunnels. A large array of guns ranging in size from 8-inch to 13-mm., and seven tanks fringed the armament of the Japanese defenders. Of all the beaches assaulted in World War II, only Iwo Jima was more strongly fortified or more stubbornly defended than Tarawa.

The capture of Makin took three days and cost more in naval casualties than in ground troops. Despite its great superiority in men and weapons, the 27th Division had considerable difficulty overcoming the 700 defenders. Combat casualties numbered 218 (66 killed and 152 wounded), as compared to an estimated 395 Japanese killed in action, a ratio of 6 to 1. When the American losses incurred in the sinking of the *Liscome Bay* are added to this total, however, the balance is on the other side. With the 642 men that went down with the carrier, American casualties exceeded the strength of the entire Japanese garrison on Makin.

If Makin had been, as one naval historian wrote, "a pushover for the ground troops," [13] Tarawa was a grim and deadly struggle, probably the toughest fight thus far in Marine Corps history. In the same length of time it took the 27th Division to capture Makin, the 2d Marine Division stormed the heavily fortified beaches of Tarawa, reduced its cement and steel emplacements one by one, and killed virtually every Japanese soldier on the island. The cost was terrific—3,301 casualties, of whom over 1,000 were killed in action or died later of wounds.

Was the island worth the price? General Holland Smith, Marine commander of the expeditionary force, thought not. Tarawa, he declared later, had "no particular strategic importance" and should have been bypassed and neutralized from bases to the east and south. Its capture, he charged, was "a terrible waste of life and effort." [14] Few of General Smith's colleagues agreed with this judgment. Strategically and tactically, they held, the campaign in the Gilberts proved of great value. Without advance bases in the Gilberts, operations against the Marshalls would have been enormously difficult and infinitely more complicated and hazardous. Moreover, the lessons learned at Tarawa—one officer compiled a list of one hundred mistakes made during the operation—were of inestimable value in subsequent assaults. The most important of these was the conclusive proof it offered, as Admiral Hill wrote, that naval task forces "had the power to move into an area, obtain complete naval air control of that area, and remain there with acceptable losses throughout the entire assault and preliminary consolidation phases." [15] Had this fact not been demonstrated—and up to this time it had not been—the entire Central Pacific

---

[13] Morison, *Aleutians, Gilberts and Marshalls,* p. 120.

[14] Smith, *Coral and Brass,* pp. 111–12; Crowl and Love, *Seizure of the Gilberts and Marshalls,* p. 157.
[15] Ltr, Adm Hill to Maj Gen Harry J. Malony, Chief, Mil Hist, 14 Feb 49, OCMH.

LANDING CRAFT MOVING IN ON BUTARITARI ISLAND. *Note LST's standing offshore at top, and reef side of island at bottom.*

offensive might well have ended before it began.

CARTWHEEL Completed

General MacArthur and Admiral Halsey, meanwhile, had been pushing forward in New Guinea and the Solomons. Having taken Lae and Finschhafen, and begun his drive up the Markham Valley, MacArthur had still to gain control of the Vitiaz and Dampier Straits before he could breach the Bismarcks barrier. On his part, Halsey was to move into the northern Solomons from where he would be in position to unite with MacArthur in the final phase of CARTWHEEL.

Before the New Georgia fighting was over, South Pacific aircraft had begun an intensified campaign to neutralize Japanese airfields in southern Bougainville and in the Shortlands while ground and naval forces prepared for the invasion to follow.[16] By 1 November, D-day for the landing, all fields in the Bougainville area had been rendered inoperational.

The neutralization of Japanese air power in the northern Solomons coincided with the arrival of strong air reinforcements at Rabaul, just at the moment when the Bougainville invasion was getting under way. To the 200 aircraft based at Rabaul were added, at the beginning of November, 173 carrier planes from the *Combined Fleet* at Truk. This move was part of a Japanese plan known as Operation *RO*, which had as its purpose the delay of the Allied drive toward the "absolute national defense line." Originator of the plan was Admiral Koga, Yamamoto's successor, who hoped that by concentrating all available naval, land, and carrier air forces at Rabaul he could cut the Allied line of communications and thus retain control of the straits between New Guinea and New Britain. It was admittedly a risky scheme, for without their aircraft the carriers were useless and without the carriers the *Combined Fleet* was helpless to stop the U.S. Pacific Fleet. But Koga, having satisfied himself that Nimitz did not intend to move into the Marshalls, took the risk. He had failed in his attempt to catch the U.S. Fleet in the Wake area and now was determined to catch it in the northern Solomons. It was a bad gamble and Koga lost not only his planes but also his chance to stop the Central Pacific offensive in its tracks. Here, at the very outset, was demonstrated in striking fashion the advantages of the twin drive through the South–Southwest Pacific and Central Pacific Areas.

The Bougainville campaign had begun on 27 October with the seizure of the Treasury Islands by New Zealand and American troops.[17] That same day marines landed on Choiseul to the southwest in a feint toward the east coast of Bougainville. The real invasion, when it came on 1 November, was actually made on the west coast, midway up the island, at Empress Augusta Bay, and it caught the Japanese by surprise. Despite

---

[16] For an account of the Bougainville campaign, see Miller, *CARTWHEEL*, ch. XII; Maj. John N. Rentz, USMC, *Bougainville and the Northern Solomons*, Historical Section, Headquarters, U.S. Marine Corps (Washington, 1948); Morison, *Breaking the Bismarcks Barrier*, chs. XVI–XXI; Craven and Cate, *AAF IV*, ch. VIII.

[17] For an account of New Zealand operations in the Treasuries as well as on Vella Lavella and Green Island, see Oliver A. Gillespie, *The Pacific*, "Official History of New Zealand in the Second World War, 1939–45" (Wellington, New Zealand: War History Branch, Department of Internal Affairs, 1952), ch. V.

local opposition from a small well dug-in garrison at Cape Torokina, between the two southernmost landing beaches, the 3d Marine Division made good its landing and by the end of D-day held a narrow beachhead 4,000 yards in length along the shore of Empress Augusta Bay.

Japanese air and naval reaction to the Allied invasion of Bougainville was prompt and violent. On 1 November, after a vain effort to send in ground reinforcements to destroy the American force in Empress Augusta Bay, a naval task force (2 heavy and 2 light cruisers accompanied by 6 destroyers) under Vice Adm. Sentaro Omori was sent down from Rabaul. It was intercepted by Rear Adm. Aaron S. Merrill's Task Force 39 off Cape Torokina and turned back after a battle that lasted most of the night.[18] A strong attempt by the Japanese next morning, 2 November, to knock out Merrill's cruisers from the air and thus isolate the beachhead was foiled by planes from New Georgia. Further attempts were discouraged by General Kenney's aircraft from the Southwest Pacific, whose raids against Rabaul kept the Japanese busy defending their own base. Here again the co-ordinated action of adjacent Allied theaters paid large dividends.

Meanwhile, Admiral Koga had assembled at Truk a formidable force of 7 heavy cruisers, 1 light cruiser, 4 destroyers, and about a half dozen auxiliary vessels. These he sent south under Vice Adm. Takeo Kurita to Rabaul, where they arrived safely in the early morning of 5 November. The threat presented by this force was a serious one. With Merrill's cruisers temporarily out of action after four engagements in two days, Halsey did not have a single heavy cruiser to send against Kurita. This was, he later wrote, "the most desperate emergency that confronted me in my entire term as COMSOPAC." [19] But south of Guadalcanal, refueling after 1–2 November strikes in the northern Solomons, was Rear Adm. Frederick C. Sherman's fast carrier force (*Saratoga* and *Princeton*), lent by Nimitz for the invasion. Another carrier force had been promised by Nimitz, who was himself in the midst of last-minute preparations for the Gilberts, but it would not arrive until the 7th.

Though reluctant to use the fast carriers against a strong base like Rabaul and fearful of the damage or loss he might incur in such a mission, Admiral Halsey could see no other way of meeting the threat posed by Kurita's force. Having made up his mind, he acted with characteristic dispatch. Sherman was to proceed immediately toward Rabaul, and, on the morning of the 5th, launch an all-out attack on Kurita's ships from a point about 230 miles to the southeast. Aircraft from New Georgia would provide cover during the approach and retirement, and MacArthur's aircraft would follow up with an attack on Rabaul that afternoon.

Halsey's boldness paid off handsomely. The weather was perfect and the plan was carried out without a hitch. At the cost of ten planes and fifteen men, Sherman inflicted such heavy damage on the

---

[18] Task Force 39 consisted of Cruiser Division 12 (four cruisers) and Destroyer Divisions 45 and 46 (four destroyers each).

[19] Halsey and Bryan, *Admiral Halsey's Story*, pp. 180–81.

enemy fleet that Koga pulled it back to Truk late on the afternoon of the 5th. Kenney's follow-up with 27 B–24's and 58 P–38's met little opposition, for the Japanese were out looking for Sherman and the Southwest Pacific aircraft were able to bomb installations and docks at Rabaul without serious opposition.

Japanese air power at Rabaul fared no better than the surface forces but accomplished a good deal more destruction. Ever since the landing at Torokina, Japanese aircraft had hammered away at targets in the Bougainville area and had fought an incessant battle with Allied aircraft from New Georgia. In a sense, this was the real battle of Bougainville, for had the Japanese won control of the air they could have cut off the beachhead area and brought in sufficient troops to drive out the marines. Thus, the Allied command exerted every effort to maintain local air superiority and to keep open the line of communication. South Pacific aircraft flew countless missions over Bougainville and struck repeatedly at the enemy's air bases. In one day, there were more than 700 takeoffs and landings at the Munda field alone. The contribution of General Kenney's air force was to bomb the fields at Rabaul, which he did at every opportunity.

The arrival of the additional carrier group (*Essex, Bunker Hill,* and *Independence*) from the Central Pacific on 7 November offered Halsey a golden opportunity.[20] Encouraged by Sherman's success, he sent both carrier groups to Rabaul on a double strike. Sherman delivered his attack on the morning of the 11th, damaged some ships, and escaped without detection. The second force, led by Rear Adm. Alfred L. Montgomery, launched its strike simultaneously, but had to fight its way out. It would have been better for the Japanese, perhaps, had they not found Montgomery, for they lost thirty-five planes in a vain effort to hit the carriers.

If Admiral Koga had needed any further proof that Operation *RO* was a failure, the events of 11 November must have convinced him. The next day he ordered the remaining 120 carrier planes back to Truk before they should all be lost. Thus, on the eve of the Gilberts invasion, the one force that the Allies feared most, the *Combined Fleet,* was helpless to interfere. It would be months before the carrier losses could be replaced and the cruisers damaged at Rabaul put in action again. The failure of the *RO* operation also marked the end of Rabaul's importance as the base for Japanese operations against any Allied advance in the Solomons and New Guinea. With land-based aircraft at close striking range, the Allies were able to neutralize the once great Japanese bastion and bypass it without danger. For the Japanese, the large garrison and formidable defenses at Rabaul ultimately proved a liability, rather than an asset.

Air and naval victory assured the success of the Bougainville invasion and greatly eased the task of the ground forces. Reinforcements and supplies began to come in on 8 November and before the end of the month the Army's 37th Division was sharing the beachhead with the 3d Marine Division. Air raids were still frequent, and the Japanese had

---

[20] Like Sherman's group, this group of carriers was scheduled for the invasion of the Gilberts and had come to the South Pacific to escort Admiral Hill's Southern Attack Force (2d Marine Division) to the target. See below, pp. 589–90.

ADMIRAL HALSEY, MAJ. GEN. ROBERT S. BEIGHTLER, AND MAJ. GEN. ROY S.
GEIGER *(seated, left to right) discuss a map problem at the 37th Division command post on
Bougainville.*

succeeded in putting ashore first a regiment and then other troops that made
the going hard for the Americans. By 15
December, when General Griswold's
XIV Corps took over from I Marine
Amphibious Corps, there were 44,000
men within a defended semicircular
perimeter about 23,000 yards in length.
As in New Georgia, Halsey made General Harmon his deputy for ground
operations on Bougainville, and by the
end of the month the American Division
had begun to replace the 3d Marine
Division. Bougainville was now virtually
an Army show.

The blow that finally broke the Japanese hold on the Vitiaz-Dampier bottle-
neck and gave the Allies clear passage
through the Bismarck barrier was delivered by MacArthur's forces at the turn
of the year.[21] It was a one-two punch,
a right at Cape Gloucester in western
New Britain to gain control of Dampier
Strait and a left at Saidor on the north
shore of the Huon Peninsula. Both operations had been on the books for some
time, but the New Britain plan was the
older one and dated from the days when
Rabaul was the great objective. The
Saidor plan was of more recent vintage,

---

[21] This account of the New Britain and Saidor
operations is based on Miller, *CARTWHEEL*, pp.
272–306; Morison, *Breaking the Bismarcks Barrier*,
pp. 369–91; Craven and Cate, *AAF IV*, pp. 328–57;
Lt. Col. Frank O. Hough and Maj. John A. Crown,
USMC, *The Campaign on New Britain*, Historical Branch, Headquarters, U.S. Marine Corps
(Washington, 1953).

GENERAL GRISWOLD AND GENERAL HARMON *(center) being briefed on the tactical situation by 3d Marine Division officers.*

having been proposed in September by General Chamberlin, and was related to the Australian drive up the New Guinea coast from Finschhafen to Sio. The Cape Gloucester operation looked east, the Saidor west and north, but both formed part of the single plan to breach the Bismarcks barrier and both were conducted by General Krueger's ALAMO Force.

Planning for New Britain had begun in August but it was not until 22 September that MacArthur issued the directive for the operation to General Krueger. Under this directive, General Krueger's ALAMO Force (U.S. Sixth Army) was required to conduct extensive airborne and amphibious operations designed to gain control of two large offshore islands

(Rooke and Long) and virtually half of New Britain. D-day was optimistically set for 20 November, and General Krueger was directed at the same time to prepare for the capture of Rabaul in co-operation with South Pacific forces.

The extensive operations envisaged in this plan, combined with the rapid progress of the advance in New Guinea and the fact that the Joint Chiefs of Staff had already decided to bypass Rabaul, produced a thorough review of the New Britain project. General Kenney thought the operation entirely unnecessary, and told MacArthur that a field at Cape Gloucester would not provide any more air support than could be provided with the bases already in Allied hands. An airfield at Saidor, he con-

SUPPLY ROAD ON BOUGAINVILLE *built by Army engineers. Note how coconut logs are used to support steep bank and underside of road.*

ceded, might be necessary.[22] General Chamberlin, MacArthur's G–3, did not dispute this point, but observed that possession of western New Britain would strengthen the Allied position in the area and facilitate operations in New Ireland and the Admiralties. Admirals Carpender and Barbey also favored control of both sides of the Vitiaz-Dampier barrier; it was the seizure of Gasmata on the southwest shore of New Britain that bothered them. That operation, they felt, would take their ships too close to Japanese bases at Rabaul.

The result of this review was a revised plan, issued on 10 November, which called only for the occupation of Cape Gloucester, the adjacent islands, and "minimum portions" of western New Britain. But now the naval commanders were dissatisfied. They apparently wanted a PT base on the south shore and none was provided for in the plan. Obligingly, MacArthur authorized the seizure of Arawe, believed to be weakly defended, as an additional objective on General Kenney's assurance that air support could be provided.[23]

Fixing a target date for the invasion proved no easy matter and was compli-

---

[22] Miller, *CARTWHEEL*, p. 273; Kenny, *General Kenny Reports*, pp. 326–27. Kenny's objections are outlined in his letter to MacArthur, 10 Oct 43, in GHQ SWPA G–3 Jnl, 11 Oct 43.

[23] There is some dispute about the reasons for going into Arawe. See Miller, *CARTWHEEL*, p. 274 n.

cated by airfield construction schedules, tide, weather, and the phases of the moon. The first date selected, 20 November, was quickly discarded, and on Chamberlin's recommendation 4 December was chosen. Krueger objected and asked for either more time or more ships. Since the ships were not available, he got more time, and the dates finally selected were 15 December for Arawe and 26 December for Cape Gloucester. The same ships that were used for Arawe would carry the invasion force to Cape Gloucester.

The assault units for the New Britain operation were American and were assigned to ALAMO Force. (The New Guinea Force, it will be remembered, was composed almost entirely of Australian units.) Arawe was to be taken by a force built around the 112th Cavalry Regiment and the 148th Field Artillery Battalion under Brig. Gen. Julian W. Cunningham. The assault force for the Cape Gloucester landing was a much stronger one, consisting of the 1st Marine Division, veteran of the Guadalcanal Campaign, the 12th Marine Defense Battalion, the Army's 2d Engineer Special Brigade, and miscellaneous service and supporting units. In ALAMO Force reserve was the 32d Division, which had fought at Buna.

Planning for the Saidor operation was less complicated, partly because the problems presented were simpler and partly because the operation was decided upon at the last moment. The advantages of an Allied base at Saidor derived from its location. Not only would it give MacArthur control of Vitiaz Strait and virtually the entire north shore of the Huon Peninsula, but it would also provide a base for further advances along the New

Guinea coast. Bogadjim was only about fifty miles away; Madang another twenty. Moreover, the bulk of Adachi's *18th Army* was divided between Madang and Sio, toward which the Australians were already driving. The capture of Saidor would place Allied forces between the two main Japanese concentrations.

Though an outline plan for the Saidor invasion was ready by 11 December, it was not until the 17th, two days after the Arawe landing, that MacArthur ordered Krueger to proceed with the operation, in co-operation with Australian operations in the Ramu Valley and against Sio. The assault force was to come from the 32d Division, ALAMO Force reserve for western New Britain. D-day was tentatively set for 2 January 1944, with the understanding that the exact date of the landing would depend upon the situation at Cape Gloucester. This proviso was necessary because there were not enough landing craft in the theater for both operations and Krueger would have to use the same vessels for both landings.

General Krueger, a cautious and conservative commander, was apprehensive about the Saidor landing. The schedule was admittedly a tight one. Moreover, the ALAMO Force would be involved in three separate operations simultaneously at a time when New Guinea Force was engaged on two separate fronts. There was little margin for error or for the unexpected, and the job of keeping these forces supplied would be difficult. For these reasons, Krueger urged postponement of the Saidor operation, but to no avail. The Allied advance had gained a momentum MacArthur was unwilling to lose. He therefore ordered Krueger to proceed as planned with the assurance that supplies would be forthcoming. On

30 December, the target date 2 January was confirmed.[24]

By the time all arrangements for the Saidor invasion had been completed, ALAMO Force had established itself firmly in western New Britain. At Arawe, the 112th Cavalry had landed on 15 December and secured a beachhead. Opposition was light initially, but the Japanese quickly ordered reinforcements to Arawe and by the end of the year the Americans faced the prospect of an arduous fight to clear the area. Two weeks were required for that job, but it was not until mid-February that the Japanese finally withdrew. Once won, the area proved of little value to the Allies and no PT base was ever built there.

At Cape Gloucester the Japanese offered little resistance to the assault forces when they came ashore on 26 December. Only when the Marine troops reached the airdrome area west of the landing beaches did they meet any opposition, and that was quickly overcome. Driving rain, jungle undergrowth, and swamp presented more difficulties than did the enemy. The most serious fighting came after the capture of the airfield on 30 December, but by the middle of January it was over and the marines spent the rest of their time in the Cape Gloucester area in mopping up. How heavy had been the fighting is indicated by the casualties in the 1st Marine Division and attached units: 328 killed and 844 wounded in action. By the end of February the Japanese had

---

[24] General Krueger did not recall that he had urged postponent of the Saidor operation. Ltr, Krueger to Col Hoover, 22 Jul 59, OCMH. That he did so is indicated by Miller, *CARTWHEEL*, page 299, citing Krueger's letter to MacArthur on 28 December 1943, sub: Deferment of MICHAELMAS [Saidor], GHQ SWPA G–3 Jnl, 29 Dec 43.

withdrawn to Rabaul and left the Americans in complete possession. Ultimately two strips were built, but they were no longer needed. Like Arawe, Cape Gloucester had little strategic significance, for its conquest came at a time when the war was moving rapidly past the Bismarck barrier. Yet both operations did serve the purpose of providing additional security on the right flank of the drive up the New Guinea coast.

The Saidor invasion force spent New Year's Eve and the first day of the year aboard landing craft. On the 2d, the troops were put ashore with an efficiency and dispatch that bore witness to the value of training and experience over the past few months. There was virtually no opposition and the only untoward incident came early the next morning when the Americans fired on their own ships in the dim light of dawn. Fortunately there was no damage. The few Japanese in the vicinity of Saidor were quickly disposed of, after which engineers and service troops moved in to clear the way for the construction of an airfield, roads, docks, and other installations. On 10 February, when the Australians at Sio had advanced up the coast to make contact with the Saidor Force, General Krueger announced that the campaign was over. It took a month more for the Australians in the Ramu Valley to complete their drive and on 21 March, elements of the 7th Australian and 32d U.S. divisions finally met. On 13 April, Bogadjim fell and all of the Huon Peninsula with the Markham and Ramu Valleys lay in Allied hands.

The end of Japanese resistance at Bogadjim marked the completion of CARTWHEEL. In a period of ten months, two more than MacArthur had originally estimated it would take, forces of the South and Southwest Pacific had advanced up the coast of New Guinea and through the Solomons in successive stages in a series of mutually supporting and co-ordinated operations and now stood in position to breach the Bismarck barrier. Despite the unique command arrangements by which MacArthur exercised strategic control and Halsey the command of South Pacific forces, co-operation between the two theaters had been excellent. Not once had there been any disagreement that had not been settled quickly with good will on both sides, or any failure to co-ordinate operations in the two theaters and to provide support when it was needed.

The original design of CARTWHEEL had been to place the forces of the South and Southwest Pacific in position to converge on Rabaul. But that objective had been changed by the Joint Chiefs of Staff while operations were in progress. Rabaul was not to be captured but neutralized. Thus, as the forces of the South and Southwest Pacific came within fighter range of Rabaul, they initiated an intensive air campaign against the Japanese base and by February 1944 had rendered it virtually impotent. Thereafter, as MacArthur resumed his advance through the Bismarck Archipelago and thence westward along the New Guinea coast toward the Philippines, Allied aircraft kept a careful watch on Rabaul. Though never reduced, the Japanese garrison there maintained a precarious existence until the war's end brought relief.

CHAPTER XXIX

Prospects for the Future

In battle there are not more than two methods of attack—the direct and indirect; yet these two in combination give rise to an endless series of maneuvers. . . . Who can exhaust the possibilities of their combination?

SUN TZU

By the end of the year 1943, the first aim of Allied strategy, set in July 1942, had been achieved. In comparison to the enormous territorial gains of the Japanese during the opening months of the war, the accomplishments of the Allies did not seem impressive. But appearances were deceptive. Every Allied advance had been bitterly contested and the way from Buna and Guadalcanal to the Bismarck barrier, from Hawaii and Midway, to Tarawa, was littered with the remnants of Japanese air and naval power. The Japanese were far from defeated; their military machine was still powerful and capable of inflicting great damage. But they could never again attain their earlier material superiority. Allied factories and shipyards were going at full speed, producing ships, planes, munitions, and supplies at a rate the Japanese could never hope to match.

But the Allies had paid dearly in human lives for their success. American battle casualties alone, not including those of the Allies in the Pacific—the Dutch, the Australians, the British, and the Filipinos—during the first two years of the war totaled over 75,000. (*Tables 11 and 12*) More than half of these casualties were suffered by the Army; the Navy lost about 18,000 men and the Marine Corps over 12,000. Total deaths during this period were 35,888—20,022 for the Army; 11,793, Navy; and 4,073 marines. The largest single loss for the Army came during the Philippine Campaign in 1942; for the Navy and marines, during the six months of the Guadalcanal Campaign. One hopeful sign for the future was the decline in casualties for 1943 as compared to the first year of the war; another was the remarkable number of wounded men returned to duty —a tribute to the medical aid men and advances in military medicine.

The Allies had come a long way since Pearl Harbor, not in distance, but in power, and confidence in the use of that power. The distances to be traversed before they came within striking range of the enemy's inner zone—Japan, Korea, Formosa, Sakhalin, Manchuria, and north China—were great, but the Allies had the means now and the experience to move more rapidly and with longer strides. The accomplishments of 1942 and 1943 had been notable; those for

TABLE 11—ARMY (AND AAF) BATTLE CASUALTIES, PACIFIC AREAS
DECEMBER 1941–DECEMBER 1943

Date	Total Battle Casualties	Total Deaths	Killed in Action	Total Wounded	Died of Wounds	Total Captured	Died POW	Missing in Action
December 1941 to December 1943	47,213	20,022	6,429	10,337	497	27,104	16,996	3,343
1941, December	1,078	489	464	558	20	23	5	33
1942	35,188	15,619	3,033	2,588	153	26,964	16,957	2,603
January	810	507	478	282	23	48	5	2
February	993	385	290	172	10	524	83	7
March	205	133	116	65	3	13	4	11
April	1,146	1,040	377	99	20	636	609	34
May	28,648	11,995	536	160	38	25,697	10,225	2,255
June	75	57	49	13	1	5	3	8
July	127	106	65	18	4	15	9	29
August	141	101	44	23	2	5	5	69
September	144	90	61	36	3	3	3	44
October	145	98	68	50	4	3	3	24
November	1,024	453	574	581	17	0	0	69
December	1,730	654	575	1,089	28	15	8	51
1943	10,947	3,914	2,932	7,191	324	117	34	707
January	1,782	667	555	1,152	53	15	6	60
February	276	141	62	121	7	11	3	82
March	203	98	72	106	5	4	0	21
April	200	92	79	110	7	5	3	6
May	204	98	45	93	4	17	2	49
June	305	181	129	119	5	8	0	49
July	3,620	990	793	2,735	128	4	3	88
August	1,561	440	328	1,176	60	5	2	52
September	740	242	182	496	19	16	2	46
October	377	199	151	160	5	12	2	54
November	1,120	474	380	651	10	7	4	82
December	559	292	156	272	21	13	7	118

Source: Dept of Army, Battle Casualties and Nonbattle Casualties in World War II, Final Report, pp. 42–43.

1944 and 1945 promised to be even more so. (Map 14)

The Pattern of Pacific Warfare

As the war in the Pacific moved into its third year, the pattern of future operations could be clearly discerned. There would be no more frontal attacks against a strongly entrenched enemy if they could be avoided, no inch-by-inch trek through the jungle or island-by-island advance across an ocean dotted with myriad atoll and island groups. Instead,

TABLE 12—BATTLE CASUALTIES, NAVY AND MARINE CORPS
DECEMBER 1941–DECEMBER 1943

Battles or Campaigns	Service	Total	Returned to Duty	Killed in Action	Wounded, Died Later	Died POW	Discharged
Total, All Battles	Navy	18,130	5,802	10,874	183	736	535
	Marine	12,333	7,226	3,390	223	460	1,034
	Total	30,463	13,028	14,264	406	1,196	1,569
Pearl Harbor 7 Dec 41	Navy	2,410	606	1,744	17	2	41
	Marine	144	37	99	2	—	6
	Total	2,554	643	1,843	19	2	47
Philippines 7 Dec 41–6 May 42	Navy	1,043	71	337	2	630	3
	Marine	542	39	89	—	413	1
	Total	1,585	110	426	2	1,043	4
Netherlands East Indies Dec 41–Mar 42	Navy	1,908	139	1,656	12	94	7
	Marine	43	—	36	—	7	—
	Total	1,951	139	1,692	12	101	7
Early Raids Dec 41–July 42	Navy	74	28	40	—	4	2
	Marine	2	1	—	1	—	—
	Total	76	29	40	1	4	2
Coral Sea May 42	Navy	674	119	537	6	1	11
	Marine	31	10	19	2	—	—
	Total	705	129	556	8	1	11
Midway June 42	Navy	490	165	301	8	1	15
	Marine	57	16	39	1	—	1
	Total	547	181	340	9	1	16
Guadalcanal 7 Aug 42–Jan 43	Navy	6,664	2,393	3,967	69	4	231
	Marine	4,032	2,511	1,050	82	12	377
	Total	10,696	4,904	5,017	151	16	608
Central & Northern Solomons Feb 43–Dec 43	Navy	3,149	1,673	1,246	56	—	174
	Marine	2,932	1,780	781	68	26	277
	Total	6,081	3,453	2,027	124	26	451

TABLE 12—BATTLE CASUALTIES, NAVY AND MARINE CORPS
DECEMBER 1941–DECEMBER 1943—*Continued*

Battles or Campaigns	Service	Total	Returned to Duty	Killed in Action	Wounded, Died Later	Died POW	Discharged
Tarawa	Navy	1,043	293	724	3	—	23
Nov 43	Marine	3,076	1,882	950	34	—	210
	Total	4,119	2,175	1,674	37	—	233
New Britain	Navy	382	208	145	9	—	20
Dec 43	Marine	1,421	904	325	33	2	157
	Total	1,803	1,112	470	42	2	177
Aleutians Area	Navy	293	107	177	1	—	8
	Marine	53	46	2	—	—	5
	Total	346	153	179	1	—	13

Source: *Hist of Medical Dept, U.S. Navy in World War II,* III, pp. 170–74.

Allied forces would advance by "kangaroo leaps" limited only by the range of land-based air cover or carrier-borne aircraft, seeking always to deceive and surprise the enemy by striking first in the Central Pacific and then in the Southwest. By following two paths, the Allies would keep the Japanese off balance and divided. Trying to defend everywhere at once, the Japanese would be unable to concentrate anywhere, their bypassed garrisons doomed to "wither on the vine," isolated and strategically impotent.

In the South–Southwest Pacific, the central fact controlling operations was the range of fighter aircraft. This fact provides the clue to the selection of objectives, to the timetable, and to the limits of the advance. Aircraft carriers could have overcome this limitation, but MacArthur had none and Halsey had them only briefly. And even if they had been available it is doubtful that they would have been used in mid-1943, for current naval doctrine did not encourage their employment in an area and against objectives such as those presented in the South and Southwest Pacific.

Atoll warfare in the Central Pacific presented problems distinctly different from those encountered in the Solomons and New Guinea. The distances to be covered were greater and the objectives were tiny islands surrounded by fringing coral reefs. The assault forces would therefore have to venture far beyond the limits of land-based air cover, exposed to enemy air and surface attack, to seize strongly defended islands too small for maneuver or for mass assault. Such operations would have to be conducted swiftly, and would require air and naval forces strong enough to establish air and naval supremacy and even take on the main body of the Japanese fleet if need be. Also, because of the distance from

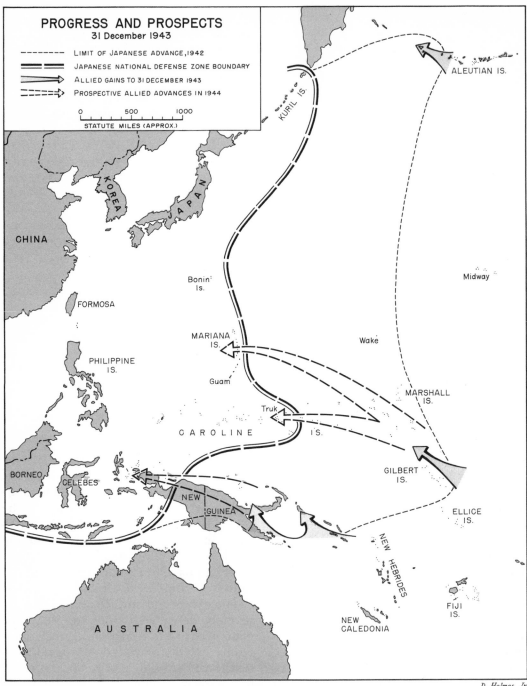

PROGRESS AND PROSPECTS
31 December 1943

--------- LIMIT OF JAPANESE ADVANCE, 1942
━━━ ━━━ JAPANESE NATIONAL DEFENSE ZONE BOUNDARY
━━━▶ ALLIED GAINS TO 31 DECEMBER 1943
━ ━ ━▷ PROSPECTIVE ALLIED ADVANCES IN 1944

0   500   1000
STATUTE MILES (APPROX.)

ALEUTIAN IS.

KURIL IS.

KOREA

JAPAN

CHINA

Bonin
Is.

Midway

FORMOSA

MARIANA
IS.

Wake

PHILIPPINE
IS.

Guam

MARSHALL
IS.

Truk

CAROLINE   IS.

BORNEO

CELEBES

NEW

GUINEA

GILBERT
IS.

ELLICE
IS.

NEW
HEBRIDES

AUSTRALIA

FIJI
IS.

NEW
CALEDONIA

D. Holmes, Jr.

MAP 14

rear bases and the duration of the operation these forces would have to be logistically self-contained, that is, they would have to carry with them all the supplies and facilities necessary to support the assault troops during and after the landing, maintain and service the fleet, garrison the island after it was taken, and, finally, convert it into an Allied base in time for the next operation.

Whether operations conducted under the conditions existing in the Central Pacific could be carried out at all had still been a question in mid-1943. Experience in the Solomons and New Guinea was valuable but not always relevant to the problems faced by Admiral Nimitz. Not once had MacArthur or Halsey ventured far from land-based air support and never did they have to face the possibility of engaging the main strength of the *Combined Fleet*. In their progressive step-by-step advance, they had always had bases near the front where they could keep reserves of manpower and supplies. If necessary, they could fall back on these bases. But the Gilberts lay more than 700 miles from the nearest Allied airfield in the Ellice Islands and more than 2,000 from the main base in Hawaii. The geography of the two areas differed also, and this fact had a marked effect on the nature of operations in each. The South–Southwest Pacific Areas consisted of seas and straits enclosed by New Guinea, itself a subcontinent, and the numerous islands of the Solomons chain and the Bismarck Archipelago. The Central Pacific Area, by contrast, consisted largely of open ocean, dotted with tiny islands. It was a region particularly suited for naval operations on a grand scale.

By the end of 1943, the problems posed by operations in the Central Pacific had been largely solved. As in the Solomons and New Guinea, the concerted and coordinated action of ground, sea, and air forces under a single commander was the essential ingredient of success in the Central Pacific Area. But though the ingredients were the same, the proportions were different. The decisive combat element in the Central Pacific was the large aircraft carrier. The great lesson of the Gilbert Islands campaign in the fall of 1943 was the demonstration that aircraft carriers, in groups but not singly, could venture deep into the territory of the enemy, within range of his air and naval forces without land-based air cover. This fact alone made possible the great forward strides that marked the progress of the war in the Central Pacific.

The second decisive element of Central Pacific warfare was the floating supply base. Consisting of oilers, tenders, repair and salvage ships, tugs, hospital ships, and a large variety of miscellaneous vessels, the mobile base was capable of supporting and defending itself while providing the supplies and services required for extended operations far from the home base. In short, it was the logistical companion of the fast carrier force, the "seven-league boots" of the Pacific Fleet. Clear also in the pattern of Pacific warfare was the large role assigned to naval gunfire and close air support before and during the landing, and to the amphibious tractor, the indispensable vehicle for carrying troops across fringing coral reefs and strongly defended beaches.

The technique of amphibious operations that emerged from experience in the Pacific in 1942 and 1943 remained virtually unchanged throughout the rest of the year. First, the objective was isolated and its defenses softened by air and naval operations in which the fast carrier forces played a major role when the objective was beyond range of land-based fighter aircraft. Simultaneously, other targets were attacked to deceive the enemy as to the true objective. The approach of the assault force signaled the opening of an air-naval bombardment of the area in which the landing was to be made. Then the landing force moved from the ship to shore under cover of air and naval gunfire. The landing itself was made in waves or echelons, with rocket-firing landing craft in the lead, followed by amphibian tanks carrying the assault troops directly from the water on to the beaches and then inland. Finally, came the landing craft with more infantry, artillery, and supporting troops. Whenever possible, small neighboring islands were occupied in advance to provide sites for the emplacement of artillery, as in New Georgia. Supplies followed the assault troops closely and, while the beachhead area was staked out, the advance inland proceeded without pause, air and naval forces providing support when necessary, until the objective was finally secured.

The Prospects for Japan

While the Allies were fighting their way closer to the absolute national defense line, the Japanese were desperately reorganizing their forces in preparation for the impending assault on their vital stronghold to the south and east.[1] Late in December 1943, as it became apparent

that the goals set at the Imperial Conference of 30 September would not be realized, *Imperial General Headquarters* had taken a fresh look at Japan's situation. Of the five possible courses the Japanese assumed were open to the Allies,[2] they attached greatest importance to the Allied offensives in the Pacific and in Burma. The latter they viewed seriously not because of any great Allied successes in that area but rather because Thailand and French Indochina were politically the weakest links in the Japanese defense system. The Allies, they therefore assumed, would take advantage of this weakness to break through the absolute national defense line in Southeast Asia, a move that would greatly strengthen the Nationalist regime in China.

It was the Allied offensive in the Pacific that worried the Japanese most. The effects of MacArthur's and Halsey's operations were serious enough, but Nimitz' invasion of the Gilberts had added a new dimension to the Pacific war. Heretofore, Allied advances had been limited by the range of land-based fighters; with the introduction of the carrier striking force of the Central Pacific, there was virtually no limit to the extent of an Allied advance. Theoretically, the Americans could land anywhere that the carriers could go. This was a lesson the Japanese grasped immediately and to

---

[1] For a description of this line and its role in Japanese strategy, see above, Chapter XXVII. This section is based on the sources cited in note 1 of that chapter.

[2] These five courses, or lines of advance, were:

1. From the Aleutians westward to the Kurils.

2. Across the Central Pacific toward the Japanese home islands or the Philippines-Formosa area.

3. North and west to the Philippines by way of New Guinea.

4. From the Indian Ocean area toward Java and Sumatra.

5. Toward Malaya and Thailand and Burma.

Imperial GHQ Army High Command Record, Japanese Studies in World War II, 72, p. 115.

which they gave due weight in their plans for defense.

Despite their concern over the Central Pacific area, the Japanese planners believed that the Allied offensive to the south posed a greater threat in the immediate future. This conclusion stemmed from their estimate that the Allies would seek control of the Philippines-Formosa area before invading the home islands, and that of the two routes to the Philippines—the Central and the Southwest Pacific—the Allies would probably take the southern route because it involved fewer risks. Thus, the Philippines became for the Japanese the key to the defense of the home islands; northwest New Guinea the final battleground for control of the vital road to the inner empire.

To meet the challenge in the Southern Area, *Imperial General Headquarters* began in December to consider a plan to reorganize and consolidate the forces in western New Guinea and the Philippines. The principal feature of this plan was to place all operations in this region under the single control of Field Marshal Terauchi, commander in chief of the *Southern Army*. With headquarters in Manila, Terauchi would, in addition to the forces in Southeast Asia, command the *2d Area Army,* which had been established under General Anami as a separate theater only a few months earlier, the *14th Army* in the Philippines, and the *3d* and *4th Air Armies*. This move, the planners at *General Headquarters* believed, would shift Terauchi's attention from the Asiatic mainland to the Pacific, now considered the more important theater, and at the same time insure the most effective use of the limited air and shipping resources of the empire. Also, by placing the air forces under the direct control of *Southern Army* and restricting *14th* and *2d Area Army* to army troops, *Imperial General Headquarters* hoped to strengthen the ground defenses of this critical sector.[3] This was the plan, but before it could be put into effect events in the Central Pacific during January and February focused attention on that area. Thus, when the reorganization did come in March of 1944, it was accompanied by a new and unified command in the Central Pacific Area that greatly resembled the American command.

For the Japanese, the Allied successes in the Pacific during the fall and winter of 1943 meant the end of all hopes for a great counteroffensive the following spring. With MacArthur and Nimitz through the outer defenses of the absolute national defense line, it was doubtful if that vital line could be held. How far the Japanese position had deteriorated may be judged from an *Imperial General Headquarters* estimate late in December that it would probably be impossible, even under the most favorable circumstances, to mount an offensive against the Allies before 1946.[4] For the first time also, *Imperial General Headquarters* accepted the possibility of an Allied penetration of the absolute national defense line and began to plan for the expected attack against the Philippines. It was there, thought the Japanese planners in common with General MacArthur and many Allied planners, that the decisive battle of the war would be fought.

---

[3] Hattori. The Greater East Asia War, III, 83; *Imperial GHQ* Army High Command Record, p. 117.
[4] Hattori, The Greater East Asia War, III, 83–85.

Long-Range Plans for the Defeat of Japan

The question of the Philippines was but one of a number of problems, and by no means the most urgent, that faced the President and his military advisers aboard the battleship *Iowa* on their way to Cairo and Tehran for what proved to be perhaps the most important of the wartime conferences and the last in which military considerations dominated political and postwar problems.[5] It was at this conference, during the meetings with Stalin at Tehran, that agreement was finally reached to launch the long-deferred cross-Channel invasion (OVERLORD) the following May, in co-ordination with a Soviet offensive on the Eastern Front, and a landing in southern France (ANVIL). Operations in the Mediterranean were to be limited to an advance in Italy to the Pisa-Rimini line, and the projected campaign to clear all of Burma was deferred indefinitely by canceling its amphibious phase in order to secure landing craft for ANVIL.[6]

For President Roosevelt and his advisers, the Cairo Conference marked a turning point in the role reserved for China in the struggle against Japan. By deferring the campaign to clear Burma, the Allies tacitly admitted that operations on the mainland of Asia were no longer considered decisive and, in effect, consigned the Generalissimo to a secondary role.[7] The emergence of this view, due partly at least to the recent successes won in the Pacific and the prospect of even greater gains in the future, coincided with the growing conviction that the main effort against Japan should be made in the Pacific, a view that received formal approval of the Combined Chiefs of Staff at Cairo.[8] The cancellation of operations in Southeast Asia was a heavy blow to those who had fought hard for it. But to balance this loss and the declining importance of China, they could now look forward to Soviet assistance in Asia, for at Tehran Stalin had given his assurance that he would join the Allies in their war against Japan after Germany had been defeated.

It was at Cairo also that the war aims of the powers allied against Japan were defined. Known as the Cairo Declaration, these aims held out little promise for an early peace with Japan, whose aggression the Allies pledged themselves to punish. The territory Japan had unlawfully annexed was to be returned to its rightful owners. Manchuria and Formosa were to go to China, Korea was to receive its independence, and the Pacific islands the Japanese had seized since 1941 were to be restored to their former status.

---

[5] The conference was conducted in three installments, at Cairo with the British and Chinese representatives between 22 and 26 November, with the British and Russians at Tehran from 28 to 30 November, and again at Cairo with the British alone from 2 to 7 December. The code name for the entire series of meetings is SEXTANT, but the meetings with the Russians at Tehran were given a special code name, EUREKA. Minutes and decisions of the three meetings are bound in the official SEXTANT Conference Book.

[6] For a full discussion of these and related decisions, see Matloff, *Strategic Planning for Coalition Warfare*, Gordon A. Harrison, *Cross-Channel Attack*, UNITED STATES ARMY IN WORLD WAR II (Washington, 1951), pp. 118–27; Leighton and Coakley, Global Logistics, 1943–45, chs. XII and XIII; Greenfield, gen. ed., *Command Decisions*, pp. 182–210, 285–303.

[7] Charles F. Romanus and Riley Sunderland, *Stilwell's Command Problems*, UNITED STATES ARMY IN WORLD WAR II (Washington, 1956), pp. 79–82; Matloff, Strategic Planning, 1943–44, ch. XVI.

[8] CCS 417, 2 Dec 43, sub: Over-all Plan for Defeat of Japan.

Considerable progess was made at the Cairo-Tehran Conference on plans for the Pacific, though this achievement has been obscured by the agreements reached on OVERLOAD and ANVIL and the differences with the British and Chinese. Two major problems relating to the Pacific had still to be settled when the planners boarded the *Iowa* on 13 November—(1) final decision on the specific objectives set for the coming year, and (2) approval of a plan for the ultimate defeat of Japan.[9] Work on a long-range plan for the defeat of Japan had begun in August 1942 and by May 1943 had produced a number of studies and a plan which considered the alternate routes to Japan and the means by which she might be brought to her knees—invasion, blockade, and aerial bombardment. In the view of the Combined Chiefs, who considered it during the Washington Conference in May (TRIDENT), this plan, though a promising start, still needed a good deal of work.[10] During the next three months, a team of American and British planners working together first in London and then Washington, produced a 103-page document—"The Mile of Pink," it was called—entitled Appreciation and Plan for the Defeat of Japan.[11]

This latest effort represented a considerable advance over the plan presented in May. The planners had faced realistically the objective of the war with Japan and discarded the announced aim of unconditional surrender. The Japanese, they held, would never surrender until the home islands were invaded and every last-ditch defender driven from his place. The difficulties of mounting such an operation would be formidable and the cost prohibitive. A more reasonable objective, the planners believed, would be "the destruction of Japanese capacity to resist," but they recognized that to accomplish this it might well prove necessary to invade.

Invasion was a last resort. There were two other ways by which Japan might be defeated—naval blockade and air bombardment. Of these, the planners seemed to place more hope on the latter, which, in any case, was a necessary prelude to invasion. Since the most desirable bases from which to bomb Japan lay in China and Formosa, that area described as the northern littoral of the South China Sea therefore became in their judgment the main intermediate objective short of Japan. There were various routes by which this area could be reached—across the Central Pacific (or along the New Guinea–Philippines axis) and into the South China Sea by way of the Celebes and Sulu Seas or across the northern tip of Luzon; from the west through the Straits of Malacca (including the capture of Singapore) and up through the Indies; or overland across China. Of these, the planners thought the Central Pacific approach most promising. The other routes offered advantages and should not be neglected, but the main effort in the east when it came should be made from

---

[9] In the preparation of this section on the development of long-range plans for the defeat of Japan, the author has been greatly assisted by an excellent summary of the subject by his colleague, Maj. Henry G. Morgan, which made the task of unraveling this complicated story much lighter than it would otherwise have been.

[10] Mins, CCS Mtg, 20 May 43; JPS 67/4, 28 April 43, Strategic Plan for Defeat of Japan; Mins, JPS Mtg, 19 Aug 42. For a discussion of the plan submitted at TRIDENT, see above, pp. 457–60.

[11] CPS 83, 8 Aug 43, Appreciation and Plan for the Defeat of Japan. Background papers on the development of this plan are filed in ABC 381 Japan (8–27–42) sec. 3.

CAIRO CONFERENCE. *Generalissimo Chiang Kai-shek sits with President Roosevelt, Prime Minister Churchill, and Madame Chiang. Standing, from left: General Shang Chen, Lt. Gen. Lin Wei, Generals Somervell, Stilwell, and Arnold, Field Marshal Dill, Lord Louis Mountbatten, and Lt. Gen. Sir Adrian Carton de Wiart.*

the Central Pacific. The schedule set by the combined planners would have placed Allied forces in the intermediate objective area in 1946, with the invasion of Japan, if that proved necessary, to begin in 1947 or later.

Though there were several unresolved differences between the American and British planners, the plan in abbreviated form (including a statement of the differences) was submitted to the Combined Chiefs when they met at Quebec (QUADRANT) in August 1943. The U.S. Chiefs met separately to discuss the plan and added their own comments.[12] Thus,

when the matter was finally considered by the Combined Chiefs most of the criticisms had already been put forward. No one was happy about the length of time it would take to reach Japan, and there was no unanimity on the relative weight attached to the various lines of advance, the British arguing strongly for the capture of Singapore and the opening of the Malacca Straits. To speed up the tempo of operations, the Americans proposed that the plan be keyed to the European war with the objective of defeating Japan within twelve months after the collapse of Germany. The British

---

[12] These comments and the statement of differences between the British and American planners are con-

tained in CCS 313 and 313/1, 18 and 20 Aug 43, sub: Appreciation and Plan for Defeat of Japan.

TEHRAN CONFERENCE. *In the front row: Marshal Stalin, President Roosevelt, and Prime Minister Churchill. Standing, from the left: Harry Hopkins, Foreign Minister Molotov, W. Averell Harriman, Sir Archibald Clark Kerr, Ambassador to the USSR, and Anthony Eden, Foreign Secretary.*

agreed in principle, but thought the twelve month goal unrealistic and only accepted it on the condition that forces would be deployed in the Pacific as rapidly as the situation in Europe allowed. Thus, the final report of the Conference stated that "operations should be framed to force the defeat of Japan as soon as possible after the defeat of Germany . . . on the basis of accomplishing this within twelve months of that event." [13] With respect to the plan itself, the Combined

Chiefs noted only that they had made a preliminary study of the "Appreciation" but, because the issues were too large and complicated to be discussed in the time remaining for the conference, the points of difference should be examined further by the planners and taken up at the next meeting of the Combined Chiefs.

One other element in the development of a long-range plan for the defeat of Japan introduced at the Quebec Conference was the possibility of employing the 1,500-mile range B-29, expected to be available soon for operations. This possibility was raised, not in the "Appreciation" of the combined planners,

[13] CCS 319/5, 24 Aug 43, sub: Rpt to President and Prime Minister; Mins, 2d Plenary Session, 23 Aug 43; CCS Mtg, 24 Aug 43. All in QUADRANT Conference Book. See also Hayes, The War Against Japan, ch. XVIII, and Matloff, Strategic Planning, 1943–44, ch. X.

but in a separate study, hastily prepared by the Air Force planners and submitted by General Arnold toward the close of the conference, probably to support the American case for defeating Japan twelve months after Germany's defeat. Briefly, the air plan called for an aerial offensive against Japan that would destroy her ability to resist by the fall of 1945, that is, within twelve months of the estimated date for the defeat of Germany. This result was to be achieved by B–29's based in the Changsha area of China (1,500 miles from the industrial center of Japan), building up from four groups in June 1944 to twenty groups the following May. Though there were obviously many problems to be solved in connection with the plan, especially in the matter of logistics, it opened up fresh possibilities and the Combined Chiefs directed their planners to report on this scheme by 15 September and to have ready a month later a new plan that would accomplish the defeat of Japan twelve months after the fall of Germany.[14]

The three months intervening between the conference at Quebec and Cairo were busy ones for the American and British planners engaged in the task of developing the long-range plan. Study of the air plan was completed on the appointed date, and the results submitted to the Combined Chiefs. There were differences in the emphasis placed on various factors by the British and Americans, but no disagreement on the main conclusion that for logistical reasons the air plan was not feasible. The Combined Chiefs therefore decided to abandon the

plan but not their efforts to find additional ways in which to utilize the possibilities of air bombardment to bring about the defeat of Japan.[15]

Meanwhile, another team of planners of the Joint War Plans Committee had been working on the long-range plan designed to produce Japan's downfall a year after Germany's. The first fruits of its work, submitted on 25 October, held out little hope for meeting the assigned deadline. The planners were convinced that the Japanese would not surrender unconditionally without invasion, at least at a reasonably early date. Given the existing schedule of operations, the planners could not see how Allied forces could by the fall of 1945 achieve the prerequisites for invasion—bases from which to bomb the center of Japan, the elimination of Japanese air and naval power, and the destruction of Japanese shipping. As the planners saw it, there were four possible courses of action:

1. The invasion of Hokkaido, northernmost of the Japanese home islands, in the summer of 1945 (presumably by forces of the Central Pacific).

2. The capture of Formosa in the spring of 1945 by way of the Pacific (presumably by forces of the Central Pacific).

3. The capture of Singapore by the end of 1945, followed by a co-ordinated assault against Formosa from the Pacific and South China Sea in the winter of 1945–46.

4. A diversionary assault against northern Sumatra in the Netherlands East Indies in the spring of 1945 (or earlier), followed by the capture of

---

[14] CCS 323, 20 Aug 43, sub: Air Plan for Defeat of Japan; Mins, CCS Mtg, 21 Aug 43; CPS 86/D, 26 Aug 43, sub: Preparation of Studies on Defeat of Japan.

[15] Mins, CCS Mtg, 17 Sep 43; JPS Mtg, 15 Sep 43; CPS 86/1, 13 Sep 43, sub: Studies on Defeat of Japan; JPS 271, 11 Sep 43, same sub.

Formosa from the Pacific in the winter of 1945–46. In each case, it was assumed that operations already planned in the Southwest Pacific, Southeast Asia, and China would be carried out as scheduled in order to support the main effort and to maintain pressure on the Japanese.[16]

Though the first alternative, the invasion of Hokkaido in the summer of 1945, came closest to meeting the requirements set by the Combined Chiefs, the planners preferred the second course, which, they held, combined the promise of Japan's early defeat with minimum risks. Thus, the schedule of operations they presented called for the capture of Formosa in the spring of 1945, or as soon thereafter as possible, followed by the invasion of Hokkaido in the summer of 1946 and of Honshu, the main island of Japan, in the fall. This was the most optimistic forecast the planners would make, but they recognized that any one of a number of factors might alter their calculations— the speed of current and projected operations in the Southwest and Central Pacific, the effectiveness of submarine operations against Japanese shipping, the possibility of bypassing strongly held Japanese positions such as Truk, and the extent of British and Russian assistance. The planners were aware also that the effectiveness of B–29 operations, which they scheduled for 1944 or early 1945, and carrier-based air attacks against Japan, both as yet untried methods of warfare, might well alter the timetable and make possible the defeat of Japan at an earlier date than the fall of 1946.

As the long-range plan made its way up the echelons of planning committees toward the Chiefs of Staff, criticisms and

differences multiplied. Almost all those who read it expressed dissatisfaction with some aspect of the plan, often disagreeing with one another in their objections, but out of this critical examination there emerged a clearer understanding of the problems involved and of the various points of view regarding the final defeat of Japan. First to comment was the senior team of the Joint War Plans Committee. More optimistic than those who had prepared the plan, this group believed that there was a real possibility of defeating Japan by October 1945 and that the plan should be revised to provide for this possibility. It also preferred the first alternative—the capture of Hokkaido in the summer of 1945—and thought the large role assigned the British Fleet in the Pacific unrealistic. Unless British naval forces were refitted and organized into self-contained and self-supporting units before they were transferred into the Pacific, the senior team of the JWPC held, they would drain off U.S. resources and constitute a liability rather than an asset in the final operations against Japan.[17]

The Joint Staff Planners, parent body of the War Plans Committee, also took exception to the plan, especially its emphasis on the necessity for invasion. Both the naval and air representatives felt that the role of air bombardment by B–29's and carrier-based aircraft in the final defeat of Japan had been minimized. "When the full weight of our air and naval power is deployed against her (Japan)," said Rear Adm. Bernhard H.

---

[16] CPS 86/2, 25 Oct 43, sub: The Defeat of Japan Within Twelve Months after the Defeat of Germany.

[17] JWPC 120, 26 Oct 43, sub: Comments on Defeat of Japan Within Twelve Months After Defeat of Germany. The views of this group and of others who commented on the plan are ably summarized in Hayes, The War Against Japan, II, 114ff.

Bieri, "we may find the road much easier than anticipated."[18] The joint planners were dubious also about the date set for the invasion of Hokkaido and of the necessity for taking Formosa. And, like the JWPC team, they were skeptical of the effectiveness of British naval forces in the Pacific at any early date, except perhaps in MacArthur's area. The plan, they decided, should be revised to provide for the capture of Hokkaido in the summer of 1945 and, if possible, of Honshu the following spring.[19]

The task of revising the plan to meet these and other criticisms was accomplished quickly in the Joint War Plans Committee. By 2 November it was in the hands of the Joint Staff Planners who forwarded it to the Joint Chiefs the next day.[20] As revised, the plan still maintained that invasion would be necessary and called for the seizure of Hokkaido in 1945 and of Honshu the following spring. Central and Southwest Pacific operations were to continue as scheduled, with MacArthur aiming for the Philippines and Nimitz for the Marianas, where B-29's would be based. In China, first priority would go to the development of airfields for the B-29, and preparations were to be made to occupy the Kurils in the event the Soviet Union came into the war. Elsewhere, operations would continue for the purpose of maintaining pressure on the enemy and securing maximum attrition of his forces and shipping.

The Joint Chiefs, beset with other problems that would come up at the Cairo and Tehran meetings, deferred consideration of the plan, sending it instead to the Joint Strategic Survey Committee for comment. These senior officers found much to criticize in this latest effort of the planners. They thought it cautious and unimaginative, overestimating the capabilities of the Japanese and underestimating the potentialities of Allied power. They doubted that invasion would be necessary and thought Japan could be defeated by a combination of naval blockade and air bombardment. The main effort, they declared flatly, should be made in the Central Pacific; there lay "the key to the early defeat of Japan." The JSSC found further cause for optimism in the belief that German resistance might collapse as early as the spring of 1944, and that Soviet intervention in Asia would follow soon after. A new plan should therefore be made, said the JSSC, one more bold and imaginative that would reflect the bright prospects facing the Allies in Europe and Asia.[21]

The first chance the Joint Chiefs had to consider the plan for the defeat of Japan was on 15 November, while they were en route to Cairo. They were not enthusiastic. The emphasis on Hokkaido came as a distinct surprise and Admiral King wondered how the planners expected to reach it. Why not go instead to Kyushu, southernmost of the Japanese home islands and closer to objectives already under consideration? Some doubt

---

[18] Mins, JPS Mtg, 27 Oct 43.

[19] Memo, U.S. Members of CPS, 1 Nov 43, sub: The Defeat of Japan Within Twelve Months After Defeat of Germany, cited in Hayes, The War Against Japan, p. 115.

[20] JWPC 120/2, 2 Nov 43, sub: The Defeat of Japan Within Twelve Months After Defeat of Germany; JCS 564, 4 Nov 43, same sub; Mins, JPS Mtg, 3 Nov 43.

[21] JCS 533/5, 8 Nov 43, sub: Recommended Line of Action at Next U.S.-British Conferences; Memo, Vice Adm Russell Willson for Adm King, 11 Nov 43, sub: Plans for Defeat of Japan, ABC 334; JCS Mins (2-14-42) sec. 5.

was expressed also of the possibility of invading and defeating Japan in a single year. The planners, Marshall felt, had not given enough weight to the vulnerability of Japan's oil resources to the south or to the possibility of bypassing strongly defended bases like Truk.[22]

Like their senior advisers of the Joint Strategic Survey Committee, the Joint Chiefs believed that invasion might not be necessary and that the long-range plan should be based on the assumption that Japan's defeat could be accomplished by blockade and bombardment. It should take into consideration Soviet intervention and provide for the employment of British naval forces in the Pacific. And finally, stipulated the Joint Chiefs, the plan should be flexible and capable of rapid adjustment to meet sudden and unexpected developments, such as the early surrender of Germany or defeat of the Japanese Fleet.

During the next two weeks, while their superiors were meeting at Cairo and Tehran, the planners set about the task of fashioning a new long-range plan. In doing so, they would have to weigh a number of imponderables and reshuffle the factors in an ever-shifting equation —the date of Germany's defeat, Soviet entry into the war against Japan, the employment of British air and naval forces, the role of China, the effectiveness of B–29 and carrier-based aircraft, whether the main effort should be made in the Central Pacific, which Japanese island should be invaded, or whether, in fact, the invasion of Japan would be necessary at all. There were no clear answers to any of these problems, but the planners were not expected to pro-

duce a blueprint worked out to the last detail. All they could do was work out a practical and realistic program that would be flexible enough to take into account the unknowns in the equation. Thus, they started with three assumptions: first, that invasion of Japan might not be necessary but that the plan must be capable of expansion to meet the contingency of invasion; second, that Germany might be defeated as early as the spring of 1944; and third, that the Soviet Union might enter the war against Japan soon after Germany's defeat.

On the assumption that Japan could be defeated by sea and air blockade and intensive air bombardment from progressively advanced bases, the objective of the plan finally drawn up was to obtain positions from which to bomb Japan and, if it should prove necessary, mount an invasion of the home islands. Such positions, the planners believed, could best be achieved by making the main effort in the Pacific, utilizing both the Central and Southwest Pacific routes so as to converge on the Formosa–Luzon–China coast area by the spring of 1945. As between the two lines of advance, they carefully avoided giving one priority over the other and specified that operations along each would be mutually supporting. But they believed also that the Central Pacific route was potentially the more decisive. Thus, in case of conflicts in timing and allocation of resources between MacArthur and Nimitz, "due weight," said the planners, should be given to the fact that operations along the central route promised "a more rapid advance toward Japan and her vital lines of communication; the earlier acquisition of strategic air bases closer to the Japanese homeland; and, of great-

---

[22] Mins, JCS Mtg, 15 Nov 43.

est importance, are more likely to precipitate a decisive engagement with the
Japanese Fleet." [23] Operations in other
areas would be subsidiary to those in the
Central and Southwest Pacific, but the
planners took note of the possibility that
if the Soviet Union entered the war operations in the North Pacific Area might
well assume an increased importance.
In any case, the schedule of operations
was to remain flexible and every preparation made to exploit any opportunity
that might develop.

The forces required for the defeat of
Japan were carefully considered in the
plan. The key was the date of Germany's
collapse and the prompt redeployment
of forces from Europe to the Pacific. A
total of forty divisions, including five
Marine divisions, plus supporting troops
would ultimately be deployed against
Japan, the planners estimated. Aircraft
also would be brought over from Europe
for the final phase of the Japanese war,
but the major strategic air weapon, the
B–29, was already scheduled for early
shipment to China and the Marianas,
when bases were ready. Naval forces,
except for the employment of British
units, was not a problem, since the largest part of U.S. naval power was incorporated in the Pacific Fleet.

The reaction to the revised plan, which
was completed by 2 December, was encouraging. The elder statesmen of the
Joint Strategic Survey Committee, who
had been so critical of the earlier plan,
found this one much more to their
liking. Only the failure of the planners
to establish a clear priority as between
the Central and the Southwest Pacific
disturbed them. "The history of our

discussions with the British concerning
the strategic concept for Europe," they
pointed out, in a clear reference to the
debates over Mediterranean strategy,
"clearly demonstrates the continuous difficulties which arise when the primacy
of the operations in one part of the theater is not clearly set forth and accepted
—but remains the subject of debate
whenever operations are being considered in another part of the same theater."
For this reason, they felt, a clear priority
should be given to one of the two lines
of advance, and, as the foremost cham-
pions of the Central Pacific, they had no
doubt as to where the primary effort was
to be made.[24]

The Joint Chiefs, when they met to
discuss the plan on 3 December, considered the advice of their senior advisers
and then asked General Sutherland, who
had accompanied the planners to Cairo,
for his views. Speaking for MacArthur,
Sutherland argued eloquently for the
priority of Southwest Pacific operations
and for RENO III.[25] But the Joint Chiefs
were unconvinced by the arguments of
either the JSSC or Sutherland. They
were not yet ready to commit themselves
to any one line of advance or to a single
concept for the defeat of Japan, preferring to leave themselves free to exploit
any opportunity that might arise. In this
respect, the work of the planners had
been well done. As General Handy
pointed out to Marshall, the planners
had considered all viewpoints and, while
placing the main effort against Japan in
the Pacific, had avoided assigning priority to operations in any one area. This,
he observed, was one great advantage of

---

[23] CCS 417, 2 Dec 43, sub: Over-all Plan for Defeat
of Japan.

[24] JCS 614, 2 Dec 43, sub: Plan for Defeat of Japan.
[25] Mins, JCS Mtg, ann. 3 Dec 43. For a summary of
these arguments, see above, pp. 538–42.

the plan. It was flexible and allowed the Joint Chiefs "to create a main effort by the commitment of forces to one or the other axis" whenever they chose. "In effect," Handy concluded, "it gives the Joint Chiefs of Staff almost complete liberty of action in the Pacific without reference to the British Chiefs of Staff." [26] On this note, the Joint Chiefs accepted the plan and recommended its approval.

The British Chiefs of Staff, for different reasons, also favored the plan. By placing the main effort against Japan in the Pacific, the plan provided a strong argument against expanded operations in Burma, which the British had steadfastly opposed. This subject led to further discussions between the U.S. and British Chiefs and resulted in a revision intended to clarify the plan with respect to operations in southeast Burma.[27] With this amendment and others of a minor nature, the Combined Chiefs of Staff approved the over-all plan for the defeat of Japan in principle "as a basis for further investigation and preparation." [28] Though this was short of unqualified approval, it provided for the first time an approved guide for short-range strategic planning and for long-range objectives.

Operations for 1944

Fixing the schedule of operations in the Pacific for 1944 proved to be less difficult than charting a plan for the defeat of Japan. Since the Quebec Conference in August 1943, at which the Combined Chiefs had approved a program for 1943–

1944, there had been considerable discussion of objectives for 1944, both in the theater and in Washington. Finally, on 4 November, General Sutherland had arrived in Washington to persuade the Joint Chiefs of Staff to approve MacArthur's 5-phase plan (Reno III) for placing forces of the Southwest Pacific on Mindanao by 1 February 1945.[29]

The reaction to Sutherland's arguments had not been favorable. To the joint planners, Reno III seemed to place too great an emphasis on the Southwest Pacific line of advance at the expense of the Central Pacific, and thereby challenged the accepted concept of concurrent and mutually supporting operations along both axes of advance. They therefore proposed a schedule for 1944 that would take MacArthur's forces only as far as the Vogelkop Peninsula, omitting the last two phases of Reno, and Nimitz' forces to the Palaus and perhaps to the Marianas. The question of the Philippines they left open, not because of any doubts about the ability of U.S. forces to undertake such a campaign but because they were unwilling to commit themselves so far in advance. As a matter of fact, they were most optimistic about progress during the coming year. Ground, air, and naval forces in the Pacific, already formidable, would be greatly strengthened during the next twelve months, and shipping, which had been so critical in the first two years of the war, could be expected to become more plentiful. Thus, the joint planners hoped that operations in 1944 would so weaken Japan as to "permit the eventual invasion of Honshu not later than the spring of 1946, in order to force her

---

[26] Memo, Handy for Marshall, 3 Dec 43, no sub, OPD Exec Files.

[27] CCS 417/1, 5 Dec 43, sub: Over-all Plan for Defeat of Japan.

[28] Mins, CCS Mtg, 6 Dec 43.

[29] See above, pp. 536–37.

unconditional surrender at the earliest practicable date." [30]

On 15 November, en route to Cairo, the Joint Chiefs considered briefly the plans for operations in 1944. Admiral Leahy immediately asked whether the recommendations of the planners "tie in with the plans for the Southwest Pacific Command." [31] The response, furnished by one of the naval planners, indicated that there had been "adjustments" in MacArthur's plans because of a lack of resources, but the extent of these adjustments was not indicated. To General Arnold's query concerning conflicts between the Southwest and Central Pacific, Admiral King replied that "dividends would be greater" in Nimitz' area and that "nothing should interfere" with operations there. [32]

No decision was reached at the meeting, and the problem was returned to the planners for further consideration in the light of the recently completed long-range plan for the defeat of Japan. By the 17th, when the Joint Chiefs met again to discuss the Pacific, the planners had completed their work. The reference to Honshu was removed as premature, and provision was made for the employment of B–29's scheduled to become available in the near future, to operate from China airfields beginning on 1 May 1944. The reaction of the Joint Chiefs to this revision was, on the whole, favorable. There was some discussion of specific objectives such as Truk and the Palaus, but these did not constitute serious objections. After all,

Admiral Cooke reminded the Chiefs, the objectives set out in the plan were not intended as an ironclad schedule but rather as a guide for planning purposes and as a forecast of what could be accomplished during the year. The planners, like their Chiefs, intended to remain flexible and to take advantage of any opportunities that might arise to speed up the war against Japan. Despite these assurances, the Palaus operation was deleted at Admiral King's insistence. Truk and Ponape remained in the plan, though General Marshall, who had raised questions about both, remained doubtful of the necessity for going to either place. [33]

The B–29 program, which had played so large a part in the development of the long-range plan for the defeat of Japan, also largely affected the selection of at least one of the objectives for 1944. Admiral King had long favored the Marianas, but even in naval circles there had been no great enthusiasm for the early invasion of these islands. The problem of finding adequate bases for the B–29 when it became available altered the picture radically. China was the first choice, but the logisticians doubted that the effort could be supported from China and the planners were skeptical of Chinese ability to hold the bases once they were built. The prospect of basing the B–29's in the Marianas, when it appeared that the islands could be occupied by the end of 1944, was seized upon by the Air Force planners after the Quebec Conference in August 1943. Thereafter, they supported Admiral King strongly whenever the Marianas question arose, arguing

---

[30] JCS 581, 9 Nov 43, sub: Specific Opns for Defeat of Japan, 1944; JWPC 115/1, 7 Nov 43, same sub.
[31] It is doubtful that the Joint Chiefs had actually examined RENO III at this time.
[32] Mins, JCS Mtg, 15 Nov 43.

[33] Mins, JCS Mtg, 17 Nov 43; JCS 581/1, 16 Nov 43, sub: Specific Opns for Defeat of Japan, 1944.

that other Central Pacific objectives be bypassed and neutralized in order to advance the date for the occupation of these islands. By October, this idea had won wide support among the Joint Staff Planners, who held that "plans for the acceleration of the defeat of Japan would place emphasis upon the seizure of the Marianas at the earliest possible date, with the establishment of heavy bomber bases as the primary mission." [34] Thus, the plans considered by the Joint Chiefs aboard the *Iowa* called for the "seizure of Guam and the Japanese Marianas" in October 1944.

There was no question now about the desirability of the operation, only about the timing. The sooner the islands were taken, the sooner would the B–29's begin operations. The plan, it is true, called for the B–29's to begin bombing Japan from Chinese fields in May but the logisticians of the Joint Staff Planners were doubtful that this commitment would be met. General Arnold, therefore, insisted that the plan include the statement that B–29 bases in the Marianas would be ready in time to permit very long range bombing of Japan from the Pacific by the end of the year. [35]

The shipboard discussion of 17 November 1943 was the last consideration by the Joint Chiefs of the proposed schedule against Japan in 1944 before

GENERAL MARSHALL *at Southwest Pacific headquarters. From left: Unidentified officer, Generals Kenney, Chamberlin, Krueger, Marshall, and MacArthur.*

their conference with the British and Chinese. They gave it their approval then, and laid it aside for other matters that would occupy much more of their time during the coming meetings. It was not until 6 December, after the decision on OVERLORD and ANVIL had been made and the Burma offensive deferred, that the plan for operations in 1944 was formally considered by the Combined Chiefs at Cairo. Already, the long-range plan for the defeat of Japan had been approved, in principle, and there was little discussion. The most controversial part of the plan dealing with operations in Southeast Asia had already been settled, and the British had no disposition to quarrel with the U.S. Chiefs of

---

[34] JPS 288, 4 Oct 43, sub: Plans for Defeat of Japan Within Twelve Months After Defeat of Germany; JPS 264, 6 Sep 43, Outline Plan for Seizure of the Marianas, Including Guam. For fuller accounts of the development of the B–29 and its relation to strategy, see Craven and Cate, *AAF II*, ch. V, pp. 3–33; Arnold, *Global Mission*, pp. 245, 477 *passim;* Matloff, Strategic Planning, 1943–44, ch. XVI; Crowl, *Campaign in the Marianas*, ch. 1.

[35] Mins, JCS Mtg, 17 Nov 43; JCS 581/3, Rpt by Joint Logistics Committee, 4 Dec 43, sub: Specific Opns for Defeat of Japan, 1944.

TABLE 13—SPECIFIC OPERATIONS FOR THE DEFEAT OF JAPAN, 1944

Date	Central Pacific	Southwest Pacific	China Southeast Asia
1–31 January	Seizure of the Marshalls, including Eniwetok and Kusaie	Complete seizure of western New Britain. Continue neutralization of Rabaul	
15 January to 15 March			Operations in upper Burma, Arakan region, and China
1 February		Seizure of Hansa Bay Area, New Guinea	
20 March		Capture of Kavieng	
20 April		Seizure of Manus in the Admiralty Islands	
1 May	Seizure of Ponape		B–29 operations from China bases against Japanese inner zone
1 June		Seizure of Hollandia and the Humboldt Bay region in New Guinea	
20 July	Seizure of the Truk area in the eastern Carolines	B–29 operations from Australia against vital targets in the Netherlands Indies	
15 August		Advance westward along north coast of New Guinea to and including the Vogelkop Peninsula	
1 October	Seizure of Guam and the Japanese Marianas		
1 November (end of monsoon)			Intensification of offensive operations in the Southeast Asia Command
31 December	Initiate B–29 bombing from Marianas bases against vital targets in Japanese inner zone		

Source: CCS 397, 3 Dec 43.

Staff about a theater the Americans regarded as their own unique responsibility. Approval therefore, was almost perfunctory, and next day the conference ended.[36] The President and most of the staff boarded the *Iowa* for the journey back to Washington, but Generals Marshall and Arnold, accompanied by the chief Army and Navy planners, General Handy and Admiral Cooke, returned home by way of the Pacific.

The plan approved at Cairo set an ambitious program for 1944 and represented a real advance over the plan adopted only five months earlier at Quebec.[37] Under the new schedule, MacArthur's forces were to complete the seizure of western New Britain in January, then go on to gain control of the Hansa Bay area and the Bismarck Archipelago by May. *(Table 13)* From there, they would continue to advance westward along the New Guinea coast as far as the Vogelkop Peninsula.

Nimitz' forces during this same period were to take the Marshalls, Ponape, Truk, and, finally, the Marianas. Thus, by the end of the year, Allied forces in the Pacific would hold a line from the tip of New Guinea to the Marianas, from where B–29's were scheduled to begin operations by 31 December.

In contrast to the accelerated program for the Pacific, the schedule approved at Cairo for Southeast Asia and China was less ambitious than that adopted at Quebec. Operations in Burma, originally set for November 1943, were deferred to

early 1944, and the plan to recapture Burma itself was abandoned altogether. Only in the case of B–29 operations was the program for China advanced. Under the new plan, very long range bombing from China bases would begin in May, rather than October 1944, as estimated at Quebec.

These were the exceptions for the coming year, placed in the setting of the larger plan for the final defeat of Japan. Their realization would depend on many factors beyond the control of those who had fashioned the plans—the reaction of the Japanese, production on the home front, the fortunes of war in Europe and elsewhere, and even the vagaries of wind and weather. Nor would those who had set these goals seek the prize themselves; that was the task of the theater commanders and the men who would lead the air-ground-naval team into battle. What they accomplished and what they believed they could or should do would have a vital bearing on events during the year and on the ultimate defeat of Japan. They had been given a plan corresponding generally with their own views and an accelerated program that would bring U.S. forces within reach of Japan's inner zone. Reality was to exceed even those expectations. Before the year was out MacArthur's forces were firmly established in the central Philippines and preparing to land on Luzon, Marianas-based B–29's were bombing the cities of Japan, the Japanese Navy had been virtually defeated, and carrier forces of the Pacific Fleet had penetrated Japan's inner zone. There was no doubt about Japan's defeat—only when, how, and under whose command. These were the major questions of strategy still to be decided for the Pacific.

---

[36] Mins, CCS Mtg, 6 Dec 43. The plan finally approved became CCS 397 (Rev), 3 Dec 43, sub: Specific Opns for Defeat of Japan, 1944.

[37] See above, Chapter XXV, for a discussion of the Quebec Conference.

Appendix A

For General Wavell from Chiefs of Staff:

By agreement among the Governments of Australia, Netherlands, United Kingdom and United States, hereinafter referred to as the ABDA Governments.

1. *Area.*—A strategic area has been constituted to comprise initially all land and sea areas including general regions of Burma, Malaya, Netherlands East Indies and Philippine Islands more precisely defined in Annexure 1. This area will be known as ABDA area.

2. *Forces.*—You have been designated as Supreme Commander of ABDA area and of all armed forces afloat ashore and in air of ABDA Governments which are or will be (a) stationed in area (b) located in Australian territory when such forces have been allotted by respective Governments for service in or in support of the ABDA area. You are not authorized to transfer from territories of any ABDA Government land forces of the Government without consent of local commander or his Government.

3. The Deputy Supreme Commander and if required a Commander of the Combined Naval Forces and the Commander of Combined Air Forces will be jointly designated by the ABDA Governments.

4. No Government will materially reduce its armed forces assigned to your area nor any commitment made by it for reinforcing its forces in your area except after giving to other Governments and to you timely information pertaining thereto.

5. *Strategic concept and policy.*—The basic strategic concept of the ABDA Governments for conduct of war in your area is not only in immediate future to maintain as many key positions as possible but to take offensive at the earliest opportunity and ultimately to conduct an all-out offensive against Japan. The first essential is to gain general air superiority at the earliest moment through employment of concentrated air power. The piece-meal employment of air forces should be minimised. Your operations should be so conducted as to further preparations for the offensive.

6. General strategic policy will be therefore:—
   (a) to hold Malaya barrier defined as line Malay Peninsula, Sumatra, Java, North Australia as basic defensive position of ABDA area and to operate sea, land and air forces in as great depth as possible forward of barrier in order to oppose Japanese southward advance;
   (b) to hold Burma and Australia as essential support positions for the area and Burma as essential to support of China and to defense of India;
   (c) to re-establish communications through Dutch East Indies with Luzon and to support Philippines garrison;
   (d) to maintain essential communications within the area.

7. *Duties, responsibilities and authorities of Supreme Commander.*—You will coordinate in ABDA area strategical operations of all armed forces of ABDA

Governments where desirable to arrange formation of task forces whether national or inter-national for executing specific operations and appointing any officers irrespective of seniority or nationality to command such task forces.

8. While you will have no responsibilities in respect of the internal administration of the respective forces under your command you are authorised to direct and coordinate the creation and development of administrative facilities and the broad allocation of war materials.

9. You will dispose of reinforcements which from time to time may be despatched to the area by ABDA Governments.

10. You are authorized to require from commanders of the armed forces under your command such reports as you deem necessary in discharging your responsibilities as supreme commander.

11. You are authorised to control the issue of all communiques concerning the forces under your command.

12. Through channels specified in paragraph 18 you may submit recommendations to the ABDA Governments on any matters pertaining to the furthering of your mission.

13. *Limitations.*—Your authority and control with respect to the various portions of ABDA area and to forces assigned thereto will normally be exercised through commanders duly appointed by their respective Governments. Interference is to be avoided in administrative processes of armed forces of any of the ABDA Governments including free communication between them and their respective Governments. No alterations or revision is to be made in basic tactical organizations of such forces and each national component of a task force will normally operate under its own commander and will not be sub-divided into small units for attachment to other national components of task forces except in cases of urgent necessity. In general your instructions and orders will be limited to those necessary for effective coordination of forces in execution of your mission.

14. *Relations with ABDA Governments.*—The ABDA Governments will jointly and severally support you in the execution of duties and responsibilities as herein defined and in the exercising of authority herein delegated and limited. Commanders of all sea, land and air forces within your area will be immediately informed by their respective Governments that from a date to be notified all orders and instructions issued by you in conformity with the provision of this directive will be considered by such commanders as emanating from their respective governments.

15. In the unlikely event that any of your immediate subordinates after making due representation to you still considers obedience to your orders would jeopardise national interests of his country to an extent unjustified by the general situation in ABDA area he has the right subject to your being immediately notified of such intention to appeal direct to his own Government before carrying out orders. Such appeals will be made by most expeditious methods and copies of appeals will be communicated simultaneously to you.

16. *Staff and assumption of command.*—Your staff will include officers of each of ABDA Powers.

You are empowered to communicate immediately with national commanders in area with view to obtaining staff officers essential your earliest possible assumption of command. Your additional staff requirements will be communicated as soon as possible to ABDA Governments through channels of communication described in paragraph 18.

17. You will report when you are in position effectively carry essential functions of supreme command so your assumption of command may be promulgated to all concerned.

18. *Superior Authority.*—As supreme commander of ABDA area you will always be responsible to ABDA Governments through agency defined in Annexure II.

ANNEXURE I.—BOUNDARIES OF ABDA AREA

The ABDA area is bounded as follows:—

North.—By boundary between India and Burma, thence eastward along Chinese frontier and coastline to latitude 030 degrees north, thence along parallel 030 degrees north to meridian 140 degrees east. (Note.—Indo-China and Thailand are NOT included in this area.)

East.—By meridian 140 degrees east from 030 degrees to the Equator, thence east to longitude 141 degrees east, thence south to the boundary of Dutch New Guinea (and to) coast on south coast, thence east along southern New Guinea coast to meridian 143 degrees east, then south down this meridian to the coast of Australia.

South.—By the northern coast of Australia from meridian 143 degrees east westward to meridian 114 degrees east, thence north-westward to latitude 015 degrees south, longitude 092 degrees east.

West.—By meridian 092 degrees east.

2. Forces assigned to ABDA and adjacent areas are authorised to extend their operations into other areas as may be required.

ANNEXURE II

1. On all important military matters not within the jurisdiction of supreme commander of ABDA area, U. S. Chiefs of Staff and representatives in Washington of British Chiefs of Staff will constitute agency for developing and submitting recommendations for decisions by President of U. S. and by British Prime Minister and Minister of Defence. Among chief matters on which decision will be required are:—

   (*a*) Provision of reinforcements.
   (*b*) Major changes in policy.
   (*c*) Departures from supreme commander's directive.

2. This agency will function as follows:—

   (*a*) Any proposals coming either from Supreme Commander or from any of the ABDA Governments will be submitted to Chiefs of Staff Committee both in Washington and in London.
   (*b*) The Chiefs of Staff Committee in London will immediately telegraph to their representatives in Washington to say whether or not they will be telegraphing any opinion.

(c) On receipt of these opinions the U.S.A. C's of S. and representatives in Washington of British C's of S. will develop and submit their recommendations to President and by telegraphing to Prime Minister and Minister of Defence. Prime Minister will then inform the President whether he is in agreement with these recommendations.

3. Since London has machinery for consulting Dominion Governments and since Dutch Government is in London the British Government will be responsible for obtaining their views and agreement for including these in the final telegrams to Washington.

4. Agreement having been reached between President and Prime Minister and Minister of Defence the orders to Supreme Commander will be despatched from Washington in the name of both of them.

Appendix B

General Outline of Policy of Future War Guidance,
Adopted by Liaison Conference, 7 March 1942, and
Report of Prime Minister and Chiefs of Staff to Emperor
13 March 1942

1. In order to bring BRITAIN to submission and to demoralize the UNITED STATES, positive measures shall be taken by seizing opportunities to expand our acquired war gains, and by building a political and military structure capable of withstanding a protracted war.

2. By holding the occupied areas and major communication lines, and by expediting the development and utilization of key resources for national defense; efforts shall be made to establish a self-sufficient structure, and to increase the nation's war potential.

3. More positive and definite measures of war guidance shall be adopted by taking the following situations into consideration: Our national power, the progress of operations, the German-Soviet war situation, the relations between the UNITED STATES and the SOVIET UNION, and the trend in CHUNGKING.

4. Our policy toward the SOVIET UNION shall be based on the "Plan for Expediting the Termination of the War against the UNITED STATES, BRITAIN, the NETHERLANDS, and CHIANG Kai-shek," adopted on 5 Nov 41; and the "Measures to be Immediately Effected in Line with the Development of the Situation," adopted on 10 Jan 42. However, under the present circumstances, no efforts shall be made to mediate a peace between GERMANY and the SOVIET UNION.

5. Our policy toward CHUNGKING shall be based on the "Matters Concerning Measures to be taken toward CHUNGKING, in Line with the Development of the Situation," adopted on 24 Dec 41.

6. Cooperation with GERMANY and ITALY shall be based on the "Plan for Expediting the Termination of the War against the UNITED STATES, BRITAIN, the NETHERLANDS and CHIANG Kai-shek," adopted on 15 Nov 41.

Report to the Throne

We humbly report to Your Majesty on behalf of the Imperial General Headquarters and the Government.

At this point, when our initial operations are about to come to a favorable end by dint of the august virtue of Your Majesty, the Imperial General Headquarters and the Government have, after a careful appraisal, since the latter part of February, of our acquired war gains and their effect, the changes in the world situation, and the present war potentialities of our Empire, agreed on the "General Outline on Future War Guidance." We will now give our explanations.

1. Regarding the general outline on war guidance to be effected hereafter in the war against the UNITED STATES and BRITAIN:

Various measures must be planned and executed in anticipation of a protracted war. It will not only be most difficult to defeat the UNITED STATES and BRITAIN in a short period, but, the war cannot be brought to an end through compromise.

It is essential to further expand the political and military advantages achieved through glorious victories since the opening of hostilities, by utilizing the present war situation to establish a political and strategic structure capable of withstanding a protracted war. We must take every possible step, within the limits of our national power, to force the UNITED STATES and BRITAIN to remain on the defensive. Any definite measure of vital significance to be effected in this connection will be given thorough study, and will be presented to Your Majesty for approval each time.

2. Regarding the need for building national power and fighting power for the successful prosecution of a protracted war.

We deem it highly essential to constantly maintain resilience in our national defense, and build up the nation's war potential so that we will be capable of taking the steps necessary to cope with the progress of situation.

If a nation should lose its resilience in national defense while prosecuting a war, and become unable to rally from an enemy blow; the result would be short of her desired goal, no matter what victory she might achieve in the process. This is amply proved in the precious lessons learned from the annals of war.

Consequently, in our Empire's war guidance policy, we have especially emphasized that, while taking steps to bring the enemy to submission, we must fully build up the nation's war potential to cope with a protracted war.

3. Regarding the adoption of a new and more positive measure of war guidance.

We have made it clear that the question of whether to adopt new and more positive measures for war guidance for the attainment of the objective of the Greater East Asia War should be decided after careful study, not only of the war gains acquired so far, but other factors of extensive and profound significance; such as, the enemy's national power and our's, especially the increase in the fighting power on both sides; the progress of our operations, our relations with the SOVIET UNION and CHINA, the German-Soviet war, and various other factors.

By "more positive measures of war guidance" we mean such measures as the invasion of INDIA and AUSTRALIA.

4. Regarding the measures to be immediately taken toward the SOVIET UNION.

We have made it clear that the measures to be taken toward the SOVIET UNION will be based on the established policy which was adopted earlier at a liaison conference. The essentials of that policy are as follows:

    a. Utmost efforts shall be made to prevent the expansion of hostilities.

    b. JAPAN shall endeavor to the utmost to prevent war with the SOVIET UNION while operations are being conducted in the Southern Area.

c. While maintaining peace between JAPAN and the SOVIET UNION, efforts shall be made to prevent the UNITED STATES and BRITAIN from strengthening their cooperation with the SOVIET UNION, and to alienate the latter from the former, if possible. However, this does not imply that our military preparations against the SOVIET UNION will be neglected, and it is our belief that all possible operations preparations should be made to achieve a quick and decisive victory in case of war.

With regard to the peace between GERMANY and the SOVIET UNION, not only does a compromise seem utterly hopeless, under the present circumstances, but we fear that our mediatory efforts at this point would be detrimental to Japanese-German relations, and would also mean risking a complication in Japanese-Soviet relations. Consequently, we have made it clear that we have no intention of taking any positive steps toward mediation.

5. Regarding the measures to be immediately taken toward Chungking:

We have made it clear that measures toward Chungking will be based on the policy which was adopted at the earlier conference that, "taking advantage of the restlessness in the Chungking Regime which was caused by our application of strong pressure on a vulnerable spot of theirs; our measures toward Chungking shall be shifted, at a proper time, from intelligence activities to activities to bring the regime to submission. The time and method therefore shall be decided at a liaison conference."

Meanwhile, the campaign in BURMA is progressing faster than originally expected, and RANGOON is already in our hands. We believe that our progress in BURMA is already having serious effects on the Chungking Regime, but since we greatly fear that any attempt to bring the Chungking Regime to submission, at too early a stage, would produce an adverse result, our intention is to postpone it to a date that will be decided later.

6. Regarding measures to be taken toward GERMANY and ITALY.

Since we keenly realized that strengthening cooperation with GERMANY and ITALY will become increasingly necessary to achieve our war aims, we have decided that we must adhere closely to the established policy regarding cooperation with GERMANY and ITALY.

We hereby respectfully report to Your Majesty.

13 Mar 42

Prime Minister TOJO Hideki
Chief of the Naval General Staff NAGANO Osami
Chief of the Army General Staff SUGIYAMA Gen

Appendix C

DIRECTIVE TO THE SUPREME COMMANDER IN THE
SOUTHWEST PACIFIC AREA
(CCS 57/1)

BY AGREEMENT AMONG THE GOVERNMENTS OF AUSTRALIA, NEW ZEALAND, UNITED KINGDOM, AND THE UNITED STATES.

1. The SOUTHWEST PACIFIC AREA has been constituted as defined in Annex One. Definitions of other areas of the PACIFIC Theater are as shown therein.

2. You are designated as the Supreme Commander of the SOUTHWEST PACIFIC Area, and of all armed forces which the governments concerned have assigned, or may assign to this area.

3. As Supreme Commander you are not eligible to command directly any national force.

4. In consonance with the basic strategic policy of the governments concerned your operations will be designed to accomplish the following:

   a. Hold the key military regions of Australia as bases for future offensive action against Japan, and in order to check the Japanese conquest of the SOUTHWEST PACIFIC AREA.

   b. Check the enemy advance toward Australia and its essential lines of communication by the destruction of enemy combatant, troop, and supply ships, aircraft, and bases in Eastern Malaysia and the New Guinea–Bismarck–Solomon Islands Region.

   c. Exert economic pressure on the enemy by destroying vessels transporting raw materials from the recently conquered territories to Japan.

   d. Maintain our position in the Philippine Islands.

   e. Protect land, sea, and air communications within the SOUTHWEST PACIFIC Area, and its close approaches.

   f. Route shipping in the SOUTHWEST PACIFIC Area.

   g. Support the operations of friendly forces in the PACIFIC OCEAN Area and in the INDIAN Theater.

   h. Prepare to take the offensive.

5. You will not be responsible for the internal administration of the respective forces under your command, but you are authorized to direct and coordinate the creation and development of administrative facilities and the broad allocation of war materials.

6. You are authorized to control the issue of all communiques concerning the forces under your command.

7. When task forces of your command operate outside the SOUTHWEST PACIFIC Area, coordination with forces assigned to the areas in which operating will be effected by the Joint Chiefs of Staff, or the Combined Chiefs of Staff, as appropriate.

8. Commanders of all armed forces within your Area will be immediately informed by their respective governments that, from a date to be notified, all orders and instructions issued by you in conformity with this directive will be considered by such commanders as emanating from their respective governments.

9. Your staff will include officers assigned by the respective governments concerned, based upon requests made directly to the national commanders of the various forces in your Area.

10. The governments concerned will exercise direction of operations in the SOUTHWEST PACIFIC Area as follows:

a. The Combined Chiefs of Staff will exercise general jurisdiction over grand strategic policy and over such related factors as are necessary for proper implementation, including the allocation of forces and war materials.

b. The Joint U.S. Chiefs of Staff will exercise jurisdiction over all matters pertaining to operational strategy. The Chief of Staff, U.S. Army will act as the Executive Agency for the Joint U.S. Chiefs of Staff. All instructions to you will be issued by or through him.

ANNEX ONE

DIVIDING LINE BETWEEN INDIAN THEATER AND PACIFIC THEATER

From CAPE KAMI in the LUICHOW PENINSULA around the coast of the TONKIN GULF, INDO-CHINA, THAILAND, and MALAYA to SINGAPORE: from SINGAPORE south to the north coast of SUMATRA, thence around the east coast of SUMATRA (leaving the SUNDA STRAIT to the eastward of the line) to a point on the coast of SUMATRA at Longitude 104° East, thence south to Latitude 08° South, thence southeasterly towards ONSLOW, AUSTRALIA, and on reaching Longitude 110° East, due south along that meridian. The PACIFIC THEATER extends eastward of this dividing line to the continents of NORTH and SOUTH AMERICA.

DEFINITION OF SOUTHWEST PACIFIC AREA

The westerly boundary of the SOUTHWEST PACIFIC Area is the westerly boundary of the PACIFIC Theater, the Area including necessary naval and air operational areas off the West Coast of AUSTRALIA. The north and east boundaries of the SOUTHWEST PACIFIC Area run as follows: From CAPE KAMI (LUICHOW PENINSULA) south to Latitude 20° North; thence east to Longitude 130° East; thence south to the Equator; thence east to Longitude 165° East; south to Latitude 10° South; southwesterly to Latitude 17° South, Longitude 160° East; thence south.

DEFINITION OF SOUTHEAST PACIFIC AREA

From the MEXICAN–GUATEMALA western boundary southwesterly to Latitude 11° North, Longitude 110° West; thence south.

DEFINITION OF THE PACIFIC OCEAN AREA

The PACIFIC OCEAN Area includes all of the PACIFIC Theater not included in the SOUTHWEST and SOUTHEAST PACIFIC Areas, and is sub-divided into the:

NORTH PACIFIC AREA, North of Latitude 42° North;

CENTRAL PACIFIC AREA, between the Equator and Latitude 42° North;

SOUTH PACIFIC AREA, South of the Equator.

Appendix D

BY AGREEMENT AMONG THE GOVERNMENTS OF
AUSTRALIA, NEW ZEALAND, UNITED KINGDOM,
AND THE UNITED STATES.

1. The PACIFIC OCEAN Area, comprising the NORTH, CENTRAL and SOUTH PACIFIC Areas, has been constituted, as defined in Annex 1.[1]

2. You are designated as the Commander in Chief of the PACIFIC OCEAN Area, and of all armed forces which the governments concerned have assigned or may assign to this area.

3. The governments concerned will appoint a commander of the SOUTH PACIFIC Area, who, as such, will not be eligible to command directly any national force. Acting under your authority and general direction he will exercise command of the combined armed forces which may at any time be assigned that area. You will exercise direct command of the combined armed forces in the NORTH and CENTRAL PACIFIC Areas.

4. In consonance with the basic strategic policy of the governments concerned your operations will be designed to accomplish the following:

a. Hold the island positions between the United States and the SOUTH-WEST PACIFIC Area necessary for the security of the line of communications between those regions; and for supporting naval, air and amphibious operations against Japanese forces.

b. Support the operations of the forces in the SOUTHWEST PACIFIC Area.

c. Contain Japanese forces within the PACIFIC Theater.

d. Support the defense of the continent of North America.

e. Protect the essential sea and air communications.

f. Prepare for the execution of major amphibious offensives against positions held by Japan, the initial offensives to be launched from the SOUTH PACIFIC Area and SOUTHWEST PACIFIC Area.

5. You will not be responsible for the internal administration of the respective forces under your command. You are authorized to direct and coordinate the creation and development of administrative facilities and the broad allocation of war materials.

6. You are authorized to control the issue of all communiques concerning the forces under your command.

7. When task forces of your command operate outside the PACIFIC OCEAN Area, coordination with forces assigned to the area in which operating will be

---

[1] See Annex One to Appendix C, above.

effected by the Joint Chiefs of Staff or the Combined Chiefs of Staff, as appropriate.

8. Commanders of all armed forces within your Area will be immediately informed by their respective governments that, from a date to be notified, all orders and instructions issued by you in conformity with this directive will be considered by such commanders as emanating from their respective governments.

9. Your staff will include officers assigned by the governments concerned, based upon requests made directly to the national commanders of the various forces in your Area.

10. The governments concerned will exercise direction of operations in the PACIFIC OCEAN Area as follows:

a. The Combined Chiefs of Staff will exercise general jurisdiction over grand strategic policy and over such related factors as are necessary for proper implementation, including the allocation of forces and war material.

b. The Joint U.S. Chiefs of Staff will exercise jurisdiction over all matters pertaining to operational strategy. The Commander in Chief, U.S. Fleet, will act as the Executive Agency for the Joint U.S. Chiefs of Staff. All instructions to you will be issued by or through him.

Appendix E

1. OBJECTIVE: Offensive operations will be conducted with the ultimate objective of seizure and occupation of the NEW BRITAIN–NEW IRELAND–NEW GUINEA Area.

2. PURPOSE: To deny the area to JAPAN.

3. TASKS:

a. TASK ONE. Seizure and occupation of SANTA CRUZ ISLANDS, TULAGI, and adjacent positions.

b. TASK TWO. Seizure and occupation of the remainder of the SOLOMON ISLANDS, of LAE, SALAMAUA, and Northeast Coast of NEW GUINEA.

c. TASK THREE. Seizure and occupation of RABAUL and adjacent positions in the NEW GUINEA–NEW IRELAND Area.

4. GENERAL INSTRUCTIONS:

a. The composition of the forces to be used, the timing of the tasks, and the passage of command will be determined by the U.S. Chiefs of Staff.

b. For planning purposes a target date for TASK ONE is tentatively set as August 1, 1942.

(c) Direct command of the tactical operations of the amphibious forces will remain with the Naval task force commander throughout the conduct of all three tasks.

(d) The withdrawal of the naval attached units of the U.S. Fleet may be ordered by the U.S. Chiefs of Staff upon the completion of any particular phase of the operation in the event that:

(1) conditions develop which unduly jeopardize the aircraft carriers:

(2) an emergency arises in other Pacific areas which dictates such withdrawal.

(e) The eastern and western boundaries of the SOUTHWEST PACIFIC AREA and of the SOUTH PACIFIC AREA respectively will, as of August 1, 1942, be longitude one hundred fifty-nine degrees east from the equator southward.

5. FORCES

(a) Ground, air, and naval forces now under the command of the Supreme Commander, Southwest Pacific Area.

(b) At least two aircraft carriers with accompanying cruisers and destroyers, and the South Pacific Amphibious Force, with necessary transport divisions.

(c) Marine air squadrons and available land-based air support in South Pacifiic Area.

(d) Army occupational forces now in the South Pacific Area to be utilized to garrison TULAGI and adjacent island positions; troops from AUSTRALIA to provide other garrisons required.

6. COMMAND.

(a) TASK ONE. Seizure and occupation of SANTA CRUZ ISLANDS, TULAGI, and adjacent positions.

(1) Task Force Commander will be designated by the Commander in Chief, U.S. Pacific Fleet.

(2) Necessary Naval reinforcements and land-based air support will be attached by the Supreme Commander, Southwest Pacific Area, who will also provide for interdiction of enemy air and naval activities westward of the operating area.

b. TASK TWO. Seizure and occupation of the remainder of the SOLOMON ISLANDS and of LAE, SALAMAUA, and Northeast Coast of NEW GUINEA. The task forces engaged in this operation will be under the direction of the Supreme Commander, Southwest Pacific Area.

c. TASK THREE. Seizure and occupation of RABAUL and adjacent positions in the NEW GUINEA–NEW IRELAND Area. The task forces engaged in this operation will be under the direction of the Supreme Commander, Southwest Pacific Area.

Appendix F

Letter of Instructions to Maj. Gen. Millard F. Harmon,
Commanding General, U.S. Army Forces in the South Pacific,
7 July 1942

1. The establishment of the Pacific Ocean Area as an area of United States strategical responsibility under the command of the Commander-in-Chief, U.S. Pacific Fleet, became effective on May 8, 1942. The Commander-in-Chief, U.S. Pacific Fleet, has been designated the "Commander-in-Chief, Pacific Ocean Area". Under the Commander-in-Chief, Pacific Ocean Area, a U.S. Naval officer has been designated as "Commander, South Pacific Area". The South Pacific Force under COMSOPAC include the following:

a. All base and local defense forces (ground, naval and air) now assigned or to be assigned to forces in the South Pacific Area. The New Zealand Chiefs of Staff are responsible for the land defense of New Zealand, subject to such strategic decisions affecting this responsibility as may be made by the Commander-in-Chief, Pacific Fleet, for the conduct of naval operations in the Pacific Ocean Areas.

b. Assigned New Zealand, Free French, Dutch and other United Nations Naval forces.

c. Such fleet types and aircraft as may be assigned by the Commander-in-Chief, U.S. Pacific Fleet.

2. COMMAND.

a. By direction of the President, you are designated as the "Commanding General, United States Army Forces in the South Pacific Area" (except CANTON Island) under the "Commander, South Pacific Area". Your short title will be COMGENSOPAC. As Commanding General of the United States Army Forces in the South Pacific Area, you will be responsible for the administration and training of all U.S. Army ground and air troops within the area, and will assist the Commander of the South Pacific Area in the preparation and execution of plans for the employment of Army forces in that area. Your responsibilities with regard to supply are covered in Paragraph 3, below.

b. You will survey and analyze the means provided each Army command in the South Pacific Area for the execution of its assigned mission and, based thereon, submit for approval by the War Department, your recommendations for the rearrangement, reduction or augmentation of the personnel and material now allocated to each base command with a view to establishing a balanced, cohesive and efficient Army contingent for the execution of separate base command missions and for the effective defense of the South Pacific Area as a whole. In this connection you are advised that for the present, operations in the South Pacific Area are restricted to those necessary to support the strategic defensive. Requirements for the present for this area will be held to the minimum consistent with that role.

3. a. Two mobile Army Air Forces, each comprising one heavy bombardment

group, have been established for operations in the Pacific and Southwest Pacific Areas, as may be directed by the Joint Chiefs of Staff. These mobile air forces will comprise.

(1) A Hawaiian mobile air force, from units duly assigned to the Hawaiian Department, which will normally base and operate in Hawaii;

(2) An Australian mobile air force, from units duly assigned to the Southwest Pacific Area, which will normally base and operate in Australia.

b. In cooperation with the Commanding General, Hawaiian Department, and the Commanding General, Southwest Pacific Area, you will assist the Commander, South Pacific Area in the preparation of advance plans for the employment, protection and supply of these two mobile air striking forces so as to facilitate their employment in the South Pacific Area, if and when they are ordered to that area.

4. SUPPLY.

a. As Commanding General, U.S. Army Forces in the South Pacific Area, you will be responsible for the supply of all bases in that area for which the Army is responsible. The basic supply directive is WD letter, file Ag 400 (4–27–42) MC–SP–M, April 28, 1942, subject: "Supply of Overseas Department, Theaters, and Separate Bases". See Inclosure No. 2 attached. You are charged with the duties of overseas department, theater and separate base commanders as prescribed in paragraph 6 a of Inclosure No. 2 except as modified below.

b. The San Francisco Port of Embarkation is assigned the responsibility for supply of your forces.

c. Where possible, delivery of supplies will be made in full shipload lots to the respective bases in accordance with directives of COMSOPAC for supplies procured by the Joint Purchasing Board, and of the Commanding General, San Francisco Port of Embarkation, for supplies furnished by him. Where redistribution of supplies is necessary, COMGENSOPAC will notify the Commanding General, San Francisco Port of Embarkation of the destination of these supplies as directed by COMSOPAC. War Department letter, AG 400 (6–22–42) MS–SP–M, June 25, 1942, subject: "Supply of United States Army Forces in the South Pacific Area" is revoked upon your assumption of command (see Inclosure No. 3).

d. The responsibility for Class III supplies of all categories at Army bases in the Area rests with the Navy. To this end, COMGENSOPAC will keep COMSOPAC fully informed of the need for this class of supply.

e. You are specifically charged to:

(1) Secure information from Army Task Force Commanders as to what supplies can be procured at each base, and pass this information on to COMSOPAC, so that these supplies need not be furnished by the Joint Purchasing Board or Army sources at San Francisco Port of Embarkation.

(2) Receive strength reports from each base and relay them to the Commanding General, San Francisco Port of Embarkation and to COMSOPAC.

(3) Arrange for the automatic supply to all bases of Class I supplies which can be procured by the New Zealand Joint Purchasing Board. The actual distribution of these supplies will be made as directed by COMSOPAC.

(4) Notify the Commanding General, San Francisco Port of Embarkation of the Class I supplies which are being furnished locally.

(5) Have all requisitions for Class II and IV supplies routed through your headquarters. Arrange to furnish those supplies of these classes which can be secured locally in the same manner as in (c) above.

(6) Forward requisitions for Class II and IV supplies to the Commanding General, San Francisco Port of Embarkation for the balance of these classes of supply with specific instructions as to priority of shipments together with full information as to the basis of the requisition.

(7) Secure from Army Task Force Commanders information as to any exportable surplus of local produce available at each base. Inform COM-SOPAC.

5. You will proceed under air-travel orders to Auckland, New Zealand, making such inspections of your command enroute as you see fit. Upon arrival at Auckland, you will establish your headquarters and make all preparations to assume command of the forces to which you have been assigned. When you are ready to assume command, you will report to the Commander, South Pacific Area and by secret radio the War Department.

By direction of the Commander-in-Chief.

G. C. MARSHALL,
Chief of Staff.

OFFICIAL:

THOS T. HANDY,
Brigadier General,
Assistant Chief of Staff.

Appendix G

I. Operational Objective

The objective of the South Pacific Operations is to establish supremacy in the South Pacific Area. In order to accomplish this aim the Army and Navy will, under closely concerted operations, occupy and secure the following strategic points without delay, and thus, gain sound strategic superiority:

A. Solomon Archipelago Area—Securement of the Solomon Archipelago (Area North of New Georgia Island and Ysabel Island).

B. Eastern New Guinea Area—Occupy and secure Eastern New Guinea, especially the strategic points in Northeastern New Guinea and prepare for subsequent operations.

II. Operational Strategy

A. Solomon Archipelago Area

1. During the period from about the latter part of January to the early part of February, the Army and Navy will, by every possible means, evacuate the units in Guadalcanal. The evacuation operation will be enforced in accordance with a separately drawn up agreement.

2. The defenses of the areas to be secured, as specified in paragraph I Operation Objective, will be strengthened without delay. For this reason, the Army and Navy will be allotted the task of defense as follows:

| Northern Solomon Archipelago | { Shortland Islands Bougainville Island Buka Island } | Army |

| New Georgia Island Ysabel Island | Navy | An Army unit, with about two infantry battalions as its nucleus, will be placed under the command of the Navy. |

3. The Navy units will continue air operations against the Guadalcanal Area and will cut off the enemy lines of supply in coordination with submarine operations.

B. New Guinea Area

1. The operational bases at Lae, Salamaua, Madang and Wewak will be reinforced without delay. Furthermore, the strategic points in the northeastern part of New Guinea, generally the area north of the Owen Stanley Range will be occupied, and preparations will be made for subsequent operations directed mainly against the Port Moresby area. The details on subsequent operations will be determined separately.

2. The units in the Buna area will, at an opportune time and as the occasion may demand, withdraw to the Salamaua area and secure necessary positions.

III. Air Operations

A. Operational Plans

1. The allotted assignments for the Army and Naval Air Forces will be as follows:

a. Army Air Force—Will support and cooperate with land and defense operations of the units in New Guinea, and protect the lines of communications in the New Guinea Area. Furthermore, as much as possible, under close cooperation with the Navy, the Army Air Force will enforce aerial supremacy combat in the Eastern New Guinea Area.

b. Naval Air Force—Will be responsible for air operations of those areas in the Solomon Archipelago and New Guinea Area not delegated to the Army Air Force.

c. The Army and Naval Air Forces will mutually support the local units in the air defense of those areas.

2. During the execution of the Operation, the Army Air Force will, without reference to Item A–1 of the foregoing, support the Naval Air Force with its main force (all fighter units will take part), and will annihilate enemy air power. Furthermore, the Army Air Force will support land operations and protect the lines of communications.

3. The Army and Naval Air Forces will, by taking advantage of the opportune moment and in close cooperation, simultaneously take part in the same operation and exert efforts to display their all-out joint might. . . .

IV. Commander and Strength

Navy:

Commander—Commander in Chief, Combined Fleet

Strength—Greater part of the Combined Fleet

Army:

Commander—Commander of 8th Area Army

Strength—8th Area Army

V. Chain of Command

It will be the joint chain of command of the Army and Navy. However, when the Army units and Navy land combat units are taking part in land operations in the same area at the same time, the senior commander will be, at times, ordered to assume the over-all command of the land operations.

VI. Communications

Communications will be carried out in accordance with the Army and Navy Central Agreement on Communications for the South Pacific Area Operation as per enclosure. . . .

X. Exchange of Intelligence

A. When necessary, the Army and Navy will exchange their staff officers for the purpose of liaison work.

B. The local Army and Navy forces will mutually exchange vital information valuable to the Army and Navy, and will maintain prompt liaison of such information.

XI. Information

Until further notice, Imperial General Headquarters will release all information.

XII. Agreement between Army-Navy Commanders

The following Army and Navy commanders will, at their discretion, conclude an operation agreement.

Commander in Chief of
Combined Fleet

and

Commander of
8th Area
Army

Commander in Chief of
South East Area Fleet

Subsequent agreements between the commanders of the Army and Navy forces concerned will be decided in accordance with the agreements of the aforementioned Army-Navy commanders.

Supplement

I. Objective

During the period from about the latter part of January to the early part of February, the Army and Navy will, by every possible means, evacuate the units in Guadalcanal.

II. Operational Strategy

A. In order to accelerate preparations for evacuation operations and at the same time facilitate the concealment of the plan, present preparations for another offensive operation on Guadalcanal will be accelerated.

B. Without delay, the combat zone of the 17 Army will be readjusted and reduced to the strategic lines in the rear.

C. Until the evacuation operation is effected, continue and increase supplies to the units by various means and maintain the fighting power of units in Guadalcanal. Furthermore, when transporting supplies, the transports will as much as possible, evacuate the casualties from Guadalcanal. The above task of transporting supplies and evacuation of casualties to the rear will mainly be the responsibility of the Navy.

D. The Army and Navy will, in cooperation, equip the air bases in the Solomon Archipelago Area without delay, and will, at an opportune time, station their air units. Thus, the Army and Navy will strengthen their air attacks against the Guadalcanal Area.

E. Along with the enforcement of the air operation mentioned in the above Item D, the Army and Navy will, by every possible means, evacuate the units in Guadalcanal to the strategic points in the rear by utilizing all available warships and other types of vessels.

F. Observe strict caution in maintaining secrecy of this operation.

Appendix H

Conduct of the War in the Pacific Theater in 1943,
Memorandum by U.S. Joint Chiefs of Staff,
22 January 1943 (CCS 168)

1. Japan has expanded the scope of her occupation so that it includes not only her former holdings of (1) Korea and Manchuria on the mainland of Asia and (2) a considerable part of China (including all of the coast), but in the past year, (3) all of Indo-China, Malaysia, Thailand, most of Burma, and as well, (4) all of the Philippines and (5) the Dutch East Indies.

2. The ultimate defeat of Japan proper will be accomplished by measures which greatly resemble those which would be effective against the British Isles —blockade (attack on ships and shipping), bombing (attack on forces, defenses, industries, and morale), and assault (attack via the sea.) Of these measures, attacks on ships and shipping along enemy lines of communications are inherent in all offensive operations; it is our purpose during 1943 to work toward positions from which Japan can be attacked by land based air; assault on Japan is remote and may well not be found necessary. Allied offensive measures in 1943 comprise continued and intensified attacks on enemy ships and shipping, in the cutting or threatening to cut enemy lines of communication between Japan and Japanese holdings, and in attacks on enemy sea, air, and ground forces by obliging them to fight to retain their holdings and to maintain their lines of communication.

3. The scope and intensity of the Allied war effort in the Pacific during 1943, while conditioned on the premise that Germany is the principal enemy, requires that sufficient means be in hand surely to counter enemy potentialities (para. 4 to follow) and, further, must take care that the means in hand are actively employed to best advantage. The general capabilities of the Allied effort in the Pacific in 1943 comprise:

(a) Keep Japan from further expansion, and from consolidating and exploiting her current holdings.

(b) Maintain the vital Midway-Hawaii line (key to the Pacific).

(c) Secure the line of communications to Australia and New Zealand.

(d) Block enemy approaches to Australia (1) from the Northward via Rabaul (2) from the Northwestward via the Malay barrier.

(e) Attain positions which menace enemy line of communication with the Dutch East Indies, the Philippines, and the South China Sea.

(f) Open the line of communications with China via Burma—in order to make use of Chinese geographical position (as to attack enemy line of communication in Formosa Straits and along the coast of China, perhaps to bomb Japan).

(g) Make ready to support Russia in case of war with Japan.

(h) Continue and intensify attrition of enemy strength by land, air, and sea (including submarine) action.

4. Japan's potentialities for offensive action during 1943 embrace:

(a) the Maritime Provinces (Eastern Siberia) –Russia;

(b) Alaska via the Aleutians;

(c) the Midway-Hawaii line—key to the Pacific

(d) the Hawaii–Samoa–Fiji–New Caledonia line, which covers the line of communications to Australia and New Zealand;

(e) Australia and New Zealand—via the Bismark Archipelago and/or the Solomons;

(f) Australia—via the Malay barrier;

(g) India—via Burma;

(h) China;

(i) *Of the above,* (a) is static unless and until war takes place between Russia and Japan; (b) has proved, and will continue, unprofitable to Japan; (c) has been tried and may be tried again but is unlikely to succeed; (d) is now unprofitable except via the Gilbert and Ellice Islands toward Samoa (the Jaluit-Samoa line); (e) is now under contest by United Nations forces; (f) is unprofitable except to forestall Allied advance from N.W. Australia; (g) is feasible except that enemy position is already well extended; (h) same as (g) —profitable chiefly to forestall Allied action.

5. Allied seizure and occupation, now in progress, of the New Caledonia/New Guinea line has for objectives:

(a) security of the line of communications from U.S. to Australia and New Zealand;

(b) blocking of enemy approaches to Eastern Australia;

(c) points d'appui for further action;

(d) attrition of enemy forces which oppose our occupation.

6. Additional to the objectives attained by the seizure and occupation of the New Caledonia/New Guinea line (para. 5 above), the other feasible objectives for us appear to be:

(a) Japan via the Maritime Provinces (Eastern Siberia) noted only for record to offset 4 (a) above.

(b) Japan via the Aleutians and Kuriles—from Alaska.

(c) Advance from Midway towards Truk-Guam line via Wake and North-westerly Marshall Islands.

(d) Advance on the Samoa-Jaluit line via Ellice and Gilbert Islands.

(e) Advance from Rabaul area on Truk-Guam line.

(f) Dutch East Indies via Malay barrier (as Timor).

(g) participation in ANAKIM.

(h) *Of the above* (which are set down to match the items of para. 4 above):

(a) is merely potential unless and until war takes place between Japan and Russia;

(b) is unprofitable with means in sight in 1943 and is best undertaken, if at all, in connection with (a);

(c) is most useful, not only as to

(1) retention of initiative;

(2) partial counter to enemy potentialities of para. 4 (c); and, particularly,

(3) to draw off enemy forces involved in holding Rabaul area;

(d) is effective

(1) to forestall enemy potentialities in para. 4 (d) ;

(2) to make the line of communications to Australia and New Zealand fully secure; and

(3) to draw off enemy forces involved in Rabaul area;

(e) cannot be done until after consolidation of the Rabaul area upon completion of operations now in hand—see para. 5 above—but should, perhaps must, eventually be undertaken;

(f) useful on limited scale

(1) to counter enemy potentialities of par. 4 (f) ;

(2) to draw off enemy forces elsewhere in the Pacific;

(3) to employ forces available in Australia (after completion of para. 5) which would not otherwise be employable; N.B.—Attacks are not to be developed fully, as this might lead to extensive operations of the nature of frontal attacks.

(g) not effective before November though forces contributed would likely have to be made available in October—but—ANAKIM is of such importance in respect of its objective (bringing Chinese manpower and geographic position to bear on Japanese forces and positions) as to merit that priority which may be found indispensable to mount it.

7. Referring now to the general capabilities of Allied action listed in para. 3 above, set off against enemy potentialities in para. 4 above, we intend, as to the feasible objectives of par. 6 above—additional to those of par. 5 above—to:

(a) and (b) —make the Aleutians as secure as may be—which will implement 3 (a) (g) (h) ; N.B.—Germany can be expected to intensify pressure on Japan to attack Russia in Siberia (Maritime Provinces) .

c. undertake advance from Midway towards Truk-Guam line as practicable —to implement 3 (a) (b) (e) (h) and, particularly, when 6 (e) is undertaken;

(d) undertake advance along Samoa-Jaluit line to implement 3 (a) (c) (h) ;

(e) refrain from advance from Rabaul area towards Truk-Guam line unless and until forces are in hand to enable it to be carried through and followed up. Noted that it implements 3 (a) , (b) , (d) (1) , (e) , (h) ;

(f) undertake advance on the Malay barier (as Timor) on limited scale to counter enemy capabilities and divert his forces—to implement 3 (a) , (d) (2) , (e) , (h) ;

(g) participate in ANAKIM as may be found indispensable to mounting it.

Appendix I

The Elkton Plan
FOR
The Seizure and Occupation of
The New Britain–New Ireland–New Guinea Area,
Prepared by GHQ, SWPA, 28 February 1943

SECTION I—GENERAL

1. a. General Task.

The Joint Directive for offensive operations in the Southwest Pacific is set forth by the Joint Chiefs of Staff in the following form:

Objective

"Seizure and occupation of the NEW BRITAIN–NEW IRELAND–NEW GUINEA area."

Purpose

"To deny the area to JAPAN."

Tasks

Task One   "Seizure and occupation of SANTA CRUZ ISLANDS, TULAGI, and adjacent positions."

Task Two   "Seizure and occupation of remainder of SOLOMONS, LAE, SALAMAUA, and northeast coast of NEW GUINEA."

Task Three   "Seizure and occupation of RABAUL and adjacent positions in NEW BRITAIN–NEW IRELAND area."

b. Analysis of Task.

(1) Task 1 above may be considered accomplished.

(2) Tasks 2 and 3 require the employment of two general axes of advance: on the west, along the line northeast coast of NEW GUINEA–NEW BRITAIN; on the east, through the SOLOMONS; culminating in the capture of RABAUL. In addition Task 3 requires seizure and occupation of positions in the NEW BRITAIN–NEW IRELAND area adjacent to RABAUL.

(3) The northeast coast of NEW GUINEA (northwest of BUNA), the SOLOMONS (northwest of GUADALCANAL), NEW IRELAND, and NEW BRITAIN are in the hands of the enemy. The sea and land areas south of the line BUNA-GUADALCANAL are generally under our control. The defenses of both sides are concentrated in and around airfields, the remainder of the land areas generally being unoccupied.

Tasks 2 and 3 generally require the following steps:

(1) Seizure of operating airdromes in the HUON PENINSULA area to provide necessary direct land-based air support for subsequent operations along the line of NEW BRITAIN.

(2) Seizure of operating airdromes in NEW GEORGIA to provide necessary direct land-based air support for subsequent operations along the line SOLOMONS–NEW IRELAND.

(3) Seizure of operating airdromes in NEW BRITAIN on the west and BOUGAINVILLE ISLAND on the east, to provide direct land-based air support for subsequent operations against KAVIENG and RABAUL.

(4) The capture of KAVIENG and the isolation of RABAUL by air and naval action. (The capture of KAVIENG may be delayed until after Step (5) if the situation justifies.)

(5) The capture of RABAUL after necessary reduction of enemy strength by combined attack to eliminate the center of enemy resistance.

2. Scheme of Maneuver.

a. The scheme of maneuver is based on seizure of HUON PENINSULA followed by converging attacks:

(1) Through NEW BRITAIN.

(2) Through the SOLOMONS to KAVIENG.

Both culminating in a combined assault on RABAUL.

The attack along the NEW GUINEA coast to capture operating airdromes in the HUON PENINSULA must precede the attack through the SOLOMONS, then both attacks proceed toward the objective, RABAUL, as a converging mutually supporting operation. Preceded by strong land-based air action and covered by our fleet to prevent major hostile naval interruption; the forces along the western axis operate against successive objectives to capture air operating bases in western NEW BRITAIN by air-borne and small craft operations and thence by amphibious operations to the capture of RABAUL; the forces along the eastern axis progress northwestward by amphibious operations through successive objectives to a meeting with western forces in a combined attack on RABAUL. Throughout the operations the employment of aviation of both forces is coordinated by the Commander in Chief, Southwest Pacific Area, in support of either force requiring the maximum assistance at the moment. The Fleet seeks decisive combat with hostile naval forces.

To insure the security of the Southwest Pacific Line of Communications, the defense of TORRES STRAIT area will be undertaken along the line DARWIN-MERAUKE by the action of ground, air, and naval units. MERAUKE will be occupied as an air operating base.

While the operations to secure successive objectives are considered separately, this does not indicate the timing necessarily. The timing will exploit favorable conditions and take advantage of the momentum achieved by either advance.

b. Diversions.

Request will be made on the Joint Chiefs of Staff for a diversion in the INDIAN OCEAN by Indian Theater Forces and/or in the North PACIFIC (ALEUTIAN ISLANDS) by North PACIFIC FORCES, to precede our operations and draw away hostile air and naval forces from the Southwest PACIFIC and supporting areas.

3. Organization.
   a. General Chart.

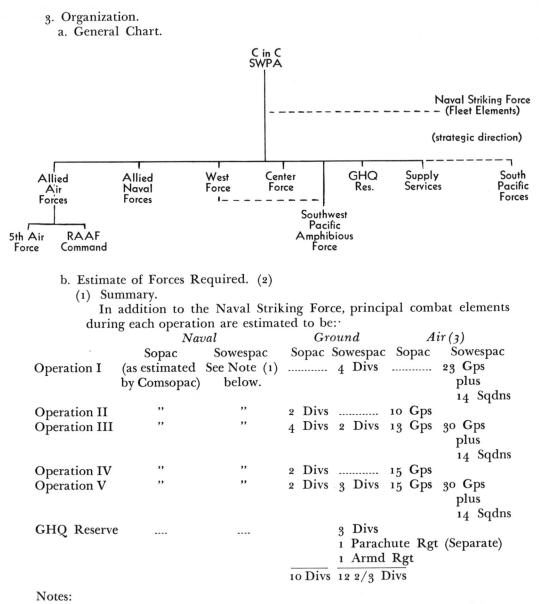

   b. Estimate of Forces Required. (2)
     (1) Summary.
       In addition to the Naval Striking Force, principal combat elements during each operation are estimated to be:·

	Naval		Ground		Air (3)	
	Sopac	Sowespac	Sopac	Sowespac	Sopac	Sowespac
Operation I	(as estimated by Comsopac)	See Note (1) below.	....	4 Divs	....	23 Gps plus 14 Sqdns
Operation II	”	”	2 Divs	....	10 Gps	
Operation III	”	”	4 Divs	2 Divs	13 Gps	30 Gps plus 14 Sqdns
Operation IV	”	”	2 Divs	....	15 Gps	
Operation V	”	”	2 Divs	3 Divs	15 Gps	30 Gps plus 14 Sqdns
GHQ Reserve	....	....	3 Divs 1 Parachute Rgt (Separate) 1 Armd Rgt			
			10 Divs	12 2/3 Divs		

Notes:
     (1) Preliminary estimate by Commander, Allied Naval Forces, of forces required for this campaign:

               2 Cru Divs
               2 Desrons
               1 Des Div
               4 PT Squadrons
              12 Submarines

in addition to the Naval forces normally required for the defense of the Southwest Pacific Area. The Commander in Chief, SWPA, considers that the minimum requirements are:

                                1 Cru Div
                                1 Desron
                                1 Des Div
                                4 PT Squadrons

in addition to the Naval forces now assigned the SWPA.

    (2) For land and air forces required for defense in the Southwest Pacific Area, see Enclosures 2 and 3.

    (3) Groups of four squadrons each, at maximum strength.

    (4) 2 Infantry Divisions (One garrisons TORRES STRAIT initially)
       1 Air-borne Division
       1 Parachute Regiment (Separate)
       1 Armored Regt. (Australian Brigade)
    (2) Totals.

       In view of the determined opposition expected and reduction of Land Force estimates to an absolute minimum, Land Forces assigned to an operation must be considered as permanently committed therein. Land Forces will require an estimated total of 22 2/3 Divisions. Air Forces will require approximately 30 Groups in the Southwest Pacific Area and 15 Groups in the South Pacific Area. Estimated capacity of amphibious equipment required is:

Operation	Sowespac	Sopac
I	1 Div	
II		1 Div
III	1 Div	2 Div
IV		2 Divs
V	2 Divs	1 Div

Southwest Pacific Area will employ small shore-to-shore equipment for one Division in Operation I. Remaining operations require amphibious equipment.

  4. Allotment of Tasks.
    a. Naval Striking Force.
      (1) Composition
      Elements of the U.S. Fleet and attached naval units.
      (2) Tasks.
      Cover the operations, prevent interference therewith by major enemy naval forces, and seek decisive action with hostile fleet.
    b. Allied Air Forces.
      (1) Composition.
      Fifth Air Force, R.A.A.F. Command and air elements Southwest Pacific Force not required for defense of installations, facilities, or shipping in the Southwest Pacific Area.
      (2) Tasks.
       (a) Destroy hostile aviation in general supporting areas of Northern

SOLOMONS, NEW IRELAND, eastern NEW BRITAIN, and the north coast NEW GUINEA. Destroy naval forces and shipping.

(b) Support the operations of the Southwest Pacific Task Forces.

(c) Support the defense of our forward bases and TORRES STRAIT.

(d) Provide transport aviation support for our operations.

(e) Be prepared to provide air support for operations of the South Pacific Area and the Naval Striking Force.

c. Allied Naval Forces.

(1) Composition.

Task Force 42, Task Force 44, PT Squadrons and escort vessels.

(2) Tasks.

(a) Support the operations of the Southwest Pacific Task Forces.

(b) Support the defense of forward bases in the Southwest Pacific Area and of TORRES STRAIT, and protect lines of communication.

d. West Force.

(1) Composition.

A self-contained Task Force organized and equipped for ground and shore-to-shore operations.

(2) Tasks

By air-borne, overland and overwater operations, capture LAE and MADANG and secure in the HUON PENINSULA–MARKHAM VALLEY areas air bases required for subsequent operations.

e. Center Force.

(1) Composition.

A Task Force organized and equipped for airborne and overwater operations in NEW BRITAIN.

(2) Tasks.

(a) Supported by air and light naval forces, capture and consolidate airfields in western NEW BRITAIN to include the general line GAS-MATA-TALASEA by combined air-borne and overwater operations.

(b) Supported by air and naval forces and in conjunction with ground forces of the South Pacific Area, capture RABAUL by an overwater operation.

f. Southwest Pacific Amphibious Force.

(1) Composition.

Escort vessels, transport vessels and landing craft.

(2) Tasks.

Embark, conduct, and land Southwest Pacific Task Forces in succession for the capture of MADANG, Western NEW BRITAIN, and RABAUL.

g. Supply Services.

(1) Composition.

USASOS and the Australian Lines of Communication.

(2) Tasks.

(a) Provide logistic support for the operations.

(b) Establish an intermediate base in MILNE BAY LOUISIADES area for logistic support of subsequent operations.

h. South 'Pacific Force.
    (1) Composition.
       as assigned.
    (2) Tasks.
      (a) Seize and occupy the NEW GEORGIA, BOUGAINVILLE, KAV-
IENG areas in successive operations.
      (b) Provide and land a secondary attack force for the capture of
RABAUL.

Appendix J

Japanese Army-Navy Central Agreement on
Southeast Area Operations, With Supplement
15 March 1943

I. Operational Objectives

The objective of Southeast Area operations lies in securing or occupying the strategic areas in the theater and thus establishing a superior and impregnable strategic position.

II. Operational Strategy

A. Plan for directing the operations

The Army and Navy forces shall literally operate as one unit, and the primary operation of the two forces will be directed against New Guinea, in order to establish bases for further operations in this theater. In the meantime, defensive measures will be intensified in the Solomon Islands and Bismarck Archipelago to secure the important areas already occupied and to destroy the enemy whenever he attacks.

B. Operation in New Guinea

1. Secure the key points around Lae and Salamaua against enemy air and ground offensives. The Army and Navy units will employ all means at their command in securing the supply situation for the units in these areas, and will thus increase their combat potentiality.

2. Air operations will be intensified to destroy the enemy air strength. At the same time, primary importance in air operations will be attached to the sustained effort of cutting off enemy lines of communications and reinforcement extending to the eastern coast of New Guinea. Furthermore, nothing will be left to be desired in respect to the air cover that our own lines of communications and supply will receive.

3. To carry out the operations in New Guinea, the Army and Navy will cooperate in the effort of quickly completing and strengthening the group of necessary air, air defense and lines of communication, and supply bases in New Guinea and New Britain. Simultaneously, vitally necessary roads will be built, mostly by Army units, and special effort will be made in expediting the establishment of military supply dumps and thus completing the establishment of operational bases on New Guinea and on the western part of New Britain.

4. Along with the preparation and expansion of bases mentioned in the preceding paragraph, troops and equipment in the vicinity of Lae and Salamaua will be increased, in order to strengthen the security of these areas. Completion of other facilities will also be expedited in preparation for the forthcoming operation, which will be directed primarily against Port Moresby. Agreement on subsequent operations will be made separately.

C. Operations in the Solomon Area

1. The defense of the key points north of New Georgia Island and Isabel Island will be strengthened, and present conditions secured and expanded,

so that enemy attacks can be repulsed at any time. Ground defense of this area will be shared by the Army and Navy as follows: Army—Northern portion of the Solomon Islands. Navy—Central portion of the Solomon Islands (New Georgia Island, Isabel Island, and adjacent islands) (some Army units will be placed under the Navy commander in accordance with agreement between the local Army and Navy commanders).

2. The operations of the naval air forces and submarines will be directed to check enemy efforts to send reinforcements and supplies to the Guadalcanal area and to crush the enemy strength.

3. The Army and Navy units will cooperate in building the necessary roads on Bougainville Island as well as in establishing as quickly as possible a supply line extending to the Solomon Islands.

4. Operations in the Bismarck Archipelago

The Army and Navy will cooperate in strengthening the defenses on New Britain Island, especially the defenses in the western part of the island and around Surumi. Also, in order to maintain supply lines to New Guinea, they will be charged with the task of completing land and sea lines of communication bases.

III. Air Operations

A. Every effort will be made by both the Army and Navy to rapidly increase their air strength and maintain their combat strength. Thus an increase in air strength will be achieved as planned, and it will be fully prepared in bringing the overall operation to a successful end.

B. In directing air operations, emphasis will be placed on achieving cooperation between Army and Navy air strength.

C. Allocation of air responsibility between Army and Navy air units during the operation, especially up to around September 1943, will be as follows:

1. Army air units

a. Will cooperate with the Navy in protecting the lines of communications and supply in the New Guinea area and in the Bismarck Archipelago.

b. Will shut off enemy land transportation in the New Guinea area as well as support our ground and defense operations in the New Guinea area.

c. Will cooperate with the Navy in aerial supremacy battles in the New Guinea area.

d. Will cooperate with the Navy in cutting off the enemy's sea lanes north of Buna.

2. Navy air units

a. Will intercept enemy surface transportation around New Guinea, as well as cooperate with the Army in aerial supremacy combat in the same area.

b. Will take part in the air operation in the Solomon area. Such an operation will consist of aerial supremacy combat, interception of enemy transportation, interception of enemy aircraft, ground support, and covering lines of communications and supply.

c. Will protect lines of communications and supply in Bismarck Archipelago area.

d. Will cooperate as much as possible, with the Army in protecting the lines of communications and supply in the New Guinea area.

e. In the defense of the Bismarck Archipelago, the Navy air units will be assigned the primary responsibility, and will receive the cooperation of the Army air units in the locality. Besides, the local air defense will be made by mutual cooperation of army and navy units in the locality.

3. Army and Navy air units will be called upon to supply the Army and Navy units in the New Guinea area via air whenever it is deemed necessary. . . .

IV. Commanders, and Strength

Navy:

Commander—Commander in Chief of Combined Fleet

Unit   —Main force of Combined Fleet

Army:

Commander—Commanding General of the 8th Area Army

Unit   —Eighth Area Army

V. Chain of Command

Operations in this theater are basically conducted under cooperation between the Army and Navy. However, in the event that the Army and Navy are engaged in land operations in the same area at the same time, the senior commander of the area from among the Army and Navy will, as the occasion may demand, command the operation. . . .

VIII. Transport and Escort

A. For the time being, Palau will be the relay point for forwarding of supplies (reinforcements) as well as for concentrating Army units in the Southeast Area. With use of its vessels the Navy will, when deemed necessary, cooperate as much as possible with the Army in transporting the foregoing Army units and supplies. In each instance, the Army Department and Navy Section of Imperial General Headquarters will, when the above cooperation is effected, determine the details.

B. Depending on operational conditions in the local operations, the Navy will assist the Army or will even carry the full burden of transporting materiel and Army units not covered in the preceding paragraph. Matters pertaining to such transportation will be studied and agreed upon by the Army and Navy commanders concerned.

C. The transport ships (including empty transports) returning from the Southeast Area will, insofar as is possible, return home directly from the point of departure. For the time being, however, Palau will be used as a relaying port, and the transports will, as much as possible, navigate in convoy formation. The local Army and Navy commanders concerned will determine the details on the navigation of the convoy.

D. The Navy will provide the necessary escort for convoys (including empty ships) on return voyages as well as for convoys transporting Army units and supply materiel to the fronts. In carrying out the escort procedure, the Army Department and the Navy Section of Imperial General Headquarters, or the Army and Navy commanders concerned will, as specified in the preceding paragraphs, determine the details on the convoy escort. . . .

Supplement

The Agreement Between the Army and Navy Commander
1. Assignment of air bases to be used by Army and Navy.
   a. Primarily Army:.
      Rabaul (South) Wake Island, Lorengau, Finschhafen
   b. Primarily Navy:
      Rabaul (East) Kavieng, Surumi
   c. Jointly used by Army and Navy:
      Rabaul (West, Bamo, Tuluvu, Lae, Madang, Wewak, Babo, Hollandia
   2. The local Army and Navy commanders will decide as to which airfield or airfiields will be designated for joint use in the Lae, Madang and Wewak airfield group, and as to which branch of service will use the new airfields, pending construction.
   3. In addition, the Army will use Palau as a shelter airfield for one bomber regiment.
   4. Army will, until the air bases necessary for its own use are constructed and for operational and supply reasons, provide necessary ground duty units and facilities for air security to the following Navy air bases: Mindanao, Manado, Ambon, Namlea, Boela, Palau, Kendari and Makassar.
   5. The Army and Navy will, according to operational circumstances, mutually facilitate and utilize the respective air bases and will mutually render assistance in supply and in air base maintenance.
   6. Summary

Bringing the operations in the Southeast Area, especially in New Guinea, to a successful end is a matter of vital importance to the national defense of our Imperial homeland. Therefore, there are ample reasons to fear that poor planning or execution of the operation would lead to grave consequences. Furthermore, in order to maintain the impregnable strategical position of the Southeast Area at large, it is absolutely a minimum prerequisite to securely hold the present positions in New Guinea, Solomon Island and Bismarck Archipelago Areas. Serious failure in any of these areas would jeopardize the entire Southern Region.

Arriving at the foregoing estimation of the situation, the Army Department and the Navy Section of Imperial General Headquarters have agreed to exert all their efforts and bring the Southeast Area Operation to a successful end at all costs, under the plan singularly followed by both the Army Department and Navy Section of Imperial General Headquarters and the frontline echelons. It is based upon the joint strategical plan sanctioned by the Emperor on March 5th and on the strategical study conducted in the presence of His Majesty.

7. These are the steps to be taken as immediate measures by the Army Department and Navy Section of Imperial General Headquarters.
   a. Strengthening of respective Air Arms.

In the Southeast Area both branches of service will hastily increase their air strength or bring up the air units presently there to full strength, designate their areas of responsibility and increase and strengthen their air bases in those areas, and thus complete their preparations for air operations.

b. Supply, especially to these units in eastern New Guinea, must be carried out under a joint Army-Navy effort and with all available means at their command. To accomplish this objective, the following measures will be taken without delay.

(1) Both services will quickly increase the number of barges and other surface craft in the Southeast Area.

(2) Under joint Army-Navy effort, the facilities of the line of communications of small surface craft will be completed, and the transportation of supplies by small surface craft will be expedited. Furthermore, the Navy will, with a group of Naval vessels, enforce emergency transportation of supplies. The Army will exert every effort in maintaining the land lines of communications. Also, supply by air will be stepped up.

(3) However, in the event that it becomes impossible to cope with the situation with the aforementioned measures, which are to be enforced with every means available, the Navy will carry out the task of supply with every available means at its command.

c. The Army will, without loss of time, send new contingents of air defense troops required in the establishment of air bases and strengthen the defensive facilities in the New Guinea area. Furthermore, the Army, in addition to the foregoing assignments covered in the earlier plan, will put the Army transports at its disposal to maximum use and transport the newly-reinforced units to the Southeast Area. The Navy will assist in the transporting as much as possible.

8. Since how to supply our troops stationed in the zone within the radius of enemy aircraft has a decisive effect on the future course of the war, concrete plans will be made quickly and various means to insure its execution will be expedited, together with organizing the necessary materiel.

9. The Army Department and Navy Section of Imperial General Headquarters will formulate a joint concrete plan to direct their operations.

10. The Army-Navy Central Agreement on the South Pacific Ocean Area Operation, which is in effect at present, will be revised on the basis of the foregoing plans.

11. The Army Department and Navy Section of Imperial General Headquarters will direct their respective front line echelons in accordance with the preceding plan formulated at Imperial General Headquarters and will strive to achieve complete harmony and cooperation in directing operations. As a most practicable measure to realize this central plan, the Army Department and the Navy Section will simultaneously call their respective chiefs of staff of the local Army and Fleet back to Tokyo toward the end of March and issue the necessary instructions on the foregoing matters.

Appendix K

Joint Chiefs of Staff Directive:
Offensive Operations in the South and Southwest
Pacific Areas During 1943, 28 March 1943
(JCS 238/5/D)

1. The Joint Chiefs of Staff directive communicated in COMINCH dispatch 022100 of July 1942 is cancelled and the following directive is substituted therefor.

2. Command.

    a. The operations outlined in this directive will be conducted under the direction of the Supreme Commander, Southwest Pacific Area.

    b. Operations in the Solomon Islands will be under the direct command of the Commander, SOPAC Area, operating under general directives of the Supreme Commander, Southwest Pacific Area.

    c. Units of the Pacific Ocean Area, other than those assigned by the Joint Chiefs of Staff to task forces engaged in these operations, will remain under the control of the Commander in Chief, Pacific Ocean Area (CINCPAC).

3. Forces will be allocated for these operations as determined by the Joint Chiefs of Staff.

4. Tasks.

    a. Establish airfields on Kiriwina and Woodlark Islands.

    b. Seize Lae-Salamaua-Finschhafen-Madang Area and occupy Western New Britain.

    c. Seize and occupy Solomon Islands to include the southern portion of Bougainville.

5. Purposes. To inflict losses on Japanese forces, to deny these areas to Japan, to contain Japanese forces in the Pacific Theater by maintaining the initiative, and to prepare for ultimate seizure of Bismarck Archipelago.

6. Plans. Supreme Commander, Southwest Pacific Area, will submit general plans including composition of task forces, sequence and timing of major offensive operations to the Joint Chiefs of Staff.

Appendix L

JOINT CHIEFS OF STAFF DIRECTIVE:
UNIFIED COMMAND FOR U.S. JOINT OPERATIONS
20 APRIL 1943 (JCS 263/2/D)

Definition

1. Unified command as employed for U.S. Joint Operations is that command organization in which a force composed of units of the Army and of the Navy operates as a single command unit under an officer specifically assigned by higher authority to the command thereof.

Commander

2. A commander for U.S. Joint Operations, with appropriate title, is designated by and is responsible to the Joint Chiefs of Staff. His selection from the ground or air arm of the Army, or from the Navy by the Joint Chiefs of Staff will be guided by the nature of the contemplated operation and by the end to be attained.

Exercise of Command

3. When the Joint Force Commander has been designated and the units composing his force assigned, his command responsibilities are the same as if the forces involved were all Army or all Navy. He will exercise his command of the Army and Navy forces assigned, through the commanders of these forces or of the task forces concerned. Normally in operations, this will consist of the assignment of their respective missions. In carrying out its mission the tactics and technique of the force concerned are the responsibility of the commander of that force. The participation in matters of administration on the part of the Joint Force Commander will be kept to a minimum, and disciplinary matters will in so far as practicable be handled through the commander of the service concerned. Directives or instructions of major importance relating to separate services of a Joint Force will be sent to the Joint Force Commander by the Joint Chiefs of Staff rather than by the individual Chiefs of Staff of the Services concerned.

Organization

4. (a) A joint force commander will not function in a dual capacity as joint force commander and as commander of a component of his force, unless so directed by the Joint Chiefs of Staff.

   (b) A joint staff of appropriate size will be organized to assist the Joint Force Commander. It will comprise representatives of each of the several component parts of his force in such a manner as to insure an understanding of their several capabilities, needs, and limitations, together with the knowledge essential to maximum efficiency in integration of their efforts.

Subsidiary Joint Forces

5. The principles and system of unified command as outlined above will be extended, as appropriate, to subsidiary joint forces when so directed by the commander of the joint force of which they are a part.

Appendix M

Joint Chiefs of Staff Memorandum:
Strategic Plan for the Defeat of Japan
Approved by the Combined Chiefs of Staff, 19 May 1943
(JCS 287/1 and CCS 220)

1. A brief discussion of a strategic plan for the defeat of JAPAN is contained in Enclosure "A."

2. The plan is based on the following overall strategic concept for the prosecution of the war.

a. In cooperation with RUSSIA and other Allies to force an unconditional surrender of the AXIS in EUROPE.

b. Simultaneously, in cooperation with the other PACIFIC powers concerned, to maintain and extend unremitting pressure against JAPAN with the purpose of continually reducing her Military power and attaining positions from which her ultimate unconditional surrender can be forced.

c. Upon the defeat of the AXIS in EUROPE, in cooperation with other PACIFIC powers and, if possible, with RUSSIA, to direct the full resources of the UNITED STATES and GREAT BRITAIN to force an unconditional surrender of JAPAN. If, however, conditions develop which indicate that the war as a whole can be brought more quickly to a successful conclusion by the earlier mounting of a major offensive against JAPAN, the strategical concept set forth herein may be reversed.

3. In view of the long period covered and the inevitable changes in conditions that cannot be foreseen, it is not practicable to divide the plan into definitely coordinated phases. With this reservation in regard to timing and coordination, the plan is expressed as follows:

PHASE I

a. CONTINUE AND AUGMENT EXISTING UNDERTAKINGS IN AND FROM CHINA.

Chinese Forces assisted by U.S. Forces.

b. RECAPTURE BURMA.

British Forces assisted by U.S. and Chinese Forces.

c. OPEN A LINE OF COMMUNICATIONS TO THE CELEBES SEA.

United States Forces.

PHASE II

a. OPERATIONS TO OPEN THE STRAIT OF MALACCA AND TO COMPEL WIDE DISPERSION OF ENEMY FORCES.

British Forces.

b. RECAPTURE THE PHILIPPINES.

United States Forces.

c. PREPARE TO CAPTURE HONG KONG.

Chinese Forces.

PHASE III
a. CONTINUE OPERATIONS TO OPEN THE STRAIT OF MALACCA AND TO COMPEL WIDE DISPERSION OF ENEMY FORCES.
British Forces.
b. SECURE CONTROL OF THE NORTHERN PART OF THE SOUTH CHINA SEA, AND ASSIST IN THE CAPTURE OF HONG KONG.
United States Forces.
c. CAPTURE HONG KONG.
Chinese Forces.
PHASE IV
ESTABLISH AIR BASES IN JAPANESE OCCUPIED CHINA FROM WHICH TO LAUNCH AN OVERWHELMING BOMBING OFFENSIVE AGAINST JAPAN.
Chinese Forces, assisted by British and U.S. Forces.
PHASE V
CONDUCT AN OVERWHELMING AIR OFFENSIVE AGAINST JAPAN.
U.S. Forces, assisted by British and Chinese Forces.
PHASE VI
INVADE JAPAN.
U.S. Forces, assisted by British and Chinese Forces.

ENCLOSURE "A"
STRATEGIC PLAN FOR THE DEFEAT OF JAPAN

4. Objective of the plan.
THE UNITED NATIONS war objective is the unconditional surrender of the AXIS Powers. The accomplishment of this objective may require the invasion of JAPAN.

5. Most probable Japanese courses of action.
JAPAN's most probable courses of action are to direct her major effort toward securing and exploiting the territory she controls, and eliminating CHINA from the war.

6. The invasion of JAPAN.
Since the invasion of JAPAN is a vast undertaking, it should not be attempted until Japanese power and will to resist have been so reduced that favorable conditions for invasion obtain. Under these conditions the invasion of JAPAN is considered feasible.

It is probable that the reduction of JAPAN'S power and will to resist may only be accomplished by a sustained, systematic, and large-scale air offensive against JAPAN itself.

7. An overwhelming air offensive against JAPAN.
An air offensive on the required scale can only be conducted from bases in CHINA.

8. Recapture BURMA.

The attainment of bases in CHINA for the air offensive against JAPAN is dependent on the continuation of CHINA in the war, and on the establishment of adequate supply routes, not only to maintain CHINA, but also to maintain UNITED NATIONS forces which are to operate in and from CHINA. The recapture of BURMA is a prerequisite to the attainment of adequate bases in CHINA. The capacity of the Burma Road supplemented by the air route from INDIA is inadequate to support the air and ground forces required to implement an air offensive on the required scale. The seizure of a port in CHINA to augment the supply routes through BURMA is essential.

9. The seizure of a port in CHINA.

HONG KONG is the most suitable port which may be seized initially. Its seizure requires an offensive from the interior of CHINA by forces supported through BURMA, and, probably, by supplementary amphibious operations. Control of the SOUTH CHINA SEA by the UNITED NATIONS will be necessary to prevent JAPAN from successfully opposing these measures.

10. A line of communications to HONG KONG.

The most feasible sea route from the UNITED STATES to HONG KONG is through the CELEBES and SULU SEAS; that from the UNITED KINGDOM is through the STRAIT OF MALACCA. The establishment of these routes will require the neutralization of Japanese bases in the northern EAST INDIES, the PHILIPPINES, FORMOSA, and on the Asiatic mainland south of HONG KONG. Control of these areas will prevent JAPAN from supporting her forces in the NETHERLANDS EAST INDIES and will deny her the economic advantages she receives from that area. Operations to open a line of communications to HONG KONG and to control the SOUTH CHINA SEA are considered feasible.

11. A line of communications from HAWAII to the CELEBES SEA.

This line of communications to the CELEBES SEA will be established by advancing in the CENTRAL and SOUTHWEST PACIFIC areas with a view to shortening the sea route, providing for its security, and denying to the enemy bases and means by which he may interfere with the line of communications.

12. A line of communications through the STRAIT OF MALACCA.

Although the supply of forces in CHINA will come mainly from the UNITED STATES, operations to open the STRAIT OF MALACCA, after the reconquest of BURMA, are a vital part of the plan. The enemy must be continuously compelled to disperse his forces throughout the PACIFIC and ASIATIC areas thus exposing them to attrition on an additional front in SOUTH-EASTERN ASIA. This area is one of British strategic responsibility, and is a suitable and feasible undertaking for British Commonwealth Forces.

13. Control of the seas.

Since control of the seas in the western PACIFIC by the UNITED NATIONS may force the unconditional surrender of JAPAN before invasion and even before JAPAN is subjected to an intensive air offensive, every means to gain this control will be undertaken by the UNITED STATES. The establishment of the line of communications to the CELEBES SEA will be used as the vehicle to gain this end. The selection of intermediate objectives which will compel the enemy to expose his naval forces will be the greatest single factor in determining the enemy positions to be seized.

Attrition of enemy shipping, air, and naval resources will be a continuing objective. Raids on Japanese lines of communication, and carrier-based air raids on Japanese positions extending to JAPAN itself, will be implemented as our naval strength increases.

Appendix N

EXTRACT FROM THE FINAL REPORT OF THE COMBINED CHIEFS OF
STAFF TO THE PRESIDENT AND PRIME MINISTER AT THE
TRIDENT CONFERENCE, APPROVED 25 MAY 1943
(CCS 242/6)

In a previous memorandum (C.C.S. 242) the Combined Chiefs of Staff presented certain agreed conclusions reached during the present conference regarding operations in the three main theaters. These conclusions have been amended to accord with the views expressed by the President and the Prime Minister. The amended conclusions, and others reached since the previous memorandum was submitted, have now been related to resources available, and a final agreed summary of conclusions is submitted herein.

I. OVERALL OBJECTIVE

In conjunction with RUSSIA and other allies to bring about at the earliest possible date, the unconditional surrender of the AXIS Powers.

II. OVERALL STRATEGIC CONCEPT FOR THE PROSECUTION OF THE WAR

1. In cooperation with RUSSIA and other allies to bring about at the earliest possible date, the unconditional surrender of the AXIS in EUROPE.

2. Simultaneously, in cooperation with other PACIFIC Powers concerned, to maintain and extend unremitting pressure against JAPAN with the purpose of continually reducing her Military power and attaining positions from which her ultimate surrender can be forced. The effect of any such extension on the overall objective to be given consideration by the Combined Chiefs of Staff before action is taken.

3. Upon the defeat of the AXIS in EUROPE, in cooperation with other PACIFIC Powers and, if possible, with RUSSIA, to direct the full resources of the UNITED STATES and GREAT BRITAIN to bring about at the earliest possible date the unconditional surrender of JAPAN.

III. BASIC UNDERTAKINGS IN SUPPORT OF OVERALL STRATEGIC CONCEPT

Whatever operations are decided on in support of the overall strategic concept, the following established undertakings will be a first charge against our resources, subject to review by the Combined Chiefs of Staff in keeping with the changing situation.

1. Maintain the security and war making capacity of the WESTERN HEMISPHERE and the BRITISH ISLES.

2. Support the war making capacity of our forces in all areas.

3. Maintain vital overseas lines of communication, with particular emphasis on the defeat of the U-boat menace.

4. Intensify the air offensive against the AXIS Powers in EUROPE.

5. Concentrate maximum resources in a selected area as early as practicable for the purpose of conducting a decisive invasion of the AXIS citadel.

6. Undertake such measures as may be necessary and practicable to aid the war effort of RUSSIA.

7. Undertake such measures as may be necessary and practicable in order to aid the war effort of CHINA as an effective ally and as a base for operations against JAPAN.

8. To prepare the ground for the active or passive participation of TURKEY in the war on the side of the Allies.

9. To prepare the French Forces in AFRICA to fulfill an active role in the war against the AXIS Powers.

IV. SPECIFIC OPERATIONS FOR 1943/44 IN EXECUTION OF OVER-ALL STRATEGIC CONCEPT. . . .

3. Operations for the defeat of JAPAN.

We have directed the Combined Staff Planners to prepare an appreciation leading up to a plan for the defeat of JAPAN, including an estimate of the forces required.

a. Operations in the BURMA-CHINA Theater.

The Combined Chiefs of Staff have agreed on:

(1) The concentration of available resources, as first priority within the ASSAM-BURMA Theater, on the building up and increasing of the air route to CHINA to a capacity of 10,000 tons a month by early Fall, and the development of air facilities in ASSAM with a view to:

(a) Intensifying air operations against the Japanese in BURMA;

(b) Maintaining increased American air forces in CHINA; and

(c) Maintaining the flow of airborne supplies to CHINA.

(2) Vigorous and aggressive land and air operations at the end of the 1943 monsoon from ASSAM into BURMA via LEDO and IMPHAL, in step with an advance by Chinese forces from YUNNAN, with the object of containing as many Japanese forces as possible, covering the air route to CHINA, and as an essential step towards the opening of the BURMA road.

(3) The capture of AKYAB and of RAMREE ISLAND by amphibious operations, with possible exploitation.

(4) The interruption of Japanese sea communications into BURMA.

(5) The continuance of administrative preparations in INDIA for the eventual launching of an overseas operation of about the size of ANAKIM.

b. Operations in the PACIFIC.

Various courses of action have been examined by the Combined Chiefs of Staff and the operations they have agreed to undertake have the following objects:

(1) Conduct of air operations in and from CHINA.

(2) Ejection of the Japanese from the ALEUTIANS.

(3) Seizure of the MARSHALL and CAROLINE ISLANDS.

(4) Seizure of the SOLOMONS, the BISMARCK ARCHIPELAGO, and Japanese held NEW GUINEA.

(5) Intensification of operations against enemy lines of communication.

Appendix O

EXTRACT FROM THE FINAL REPORT OF THE COMBINED CHIEFS
OF STAFF TO THE PRESIDENT AND PRIME MINISTER AT THE
QUADRANT CONFERENCE, 24 AUGUST 1943 (CCS 319/5)

1. In previous memoranda (C.C.S. 319 and C.C.S. 319/2) the Combined Chiefs of Staff presented certain agreed conclusions reached during the present Conference regarding operations in the main theaters of war. These amended conclusions have been related to resources available, and an agreed summary is submitted herewith.

I. OVER-ALL OBJECTIVE

2. In conjunction with RUSSIA and other Allies to bring about at the earliest possible date, the unconditional surrender of the AXIS powers.

II. OVER-ALL STRATEGIC CONCEPT FOR THE PROSECUTION OF THE WAR

3. In cooperation with RUSSIA and other Allies to bring about at the earliest possible date, the unconditional surrender of the AXIS in EUROPE.

4. Simultaneously, in cooperation with other PACIFIC Powers concerned to maintain and extend unremitting pressure against JAPAN with the purpose of continually reducing her Military power and attaining positions from which her ultimate surrender can be forced. The effect of any such extension on the over-all objective to be given consideration by the Combined Chiefs of Staff before action is taken.

5. Upon the defeat of the AXIS in EUROPE, in cooperation with other PACIFIC Powers and, if possible, with RUSSIA, to direct the full resources of the UNITED STATES and GREAT BRITAIN to bring about at the earliest possible date the unconditional surrender of JAPAN.

III. BASIC UNDERTAKINGS IN SUPPORT OF OVER-ALL STRATEGIC CONCEPT.

6. Whatever operations are decided on in support of the overall strategic concept, the following established undertakings will be a first charge against our resources, subject to review by the Combined Chiefs of Staff in keeping with the changing situation.

    a. Maintain the security and war-making capacity of the WESTERN HEMISPHERE and the BRITISH ISLES.

    b. Support the war-making capacity of our forces in all areas.

    c. Maintain vital overseas lines of communication, with particular emphasis on the defeat of the U-boat menace.

    d. Continue the disruption of AXIS sea communications.

    e. Intensify the air offensive against the AXIS Powers in EUROPE.

    f. Concentrate maximum resources in a selected area as early as practicable for the purpose of conducting a decisive invasion of the AXIS citadel.

    g. Undertake such measures as may be necessary and practicable to aid the war effort of Russia.

h. Undertake such measures as may be necessary and practicable in order to aid the war effort of CHINA as an effective Ally and as a base for operations against JAPAN.

i. To prepare the ground for the active or passive participation of TURKEY in the war on the side of the Allies. (See also paragraph 62.)

j. To prepare the French Forces in AFRICA to fulfill an active role in the war against the AXIS Powers.

IV. EXECUTION OF THE OVER-ALL STRATEGIC CONCEPT

The War Against JAPAN

20. Long-term strategy

We have made a preliminary study of long-term strategy for the defeat of JAPAN and are of the opinion that the following factors require particular emphasis:

a. The dependence of JAPAN upon air power, naval power, and shipping for maintaining her position in the Pacific and Southeast Asia.

b. The consequent need for applying the maximum attrition to JAPAN's air force, naval forces, and shipping by all possible means in all possible areas.

c. The advantage to be gained and the time to be saved by a more extensive use of the superior air resources at the disposal of the United Nations, both in the strategic field and in conjunction with operations on land.

21. We consider that great advantage may be obtained, by modern and untried methods, from the vast resources which, with the defeat of Germany, will become available to the United Nations. We have in mind:

a. A project rapidly to expand and extend the striking power of the United Nations air forces in CHINA as well as of the ground troops for their defense by employing the large numbers of load carrying aircraft available to open an "air road" to CHINA.

b. The employment of lightly equipped jungle forces, dependent largely upon air supply lines.

c. The use of special equipment, such as artificial harbors, HABBAKUKS, etc., to enable the superior power of the United Nations to be deployed in unexpected and undeveloped areas.

22. From every point of view operations should be framed to force the defeat of JAPAN as soon as possible after the defeat of GERMANY. Planning should be on the basis of accomplishing this within twelve months of that event. Decisions as to specific operations which will insure a rapid course of events must await further examination on the lines indicated above.

23. The deployment of forces and the operations to be undertaken in the war against JAPAN must be in accord with the over-all objective and strategic concept reaffirmed in Sections I and II above (paragraphs 2–5).

24. We are agreed that the reorientation of forces from the European Theater to the PACIFIC and FAR EAST should be started as soon as the German situation, in our opinion, so allows.

25. The principle has been accepted that the forces to carry out operations

from the East, including the SOUTHWEST PACIFIC, shall be provided by the UNITED STATES, and for operations from the West by GREAT BRITAIN, except for special types not available to GREAT BRITAIN which will be provided by the UNITED STATES. The employment of Dominion forces will be a matter of discussion between all Governments concerned.

26. Specific operations 1943–44

We have found it impracticable during QUADRANT to arrive at all the necessary decisions for operations in the war against JAPAN in 1943–44. We therefore propose that, as soon as the necessary further examinations have been made, a Combined Chiefs of Staff Conference should be held wherever may be most convenient, unless agreement is reached through the ordinary channels. There are, nevertheless, certain decisions which we feel able to make at once.

27. Operations in the Pacific 1943–44.

We approve the proposals of the United States Chiefs of Staff for operations in the PACIFIC in 1943–44 as follows:

28. Gilberts

The seizure and consolidation of the GILBERTS preparatory to a further advance into the MARSHALLS.

29. Marshalls

The seizure of the MARSHALL ISLANDS (including WAKE and KUSAIE) preparatory to a westward advance through the central PACIFIC.

30. Ponape

The capture of PONAPE preparatory to operations against the TRUK area.

31. Carolines (Truk area)

The seizure of the eastern CAROLINES as far west as WOLEAI and the establishment of a fleet base at TRUK.

32. Palau Islands

The capture of the PALAUS including YAP.

33. Operations against Guam and the Japanese Marianas

The seizure of GUAM and the Japanese MARIANAS.

34. Paramushiru.

Consideration of operations against PARAMUSHIRU and the KURILES.

35. Operations in the New Guinea–Bismarcks–Admiralty Islands subsequent to current operations

The seizure or neutralization of eastern NEW GUINEA as far west as WEWAK and including the ADMIRALTY ISLANDS and BISMARCK ARCHIPELAGO. RABAUL is to be neutralized rather than captured.

36. Operations in NEW GUINEA subsequent to the WEWAK-KAVIENG Operation

An advance along the north coast of NEW GUINEA as far west as VOGELKOP, by step-by-step airborne-waterborne advances.

37. Operations in INDIA-BURMA-CHINA Theater, 1943–44

To carry out operations for the capture of UPPER BURMA in order to improve the air route and establish overland communications with CHINA. Target date mid-February 1944.

It is recognized that the extent of these operations is dependent upon logistic considerations as affected by recent floods.

38. To continue preparations for an amphibious operation in the Spring of 1944. Pending a decision on the particular operation, the scale of these preparations should be of the order of those contemplated at TRIDENT for the capture of AKYAB and RAMREE.

39. To continue the preparation of INDIA as a base for the operations eventually contemplated in the Southeast Asia Command.

40. To continue to build up and increase the air routes and air supplies of CHINA, and the development of air facilities, with a view to:

    a. Keeping CHINA in the war.

    b. Intensifying operations against the Japanese.

    c. Maintaining increased U.S. and Chinese Air Forces in CHINA.

    d. Equipping Chinese ground forces.

41. We have decided that our main effort should be put into offensive operations with the object of establishing land communications with CHINA and improving and securing the air route. Priorities cannot be rigid and we therefore propose to instruct the Supreme Commander in formulating his proposals to regard this decision as a guide and to bear in mind the importance of the longer term development of the lines of communication.

Appendix P

By direction of the President you are hereby informed that the Commanding General, Hawaiian Department has been designated as "Commanding General, U.S. Army Forces, Central Pacific Area" (including Canton Island) under the "Commander-in-Chief, Pacific Ocean Area". His short title will be COMGEN-CENTPAC. For this purpose the Central Pacific Area is as has been delineated to the Commander-in-Chief, Pacific Ocean Area. As Commanding General, U.S. Army Forces, Central Pacific Area, he will be responsible for the administration and training of all U.S. Army Ground and Air Troops within the area, and will be subject to the direction of the Commander-in-Chief of the Pacific Ocean Area in the preparation and execution of plans for the employment of Army Forces in that area. Responsibility with regard to supply remains unchanged.

By order of the Secretary of War:

J. A. ULIO
Major General
The Adjutant General

Appendix Q

JAPANESE GENERAL OUTLINE
OF THE FUTURE WAR DIRECTION POLICY,
ADOPTED AT THE IMPERIAL CONFERENCE,
30 SEPTEMBER 1943

Policy

(1) JAPAN will speedily establish a strategic position to gain victory over the UNITED STATES and BRITAIN while crushing enemy offensives in order to decide the issue of war during this year or the next, and at the same time, rapidly build up the decisive battle strength, especially air power, and prosecute the war against the UNITED STATES and BRITAIN on our own initiative.

(2) JAPAN will further strengthen co-operation with GERMANY and strive relentlessly for the successful conclusion of the joint war and will also take the initiative in improving relations with the SOVIET UNION.

(3) JAPAN will promptly establish the domestic structure for the decisive battle and will further solidify the unity of Greater East Asia.

Procedure

(1) The strategic posture to meet the Anglo-American invasion will be established, at the latest by around the middle of 1944 by surmounting all difficulties, and in the meantime the enemy offensive forces will be attacked and destroyed whenever occasion arises.

The strategic areas to be held at all costs in the PACIFIC and the INDIAN Ocean areas in prosecuting the war will be the KURILES, the BONINS, the Inner South Seas (central and western parts), and the area covering western NEW GUINEA, the SUNDA Islands, and BURMA.

Sea communications within the absolute national defense sphere will be safeguarded throughout the duration of the war.

(2) JAPAN will strive to the utmost to prevent the outbreak of the war with the SOVIET UNION and will take the initiative in improving the Soviet-Japanese relations and will also endeavor to mediate for peace between the SOVIET UNION and GERMANY at proper opportunities.

(3) JAPAN will maintain unremitting pressure against CHUNGKING and will take the earliest possible opportunity to settle the Chinese problem while checking especially the enemy air forces based in CHINA from bombing our homeland and disrupting our sea traffic.

(4) JAPAN will take every possible measure to strengthen co-operation with GERMANY. However, every precaution will be exercised to prevent the outbreak of war with the SOVIET UNION.

(5) JAPAN will win the confidence of the nations and the peoples of Greater East Asia and will guide them in order to receive and further encourage their co-operation with JAPAN'S war efforts. Vigilance will be exercised over enemy

political strategem toward the nations and the peoples of Greater East Asia, and necessary steps will be taken to forestall such enemy endeavors.

(6) The Imperial General Headquarters and the Government will further strengthen co-operation in their joint endeavor and will direct the war with renewed vigor.

(7) Resolute measures will be taken to build up the decisive military capability, especially the air power. The dauntless spirit to face the national crisis will be encouraged in order to bring the total national power into full play.

(8) The propaganda effort against the enemy will be conducted under a consistent policy, and will be directed mainly toward propagation of the Axis cause, diffusion of JAPAN's policy in Greater East Asia, demoralizing our major enemy, the UNITED STATES, alienation of the UNITED STATES, BRITAIN, CHINA and the SOVIET UNION, and helping INDIA achieve her independence.

Appendix R

JAPANESE ARMY-NAVY CENTRAL AGREEMENT CONCERNING
THE CENTRAL AND SOUTH PACIFIC OPERATIONS,
WITH SUPPLEMENT, 30 SEPTEMBER 1943

I. Operational Objectives

The objectives of the Southeast Area Operations are to destroy the attacking enemy in strategic sectors in this area and to plan to hold out as long as possible, thereby expediting future operations.

II. Operational Direction

The Army and Navy will closely cooperate to destroy the attacking enemy at all times at strategic sectors in the Southeast Area, extending east from Eastern New Guinea to the Solomon Islands, and thereby endeavor to hold out as long as possible. In order to accomplish this:

A. Defenses of the strategic sectors in the Bougainville–Bismarck Archipelago Area, centering around the vicinity of Rabaul, will be strengthened, and efforts will be made to hold them as long as possible. Moreover, supplies for strategic sectors on both shores of Dampier Strait as well as those in the Northern New Guinea Area will be secured as much as possible and efforts will be made to maintain them.

B. Efforts will be made to destroy with air and sea strength the attacking enemy before he makes a landing. In the event that the enemy does make a landing the enemy will be destroyed in the initial stage, thereby endeavoring to check his counterattack plan.

C. Large quantities of munitions will be amassed in the above strategic sectors and, in particular, supply transportation to the New Guinea Area will be speedily expedited.

III. Air Operations

A. The Army and Navy will utilize all available means to intensify their air operations, and will especially endeavor to display combined Army and Navy air strength and thereby conduct thoroughly satisfactory operations.

B. In air operations direction, overall operational policy will be considered, in particular search and patrol operations will be intensified and in the event of enemy landing operation, efforts will be made to destroy him resolutely at sea. . . .

IV. Commanders and Forces to be used

    1. Army:
    Commander—Commander of the 8th Area Army
    Strength—8th Area Army

    2. Navy:
    Commander—Commander in Chief of the Combined Fleet
    Strength—Bulk of the Combined Fleet

V. Command Relation

The Army and Navy will coordinate. Nevertheless, in the event that both the

Army and Navy units simultaneously conduct localized ground operations, the senior ranking officer may be ordered to assume unified operational command.

VI. Communications, Air Security and Weather

In accordance with the appendix, Army-Navy Central Agreement Concerning Communications, Air Security and Weather in the Southeast Area Operation.

VII. Supply

The Army and Navy will cooperate in regard to the supply of the Eastern New Guinea Area, particularly in the Dampier Strait and Madang Area, as well as to the Bougainville Island Area. Supply will be maintained as much as possible by the use of small craft and emergency transportation by naval craft.

VIII. Transportation and Escort

A. The Navy will cooperate with its naval vessels as much as possible for the transportation to concentrate and replenish Army forces in the Southeast Area. Whenever this is to be done, it will be conferred upon and decided at the Army and Navy Sections, Imperial General Headquarters.

B. In the transportation of Army units and supplies for local operations other than those mentioned in the above paragraph, the Army and Navy will cooperate and ships and naval vessels will be used. In regard to this, the Army and Navy commanders concerned will confer and decide.

C. Ships returning from the Southeast Area will be made as much as possible to proceed on a direct course from their point of departure. Nevertheless, for the time being, they will use Palau as a relay point and endeavor to proceed in a convoy. In regard to the above, the local Army and Navy commanders will confer and decide.

D. The Navy will furnish escorts for the transportation of Army units and supplies as well as for the return from such mission.

In regard to the execution of the above, the Army and Navy Sections, Imperial General Headquarters, or the Army and Navy commanders concerned will confer and decide in accordance with the provisions set down in the foregoing paragraphs.

IX. Public Information

It will be unified and handled by Imperial General Headquarters until further notice.

X. Designation of Operations

Solomon–Bismarck Archipelago Operation—Operation Ka.

New Guinea Area Operation—Operation To.

XI. Agreements Between Army and Navy Commanders

The following Army and Navy commanders will conclude agreements at their discretion: Commander in Chief of the Combined Fleet and the 8th Area Army Commander; Southeast Area Fleet Commander and the 8th Area Army Commander.

Supplement

This agreement stipulates the outline of operational direction throughout all of the Central and South Pacific Area this year and next year, and matters of special necessity. Agreements on matters pertaining to operations in the southeast area of the Central and South Pacific Areas and other areas will be made separately according to necessity.

I. Operational Policy

The Imperial Army and Navy will cooperate closely and annihilate the attacking enemy at strategic sectors of the Southeast Area and will plan to hold out as long as possible. During this time, the backbone for counteroffensives from the area North of Australia to strategic sectors in the Central Pacific Area will be completed, fighting strength for the counteroffensive will be prepared, and a thorough counteroffensive will be launched against the attacking enemy. Efforts will be made to annihilate the enemy beforehand and break down his fighting spirit.

II. Outline of Operational Direction

1. Plans will be made to hold out as long as possible by destroying the enemy attacking in the strategic sector of the Southeast Area, extending from Eastern New Guinea east to the Solomon Islands.

2. With the deadline generally set at spring of 1944, operational bases extending from strategic sectors in the area North of Australia to strategic sectors in the Caroline and Mariana Islands Area will be completed and their defenses strengthened, and such measures for counteroffensives as the construction of operational bases in the Philippines Area and preparation of land, sea and air counteroffensive strength will be speedily strengthened.

3. In the event of an enemy attack, all types of fighting strength will be concentrated against the enemy's attack front with bases in the aforementioned strategic sectors as the main support. Efforts will be made to destroy the enemy beforehand and thwart his attack plan.

4. Efforts will be made to conduct aggressive operations from the area north of Australia after the midde of 1944 if the situation permits. In regard to the direction of attack, separate studies and the necessary preparations will be made.

III. Southeast Area

Current operations in the Southeast Area will be based on the appendix, "Army-Navy Central Agreement Concerning Southeast Area Operation."

IV. Area North of Australia

1. The Army and Navy will cooperate and speedily strengthen operational preparations in the area North of Australia, such as the preparation of bases, strengthening of defenses, storing of munitions, sea transport and establishment of line of communications bases with a deadline set about spring of 1944.

2. The foregoing operational preparations will be accelerated so as to leave nothing to be desired in the current defenses of the area North of Australia and particularly so that these operations will become the backbone for a counteroffensive according to charges in operation in the Southeast Area. . . .

4. For the strengthening of operational preparations in the area North of Australia, the Navy will escort the Army forces and munitions to said area. Moreover, the Army and Navy will cooperate and as much as possible provide cover for supplies and the above transport by means of air strength.

Matters pertaining to the carrying out of the above will be conferred upon and decided by the Army and Navy commanders concerned.

V. Central Pacific Area

1. With the spring of 1944 as the deadline, the Navy will speedily strengthen operational preparations in the Caroline and Mariana Islands Area. The Army will dispatch the necessary Army force and elements of line of communications organs to the Central Pacific Area, where they will be placed under the command of the Navy commander. Thus, the Army will cooperate with the Navy in strengthening operational preparations.

2. The Army will be responsible for the aforementioned transportation of Army forces while the Navy will be responsible for the subsequent constant transportation of supply materials (replacements) and evacuation of patients.

The Army will be responsible for weapons and clothing in the constant supply of materials for Army forces, while the Navy will be chiefly responsible for such things as other provisions and construction materials. The details for providing for the above supplies and other materials for the operations will be conferred upon and decided on each occasion by the Army and Navy Section of Imperial General Headquarters. . . .

    2. Commanders

      Southeast Area Operation:

        Army—Commander of the 8th Area Army

        Navy—Commander in Chief of the Combined Fleet

          (Commander of the Southeast Area Fleet)

      North of Australia Area Operation:

        Army—Commander in Chief of the Southern Central Army

          (Commander of the 19th Army)

        Navy—Commander in Chief of the Combined Fleet

          (Commander of the Southwest Area Fleet)

      Central Pacific Area Operation:

      Commander in Chief of the Combined Fleet.

Appendix S

SUMMARY OF RENO III, OUTLINE PLAN FOR OPERATIONS
OF THE SOUTHWEST PACIFIC AREA TO REOCCUPY THE SOUTHERN
PHILIPPINES, PREPARED BY GHQ, SWPA, 20 OCTOBER 1943

Our strategic objective is the isolation of Japan from the Malay-NEI area. Present tasks are to:

1. Seize or neutralize E NG as far W as Wewak, and including the Admiralties and the Bismarck Archipelago. Neutralize, rather than capture Rabaul.
2. Advance along the N coast of NG as far W as the Vogelkop by AB-amphib jumps.
3. Prepare to seize Mindanao by AB-amphib opns.

Our eventual task is to reoccupy the S PI, and by subsequent opns isolate Japan from the Malaya-NEI area.

Accomplishment of the tasks presently assigned by Quadrant decisions initially requires opns along 2 general axes.

1. NW along the NG coast from Vitiaz St in order to advance land-based air.
2. W through the N Solomons—New Ireland, including the Admiralties, to a junction with the W axis in order to complete the isolation of Rabaul and obtain necessary bases for naval support of opns along the axis.

The eventual task requires seizure of Mindanao, followed by opns in conjunction with other Theaters to sever sea and air communications between Japan and Malaya-NEI area. These opns require attacks against strongly defended air and naval bases. Our advantages lie in superior equipment and potentially superior strength in the air and on the sea, but amphib equipment will be limited pending cessation of the offensive in Europe. On the assumption that the Japanese will maintain their strategic defense, our advantages must be fully utilized to deal him a succession of blows precluding his recouping of air and sea forces after each of his defeats and so permit destruction of his bases in detail.

The general scheme of maneuver is to advance our land-based bomber line rapidly W along the land masses on NG and the PI by successive occupation of the minimum bases required. Hostile strength is by-passed wherever practicable to avoid costly and time-consuming opns; our flanks are protected by air opns; and necessary advanced naval bases are established under protection of land-based aviation in order to extend the range of naval action. Destructive air attacks are employed to soften up objectives and to gain air superiority. Hostile naval forces and shipping are destroyed along our line of advance to prevent reinforcement. Ground forces are displaced forward by air and amphib movements. Air and naval forces are established at each objective and the process is then repeated, neutralizing by air and sea action hostile concentrations that may be by-passed. The number of objectives is decreased and the length of bound increased by use of a/c carriers to provide close air support. The same result is aided by extending the destructive effort of bombers through use of air envelopment to advance the fighter line through inland fields established and maintained by air support.

Sequence and timing are based on present enemy dispositions and are subject to change dependent upon enemy reaction and success of our opns. Timing is also dependent upon the availability of means, particularly amphib forces, and the timing given herein is based on an estimate of means to be available as a result of quadrant.

Logistic support is provided by the SOS of Sopac and SWPA. As opns progress to the NW, ports and supply bases are advanced by corresponding bounds. Heavy shipping is used wherever unloading facilities are available and amphib craft are used for assault elements and where the use of heavy shipping is impracticable. Trans-Pacific shipping is diverted directly to newly established bases along the line of advance. Bulk petroleum is transported forward in small tankers to points where the tactical situation permits the installation of bulk storage tanks.

Known requirements in items of special equipment, major units, air and service units, are set forth in the "1944 Troop Basis, GHQ, SWPA, 9 October 1943."

Phase I

Naval bases are required in the Bismarcks to support subsequent opns into W NG. Direct attack to capture Rabaul will be costly and time-consuming. Anchorages and potential air and naval bases exist at Kavieng and in the Admiralties. With the capture and development of such bases, Rabaul can be isolated from the NE. Direct attack into the Wewak area would also be costly in means and time. Presently occupied a/mes do not provide sufficient protection to bypass the area, but potential air bases exist in the Hansa Bay area, from which the isolation of Rabaul can be completed and opns to the W of Wewak be protected.

Scheme of Maneuver:

A. Target date 1 Feb 44. SWPA forces seize the Hansa Bay area by amphib opns with AB support. Direct air support is provided from the Vitiaz St–Ramu Valley a/mes. Shore-to-shore opns secure the mouth of the Sepik to contain enemy forces in the Wewak area. Advance bases are established for the support of opns in the Humboldt Bay area. Hostile forces in the Madang-Alexishafen area are isolated and the area later occupied by holding forces from the Huon Peninsula–Ramu Valley.

B. Target date 1 Mar 44. Kavieng is occupied by an amphib opn of Sopac Forces. The opn is preceded by intensive air and naval neutralization of the Rabaul area and has the direct support of heavy elements of the PacFlt. Air support comes from W New Britain and from carriers. General air support is from NG, Nor-Sols, and Kiriwina and Woodlark. Interference from hostile flt is covered by opns of Cenpac and in the Mandates and by the PacFlt. Air elements are then established for support of opns against the Carolines and Rabaul.

Light naval forces are established for support of opns to the W and to help blockade Rabaul.

C. Target date 1 Mar 44. The Admiralties are taken by amphib opns of SWPA Forces staging through Vitiaz St. Direct air support comes from the Vitiaz St area and from CVEs. General air support from the Markham-Ramu area. Air and naval forces are established in the Admiralties, and base facilities developed, for the support of opns along the N coast of NG.

D. When the blockade has sufficiently reduced the defensive capacity of the enemy garrison, Rabaul is occupied at a date and by forces later to be determined, and appropriate base facilities are established.
Forces required:

Garrison	Assault	Air	Naval	
2 US inf div	7 US inf div	HB 5 grps	15 APD	2 CV
6 Austn divs	2 US Para RCTs	MB 10 grps	16 APA	9 CVE
1 NZ div	3 MarDefBns	LB 11½ grps	5 AKA	4 CA
1 Aust armd bde		Day F 16½ grps	85 LST	4 CL
		Night F 14 grps	60 LCI	58 DD
		Trp Carr 6¼ grps	105 LCT	164 PT
		Photo & Recce 8½ grps	(and small craft)	

Naval strategic support will be elements of the US Pac Flt as designated by the JCS.

Phase II
(Initiated 1 Jun 44)

Advanced air and naval bases are required at an intermediate point on the N coast of NG for the support of opns into Geelvink Bay and protection of the L/C thereto. Air bases in Wewak are too distant from the Geelvink area to support attacks and are held in great strength by the Japanese. Costly and time-consuming opns will be avoided by by-passing and neutralizing the Wewak area. Partially developed sites exist in the Humboldt Bay area which may be improved to meet essential requirements. The concentration of hostile a/mes in the Banda Sea area requires establishment of flank protection and support for opns into Geelvink Bay. Occupation of the Aroe-Kai-Tanimbar Islands provides a difficult but feasible means of securing this protection and support.

Scheme of Maneuver:

A. Humboldt Bay, target date 1 Jun 44. An amphib opn from NG bases with AB support seizes objectives in the Aitape–Humboldt Bay area, by-passing Wewak. Air support is provided from the Markham–Ramu Valley, Hansa Bay, and the Admiralties. Close support comes from CVEs. Inland air bases are established in the upper Digoe-Fly Rivers by air transport as practicable. Adv bases are established in the Humboldt Bay area for support of opns into the Geelvink-

Vogelkop area. Forces in the Aitape area initiate infiltration opns from the W toward Wewak and finally occupy it when hostile resistance has deteriorated.

B. Arafura Sea. 1 Jun 44. Preceded by aerial neutralization of Timor a/mes, the Aroe-Kai-Tanimbar Islands are occupied by an amphib assault of Austn troops supported by AB elements. General air support is provided from Darwin area, convoy cover from Merauke–Horn Is–Arnhem Bay, and by CVEs. Air bases are promptly developed.

Forces required:

Garrison	Assault	Air Grps	Naval	
6 Austn inf divs	4 US inf divs	8 HB	2 CV	15 APD
1 NZ inf div	2 Austn inf divs	12 MB	7 CVE	5 APA
5 US inf divs	1 US AB div	11¾ LB	4 CA	84 LST
1 Austn armd bde	2 para RCTs	22½ Night F	6 CL	60 LCI
	1 MarDefBn	18½ F	83 DD	145 LCT
		8¼ Trp Carrier	8 PF	
		11 Photo Recce	168 PT	

Naval strategic support will be from the US PacFlt as designated by the JCS to insure noninterference by hostile heavy flt elements.

Phase III
Initiated 15 Aug 44)

Major naval and air bases are required in W NG to support opns to the NW. Potential sites are available in the Geelvink Bay–Vogelkop area. Opns require protection against major enemy flt elements by the US Flt.

Scheme of Maneuver:

A. Geelvink Bay, 15 Aug 44. Anchorages, a/mes, and potential base sites are seized by an AB overseas landing, staged in NG. Babo and Nabire are neutralized by air staged through Aroe-Kai-Tanimbar. Direct air support is provided from the Humboldt Bay area through inland air bases established and maintained in favorable locations by air transport, and also by CVEs. Major air and naval base development is instituted for support of opns against Mindanao.

B. Vogelkop Area, 1 Oct. 44. The Sorong and Kabui Bay areas are occupied by an amphib opn with AB support. This opn is launched as soon as air support is available from Geelvink Bay bases. The Klamono oil field is occupied and intensively developed as a source of bunker fuel.

Forces required:

Garrison	Combat	Air Groups
7 Austn inf divs		
1 NZ inf div		
4 US inf divs		
1 Austn armd bde		

Naval Combat	Amphib Craft
2 CV	15 APD
6 CVE	16 APA
4 CA	5 AKA
6 CL	54 LST
64 DD	60 LCI
183 PT	175 LCT

Phase IV
(Initiated 1 Dec 44)

Advance into Mindanao requires a broadening of the front for deployment of air forces, protection for flanks, and establishment of advance bases for support of sea and AB movements. These requirements can be met by establishing air and light naval elements on Halmahera and/or Morotai. Menado must at least be denied to the enemy and Palau must be occupied by either Cenpac or SWPA forces. The Ambon area must be neutralized by air action, but may have to be occupied if hostile strength in the NEI requires such action.

Scheme of Maneuver:

A. Halmahera-Menado, target date 1 Dec 44. A/mes or sites therefore on Halmahera and/or Morotai are occupied and Menado seized by amphib opns from Geelvink Bay, supported by AB elements. Air and naval forces are established for flank protection and support of subsequent opns to seize and occupy Mindanao.

B. Ambon (contingent opn), 1 Dec 44. In the event that hostile strength in the E NEI jeopardizes opns on Mindanao, it may be necessary to establish air and naval forces on Ambon. If required, this opn will be amphib, staged from Geelvink via the Dampier Strs, will seize enemy air bases on Ceram and Boeroe and capture Ambon. Enemy air forces on Timor are neutralized from Darwin, and general air support comes from Aroe-Kai-Tanimbar-Geelvink-Vogelkop areas.

C. Palau, 1 Dec 44, or 15 Jan 45 if Ambon is occupied. In the event that SWPA forces are assigned the task of occupying Palau, that group is seized by amphib opns with the direct support of the PacFlt, including strong carrier elements. Naval air elements are established on Palau for protection of the axis of advance against enemy air attacks from the N.

Completion of Phase III accomplishes the tasks presently assigned to the SWPA by the Quadrant decisions. Estimates of forces required to accomplish Phases IV and V of this plan are of problematical value in view of the certainty of major changes in the Pacific situation and in the availability and types of means available for the carrying out of Phase III. A tentative estimate of divs for Phases IV and V have been shown in Annex 3, but only as a basis for 44 troop estimates. For Phase IV these are:

Garrison	Combat
5 Austn inf divs	7 US inf divs
4 US inf divs	1 Para RCT
1 Austn armd bde	1 MarDefBn
	2 US inf divs for possible opns in Jan 45

No estimates of naval or air means can be given at this time.

Phase V

(Initiated 1 Feb 45)

Occupation of Mindanao requires an attack by major forces of all components over a widely spread area in order to achieve surprise and disperse the defensive effort. Employment of air envelopment on a major scale, using equipment now in prospect, becomes feasible upon establishment of adequate bases in the Geelvink-Vogelkop area. Present guerrilla organization provides necessary terminal facilities. Prompt and ample seaborne reinforcement of initial assault is essential. Consolidation of the S PI requires occupation of covering positions in the islands to the SW and N of Mindanao and the establishment of major forces thereon preparatory to subsequent opns. Inasmuch as the enemy must defend Mindanao with all the means at his disposal, prompt consolidation and subsequent exploitation should meet a minimum of effective opposition.

Scheme of Maneuver (see also map in Annex 2-e)

A. Occupation of Mindanao, target date 1 Feb 45. Beachheads and a/mes through the N and NW portions of Mindanao are seized by major combined AB-amphib opns with carrier based air support. An AB invasion in strength is staged in New Britain and E NG via W NG. Guerrilla forces are employed to seize a/mes on which to land AB forces. Landing opns seize beachheads in the proximity of a/mes. Paratroops are dropped on a/mes. Light air elements are flown in to support the advance of occupation forces and protect subsequent landings. Initial landings are promptly reinforced by air transport.

B. Consolidation of Southern PI: The Minadanao Occupation Force follows the AB invasion closely along the main line of advance to beachheads in our possession. All types of aviation are established in order to maintain air superiority and cover the occupation of Zamboanga and Davao and positions in islands to the SW and N. The L/C W of the line Palau-Vogelkop is kept open by naval elements from advanced bases in the Vogelkop area, supported by air from Palau, Menado, and Halmahera-Morotai. Additional forces of all arms are rapidly established on Mindanao in preparation for opns to reoccupy the northern PI and to isloate Japan from the Malay-NEI.

Logistic bases are set forth on map of Annex 4–f. Ground forces required (a suggestion rather than definite estimate) :

Garrison	*Combat*
5 Austn inf divs	4 US inf divs
4 US inf divs	2 US AB divs
3 US inf divs for contingent opns	1 para RCT
1 Austn armd bde	2 MarDefBns

Forces for the consolidation are undetermined. Impossible to estimate at this time the naval and air forces required.

Appendix T

OVERALL PLAN FOR THE DEFEAT OF JAPAN:
REPORT BY THE COMBINED STAFF PLANNERS,
APPROVED IN PRINCIPLE, 2 DECEMBER 1943
(CCS 417)

PROBLEM

1. To prepare an overall plan for the defeat of Japan.

ASSUMPTIONS

2. Our studies of this subject have taken account of:

a. The possibility that invasion of the principal Japanese islands may not be necessary and the defeat of Japan may be accomplished by sea and air blockade and intensive air bombardment from progressively advanced bases. The plan must, however, be capable of expansion to meet the contingency of invasion.

b. The possibility that Germany may be defeated as early as the spring of 1944.

c. The possibility that the U.S.S.R. may enter the war against Japan early after the defeat of Germany, and our plan proposes that all possible preparations should be made to take advantage of such a development. Further progress is dependent upon staff conversations with the Soviets.

d. The possibility that a full campaign in Burma may have to be carried out following on the TARZAN operation.[1]

OVERALL OBJECTIVE

3. To obtain objectives from which we can conduct intensive air bombardment and establish a sea and air blockade against Japan, and from which to invade Japan proper if this should prove to be necessary.

GENERAL CONCEPT

4. The main effort against Japan should be made in the Pacific.

CONCEPT WITHIN THE PACIFIC

5. The advance along the New Guinea–N.E.I.–Philippine axis will proceed concurrently with operations for the capture of the Mandated Islands. These two series of operations will be mutually supporting. United Nations naval forces can be deployed to support successive operations along each axis, and to prevent interference by hostile surface units with simultaneous operations in the two areas. Transfer of forces and resources from one area to the other is contemplated. When conflicts in timing and allocation of means exist, due weight should be accorded to the fact that operations in the Central Pacific promise at

---

[1] TARZAN was the code for operations in upper Burma.

this time a more rapid advance toward Japan and her vital lines of communication; the earlier acquisition of strategic air bases closer to the Japanese homeland; and, of greatest importance, are more likely to precipitate a decisive engagement with the Japanese Fleet.

The aim should be to advance along the New Guinea–N.E.I.–Philippine axis and to complete the capture of the Mandated Islands in time to launch a major assault in the Formosa-Luzon-China area in the spring of 1945 (i.e., before the onset of the typhoon season), from a distant base.

CONCEPT WITHIN OTHER AREAS

6. Operations in the North Pacific, the South Pacific, China and the South East Asia theater should be conducted in support of the main operations in the Central and South West Pacific. In the event of the U.S.S.R. entering the war, operations in the North Pacific may assume far greater importance and may involve a major redeployment of forces.

GENERAL CONDUCT OF OPERATIONS

7. The conduct of operations should be designed to:

    a. Destroy the Japanese Fleet at an early date.

    b. Secure the maximum attrition of enemy forces.

    c. Intensify air, submarine and mining operations against enemy shipping and lines of communication.

    d. Enable us to launch shore-based and carrier-borne air attack on Japan.

    e. Keep China in the war.

    f. Insure that the sequence of operations remains flexible and that preparations are made to take all manner of short cuts made possible by developments in the situation.

    g. Take advantage of the earliest practicable reorientation of forces from the European Theater.

SPECIFIC OPERATIONS IN 1944

8. For operations planned for 1944, see schedule in C.C.S. 397, Specific Operations for the Defeat of Japan, 1944 (To be revised).[2] These operations are in accordance with the overall concept. In brief they contemplate:

Central Pacific

    a. Capture of the Mandated Islands and conduct of V.L.R. strategic bombing of Japan proper from the Marianas (Guam, Tinian and Saipan).

South West Pacific

    b. Continuing the advance along the New Guinea–N.E.I.–Philippine axis. Intensification of air bombardment of targets in the N.E.I.–Philippine area.

North Pacific

    c. Preparations to conduct very long range strategic bombing against the

---

[2] See Appendix U.

Kuriles and Northern Japan. (Preparations for the possible entry of the U.S.S.R. into the war are discussed in Annex I.)

South East Asia Theater

d. Operations for the capture of Upper Burma in the spring of 1944 in order to improve the air route and establish overland communications with China, and an amphibious operation at approximately the same time. Continuance of operations during the autumn of 1944 within the limits of the forces available (See Par. 14) to extend the position held in Upper Burma.

e. Should the means be available, additional ground, sea and air offensive operations, including carrier-borne raids, with the object of maintaining pressure on the enemy, forcing dispersion of his forces, and attaining the maximum attrition practicable on his air and naval forces and shipping.

China Area

f. Conducting V.L.R. air operations from the Chengtu area in China against vital targets in the Japanese inner zone.

g. Building up the U.S. Air Forces in China and the Chinese Army and air force with the objective of intensifying land and air operations in and from China.

DISPOSITION OF FORCES

Naval Forces

9. Considering the British Naval forces shown below, we believe the combined naval forces will be adequate to conduct the operations envisaged for the defeat of Japan. We show in Annex II, page 9,[3] the estimated dispositions of British Naval forces in the Indian Ocean and the Pacific after the completion of operation BUCCANEER,[4] and the subsequent build-up of British Naval forces in the Pacific during 1944 and early 1945.

10. This allocation provides for sufficient forces in the Indian Ocean to maintain our communications with the Andamans, to act as a deterrent against any attempt to recapture them by the Japanese and to carry out operations, raids, and threats against Japanese possessions in S.E. Asia. All other available units, to the extent that they can be supported and profitably employed, will be concentrated for the main effort in the Pacific.

11. Though full details have not yet been worked out, we consider that the British Naval forces shown can be supported logistically and should in general operate from advanced bases in the Bismarck and Solomons area so that they may either cover the operations along the New Guinea–N.E.I.–Philippines axis, or cooperate with the U.S. Fleet in the Central Pacific.

12. Logistic preparations should be made by the British for the increased British Naval forces expected to become available for the long distance assault contemplated in the spring of 1945. Manpower limitations will probably prevent any new bases being manned by the British until after the defeat of Germany.

---

[3] Not included.

[4] BUCCANEER is the code name for the proposed amphibious operations against the Andaman Islands.

13. Our studies have reemphasized the importance of the provision of aircraft carriers of all sorts for our future operations against Japan.

Land Forces

14. Present plans contemplate the timely deployment in the Pacific of about 40 U.S. Divisions and supporting troops. British/Indian land forces which can be made available to South East Asia command up to the end of 1944 are likely to be fully committed in carrying out the operations recommended for the season 1943/44, and subsequently extending the area of occupation in Burma and in carrying out additional operations against the enemy. This concept is subject to alteration in the light of the progress of the 1943/44 operations and of detailed examination of the forces which will be required for 1944/45, but included in the forces retained in the theater there should be at least one amphibious division.

15. After the defeat of Germany the number of additional British divisions from the European theater and the dates by which they can be made available for the war against Japan cannot yet be assessed, but it is estimated that some 9 months will be required for the necessary reorganization, passage and training. Additional British forces may prove essential for Burma. In the Pacific, the target should be to provide four British divisions based on Australia for service in that theater as early as possible after the defeat of Germany. At least two of these divisions should be amphibiously trained.

16. After providing for paragraph 15 above, additional British forces becoming available will probably be best placed in reserve at the disposal of South East Asia, ready for additional offensive operations in that area.

17. Australian and New Zealand forces should continue to be employed in Pacific operations. The employment of Canadian forces should be discussed with the Canadian Government.

18. We believe that the combined land forces to be made available as outlined in paragraphs 14, 15, 16 and 17 above will be adequate to conduct the operations envisaged for the defeat of Japan.

Assault Shipping and Landing Craft

19. Present plans contemplate an eventual U.S. assault lift of 12 divisions in the Pacific. The British should maintain in the South East Asia theater an assault lift for at least one division. As soon as the war with Germany is over the British should aim to provide in the South West Pacific as large an assault lift as possible (probably between two and three divisions simultaneously).

Air Forces

20. British and U.S. air forces are sufficient for plans at present contemplated although if the U.S.S.R. enters the war the demand on our resources for the establishment of a bomber force in the Maritime Provinces may conflict with the development of our air effort against Japan through China.

The large air forces which will be available when Germany is defeated must be redeployed against Japan as quickly as possible. The general principles which we consider should govern this redeployment are in Annex III, page 10.[5] Immediate examinations of the problems involved in the redeployment of British and U.S. air forces should be made. Studies are now under way to determine the best employment of the B-29 aircraft against Japan.

Appendix "A" to Annex III shows the U.S. and British air forces which may be available for deployment against Japan after the defeat of Germany.[6]

PREPARATION OF BASES IN INDIA

21. The preparation of the bases in India required for approved operations in the South East Asia and China theater should continue in consonance with provisions of paragraphs 4, 5 and 6.

RECOMMENDATIONS

22. It is recommended that the Combined Chiefs of Staff:

a. Approve the overall plan for the defeat of Japan and direct that the necessary preparation be initiated.

b. Approve the specific operations set out in C.C.S. 397, Specific Operations for the Defeat of Japan, 1944. (To be revised.)

NOTE ON PREPARATIONS THAT SHOULD BE MADE FOR POSSIBLE RUSSIAN ENTRY INTO THE WAR

1. We urge the U.S.S.R. to come in as early as possible; ask them to tell us when they propose to come in; what they propose to do when they come in; and what they want us to do to help.

2. Meanwhile, in so far as they do not conflict with the operations in the Central and Southwest Pacific, preparations should be made by the spring or early summer of 1944 so that we can assist her:—

a. By building up supplies by trans-Pacific shipment, sea and air.

b. By insuring that her defenses and means in Kamchatka are adequate. If she wants our forces there we should be prepared to move them in, especially air.

c. By furnishing aircraft and air units released from the European front, both from the East and the West.

3. If and when conversations with the Soviets can be arranged, plans should also be made for operations:—

a. To enter and develop bases in Kamchatka and the Maritime Provinces.

b. To seize and hold the Northern Kuriles and to open a sea route to the Maritime Provinces.

c. To supply and operate air forces from Siberian bases.

4. We must constantly review the situation so as to be ready to adjust our operations elsewhere when the U.S.S.R. comes into the war.

---

[5] Not included.
[6] Not included.

Appendix U

SPECIFIC OPERATIONS FOR THE DEFEAT OF JAPAN, 1944
3 DECEMBER 1943
(CCS 397 REV)

MEMORANDUM BY THE U.S. CHIEFS OF STAFF

1. We are agreed that every effort should be exerted to bring the U.S.S.R. into the war against Japan at the earliest practicable date, and that plans should be prepared in that event.

2. We are agreed that plans should be prepared for operations in the event that Germany is defeated earlier than the fall of 1944.

3. A schedule of proposed operations and projected target dates for planning purposes is given in the appendix to the Enclosure.[1] The operations envisaged are based on a concept of obtaining strategic objectives and bases from which to conduct further operations to force the unconditional surrender of Japan at the earliest practicable date. The operations are in consonance with the over-all objectives and over-all strategic concept agreed upon at QUADRANT and reaffirmed by the Combined Chiefs of Staff in C.C.S. 380/2, and with provisions of C.C.S 417 (Over-all Plan for the Defeat of Japan).

4. *General.* In addition to the specific objectives hereinafter indicated supporting operations should be conducted. Both the specific and supporting operations will be designed to destroy the Japanese fleet at an early date; to secure maximum attrition of enemy air forces; to intensify air, submarine, and mining operations against enemy shipping and lines of communication; to establish air and sea blockade of the main Japanese islands; to continue efforts to keep China in the war; and to enable us to launch land and carrier based air operations against Japan.

5. *North Pacific.* Plans for the North Pacific involve the augmentation of base facilities and defensive installations in the Aleutians in preparation for entry into the Kuriles and Soviet territory in the event of Russian collaboration. Naval surface and submarine action, including raids on the Japanese fishing fleet will be carried out. Preparations will be made for executing very long range strategic bombing against the Kuriles and northern Japan.

6. *Central, South and Southwest Pacific.* The advance along the New Guinea–N.E.I.–Philippine axis will proceed concurrently with operations for the capture of the Mandated Islands. A strategic bombing force will be established in Guam, Tinian, and Saipan for strategic bombing of Japan proper. Air bombardment of targets in the N.E.I.-Philippine Area and the aerial neutralization of Rabaul will be intensified.

7. *China.* Our efforts in the China Area should have as their objective the intensification of land and air operations in and from China and the build-up of the U.S.A.A.F. and the Chinese army and air forces. It shall include also

[1] See Table 12, p. 586.

the establishing, without materially affecting other approved operations, of a very long range strategic bombing force at Calcutta, with advanced bases at Chengtu to attack vital targets in the Japanese "inner zone."[2]

8. *Southeast Asia.* Operations for the capture of Upper Burma in the spring of 1944 in order to improve the air route and establish overland communications with China, and an amphibious operation at approximately the same time. Continuance of operations during the autumn of 1944 within the limits of the forces available . . . to extend the position held in Upper Burma.

Should the means be available, additional ground, sea and air offensive operations including carrier borne raids, with the object of maintaining pressure on the enemy, inducing dispersion of his forces, and attaining the maximum attrition practicable on his air and naval forces and shipping.

9. As more carriers become available, the operations set forth should be supplemented, between scheduled operational dates as practicable, with massed carrier task force strikes against selected vital targets.

10. The completion of these operations will place the United Nations in positions from which to use most advantageously the great air, ground, and naval resources which will be at our disposal after Germany is defeated.

ENCLOSURE

A schedule of operations for 1944 is set forth in the Appendix.[3] Target dates which have been determined after careful consideration of prospective means and of time and space factors, are presented for planning purposes only. We are convinced that the sequence of operations must be flexible; we must be prepared to take all manner of short cuts made possible by developments in the situation. The four primary developments which may permit short cuts are:

a. Early defeat of the Japanese Fleet.

b. Sudden withdrawal of Japanese forces from areas (as from Kiska).

c. Increase in our means such as by acceleration of the assault ship-building program and by an earlier defeat of Germany than 1 October 1944.

d. The early collaboration of the U.S.S.R. in the war against Japan.

We have directed that further study be conducted and plans made and kept up to date for the conditions assumed in *c.* and *d.*

We have directed that special attention be given to the optimum employment of the enormous air forces which will be released upon the defeat of Germany.

We have directed that a study be made for the optimum use, timing and deployment in the war against Japan in very long range bombers.

---

[2] Includes Japan proper, Manchuria, Korea, North China, Karafuto (Japanese Sakhalin), and Formosa.

[3] The schedule of operations is included in the text as Table 13, page 604.

Appendix V

GENERAL HEADQUARTERS
SOUTHWEST PACIFIC AREA

"ELKTON" III

PLAN FOR THE SEIZURE
AND OCCUPATION OF THE
LAE SALAMAUA MADANG
WESTERN NEW BRITAIN
SOLOMONS AREAS

26 APRIL 1943

"ELKTON" III
SECTION I—GENERAL

1. a. GENERAL TASK.

   (1) The Joint Chiefs of Staff directive for offensive operations is set forth in the following form:

   "2. Command.

      a. The operations outlined in this directive will be conducted under the direction of the Supreme Commander, SOUTHWEST PACIFIC AREA.

b. Operations in the SOLOMON ISLANDS will be under the direct command of the Commander, SOPAC AREA, operating under general directives of the Supreme Commander, SOUTHWEST PACIFIC AREA.

c. Units of the PACIFIC OCEAN AREA, other than those assigned by the Joint Chiefs of Staff to Task Forces engaged in these operations, will remain under the control of the Commander-in-Chief, PACIFIC OCEAN AREA (CINCPAC).

3. Forces will be allocated for these operations as determined by the Joint Chiefs of Staff.

4. Tasks.

    a. Establish airfields on KIRIWINA and WOODLARK ISLANDS.

    b. Seize LAE-SALAMAUA-FINSCHHAFEN-MADANG area and occupy WESTERN NEW BRITAIN.

    c. Seize and occupy SOLOMON ISLANDS to include the southern portion of BOUGAINVILLE.

5. Purposes.

    To inflict losses on Japanese Forces, to deny these areas to JAPAN, to contain Japanese Forces in the PACIFIC theater by maintaining the initiative, and to prepare for ultimate seizure of BISMARCK ARCHIPELAGO"

b. ANALYSIS OF THE TASK.

    (1) The sea and land areas south of the line WAU–RUSSELL ISLAND are generally under our control, with the enemy in control north of that line. The defenses of both sides are concentrated in and around airfields. The remainder of the land areas are generally unoccupied.

    (2) Task a. Requires establishment of airfields on KIRIWINA and WOODLARK ISLANDS, neither of which is occupied by our own or enemy forces.

    (3) Tasks b. and c. require the employment of two general lines of advance: on the West, along the northeast coast of NEW GUINEA to seize the HUON PENINSULA AREA as far as MADANG, and then across VITIAZ STRAIT to seize the Western NEW BRITAIN AREA; on the East, northwestward through the SOLOMONS to seize southeastern BOUGAINVILLE. The stated objectives are preliminary to the seizure of RABAUL and the occupation of the BISMARCK ARCHIPELAGO.

    (4) The establishment of airfields on WOODLARK ISLAND is a necessary preliminary to the seizure of the Southeastern BOUGAINVILLE AREA in order to provide wider employment of air power and obtain closer support for operations against BUIN-FAISI. By arrangement the occupying forces for WOODLARK ISLAND are to be furnished by the SOUTH PACIFIC AREA but the operation will be undertaken by the SOUTHWEST PACIFIC AREA. SOUTH PACIFIC will establish their own air forces on WOODLARK and control their operation. The establishment of airfields on KIRIWINA ISLAND is complementary to the occupation and consolidation of WOODLARK, and is required for the control of the air over the SOLOMON SEA and to assist our advance along the western axis. Early occupation and consolidation of both islands are mandatory. Full scale consolidation must await provision of adequate fighter cover on GOODENOUGH ISLAND. In order to maintain the initiative and contain Japanese forces in the SOUTHWEST PACIFIC theater, continuous air

activity on a pre-offensive scale and early infiltrating attacks along both axes, avoiding commitment of important forces, should be started immediately and prosecuted vigorously.

(5) Task b. requires successively the seizure of the LAE-MARKHAM VALLEY AREA, the occupation of HUON PENINSULA, the seizure and occupation of Western NEW BRITAIN, with the objective of securing airdromes to cover further advances, and the seizure and occupation of MADANG to protect the northern flank. Operations along the eastern axis require the seizure and consolidation, or neutralization, successively of NEW GEORGIA airfields, the seizure and consolidation of airfields in the BUIN-FAISI AREA, the seizure of KIETA and neutralization of BUKA.

Generally speaking, the advance into the BUIN-FAISI AREA along the eastern axis is doubtful of success pending implementation of land-based airfields on WOODLARK ISLAND to provide a wider deployment and closer support of that operation and the implementation of airfields on KIRIWINA and in the LAE AREA to neutralize supporting Japanese air bases at BUKA, RABAUL and KAVIENG. Operations to seize and occupy the western portion of NEW BRITAIN and MADANG cannot progress prior to the implementation of airfields in the LAE and/or MARKHAM VALLEY AREA. The sequence of the advance along either axis alone or one axis in relation to the other cannot be rigidly preplanned but must remain flexible in order to take advantage of the situation obtaining regardless of the arrangement of tasks a., b. and c. in the directive.

2. SCHEME OF MANEUVER.

a. The general scheme of maneuver is to improve all presently occupied forward air bases; occupy and implement air bases which can be secured without committing large forces; employ air forces from these bases to soften up and to gain air superiority over the initial attack objectives along the two axes; neutralize with appropriate aviation supporting hostile air bases and destroy hostile naval forces and shipping within range; move land forces forward covered by air and naval forces to obtain first objectives (existing and potential hostile air bases) and consolidate same; displace aviation forward onto captured airdromes.

This process is repeated to successive objectives, neutralizing by air action, or by air, land and sea action, intermediate hostile installations which are not objectives of immediate attack.

The entire movement will be covered by air attack on Japanese air and sea bases along the general perimeter BUKA, RABAUL, KAVIENG and WEWAK with the objective of interrupting and denying sea supply and/or support or reinforcement of objectives under attack.

b. In the initiation of the operations, SOUTHWEST PACIFIC FORCES, by amphibious means, first secretly infiltrate and later when pursuit coverage is available from GOODENOUGH ISLAND, move in force to occupy and consolidate WOODLARK and KIRIWINA ISLANDS. Diverting and covering air attacks on Japanese bases and infiltration ground attacks northwestward through the SOLOMONS and toward SALAMAUA and LAE will support the operation.

Preceded by strong land-based air action, the forces along the western axis operate against successive objectives to capture by air-borne and shore-to-shore operations air operating bases in the HUON PENINSULA–MARKHAM VALLEY AREA, in Western NEW BRITAIN, and along the North-eastern coast of NEW GUINEA to include MADANG: the forces along the eastern axis progress northwestward by amphibious operations, to secure airdromes in the BUIN-FAISI AREA, neutralizing or capturing enemy airdromes of NEW GEORGIA, later occupying the KIETA AREA and neutralizing hostile airfields in the vicinity of BUKA PASSAGE.

The general sequence and timing of the operations along either axis, or along one axis in relationship to the other, will be governed by conditions obtaining at the time in order that the maximum benefit can be derived from the successes of our own forces or weaknesses of the enemy. Generally speaking for planning purposes, occupation of WOODLARK and KIRIWINA ISLANDS will be simultaneous. The advance northward along the NEW GUINEA coast to secure airfields in the HUON PENINSULA–MARKHAM VALLEY AREA will precede major attack on the BUIN-FAISI AREA and will be covered by diverting air and ground infiltration attacks along the eastern axis. Following the displacement of SOUTHWEST PACIFIC Air Force into LAE AREA, the seizure of southeastern BOUGAINVILLE may progress covered by neutralizing attacks by SOUTHWEST PACIFIC Air Force on BUKA, RABAUL and KAVIENG. The remainder of the operations along both axes will be made simultaneously to the final objectives, the SOUTH PACIFIC Air Force assisting in the neutralization of the RABAUL area and thus partially freeing the SOUTHWEST PACIFIC Air Forces to neutralize hostile air action along the Northeastern NEW GUINEA coast.

c. OPERATIONS REQUIRED.

(1) SOUTHWEST PACIFIC AREA.

Operation I, NEW BRITAIN FORCES.
Establish airfields on KIRIWINA and WOODLARK.

Operation II, NEW GUINEA FORCE.

IIa	IIb	IIc
Seize LAE	Seize SALAMAUA	Seize MADANG
	Seize FINSCHHAFEN	

Operation III, NEW BRITAIN FORCE.

IIIa	IIIb
Occupy CAPE GLOUCESTER and ARAWE.	Occupy GASMATA. Neutralize TALASEA.

(2) SOUTH PACIFIC AREA.

Operation A.	Operation B.	Operation C.
Infiltration NEW GEORGIA and/or YSABEL ISLANDS.	Seize and occupy BUIN-FAISI and NEW GEORGIA.	Seize and occupy KIETA. Neutralize BUKA.

d. ESTIMATED TIMING AND SEQUENCE OF OPERATIONS.

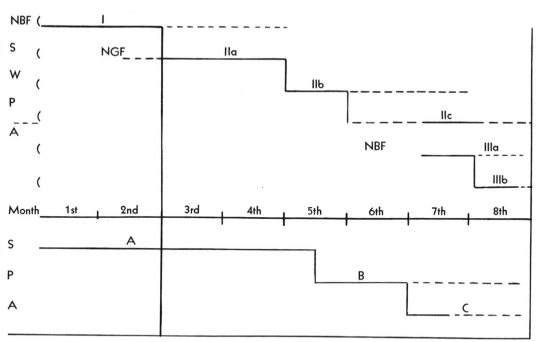

Notes:

General.

For planning purposes, it is estimated that "1st month" can be June 1943.

S.W.P.A.

Operation I.   Solid line, establishment of fighter sector KIRIWINA and WOODLARK. Dotted line, establishment of additional designated air elements.

Operation IIa.   Dotted line, seizure of operating base in MARKHAM VALLEY. Solid line, seizure of LAE.

Operation IIb.   Solid line, seizure of SALAMAUA and FINSCHHAFEN, establishment of air support for ARAWE and GLOUCES-TER operations. Dotted line, establishment of air support for MADANG and GASMATA operations.

Operation IIc.   Initial dotted line, overland approach to MADANG AREA. Solid line, combined operation to seize MADANG. Dotted line, consolidation.

Operation IIIa.   Solid line, occupation of CAPE GLOUCESTER and ARAWE. Dotted line, consolidation and development.

Operation IIIb. Solid line, occupation of GASMATA, neutralization TALA-SEA. Dotted line, consolidation and development.

S.P.A.

Operation A. Solid line, infiltration into NEW GEORGIA and/or YSABEL.

Operation B. Solid line, seizure BUIN-FAISI and NEW GEORGIA AREAS. Dotted line, consolidation and development.

Operation C. Solid line, seizure KIETA. Dotted line, neutralization BUKA.

3. ORGANIZATION.

a. GENERAL CHART.

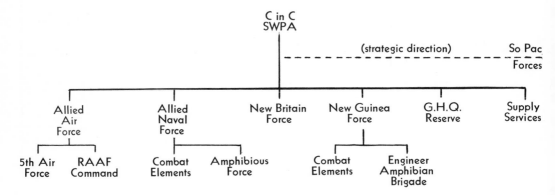

b. ESTIMATE OF THE FORCES AVAILABLE.[1]

(1) Summary

Principal combat elements available for each operation are estimated to be:

(a) SWPA:

	Naval[2]	Ground	Air[3]
Operation I	T.F. 74	1 Regimental Combat Team (U.S.)	7 Sqs HB
	T.F. 72		4 Sqs MB
	T.G. 70.1		5 Sqs LB
	T.F. 76		3 Sqs F (escort)
			10 Sqs F (int.)
			1 Sq FR
			4 Sqs TC
			1 Sq OB

Requested from SPA:

3 APD's	1 Defense Battalion (U.S. Marines)	3 Sqs F
6 LST's	1 Regimental Combat Team (U.S.)	
6 PT's		
26 LCI's (2 weeks)		

	Naval	Ground	Air
Operation II	T.F. 74	3 Inf. Divs. (Aust.)	8 Sqs HB
	T.F. 72	1 Inf. Div. (Aust.) (Reserve)	13 Sqs MB
	T.G. 70.1	1 Inf. Div. (Aust.) (Defense)	6 Sqs LB
	T.F. 76		(2 RAAF)
			16 Sqs F (int.)
			2 Sqs F (night)
			14 Sqs TC
			1 Sq FR
			1 Sq OB
Operation III	T.F. 74	1 Marine Div. (U.S.)	8 Sqs HB
	T.F. 72	1 Inf. Div. (U.S.) (Reserve)	13 Sqs MB
	T.G. 70.1		10 Sqs LB
	T.F. 76		16 Sqs F (int.)
			3 Sqs F (escort)
			2 Sqs F (night)
			18 Sqs TC
			5 Sqs OB
			4 Sqs FR
	GHQ Reserve	3 Inf. Divs. (U.S.)	
		1 Parachute Regt. (U.S.)	
		1 Armored Bde. (Aust.)	

(b) SPA

FORCES AS ESTIMATED BY COMSOPAC.

Notes:

[1] Land and Air Forces required for defense of continental AUSTRALIA and TORRES STRAIT, are shown in Inclosures 2 and 3.

[2] T.F. 74—1 Crudiv   T.F. 72—12 submarines (average)
     1 Desron   T.G. 70.1—2 PT Squadrons
     1 Desdiv

T.F. 76, SWPA Amphibious Force

Means available	LST	LCI (L)	LCT (5)	APC
1 May	3	14	9	0
1 June	8	24	20	7
1 July	15	26	20	16

(Plus units from SOPAC)

[3] Air Forces shown are available for operations in NEW GUINEA.

4. ALLOTMENT OF TASKS.

   a. SOUTH PACIFIC FORCES.

      (1) Composition.
            As assigned.
      (2) Tasks.
         (a) Seize and occupy the SOLOMON ISLANDS to include the southern portion of BOUGAINVILLE.

(b) Provide strategic naval support for the operations.

(c) Support the operations of SOUTHWEST PACIFIC FORCES as directed.

b. NEW BRITAIN FORCE.

(1) Composition.

A Task Force organized and equipped for air-borne and over-water operations in D'ENTRECASTEAUX, WOODLARK and TROBRIAND ISLANDS and Western NEW BRITAIN.

(2) Tasks.

(a) Establish airfields on KIRIWINA and WOODLARK Islands, and occupy western NEW BRITAIN, to include the general line GASMATA-TALASEA, by combined air-borne and over-water operations.

c. NEW GUINEA FORCE.

(1) Composition.

A Task Force organized and equipped for airborne, overland and shore-to-shore operations in NEW GUINEA.

(2) Tasks.

By airborne, overland and overwater operations:

(a) Seize LAE and SALAMAUA.

(b) Secure in the HUON PENINSULA–MARKHAM VALLEY AREAS, air bases required for subsequent operations.

(c) Seize the north coast of NEW GUINEA to include MADANG.

d. ALLIED AIR FORCES.

(1) Composition.

Fifth Air Force, R.A.A.F. Command and air elements SOUTHWEST PACIFIC FORCE not required for defense of installations, facilities, or shipping in the SOUTHWEST PACIFIC AREA.

(2) Tasks.

(a) Destroy hostile aviation in general supporting areas of Northern SOLOMONS, NEW IRELAND, NEW BRITAIN and the north coast of NEW GUINEA. Destroy naval forces and shipping.

(b) Support the operations of the SOUTHWEST PACIFIC Task Forces.

(c) Support the defense of SOUTHWEST PACIFIC forward bases.

(d) Provide transport aviation support for SOUTHWEST PACIFIC operations.

(e) Be prepared to provide general air support for operations in the SOUTH PACIFIC AREA.

e. ALLIED NAVAL FORCES.

(1) Composition.

Task Force 74, Task Force 72, T.F. 76, Task Group 70.1 and escort vessels.

(2) Tasks.

(a) Support the operations of the SOUTHWEST PACIFIC Task Force.

(b) Support the defense of forward bases in the SOUTHWEST PACIFIC AREA and of TORRES STRAIT, and protect lines of communication.

(c) Embark, transport and land elements of the SOUTHWEST PACIFIC Task Forces as required.

f. SUPPLY SERVICES.

(1) Composition.

USASOS and the Australian Lines of Communication.

(2) Tasks.

(a) Provide logistic support for the operations.

(b) Reinforce intermediate bases in the PORT MORESBY and MILNE BAY–LOUISIADES AREA and an advance base at ORO BAY.

(c) Establish advanced bases as required.

x. COORDINATION OF OPERATIONS.

(1) With the initiation of Operation I, the organic Air Forces of the SOUTHWEST PACIFIC and SOUTH PACIFIC AREAS will provide defensive reconnaissance as indicated in the following paragraphs, thereafter as directed by the Commander-in-Chief, SOUTHWEST PACIFIC AREA.

SWPA

(a) The SOLOMON and BISMARCK SEA AREA west of the 155° meridian East Longitude and southwest of the line BUKA PASSAGE–NEW IRELAND.

SPA

(b) East and northeastward of SOUTHWEST PACIFIC defensive reconnaissance boundaries as required, with a permissible overlap of one degree along the eastern boundary.

(c) The water area southwest of the SOLOMONS eastward of 155°E and northward of 9° South to be covered by SOUTH PACIFIC.

(d) Offensive reconnaissances of the two areas will cover such sectors as required without regard to defensive reconnaissance boundaries.

(2) Within the defensive reconnaissance areas indicated in paragraph (1), the Air and Naval Forces of the SOUTHWEST PACIFIC and SOUTH PACIFIC AREAS will attack targets of opportunity as directed by respective commanders. Within the reconnaissance area of the other Force, timely notification by each commander will be given the other of contemplated air and naval (including shipping) movements. Necessary coordination when required will be arranged by the Commander-in-Chief, SOUTHWEST PACIFIC AREA.

(3) The forces of the SOUTHWEST PACIFIC and SOUTH PACIFIC AREAS will mutually support each other generally as follows, timing being directed by the Commander-in-Chief, SOUTHWEST PACIFIC AREA:

Operation I and A. Fighter protection for occupation of WOODLARK ISLAND will be provided by SOUTHWEST PACIFIC FORCES assisted by long-range fighters of SOUTH PACIFIC FORCES, operating from airdromes of the SOUTHWEST PACIFIC AREA. Both forces will support the operation along their respective axes by intensive air action against hostile rearward air bases and by diversions employing land and light naval forces threatening nearby enemy bases.

Operation II. SOUTH PACIFIC FORCES will pin down hostile air forces along their axis of advance by air attack and infiltration north-westward without commitment to major action.

Operation B. SOUTHWEST PACIFIC Air Forces will cover the operations of SOUTH PACIFIC FORCES by neutralization of hostile air bases along the line BUKA–RABAUL–KAVIENG.

Operation III and C. When SOUTH PACIFIC Air Forces are established in southern BOUGAINVILLE, SOUTH PACIFIC Air Forces will assist SOUTHWEST PACIFIC Air Forces in the neutralization of the RABAUL–KAVIENG AREA.

(4) The SOUTHWEST PACIFIC AREA and SOUTH PACIFIC AREA will exchange daily summaries of intelligence and operations. The Commander-in-Chief, SOUTHWEST PACIFIC AREA will be furnished the plan of major operations by SOUTH PACIFIC FORCES sufficiently in advance of operations to permit necessary coordination.

(5) (a) Direct command communication will be established between General Headquarters, SOUTHWEST PACIFIC AREA, and Headquarters, SOUTH PACIFIC AREA.

(b) Direct communication on operational and intelligence matters will be established between the two air forces, and reconnaissance information interchanged by the most rapid means.

5. LOGISTIC ARRANGEMENTS.

SOUTHWEST PACIFIC AREA.

a. GENERAL.

(1) Logistic support is the responsibility of the United States Army Services of Supply and the Australian Line of Communication from the Zone of Interior (AUSTRALIA) to the intermediate bases on the YORK PENINSULA, at PORT MORESBY and MILNE BAY and to the advance base at ORO BAY and others subsequently established.

b. TRANSPORTATION.

(1) The Australian Line of Communication will be responsible for the over-water transportation of all requirements for the YORK PENINSULA north from CAIRNS (exclusive), for the TORRES STRAIT and NORTHERN TERRI-TORY FORCES (except for naval forces) and, insofar as is practicable, for the Australian Land Forces based on PORT MORESBY.

(2) The United States Army Services of Supply will be responsible for the overwater transportation of all requirements (except for Naval forces) for the intermediate base at MILNE BAY, the advance base at ORO BAY and others subsequently established, and for all military units at PORT MORESBY, except those requirements transported by the Australian Line of Communication.

(3) The Allied Naval Force will furnish overwater transportation for the NEW BRITAIN FORCE until relieved.

c. PORTS AND BASES.

(1) The Australian Line of Communication will establish port organizations on the YORK PENINSULA, in the TORRES STRAIT AREA, and in

the NORTHERN TERRITORY. In NEW GUINEA, the United States Army Services of Supply and Australian Line of Communication will maintain separate port and base organizations for the logistic support of their respective units based therein. Coordination will be effected by the Combined Operational Service Command under the Commander, NEW GUINEA FORCE.

d. UNIT RESPONSIBILITY IN FORWARD AREAS.

(1) NEW GUINEA FORCE and NEW BRITAIN FORCE will establish their own services for logistic support forward of the intermediate and advance bases.

(2) At objectives under attack, organic service elements of assault forces, reinforced where necessary by Australian Line of Communication or the United States Army Services of Supply, will provide logistic support.

(3) (a) NEW BRITAIN FORCE will provide logistic support of Allied Air Forces, serving in its area of responsibility.

(b) The United States Army Service of Supply will provide logistic support for Allied Air Forces in NEW GUINEA. Pending establishment of necessary facilities in forward areas, the NEW GUINEA FORCE will provide required logistic support.

(4) The Allied Naval Forces will continue their present system of logistic support for naval forces, except that Task Forces will furnish this support to naval forces in advance areas until the Navy system is established.

e. SOUTH PACIFIC AREA.

(1) In accordance with plans and directives of the Commander, SOUTH PACIFIC FORCES.

Appendix W

HISTORICAL RECORD INDEX CARD
GHQ SWPA

TYPE:	Mimeo Secret Outline Plan, P241–43	**DATE:**	20 Oct 43
FROM:	G–3 GHQ Planning	**FILE:**	G–3 GHQ Planning
TO:	(Not stated)	**PAGES:**	Cover, (4), 13, plus maps and charts
SUBJ:	Reno III, Outline Plan for Opns of the SWPA, 1944		

(Plan Reno III was promulgated as a result of certain Quadrant (Quebec I) Conference decisions and differs rather radically from Reno, Reno II–A, and Reno II, which have been treated separately. Attached hereto is a memo dated 31 Oct 43 saying in part:

("The accompanying Reno III Outline Plan for operations of the Southwest Pacific Area to reoccupy the Southern Philippines has been submitted to the Joint Chiefs of Staff in compliance with the enclosed directive. Pending approval this plan will be utilized as a guide by the commander to whom issued for long-range planning for the year 1944 . . . ."

(The directive mentioned is a radio, #8162/19th, presumably Oct 43, from Gen Marshall to Gen MacArthur, saying in part: ("Certain papers delivered to you by Colonel Ritchie contain quadrant decisions covering operation against the Japanese. It is requested that you forward by 1 November 1943 outline plans for your operations to seize Kavieng and Admiralty Islands and for your advances in New Guinea as far west as Vogelkop . . . . This information is necessary for the integration of operations in your area with other approved operations against the Japanese in 1943–1944, particularly those to be conducted in the Japanese Mandates."

(Herewith follows the synopsis of Reno III—Ed.)

Our strategic objective is the isolation of Japan from the Malaya-NEI area. Present tasks are to:

1. Seize or neutralize E NG as far W as Wewak and including the Admiralties and the Bismarck Archipelago.
   Neutralize, rather than capture Rabaul.
2. Advance along the N coast of NG as far W as the Vogelkop by AB-amphib jumps.
3. Prepare to seize Mindanao by AB-amphib opns.

Our eventual task is to reoccupy the S PI, and by subsequent opns isolate Japan from the Malay-NEI area.

Accomplishment of the tasks presently assigned by Quadrant decisions initially requires opns along 2 general axes.

1. NW along the NG coast from Vitiaz St in order to advance land-based air.

2. W through the N Solomons–New Ireland, including the Admiralties, to a junction with the W axis in order to complete the isolation of Rabaul and obtain necessary bases for naval support of opns along the axis.

The eventual task requires seizure of Mindanao, followed by opns in conjunction with other Theaters to sever sea and air communications between Japan and the Malaya-NEI area. These opns require attacks against strongly defended air and naval bases. Our advantages lie in superior equipment and potentially superior strength in the air and on the sea, but amphib equipment will be limited pending cessation of the offensive in Europe. On the assumption that the Japanese will maintain their strategic defense, our advantages must be fully utilized to deal him a succession of blows precluding his recouping of air and sea forces after each of his defeats and so permit destruction of his bases in detail.

The general scheme of maneuver is to advance our land-based bomber line rapidly W along the land masses of NG and the PI by successive occupation of the minimum bases required. Hostile strength is by-passed wherever practicable to avoid costly and time-consuming opns; our flanks are protected by air opns; and necessary advanced naval bases are established under protection of land-based aviation in order to extend the range of naval action. Destructive air attacks are employed to soften up objectives and to gain air superiority. Hostile naval forces and shipping are destroyed along our line of advance to prevent reinforcement. Ground forces are displaced forward by air and amphib movements. Air and naval forces are established at each objective and the process is then repeated, neutralizing by air and sea action hostile concentrations that may be by-passed. The number of objectives is decreased and the length of bound increased by the use of a/c carriers to provide close air support. The same result is aided by extending the destructive effort of bombers through use of air envelopment to advance the fighter line through inland fields established and maintained by air support.

Sequence and timing are based on present enemy dispositions and are subject to change dependent upon enemy reaction and success of our opns. Timing is also dependent upon the availability of means, particularly amphib forces, and the timing given herein is based on an estimate of means to be available as a result of quadrant.

Logistic support is provided by the SOS of Sopac and SWPA. As opns progress to the NW, ports and supply bases are advanced by corresponding bounds. Heavy shipping is used wherever unloading facilities are available and amphib craft are used for assault elements and where the use of heavy shipping is impracticable. Trans-Pacific shipping is diverted directly to newly established bases along the line of advance. Bulk petroleum is transported forward in small tankers to points where the tactical situation permits the installation of bulk storage tanks.

Known requirements in items of special equipment, major units, air and service units, are set forth in the "1944 Troop Basis, GHQ, SWPA, 9 October 1943." (Requirements for each phase of the opns are set forth below—Ed.)

Phase I

Naval bases are required in the Bismarcks to support subsequent opns into W NG. Direct attack to capture Rabaul will be costly and time-consuming. Anchorages and potential air and naval bases exist at Kavieng and in the Admiralties. With the capture and development of such bases, Rabaul can be isolated from the NE. Direct attack into the Wewak area would also be costly in means and time. Presently occupied a/mes do not provide sufficient protection to by-pass the area, but potential air bases exist in the Hansa Bay area, from which the isolation of Rabaul can be completed and opns to the W of Wewak be protected. Scheme of Maneuver:

A. Target date 1 Feb 44. SWPA forces seize the Hansa Bay area by amphib opns with AB support. Direct air support is provided from the Vitiaz St–Ramu valley a/mes. Shore-to-shore opns secure the mouth of the Sepik to contain enemy forces in the Wewak area. Advance bases are established for the support of opns in the Humboldt Bay area. Hostile forces in the Madang-Alexishafen area are isolated and the area later occupied by holding forces from the Huon Peninsula–Ramu Valley.

B. Target date 1 Mar 44. Kavieng is occupied by an amphib opn of Sopac Forces. The opn is preceded by intensive air and naval neutralization of the Rabaul area and has the direct support of heavy elements of the PacFlt. Air support comes from W New Britain and from carriers. General air support is from NG, Nor-Sols, and Kiriwina and Woodlark. Interference from hostile flt is covered by opns of Cenpac and in the Mandates and by the PacFlt. Air elements are then established for support of opns against the Carolines and Rabaul. Light naval forces are established for support of opns to the W and to help blockade Rabaul.

C. Target date 1 Mar 44. The Admiralties are taken by amphib opns of SWPA Forces staging through Vitiaz St. Direct air support comes from the Vitiaz St area and from CVEs. General air support from the Markham-Ramu area. Air and naval forces are established in the Admiralties, and base facilities developed, for the support of opns along the N coast of NG.

D. When the blockade has sufficiently reduced the defensive capacity of the enemy garrison, Rabaul is occupied at a date and by forces later to be determined, and appropriate base facilities are established.

Forces required:

Garrison	Assault	Air	Naval	
2 US inf divs	7 US inf divs	HB 5 grps	15 APD	2 CV
6 Austn divs	2 US Para RCTs	MB 10 grps	16 APA	9 CVE
1 NZ div	3 MarDefBns	LB 11½ grps	5 AKA	4 CA
1 Austn armd bde		Day F 16½ grps	85 LST	4 CL
		Night F 14 grps	60 LCI	58 DD
		Trp Carr 6¼ grps	105 LCT	164 PT
		Photo & Recce 8½ grps	(and small craft)	

Naval strategic support will be elements of the US Pac Flt as designated by the JCS. Location and types of bases for logistic support are mapped in Annex 4–b, and the scheme of maneuver is mapped in Annex 2–a.

Phase II
(Initiated 1 Jun 44)

Advanced air and naval bases are required at an intermediate point on the N coast of NG for the support of opns into Geelvink Bay and protection of the L/C thereto. Air bases in Wewak are too distant from the Geelvink area to support attacks and are held in great strength by the Japanese. Costly and time-consuming opns will be avoided by by-passing and neutralizing the Wewak area. Partially developed sites exist in the Humboldt Bay area which may be improved to meet essential requirements. The concentration of hostile a/mes in the Banda Sea area requires establishment of flank protection and support for opns into Geelvink Bay. Occupation of the Aroe-Kai-Tanimbar Islands provides a difficult but feasible means of securing this protection and support. Scheme of Maneuver (see also map, Annex 2–b) :

A. Humboldt Bay, target date 1 Jun 44. An amphib opn from NG bases with AB support seizes objectives in the Aitape–Humboldt Bay area, by-passing Wewak. Air support is provided from the Markham–Ramu Valley, Hansa Bay, and the Admiralties. Close support comes from CVEs. Inland air bases are established in the upper Digoe-Fly Rivers by air transport as practicable. Adv bases are established in the Humboldt Bay area for support of opns into the Geelvink-Vogelkop area. Forces in the Aitape area initiate infiltration opns from the W toward Wewak and finally occupy it when hostile resistance has deteriorated.

B. Arafura Sea. 1 Jun 44. Preceded by aerial neutralization of Timor a/mes, the Aroe-Kai-Tanimbar Islands are occupied by an amphib assault of Austn troops supported by AB elements. General air support is provided from Darwin area, convoy cover from Merauke–Horn Is–Arnhem Bay, and by CVEs. Air bases are promptly developed.

Forces required:

Garrison	Assault	Air Grps	Naval	
6 Austn inf divs	4 US inf divs	8 HB	2 CV	15 APD
1 NZ inf div	2 Austn inf divs	12 MB	7 CVE	5 APA
5 US inf divs	1 US AB div	11¾ LB	4 CA	84 LST
1 Austn armd bde	2 para RCTs	22½ Night F	6 CL	60 LCI
	1 MarDefBn	18½ F	83 DD	145 LCT
		8¼ Trp Carr	8 PT	
		11 Photo Recce	168 PT	

Naval strategic support will be from the US PacFlt as designated by the JCS to insure noninterference by hostile heavy flt elements. Locations and types of bases for logistic support are in Annex 4–c.

Phase III

(Initiated 15 Aug 44)

Major naval and air bases are required in W NG to support opns to the NW. Potential sites are available in the Geelvink Bay–Vogelkop area. Opns require protection against major enemy flt elements by the US Flt. Scheme of Maneuver (see also map, Annex 2–c) :

A. Geelvink Bay. 15 Aug 44. Anchorages, a/mes, and potential base sites are seized by an AB overseas landing, staged in NG. Babo and Nabire are neutralized by air staged through Aroe-Kai-Tanimbar. Direct air support is provided from the Humboldt Bay area through inland air bases established and maintained in favorable locations by air transport, and also by CVEs. Major air and naval base development is instituted for support of opns against Mindanao.

B. Vogelkop Area, 1 Oct 44. The Sorong and Kabui Bay areas are occupied by an amphib opn with AB support. This opn is launched as soon as air support is available from Geelvink Bay bases. The Klamono oil field is occupied and intensively developed as a source of bunker fuel.

Forces required (see also Annexes 3–2, –b, and –c) :

Garrison	*Combat*	*Air Groups*
7 Austn inf divs		
1 NZ inf div		
4 US inf divs		
1 Austn armd bde		

Naval Combat	*Amphib Craft*
2 CV	15 APD
6 CVE	16 APA
4 CA	5 AKA
6 CL	54 LST
64 DD	60 LCI
183 PT	175 LCT

Phase IV

(Initiated 1 Dec 44)

Advance into Mindanao requires a broadening of the front for deployment of air forces, protection for flanks, and establishment of advance bases for support of sea and AB movements. These requirements can be met by establishing air and light naval elements on Halmahera and/or Morotai. Menado must at least be denied to the enemy and Palua must be occupied by either Cenpac or SWPA forces. The Ambon area must be neutralized by air action, but may have to be occupied if hostile strength in the NEI requires such action. Scheme of Maneuver (see also map in Annex 2–d) :

A. Halamhera-Menado, target date 1 Dec 44. A/mes or sites therefor on Halamahera and/or Morotai are occupied and Menado seized by amphib opns from Geelvink Bay, supported by AB elements. Air and naval forces are established for flank protection and support of subsequent opns to seize and occupy Mindanao.

B. Ambon (contingent opn), 1 Dec. 44. In the event that hostile strength in the E NEI jeopardizes opns on Mindanao, it may be necessary to establish air and naval forces on Ambon. If required, this opn will be amphib, staged from Geelvink via the Dampier Strs, will seize enemy air bases on Ceram and Boeroe and capture Ambon. Enemy air forces on Timor are neutralized from Darwin, and general air support comes from Aroe-Kai-Tanimbar-Geelvink-Vogelkop areas.

C. Palau, 1 Dec 44, or 15 Jan 45 if Ambon is occupied. In the event that SWPA forces are assigned the task of occupying Palau, that group is seized by amphib opns with the direct support of the PacFlt, including strong carrier elements. Naval air elements are established on Palau for protection of the axis of advance against enemy air attacks from the N.

For location of bases for logistic support see Annex 4–e. Completion of Phase III accomplishes the tasks presently assigned to the SWPA by the quadrant decisions. Estimates of forces required to accomplish Phases IV and V of this plan are of problematical value in view of the certainty of major changes in the Pacific situation and in the availability and types of means available for the carrying out of Phase III. A tentative estimate of divs for Phases IV and V have been shown in Annex 3, but only as a basis for 44 troop estimates. For Phase IV these are:

Garrison	*Combat*
5 Austn inf divs	7 US inf divs
4 US inf divs	1 Para RCT
1 Austn armd bde	1 MarDefBn
	2 US divs for possible opns in Jan 45

No estimates of naval or air means can be given at this time.

Phase V

(Initiated 1 Feb 45)

Occupation of Mindanao requires an attack by major forces of all components over a widely spread area in order to achieve surprise and disperse the defensive effort. Employment of air envlopment on a major scale, using equipment now in prospect, becomes feasible upon establishment of adquate bases in the Geelvink-Vogelkop area. Present guerrilla organization provides necessary terminal facilities. Prompt and ample seaborne reinforcement of initial assault is essential. Consolidation of the S PI requires occupation of covering position in the islands to the SW and N of Mindanao and the establishment of major forces thereon preparatory to subsequent opns. "Inasmuch as the enemy must defend Mindanao with all the means at his disposal, prompt consolidation and subsequent exploitation should meet a minimum of effective opposition." Scheme of Maneuver (see also map in Annex 2–e) :

A. Occupation of Mindanao, target date 1 Feb 45. Beachheads and a/mes through the N and NW portion of Mindanao are seized by major combined AB-amphib opns with carrier based air support. An AB invasion in strength is staged in New Britain and E NG via W NG. Guerrilla forces are employed to seize a/mes on which to land AB forces. Landing opns seize beachheads in the proximity of a/mes. Paratroops are dropped on a/mes. Light air elements are flown in to support the advance of occupation forces and protect subsequent landings. Initial landings are prompty reinforced by air transport.

B. Consolidation of Southern PI: The Mindanao Occupation Force follows the AB invasion closely along the main line of advance to beachheads in our possession. All types of aviation are established in order to maintain air superiority and cover the occupation of Zamboanga and Davao and positions in islands to the SW and W. The L/C W of the line Palau-Vogelkop is kept open by naval elements from advanced bases in the Vogelkop area, supported by air from Palau, Menado, and Halmahera-Morotai. Additional forces of all arms are rapidly established on Mindanao in preparation for opns to reoccupy the northern PI and to isolate Japan from the Malay-NEI. Logistic bases are set forth on map of Annex 4–f. Ground forces required (a suggestion rather than definite estimate) :

Garrison	Combat
5 Austn inf divs	4 US inf divs
4 US inf divs	2 US AB divs
3 US inf divs for contingent opns	1 para RCT
1 Austn armd bde	2 MarDefBns

Forces for the consolidation are undetermined. Impossible to estimate at this time the naval and air forces required.

(Annex 1 gives a map outline of the phases of opns as outlined above. An undated map attached to Annex 1 starts Phase I of the opns in the Vogelkop-Geelvink Area on 15 Jun 44, and must be dated after Apr 44 since it lists the Wadke-Sarmi Opn as a "Current Operation." It also lists the Marianas Opns of Cenpac to start on 15 Jun 44. (Annex 2–a through 2–f (3) outlines the scheme of maneuver for ground forces and the location of the air forces throughout each phase of the operations.) (Annex 3 lists the combat elements required for navy, air, and ground forces. Information from this Annex has been integrated into the synopsis above. (Annexes 4–a through 4–f give the location and types of bases for logistic support of each phase of the opns planned in Reno III. (Supplement "A," G–2 Estimate of the Enemy Situation," is under a separate cover. (Supplement "B" is a chart showing the detailed use of ground, air and naval forces for each objective area, giving type and number of units for each opn. (Supplement "C" is a time and location schedule of each division utilized in the planned opns—Ed.)

Guide to Footnotes

The footnotes in this volume are designed to accomplish two objectives: (1) to indicate the nature of the evidence on which the author based his account, and (2) to enable the scholar and researcher to identify the document and to locate it among the mass of World War II records, with the assistance of the archivist, in as brief a time as possible. These objectives were not always consistent with brevity, but the author has used every device to reduce the length of the footnotes and to keep their number to the minimum. Thus, collective footnotes summarizing the sources for a particular subject or section of a chapter have been employed wherever possible; information not essential to identification or location has been omitted; and abbreviations and code names, rigorously eschewed in the text, have been used liberally in the footnotes. Though these short cuts should not present any difficulty for the reader familiar with military records and abbreviations, a word of explanation for the uninitiated may be helpful.

The information normally required to identify and locate a document in any of the various military archival depositories includes (a) a description of the type of document, (b) the originator, (c) the recipient, (d) date, (e) subject, and (f) file reference. With important exceptions, to be noted below, the author has made every effort to provide this information, in the order named, in the citations to this volume. The following explanation should make clear the pur-

pose of each item in the footnote:

1. *Kind of Document.* The nature of the sources used in the preparation of this volume varies widely, both as to type and official character, and has to be taken into account in evaluating the evidence. There is a wide gap between an informal memorandum or personal note and a directive from the Joint Chiefs of Staff or an order from a theater commander. Thus, the first item in the citation indicates, usually in abbreviated form, the type of document cited. Those most frequently used in the preparation of this volume are (a) official reports, orders, plans, and directives of theater headquarters, the War Department, and the Joint and Combined Chiefs of Staff; (b) minutes of meetings and conferences, ranging from those of senior staff officers and commanders, such as the Pacific Military Conference in March 1943, to the wartime meetings of the Combined Chiefs of Staff with the President and Prime Minister (recorded in bound, printed volumes called Conference Books); (c) estimates, studies, and plans developed in the theater, by staff agencies in the War and Navy Departments, and by committees of the Joint and Combined Chiefs of Staff; (d) official correspondence within and between headquarters, agencies, and overseas commands in the form of radio messages, letters and memoranda; (e) informal and often revealing exchanges of view within and between agencies, offices, and commands, expressed usually in memoranda, records of conversations, notes on meet-

ings, and comments on studies and drafts of plans; and finally, (f) notes, routing slips, and memoranda for the record, filed with the official correspondence.

2. *Originator.* The originator of a document may be a single person, an office, a headquarters, or an agency. Military staff officers are dedicated to anonymity and official documents are issued in the name of a commander or an office. Thus, the identity of the actual author of the document is often difficult to determine, and, in any case, is likely to be of little importance. Where it is significant, the citation so indicates.

3. *Recipient.* A document may be addressed to a specific individual, a headquarters, an agency, to no one in particular, or to everyone concerned, depending on the nature of the source. Thus, the establishment or clarification of policy by the War Department or Joint Chiefs of Staff would have no specific addressee, and a memo for record no recipient but the files.

4. *Date.* In some cases, such as radio messages, the time may be an important element in the identification of a document. When it is, this information is included in the citation. The military system for dates (7 December 1941) and times (the 24-hour clock—0900 for 9:00 a.m. and 2100 for 9:00 p.m.) is used throughout, in the text as well as the footnotes. Navy radio messages are usually identified by the month and a date-time group, a 6-number group of which the first two represent the day of the month and the last four the time the message was sent.

5. *Subject.* Military usage dictates a subject heading for certain types of documents, notably memoranda; others, such as letters, reports, and studies, may or

may not have one, and some documents such as radio messages never do. When the document cited has a subject heading, this information is included in the footnote in abbreviated form as an aid to identification.

6. *Location.* Under the Army decimal system for filing, a document can usually be located by its file number.* This number is invariably preceded by a letter symbol identifying the record group (or office of origin) in which the file is located. The letter symbols most often used in the present volume are (a) AG, denoting the central files of The Adjutant General's Office, record keeper for the Army; (b) OCS or WDCSA, the files of the Chief of Staff; (c) WPD and OPD, the War Plans Division of the War Department General Staff and its successor, the Operations Division; (d) ABC, the records of the Strategy and Policy Group of the Operations Division; (e) JB, the Joint Board; (f) OPD Exec, the special collection maintained by the Executive Office of OPD; (g) SWPA, the Southwest Pacific Area; (h) POA, Pacific Ocean Areas; and (i) PTO, the Pacific Theater of Operations, a file designation and not a theater command. This system and the abbreviations may vary somewhat among offices and agencies, and in different periods of time (the WPD records, for example, do not employ the decimal system), but the letter symbol and number usually provide sufficient information to locate the relevant file quickly.

The files themselves are often volumi-

---

* For a description of the system, see *War Department Decimal File System*, compiled under the direction of The Adjutant General of the Army, revised edition (Washington, 1943), and supplements.

nous, consisting of several volumes (called sections), and any one numbered file may be subdivided in a variety of ways—by date, theater, country, and the like. Thus the entire file reference, including symbol, number, date, area, and section, is necessary to locate the document. Once the particular document is found, the researcher's task is easy. Most of the files are indexed, and some offices, such as the Operations Division, assigned a case number to each document showing the relative position of that document in the file. This information is indicated in the footnote whenever necessary. Thus WPD 4439–5 refers to the fifth case in the War Plans Division file 4439 (an arbitrarily assigned number for a subject heading).

Certain exceptions must be noted. Among these, perhaps the most important for this volume are the documents originating with the Joint Board, the Joint and Combined Chiefs of Staff, and their committees. These are usually identified by a letter symbol indicating the committee of origin (JPS for Joint Staff Planners, JSSC for Joint Strategic Survey Committee, JWPC for Joint War Plans Committee, CPS for Combined Staff Planners) or the Joint and Combined Chiefs themselves. The letter symbol is followed by a number representing a subject, and frequently by a slash and another number, indicating the numbered version of that particular document. Thus, JPS 67/4, represents the fifth version of a study (assigned the number 67) prepared by the Joint Staff Planners.

The reader should be aware also that a study may be known by different numbers, acquired as it makes its way up the hierarchy of joint and combined committees. A typical example is the strategic plan for the defeat of Japan developed in the spring of 1943. Starting in the Joint U.S. Strategic Committee as JUSSC 40/2, it became JPS 67/4 after the Joint Staff Planners had worked it over. The Joint Chiefs took the plan with them to TRIDENT as JCS 287/1, and it emerged finally from the Combined Chiefs of Staff in May 1943 as CCS 220. Though the final version differed from the first, it is still recognizable as basically the same study.

Joint and combined papers require no further identification than the number, date, and subject or title. Citations of these documents, therefore, ordinarily omit originator, recipient, and file reference. The last item is omitted also in footnote references to radio messages and certain other types of documents. Navy messages are identified usually by date-time groups, and Army messages filed in the Classified Message Center of The Adjutant General's Office (and elsewhere) by the date and CM–IN or CM–OUT number assigned by that office. Finally, it has not been necessary to furnish file references for letters, directives, and other types of documents issued by The Adjutant General since these can be readily identified and located in central files by date and AG symbol.

Frequent use has been made of Japanese sources throughout this volume. No particular difficulty should be encountered in footnote references to these sources since most of them refer either to (a) studies in the collection designated Japanese Studies in World War II (described fully in The Sources), by number and title; or (b) works published in Japan and translated for the author.

No file references are required since both English and Japanese versions are available in the Office of the Chief of Military History.

The reader will note numerous references to letters of recent origin addressed to the Chief of Military History. These letters represent, in effect, the comments of many of the wartime commanders and staff officers on the present volume in manuscript form. In their response to requests for comment, many of these officers furnished information not available in the official records. This information was used by the author in revising the volume, and the letters themselves are retained in a single file in OCMH as constituting a valuable source for the war in the Pacific.

One further type of source, manuscript histories, must be noted. These are of two kinds: those intended for publication in the present series or elsewhere; and those prepared by an office or headquarters and not intended for publication. The latter vary widely in size, quality, and form, and are described in the bibliography. Where author and title are indicated, the manuscript is cited in the usual manner. Frequently, authorship is not given or known, and the manuscript is identified by title and office of origin, with appropriate volume and page references. In each case, the location of the manuscript, or of the copy used by the present author, is indicated, since such manuscripts are like documents in that they can be found only in specific record collections or files.

The citation of published works and official records will present no problem to the reader; these are cited in the customary fashion and a list of most of the published sources used by the author or useful for background will be found in the bibliography.

The Sources

The student of World War II is confronted with an enormous body of records and an imposing list of published works and official documents. For the World War II years alone, the Army, it has been estimated, has more than 17,000 tons of records, with an undetermined but large quantity of prewar records essential to an understanding of the wartime period. When to this total is added the extant records of the Navy, which has its own vast records depots filled with World War II records; the Air Force, which has moved many of the records to its own depots; and the Marine Corps, the result is a truly staggering mass of paper.

Obviously a large part of this material is of a purely routine nature, important for accounting purposes and orderly administration but of little interest to the student of war. He can further reduce the total appreciably by eliminating the records of housekeeping activities of the numerous military installations established during the war at home and abroad. The scope of his inquiry and the historian's own interests serve also to eliminate large bodies of records from consideration. If his research is focused on matters of strategy and organization, as this volume is, he can safely ignore the records and reports of all units but those on the highest level; if it is focused on military operations, then the records and reports of the units involved become his primary sources.[1]

Introduction: Guide to the Records

Though the largest part of the total body of military records can be safely eliminated by the historian so far as his purposes are concerned, the remainder constitutes a body of considerable magnitude. Fortunately, there are a number of archival aids to enable him to identify the materials he needs and locate them in the various records depositories. The most valuable of these aids is the 2-volume *Federal Records of World War II* (Washington, 1951) prepared by the National Archives. The second volume of this work deals exclusively with military agencies and contains not only descriptions of the records and their location as of 1950, but also brief histories of the organizations that created them, including the overseas commands. It is the indispensable guide for all those entering for the first time the strange world of military archives.[2]

Federal Records of World War II provides only the most general description of the vast body of records it surveys. For more specific descriptions, the student must turn to the inventories and guides prepared from time to time by the National Archives and listed in the *Guide to the Records in the National*

[1] An excellent brief account of the problems involved in the use of military records is Paul P. Van

Riper, "A Survey of Materials for the Study of Military Management," *American Political Science Review*, XLIX, No. 3 (September, 1955), 828–50.

[2] For a general description of the problems involved in the use of federal records, see Philip C. Brooks, "The Historian's Stake in Federal Records," *Mississippi Valley Historical Review*, XLIII, No. 2 (September, 1956), 259–74.

Archives (Washington, 1948) and the latest edition of the *Publications of the National Archives and Records Service* (Washington, January 1961).[3]

The Army and Navy have their own guides to the records. These are not listed in any single publication as are those of the National Archives, but can ordinarily be obtained without difficulty from the originating agencies, both of which make provision for assistance, within the limits of existing laws and regulations, to students of military affairs.[4]

The major depository of records for the World War II period, in addition to the services themselves, which still hold some of the most important records of the war, is the World War II Records Division of the National Archives in Alexandria, Virginia. Formerly the Departmental Records Branch of the Adjutant General's Office, the World War II Records Division was transferred with its records to the National Archives in 1958. At the time of its transfer, the Army's Departmental Records Branch was a joint records depository serving headquarters agencies of both the Army and the Air Force, as well as the former War Department, and the present Office, Secretary of Defense. This new division of the National Archives, still located temporarily in Alexandria, Virginia, will henceforth administer all permanent records of the World War II and postwar periods transferred to the National Archives. Records for the earlier period are already located in the Archives Building in Washington and are administered by the War Records Division.

The Army's former depository of prewar and World War II records at Kansas City, containing largely unit and operational records, and the Navy's depositories comprising similar records located in Alexandria, Va., and Mechanicsburg, Pa., are now administered by the GSA Federal Records Centers in those areas. The Navy continues to control the holdings of its Operational Archives Branch in Arlington, Va., while the Historical Branch, G–3, Headquarters, U.S. Marine Corps, maintains the archives for the Marine Corps.

The Records

Research for the present study of strategy and command in the Pacific has ranged widely over the records from the highest levels to the comparatively low level of division and corps in the theater, and from the early 1900's down to 1944. Through these records, the author has had an unrivaled opportunity to trace the approach of war and the emergence of American and Japanese Strategy before Pearl Harbor, and to follow closely the progress of the war from the lofty heights of the Combined Chiefs of Staff and the Japanese *Imperial General Headquarters*, from the viewpoint of the Army and Navy, from the vantage point of the

---

[3] See also Elizabeth Bethel, "Early Records of the War Department General Staff," *American Archivist* (October, 1945), 241–7, and E. L. Huber, "War Department Records in the National Archives," Military Affairs (Winter, 1942), 247–54.

[4] Among the Army's publications are Guide to the Records of the Adjutant General's Department, 1940–45 (1950); Guide to the Records of the Office of the Secretary of War, 1939–46 (1949); Descriptive List of Studies of the USAF Historical Division (1956); Inventory of Certain Records of United States Army Forces in the Far East and United States Forces in the Philippines, July 1941–May 1942 (1952). The Navy's contribution is a short pamphlet entitled A Brief Guide to U.S. Naval History Sources in the Washington, D.C. Area (1957).

theater commanders, and, finally, from the level of the commanders on the field of battle. Wherever possible, he has viewed the war from both sides and sought to find in the records the reasons for both American and Japanese actions. In some matters, the record was voluminous; in others, so sparse as to require requests for information from the participants.

It is obviously impossible to describe here all the records used directly or indirectly in the preparation of this volume. For that, the reader will have to rely on the footnotes and the various guides noted above.[5] This discussion, therefore, is confined to those record collections considered most valuable for the study of Pacific strategy.

The sources for the study of strategy in the prewar period are best considered separately since they are maintained and organized somewhat differently from those dealing with World War II. It is useful also, because of the reorganization after World War I, to divide these records into two general categories: (a) those for the period 1900 to 1919, and (b) those covering the years 1919 to 1942. During the earlier period strategic planning was the function mainly of the two war colleges, the General Board of the Navy, and the Joint Army-Navy Board; in the latter period, of the War Plans Divisions of the two services, and of the reorganized Joint Board and its Joint Planning Committee, with the General Board playing a minor role.

The Joint Board kept few records. Those for the years 1903 to 1919 occupy altogether about half a file drawer in the National Archives, where they can be used without restriction. Sparse as they are, these records, including correspondence, minutes of meetings, memoranda, strategic studies and plans, contain valuable material.

The General Board of the Navy dealt with a variety of matters of the first importance and its records constitute an indispensable source for the study of strategy during these years. Still classified, these records are located in the Navy's Operational Archives Branch in Arlington and are controlled by the Naval History Division. The general records of the Navy Department for these years (Record Group 80) are located in the Navy Branch, War Records Division, National Archives. These are well indexed and in the custody of archivists whose intimate knowledge of the records greatly simplifies the task of research.

Records of the early planning activities of the War Department General Staff became part of the records of the Army War College. These as well as the records of the Office of the Chief of Staff, and other staff divisions, altogether over 4,000 cubic feet of records, constitute Record Group 165 of the National Archives holdings.[6] Frequently overlooked by the student of military affairs, this collection contains the Army's plans for a variety of situations, strategic studies, comments on plans developed by other agencies, memoranda, and other documents of interest and value in any survey

---

[5] He may also wish to consult the bibliographical note in each of the companion volumes of the Pacific subseries listed on p. iv, which describes not only the operational records but also those pertaining to the strategic background of each campaign.

[6] This collection is described in Preliminary Checklist of the Records of the War Department General Staff, prepared by Elizabeth Bethel, copy in OCMH.

of military strategy in the period 1903 to 1919.

The record for the years after World War I, especially those immediately preceding Pearl Harbor, are indispensable to an understanding of the war. Fortunately, the records become fuller with the passage of time. Those for the Joint Board from 1919 to 1941, for example, are fully ten times more voluminous than for the earlier period. A large part of this material has been declassified, and transferred to the National Archives of the Joint Chiefs of Staff. The same material, with the valuable addition of supporting memoranda and studies reflecting the points of view of the Army and Navy, can be found in the World War II Records Division of the National Archives in Alexandria. Though not the official record of the Joint Board, this collection represents the file of the Army members of the Joint Planning Committee and is in some ways a more valuable source than the original.

The records of the Army War Plans Division constitute the best single collection for the prewar period. Located in the World War II Records Division and carefully indexed by subject with cross references, this large body of material throws light on every major issue facing the Army during these years. The files are organized on a numerical system (not the Army decimal file system) in which each number designates a particular subject. For identification the numbers are preceded by the symbol WPD, and within each file the documents are arranged chronologically by case number. The War Plans Division also maintained a full set of joint and Army plans, supported by Development Files. Most of these are now in a special Obsolete War Plans collection in the World War II Records Division.

With the entry of the United States into war, existing agencies for planning were reorganized and greatly enlarged, and new agencies established. Planning activities increased sharply and the volume of records grew at a rapid rate. Fortunately for the student, strategic planning in the Army was concentrated in the War Plans Division (redesignated the Operations Division in March 1942), which maintained excellent records of not only its own activities but also those of joint and combined committees. These records, on which the author relied almost entirely for the story of the higher direction of the war in the Pacific, contain virtually a complete set of Joint and Combined Chiefs of Staff papers, radio messages to and from the theater commanders, official correspondence, memoranda, and strategic studies and plans, together with the background and supporting documents.

The records of the Operations Division, practically all of which (with the exception noted below) have been retired to the World War II Records Division of the National Archives, are maintained in separate groups. The radio messages, the largest and most complete collection outside the permanent central file (microfilmed) of the Department of the Army, form the OPD Message Center File. In it, are the incoming and outgoing messages, arranged by number, for the entire period of the war. In many ways, this collection is more convenient to use than the official file of the Staff Communications Office, Office of the Chief of Staff, which, in addition, maintained a Chief of Staff Log of messages between General Marshall and the theater commanders. This log contains also the records of radio-telephone conversations (telecons) as well as the daily reports from the theaters.

The OPD Central File is the largest and most valuable of the Operations Division's wartime records, probably the most important single collection of World War II Army records dealing with strategy and policy. It is organized into two groups based on classification, and within each by subject under the Army decimal system, and by case number. In each case the number is preceded by the identifying symbol OPD. Joint and combined records, including those of the subordinate committees and of the wartime meetings with the Allies, together with the studies and memoranda prepared by officers in the Operations Division, form still another separate collection of the wartime OPD records — perhaps the most important outside the Joint Chiefs of Staff. It was collected by the Strategy and Policy Group of OPD, and unlike other records of OPD is identified by the symbol ABC, combined with a number assigned according to the Army decimal system. The Executive Office of OPD maintained an informal collection of records on matters of a particularly sensitive nature that required special handling. These were not maintained or organized in any systematic way, but there exists an index of the files in the collection. Located in the Office of the Chief of Military History at the time the author used them, the Executive Office Files were scheduled for early transfer to the World War II Records Division in Alexandria.

There is no convenient collection of records for the overseas commands comparable to that of the Operations Division. Some of them are in the Washington area, some in records centers in different parts of the country, and some remain in the theater under control of successor commands. The records of the overseas commands have been further scattered by distribution among the Army, Navy, and Air Force. The main collections in the Federal Records Center Annex, Kansas City, are those of General Headquarters, Southwest Pacific Area, and its subordinate commands, of Headquarters, South Pacific Area, and of the Hawaiian Department and its successor commands. The records of Admiral Nimitz' headquarters are divided between the naval depository in Arlington and the Federal Records Center in Mechanicsburg, Pennsylvania. Some operational records are also in the GSA Center in Alexandria. Marine Corps records, as indicated earlier, are retained for the most part in the Historical Branch, G–3, Headquarters, U.S. Marine Corps.

The records of General MacArthur's command are of perhaps chief interest to the student of Army planning in the Pacific. Initially, these were divided between the United States and Australia, those for Allied Land Forces (and certain other specified records) going to the latter. Since most U.S. ground forces served under Sixth Army (ALAMO Force), this distribution left the bulk of the ground operational records for the Americans, and these are divided between the World War II Records Division in Alexandria and in the Federal Records Center Annex in Kansas City. The records of the Allied Air Forces, General Kenney's command, were returned to the United States and are filed with those of the Fifth Air Force and the Far East Air Force in Kansas City, where the records of the Seventh and Thirteenth Air Forces are located. Selected portions of these records have since been moved to the Air Historical Office at Maxwell Field, Montgomery, Alabama.

The early records of MacArthur's command in the Philippines, U.S. Army Forces in the Far East, were retained as a special collection in The Adjutant General's Office, since transferred to the World War II Records Division. A portion of the headquarters files of GHQ went to Kansas City, but the important G–3 Journals are in the World War II Records Division. Not all of the records of MacArthur's wartime command have been returned to the United States, or, if they have, their location seems to be unknown. Among these records are the files of the Chief of Staff and of the G–3 Planning Division.

Special mention should be made of the notes taken by the Historical Section of MacArthur's headquarters. These consist of many thousands of cards containing précis of the plans, studies, and important correspondence of the headquarters for the entire period of the war, organized chronologically and by subject, with cross references. A part of this collection is now in the possession of the Office of the Chief of Military History, which has also a further selection, typed and bound in a volume entitled Historical Record Index Cards, GHQ SWPA.

The records of U.S. Army Forces in the South Pacific Area, General Harmon's command, and of the Army headquarters in Hawaii are distributed between the Federal Records Center Annex in Kan-

sas City and the World War II Records Division, with the bulk of the files in Kansas City but the more important ones in Alexandria. The letters of Generals Harmon and Richardson to Marshall and officers in the Operations Division are also in the OPD files, with copies in the Central Files of The Adjutant General's Office, which also contain much of the wartime correspondence of the Army headquarters in the Pacific. These files, too, are in the World War II Records Division. While there may appear to be a division of the records of Army overseas commands between the Kansas City Federal Records Center Annex and the World War II Records Division, the records in custody of the latter are mainly those which were forwarded to higher headquarters during the war. The retained organizational copies will be found in Kansas City.

Manuscript Histories

There are a great number of unpublished manuscripts available to the student of World War II. Often these works were prepared by highly qualified scholars as part of an official program that was never intended for publication. Even when their authors were not so qualified, these manuscripts represent a careful survey of a large body of records, backed by official sanction, and often with the co-operation of participants in the events described. Thus, they may not only prove valuable as a guide to the records, but may supplement the records themselves.

The number of manuscript histories dealing with World War II is very large indeed. Virtually every major agency in the War Department and every major command in the United States and overseas prepared a history of its activities during World War II. The Naval History Division alone has almost 300 such unpublished histories. The Army's Office of the Chief of Military History has many more, and has eased the task of the researcher by preparing a series of Historical Manuscript Accession Lists.[7] The Air Force, too, has a large number of these manuscripts, and, like OCMH, publishes periodically a guide to these and other studies.

By far the most valuable and, professionally, among the most competent of the unpublished histories are those prepared by the Historical Division of the Joint Chiefs of Staff. For Pacific strategy, the two volumes of Lt. Grace P. Hayes are unsurpassed.[8] Carefully and fully documented, well organized and presented, these two volumes present a detailed and accurate account of the role of the Joint Chiefs of Staff in the Pacific war. Though the narrative is focused on the Joint Chiefs and their committees, it contains much Army and Navy material as well. Like all the manuscripts prepared by the Historical Division of the Joint Chiefs, Lieutenant Hayes' two volumes are classified and available only to those with proper clearance and access.

Two other manuscripts in the Joint Chiefs historical series should be noted in connection with Pacific strategy and command. The first is the projected 3-volume work of Vernon E. Davis on the organization of the Joint Chiefs, two volumes of which are completed.[9] This work, even in its incomplete form, is the most accurate and detailed description of the organization of the high command in World War II known to this author. Its publication would be a real service to scholars. The unfinished manuscript of the late Capt. Tracy B. Kittredge, USN, Evolution of Global Strategy, also contains much of interest and value to the student of Pacific strategy, especially for the prewar period. Captain Kittredge, a lifelong student of naval affairs, was on the staff of U.S. Naval Forces, Europe, before he joined the Joint Chiefs of Staff Historical Division, and during that period prepared an account of U.S.-British Naval Cooperation, 1939–1945, that cannot be ignored by any student of World War II strategy. A copy is on file in OCMH.

Space prohibits discussion of the numerous manuscripts prepared by staff agencies in Washington and filed now in the historical offices of the Army and Navy. The Navy manuscripts are especially useful for the Pacific war, but many of the Army manuscripts also contain material dealing with the Pacific.

Histories were prepared also in the overseas commands, and these constitute a primary source for the student of the war in the Pacific since they are based on theater records and represent the theater point of view. The program in MacArthur's area was perhaps the most ambitious, though the results in terms of quality are disappointing. In addition to a 2-volume over-all history covering Allied and Japanese operations in the Southwest Pacific, it produced adminis-

---

[7] The student of Pacific commands will be interested primarily in No. 5 of this series, dated 1 August 1957.

[8] Vol. I: Pearl Harbor Through TRIDENT (1953); Vol. II: The Advance to Victory (1954).

[9] Vol. I: Origins of the Joint and Combined Chiefs of Staff; Vol. II: Development of the JCS Committee Structure.

trative histories of USAFFE, the Services of Supply, and intelligence activities as well as a number of monographs, all on file in the Office of Military History. Greatest interest, perhaps, attaches to the two over-all volumes, known as the MacArthur History. Prepared after the war under the direction of Maj. Gen. Charles A. Willoughby, these volumes are based on extensive research in Allied and Japanese records. A very limited number of copies — five in all — were printed in Japan, and one of these, with thirty-two footlockers of supporting material, is on file in the World War II Records Division in Alexandria.

Historians were assigned also to General Harmon's headquarters, and they prepared during the war a multivolume narrative covering both the organizational and operational aspects of the war in the South Pacific. Though prepared independently, it was incorporated into the history prepared in Hawaii by the historical section of General Richardson's headquarters. This larger work consists of many parts, including a narrative account of Army forces in the theater, a record of Army-Navy relations and of Army participation in operations, and separate histories of staff sections and the major subordinate commands.[10]

In a separate category from manuscripts prepared by historians in uniform are those written by senior commanders as a record of their contribution to victory. In a sense, these are not histories at all, though they are cast in historical form, but primary sources. Their value,

however, is undeniable. There are three such narratives, one by the first commander of Army forces in Australia, one by General Harmon, and one by Admiral Halsey—all on file in OCMH.[11]

The Japanese

The Japanese side of the war, though not as fully documented as the German, is fairly well understood and becoming better known with each passing year. Aside from the documents captured by Allied forces on the field of battle,[12] there are a number of other sources from which the Japanese story can be reconstructed. The chief of these, in the absence of records destroyed by the air raids over Japan and by the Japanese themselves, is the series of monographs known as Japanese Studies in World War II. Prepared by former Japanese Army and Navy officers in Tokyo after the war working under the direction of the Historical Section, G–2, of the Far East Command, these monographs cover almost every aspect of the war in considerable detail. Where available, records were used in their preparation, but more frequently the studies are

---

[10] History of United States Army Forces, Middle Pacific and Predecessor Commands During World War II, 7 December 1941–2 September 1945, Hist Sec G–2, USAFMIDPAC, 33 volumes. Copy in OCMH.

[11] Maj. Gen. Julian F. Barnes, The Organization and Activities of the U.S. Army Forces in Australia; Lt. Gen. Millard F. Harmon, The Army in the South Pacific, Admiral William F. Halsey, Jr., Narrative Account of the South Pacific Campaign, 20 April 1942–15 June 1944.

[12] Captured documents are not covered here, though the author has made occasional use of them. There is no single collection of such documents known to the author, but they can usually be found filed with G–2 and G–3 Journals and in the intelligence reports of the various commands in the theater and in Washington. The largest collection of such material is in the G–2 Library, War Department General Staff. The most important are noted in the bibliographical notes of the volumes in the Pacific subseries.

based on recollections of the officers involved, on personal diaries, and on information furnished the authors. The subjects covered range widely and include politico-military matters as well as strategy, logistics, and administration and operations of Japanese ground, air, and naval forces.[13]

In addition to these studies, the Far East Command assembled from a variety of sources a unique collection of *Imperial General Headquarters* directives and orders for the wartime period. Altogether, there are seventeen volumes in the collection, nine of which contain directives of Army Section and Navy Section of *Imperial General Headquarters* and the rest, Army and Navy orders. In addition, the Historical Section of the Far East Command prepared another eight volumes of interrogations and statements of Japanese wartime officials.[14] All in all, the contribution of the Far East Command to the study of the Japanese side of the war represents the most valuable single collection of Japanese material in existence.

The same officers who produced the Japanese Studies in World War II also prepared a history of Japanese Operations in the Southwest Pacific Area, which forms the second volume of the MacArthur History. Though limited to only one area of the Pacific, this work is probably the most valuable Japanese account of the war. It is based on the

monographs in the Japanese Studies and in its documentation furnished an excellent guide to the series.

Another major contribution to the study of the war in the Pacific is the work of the U.S. Strategic Bombing Survey (USSBS). The result of this survey, undertaken after the war in both Germany and Japan to measure the effect of strategic bombardment, was a series of published reports dealing with all aspects of the Japanese war effort, a Summary Report (Pacific War), and two volumes of interrogations of Japanese officials.[15] The last represent only a portion of the interrogations conducted by USSBS; the remainder are in the National Archives with USSBS records. Japanese shipping losses during the war are covered in another publication, the work of the Joint Army-Navy Assessment Committee, published by the Navy Department in 1947 and revised since.

For the prewar period, the best single source for the study of the steps by which Japan entered the war is the International Military Tribunal for the Far East. The testimony and exhibits of the Tribunal, stored in the World War II Records Division, represent an invaluable collection of primary source material for almost every phase of Japanese history in the decade preceding Pearl Harbor. The judgment of the Tribunal issued in November 1948, itself a multivolume work, is an additional source of considerable value. Nor should the stu-

---

[13] For a list of these monographs, see the accession list prepared by OCMH, which has on file copies of both the Japanese and English versions. There are about 180 volumes in the series, a number of which have been reproduced for limited distribution. The series is unclassified and available for use in OCMH.

[14] Personal History Statements, 2 vols.; Interrogations of Japanese Officials on World War II, 2 vols.; Statements of Japanese Officials on World War II, 4 vols.

---

[15] Among the titles of USSBS publications are: *Air Campaigns of the Pacific War* (1947); *Employment of Forces Under the Southwest Pacific Command* (1947); *The Campaigns of the Pacific War* (1946), which deals exclusively with naval engagements; *Japanese Air Power* (1946); and *Oil in Japan's War* (1946).

dent overlook the thirty-nine volumes of the *Hearings Before the Joint Committee on the Investigation of the Pearl Harbor Attack* (79th Cong., 2d sess.), which contain many Japanese documents, including the diary of Prince Konoye.

One further collection of Japanese records should be noted, though this was not examined by the author. This is a collection seized by U.S. authorities after the war and containing records of the Japanese Army and Navy Ministries dating from the turn of the century. Before these records were returned to Japan in the fall of 1958, microfilm copies of certain documents were made by the Naval History Division and of others by a group of scholars under a grant from the Ford Foundation. The latter documents are on file in the National Archives.[16]

The student of the Pacific War interested in the Japanese story will find a number of published works by participants and by observers of the Japanese scene of considerable value. The most important of these is the 4-volume work of Takushiro Hattori, a wartime colonel and one of the chief Army planners in the general staff.[17] Hattori was also head of the group of ex-Army officers who worked on the second volume of the MacArthur History and his work represents a fuller version of that volume, unedited by American hands. In this sense, it is more revealing than the Japanese history prepared by the Far East

Command and can be considered virtually a primary source for the Pacific war. Useful also for a high-level view of the war as seen from Tokyo is Saburo Hayashi's *KOGUN: The Japanese Army in the Pacific War* (Quantico, Va.: The Marine Corps Association, 1959) and a description of Japan during the war years entitled *The Lost War* (New York: Alfred A. Knopf, 1946) by Masuo Kato. Available also in English are several excellent accounts of Japanese naval operations, including a particularly fine study, *Midway: The Battle that Doomed Japan* (Annapolis: U.S. Naval Institute, 1955) by Mitsuo Fuchida and Masatake Okumiya.[18]

The library of secondary works and reference books on Japanese military and political institutions is large, and has no place in the present survey. But it may not be inappropriate to call attention to several works particularly helpful to an understanding of the role of *Imperial General Headquarters* in the formulation of policy and strategy and of the military in the national life of Japan. The most recent of these is Yale Candee Maxon's *Control of Japanese Foreign Policy: A Study of Civil-Military Rivalry* (Berkeley: University of California Press, 1957), which draws heavily on Japan's World War II experience. Other excellent studies in the same field are Hugh Byas, *Government by Assassination* (New York: Alfred A. Knopf, 1942); Hillis Lory, *Japan's Military Masters* (New York: The Viking Press, 1943); and Kenneth W. Colegrove, *Mili-*

---

[16] The original collection, comprising 7,000 linear feet, is described by James W. Morley, "Check List of Seized Japanese Records in the National Archives," *Far Eastern Quarterly* (May, 1950).

[17] The Complete History of the Greater East Asia War, 4 vols. (*Dai Toa Senso Zenshi*, Tokyo: Masu Publishing Co., 1953). The four volumes were translated for OCMH and are on file there.

---

[18] See also Masatake Okumiya and Jiro Horikoshi, *Zero!* (New York: Ballantine Books, 1956); and Mochitsura Hashimoto, *Sunk: The Story of the Japanese Submarine Fleet, 1942–1945* (London: Cassell & Co., Ltd., 1954).

tarism in Japan (Boston and New York: World Peace Foundation, 1936).[19] For a description of Japan's wartime economy, the student will find Jerome B. Cohen's *Japan's Economy in War and Reconstruction* (Minneapolis: University of Minnesota Press, 1949) thoroughly reliable and complete.

Reference Works

Certain standard reference works will also be useful. To find his way in the vast Pacific Ocean and in areas of the world with which he may be unfamiliar, the student can turn to an atlas—any standard atlas will do. But this is only an introduction; for a more detailed guide he will have to turn elsewhere. Maps in abundance will be found in all the volumes of the Pacific subseries of UNITED STATES ARMY IN WORLD WAR II and in other series. The Allied Geographic Section, G–2 of GHQ SWPA, published during the war well over one hundred Terrain Studies, Terrain Handbooks, and Special Reports covering all areas of the entire region encompassed in General MacArthur's command. The standard reference work on the Pacific is R. W. Robson, *The Pacific Islands Handbook, 1944*, published in a North American edition by the MacMillan Company (New York, 1946). The 1944 edition includes a chronology of the war and its effect on each of the islands in the Pacific. In addition, the student may wish to consult for historical background, as well as geographic information, the extremely

readable and thoroughly reliable works of Douglas L. Oliver, *The Pacific Islands* (Cambridge: Harvard University Press, 1952), the *Geography of the Pacific* (New York: John Wiley & Sons, 1951) edited by O. W. Freeman, *The Pacific World* (New York: W. W. Norton & Co., 1944) edited by Fairfield Osborn, or Joseph C. Furnas, *Anatomy of Paradise* (New York: W. Sloan Associates, 1948). The best studies of exploration are J. C. Beaglehole, *The Exploration of the Pacific* (London: A. & C. Black, Ltd., 1934) and James A. Williamson, *Cook and the Opening of the Pacific* (New York: The Macmillan Company, 1948).

Most of the chronologies of World War II are of limited usefulness for military purposes. There are, however, several important exceptions: Mary H. Williams, compiler, *Chronology: 1941–1945*, UNITED STATES ARMY IN WORLD WAR II (Washington, 1959); *United States Naval Chronology, World War II*, prepared by the Naval History Division (Washington, 1955); Chronology of World War II, prepared by the Air War College at Maxwell Field, and, finally, Chronology of Events in the Southwest Pacific Area, prepared in General MacArthur's headquarters. Information about Army units serving in the Pacific can be found in Order of Battle of U.S. Army Ground Forces in World War II: Pacific Theater of Operations. Prepared in the Office of Military History, this volume is as yet unpublished but a limited number of copies are available.

Statistical data on a variety of subjects have been compiled but are not yet consolidated in any single work. Army strength and casualties figures can be

---

[19] Two reference books, often overlooked though readily available, are *The Japan Year Book*, and the War Department *Handbook on Japanese Military Forces* (TM–E 30 –480).

found in Strength of the Army (STM–30), prepared in The Adjutant General's Office, and in Army Battle Casualties and Non-Battle Deaths in World War II, Final Report, prepared under the direction of the Office of the Comptroller, Department of the Army. Naval casualties, including Marine, can be obtained from *The History of the Medical Department of the United States Navy in World War II*, 2 vols. (Washington, 1953–54). Other statistical collections containing material on the Pacific are Statistical Review, World War II (1946), prepared by the Control Division Army Service Forces, and a volume in preparation for the Army series and available in incomplete form in OCMH, as are the other references noted above. This last work is tentatively titled Statistics and is being prepared under the direction of Theodore E. Whiting in the Office of the Comptroller.

Official Publications

Official publications dealing with the war include the published histories of each of the services and of the Allies, the reports of the wartime chiefs and major commanders, and official collections of documents. There is little need to note here the numerous titles of the official historical programs; they are readily available and not all of them are relevant to this study. The Pacific volumes of the present series, UNITED STATES ARMY IN WORLD WAR II, prepared in the Office of the Chief of Military History and published by the Government Printing Office, have already been noted, but there are additional volumes in this series the student will find extremely helpful in his study of strategy,

as did the author: Ray S. Cline, *Washington Command Post: The Operations Division* (1951); Stetson Conn and Byron Fairchild, *The Framework of Hemisphere Defense* (1960); Richard M. Leighton and Robert W. Coakley, *Global Logistics and Strategy, 1940–1943* (1953) and a second volume in preparation covering the years 1943–1945; Maurice Matloff and Edwin M. Snell, *Strategic Planning for Coalition Warfare, 1941–1942* (1953), and a second volume, for the years *1943–1944* (1959), by Mr. Matloff alone; Mark Skinner Watson, *Chief of Staff: Prewar Plans and Preparations* (1950); Charles F. Romanus and Riley Sunderland, *Stilwell's Mission to China* (1953) and *Stilwell's Command Problems* (1956). One other publication of the Office of the Chief of Military History should be noted, *Command Decisions*, a collection of essays by present and former members of the office, published originally by Harcourt, Brace and Company (New York, 1959), and, with an introduction by Kent R. Greenfield and several additional essays, by the Government Printing Office in 1960.

The historical program of the U.S. Air Force produced seven volumes dealing with World War II when the Air Forces was a part of the Army. Unlike the Army series, of which it was a part, the "Army Air Forces in World War II" was published by the University of Chicago Press. Each volume in the series is the work of many hands, ably brought together by the editors, Wesley Frank Craven and James Lea Cate. Four of the seven volumes contain material bearing on the Pacific: *Plans and Early Operations: January 1939 to August 1942* (1948), *The Pacific—Guadalcanal to Saipan: August 1942 to July 1944*

(1950), *The Pacific: Matterhorn to Nagasaki, June 1944 to August 1945* (1953), and *Men and Planes* (1955).

The Navy's historical program for World War II did not contemplate the publication of a series, but by arrangement with Samuel Eliot Morison, then Professor of History at Harvard, a semi-official "History of United States Naval Operations in World War II" was undertaken, to be published by Little, Brown and Company in Boston. At the present writing, this series of fourteen volumes is almost completed, with only one volume remaining to be written.[20] Though largely replaced by Admiral Morison's work, the classified volumes published by the Office of Naval Intelligence during the war are still useful. These volumes, written by competent historians in uniform, form the series known as ONI Combat Narratives and cover virtually every naval engagement for the first two years of the war. The Navy has also published two volumes dealing with logistics in the Pacific that the student of the war will find most useful: Rear Adm. Worrall R. Carter, USN (Ret.), *Beans, Bullets, and Black Oil: The Story of Fleet Logistics Afloat . . .* (Washington, 1953); and *Building the Navy's Bases in World War II*, 2 vols. (Washington, 1947).

The Historical Branch of the Marine Corps has to its credit a long list of publications on World War II. Its program was envisaged as consisting of two phases —first, the preparation of monographs on each campaign in which the Marine Corps participated, and second, a 5-volume series entitled "History of U.S. Marine Corps Operations in World War II," all to be published by the Government Printing Office. The first phase, which produced fifteen monographs, has been completed and an excellent start was made on the second phase with the publication in 1958 of the first volume of the series carrying the Marine story through the Guadalcanal Campaign.

The official historical programs of our Allies during World War II have produced a number of volumes on the Pacific war. Of first importance is the British series "History of the Second World War" edited by J. R. M. Butler and published by Her Majesty's Stationery Office. To date, two volumes of a projected five have been published on the war against Japan, and four of a projected six on grand strategy. Though undocumented, these volumes are among the best yet published on the war.[21] The Australian series, like the British, is organized into separate sub-series by service but does not include a series on strategy. Two of the Army volumes, one on air operations and one on the Navy have been published thus far in Canberra, with a total of three

---

[20] The volumes dealing with the Pacific war are: *The Rising Sun in the Pacific, 1931–April 1942* (1948), *Coral Sea, Midway and Submarine Actions, May 1942–August 1942* (1950), *The Struggle for Guadalcanal, August 1942–February 1943* (1950), *Breaking the Bismarcks Barrier, 22 July 1942–1 May 1944* (1950), *Aleutians, Gilberts and Marshalls, June 1942–April 1944* (1951), *New Guinea and the Marianas, March 1944–August 1944* (1953), *Leyte, 1944* (1958), and *Liberation of the Philippines: Luzon, Mindanao, the Visayas, 1944–1945* (1959).

[21] The two volumes on Japan are: *The Loss of Singapore* (London, 1957) and *India's Most Dangerous Hour* (1958), both by Maj. Gen. S. Woodburn Kirby, *et al.* The most useful of the strategy volumes for the Pacific war are: J. R. M. Butler, *Grand Strategy: September 1939–June 1941* (1957) and John Ehrman, *Grand Strategy, August 1943–September 1944* (1956). One other volume in the British series that should be consulted is S. W. Roskill, *The War at Sea*, projected in three volumes of which two have been published.

more still to come. The official history of New Zealand forces in the war against Japan projects only one volume for the Pacific and this has already been published. Finally, the Dutch have published an account of their own operations in the Netherlands Indies in five volumes, two of which deal with the prewar period.[22]

The number of official publications issued by the services and other agencies of the government during and immediately after the war is enormous. These cover such a wide variety of subjects and are so uneven in quality and reliability that it would be impractical to discuss them here. But no survey of the sources for the prewar period would be complete without noting the contributions of the State Department in its Foreign Relations volumes dealing with Japan and the Far East and in the wartime *Peace and War, United States Foreign Policy, 1931–1941* (Washington, 1943). These contain documents of prime importance to a study of U.S. entry into the war and complement the published volumes of the Pearl Harbor investigation, which no student can afford to ignore.[23] The reports of the wartime commanders must be noted also. Unfortunately, the American commanders in the Pacific did not

prepare final reports comparable to those of General Eisenhower for the European theater, but there are reports from some of the British commanders engaged in operations against the Japanese, notably those of General Wavell on "ABDA-COM" (1942) in OCMH, and of Maj. Gen. E. M. Maltby, "Operations in Hong Kong, 8–25 December 1941," *Supplement to the London Gazette*, January 29, 1948. Nor should the student overlook the reports of Generals Marshall and Arnold to the Secretary of War, and of Admiral King to the Secretary of the Navy. These appeared in several forms and were widely distributed, appearing finally in a single volume, edited by Walter Millis, as *The War Reports of General of the Army George C. Marshall, General of the Army H. H. Arnold, and Fleet Admiral Ernest J. King* (Philadelphia and New York: J. B. Lippincott Company, 1947).

Memoirs and Biography

Second to the records in importance are the memoirs and biographical literature of the war. On the highest level are *The Public Papers and Addresses of Franklin D. Roosevelt*, 13 vols. (New York: Random House, 1938–1950) and biographies of Roosevelt and the Roosevelt era. The most valuable of the biographies is Robert E. Sherwood's *Roosevelt and Hopkins: An Intimate History* (New York: Harper & Brothers, 1948). The volumes of Winston Churchill's "The Second World War" contain much valuable material on the Pacific. Though Henry L. Stimson did not figure prominently in the shaping of U.S. strategy, his book, written with McGeorge Bundy, *On Active Service in Peace and War*

---

[22] The Australian volumes are Lionel Wigmore, *The Japanese Thrust* (Canberra: Australian War Memorial, 1957), Dudley McCarthy, *Southwest Pacific Area — First Year: Kokoda To Wau* (1959), G. Hermon Gill, *Royal Australian Navy, 1939–42* (1957), and George Odgers, *Air War Against Japan* (1957). The New Zealand official history by Oliver A. Gillespie, is entitled simply *The Pacific* (Wellington: War History Branch, Department of Internal Affairs, 1952); the 5-volume Dutch series *"Nederlands-Indie Contra Japan"* (1949–1957).

[23] *Pearl Harbor Attack: Hearing Before the Joint Committee on the Investigation of the Pearl Harbor Attack*, 39 pts., 79th Cong., 2d sess. (Washington, 1946).

(New York: Harper & Brothers, 1948), will prove most useful.

On the military side of the high command, three of the members of the Joint Chiefs of Staff, Admiral Leahy, Admiral King, and General Arnold have written their memoirs.[24] Of these, the most useful for the Pacific war is King's volume. General Marshall never wrote his memoirs, but a definitive 3-volume biography undertaken with Marshall's consent and co-operation, is in preparation by Forrest C. Pogue, Research Director of the George C. Marshall Foundation. Until it appears, the student will have to rely on two journalistic biographies: William Frye, *Marshall, Citizen Soldier* (New York: Bobbs-Merrill, 1947), and Robert Payne, *The Marshall Story* (New York: Prentice-Hall, 1951). Finally, the student will find worthwhile material on the Pacific in that portion of General Eisenhower's *Crusade in Europe* (New York: Doubleday and Company, 1948), dealing with his tour of duty in the Operations Division of the War Department General Staff, to which he was assigned in December 1941 primarily because of his earlier association with General MacArthur.

The senior commanders in the Pacific are well represented in the memoirs and biographical literature of the war. As one would expect, General MacArthur has been the favorite subject of the biographers. Two of these were officers on his staff, closely associated with him during the war and after, and their volumes may

be considered virtually as authorized biographies.[25] Less favorable to MacArthur is the work of the journalist-historian team of Richard H. Rovere and Arthur M. Schlesinger, Jr., written at the time of MacArthur's relief in 1951 and called *The General and the President, and the Future of American Foreign Policy* (New York: Farrar, Straus and Young, 1951). John Gunther has turned his talents also to *The Riddle of MacArthur* (New York: Harper & Brothers, 1951) to produce a fairly well-balanced and impartial account of the general. Other journalists such as Clark Lee and Frazier Hunt have tried their hand on this difficult subject, and the results, though readable, do not add much to our understanding of the complex character of General MacArthur. The only other Pacific area commander whose story has appeared in print to date is Admiral Halsey, who collaborated with Joseph Byran to write *Admiral Halsey's Story* (New York: Whittlesey House, 1947).

Below the level of theater commander, the number of memoirs increases substantially. Virtually all of MacArthur's senior subordinates have told their stories, perhaps because they were so inadequately told during the war. General Brereton, who commanded the Far East Air Force in the Philippines, produced *The Brereton Diaries* (New York: William Morrow and Company, 1946); Wainwright, with the assistance of Bob Considine, *General Wainwright's Story*

[24] Fleet Adm. William D. Leahy, *I Was There* (New York: Whittlesey House, 1950); Ernest J. King and Walter Muir Whitehill, *Fleet Admiral King* (New York: W. W. Norton & Co., 1952); Henry H. Arnold, *Global Mission* (New York: Harper & Brothers, 1949).

[25] Maj. Gen. Charles A. Willoughby and John Chamberlin, *MacArthur 1941–1951* (New York: McGraw-Hill Book Co., Inc., 1954); Courtney Whitney, *MacArthur: His Rendezvous with Destiny* (New York: Alfred A. Knopf, 1956).

(New York: Doubleday and Company, 1945). General Kenney, Allied Air Forces Commander, told his story in *General Kenney Reports* (New York: Duell, Sloan and Pearce, 1949), and the major ground force commanders, Generals Krueger and Eichelberger, theirs in *From Down Under to Nippon* (Washington: Combat Forces Press, 1953) and *Our Jungle Road to Tokyo* (New York: The Viking Press, 1950).

For some unexplained reason, naval commanders are conspiciously absent from the list. We have no memoirs from Admiral Nimitz, Admiral Spruance, Admiral Sherman, or any of the other senior naval officers in the Pacific except Halsey. There is a biography, *The Magnificent Mitscher* (New York: W. W. Norton and Company, 1954), by Theodore Taylor and an account by the Marine General Holland M. Smith, with Percy Finch, entitled *Coral and Brass* (New York: Charles Scribner's Sons, 1949).

Unit Histories

The histories of units, ranging in size from separate regiments and lower to field armies and army groups, are most useful for operational and administrative history, and in some cases they may prove of value for other purposes. Virtually all separate units prepared a history of one kind or another during the war, since regulations required them to do so. These are on file in the World War II Records Division and the Kansas City Federal Records Center Annex, where they can be consulted readily.

In addition to these unpublished histories, there are a great number of published histories of units and, for the Navy, of ships of all types. To list them

would be a tedious and unrewarding exercise, and there is no need to do so for there are several excellent bibliographies to these histories. The student can consult these for any unit or vessels in which he may be interested. Major credit for the preparation of the bibliographies belongs to C. E. Dornbusch of the New York Public Library, who has made a specialty of unit histories and gathered for the library the largest collection of such histories outside Washington.[26]

General Works and Special Studies

The task of the student of World War II is made more difficult by the fact that much of the most useful material on the Pacific war appears in article form in journals that are not indexed in such standard references as the *Reader's Guide to Periodical Literature*.[27] Some of it, however, can be found in the *National Defense Review*, issued by the Army Library from 1947 to 1955, and the Periodical Index of the Air University Library. For articles and books published during the war years, there are two useful guides, one compiled by Henry O. Spier entitled *World War II*

---

[26] For Army units, see Unit Histories of World War II (1950), issued by the Office of the Chief of Military History; Unit Histories of World War II and After: United States Army (1953), issued by The Adjutant General; and C. E. Dornbusch, complier, Histories of American Army Units, World Wars I and II and Korean Conflict (1956). For naval and Marine units, see Post-War Souvenir Books and Unit Histories of the Navy, Marine Corps, and Construction Battalions (1953), compiled by Mr. Dornbusch and issued by the Naval History Division.

[27] See Max L. Marshall, A Survey of Military Periodicals, an M.A. thesis prepared at the University of Missouri, 1952, which describes eighty-nine military periodicals. A copy can be found in the Army Library in the Pentagon.

in Our Magazines and Books, September 1939–September 1945 (New York: The Stuyvesant Press Corp., 1945), and one by the Legislative Reference Service, Library of Congress, a serial entitled Bibliographies of the World at War, issued in 1942 and 1943.

Valuable also are the bibliographical sections of various military journals. *Military Affairs,* the quarterly journal of the American Military Institute with headquarters in Washington, contains in each issue a section entitled "Military Library," and *Military Review,* the monthly journal of the Command and General Staff College, abstracts the leading articles from military journals throughout the world. Naval literature is covered in *The American Neptune* under the title "Recent Writings in Maritime History," prepared by Prof. Robert G. Albion of Harvard.

For general works on World War II the student will find useful the *Harvard Guide to American History* (Cambridge: Harvard University Press, 1955). The *Writings on American History,* published annually by the American Historical Association, contains a fairly full listing of works on military subjects. There are also several naval bibliographies which list background materials for World War II, especially the Pacific area.[28]

Though there are few general accounts of the Pacific war covering both the high-level story and the operations of all services, there are a number of works recounting the contributions of a single service or type of unit. In this category, the Army, including the Air Forces, comes off a poor third to the Marines and the Navy.[29] For the Marines, we have at least two excellent unofficial histories, Frank O. Hough, *The Island War* (Philadelphia and New York: J. B. Lippincott Co., 1947) and Fletcher Pratt, *The Marines' War* (New York: W. Sloane Associates, 1946), a scholarly study written at Princeton University by Jeter A. Isely and Philip A. Crowl, *The U.S. Marines and Amphibious War, Its Theory, and Its Practice in the Pacific* (Princeton, N. J.: Princeton University Press, 1951), a *History of Marine Corps Aviation in World War II* (Washington: Combat Forces Press, 1952) by Robert Sherrod, a number of fine division histories, and such outstanding examples of combat narrative as Herbert L. Merillat's *The Island* (Boston: Houghton Mifflin Co., 1944) and Richard Tregaskis' *Guadalcanal Diary* (New York: Random House, Inc., 1943).

The catalogue of naval histories dealing with the Pacific war offers for understandable reasons, a large and varied fare. In addition to the excellent treatment of the Navy in World War II in

---

[28] *A Selected and Annotated Bibliography on United States Naval History, Naval Biography, Naval Strategy and Tactics,* prepared by the Naval History Division (Washington, 1956); Robert G. Albion, Maritime and Naval History: An Annotated Bibliography (1951) (a revised edition was published in mimeographed form in 1955 by the Marine Historical Association, Mystic, Conn.); Werner B. Ellinger and Herbert Rosinski, *Sea Power in the Pacific, 1936–1941* (Princeton, N.J.: Princeton University Press, 1942).

[29] One should note for its value Brig. Gen. William F. Heavy, *Down Ramp! The Story of the Army Amphibian Engineers* (Washington: Infantry Journal Press, 1947), and for its readability and accuracy Walter D. Edmonds, *They Fought With What They Had, The Story of the Army Air Forces in the Southwest Pacific, 1941–1942* (Boston: Little, Brown and Co., 1951).

general histories of the Navy,[30] the student can consult the 5-volume series *Battle Report* (New York: Rinehart and Company, 1944–1949) by Walter Karig and others, though he would be better advised to turn to the Morison series. A provocative discussion of the role of the Navy, useful even if the reader does not agree, is William D. Puleston's *Influence of Sea Power in World War II* (New Haven: Yale University Press, 1947). More scholarly and, in its field, a pioneering work, is the study of Duncan Ballantine, *U.S. Naval Logistics in the Second World War* (Princeton, N.J.: Princeton University Press, 1947). Then there are separate histories of naval aviation, destroyers, and submarines, all of them detailed and accurate. The first of these is traced in two separate works, the scholarly and readable study of Archibald D. Turnbull and Clifford L. Lord, *History of United States Naval Aviation* (New Haven: Yale University Press, 1949) and Frederick C. Sherman's *Combat Command: The American Aircraft Carriers in the Pacific War* (New York: E. P. Dutton & Co., 1950). Theodore Roscoe had written a volume on *United States Destroyer Operations in World War II* (Annapolis: U.S. Naval Institute, 1953) and another, *United States Submarine Operations in World War II* (Annapolis: U.S. Naval Institute, 1949), both large, handsome volumes that treat their subjects with loving care and attention to detail. For those who wish to

pursue submarine operations further, there is the work of Charles A. Lockwood, *Sink 'em All: Submarine Warfare in the Pacific* (New York: E. P. Dutton & Co., 1951) and Edward L. Beach, *Submarine!* (New York: Henry Holt & Co., 1952.

For those who wish to investigate the problems associated with the Pearl Harbor attack, there are two surveys of the literature in the field, one by the present author, "Pearl Harbor in Perspective" *U.S. Naval Institute Proceedings* (April, 1955), and the other by Wayne S. Cole, "American Entry into World War II: A Historiographical Appraisal," *The Mississippi Valley Historical Review* (March, 1957). The basic documents for the study of the attack have been noted above under official publications and Japanese records—the Pearl Harbor hearings and the records of the International Military Tribunal for the Far East. The best account of American foreign policy in the years immediately preceding the Japanese attack is the 2-volume work of William L. Langer and S. Everett Gleason, *The Challenge to Isolation 1937–1940* (New York: Harper & Brothers, 1952) and *The Undeclared War* (New York: Harper & Brothers, 1953). On the Japanese side, Herbert Feis, *Road to Pearl Harbor, The Coming of the War Between the United States and Japan* (Princeton, N.J.: Princeton University Press, 1950), provides the best summary of the available Japanese evidence.

The grand strategy of the war, like the question of war guilt, has come under the close scrutiny of many military critics and scholars and is the subject of continued controversy. On this level, it is difficult to separate Pacific strategy from the strategy of global war, and most

---

[30] Dudley W. Knox, *A History of the United States Navy* (New York: G. P. Putnam's Sons, 1948) and E. B. Potter, editor, *et al.*, *The United States and World Sea Power* (Englewood Cliffs: Prentice-Hall, Inc., 1955). See also John Creswell, *Sea Warfare, 1939–1945* (London and New York: Longmans, Green, & Co., Inc., 1950).

writers have made no effort to do so. As a matter of fact, some of the most controversial questions of Pacific strategy, such as the Europe-first concept, are intimately related to the larger problems of strategy. These questions are discussed in the official histories, general histories of the war, and memoirs noted above, but other works dealing specifically with strategy should be noted here. An excellent introduction to the subject can be found in three small books, all of them readable and based on wide knowledge—one by the former Chief Historian of the Army, Kent Roberts Greenfield, *The Historian and the Army* (New Brunswick: Rutgers University Press, 1954), one by Professor Morison, *Strategy and Compromise* (Boston: Little, Brown & Co., 1958), and the third by the British military historian, Alfred H. Burne, *Strategy in World War II* (Harrisburg, Pa.: Military Service Publishing Company, 1947). Most of the writing on Pacific strategy alone is found in military periodicals such as the *United States Naval Institute Proceedings*, *Army* (and its predecessors, *Combat Forces Journal* and the *Infantry Journal*), *Military Review*, *Military Affairs*, *Marine Corps Gazette*, the British *Journal of the Royal Service Institute*, and others. The list of these articles is too long for a general survey such as this one, but no study of the Pacific war should overlook this important source.

Basic Military Map Symbols*

Symbols within a rectangle indicate a military unit, within a triangle an observation post, and within a circle a supply point.

Military Units—Identification

Antiaircraft Artillery . . . .

Armored Command . . . .

Army Air Forces . . . .

Artillery, except Antiaircraft and Coast Artillery . . . .

Cavalry, Horse . . . .

Cavalry, Mechanized . . . .

Chemical Warfare Service . . . .

Coast Artillery . . . .

Engineers . . . .

Infantry . . . .

Medical Corps . . . .

Ordnance Department . . . .

Quartermaster Corps . . . .

Signal Corps . . . .

Tank Destroyer . . . .

Transportation Corps . . . .

Veterinary Corps . . . .

Airborne units are designated by combining a gull wing symbol with the arm or service symbol:

Airborne Artillery . . . .

Airborne Infantry . . . .

*For complete listing of symbols in use during the World War II period, see FM 21–30, dated October 1943, from which these are taken.

Size Symbols

The following symbols placed either in boundary lines or above the rectangle, triangle, or circle inclosing the identifying arm or service symbol indicate the size of military organization:

Squad . . . . ●

Section . . . . ● ●

Platoon . . . . ● ● ●

Company, troop, battery, Air Force flight I

Battalion, cavalry squadron, or Air Force squadron . . . . I I

Regiment or group; combat team (with abbreviation CT following identifying numeral) . . . . I I I

Brigade, Combat Command of Armored Division, or Air Force Wing X

Division or Command of an Air Force XX

Corps or Air Force XXX

Army XXXX

Group of Armies XXXXX

EXAMPLES

The letter or number to the left of the symbol indicates the unit designation; that to the right, the designation of the parent unit to which it belongs. Letters or numbers above or below boundary lines designate the units separated by the lines:

Company A, 137th Infantry . . . . A⊠137

8th Field Artillery Battalion . . . . ⊡8

Combat Command A, 1st Armored Division . . . . A⬭I

Observation Post, 23d Infantry . . . . ▲23

Command Post, 5th Infantry Division . . . . ⊠5

Boundary between 137th and 138th Infantry . . . . —I37 / III / I38—

Weapons

Machine gun . . . . ●→

Gun . . . . ●

Gun battery . . . . ⊔⊔⊔

Howitzer or Mortar . . . . ◆

Tank . . . . ◇

Self-propelled gun . . . . ▣

UNITED STATES ARMY IN WORLD WAR II

The multivolume series, UNITED STATES ARMY IN WORLD WAR
II, consists of a number of subseries which are planned as follows: The War
Department, The Army Air Forces, The Army Ground Forces, The Army
Service Forces, The Western Hemisphere, The War in the Pacific, The
Mediterranean Theater of Operations, The European Theater of Operations,
The Middle East Theater, The China–Burma–India Theater, The Technical
Services, Special Studies, and Pictorial Record.

The following volumes have been published or are in press: *

The War Department

Chief of Staff: Prewar Plans and Preparations
Washington Command Post: The Operations Division
Strategic Planning for Coalition Warfare:1941–1942
Strategic Planning for Coalition Warfare: 1943–1944
Global Logistics and Strategy:1940–1943
The Army and Economic Mobilization
The Army and Industrial Manpower

The Army Ground Forces

The Organization of Ground Combat Troops
The Procurement and Training of Ground Combat Troops

The Army Service Forces

The Organization and Role of the Army Service Forces

The Western Hemisphere

The Framework of Hemisphere Defense

The War in the Pacific

The Fall of the Philippines
Guadalcanal: The First Offensive
Victory in Papua
CARTWHEEL: The Reduction of Rabaul
Seizure of the Gilberts and Marshalls
Campaign in the Marianas
The Approach to the Philippines
Leyte: The Return to the Philippines

---

* The volumes on the Army Air Forces, published by the University of Chicago Press, are not
included in this list.

Special Studies

Chronology: 1941–1945
Military Relations Between the United States and Canada: 1939–1945
Rearming the French
Three Battles: Arnaville, Altuzzo, and Schmidt
The Women's Army Corps

Pictorial Record

The War Against Germany and Italy: Mediterranean and Adjacent Areas
The War Against Germany: Europe and Adjacent Areas
The War Against Japan

Index

U. S. GOVERNMENT PRINTING OFFICE: 1962—O 592496